Bioethics

BLACKWELL PHILOSOPHY ANTHOLOGIES

Each volume in this outstanding series provides an authoritative and comprehensive collection of the essential primary readings from philosophy's main fields of study. Designed to complement the *Blackwell Companions to Philosophy* series, each volume represents an unparalleled resource in its own right, and will provide the ideal platform for course use.

1 Cottingham: *Western Philosophy: An Anthology*
2 Cahoone: *From Modernism to Postmodernism: An Anthology* (expanded second edition)
3 LaFollette: *Ethics in Practice: An Anthology* (second edition)
4 Goodin and Pettit: *Contemporary Political Philosophy: An Anthology*
5 Eze: *African Philosophy: An Anthology*
6 McNeill and Feldman: *Continental Philosophy: An Anthology*
7 Kim and Sosa: *Metaphysics: An Anthology*
8 Lycan: *Mind and Cognition: An Anthology* (second edition)
9 Kuhse and Singer: *Bioethics: An Anthology*
10 Cummins and Cummins: *Minds, Brains, and Computers – The Foundations of Cognitive Science: An Anthology*
11 Sosa and Kim: *Epistemology: An Anthology*
12 Kearney and Rasmussen: *Continental Aesthetics – Romanticism to Postmodernism: An Anthology*
13 Martinich and Sosa: *Analytic Philosophy: An Anthology*
14 Jacquette: *Philosophy of Logic: An Anthology*
15 Jacquette: *Philosophy of Mathematics: An Anthology*
16 Harris, Pratt, and Waters: *American Philosophies: An Anthology*
17 Emmanuel and Goold: *Modern Philosophy – From Descartes to Nietzsche: An Anthology*
18 Scharff and Dusek: *Philosophy of Technology – The Technological Condition: An Anthology*
19 Light and Rolston: *Environmental Ethics: An Anthology*
20 Taliaferro and Griffiths: *Philosophy of Religion: An Anthology*
21 Lamarque and Olsen: *Aesthetics and the Philosophy of Art – The Analytic Tradition: An Anthology*
22 John and Lopes: *Philosophy of Literature – Contemporary and Classic Readings: An Anthology*
23 Cudd and Andreasen: *Feminist Theory: A Philosophical Anthology*

Bioethics

An Anthology

Edited by

Helga Kushe (Monash Univerity)

and Peter Singer (Princeton University)

BLACKWELL PUBLISHING
350 Main Street, Malden, MA 02148-5020, USA
108 Cowley Road, Oxford OX4 1JF, UK
550 Swanston Street, Carlton, Victoria 3053, Australia

First published 1999
Reprinted 2000, 2001, 2002, 2003 (twice), 2004

Library of Congress Cataloging-in-Publication Data

Bioethics: an anthology / edited by Helga Kuhse and Peter Singer.
p. cm.— (Blackwell philosophy anthologies; 9)
Includes bibliographical references and index.
ISBN 0–631–20310–9 (hbk.: alk. paper) — ISBN 0–631–20311–7
(pbk.: alk. paper)
1. Medical ethics. 2. Bioethics. I. Kuhse, Helga. II. Singer, Peter.
III. Series.
R724. B4582 1999
174.'2—dc21 98–56161
CIP

A catalogue record for this title is available from the British Library.

Set in 9 on 11pt Ehrhardt
by Kolam Information Services Pvt Ltd, Pondicherry, India
Printed and bound in the United Kingdom
by TJ International Ltd, Padstow, Cornwall

The publisher's policy is to use permanent paper from mills that operate a sustainable forestry policy, and which has been manufactured from pulp processed using acid-free and elementary chlorine-free practices. Furthermore, the publisher ensures that the text paper and cover board used have met acceptable environmental accreditation standards.

For further information on
Blackwell Publishing, visit our website:
http://www.blackwellpublishing.com

Contents

Introduction

Helga Kuhse and Peter Singer

The term "bioethics" was coined by Van Rensselaer Potter, who used it to describe his proposal that we need an ethic that can incorporate our obligations, not just to other humans, but to the biosphere as a whole.[1] Although the term is still occasionally used in this sense of an ecological ethic, it is now much more commonly used in the narrower sense of the study of ethical issues arising from the biological and medical sciences. So understood, bioethics has become a specialized, although interdisciplinary, area of study. The essays included in this book give an indication of the range of issues which fall within its scope – but it is only an indication. There are many other issues that we simply have not had the space to cover.

Bioethics can be seen as a branch of ethics, or more specifically, of applied ethics. For this reason some understanding of the nature of ethics is an essential preliminary to any serious study of bioethics. The remainder of this introduction will seek to provide that understanding.

One question about the nature of ethics is especially relevant to bioethics: to what extent is reasoning or argument possible in ethics? Many people assume without much thought that ethics is subjective. The subjectivist holds that what ethical view we take is a matter of opinion or taste that is not amenable to argument. But if ethics were a matter of taste, why would we even attempt to argue about it? If Helen says "I like my coffee sweetened," whereas Paul says "I like my coffee unsweetened," there is not much point in Helen and Paul arguing about it. The two statements do not contradict each other. They can both be true. But if Helen says "Doctors should never assist their patients to die" whereas Paul says "Sometimes doctors should assist their patients to die," then Helen and Paul are disagreeing, and there does seem to be a point in their trying to argue about the issue of physician-assisted suicide.

It seems clear that there is some scope for argument in ethics. If I say "It is always wrong to kill a human being" and "Abortion is not always wrong" then I am committed to denying that abortion kills a human being. Otherwise I have contradicted myself, and in doing so I have not stated a coherent position at all. So consistency, at least, is a requirement of any defensible ethical position, and thus sets a limit to the subjectivity of ethical judgements. The requirement of factual accuracy sets another limit. In discussing issues in bioethics, the facts are often complex. But we cannot reach the right ethical decisions unless we are well-informed about the relevant facts. In this respect ethical decisions are unlike decisions of taste. We can enjoy a taste without knowing what we are eating; but if we assume that it is wrong to resuscitate a terminally ill patient against her wishes, then we cannot know whether an instance of resuscitation was morally right or wrong without knowing something about the patient's prognosis and whether the patient has expressed any wishes about being resuscitated. In that sense, there is no equivalent in ethics to the immediacy of taste.

Ethical relativism, sometimes also known as cultural relativism, is one step away from ethical subjectivism, but it also severely limits the scope of ethical argument. The ethical relativist holds that it is not individual attitudes that determine what is right or wrong, but the attitudes of the culture in which one lives. Herodotus tells how Darius, King of Persia, summoned the Greeks from the western shores of his kingdom before him, and asked them how much he would have to pay them to eat their fathers' dead bodies. They were horrified by the idea and said they would not do it for any amount of money, for it was their custom to cremate their dead. Then Darius called upon Indians from the eastern frontiers of his kingdom, and asked them what would make them willing to burn their fathers' bodies. They cried out and asked the King to refrain from mentioning so shocking an act. Herodotus comments that each nation thinks its own customs best. From here it is only a short step to the view that there can be no objective right or wrong, beyond the bounds of one's own culture. This view found increased support in the nineteenth century as Western anthropologists came to know many different cultures, and were impressed by ethical views very different from those that were standardly taken for granted in European society. As a defence against the automatic assumption that Western morality is superior and should be imposed on "savages", many anthropologists argued that, since morality is relative to culture, no culture can have any basis for regarding its morality as superior to any other culture.

Although the motives with which anthropologists put this view forward were admirable, they may not have appreciated the implications of the position they were taking. The ethical relativist maintains that a statement like "It is good to enslave people from another tribe if they are captured in war" means simply "In my society, the custom is to enslave people from another tribe if they are captured in war." Hence if one member of the society were to question whether it really was good to enslave people in these circumstances, she could be answered simply by demonstrating that this was indeed the custom – for example, by showing that for many generations it had been done after every war in which prisoners were captured. Thus there is no way for moral reformers to say that an accepted custom is wrong – "wrong" just means "in accordance with an accepted custom".

On the other hand, when people from two different cultures disagree about an ethical issue, then according to the ethical relativist there can be no resolution of the disagreement. Indeed, strictly there is no disagreement. If the apparent dispute were over the issue just mentioned, then one person would be saying "In my country it is the custom to enslave people from another tribe if they are captured in war" and the other person would be saying "In my country it is not the custom to allow one human being to enslave another." This is no more a disagreement than such statements as "In my country people greet each other by rubbing noses" and "In my country people greet each other by shaking hands." If ethical relativism is true, then it is impossible to say that one culture is right and the other is wrong. Bearing in mind that some cultures have practised slavery, or the burning of widows on the funeral pyre of their husbands, this is hard to accept.

A more promising alternative to both ethical subjectivism and cultural relativism is universal prescriptivism, an approach to ethics developed by the Oxford philosopher R. M. Hare. Hare argues that the distinctive property of ethical judgements is that they are universalizable. In saying this, he means that if I make an ethical judgement, I must be prepared to state it in universal terms, and apply it to all relevantly similar situations. By "universal terms" Hare means those terms that do not refer to a particular individual. Thus a proper name cannot be a universal term. If, for example, I were to say "Everyone should do what is in the interests of Mick Jagger" I would not be making a universal judgement, because I have used a proper name. The same would be true if I were to say that everyone must do what is in *my* interests, because the personal pronoun "my" is here used to refer to a particular individual, myself.

It might seem that ruling out particular terms in this way does not take us very far. After all, one can always describe oneself in universal terms. Perhaps I can't say that everyone should do what is in my interests, but I could say that everyone must do whatever is in the interests of people who . . . and then give a minutely detailed description of myself, including the precise location of all my freckles. The effect would be the same as saying that everyone should do what is in my interests, because there would be no one except me who matches that description. But Hare meets this problem very effectively by saying that to prescribe an ethical judgement universally means being prepared to prescribe it for all possible circumstances, including hypothetical ones. So if I were to say that everyone should do what is in the interests of a person with a particular pattern of freckles, I must be prepared to prescribe that in the hypothetical situation in which I do not have this pattern of freckles, but someone else does, I should do what is in the interests of that person. Now of course I may *say* that I should do that, since I am confident that I shall never be in such a situation, but this simply means that I am being dishonest. I am not genuinely prescribing the principle universally.

The effect of saying that an ethical judgement must be universalizable for hypothetical as well as actual circumstances is that whenever I make an ethical judgement, I can be challenged to put myself in the position of the parties affected, and see if I would still be able to accept that judgement. Suppose, for example, that I own a small factory and the cheapest way for me to get rid of some waste is to pour it into a nearby river. I do not take water from this river, but I know that some villagers living downstream do and the waste may make them ill. The requirement that ethical judgements should be universalizable will make it difficult for me to justify my conduct, because if I imagine myself in the hypothetical situation of being one of the villagers, rather than the factory-owner, I would not accept that the profits of the factory-owner should outweigh the risk of adverse effects on my health and that of my children. In this way Hare's approach requires us to take into account the interests and preferences of all others affected by our actions. Hence it allows for an element of reasoning in ethical deliberation.

Since the rightness or wrongness of our actions will, on this view, depend on the way in which they affect others, Hare's universal prescriptivism leads to a form of consequentialism – that is, the view that the rightness of an action depends on its consequences. The best-known form of consequentialism is the classical utilitarianism developed in the late eighteenth century by Jeremy Bentham and popularized in the nineteenth century by John Stuart Mill. They held that an action is right if it leads to a greater surplus of happiness over misery than any possible alternative, and wrong if it does not. By "greater surplus of happiness", the classical utilitarians had in mind the idea of adding up all the pleasure or happiness that resulted from the action and subtracting from that total all the pain or misery to which the action gave rise. Naturally, in some circumstances, it might be possible only to reduce misery, and then the right action should be understood as the one that will result in less misery than any possible alternative.

The utilitarian view is striking in many ways. It puts forward a single principle that it claims can provide the right answer to all ethical dilemmas, if only we can predict what the consequences of our actions will be. It takes ethics out of the mysterious realm of duties and rules, and bases ethical decisions on something that almost everyone understands and values. Moreover, utilitarianism's single principle is applied universally, without fear or favour. Bentham said: "Each to count for one and none for more than one," by which he meant that the happiness of a common tramp counted for as much as that of a noble, and the happiness of an African was no less important than that of a European.

Many twentieth-century consequentialists – including Hare – agree with Bentham to the extent that they think the rightness or wrongness of an action must depend on its consequences, but they have abandoned the idea that maximizing net happiness is the ultimate goal. Instead they argue that we should seek to bring about whatever will satisfy the greatest number of desires or preference. This variation, which is known as "preference utilitarianism", does not regard anything as good, except in so far as it is wanted or desired. More intense or strongly held preferences would get more weight than weak preferences.

Consequentialism offers one important answer to the question of how we should decide what is right and what is wrong, but many ethicists reject it. The denial of this view was dramatically presented by Dostoevsky in *The Karamazov Brothers*:

> imagine that you are charged with building the edifice of human destiny, the ultimate aim of which is to bring people happiness, to give them peace and contentment at last, but that in order to achieve this it is essential and unavoidable to torture just one little speck of creation, that same little child beating her chest with her little fists, and imagine that this edifice has to be erected on her unexpiated tears. Would you agree to be the architect under those conditions? Tell me honestly![2]

The passage suggests that some things are always wrong, no matter what their consequences. This has, for most of Western history, been the prevailing approach to morality, at least at the level of what has been officially taught and approved by the institutions of Church and State. The ten commandments of the Hebrew scriptures served as a model for much of the Christian era, and the Roman Catholic Church built up an elaborate system of morality based on rules to which no exceptions were allowed.

Another example of an ethic of rules is that of Immanuel Kant. Kant's ethic is based on his "categorical imperative" which he states in several distinct formulations. One is that we must always act so that we can will the maxim of our action to be a universal law. This can be interpreted as a form of Hare's idea of universalizability, which we have already encountered. Another is that we must always treat other people as ends, never as means. While these formulations of the categorical imperative might be applied in various ways, in Kant's hands they lead to inviolable rules, for example, against making promises that we do not intend to keep. Kant also thought that it was always wrong to tell a lie. In response to a critic who suggested that this rule has exceptions, Kant said that it would be wrong to lie even if someone had taken refuge in your house, and a person seeking to murder him came to your door and asked if you knew where he was. Modern Kantians often reject this hard-line approach to rules, and claim that Kant's categorical imperative did not require him to hold so strictly to the rule against lying.

How would a consequentialist – for example, a classical utilitarian – answer Dostoevsky's challenge? If answering honestly – and if one really could be certain that this was a sure way, and the only way, of bringing lasting happiness to all the people of the world – utilitarians would have to say yes, they would accept the task of being the architect of the happiness of the world at the cost of the child's unexpiated tears. For they would point out that the suffering of that child, wholly undeserved as it is, will be repeated a million-fold over the next century, for other children, just as innocent, who are victims of starvation, disease and brutality. So if this one child must be sacrificed to stop all this suffering then, terrible as it is, the child must be sacrificed.

Fantasy apart, there can be no architect of the happiness of the world. The world is too big and complex a place for that. But we may attempt to bring about less suffering and more happiness, or satisfaction of preferences, for people or sentient beings in specific places and circumstances. Alternatively, we might follow a set of principles or rules – which could be of varying degrees of rigidity or flexibility. Where would such rules come from? Kant tried to deduce them from his categorical imperative, which in turn he had reached by insisting that the moral law must be based on reason alone, without any content from our wants or desires. But the problem with trying to deduce morality from reason alone has always been that it becomes an empty formalism that cannot tell us what to do. To make it practical, it needs to have some additional content, and Kant's own attempts to deduce rules of conduct from his categorical imperative are unconvincing.

Others, following Aristotle, have tried to draw on human nature as a source of moral rules. What is good, they say, is what is natural to human beings. They then contend that it is natural and right for us to seek certain goods, such as knowledge, friendship, health, love and procreation, and unnatural and wrong for us to act contrary to these goods. This "natural law" ethic is open to criticism on several points. The word "natural" can be used both descriptively and evaluatively, and the two senses are often mixed together so that value judgements may be smuggled in under the guise of a description. The picture of human nature presented by proponents of natural law ethics usually selects only those characteristics of our nature that the proponent considers desirable. The fact that our species, especially its male members, frequently go to war, and are also prone to commit individual acts of violence against others, is no doubt just as much part of our nature as our desire for knowledge, but no natural law theorist therefore views these activities as good. More generally, natural law theory has its origins in an Aristotelian idea of the cosmos, in which everything has a goal or "end", which can be deduced from its nature. The "end" of a knife is to cut; the assumption is that human beings also have an "end", and we will flourish when we live in accordance with the end for which we are suited. But this is a pre-Darwinian view of nature. Since Darwin, we know that we do not exist for any purpose, but are the result of natural selection operating on random mutations over millions of years. Hence there is no reason to believe that living according to nature will produce a harmonious society, let alone the best possible state of affairs for human beings.

Another way in which it has been claimed that we can come to know what moral principles or rules we should follow is through our intuition. In practice this usually means that we adopt conventionally accepted moral principles or rules, perhaps with some adjustments in order to avoid inconsistency or arbitrariness. On this view, a moral theory should, like a scientific theory, try to match the data; and the data that a moral theory must match is provided by our moral intuitions. As in science, if a plausible theory matches most, but not all, of the data, then the anomalous data might be rejected on the grounds that it is more likely that there was an error in the procedures for gathering that particular set of data than that the theory as a whole is mistaken. But ultimately the test of a theory is its ability to explain the data. The problem with applying this model of scientific justification to ethics is that the "data" of our moral intuitions is unreliable, not just at one or two specific points, but as a whole. Here the facts that cultural relativists draw upon are relevant (even if they do not establish that cultural relativism is the correct response to it). Since we know that our intuitions are strongly influenced by such things as culture and religion, they are ill-suited to serve as the fixed points against which an ethical theory must be tested. Even where there is cross-cultural agreement, there may be some aspects of our intuitions on which *all* cultures unjustifiably favour our own interests over those of others. For example, simply because we are all human beings, we may have a systematic bias that leads us to give an unjustifiably low moral status to non-human animals. Or, because in virtually all known human societies, men have taken a greater leadership role than women, the moral intuitions of all societies may not adequately reflect the interests of females.

Some philosophers think that it is a mistake to base ethics on principles or rules. Instead they focus on what it is to be a good person – or, in the case of the problems with which this book is concerned, perhaps on what it is to be a good nurse or doctor or researcher. They seek to describe the virtues that a good person, or a good member of the relevant profession, should possess. Moral education then consists of teaching these virtues and discussing how a virtuous person would act in specific situations. The question is, however, whether we can have a notion of what a virtuous person would do in a specific situation without making a prior decision about what it is right to do. After all, in any particular moral dilemma, different virtues may be applicable, and even a particular virtue will not always give unequivocal guidance. For instance, if a terminally ill patient repeatedly asks a nurse or doctor for assistance in dying, what response best exemplifies the virtues of a health-care professional? There seems no answer to this question, short of an inquiry into whether it is right or wrong to help a patient in such circumstances to die. But in that case we seem bound, in the end, to come back to discussing such issues as whether it is right to follow moral rules or principles, or to do what will have the best consequences.

In recent years some feminists have offered new criticisms of conventional thought about ethics. They argue that the approaches to ethics taken by the influential philosophers of the past – all of whom have been male – give too much emphasis to abstract principles and the role of reason, and give too little attention to personal relationships and the part played by emotion. One outcome of these criticisms has been the development of an "ethic of care", which is not so much a single ethical theory as a cluster of ways of looking at ethics which put an attitude of caring for others at the centre, and seek to avoid reliance on abstract ethical principles. The ethic of care has seemed especially applicable to the work of those involved in direct patient care, and has recently been taken up by a number of nursing theorists as offering a more suitable alternative to other ideas of ethics. Not all feminists, however, support this development. Some worry that the adoption of a "care" approach by nurses may reflect, and even reinforce, stereotypes of women as more emotional and less rational than men. They also fear that it could lead to women continuing to carry a disproportionate burden of caring for others, to the exclusion of adequately caring for themselves.

In this discussion of ethics we have not mentioned anything about religion. This may seem odd, in view of the close connection that there has often been between religion and ethics, but it reflects our belief that, despite this historical connection, ethics and religion are fundamentally independent. Logically, ethics is prior to religion. If religious believers wish to say that a deity is good, or praise her or his creation or deeds, they must have a notion of goodness that is independent of their conception of the deity and what she or he does. Otherwise they will be saying that the deity is good, and when asked what they mean by "good", they will have to refer back to the deity, saying perhaps that "good" means "in accordance with the wishes of the deity". In that case, sentences such as "God is good" would be a meaningless tautology. "God is good" could mean no more than "God is in accordance with God's wishes." As we have already seen, there are ideas of what it is for something to be "good" that are not rooted in any religious belief. While religions typically encourage or instruct their followers to obey a particular ethical code, it is obvious that others who do not follow any religion can also think and act ethically.

To say that ethics is independent of religion is not to deny that theologians or other religious believers may have a role to play in bioethics. Religious traditions often have long histories of dealing with ethical dilemmas, and the accumulation of wisdom and experience that they represent can give us valuable insights into particular problems. But these insights should be subject to criticism in the way that any other proposals would be. If in the end we accept them, it is because we have judged them sound, not because they are the utterances of a pope, a rabbi, a mullah or a holy person.

Ethics is also independent of the law, in the sense that the rightness or wrongness of an act cannot be settled by its legality or illegality. Whether an act is legal or illegal may often be relevant to whether it is right or wrong, because it is arguably wrong to break the law, other things being equal. Many people have thought that this is especially so in a democracy, in which everyone has a say in making the law. Another reason why the fact that an act is illegal may be a reason against doing it is that the legality of an act may affect the consequences that are likely to flow from it. If active voluntary euthanasia is illegal, then doctors who practise it risk going to gaol, which will cause them and their families to suffer, and also mean that they will no longer be able to help other patients. This can be a powerful reason for not practising voluntary euthanasia when it is against the law, but if there is only a very small chance of the offence becoming known or being proved, then the weight of this consequentialist reason against breaking the law is reduced accordingly. Whether we have an ethical obligation to obey the law, and if so, how much weight should be given to it, is itself an issue for ethical argument.

Though ethics is independent of the law, in the sense just specified, laws are subject to evaluation from an ethical perspective. Many debates in bioethics focus on questions about what practices should be allowed – for example, should we allow embryo experimentation, or surrogate pregnancy, or cloning? – and committees set up to advise on the ethical, social and legal aspects of these questions often recommend legislation to prohibit the activity in question, or to allow it to be practised under some form of regulation. Discussing a question at the level of law and public policy, however, raises somewhat different considerations than a discussion of personal ethics, because the consequences of adopting a public policy generally have much wider ramifications than the consequences of a personal choice. That is why some health-care professionals feel justified in assisting a terminally ill patient to die, while at the same time opposing the legalization of physician-assisted suicide. Paradoxical as this position may appear – and it is certainly open to criticism – it is not straightforwardly inconsistent.

We have structured this anthology along broadly the same lines as *A Companion to Bioethics*, which we also edited for the same publisher. The *Anthology*, therefore, can serve as a set of readings to illustrate the themes that our contributors have discussed in the original essays they wrote for the *Companion*. But we did not allow the structure of the *Companion* to dictate the inclusion of readings to us, where we were unable to find a suitable selection of essays that would illuminate a topic, or where we thought that a previously covered topic should be expanded. Hence, although this anthology generally parallels the topics of the essays in the *Companion*, the match is not total.

Naturally, many of the essays we have selected reflect the times in which they were written. Since bioethics often comments on developments in fast-moving areas of medicine and the biological sciences, the factual content of articles in bioethics can become obsolete quite rapidly. But an article that has dated in regard to its facts often makes ethical points that are still valid, or worth considering, so we have not excluded older articles for this reason.

Other articles are dated in a different way. During the past few decades we have become more sensitive about the ways in which our language may exclude women, or reflect our prejudices regarding race or sexuality. We see no merit in trying to disguise past practices on such matters, so we have not excluded otherwise valuable works in bioethics on these grounds. If they are jarring to the modern reader, that may be a salutary reminder of the extent to which we all are subject to the conventions and prejudices of our times.

References

1 See Van Rensselaer Potter, *Bioethics: Bridge to the Future* (Englewood Cliffs, NJ: Prentice-Hall, 1971).

2 *The Karamazov Brothers*, trans. Ignat Avsey (Oxford: Oxford University Press, 1994), vol. I, part 2, bk 5, ch. 4. First published in 1879.

PART I

Before Birth

Abortion

1

Abortion and Health Care Ethics

John Finnis

If the unborn are human persons, the principles of justice and non-maleficence (rightly understood) prohibit every abortion; that is, every procedure or technical process carried out with the intention of killing an unborn child or terminating its development. In the first part of this chapter I argue that the only reasonable judgement is that the unborn are indeed human persons. In the second I explore the ways in which the principles of justice and non-maleficence bear on various actions and procedures which harm or may well harm the unborn. The right understanding of those principles, in the context of 'the four principles' [i.e. autonomy, beneficence, non-maleficence and justice], is sketched in an earlier chapter, 'Theology and the Four Principles: A Roman Catholic View I' but the considerations which I set out in the present chapter in no way depend on Catholic faith; they are philosophical and natural-scientific considerations valid and, in my view, properly decisive for everyone, quite independently of any religious premises.

Most People Begin at Fertilization

Leaving aside real or supposed divine, angelic and extraterrestrial beings, the one thing common to all who, in common thought and speech, are regarded as *persons* is that they are *living human individuals*. This being so, anyone who claims that some set of living, whole, bodily human individuals are not persons, and ought not to be regarded and treated as persons, must demonstrate that the ordinary notion of a person is misguided and should be replaced by a different notion. Otherwise the claim will be mere arbitrary discrimination. But no such demonstration has ever been provided, and none is in prospect.

Among the most serious attempts to provide a demonstration is Michael Tooley's argument that personhood is gradually acquired by development; it concludes that not only the unborn but also newborn babies are not persons.[1]

But Tooley's argument begs the question by simply *assuming* two basic but unargued premises: (a) that abortion is morally acceptable, and (b) that an active potentiality or capacity which is not being actually exercised cannot be the defining property of personhood even when it is a capacity really possessed by an individual.[2–4]

Some contemporary neo-Aristotelians, notably Joseph Donceel, have argued that personhood is dependent on sense organs and a brain, and that the early embryo, though a living human individual, is only a pre-personal entity which changes into a person (is 'ensouled'), not gradually but by a sudden, substantial change that occurs when the brain first begins to develop; *thereafter*, the personal soul shapes the development of the whole entity.[5] (By 'substantial change' is meant the change which occurs when an individual entity of one kind changes into an individual entity of a different kind, as typically occurs, for example, in a chemical reaction.) But Donceel's view, like its mediaeval predecessors, is inconsistent with the biological data and with itself.[3,6,7] The beginning of the brain's development does not yet provide a

From Raanan Gillon (ed.), *Principles of Health Care Ethics* (Chichester: John Wiley, 1994), pp. 547–57.

bodily basis for intellectual activities, but provides only the precursor of such a basis; so if this precursor is sufficient for 'ensoulment', there is no reason why earlier precursors should fail to suffice. In fact each embryonic human individual has from the outset a specific developmental tendency (involving a high degree of organization) which includes the epigenetic primordia of all its organs. The hypothesis of a substantial change by ensoulment at some time after the forming of the zygote is an unnecessary multiplication of entities, to be eliminated by Occam's razor, i.e. the scientific principle of economy in explanations.

The biological basis for the mediaeval view that specifically human ensoulment takes place some weeks after conception has completely disappeared. Mediaeval Aristotelians such as Thomas Aquinas depended upon the biology then current, which taught that life originates from semen and menstrual blood, that neither of these is alive, and that the very limited active instrumental power in the semen organizes the blood into a body which can begin to grow and nourish itself first in a plant-like way and then in an animal-like way. If the mediaeval Aristotelians had known about the organic life which organizes the roughly one billion items of molecular information in the one-cell conceptus with a self-directing dynamic integration that will remain continuously and identifiably identical until death, they would have concurred with the view of their successors (and almost everyone else) since the eighteenth century.[8] On this later view the fertilized human ovum is specifically human (not merely vegetable), and even the youngest human embryo already has a body which in its already specified (but quite undeveloped) capacities, its epigenetic primordia, is apt for understanding, knowing and choosing. Rather as you or I have the capacity to speak Tibetan or Icelandic, though we lack the ability to do so, so even the youngest human embryo *already* has the biological capacity appropriate to supporting specifically human operations such as self-consciousness, rationality and choice (given only time and metabolic transformations of air, water and other sustenance). The active potential which he or she already has includes the very capacities which are distinctive of persons.[9] So he or she is a human being and human person with potential, not a merely potential human person or potential human being.

The most serious contemporary effort to show that there is no lasting human *individual* (and therefore no person) until about two weeks after conception, is by Norman Ford.[10] Unlike Tooley and Donceel, Ford holds that personhood begins when an individual with a truly human nature emerges. But the conclusions of his argument are so radically opposed to any biological understanding of human development that they turn out to offer no serious alternative to the standard view: an individual with a truly human nature begins at fertilization. (For detailed analysis, refutations and bibliography, see references 3, 11–13.) Still, Ford's argument is worth tracing, because it attempts to take seriously certain claims often unreflectively uttered, such as that until implantation, or the formation of the primitive streak, or the loss of toti- or pluri-potentiality among the embryo's cells, or the end of the period during which twinning may naturally occur, the conceptus is 'not individuated'.

Ford proposes that at fertilization an ontologically individual and biologically human entity, the zygote, begins, but that (whatever biologists may think) this is never the same individual as the one which (with the same genetic constitution and gender) will begin about 16 days later and will thereafter survive as one and the same individual until death perhaps many decades later. For, according to Ford, the ontologically individual and human zygote is replaced at the first mitotic division by two ontologically individual beings, which in turn are replaced by four, the four by eight, the eight by 12 and 16, these by 32 and 64, and so forth, until by day 14 there are many thousands of ontologically entirely distinct individual human beings (even though all biologists think there is still, unless there has been twinning, only one individual human being). Then these thousands of individuals all suddenly cease to exist when God forms them into 'one living body'.

What drives Ford towards this remarkable conclusion is, on the one hand, his imagination, which finds nothing that looks human in shape until the spatial axes of future somatic development emerge around day 15, and on the other hand the classic puzzle about twinning and mosaics (hypothetical combination of two embryos into one). However, his own theory makes twinning unintelligible, since it occurs at a time, around day six or seven, when, on his view, there is not one individual to become two, but hundreds to become . . . how many? (Ford does not even try to apply his theory to the facts about twinning, facts which he has earlier treated as decisive against the standard view.)

What, then, should be said about twinning, and about the assumed possibility of human mosaics? Simply that, biologically, one always finds just individuals. If these split, or combine to form a mosaic, one then simply finds one or more different individuals. Twinning is an unusual way of being generated; the relationship between the earlier and the later generated individuals is an unusual form of parentage. Being absorbed into a mosaic would presumably be an unusual way of dying. Common thought and language has not had to categorize these events, but there is little or no intrinsic difficulty in doing so.

Nor should one here substitute one's imagination for one's reason. Domination of thought and argument by imagination and conventional associations occurs at various places in the debate. Many people, for example, allow themselves to be dominated by the assumption that no single organ can be larger than all the other organs of an animal, and/or that no major organ can be transient and disposable; they therefore refuse to take seriously the biological data and philosophical considerations which establish that the placenta is an organ of the embryo. Or again, many people (not least some theologians) argue that personhood or ensoulment cannot begin at conception, because they feel it intolerable to suppose that a high proportion of human persons never get beyond the earliest stage of existence as persons. Now that supposition may indeed challenge the imagination. But it is not intolerable to reason, for (a) in every era hitherto, *infant* mortality has been very high, often as high as the rate of pregnancy losses in modern western society; (b) many pregnancy losses are due to chromosomal defects so severe that the losses are not of human beings, but only of beings which (like hydatidiform moles) had a human genome but lacked the epigenetic primordia of a human body normal enough to be the organic basis of at least some intellectual act; and (c) as Ford himself reflects[11] (p. 181), it is presumptuous to suppose that we know how God provides for those who never have any intellectual life, and what are the limits of his provision.

Any entity which, remaining the same individual, will develop into a paradigmatic instance of a substantial kind already is an instance of that kind. The one-cell human organism originating with the substantial change which occurs upon the penetration of a human ovum by a human sperm typically develops, as one and the same individual, into a paradigmatic instance of the rational bodily person, the human person; in every such case, therefore, it is already an actual instance of the human person. In the atypical case where a *genetically* human zygote lacks the epigenetic primordia needed to develop any brain, there is no human being and so no human person, no unborn child.[14] And there is another atypical range of cases: some people, including some or all identical twins, were never activated ova, because their life began during the two or three weeks after fertilization, by others dividing or perhaps also others combining.

In all this, what is decisive is not the possession of a unique human genome, but rather the organic integration of a single, whole bodily individual organism. That organic integration, whether the developing organism has one cell or many and whether those cells are toti-potential, pluri-potential or fully specialized, is found from the inception of fertilization. On all biologically and philosophically pertinent criteria that event marks substantial change (in the sense explained above), and no subsequent development or event can be identified plausibly as a genuine substantial change. If there remain biologically and/or philosophically unresolved questions about identity (individuation) in the exceptional cases of embryos which are about to twin, this no more affects the identity of the remaining 97 per cent of embryos than the puzzles about the identity of some adult Siamese twins affect the identity of the rest of us.

Of course, our imagination balks at equating the intelligent adult with a one-cell zygote smaller than a full stop and weighing only 2 mg. But imagination also balks at differentiating between a full-term child just before and just after birth. And *reason* can find no event or principle or criterion by which to judge that the typical adult or newborn child or full-term or mid-term unborn child is anything other than one and the same individual human being – human person – as the one-cell, 46-chromosome zygote whose emergence was the beginning of the personal history of that same child and adult.

In short, science and philosophy concur in the conclusion: every living human individual must be regarded as a person.

Justice, Beneficence and Non-maleficence for Mother and Child

Every attempt to harm an innocent human person violates the principles of non-maleficence and justice, and is always wrong. Every procedure adopted with the intention of killing an unborn child, or of terminating its development, is an attempt to harm, even if it is adopted only as a means to some beneficent end (purpose) and even if it is carried out with very great reluctance and regret. Such procedures are often called 'direct abortions'. But here 'direct' does not refer to physical or temporal immediacy, but to the reasons for the procedure: whatever is chosen as an end or (however reluctantly) as a means is 'directly' willed.[15–17] What is only an unintended side-effect is 'indirectly' willed. Using this terminology, one can rightly say that 'direct abortion' is always wrong, while 'indirect abortion' is not always wrong. But it would be clearer to reserve the word 'abortion' (or 'induced abortion' or 'therapeutic abortion') for procedures adopted with the intent to kill or terminate the development of the fetus, and to call by their own proper names any therapeutic procedures which have amongst their foreseen but unintended results the termination of pregnancy and death of the fetus.

The ethics governing therapeutic procedures which impact fatally on the unborn can be summarized as follows:

1 The direct killing of the innocent – that is, killing either as an end or as a chosen means to some other end – is always gravely wrong. This moral norm excludes even the choice to kill one innocent person as a means of saving another or others, or even as a means of preventing the murder of another or others.
2 Every living human individual is equal to every other human person in respect of the right to life. Since universal propositions are true equally of every instance which falls under them, *equality in right to life* is entailed by the truth of two universal propositions: (a) every living human individual must be regarded and treated as a person, and (b) every innocent human person has the right never to be directly killed.
3 The unborn can never be considered as aggressors, still less as unjust aggressors. For the concept of aggression involves action. But it is only the very existence and the vegetative functioning of the unborn (and not its animal activities, its movements, its sensitive reactions to pain, etc., real as these are) that can give rise to problems for the life or health of the mother. So the concept of aggression extends only by metaphor to the unborn. Moreover, the unborn child, being in its natural place through no initiative and no breach of duty of its own, cannot be reasonably regarded as intruder, predator or aggressor; its relation to its mother is just that: mother and child.[18]
4 Provided that bringing about death or injury is not chosen as a means of preserving life, an action which is necessary to preserve the life of one person can be permissible even if it is certain also to bring about the death or injury of another or others.
5 Not every indirect killing is permissible; sometimes, though indirect, it is unjust, e.g. because there is a non-deadly alternative to the deadly procedure which could be used for preserving life.

A just law and a decent medical ethic forbidding the killing of the unborn cannot admit an exception 'to save the life of the mother'. Many of the laws in Christian nations used to include exactly that exception (and no others), but there are two decisive reasons why a fully just law and medical ethic cannot include a provision formulated in that sort of way. First, that sort of formulation implies that, in this case at least, killing may rightly be chosen as a means to an end. Second, by referring only to the mother, any such formulation implies that her life should *always* be preferred, which is unfair.

However, a just law and a decent medical ethic cannot delimit permissible killing by limiting its prohibition to 'direct killing' (or 'direct abortion'). For this would leave unprohibited the cases where indirect killing is unjust (e.g. because it could have been delayed until the time when the unborn child would survive the operation; or because it was done to relieve the mother of a condition which did not threaten her life).

Where the life of mother or of the unborn child is at stake, the requirements both of a decent medical ethic (including the four principles) and of just law can be expressed in the following proposition:

> If the life of either the mother or the child can be saved only by some medical procedure which will adversely affect the other, then it is permissible to undertake such a procedure with the intention of saving life, provided that the procedure is the most effective available to increase the overall probability that one or the

other (or both) will survive, i.e. to increase the *average probability* of their survival.

This proposition does not say or imply that killing as a means can be permissible. It does not give an unfair priority to either the mother or the child. It excludes any indirect killing which would be unfair.

Nevertheless, it may seem at first glance that the proposition would admit direct abortion in certain cases. For people often assume, and many Catholic theologians argue, that any procedure is direct abortion if in the process of cause and effect it *at once* or *first* brings about the damage to the unborn child.

But even amongst Catholic theologians who reject every kind of compromise with secular consequentialism and proportionalism, there are some who propose an alternative understanding of direct killing, using the framework of Thomas Aquinas's analysis of acts with two effects and of Pope Pius XII's interpretation of 'direct killing' as an action which aims at the destruction of an innocent human life either as an end or as a means.[19, 20] The directness which is in choosing a means is to be understood, according to these theologians, not by reference to immediacy or priority in the process of cause and effect, as such, but by reference to the intelligible content of a choice to do something inherently suited to bring about intended benefit.

The proposition I have set out above requires that any procedure which adversely affects the life of either the mother or the unborn child be intended *and inherently suited* to preserving life (both lives) so far as is possible. It thus falls within an acceptable understanding of Catholic teaching on direct abortion. At the same time it demands that any such procedure satisfy the requirements of justice (fairness) which are conditions for the moral permissibility of indirect abortion. The most obvious and likely application of the proposition is in cases where four conditions are satisfied: some pathology threatens the lives of both the pregnant woman and her child; it is not safe to wait, or waiting will very probably result in the death of both; there is no way to save the child; and an operation that can save the mother's life will result in the child's death. Of these cases the example most likely to be met in modern health care is that of ectopic pregnancy (assuming that the embryo cannot be successfully transplanted from the tube to the uterus).

Abortion to 'save the life of the mother' because she is threatening to commit suicide (or because her relatives are threatening to kill her) obviously falls outside the proposition and is a case of direct, impermissible killing. It is neither the only means of saving her life (guarding or restraining her or her relatives is another means), nor is it a means suited of its nature to saving life; of itself, indeed, the abortion in such a case does nothing but kill.

Rape

A woman who is the victim of rape is entitled to defend herself against the continuing effects of such an attack and to seek immediate medical assistance with a view to preventing conception.[21] (Such efforts to prevent conception are not necessarily acts of contraception, for they seek to prevent conception not *as* the coming to be of a new human life but rather *as* the invasion of her ovum as a final incident in the invasion of her body by her assailant's bodily substances.) But the possible presence of an unborn child changes the moral situation notably. Even if a procedure for terminating pregnancy were undertaken without any intention, even partly, to terminate the development and life of the unborn child, but *solely* to relieve the mother of the continued bodily effects of the rape, that procedure would be unjust to the unborn child, who is wholly innocent of the father's wrongdoing. For people are generally willing to accept, and expect their close friends and relatives to accept, grave burdens short of loss of life or moral integrity in order to avert certain death. So imposing certain or even probable death on the unborn child in these circumstances is an unfair discrimination against the child.

However, if a procedure such as the administration of the 'post-coital pill' is undertaken for the purpose only of *preventing* conception after rape but involves some *risk* of causing abortion *as a side-effect* (because it is not known at what stage of her cycle the woman is), there can be no universal judgement that the adoption of such a procedure is unjust to the unborn. For there are many legitimate activities which foreseeably cause some risk of serious or even fatal harm, a risk which in many cases is rightly accepted by upright and informed people as a possible side-effect of their choices to engage in those activities.[22, 23]

Prenatal Screening and Genetic Counselling

Examinations and tests done with the intention of, if need be, treating the unborn or preparing for a safe pregnancy and delivery are desirable and right when undertaken on the same criteria as other medical procedures. Examinations and tests done to allay anxiety or curiosity are justifiable only if they involve no significant risk to the child. But anyone who does or accepts a test or examination with the thought of perhaps suggesting or arranging or carrying out an abortion if the results show something undesirable, is already willing, conditionally, abortion, and so is already making himself or herself into a violator of the principles of non-maleficence and justice.

Health care personnel who respect those principles have a responsibility not only to refrain from recommending or conducting tests or examinations with a view to seeing whether or not abortion is 'medically indicated', but also the responsibility of telling a woman within their care which of the various tests she may be offered by others are done only or mainly for that immoral (but widely accepted) purpose and which are done to safeguard the health of the unborn child.[24]

Participation

Anyone who commands, directs, advises, encourages, prescribes, approves, or actively defends doing something immoral is a cooperator in it if it is done and, even if it is not in the event done, has already willed it to be done and thus already participates in its immorality. So a doctor who does not perform abortions but refers pregnant women to consultant obstetricians with a view to abortion wills the immorality of abortion.

On the other hand, some people whose activity contributes to the carrying out of an immoral act need not will the accomplishment of the immoral act; their cooperation in the evil is not a participation in the immorality as such. Their cooperation is often called 'material', to distinguish it from the so-called 'formal' (intended) cooperation of those who (for whatever reason and with whatever enthusiasm or reluctance) will the successful doing of the immoral act. Formal cooperation in immoral acts is always wrong; material cooperation is not always wrong, but will be wrong if it is unfair or a needless failure to witness to the truth about the immorality or a needless giving of a bad example. So a nurse in a general hospital who is unwilling to participate in abortions but is required by the terms of her employment to prepare patients for surgical operations (cleaning, shaving, etc.) may prepare patients for abortion without ever willing the killing or harming of the unborn child; she does only whatever she does towards any morally good operation; so her co-operation can be morally permissible *if* in all the circumstances it is not unfair and a needless occasion of scandal (morally corrupting example to others). The surgeon, on the other hand, must will the harm to the unborn, since that is the point of the immoral abortion and he or she must will the operation's success; so he or she is a participant, indeed a primary participant, in immorality, even if he or she too is doing so only in order to retain employment or gain medical qualifications.[25] Hospital managers who want every patient to give written and full consent to operations must want women who come to the hospital for abortions to consent precisely to abortion; so these managers willy-nilly encourage the women's immoral willing of abortion; indeed, the managers' immoral commitment of will may well be greater than that of women whose consent is given in a state of emotional upheaval and distress.

All health care personnel have a moral right (and duty) of non-participation in wrongdoing. This right is not in essence one of 'conscientious objection', since it is founded not on the sheer fact of having made a good-faith judgement of conscience – which might be mistaken – but on the basic human duty and corresponding right not to participate in what really is a moral evil. But where the state recognizes a legal right of 'conscientious objection' to participation in abortion, health care personnel have the moral right and duty to avail themselves of that legal right wherever they would otherwise incur any kind of legal obligation or institutional responsibility to cooperate 'formally' (i.e. intentionally) in abortion. They should take the appropriate steps in good time (but even if they have culpably failed to take those steps, should still refuse all formal cooperation in any of the immoral activities now so widespread in the practice of health care).

Embryo Experimentation

What has been said above about abortion applies, of course to embryos living *in vitro* – understanding by 'embryo' any human individual from the beginning of fertilization. Any form of experimentation on or observation of an embryo which is likely to damage that embryo (or any other embryo which it might engender by twinning), or to endanger it by delaying the time of its transfer and implantation, is maleficent or unjust or both, unless the procedures are intended to benefit that individual itself. Any form of freezing or other storage done without genuine and definite prospect of a subsequent transfer, unimpaired, to the proper mother is unjust unless done as a measure to save the embryo in an unexpected emergency. Any procedure whereby embryos are brought into being with a view to selecting among them the fittest or most desirable for transfer and implantation involves a radically unjust and maleficent intention, however good its further motivations.[26–28]

Benevolence and Autonomy

The open acceptance of abortion into reputable medical practice during the past quarter of a century – an ethical and civilizational collapse of historic magnitude and far-reaching effects – creates a profound challenge for all who remain willing to adhere to the proper meaning of non-maleficence and justice. They need a proper sense of their own autonomy, as upright moral subjects who preserve and respect the truth amid a social fabric of untruths and rationalizations. They also need to retain and live out a full respect for the principle of beneficence. By refusing their participation in abortion they show beneficence to the unborn (even though these will almost certainly be killed by others); and to the mothers of the unborn (however little they appreciate it at the time); and to all whose lives are endangered by the spread of an ethos of 'ethical killing' in the name of compassion or autonomy. They retain a full responsibility for the compassionate care of pregnant women and for women whose pregnancy was terminated by abortion, no less than of women threatened by or suffering in or after miscarriage or stillbirth. They should be aware of the very real special needs and vulnerabilities of those who have had an induced abortion, even though those needs and sequelae are widely denied by those who promote abortion and produce rationalizations for doing and undergoing it.

References

1 Tooley, M. 1983. *Abortion and Infanticide*. Oxford: Clarendon Press.

2 Hurst, G. 1977. *Beginning Lives*, pp. 107–11. Oxford: Basil Blackwell/Open University.

3 Grisez, G. 1989. When do people begin? *Proceedings of the American Catholic Philosophical Association*, **63**: 27–47.

4 Atkinson G. M. 1977. Persons in the whole sense. *American Journal of Jurisprudence*, **22**: 86–117.

5 Donceel, J. F. 1970. Immediate animation and delayed hominization. *Theological Studies*, **31**: 76–105.

6 Ashley, B. 1976. A critique of the theory of delayed hominization, pp. 113–33, *in* McCarthy, D. G. and Moraczewski, A. S. (eds), *An Ethical Evaluation of Fetal Experimentation: an interdisciplinary study*. Pope John XXIII Medical-Moral Research and Education Center, St Louis, MO.

7 Gallagher, J. 1985. Is the human embryo a person? *Human Life Institute Reports*, No. 4, pp. 22–6. Human Life Research Institute, Toronto.

8 Heaney, S. J. 1992. Aquinas and the presence of the human rational soul in the early embryo. *Thomist*, **56**: 19–48.

9 Wade, F. C. 1975. Potentiality in the abortion discussion. *Review of Metaphysics*, **29**: 239–55.

10 Ford, N. M. 1988. *When did I begin?* Cambridge: Cambridge University Press.

11 Fisher, A. O. P. 1991. Individuogenesis and a recent book by Fr. Norman Ford. *Rivista di Studi sulla Persona e la Famiglia Anthropotes*, no. 2: 199–244.

12 Fisher, A. 1991. 'When did I begin?' revisited. *Linacre Quarterly*, August, pp. 59–68.

13 Tonti-Filippini, N. 1989. A critical note. *Linacre Quarterly*, **56**: 36–50.

14 Suarez, A. 1990. Hydatidiform moles and teratomas confirm the human identity of the preimplantation embryo. *Journal of Medicine and Philosophy*, **15**: 627–35.

15 Pius XII, Pope. 1944. Address of 12 November 1944. *Discorsi & Radiomessaggi*, **6**: 191–2.

16 Congregation for the Doctrine of the Faith. 1974. *De abortu procurato*, para. 7. Declaration on

Abortion of 18 November. London: Catholic Truth Society.
17 Finnis, J. 1991. *Moral Absolutes*, pp. 40, 67–77. Washington, DC: Catholic University of America Press.
18 Finnis, J. 1973. The rights and wrongs of abortion: a reply to Judith Thomson. *Philosophy and Public Affairs*, **2**: 117 at 138–43; reprinted in Dworkin, R. 1977. *The Philosophy of Law*. Oxford: Clarendon Press.
19 Zalba, M. 1977. 'Nihil prohibet unius actus esse duos effectus' (Summa theologica 2–2, q.64, a.7) Numquid applicari potest principium in abortu therapeutico? Atti del Congresso Internazionale (Roma-Napoli, 17/24 Aprile 1974), *Tommaso d'Aquino nel suo Settimo Centenario*, vol. 5, *L'Agire Morale*, pp. 557–68, esp. 567–8. Naples: Edizioni Domenicane Italiane.
20 Grisez, G. and Boyle, J. M. 1979. *Life and Death with Liberty and Justice*, pp. 404–7. South Bend, IN, and London: Notre Dame University Press.
21 Catholic Archbishops of Great Britain. 1980. *Abortion and the Right to Live*, para. 21. London: Catholic Truth Society.
22 Catholic Bishops' Joint Committee on Bio-ethical Issues. 1986. The morning-after pill: some practical and moral questions about post-coital 'contraception'. *Briefing*, **16**: 33–9.
23 Catholic Bishops' Joint Committee on Bio-ethical Issues. 1986. The morning-after pill–a reply. *Briefing*, **16**: 254–5.
24 Sutton, A. 1990. *Prenatal Diagnosis: Confronting the Ethical Issues*, pp. 1–188. London: Linacre Centre.
25 Grisez, G. 1984. *Christian Moral Principles*, pp. 300–3. Chicago, IL: Franciscan Herald Press.
26 Fisher, A., O. P. 1989. *IVF: The Critical Issues*. Melbourne: Collins Dove.
27 Catholic Bishops' Joint Committee on Bioethical Issues. 1983. *In Vitro Fertilisation: Morality and Public Policy*, part II. Abingdon: Joint Committee on Bioethical Issues.
28 Congregation for the Doctrine of the Faith. 1987. *Donum Vitae. Instruction on respect for human life in its origin and the dignity of procreation*. London: Catholic Truth Society.

2

Abortion and Infanticide[1]

Michael Tooley

This essay deals with the question of the morality of abortion and infanticide. The fundamental ethical objection traditionally advanced against these practices rests on the contention that human fetuses and infants have a right to life. It is this claim which will be the focus of attention here. The basic issue to be discussed, then, is what properties a thing must possess in order to have a serious right to life. My approach will be to set out and defend a basic moral principle specifying a condition an organism must satisfy if it is to have a serious right to life. It will be seen that this condition is not satisfied by human fetuses and infants, and thus that they do not have a right to life. So unless there are other substantial objections to abortion and infanticide, one is forced to conclude that these practices are morally acceptable ones. In contrast, it may turn out that our treatment of adult members of other species – cats, dogs, polar bears – is morally indefensible. For it is quite possible that such animals do possess properties that endow them with a right to life.

I Abortion and Infanticide

One reason the question of the morality of infanticide is worth examining is that it seems very difficult to formulate a completely satisfactory liberal position on abortion without coming to grips with the infanticide issue. The problem the liberal encounters is essentially that of specifying a cutoff point which is not arbitrary: at what stage in the development of a human being does it cease to be morally permissible to destroy it? It is important to be clear about the difficulty here. The conservative's objection is not that since there is a continuous line of development from a zygote to a newborn baby, one must conclude that if it is seriously wrong to destroy a newborn baby it is also seriously wrong to destroy a zygote or any intermediate stage in the development of a human being. His point is rather that if one says it is wrong to destroy a newborn baby but not a zygote or some intermediate stage in the development of a human being, one should be prepared to point to a *morally relevant* difference between a newborn baby and the earlier stage in the development of a human being.

Precisely the same difficulty can, of course, be raised for a person who holds that infanticide is morally permissible. The conservative will ask what morally relevant differences there are between an adult human being and a newborn baby. What makes it morally permissible to destroy a baby, but wrong to kill an adult? So the challenge remains. But I will argue that in this case there is an extremely plausible answer.

Reflecting on the morality of infanticide forces one to face up to this challenge. In the case of abortion a number of events – quickening or viability, for instance – might be taken as cutoff points, and it is easy to overlook the fact that none of these events involves any morally significant change in the developing human. In contrast, if one is going to defend infanticide, one has to get very clear

From Philosophy & Public Affairs, vol. 2, no. 1 (1972), pp. 37–65.

about what makes something a person, what gives something a right to life.

One of the interesting ways in which the abortion issue differs from most other moral issues is that the plausible positions on abortion appear to be extreme positions. For if a human fetus is a person, one is inclined to say that, in general, one would be justified in killing it only to save the life of the mother.[2] Such is the extreme conservative position.[3] On the other hand, if the fetus is not a person, how can it be seriously wrong to destroy it? Why would one need to point to special circumstances to justify such action? The upshot is that there is no room for a moderate position on the issue of abortion such as one finds, for example, in the Model Penal Code recommendations.[4]

Aside from the light it may shed on the abortion question, the issue of infanticide is both interesting and important in its own right. The theoretical interest has been mentioned: it forces one to face up to the question of what makes something a person. The practical importance need not be labored. Most people would prefer to raise children who do not suffer from gross deformities or from severe physical, emotional, or intellectual handicaps. If it could be shown that there is no moral objection to infanticide the happiness of society could be significantly and justifiably increased.

Infanticide is also of interest because of the strong emotions it arouses. The typical reaction to infanticide is like the reaction to incest or cannibalism, or the reaction of previous generations to masturbation or oral sex. The response, rather than appealing to carefully formulated moral principles, is primarily visceral. When philosophers themselves respond in this way, offering no arguments, and dismissing infanticide out of hand it is reasonable to suspect that one is dealing with a taboo rather than with a rational prohibition.[5] I shall attempt to show that this is in fact the case.

II Terminology: "Person" versus "Human Being"

How is the term "person" to be interpreted? I shall treat the concept of a person as a purely moral concept, free of all descriptive content. Specifically, in my usage the sentence "X is a person" will be synonymous with the sentence "X has a (serious) moral right to life."

This usage diverges slightly from what is perhaps the more common way of interpreting the term "person" when it is employed as a purely moral term, where to say that X is a person is to say that X has rights. If everything that had rights had a right to life, these interpretations would be extensionally equivalent. But I am inclined to think that it does not follow from acceptable moral principles that whatever has any rights at all has a right to life. My reason is this. Given the choice between being killed and being tortured for an hour, most adult humans would surely choose the latter. So it seems plausible to say it is worse to kill an adult human being than it is to torture him for an hour. In contrast, it seems to me that while it is not seriously wrong to kill a newborn kitten, it is seriously wrong to torture one for an hour. This *suggests* that newborn kittens may have a right not to be tortured without having a serious right to life. For it seems to be true that an individual has a right to something whenever it is the case that, if he wants that thing, it would be wrong for others to deprive him of it. Then if it is wrong to inflict a certain sensation upon a kitten if it doesn't want to experience that sensation, it will follow that the kitten has a right not to have sensation inflicted upon it.[6] I shall return to this example later. My point here is merely that it provides some reason for holding that it does not follow from acceptable moral principles that if something has any rights at all, it has a serious right to life.

There has been a tendency in recent discussions of abortion to use expressions such as "person" and "human being" interchangeably. B. A. Brody, for example, refers to the difficulty of determining "whether destroying the foetus constitutes the taking of a human life," and suggests it is very plausible that "the taking of a human life is an action that has bad consequences for him whose life is being taken."[7] When Brody refers to something as a human life he apparently construes this as entailing that the thing is a person. For if every living organism belonging to the species *Homo sapiens* counted as a human life, there would be no difficulty in determining whether a fetus inside a human mother was a human life.

The same tendency is found in Judith Jarvis Thomson's article, which opens with the statement: "Most opposition to abortion relies on the premise that the fetus is a human being, a person, from the moment of conception."[8] The same is true of Roger Wertheimer, who explicitly says: "First off I should note that the expressions 'a human life,' 'a human being,' 'a person' are virtually interchangeable in this context."[9]

The tendency to use expressions like "person" and "human being" interchangeably is an unfortunate one. For one thing, it tends to lend covert support to antiabortionist positions. Given such usage, one who holds a liberal view of abortion is put in the position of maintaining that fetuses, at least up to a certain point, are not human beings. Even philosophers are led astray by this usage. Thus Wertheimer says that "except for monstrosities, every member of our species is indubitably a person, a human being, at the very latest at birth."[10] Is it really *indubitable* that newborn babies are persons? Surely this is a wild contention. Wertheimer is falling prey to the confusion naturally engendered by the practice of using "person" and "human being" interchangeably. Another example of this is provided by Thomson: "I am inclined to think also that we shall probably have to agree that the fetus has already become a human person well before birth. Indeed, it comes as a surprise when one first learns how early in its life it begins to acquire human characteristics. By the tenth week, for example, it already has a face, arms and legs, fingers and toes; it has internal organs, and brain activity is detectable."[11] But what do such physiological characteristics have to do with the question of whether the organism is a person? Thomson, partly, I think, because of the unfortunate use of terminology, does not even raise this question. As a result she virtually takes it for granted that there are some cases in which abortion is "positively indecent."[12]

There is a second reason why using "person" and "human being" interchangeably is unhappy philosophically. If one says that the dispute between pro- and anti-abortionists centers on whether the fetus is a human, it is natural to conclude that it is essentially a disagreement about certain facts, a disagreement about what properties a fetus possesses. Thus Wertheimer says that "if one insists on using the raggy fact-value distinction, then one ought to say that the dispute is over a matter of fact in the sense in which it is a fact that the Negro slaves were human beings."[13] I shall argue that the two cases are not parallel, and that in the case of abortion what is primarily at stake is what moral principles one should accept. If one says that the central issue between conservatives and liberals in the abortion question is whether the fetus is a person, it is clear that the dispute may be either about what properties a thing must have in order to be a person, in order to have a right to life – a moral question – or about whether a fetus at a given stage of development as a matter of fact possesses the properties in question. The temptation to suppose that the disagreement must be a factual one is removed.

It should now be clear why the common practice of using expressions such as "person" and "human being" interchangeably in discussions of abortion is unfortunate. It would perhaps be best to avoid the term "human" altogether, employing instead some expression that is more naturally interpreted as referring to a certain type of biological organism characterized in physiological terms, such as "member of the species *Homo sapiens*." My own approach will be to use the term "human" only in contexts where it is not philosophically dangerous.

III The Basic Issue: When is a Member of the Species *Homo sapiens* a Person?

Settling the issue of the morality of abortion and infanticide will involve answering the following questions: What properties must something have to be a person, i.e., to have a serious right to life? At what point in the development of a member of the species *Homo sapiens* does the organism possess the properties that make it a person? The first question raises a moral issue. To answer it is to decide what basic[14] moral principles involving the ascription of a right to life one ought to accept. The second question raises a purely factual issue, since the properties in question are properties of a purely descriptive sort.

Some writers seem quite pessimistic about the possibility of resolving the question of the morality of abortion. Indeed, some have gone so far as to suggest that the question of whether the fetus is a person is in principle unanswerable: "we seem to be stuck with the indeterminateness of the fetus' humanity."[15] An understanding of some of the sources of this pessimism will, I think, help us to tackle the problem. Let us begin by considering the similarity a number of people have noted between the issue of abortion and the issue of Negro slavery. The question here is why it should be more difficult to decide whether abortion and infanticide are acceptable than it was to decide whether slavery was acceptable. The answer seems to be that in the case of slavery there are moral principles of a quite uncontroversial sort that settle the issue. Thus most people would agree to some such principle as the following: No organism that has experiences, that is capable of thought and of using language, and that has harmed no one, should be made a slave. In the case of abortion, on the other hand, conditions that are generally agreed to be sufficient grounds for ascribing a right to life to something do not suffice to settle the issue. It is easy to specify other, purportedly sufficient conditions that will settle the issue, but no one has been successful in putting forward considerations that will convince others to accept those additional moral principles.

I do not share the general pessimism about the possibility of resolving the issue of abortion and infanticide because I believe it is possible to point to a very plausible moral principle dealing with the question of *necessary* conditions for something's having a right to life, where the conditions in question will provide an answer to the question of the permissibility of abortion and infanticide.

There is a second cause of pessimism that should be noted before proceeding. It is tied up with the fact that the development of an organism is one of gradual and continuous change. Given this continuity, how is one to draw a line at one point and declare it permissible to destroy a member of *Homo sapiens* up to, but not beyond, that point? Won't there be an arbitrariness about any point that is chosen? I will return to this worry shortly. It does not present a serious difficulty once the basic moral principles relevant to the ascription of a right to life to an individual are established.

Let us turn now to the first and most fundamental question: What properties must something have in order to be a person, i.e., to have a serious right to life? The claim I wish to defend is this: An organism possesses a serious right to life only if it possesses the concept of a self as a continuing subject of experiences and other mental states, and believes that it is itself such a continuing entity.

My basic argument in support of this claim, which I will call the self-consciousness requirement, will be clearest, I think, if I first offer a simplified version of the argument, and then consider a modification that seems desirable. The simplified version of my argument is this. To ascribe a right to an individual is to assert something about the prima facie obligations of other individuals to act, or to refrain from acting, in certain ways. However, the obligations in question are conditional ones, being dependent upon the existence of certain desires of the individual to whom the right is ascribed. Thus if an individual asks one to destroy something to which he has a right, one does not violate his right to that thing if one proceeds to destroy it. This suggests the following analysis: "A has a right to X" is roughly synonymous with "If A desires X, then others are under a prima facie obligation to refrain from actions that would deprive him of it."[16]

Although this analysis is initially plausible, there are reasons for thinking it not entirely correct. I will consider these later. Even here, however, some expansion is necessary, since there are features of the concept of a right that are important in the present context, and that ought to be dealt with more explicitly. In particular, it seems to be a conceptual truth that things that lack consciousness, such as ordinary machines, cannot have rights. Does this conceptual truth follow from the above analysis of the concept of a right? The answer depends on how the term "desire" is interpreted. If one adopts a completely behavioristic interpretation of "desire," so that a machine that searches for an electrical outlet in order to get its batteries recharged is described as having a desire to be recharged, then it will not follow from this analysis that objects that lack consciousness cannot have rights. On the other hand, if "desire" is interpreted in such a way that desires are states necessarily standing in some sort of relationship to states of consciousness, it will follow from the analysis that a machine that is not capable of being conscious, and consequently of having desires, cannot have any rights. I think those who defend analyses of the concept of a right along the lines of this one do have in mind an interpretation of the term "desire" that involves reference to something more than behavioral dispositions. However, rather than relying on this, it seems preferable to make such an interpretation explicit. The following analysis is a natural way of doing that: "A has a right to X" is roughly synonymous with "A is the sort of thing that is a subject of experiences and other mental states, A is capable of desiring X, and if A does desire X, then others are under a prima facie obligation to refrain from actions that would deprive him of it."

The next step in the argument is basically a matter of applying this analysis to the concept of a right to life. Unfortunately the expression "right to life" is not entirely a happy one, since it suggests that the right in question concerns the continued existence of a biological organism. That this is incorrect can be brought out by considering possible ways of violating an individual's right to life. Suppose, for example, that by some technology of the future the brain of an adult human were to be completely reprogrammed, so that the organism wound up with memories (or rather, apparent memories), beliefs, attitudes, and personality traits completely different from those associated with it before it was subjected to reprogramming. In such a case one would surely say that an individual had been destroyed, that an adult human's right to life had been violated, even though no biological organism had been killed. This example shows that the expression "right to life" is misleading, since what one is really concerned about is not just the continued existence of a biological organism, but the right of a subject of experiences and other mental states to continue to exist.

Given this more precise description of the right with which we are here concerned, we are now in a position to apply the analysis of the concept of a right stated above. When we do so we find that the statement "A has a right to continue to exist as a subject of experiences and other mental states" is roughly synonymous with the statement "A is a subject of experiences and other mental states, A is capable of desiring to continue to exist as a subject of experiences and other mental states, and if A does desire to continue to exist as such an entity, then others are under a prima facie obligation not to prevent him from doing so."

The final stage in the argument is simply a matter of asking what must be the case if something is to be capable of having a desire to continue existing as a subject of experiences and other mental states. The basic point here is that the desires a thing can have are limited by the concepts it possesses. For the fundamental way of describing a given desire is as a desire that a certain proposition be true.[17] Then, since one cannot desire that a certain proposition be true unless one understands it, and since one cannot understand it without possessing the concepts involved in it, it follows that the desires one can have are limited by the concepts one possesses. Applying this to the present case results in the conclusion that an entity cannot be the sort of thing that can desire that a subject of experiences and other mental states exist unless it possesses the concept of such a subject. Moreover, an entity cannot desire that it itself *continue* existing as a subject of experiences and other mental states unless it believes that it is now such a subject. This completes the justification of the claim that it is a necessary condition of something's having a serious right to life that it possess the concept of a self as a continuing subject of experiences, and that it believe that it is itself such an entity.

Let us now consider a modification in the above argument that seems desirable. This modification concerns the crucial conceptual claim advanced about the relationship between ascription of rights and ascription of the corresponding desires. Certain situations suggest that there may be exceptions to the claim that if a person doesn't desire something, one cannot violate his right to it. There are three types of situations that call this claim into question: (i) situations in which an individual's desires reflect a state of emotional disturbance; (ii) situations in which a previously conscious individual is temporarily unconscious; (iii) situations in which an individual's desires have been distorted by conditioning or by indoctrination.

As an example of the first, consider a case in which an adult human falls into a state of depression which his psychiatrist recognizes as temporary. While in the state he tells people he wishes he were dead. His psychiatrist, accepting the view that there can be no violation of an individual's right to life unless the individual has a desire to live, decides to let his patient have his way and kills him. Or consider a related case in which one person gives another a drug that produces a state of temporary depression; the recipient expresses a wish that he were dead. The person who administered the drug then kills him. Doesn't one want to say in both these cases that the agent did something seriously wrong in killing the other person? And isn't the reason the action was seriously wrong in each case the fact that it violated the individual's right to life? If so, the right to life cannot be linked with a desire to live in the way claimed above.

The second set of situations are ones in which an individual is unconscious for some reason – that is, he is sleeping, or drugged, or in a temporary coma. Does an individual in such a state have any desires? People do sometimes say that an unconscious individual wants something, but it might be argued that if such talk is not to be simply false it must be interpreted as actually referring to the desires the individual *would* have if he were now conscious. Consequently, if the analysis of the concept of a right proposed above were correct, it would follow that one does not violate an individual's right if one takes his car, or kills him, while he is asleep.

Finally, consider situations in which an individual's desires have been distorted, either by inculcation of irrational beliefs or by direct conditioning. Thus an individual may permit someone to kill him because he has been convinced that if he allows himself to be sacrificed to the gods he will be gloriously rewarded in a life to come. Or an individual may be enslaved after first having been conditioned to desire a life of slavery. Doesn't one want to say that in the former case an individual's right to life has been violated, and in the latter his right to freedom?

Situations such as these strongly suggest that even if an individual doesn't want something, it is still possible to violate his right to it. Some modification of the earlier account of the concept of a right thus seems in order. The analysis given covers, I believe, the paradigmatic cases of violation of an individual's rights, but there are other, secondary cases where one also wants to say that someone's right has been violated which are not included.

Precisely how the revised analysis should be formulated is unclear. Here it will be sufficient merely to say that, in view of the above, an individual's right to X can be violated not only when he desires X, but also when he *would* now desire X were it not for one of the following: (i) he is in an emotionally unbalanced state; (ii) he is temporarily unconscious; (iii) he has been conditioned to desire the absence of X.

The critical point now is that, even given this extension of the conditions under which an individual's right to something can be violated, it is still true that one's right to something can be violated only when one has the conceptual capability of desiring the thing in question. For example, an individual who would now desire not to be a slave if he weren't emotionally unbalanced, or if he weren't temporarily unconscious, or if he hadn't previously been conditioned to want to be a slave, must possess the concepts involved in the desire not to be a slave. Since it is really only the conceptual capability presupposed by the desire to continue existing as a subject of experiences and other mental states, and not the desire itself, that enters into the above argument, the modification required in the account of the conditions under which an individual's rights can be violated does not undercut my defense of the self-consciousness requirement.[18]

To sum up, my argument has been that having a right to life presupposes that one is capable of desiring to continue existing as a subject of experiences and other mental states. This in turn presupposes both that one has the concept of such a continuing entity and that one believes that one is oneself such an entity. So an entity that lacks such a consciousness of itself as a continuing subject of mental states does not have a right to life.

It would be natural to ask at this point whether satisfaction of this requirement is not only necessary but also sufficient to ensure that a thing has a right to life. I am inclined to an affirmative answer. However, the issue is not urgent in the present context, since as long as the requirement is in fact a necessary one we have the basis of an adequate defense of abortion and infanticide. If an organism must satisfy some other condition before it has a serious right to life, the result will merely be that the interval during which infanticide is morally permissible may be somewhat longer. Although the point at which an organism first achieves self-consciousness and hence the capacity of desiring to continue existing as a subject of experiences and other mental states may be a theoretically incorrect cutoff point, it is at least a morally safe one: any error it involves is on the side of caution.

IV Some Critical Comments on Alternative Proposals

I now want to compare the line of demarcation I am proposing with the cutoff points traditionally advanced in discussions of abortion. My fundamental claim will be that none of these cutoff points can be defended by appeal to plausible, basic moral principles. The main suggestions as to the point past which it is seriously wrong to destroy something that will develop into an adult member of the species *Homo sapiens* are these: (a) conception; (b) the attainment of human form; (c) the achievement of the ability to move about spontaneously; (d) viability; (e) birth.[19] The corresponding moral principles suggested by these cutoff points are as follows. (1) It is seriously wrong to kill an organism, from a zygote on, that belongs to the species *Homo sapiens*. (2) It is seriously wrong to kill an organism that belongs to *Homo sapiens* and that has achieved human form. (3) It is seriously wrong to kill an organism that is a member of *Homo sapiens* and that is capable of spontaneous movement. (4) It is seriously wrong to kill an organism that belongs to *Homo sapiens* and that is capable of existing outside the womb.

(5) It is seriously wrong to kill an organism that is a member of *Homo sapiens* that is no longer in the womb.

My first comment is that it would not do *simply* to omit the reference to membership in the species *Homo sapiens* from the above principles, with the exception of principle (2). For then the principles would be applicable to animals in general, and one would be forced to conclude that it was seriously wrong to abort a cat fetus, or that it was seriously wrong to abort a motile cat fetus, and so on.

The second and crucial comment is that none of the five principles given above can plausibly be viewed as a *basic* moral principle. To accept any of them as such would be akin to accepting as a basic moral principle the proposition that it is morally permissible to enslave black members of the species *Homo sapiens* but not white members. Why should it be seriously wrong to kill an unborn member of the species *Homo sapiens* but not seriously wrong to kill an unborn kitten? Difference in species is not per se a morally relevant difference. If one holds that it is seriously wrong to kill an unborn member of the species *Homo sapiens* but not an unborn kitten, one should be prepared to point to some property that is morally significant and that is possessed by unborn members of *Homo sapiens* but not by unborn kittens. Similarly, such a property must be identified if one believes it seriously wrong to kill unborn members of *Homo sapiens* that have achieved viability but not seriously wrong to kill unborn kittens that have achieved that state.

What property might account for such a difference? That is to say, what *basic* moral principles might a person who accepts one of these five principles appeal to in support of his secondary moral judgment? Why should events such as the achievement of human form, or the achievement of the ability to move about, or the achievement of viability, or birth serve to endow something with a right to life? What the liberal must do is to show that these events involve changes, or are associated with changes, that are morally relevant.

Let us now consider reasons why the events involved in cutoff points (b) through (e) are not morally relevant, beginning with the last two: viability and birth. The fact that an organism is not physiologically dependent upon another organism, or is capable of such physiological independence, is surely irrelevant to whether the organism has a right to life. In defense of this contention, consider a speculative case where a fetus is able to learn a language while in the womb. One would surely not say that the fetus had no right to life until it emerged from the womb, or until it was capable of existing outside the womb. A less speculative example is the case of Siamese twins who have learned to speak. One doesn't want to say that since one of the twins would die were the two to be separated, it therefore has no right to life. Consequently it seems difficult to disagree with the conservative's claim that an organism which lacks a right to life before birth or before becoming viable cannot acquire this right immediately upon birth or upon becoming viable.

This does not, however, completely rule out viability as a line of demarcation. For instead of defending viability as a cutoff point on the ground that only then does a fetus acquire a right to life, it is possible to argue rather that when one organism is physiologically dependent upon another, the former's right to life may conflict with the latter's right to use its body as it will, and moreover, that the latter's right to do what it wants with its body may often take precedence over the other organism's right to life. Thomson has defended this view: "I am arguing only that having a right to life does not guarantee having either a right to the use of or a right to be allowed continued use of another person's body – even if one needs it for life itself. So the right to life will not serve the opponents of abortion in the very simple and clear way in which they seem to have thought it would."[20] I believe that Thomson is right in contending that philosophers have been altogether too casual in assuming that if one grants the fetus a serious right to life, one must accept a conservative position on abortion.[21] I also think the only defense of viability as a cutoff point which has any hope of success at all is one based on the considerations she advances. I doubt very much, however, that this defense of abortion is ultimately tenable. I think that one can grant even stronger assumptions than those made by Thomson and still argue persuasively for a semiconservative view. What I have in mind is this. Let it be granted, for the sake of argument, that a woman's right to free her body of parasites which will inhibit her freedom of action and possibly impair her health is stronger than the parasite's right to life, and is so even if the parasite has as much right to life as an adult human. One can still argue that abortion ought not to be permitted. For if A's right is stronger than B's, and it is impossible to satisfy both, it does not follow that A's should be satisfied rather than B's. It may be possible to compensate A if his right isn't satisfied, but impossible to compensate B if his right isn't satisfied. In such a case the best thing to do may be to satisfy B's claim and to compensate A. Abortion may be a case in point. If the fetus has a right to life and the right is not satisfied, there is certainly no way the fetus can be compensated. On the other hand, if the woman's right to rid her body of harmful and annoying parasites is not satisfied, she can be compensated. Thus it would seem that the just thing to do would be to prohibit abortion, but to compensate women for the burden of carrying a parasite to term. Then, however, we are back at a (modified) conservative position.[22] Our conclusion must be that it appears unlikely there is any satisfactory defense either of viability or of birth as cutoff points.

Let us now consider the third suggested line of demarcation, the achievement of the power to move about spontaneously. It might be argued that acquiring this power is a morally relevant event on the grounds that there is a connection between the concept of an agent and the concept of a person, and being motile is an indication that a thing is an agent.[23]

It is difficult to respond to this suggestion unless it is made more specific. Given that one's interest here is in defending a certain cutoff point, it is natural to interpret the proposal as suggesting that motility is a necessary condition of an organism's having a right to life. But this won't do, because one certainly wants to ascribe a right to life to adult humans who are completely paralyzed. Maybe the suggestion is rather that motility is a sufficient condition of something's having a right to life. However, it is clear that motility alone is not sufficient, since this would imply that all animals, and also certain machines, have a right to life. Perhaps, then, the most reasonable interpretation of the claim is that motility together with some other property is a sufficient condition of something's having a right to life, where the other property will have to be a property possessed by unborn members of the species *Homo sapiens* but not by unborn members of other familiar species.

The central question, then, is what this other property is. Until one is told, it is very difficult to evaluate either the moral claim that motility together with that property is a sufficient basis for ascribing to an organism a right to life or the factual claim that a motile human fetus possesses that property while a motile fetus belonging to some other species does not. A conservative would presumably reject motility as a cutoff point by arguing that whether an organism has a right to life depends only upon its potentialities, which are of course not changed by its becoming motile. If, on the other hand, one favors a liberal view of abortion, I think that one can attack this third suggested cutoff point, in its unspecified form, only by determining what properties are necessary, or what properties sufficient, for an individual to have a right to life. Thus I would base my rejection of motility as a cutoff point on my claim, defended above, that a necessary condition of an organism's possessing a right to life is that it conceive of itself as a continuing subject of experiences and other mental states.

The second suggested cutoff point – the development of a recognizably human form – can be dismissed fairly quickly. I have already remarked that membership in a particular species is not itself a morally relevant property. For it is obvious that if we encountered other "rational animals," such as Martians, the fact that their physiological makeup was very different from our own would not be grounds for denying them a right to life.[24] Similarly, it is clear that the development of human form is not in itself a morally relevant event. Nor do there seem to be any grounds for holding that there is some other change, associated with this event, that is morally relevant. The appeal of this second cutoff point is, I think, purely emotional.

The overall conclusion seems to be that it is very difficult to defend the cutoff points traditionally advanced by those who advocate either a moderate or a liberal position on abortion. The reason is that there do not seem to be any basic moral principles one can appeal to in support of the cutoff points in question. We must now consider whether the conservative is any better off.

V Refutation of the Conservative Position

Many have felt that the conservative's position is more defensible than the liberal's because the conservative can point to the gradual and continuous development of an organism as it changes from a zygote to an adult human being. He is then in a position to argue that it is morally arbitrary for the liberal to draw a line at some point in this continuous process and to say that abortion is permissible before, but not after, that particular point. The liberal's reply would presumably be that the emphasis upon the continuity of the process is misleading. What the conservative is really doing is simply challenging the liberal to specify the properties a thing must have in order to be a person, and to show that the developing organism does acquire the properties at the point selected by the liberal. The liberal may then reply that the difficulty he has meeting this challenge should not be taken as grounds for rejecting his position. For the conservative cannot meet this challenge either; the conservative is equally unable to say what properties something must have if it is to have a right to life.

Although this rejoinder does not dispose of the conservative's argument, it is not without bite. For defenders of the view that abortion is always wrong have failed to face up to the question of the basic moral principles on which their position rests. They have been content to assert the wrongness of killing any organism, from a zygote on, if that organism is a member of the species *Homo sapiens*. But they have overlooked the point that this cannot be an acceptable *basic* moral principle, since difference in species is not in itself a morally relevant difference. The conservative can reply, however, that it is possible to defend his position – but not the liberal's – *without* getting clear about the properties a thing must possess if it is to have a right to life. The conservative's defense will rest upon the following two claims: first, that there is a property, even if one is unable to specify what it is, that (i) is possessed by adult humans, and (ii) endows any organism possessing it with a serious right to life. Second, that if there are properties which satisfy (i) and (ii) above, at least one of those properties will be such that any organism potentially possessing that property has a serious right to life even now, simply by virtue of that potentiality, where an organism possesses a property potentially if it will come to have that property in the normal course of its development. The second claim – which I shall refer to as the potentiality principle – is critical to the conservative's defense. Because of it he is able to defend his position without deciding what properties a thing must possess in order to have a right to life. It is enough to know that adult members of *Homo sapiens* do have such a right. For then one can conclude that any organism which belongs to the species *Homo sapiens*, from a zygote on, must also have a right to life by virtue of the potentiality principle.

The liberal, by contrast, cannot mount a comparable argument. He cannot defend his position without offering at least a partial answer to the question of what properties a thing must possess in order to have a right to life.

The importance of the potentiality principle, however, goes beyond the fact that it provides support for the conservative's position. If the principle is unacceptable, then so is his position. For if the conservative cannot defend the view that an organism's having certain potentialities is sufficient grounds for ascribing to it a right to life, his claim that a fetus which is a member of *Homo sapiens* has a right to life can be attacked as follows. The reason an adult member of *Homo sapiens* has a right to life, but an infant ape does not, is that there are certain psychological properties which the former possesses and the latter lacks. Now, even if one is unsure exactly what these psychological properties are, it is clear that an organism in the early stages of development from a zygote into an adult member of *Homo sapiens* does not possess these properties. One need merely compare a human fetus with an ape fetus. What mental states does the former enjoy that the latter does not? Surely it is reasonable to hold that there are no significant differences in their respective mental lives – assuming that one wishes to ascribe any mental states at all to such organisms. (Does a zygote have a mental life? Does it have experiences? Or beliefs? Or desires?) There are, of course, physiological differences, but these are not in themselves morally significant. *If* one held that potentialities were relevant to the ascription of a right to life, one could argue that the physiological differences, though not morally significant in themselves, are morally significant by virtue of their causal consequences: they will lead to later psychological differences that are morally relevant, and for this reason the physiological differences are themselves morally significant. But if the potentiality principle is not available, this line of argument cannot be used, and there will then be no differences between a human fetus and an ape fetus that the conservative can use as grounds for ascribing a serious right to life to the former but not to the latter.

It is therefore tempting to conclude that the conservative view of abortion is acceptable if and only if the potentiality principle is acceptable. But to say that the conservative position can be defended if the potentiality principle is acceptable is to assume that the argument is over once it is granted that the fetus has a right to life, and, as was noted above, Thomson has shown that there are serious grounds for questioning this assumption. In any case, the important point here is that the conservative position on abortion is acceptable *only if* the potentiality principle is sound.

One way to attack the potentiality principle is simply to argue in support of the self-consciousness requirement – the claim that only an organism that conceives of itself as a continuing subject of experiences has a right to life. For this requirement, when taken together with the claim that there is at least one property, possessed by adult humans, such that any organism possessing it has a serious right to life, entails the denial of the potentiality principle. Or at least this is so if we add the uncontroversial empirical claim that an organism that will in the normal course of events develop into an adult human does not from the very beginning of its existence possess a concept of a continuing subject of experiences together with a belief that it is itself such an entity.

I think it best, however, to scrutinize the potentiality principle itself, and not to base one's case against it simply on the self-consciousness requirement. Perhaps the first point to note is that the potentiality principle should not be confused with principles such as the following: the value of an object is related to the value of the things into which it can develop. This "valuation principle" is rather vague. There are ways of making it more precise, but we need not consider these here. Suppose now that one were to speak not of a right to life, but of the value of life. It would then be easy to make the mistake of thinking that the valuation principle was relevant to the potentiality principle – indeed, that it entailed it. But an individual's right to life is not based on the value of his life. To say that the world would be better off if it contained fewer people is not to say that it would be right to achieve such a better world by killing some of the present inhabitants. *If* having a right to life were a matter of a thing's value, then a thing's potentialities, being connected with its expected value, would clearly be relevant to the question of what rights it had. Conversely, once one realizes that a thing's rights are not a matter of its value, I think it becomes clear that an organism's potentialities are irrelevant to the question of whether it has a right to life.

But let us now turn to the task of finding a direct refutation of the potentiality principle. The basic issue is this. Is there any property J which satisfies the following conditions: (1) There is a property K such that any individual possessing property K has a right to life, and there is a scientific law L to the effect that any organism possessing property J will in the normal course of events come to possess property K at some later time. (2) Given the relationship between property J and property K just described, anything possessing property J has a right to life. (3) If property J were not related to property K in the way indicated, it would not be the case that anything possessing property J thereby had a right to life. In short, the question is whether there is a property J that bestows a right to life on an organism *only because* J stands in a certain causal relationship to a second property K, which is such that anything possessing that property *ipso facto* has a right to life.

My argument turns upon the following critical principle: Let C be a causal process that normally leads to outcome E. Let A be an action that initiates process C, and B be an action involving a minimal expenditure of energy that stops process C before outcome E occurs. Assume further that actions A and B do not have any other consequences, and that E is the only morally significant outcome of process C. Then there is no moral difference between intentionally performing action B and intentionally refraining from performing action A, assuming identical motivation in both cases. This principle, which I shall refer to as the moral symmetry principle with respect to action and inaction, would be rejected by some philosophers. They would argue that there is an important distinction to be drawn between "what we owe people in the form of aid and what we owe them in the way of non-interference,"[25] and that the latter, "negative duties," are duties that it is more serious to neglect than the former, "positive" ones. This view arises from an intuitive response to examples such as the following. Even if it is wrong not to send food to starving people in other parts of the world, it is more wrong still to kill someone. And isn't the conclusion, then, that one's obligation to refrain from killing someone is a more serious obligation than one's obligation to save lives?

I want to argue that this is not the correct conclusion. I think it is tempting to draw this conclusion if one fails to consider the motivation that is likely to be associated with the respective actions. If someone performs an action he knows will kill someone else, this will usually be grounds for concluding that he wanted to kill the person in question. In contrast, failing to help someone may indicate only apathy, laziness, selfishness, or an amoral outlook: the fact that a person knowingly allows another to die will not normally be grounds for concluding that he desired that person's death. Someone who knowingly kills another is more likely to be seriously defective from a moral point of view than someone who fails to save another's life.

If we are not to be led to false conclusions by our intuitions about certain cases, we must explicitly assume identical motivations in the two situations. Compare, for example, the following: (1) Jones sees that Smith will be killed by a bomb unless he warns him. Jones's reaction is: "How lucky, it will save me the trouble of killing Smith myself." So Jones allows Smith to be killed by the bomb, even though he could easily have warned him. (2) Jones wants Smith dead, and therefore shoots him. Is one to say there is a significant difference between the wrongness of Jones's behavior in these two cases? Surely not. This shows the mistake of drawing a distinction between positive duties and negative duties and holding that the latter impose stricter obligations than the former. The difference in our intuitions about situations that involve giving aid to others and corresponding situations that involve not interfering with others is to be explained by reference to probable differences in the motivations operating in the two situations, and not by reference to a distinction between positive and negative duties. For once it is specified that the motivation is the same in the two situations, we realize that inaction is as wrong in the one case as action is in the other.

There is another point that may be relevant. Action involves effort, while inaction usually does not. It usually does not require any effort on my part to refrain from killing someone, but saving someone's life will require an expenditure of energy. One must then ask how large a sacrifice a person is morally required to make to save the life of another. If the sacrifice of time and energy is quite large it may be that one is not morally obliged to save the life of another in that situation. Superficial reflection upon such cases might easily lead us to introduce the distinction between positive and negative duties, but again it is clear that this would be a mistake. The point is not that one has a greater duty to refrain from killing others than to perform positive actions that will save them. It is rather that positive actions require effort, and this means that in deciding what to do a person has to take into account his own right to do what he wants with his life, and not only the other person's right to life. To avoid this confusion, we should confine ourselves to comparisons between situations in which the positive action involves minimal effort.

The moral symmetry principle, as formulated above, explicitly takes these two factors into account. It applies only to pairs of situations in which the motivations are identical and the positive action involves minimal effort. Without these restrictions, the principle would be open to serious objection; with them, it seems perfectly acceptable. For the central objection to it rests on the claim that we must distinguish positive from negative duties and recognize that negative duties impose stronger obligations than positive ones. I have tried to show how this claim derives from an unsound account of our moral intuitions about certain situations.

My argument against the potentiality principle can now be stated. Suppose at some future time a chemical were to be discovered which when injected into the brain of a kitten would cause the kitten to develop into a cat possessing a brain of the sort possessed by humans, and consequently into a cat having all the psychological capabilities characteristic of adult humans. Such cats would be able to think, to use language, and so on. Now it would surely be morally indefensible in such a situation to ascribe a serious right to life to members of the species *Homo sapiens* without also ascribing it to cats that have undergone such a process of development: there would be no morally significant differences.

Secondly, it would not be seriously wrong to refrain from injecting a newborn kitten with the special chemical, and to kill it instead. The fact that one could initiate a causal process that would transform a kitten into an entity that would eventually possess properties such that anything possessing them *ipso facto* has a serious right to life does not mean that the kitten has a serious right to life even before it has been subjected to the process of injection and transformation. The possibility of transforming kittens into persons will not make it any more wrong to kill newborn kittens than it is now.

Thirdly, in view of the symmetry principle, if it is not seriously wrong to refrain from initiating such a causal process, neither is it seriously wrong to interfere with such a process. Suppose a kitten is accidentally injected with the chemical. As long as it has not yet developed those properties that in themselves endow something with a right to life, there cannot be anything wrong with interfering with the causal process and preventing the development of the properties in question. Such interference might be accomplished either by injecting the kitten with some "neutralizing" chemical or simply by killing it.

But if it is not seriously wrong to destroy an injected kitten which will naturally develop the properties that bestow a right to life, neither can it be seriously wrong to destroy a member of *Homo sapiens* which lacks such properties, but will naturally come to have them. The potentialities are the same in both cases. The only difference is that in the case of a human fetus the potentialities have been present from the beginning of the organism's development, while in the case of the kitten they have been present only from the time it was injected with the special chemical. This difference in the time at which the potentialities were acquired is a morally irrelevant difference.

It should be emphasized that I am not here assuming that a human fetus does not possess properties which in themselves, and irrespective of their causal relationships to other properties, provide grounds for ascribing a right to life to whatever possesses them. The point is merely that if it is seriously wrong to kill something, the reason cannot be that the thing will later acquire properties that in themselves provide something with a right to life.

Finally, it is reasonable to believe that there are properties possessed by adult members of *Homo sapiens* which establish their right to life, and also that any normal human fetus will come to possess those properties shared by adult humans. But it has just been shown that if it is wrong to kill a human fetus, it cannot be because of its potentialities. One is therefore forced to conclude that the conservative's potentiality principle is false.

In short, anyone who wants to defend the potentiality principle must either argue against the moral symmetry principle or hold that in a world in which kittens could be transformed into "rational animals" it would be seriously wrong to kill newborn kittens. It is hard to believe there is much to be said for the latter moral claim. Consequently one expects the conservative's rejoinder to be directed against the symmetry principle. While I have not attempted to provide a thorough defense of that principle, I have tried to show that what seems to be the most important objection to it – the one that appeals to a distinction between positive and negative duties – is based on a superficial analysis of our moral intuitions. I believe that a more thorough examination of the symmetry principle would show it to be sound. If so, we should reject the potentiality principle, and the conservative position on abortion as well.

VI Summary and Conclusions

Let us return now to my basic claim, the self-consciousness requirement: An organism possesses a serious right to life only if it possesses the concept of a self as a continuing subject of experiences and other mental states, and believes that it is itself such a continuing entity. My defense of this claim has been twofold. I have offered a direct argument in support of it, and I have tried to show that traditional conservative and liberal views on abortion and infanticide, which involve a rejection of it, are unsound. I now want to mention one final reason why my claim should be accepted. Consider the example mentioned in section II – that of killing, as opposed to torturing, newborn kittens. I suggested there that while in the case of adult humans most people would consider it worse to kill an individual than to torture him for an hour, we do not usually view the killing of a newborn kitten as morally outrageous, although we would regard someone who tortured a newborn kitten for an hour as heinously evil. I pointed out that a possible conclusion that might be drawn from this is that newborn kittens have a right not to be tortured, but do not have a serious right to life. If this is the correct conclusion, how is one to explain it? One merit of the self-consciousness requirement is that it provides an explanation of this situation. The reason a newborn kitten does not have a right to life is explained by the fact that it does not possess the concept of a self. But how is one to explain the kitten's having a right not to be tortured? The answer is that a desire not to suffer pain can be ascribed to something without assuming that it has any concept of a continuing self. For while something that lacks the concept of a self cannot desire that a self not suffer, it can desire that a given sensation not exist. The state desired – the absence of a particular sensation, or of sensations of a certain sort – can be described in a purely phenomenalistic language, and hence without the concept of a continuing self. So long as the newborn kitten possesses the relevant phenomenal concepts, it can truly be said to desire that a certain sensation not exist. So we can ascribe to it a right not to be tortured even though, since it lacks the concept of a continuing self, we cannot ascribe to it a right to life.

This completes my discussion of the basic moral principles involved in the issue of abortion and infanticide. But I want to comment upon an important factual question, namely, at what point an organism comes to possess the concept of a self as a continuing subject of experiences and other mental states, together with the belief that it is itself such a continuing entity. This is obviously a matter for detailed psychological investigation, but everyday observation makes it perfectly clear, I believe, that a newborn baby does not possess the concept of a continuing self, any more than a newborn kitten possesses such a concept. If so, infanticide during a time interval shortly after birth must be morally acceptable.

But where is the line to be drawn? What is the cutoff point? If one maintained, as some philosophers have, that an individual possesses concepts only if he can express these concepts in language, it would be a matter of everyday observation whether or not a given organism possessed the concept of a continuing self. Infanticide would then be permissible up to the time an organism learned how to use certain expressions. However, I think the claim that acquisition of concepts is dependent on acquisition of language is mistaken. For example, one wants to ascribe mental states of a conceptual sort – such as beliefs and desires – to organisms that are incapable of learning a language. This issue of prelinguistic understanding is clearly outside the scope of this discussion. My point is simply that *if* an organism can acquire concepts without thereby acquiring a way of expressing those concepts linguistically, the question of whether a given organism possesses the concept of a self as a continuing subject of experiences and other mental states, together with the belief that it is itself such a continuing entity, may be a question that requires fairly subtle experimental techniques to answer.

If this view of the matter is roughly correct, there are two worries one is left with at the level of practical moral decisions, one of which may turn out to be deeply disturbing. The lesser worry is where the line is to be drawn in the case of infanticide. It is not troubling because there is no serious need to know the exact point at which a human infant acquires a right to life. For in the vast majority of cases in which infanticide is desirable, its desirability will be apparent within a short time after birth. Since it is virtually certain that an infant at such a stage of its development does not possess the concept of a continuing self, and thus does not possess a serious right to life, there is excellent reason to believe that infanticide is morally permissible in most cases where it is otherwise desirable. The practical moral problem can thus be satisfactorily handled by choosing some period of time, such as a week after birth, as the interval during which infanticide will be permitted. This interval could then be modified once psychologists have established the point at which a human organism comes to believe that it is a continuing subject of experiences and other mental states.

The troubling worry is whether adult animals belonging to species other than *Homo sapiens* may not also possess a serious right to life. For once one says that an organism can possess the concept of a continuing self, together with the belief that it is itself such an entity, without having any way of expressing that concept and that belief linguistically, one has to face up to the question of whether animals may not possess properties that bestow a serious right to life upon them. The suggestion itself is a familiar one, and one that most of us are accustomed to dismiss very casually. The line of thought advanced here suggests that this attitude may turn out to be tragically mistaken. Once one reflects upon the question of the *basic* moral principles involved in the ascription of a right to life to organisms, one may find himself driven to conclude that our everyday treatment of animals is morally indefensible, and that we are in fact murdering innocent persons.

Notes

1 I am grateful to a number of people, particularly the editors of *Philosophy & Public Affairs*, Rodelia Hapke and Walter Kaufmann, for their helpful comments. It should not, of course, be inferred that they share the views expressed in this paper.

2 Judith Jarvis Thomson, in her article "A Defense of Abortion," *Philosophy & Public Affairs*, I, no. I (Fall

1971): 47–66, has argued with great force and ingenuity that this conclusion is mistaken. I will comment on her argument later in this paper.

3 While this is the position conservatives tend to hold, it is not clear that it is the position they ought to hold. For if the fetus is a person it is far from clear that it is permissible to destroy it to save the mother. Two moral principles lend support to the view that it is the fetus which should live. First, other things being equal, should not one give something to a person who has had less rather than to a person who has had more? The mother has had a chance to live, while the fetus has not. The choice is thus between giving the mother more of an opportunity to enjoy life while giving the fetus none at all and giving the fetus an opportunity to enjoy life while not giving the mother a further opportunity to do so. Surely fairness requires the latter. Secondly, since the fetus has a greater life expectancy than the mother, one is in effect distributing more goods by choosing the life of the fetus over the life of the mother.

The position I am here recommending to the conservative should not be confused with the official Catholic position. The Catholic Church holds that it is seriously wrong to kill a fetus directly even if failure to do so will result in the death of *both* the mother and the fetus. This perverse value judgment is not part of the conservative's position.

4 Section 230.3 of the American Law Institute's *Model Penal Code* (Philadelphia, 1962). There is some interesting, though at time confused, discussion of the proposed code in *Model Penal Code–Tentative Draft No. 9* (Philadelphia, 1959), pp. 146–62.

5 A clear example of such an unwillingness to entertain seriously the possibility that moral judgments widely accepted in one's own society may nevertheless be incorrect is provided by Roger Wertheimer's superficial dismissal of infanticide on pages 69–70 of his article "Understanding the Abortion Argument," *Philosophy & Public Affairs*, I, no. I (Fall 1971): 67–95.

6 Compare the discussion of the concept of a right offered by Richard B. Brandt in his *Ethical Theory* (Englewood Cliffs, NJ, 1959), pp. 434–41. As Brandt points out, some philosophers have maintained that only things that can *claim* rights can have rights. I agree with Brandt's view that "inability to claim does not destroy the right" (p. 440).

7 B. A. Brody, "Abortion and the Law," *Journal of Philosophy*, LXVIII, no. 12 (17 June 1971): 357–69. See pp. 357–8.

8 Thomson, "A Defense of Abortion," p. 47.

9 Wertheimer, "Understanding the Abortion Argument," p. 69.

10 Ibid.

11 Thomson, "A Defense of Abortion," pp. 47–48.

12 *Ibid.*, p. 65.

13 Wertheimer, "Understanding the Abortion Argument," p. 78.

14 A moral principle accepted by a person is *basic for him* if and only if his acceptance of it is not dependent upon any of his (nonmoral) factual beliefs. That is, no change in his factual beliefs would cause him to abandon the principle in question.

15 Wertheimer, "Understanding the Abortion Argument," p. 88.

16 Again, compare the analysis defended by Brandt in *Ethical Theory*, pp. 434–41.

17 In everyday life one often speaks of desiring things, such as an apple or a newspaper. Such talk is elliptical, the context together with one's ordinary beliefs serving to make it clear that one wants to eat the apple and read the newspaper. To say that what one desires is that a certain proposition be true should not be construed as involving any particular ontological commitment. The point is merely that it is sentences such as "John wants it to be the case that he is eating an apple in the next few minutes" that provide a completely explicit description of a person's desires. If one fails to use such sentences one can be badly misled about what concepts are presupposed by a particular desire.

18 There are, however, situations other than those discussed here which might seem to count against the claim that a person cannot have a right unless he is conceptually capable of having the corresponding desire. Can't a young child, for example, have a right to an estate, even though he may not be conceptually capable of wanting the estate? It is clear that such situations have to be carefully considered if one is to arrive at a satisfactory account of the concept of a right. My inclination is to say that the correct description is not that the child now has a right to the estate, but that he will come to have such a right when he is mature, and that in the meantime no one else has a right to the estate. My reason for saying that the child does not now have a right to the estate is that he cannot now do things with the estate, such as selling it or giving it away that he will be able to do later on.

19 Another frequent suggestion as to the cutoff point not listed here is quickening. I omit it because it seems clear that if abortion after quickening is wrong, its wrongness must be tied up with the motility of the fetus, not with the mother's awareness of the fetus' ability to move about.

20 Thomson, "A Defense of Abortion," p. 56.

21 A good example of a failure to probe this issue is provided by Brody's "Abortion and the Law."

22 Admittedly the modification is a substantial one, since given a society that refused to compensate women, a woman who had an abortion would not be doing anything wrong.

23 Compare Wertheimer's remarks, "Understanding the Abortion Argument," p. 79.

24 This requires qualification. If their central nervous systems were radically different from ours, it might be thought that one would not be justified in ascribing to them mental states of an experiential sort. And then, since it seems to be a conceptual truth that only things having experiential states can have rights, one would be forced to conclude that one was not justified in ascribing any rights to them.

25 Philippa Foot, "The Problem of Abortion and the Doctrine of the Double Effect," *Oxford Review*, 5 (1967): 5–15. See the discussion on pp. IIff.

3

A Defense of Abortion[1]

Judith Jarvis Thomson

Most opposition to abortion relies on the premise that the fetus is a human being, a person, from the moment of conception. The premise is argued for, but, as I think, not well. Take, for example, the most common argument. We are asked to notice that the development of a human being from conception through birth into childhood is continuous; then it is said that to draw a line, to choose a point in this development and say "before this point the thing is not a person, after this point it is a person" is to make an arbitrary choice, a choice for which in the nature of things no good reason can be given. It is concluded that the fetus is, or anyway that we had better say it is, a person from the moment of conception. But this conclusion does not follow. Similar things might be said about the development of an acorn into an oak tree, and it does not follow that acorns are oak trees, or that we had better say they are. Arguments of this form are sometimes called "slippery slope arguments" – the phrase is perhaps self-explanatory – and it is dismaying that opponents of abortion rely on them so heavily and uncritically.

I am inclined to agree, however, that the prospects for "drawing a line" in the development of the fetus look dim. I am inclined to think also that we shall probably have to agree that the fetus has already become a human person well before birth. Indeed, it comes as a surprise when one first learns how early in its life it begins to acquire human characteristics. By the tenth week, for example, it already has a face, arms and legs, fingers and toes; it has internal organs, and brain activity is detectable.[2] On the other hand, I think that the premise is false, that the fetus is not a person from the moment of conception. A newly fertilized ovum, a newly implanted clump of cells, is no more a person than an acorn is an oak tree. But I shall not discuss any of this. For it seems to me to be of great interest to ask what happens if, for the sake of argument, we allow the premise. How, precisely, are we supposed to get from there to the conclusion that abortion is morally impermissible? Opponents of abortion commonly spend most of their time establishing that the fetus is a person, and hardly any time explaining the step from there to the impermissibility of abortion. Perhaps they think the step too simple and obvious to require much comment. Or perhaps instead they are simply being economical in argument. Many of those who defend abortion rely on the premise that the fetus is not a person, but only a bit of tissue that will become a person at birth; and why pay out more arguments than you have to? Whatever the explanation, I suggest that the step they take is neither easy nor obvious, that it calls for closer examination than it is commonly given, and that when we do give it this closer examination we shall feel inclined to reject it.

I propose, then, that we grant that the fetus is a person from the moment of conception. How does the argument go from here? Something like this, I take it. Every person has a right to life. So the fetus has a right to life. No doubt the mother has a right to decide what shall happen in and to her body; everyone would grant that. But surely a person's

From *Philosophy & Public Affairs,* vol. 1, no. 1 (1971) pp. 47–66.

right to life is stronger and more stringent than the mother's right to decide what happens in and to her body, and so outweighs it. So the fetus may not be killed; an abortion may not be performed.

It sounds plausible. But now let me ask you to imagine this. You wake up in the morning and find yourself back to back in bed with an unconscious violinist. A famous unconscious violinist. He has been found to have a fatal kidney ailment, and the Society of Music Lovers has canvassed all the available medical records and found that you alone have the right blood type to help. They have therefore kidnapped you, and last night the violinist's circulatory system was plugged into yours, so that your kidneys can be used to extract poisons from his blood as well as your own. The director of the hospital now tells you, "Look, we're sorry the Society of Music Lovers did this to you – we would never have permitted it if we had known. But still, they did it, and the violinist now is plugged into you. To unplug you would be to kill him. But never mind, it's only for nine months. By then he will have recovered from his ailment, and can safely be unplugged from you." Is it morally incumbent on you to accede to this situation? No doubt it would be very nice of you if you did, a great kindness. But do you *have* to accede to it? What if it were not nine months, but nine years? Or longer still? What if the director of the hospital says, "Tough luck, I agree, but you've now got to stay in bed, with the violinist plugged into you, for the rest of your life. Because remember this. All persons have a right to life, and violinists are persons. Granted you have a right to decide what happens in and to your body, but a person's right to life outweighs your right to decide what happens in and to your body. So you cannot ever be unplugged from him." I imagine you would regard this as outrageous, which suggests that something really is wrong with that plausible-sounding argument I mentioned a moment ago.

In this case, of course, you were kidnapped; you didn't volunteer for the operation that plugged the violinist into your kidneys. Can those who oppose abortion on the ground I mentioned make an exception for a pregnancy due to rape? Certainly. They can say that persons have a right to life only if they didn't come into existence because of rape; or they can say that all persons have a right to life, but that some have less of a right to life than others, in particular, that those who came into existence because of rape have less. But these statements have a rather unpleasant sound. Surely the question of whether you have a right to life at all, or how much of it you have, shouldn't turn on the question of whether or not you are the product of a rape. And in fact the people who oppose abortion on the ground I mentioned do not make this distinction, and hence do not make an exception in the case of rape.

Nor do they make an exception for a case in which the mother has to spend the nine months of her pregnancy in bed. They would agree that would be a great pity, and hard on the mother; but all the same, all persons have a right to life, the fetus is a person, and so on. I suspect, in fact, that they would not make an exception for a case in which, miraculously enough, the pregnancy went on for nine years, or even the rest of the mother's life.

Some won't even make an exception for a case in which continuation of the pregnancy is likely to shorten the mother's life; they regard abortion as impermissible even to save the mother's life. Such cases are nowadays very rare, and many opponents of abortion do not accept this extreme view. All the same, it is a good place to begin: a number of points of interest come out in respect to it.

1. Let us call the view that abortion is impermissible even to save the mother's life "the extreme view." I want to suggest first that it does not issue from the argument I mentioned earlier without the addition of some fairly powerful premises. Suppose a woman has become pregnant, and now learns that she has a cardiac condition such that she will die if she carries the baby to term. What may be done for her? The fetus, being a person, has a right to life, but as the mother is a person too, so has she a right to life. Presumably they have an equal right to life. How is it supposed to come out that an abortion may not be performed? If mother and child have an equal right to life, shouldn't we perhaps flip a coin? Or should we add to the mother's right to life her right to decide what happens in and to her body, which everybody seems to be ready to grant – the sum of her rights now outweighing the fetus' right to life?

The most familiar argument here is the following. We are told that performing the abortion would be directly killing[3] the child, whereas doing nothing would not be killing the mother, but only letting her die. Moreover, in killing the child, one would be killing an innocent person, for the child has committed no crime, and is not aiming at his mother's death. And then there are a variety of ways in which this might be continued.

(1) But as directly killing an innocent person is always and absolutely impermissible, an abortion may not be performed. Or, (2) as directly killing an innocent person is murder, and murder is always and absolutely impermissible, an abortion may not be performed.[4] Or, (3) as one's duty to refrain from directly killing an innocent person is more stringent than one's duty to keep a person from dying, an abortion may not be performed. Or, (4) if one's only options are directly killing an innocent person or letting a person die, one must prefer letting the person die, and thus an abortion may not be performed.[5]

Some people seem to have thought that these are not further premises which must be added if the conclusion is to be reached, but that they follow from the very fact that an innocent person has a right to life.[6] But this seems to me to be a mistake, and perhaps the simplest way to show this is to bring out that while we must certainly grant that innocent persons have a right to life, the theses in (1) through (4) are all false. Take (2), for example. If directly killing an innocent person is murder, and thus is impermissible, then the mother's directly killing the innocent person inside her is murder, and thus is impermissible. But it cannot seriously be thought to be murder if the mother performs an abortion on herself to save her life. It cannot seriously be said that she *must* refrain, that she *must* sit passively by and wait for her death. Let us look again at the case of you and the violinist. There you are, in bed with the violinist, and the director of the hospital says to you, "It's all most distressing, and I deeply sympathize, but you see this is putting an additional strain on your kidneys, and you'll be dead within the month. But you *have* to stay where you are all the same. Because unplugging you would be directly killing an innocent violinist, and that's murder, and that's impermissible." If anything in the world is true, it is that you do not commit murder, you do not do what is impermissible, if you reach around to your back and unplug yourself from that violinist to save your life.

The main focus of attention in writings on abortion has been on what a third party may or may not do in answer to a request from a woman for an abortion. This is in a way understandable. Things being as they are, there isn't much a woman can safely do to abort herself. So the question asked is what a third party may do, and what the mother may do, if it is mentioned at all, is deduced, almost as an afterthought, from what it is concluded that third parties may do. But it seems to me that to treat the matter in this way is to refuse to grant to the mother that very status of person which is so firmly insisted on for the fetus. For we cannot simply read off what a person may do from what a third party may do. Suppose you find yourself trapped in a tiny house with a growing child. I mean a very tiny house, and a rapidly growing child – you are already up against the wall of the house and in a few minutes you'll be crushed to death. The child on the other hand won't be crushed to death; if nothing is done to stop him from growing he'll be hurt, but in the end he'll simply burst open the house and walk out a free man. Now I could well understand it if a bystander were to say, "There's nothing we can do for you. We cannot choose between your life and his, we cannot be the ones to decide who is to live, we cannot intervene." But it cannot be concluded that you too can do nothing, that you cannot attack it to save your life. However innocent the child may be, you do not have to wait passively while it crushes you to death. Perhaps a pregnant woman is vaguely felt to have the status of house, to which we don't allow the right of self-defense. But if the woman houses the child, it should be remembered that she is a person who houses it.

I should perhaps stop to say explicitly that I am not claiming that people have a right to do anything whatever to save their lives. I think, rather, that there are drastic limits to the right of self-defense. If someone threatens you with death unless you torture someone else to death, I think you have not the right, even to save your life, to do so. But the case under consideration here is very different. In our case there are only two people involved, one whose life is threatened, and one who threatens it. Both are innocent: the one who is threatened is not threatened because of any fault, the one who threatens does not threaten because of any fault. For this reason we may feel that we bystanders cannot intervene. But the person threatened can.

In sum, a woman surely can defend her life against the threat to it posed by the unborn child, even if doing so involves its death. And this shows not merely that the theses in (1) through (4) are false; it shows also that the extreme view of abortion is false, and so we need not canvass any other possible ways of arriving at it from the argument I mentioned at the outset.

2. The extreme view could of course be weakened to say that while abortion is permissible to

save the mother's life, it may not be performed by a third party, but only by the mother herself. But this cannot be right either. For what we have to keep in mind is that the mother and the unborn child are not like two tenants in a small house which has, by an unfortunate mistake, been rented to both: the mother *owns* the house. The fact that she does adds to the offensiveness of deducing that the mother can do nothing from the supposition that third parties can do nothing. But it does more than this: it casts a bright light on the supposition that third parties can do nothing. Certainly it lets us see that a third party who says "I cannot choose between you" is fooling himself if he thinks this is impartiality. If Jones has found and fastened on a certain coat, which he needs to keep him from freezing, but which Smith also needs to keep him from freezing, then it is not impartiality that says "I cannot choose between you" when Smith owns the coat. Women have said again and again "This body is *my* body!" and they have reason to feel angry, reason to feel that it has been like shouting into the wind. Smith, after all, is hardly likely to bless us if we say to him, "Of course it's your coat, anybody would grant that it is. But no one may choose between you and Jones who is to have it."

We should really ask what it is that says "no one may choose" in the face of the fact that the body that houses the child is the mother's body. It may be simply a failure to appreciate this fact. But it may be something more interesting, namely the sense that one has a right to refuse to lay hands on people, even where it would be just and fair to do so, even where justice seems to require that somebody do so. Thus justice might call for somebody to get Smith's coat back from Jones, and yet you have a right to refuse to be the one to lay hands on Jones, a right to refuse to do physical violence to him. This, I think, must be granted. But then what should be said is not "no one may choose," but only "*I* cannot choose," and indeed not even this, but "*I* will not *act*," leaving it open that somebody else can or should, and in particular that anyone in a position of authority, with the job of securing people's rights, both can and should. So this is no difficulty. I have not been arguing that any given third party must accede to the mother's request that he perform an abortion to save her life, but only that he may.

I suppose that in some views of human life the mother's body is only on loan to her, the loan not being one which gives her any prior claim to it. One who held this view might well think it impartiality to say "I cannot choose." But I shall simply ignore this possibility. My own view is that if a human being has any just, prior claim to anything at all, he has a just, prior claim to his own body. And perhaps this needn't be argued for here anyway, since, as I mentioned, the arguments against abortion we are looking at do grant that the woman has a right to decide what happens in and to her body.

But although they do grant it, I have tried to show that they do not take seriously what is done in granting it. I suggest the same thing will reappear even more clearly when we turn away from cases in which the mother's life is at stake, and attend, as I propose we now do, to the vastly more common cases in which a woman wants an abortion for some less weighty reason than preserving her own life.

3. Where the mother's life is not at stake, the argument I mentioned at the outset seems to have a much stronger pull. "Everyone has a right to life, so the unborn person has a right to life." And isn't the child's right to life weightier than anything other than the mother's own right to life, which she might put forward as ground for an abortion?

This argument treats the right to life as if it were unproblematic. It is not, and this seems to me to be precisely the source of the mistake.

For we should now, at long last, ask what it comes to, to have a right to life. In some views having a right to life includes having a right to be given at least the bare minimum one needs for continued life. But suppose that what in fact *is* the bare minimum a man needs for continued life is something he has no right at all to be given? If I am sick unto death, and the only thing that will save my life is the touch of Henry Fonda's cool hand on my fevered brow, then all the same, I have no right to be given the touch of Henry Fonda's cool hand on my fevered brow. It would be frightfully nice of him to fly in from the West Coast to provide it. It would be less nice, though no doubt well meant, if my friends flew out to the West Coast and carried Henry Fonda back with them. But I have no right at all against anybody that he should do this for me. Or again, to return to the story I told earlier, the fact that for continued life that violinist needs the continued use of your kidneys does not establish that he has a right to be given the continued use of your kidneys. He certainly has no right against you that *you* should give him continued use of your kidneys. For nobody has any right to use your kidneys unless you give him such a right; and nobody has the right against you that you shall give him this right – if you do allow him to go on using your kidneys, this is a kindness on your part, and not something he can claim from you as his due. Nor has he any right against anybody else that *they* should give him continued use of your kidneys. Certainly he had no right against the Society of Music Lovers that they should plug him into you in the first place. And if you now start to unplug yourself, having learned that you will otherwise have to spend nine years in bed with him, there is nobody in the world who must try to prevent you, in order to see to it that he is given something he has a right to be given.

Some people are rather stricter about the right to life. In their view, it does not include the right to be given anything, but amounts to, and only to, the right not to be killed by anybody. But here a related difficulty arises. If everybody is to refrain from killing that violinist, then everybody must refrain from doing a great many different sorts of things. Everybody must refrain from slitting his throat, everybody must refrain from shooting him – and everybody must refrain from unplugging you from him. But does he have a right against everybody that they shall refrain from unplugging you from him? To refrain from doing this is to allow him to continue to use your kidneys. It could be argued that he has a right against us that *we* should allow him to continue to use your kidneys. That is, while he had no right against us that we should give him the use of your kidneys, it might be argued that he anyway has a right against us that we shall not now intervene and deprive him of the use of your kidneys. I shall come back to third-party interventions later. But certainly the violinist has no right against you that *you* shall allow him to continue to use your kidneys. As I said, if you do allow him to use them, it is a kindness on your part, and not something you owe him.

The difficulty I point to here is not peculiar to the right to life. It reappears in connection with all the other natural rights; and it is something which an adequate account of rights must deal with. For present purposes it is enough just to draw attention to it. But I would stress that I am not arguing that people do not have a right to life – quite to the contrary, it seems to me that the primary control we must place on the acceptability of an account of rights is that it should turn out in that account to be a truth that all persons have a right to life. I am arguing only that having a right to life does not guarantee having either a right to be given the use of or a right to be allowed continued use of another person's body – even if one needs it for life itself. So the right to life will not serve the opponents of abortion in the very simple and clear way in which they seem to have thought it would.

4. There is another way to bring out the difficulty. In the most ordinary sort of case, to deprive someone of what he has a right to is to treat him unjustly. Suppose a boy and his small brother are jointly given a box of chocolates for Christmas. If the older boy takes the box and refuses to give his brother any of the chocolates, he is unjust to him, for the brother has been given a right to half of them. But suppose that, having learned that otherwise it means nine years in bed with that violinist, you unplug yourself from him. You surely are not being unjust to him, for you gave him no right to use your kidneys, and no one else can have given him any such right. But we have to notice that in unplugging yourself, you are killing him; and violinists, like everybody else, have a right to life, and thus in the view we were considering just now, the right not to be killed. So here you do what he supposedly has a right you shall not do, but you do not act unjustly to him in doing it.

The emendation which may be made at this point is this: the right to life consists not in the right not to be killed, but rather in the right not to be killed unjustly. This runs a risk of circularity, but never mind: it would enable us to square the fact that the violinist has a right to life with the fact that you do not act unjustly toward him in unplugging yourself, thereby killing him. For if you do not kill him unjustly, you do not violate his right to life, and so it is no wonder you do him no injustice.

But if this emendation is accepted, the gap in the argument against abortion stares us plainly in the face: it is by no means enough to show that the fetus is a person, and to remind us that all persons have a right to life – we need to be shown also that killing the fetus violates its right to life, i.e., that abortion is unjust killing. And is it?

I suppose we may take it as a datum that in a case of pregnancy due to rape the mother has not given the unborn person a right to the use of her body for food and shelter. Indeed, in what pregnancy could it be supposed that the mother has given the unborn person such a right? It is not as if there were unborn persons drifting about the world, to whom a woman who wants a child says "I invite you in."

But it might be argued that there are other ways one can have acquired a right to the use of another person's body than by having been invited to use it by that person. Suppose a woman voluntarily indulges in intercourse, knowing of the chance it will issue in pregnancy, and then she does become pregnant; is she not in part responsible for the presence, in fact the very existence, of the unborn person inside her? No doubt she did not invite it in. But doesn't her partial responsibility for its being there itself give it a right to the use of her body?[7] If so, then her aborting it would be more like the boy's taking away the chocolates, and less like your unplugging yourself from the violinist – doing so would be depriving it of what it does have a right to, and thus would be doing it an injustice.

And then, too, it might be asked whether or not she can kill it even to save her own life: If she voluntarily called it into existence, how can she now kill it, even in self-defense?

The first thing to be said about this is that it is something new. Opponents of abortion have been so concerned to make out the independence of the fetus, in order to establish that it has a right to life, just as its mother does, that they have tended to overlook the possible support they might gain from making out that the fetus is *dependent* on the mother, in order to establish that she has a special kind of responsibility for it, a responsibility that gives it rights against her which are not possessed by any independent person – such as an ailing violinist who is a stranger to her.

On the other hand, this argument would give the unborn person a right to its mother's body only if her pregnancy resulted from a voluntary act, undertaken in full knowledge of the chance a pregnancy might result from it. It would leave out entirely the unborn person whose existence is due to rape. Pending the availability of some further argument, then, we would be left with the conclusion that unborn persons whose existence is due to rape have no right to the use of their mothers' bodies, and thus that aborting them is not depriving them of anything they have a right to and hence is not unjust killing.

And we should also notice that it is not at all plain that this argument really does go even as far as it purports to. For there are cases and cases, and the details make a difference. If the room is stuffy, and I therefore open a window to air it, and a burglar climbs in, it would be absurd to say, "Ah, now he can stay, she's given him a right to the use of her house – for she is partially responsible for his presence there, having voluntarily done what enabled him to get in, in full knowledge that there are such things as burglars, and that burglars burgle." It would be still more absurd to say this if I had had bars installed outside my windows, precisely to prevent burglars from getting in, and a burglar got in only because of a defect in the bars. It remains equally absurd if we imagine it is not a burglar who climbs in, but an innocent person who blunders or falls in. Again, suppose it were like this: people-seeds drift about in the air like pollen, and if you open your windows, one may drift in and take root in your carpets or upholstery. You don't want children, so you fix up your windows with fine mesh screens, the very best you can buy. As can happen, however, and on very, very rare occasions does happen, one of the screens is defective; and a seed drifts in and takes root. Does the person-plant who now develops have a right to the use of your house? Surely not – despite the fact that you voluntarily opened your windows, you knowingly kept carpets and upholstered furniture, and you knew that screens were sometimes defective. Someone may argue that you are responsible for its rooting, that it does have a right to your house, because after all you *could* have lived out your life with bare floors and furniture, or with sealed windows and doors. But this won't do – for by the same token anyone can avoid a pregnancy due to rape by having a hysterectomy, or anyway by never leaving home without a (reliable!) army.

It seems to me that the argument we are looking at can establish at most that there are *some* cases in which the unborn person has a right to the use of its mother's body, and therefore *some* cases in which abortion is unjust killing. There is room for much discussion and argument as to precisely which, if any. But I think we should sidestep this issue and leave it open, for at any rate the argument certainly does not establish that all abortion is unjust killing.

5. There is room for yet another argument here, however. We surely must all grant that there may be cases in which it would be morally indecent to detach a person from your body at the cost of his life. Suppose you learn that what the violinist needs is not nine years of your life, but only one hour: all you need do to save his life is to spend one hour in that bed with him. Suppose also that letting him use your kidneys for that one hour would not affect your health in the slightest.

Admittedly you were kidnapped. Admittedly you did not give anyone permission to plug him into you. Nevertheless it seems to me plain you *ought* to allow him to use your kidneys for that hour – it would be indecent to refuse.

Again, suppose pregnancy lasted only an hour, and constituted no threat to life or health. And suppose that a woman becomes pregnant as a result of rape. Admittedly she did not voluntarily do anything to bring about the existence of a child. Admittedly she did nothing at all which would give the unborn person a right to the use of her body. All the same it might well be said, as in the newly emended violinist story, that she *ought* to allow it to remain for that hour – that it would be indecent in her to refuse.

Now some people are inclined to use the term "right" in such a way that it follows from the fact that you ought to allow a person to use your body for the hour he needs, that he has a right to use your body for the hour he needs, even though he has not been given that right by any person or act. They may say that it follows also that if you refuse, you act unjustly toward him. This use of the term is perhaps so common that it cannot be called wrong; nevertheless it seems to me to be an unfortunate loosening of what we would do better to keep a tight rein on. Suppose that box of chocolates I mentioned earlier had not been given to both boys jointly, but was given only to the older boy. There he sits, stolidly eating his way through the box, his small brother watching enviously. Here we are likely to say "You ought not to be so mean. You ought to give your brother some of those chocolates." My own view is that it just does not follow from the truth of this that the brother has any right to any of the chocolates. If the boy refuses to give his brother any, he is greedy, stingy, callous – but not unjust. I suppose that the people I have in mind will say it does follow that the brother has a right to some of the chocolates, and thus that the boy does act unjustly if he refuses to give his brother any. But the effect of saying this is to obscure what we should keep distinct, namely the difference between the boy's refusal in this case and the boy's refusal in the earlier case, in which the box was given to both boys jointly, and in which the small brother thus had what was from any point of view clear title to half.

A further objection to so using the term "right" that from the fact that A ought to do a thing for B, it follows that B has a right against A that A do it for him, is that it is going to make the question of whether or not a man has a right to a thing turn on how easy it is to provide him with it; and this seems not merely unfortunate, but morally unacceptable. Take the case of Henry Fonda again. I said earlier that I had no right to the touch of his cool hand on my fevered brow, even though I needed it to save my life. I said it would be frightfully nice of him to fly in from the West Coast to provide me with it, but that I had no right against him that he should do so. But suppose he isn't on the West Coast. Suppose he has only to walk across the room, place a hand briefly on my brow – and lo, my life is saved. Then surely he ought to do it, it would be indecent to refuse. Is it to be said "Ah, well, it follows that in this case she has a right to the touch of his hand on her brow, and so it would be an injustice in him to refuse"? So that I have a right to it when it is easy for him to provide it, though no right when it's hard? It's rather a shocking idea that anyone's rights should fade away and disappear as it gets harder and harder to accord them to him.

So my own view is that even though you ought to let the violinist use your kidneys for the one hour he needs, we should not conclude that he has a right to do so – we should say that if you refuse, you are, like the boy who owns all the chocolates and will give none away, self-centered and callous, indecent in fact, but not unjust. And similarly, that even supposing a case in which a woman pregnant due to rape ought to allow the unborn person to use her body for the hour he needs, we should not conclude that he has a right to do so; we should conclude that she is self-centered, callous, indecent, but not unjust, if she refuses. The complaints are no less grave; they are just different. However, there is no need to insist on this point. If anyone does wish to deduce "he has a right" from "you ought," then all the same he must surely grant that there are cases in which it is not morally required of you that you allow that violinist to use your kidneys, and in which he does not have a right to use them, and in which you do not do him an injustice if you refuse. And so also for mother and unborn child. Except in such cases as the unborn person has a right to demand it – and we were leaving open the possibility that there may be such cases – nobody is morally *required* to make large sacrifices, of health, of all other interests and concerns, of all other duties and commitments, for nine years, or even for nine months, in order to keep another person alive.

6. We have in fact to distinguish between two kinds of Samaritan: the Good Samaritan and what we might call the Minimally Decent Samaritan. The story of the Good Samaritan, you will remember, goes like this:

> A certain man went down from Jerusalem to Jericho, and fell among thieves, which stripped him of his raiment, and wounded him, and departed, leaving him half dead.
>
> And by chance there came down a certain priest that way; and when he saw him, he passed by on the other side.
>
> And likewise a Levite, when he was at the place, came and looked on him, and passed by on the other side.
>
> But a certain Samaritan, as he journeyed, came where he was; and when he saw him he had compassion on him.
>
> And went to him, and bound up his wounds, pouring in oil and wine, and set him on his own beast, and brought him to an inn, and took care of him.
>
> And on the morrow, when he departed, he took out two pence, and gave them to the host, and said unto him, "Take care of him; and whatsoever thou spendest more, when I come again, I will repay thee."
>
> (Luke 10: 30–35)

The Good Samaritan went out of his way, at some cost to himself, to help one in need of it. We are not told what the options were, that is, whether or not the priest and the Levite could have helped by doing less than the Good Samaritan did, but assuming they could have, then the fact they did nothing at all shows they were not even Minimally Decent Samaritans, not because they were not Samaritans, but because they were not even minimally decent.

These things are a matter of degree, of course, but there is a difference, and it comes out perhaps most clearly in the story of Kitty Genovese, who, as you will remember, was murdered while thirty-eight people watched or listened, and did nothing at all to help her. A Good Samaritan would have rushed out to give direct assistance against the murderer. Or perhaps we had better allow that it would have been a Splendid Samaritan who did this, on the ground that it would have involved a risk of death for himself. But the thirty-eight not only did not do this, they did not even trouble to pick up a phone to call the police. Minimally Decent Samaritanism would call for doing at least that, and their not having done it was monstrous.

After telling the story of the Good Samaritan, Jesus said "Go, and do thou likewise." Perhaps he meant that we are morally required to act as the Good Samaritan did. Perhaps he was urging people to do more than is morally required of them. At all events it seems plain that it was not morally required of any of the thirty-eight that he rush out to give direct assistance at the risk of his own life, and that it is not morally required of anyone that he give long stretches of his life – nine years or nine months – to sustaining the life of a person who has no special right (we were leaving open the possibility of this) to demand it.

Indeed, with one rather striking class of exceptions, no one in any country in the world is *legally* required to do anywhere near as much as this for anyone else. The class of exceptions is obvious. My main concern here is not the state of the law in respect to abortion, but it is worth drawing attention to the fact that in no state in this country is any man compelled by law to be even a Minimally Decent Samaritan to any person; there is no law under which charges could be brought against the thirty-eight who stood by while Kitty Genovese died. By contrast, in most states in this country women are compelled by law to be not merely Minimally Decent Samaritans, but Good Samaritans to unborn persons inside them. This doesn't by itself settle anything one way or the other, because it may well be argued that there should be laws in this country – as there are in many European countries – compelling at least Minimally Decent Samaritanism.[8] But it does show that there is a gross injustice in the existing state of the law. And it shows also that the groups currently working against liberalization of abortion laws, in fact working toward having it declared unconstitutional for a state to permit abortion, had better start working for the adoption of Good Samaritan laws generally, or earn the charge that they are acting in bad faith.

I should think, myself, that Minimally Decent Samaritan laws would be one thing, Good Samaritan laws quite another, and in fact highly improper. But we are not here concerned with the law. What we should ask is not whether anybody should be compelled by law to be a Good Samaritan, but whether we must accede to a situation in which somebody is being compelled – by nature, perhaps – to be a Good Samaritan. We have, in other words, to look now at third-party interventions. I have been arguing that no person is morally required to make large sacrifices to sustain the life of another who has no right to demand them, and this even where the sacrifices do not include life itself; we are not morally required to be Good Samaritans or anyway Very Good Samaritans to one another. But what if a man cannot extricate himself from such a situation? What if he appeals to us to extricate him? It seems to me plain that there are cases in which we can, cases in which a Good Samaritan would extricate him. There you are, you were kidnapped, and nine years in bed with that violinist lie ahead of you. You have your own life to lead. You are sorry, but you simply cannot see giving up so much of your life to the sustaining of his. You cannot extricate yourself, and ask us to do so. I should have thought that – in light of his having no right to the use of your body – it was obvious that we do not have to accede to your being forced to give up so much. We can do what you ask. There is no injustice to the violinist in our doing so.

7. Following the lead of the opponents of abortion, I have throughout been speaking of the fetus merely as a person, and what I have been asking is whether or not the argument we began with, which proceeds only from the fetus' being a person, really does establish its conclusion. I have argued that it does not.

But of course there are arguments and arguments, and it may be said that I have simply fastened on the wrong one. It may be said that what is important is not merely the fact that the fetus is a person, but that it is a person for whom the woman has a special kind of responsibility issuing from the fact that she is its mother. And it might be argued that all my analogies are therefore irrelevant – for you do not have that special kind of responsibility for that violinist, Henry Fonda does not have that special kind of responsibility for me. And our attention might be drawn to the fact that men and women both *are* compelled by law to provide support for their children.

I have in effect dealt (briefly) with this argument in section 4 above; but a (still briefer) recapitulation now may be in order. Surely we do not have any such "special responsibility" for a person unless we have assumed it, explicitly or implicitly. If a set of parents do not try to prevent pregnancy, do not obtain an abortion, and then at the time of birth of the child do not put it out for adoption, but rather take it home with them, then they have assumed responsibility for it, they have given it rights, and they cannot *now* withdraw support from it at the cost of its life because they now find it difficult to go on providing for it. But if they have taken all reasonable precautions against having a child, they do not simply by virtue of their biological relationship to the child who comes into existence have a special responsibility for it. They may wish to assume responsibility for it, or they may not wish to. And I am suggesting that if assuming responsibility for it would require large sacrifices, then they may refuse. A Good Samaritan would not refuse – or anyway, a Splendid Samaritan, if the sacrifices that had to be made were enormous. But then so would a Good Samaritan assume responsibility for that violinist; so would Henry Fonda, if he is a Good Samaritan, fly in from the West Coast and assume responsibility for me.

8. My argument will be found unsatisfactory on two counts by many of those who want to regard abortion as morally permissible. First, while I do argue that abortion is not impermissible, I do not argue that it is always permissible. There may well be cases in which carrying the child to term requires only Minimally Decent Samaritanism of the mother, and this is a standard we must not fall below. I am inclined to think it a merit of my account precisely that it does *not* give a general yes or a general no. It allows for and supports our sense that, for example, a sick and desperately frightened fourteen-year-old schoolgirl, pregnant due to rape, may of *course* choose abortion, and that any law which rules this out is an insane law. And it also allows for and supports our sense that in other cases resort to abortion is even positively indecent. It would be indecent in the woman to request an abortion, and indecent in a doctor to perform it, if she is in her seventh month, and wants the abortion just to avoid the nuisance of postponing a trip abroad. The very fact that the arguments I have been drawing attention to treat all cases of abortion, or even all cases of abortion in which the mother's life is not at stake, as morally on a par ought to have made them suspect at the outset.

Secondly, while I am arguing for the permissibility of abortion in some cases, I am not arguing for the right to secure the death of the unborn child. It is easy to confuse these two things in that up to a certain point in the life of the fetus it is not able to survive outside the mother's body; hence removing it from her body guarantees its death. But they are importantly different. I have argued that you are not morally required to spend nine months in bed, sustaining the life of that violinist; but to say this is by no means to say that if, when you unplug yourself, there is a miracle and he survives, you then have a right to turn round and slit his throat. You may detach yourself even if this costs him his life; you have no right to be guaranteed his death, by some other means, if unplugging yourself does not kill him. There are some people who will feel dissatisfied by this feature of my argument. A woman may be utterly devastated by the thought of a child, a bit of herself, put out for adoption and never seen or heard of again. She may therefore want not merely that the child be detached from her, but more, that it die. Some opponents of abortion are inclined to regard this as beneath contempt – thereby showing insensitivity to what is surely a powerful source of despair. All the same, I agree that the desire for the child's death is not one which anybody may gratify, should it turn out to be possible to detach the child alive.

At this place, however, it should be remembered that we have only been pretending throughout that the fetus is a human being from the moment of conception. A very early abortion is surely not the killing of a person, and so is not dealt with by anything I have said here.

Notes

1 I am very much indebted to James Thomson for discussion, criticism, and many helpful suggestions.

2 Daniel Callahan, *Abortion: Law, Choice and Morality* (New York, 1970), p. 373. This book gives a fascinating survey of the available information on abortion. The Jewish tradition is surveyed in David M. Feldman, *Birth Control in Jewish Law* (New York, 1968), Part 5, the Catholic tradition in John T. Noonan, Jr., "An Almost Absolute Value in History," in *The Morality of Abortion*, ed. John T. Noonan, Jr. (Cambridge, Mass., 1970).

3 The term "direct" in the arguments I refer to is a technical one. Roughly, what is meant by "direct killing" is either killing as an end in itself, or killing as a means to some end, for example, the end of saving someone else's life. See note 6, below, for an example of its use.

4 Cf. *Encyclical Letter of Pope Pius XI on Christian Marriage*, St. Paul Editions (Boston, n.d.), p. 32: "however much we may pity the mother whose health and even life is gravely imperiled in the performance of the duty allotted to her by nature, nevertheless what could ever be a sufficient reason for excusing in any way the direct murder of the innocent? This is precisely what we are dealing with here." Noonan (*The Morality of Abortion*, p. 43) reads this as follows: "What cause can ever avail to excuse in any way the direct killing of the innocent? For it is a question of that."

5 The thesis in (4) is in an interesting way weaker than those in (1), (2), and (3): they rule out abortion even in cases in which both mother *and* child will die if the abortion is not performed. By contrast, one who held the view expressed in (4) could consistently say that one needn't prefer letting two persons die to killing one.

6 Cf. the following passage from Pius XII, *Address to the Italian Catholic Society of Midwives*: "The baby in the maternal breast has the right to life immediately from God – Hence there is no man, no human authority, no science, no medical, eugenic, social, economic or moral 'indication' which can establish or grant a valid juridical ground for a direct deliberate disposition of an innocent human life, that is a disposition which looks to its destruction either as an end or as a means to another end perhaps in itself not illicit. – The baby, still not born, is a man in the same degree and for the same reason as the mother" (quoted in Noonan, *The Morality of Abortion*, p. 45).

7 The need for a discussion of this argument was brought home to me by members of the Society for Ethical and Legal Philosophy, to whom this paper was originally presented.

8 For a discussion of the difficulties involved, and a survey of the European experience with such laws, see *The Good Samaritan and the Law*, ed. James M. Ratcliffe (New York, 1966).

4

Why Abortion is Immoral

Don Marquis

The view that abortion is, with rare exceptions, seriously immoral has received little support in the recent philosophical literature. No doubt most philosophers affiliated with secular institutions of higher education believe that the anti-abortion position is either a symptom of irrational religious dogma or a conclusion generated by seriously confused philosophical argument. The purpose of this essay is to undermine this general belief. This essay sets out an argument that purports to show, as well as any argument in ethics can show, that abortion is, except possibly in rare cases, seriously immoral, that it is in the same moral category as killing an innocent adult human being.

The argument is based on a major assumption. Many of the most insightful and careful writers on the ethics of abortion – such as Joel Feinberg, Michael Tooley, Mary Anne Warren, H. Tristram Engelhardt, Jr, L. W. Sumner, John T. Noonan, Jr, and Philip Devine – believe that whether or not abortion is morally permissible stands or falls on whether or not a fetus is the sort of being whose life it is seriously wrong to end. The argument of this essay will assume, but not argue, that they are correct.

Also, this essay will neglect issues of great importance to a complete ethics of abortion. Some anti-abortionists will allow that certain abortions, such as abortion before implantation or abortion when the life of a woman is threatened by a pregnancy or abortion after rape, may be morally permissible. This essay will not explore the casuistry of these hard cases. The purpose of this essay is to develop a general argument for the claim that the overwhelming majority of deliberate abortions are seriously immoral.

From Journal of Philosophy, LXXXVI, 4 (April 1989), pp. 183–202. Reproduced by courtesy of Columbia University and the author.

I

A sketch of standard anti-abortion and pro-choice arguments exhibits how those arguments possess certain symmetries that explain why partisans of those positions are so convinced of the correctness of their own positions, why they are not successful in convincing their opponents, and why, to others, this issue seems to be unresolvable. An analysis of the nature of this standoff suggests a strategy for surmounting it.

Consider the way a typical anti-abortionist argues. She will argue or assert that life is present from the moment of conception or that fetuses look like babies or that fetuses possess a characteristic such as a genetic code that is both necessary and sufficient for being human. Anti-abortionists seem to believe that (1) the truth of all of these claims is quite obvious, and (2) establishing any of these claims is sufficient to show that abortion is morally akin to murder.

A standard pro-choice strategy exhibits similarities. The pro-choicer will argue or assert that fetuses are not persons or that fetuses are not rational agents or that fetuses are not social beings. Pro-choicers seem to believe that (1) the truth of any of these claims is quite obvious, and (2) establishing any of these claims is sufficient to show that an abortion is not a wrongful killing.

In fact, both the pro-choice and the anti-abortion claims do seem to be true, although the "it looks like a baby" claim is more difficult to establish the earlier the pregnancy. We seem to have a standoff. How can it be resolved?

As everyone who has taken a bit of logic knows, if any of these arguments concerning abortion is a good argument, it requires not only some claim characterizing fetuses, but also some general moral principle that ties a characteristic of fetuses to having or not having the right to life or to some other moral characteristic that will generate the obligation or the lack of obligation not to end the life of a fetus. Accordingly, the arguments of the anti-abortionist and the pro-choicer need a bit of filling in to be regarded as adequate.

Note what each partisan will say. The anti-abortionist will claim that her position is supported by such generally accepted moral principles as "It is always prima facie seriously wrong to take a human life" or "It is always prima facie seriously wrong to end the life of a baby." Since these are generally accepted moral principles, her position is certainly not obviously wrong. The pro-choicer will claim that her position is supported by such plausible moral principles as "Being a person is what gives an individual intrinsic moral worth" or "It is only seriously prima facie wrong to take the life of a member of the human community." Since these are generally accepted moral principles, the pro-choice position is certainly not obviously wrong. Unfortunately, we have again arrived at a standoff.

Now, how might one deal with this standoff? The standard approach is to try to show how the moral principles of one's opponent lose their plausibility under analysis. It is easy to see how this is possible. On the one hand, the anti-abortionist will defend a moral principle concerning the wrongness of killing which tends to be broad in scope in order that even fetuses at an early stage of pregnancy will fall under it. The problem with broad principles is that they often embrace too much. In this particular instance, the principle "It is always prima facie wrong to take a human life" seems to entail that it is wrong to end the existence of a living human cancer-cell culture, on the grounds that the culture is both living and human. Therefore, it seems that the anti-abortionist's favored principle is too broad.

On the other hand, the pro-choicer wants to find a moral principle concerning the wrongness of killing which tends to be narrow in scope in order that fetuses will *not* fall under it. The problem with narrow principles is that they often do not embrace enough. Hence, the needed principles such as "It is prima facie seriously wrong to kill only persons" or "It is prima facie wrong to kill only rational agents" do not explain why it is wrong to kill infants or young children or the severely retarded or even perhaps the severely mentally ill. Therefore, we seem again to have a standoff. The anti-abortionist charges, not unreasonably, that pro-choice principles concerning killing are too narrow to be acceptable; the pro-choicer charges, not unreasonably, that anti-abortionist principles concerning killing are too broad to be acceptable.

Attempts by both sides to patch up the difficulties in their positions run into further difficulties. The anti-abortionist will try to remove the problem in her position by reformulating her principle concerning killing in terms of human beings. Now we end up with: "It is always prima facie seriously wrong to end the life of a human being." This principle has the advantage of avoiding the problem of the human cancer-cell culture counterexample. But this advantage is purchased at a high price. For although it is clear that a fetus is both human and alive, it is not at all clear that a fetus is a human *being*. There is at least something to be said for the view that something becomes a human being only after a process of development, and that therefore first trimester fetuses and perhaps all fetuses are not yet human beings. Hence, the anti-abortionist, by this move, has merely exchanged one problem for another.[2]

The pro-choicer fares no better. She may attempt to find reasons why killing infants, young children, and the severely retarded is wrong which are independent of her major principle that is supposed to explain the wrongness of taking human life, but which will not also make abortion immoral. This is no easy task. Appeals to social utility will seem satisfactory only to those who resolve not to think of the enormous difficulties with a utilitarian account of the wrongness of killing and the significant social costs of preserving the lives of the unproductive.[3] A pro-choice strategy that extends the definition of "person" to infants or even to young children seems just as arbitrary as an anti-abortion strategy that extends the definition of "human being" to fetuses. Again, we find symmetries in the two positions and we arrive at a standoff.

There are even further problems that reflect symmetries in the two positions. In addition to counterexample problems, or the arbitrary application problems that can be exchanged for them, the standard anti-abortionist principle "It is prima facie seriously wrong to kill a human being," or one of its variants, can be objected to on the grounds of ambiguity. If "human being" is taken to be a *biological* category, then the anti-abortionist is left with the problem of explaining why a merely biological category should make a moral difference. Why, it is asked, is it any more reasonable to base a moral conclusion on the number of chromosomes in one's cells than on the color of one's skin?[4] If "human being", on the other hand, is taken to be a *moral* category, then the claim that a fetus is a human being cannot be taken to be a premise in the anti-abortion argument, for it is precisely what needs to be established. Hence, either the anti-abortionist's main category is a morally irrelevant, merely biological category, or it is of no use to the anti-abortionist in establishing (noncircularly, of course) that abortion is wrong.

Although this problem with the anti-abortionist position is often noticed, it is less often noticed that the pro-choice position suffers from an analogous problem. The principle "Only persons have the right to life" also suffers from an ambiguity. The term "person" is typically defined in terms of psychological characteristics, although there will certainly be disagreement concerning which characteristics are most important. Supposing that this matter can be settled, the pro-choicer is left with the problem of explaining why *psychological* characteristics should make a *moral* difference. If the pro-choicer should attempt to deal with this problem by claiming that an explanation is not necessary, that in fact we do treat such a cluster of psychological properties as having moral significance, the sharp-witted anti-abortionist should have a ready response. We do treat being both living and human as having moral significance. If it is legitimate for the pro-choicer to demand that the anti-abortionist provide an explanation of the connection between the biological character of being a human being and the wrongness of being killed (even though people accept this connection), then it is legitimate for the anti-abortionist to demand that the pro-choicer provide an explanation of the connection between psychological criteria for being a person and the wrongness of being killed (even though that connection is accepted).[5]

Feinberg has attempted to meet this objection (he calls psychological personhood "commonsense personhood"):

> The characteristics that confer commonsense personhood are not arbitrary bases for rights and duties, such as race, sex or species membership; rather they are traits that make sense out of rights and duties and without which those moral attributes would have no point or function. It is because people are conscious; have a sense of their personal identities; have plans, goals, and projects; experience emotions; are liable to pains, anxieties, and frustrations; can reason and bargain, and so on – it is because of these attributes that people have values and interests, desires and expectations of their own, including a stake in their own futures, and a personal well-being of a sort we cannot ascribe to unconscious or nonrational beings. Because of their developed capacities they can assume duties and responsibilities and can have and make claims on one another. Only because of their sense of self, their life plans, their value hierarchies, and their stakes in their own futures can they be ascribed fundamental rights. There is nothing arbitrary about these linkages. ("Abortion", p. 270)

The plausible aspects of this attempt should not be taken to obscure its implausible features. There is a great deal to be said for the view that being a psychological person under some description is a necessary condition for having duties. One cannot have a duty unless one is capable of behaving morally, and a being's capability of behaving morally will require having a certain psychology. It is far from obvious, however, that having rights entails consciousness or rationality, as Feinberg suggests. We speak of the rights of the severely retarded or the severely mentally ill, yet some of these persons are not rational. We speak of the rights of the temporarily unconscious. The New Jersey Supreme Court based their decision in the Quinlan case on Karen Ann Quinlan's right to privacy, and she was known to be permanently unconscious at that time. Hence, Feinberg's claim that having rights entails being conscious is, on its face, obviously false.

Of course, it might not make sense to attribute rights to a being that would never in its natural history have certain psychological traits. This modest connection between psychological personhood and moral personhood will create a place for Karen Ann Quinlan and the temporarily unconscious. But then it makes a place for fetuses also. Hence, it does not serve Feinberg's pro-choice purposes. Accordingly, it seems that the pro-choicer will have as much difficulty bridging the gap between psychological personhood and personhood in the moral sense as the anti-abortionist has bridging the gap between being a biological human being and being a human being in the moral sense.

Furthermore, the pro-choicer cannot any more escape her problem by making person a purely moral category than the anti-abortionist could escape by the analogous move. For if person is a moral category, then the pro-choicer is left without the resources for establishing (noncircularly, of course) the claim that a fetus is not a person, which is an essential premise in her argument. Again, we have both a symmetry and a standoff between pro-choice and anti-abortion views.

Passions in the abortion debate run high. There are both plausibilities and difficulties with the standard positions. Accordingly, it is hardly surprising that partisans of either side embrace with fervor the moral generalizations that support the conclusions they preanalytically favor, and reject with disdain the moral generalizations of their opponents as being subject to inescapable difficulties. It is easy to believe that the counterexamples to one's own moral principles are merely temporary difficulties that will dissolve in the wake of further philosophical research, and that the counterexamples to the principles of one's opponents are as straightforward as the contradiction between *A* and *O* propositions in traditional logic. This might suggest to an impartial observer (if there are any) that the abortion issue is unresolvable.

There is a way out of this apparent dialectical quandary. The moral generalizations of both sides are not quite correct. The generalizations hold for the most part, for the usual cases. This suggests that they are all *accidental* generalizations, that the moral claims made by those on both sides of the dispute do not touch on the *essence* of the matter.

This use of the distinction between essence and accident is not meant to invoke obscure metaphysical categories. Rather, it is intended to reflect the rather atheoretical nature of the abortion discussion. If the generalization a partisan in the abortion dispute adopts were derived from the reason why ending the life of a human being is wrong, then there could not be exceptions to that generalization unless some special case obtains in which there are even more powerful countervailing reasons. Such generalizations would not be merely accidental generalizations; they would point to, or be based upon, the essence of the wrongness of killing, what it is that makes killing wrong. All this suggests that a necessary condition of resolving the abortion controversy is a more theoretical account of the wrongness of killing. After all, if we merely believe, but do not understand, why killing adult human beings such as ourselves is wrong, how could we conceivably show that abortion is either immoral or permissible?

II

In order to develop such an account, we can start from the following unproblematic assumption concerning our own case: it is wrong to kill *us*. Why is it wrong? Some answers can be easily eliminated. It might be said that what makes killing us wrong is that a killing brutalizes the one who kills. But the brutalization consists of being inured to the performance of an act that is hideously immoral; hence, the brutalization does not explain the immorality. It might be said that what makes killing us wrong is the great loss others would experience due to our absence. Although such hubris is understandable, such an explanation does not account for the wrongness of killing hermits, or those whose lives are relatively independent and whose friends find it easy to make new friends.

A more obvious answer is better. What primarily makes killing wrong is neither its effect on the murderer nor its effect on the victim's friends and relatives, but its effect on the victim. The loss of one's life is one of the greatest losses one can suffer. The loss of one's life deprives one of all the experiences, activities, projects, and enjoyments that would otherwise have constituted one's future. Therefore, killing someone is wrong, primarily because the killing inflicts (one of) the greatest possible losses on the victim. To describe this as the loss of life can be misleading, however. The change in my biological state does not by itself make killing me wrong. The effect of the loss of my biological life is the loss to me of all those activities, projects, experiences, and enjoyments which would otherwise have constituted my future personal life. These activities, projects, experiences, and enjoyments are either valuable for their own sakes or are means to something else that is valuable for its own sake. Some parts of my future are not valued by me now, but will come to be valued by me as I grow older and as my values and capacities change. When I am killed, I am deprived both of what I now value which would have been part of my future personal life, but also what I would come to value. Therefore, when I die, I am deprived of all of the value of my future. Inflicting this loss on me is ultimately what makes killing me wrong. This being the case, it would seem that what makes killing *any* adult human being prima facie seriously wrong is the loss of his or her future.[6]

How should this rudimentary theory of the wrongness of killing be evaluated? It cannot be faulted for deriving an 'ought' from an 'is', for it does not. The analysis assumes that killing me (or you, reader) is prima facie seriously wrong. The point of the analysis is to establish which natural property ultimately explains the wrongness of the killing, given that it is wrong. A natural property will ultimately explain the wrongness of killing, only if (1) the explanation fits with our intuitions about the matter and (2) there is no other natural property that provides the basis for a better explanation of the wrongness of killing. This analysis rests on the intuition that what makes killing a particular human or animal wrong is what it does to that particular human or animal. What makes killing wrong is some natural effect or other of the killing. Some would deny this. For instance, a divine-command theorist in ethics would deny it. Surely this denial is, however, one of those features of divine-command theory which renders it so implausible.

The claim that what makes killing wrong is the loss of the victim's future is directly supported by two considerations. In the first place, this theory explains why we regard killing as one of the worst of crimes. Killing is especially wrong, because it deprives the victim of more than perhaps any other crime. In the second place, people with AIDS or cancer who know they are dying believe, of course, that dying is a very bad thing for them. They believe that the loss of a future to them that they would otherwise have experienced is what makes their premature death a very bad thing for them. A better theory of the wrongness of killing would require a different natural property associated with killing which better fits with the attitudes of the dying. What could it be?

The view that what makes killing wrong is the loss to the victim of the value of the victim's future gains additional support when some of its implications are examined. In the first place, it is incompatible with the view that it is wrong to kill only beings who are biologically human. It is possible that there exists a different species from another planet whose members have a future like ours. Since having a future like that is what makes killing someone wrong, this theory entails that it would be wrong to kill members of such a species. Hence, this theory is opposed to the claim that only life that is biologically human has great moral worth, a claim which many anti-abortionists have seemed to adopt. This opposition, which this theory has in common with personhood theories, seems to be a merit of the theory.

In the second place, the claim that the loss of one's future is the wrong-making feature of one's being killed entails the possibility that the futures of some actual nonhuman mammals on our own planet are sufficiently like ours that it is seriously wrong to kill them also. Whether some animals do have the same right to life as human beings depends on adding to the account of the wrongness of killing some additional account of just what it is about my future or the futures of other adult human beings which makes it wrong to kill us. No such additional account will be offered in this essay. Undoubtedly, the provision of such an account would be a very difficult matter. Undoubtedly, any such account would be quite controversial. Hence, it surely should not reflect badly on this sketch of an elementary theory of the wrongness of killing that it is indeterminate with respect to some very difficult issues regarding animal rights.

In the third place, the claim that the loss of one's future is the wrong-making feature of one's being killed does not entail, as sanctity of human life theories do, that active euthanasia is wrong. Persons who are severely and incurably ill, who face a future of pain and despair, and who wish to die will not have suffered a loss if they are killed. It is, strictly speaking, the value of a human's future which makes killing wrong in this theory. This being so, killing does not necessarily wrong some persons who are sick and dying. Of course, there may be other reasons for a prohibition of active euthanasia, but that is another matter. Sanctity-of-human-life theories seem to hold that active euthanasia is seriously wrong even in an individual case where there seems to be good reason for it independently of public policy considerations. This consequence is most implausible, and it is a plus for the claim that the loss of a future of value is what makes killing wrong that it does not share this consequence.

In the fourth place, the account of the wrongness of killing defended in this essay does straightforwardly entail that it is prima facie seriously wrong to kill children and infants, for we do presume that they have futures of value. Since we do believe that it is wrong to kill defenseless little babies, it is important that a theory of the wrongness of killing easily account for this. Personhood theories of the wrongness of killing, on the other hand, cannot straightforwardly account for the wrongness of killing infants and young children.[7] Hence, such theories must add special ad hoc accounts of the wrongness of killing the young. The plausibility of such ad hoc theories seems to be a function of how desperately one wants such theories to work. The claim that the primary wrong-making feature of a killing is the loss to the victim of the value of its future accounts for the wrongness of killing young children and infants directly; it makes the wrongness of such acts as obvious as we actually think it is. This is a further merit of this theory. Accordingly, it seems that this value of a future-like-ours theory of the wrongness of killing shares strengths of both sanctity-of-life and personhood accounts while avoiding weaknesses of both. In addition, it meshes with a central intuition concerning what makes killing wrong.

The claim that the primary wrong-making feature of a killing is the loss to the victim of the value of its future has obvious consequences for the ethics of abortion. The future of a standard fetus includes a set of experiences, projects, activities, and such which are identical with the futures of adult human beings and are identical with the futures of young children. Since the reason that is sufficient to explain why it is wrong to kill human beings after the time of birth is a reason that also applies to fetuses, it follows that abortion is prima facie seriously morally wrong.

This argument does not rely on the invalid inference that, since it is wrong to kill persons, it is wrong to kill potential persons also. The category that is morally central to this analysis is the category of having a valuable future like ours; it is not the category of personhood. The argument to the conclusion that abortion is prima facie seriously morally wrong proceeded independently of the notion of person or potential person or any equivalent. Someone may wish to start with this analysis in terms of the value of a human future, conclude that abortion is, except perhaps in rare circumstances, seriously morally wrong, infer that fetuses have the right to life, and then call fetuses "persons" as a result of their having the right to life. Clearly, in this case, the category of person is being used to state the *conclusion* of the analysis rather than to generate the *argument* of the analysis.

The structure of this anti-abortion argument can be both illuminated and defended by comparing it to what appears to be the best argument for the wrongness of the wanton infliction of pain on animals. This latter argument is based on the assumption that it is prima facie wrong to inflict pain on me (or you, reader). What is the natural property associated with the infliction of pain which makes such infliction wrong? The obvious answer seems to be that the infliction of pain causes suffering and that suffering is a misfortune. The suffering caused by the infliction of pain is what makes the wanton infliction of pain on me wrong. The wanton infliction of pain on other adult humans causes suffering. The wanton infliction of pain on animals causes suffering. Since causing suffering is what makes the wanton infliction of pain wrong and since the wanton infliction of pain on animals causes suffering, it follows that the wanton infliction of pain on animals is wrong.

This argument for the wrongness of the wanton infliction of pain on animals shares a number of structural features with the argument for the serious prima facie wrongness of abortion. Both arguments start with an obvious assumption concerning what it is wrong to do to me (or you, reader). Both then look for the characteristic or the consequence of the wrong action which makes the action wrong. Both recognize that the wrong-making feature of these immoral actions is a property of actions sometimes directed at individuals other than postnatal human beings. If the structure of the argument for the wrongness of the wanton infliction of pain on animals is sound, then the structure of the argument for the prima facie serious wrongness of abortion is also sound, for the structure of the two arguments is the same. The structure common to both is the key to the explanation of how the wrongness of abortion can be demonstrated without recourse to the category of person. In neither argument is that category crucial.

This defense of an argument for the wrongness of abortion in terms of a structurally similar argument for the wrongness of the wanton infliction of pain on animals succeeds only if the account regarding animals is the correct account. Is it? In the first place, it seems plausible. In the second place, its major competition is Kant's account. Kant believed that we do not have direct duties to animals at all, because they are not persons. Hence, Kant had to explain and justify the wrongness of inflicting pain on animals on the grounds that "he who is hard in his dealings with animals becomes hard also in his dealing with men."[8] The problem with Kant's account is that there seems to be no reason for accepting this latter claim unless Kant's account is rejected. If the alternative to Kant's account is accepted, then it is easy to understand why someone who is indifferent to inflicting pain on animals is also indifferent to inflicting pain on humans, for one is indifferent to what makes inflicting pain wrong in both cases. But, if Kant's account is accepted, there is no intelligible reason why one who is hard in his dealings with animals (or crabgrass or stones) should also be hard in his dealings with men. After all, men are persons: animals are no more persons than crabgrass or stones. Persons are Kant's crucial moral category. Why, in short, should a Kantian accept the basic claim in Kant's argument?

Hence, Kant's argument for the wrongness of inflicting pain on animals rests on a claim that, in a world of Kantian moral agents, is demonstrably false. Therefore, the alternative analysis, being more plausible anyway, should be accepted. Since this alternative analysis has the same structure as the anti-abortion argument being defended here, we have further support for the argument for the immorality of abortion being defended in this essay.

Of course, this value of a future-like-ours argument, if sound, shows only that abortion is prima facie wrong, not that it is wrong in any and all circumstances. Since the loss of the future to a standard fetus, if killed, is, however, at least as great a loss as the loss of the future to a standard adult human being who is killed, abortion, like ordinary killing, could be justified only by the most compelling reasons. The loss of one's life is almost the greatest misfortune that can happen to one. Presumably abortion could be justified in some circumstances, only if the loss consequent on failing to abort would be at least as great. Accordingly, morally permissible abortions will be rare indeed unless, perhaps, they occur so early in pregnancy that a fetus is not yet definitely an individual. Hence, this argument should be taken as showing that abortion is presumptively very seriously wrong, where the presumption is very strong – as strong as the presumption that killing another adult human being is wrong.

III

How complete an account of the wrongness of killing does the value of a future-like-ours account have to be in order that the wrongness of abortion is a consequence? This account does not have to be an account of the necessary conditions for the wrongness of killing. Some persons in nursing homes may lack valuable human futures, yet it may be wrong to kill them for other reasons. Furthermore, this account does not obviously have to be the sole reason killing is wrong where the victim did have a valuable future. This analysis claims only that, for any killing where the victim did have a valuable future like ours, having that future by itself is sufficient to create the strong presumption that the killing is seriously wrong.

One way to overturn the value of a future-like-ours argument would be to find some account of the wrongness of killing which is at least as intelligible and which has different implications for the ethics of abortion. Two rival accounts possess at least some degree of plausibility. One account is based on the obvious fact that people value the experience of living and wish for that valuable experience to continue. Therefore, it might be said, what makes killing wrong is the discontinuation of that experience for the victim. Let us call this the *discontinuation account*.[9] Another rival account is based upon the obvious fact that people strongly desire to continue to live. This suggests that what makes killing us so wrong is that it interferes with the fulfillment of a strong and fundamental desire, the fulfillment of which is necessary for the fulfillment of any other desires we might have. Let us call this the *desire account*.[10]

Consider first the desire account as a rival account of the ethics of killing which would provide the basis for rejecting the anti-abortion position. Such an account will have to be stronger than the value of a future-like-ours account of the wrongness of abortion if it is to do the job expected of it. To entail the wrongness of abortion, the value of a future-like-ours account has only to provide a sufficient, but not a necessary, condition for the wrongness of killing. The desire account, on the other hand, must provide us also with a necessary condition for the wrongness of killing in order to generate a pro-choice conclusion on abortion. The reason for this is that presumably the argument from the desire account moves from the claim that what makes killing wrong is interference with a very strong desire to the claim that abortion is not wrong because the fetus lacks a strong desire to live. Obviously, this inference fails if someone's having the desire to live is not a necessary condition of its being wrong to kill that individual.

One problem with the desire account is that we do regard it as seriously wrong to kill persons who have little desire to live or who have no desire to live or, indeed, have a desire not to live. We believe it is seriously wrong to kill the unconscious, the sleeping, those who are tired of life, and those who are suicidal. The value-of-a-human-future account renders standard morality intelligible in these cases; these cases appear to be incompatible with the desire account.

The desire account is subject to a deeper difficulty. We desire life, because we value the goods of this life. The goodness of life is not secondary to our desire for it. If this were not so, the pain of one's own premature death could be done away with merely by an appropriate alteration in the configuration of one's desires. This is absurd. Hence, it would seem that it is the loss of the goods of one's future, not the interference with the fulfillment of a strong desire to live, which accounts ultimately for the wrongness of killing.

It is worth noting that, if the desire account is modified so that it does not provide a necessary, but only a sufficient, condition for the wrongness of killing, the desire account is compatible with the value of a future-like-ours account. The combined accounts will yield an anti-abortion ethic. This suggests that one can retain what is intuitively plausible about the desire account without a challenge to the basic argument of this paper.

It is also worth noting that, if future desires have moral force in a modified desire account of the wrongness of killing, one can find support for an anti-abortion ethic even in the absence of a value of a future-like-ours account. If one decides that a morally relevant property, the possession of which is sufficient to make it wrong to kill some individual, is the desire at some future time to live – one might decide to justify one's refusal to kill suicidal teenagers on these grounds, for example – then, since typical fetuses will have the desire in the future to live, it is wrong to kill typical fetuses. Accordingly, it does not seem that a desire account of the wrongness of killing can provide a justification of a pro-choice ethic of abortion which is nearly as adequate as the value of a human-future justification of an anti-abortion ethic.

The discontinuation account looks more promising as an account of the wrongness of killing. It seems just as intelligible as the value of a future-like-ours account, but it does not justify an anti-abortion position. Obviously, if it is the continuation of one's activities, experiences, and projects, the loss of which makes killing wrong, then it is not wrong to kill fetuses for that reason, for fetuses do not have experiences, activities, and projects to be continued or discontinued. Accordingly, the discontinuation account does not have the anti-abortion consequences that the value of a future-like-ours account has. Yet, it seems as intelligible as the value of a future-like-ours account, for when we think of what would be wrong with our being killed, it does seem as if it is the discontinuation of what makes our lives worthwhile which makes killing us wrong.

Is the discontinuation account just as good an account as the value of a future-like-ours account? The discontinuation account will not be adequate at all, if it does not refer to the *value* of the experience that may be discontinued. One does not want the discontinuation account to make it wrong to kill a patient who begs for death and who is in severe pain that cannot be relieved short of killing. (I leave open the question of whether it is wrong for other reasons.) Accordingly, the discontinuation account must be more than a bare discontinuation account. It must make some reference to the positive value of the patient's experiences. But, by the same token, the value of a future-like-ours account cannot be a bare future account either. Just having a future surely does not itself rule out killing the above patient. This account must make some reference to the value of the patient's future experiences and projects also. Hence, both accounts involve the value of experiences, projects, and activities. So far we still have symmetry between the accounts.

The symmetry fades, however, when we focus on the time period of the value of the experiences, etc., which has moral consequences. Although both accounts leave open the possibility that the patient in our example may be killed, this possibility is left open only in virtue of the utterly bleak future for the patient. It makes no difference whether the patient's immediate past contains intolerable pain, or consists in being in a coma (which we can imagine is a situation of indifference), or consists in a life of value. If the patient's future is a future of value, we want our account to make it wrong to kill the patient. If the patient's future is intolerable, whatever his or her immediate past, we want our account to allow killing the patient. Obviously, then, it is the value of that patient's future which is doing the work in rendering the morality of killing the patient intelligible.

This being the case, it seems clear that whether one has immediate past experiences or not does no work in the explanation of what makes killing wrong. The addition the discontinuation account makes to the value of a human future account is otiose. Its addition to the value-of-a-future account plays no role at all in rendering intelligible the wrongness of killing. Therefore, it can be discarded with the discontinuation account of which it is a part.

IV

The analysis of the previous section suggests that alternative general accounts of the wrongness of killing are either inadequate or unsuccessful in getting around the anti-abortion consequences of the value of a future-like-ours argument. A different strategy for avoiding these anti-abortion consequences involves limiting the scope of the value of a future argument. More precisely, the strategy involves arguing that fetuses lack a property that is essential for the value-of-a-future argument (or for any anti-abortion argument) to apply to them.

One move of this sort is based upon the claim that a necessary condition of one's future being valuable is that one values it. Value implies a valuer. Given this one might argue that, since fetuses cannot value their futures, their futures are not valuable to them. Hence, it does not seriously wrong them deliberately to end their lives.

This move fails, however, because of some ambiguities. Let us assume that something cannot be of value unless it is valued by someone. This does not entail that my life is of no value unless it is valued by me. I may think, in a period of despair, that my future is of no worth whatsoever, but I may be wrong because others rightly see value – even great value – in it. Furthermore, my future can be valuable to me even if I do not value it. This is the case when a young person attempts suicide, but is rescued and goes on to significant human achievements. Such young people's futures are ultimately valuable to them, even though such futures do not seem to be valuable to them at the moment of attempted suicide. A fetus's future can be valuable to it in the same way. Accordingly, this attempt to limit the anti-abortion argument fails.

Another similar attempt to reject the anti-abortion position is based on Tooley's claim that an entity cannot possess the right to life unless it has the capacity to desire its continued existence. It follows that, since fetuses lack the conceptual capacity to desire to continue to live, they lack the right to life. Accordingly, Tooley concludes that abortion cannot be seriously prima facie wrong ("Abortion and Infanticide" pp. 46–7 [31–2 in this volume]).

What could be the evidence for Tooley's basic claim? Tooley once argued that individuals have a prima facie right to what they desire and that the lack of the capacity to desire something undercuts the basis of one's right to it (pp. 44–5 [29–30 in this volume]). This argument plainly will not succeed in the context of the analysis of this essay, however, since the point here is to establish the fetus's right to life on other grounds. Tooley's argument assumes that the right to life cannot be established in general on some basis other than the desire for life. This position was considered and rejected in the preceding section of this paper.

One might attempt to defend Tooley's basic claim on the grounds that, because a fetus cannot apprehend continued life as a benefit, its continued life cannot be a benefit or cannot be something it has a right to or cannot be something that is in its interest. This might be defended in terms of the general proposition that, if an individual is literally incapable of caring about or taking an interest in some *X*, then one does not have a right to *X* or *X* is not a benefit or *X* is not something that is in one's interest.[11]

Each member of this family of claims seems to be open to objections. As John C. Stevens[12] has pointed out, one may have a right to be treated with a certain medical procedure (because of a health insurance policy one has purchased), even though one cannot conceive of the nature of the procedure. And, as Tooley himself has pointed out, persons who have been indoctrinated, or drugged, or rendered temporarily unconscious may be literally incapable of caring about or taking an interest in something that is in their interest or is something to which they have a right, or is something that benefits them. Hence, the Tooley claim that would restrict the scope of the value of a future-like-ours argument is undermined by counterexamples.[13]

Finally, Paul Bassen[14] has argued that, even though the prospects of an embryo might seem to be a basis for the wrongness of abortion, an embryo cannot be a victim and therefore cannot be wronged. An embryo cannot be a victim, he says, because it lacks sentience. His central argument for this seems to be that, even though plants and the permanently unconscious are alive, they clearly cannot be victims. What is the explanation of this? Bassen claims that the explanation is that their lives consist of mere metabolism and mere metabolism is not enough to ground victimizability. Mentation is required.

The problem with this attempt to establish the absence of victimizability is that both plants and the permanently unconscious clearly lack what Bassen calls "prospects" or what I have called "a future life like ours." Hence, it is surely open to one to argue that the real reason we believe plants and the permanently unconscious cannot be victims is that killing them cannot deprive them of a future life like ours; the real reason is not their absence of present mentation.

Bassen recognizes that his view is subject to this difficulty, and he recognizes that the case of children seems to support this difficulty, for "much of what we do for children is based on prospects." He argues, however, that, in the case of children and in other such cases, "potentiality comes into play only where victimizability has been secured on other grounds" (p. 333).

Bassen's defense of his view is patently question-begging, since what is adequate to secure victimizability is exactly what is at issue. His examples do not support his own view against the thesis of this essay. Of course, embryos can be victims: when their lives are deliberately terminated, they are deprived of their futures of value, their prospects. This makes them victims, for it directly wrongs them.

The seeming plausibility of Bassen's view stems from the fact that paradigmatic cases of imagining someone as a victim involve empathy, and empathy requires mentation of the victim. The victims of flood, famine, rape, or child abuse are all persons with whom we can empathize. That empathy seems to be part of seeing them as victims.[15]

In spite of the strength of these examples, the attractive intuition that a situation in which there is victimization requires the possibility of empathy is subject to counterexamples. Consider a case that Bassen himself offers: "Posthumous obliteration of an author's work constitutes a misfortune for him only if he had wished his work to endure" (p. 318). The conditions Bassen wishes to impose upon the possibility of being victimized here seem far too strong. Perhaps this author, due to his unrealistic standards of excellence and his low self-esteem, regarded his work as unworthy of survival, even though it possessed genuine literary merit. Destruction of such work would surely victimize its author. In such a case, empathy with the victim concerning the loss is clearly impossible.

Of course, Bassen does not make the possibility of empathy a necessary condition of victimizability; he requires only mentation. Hence, on Bassen's actual view, this author, as I have described him, can be a victim. The problem is that the basic intuition that renders Bassen's view plausible is missing in the author's case. In order to attempt to avoid counterexamples, Bassen has made his thesis too weak to be supported by the intuitions that suggested it.

Even so, the mentation requirement on victimizability is still subject to counterexamples. Suppose a severe accident renders me totally unconscious for a month, after which I recover. Surely killing me while I am unconscious victimizes me, even though I am incapable of mentation during that time. It follows that Bassen's thesis fails. Apparently, attempts to restrict the value of a future-like-ours argument so that fetuses do not fall within its scope do not succeed.

V

In this essay, it has been argued that the correct ethic of the wrongness of killing can be extended to fetal life and used to show that there is a strong presumption that any abortion is morally impermissible. If the ethic of killing adopted here entails, however, that contraception is also seriously immoral, then there would appear to be a difficulty with the analysis of this essay.

But this analysis does not entail that contraception is wrong. Of course, contraception prevents the actualization of a possible future of value. Hence, it follows from the claim that if futures of value should be maximized that contraception is prima facie immoral. This obligation to maximize does not exist, however; furthermore, nothing in the ethics of killing in this paper entails that it does. The ethics of killing in this essay would entail that contraception is wrong only if something were denied a human future of value by contraception. Nothing at all is denied such a future by contraception, however.

Candidates for a subject of harm by contraception fall into four categories: (1) some sperm or other, (2) some ovum or other, (3) a sperm and an ovum separately, and (4) a sperm and an ovum together. Assigning the harm to some sperm is utterly arbitrary, for no reason can be given for making a sperm the subject of harm rather than an ovum. Assigning the harm to some ovum is utterly arbitrary, for no reason can be given for making an ovum the subject of harm rather than a sperm. One might attempt to avoid these problems by insisting that contraception deprives both the sperm and the ovum separately of a valuable future like ours. On this alternative, too many futures are lost. Contraception was supposed to be wrong, because it deprived us of one future of value, not two. One might attempt to avoid this problem by holding that contraception deprives the combination of sperm and ovum of a valuable future like ours. But here the definite article misleads. At the time of contraception, there are hundreds of millions of sperm, one (released) ovum and millions of possible combinations of all of these. There is no actual combination at all. Is the subject of the loss to be a merely possible combination? Which one? This alternative does not yield an actual subject of harm either. Accordingly, the immorality of contraception is not entailed by the loss of a future-like-ours argument simply because there is no nonarbitrarily identifiable subject of the loss in the case of contraception.

VI

The purpose of this essay has been to set out an argument for the serious presumptive wrongness of abortion subject to the assumption that the moral permissibility of abortion stands or falls on the moral status of the fetus. Since a fetus possesses a property, the possession of which in adult human beings is sufficient to make killing an adult human being wrong, abortion is wrong. This way of dealing with the problem of abortion seems superior to other approaches to the ethics of abortion, because it rests on an ethics of killing which is close to self-evident, because the crucial morally relevant property clearly applies to fetuses, and because the argument avoids the usual equivocations on "human life," "human being," or "person". The argument rests neither on religious claims nor on Papal dogma. It is not subject to the objection of "speciesism." Its soundness is compatible with the moral permissibility of euthanasia and contraception. It deals with our intuitions concerning young children.

Finally, this analysis can be viewed as resolving a standard problem – indeed, *the* standard problem – concerning the ethics of abortion. Clearly, it is wrong to kill adult human beings. Clearly, it is not wrong to end the life of some arbitrarily chosen single human cell. Fetuses seem to be like arbitrarily chosen human cells in some respects and like adult humans in other respects. The problem of the ethics of abortion is the problem of determining the fetal property that settles this moral controversy. The thesis of this essay is that the problem of the ethics of abortion, so understood, is solvable.

Notes

1 Feinberg, "Abortion," in *Matters of Life and Death: New Introductory Essays in Moral Philosophy*, Tom Regan, ed. (New York: Random House, 1986), pp. 256–93; Tooley, "Abortion and Infanticide," *Philosophy and Public Affairs*, II, 1 (1972): 37–65, Tooley, *Abortion and Infanticide* (New York: Oxford, 1984); Warren, "On the Moral and Legal Status of Abortion," *The Monist*, 1. VII, 1 (1973): 43–61; Engelhardt, "The Ontology of Abortion," *Ethics*, I. XXXIV, 3 (1974): 217–34; Sumner, *Abortion and Moral Theory* (Princeton: University Press, 1981); Noonan, "An Almost Absolute Value in History," in *The Morality of Abortion: Legal and Historical Perspectives*, Noonan, ed. (Cambridge: Harvard, 1970); and Devine, *The Ethics of Homicide* (Ithaca: Cornell, 1978).

2 For interesting discussions of this issue, see Warren Quinn, "Abortion: Identity and Loss," *Philosophy and Public Affairs*, XIII, 1 (1984): 24–54; and Lawrence C. Becker, "Human Being: The Boundaries of the Concept," *Philosophy and Public Affairs*, IV, 4 (1975): 334–59.

3 For example, see my "Ethics and The Elderly: Some Problems," in Stuart Spicker, Kathleen Woodward, and David Van Tassel, eds., *Aging and the Elderly: Humanistic Perspectives in Gerontology* (Atlantic Highlands, NJ: Humanities, 1978), pp. 341–55.

4 See Warren, "On the Moral and Legal Status of Abortion," and Tooley, "Abortion and Infanticide."

5 This seems to be the fatal flaw in Warren's treatment of this issue.

6 I have been most influenced on this matter by Jonathan Glover, *Causing Death and Saving Lives* (New York: Penguin, 1977), ch. 3; and Robert Young, "What Is So Wrong with Killing People?" *Philosophy*, LIV, 210 (1979): 515–28.

7 Feinberg, Tooley, Warren, and Engelhardt have all dealt with this problem.

8 Kant "Duties to Animals and Spirits," in *Lectures on Ethics*, trans. Louis Infeld (New York: Harper, 1963), p. 239.

9 I am indebted to Jack Bricke for raising this objection.

10 Presumably a preference utilitarian would press such an objection. Tooley once suggested that his account has such a theoretical underpinning. See his "Abortion and Infanticide," pp. 44–5.

11 Donald VanDeVeer seems to think this is self-evident. See his "Whither Baby Doe?" in *Matters of Life and Death*, p. 233.

12 "Must the Bearer of a Right Have the Concept of That to Which He Has a Right?" *Ethics*, XCV, 1 (1984): 68–74.

13 See Tooley again in "Abortion and Infanticide," pp. 47–9.

14 "Present Sakes and Future Prospects: The Status of Early Abortion," *Philosophy and Public Affairs*, XI, 4 (1982): 322–6.

15 Note carefully the reasons he gives on the bottom of p. 316.

5

Abortion and the Golden Rule

R. M. Hare

I

If philosophers are going to apply ethical theory successfully to practical issues, they must first have a theory. This may seem obvious; but they often proceed as if it were not so. A philosopher's chief contribution to a practical issue should be to show us which are good and which are bad arguments; and to do this he has to have some way of telling one from the other. Moral philosophy therefore needs a basis in philosophical logic – the logic of the moral concepts. But we find, for example, Professor Judith Jarvis Thomson, in an article on abortion which has been justly praised for the ingenuity and liveliness of her examples, proceeding as if this were not necessary at all.[1] She simply parades the examples before us and asks what we would say about them. But how do we know whether what we feel inclined to say has any secure ground? May we not feel inclined to say it just because of the way we were brought up to think? And was this necessarily the right way? It is highly diverting to watch the encounter in the same volume between her and Mr John Finnis, who, being a devout Roman Catholic, has intuitions which differ from hers (and mine) in the wildest fashion.[2] I just do not know how to tell whether Mr Finnis is on safe ground when he claims that suicide is "a paradigm case of an action that is always wrong"; nor Professor Thomson when she makes the no doubt more popular claim that we have a right to decide what happens in and to our own bodies.[3] How would we choose between these potentially conflicting intuitions? Is it simply a contest in rhetoric?

In contrast, a philosopher who wishes to contribute to the solution of this and similar practical problems should be trying to develop, on the basis of a study of the moral concepts and their logical properties, a theory of moral reasoning that will determine which arguments we ought to accept. Professor Thomson might be surprised to see me saying this, because she thinks that I am an emotivist,[4] in spite of the fact that I devoted two of the very first papers I ever published to a refutation of emotivism.[5] Her examples are entertaining, and help to show up our prejudices; but they will do no more than that until we have a way of telling which prejudices ought to be abandoned.

II

I shall abjure two approaches to the question of abortion which have proved quite unhelpful. The first puts the question in terms of the "rights" of the fetus or the mother; the second demands, as a necessary condition for solving the problem, an answer to the question, Is the fetus a person? The first is unhelpful at the moment because nobody has yet proposed an even plausible account of how we might argue conclusively about rights. Rights are the stamping-ground of intuitionists, and it would be difficult to find any claim confidently asserted to a right which could not be as

From *Philosophy & Public Affairs*, vol. 4, no. 3 (1975), pp. 201–22. This is a revised version of the Hurst Lecture given at American University, Washington, DC, in 1974.

confidently countered by a claim to another right, such that both rights cannot simultaneously be complied with. This is plainly true in the present controversy, as it is in the case of rights to property – one man has a right not to starve, another a right to hold on to the money that would buy him food. Professor Thomson evidently believes in property rights, because she curiously bases the right of a woman to decide what happens in and to her own body on her ownership of it. We might ask whether, if this is correct, the property is disposable; could it be held that by the marriage contract a wife and a husband yield up to each other some of their property rights in their own bodies? If so, might we find male chauvinists who were prepared to claim that, if the husband wants to have an heir, the wife cannot claim an absolute liberty to have an abortion? As a question of law, this could be determined by the courts and the legislature; but as a question of morals . . .?

In the law, cash value can be given to statements about rights by translating them into statements about what it is or is not lawful to do. An analogous translation will have to be effected in morals, with "right" (adjective), "wrong," and "ought" taking the place of "lawful" and "unlawful," before the word "rights" can be a dependable prop for moral arguments. It may be that one day somebody will produce a theory of rights which links the concept firmly to those of "right," "wrong," and "ought" – concepts whose logic is even now a *little* better understood. The simplest such theory would be one which said that *A* has a right, in one sense of the word, to do *X* if and only if it is not wrong for *A* to do *X*; and that *A* has a right, in another sense, to do *X* if and only if it is wrong to prevent *A* from doing *X*; and that *A* has a right to do *X* in a third sense if and only if it is wrong not to assist *A* to do *X* (the extent of the assistance, and the persons from whom it is due, being unspecified and, on many occasions of the use of this ambiguous word "rights," unspecifiable). It is often unclear, when people claim that women have a right to do what they like with their own bodies, which of these senses is being used. (Does it, for example, mean that it is not wrong for them to terminate their own pregnancies, or that it is wrong to stop them doing this, or that it is wrong not to assist them in doing this?) For our present purposes it is best to leave these difficulties on one side and say that *if* at some future time a reliable analysis of the various senses of "rights" in terms of "wrong" or "ought" is forthcoming, then arguments about rights will be restatable in terms of what it is wrong to do, or what we ought or ought not to do. Till that happy day comes, we shall get the issues in better focus if we discuss them directly in terms of what we ought or ought not to do, or what it would be right or wrong to do, to the fetus or the mother in specified circumstances.

III

The other unhelpful approach, that of asking whether the fetus is a person, has been so universally popular that in many of the writings it is assumed that this question is the key to the whole problem. The reason for this is easy to see; if there is a well-established moral principle that the intentional killing of other innocent persons is always murder, and therefore wrong, it looks as if an easy way to determine whether it is wrong to kill fetuses is to determine whether they are persons, and thus settle once for all whether they are subsumable under the principle. But this approach has run into well-known difficulties, the basic reason for which is the following. If a normative or evaluative principle is framed in terms of a predicate which has fuzzy edges (as nearly all predicates in practice have), then we are not going to be able to use the principle to decide cases on the borderline without doing some more normation or evaluation. If we make a law forbidding the use of wheeled vehicles in the park, and somebody thinks he can go in the park on roller skates, no amount of cerebration, and no amount of inspection of roller skates, are going to settle for us the question of whether roller skates are wheeled vehicles "within the meaning of the Act" if the Act has not specified whether they are; the judge has to decide whether they are *to be* counted as such. And this is a further determination of the law.[6] The judge may have very good reasons of public interest or morals for his decision; but he cannot make it by any physical or metaphysical investigation of roller skates to see whether they are *really* wheeled vehicles. If he had not led too sheltered a life, he knew all he needed to know about roller skates before the case ever came into court.

In the same way the decision to say that the fetus becomes a person at conception, or at quickening, or at birth, or whenever takes your fancy, and that thereafter, because it is a person, destruction of it is murder, is inescapably a moral decision, for which we have to have moral reasons. It is not necessary, in order to make this point, to insist that the word "person" is a moral word; though in many contexts there is much to be said for taking this line. It is necessary only to notice that "person," even if descriptive, is not a fully determinate concept; it is loose at the edges, as the abortion controversy only too clearly shows. Therefore, if we decide that, "within the meaning of" the principle about murder, a fetus becomes a person as soon as it is conceived, we are deciding a moral question, and ought to have a moral reason for our decision. It is no use looking more closely at the fetus to satisfy ourselves that it is *really* a person (as the people do who make so much of the fact that it has arms and legs); we already have all the information that we need about the fetus. What is needed is thought about the moral question, How ought a creature, about whose properties, circumstances, and probable future we are quite adequately informed, to be treated? If, in our desire to get out of addressing ourselves to this moral question – to get it settled for us without any moral thought on our part – we go first to the physicians for information about whether the fetus is really a person, and then, when they have told us all they can, to the metaphysicians, we are only indulging in the well-known vice of philosophers (which my fellow linguistic philosophers, at any rate, ought to be on their guard against, because that is the mainstay of our training) – the vice of trying to settle substantial questions by verbal maneuvers.

I am not saying that physiological research on the fetus has no bearing on moral questions about abortion. If it brought to light, for example, that fetuses really do suffer on the same scale as adults do, then that would be a good moral reason for not causing them to suffer. It will not do to show that they wriggle when pricked, for so do earthworms; and I do not think that the upholders of the rights of unborn children wish to extend these rights to earthworms. Encephalograms are better; but there are enormous theoretical and practical difficulties in the argument from encephalograms to conscious experiences. In default of these latter, which would have to be of such a sort as to distinguish fetuses radically from other creatures which the anti-abortionists would not lift a finger to protect, the main weight of the anti-abortionist argument is likely to rest, not on the sufferings of the fetus, but on harms done to the interests of the person into whom the fetus would normally develop. These will be the subject of most of the rest of this paper.

Approaching our moral question in the most general way, let us ask whether there is *anything* about the fetus *or* about the person it may turn into that should make us say that we ought not to kill it. If, instead of asking this question, somebody wants to go on asking, indirectly, whether the fetus is a person, and whether, *therefore*, killing it is wrong, he is at liberty to do so; but I must point out that the reasons he will have to give for saying that it is a person, and that, therefore, killing it is wrong (or that it is not a person and, therefore, killing it is not wrong) will be the very same moral reasons as I shall be giving for the answer to my more direct question. Whichever way one takes it, one cannot avoid giving a reasoned answer to this moral question; so why not take it the simplest way? To say that the fetus is (or is not) a person gives *by itself* no moral reason for or against killing it; it merely incapsulates any reasons we may have for including the fetus within a certain category of creatures that it is, or is not, wrong to kill (i.e. persons or nonpersons). The word "person" is doing no work here (other than that of bemusing us).

IV

Is there then anything about the fetus which raises moral problems about the legitimacy of killing it? At this point I must declare that I have no axe to grind – I am not a fervent abortionist nor a fervent anti-abortionist – I just want fervently to get to the root of the matter. It will be seen, as the argument goes on, that the first move I shall make is one which will give cheer to the anti-abortionists; but, before they have had time to celebrate, it will appear that this move brings with it, inescapably, another move which should encourage the other side. We shall end up somewhere in between, but perhaps with a clearer idea of how, in principle, to set about answering questions about particular abortions.

The single, or at least the main, thing about the fetus that raises the moral question is that, if not terminated, the pregnancy is highly likely to result in the birth and growth to maturity of a person just like the rest of us. The word "person" here reenters the argument, but in a context and with a meaning that does not give rise to the old troubles; for it is clear at least that we ordinary adults are persons. If we knew beyond a peradventure that a fetus was going to miscarry anyway, then little would remain of the moral problem beyond the probably minimal sufferings caused to the mother and just possibly the fetus by terminating the pregnancy now. If, on the other hand, we knew (to use Professor Tooley's science-fiction example)[7] that an embryo kitten would, if not aborted but given a wonder drug, turn into a being with a human mind like ours, then that too would raise a moral problem. Perhaps Tooley thinks not; but we shall see. It is, to use his useful expression, the "potentiality" that the fetus has of becoming a person in the full ordinary sense that creates the problem. It is because Tooley thinks that, once the "potentiality principle" (see below) is admitted, the conservatives or extreme anti-abortionists will win the case hands down, that he seeks reasons for rejecting it; but, again, we shall see.

We can explain why the potentiality of the fetus for becoming a person raises a moral problem if we appeal to a type of argument which, in one guise or another, has been the formal basis of almost all theories of moral reasoning that have contributed much that is worthwhile to our understanding of it. I am alluding to the Christian (and indeed pre-Christian) "Golden Rule," the Kantian Categorical Imperative, the ideal observer theory, the rational contractor theory, various kinds of utilitarianism, and my own universal prescriptivism.[8] I would claim that the last of these gives the greatest promise of putting what is common to all these theories in a perspicuous way, and so revealing their justification in logic; but it is not the purpose of this paper to give this justification. Instead, since the problem of abortion is discussed as often as not from a Christian standpoint, and since I hope thereby to find a provisional starting point for the argument on which many would agree, I shall use that form of the argument which rests on the Golden Rule that we should do to others as we wish them to do to us.[9] It is a logical extension of this form of argument to say that we should do to others what *we are glad was* done to us. Two (surely readily admissible) changes are involved here. The first is a mere difference in the two tenses which cannot be morally relevant. Instead of saying that we should do to others as we wish them (in the future) to do to us, we say that we should do to others as we wish that they had done to us (in the past). The second is a change from the hypothetical to the actual: instead of saying that we should do to others as we wish that they had done to us, we say that we should do to others as we are glad that they did do to us. I cannot see that this could make any difference to the spirit of the injunction, and logical grounds could in any case be given, based on the universal prescriptivist thesis, for extending the Golden Rule in this way.

The application of this injunction to the problem of abortion is obvious. If we are glad that nobody terminated the pregnancy that resulted in *our* birth, then we are enjoined not, *ceteris paribus*, to terminate any pregnancy which will result in the birth of a person having a life like ours. Close attention obviously needs to be paid to the "*ceteris paribus*" clause, and also to the expression "like ours." The "universalizability" of moral judgements, which is one of the logical bases of the Golden Rule, requires us to make the same moral judgment about qualitatively identical cases, and about cases which are *relevantly* similar. Since no cases in this area are going to be qualitatively *identical*, we shall have to rely on relevant similarity. Without raising a very large topic in moral philosophy, we can perhaps avoid the difficulty by pointing out that the relevant respects here are going to be those things about our life which make us glad that we were born. These can be stated in a general enough way to cover all those persons who are, or who are going to be or would be, glad that they were born. Those who are not glad they were born will still have a reason for not aborting those who would be glad; for even the former wish that, if they had been going to be glad that they were born, nobody should have aborted them. So, although I have, for the sake of simplicity, put the injunction in a way that makes it apply only to the abortion of people who will have a life just like that of the aborter, it is generalizable to cover the abortion of any fetus which will, if not aborted, turn into someone who will be glad to be alive.

I now come back to Professor Tooley's wonder kitten. He says that if it became possible by administering a wonder drug to an embryo kitten to cause it to turn into a being with a human mind like ours, we should still not feel under any obligation either to administer the drug to kittens or to refrain from aborting kittens to whom the drug had been administered by others. He uses this as an argument against the "potentiality principle," which says that if there are any properties which are possessed by adult human beings and which endow any organisms possessing them with a serious right to life, then "at least one of those properties will be such that any organism *potentially* possessing that property has a serious right to life even now, simply by virtue of that potentiality, where an organism possesses a property potentially if it will come to have that property in the normal course of its development."[10] Putting this more briefly and in terms of "wrong" instead of "rights," the potentiality principle says that if it would be wrong to kill an adult human being because he has a certain property, it is wrong to kill an organism (e.g. a fetus) which will come to have that property if it develops normally.

There is one minor objection to what Tooley says which we can pass over quickly. The administration of wonder drugs is not normal development, so Tooley ought not to have used the words "in the normal course of its development"; they spoil his "kitten" example. But let us amend our summary of his principle by omitting the words "if it develops normally" and substituting "if we do not kill it." I do not think that this substitution makes Tooley's argument any weaker than it is already.

Now suppose that I discovered that I myself was the result of the administration of the wonder drug to a kitten embryo. To make this extension of the example work, we have to suppose that the drug is even more wonderful and can make kitten embryos grow into beings with human bodies as well as minds; but it is hard to see how this could make any moral difference, especially for Tooley, who rests none of his argument on bodily shape. If this happened, it would not make my reasons for being glad that I was not aborted cease to apply. I certainly prescribe that they should not have aborted an embryo kitten which the wonder drug was going to turn into *me*. And so, by the Golden Rule, I must say that I should not abort an embryo kitten to whom the wonder drug had been administered and which therefore was going to turn into a creature just like me. And, for what it is worth, this is what I would say. The fact that I confidently assert this, whereas Tooley confidently asserts the opposite – so confidently, in fact, that he thinks that this single example is enough to establish his entire case against the potentiality principle, and produces no other – just shows how inadequate intuitions are as a guide to moral conclusions. The fantastic nature of his example (like that of some of Professor Thomson's) makes it even more difficult to be certain that we are saying what we *should* say about it. Our intuitions are the result of our upbringing, and we were not brought up on cases where kittens can be turned into beings with human minds, or where people get kidnapped and have distinguished violinists with kidney failure plugged into their bloodstreams, as in Professor Thomson's example.

The problem becomes more difficult if we ask whether the same argument could be used to establish that it would be wrong, if this wonder drug were invented, not to administer it to all the embryo kittens one could get hold of. I shall postpone discussion of this problem until we have discussed the similar problem of whether the potentiality principle, once established, will not force upon us an extreme conservative position not only about abortion but also about contraception, and even forbid chastity. If we allow the potentiality of procreating human beings to place upon us obligations to procreate them, shall we not have a duty to procreate all the human beings that we can, and will not even monks and nuns have to obey King Lear's injunction to "let copulation thrive"?[11] To the general problem which this raises I shall return. We shall see that it is simply the familiar problem about the right population policy, which has to be faced whatever view we take of the present question.

V

I propose to take it as established, that the potentiality principle is *not* refuted by Tooley's one example, and that it therefore holds the field until somebody produces a better argument against it – which I do not expect to happen, because the potentiality principle itself can be based on the Golden Rule, as the examples already considered show, and the Golden Rule has a secure logical foundation which I have already mentioned, though I have not had room to expound it.

Why does Tooley think that, if the potentiality principle is once granted, the extreme conservative position on abortion becomes impregnable? Obviously because he has neglected to consider some other potential beings. Take, to start with, the next child that this mother will have if this pregnancy is terminated but will not have if this pregnancy is allowed to continue. Why will she not have it? For a number of alternative reasons. The most knockdown reason would be that the mother would die or be rendered sterile if this pregnancy were allowed to continue. Another would be that the parents had simply decided, perhaps for morally adequate reasons, that their family would be large enough if and when this present fetus was born. I shall be discussing later the morality of family limitation; for the moment I shall assume for the sake of argument that it is morally all right for parents to decide, after they have had, say, fifteen children, not to have any more, and to achieve this modest limitation of their family by remaining completely chaste.

In all these cases there is, in effect, a choice between having this child now and having another child later. Most people who oppose abortion make a great deal of the wrongness of stopping the birth of this child but say nothing about the morality of stopping the birth of the later child. My own intuition (on which I am by no means going to rely) is that they are wrong to make so big a distinction. The basis of the distinction is supposed to be that the fetus already exists as a single living entity all in one place, whereas the possible future child is at the moment represented only by an unfertilized ovum and a sperm which may or may not yet exist in the father's testes. But will this basis support so weighty a distinction?

First, why is it supposed to make a difference that the genetic material which causes the production of the future child and adult is in two different places? If I have a duty to open a certain door, and two keys are required to unlock it, it does not seem to me to make any difference to my duty that one key is already in the lock and the other in my trousers. This, so far, is an intuition, and I place no reliance on it; I introduce the parallel only to remove some prejudices. The real argument is this: when I am glad that I was born (the basis, it will be remembered, of the argument that the Golden Rule therefore places upon me an obligation not to stop others being born), I do not confine this gladness to gladness that they did not abort me. I am glad, also, that my parents copulated in the first place, without contraception. So from my gladness, in conjunction with the extended Golden Rule, I derive not only a duty not to abort, but also a duty not to abstain from procreation. In the choice situation that I have imagined, in which it is either this child or the next one but not both, I cannot perform both these duties. So, in the words of a wayside pulpit report to me by Mr Anthony Kenny, "if you have conflicting duties, one of them isn't your duty." But which?

I do not think that any general answer can be given to this question. If the present fetus is going to be miserably handicapped if it grows into an adult, perhaps because the mother had rubella, but there is every reason to suppose that the next child will be completely normal and as happy as most people, there would be reason to abort this fetus and proceed to bring to birth the next child, in that the next child will be much gladder to be alive than will this one. The Golden Rule does not directly guide us in cases where we cannot help failing to do to *some* others what we wish were done to us, because if we did it to some, we should thereby prevent ourselves from doing it to others. But it can guide us indirectly, if further extended by a simple maneuver, to cover what I have elsewhere called "multilateral" situations. We are to do to the others affected, taken together, what we wish were done to us if we had to be all of them by turns in random order.[12] In this case, by terminating this pregnancy, I get, on this scenario, no life at all in one of my incarnations and a happy life in the other; but by not terminating it, I get a miserable life in one and no life at all in the other. So I should choose to terminate. In order to reach this conclusion it is not necessary to assume, as we did, that the present fetus will turn into a person who will be positively miserable; only that that person's expectation of happiness is so much less than the expectation of the later possible person that the other factors (to be mentioned in a moment) are outweighed.

In most cases, the probability that there will be another child to replace this one is far lower than the probability that this fetus will turn into a living child. The latter probability is said in normal cases to be about 80 percent; the probability of the next child being born may be much lower (the parents may separate; one of them may die or become sterile; or they may just change their minds about having children). If I do not terminate in such a normal case, I get, on the same scenario, an 80 percent chance of a normal happy life in one incarnation and no chance at all of any life in the other; but if I do terminate, I get a much lower chance of a normal happy life in the second incarnation and no chance at all in the first. So in this case I should not terminate. By applying this kind of scenario to different cases, we get a way of dramatizing the application of the Golden Rule to them. The cases will all be different, but the relevance of the differences to the moral decision becomes clearer. It is these differences in probabilities of having a life, and of having a happy one, that justify, first of all the presumptive policy, which most people would follow, that abortions in general ought to be avoided, and secondly the exceptions to this policy that many people would now allow – though of course they will differ in their estimation of the probabilities.

I conclude, therefore, that the establishment of the potentiality principle by no means renders impregnable the extreme conservative position, as Tooley thinks it does. It merely creates a rebuttable or defeasible presumption against abortion, which is fairly easily rebutted if there are good indications. The interests of the mother may well, in many cases, provide such good indications, although, because hers is not the only interest, we have also to consider the others. Liberals can, however, get from the present form of argument all that they could reasonably demand, since in the kinds of cases in which they would approve of termination, the interests of the mother will usually be predominant enough to tip the balance between those of the others affected, including potential persons.

The effect of this argument is to bring the morality of contraception and that of abortion somewhat closer together. Important differences will remain, however. There is the fact that the fetus has a very good chance of turning into a normal adult if allowed to develop, whereas the chance that a single coitus will have that result is much lower. Further, if a general duty to produce children be recognized (as the view I have suggested requires), to kill a fetus means the nonfulfilment of this duty for a much longer period (the period from its begetting to the begetting of the next child, if any); whereas, if you do not beget a child now, you may five minutes later. Thirdly, parents become attached to the child in the womb (hence the argument, "We should all think differently if wombs were transparent") and therefore an abortion may (whatever the compensating good) do some harm to them in addition to that (if any) done to the prospective child that is aborted; this is not so if they merely refrain from procreation. These differences are enough to account for the moral gap between contraception and abortion which will be found in the intuitions of most people; one has to be very extreme in one's views either to consider contraception as sinful as abortion or to think of abortion as *just* another alternative to contraception.

VI

We must now consider some possible objections to this view. Some of these rest on supposed conflicts with received opinion. I shall not deal at great length with these, for a number of reasons. The first is that it would be hard at the moment to point to any at all generally received opinion about abortion. But even if we could, it is a difficult question in moral philosophy, which I have discussed at length elsewhere,[13] how much attention should be paid to received opinon on moral issues. I shall sum up my view, without defending it. There are two levels of moral thinking. The first (level 1) consists in the application of learnt principles, which, in order to be learnt, have to be *fairly* general and simple; the second (level 2) consists in the criticism, and possibly the modification, of these general principles in the light of their effect in particular cases, actual and imagined. The purpose of this second, reflective kind of thinking is to select those general principles for use in the first kind of thinking which will lead to the nearest approximation, if generally accepted and inculcated, to the results that would be achieved if we had the time and the information and the freedom from self-deception to make possible the practice of level-2 thinking in every single case. The intuitions which many moral philosophers regard as the final court of appeal are the result of their upbringing – i.e. of the fact that just these level-1 principles were accepted by those who most influenced them. In discussing abortion, we ought to be doing some level-2 thinking; it is therefore quite futile to appeal to those level-1 intuitions that we happen to have acquired. It is a question, not of what our intuitions *are*, but of what they *ought to be* – a question which can usefully be dramatized by asking, What opinions about abortion ought we to be teaching to our children?

This may help to answer two objections which often crop up. The first claims that common opinion makes a larger moral distinction between failure to procreate and killing a fetus than the present view would warrant. Sometimes this distinction is said to be founded on the more general one between omissions and acts. There are strong arguments against the moral relevance of this last distinction;[14] and if we are always careful to compare like with like in our examples, and apply the Golden Rule to them, we shall not obtain any morally relevant difference between acts and omissions, provided that we are engaged in level-2 thinking. However, it may well be that the level-1 principles, which we selected as a result of this thinking, *would* use the distinction between acts and omissions. The reason for this is that, although this distinction is philosophically very puzzling and even suspect, it is operable by the ordinary man at the common-sense level; moreover, it serves to separate from each other classes of cases which a more refined thinking would also separate, but would do so only as a result of a very protracted investigation which did not itself make use of the act-omission distinction. So the act-omission distinction serves as a useful surrogate for distinctions which really are morally relevant, although it itself is not. Thus there may be no morally relevant distinction, so far as the Golden Rule goes, between killing and failing to keep alive *in otherwise identical cases*; but if people have ingrained in them the principle that it is wrong to kill innocent adults, but not always so wrong to fail to keep them alive, they are more likely in practice to do the right thing than if their ingrained principles made no such distinction. This is because most cases of killing differ from most cases of failing to keep alive in *other* crucial ways, such that the former are very much more likely to be wrong than the latter. And in the case of abortion and failure to procreate, it is *possible* (I do not say that it is so) that the best level-1 principles for practical use would make bigger distinctions at birth and at conception than a refined level-2 thinking could possibly support. The reason is that conception and birth are dividing lines easily discerned by the ordinary man, and that therefore a level-1 principle which uses these dividing lines in order to draw the moral line (what moral line?) *may* lead in practice to the morally best results. But if we are arguing (as we are) whether or not this is so, appeals to the intuitions of the ordinary man are entirely beside the point.

Secondly, we have the "thin end of the wedge" or "slippery-slope" objection. If we sanction contraception, why not abortion; and if abortion, why not infanticide; and if infanticide, why not the murder of adults? As an argument against the too ready abandonment of accepted general level-1 principles this argument has some force; for, psychologically speaking, if the ordinary man or the ordinary doctor has got hold of some general principles about killing, which serve well enough in the ordinary run, and then somebody tells him that these principles ought not to be followed universally, it may well be that he will come to disregard them in cases where he ought not. The argument can be overplayed – I do not think that many doctors who have come to accept abortion are thereby made any more prone to murder their wives; but at this level the argument has *some* force, especially if, in the upbringing of the ordinary man and the ordinary doctor, enormous stress has been laid on general principles of great rigidity – such principles are naturally susceptible to thin ends of wedges. But when we are disputing at level 2 about what our level-1 principles ought to be, the argument has little force. For it may be that we could devise other, equally simple principles which would be wedge-resistant and would draw lines in different places; it may be that we *ought* to do this, if the new places were more likely, if generally recognized, to lead most often to the right results in practice. Tooley recommends such a moral line very shortly *after* birth, and his arguments have a great attraction.[15] For the present, it is enough to say that if the line proved wedge-resistant and if it separated off, in a workable manner, nearly all the cases that would be pronounced wrong by level-2 thinking from nearly all those which would be pronounced permissible, then it would be no argument against this proposal that it conflicted with people's intuitions. These intuitions, like earlier ones which made a big distinction at quickening, are the results of attempts to simplify the issues for a laudable practical purpose; they cannot without circularity be used in an appraisal of themselves. As Tooley implies, we have to find real moral reasons for distinguishing cases. If, as is sure to happen, the distinctions that result are very complicated, we have to simplify them for ordinary use as best we can; and there is no reason to assume that the simplifications which will be best are those which have been current hitherto – certainly not in a context in which circumstances have changed as radically as they have with regard to abortion.

VII

It might be objected, as we have seen, that the view I have advocated would require unlimited procreation, on the ground that not to produce any single child whom one might have produced lays one open to the charge that one is not doing to that child as one is glad has been done to oneself (viz. causing him to be born). But there are, even on the present view, reasons for limiting the population. Let us suppose that fully-grown adults were producible ad lib., not by gestation in human mothers or in the wombs of cats or in test tubes, but instantaneously by waving a wand. We should still have to formulate a population policy for the world as a whole, and for particular societies and families. There would be a point at which the additional member of each of these units imposed burdens on the other members great enough in sum to outweigh the advantage gained by the additional member. In utilitarian terms, the classical or total utility principle sets a limit to population which, although higher than the average utility principle, is nevertheless a limit.[16] In terms of the Golden Rule, which is the basis of my present argument, even if the "others" to whom we are to do what we wish, or what we are glad, to have done to us are to include potential people, good done to them may be outweighed by harm done to other actual or potential people. If we had to submit to all their lives or nonlives in turn, we should have a basis for choosing a population policy which would not differ from that yielded by the classical utility principle. How restrictive this policy would be would depend on assumptions about the threshold effects of certain increases in population size and density. I think myself that even if potential people are allowed to be the objects of duties, the policy will be fairly restrictive; but this is obviously not the place to argue for this view.

One big gap in the argument of this paper is my failure to deal with the question of whether, when we are balancing the interests of the potential person into whom this fetus will turn against the interests of other people who might be born, we ought to limit the second class to other members of the same family, or include in it *any* potential person who might in some sense "replace" the first-mentioned potential person. This major question would seem to depend for its answer on a further question: To what extent will the birth or non-birth of *this* person make more or less likely the birth or non-birth of the others? This is a demographic question which at the moment baffles me; but it would obviously have to be gone into in any exhaustive account of the morality of abortion. I have, however, written (possibly too hastily) as if only other potential members of the same family need be considered. That was enough to illustrate the important principle that I was trying to explain.

VIII

Lastly, a logician might object that these potential people do not exist, and cannot be identified or individuated, and therefore cannot be the objects of duties. If I had put my own view in terms of rights or interests, the same objection could be expressed by saying that only actual people have these. Two points can be made against this objection at once. The first is a perhaps superficial one: it would be strange if there were an act whose very performance made it impossible for it to be wrong. But if the objection were correct, the act of aborting a possible person would be such an act; by preventing the existence of the object of the wrongdoing, it would remove its wrongness. This seems too easy a way of avoiding crime.

Secondly, there seems to be no objection in principle to condemning hypothetical acts: it would have been wrong for Nixon to stay on any longer in the presidency. And it seems a fairly safe principle that if it makes sense to make value-judgments about an act that was done, it makes equal sense to make opposite judgments about the hypothetical omission to do that act. "Nixon did right to resign" makes sense; and so, therefore, does "Nixon would have done wrong not to resign." But we do commend actions which resulted in our own existence – every Sunday in thousands of churches we give thanks for our creation as well as for our preservation and all the blessings of this life; and Aristotle says that we ought to show the same gratitude to our earthly fathers as "causes of our being."[17] So it is at least meaningful to say of God or of our fathers that if they had not caused us to exist, they would not have been doing as well for us as they could. And this is all that my argument requires.

Coming now to the purely logical points, we notice that the nonactuality of the potential person (the supposed object of the duty to procreate or not abort) is a separate issue from his nonidentifiability. Unfortunately "identifiable" is an ambiguous word; in one sense I can identify the next man to occupy my carrel at the library by describing him thus, but in another sense I cannot identify him because I have no idea who he is. The person who will be born if these two people start their coitus in precisely five minutes is identified by that description; and so, therefore, is the person who would have been born if they had started it five minutes ago. Moreover (this is an additional point) if we had enough mechanical and other information, we could specify the hair color and all the other traits of that person, if we wished, with as much precision as we could the result of a lottery done on a computer whose randomizing mechanism we could minutely inspect. In this sense, therefore, the potential person is identifiable. We do not know who he will be, in the sense that we do not know what actually now existing person he will be, because he will not be identical with any actually now existing person. But it is hard to see how his inability to meet this logically unmeetable demand for identifiability with some already existing person affects the argument; he is identifiable in the sense that identifying reference can be made to him. So it cannot be nonidentifiability that is the trouble.

Is it then nonactuality? Certainly not *present* nonactuality. We can do harm to and wrong succeeding generations by using up all the world's resources or by releasing too much radioactive material. But suppose that this not merely made them miserable, but actually stopped them being born (e.g. that the radioactive material made everybody sterile all at once). As before it seems that we can be thankful that our fathers did not do this, thereby stopping us coming into existence; why cannot we say, therefore, that if we behave as well as our fathers, we shall be doing well by our children or grandchildren, or that if we were to behave in this respect worse than our fathers, we would be doing worse by our children or grandchildren. It seems strange to say that if we behaved only a little worse, so that the next generation was half the size it would have been, we had done badly for that generation, but that if we behaved much worse, so that the succeeding generation was reduced to nil, we had not done badly for it at all.

This is obviously a very perplexing matter, and needs much more discussion. All I can hope to do here is to cast doubt on the assumption that some people accept without question, viz. that one cannot harm a person by preventing him coming into existence. True, he does not exist to be harmed; and he is not *deprived* of existence, in the sense of having it taken away from him, though he is *denied* it. But if it would have been a good for him to exist (because this made possible the goods that, once he existed, he was able to enjoy), surely it was a harm to him not to exist, and so not to be able to enjoy these goods. He did not suffer; but there were enjoyments he could have had and did not.

IX

I conclude, then, that a systematic application of the Christian Golden Rule yields the following precepts about abortion. It is prima facie and in general wrong in default of sufficient countervailing reasons. But since the wrongness of it consists, in the main, of stopping a person coming into existence and not in any wrong done to the fetus as such, such countervailing reasons are not too hard to find in many cases. And if the termination of this pregnancy facilitates or renders possible or probable the beginning of another more propitious one, it really does not take much to justify it.

I have not discussed what the law on abortion ought to be; that question would have to be the subject of another paper. I have been speaking only about the morality of terminating individual pregnancies. I will end as I began by saying that my argument has been based on a developed ethical theory, though I have not had room to expound this theory (I have done it in my books). This theory provides the logical basis of the Golden Rule. Though not *founded on* a utilitarian principle, it also provides the basis for a certain sort of utilitarianism that escapes the vices which have been decried in some other sorts.[18] But I shall not now try to defend these last assertions. If they are challenged, and if the view that I have advanced in this paper is challenged, the issue can only be fought out on the terrain of ethical theory itself. That is why it is such a pity that so many people – even philosophers – think that they can discuss abortion without making up their minds about the fundamental problems of moral philosophy.

Notes

1 Judith Jarvis Thomson, "A Defense of Abortion," *Philosophy & Public Affairs*, I, no. 1 (Fall 1971). Reprinted in *The Rights and Wrongs of Abortion*, ed. Marshall Cohen, Thomas Nagel, and Thomas Scanlon (Princeton, NJ, 1974), hereafter cited as *RWA*.

2 John Finnis, "The Rights and Wrongs of Abortion: A Reply to Judith Thomson," *Philosophy & Public Affairs*, 2, no. 2 (Winter 1973); reprinted in *RWA*.

3 Finnis, "Rights and Wrongs," p. 129; *RWA*, p. 97. Thomson, "Defense," pp. 53f.; *RWA*, pp. 9f.

4 Judith Jarvis Thomson and Gerald Dworkin, *Ethics* (New York, 1968), p. 2. Cf. David A. J. Richards, "Equal Opportunity and School Financing: Towards

a Moral Theory of Constitutional Adjudication," *Chicago Law Review*, 41 (1973): 71, for a similar misunderstanding. I am most grateful to Professor Richards for clearing up this misunderstanding in his article, "Free Speech and Obscenity Law," *University of Pennsylvania Law Review*, 123 (1974), fn. 255.

5 "Imperative Sentences," *Mind*, 58 (1949), reprinted in my *Practical Inferences* (London, 1971); "Freedom of the Will," *Aristotelian Society Supp.* 25 (1951), reprinted in my *Essays on the Moral Concepts* (London, 1972).

6 Cf. Aristotle, *Nicomachean Ethics*, 5, $1137^{b}20$. I owe the roller-skate example to H. L. A. Hart.

7 "Abortion and Infanticide," *Philosophy & Public Affairs*, 2, no. 1 (Fall 1972): 60; *RWA*, p. 75. It will be clear what a great debt I owe to this article.

8 See my "Rules of War and Moral Reasoning," *Philosophy & Public Affairs*, 1, no. 2 (Winter 1972), fn. 3; reprinted in *War and Moral Responsibility*, ed. Marshall Cohen, Thomas Nagel, and Thomas Scanlon (Princeton, NJ, 1974). See also my review of John Rawls, *A Theory of Justice*, in *Philosophical Quarterly*, 23 (1973): 154f.; and my "Ethical Theory and Utilitarianism" in *Contemporary British Philosophy*, series 4, ed. H. D. Lewis (London, 1976).

9 St Matthew 7:12. There have been many misunderstandings of the Golden Rule, some of which I discuss in my "Euthanasia: A Christian View," *Proceedings of the Center for Philosophic Exchange*, vol. 6 (SUNY at Brockport, 1975).

10 Tooley, "Abortion and Infanticide," pp. 55–6; *RWA*, pp. 70–1 (my italics)

11 Act IV, scene 6.

12 See C. I. Lewis, *An Analysis of Knowledge and Valuation* (La Salle, 1946), p. 547; D. Haslett, *Moral Rightness* (The Hague, 1974), ch. 3. Cf. my *Freedom and Reason* (Oxford, 1963), p. 123.

13 See "The Argument from Received Opinion," in my *Essays on Philosophical Method* (London, 1971); "Principles," *Aristotelian Society*, 72 (1972–3); and my "Ethical Theory and Utilitarianism."

14 Tooley, "Abortion and Infanticide," p. 59; *RWA*, p. 74. See also Janathan Glover's book on the morality of killing, *Causing Death and Saving Lives* (Harwardsworth, 1977).

15 Tooley, p. 64; *RWA*, p. 79. If the potentiality principle be granted, the number of permissible infanticides is greatly reduced, but not to nothing. See my "Survival of the Weakest" in *Documentation in Medical Ethics*, 2 (1973); reprinted in *Moral Problems in Medicine*, ed. Samuel Gorovitz et al., 2nd edn (New York, 1982).

16 See my review of Rawls, pp. 244f.

17 *Nicomachean Ethics*, 8, $1161^{a}17$, $1163^{a}6$, $1165^{a}23$.

18 See my "Ethical Theory and Utilitarianism."

Mother–Fetus Conflict

6

Are Pregnant Women Fetal Containers?

Laura M. Purdy

Introduction

Let me relieve your curiosity right away: yes, pregnant women are fetal containers.[1] That is, they have fetuses in their bodies. But the implication from this fact drawn by some people from the phrase – that women are nothing but cheap clay pots supporting infinitely precious flowers – is very far from being the case.[2]

Women carry fetuses in their bodies, it is true. It is equally true, however, that fetuses are part of women's bodies. The champions of fetus and woman in this latest round of the war about women's reproductive rights would argue that these claims are inconsistent. For one of the legacies of the abortion battle has been the assumption that if fetuses are part of women's bodies, they are not separate entities and women should therefore have the final say about what happens to them.

The Problem

Women, like men, want to control what happens to and in our bodies. Women's ability to do this is being threatened by proponents of the view that our choices should be subordinated to the welfare of fetuses within us.

Respect for our right, as moral agents, to control our bodies, is a keystone of liberal society. The paradigm cases of such control consist of situations common to both women and men. Those, like pregnancy, that are experienced only by women, have a way of being regarded as special cases and thrown into question. Such debate is perhaps innocuous when it involves moral claims. However, when, as here, it moves to the legal realm and can lead to coercion or punishment, its implications become much more serious.

Cases where women's decisions about their pregnancies have been overridden by doctors and judges are accumulating. Some involve drug use. For example, one woman was charged with child abuse last year after giving birth to her second cocaine-addicted baby; her child was placed in foster care. In another case, a woman was jailed for a week after she gave birth to a brain-damaged baby: she was accused, among other things, of drug abuse. In a third case, a woman arrested for cheque forgery was found to be using cocaine; a judge sent her to jail for four months to protect her fetus.[3] Others involve involuntary Caesareans. In one such case, a Nigerian woman's husband was thrown out of the hospital and she was strapped to the table for the surgery.[4] In another, a terminally-ill cancer patient was forced to submit to surgery in order to give a marginally viable fetus a chance at life; both were dead in two days.[5] And so forth. Relatively little publicity has accompanied such cases.[6] Yet if the same things were being done to the average middle-class white man on the street, there would be public outrage. Is there then some morally relevant difference between that man in the street and pregnant women that would justify such different legal treatment?

The Fetus's Place

Fetuses live in women's bodies. This means both that what happens in and to those bodies can

From *Bioethics*, vol. 4, no. 4 (1990), pp. 273–91.

adversely affect fetuses and that the only way to get at a fetus is through the body that houses it.

It is now well-known that fetuses can be harmed by a variety of causes that operate before or after conception. Genetic defects, exposure to radiation or toxic substances, maternal ill-health and birth itself can lead to a diseased or handicapped baby. Research has helped us to understand and deal with some of the difficulties afflicting fetal development and birth, and this area is currently the subject of intensive scrutiny and experimentation. The list of worries is long. Consider, just for a start, maternal infections such as rubella, herpes, syphilis and AIDS. Pregnant women may also suffer from a variety of diseases such as diabetes, thyroid disease, hypertension and cancer; they may also be exposed to toxic chemicals like anaesthetic gases, chemotherapeutic drugs, benzene and dioxin.[7]

Because fetuses are so vulnerable, protecting them requires a comprehensive approach. Women must avoid harmful substances, act to meet fetal needs and, at times, submit to bodily invasions. They must exercise self-discipline about so-called 'life-style' choices, keeping away from substances such as alcohol, tobacco, drugs – and no doubt hot fudge sundaes. They also need to stay away from toxic environments, including work and living places. It is also important that they get good prenatal care, eat a healthy diet, and exercise appropriately. Finally, they must make good judgements about recommended medical treatment for themselves and their fetuses.[8]

This list demonstrates how entwined fetal interests are with women's lives, and at how many points those interests might diverge. Furthermore, the more thoroughgoing our understanding of the process of pregnancy and the bolder our technology, the more acute the potential conflicts.

The existence of such conflict is denied by many of those who are thinking about the problem. Some writers conflate fetuses and children, unable to see any morally relevant differences between them: they seem oblivious to the fact that fetuses live in women's bodies. The implications of that fact are therefore ignored or dismissed.[9] They fail to recognize that women's rights might sometimes trump considerations about fetal welfare.

We should not forget that the sacrifices exacted by a well-run pregnancy may be considerable; they deserve recognition and perhaps even compensation; some may be too great to be required at all. Forgoing small pleasures like an occasional drink is just the beginning. Imagine a bad cold – let alone more serious illness – without pain relief. Imagine, too, foregoing the therapy that will cure your disease – or being denied, as was Angela Carder, the only drugs that may prolong your life. What is it like to be a cocaine addict voluntarily – or involuntarily – going cold turkey? Imagine losing a good job because it endangers your fetus. Imagine knowing that you need unavailable prenatal care – or that its lack increases the probability that you will need dangerous treatment. Picture being required to undergo risky therapy for the sole benefit of another. Our anger rightly flares in response to those who take these situations for granted.

And yet it seems to me that those in the opposing camp are not altogether free of the same tendency to deny the reality of conflict or dismiss rather too quickly fetus's interests.

Barbara Katz Rothman, for instance, writes that

> The perception of the fetus as a person separate from the mother draws its roots from patriarchal ideology, and can be documented at least as far back as the early use of the microscope to see the homunculus. But until recently, the effects of this ideology on the management of pregnancy could only be indirect. For all practical purposes, the mother and fetus had to be treated as one unit while the fetus lay hidden inside the mother.[10]

She goes on to argue that medical technology emphasizes and makes concrete patriarchal notions about the relationship beween woman and fetus. Woman and fetus are seen as conceptually separate, joined only by an unimportant physical bond. A woman-centred view of pregnancy is, on the contrary, holistic: 'the baby is not planted within the mother, but flesh of her flesh, part of her . . .'[11] In consequence, the vision of warring interests and rights collapses.

What takes its place? Rothman suggests an analogy between persons at various ages and the relationship between woman and fetus: 'our old selves, our ageing selves, are part of our young selves, and yet become someone very different. Can I in my old age come to sue myself for behavior I engaged in when younger . . .'[12]

Now it may well be true that a patriarchal lens colours our view of pregnancy, obscuring the fact that fetuses are part of women's bodies. However, it does not follow that diverse interests cannot coexist in one bit of flesh. Consider Siamese twins: the surgery necessary to separate them may mutilate or kill one or both. Do we really want to say that the loss is an illusion, that there can be no conflict of interest here?

Likewise, it is undeniable that decisions a woman makes now may affect the child she later bears. Where she chooses – perhaps for good reason – to ignore physicians' recommendations, any resulting baby will share the consequences with her. A choice that is good for her may harm her fetus; one person enjoys a benefit whereas the other (eventually) bears a burden. Just societies attempt to minimize such situations.

This contrasts with Rothman's image of the self. We may feel less or more connected with our earlier selves throughout life, but we are nonetheless one person. If we are lucky, others cared enough to help us temper our youthful exuberance and rebellion with some attention to long-term consequences. To the extent that we did not, we may now be paying the costs of long-gone pleasures. But the pleasures – even if we now regret them – were *ours*, not someone else's. A woman might enjoy her nightly beer, but it is not she who reaps Fetal Alcohol Syndrome. So the fact of being one flesh now does not preclude two different fates.[13]

Christine Overall attempts to diminish the impact of this conclusion by arguing that maternal and fetal interests tend to be in harmony: what is good for the one is also good for the other. This may often be true, but it does not help us when women, for whatever reason, fail to act in their own interest or when those interests truly diverge.[14]

The Social Context of Conflict

How can we begin to sort out the moral problems created by this situation? Surely we should start with the assumption that women have at least the same basic rights as other people. Universalizability requires that to the extent situations are parallel, women's interests should garner the same degree of respect as anybody else's. Where treatment diverges, it must be possible to point to a morally relevant difference in the situation. And the connection between that difference and the treatment must be tightly argued and show the same respect for women as middle-class white men would expect.

The question before us is a special case of the first general moral question: what do we owe others? More particularly, what do we owe others who do not yet exist? And, most particularly, what legally enforceable duties towards such future persons can be exacted of us?

Several different levels of obligation are recognized, depending on the nature of the relationship between the individuals in question. Various types of agreements (marriage, for instance), as well as biological relationships (such as parenthood) raise our expectations of what is morally owed; the law tends to reflect this understanding.

The closest analogy to the relationship between woman and fetus is the one between relatives. It is therefore more than a little interesting that a court refused to order involuntary bone marrow surgery on Shimp in order to increase the probability of his leukaemic cousin McFall's survival.[15]

Perhaps the proper rejoinder is that Shimp and McFall were merely cousins – surely the closer relationship between women and fetus can justify greater demands on the former. But, as Kolder, Gallagher and Parsons argue, 'the closest legal analogy would be an organ "donation" ordered over the explicit refusal of a competent adult, and such an order would be profoundly at odds with our legal tradition.'[16] George Annas notes that 'no mother has ever been legally required to undergo surgery or general anaesthesia (e.g. bone marrow or kidney transplant) to save the life of her dying child. It would be ironic, to say the least, if she could be forced to submit to more invasive surgical procedures for the sake of her fetus than for her child.'[17]

Annas assumes that a woman's duty toward her fetus must be no more demanding – in fact, less so – than a parent's duty toward her child. Fetuses, after all, are not yet persons, and the call of persons upon us is stronger than that of non-persons. Those who insist that women owe their fetuses at least the equivalent of transplants, are, on the contrary, assuming that women owe their fetuses *more* than their children.

Pregnancy is, of course, unlike any other relationship in human experience: analogies go only so far, and then we venture onto new territory. The uniquely close relationship between woman and fetus has been taken to have serious moral implications. Those who are prepared to subordinate the welfare of women to that of their fetuses see this close relationship as justification for demands on women that exceed those required for children.

However, proponents of this view don't seem to feel the need for argument showing just how and why this is the case; nor do they address the question of limits.

That this uniquely close relationship has compelling moral consequences is also taken for granted by those who think it justifies women's overriding say about their fetuses. But the case is little more developed than the previous one.

This as yet undefined characteristic that takes reasoning about pregnancy out of the realm of the relatively settled assumptions about parents and children seems to me to be disturbingly amorphous. Perhaps that is why we are seeing such contradictory implications drawn from it. Future research may help us to see the matter more clearly, but for now I think it would be a good deal safer to retreat to better explored ground.

The following points seem to me to be relevant to our discussion. First, dependence is a pervasive characteristic of human society. Secondly, because of their location and state, fetuses are dependent on women in an unusally fundamental and continuous way. Thirdly, fetuses are not moral persons. Fourthly, they will probably become such persons some time after birth.

I take it that we have a moral duty to take some steps to meet the needs of those who are dependent on us. I also take it that the morally relevant feature of pregnancy is not that fetuses are not now moral persons, but that they will be affected after birth by what happens now. So I think that Annas is wrong to assume that women might owe fetuses less than children here because they are not persons. But I think that there are no grounds for holding that woman owe them more than children either.

If we ought to try to prevent disease or handicap in our children, the same duty holds for our fetuses, even if they are not yet persons. To achieve that end, no more and no less sacrifice ought to be legally expected of us in the two cases. Thus if parents are not required to submit to bodily invasions to save a dying child, then a woman should not be expected to do so for the benefit of a fetus; the converse is also true.

Personhood becomes relevant only where preventing death is at issue. Because fetuses are not persons, it may be morally permissible to abort them. This means that a woman could avoid some demands by aborting her fetus, whereas she cannot kill a child. In this way, pregnancy requires less of her than parenthood.

Other factors may also help us differentiate between pregnancy and parenthood. One is that the fetus's probability of survival to personhood is somewhat lower. Another is that in some cases we are much less certain of how a fetus will be affected by a given state of affairs. This uncertainty increases the burden of proof on those who would override a pregnant woman's decision about what to do.

Given the foregoing, if judges refuse to order bodily invasions of parents for their children's benefit, they certainly should not be ordering them of women for their fetus's benefit. And they are refusing to order such invasions of parents. Consider, for instance, *In re George*, a case where a leukaemic adoptee wanted access to his adoption records in order to see whether he could find a good bone marrow donor. The judge contacted his father, who was unwilling either to acknowledge paternity or be tested for compatibility. The judge would not even give the petitioner his father's name.[18] It should also be noted that the invasions so far contemplated (and denied) by the courts have been of substantially lesser magnitude then the Caesareans now being ordered for women.

Not only are the orders legally inconsistent with precedent, but the manner of their making violates established procedures. Despite a general legal trend toward increased respect for our right to determine what shall happen to us and our bodies, women are deprived of the safeguards routinely afforded the unconscious, criminals, and individuals with mental problems. Indeed, 'court-ordered medical treatment – even of the incompetent or of those whose legal rights are limited – is imposed only after detailed fact finding conducted through full adversarial hearings with scrupulous attention to procedural rights.'[19] The reference to incompetents is not inapposite, as some cases overriding competent women's decisions rely for precedent on those where she is judged incompetent, suggesting that pregnancy renders women incompetent or constitutes a waiver of autonomy.[20] Yet proposed surgical searches of criminal defendants, sterilization of the mentally retarded or even mind-altering drug therapy for mental patients are supposed to be conducted only after a full legal hearing.[21]

These violations tend to be protected from appellate review because the case is moot or because the losing party is unable or unwilling to pursue such a remedy. Moreover, the time constraints on cases of this kind limit the potential for amicus briefs filed by outside experts. These factors, Gallagher contends, have serious repercussions on the resulting law: 'the procedural shortcomings rampant in these cases are not mere technical deficiencies. They undermine the authority of the decisions themselves, posing serious questions as to whether judges can, in the absence of genuine notice, adequate representation, explicit standards of proof, and right of appeal, realistically frame principled and useful legal responses to the dilemmas with which they are being confronted.'[22]

George Annas elaborates on the inadequate social context of such emergency decision making, arguing that

> In the vast majority of cases, judges were called on an emergency basis and ordered interventions within hours. The judge usually went to the hospital. Physicians should know what most lawyers and almost all judges know: When a judge arrives at a hospital in response to an emergency call, he or she is acting much more like a lay person than a jurist. Without time to analyze the issues, without representation for the pregnant woman, without briefing or thoughtful reflection on the situation, in almost total ignorance of the relevant law, and in an unfamiliar setting faced by a relatively calm physician and a woman who can easily be labelled 'hysterical', the judge will almost always order whatever the physician advises.[23]

These procedures might help explain why of the twenty-one cases where involuntary treatment orders had been sought as of May 1987, they were successfully obtained in 86 percent of the cases, and were received within six hours in 88 percent of them. That especially powerless women are at risk is suggested by the additional fact that 81 percent of the women were black, Asian or Hispanic.[24]

The casual nature of these decision procedures, as well as the gravity of the intrusion, differentiates these cases from others cited by Robertson in their defence.[25] Overturning an adult's decision about a matter affecting her own body legally requires physicians to 'meet an exacting standard of proof: establishing both the necessity of the procedure and the fact that no less drastic means are available. Their burden increases with the degree of invasiveness, risk, or indignity involved.'[26] Even cursory scrutiny of existing cases suggests that physicians' decisions are not subjected to even the most minimally demanding version of this charge.

Until medicine becomes less of an art and more of a science, it is not clear whether it is possible even in principle to meet that standard of proof. Disagreements about the best way to handle many situations abound. For example, there is serious debate about whether Caesareans are indicated when a woman is pregnant with triplets.[27] It is also well known that Caesarean rates generally vary widely, suggesting that decisions to cut are influenced by non-medical factors.[28]

Even where there is broad agreement about the necessity for treatment, judgements are not certain. For example, a condition known as 'placenta previa', where the placenta blocks the exit of the uterus, is widely considered a clear indication for a Caesarean section. However, although ultrasonography is usually accurate in diagnosing this condition, it is not foolproof: less dangerous partial cases may be difficult to distinguish from complete ones. Furthermore, the placenta can move before delivery.[29] In fact, despite dire predictions for both woman and baby, a substantial percentage of the women for whom they were ordered subsequently gave birth to healthy babies without surgery. Thus, of the cases surveyed by Kolder, Gallagher and Parson, there were fifteen court orders for Caesareans; in two of those cases the patient agreed in the end to have the operation; yet in six other cases, vaginal birth proved harmless.[30] Yet this reality has not prevented a judge from ordering 'that if the pregnant woman did not admit herself to the hospital by a specified time and date, she would be picked up and transported there by the police and would have to submit to "whatever the medical personnel deemed appropriate, including Caesarean section and medication".'[31]

In general, the widely varying opinions about treatment, and the unreliable nature of the technologies, such as fetal monitoring, upon which those criteria for action are based, appropriately give rise to considerable scepticism about physician recommendations. It is well known, for example, that fetal monitoring yields ambiguous results and there is much disagreement about their interpretation. Worse still, the Apgar scores used to rate fetal monitoring are themselves plagued by false positives, so that large numbers of children with low scores later do well. Even if such monitoring were accurate, however, many false positives would occur because of the special problems involved in screening for rare conditions. Many such practices, including keeping women prone during labour, have a tendency to precipitate the need for further intervention.[32] It is not just ignorance, but education that might cause a woman to think twice about doing as her doctor orders.

Another important related issue is that many decisions made by physicians are value judgements, not medical decisions at all. For example, Rhoden notes that physicians' approach to risk may not be the only reasonable one. Thus American obstetricians tend to adopt a maximin approach that 'focuses on the worst possible outcome in a situation of uncertainty (here, fetal death or damage), and takes action to prevent that outcome, regardless of the outcome's actual probability of occurrence.'[33] Not only is this strategy not the only reasonable one, but the judgement that fetal death is the worst possible outcome is a moral judgement, not a medical one: we might prefer the conclusion that the worst outcome is maternal morbidity or mortality. The problem is exacerbated by the fact that most doctors have little or no training in moral reasoning, and even if they do, we may not share their values. In any case, the medical establishment's track record on women's interests is mixed at best.

Finally, this analysis has so far assumed that the overall social context is just. This is not true: unfair assumptions about women and their importance are embedded in judgements about what actions constitute 'least restrictive alternatives' and 'least drastic intrusions' required for overriding principles about bodily integrity and privacy and blind us to alternatives.

Take for instance the question of medical care. First, a narrow case: studies show that birthing women monitored by nurses with stethoscopes and those monitored with fetal monitors had equally healthy babies, although the former had fewer Caesareans.[34] Hence such human monitoring ought to be required where we otherwise risk invading women's bodies – even if it costs more.

More generally, perinatal mortality is most commonly caused by prematurity.[35] Prematurity is well known to be strongly associated with poor prenatal care. Yet, 23 percent of pregnant women received late or no prenatal care in 1982. Such women, writes Schott, 'are three times more likely to have babies of low birth weight, the single most important contributor to infant mortality. Low birthweight babies are also susceptible to a host of medical problems and disabilities.'[36] Poverty, lack of education, minority status and geographical location are serious barriers to such care. For instance, according to Schott, in the USA it now costs an average of $5,000 to have a child. This amount may be more than a family without health insurance can pay. In 1978, twenty-six million Americans didn't have insurance; in 1984, thirty-seven million didn't have it, an increase of more than 30 percent. This means that some 36 percent of the women of childbearing age do not have insurance.[37]

Current medical welfare programmes are not always sufficient to guarantee adequate care. Poor and minority women face special obstacles: they may have difficulty getting time off work, paying for childcare, arranging transportation to a clinic; they may also be subjected to indignities and outrages like involuntary sterilization once there. As federal funds are repeatedly cut, care may become completely unavailable. By 1985, the percentage of poor receiving Medicaid had dropped to 46 percent, down from 63 percent in 1975. Even if a woman has Medicaid, however, she is by no means guaranteed care: in some areas there are no obstetrics physicians who accept Medicaid patients; overall, only 56 percent of such physicians do so.[38]

Under these circumstances, invading women's bodies to impose last-minute, heroic care is stupid, mean, and unfair. It is reminiscent of proposals to dose us with contraceptives to lower the birth rate, before eradicating the pronatalist pressures and occupational discrimination that contribute significantly to overpopulation in the first place. Until we as a society act to make good, inexpensive, convenient, and respectful care a priority, punishing women for lack of prenatal care reeks of hypocrisy. It is especially inappropriate in a society where no one is required to provide the poor with care if they lack funds. Consequently, a woman may be denied life-saving treatment, yet later be subjected to life-threatening risk to attempt to save her fetus.[39] This state of affairs is all the more angering because it is cheaper to furnish good prenatal care than Caesareans, gaol, neonatal intensive care, or lifetime care for damaged babies. According to Schott, full prenatal care costs about $600 per patient; the cost of neonatal intensive care for a low birthweight baby costs about $10,000–$15,000.[40] Such care can, of course, cost vastly more, and these figures, in any case, take into account neither lifetime costs of disability nor pain and suffering.

Toxic exposure in the workplace raises similar considerations. Many women of childbearing age are now exposed to dangerous substances. Should they all be required to remove themselves from these environments, even at the cost of losing their job? Most women work because they must, and a well-paying safe job may be hard to find; many are in any case inaccessible to the poor and uneducated. Eradicating discrimination against women in general, and recognizing the special contribution and needs of pregnant women, would relieve them of these difficult choices.

This particular problem would also disappear if employers were required to clean up workplaces. Some employers object that the expense of doing so is prohibitive. But then they are just passing on the cost of doing safe business to women, who are among those members of society least able to bear it as they earn the least. The dilemma facing women is therefore not inevitable: it is caused by employers' desire to save money and society's willingness to let them do so at women's expense. Alleged concern about fetuses rings hollow when people attempt to pass the entire burden of protecting them onto women.[41] Such 'concern' is especially suspect when it keeps women from only high-paying jobs, not the traditionally feminine ones that may well pose equally serious risks. Lack of interest in possible damage to sperm simply reinforces this suspicion.

The focus on getting women out of certain workplaces is especially odd when we discover that there have been no lawsuits by children with birth defects caused by occupational exposures of their parents. Furthermore, there are good reasons for believing that none is likely to be successful:

> Scientifically conclusive evidence that a particular workplace exposure caused or contributed to an injury is rare . . . a court of law or a worker's compensation board may be unwilling to rely solely, or even substantially, on the results of epidemiologic or toxicologic investigations to support claims for compensation . . . Therefore, for the most part, reproductively damaged workers have very limited access to redress against their employers through the courts.[42]

Odder still is the fact that, so far, more men than women have filed legal charges of reproductive damage caused by occupational exposures.[43] Environmental pollution raises similar issues.

Some environmental exposures arise from personal habits. Like men, women drink, smoke, and take drugs. It is now obvious that these substances affect fetuses. Disease and serious handicap are among the consequences for babies.[44] Shielding them from these substances is therefore highly desirable. What about the pregnant women who use them? Non-addicted women can reasonably be expected to stop if they are pregnant or trying to get pregnant, although the moral basis for such responsibility is shaky while corporations still spew dangerous pollutants into the air.[45] However, at present we depend mostly on moral exhortation, backed up with coercion. This approach is notoriously ineffective, yet society is unwilling to make the changes that would help people to reduce their reliance on such crutches and find alternative pleasures that are less harmful. Steps could be taken to lessen the likelihood that young women (and men) would adopt these habits in the first place. How about banning the cigarette and alcohol advertising that helps ensnare them? And, instead of subsidizing tobacco growers, the government could help fund wholesome alternative sources of fun like swimming pools, ski camps and cultural centres. This issue is symptomatic of the general reluctance to undertake fundamental reform that would help eradicate problems at their root instead of punishing those caught in difficult situations. Schott demonstrates convincingly in her article on the Pamela Rae Stewart case that the apparently self-centred and callous behaviour emphasized by the media can be shown to be reasonable in the circumstances; such circumstances could have been in large part prevented by better physician–patient communication and a more supportive society.

This point suggests the importance of raising some very basic questions about our society. Why is addiction growing? Why, in the eyes of so many, is being smashed or stoned a prerequisite for having a good time? I suspect that our social and political principles and arrangements have a great deal to do with what is happening. It seems that we have available to us relatively few sources of genuine pleasure and satisfaction. Furthermore, even those who are relatively well off are constantly enticed by goods they cannot have. Few of us have any real sense of economic security. Among industrialized countries, the United States is among the least developed in terms of social programmes, and the growth of drug use in the 1980s coincides with reductions in those already inadequate programmes; poverty is increasing. Furthermore, the philosophy of individualism, egoism and self-sufficiency coupled with a system of hierarchy and privilege that for the most part excludes women and men of colour, is singularly hostile to human welfare. Austere and unsympathetic, this world-view prefers narrowly-defined notions of freedom and justice to concerns about human happiness. It also tends to hold those on the bottom responsible for their acts, no matter how difficult the circumstances, and prefers punishment to making social and political arrangements that help people to act morally in the first place. Consider, for example, the dearth of drug treatment programmes for pregnant women: there are six-month waiting lists for the few clinics that accept them in California.[46] Given the powerful grip drugs can have on people, how can we justifiably punish such women for not quitting when they get so little help?

If there is any truth in these speculations, then we are going to be faced with a choice between increasingly harsh and inequitable treatment of women or fundamental social change. The general social bias against fair consideration of women's interests already evident in much of medicine is likely, in the absence of such change, to lead to further high-handed treatment if contemporary trends continue. For example, physicians did an involuntary Caesarean on a woman *without* seeking a court order in 1984.[47] That same year, a hospital sought and got a court order granting it temporary custody of a Nigerian woman's triplet fetuses and authorization of a Caesarean section against her will. Yet the woman was not even informed of these events.[48]

Taken to their logical conclusion, current attitudes and practices could lead to still more fundamental subordination of women in the interests (or alleged interests) of others. Schott suggests that:

> for a pregnant woman, the existence of a fetal harm law would make nearly every action potentially criminal. Her day-to-day movements, diet, sexual practices, recreation and other activities would be subjected to the exacting and suspicious scrutiny of doctors, the public and possibly a jury. A woman might find it difficult to explain the forces influencing her actions, and to convince a jury that she was not motivated by hostility toward her fetus.[49]

These developments would broadcast a clear message about the relative weight of pregnant women's interests in comparison with those of fetuses. Peeping out from under such judgements would be the assumption that women in general are self-centred, thoughtless individuals who cannot be expected to behave morally.[50]

These possibilities are less farfetched than they might seem at first blush. When Kolder et al. examined the attitudes of heads of fellowship programmes in maternal-fetal medicine they discovered the following statistics. First, in a sample of 57, 46 percent thought that women who endanger a fetus by refusing medical advice should be held against their will 'so that compliance could be assured.' Second, 47 percent wanted additional potentially life-saving procedures ordered by courts if women refuse them. Last, but not least, 26 percent 'advocated state surveillance of women in the third trimester who stay outside the hospital system'. Because of erratic patterns of answers, only 24 percent consistently supported women's right to refuse medical advice.[51] *The Handmaid's Tale* looms ever closer!

In conclusion, court orders violating a woman's decisions about her own care are dubious at best. Both the procedures leading to the orders, and the orders themselves constitute and perpetuate a legal double standard for pregnant women. The facts upon which these decisions are based are less certain than they seem, and the non-medical judgements involved are, at best, ones about which reasonable people might disagree and, at worst, are biased against women. All of this constitutes another proof that women are still second-class citizens who are tacitly excluded from supposedly universal rights whenever convenient. Americans have more say over what will happen to their bodies after death than many women do over their bodies while they are alive. Yet, as Rhoden points out, 'by way of comparison, an organ taken from a cadaver can save a life just as an emergency Caesarean can.'[52]

Hence it is seriously unjust to subject women to the kinds of treatment lately visited on them. Although women in difficult circumstances have a moral duty to do what they can for their fetuses, society ought not to hold them responsible for situations that are in large part due to its own moral inadequacies. It is especially dubious for society to do so when it shows so little concern for the well-being of existing children.[53]

I do not say any of this lightly: I have argued elsewhere – and still believe – that it is seriously wrong to knowingly bring a diseased or handicapped child into the world.[54] Other things being equal, I think that a woman's right to control her body can in some cases be less morally compelling than her child's interest in not going through life with major damage.

Should this moral state of affairs ever be reflected in a legal duty to submit to medical coercion or punishment for having refused to follow medical advice? Recognizing any limit on women's right to control their bodies would be cause for considerable anxiety. A good deal of our current social and political edifice appears to have been constructed on the premise that even the most vital of women's interests deserve little consideration. Thus for example, it is still far from clear that all are persuaded that marital prerogative or privacy do not justify wife-beating or rape. The research for this paper was eye-opening with respect to the contempt with which some of women's most basic interests can be treated. Because women's interests are in constant danger of being undervalued, I believe that in cases of conflict our inclination should be to grant them priority. It would follow from this that no legal duty to submit to medical advice should be recognized.

Suppose, though, that we manage to create a humane and fair society, one where women's interests are fully recognized, where discrimination based on race, class, sexual orientation and the like are eradicated, and much greater concern for human welfare informs social and political arrangements.

We might want to consider expecting more of each other, both morally and legally. One form such expectations might take would be to assume that people should be willing to sacrifice expendable parts of their bodies (bone marrow, paired organs) to save the lives of others. A still more demanding expectation would be that people make such sacrifices to prevent serious illness or handicap on the part of others. Although the first of these would not affect pregnant women especially, because fetuses aren't persons, the second would have a disproportionate impact on such women, despite the fact that for all the reasons suggested in this paper, a humane world would invite many fewer conflicts of interest between women and their fetuses.

Perhaps for this, or some other reason, we would reject the prospect of enforcing such expectations legally; perhaps medical science will advance sufficiently to render the point moot. If not, might we then have to countenance the possibility of a legal duty on women's part to submit to medical care? As many commentators have noticed, a duty of this kind might be counterproductive, leading women to avoid the medical establishment altogether. In that case, only extreme and unacceptable invasions of our civil liberties could then guarantee women's compliance.[55] Women might also maintain control of their bodies by being willing to see seriously damaged newborns die or be killed.

A more caring society would be very desirable: its coming should be encouraged by all those who are dissatisfied with the chill of the classical liberal approach to relationships. It is time for thinking about what forms such caring might reasonably take, together with their implications for our contemporary values. In the meantime, the contrast between this vision and our current world should be enough to fuel the fight against the invasions of women's bodies now occurring.

Notes

1 This paper was given at the December 1989 meeting of the Society for Philosophy and Public Policy; I would like to thank commentators Joan Callahan and Mary Anne Warren for their helpful comments. I would also like to thank Dianne Romain for her criticism of an earlier version, as well as Denise McCoskey and the two anonymous readers for *Bioethics*.

2 The flower-pot theory is elucidated by Caroline Whitbeck, 'Theories of Sex Difference', *Philosophical Forum*, 5, 1973, 1–2.

3 *Time* (May 22, 1989), 45.

4 Janet Gallagher, 'Prenatal Invasions and Interventions: What's Wrong with Fetal Rights', *Harvard Women's Law Journal*, 10 (1987), 9.

5 See Mary Mahowald, 'Beyond Abortion: Refusal of Caesarean Section', *Bioethics*, 32 (April 1989), 106.

6 See for instance, Gallagher, p. 10.

7 For a more detailed look at fetal hazards, see Margery W. Shaw, 'Conditional Prospective Rights of the Fetus', *Journal of Legal Medicine*, 5(1), (March 1984), 63–116.

8 For a fuller description of the effects on women of recognizing fetal rights, John Robertson, 'The Right to Procreate and in Utero Fetal Therapy', *Journal of Legal Medicine*, 3(3) (1982), 355.

9 Among the writers who appear to be unaware of the implications of their recommendations, see Shaw and E. W. Keyserlingk, 'A Right of the Unborn Child to

Prenatal Care – the Civil Law Perspective', *Revue de Droit*, 13 (Winter 1982), 49–90. For others who dismiss women's rights to bodily integrity and determination see Eike-Henner W. Kluge, 'When Caesarean Action Operations Imposed by a Court are Justified', *Journal of Medical Ethics* (1988), 206–11; Jeffrey Parness 'The Abuse and Neglect of the Human Unborn', *Family Law Quarterly*, 20 (1986), 197–212 and 'The Duty to Prevent Handicaps: Laws Promoting the Prevention of Handicaps to Newborns', *Western New England Law Review* 5 (1983), 431–64; Robertson, and a commentator in the *Whittier Law Review*, 9 (Summer 1987), 363–91.

10 Barbara Katz Rothman, *Recreating Motherhood: Ideology and Technology in a Patriarchal Society* (New York: W. W. Norton, 1989), p. 157.

11 Ibid., 161

12 Ibid.

13 I come to this conclusion with great regret, given Mary Anne Warren's attractive proposal that '*there is room for only one person with full and equal rights inside a single human skin*' 'The Moral Significance of Birth', *Hypatia*, 4, (3) (Fall 1990), 46–65.

14 Christine Overall, *Ethics and Human Reproduction* (Boston, MA: Allen and Unwin, 1987), pp. 99–100.

15 See Nancy K. Rhoden, 'The Judge in the Delivery Room: The Emergence of Court-Ordered Cesareans', *California Law Review*, 74 (6), part 2 (1986), 19.

16 Veronika E. B. Kolder, Janet Gallagher, and Michael T. Parsons, 'Court-Ordered Obstetrical Interventions', *New England Journal of Medicine*, 316 (19) (May 7, 1987), 1194.

17 George J. Annas, 'Forced Cesareans: The Most Unkindest Cut of All', *Hastings Center Report* (June 1982), 17. Rhoden offers an interesting analogy for our consideration: suppose a 'recalcitrant father were very obese and securely wedged in the door, and gaining access to the sick child to provide treatment required cutting through the father', 1968.

18 Rhoden, 1978.

19 Ibid., 20.

20 Ibid., 37. See also Rosalind Ekman Ladd, 'Women in Labor: Some Issues About Informed Consent', *Hypatia*, 4 (3) (Fall 1990), 37–45.

21 Ibid., 20.

22 Ibid., 49.

23 George J. Annas, 'Protecting the Liberty of Pregnant Patients', *New England Journal of Medicine*, 316 (19) (May 7, 1987), 1213–14; 1213.

24 Kolder, Gallagher, and Parsons, 1192.

25 Robertson, 353–4.

26 Gallagher, 20–1.

27 Gallagher, 9. This information comes from V. Kolder, *Women's Health Law: A Feminist Perspective* (August, 1985), pp. 1–2, unpublished manuscript on file at the *Harvard Women's Law Journal.*

28 Gallagher, 50–1.

29 Rhoden discusses this problem and others, 2011–17.

30 Kolder, Gallagher and Parsons, 1193, 1195.

31 Gallagher, 47, In this particular case, the woman fled into hiding with her entire family and two weeks later gave birth normally to a healthy, nine pound, two ounce baby. This matter of Caesareans is far from trivial.

An interesting sidelight on the safety of Caesareans is provided by a nineteenth-century medical historian who comments that a 'pregnant woman in labour had a 50 percent chance of survival post-Cesarean if she performed her own surgery, or if gored by a bull, compared to a 10 percent reported survival rate if attended to by a New York surgeon'. (Cited by Rhoden, 1951.)

This historical tidbit is now outdated, but the risks of Caesareans compared to natural childbirth remain considerable. Gallagher cites figures showing that the operation still involves a much higher risk of the woman's death: it is from three to thirty times the rate associated with vaginal delivery. Furthermore, all the subjects had much more pain, weakness and difficulty holding and caring for their new babies. The latter would support studies that suggest that Caesareans make it more difficult for mother and baby to bond. Many more women also get sick – 10 to 65 percent of the women developed infections like intrauterine cystitis, peritonitis, abscess, gangrene, sepsis, urinary tract infections, and respiratory infections; women delivering normally experience five to 10 times less infection (Gallagher, 50, notes 210–13). Among its risks, a Caesarean apparently sextuples the risk of developing placenta previa in subsequent pregnancies (Rhoden, 1958, n. 51).

Caesarean delivery is not completely unproblematic for babies either. Apart from the aforementioned consequences of possible difficult bonding, they are more at risk physically, too. Gallagher cites a National Institutes of Health Caesarean Birth Task Force report that stated that the most serious worry is respiratory distress, especially when previous Caesareans render a new, earlier operation necessary. It may be that vaginal delivery performs a helpful function by compressing the lungs (50, notes 212 and 213).

Gallagher argues that despite decreased rates of perinatal mortality cannot necessarily be attributed to the increasing rate of Caesareans. She quotes Dr Helen Marieskind who lists more plausible contributing factors such as improved sanitation and nutrition, increased access to health care, and use of contraception and abortion (p. 50).

32 Rhoden, 2011–17; Gallagher, 51.

33 Rhoden, 2013. She gives several specific examples of such strategies.

34 See Rothman, 157.

35 Rhoden, 2013.

36 Lee A. Schott, 'The Pamela Rae Stewart Case and Fetal Harm: Prosecution or Prevention?' *Harvard Women's Law Journal*, 11 (1988), 242.

37 Ibid.
38 Ibid., 241–2.
39 See George J. Annas, 'AIDS, Judges, and the Right to Medical Care', *Hastings Center Report*, 18, no. 4 (August/September 1988), 21.
40 Schott, 242.
41 Of course, if women are impoverished by these policies, fetuses will ultimately also suffer.
42 Office of Technology Assessment, cited by Donna M. Randall, 'Fetal Protection Policies: A Threat to Employee Rights?' *Employee Responsibilities and Rights Journal*, 1 (2) (1988), 123–4.
43 Ibid.
44 See Marty Jessup and Robert Roth 'Clinical and Legal Perspectives on Prenatal Drug and Alcohol Use: Guidelines for Individual and Community Response', *Medicine and Law*, 7(4) (November 4, 1988), 377–89.
45 See Gallagher, 56–7, n. 242.
46 *Time* (May 22, 1989), 45.
47 Gallagher, 46.
48 Ibid., 9.
49 Lee A. Schott, 'The Pamela Rae Stewart Case and Fetal Harm: Prosecution or Prevention?' *Harvard Women's Law Journal*, 11 (1988), 239.
50 Ibid.
51 Kolder et al., 1193–4.
52 Rhoden, 1982.
53 I am indebted to Joan Callahan for reminding me of this point.
54 See 'Genetic Disease: Can Having Children Be Immoral?' *Moral Problems in Medicine*, ed. Samuel Gorovitz et al., (Englewood Cliffs, NJ: Prentice-Hall, 2nd edn, 1982), pp. 377–84.
55 Thanks to Mary Anne Warren for this point.

PART II

Issues in Reproduction

Assisted Reproduction

7

Case Study: Becoming IVF Parents

Jan and Len Brennan

1 Jan Brennan

The reason for my infertility is through a wrong diagnosis when I was 19 years of age. I was treated for four weeks for something that was described as ovulation pains and treated with liquid aspirin. It was not until I was referred to a gynaecologist that it was discovered that in actual fact I had a massive infection in the Fallopian tubes and surrounding area. As a consequence both Fallopian tubes had to be removed and I nearly lost my life.

At the age of 19, although very upset and depressed at the thought of never being able to have children of my own, I do not think I fully realized the implications and the effect being infertile would have on my life. Besides I was cheerfully told by a nurse who was tending to me after my operation "at least you can always go in for breeding dogs!"

It was not until several years later and I had decided to marry that the fact I could not have children really hit home: the feeling of 'why me', as I am sure anyone who suffers from some form of disability experiences, but most of all the feeling of being useless as a woman because I could not have a baby. I found these feelings especially hard to cope with when friends announced with great excitement "Guess what, I'm pregnant." I would feel very happy for them of course but I always felt an emptiness and a sadness and a sense of great loss, that I would never be able to say those words and feel the excitement that they did. Ever since early childhood I had decided that more than anything else in the world, I wanted to be a Mum and have my own family.

There were many times when I felt that the fact I could not have children would have a detrimental effect on Len's love for me and would often wonder to myself if he would continue to love me as much in the future, and whether our relationship, although very strong and deep, would perhaps suffer through the feelings caused by my infertility. I felt too that perhaps he would think of me as not a complete woman and not very feminine because the most basic function of a woman's body had been taken away from me.

All my friends have children or are able to have them and although they did sympathize with me and try to understand how I felt, it is impossible to understand fully what it really is like. For this reason I felt very isolated and alone. I felt as though I was the only person in the world suffering from infertility. The formation of the IVF Friends Support Group has helped to alleviate these feelings and has made me realize just how many other couples are in our situation and have the same feelings as Len and me.

It saddens us greatly when we hear or read of children being dumped or bashed or abused, and I feel outrage at the fact that there are so many loving couples desperately wanting children to nurture and love and yet there are people who do not want their children. To them kids are a nuisance, a burden, an imposition; not a miracle of

From M. Brumby (ed.), *Proceedings of the Conference on* in vitro *Fertilization: Problems and Possibilities* (Clayton: Monash University Centre for Human Bioethics, 1982), pp. 12–16.

creation, a child to bestow love and understanding upon.

I have heard it said that wanting a child of our own is indulging our egos and that there are plenty of children waiting to be adopted. This is not true. We did not want a child of our own just because it might look like me or Len, or for any other reason, apart from the very simple one of a child of our own, whether adopted or not, to love and cherish. If there were plenty of children for adoption, there would not be the long waiting list of patients for IVF treatment, or AI, or other methods of treating infertility.

In 1978 we were referred to Professor Leeton to see if there was anything that could be done to enable us to have a child. At this stage Professor Leeton could offer us little hope and asked us to ring him periodically to check if any new developments had arisen.

It was not until the birth of the first IVF baby in the world that Len and I thought that here at last there might be a chance of us overcoming our problem. In March 1979 we received a letter from Professor Leeton asking us if we would like to begin IVF treatment. We were elated and felt so very lucky that we had the opportunity to participate in the IVF programme. We would never have dreamt that this treatment we were about to undergo would ever be questioned morally or ethically and to this day we do not see anything suspect about the IVF programme, which has only brought happiness to many couples, and a chance to have their much wanted baby.

In June 1979 we had our first attempt at IVF; unfortunately my ovulation time was uncertain and we were sent home. In August 1979, I went to theatre and a mature egg was collected but failed to be fertilized. Our third attempt in November of the same year proved unsuccessful too. A laparoscopy was performed but I had already ovulated and the egg had gone. In June 1980 we at last had some success. An egg was collected and fertilized and was transferred to my womb. Sadly it failed to embed and pregnancy did not occur. October 1980 was to be our month. Two eggs were transferred to my womb. On Tuesday 11th November it was confirmed I was pregnant with twins.

The emotions during these treatments ranged from feelings of elation and hope to depression and the feeling of not being able to cope with the intense emotions experienced. The hardest thing of all I found to cope with was the waiting. Waiting to go to theatre, for an egg to be fertilized and transferred, waiting to see if you became pregnant. It was a combination of hope that maybe next time it would be successful, determination and the longing to have our own child that kept us bouncing back up after each low and being prepared to try again. I must mention here at this point too, that if it had not been for the wonderful support and understanding of Len I would probably have faltered many times. It was Len's love and his unfailing conviction that I would become pregnant and that it was only a matter of time before the treatment would be successful and my own determination that made each treatment a little easier to cope with and to eventually have our prayers answered.

During the time of our treatments I could think of nothing else. It was with me nearly every waking hour, even though between attempts I did try to have a break to recover. I tried during this time to really help myself to become pregnant and give myself every possible chance. I lost weight, tried to eat a healthy diet and gave up smoking. I felt by doing this, I, at least, was perhaps contributing something to achieving our pregnancy.

The two treatments in which I had transfers were obviously the most trying times. I felt that once the embryo was inside my womb that I might have some force or control over it and will it to embed in the walls of my uterus. I would talk to it and think loving thoughts towards it and pray with all my might that we would have our little baby. I felt very special and very privileged to think that I had a potential human life hopefully developing within me. For the first 24 hours after the transfer I was afraid to move, sneeze or cough just in case I upset something. I was even afraid to go to the toilet because being vertical might cause our little cluster of cells to come tumbling out.

My feelings when I was told over the phone by Sister Jillian Wood that my hormones were nice and high and it was almost certain I was pregnant were ones of disbelief, amazement, joy and thousands of other feelings combined. Three days later our pregnancy was confirmed. We were both stunned and grinned from ear to ear each time we looked at each other. To be pregnant with twins was something in our wildest dreams we had never dared to hope for. I think this feeling of disbelief that I was pregnant continued right through until Pippin was born. We just could not believe our luck and thought that at any time we would wake up and learn that we had dreamt it all. I can remember some mornings on waking up

I would look under the bedclothes just to make sure I still had my fat tummy.

Now that I was having a baby the waiting really began. Because of the IVF treatments we had been through we had learnt much about conception and pregnancy. I think we realized more than most couples who fall pregnant just how many things can go wrong, the chances of miscarrying in early pregnancy, and how everything has to be just right before a pregnancy goes to full term. Every child conceived, be it by IVF or normally, is a very special miracle and Len and I would often marvel at the wonder of it all.

At approximately the eighth week of pregnancy, I awoke one morning and discovered I was spotting blood. To say we were frightened and worried sick was an understatement. I was admitted to hospital for complete rest for eight days. Once again during this time I was scared to even move and we prayed with all our strength that all was well. On leaving hospital I was sent to have an ultrasound. It showed that one of our twins had died. We were both very upset at our loss and were now even more frightened that our remaining baby might miscarry also. We were distraught to think that we had at last achieved our dream and now it seemed that it might be taken away from us. With this I doubt I could have ever coped. But our little embryo was made of sterner stuff and continued to flourish.

We continued taking things very carefully and Len took over most of the domestic duties as well as his own work. Once again I could never have managed without him. He was a tower of strength. Things appeared to be going well and we were just starting to relax and enjoy our pregnancy when at fourteen weeks, I suddenly began to bleed. This time it was more than just spotting. Once again we were thrown into turmoil and I was re-admitted to hospital. I cannot describe our feelings at this stage. We were desperate that everything would be alright with our little baby. A scan in the hospital proved to our enormous relief that our baby was fit and well and jumping about like a little cricket. After this trauma, our pregnancy continued in every way like any other pregnancy except that I was monitored more closely throughout the duration.

I was so proud of our pregnancy I wanted the whole world to know and wanted to shout it from the roof tops. I was so proud of my expanding tummy that when I went shopping I stuck it out further and felt like saying "Hey look at me, isn't it wonderful!" I was so happy I went everywhere with a grin on my face, I wanted to share my happiness with everyone.

Eventually the 23rd July, that magic day, arrived and our beautiful baby daughter was at last born. She was placed on my tummy to hold, a little blue but absolutely wonderful. Len was cuddling us both and tears of joy and happiness were shed. We were overwhelmed at this little miracle we had been given. Ten fingers, ten toes and wide alert blue eyes. Beautiful auburn hair. We have never been so thankful.

Since Pippin's birth she has been an eternal source of happiness and delight. We love her so dearly and are so very proud of our little girl. How empty our lives would have been without her, how pointless I would have felt my existence if I had been denied this opportunity of being Pippin's Mum and the opportunity to show her just how much we love her and how she means more than anything else in the world to us.

Pippin is now just over 7 months of age and has grown all too quickly as seems to be the habit of babies. I still look at her in wonder and awe and think back to all those times I despaired of ever having her, and all the ups and downs and the miracle of her conception and birth. We will be eternally grateful to the IVF team whose dedicated work made it all possible. They are wonderful people, dedicated, hard-working, and their only aim is to help childless couples achieve a much wanted pregnancy. In this we can't see any ethical or moral problems and can only hope and pray for the sake of other couples that the IVF programme be allowed to continue in its present form.

2 Len Brennan

Jan is not only my wife and lover but also my closest and dearest friend. I would go to any lengths to help her achieve what she wants out of life. I realize how important and natural children are in your life. They are the purpose of life, the fruit of your love for each other and a basic instinct of nature.

I have enjoyed going through the five IVF treatments with Jan because we have done it together. It has involved effort on my part and courage on Jan's. I guess it has involved over 300 daily trips from Dandenong to the city, most of which were early-morning dashes before work, with urine samples, to have blood samples taken and the like. I think if either one of us had shown signs of weakening the other would have fallen by the wayside. Upon reflection it put an enormous strain on our relationship. We seemed to have no time for ourselves, we seemed to be always rushing somewhere which disrupted our normal happy homelife. It also affected my business due to lost time. I can only say that it has all been worthwhile, and I would do it all over again.

The most moving experience in my life was to be present at Pippin's birth, the first one in my life. I was totally overwhelmed at the moment of birth. A combination of relief, excitement, wonder and awe, at the miracle of life and the beginning of a new generation.

Now that we have our little baby girl, one of the few in the world to do so, there is talk of the whole programme coming to a halt. It will not affect us if it does, but we know exactly how all those other couples will feel. They have watched Jan's pregnancy start and proceed to fruition. It has helped to give them the courage to go on and try to achieve their own much wanted pregnancy which only the IVF process can give them. To consider stopping the IVF programme, even temporarily, is out of the question, as there are many couples depending on it. It is the only glimmer of hope that they have. The whole IVF process as carried out at Queen Victoria is totally open and above reproach. The IVF process should be established as an everyday treatment freely available to all infertile couples without restrictions or reservations.

It has been said that IVF babies are conceived without love, this is not so. I cannot speak for everyone, but many couples like ourselves put in as much love-making as is possible, making sperm collection a close and intimate time (providing you can drive the wedge under the door hard enough). Jan and I consider Pippin was conceived with more awareness, enthusiasm and anticipation than most natural conceptions.

I had a strict Catholic upbringing and I can say that my conscience was clear of conflict as far as the Church and IVF treatment were concerned. I considered that we had a mechanical breakdown in our reproductive equipment, and a mechanical repair was necessary by the IVF medical team, to enable us to achieve something natural and beautiful and an essential part of life. It does not even compare with the emotional conflict the Church placed on me many years ago in my first marriage when faced with growing family numbers, financial problems and an emotional burden. It appeared to us that a contraceptive to limit childbirth was imperative, but the Church's attitude had been made clear at that time, and had burdened us with enormous emotional and religious conflict. I feel sure that this had been a large contributing factor towards the failure of that marriage. I do not condemm the Church, only the inflexibility of its teachings. I still remain a Catholic and Pippin has been baptized one also. I just hope that the Church can bend with the winds of time.

The IVF programme on the other hand is totally opposite in context. Jan and I wanted to produce a child, not stop one. A child to be a pleasure not a burden, a child that will add to the world not distract from it, to have a family and be a family which you need to be to take your place in society. We wanted the right to life.

With the IVF treatment they merely take the two halves from each of us and place them together for 48 hours until fertilized, then place the embryo back where it belongs. Nothing is altered, changed or tampered with. The ingredients only belong to Jan and me. We feel even the egg's and the sperms' modesty is preserved, as they are placed together and are immediately put in an incubator and lovingly referred to as 'doing their own thing' in the privacy of the incubator and away from prying eyes.

We both agree that guidelines should and must be set on freezing, genetic engineering, etc., but let us not get too carried away and spoil the years of research and hard work of the medical team or the dreams and hopes of the participants in the future.

8

IVF: A Debate

A Pandora's Box of Social and Moral Problems

Margaret Tighe

Seeing an IVF baby and its doting parents on television, one cannot help but be moved at the joyful scene. Why then oppose IVF when, we are told, it is the creation of new life – something which can only bring human happiness?

But: *All that glisters is not gold*; and in order to decide whether or not we should allow science and technology to be used to create man or woman we should reflect well upon the awesome ramifications for society as a whole of allowing such procedures.

Back in 1980, when the birth of the first Australian test-tube baby was announced by the Monash IVF team in Melbourne, Right to Life Victoria was the first voice raised in opposition to it and it remains opposed to it today. The reason for this is quite simple – the whole procedure involves an inherent lack of respect for human life.

With the development of human embryos taking place in laboratories we have entered a new and frightening age where we have a category of human beings treated as consumer products. As a result, human embryos can now be discarded, dissected, frozen and stored and eventually disposed of, genetically manipulated and experimented upon – all at the whim of scientists.

The four sections of this chapter are reprinted with permission from Karen Dawson, *Reproductive Technology* (South Melbourne: VCTA Publishing, 1994), pp. 84–90, 94–102.

The Beginning of Human Life and the Status of the Embryo

Medical science has shown us quite clearly that human life begins at fertilization. From that time when the father's sperm begins to penetrate the mother's ovum, a new life has begun and, unless man or nature intervenes, has commenced the journey of life only requiring time, optimum conditions and natural development to become a fully-fledged member of the human family – male or female – with all of the characteristics unique to that person.

It has been argued that, although a human being, the embryo is not a person and that it is only the attainment of personhood that qualifies a human being for entitlement to the full measure of rights, which at least until now have been known as human – not person – rights.

Amongst those who take the view that there are some human beings who cannot be considered to be persons – in the sense of having full human rights – there is a wide variety of criteria used to distinguish the classes.

These criteria include syngamy, implantation, the development of various organs (e.g. primitive streak, brain, nervous system), the attainment of *viability* (currently about 20 weeks from fertilization), birth, the presence of interests and preferences, a sense of future or the development of morally relevant characteristics (such as rationality and sensation).

The very diversity and subjectivity of these criteria should be sufficient to make one suspicious of the concept of a human being who is not a person.

Broadly, these various criteria are in one of two camps: notions related to survival prospects; and those concerned with qualitative considerations.

Of the former, there are many who have argued that implantation is a milestone, not only in the life of the embryo but in the development of its status.

Embryos prior to implantation or unimplanted embryos in laboratories have been viewed as less than human, or as human but not persons – simply because they do not have the survival prospects offered by successful implantation.

Since the process of implantation is essentially the establishment of a lifeline, this is tantamount to a view that a person lost at sea is not a person unless or until he manages to secure a hold on a lifeline, which is an absurd argument.

The imminence or otherwise of death does not affect the status or rights of a human being while he continues to live. So implantation (and viability) are not relevant to the status of the human embryo or fetus.

Since it is only a matter of time before scientists will be able to sustain life *ex utero* beyond the implantation stage through the development of an artificial uterus, we will soon have the capacity to grow human beings to any stage.

Since these people may not ever be born they may never acquire the status, the rights, of born persons, and may spend their whole lives as slaves of science.

We maintain that the human embryo is fully human or a person from his beginning, enjoying full human rights, including the right to his life, equally with every other human being, regardless of the stage or quality of his development.

IVF: A Slippery Slope

Since the world's first test-tube baby was born in the UK in 1978, with Australia soon to follow, the demands of IVF scientists have become more and more voracious.

For example, in Victoria legislation allows the production of and experimentation upon human embryos up to 22 hours after fertilization has begun. Following the passage of this law, prominent IVF scientist Professor Carl Wood of Monash University predicted it was only a matter of time until the 22-hour limit would be extended to 14 days. Only a few years later, a government-appointed IVF committee is now seriously proposing allowing the 14-day limit!

In the early days of IVF, scientists – no doubt mindful of the community's unease – stoutly declared themselves to be opposed to embryo freezing and storage and other forms of experimentation. Examination of press statements of IVF scientists since 1980 reveals a gradual increase in demands of greater access to more embryos for experimentation with newer and more extraordinary scientific feats being performed increasingly.

We have always been told that IVF is only concerned with treating infertility and to oppose it is to be uncaring of childless couples. Yet more than a decade of IVF has seen a virtual Pandora's box of horrendous possibilities for human manipulation develop.

Towards a Perfect Child

Genetic diseases can now be identified through laboratory reproduction with the means of screening out imperfect embryos. Eventually the IVF procedure could become mandatory for those couples likely to produce defective children. I could envisage them being coerced by the state (concerned at the cost of raising disabled children) into submitting their embryos for examination prior to implantation. In short – a licence to breed.

Perhaps habitual offenders might also be subjected to the same embryo screening procedures for their offspring to remove undesirable traits. The state, of course, would decide on what are undesirable traits!

With the transplanting of fetal tissue from aborted babies being promoted as a cure for certain diseases, baby farming – or growing of embryos with subsequent harvesting of organs – is not beyond the realms of possibility.

IVF and Custom-made Babies

An article in the *Sydney Morning Herald* of February 16 1993 reported that... *the technology to determine the sex of a child may soon be within our reach.* A clinic for this purpose, the London Gender Clinic, is already established in the UK, with pregnancy through IVF being a necessary part of the treatment. Indeed it is IVF that has opened the way to choosing not only the sex of one's child but also (in the future) its genetic makeup.

IVF has even made it possible for women well past their middle age to bear children – a most undesirable development. Recent reports tell us of a 60-year-old Italian woman bearing a child using the husband's sperm and a donor egg. There have also been several instances in the United States and South Africa of grandmothers giving birth to their grandchild: the biological parents submitting to IVF and the resultant embryo being transplanted in the womb of the grandmother because the biological mother had no womb.

Some suggest that a woman will be able to store her eggs – taken from her when she is young and fertile – thereby postponing childbirth until well after her career has been established. Pregnancy would have to be achieved through IVF in this instance.

Infertility: What about Prevention?

Infertility is a distressing problem for any couple and the condition certainly deserves the attention of medical science. But the price we are being asked to pay in order to deliver a relatively few babies into the arms of approximately 10 per cent of infertile couples is far too high.

More attention should be given to research into other ways of overcoming and preventing the problem. There has been a conspiracy of silence as to the causes of infertility and little or nothing done to educate young women in particular about this. In evidence to the Senate Select Committee into Human Embryo Experimentation in 1985, an expert in *women's* health, Dr Stefania Siedlecky, said that the major causes of infertility were wearing IUDs (contraceptive intra-uterine devices), abortion and sterilization.

Sexually transmitted diseases notoriously can cause infertility.

IVF Embryos Treated as Property

Basically IVF involves the treating of human beings as manufactured objects. To go to such extraordinary lengths to produce custom-made babies when approximately 100 000 unborn babies are casually aborted in Australia each year is wantonness in the extreme.

With human life now being generated in laboratories, with accompanying stockpiling of human embryos, donor eggs and sperm, the possibility now exists to create a whole class of human beings who can be treated as property and subjected to treatment which if applied to older humans would be seen as a gross abuse of human rights.

The Catholic Church and Reproductive Technology

Nicholas Tonti-Filippini

The birth of the world's first *test-tube baby*, Louise Brown, in 1978 in the United Kingdom raised some fundamental questions for the Catholic Church. Louise Brown had been created in a laboratory at the hands of a scientist who brought sperm and ova together in a Petri dish. What was Louise Brown when she was just a one-cell embryo? Could she be considered legitimately as the subject of an experiment at that first stage of her development? Was it morally acceptable for a scientist to take over the process of beginning a new life and to take it out of the normal context of the expression of sexual love by her parents?

A worldwide process of consultation was undertaken on these points as the Church sought to come to terms with the new possibilities. The Congregation for the Doctrine of the Faith had the task of reaching an understanding of a faithful response to the problems. Nine years later that process of consultation was brought to a conclusion with the publication of a document entitled *Instruction on respect for human life in its origin and on the dignity of procreation: replies to certain questions of the day*. The first words of the document are 'The gift of life' and the tradition has been to name Church documents by the first words. Hence the document is known generally as

Donum vitae, Latin being the language of the official publication.

The Church welcomed Louise Brown as a great gift, a gift to her infertile parents, a gift to the world of another person unique as a human individual, formed, even as that first cell, with the capacity for development to human adulthood with all the many attributes of a human person with which she would love, wonder, doubt and reason.

How could there be doubts and criticisms of the scientific processes that had as their goal such a beautiful product? But doubts there were.

The first problem was with the fact that Louise was a survivor of a process which had resulted and still results in the deliberate destruction of many others like her. The technology was not just applied to treating infertility. A whole new practical science rapidly developed, the science of experimental human embryology. The creation of human embryos in the laboratory made them available as experimental objects. Human embryos became accessible to scientific manipulation.

In Australia some pioneering work was done on developing the use of superovulants so that many embryos could be produced in a cycle and hence a surplus of embryos was created. As a consequence there were to be many who were created in the same way as Louise but who would never be transferred to their mothers' wombs where they could develop safely and without scientific manipulation.

In attaching great value to each human life, the Church sees the acts which result in a human life as themselves sacred. The traditional teaching sees married couples as co-creators with God of a new life. Ideally a child was seen as coming into existence as a result of the expression of love of his or her parents for each other. The child is thus an embodiment of that expression of love and an extension of the parents' love for each other. The Church gives sexual expression a very high status, it is the altar on which a family is founded. Sexual expression is the means by which a couple strengthen their understanding and their love for each other and the bond between them.

In vitro fertilization (IVF) took the origin of a child away from that expression of love and located it in the hands of an outsider where the child rather than being the embodiment of an expression of love, comes into existence as the object of a manufacturing process, as a product.

In *Donum vitae* this concern is expressed in the following way:

> IVF and ET is brought about outside the bodies of the couple through actions of third parties whose competence and technical activity determine the success of the procedure. Such fertilization entrusts the life and identity of the embryo into the power of doctors and biologists and establishes the domination of technology over the origin and destiny of the human person. Such a relationship of domination is in itself contrary to the dignity and equality that must be common to parents and children.

Thus the concern is that fertilization in the laboratory establishes an unequal relationship between the new human individual and the technologist. The technologist adopts a dominant role of control over the new life, which he or she regards not as a person but as something he or she has made. That dominance finds practical expression in the rapid moves which were made to exploit the vulnerability of human embryos by using them for experiments.

In order to justify that dominance, many technologists have tried to find new words to describe the early human embryo such as *pre-embryo* or *fertilized egg*. They have argued that the first cells which are the beginning of a human life should not be given human status and should not enjoy the protection owed to each human individual. They have tried to make moral distinctions between the early stages of development of a human being and the later stages.

The Church rejects these distinctions. The Church sees every human life at every stage as equally worthy of protection and the more vulnerable a human being is at a particular stage, the more strenuous should be the community's efforts to protect him or her.

From the time that an ovum is fertilized, a new life is begun which is neither that of the father nor of the mother. Rather, he or she is a new human being who needs only nourishment and a favourable environment to grow to human adulthood. A human embryo could not later be made human, if it were not human already. Modern genetic science brings valuable confirmation of this understanding. Science has demonstrated that, from the first instant, the programme is fixed as to what this living being will be, a man or a woman.

With the formation of the first embryonic cell a new individual person comes into being with his or her characteristic aspects already determined. From that first moment has begun the adventure of a human life, and each of his or her great capacities requires only time to find a place and to be in a position to act as a human person.

Thus from that first moment, that new human being demands the unconditioned respect that is morally due to a human being in his or her bodily and spiritual totality.

There are then two basic principles which the Church would like to see applied to reproductive technology. Firstly, human life from its first beginning with the formation of the first cell should be treated with the unconditional respect owed to all human beings. Secondly, reproductive assistance to a married couple in order to help them overcome infertility should not displace their sacred role as the originators of a new life by their expression of love for each other in the complete gift of sexual expression. It is only within the bond of that love that a child can come into existence in circumstances of respect for his or her dignity and equal status as a human being.

Thus the Church does not approve of *in vitro* fertilization nor can it approve of destructive experiments on human embryos.

The Church does not reject experiments on human embryos which are genuinely therapeutic, if they are genuinely designed to assist the embryo to overcome the effects of an illness or disease.

The Church resists genetic diagnosis for genetic selection of embryos, such as for producing human beings selected according to sex or other predetermined qualities and eliminating others.

Similarly the Church rejects the practice of embryo freezing on the grounds that it exposes human beings to grave risks of death or harm to their physical integrity and deprives them, at least temporarily, of material shelter and gestation by placing them in a situation in which further offences and manipulation are possible.

Surrogate motherhood is rejected on the grounds that it represents a failure to meet the obligations of maternal love, of marital fidelity, and of responsible motherhood. Surrogacy offends the dignity and the right of every child to have been conceived by his or her parents, carried in his or her mother's womb, and brought into the world and brought up by his or her own parents. Surrogacy sets up, to the detriment of families, a division between the physical, psychological and moral elements which constitute families.

The Church not only offers this advice to infertile couples and reproductive technologists, it also argues that society in general has obligations to ensure the protection of the life, dignity and equal status of every human being at every stage of life.

The Church asserts that the task of civil law is to ensure the common good of people through the recognition and defence of fundamental human rights, and through the promotion of peace and public morality. The inalienable rights of the person must be recognized and respected by civil society and the political authority. These human rights depend neither on single individuals nor on parents, nor are they conferred by the society or the state; they belong to each human being because he or she is a human being equal in worth and dignity to every other human being.

Reference

Sacred Congregation for the Doctrine of the Faith, March 1987, *Instruction on Respect for Human Life in its Origin and on the Dignity of Procreation: Replies to Certain Questions of the Day* (Homebush NSW: St Paul Publications.)

Human Embryo Research: A Global Social Experiment

Robyn Rowland

The question of when an embryo becomes an individual has been a matter of much debate. At a conference in Europe in 1988 Niall Tierney of the Irish Department of Health said that 'identity and integrity must be protected from the single cell stage.' On the other hand Anne McLaren,

Head of the Mammalian Development Unit of Britain's Medical Research Council, argued that individuality begins only after 14 days, the deadline already set by Britain's Warnock Committee on experimentation. She argued that at this stage the genetic uniqueness of the embryo is determined and therefore its identity begins. Other scientists argue that experimentation should be allowed to continue until a central nervous system is developed and the foetus experiences pain.

For many of us, however, the ethical issues of embryo experimentation do not revolve around when life or identity begins. Rather, it concerns:

- the origin of the embryos and the effect on the women from whom they come
- the eugenics implications of screening for imperfection
- the social implications of embryo donation on the structures of family and family relationships.

The most obvious source of possible egg and therefore embryo donors are women on *in vitro* fertilization (IVF) programmes. Under the superovulation treatment, women are given hormones to make their bodies produce more than the normal one egg per cycle. These eggs are fertilized, but only three of 14 to 45 eggs will be implanted. For each woman's attempt at IVF, then, there may be an excess of 10 or more fertilized embryos. Couples will ultimately face the dilemma of what to do with these embryos if their attempt at IVF is successful. If their attempts are unsuccessful, as in most cases, their embryos may be fully utilized. But if the procedure is successful, a couple may produce one or two children and still have embryos frozen. Their personal dilemma is whether to donate these, have them discarded or donate them for research.

While pro-research writers often cite polls that supposedly show general support for IVF and experimentation, surveys of women undertaking IVF indicate that they are far from convinced of the value of embryo research. One such survey carried out in Perth found that donation of embryos for experimentation was not acceptable to 35 per cent of respondents while a further 35 per cent of couples was undecided. A study in the Netherlands found that 59 per cent of IVF women rejected experimentation on spare embryos and a further 23 per cent was unsure. As one IVF client, Dr Barbara Burton, said in her representations to the Australian Federal Select Committee on Human Embryo Experimentation, she supported embryo experimentation provided that these embryos came from *normally fertile couples*. One IVF client had told her:

> I want them to do research, but not on my embryos.[1]

This is entirely understandable because people on IVF envisage every embryo as their own potential child; so the thought of experimentation on these embryos is often distasteful to them. These studies are also more educative than others in that general polls of the population do not take into account the lack of knowledge that most people have about IVF and embryo research procedures.

Doctors are increasingly turning to another source of eggs: donor women. At the moment these are primarily women seeking sterilization. The procedures are by no means as simple as they are depicted. Women who donate eggs are usually superovulated using the same drugs as those used for IVF.

And here we might consider briefly IVF itself.

IVF: A Failed Technology

In vitro fertilization is a problematic technology. Although experimental, it is often described as a simple process or as a therapy. The World Health Organization, however, still designates it as experimental. After 14 years IVF is still a failed technology with failures in Australia, the United Kingdom, the United States, Canada and Germany of between 85 per cent and 90 per cent per attempt. Furthermore, birthrates are averaged over clinics so that the failure of some clinics to obtain any births is often camouflaged. Individual clinic rates are not given, depriving couples of the information needed to assess where their best chances lie. Other measures of the failure of IVF include:

- the spontaneous abortion rate (20 per cent)
- the ectopic pregnancy rate (6 per cent: higher than after natural conception)
- multiple births (21 per cent, even with the policy of replacing only three embryos)
- the high incidence of pre-term births and low birthweight babies.[2]

IVF may also be potentially dangerous. The literature on one drug often used in the procedure, clomiphene citrate, reveals:

- possible birth abnormalities
- chromosomal abnormalities in the eggs produced
- a long life span of the drug in the body
- visual problems in both mothers and children
- unpleasant side effects including nausea, dizziness and emotional instability
- hyperstimulation (during which the ovaries swell enormously and the woman's physical system is traumatized) which can be fatal.

Klein and Rowland (1988)[3] published a summary of the scientific incidence of the hazards of this drug, to the vilification of practitioners. Following three cases of ovarian cancer after clomiphene use, Fishel and Jackson (1989) concluded in the *British Medical Journal* that 'it is not until the fourth decade that the incidence of ovarian carcinoma can be fully assessed.'[4]

The Federal Drug Administration in the United States last year finally demanded that drug companies carry a warning of potential cancer for some fertility drugs and, following this, the Royal College of Obstetricians and Gynaecologists in Australia advised doctors to warn clients of the possible links with cancer from some of these drugs.

These dangers exist for women on IVF, yet women who are asked to donate eggs face the same risks. Rarely are they given information about these drugs so that they can make informed decisions.

IVF is expensive, unsuccessful and potentially hazardous. It has led us to confront difficult dilemmas concerning embryo research. Issues revolve around embryo experimentation itself, whether from the screening of embryos through the use of embryo biopsy followed by implantation, or from the manipulation of embryos through donation.

Embryo Biopsy

Embryo biopsy techniques at the moment involve the removal of one cell of a developing embryo for screening before the embryo starts differentiating into various potential body parts. The purpose of this procedure, we are told, is to eliminate genetic disease. This sounds positive and anyone questioning the research is therefore seen as scaremongering and being unkind to those with genetic disorders. But it is worth thinking about the social implications of procedures that can screen for certain diseases. For example, the cost of the implementation of these techniques on a broader scale is not considered. At the moment, few people are using these experimental processes: studies at Hammersmith Hospital in London, for example, concern the elimination of embryos carrying cystic fibrosis. If the technique becomes more successful, however, who will have access to this technique? And who will pay?

Genetic screening reveals a plethora of difficult decisions for our society. Only about 3 per cent of genetic diseases will be able to be diagnosed at this stage of development. As more resources go towards screening technologies, fewer and fewer resources may be available for those who have existing disabilities or genetic problems. Will those who should have been screened out come to be seen as a mistake? Women may be pressured to use screening technology, then blamed if they don't and the child is not perfect. We could argue that as a society we have a greater responsibility to those already with us to ensure their greater wellbeing and quality of life than we do to assist people to create children that are made to order.

The techniques themselves are still experimental. Embryo biopsy assumes there is a discreteness in the act itself: that the research done has no impact on the development of the embryo. This assumption is similarly applied in genetics, where the assumption behind supposedly single-gene-determined diseases is that if genetic manipulation takes place it will not affect any of the other building blocks around it in the human cell.

The embryo research currently being developed will lead to the ability to genetically manipulate embryos. Instead of having to discard embryos that are supposedly undesirable, scientists will argue that they may be able to rectify the fault. As with all of these experimental procedures, the woman becomes a living laboratory in order to carry the embryo to term. As Mike Rayner, an embryologist at Oxford has written: 'If the [screening] technique is to be practicable, a high proportion of screened embryos must be capable of developing into babies.' And it is only when women carry these embryos, fetuses and finally children to term that we will know the outcome of the experiment.

The eugenics implications of screening technologies are obvious. Unlike the principles of Nazi Germany, where eugenics laws were enacted violently, the new eugenics aims to perfect human beings more subtly and graciously. Nevertheless, the theory and the attitudes are similar. Now we have people who are black wanting to carry children from white eggs, thereby attempting to resolve the problems of racism and violence by whitening the population.

As with all science, the use of it is determined not by the researchers but by those who own the research. Multinational companies are thriving on eugenics.

Embryo Donation and Surrogacy

The science and technology involved in embryo work has also led us to social and emotional experimentation. Although embryo donation can result in embryo research, which can then involve embryo selection and screening, embryo donation also leads us to surrogacy, the creation of older mothers, the possibility of sex selection and, as we have seen recently in the United Kingdom, the possibility of the maturing of immature eggs, either from slices of a woman's ovaries or from the ovaries of fetuses.

Embryo donation sounded so simple. It was intended that people who had spare embryos could donate those embryos to another infertile couple to give them the chance to have a child. However, like all of these developments, what we were offered as a social good has become a scientific imperative. So-called family or altruistic surrogacy is now being pushed by members of the medical profession, particularly in Victoria. Professor John Leeton assures us that: 'IVF surrogacy is superior to any other sort of surrogacy . . . because the risk of the surrogate mother bonding to the child after pregnancy is less.'

Professor Leeton has argued that these procedures allow people to construct families; but what sort of families are actually produced? Because of the ability to create embryos outside of the body and donate either these embryos or eggs and sperm, a child created through IVF may be connected at conception to five different adults. The child may never know this, however, because birth certificates record the mother and father as those who claim to be the parents and therefore do not reflect the complexity of current reproductive technology.

The manipulation of gametes has also allowed research to explore the possibility of maturing immature eggs outside of a woman's body by using slices of her ovary.

Dr Brinsmead from Newcastle University has raised the possibility of *fetal mothers*, where the immature eggs from a fetus would be matured, fertilized and implanted in a woman, possibly creating a child (Rowland, 1992). Now we hear in Britain that the technique has been developed. In addition, embryo biopsy enables scientists to detect the sex of the embryo. Sex selection is now firmly on the agenda.

The Future of Reproductive Technology

Interconnected with embryo experimentation, genetic engineering and surrogacy, *in vitro* fertilization has created massive social problems. In 14 years we have moved from the first IVF baby, which generated an image of happy families, to the point where:

- an Italian woman uses donor eggs and IVF to become pregnant at 62
- a 59-year-old British woman has twins
- a 21-year-old daughter gives birth to a child from her 48-year-old mother's embryo in order to give it to her mother
- a South African woman has triplets for her daughter, saying she feels no maternal bond with them
- in the United States, birth mother Anna Johnson loses a court battle to gain visitation rights to her child because the egg and the sperm used in her surrogacy arrangement did not come from her body.

These things are all happening already; but where might reproductive technology take us in the future?

- In Italy, experiments have taken place attempting to keep three uteruses operating in a laboratory setting. Embryos were implanted into them with the intention of generating life outside the body.
- With embryo donation and surrogacy, racial experimentation can take place where, for

example, Third World women could carry to term children for white commissioning couples using that couple's white embryo.

- The eggs of women declared brain dead or donated (so to speak) after death could be fertilized to create children.
- Women who are brain dead have been discussed as possible surrogate mothers, ideal because they will never make a claim on their children.
- The eggs from a fetal ovary could be matured *in vitro*, fertilized and implanted, resulting in what one writer has called a foetal mother.

We are involved in a massive social experiment; and children are being born from this research. These children will not be children forever, but will be adults with definite opinions about the ethics of reproductive technology.

The social experiment is enormous.

References

R. Rowland, *Living Laboratories: Women and Reproductive Technology* (Sydney: Sun Books, Pan Macmillan, 1992.)

National Perinatal Statistics Unit 1993, *IVF and GIFT Pregnancies in Australia and New Zealand.*

R. Klein and R. Rowland, 'Women as test sites for fertility drugs: clomiphene citrate and hormonal cocktails, *Reproductive and Genetic Engineering: Journal of International Feminist Analysis*, 1 (1988), 251–73

S. Fishel and P. Jackson, 'Follicular stimulation for high-tech pregnancies: are we playing it safe?' *British Medical Journal*, 298 (1989), 309–11.

New Assisted Reproductive Technology

Peter Singer

In 1978 Lesley Brown gave birth to a daughter whom she named Louise. Louise Brown was the first person able to trace her life back to an embryo that had existed, for a time, outside her mother's body. She had grown from an egg that Patrick Steptoe, an obstetrician, had removed from Lesley Brown's ovary. Without the help of Steptoe and his colleague, the biological scientist Robert Edwards, Louise Brown could not have been born. At the time that the Browns went to see Steptoe, Lesley Brown was 29 years old. She was infertile because her Fallopian tubes were blocked. The couple had been wanting to have children for several years. The new reproductive technology made this possible. But having a live and viable embryo in a glass dish in a laboratory also made many other things possible.

The standard procedure for *in vitro* fertilization (IVF) soon became relatively routine. As of September 1993, the best estimate is that about 54 000 babies have been born as a result of IVF, and another 9500 from a related procedure known as GIFT. In the overwhelming majority of these cases, the couple could not have had children without using one of these techniques.

That is the positive side of IVF. But what are the limits of the technology? Consider, alongside the case of the Browns, the story of an Italian woman named Liliana Cantadori. In August 1992 Liliana Cantadori had a son. This made her very happy, because she had been trying for 17 years to have a child. Just another standard IVF success story? Not quite, because those many years of trying to have a child had only begun with Mrs Cantadori's marriage, at the advanced age of 44. She and her husband Orlando had at the time wanted to have a child, and thought it would be possible: her husband's grandmother had had a child at 50. Liliana in fact became pregnant twice, but both times there was a miscarriage. She consulted specialists, but in vain. Time passed, but she did not give up hoping to have a child. She heard of a woman in her fifties who had been helped to have a child by IVF, and consulted Professor Carlo Flamigni, in Bologna, Italy's leading practitioner of IVF. She told him she was 52, and he agreed to help her to have a child. She used a donated egg and her husband's sperm, and had hormone treatment. She was told that the pregnancy could be dangerous, but she was willing to take the risk. Shortly after the birth both the mother and her son were reported to be in good health.

The cases of the Browns and the Cantadoris indicate that the new reproductive technology, like almost any technology, can be used in different ways. The choice is up to us, both individually and collectively, to make an ethical decision about how we should use it – or even not to use it at all.

On what basis would we make such a decision? One way is to consider all the objections that have been put forward about the use of IVF, and try to establish how much substance they have.

The Argument from Nature: Natural vs Unnatural Reproduction

It is sometimes said that IVF is wrong because it is *unnatural*. But what is the sense of the word *natural* being used here? Sometimes when we talk about something as natural we mean that it would happen without any human intervention. In this sense the life cycle of a forest in a national park may be natural, but no medical treatment can be natural. So while it is true that any form of assisted reproduction is unnatural in this sense, so is wearing glasses or having an anaesthetic.

In this sense, there can be nothing wrong with acting *against nature*; in fact, it would be impossible for us to avoid doing so.

In other cases, when we say that something is unnatural we mean that it is contrary to our own *human nature*. This is the sense intended by advocates of natural law ethics, which is influential within the Roman Catholic Church. But what is human nature? Is it so fixed that IVF (like contraception, in the view of the Catholic Church) is contrary to it? If anything at all is distinctive of human beings, and characterizes our nature, surely it is our ability to use our ingenuity to overcome impediments to getting what we want. In this sense, the birth of Louise Brown was entirely in accord with human nature – perhaps more so than every previous birth, because those earlier births had used means that we share with nonhuman animals, not means that are possible only for a being with our distinctive abilities.

The Argument from Overpopulation: Do We Really Need IVF?

Taking our planet as a whole, we surely do not need IVF. The population is nearing six billion, and that is enough, more than enough. But to argue from this fact to the conclusion that we should not allow infertile couples to use IVF, while other couples are free to have families as large as they wish, is to place an unfair burden on the infertile.

It is sometimes said that infertile couples should adopt orphaned children from poorer countries. This does sometimes happen, and it is an excellent thing when it works well. But it is not always easy to organize, and some infertile couples may have a strong desire to have their own children, or at least the children of one of the partners.

Again, it seems unfair to prevent such couples using assisted reproduction if other couples are under no pressure to adopt Third World children rather than have their own.

The Argument from Scarce Resources: is IVF too Expensive?

It is very difficult to discuss whether IVF offers value for money, because we must first ask: compared with what? Compared with what we could do to help save people in Third World countries, to spend money on IVF seems scandalous. For the cost of one IVF treatment we could provide oral rehydration therapy for hundreds of children dying from diarrhoea in developing nations. But then, with the money spent on growth hormones for one abnormally short child, we could also save a lot of lives; and the money available from doing fewer heart transplant operations would save more still. When no one else in need of medical treatment is held to so strict a standard, it seems unfair to apply the comparison only to infertile couples in need of IVF.

IVF remains a very small proportion of the total amount spent on medical care; and it is not clear that it represents worse value for money than many other forms of medical care that are paid for from the public purse, without serious argument.

What we really need is a rational basis for deciding which forms of medical care are good value and which are not. Until that is done, it is very difficult to reach any decision about how IVF ranks among the many different forms of treatment available at public expense.

The Feminist Argument: Does IVF Exploit Women?

Some feminists have claimed that the male scientists who are responsible for IVF ignore physical and psychological risks to the women who participate in the programme. At their most extreme, these claims go so far as to suggest that in some way the new birth technologies are aimed at making women unnecessary! These latter claims are far-fetched. The more moderate version is more plausible, but it is not an argument for prohibiting IVF, any more than it is an argument for prohibiting other medical procedures that carry some risk to the patient. Instead, it is an argument for the provision of full information about what is and is not known about the risks involved. Then women going onto the programme can make up their own minds.

To suggest that women are unable to make their own decision on this difficult matter is a highly paternalistic position for feminists to take, and one strongly resented by many women on the IVF programme.

The Argument against Embryo Experimentation

The early development of IVF involved experimentation on human embryos. Strictly speaking, IVF could continue without further embryo experimentation, but experimentation may be desirable in order to increase the success rate of the procedure. Experimentation can also be carried out for quite different purposes: to increase our knowledge of fertilization and early human development, perhaps to develop new contraceptives, diagnose genetic abnormalities, or even, in future, to find ways of overcoming some human diseases. All of this raises an important question: is there anything wrong with experimenting on human embryos?

To answer this question, we should consider exactly what a human embryo is. Of course, it changes as it develops, but at all the stages at which it can now be kept alive outside the body, it lacks any of the anatomical features of a human being, including, most importantly, a brain and a nervous system. Hence it could not possibly suffer in any way from the experimentation. In this respect, experimenting on a human embryo is not to be compared in significance with experimenting on a living, sentient mouse. It may be true that the embryo is biologically human – that is, a member of the species *Homo sapiens* – and the mouse is not, but what is the moral significance of mere species membership, if there are no morally relevant properties that go with it?

One morally relevant fact about a human embryo is that it comes from human parents, and they may have views about whether it should be used in experimentation. There is an objection to embryo experimentation without the consent of those from whom the egg and the sperm came, but no objection at all if they have given their free and informed consent.

But, it may be objected, the embryo has the potential to become a human being. That claim is not really so straightforward as it seems, because the embryo in the laboratory needs a lot of assistance in order to have any chance at all of becoming a human being, and even with that assistance, its chances are at best about 10 per cent. Imagine that we have an egg, and we have a single sperm collected in a special syringe ready for injection into the egg. (This technique is used to assist men who are infertile because they have insufficient sperm, or sperm that does not move normally.) The egg-and-sperm also have the potential to become a human being, and that potential is not very different from that of the embryo. Yet no one, not even the most avid right-to-life campaigners, thinks that it would be wrong to experiment on the egg and the sperm, when separate. It is very difficult to understand why people should value the potential of the embryo, but not the egg-and-sperm.

The major relevance of the potential of an embryo is that, if the embryo survives experimentation, it is possible that a damaged human being could be born. This is a reason for taking great care over experimentation that does not destroy the embryo. On the other hand it is not a reason against carrying out experimentation that destroys the embryo.

Conclusion

None of the major objections to the present practice of IVF is sufficiently strong to show that continuing with the practice of IVF is wrong. There are, of course, limits to what we ought to do in this area. I have not been able to discuss all the possible present and future ramifications of the technique. Maybe there should be an age limit, so we do not have mothers in their seventies with teenage children (though there is nothing to stop men from fathering children at any age). Certainly there should be some constraints on genetic manipulation of embryos, should that become possible. Each further development needs to be discussed on its merits. To assisted reproduction in itself, there seems to me to be no intrinsic objection.

9

Surrogate Mothering: Exploitation or Empowerment?

Laura M. Purdy

Introduction

'Pregnancy is barbaric'[1] proclaimed Shulamith Firestone in the first heady days of the new women's movement; she looked forward to the time when technology would free women from the oppression of biological reproduction. Yet as reproductive options multiply, some feminists are making common cause with conservatives for a ban on innovations. What is going on?

Firestone argued that nature oppresses women by leaving them holding the reproductive bag, while men are free of such burden; so long as this biological inequality holds, women will never be free (pp. 198–200) It is now commonplace to point out the naivety of her claim: it is not the biological difference per se that oppresses women, but its social significance. So we need not change biology, only attitudes and institutions.

This insight has helped us to see how to achieve a better life for women, but I wonder if it is the whole story. Has Firestone's brave claim no lesson at all for us?

Her point was that being with child is uncomfortable and dangerous, and it can limit women's lives. We have become more sensitive to the ways in which social arrangements can determine how much these difficulties affect us. However, even in feminist utopias, where sex or gender are considered morally irrelevant except where they may entail special needs, a few difficulties would remain. Infertility, for instance, would exist, as would the desire for a child in circumstances where pregnancy is impossible or undesirable.

At present, the problem of infertility is generating a whole series of responses and solutions. Among them are high-tech procedures like IVF, and social arrangements like surrogate motherhood. Both these techniques are also provoking a storm of concern and protest. As each raises a distinctive set of issues, they need to be dealt with separately, and I shall here consider only surrogate motherhood.

One might argue that no feminist paradise would need any practice such as this. As Susan Sherwin argues, it could not countenance 'the capitalism, racism, sexism, and elitism of our culture [that] have combined to create a set of attitudes which views children as commodities whose value is derived from their possession of parental chromosomes.'[2] Nor will society define women's fulfilment as only in terms of their relationship to genetically-related children. No longer will children be needed as men's heirs or women's livelihood.

We will, on the contrary, desire relationships with children for the right reasons: the urge to nurture, teach and be close to them. No longer will we be driven by narcissistic wishes for clones or immortality to seek genetic offspring no matter what the cost. Indeed, we will have recognized that children are the promise and responsibility of the whole human community. And child-rearing practices will reflect these facts, including at least a more diffuse family life that allows children to have significant relationships with others. Perhaps child-bearing will be communal.

This radically different world is hard to picture realistically, even by those like myself who –

From *Bioethics*, vol. 3, no. 1 (1989), pp. 18–34.

I think – most ardently wish for it. The doubts I feel are fanned by the visions of so-called 'cultural feminists' who glorify traditionally feminine values. Family life can be suffocating, distorting, even deadly.[3] Yet there is a special closeness that arises from being a child's primary caretaker, just as there can be a special thrill in witnessing the unfolding of biologically-driven traits in that child. These pleasures justify risking neither the health of the child[4] nor that of the mother; nobody's general well-being should be sacrificed to them, nor do they warrant high social investment. However, they are things that, other things being equal, it would be desirable to preserve so long as people continue to have anything like their current values. If this is so, then evaluating the morality of practices that open up new ways of creating children is worthwhile.[5]

Moral or Immoral?

What is surrogate mothering exactly? Physically, its essential features are as follows: a woman is inseminated with the sperm of a man to whom she is not married. When the baby is born she relinquishes her claim to it in favour of another, usually the man from whom the sperm was obtained. As currently practiced, she provides the egg, so her biological input is at least equal to that of the man. 'Surrogate' mothering may not therefore be the best term for what she is doing.[6]

By doing these things she also acts socially – to take on the burden and risk of pregnancy for another, and to separate sex and reproduction, reproduction and child-rearing, and reproduction and marriage. If she takes money for the transaction (apart from payment of medical bills), she may even be considered to be selling a baby.

The bare physical facts would not warrant the welter of accusation and counter-accusation that surrounds the practice.[7] It is the social aspects that have engendered the acrimony about exploitation, destruction of the family, and baby-selling. So far we have reached no consensus about the practice's effect on women or its overall morality.

I believe that the appropriate moral framework for addressing questions about the social aspects of contracted pregnancy is consequentialist.[8] This framework requires us to attempt to separate those consequences that invariably accompany a given act from those that accompany it only in particular circumstances. Doing this compels us to consider whether a practice's necessary features lead to unavoidable overridingly bad consequences. It also demands that we look at how different circumstances are likely to affect the outcome. Thus a practice which is moral in a feminist society may well be immoral in a sexist one. This distinction allows us to tailor morality to different conditions for optimum results without thereby incurring the charge of malignant relativism.

Before examining arguments against the practice of contracted pregnancy, let us take note of why people might favour it. First, as noted before, alleviating infertility can create much happiness. Secondly, there are often good reasons to consider transferring burden and risk from one individual to another. Pregnancy may be a serious burden or risk for one woman, whereas it is much less so for another. Some women love being pregnant, others hate it; pregnancy interferes with work for some, not for others; pregnancy also poses much higher levels of risk to health (or even life) for some than for others. Reducing burden and risk is a benefit not only for the woman involved, but also for the resulting child. High-risk pregnancies create, among other things, serious risk of prematurity, one of the major sources of handicap in babies. Furthermore, we could prevent serious genetic diseases by allowing carriers to avoid pregnancy. A third benefit of 'surrogate mothering' is that it makes possible the creation of non-traditional families. This can be a significant source of happiness to single women and gay couples.

All of the above presuppose that there is some advantage in making possible at least partially genetically-based relationships between parents and offspring. Although, as I have argued above, we might be better off without this desire, I doubt that we will soon be free of it. Therefore, if we can satisfy it at little cost, we should try to do so.

Is Surrogate Mothering Always Wrong?

Despite the foregoing advantages, some feminists argue that the practice is *necessarily* wrong: it is wrong because it must betray women's and society's basic interests.[9]

What, if anything is wrong with the practice? Let us consider the first three acts I described earlier: transferring burden and risk, separating sex and reproduction, and separating reproduction and child-rearing. Separation of reproduction and marriage will not be dealt with here.

Is it wrong to take on the burden of pregnancy for another? Doing this is certainly supererogatory, for pregnancy can threaten comfort, health, even life. One might argue that women should not be allowed to take these risks, but that would be paternalistic. We do not forbid mountain-climbing or riding a motorcycle on these grounds. How could we then forbid a woman to undertake this particular risk?

Perhaps the central issue is the transfer of burden from one woman to another. However, we frequently do just that – much more often than we recognize. Anyone who has her house cleaned, her hair done, or her clothes dry-cleaned is engaging in this procedure;[10] so is anyone who depends on agriculture or public works such as bridges.[11] To the objection that in this case the bargain includes the risk to life and limb, as well as use of time and skills, the answer is that the other activities just cited entail surprisingly elevated risk rates from exposure to toxic chemicals or dangerous machinery.[12]

Furthermore, it is not even true that contracted pregnancy merely shifts the health burden and risks associated with pregnancy from one woman to another. In some cases (infertility, for example,) it makes the impossible possible; in others (for women with potentially high-risk pregnancies) the net risk is lowered.[13] As we saw, babies benefit, too, from better health and fewer handicaps. Better health and fewer handicaps in both babies and women also means that scarce resources can be made available for other needs, thus benefiting society in general.

I do think that there is, in addition, something suspect about all this new emphasis on risk. Awareness of risks inherent in even normal pregnancy constitutes progress: women have always been expected to forge ahead with child-bearing oblivious to risk. Furthermore, child-bearing has been thought to be something women owed to men or to society at large, regardless of their own feelings about a given – or any – pregnancy. When women had little say about these matters, we never heard about risk.[14] Why are we hearing about risk only now, now that women finally have some choices, some prospect of remuneration?[15] For that matter, why is our attention not drawn to the fact that surrogacy is one of the least risky approaches to non-traditional reproduction?[16]

Perhaps what is wrong about this kind of transfer is that it necessarily involves exploitation. Such exploitation may take the form of exploitation of women by men and exploitation of the rich by the poor. This possibility deserves serious consideration, and will be dealt with shortly.

Is there anything wrong with the proposed separation of sex and reproduction? Historically, this separation – in the form of contraception – has been beneficial to women and to society as a whole. Although there are those who judge the practice immoral. I do not think we need belabour the issue here.

It may be argued that not all types of separation are morally on a par. Contraception is permissible, because it spares women's health, promotes autonomy, strengthens family life, and helps make population growth manageable. But separation of sex and reproduction apart from contraception is quite another kettle of fish: it exploits women, weakens family life, and may increase population. Are these claims true and relevant?

Starting with the last first, if we face a population problem, it would make sense to rethink overall population policy, not exploit the problems of the infertile.[17] If family strengthing is a major justification for contraception, we might point out that contracted pregnancy will in some cases do the same. Whether or not having children can save a failing marriage, it will certainly prevent a man who wants children from leaving a woman incapable of providing them. We may bewail his priorities, but if his wife is sufficiently eager for the relationship to continue it would again be paternalistic for us to forbid 'surrogacy' in such circumstances. That 'surrogacy' reduces rather than promotes women's autonomy may be true under some circumstances, but there are good grounds for thinking that it can also enhance autonomy. It also remains to be shown that the practice systematically burdens women, or one class of women. In principle, the availability of new choices can be expected to nourish rather than stunt women's lives, so long as they retain control over their bodies and lives. The claim that contracted pregnancy destroys women's individuality and constitutes alienated labour, as Christine Overall argues, depends not only on a problematic Marxist analysis, but on the assumption that other jobs available to women are seriously less alienating.[18]

Perhaps what is wrong here is that contracted pregnancy seems to be the other side of the coin of prostitution. Prostitution is sex without reproduction; 'surrogacy' is reproduction without sex. But it is difficult to form a persuasive argument that goes beyond mere guilt by association. Strictly speaking, contracted pregnancy is not prostitution; a broad-based Marxist definition would include it, but also traditional marriage. I think that in the absence of further argument, the force of this accusation is primarily emotional.

Perhaps the dread feature contracted pregnancy shares with prostitution is that it is a lazy person's way of exploiting their own 'natural resources'. But I suspect that this idea reveals a touchingly naive view of what it takes to be a successful prostitute, not to mention the effort involved in running an optimum pregnancy. Overall takes up this point by asserting that it

> is not and cannot be merely one career choice among others. It is not a real alternative. It is implausible to suppose that fond parents would want it for their daughters. We are unlikely to set up training courses for surrogate mothers. Schools holding 'career days' for their future graduates will surely not invite surrogate mothers to address the class on advantages of 'vocation'. And surrogate motherhood does not seem to be the kind of thing one would put on one's curriculum vitae. (p. 126)

But this seems to me to be a blatant *ad populum* argument.

Such an objection ought, in any case, to entail general condemnation of apparently effortless ways of life that involved any utilization of our distinctive characteristics.

We surely exploit our personal 'natural resources' whenever we work. Ditchdiggers use their bodies, professors use their minds. Overall seems particularly to object to some types of 'work': contracted pregnancy 'is no more a real job option than selling one's blood or one's gametes or one's bodily organs can be real job options' (p. 126). But her discussion makes clear that her denial that such enterprises are 'real' jobs is not based on any social arrangements that preclude earning a living wage doing these things, but rather on the moral judgement that they are wrong. They are wrong because they constitute serious 'personal and bodily alienation'. Yet her arguments for such alienation are weak. She contends that women who work as 'surrogates' are deprived of any expression of individuality (p. 126), are interchangeable (p. 127), and that they have no choice about whose sperm to harbour (p. 128). It is true that, given a reasonable environment (partly provided by the woman herself), bodies create babies without conscious effort. This fact, it seems to me, has no particular moral significance: many tasks can be accomplished in similar ways yet are not thought valueless.[19]

It is also usually true that women involved in contracted pregnancy are, in some sense, interchangeable. But the same is true, quite possibly necessarily so, of most jobs. No one who has graded mounds of logic exams or introductory ethics essays could reasonably withhold their assent to this claim, even though college teaching is one of the most autonomous careers available. Even those of us lucky enough to teach upper-level courses that involve more expression of individual expertise and choice can be slotted into standardized job descriptions. Finally, it is just false that a woman can have no say about whose sperm she accepts: this could be guaranteed by proper regulation.

I wonder whether there is not some subtle devaluing of the physical by Overall. If so, then we are falling into the trap set by years of elitist equations of women, nature and inferiority.

What I think is really at issue here is the disposition of the fruit of contracted pregnancy: babies. However, it seems to be generally permissible to dispose of or barter what we produce with both our minds and our bodies – except for that which is created by our reproductive organs. So the position we are considering may just be a version of the claim that it is wrong to separate reproduction and child-rearing.

Why? It is true that women normally expect to become especially attached to the product of this particular kind of labour, and we generally regard such attachment as desirable. It seems to be essential for successfully rearing babies the usual way. But if they are to be reared by others who are able to form the appropriate attachment, then what is wrong if a surrogate mother fails to form it? It seems to me that the central question here is whether this 'maternal instinct' really exists, and, if it does, whether suppressing it is always harmful.

Underlying these questions is the assumption that bonding with babies is 'natural' and therefore 'good'. Perhaps so: the evolutionary advantage of such a tendency would be clear. It would be simple-minded, however, to assume that our habits are biologically determined: our culture is permeated with pronatalist bias.[20] 'Natural' or not, whether a tendency to such attachment is desirable could reasonably be judged to depend on circumstance. When infant mortality is high[21] or responsibility for child-rearing is shared by the community, it could do more harm than good. Beware the naturalistic fallacy![22]

But surely there is something special about gestating a baby. That is, after all, the assumption behind the judgement that Mary Beth Whitehead, not William Stern, had a stronger claim to Baby M. The moral scoreboard seems clear: they both had the same genetic input, but she gestated the baby, and therefore has a better case for social parenthood.[23]

We need to be very careful here. Special rights have a way of being accompanied by special responsibilities: women's unique gestational relationship with babies may be taken as reason to confine them once more to the nursery. Furthermore, positing special rights entailed directly by biology flirts again with the naturalistic fallacy and undermines our capacity to adapt to changing situations and forge our destiny.[24]

Furthermore, we already except many varieties of such separation. We routinely engage in sending children to boarding school, foster parenting, daycare, and so forth; in the appropriate circumstances, these practices are clearly beneficial. Hence, any blanket condemnation of separating reproduction and child-rearing will not wash; additional argument is needed for particular classes of cases.

John Robertson points out that the arguments against separating reproduction and child-rearing used against contracted pregnancy are equally valid – but unused – with respect to adoption.[25] Others, such as Herbert Krimmel, reject this view by arguing that there is a big moral difference between giving away an already existing baby and deliberately creating one to give away. This remains to be shown, I think. It is also argued that as adoption outcomes are rather negative, we should be wary of extending any practice that shares its essential features. In fact, there seems to be amazingly little hard information about adoption outcomes. I wonder if the idea that they are bad results from media reports of offspring seeking their biological forebears. There is, in any case, reason to think that there are differences between the two practices such that the latter is likely to be more successful than the former.[26]

None of the social descriptions of surrogacy thus seem to clearly justify the outcry against the practice. I suspect that the remaining central issue is the crucial one: surrogacy is baby-selling and participating in this practice exploits and taints women.

Is Surrogacy Baby-selling?

In the foregoing, I deliberately left vague the question of payment in contracted pregnancy. It is clear that there is a recognizable form of the practice that does not include payment; however, it also seems clear that controversy is focusing on the commercial form. The charge is that it is baby-selling and that this is wrong.

Is paid 'surrogacy' baby-selling? Proponents deny that it is, arguing that women are merely making available their biological services. Opponents retort that as women are paid little or nothing if they fail to hand over a live, healthy child, they are indeed selling a baby. If they are merely selling their services they would get full pay, even if the child were born dead.

It is true women who agree to contracts relieving clients of responsibility in this case are being exploited. They, after all, have done their part, risked their risks, and should be paid – just like the physicians involved. Normal child-bearing provides no guarantee of a live, healthy child – why should contracted pregnancy?

There are further reasons for believing that women are selling their services, not babies. Firstly, we do not consider children property. Therefore, as we cannot sell what we do not own, we cannot be selling babies. What creates confusion here is that we do think we own sperm and ova. (Otherwise, how could men sell their sperm?) Yet we do not own what they become, persons. At what point, then, does the relationship cease to be describable as 'ownership'?

Resolution of this question is not necessary to the current discussion. If we can own babies, there seems to be nothing problematic about selling them. If ownership ceases at some time before birth (and could thus be argued to be unconnected with personhood), then it is not selling of babies that is going on.

Although this response deals with the letter of the objection about baby-selling, it fails to heed its spirit, which is that we are trafficking in persons, and that such trafficking is wrong. Even if we are not 'selling', something nasty is happening.

The most common analogy, with slavery, is weak. Slavery is wrong according to any decent moral theory: the institution allows people to be treated badly. Their desires and interests, whose satisfaction is held to be essential for a good life, are held in contempt. Particularly egregious is the callous disregard of emotional ties to family and self-determination generally. But the institution of surrogate mothering deprives babies of neither.[27] In short, as Robertson contends, 'the purchasers do not buy the right to treat the child . . . as a commodity or property. Child abuse and neglect laws still apply' (p. 655).

If 'selling babies' is not the right description of what is occurring, then how are we to explain what happens when the birth mother hands the child over to others? One plausible suggestion is that she is giving up her parental right to have a relationship with the child.[28] That it is wrong to do this for pay remains to be shown. Although it would be egoistic and immoral to 'sell' an ongoing, friendly relationship (doing so would raise questions about whether it was friendship at all), the immorality of selling a relationship with an organism your body has created but with which you do not yet have a unique social bond, is a great deal less clear.[29]

People seem to feel much less strongly about the wrongness of such acts when motivated by altruism; refusing compensation is the only acceptable proof of such altruism. The act is, in any case, socially valuable. Why then must it be motivated by altruistic considerations? We do not frown upon those who provide other socially valuable services even when they do not have the 'right' motive. Nor do we require them to be unpaid. For instance, no one expects physicians, no matter what their motivation, to work for beans. They provide an important service; their motivation is important only to the extent that it affects quality.

In general, workers are required to have appropriate skills, not particular motivations.[30] Once again, it seems that there is a different standard for women and for men.

One worry is that women cannot be involved in contracted pregnancy without harming themselves, as it is difficult to let go of a child without lingering concern. So far, despite the heavily-publicized Baby M case, this appears not to be necessarily true.[31]

Another worry is that the practice will harm children. Children's welfare is, of course, important. Children deserve the same consideration as other persons, and no society that fails to meet their basic needs is morally satisfactory. Yet I am suspicious of the objections raised on their behalf in these discussions: recourse to children's alleged well-being is once again being used as a trump card against women's autonomy.

First, we hear only about possible risks, never possible benefits, which, as I have been arguing, could be substantial.[32] Second, the main objection raised is the worry about how children will take the knowledge that their genetic mother conceived on behalf of another. We do not know how children will feel about having had such 'surrogate' mothers. But as it is not a completely new phenomenon we might start our inquiry about this topic with historical evidence, not pessimistic speculation. In any case, if the practice is dealt with in an honest and common-sense way, particularly if it becomes quite common (and therefore 'normal'), there is likely to be no problem. We are also hearing about the worries of existing children of women who are involved in the practice: there are reports that they fear their mother will give them away, too. But surely we can make clear to children the kinds of distinctions that distinguish the practice from slavery or baby-selling in the first place.

Although we must try to foresee what might harm children, I cannot help but wonder about the double standards implied by this speculation. The first double standard occurs when those who oppose surrogacy (and reproductive technologies generally) also oppose attempts to reduce the number of handicapped babies born.[33] In the latter context, it is argued that despite their problems handicapped persons are often glad to be alive. Hence it would be paternalistic to attempt to prevent their birth.

Why then do we not hear the same argument here? Instead, the possible disturbance of children born of surrogacy is taken as a reason to prevent their birth. Yet this potential problem is both more remote and most likely involves less suffering than such ailments as spina bifida, Huntington's Disease or cystic fibrosis, which some do not take to be reasons to refrain from child-bearing.[34]

Considering the sorts of reasons why parents have children, it is hard to see why the idea that one was conceived in order to provide a desperately-wanted child to another is thought to be problematic. One might well prefer that to the idea that one was an 'accident', adopted, born because contraception or abortion were not available, conceived to cement a failing marriage, to continue a family line, to qualify for welfare aid, to sex-balance a family, or as an experiment in child-rearing. Surely what matters for a child's well-being in the end is whether it is being raised in a loving, intelligent environment.

The second double standard involves a disparity between the interests of women and children. Arguing that surrogacy is wrong because it may upset children suggests a disturbing conception of the moral order. Women should receive consideration at least equal to that accorded children. Conflicts of interest between the two should be resolved according to the same rules we use for any other moral subjects. Those rules should never prescribe sacrificing one individual's basic interest at the mere hint of harm to another.

In sum, there seems to be no reason to think that there is anything necessarily wrong with 'surrogate mothering', even the paid variety. Furthermore, some objections to it depend on values and assumptions that have been the chief building blocks of women's inequality. Why are some feminists asserting them? Is it because 'surrogacy' as currently practiced often exploits women?

Is 'Surrogate Mothering' Wrong in Certain Situations?

Even if 'surrogate mothering' is not necessarily immoral, circumstances can render it so. For instance, it is obviously wrong to coerce women to engage in the practice. Also, certain conditions are unacceptable. Among them are clauses in a contract that subordinate a woman's reasonable desires and judgements to the will of another contracting party,[35] clauses legitimating inadequate pay for the risks and discomforts involved, and clauses that penalize her for the birth of a handicapped or dead baby through no fault of her own. Such contracts are now common.[36]

One popular solution to the problem of such immoral contracts is a law forbidding all surrogacy agreements; their terms would then be unenforceable. But I believe that women will continue to engage in surrogate mothering, even if it is unregulated, and this approach leaves them vulnerable to those who change their mind, or will not pay. Fair and reasonable regulations are essential to prevent exploitation of women. Although surrogate mothering may seem risky and uncomfortable to middle-class persons safely ensconced in healthy, interesting, relatively well-paid jobs, with adequate regulation it becomes an attractive option for some women. That these women are more likely than not to be poor is no reason to prohibit the activity.

As I suggested earlier, poor women now face substantial risks in the workplace. Even a superficial survey of hazards in occupations available to poor women would give pause to those who would prohibit surrogacy on the grounds of risk.[37]

Particularly shocking is the list of harmful substances and conditions to which working women are routinely exposed. For instance, cosmeticians and hairdressers, dry-cleaners and dental technicians are all exposed to carcinogens in their daily work. (Stellman, Appendixes 1 and 2) Most low-level jobs also have high rates of exposure to toxic chemicals and dangerous machinery, and women take such jobs in disproportionate numbers. It is therefore unsurprising that poor women sicken and die more often than other members of society.[38]

This is not an argument in favour of adding yet another dangerous option to those already facing such women. Nor does it follow that the burdens they already bear justify the new ones. On the contrary, it is imperative to clean up dangerous workplaces. However, it would be utopian to think that this will occur in the near future. We must therefore attempt to improve women's lot under existing conditions. Under these circumstances it would be irrational to prohibit surrogacy on the grounds of risk when women would instead have to engage in still riskier pursuits.

Overall's emphatic assertion that contracted pregnancy is not a 'real choice' for women is unconvincing. Her major argument, as I suggested earlier, is that it is an immoral, alienating option. But she also believes that such apparently expanded choices simply mask an underlying contraction of choice (p. 124). She also fears that by 'endorsing an uncritical freedom of reproductive choice, we may also be implicitly endorsing all conceivable alternatives that an individual might adopt; we thereby abandon the responsibility for evaluating substantive actions in favour of advocating merely formal freedom of choice' (p. 125). Both worries are, as they stand, unpersuasive.

As I argued before, there is something troubling here about the new and one-sided emphasis on risk. If nothing else, we need to remember that contracted pregnancy constitutes a low-tech approach to a social problem, one which would slow the impetus toward expensive and dangerous high-tech solutions.[39]

A desire for children on the part of those who normally could not have them is not likely to disappear anytime soon. We could discount it, as many participants in debate about new reproductive technologies do. After all, nobody promised a rose garden to infertile couples, much less to homosexuals or to single women. Nor is it desirable to propagate the idea that having children is essential for human fulfilment.

But appealing to the sacrosancity of traditional marriage or of blood ties to prohibit otherwise acceptable practices that would satisfy people's desires hardly makes sense, especially when those practices may provide other benefits. Not only might contracted pregnancy be less risky and more enjoyable than other jobs women are forced to take, but there are other advantages as well. Since being pregnant is not usually a full-time occupation, 'surrogate mothering' could buy time for women to significantly improve their lot: students, aspiring writers, and social activists could make real progress toward their goals.

Women have until now done this reproductive labour for free.[40] Paying women to bear children should force us all to recognize this process as the socially useful enterprise that it is, and children as socially valuable creatures whose upbringing and welfare are critically important.

In short, 'surrogate mothering' has the potential to empower women and increase their status in society. The darker side of the story is that it also has frightening potential for deepening their exploitation. The outcome of the current warfare over control of new reproductive possibilities will determine which of these alternatives comes to pass.

Notes

1 Shulamith Firestone, *The Dialectic of Sex* (New York: Bantam Books, 1970), p. 198. A version of this paper was given at the Eastern SWIP meeting, 26 March 1988. I would like especially to thank Helen B. Holmes and Sara Ann Ketchum for their useful comments on this paper; they are, of course, in no way responsible for its perverse position! Thanks also to the editors and referees of *Bioethics* for their helpful criticisms.

2 Susan Sherwin, 'Feminist Ethics and *In Vitro* Fertilization,' *Science, Moralty and Feminist Theory*, ed. Marsha Hanen and Kai Nielsen, *Canadian Journal of Philosophy*, supplementary volume 13 (1987), p. 277.

3 Consider the many accounts of the devastating things parents have done to children, in particular.

4 See L. M. Purdy 'Genetic Diseases: Can Having Children be Immoral?' *Moral Problems in Medicine*, ed. Samuel Gorovitz (Eglewood Cliffs, NJ: Prentice-Hall, 1983), pp. 377–84.

5 Another critical issue is that no feminist utopia will have a supply of 'problem' children whom no one wants. Thus the proposal often heard nowadays that people should just adopt all those handicapped, non-white kids will not do. (Nor does it 'do' now.)

6 I share with Sara Ann Ketchum the sense that this term is not adequate, although I am not altogether happy with her suggestion that we call it 'contracted motherhood' ('New Reproductive Technologies and the Definition of Parenthood: A Feminist Perspective', paper given at the 1987 *Feminism and Legal Theory Conference*, at the University of Wisconsin at Madison, summer 1987, pp. 44ff.) It would be better, I think, to reserve terms like 'mother' for the social act of nurturing. I shall therefore substitute the terms 'contracted pregnancy' and 'surrogacy' (in scare quotes).

7 This is not to say that no one would take the same view as I: the Catholic Church, for instance, objects to the masturbatory act required for surrogacy to proceed.

8 The difficulty in choosing the 'right' moral theory to back up judgments in applied ethics, given that none are fully satisfactory, continues to be vexing. I would like to reassure those who lose interest at the mere sight of consequentialist – let alone utilitarian – judgement, that there are good reasons for considering justice an integral part of moral reasoning, as it quite obviously has utility.

A different issue is raised by the burgeoning literature on feminist ethics. I strongly suspect that utilitarianism could serve feminists well, if properly applied. (For a defence of this position, see my paper 'Do Feminists Need a New Moral Theory', given at the University of Minnesota, Duluth, at the conference *Explorations in Feminist Ethics: Theory and Practice*, 8–9 October 1988.)

9 See for example Gena Corea, *The Mother Machine*, and Christine Overall, *Ethics and Human Reproduction* (Winchester, MA: Allen & Unwin, 1987).

10 These are just a couple of examples in the sort of risky service that we tend to take for granted.

11 Modern agricultural products are brought to us at some risk by farm workers. Any large construction project will also result in some morbidity and mortality.

12 Even something so mundane as postal service involves serious risk on the part of workers.

13 The benefit to both high-risk women, and to society is clear. Women need not risk serious deterioration of health or abnormally high death rates.

14 See Laura Purdy, 'The Morality of New Reproductive Technologies', *Journal of Social Philosophy* (Winter 1987), 38–48.

15 For elaboration of this view, consider Jane Ollenburger and John Hamlin, '"All Birthing Should be Paid Labor" – A Marxist Analysis of the Commodification of Motherhood', in *On the Problem of Surrogate Parenthood: Analyzing the Baby M Case*, ed. Herbert Richardson, (Lewistong, NY: Edwin Mellen Press, 1987).

16 Compare the physical risk with that of certain contraceptive technologies, and high-tech fertility treatments like IVF.

17 Infertility is often a result of social arrangements. This process would therefore be especially unfair to those who have already been exposed to more than their share of toxic chemicals or other harmful conditions.

18 Christine Overall, *Ethics and Human Reproduction*, (Winchester, MA: Allen & Unwin, 1987), ch. 6. Particularly problematic are her comments about women's loss of individuality, as I will be arguing shortly.

19 Men have been getting handsome pay for sperm donation for years; by comparison with child-bearing, such donation is a lark. Yet there has been no outcry about its immorality. Another double standard?

20 See Ellen Peck and Judith Senderowitz, *Pronatalism: The Myth of Mom and Apple Pie* (New York: Thomas Y. Crowell, 1974).

21 As it has been at some periods in the past: see for example information about family relationships in Philippe Ariès, *Centuries of Childhood: A Social History of Family Life*, trans. Robert Baldick (New York, 1982), and Lloyd DeMause's work.

22 Consider the arguments in ch. 8 of *Women's Work*, by Ann Oakley, (New York: Vintage Books, 1974).

23 One of the interesting things about the practice of contracted pregnancy is that it can be argued to both strengthen and weaken the social recognition of biological relationships. On the one hand, the pregnant woman's biological relationship is judged irrelevant beyond a certain point; on the other, the reason for not valuing it is to enhance that of the sperm donor. This might be interpreted as yet another case where men's interests are allowed to overrule women's. But it might also be interpreted as a salutary step toward awareness that biological ties can and sometimes should be subordinated to social ones. Deciding which interpretation is correct will depend on the facts of particular cases, and the arguments taken to justify the practice in the first place.

24 Science fiction, most notably John Wyndham's *The Midwich Cuckoos*, provides us with thought-provoking material.

25 John Robertson, 'Surrogate Mothers: Not so Novel After All', *Hastings Center Report*, vol. 13, no. 5 (October 1983). This article is reprinted in *Bioethics*, ed. Rem B. Edwards and Glen C. Graber (San Diego, CA: Harcourt, Brace Jovanovich, 1988). Krimmel's article ('The Case Against Surrogate Parenting') was also originally published in the *Hastings Center Report* and is reprinted in *Bioethics*. References here are to the latter.

26 One major difference between adoption and contracted pregnancy is that the baby is handed over virtually at birth, thus ensuring that the trauma sometimes experienced by older adoptees is not experienced. Although children of contracted pregnancy might well be curious to know about their biological mother, I do not see this as a serious obstacle to the practice, since we could change our policy about this. There is also reason to believe that carefully-screened women undertaking a properly-regulated contracted pregnancy are less likely to experience lingering pain of separation. First, they have deliberately chosen to go through pregnancy, knowing that they will give the baby up. The resulting sense of control is probably critical to both their short- and long-term well-being. Second, their pregnancy is not the result of trauma. See also Monica B. Morris, 'Reproductive Technology and Restraints', *Transaction/SOCIETY* (March/April 1988), 16–22, esp. p. 18.

27 There may be a problem for the woman who gives birth, as the Baby M case has demonstrated. There is probably a case for a waiting period after the birth during which the woman can change her mind.

28 Heidi Malm suggested this position in her comment on Sara Ann Ketchum's paper 'Selling Babies and Selling Bodies: Surrogate Motherhood and the Problem of Commodification', at the Eastern Division *APA* meetings, 30 December 1987.

29 Mary Anne Warren suggests, alternatively, that this objection could be obviated by women and children retaining some rights and responsibilities toward each other in contracted pregnancy. Maintaining a relationship of sorts might also, she suggests, help forestall and alleviate whatever negative feelings children might have about such transfers. I agree that such openness is probably a good idea in any case. (Referee's comment.)

30 Perhaps lurking behind the objections of surrogacy is some feeling that it is wrong to earn money by letting your body work, without active effort on

your part. But this would rule out sperm selling, as well as using women's beauty to sell products and services.

31 See, for example, James Rachels, 'A Report from America: The Baby M Case', *Bioethics*, vol. 1, n. 4 (October 1987), 365. He reports that there have been over 600 succesful cases; see also the above note on adoption.

32 Among them the above-mentioned one of being born healthier.

33 To avoid the difficulties about abortion added by the assumption that we are talking about existing fetuses, let us consider here only the issue of whether certain couples should risk pregnancy.

34 There is an interesting link here between these two aspects of reproduction, as the promise of healthier children is, I think, one of the strongest arguments for contracted pregnancy.

35 What this may consist of naturally requires much additional elucidation.

36 See Susan Ince, 'Inside the Surrogate Industry', *Test- Tube Women*, ed. Rita Arditti, Renate Duelli Klein, and Shelley Minden (London: Pandora Press, 1984).

37 See, for example, Jeanne Mager Stellman, *Women's Work, Women's Health* (New York: Pantheon, 1977).

38 See George L. Waldbott, *Health Effects of Environmental Pollutants*, (St. Louis: C. V. Mosby, 1973); Nicholas Ashford, *Crisis in the Workplace: Occupational Disease and Injury* (Cambridge: MIT Press, 1976); *Cancer and the Worker* (New York Academy of Science, 1977); *Environmental Problems in Medicine*, ed. William D. McKee (Springfield, IL: Charles C. Thomas, 1977).

39 These are the ones most likely to put women in the clutches of the paternalistic medical establishment. Exploitation by commercial operations such as that of Noel Keane could be avoided by tight regulation or prohibition altogether of for-profit enterprises.

40 The implications of this fact remain to be fully understood; I suspect that they are detrimental to women and children, but that this is a topic for another paper

10

A Response to Purdy

Susan Dodds and Karen Jones

In 'Surrogate Motherhood: Exploitation or Empowerment?', Laura Purdy is primarily concerned with discussing whether there is something about contracts for surrogate motherhood which makes the practice necessarily wrong. More specifically, in Purdy's consequentialist framework, the question is whether contracts for surrogate motherhood are 'invariably accompanied' by consequences which are 'unavoidable' and 'overridingly bad'. The question of whether there is something necessarily wrong about surrogacy contracts is not one we have attempted to answer in 'Surrogacy and Autonomy' [*Bioethics*, 3/1 (1989), pp. 1–17]. Strategically, centering on this question is dangerous in that once it is established that there is nothing *necessarily* wrong with surrogate motherhood contracts, it is easy to overlook the real, although *contingent*, features of our contemporary society (and of the realistic alternatives for the foreseeable future) that make surrogate motherhood contracts morally wrong. By focusing on what is necessarily wrong, we risk being falsely reassured as to the permissibility of surrogacy in *this* world. Most of the concerns raised by feminists regarding surrogacy are specifically about surrogacy in exchange for money in a classist, patriarchical society. In showing that there is nothing about the practice which makes it necessarily wrong, Purdy allows these feminist concerns to be marginalized, relegated to footnotes in the debate (e.g. Purdy's note 26). The public IVF debate is presently guilty of similar omissions.

Of equal importance are the theoretical reasons for supposing that the question of whether the practice of surrogacy is necessarily wrong is the wrong question to ask, especially given the consequentialist framework Purdy uses to determine what it is for an act or practice to be necessarily wrong. Purdy explains acts which are necessarily wrong in terms of invariably accompanying features which lead to unavoidable and overridingly bad consequences, but it is not obvious that a consequentialist should even find the question of the *necessarily* wrong features of surrogacy answerable. If we are agnostic about the nature of men and women – as we have good reason to be – then we cannot now know whether the good consequences of having surrogacy in the ideal, non-sexist world would outweigh the bad. For instance, we cannot now tell how a woman would feel about parting with a child to which she had given birth, nor can we claim to know whether the desire to have children to whom one is genetically related would continue in a feminist utopia. We shall see later that Purdy considers some rather peculiar features as being the essential features of surrogacy. It is not clear, however, that these are the main features that should be used by a consequentialist in assessing the rightness or wrongness of surrogacy in an ideal world. First, it is worthwhile bringing out the connection between Purdy's focus on necessary features of surrogacy, her definition of what it is to be a necessarily wrong practice and the individualistic approach she takes to the issue.

It is the immediate players in a surrogacy contract that receive most of Purdy's attention. For example, in considering the effects of surrogate mothering on children, she considers only the effects on children who are the result of a surrogacy contract and on the other children of the

From *Bioethics*, vol. 3, no. 1 (1989), pp. 35–9.

surrogate mother. Whether the practice of surrogacy might foster attitudes detrimental to children as a group is not considered. Presumably this is because these effects will depend on the broader social circumstances in which surrogacy occurs, and thus are not *necessary* consequences of those contracts. The issue is, however, vitally relevant to the moral assessment of surrogacy contracts, yet it is omitted from discussion, even when Purdy turns her attention to circumstantial consequences affecting the morality of surrogacy. Likewise, Purdy overlooks the way the practice of contracted pregnancy might affect attitudes to women as a *group*, rather than particular women who become surrogate mothers. Again, this is because the possible harms are not necessary features of surrogate motherhood contracts. Her discussion of the harms which might result from the institution of surrogacy is too individualistic in scope and this is owed directly to her focus on the question of necessarily bad consequences.

Moreover, Purdy's discussion of the possible harms of surrogacy is too narrow. The risks Purdy identifies for the woman who contracts to become a surrogate mother are physical risks. These are important; but of greater importance, because not found in ordinary pregnancy, is the psychological harm that can result from being forced to give up a child one gave birth to when one wanted to raise that child.

Let us look more closely at what Purdy offers as possible necessary features of contracted pregnancy which could make the practice necessarily wrong. These are four: surrogacy might necessarily yield bad consequences because it transfers the burden and risk of pregnancy from one person to another; because it separates sex and reproduction; because it separates reproduction and child-rearing, or because it involves baby-selling. Firstly, transferring the burden of pregnancy. Is this wrong? Purdy argues that as it is routine to transfer burdens and risks, there can be nothing particularly wrong in the way surrogacy does so. Anyone who has had any services performed by another does this, likewise anyone who buys goods. There are a number of things to be said here. The rightness or otherwise of transferring burdens and risks depends on more features than Purdy takes into account. It depends on whether there was an obligation to undertake the risks on the part of the person transferring them to someone else. This could arguably be the case in, for instance, jury duty or military service, where being a citizen, and reaping the benefits which accrue to citizens, creates an obligation to take on the risks associated with jury duty or military service. However, women can hardly be said to have an obligation to have children, so there cannot be this pre-existing obligation not to transfer the burden. The rightness of transferring burdens and risks depends also on the extent of the risk involved and on the motivation of the person undertaking the risk. Purdy dismisses the motivation of a surrogate mother as being irrelevant, arguing that we consider it irrelevant for all other occupations. We have argued, however that motivation can be important in determining the permissibility of paternalism based on consideration of the agent's dispositional autonomy. Certainly, it would be *paternalistic* to interfere with a woman's choice to become a surrogate mother, but this does not mean that it must be *wrong* to do so.

Both in her discussion of whether surrogacy contracts have necessary bad consequences, and in her decision of whether such contracts might be wrong in certain circumstances, Purdy seems to assume that if it can be shown that prohibiting women from undertaking certain risks is paternalistic, the presence of paternalism is sufficient to show that the prohibition is morally wrong. However, especially for consequentialists, argument is needed to establish the wrongness of paternalism in the circumstances in question, given the likely consequences. Without this argument, the observation that an interference is paternalistic has no more than emotive force. Purdy contents herself with the observation that, for example, we do not forbid riding motorcycles on the grounds that riders are subject to physical risks of accident and injury. What she fails to notice, however, is that in many places it is considered acceptable to prohibit riding motorcycles without crash helmets, for paternalistic reasons. This shows that it requires argument to move from the fact of a policy being paternalistic to the wrongness of that policy. Purdy gives no such argument.

It is worthwhile asking whether surrogacy contracts are really about transferring burdens and risks between women. It seems that they could be about this. For example, a woman whose heart condition makes pregnancy very risky to her life could be helped by her healthy, fertile sister to have a baby. However, in contracted surrogacy for remuneration, it appears that something else is happening. The woman who will become the social mother of the child born as result of a surrogacy contract seems a minor player in the surrogacy drama (at least as surrogacy is now practised). She is not required to sign the original contract. The contract is entered into by the commissioning father, the surrogate mother, and the surrogate's husband if she has one (see Kentucky contract, K. Brophy, *Journal of Family Law*, 20 (1981–2), pp. 263–91). Surrogacy as it is actually practised seems to be more about enabling *men* to have children genetically related to themselves than it is about women agreeing to transfer burdens or risks, or making the impossible possible. (We note with concern William Stern's stress on genetic connection and blood lines in the 'Baby M' case.)

Purdy also examines whether surrogacy is necessarily wrong because it separates sex and reproduction and child-rearing. Surrogacy involves the separation of sex and reproduction, but so do many other things, e.g. contraception, homosexuality, prostitution. Purdy's dismissal of the relevance of this objection to surrogacy would not satisfy those traditionalists who object to the separation of sex and reproduction, and to the rest of us the issue seems curiously irrelevant. Surrogacy is about much more than separating sex and reproduction, and it is here that the real moral objections lie (e.g. issues of commodification and exploitation of women and children, of harms and risks, autonomy and paternalism). Purdy rightly points out that there are problems with arguments against separating child-bearing and child-rearing. Such arguments tend to be biologically reductionist. However, again, the issue is not whether this is wrong, but whether it is wrong to make a woman give up her child-bearing rights and responsibilities when she does not want to. The question is one of autonomy and harm, not whether, considered in a vacuum, it is ever wrong to separate child-bearing and child-rearing. The parallel here is not, as Purdy assumes, with adoption, but with acrimonious custody disputes.

The last possibility Purdy considers for the necessary wrongness of surrogacy contracts is that the practice entails baby-selling. Her argument, that surrogate mothers must be selling their services rather than babies on the grounds that 'we do not consider children property... (t)herefore as we cannot sell what we do not own, we cannot be selling babies,' is seriously flawed. First, there is a conceptual question relating to the normative sense of property being employed here: we are to say that the slave-trader is not *really* selling persons because we do not consider persons property? Rather we should say that persons ought not be treated as potentially the property of others, and thus slave-trading ought to be prohibited (and not merely on the grounds that the institution of slavery tend to treat persons badly). Secondly, there is the problem of her jump from the idea that children are not considered property to the idea that we cannot sell what we do not own. We may be morally bound to abstain from selling what we do not own, but there is no conceptual problem with my selling the car I stole from you. We do not believe that surrogacy necessarily entails baby-selling; however, Purdy ought to have offered a better argument for the position.

Perhaps Purdy would say that these arguments are unfair. She suggests that some changes might be necessary in the present contracts. However, she does not really tell us what sorts of changes are needed, and this is a dangerous omission. Even if, as she suggests, surrogacy contracts are altered to allow for a cooling-off period, custody disputes could presumably result. Is Purdy suggesting that these features of surrogacy be changed or not? She does not tell us, yet she leaves us with the vague hope that the existence of the practice of paying women to bear children might empower all women, because it would then force reproductive labour to be recognized as productive labour. We have some evidence that this hope is probably just wishful thinking (other areas of traditionally unpaid 'women's work' – childcare, domestic labour – have become professionalized with, at best, marginal effects on the recognition of those who perform the tasks). Purdy's hope is, nonetheless, too vague to even begin to assess until Purdy tells us precisely what she means by contracts for surrogate motherhood, given that she does not mean surrogacy as it is presently practised.

11

An Ethical Debate: Should Older Women be Offered *in vitro* Fertilization?

The Interests of the Potential Child

Tony Hope, Gill Lockwood, Michael Lockwood

In most discussions of the ethics of fertility treatment it is claimed that the interests of the potential child are of major if not paramount importance. The practical significance of this consideration has been grossly overestimated. Contrary to conventional wisdom, the interests of the potential child hardly ever constitute an adequate reason for withholding fertility treatment.

Modern fertility treatments became the focus of much media attention in 1993 after the widely publicized case in which a 59-year-old woman was enabled to give birth to twins by means of *in vitro* fertilization with donated eggs and her partner's sperm. Fertility treatments raise a wide range of ethical and social issues. We focus on one specific issue: the interests and welfare of the potential child. These factors are often cited as important reasons for withholding fertility treatment. We contend that they are almost never relevant, and moreover, we support a wider provision of fertility treatment.

The Human Fertilization and Embryology Act 1991 states that "centres considering treatment must take into account the welfare of any child who may be born." Robert Winston, professor of fertility studies at the Hammersmith Hospital, argued that it is wrong to offer *in vitro* fertilization to most postmenopausal women.[1] One of his reasons concerned the potential child. Hugh Whittall of the Human Embryology and Fertilisation Authority said that although there was no upper age limit for treatment in law, concerns for the potential children ruled out treating elderly women.[2] The welfare of the child was raised by Dame Jill Knight, Member of Parliament for Edgbaston, in connection with using eggs from aborted fetuses. She said that she did not understand how the medical profession could consider producing children from a mother who never existed, and she asked what the effect on the child would be when he or she realized that basic truth.[3]

Conception and Adoption – a Fair Analogy?

A parallel is often drawn between assisted conception and adoption, with the underlying implication being that couples seeking fertility treatment should somehow prove their fitness as potential parents. We consider this to be a false analogy.

In the case of adoption the child already exists. Hence, the question being asked is: among all the couples who would like to adopt a child, which would make the most suitable parents for this child? The criteria for adoption will inevitably be determined by supply and demand. To put it bluntly, if there are only 10 babies for adoption

The three sections in this chapter are reprinted with permission from the *British Medical Journal*, 310 (3 June 1995), pp. 1455–7.

and 5000 couples wishing to adopt, then the authorities can afford to be very particular about their criteria for accepting couples as adoptive parents.

The situation for a couple seeking help with conception is totally different. If we focus on the interests of the potential child the question that needs to be asked is: are the interests of this potential child better served if he or she is born to these parents or if he or she never exists at all? The possibility of "this" potential child being born to any other (possibly better) parents does not arise. This, crucially, is where the analogy with adoption breaks down.

Of course it is difficult to say when it would be better not to exist; the intrinsic worth of an individual's life cannot readily be quantified, least of all when that life has not yet started. We suggest, however, that the level of parenting would have to be very low for it to be preferable not to exist at all rather than exist as a child of those parents. Society's reluctance to step in and take a child into care except under the most dire circumstances of appalling parenting confirms this.

With regard to the 59-year-old woman who gave birth to twins, a frequently reported objection is that the children's mother is likely to die when they are still quite young. No doubt, other things being equal, it is preferable to have a mother who survives well into one's own adulthood. But to put this forward as a sufficient reason for denying fertility treatment is tantamount to claiming that it is better never to have existed than for one's mother to have died when one is still quite young.

This is not the stance we should normally adopt in other contexts. Many serious medical conditions experienced by young women are also associated with difficulties in conceiving or bearing children. Yet these women's desire for children and need for fertility treatment is often regarded most sympathetically precisely because of their diminished life expectancy.

Interests of Society Masquerading as Interests of the Potential Child

It might be argued that if we cannot help every couple who wants help – because of limited resources – then we should choose between "competing" couples, on the basis of seeking to maximize the number of happy children made per pound spent. If it is true that the children of younger parents usually enjoy a higher level of wellbeing than those of older parents, then we are likely to purchase more wellbeing by helping younger rather than older prospective parents.

In whose interests, however, are we acting? Selecting couples for *in vitro* fertilization resembles other procedures that entail problems of allocating resources. For example, a hospital might delay admission of a patient who requires non-urgent surgery in order to admit a patient requiring an urgent operation. No one would maintain that it was in the best interests of the first patient for his or her surgery to be delayed, but the justification for acting against those interests is that others in the society benefit thereby and that, all things considered, the decision is fair.

There are two main dangers in failing to distinguish between the interests of the particular potential child and those of the potential children who might come into existence if resources were used to help other couples instead. The first danger is that we might, wrongly, refuse to help a couple even when not helping them would not in fact benefit other couples – for example, when the treatment is funded by private resources that would not be available to other couples. The second danger is that society might fail to provide sufficient funds for assisted reproduction. It would clearly be wrong in general to fund assisted conception for an individual couple if it would be better for that couple's potential child not to exist. But it is a very different matter for society to provide insufficient funds for treatments that would confer a genuine benefit. Society may decide as a matter of policy that it will not fund medicine, gynaecology, or fertility treatment beyond a certain level, but that decision requires justification.

Conclusion

We conclude therefore that except in most unusual circumstances it is not right to withhold fertility treatment on the grounds of the interests of the potential child. Society may feel entitled to refuse fertility treatment because of cost or because it does not regard infertility as a priority health concern, but it should not feel comfortable justifying such failure of provision in terms of the interests of the potential child.

References

1 Mihill, C. UK fertility doctors rule out test tube babies for older women because of fears for children's welfare. *Guardian* (1993 Jul. 20).

2 *Guardian* (1993 Jul 20).

3 Laurance, J. New fertility treatment facing ban *Times* (1994 Jan 3).

Can Older Women Cope with Motherhood?

Jennifer Jackson

The reasons put about for refusing *in vitro* fertilization to postmenopausal women may seem feeble – as if people first of all feel uncomfortable about such treatment then cast around for reasons to justify their misgivings.

Some consider that these older women are less likely to benefit than younger women in the competition for treatment. But I do not want to go into the vexed issue of "fair shares". Resources aside, underlying people's misgivings is the thought that even though technology can fit such women for pregnancy, it does not fit them for parenthood – they are too old to be adequate parents to young children.

Is it wrong for a woman to seek to become a mother if she knows, or should know, that she will not be able to cope well with motherhood? It is wrong if her becoming a mother is unjust – as it infringes the resultant child's rights. But the child is not wronged since it cannot be born to better parents.

Yet even if such women are not acting unjustly they may still be acting wrongly. There are other vices besides injustice, such as taking on a commitment as binding and permanent as motherhood when there are good reasons for anticipating that one will fail to cope. If the women who seek *in vitro* fertilization are acting irresponsibly it is wrong for health professionals to assist them.

Women who become pregnant without medical help are not vetted by their doctors to see whether they are fit for motherhood before being allowed to proceed with their pregnancies. But it is one thing to draw the line at forcibly preventing people from acting fecklessly, another to help or enable them to do so. If my general practitioner, having earnestly remonstrated with me about my drinking, meets me in the pub the next day, I do not expect him to snatch my glass from my lips, but neither do I expect him to offer to buy me a refill. If someone is bent on acting irresponsibly others may be powerless to intervene. They are certainly under no obligation to give help.

Health professionals are not supposed to provide services indiscriminately, even to their paying patients. They are supposed to be providing their services in a cause – to protect and promote good health and wellbeing: that is their vocation. Hence, if gynaecologists know that older women are likely to be inadequate mothers it is wrong for them to offer their facilities for *in vitro* fertilization to these women.

Of course it may not be reasonable to suppose that older women cannot cope with motherhood. We are, after all, perfectly happy about older men becoming fathers. A century ago when life expectancy for women in Britain was 47 years (as against the current 78 years) nobody objected to women embarking on motherhood in their late twenties. Nowadays, a woman who embarks on motherhood in her fifties has a better chance of seeing her children grow up.

All the same there may be reasons against changing a practice that do not surface if we examine a question only in relation to individual cases. The "case focused" approach dominates medical ethics. The ethical significance of practices deserves more investigation.

In vitro Fertilization is Rarely Successful in Older Women

Susan Bewley

The two most extreme views of infertility are that (*a*) it is an unfortunate circumstance but not a medical disorder worthy of treatment and (*b*) it is a distressing physical malfunction leaving people unable to fulfil a fundamental human potential. Disease or not, infertility is associated with distress and is currently widely investigated and treated. The disagreement thus seems to be not whether doctors have an obligation to infertile women but the extent of that obligation.

Debates on infertility, as on abortion, are clouded by different ethical value systems and deep prejudices about "deserving women" and "potential children". Age is not an issue unless doctors have a prior obligation to help. If they do then very good reasons, apart from prejudice, have to exist to deny treatment to a particular woman. What criteria may legitimately be used to decide whether a particular woman is denied treatment (in this case, *in vitro* fertilization)? Only three real arguments relate to risk-harm benefit, the interests of the potential child, and rationing of resources.

For doctors who believe in "first of all do no harm" the most powerful argument relates to the risk–benefit ratio of treating a particular individual. The chance of successful *in vitro* fertilization (which itself carries risks) in women aged over 45–50 is remote. A woman may die in pregnancy or childbirth, and there is a risk of creating harm (an orphan). If doctors applied the same criteria and refused infertility treatment to some women with medical disorders such as breast cancer and cardiac disease then they would be consistent. An overall, arbitrary age limit would not be possible as the facts for each patient would be different. Some ethicists claim that the issue of being an orphan is of "no harm" (because you cannot harm something that does not exist) rather than "not enough harm" usually to deny infertility treatment. If the success rates of *in vitro* fertilization improve, and it is shown that a higher age is not a high personal risk and that old parents are not very damaging, then risk–benefit objections to treating older women must be dropped.

For those who believe in maximizing the interests of mother, child, and society (and this view of medical ethics that is based on interests is not universally accepted) a problem exists about weighing future children in the calculations. Do potential children count for something, and if so, what and how much? If potential children do count and it were conclusively shown that certain classes or racial groups had an adverse association with parenting skills then would these become legitimate reasons for denying infertility treatment? Most people would be uncomfortable with this view, and we therefore should not invoke such arguments in the debate. If we consider that the interests of the potential child in fact count for nothing, as the child does not yet exist, then logically there would be no cases in which treatment could be refused, however old the potential parents.

Whatever the underlying ethical value system, the last argument relates to effective rationing. There is limited money for infertility treatment, and women over a certain age (for whom treatment becomes less effective) are just not going to get it. This at least would be an honest approach to rationing. Older women would be discriminated against, which is unjust, but there is a countervailing reason. There can be no objection, however, to these women spending their money in the private sector, whatever their age. The ability of richer women to have children when poorer ones cannot seems to reduce children to commodities, which may have adverse knock-on social consequences.

Most ethical debates turn on the medical facts. Improvements in success rates will make it increasingly difficult to sustain objections to offering older women *in vitro* fertilization. At present, it is merely the inefficacy of treatment that allows otherwise weak objections to maternal age to hold together.

Prenatal Screening, Sex Selection and Cloning

12

Genetics and Reproductive Risk: Can Having Children be Immoral?

Laura M. Purdy

Is it morally permissible for me to have children? A decision to procreate is surely one of the most significant decisions a person can make. So it would seem that it ought not be made without some moral soul-searching.

There are many reasons why one might hesitate to bring children into this world if one is concerned about their welfare. Some are rather general, such as the deteriorating environment or the prospect of poverty. Others have a narrower focus, such as continuing civil war in one's country or the lack of essential social support for child-rearing in the United States. Still others may be relevant only to individuals at risk of passing harmful diseases to their offspring.

There are many causes of misery in this world, and most of them are unrelated to genetic disease. In the general scheme of things, human misery is most efficiently reduced by concentrating on noxious social and political arrangements. Nonetheless, we should not ignore preventable harm just because it is confined to a relatively small corner of life. So the question arises, Can it be wrong to have a child because of genetic risk factors?[1]

Unsurprisingly, most of the debate about this issue has focused on prenatal screening and abortion: much useful information about a given fetus can be made available by recourse to prenatal testing. This fact has meant that moral questions about reproduction have become entwined with abortion politics, to the detriment of both. The abortion connection has made it especially difficult to think about whether it is wrong to prevent a child from coming into being, because doing so might involve what many people see as wrongful killing; yet there is no necessary link between the two. Clearly, the existence of genetically compromised children can be prevented not only by aborting already existing fetuses but also by preventing conception in the first place.

Worse yet, many discussions simply assume a particular view of abortion without recognizing other possible positions and the difference they make in how people understand the issues. For example, those who object to aborting fetuses with genetic problems often argue that doing so would undermine our conviction that all humans are in some important sense equal.[2] However, this position rests on the assumption that conception marks the point at which humans are endowed with a right to life. So aborting fetuses with genetic problems looks morally the same as killing "imperfect" people without their consent.

This position raises two separate issues. One pertains to the legitimacy of different views on abortion. Despite the conviction of many abortion activists to the contrary, I believe that ethically respectable views can be found on different sides of the debate, including one that sees fetuses as developing humans without any serious moral claim on continued life. There is no space here to

From *Reproducing Persons: Issues in Feminist Bioethics* (Ithaca, NY: Cornell University Press, 1996), pp. 39–49. Used by permission of Cornell University Press. This essay is loosely based on "Genetic Diseases: Can Having Children Be Immoral?" originally published in *Genetics Now*, ed. John L. Buckley (Washington, DC: University Press of America, 1978), and subsequently anthologized in a number of medical ethics texts. Thanks to Thomas Mappes and David DeGrazia for their helpful suggestions about updating the article.

address the details, and doing so would be once again to fall into the trap of letting the abortion question swallow up all others. However, opponents of abortion need to face the fact that many thoughtful individuals do *not* see fetuses as moral persons. It follows that their reasoning process, and hence the implications of their decisions, are radically different from those envisioned by opponents of prenatal screening and abortion. So where the latter see genetic abortion as murdering people who just don't measure up, the former see it as a way to prevent the development of persons who are more likely to live miserable lives, a position consistent with a world-view that values persons equally and holds that each deserves a high-quality life. Some of those who object to genetic abortion appear to be oblivious to these psychological and logical facts. It follows that the nightmare scenarios they paint for us are beside the point: many people simply do not share the assumptions that make them plausible.

How are these points relevant to my discussion? My primary concern here is to argue that conception can sometimes be morally wrong on grounds of genetic risk, although this judgment will not apply to those who accept the moral legitimacy of abortion and are willing to employ prenatal screening and selective abortion. If my case is solid, then those who oppose abortion must be especially careful not to conceive in certain cases, as they are, of course, free to follow their conscience about abortion. Those like myself who do not see abortion as murder have more ways to prevent birth.

Huntington's Disease

There is always some possibility that reproduction will result in a child with a serious disease or handicap. Genetic counselors can help individuals determine whether they are at unusual risk and, as the Human Genome Project rolls on, their knowledge will increase by quantum leaps. As this knowledge becomes available, I believe we ought to use it to determine whether possible children are at risk *before* they are conceived.

In this chapter I want to defend the thesis that it is morally wrong to reproduce when we know there is a high risk of transmitting a serious disease or defect. This thesis holds that some reproductive acts are wrong, and my argument puts the burden of proof on those who disagree with it to show why its conclusions can be overridden. Hence it denies that people should be free to reproduce mindless of the consequences.[3] However, as moral argument, it should be taken as a proposal for further debate and discussion. It is not, by itself, an argument in favor of legal prohibitions of reproduction.[4]

There is a huge range of genetic diseases. Some are quickly lethal; others kill more slowly, if at all. Some are mainly physical, some mainly mental; others impair both kinds of function. Some interfere tremendously with normal functioning, others less. Some are painful, some are not. There seems to be considerable agreement that rapidly lethal diseases, especially those, such as Tay-Sachs, accompanied by painful deterioration, should be prevented even at the cost of abortion. Conversely, there seems to be substantial agreement that relatively trivial problems, especially cosmetic ones, would not be legitimate grounds for abortion.[5] In short, there are cases ranging from low risk of mild disease or disability to high risk of serious disease or disability. Although it is difficult to decide where the duty to refrain from procreation becomes compelling, I believe that there are some clear cases. I have chosen to focus on Huntington's Disease to illustrate the kinds of concrete issues such decisions entail. However, the arguments are also relevant to many other genetic diseases.[6]

The symptoms of Huntington's Disease usually begin between the ages of 30 and 50:

> Onset is insidious. Personality changes (obstinacy, moodiness, lack of initiative) frequently antedate or accompany the involuntary choreic movements. These usually appear first in the face, neck, and arms, and are jerky, irregular, and stretching in character. Contradictions of the facial muscles result in grimaces; those of the respiratory muscles, lips, and tongue lead to hesitating, explosive speech. Irregular movements of the trunk are present; the gait is shuffling and dancing. Tendon reflexes are increased.... Some patients display a fatuous euphoria; others are spiteful, irascible, destructive, and violent. Paranoid reactions are common. Poverty of thought and impairment of attention, memory, and judgment occur. As the disease progresses, walking becomes impossible, swallowing difficult, and dementia profound. Suicide is not uncommon.[7]

The illness lasts about fifteen years, terminating in death.

Huntington's Disease is an autosomal dominant disease, meaning it is caused by a single defective gene located on a non-sex chromosome. It is passed from one generation to the next via affected individuals. Each child of such an affected person has a 50 percent risk of inheriting the gene and thus of eventually developing the disease, even if he or she was born before the parent's disease was evident.[8]

Until recently, Huntington's Disease was especially problematic because most affected individuals did not know whether they had the gene for the disease until well into their child-bearing years. So they had to decide about child-bearing before knowing whether they could transmit the disease or not. If, in time, they did not develop symptoms of the disease, then their children could know they were not at risk for the disease. If unfortunately they did develop symptoms, then each of their children could know there was a 50 percent chance that they too had inherited the gene. In both cases, the children faced a period of prolonged anxiety as to whether they would develop the disease. Then, in the 1980s, thanks in part to an energetic campaign by Nancy Wexler, a genetic marker was found that, in certain circumstances, could tell people with a relatively high degree of probability whether or not they had the gene for the disease.[9] Finally, in March 1993, the defective gene itself was discovered.[10] Now individuals can find out whether they carry the gene for the disease, and prenatal screening can tell us whether a given fetus has inherited it. These technological developments change the moral scene substantially.

How serious are the risks involved in Huntington's Disease? Geneticists often think a 10 percent risk is high.[11] But risk assessment also depends on what is at stake: the worse the possible outcome, the more undesirable an otherwise small risk seems. In medicine, as elsewhere, people may regard the same result quite differently. But for devastating diseases such as Huntington's this part of the judgment should be unproblematic: no one wants a loved one to suffer in this way.[12]

There may still be considerable disagreement about the acceptability of a given risk. So it would be difficult in many circumstances to say how we should respond to a particular risk. Nevertheless, there are good grounds for a conservative approach, for it is reasonable to take special precautions to avoid very bad consequences, even if the risk is small. But the possible consequences here *are* very bad: a child who may inherit Huntington's Disease has a much greater than average chance of being subjected to severe and prolonged suffering. And it is one thing to risk one's own welfare, but quite another to do so for others and without their consent.

Is this judgment about Huntington's Disease really defensible? People appear to have quite different opinions. Optimists argue that a child born into a family afflicted with Huntington's Disease has a reasonable chance of living a satisfactory life. After all, even children born of an afflicted parent still have a 50 percent chance of escaping the disease. And even if afflicted themselves, such people will probably enjoy some thirty years of healthy life before symptoms appear. It is also possible, although not at all likely, that some might not mind the symptoms caused by the disease. Optimists can point to diseased persons who have lived fruitful lives, as well as those who seem genuinely glad to be alive. One is Rick Donohue, a sufferer from the Joseph family disease: "You know, if my mom hadn't had me, I wouldn't be here for the life I have had. So there is a good possibility I will have children."[13] Optimists therefore conclude that it would be a shame if these persons had not lived.

Pessimists concede some of these facts but take a less sanguine view of them. They think a 50 percent risk of serious disease such as Huntington's is appallingly high. They suspect that many children born into afflicted families are liable to spend their youth in dreadful anticipation and fear of the disease. They expect that the disease, if it appears, will be perceived as a tragic and painful end to a blighted life. They point out that Rick Donohue is still young and has not experienced the full horror of his sickness. It is also well-known that some young persons have such a dilated sense of time that they can hardly envision themselves at 30 or 40, so the prospect of pain at that age is unreal to them.[14]

More empirical research on the psychology and life history of suffers and potential sufferers is clearly needed to decide whether optimists or pessimists have a more accurate picture of the experiences of individuals at risk. But given that some will surely realize pessimists' worst fears, it seems unfair to conclude that the pleasures of those who deal best with the situation simply cancel out the suffering of those others when that suffering could be avoided altogether.

I think that these points indicate that the morality of procreation in such situations demands further investigation. I propose to do this by looking first at the position of the possible child, then at that of the potential parent.

Possible Children and Potential Parents

The first task in treating the problem from the child's point of view is to find a way of referring to possible future offspring without seeming to confer some sort of morally significant existence on them. I follow the convention of calling children who might be born in the future but who are not now conceived "possible" children, offspring, individuals, or persons.

Now, what claims about children or possible children are relevant to the morality of child-bearing in the circumstances being considered? Of primary importance is the judgment that we ought to try to provide every child with something like a minimally satisfying life. I am not altogether sure how best to formulate this standard, but I want clearly to reject the view that it is morally permissible to conceive individuals so long as we do not expect them to be so miserable that they wish they were dead.[15] I believe that this kind of moral minimalism is thoroughly unsatisfactory and that not many people would really want to live in a world where it was the prevailing standard. Its lure is that it puts few demands on us, but its price is the scant attention it pays to human well-being.

How might the judgment that we have a duty to try to provide a minimally satisfying life for our children be justified? It could, I think, be derived fairly straightforwardly from either utilitarian or contractarian theories of justice, although there is no space here for discussion of the details. The net result of such analysis would be to conclude that neglecting this duty would create unnecessary unhappiness or unfair disadvantage for some persons.

Of course, this line of reasoning confronts us with the need to spell out what is meant by "minimally satisfying" and what a standard based on this concept would require of us. Conceptions of a minimally satisfying life vary tremendously among societies and also within them. *De rigueur* in some circles are private music lessons and trips to Europe, whereas in others providing eight years of schooling is a major accomplishment. But there is no need to consider this complication at length here because we are concerned only with health as a prerequisite for a minimally satisfying life. Thus, as we draw out what such a standard might require of us, it seems reasonable to retreat to the more limited claim that parents should try to ensure something like normal health for their children. It might be thought that even this moderate claim is unsatisfactory as in some places debilitating conditions are the norm, but one could circumvent this objection by saying that parents ought to try to provide for their children health normal for that culture, even though it may be inadequate if measured by some outside standard.[16] This conservative position would still justify efforts to avoid the birth of children at risk for Huntington's Disease and other serious genetic diseases in virtually all societies.[17]

This view is reinforced by the following considerations. Given that possible children do not presently exist as actual individuals, they do not have a right to be brought into existence, and hence no one is maltreated by measures to avoid the conception of a possible person. Therefore, the conservative course that avoids the conception of those who would not be expected to enjoy a minimally satisfying life is at present the only fair course of action. The alternative is a *laissez-faire* approach that brings into existence the lucky, but only at the expense of the unlucky. Notice that attempting to avoid the creation of the unlucky does not necessarily lead to *fewer* people being brought into being; the question boils down to taking steps to bring those with better prospects into existence, instead of those with worse ones.

I have so far argued that if people with Huntington's Disease are unlikely to live minimally satisfying lives, then those who might pass it on should not have genetically related children. This is consonant with the principle that the greater the danger of serious problems, the stronger the duty to avoid them. But this principle is in conflict with what people think of as the right to reproduce. How might one decide which should take precedence?

Expecting people to forgo having genetically related children might seem to demand too great a sacrifice of them. But before reaching that conclusion we need to ask what is really at stake. One reason for wanting children is to experience family life, including love, companionship, watching kids grow, sharing their pains and triumphs, and helping to form members of the next generation. Other reasons emphasize the validation of parents as individuals within a continuous family line, children as a source of immortality, or perhaps even the gratification of producing partial replicas of oneself. Children may also be desired in an effort to prove that one is an adult, to try to cement a marriage, or to benefit parents economically.

Are there alternative ways of satisfying these desires? Adoption or new reproductive technologies can fulfill many of them without passing on known genetic defects. Sperm replacement has been available for many years via artificial insemination by donor. More recently, egg donation, sometimes in combination with contract pregnancy,[18] has been used to provide eggs for women who prefer not to use their own. Eventually it may be possible to clone individual humans, although that now seems a long way off. All of these approaches to avoiding the use of particular genetic material are controversial and have generated much debate. I believe that tenable moral versions of each do exist.[19]

None of these methods permits people to extend both genetic lines or realize the desire for immortality or for children who resemble both parents; nor is it clear that such alternatives will necessarily succeed in proving that one is an adult, cementing a marriage, or providing economic benefits. Yet, many people feel these desires strongly. Now, I am sympathetic to William James's dictum regarding desires: "Take any demand, however slight, which any creature, however weak, may make. Ought it not, for its own sole sake be satisfied? If not, prove why not."[20] Thus a world where more desires are satisfied is generally better than one where fewer are. However, not all desires can be legitimately satisfied, because as James suggests, there may be good reasons, such as the conflict of duty and desire, why some should be overruled.

Fortunately, further scrutiny of the situation reveals that there are good reasons why people should attempt with appropriate social support to talk themselves out of the desires in question or to consider novel ways of fulfilling them. Wanting to see the genetic line continued is not particularly rational when it brings a sinister legacy of illness and death. The desire for immortality cannot really be satisfied anyway, and people need to face the fact that what really matters is how they behave in their own lifetimes. And finally, the desire for children who physically resemble one is understandable, but basically narcissistic, and its fulfillment cannot be guaranteed even by normal reproduction. There are other ways of proving one is an adult, and other ways of cementing marriages – and children don't necessarily do either. Children, especially prematurely ill children, may not provide the expected economic benefits anyway. Nongenetically related children may also provide benefits similar to those that would have been provided by genetically related ones, and expected economic benefit is, in many cases, a morally questionable reason for having children.

Before the advent of reliable genetic testing, the options of people in Huntington's families were cruelly limited. On the one hand, they could have children, but at the risk of eventual crippling illness and death for them. On the other, they could refrain from child-bearing, sparing their possible children from significant risk of inheriting this disease, perhaps frustrating intense desires to procreate – only to discover, in some cases, that their sacrifice was unnecessary because they did not develop the disease. Or they could attempt to adopt or try new reproductive approaches.

Reliable genetic testing has opened up new possibilities. Those at risk who wish to have children can get tested. If they test positive, they know their possible children are at risk. Those who are opposed to abortion must be especially careful to avoid conception if they are to behave responsibly. Those not opposed to abortion can responsibly conceive children, but only if they are willing to test each fetus and abort those who carry the gene. If individuals at risk test negative, they are home free.

What about those who cannot face the test for themselves? They can do prenatal testing and abort fetuses who carry the defective gene. A clearly positive test also implies that the parent is affected, although negative tests do not rule out that possibility. Prenatal testing can thus bring knowledge that enables one to avoid passing the disease to others, but only, in some cases, at the cost of coming to know with certainty that one will indeed develop the disease. This situation raises with peculiar force the question of whether parental responsibility requires people to get tested.

Some people think that we should recognize a right "not to know." It seems to me that such a right could be defended only where ignorance does not put others at serious risk. So if people are prepared to forgo genetically related children, they need not get tested. But if they want genetically related children, then they must do whatever is necessary to ensure that affected babies are not the result. There is, after all, something inconsistent about the claim that one has a right to be shielded from the truth, even if the price is to risk inflicting on one's children the same dread disease one cannot even face in oneself.

In sum, until we can be assured that Huntington's Disease does not prevent people from living a minimally satisfying life, individuals at risk for the disease have a moral duty to try not to bring affected babies into this world. There are now enough options available so that this duty needn't frustrate their reasonable desires. Society has a corresponding duty to facilitate moral behavior on the part of individuals. Such support ranges from the narrow and concrete (such as making sure that medical testing and counseling is available to all) to the more general social environment that guarantees that all pregnancies are voluntary, that pronatalism is eradicated, and that women are treated with respect regardless of the reproductive options they choose.

Notes

1 I focus on genetic considerations, although with the advent of AIDS the scope of the general question here could be expanded. There are two reasons for sticking to this relatively narrow formulation. One is that dealing with a smaller chunk of the problem may help us to think more clearly, while realizing that some conclusions may nonetheless be relevant to the larger problem. The other is the peculiar capacity of some genetic problems to affect ever more individuals in the future.

2 For example, see Leon Kass, "Implications of Prenatal Diagnosis for the Human Right to Life," in *Ethical Issues in Human Genetics*, ed. Bruce Hilton et al. (New York: Plenum, 1973).

3 This is, of course, a very broad thesis. I defend an even broader version in ch. 2 of *Reproducing Persons*, "Loving Future People."

4 Why would we want to resist legal enforcement of every moral conclusion? First, legal action has many costs, costs not necessarily worth paying in particular cases. Second, legal enforcement tends to take the matter out of the realm of debate and treat it as settled. But in many cases, especially where mores or technology are rapidly evolving, we don't want that to happen. Third, legal enforcement would undermine individual freedom and decision-making capacity. In some cases, the ends envisioned are important enough to warrant putting up with these disadvantages.

5 Those who do not see fetuses as moral persons with a right to life may nonetheless hold that abortion is justifiable in these cases. I argue at some length elsewhere that lesser defects can cause great suffering. Once we are clear that there is nothing discriminatory about failing to conceive particular possible individuals, it makes sense, other things being equal, to avoid the prospect of such pain if we can. Naturally, other things rarely are equal. In the first place, many problems go undiscovered until a baby is born. Second, there are often substantial costs associated with screening programs. Third, although women should be encouraged to consider the moral dimensions of routine pregnancy, we do not want it to be so fraught with tension that it becomes a miserable experience. (See ch. 2 of *Reproducing Persons*, "Loving Future People.")

6 It should be noted that failing to conceive a single individual can affect many lives: in 1916, 962 cases could be traced from six seventeenth-century arrivals in America. See Gordon Rattray Taylor, *The Biological Time Bomb* (New York: Penguin, 1968), p. 176.

7 *The Merck Manual* (Rahway, NJ: Merck, 1972), pp. 1363, 1346. We now know that the age of onset and severity of the disease are related to the number of abnormal replications of the glutamine code on the abnormal gene. See Andrew Revkin, "Hunting Down Huntington's," *Discover* (December 1993): 108.

8 Hymie Gordon, "Genetic Counseling," *JAMA*, 217, no. 9 (August 30, 1971): 1346.

9 See Revkin, "Hunting Down Huntington's," 99–108.

10 "Gene for Huntington's Disease Discovered," *Human Genome News*, no. 1 (May 1993): 5.

11 Charles Smith, Susan Holloway, and Alan E. H. Emery, "Individuals at Risk in Families – Genetic Disease," *Journal of Medical Genetics*, 8 (1971): 453.

12 To try to separate the issue of the gravity of the disease from the existence of a given individual, compare this situation with how we would assess a parent who neglected to vaccinate an existing child against a hypothetical viral version of Huntington's.

13 *The New York Times* (September 30, 1975), p. 1. The Joseph family disease is similar to Huntington's Disease except that symptoms start appearing in the twenties. Rick Donohue was in his early twenties at the time he made this statement.

14 I have talked to college students who believe that they will have lived fully and be ready to die at those ages. It is astonishing how one's perspective changes over time and how ages that one once associated with senility and physical collapse come to seem the prime of human life.

15 The view I am rejecting has been forcefully articulated by Derek Parfit, *Reasons and Persons* (Oxford: Clarendon, 1984). For more discussion, see ch. 2 of *Reproducing Persons*, "Loving Future People."

16 I have some qualms about this response, because I fear that some human groups are so badly off that it might still be wrong for them to procreate, even if that would mean great changes in their cultures. But this is a complicated issue that needs to be investigated on its own.

17 Again, a troubling exception might be the isolated Venezuelan group Nancy Wexler found, where, because of inbreeding, a large proportion of the population is affected by Huntington's. See Revkin, "Hunting Down Huntington's."

18 Or surrogacy, as it has been popularly known. I think that "contract pregnancy" is more accurate and more respectful of women. Eggs can be provided either by a woman who also gestates the fetus or by a third party.

19 The most powerful objections to new reproductive technologies and arrangements concern possible bad consequences for women. However, I do not think that the arguments against them on these grounds have yet shown the dangers to be as great as some believe. So although it is perhaps true that new reproductive technologies and arrangements should not be used lightly, avoiding the conceptions discussed here is well worth the risk. For a series of viewpoints on this issue, including my own "Another Look at Contract Pregnancy" (ch. 12 of *Reproducing Persons*), see Helen B. Holmes, *Issues in Reproductive Technology I: An Anthology* (New York: Garland, 1992).

20 William James, *Essays in Pragmatism*, ed. A. Castell (New York: Hafner, 1948), p. 73.

13

Prenatal Screening and its Impact on Persons with Disabilities

Deborah Kaplan

The disability rights movement has "come of age" in the 1990s with the passage of the Americans with Disabilities Act and increased public attention to disability concerns. Persons with disabilities have made great advances in moving social policy away from two different models of thought on disability: (1) the "charity" approach, which presumes that the best we can do is to provide welfare and charity toward primarily custodial services for persons with less social value, and (2) the "medical" approach, which applies a medical framework toward social problems presented by disability and assumes that the best outcome is for a medical cure of the disability. A new approach, based on integrating persons with disabilities into society and accepting disability as a predictable aspect of life, has emerged during the past two decades.

Prenatal screening inherently is concerned with the existence, or avoidance, of disability in society and individuals. Are the social goals of those who have worked for the widespread use of prenatal screening consistent with those of the disability rights movement? As persons with disabilities have moved into significant policy-making positions throughout society, their views and experiences are becoming difficult to ignore.

The purpose of this article is to examine some of the policy implications of prenatal screening from a disability perspective. That perspective is based on the life experiences of persons with disabilities who have attained academic, scientific, and social roles that provide them with an opportunity to provide a new way of looking at the value of living with a disability. This article also reviews some of the most commonly given reasons for prenatal screening and extracts potential research topics from an analysis of those reasons.

From *Clinical Obstetrics and Gynecology*, vol. 36, no. 3 (September 1993), pp. 605–12. Reprinted by permission of Lippincott Williams & Wilkins.

Why Do We Engage in Prenatal Testing?

The most frequently given reason is that we are trying to "prevent" or ameliorate medical or disabling conditions that are genetically based. After a genetic syndrome or condition is diagnosed in a fetus, there are three types of prevention that can be taken as follows:

1 Prevention of the birth through abortion. Although new testing procedures sometimes permit this to take place during the first trimester of pregnancy, many such abortions still occur during the second trimester.
2 Prevention or amelioration of the disability through methods such as treatment through dietary changes or supplements for the mother (prebirth) or infant, prenatal treatment of the fetus through pharmaceutical or surgical interventions, other forms of treatment or therapy for the infant that occur after the prenatal diagnosis.
3 Prevention of family disruption through prenatal preparation by family members. This can entail obtaining information about the diagnosed condition and its consequences through reading, talking with families with children with similar disabilities or adults with the dis-

ability, or other means. It also may include finding out about available public or private resources or other forms of assistance, purchasing equipment or making home modifications, and other similar activities.

From the perspective of persons with disabilities, the second and third types of prevention are not terribly controversial, although there are some disability groups that might object to some forms of prenatal medical intervention. For example, some deaf families might reject prenatal cochlear implants, were such interventions available, because they do not regard deafness as a negative characteristic. For many persons with disabilities, however, the most disturbing type of prevention is the first, abortion. There are two general reasons for this.

The first reason is the general public controversy over abortion. People with disabilities can be found taking positions on both sides of this issue, for the same reasons as other people, and for reasons that are specific to persons with disabilities. On one side, some persons with disabilities are anti-abortion for primarily disability-based reasons, including the very personal reason that they might have never been born if their parents had had access to prenatal screening and a legal abortion. There are anecdotal accounts from adults with disabilities who were told as much by their parents. On the other side, many in the disability rights movement have a very strong belief in individual autonomy and support the concept of a woman's right to control her own body. Some disabled women and men are in favor of legal abortions because, among other reasons, women with some types of disabilities and medical conditions may be more likely to require late abortions of wanted pregnancies because of medical risks associated with particular disabilities.[1]

There is a unique disability perspective on both sides of the broader social debate that is largely unappreciated by the general public or the media. It is frustrating and difficult for persons with disabilities to understand why their varied points of view on this issue are so often ignored, discounted, or simply unreported, especially when part of the debate focuses on the quality of life for a person with a disability.[2–4]

The second reason is the clash in values or beliefs about the value of life with a disability. Many in the disability rights movement and the disabled community hold a different view from the majority of society on the affects of disability on individuals and families. The traditional belief in many cultures is that the existence of a disability is an overall negative trait.[5] We do not need to look very far to find negative images of disability in both fiction and nonfiction. Even the fairy tales and classics that are read by children contain disabled villains (such as Captain Hook) or pathetic, helpless figures (such as the little girl who cannot walk until Heidi befriends her). Horror movies are full of crazed killers who have one form of disability or another.

Generally, however, the prevailing attitude usually does not hold that disabled people themselves are bad but that the experience of the disability contributes to a lower quality of life for the individual. This often results in a widespread assumption that, if a person with a disability is experiencing difficulties, they are caused by the disability and not other factors. It also results in the disability becoming elevated as the predominant characteristic about a person, only one feature out of many that define a personality.

However, people with disabilities are finding that, with advances in the availability of assistive technology, accessible environments, and appropriate social services, these widespread negative assumptions are not necessarily true. For many persons with a variety of disabilities, their own experience of the quality of their lives is positive. Persons with very significant disabilities now attend regular schools, colleges, and universities where they receive advanced degrees, find challenging jobs, get married, and live fairly normal lives.

The emerging disability rights movement is built on the shared belief that many of the problems experienced by persons with disabilities are caused not by the disability but by the barriers that exist in society, whether they are architectural, technologic, legal, or attitudinal. This is easier to see in retrospect. For example, a person who uses a wheelchair is not "confined" to the wheelchair in an accessible environment. The wheelchair is a tool, much like a pair of glasses, that enables someone with a mobility limitation to move about wherever they please. However, until wheelchair users had the opportunity to go places freely without assistance, a wheelchair did feel like a confining piece of equipment.

The advances in the legal rights of persons with disabilities that have taken place during the past two decades have permitted persons with disabilities to gain this new perspective about their lives.

Until children with a disability could go to their local schools and obtain the services needed to benefit fully from an education, it was easier to assume that the disability was the cause of the lack of educational equality in these children's lives. Now, with a federal law mandating equality in access to education, it no longer makes sense to perceive the disability as the problem.

Why Do We Want to Prevent the Birth of Fetuses with Disabilities?

The most often given reasons are to avoid negative consequences in the following areas:

1 The economic impact on families.
2 The economic impact on society.
3 The disruption to families.
4 The "quality of life" of a child or person with a disability.
5 The not being a "perfect" child.

It is possible to identify areas that are ripe for further research by conducting an analysis of each reason. More information is needed to determine whether the assumptions behind these reasons are actually correct.

Economic impact

It is widely believed that there are disability-related costs that must be assumed by families with disabled children. Although there is plenty of anecdotal evidence of this situation, it is unclear exactly what those costs are and how predictable they are.

There is some research on the costs of raising a child with a disability. This work needs to be collected and examined to determine what are the specific costs associated with raising a child with a disability that are not associated with nondisabled children? Similarly, what costs are higher for a child with a disability? For those, what sources of support are available currently to families? Which costs must be borne by the families?

Social economic impact

Some have pointed to alarming amounts of money that are allocated by the government to pay for social programs for persons with disabilities. The inference is that "prevention" through abortion will decrease these expenditures and therefore reduce public expenditures associated with disability.

The nature of public expenditures for disability needs is changing, however. In large part, because of the advocacy of persons with disabilities, the purposes of many public programs are under examination. Persons with disabilities are challenging the custodial nature of many public programs and have advocated for program redesign, with the goal of providing incentives and support for employment and self-sufficiency as much as possible. Thus, new program priorities could be viewed as creating a social investment that is paid back by the person with a disability later in life through income taxes and other types of contributions to society, both fiscal and in other forms.

In addition, legislation like the Americans with Disabilities Act will have a significant impact on the American landscape, resulting in an environment with permanent fixtures that enable persons with disabilities to function like other people. It is unclear to what extent these changes will reduce the need for public expenditures that previously had served to compensate for social and architectural barriers that reduced the functioning abilities of persons with disabilities.

Given these caveats, there still is little research to validate the assumption that abortion-based prevention will reduce disability-related social costs significantly. To what extent are social program resources used by persons with genetic conditions? Of that group, what percentage has been reduced in recent years through genetic testing? To what extent are savings offset by public expenditures related to prenatal screening? What amount of money has been saved?

Disruption of families

Although there is an assumption that the addition of a child with a disability to a family will be disruptive, there are anecdotal accounts on both sides of this question. It is possible that the general attitude that assumes a negative impact of disability, discussed previously, may be at work here.

There are accounts of families that have been weakened by the presence of a disabled child and those that report strengthening or enrichment. Presumably, there are also families that report little or no significant impact. Aside from anecdotes, however, there is little solid evidence that can be found either to support or refute the common view.

Without solid research into this issue, we really do not know what the impact is across many different types of families. What demographic factors account for any differences in familial experiences? Are there other factors?

Of particular importance to women, we need to know to what extent mothers of disabled children are expected to disrupt their lives to make sure the needs of their children with disabilities are met. Anecdotal accounts suggest that mothers take up this role far more often than fathers.

Quality of life

There are several possible sources of information about the quality of life of a person with a disability: health and helping professionals, parents and other family members, and persons with disabilities. Professionals and family members are secondary sources of information. Persons with disabilities are primary sources of information. Because quality of life is such a subjective concept, it makes sense to get information from primary sources as much as possible. This means that research into this issue should use subjects who are disabled themselves.

There is a distinction between the quality of life of the person with a disability and that of others, such as family members. Many of the concerns voiced about the quality of life of family members were reflected previously, and possible research was suggested. However, acknowledging the interrelationships of individuals in families, it is important to recognize that the experience of the family member with a disability may be different from that of other family members.

Allowing family members to report on the quality of life of the person with a disability may be misleading because their perceptions may be wrong or may be biased by their own experiences. It is surprising and alarming, however, that the expressions of professionals and family members have been given great credence in this regard, without acknowledging their distance from the subject matter.

There is little existing research to refer to on this subject. There is a need for research to examine the subjective feelings of persons with genetically based disabilities regarding the quality of their lives. Subjects should be questioned about major facets of their lives (such as social life, employment, family relationships, and recreation); persons with no disabilities should serve as a control group, responding to the same set of questions. The results of such a survey would give us needed information about how persons with disabilities regard their own lives.

Perfection

It is difficult to know whether to consider this reason seriously. Even though the goal of guaranteeing "perfection" in an offspring is not usually the stated reason for obtaining prenatal testing, it cannot be ignored. To a certain extent, this concept of perfection is tied to our notion of "normalcy."

Potential research questions include: (1) to what degree does a desire for a normal child factor into the decision to seek prenatal screening, (2) what are the ethical implications of these goals, (3) what do we mean by "perfect" or "normal," (4) what cultural factors contribute to different perceptions about normalcy, and (5) are some disabilities acceptable to some groups and not to others?

The Quality of Life Dilemma

The most appealing and satisfying reason for permitting abortions based on genetic characteristics is altruism. We believe we are saving potential future children from pain and harm. Other justifications, based on the economic or social interests of the family, or society in general, also may be present, but they do not sound as benevolent. Perhaps it is this justification that is most troublesome to disability rights activists.

What would happen to the level of social acceptance for this technology if quality-of-life research reveals that persons with disabilities do not share the view that the quality of their life is reduced significantly because of their disabilities? Are the economic or social interests of others sufficient? What would be the policy result if it were found that persons with disabilities do not report a subjective experience of their own lives that is negative?

It is noteworthy that some of the most insistent voices questioning the rationale for prenatal screening are persons with disabilities. The perspective of persons with disabilities deserves attention because quality of life is defined most appropriately by the group that has the most direct experience with disability. Persons with disabilities and their leaders are questioning the use of prenatal screening to respond to social problems that could be resolved through other policy initiatives.

Public Perceptions of Disability

Many leaders of the disabled community (persons with disabilities, as opposed to family members or professionals who often speak "for" disabled persons) have expressed concern that genetic testing and prenatal screening has a tendency to promote negative general attitudes about disability. They worry that these negative attitudes might result in public policies or practices, such as job discrimination, barriers to obtaining health insurance coverage, cutbacks in public support programs, and other similar negative actions.[6]

Prenatal testing has arisen during a time in which persons with disabilities and their organizations have undertaken major efforts to remove "attitudinal barriers" to social acceptance. They fear that the availability of prenatal testing encourages negative attitudes in several ways:

1 A general social expectation has developed that we will be able to reduce funding of programs for persons with disabilities, whether or not the actual numbers of persons with disabilities decrease. Prenatal screening has been promoted as beneficial because it will lead to a reduction in the numbers of persons with disabilities in society. To what extent have public policy makers, under increasing pressure to make budget cuts, seized on this idea to rationalize their actions?
2 A subtle shift in perception about the causes of disability, at least for genetic disabilities, results in the blaming of parents who "caused" a disability by either not being screened or by choosing to carry a pregnancy to term after screening revealed the existence of a targeted genetic trait. To what extent has this led to family difficulties or disruptions, social ostracism, or other negative results?
3 There may be an increase in negative attitudes in general. In part, this fear comes from the language or terminology that is often used in the medical field, i.e., "bad" genes, "bad" babies, "defective" genes, and "defective" babies. Do these terms extend to persons with disabilities? Are they "bad" people or "defective" people? These are not terms that disabled people use to describe themselves. To what extent are negative images of disability related to these expressions?
4 The ability to predict the existence of a genetic condition before birth could cause increased difficulties in obtaining adequate medical insurance coverage for persons with disabilities. Do prenatally diagnosed conditions become "pre-existing conditions?" Under current economic conditions, insurance companies are using many different tactics to deny coverage to individuals who previously had no trouble with health insurance. To what extent has the availability of prenatal screening resulted in more exclusive medical insurance practices?

Underlying these concerns is a message that many disabled leaders believe is implicit in the practice of abortion based on genetic characteristics, i.e., it is better not to exist than to have a disability. This concept is rejected soundly by the disability rights movement, which is promoting a very different message, i.e., most of the problems experienced by persons with disabilities are the result of intolerance, poorly conceived social programs, and environmental or communication barriers that can be removed by changes in social policy.[7] These are two profoundly different perspectives on disability.

It should be pointed out that prenatal testing will never have a very significant impact on the number of persons with disabilities in the United States. It is estimated that there are more than 42 million persons with a variety of disabilities. Most of them are caused by trauma and age; relatively few are genetic in nature. Any public expectation that prenatal testing will lead to a meaningful reduction in the rates of disability in society is quite misplaced.

Another factor that complicates the discussion, or debate, is the fact that disability is a relative concept, as is genetic condition. All human beings have genetic characteristics that differentiate them from other people. As our base of genetic information increases, are we at risk of creating new genetic conditions with new social stigma attached to them? Are we contracting (as opposed to expanding) the category of "normal"? A recent poll suggested that 11 per cent of Americans might abort a fetus predisposed to obesity.

What is the difference between a genetic characteristic and a genetic condition? In a preliterate society, learning disabilities probably had much less impact on the ability of the individual to function or succeed. In a physical environment that is fully wheelchair accessible, with the low-cost and lightweight sports wheelchairs commonly available, we might not be so prone to describe wheelchair riders as "wheelchair bound" or "confined to a wheelchair." Prenatal screening cannot predict the severity of most genetic conditions, which adds further complications.

It is important to weigh these potential negative results of the availability of prenatal screening against its known benefits. Thus, the benefits from prenatal screening should be defined clearly and be measurable.

It is also important to evaluate whether the means that are used currently to promote prenatal screening, such as publicity, brochures, training of medical personnel, and other methods, tend to promote unacceptable negative messages about disability. If so, then alternative means or messages should be explored.[6]

Perceptions about disability may explain partly the different points of view about the validity of prenatal screening as a tool of public policy. If persons with disabilities are perceived as individuals who encounter insurmountable difficulties in life and who place a burden on society, prenatal screening may be regarded as a logical response. However, if persons with disabilities are regarded as a definable social group who have faced great oppression and stigmatization, then prenatal screening may be regarded as yet another form of social abuse.

Conclusion

To evaluate the effectiveness of prenatal screening, we must first be clear about what goals we are trying to achieve. If we are attempting to protect future human beings from experiencing a terrible quality of life, we had better be sure that there is a relationship between predictable genetic conditions and a negative life experience. If we are attempting to resolve economic or social disadvantages that are associated with genetic disabilities, we should at least explore whether this goal can be achieved through alternative methods and examine these alternatives. The disability rights movement certainly agrees that there are economic and social disadvantages that are associated with disability. However, the fact that so many persons with disabilities are engaging in ordinary lives with satisfying jobs, happy family situations, and a variety of community roles suggests that these disadvantages can be eliminated without eliminating persons with disabilities.

Disability leaders have attempted to eradicate these problems through advocacy for civil rights protection, legislation to eradicate barriers found in the environment, programs to promote and make available adaptive technology, and more effective social support programs. Prenatal screening as a widespread social practice appears to be at odds with some of the goals of the disability rights movement, and many prominent disability leaders question its value and ethical basis.[8]

At a minimum, prenatal testing strikes some as a technology that is proceeding without a firm basis in social policy. There are many questions about how we should proceed in an era in which proliferating information about human genetics makes matters more and more complex. We surely need to include the perspectives of the disabled community better in our research and exploration of policy options. The disability community is willing to join the dialogue.

References

1 Fine, M. and Asch, A. "Shared dreams: a left perspective on disability rights and reproductive rights." In: M. Fine, A. Asch (eds) *Women with Disabilities: Essays in Psychology, Culture and Politics*, (Philadelphia: Temple University Press, 1988), pp. 297–305.

2 Morris, J. "Tyrannies of perfection." *New Internationalist* 233 (July 1992): 16.

3 Saxton, M. "The implications of 'choice' for people with disabilities." *Women Wise*, *The N.H. Feminist Health Center Q.* (Winter, 1984).

4 Saxton, M. "Born and unborn: implications of the reproductive technologies for people with disabilities." In: R. Arditti, R. Duelli-Klein, and S. Minden (eds), *Test-Tube Women: What Future for Motherhood?* (Boston: Routledge and Kegan Paul, 1984).

5 Degener, T. "Female self-determination between feminist claims and 'voluntary' eugenics, between 'rights' and ethics." *Issues in Reproductive and Genetic Engineering*, 3(2) (1990): 87–99.
6 Wang, C. "Culture, meaning and disability: injury prevention campaigns and the production of stigma." *Social Science Medicine*, 35: (1992) 1093–1102.
7 Deegan, M.J. and Brooks, N.A. *Women and Disability: The Double Handicap*. (New Brunswick, NJ: Transaction, 1985).
8 Finger, A. "Claiming all of our bodies: reproductive rights and disabilities." In: R. Arditti, R. Duelli-Klein, and S. Minden (eds), *Test-Tube Women: What Future for Motherhood*? (Boston: Routledge and Kegan Paul, 1984).

14

Sex Selection: Individual Choice or Cultural Coercion?

Mary Anne Warren

Much public attention has been focused on the technology of *in vitro* fertilization (IVF), and on some of the dramatic reproductive technologies which might be developed in the future, such as the cloning of adult human beings, or the creation of heritable changes to the human genome through the genetic alteration of human germ-line cells. Meanwhile, another set of reproductive technologies is being introduced more quietly. It is now possible to preselect the sex of children, either before birth, through selective abortion, or (less reliably) before conception.

In China, India, and other parts of Asia, amniocentesis has been widely used to enable the abortion of unwanted females. Amniocentesis is usually performed at fourteen weeks or later, and the results can take several weeks to obtain. Thus, if an abortion is done, it will usually not be earlier than the latter part of the second trimester. Women who submit to such late abortions merely for sex selection[1] must either be desperate for a child of the "right" sex or subject to powerful social pressures (or both), since late abortion is much more emotionally traumatic and physically dangerous than early abortion. For these and other reasons, sex-selective abortion has been uncommon in the Western industrialized nations. Nor has it been common in parts of the world (e.g., much of Central and South America) where abortion remains illegal and clandestine. However, there are already technically feasible ways of diagnosing fetal sex at earlier stages of pregnancy, e.g., through chorion biopsy; and more techniques are likely to emerge as a side effect of the development of procedures for the early detection of fetal abnormalities. For instance, procedures being developed for isolating fetal cells from maternal blood and culturing them to provide material for genetic analysis will probably also provide a means of early sex diagnosis. Once it becomes feasible to diagnose fetal sex in the first trimester of pregnancy, sex-selective abortion may become a more acceptable option for some prospective parents.

However, a reliable method of preselecting sex prior to conception would certainly have greater appeal for more people. There are a variety of "home remedies" that have been recommended for sex selection, involving, for instance, the timing of intercourse in relation to ovulation, the mother's and/or father's diet, the positions used for intercourse, or the alteration of vaginal acidity. There is no convincing evidence that any of these do-it-yourself methods is effective. However, a more sophisticated technique has been commercially available for over a decade. Dr Ron Ericsson has operated clinics in Europe, Asia, and North America, offering to enhance the odds of having sons, through artificial insemination with semen that has been filtered in order to separate androgenic (male-producing) from gynogenic (female-producing) spermatozoa. While the effectiveness of this particular method is uncertain, the search for an effective method of preconceptive sex selection is likely to continue. Work has been done towards the development of vaccines that will cause women's immune systems selectively to attack either androgenic or gynogenic spermatozoa. IVF pre-embryos can be selected for sex by removing a cell from each, determining the chromosomal composition, and implanting only pre-embryos of the desired sex. IVF is still too expensive, too physically and emotionally trying, and too often unsuccessful to be attractive to most women merely as a means of sex selection. However, if the success rates continue to improve, and the cost comes down significantly, it may some day commonly be used to predetermine children's sex, and perhaps many of their other characteristics as well.

The prospect of the widespread use of new methods of preselecting sex is disturbing, because in practice sex selection has almost always meant the elimination of unwanted females. Even in the industrialized nations, where son preference tends to be weaker than in much of the developing world, males remain the preferred sex of the majority. Potential parents of both sexes tend to want more boys than girls, to want a male first-born, and to want a son if they plan to have just one child.

Patriarchy almost inevitably creates a preference for sons. If sons have greater earning power, then they are apt to be regarded as more valuable contributors to family income and old-age security. Sons do not require dowries – an important factor in India, where families often fear economic ruin from the birth of daughters. Where residence patterns are patrilocal, sons are more permanent members of the family; daughters leave when they marry, and neither their children nor their labor will belong to their family of origin. In patrilineal societies, it is usually only sons who pass on the paternal name. Even when the law permits daughters to do this, as in the United States, the force of custom often means that few do. In some cultures, e.g., in China, sons have religious duties towards ancestors that cannot be performed by daughters. Son preference has declined in the industrialized nations, in part because women's earning power has increased relative to men's; but it is unlikely to disappear entirely so long as women's average earnings are not equal to men's, and so long as the patrilineal inheritance of names and property persists.

The selective elimination of female children is nothing new. Female infanticide has been a common (though often covert) practice in most patriarchal cultures throughout the world, and throughout recorded history. It has sometimes been so prevalent that males have outnumbered females by more than two to one – as appears to have been the case in some parts and periods of ancient Greece.[2] Even today, in many impoverished parts of the world, female children may be abandoned at birth or allowed to die later of malnutrition or neglect. There is no other plausible explanation for the higher death rates for female infants observed, for instance, in parts of India; for if the only factors were poverty and illness, it would be male infants who experienced higher mortality rates, since they are more vulnerable to the effects of illness and malnutrition.[3] Because in twentieth-century Western industrialized nations female infanticide has been uncommon, and because women's average life-span has surpassed that of men, these nations have for some time enjoyed sex ratios that are fairly even, except when disrupted by war. Indeed, there is now a slight female majority in many nations. But the introduction of more reliable and less expensive methods of sex selection might alter these roughly even ratios.

How, then, should feminists respond to the prospect of new methods of sex selection? Sex selection has been attacked as immoral by both radical feminists and conservative antifeminists, although for different reasons. Religious conservatives often oppose sex selection for much the same reasons that they often oppose abortion: they regard all technological means of sex selection as unnatural and morally objectionable interferences with the human reproductive process; and they view sex-selective abortion as the wrongful taking of a human life. In contrast, some feminists have opposed sex selection and other new reproductive technologies, as part of the historical process by which men have progressively taken control of women's reproductive lives. Some have predicted that increases in the relative number of males will produce more violent societies, increased sexual exploitation of women and children, and a loss of personal liberty and social and political influence for women. Some have worried that women will be eliminated entirely in favor of ectogenesis machines. Both feminists and conservative antifeminists have predicted that the development of IVF and other reproductive and genetic technologies may eventually bring about the Brave New World scenario, in which totalitarian governments and medical technocrats control who will have children, and exactly what sorts of children they will have.

There is too little space here to deal with all of these objections.[4] Instead, I will consider what I take to be the most troubling objection to sex selection, and ask whether this objection provides a sufficient basis for advocating the universal legal prohibition of all artificial means of sex selection.

The primary objection to sex selection is that it will tend to increase sex ratios, i.e., to reduce the relative number of females born. We need not fear that women will be deliberately rendered extinct, since we will still be needed, e.g., for reproduction. Even if an artificial womb is developed, economic realities will (for some time, and perhaps forever) restrict its use to the wealthy, while the majority of humankind continue to be born of woman. However, if inexpensive and effective forms of sex selection become widely available, women may eventually be outnumbered by men in most of the world. The disparity is likely to be greatest in nations which are severely patriarchal, and not predominantly Roman Catholic. Without legal prohibition, the most extreme sex ratio changes would be likely to occur in India, Southeast Asia, and China, where the one-child policy – now relaxed but not abandoned – has made many couples reluctant to rear a firstborn daughter. Extreme changes might also occur in some of the predominantly Islamic nations which have the wealth to embrace high-tech methods of reproduction. The nations of Central and South America are considerably less likely to experience extreme sex ratio shifts, both because of the influence of the Roman Catholic Church (which officially opposes all of the new reproductive technologies, including sex selection), and because the preference for sons is generally weaker there.[5]

It seems highly probable that large increases in sex ratios (i.e., in the relative number of males) would be detrimental to the cause of gender justice. Other things being equal, there is power in numbers, whether within families, communities, or nations. Given that males often retain a near hegemony of economic and political power even when women are slightly in the majority, it seems unrealistic to hope for significant progress when women are greatly in the minority.

Some commentators have suggested that high sex ratios are good for women, who tend to benefit from their own scarcity. Marcia Guttentag and Paul Secord have argued that in a high-sex-ratio society women enjoy a greater range of choices in the matrimonial sweepstakes, and thus more power in heterosexual relationships.[6] If women are in short supply, they argue, then they are more highly valued, and men are more willing to commit themselves to marriage and family life.

However, Guttentag and Second also point out that women in high-sex-ratio societies tend to be more strictly confined to domesticity than women in societies with a more even sex ratio; they have fewer opportunities for economic independence, and they are often largely excluded from the political, religious, and other extradomestic institutions of the society. Feminist movements are less likely to arise in high-sex-ratio societies, because most women are absorbed into the domestic role, leaving few to demand entry into politics, the professions, or other public social roles. Wives and mothers are respected, but the flip side of that respect is contempt for women who are not wives, and wives who fail to bear sons. Women who are content with a private domestic role, wishing only that this role could be more highly valued, may find the typical high-sex-ratio society attractive. But women who value the freedom to take part in the full range of social, economic, and political institutions can only view it as a nightmare.

We cannot know that the introduction of new means of sex selection would produce such dire consequences in all societies. It is possible that the extreme forms of patriarchal domination which Guttentag and Secord observe in high-sex-ratio societies are a cause rather than an effect of high sex ratios. It is also possible that sex selection will have only slight effects on sex ratios in most nations. Some jurisdictions have already banned the use of amniocentesis for sex-selective abortion (e.g., the American state of Pennsylvania, and some Indian states). Perhaps public opinion will gradually turn against against all forms of sex selection, such that in the future they will be used only rarely. In the Western industrialized world, improved economic opportunities available to women may already have undermined son preference enough so that seriously skewed sex ratios will never be a problem.

Yet it seems probable that in some societies, without legal prohibition, sex selection will lead to much higher sex ratios, and that the net results will be detrimental to women – and probably also to men. (For instance, men in high-sex-ratio societies are apt to have more difficulty finding a female partner, and they may have to work longer and harder before being considered marriageable.) Thus, where sex ratios are apt to be severely altered by sex selection, there is a strong argument for prohibition – provided that it will not lead to still greater harm, such as a black market in unsafe sex-selection procedures that will put women at even greater medical risk.

But what about the legal and moral status of sex selection in societies which are unlikely to experience large sex-ratio shifts? Is sex selection morally objectionable regardless of the social and personal context? If we find sex selection morally troubling, should we argue for its universal prohibition, even where significant social harm seems unlikely to occur? Our answers to these questions will depend in part upon what we think that a woman is doing – or what is being done to her – when she submits to sex-selective abortion or preconceptive sex-selection procedures. Is she making a choice which ought to be be protected by her right to reproductive liberty? Is she making a choice which is not entitled to such protection? Or is she not making a choice at all, but only yielding to social coercion?

Liberals and liberal feminists tend to support the first interpretation, arguing that the preselection of the sex of a future child is as morally acceptable as the use of contraception for family planning. On this view, individuals and couples are entitled to make these family-planning decisions on the basis of their own moral and religious values, and in the light of their own social and economic situation. Radical feminists, in contrast, generally argue for the second or third interpretation. Some maintain that a woman who uses sex selection in order to have a son may be acting voluntarily, but her choice is ethically indefensible because it will militate against the legitimate rights and interests of all women. Others argue that a woman's use of sex selection is virtually always socially coerced, in so far as she would probably not have made that choice in a society where sons and daughters were equally valued. Thus, the argument continues, women cannot benefit from the legal right to make such a choice; to speak of a "right to choose" in this context is to obscure the reality of coercion.

These conflicting feminist perspectives are apparent not only in the debate over sex selection, but also in connection with *in vitro* fertilization, prenatal diagnosis, and other new reproductive technologies. It is therefore important to ask which of these perspectives on choice is more appropriate as a guide to the moral evaluation of these technologies.

It should be clear that none of these three alternatives represents a universally valid description of what is happening when a woman agrees to the use of sex-selection technology. A more realistic view is that sometimes the choice is clearly coerced, and sometimes it is clearly not coerced; and that usually it falls somewhere between the two extremes. Consider, at one extreme, a poor, young, uneducated woman in a highly patriarchal and highly son-preferring rural community in northern India. She has married into a family which values her only for her dowry and her potential to produce sons. She reasonably fears that if she fails to have sons she may be abused, repudiated, and perhaps even murdered. While she may want a daughter as a companion and helper, she knows that others in the family will view a female child as a useless drain on the family's resources, and may therefore neglect and abuse her. Even if she is not directly coerced into undergoing sex-selection procedures (as she may be), this woman may perceive no alternative to submission. To insist upon letting chance determine the sex of her children might be an act of heroism, but it is a heroism of which she feels incapable. In this situation, her "choice" to avoid bearing daughters is arguably no choice at all, and her "right" to make it is a mockery of reproductive freedom.

Now consider a well-educated woman in a prosperous industrialized nation, such as Australia. She is single, self-supporting (though not wealthy), and committed to doing what she can to remedy injustices against women and other oppressed groups. She may be a lesbian or bisexual, but that is not essential to the situation I wish to depict. What is essential is that she wishes to have a child, and expects to raise the child without a male partner. Her personal reflections have led her to conclude that she does not want to raise a son. She is not a sexist in the usual sense; that is, she does not believe that members of one sex are inherently more valuable than the other. However, she fears that if she has a son, "no amount of love and care and nonsexist training will save . . . [him] from a culture where male violence is institutionalized and revered."[7] She is unwilling to spend a large part of her life raising, at best, a well-meaning member of the ruling sex caste, and at worst, "a potential rapist, a potential batterer, a potential Big Man."[8] She believes that, given her convictions, it would be unfair to have a son, who would have no social father, and might come to feel that his mother regards him as the enemy.

This woman is hypothetical, but she is not mythical. I have met many women who would prefer to have daughters, often for reasons such as these. Her reasons for not wanting to raise a son may not be particularly good ones; but that is not the issue here. The issue is whether she can be said to be making an uncoerced choice to select her child's sex. I would argue that she can. Her decision is obviously influenced by social realities as she understands them; she might say that in a society with greater gender equality she would be happy to raise a son. But that influence does not rise to the level of coercion, since she remains free to either accept or reject sex selection, without suffering severe social sanctions, or placing herself or the child in great peril.

The lesson to be drawn from these cases is that it will not do to say either that the use of sex-selection technologies is always an exercise of individual reproductive freedom, or that it is always an illusory "choice" of no real benefit to women. Neither description can be generalized to all societies, or all circumstances within any given society. There is a continuum between maximally coerced and ideally uncoerced, voluntary, and autonomous decisions. Some women may submit to sex-selective abortion or preconceptive sex-selection treatments because they fear violence or abandonment if they refuse. Others may do so in defiance of the preponderance of social pressures acting upon them. But most cases are likely to be less clear. Most women will be influenced by the social, moral, and religious values that they have been taught, and the power dynamics of their own family and community life; but of what important decision is this not true? Many will opt for sex-selection technologies not because of coercive forces that they are powerless to resist, but because they judge that this is the best option for the child itself, in a world in which gender is still one of the most powerful determinants of opportunity.

In some societies, poor women often want sons because daughters are more costly to raise and likely to contribute less to the family's long-term economic security. If they seek to have more sons than daughters, are they being coerced or are they making a responsible reproductive decision in the light of harsh realities? Is their attitude essentially selfish or essentially altruistic? We should be wary of rash generalizations here. There may be some contemporary societies in which the economic and ideological forces that shape son preference are so powerful, and women have so little power to resist those pressures, that to permit the sale of sex-selection procedures can only make women more vulnerable to coercion. Deprived of daughters and sisters, women may become more isolated and powerless. In such circumstances, it is difficult to argue that new methods of preselecting sex will provide a net benefit to women, or an extension of their reproductive freedom. On the contrary, women's reproductive freedom may be best protected by the effective prohibition of sex selection.

But this model does not fit the situation of women in the Western industrialized nations. There, more women may choose to raise daughters in preference to sons. More women and couples will use sex selection in order to have a child of each sex. Others will prefer sons; but probably not so many as to produce large increases in sex ratios. Indeed, it is possible that in some instances sex selection will prevent severely *declining* sex ratios in the future, e.g., if natural sex ratios at birth decline due to environmental contaminants that are differentially lethal to male fetuses, or androgenic spermatozoa.

New methods of preselecting sex will probably be introduced over a period of several decades, or longer. Thus, there will be time to improve our understanding of the social consequences of small sex-ratio changes. As Guttentag and Secord point out, some of these changes might be beneficial to women. For instance, a shortage of women in underpaid female-dominated professions, such as nursing, might make it easier for members of these professions to demand improved pay and working conditions, and the redefinition of their role to better reflect their levels of responsibility and skill. Similarly, older women might find it easier to find male partners if the relative number of males were higher – a nontrivial consideration, since women's longer lives, together with men's preference for younger women, cause many women to face unwanted singleness in their later years.

The impossibility of accurately predicting the long-term social consequences of small sex-ratio changes militates against the prohibition of sex selection where large sex-ratio changes are unlikely. Individual rights and freedoms are not absolute, and must sometimes be overridden for the sake of a greater social good. For instance, the rights of property owners to do as they wish with their property are restricted for the sake of promoting environmentally sound practices and to avoid the creation of public hazards. But reproductive freedoms are crucial to women's other basic moral rights, and it is wise to resist incursions upon these freedoms, unless the arguments are extremely strong. Even if we knew that the net results of permitting sex selection would be somewhat negative, it would not immediately follow that such use should be banned, since the consequences of prohibition may be worse than those of tolerance.

The slippery slope that leads from one infringement upon reproductive liberty to others is very real. In much of the world, women do not have the legal right to contraception and safe abortion; and where these rights exist, they are often under continual threat from conservative religious factions. In some Australian states, women still do not have a legal right to abortion, although it is subsidized by the national health-care service. In the United States abortion has been a constitutional right since 1973, but access is limited by the unwillingness of the majority of state Medicaid programs and private insurers to pay for it; by state laws requiring waiting periods, medically unnecessary tests, and parental consent for minors; and by the increasing scarcity of abortion providers, who are harassed, threatened, and sometimes murdered by abortion opponents. In this situation, it is dangerous to advocate further constrictions of reproductive freedom. The legal oversight and surveillance that would be necessary to prevent women from choosing sex-selective abortion would create further risks to abortion providers, and further erode the willingness of physicians to perform abortions.

But we do not in fact know that the net results of new sex-selection methods will always be negative. Nor it is clear that the goal of preventing the use of sex selection to produce sons automatically justifies overriding the liberty of prospective parents who may wish to use sex selection to produce daughters, or to have a child of each sex. If we knew that women never submit to sex-selection treatments except under coercion, then we could reject out of hand the idea that having this option will benefit some women. But this claim is not plausible in all societies, or with respect to all women.

Feminists in each part of the world must decide which is the greater danger: the erosion of reproductive and other civil liberties through the prohibition of the development and marketing of sex-selection methods, or the reduction in the relative number of girls and women that may result from the introduction of such methods. My conclusion is that, where son preference is not overwhelmingly powerful, and where women enjoy a substantial degree of personal and economic autonomy, the first danger is likely to prove the greater. For the threat to existing reproductive freedoms is real and immediate, while the risk of harm resulting from small sex-ratio changes is uncertain, and perhaps insignificant.

Notes

1 I refer here to sex-selective abortion in the absence of medical indication or need. The ethical arguments are different when there are medical reasons for preferring the birth of a male or female child, for instance, when a male child would be likely to suffer from a severe X-linked illness, such as Duchenne's muscular dystrophy or hemophilia.

2 See Sarah B. Pomeroy, *Goddesses, Whores, Wives and Slaves* (New York: Schocken, 1975).

3 See Susila Mehta, *Revolution and the Status of Women in India* (New Delhi: Metropolitan, 1982), p. 209.

4 I discuss these and other objections to sex selection in *Gendercide: The Implications of Sex Selection* (Totowa, NJ: Rowman & Allanheld, 1985).

5 See Nancy E. Williamson, *Sons or Daughters: A Cross-Cultural Survey of Parental Preferences* (Beverly Hills, CA: Sage, 1976), p. 13.

6 Marcia Guttentag and Paul Secord, *Too Many Women? The Sex Ratio Question* (Beverly Hills, CA: Sage, 1983).

7 Sally Gearhart, "The Future – if there is One – is Female," in *Reweaving the Web of Life: Feminism and Nonviolence*, ed. Pam McAllister (Philadelphia: New Society Publishers, 1982), p. 282.

8 Ibid.

15

"Goodbye Dolly?" The Ethics of Human Cloning

John Harris

Abstract

The ethical implications of human clones have been much alluded to, but have seldom been examined with any rigour. This paper examines the possible uses and abuses of human cloning and draws out the principal ethical dimensions, both of what might be done and its meaning. The paper examines some of the major public and official responses to cloning by authorities such as President Clinton, the World Health Organization, the European Parliament, UNESCO, and others and reveals their inadequacies as foundations for a coherent public policy on human cloning. The paper ends by defending a conception of reproductive rights or "procreative autonomy" which shows human cloning to be not inconsistent with human rights and dignity.

The recent announcement of a birth[1] in the press heralds an event probably unparalleled for two millennia and has highlighted the impact of the genetic revolution on our lives and personal choices. More importantly perhaps, it raises questions about the legitimacy of the sorts of control individuals and society purport to exercise over something, which while it must sound portentous, is nothing less than human destiny. This birth, that of "Dolly", the cloned sheep, is also illustrative of the responsibilities of science and scientists to the communities in which they live and which they serve, and of the public anxiety that sensational scientific achievements sometimes provokes.

From *Journal of Medical Ethics*, vol. 23 (1997), pp. 353–60. Reprinted with permission.

The ethical implications of human clones have been much alluded to, but have seldom been examined with any rigour. Here I will examine the possible uses and abuses of human cloning and draw out the principal ethical dimensions, both of what might be done and its meaning, and of public and official responses.

There are two rather different techniques available for cloning individuals. One is by nuclear substitution, the technique used to create Dolly, and the other is by cell mass division or "embryo splitting". We'll start with cell mass division because this is the only technique for cloning that has, as yet, been used in humans.

Cell Mass Division

Although the technique of cloning embryos by cell mass division has, for some time been used extensively in animal models, it was used as a way of multiplying human embryos for the first time in October 1993 when Jerry Hall and Robert Stillman[2] at George Washington Medical Centre cloned human embryos by splitting early two-to eight-cell embryos into single embryo cells. Among other uses, cloning by cell mass division or embryo splitting could be used to provide a "twin" embryo for biopsy, permitting an embryo undamaged by invasive procedures to be available for implantation following the result of the biopsy on its twin, or to increase the number of embryos available for implantation in the treatment of infertility.[3] To what extent is such a practice unethical?

Individuals, Multiples and Genetic Variation

Cloning does not produce identical copies of the same individual person. It can only produce identical copies of the same genotype. Our experience of identical twins demonstrates that each is a separate individual with his or her own character, preferences and so on. Although there is some evidence of striking similarities with respect to these factors in twins, there is no question but that each twin is a distinct individual, as independent and as free as is anyone else. To clone Bill Clinton is not to create multiple Presidents of the United States. Artificial clones do not raise any difficulties not raised by the phenomenon of "natural" twins. We do not feel apprehensive when natural twins are born, why should we when twins are deliberately created?

If the objection to cloning is to the creation of identical individuals separated in time (because the twin embryos might be implanted in different cycles, perhaps even years apart), it is a weak one at best. We should remember that such twins will be "identical" in the sense that they will each have the same genotype, but they will never (unlike some but by no means all natural monozygotic twins) be identical in the more familiar sense of looking identical at the same moment in time. If we think of expected similarities in character, tastes and so on, then the same is true. The further separated in time, the less likely they are to have similarities of *character* (the more different the environment, the more different environmental influence on individuality).

The significant ethical issue here is whether it would be morally defensible, by outlawing the creation of clones by cell mass division, to deny a woman the chance to have the child she desperately seeks. If this procedure would enable a woman to create a sufficient number of embryos to give her a reasonable chance of successfully implanting one or two of them, then the objections to it would have to be weighty indeed. If preimplantation testing by cell biopsy might damage the embryo to be implanted, would it be defensible to prefer this to testing a clone, if technology permits such a clone to be created without damage, by separating a cell or two from the embryonic cell mass? If we assume each procedure to have been perfected and to be equally safe, we must ask what the ethical difference would be between taking a cell for cell biopsy and destroying it thereafter, and taking a cell to create a clone, and then destroying the clone? The answer can only be that destroying the cloned embryo would constitute a waste of human potential. But this same potential is wasted whenever an embryo is not implanted.

Nuclear Substitution: The Birth of Dolly

This technique involves (crudely described) deleting the nucleus of an egg cell and substituting the nucleus taken from the cell of another individual. This can be done using cells from an adult. The first viable offspring produced from fetal and adult mammalian cells was reported from an Edinburgh-based group in *Nature* on February 27, 1997.[4] The event caused an international sensation and was widely reported in the world press. President Clinton of the United States called for an investigation into the ethics of such procedures and announced a moratorium on public spending on human cloning; the British Nobel Prize winner, Joseph Rotblat, described it as science out of control, creating "a means of mass destruction",[5] and the German newspaper *Die Welt* evoked the Third Reich, commenting: "The cloning of human beings would fit precisely into Adolph Hitler's world view."[6]

More sober commentators were similarly panicked into instant reaction. Dr Hiroshi Nakajima, Director General of the World Health Organization said: "WHO considers the use of cloning for the replication of human individuals to be ethically unacceptable as it would violate some of the basic principles which govern medically assisted procreation. These include respect for the dignity of the human being and protection of the security of human genetic material."[7] The World Health Organization followed up the line taken by Nakajima with a resolution of the Fiftieth World Health Assembly which saw fit to affirm "that the use of cloning for the replication of human individuals is ethically unacceptable and contrary to human integrity and morality".[8] Federico Mayor of UNESCO, equally quick off the mark, commented: "Human beings must not be cloned under any circumstances. Moreover, UNESCO's International Bioethics Committee (IBC), which has been reflecting on the ethics of scientific progress, has maintained that the human genome must be preserved as common heritage of humanity."[9]

The European Parliament rushed through a resolution on cloning, the preamble of which asserted, (paragraph B):

> [T]he cloning of human beings . . . cannot under any circumstances be justified or tolerated by any society, because it is a serious violation of fundamental human rights and is contrary to the principle of equality of human beings as it permits a eugenic and racist selection of the human race, it offends against human dignity and it requires experimentation on humans [and which went on to claim that (clause 1)] each individual has a right to his or her own genetic identity and that human cloning is, and must continue to be, prohibited.[10]

These statements are, perhaps unsurprisingly, thin on argument and rationale; they appear to have been plucked from the air to justify an instant reaction. There are vague references to "human rights" or "basic principles" with little or no attempt to explain what these principles are, or to indicate how they might apply to cloning. The WHO statement, for example, refers to the basic principles which govern human reproduction and singles out "respect for the dignity of the human being" and "protection of the security of genetic material". How, we are entitled to ask, is the security of genetic material compromised? Is it less secure when inserted with precision by scientists, or when spread around with the characteristic negligence of the average human male?[11]

Human Dignity

Appeals to human dignity, on the other hand, while universally attractive, are comprehensively vague and deserve separate attention. A first question to ask when the idea of human dignity is invoked is: whose dignity is attacked and how? Is it the duplication of a large part of the genome that is supposed to constitute the attack on human dignity? If so we might legitimately ask whether and how the dignity of a natural twin is threatened by the existence of her sister? The notion of human dignity is often also linked to Kantian ethics. A typical example, and one that attempts to provide some basis for objections to cloning based on human dignity, was Axel Kahn's invocation of this principle in his commentary on cloning in *Nature*.[12]

> The creation of human clones solely for spare cell lines would, from a philosophical point of view, be in obvious contradiction to the principle expressed by Emmanuel Kant: that of human dignity. This principle demands that an individual – and I would extend this to read human life – should never be thought of as a means, but always also as an end. Creating human life for the sole purpose of preparing therapeutic material would clearly not be for the dignity of the life created.

The Kantian principle, crudely invoked as it usually is without any qualification or gloss, is seldom helpful in medical or bio-science contexts. As formulated by Kahn, for example, it would outlaw blood transfusions. The beneficiary of blood donation, neither knowing of, nor usually caring about, the anonymous donor uses the blood (and its donor) simply as a means to her own ends. It would also outlaw abortions to protect the life or health of the mother.

Instrumentalization

This idea of using individuals as a means to the purposes of others is sometimes termed "instrumentalization". Applying this idea coherently or consistently is not easy! If someone wants to have children in order to continue their genetic line do they act instrumentally? Where, as is standard practice in *in vitro* fertilization (IVF), spare embryos are created, are these embryos created instrumentally? If not how do they differ from embryos created by embryo splitting for use in assisted reproduction?[13]

Kahn responded in the journal *Nature* to these objections.[14] He reminds us, rightly, that Kant's famous principle states: "respect for human dignity requires that an individual is *never* used . . . *exclusively* as a means" and suggests that I have ignored the crucial use of the term "exclusively". I did not, of course, and I'm happy with Kahn's reformulation of the principle. It is not that Kant's principle does not have powerful intuitive force, but that it is so vague and so open to selective interpretation and its scope for application is consequently so limited, that its utility as one of the "fundamental principles of modern bioethical thought", as Kahn describes it, is virtually zero.

Kahn himself rightly points out that debates concerning the moral status of the human embryo are debates about whether embryos fall within the *scope* of Kant's or indeed any other moral principles concerning persons; so the principle itself is not illuminating in this context. Applied to the creation of individuals which are or will become autonomous, it has limited application. True, the Kantian principle rules out slavery, but so do a range of other principles based on autonomy and rights. If you are interested in the ethics of creating people then, so long as existence is in the created individual's own best interests, and the individual will have the capacity for autonomy like any other, then the motives for which the individual was created are either morally irrelevant or subordinate to other moral considerations. So that even where, for example, a child is engendered exclusively to provide "a son and heir" (as so often in so many cultures) it is unclear how or whether Kant's principle applies. Either other motives are also attributed to the parent to square parental purposes with Kant, or the child's eventual autonomy, and its clear and substantial interest in or benefit from existence, take precedence over the comparatively trivial issue of parental motives. Either way the "fundamental principle of modern bioethical thought" is unhelpful and debates about whether or not an individual has been used *exclusively* as a means are sterile and usually irresolvable.

We noted earlier the possibility of using embryo splitting to allow genetic and other screening by embryo biopsy. One embryo could be tested and then destroyed to ascertain the health and genetic status of the remaining clones. Again, an objection often voiced to this is that it would violate the Kantian principle, and that "one twin would be destroyed for the sake of another."

This is a bizarre and misleading objection both to using cell mass division to create clones for screening purposes, and to creating clones by nuclear substitution to generate spare cell lines. It is surely ethically dubious to object to one embryo being sacrificed for the sake of another, but not to object to it being sacrificed for nothing. In *in vitro* fertilization, for example, it is, in the United Kingdom, currently regarded as good practice to store spare embryos for future use by the mother or for disposal at her direction, either to other women who require donor embryos, or for research, or simply to be destroyed. It cannot be morally worse to use an embryo to provide information about its sibling, than to use it for more abstract research or simply to destroy it. If it is permissible to use early embryos for research or to destroy them, their use in genetic and other health testing is surely also permissible. The same would surely go for their use in creating cell lines for therapeutic purposes.

It is Better to do Good

A moral principle, which has at least as much intuitive force as that recommended by Kant, is that it is better to do some good than to do no good. It cannot, from the ethical point of view, be better or more moral to waste human material that could be used for therapeutic purposes, than to use it to do good. And I cannot but think that if it is right to *use* embryos for research or therapy then it is also right to *produce* them for such purposes.[15] Kant's prohibition does after all refer principally to use. Of course some will think that the embryo is a full member of the moral community with all the rights and protections possessed by Kant himself. While this is a tenable position, it is not one held by any society which permits abortion, post-coital contraception, or research with human embryos.

The UNESCO approach to cloning is scarcely more coherent than that of WHO; how does cloning affect "the preservation of the human genome as common heritage of humanity"? Does this mean that the human genome must be "preserved intact", that is, without variation, or does it mean simply that it must not be "reproduced asexually"? Cloning cannot be said to impact on the variability of the human genome, it merely repeats one infinitely small part of it, a part that is repeated at a natural rate of about 3.5 per thousand births.[16]

Genetic Variability

So many of the fears expressed about cloning, and indeed about genetic engineering more generally, invoke the idea of the effect on the gene pool or upon genetic variability or assert the sanctity of the human genome as a common resource or heritage. It is very difficult to understand what is allegedly at stake here. The issue of genetic variation need not detain us long. The numbers of twins produced by cloning will always be so small compared to the human gene pool in totality, that the effect on the variation of the human gene pool will be vanishingly small. We can say with confidence that the human genome and the human population were not threatened at the start of the present millennium in the year AD 1, and yet the world population was then perhaps 1 per cent of what it is today. Natural species are usually said to be endangered when the population falls to about 1000 breeding individuals; by these standards fears for humankind and its genome may be said to have been somewhat exaggerated.[17]

The resolution of the European Parliament goes into slightly more detail; having repeated the, now mandatory, waft in the direction of fundamental human rights and human dignity, it actually produces an argument. It suggests that cloning violates the principal of equality, "as it permits a eugenic and racist selection of the human race". Well, so does prenatal and pre-implantation screening, not to mention egg donation, sperm donation, surrogacy, abortion and human preference in choice of sexual partner. The fact that a technique could be abused does not constitute an argument against the technique, unless there is no prospect of preventing the abuse or wrongful use. To ban cloning on the grounds that it might be used for racist purposes is tantamount to saying that sexual intercourse should be prohibited because it permits the possibility of rape.

Genetic Identity

The second principle appealed to by the European Parliament states, that "each individual has a right to his or her own genetic identity." Leaving aside the inevitable contribution of mitochondrial DNA,[18] we have seen that, as in the case of natural identical twins, genetic identity is not an essential component of personal identity[19] nor is it necessary for "individuality". Moreover, unless genetic identity is required either for personal identity, or for individuality, it is not clear why there should be a right to such a thing. But if there is, what are we to do about the rights of identical twins?

Suppose there came into being a life-threatening (or even disabling) condition that affected pregnant women and that there was an effective treatment, the only side effect of which was that it caused the embryo to divide, resulting in twins. Would the existence of the supposed right conjured up by the European Parliament mean that the therapy should be outlawed? Suppose that an effective vaccine for HIV was developed which had the effect of doubling the natural twinning rate; would this be a violation of fundamental human rights? Are we to foreclose the possible benefits to be derived from human cloning on so flimsy a basis? We should recall that the natural occurrence of monozygotic (identical) twins is one in 270 pregnancies. This means that in the United Kingdom, with a population of about 58 million, over 200 000 such pregnancies have occurred. How are we to regard human rights violations on such a grand scale?

A Right to Parents

The apparently overwhelming imperative to identify some right that is violated by human cloning sometimes expresses itself in the assertion of "a right to have two parents" or as "the right to be the product of the mixture of the genes of two individuals". These are on the face of it highly artificial and problematic rights – where have they sprung from, save from a desperate attempt to conjure some rights that have been violated by cloning? However, let's take them seriously for a moment and grant that they have some force. Are they necessarily violated by the nuclear transfer technique?

If the right to have two parents is understood to be the right to have two social parents, then it is of course only violated by cloning if the family identified as the one to rear the resulting child is a one-parent family. This is not, of course, necessarily any more likely a result of cloning than of the use of any of the other new reproductive technologies (or indeed of sexual reproduction). Moreover if there is such a right, it is widely violated, creating countless "victims", and there is no significant evidence of any enduring harm from the violation of this supposed right. Indeed, war widows throughout the world would find its assertion highly offensive.

If, on the other hand, we interpret a right to two parents as the right to be the product of the mixture of the genes of two individuals, then the supposition that this right is violated when the nucleus of the cell of one individual is inserted into the de-nucleated egg of another, is false in the way this claim is usually understood. There is at least one sense in which a right expressed in this form might be violated by cloning, but not in any way which has force as an objection. Firstly it is false to think that the clone is the genetic child of the nucleus donor. It is not. The clone is the twin brother or sister of the nucleus donor and the genetic offspring of the nucleus donor's own parents. Thus this type of cloned individual is, and always must be, the genetic child of two separate genotypes, of two genetically different individuals, however often it is cloned or re-cloned.

Two Parents Good, Three Parents Better

However, the supposed right to be the product of two separate individuals is perhaps violated by cloning in a novel way. The de-nucleated egg contains mitochondrial DNA – genes from the female whose egg it is. The inevitable presence of the mitochondrial genome of the egg donor means that the genetic inheritance of clones is in fact richer than that of other individuals, richer in the sense of being more variously derived.[20] This can be important if the nucleus donor is subject to mitochondrial diseases inherited from his or her mother and wants a child genetically related to her that will be free of these diseases. How this affects alleged rights to particular combinations of "parents" is more difficult to imagine, and perhaps underlines the confused nature of such claims.

What Good is Cloning?

One major reason for developing cloning in animals is said to be[4] to permit the study of genetic diseases and indeed genetic development more generally. Whether or not there would be major advantages in human cloning by nuclear substitution is not yet clear. Certainly it would enable some infertile people to have children genetically related to them, it offers the prospect, as we have noted, of preventing some diseases caused by mitochondrial DNA, and could help "carriers" of X-linked and autosomal recessive disorders to have their own genetic children without risk of passing on the disease. It is also possible that cloning could be used for the creation of "spare parts" by, for example, growing stem cells for particular cell types from non-diseased parts of an adult.

Any attempt to use this technique in the United Kingdom is widely thought to be illegal. Whether it would in fact be illegal might turn on whether it is plausible to regard such cloning as the product of "fertilization". Apparently only fertilized embryos are covered by the *Human Fertilization and Embryology Act 1990*.[21] The technique used in Edinburgh which involves deleting the nucleus of an unfertilized egg and then substituting a cell nucleus from an existing individual, bypasses what is normally considered to be fertilization completely and may therefore turn out not to be covered by existing legislation. On the other hand, if as seems logical, we consider "fertilization" as the moment when all forty-six chromosomes are present and the zygote is formed, the problem does not arise.

The unease caused by Dolly's birth may be due to the fact that it was just such a technique that informed the plot of the film *The Boys from Brazil* in which Hitler's genotype was cloned to produce a *führer* for the future. The prospect of limitless numbers of clones of Hitler is rightly disturbing. However, the numbers of clones that could be produced of any one genotype will, for the foreseeable future, be limited not by the number of copies that could be made of one genotype (using serial nuclear transfer techniques, 470 copies of a single nuclear gene in cattle have been reported),[22] but by the availability of host human mothers.[23] Mass production in any democracy could therefore scarcely be envisaged. Moreover, the futility of any such attempt is obvious. Hitler's genotype might conceivably produce a "gonadically challenged" individual of limited stature, but reliability in producing an evil and vicious megalomaniac is far more problematic, for reasons already noted in our consideration of cloning by cell mass division.

Dolly Collapses the Divide between Germ and Somatic Cells

There are some interesting implications of cloning by nuclear substitution (which have been clear since frogs were cloned by this method in the 1950s) which have not apparently been noticed.[24] There is currently a worldwide moratorium on manipulation of the human germ line, while therapeutic somatic line interventions are, in principle, permitted.[13] However, inserting the mature nucleus of an adult cell into a de-nucleated egg turns the cells thus formed into germ line cells. This has three important effects. First, it effectively eradicates the firm divide between germ line and somatic line nuclei because each adult cell nucleus is in principle "translatable" into a germ line cell nucleus by transferring its nucleus and creating a clone. Secondly, it permits somatic line modifications to human cells to become germ line modifications. Suppose you permanently insert a normal copy of the adenosine deaminase gene into the bone-marrow cells of an individual suffering from severe combined immuno-deficiency (which affects the so called "bubble boy" who has to live in a protective bubble of clean air) with obvious beneficial therapeutic effects. This is a somatic line modification. If you then cloned a permanently genetically modified bone-marrow cell from this individual, the modified genome would be passed to the clone and become part of his or her genome, transmissible to her offspring indefinitely through the germ line. Thus a benefit that would have perished with the original recipient and not been passed on for the protection of her children, can be conferred on subsequent generations by cloning.[25] The third effect is that it shows the oft asserted moral divide between germ line and somatic line therapy to be even more ludicrous than was previously supposed.[15]

Immortality?

Of course some vainglorious individuals might wish to have offspring not simply with their genes but with a matching genotype. However, there is no way that they could make such an individual a duplicate of themselves. So many years later the environmental influences would be radically different, and since every choice, however insignificant, causes a life-path to branch with unpredictable consequences, the holy grail of duplication would be doomed to remain a fruitless quest. We can conclude that people who would clone themselves would probably be foolish and ill-advised, but would they be immoral and would their attempts harm society or their children significantly?

Whether we should legislate to prevent people reproducing, not 23 but all 46 chromosomes, seems more problematic for reasons we have already examined, but we might have reason to be uncomfortable about the likely standards and effects of child-rearing by those who would clone themselves. Their attempts to mould their child in their own image would be likely to be more pronounced than the average. Whether they would likely be worse than so many people's attempts to duplicate race, religion and culture, which are widely accepted as respectable in the contemporary world, might well depend on the character and constitution of the genotype donor. Where identical twins occur naturally we might think of it as "horizontal twinning", where twins are created by nuclear substitution we have a sort of "vertical twinning". Although horizontal twins would be closer to one another in every way, we do not seem much disturbed by their natural occurrence. Why we should be disturbed either by artificial horizontal twinning or by vertical twinning (where differences between the twins would be greater) is entirely unclear.

Suppose a woman's only chance of having "her own" genetic child was by cloning herself; what are the strong arguments that should compel her to accept that it would be wrong to use nuclear substitution? We must assume that this cloning technique is safe, and that initial fears that individuals produced using nuclear substitution might age more rapidly have proved groundless.[26] We usually grant the so called "genetic imperative" as an important part of the right to found a family, of procreative autonomy.[27] The desire of people to have "their own" genetic children is widely accepted, and if we grant the legitimacy of genetic aspirations in so many cases, and the use of so many technologies to meet these aspirations,[28] we need appropriately serious and weighty reasons to deny them here.

It is perhaps salutary to remember that there is no necessary connection between phenomena, attitudes or actions that make us uneasy, or even those that disgust us, and those phenomena, attitudes, and actions that there are good reasons for judging unethical. Nor does it follow that those things we are confident *are* unethical must be prohibited by legislation or regulation.

We have looked at some of the objections to human cloning and found them less than plausible, we should now turn to one powerful argument that has recently been advanced in favour of a tolerant attitude to varieties of human reproduction.

Procreative Autonomy

We have examined the arguments for and against permitting the cloning of human individuals. At the heart of these questions is the issue of whether or not people have rights to control their reproductive destiny and, so far as they can do so without violating the rights of others or threatening society, to choose their own procreative path. We have seen that it has been claimed that cloning violates principles of human dignity. We will conclude by briefly examining an approach which suggests rather that failing to permit cloning might violate principles of dignity.

The American philosopher and legal theorist, Ronald Dworkin, has outlined the arguments for a right to what he calls "procreative autonomy" and has defined this right as "a right to control their own role in procreation unless the state has a compelling reason for denying them that control".[29] Arguably, freedom to clone one's own genes might also be defended as a dimension of procreative autonomy because so many people and agencies have been attracted by the idea of the special nature of genes and have linked the procreative imperative to the genetic imperative.

> The right of procreative autonomy follows from any competent interpretation of the due process clause and of the Supreme Court's past decisions applying it.... The First Amendment prohibits government from establishing any religion, and it guarantees all citizens free exercise of their own religion. The Fourteenth Amendment, which incorporates the First Amendment, imposes the same prohibition and same responsibility on states. These provisions also guarantee the right of procreative autonomy.[30]

The point is that the sorts of freedoms which freedom of religion guarantees, freedom to choose one's own way of life and live according to one's most deeply held beliefs, are also at the heart of procreative choices. And Dworkin concludes:

> that no one may be prevented from influencing the shared moral environment, through his own private choices, tastes, opinions, and example, just because these tastes or opinions disgust those who have the power to shut him up or lock him up.[31]

Thus it may be that we should be prepared to accept both some degree of offence and some social disadvantages as a price we should be willing to pay in order to protect freedom of choice in matters of procreation and perhaps this applies to cloning as much as to more straightforward or usual procreative preferences.[32]

The nub of the argument is complex and abstract but it is worth stating at some length. I cannot improve upon Dworkin's formulation of it.

> The right of procreative autonomy has an important place... in Western political culture more generally. The most important feature of that culture is a belief in individual human dignity: that people have the moral right – and the moral responsibility – to confront the most fundamental questions about the meaning and value of their own lives for themselves, answering to their own consciences and convictions.... The principle of procreative autonomy, in a broad sense, is embedded in any genuinely democratic culture.[33]

In so far as decisions to reproduce in particular ways or even using particular technologies constitute decisions concerning central issues of value, then arguably the freedom to make them is guaranteed by the constitution (written or not) of any democratic society, unless the state has a compelling reason for denying its citizens that control. To establish such a compelling reason the state (or indeed a federation or union of states, such as the European Union, for example) would have to show that more was at stake than the fact that a majority found the ideas disturbing or even disgusting.

As yet, in the case of human cloning, such compelling reasons have not been produced. Suggestions have been made, but have not been sustained, that human dignity may be compromised by the techniques of cloning. Dworkin's arguments suggest that human dignity and indeed democratic constitutions may be compromised by attempts to limit procreative autonomy, at least where greater values cannot be shown to be thereby threatened.

In the absence of compelling arguments against human cloning, we can bid Dolly a cautious "hello". We surely have sufficient reasons to permit experiments on human embryos to proceed, provided, as with any such experiments, the embryos are destroyed at an early stage.[34] While we wait to see whether the technique will ever be established as safe, we should consider the best ways to regulate its uptake until we are in a position to know what will emerge both by way of benefits and in terms of burdens.

Acknowledgements

This paper was presented to the *UNDP/WHO/World Bank Special Programme of Research, Development and Research Training in Human Reproduction* Scientific and Ethical Review Group Meeting, Geneva, 25 April 1997, and to a hearing on cloning held by the European Parliament in Brussels, 7 May 1997. I am grateful to participants at these events for many stimulating insights. I must also thank Justine Burley, Christopher Graham and Pedro Lowenstein for many constructive comments.

References and Notes

1 The arguments concerning human dignity are developed in my "Cloning and human dignity" in *The Cambridge Quarterly of Healthcare Ethics* (1997). The issues raised by cloning were discussed in a special issue of the *Kennedy Institute of Ethics Journal*, 4, 3 (1994) and in my *Wonderwoman and Superman: The Ethics of Human Biotechnology* (Oxford: Oxford University Press, 1992), especially ch. 1.

2 Human embryo cloning reported. *Science*, 262 (1993); 652–3.

3 Where few eggs can be successfully recovered or where only one embryo has been successfully fertilized, this method can multiply the embryos available for implantation to increase the chances of successful infertility treatment.

4 Wilmut, I et al. "Viable offspring derived from fetal and adult mammalian cells." *Nature*, 385 (1997): 810–13.

5 Arlidge, J. *Guardian* (26 Feb. 1997): 6.

6 Radford, T. *Guardian*, (28 Feb. 1997): 1.

7 WHO press release (WHO/20 1997 Mar. 11).

8 WHO document (WHA50.37 1997 May 14). Despite the findings of a meeting of the Scientific and Ethical Review Group (see **Acknowledgements**) which recommended that "the next step should be a thorough exploration and fuller discussion of the [issues]."

9 UNESCO press release No. 97–29 1997 Feb. 28.

10 The European Parliament. Resolution on cloning. Motion dated March 11 1997. Passed March 13 1997.

11 Perhaps the sin of Onan was to compromise the security of his genetic material?

12 Kahn, A. "Clone mammals... clone man." *Nature*, 386 (1997): 119.

13 For use of the term and the idea of "instrumentalization" see: *Opinion of the Group of Advisers on the Ethical Implications of Biotechnology to the European Commission No. 9*, 1997 28 May. Rapporteur, Dr Anne McClaren.

14 Kahn, A. "Cloning, dignity and ethical revisionism." *Nature* 388 (1997): 320. Harris J. "Is cloning an attack on human dignity?" *Nature* 387 (1997): 754.

15 See my *Wonderwoman and Superman: The Ethics of Human Biotechnology* (Oxford: Oxford University Press, 1992), ch. 2.

16 It is unlikely that "artificial" cloning would ever approach such a rate on a global scale and we could, of course, use regulative mechanisms to prevent this without banning the process entirely. I take this figure of the rate of natural twinning from Moore K. L. and Persaud, T. V. N. *The Developing Human*, 5th ed, (Philadelphia: W. B. Saunders, 1993). The rate mentioned is 1 per 270 pregnancies.

17 Of course if *all* people were compulsorily sterilized and reproduced only by cloning, genetic variation would become fixed at current levels. This would halt the evolutionary process. How bad or good *this* would be could only be known if the course of future evolution and its effects could be accurately predicted.

18 Mitochondrial DNA individualizes the genotype even of clones to some extent.

19 Although, of course, there would be implications for criminal justice since clones could not be differentiated by so called "genetic fingerprinting" techniques.

20 Unless of course the nucleus donor is also the egg donor.

21 Margaret Brazier alerted me to this possibility.

22 Apparently Alan Trounson's group in Melbourne Australia have recorded this result. *Herald Sun* (Mar. 13, 1997).

23 What mad dictators might achieve is another matter; but such individuals are, almost by definition, impervious to moral argument and can therefore, for present purposes, be ignored.

24 Except by Pedro Lowenstein, who pointed them out to me.

25 These possibilities were pointed out to me by Pedro Lowenstein, who is currently working on the implications for human gene therapy.

26 "Science and technology." *The Economist* (Mar. 1, 1997); 101–4.

27 *Universal Declaration of Human Rights* (article 16). *European Convention on Human Rights* (article 12). These are vague protections and do not mention any particular ways of founding families.

28 These include the use of reproductive technologies such as surrogacy and Intra Cytoplasmic Sperm Injection (ICSI).
29 Dworkin, R. *Life's Dominion* (London: Harper Collins, 1993); p. 148.
30 Ibid., p. 160.
31 Dworkin, R. *Freedom's Law*, (Oxford: Oxford University Press, 1996), pp. 237–8.
32 Ronald Dworkin has produced an elegant account of the way the price we should be willing to pay for freedom might or might not be traded off against the costs. See his *Taking Rights Seriously*, (London: Duckworth, 1977), ch. 10. And his *A Matter of Principle* (Cambridge, MA: Harvard University Press, 1985), ch. 17.
33 See reference 29: 166–7.
34 The blanket objection to experimentation on humans suggested by the European Parliament resolution would dramatically change current practice on the use of spare or experimental human embryos.

PART III

The New Genetics

16

Ethical Issues in Manipulating the Human Germ Line

Marc Lappé

Abstract

This essay examines the arguments for and against working towards the objective of human germ line engineering for medical purposes. Germ line changes which result as a secondary consequence of other well-designed and ethically acceptable manipulations of somatic cells to cure an otherwise fatal disease can be seen as acceptable. More serious objections apply to intentional germ line interventions because of the unacceptability of using a person solely as a vehicle for creating uncertain genetic change in his descendants. It is also morally unacceptable to use the promise of future benefit to experiment on fetuses or embryos when other more effective technologies exist to help parents have healthy children. Using new genetic technologies to *select* desirable genotypes among gametes is less problematic and affords a promising new technique for avoiding intergenerational harm.

1 Introduction

Germ line engineering embraces any of several techniques which permit the alteration of germinal epithelium, sperm or eggs, or early products of conception such that genetic changes become permanently encoded in the sex cells of the resulting adult. Germ cell alterations can be distinguished from somatic cell ones by virtue of their intergenerational consequences. In theory, only changes directed at the germ line can produce heritable changes. In practice, some somatic cell alterations may also become transmissible, as will be discussed below.

Germ line engineering of the human genome may become technically feasible within a decade, particularly since specific techniques for directing genetic changes in somatic cells already exist (Anderson, 1985, 55–63). Genomic alteration of germ cells has already been demonstrated in animal models (Hammer et al., 1986, 269–78), and has been proposed as a rapid method for accelerating the genetic improvement of livestock (Van Raden and Freeman, 1985, 1425–31).

While such techniques mark a major advance in our ability to manipulate and control genetic material in animals, the prospect of their application to humans raises fundamental questions about the limits to human control over genetic destiny. Although few convincing rationales have been promulgated which justify using germ line engineering in humans (cf. Fowler et al., 1989, 151–65), vociferous objections to using this technology have appeared (Rifkin et al., 1983, 1360–61). It remains important to consider germ line engineering because it can provide great benefits as well as harm.

Potential justifications for germ line alterations include the correction of genetic defects not otherwise amenable to somatic cell treatment; permanent stabilization of genetic material in offspring of high risk matings (e.g., fragile X syndrome); or the elimination of the need for repeated prenatal diagnosis and selective abortion in genetically at-risk families. Germ line interventions could also permit increases in the frequency of desirable genes and/

From *Journal of Medicine and Philosophy*, vol. 16 (1991), pp. 621–39.

or the decrease of deleterious ones (*eugenic* changes) and can thereby lead to the selection and perfection of lineages of organisms with improved genetic characteristics. The present essay will examine the arguments for and against working towards such objectives in humans.

2 State of the Art

Germ line changes can be produced by any of three techniques, each with technical strengths and limitations of its own (Anonymous, 1989, 107; Tam, 1986, 187–94). The first technique entails the direct microinjection of specific sequences of DNA (cloned DNA) into the pronucleus of a one-celled fertilized egg. This procedure has been perfected in laboratory animals, and leads to a variable percentage of successfully integrated embryos (usually in the order of 10–30 per cent). The second utilizes an embryonic stem cell derived from the blastocyst stage which is manipulated in tissue culture by direct transfection with raw DNA or by using a retrovirus to carry genetic material into the cell. Effectively transfected cells can then be reintroduced to a developing embryo during the blastocyst period of development. The third technique involves the use of retroviruses to carry DNA sequences into four cell embryos, the blastocyst or the mid-gestation embryo. This technique is in theory the most precise, but is presently limited to experimental animals. A fourth technique in which sperm is treated directly with raw DNA appeared to promise a rapid method for achieving permanent genetic change, but it has not proven to be reproducible to date (Barinagg, 1989, 590–1).

3 Distinguishing Somatic from Germ Line Engineering

The multifarious methods which can alter the germ line highlight a common misconception about germ line engineering: germ line changes need *not* be accomplished by direct alteration of the sperm or ova prior to fertilization.

As a result of early genetic engineering, the traditional modes of genetic engineering may result in alterations of *both* somatic and germ line cells. This is so because any genetic change made to the embryo theoretically can be incorporated into its germ line, as long as the change was done prior to the differentiation and segregation of the sex cells from the body of the early embryo proper. Thus, if performed early enough in embryonic development, any gene-modifying technique can lead to germ line alterations. A genetically altered cell which is introduced prior to the segregation of the cellular precursors of the germinal epithelium in the neural crest (in the early somite stage embryo) has the prospect of being permanently incorporated in the sex cells. It is only after the neural plate has folded to form the neural crest that these sex cells migrate to their sites in the primordia of the germinal epithelium to assume their function as stem cells. In females, the primary oöcytes (oögonia) are fixed in number, while germ cells in males are continuously replenished on a fixed cell cycle.

In theory, therapy could also be targeted exclusively to the germ cells of either parent without producing somatic cell genetic changes or effecting a therapeutic change in the phenotype of that adult. Conversely, most somatic cell therapies are directed at a patient and are not presently intended to alter the germ line.

These three modalities can usefully be put into the following typology:

A 'Mixed' germ line/somatic cell therapy.
B 'Pure' germ line therapy.
C 'Pure' somatic cell therapy.

The category of greatest interest in this essay is *A*. Previous discussions have fairly exhaustively treated pure germ line therapy (category *B*). The ethical objections to traditional germ line therapy have centered on the limits of non-consensual research and the unacceptability of manipulations done on embryos (Fowler et al., 1989, 151–65). Broader theological objections to altering the heritable genetic material transgenerationally have also been broached (Walters, 1986, 225–7).

Much more complex ethical issues are generated when the subject is an existing patient with a bona fide need for a genetic intervention which may indirectly alter his germ cell lineage. This prospect is raised by the realization that many forms of somatic cell genetic engineering are contemplated for early treatment of embryos or fetuses. With systemic genetic disorders like adenosine deaminase deficiency, the therapeutic goal will be to convert as many autologous or transplanted cells as possible in a newborn, also raising the possibility that germ line cells in the same individual will be affected by transformed or transfected cells. The first experimental subjects may receive either transfected cells, viral vectors or primitive stem cell populations that may simultaneously convert or seed germ line precursors with the same genetic changes intended for body cells. Stem cell treatment of young children and, hypothetically, even young adults may also colonize the germinal epithelium. This possibility must be considered, for example, in somatic cell engineering of males whose own spermatocytes have been depleted or destroyed by congenital disease or chemical toxicity, since recovery of functionally azoospermic males has been demonstrated (see Lipschulz et al., 1980, 464–8). This finding suggests that primary spermatocytes may regenerate from as yet unknown precursors. The eventuality of concomitant germ cell transfection or seeding may be seen as either an unintended 'risk' or secondary 'benefit' of the somatic cell intervention, depending on the nature of the resulting heritable change. This is so in cases of concomitant germ line change because any therapeutic achievement (or errors) achieved by somatic gene therapy will then be perpetuated in future generations.

4 Proxy Consent

Because changes in the germ line potentially affect someone in addition to the recipient of the prospective germinal tissue (i.e., the offspring and future descendants of the treated individual), germ line experimentation raises novel questions of traditional research ethics. Foremost among these is the adequacy and acceptability of proxy consent. Little guidance exists for others assuming the risks for future persons of potentially flawed manipulations of the germ line. By definition, germ line alterations place irreversible changes into the genetic material. Any qualitative alterations to the phenotype that results from such changes may prove to be highly desirable or undesirable to future persons depending on the adaptive value of the resulting traits in unknown future environments. To discover whether or not such changes are in fact beneficial thus requires that we know with some certainty what the future holds and can faithfully convey those probabilities in a discussion of informed consent by proxy. Germ line interventions may therefore subject at least one or probably two generations of future persons to experimentation before the phenotypic effects of the germinal change can be said to 'test out'. As will be discussed below, such an exercise in predictive science is fraught with uncertainties.

5 Targets of Germ Line Engineering

The range of therapeutic options possible with germ line engineering includes two distinct endpoints: (1) *correction*, in which researchers would identify and repair or replace defective genes in the germ line (i.e., those whose products generate serious pathological or physiological consequences); and (2) *enhancement*, in which researchers alter the genetic makeup of the sperm or egg or their precursors to improve characteristics of offspring in 'favorable' ways (Walters, 1986, 225–7). Only the first is squarely within the domain of orthodox medicine. Note that recent improvements in cosmetic surgery and biotechnology-facilitated cloning of human genes like those for human growth hormone increase the likelihood that genetic techniques may find a place in selective improvement in physiological or physical characteristics not strictly pathological in nature.

Arguments for repair or correction of genetic defects have traditionally been justified on the basis of a moral duty to relieve human suffering when we have the capacity to do so. Using somatic gene therapy to achieve such ends raises special problems in that the treatment results in an universal and probably irreversible change in the individual's cells (as compared to a drug which may be discontinued). This problem is compounded where attempts are made to program a person's germ cells with the same genetic change targeted for somatic cell therapy. These problems are less evident when germ line changes occur secondarily.

From an ethical viewpoint, the eventuality of secondary germ cell conversion raises more intergenerational problems than does pure germ line therapy. While there would be no basis in theory to restrict procreation for a somatically engineered individual, the uncertainty of *what* genetic alterations had actually occurred in a secondarily impacted germ line would make procreation of such a person more risk-laden than when there was reasonable foreknowledge of just how the germ line was likely to have been changed.

From animal models, we know that transgenic mice can have multiple gene insertions, higher mutation rates, and greater propensity to cancer than their normally generated counterparts (see

Orian et al., 1990, 393–7). These possibilities might make the first experimental subjects of mixed somatic cell-germ line therapy reproductive pariahs until we had a basis to vouchsafe the genetic integrity of their reproductive cells.

The converse situation, wherein a person receives no benefit himself from germ line engineering but is treated only to assure his descendants are free from some genetic defect, comprises a different ethical circumstance. In principle, a carrier of deleterious genes who accepted a risk for himself in germ line therapy to permit the well-being of his offspring and future generations is morally more acceptable than when offspring were inadvertently jeopardized. Obviously, since non-procreation of a carrier of deleterious genes assures a similar outcome, the ethics are not straightforward.

6 Typology of Germ Line Alterations

At least four different outcomes can be evaluated as shown in Table 1. While all previous critiques of the acceptability of germ line therapy have dealt with Type III of interventions (i.e., those in which germ line therapy is the intended outcome), the present one considers the consequences of the Type I therapy where germ line alterations are unintended consequences of 'standard' somatic cell engineering. Consider the ethical conundrum raised by the prospect of an otherwise ethically acceptable Type I somatic cell protocol. What if the only limitation of the protocol were that it required conditions which *might* lead to implantation of stem cells in the germ line (e.g., it had to be made early in embryonic or fetal development to correct a basic hemoglobinopathy). Would we find the experiment ethically suspect? I think not, especially if the primary beneficiary of the intervention would be a healthy, genetically 'normal' child. If secondary germ line changes would be acceptable as a secondary effect of an otherwise acceptable protocol, what makes them less acceptable if they were the *primary* objective of a Type III intervention?

Consider the circumstance where the sole objective of an intervention in an otherwise healthy individual is to correct a germ line defect and *not* to treat his underlying condition (e.g., the gene coding for retinoblastoma in a still asymptomatic carrier). Assuming other conditions are met (e.g., that risks are knowable or known, and that informed consent can be given, etc.), such a procedure would be ethically questionable only to the extent that treatments to affect future persons are less justified than those to correct problems in present ones.

However, ethical acceptability is eroded where germ line therapy is intended to achieve a *eugenic* effect in the person's descendants irrespective of *any* therapeutic objective in the host or his immediate offspring. This is so because it is morally suspect to use the parent (and subsequently his children) as means to achieve societally directed ends that are not necessarily those shared or desired by the family.

7 Arguments against Germ Line Therapy

The major ethical arguments about germ line engineering thus turn on whether persons can be used as means to uncertain, or morally questionable, ends. It matters whether the objective *and* consequence of the intervention are intended to affect only a single individual, that individual and his family, future lineages from that family line, or whole groups of persons. Medical ethicists generally consider that competent persons may give

Table 1 Differences in outcome and intent in genetic engineering.

Intended target of intervention	*Germ line consequences*
1. Somatic cells	3. Germ line altered
2. Germ cells	4. Germ line unaltered

These four possible outcomes, comprise a typology of interventions:
I somatic cells are targeted but germ lines are inadvertently affected [1 → 3]
II somatic cells are altered but germ lines are not (conventional somatic gene therapy) [1 → 4]
III germ cells are targeted and altered [2 → 3]
IV germ cells are targeted but unaltered [2 → 4]

consent for interventions for which they and they alone assume risks but that they are less justified in giving consent for their own offspring when the benefit/risk ratio is closer to unity.

Because this germ line research also presupposes direct experimentation on embryos, the whole ethical debate of the acceptability of research on fertilized eggs and embryos may have to be rejoined. The core of this debate turns on the acceptability of killing genetically altered but defective embryos or allowing their creation in the first place. The related question of fetal experimentation has already received much attention and is beyond the scope of the present inquiry. These questions are part of the broader issues of assuming risks for future generations.

In one view, germ line research comprises unethical experimentation on the unborn because the early embryo can never be an acceptable subject of experimentation. Not only can it not give informed consent, but it is exquisitely vulnerable to some interventions and experimental incursions which can produce lasting harms. But with the demonstrated success of *in vitro* fertilization, the objection to using normal *gametes* under experimental conditions has been largely overcome.

A further argument against Type III research is that researchers designing germ line strategies would likely be required to sample or, in an extreme, to destroy embryonic tissue to ensure that errors would not be perpetuated into a fully developed human fetus. This assurance would either require wholesale destruction of failed attempts while still in embryo stages, or at an extreme, the killing of abnormal fetuses whose phenotypes did not correspond to initial expectations. These difficulties might be minimized if reasonably close animal models existed. If it could be shown that germ line alterations were successful in permanently correcting a major genetic defect common to a certain familial lineage, and if non-destructive sampling (e.g., via the polar body) were possible, germ line therapy in humans would be technically feasible although still morally questionable.

In the end, objectors to germ line engineering presume that it may fail (i.e., that it will project potential harm into the future), while supporters argue that any potential good of the intervention would be multiplied by their future projection. In this view, the benefits of successful germ line engineering would enjoy a longevity unachievable by somatic cell manipulation.

8 Application of the Law of Double Effect

These issues appear less vexing in the context of Type I interventions which are expressly designed to assure a better physiological state of the organism through somatic genetic therapy. As I have noted, many somatic gene therapy programs entail the use of stem cells which are introduced to a young infant or child in the hope of replacing some or all of the cells of a major organ system such as the liver or bone marrow, making it conceivable that such cell grafts could also enter the germinal epithelium, especially in males. Were this to occur, some sperm might be produced that carried the genetically altered instructions intended to correct the somatic cell defect in the genetically diseased individual.

This possibility makes it important to consider the achievement of germ cell engineering as a secondary consequence of somatic cell therapy under the 'law of double effect'. Under this provision of Catholic doctrine, an act which is otherwise ethically objectionable may be morally acceptable if it is the inevitable and unavoidable consequence of carrying out primary morally desirable intervention. Thus, if it is necessary to terminate a tubal pregnancy to save a mother's life, the fact that a fetus is by necessity also destroyed is considered a tragic but acceptable moral consequence. By analogy, if some forms of somatic cell engineering were also to alter the germ line as an indirect consequence of an ethically approved attempt at genetic engineering, they might also be an instance of double effect. Obviously, before such an inadvertently altered person would be encouraged to reproduce, careful appraisal of the genetic composition of his sperm would be mandatory. It would be unlikely, however, that all eventualities of his reproduction could be anticipated without having an embryo produced in which gene expression could be assessed. This manipulation would bring us once again to the problems entailed with research on the products of germ line engineering.

Were the technique of somatic cell therapy plus indirect germ line alteration to prove successful to both the parent *and* his offspring, it would provide appreciable impetus to do more such experimental manipulations irrespective of the ethical nuances raised by non-consenting experimentation and embryo research. (This is exactly what happened with *in vitro* experimentation.) In theory, it would be difficult to object to germ line changes arising as a consequence of somatic cell therapy since they will reduce the likelihood of future transmission of the genetic defect in question, in itself a morally praiseworthy goal.

9 Risks to Future Generations

The acceptability of such radical departures from normal procreative decisions turns to a large extent on the duty of the present generation to protect or to enhance the genetic quality of the next. The technology of genetic engineering which is now being contemplated for somatic cells is intended to affect only the present individual. Any genetic damage which is indirectly caused by manipulations of the germ line will be perpetuated independently of what is done to the phenotype of the genetically engineered patient. In this sense, it is valid to speak of intergenerational consequences of genetic engineering of the germ line.

As we have seen, Type III germ line engineering may be critiqued because it makes irrevocable decisions for future generations without a reasonable proxy or mechanism of consent, and because it alters the genetic makeup of subsequent generations in ways that by definition have unforseeable consequences (Weatherall, 1988, 13–14). Consideration of such long-range risks is outside the purview of most formal ethical review boards. For instance, institutional review boards are limited in their ability to consider long-range implications and risks of proposed experimentation (45 CFR 46). Presumably, such issues would have to be discussed at other levels of review of genetic experimentation.

While valid, the argument that we cannot know enough to secure the well-being of genetically modified individuals who become part of future generations is insufficient to ban germ line engineering. To reject all germ line alterations as 'unethical' because not all germ line-engineered individuals will be assured of normal protective options or they may be genetically unsuited to future environments is tantamount to saying no one should have children. Even the terminally impaired may accept their salvation from genetic disease as a tradeoff for their non-reproduction, a position argued previously to justify encouraging rescued female phenylketonurics to be sterilized. These arguments show the extent to which some people might go to justify germ line engineering. For this reason, it is critical to review the concept of intergenerational responsibility to determine if germ line manipulations can be justified for future persons.

10 Intergenerational Ethics

Intergenerational ethics can be broken into two subsets: those that pertain to the immediate descendants of individual couples, and those that relate to the more global impact of a wider application of the technology. For the purposes of this essay, the prospect of germ line engineering for couples at risk of transmitting serious genetic disease is considered more likely than that of systematically altering genes on a large scale. Nonetheless, the ethical issues are sufficiently similar to treat them both together. Sufficiently compelling reasons for introducing genetic changes to the germ line exist. As we have discussed previously, germ line engineering provides a vehicle for blocking the transmission of heritable forms of debilitating illness from one generation to the next. If germ line engineering were accomplished on a scale sufficiently large to affect whole populations, it could also have eugenic effects by reducing the frequency of dominantly inherited or X-linked conditions in future generations.

The root of ethical concerns about such otherwise desirable intervention hinges on the limits of eugenics generally and of experimentation to achieve long-term genetic changes. Some of these limitations have been imposed by various bodies (e.g., that on experimental manipulation on embryos recommended by the Ethics Committee of the American Fertility Society (Ethics Committee, 1986, 3–94)). Others are more diffuse, and constitute the basic ethical precepts on which pure (Type III) germ line therapy is based.

11 Experimentation for Future Benefits

Foremost among these precepts are the ethical duties imposed by what Summer Twiss of Brown University has termed, "the ethic of long-range responsibility" (Twiss, 1976, 28–30). This ethic requires that we acquire relevant predictive knowledge (about the expression of germ-line implants, for example) before we implement the technology to effect such changes. Thus, before we were to bring a germ line-altered person into being, we would have to know what that person would look like both phenotypically and genetically. Unfortunately, as I have showed, the nearest model for such a person, the transgenic mouse, has *not* shown the necessary degree of uniformity or regulatory control after being manipulated. Some germ line-altered animals fail to express their genotypes or have altered gene control mechanisms (see Orian, 1990, 393–7). This situation means that 'to get to know' how germ line therapy will work in humans will more likely than not require that we experiment on human embryos and perhaps fetuses with extreme uncertainty. Only in this way could we discover, for instance, how well genes that are inserted into germ cells function. But we would still not know how such genes act *transgenerationally*.

To make that discovery, would require that we perform a second generation of experimentation on the germ cells of the first experimental subjects (i.e., the F1 generation before it reproduced to produce the F2 generation). Such an eventuality implies that we must be able to predict future consequences with sufficient certitude to give a valid consent for such manipulations. Given present limitations, I consider this possibility unlikely. We also cannot know without experimentation if the handling and control of sex cells and the products of conception will produce harm that is ethically unaceptable. All of these uncertainties mean that we cannot meaningfully assure an extant parent the outcome of manipulation of his progency. Moreover, it will be morally problematic to get parental consent to abate any damage which the intervention may do to his or her progeny since this requires the intentional conception of a human embryo which may need to be destroyed or will bear initially invisible cellular harm. This eventually argues for respecting the minimalist duty to ensure that we refrain from acts which create unresolvable difficulties for as yet unborn persons.

These problems underscore a second limitation posed by intergenerational ethics to germ line therapy. When we are ignorant about indirect or delayed second-order consequences of any intervention, particularly when these consequences may be harmful and/or irreversible, we are obliged to exercise 'responsible restraint' in developing and implementing that technology (Twiss, 1976, 28–30).

Together, these two conditions circumscribe germ line therapy and limit the weight given to the claim that we have a moral imperative to improve future generations. Advocates of so-called 'transgenerational ethics' insist that we have at least a duty not to leave subsequent generations worse off than we are at present. However, such a requirement does not demand that we use germ line engineering to assure genetic equality for the future, since we cannot know now what their phenotype requirements will be in their contemporary environments. Simply ensuring that we do not allow deterioration of the gene pool through an infusion of new mutations (e.g., through faulty germ line intervention or exposure to mutagens) would suffice to meet this minimal requirement.

12 Genetic 'Improvement'

These last arguments anticipate a more complex issue: whether or not we have a duty to improve on the present generation to ensure 'better' genotypes in the future. Many ethicists concur that we have a minimal duty to ensure that the legacy we bequeath to the next generation leaves them at least no worse off than we were at the onset of our generation. But our obligations for future generations are much less clear than are those for present ones. Do we have a duty to promote the good of what Martin Golding calls a "distant futurity" (Golding, 1978, 507–12)? Under this construction, we have a duty to selectively reduce the genetic load passed on to future generations. This argument has formed part of the rationale for the crude attempts at eugenics over the last five decades, culminating in Hitler's notorious *Lebensborn* movement in the early 1940s. In the *Lebensborn* program, selective breeding between so-called 'Aryan' couples was conducted to perpetuate 'desirable genotypes'. This program produced no evidence of benefit to society. Hitler's eugenic program and similarly misguided attempts at eugenic sterilization in this country underscore how readily we may do harm in attempting to 'improve' the genetic makeup of future generations. Some researchers have none the less noted that certain genetic diseases are almost certainly disadvantageous for future generations. In Martin Golding's view, for instance, we have a duty to "do what we can, consistent with reason and morality, to eliminate them" (Golding, 1978, 507–12).

Some commentators stop short of advocating eugenic intervention because of the difficulty in defining the gray zone of a marginally deleterious recessive disorder. It is clearer that we do have a duty to reduce the likelihood of the perpetuation of clearly undesirable dominant or X-linked traits like Lesch-Nyhan Disease or neurofibromatosis. Germ line intervention could in theory ensure that neither the birth nor the procreation of an individual with such powerfully undesirable dominantly inherited conditions or traits would occur.

But other less technologically controversial or intrusive measures already exist to achieve the same ends. Both zygote selection (via polar body analysis) and prenatal diagnosis with selective abortion exist and could obviate the need for germ line intervention for treating individuals with such dominantly inherited conditions. The selective destruction of affected early embryos or fetuses to save their 'normal' counterparts will still raise serious ethical issues about taking human life. Importantly, these consequences would be minimized by the ability to select – or genetically engineer – the sperm or eggs.

13 'Selective' Elimination and Germ Line Engineering

Because virtually all of the technologies now available to *select* desired from undesired genotypes entail killing a potential human being, through genetic diagnosis and selective abortion, for instance, interventions at the level of germ cells may paradoxically be more morally acceptable than are those done later in embryogenesis. (This assumes of course that germ line engineering can be perfected without killing or destroying human embryos in the first place.) Moreover, while screening and selective abortion of genetically abnormal fetuses suffice for 'eliminating' most Mendelian disorders in the immediate offspring, they do not protect against fetuses which carry recessive disorders in the heterozygous state, nor against the constant reintroduction of X-linked and dominant traits by spontaneous mutation.

For many conditions, notably classic hemophilia and Duchenne muscular dystrophy, such spontaneous mutations are the dominant modes of reintroduction of the genes each generation. To ameliorate the impact of these conditions on future generations, a technique would be needed that could screen germ line cells for defective genes prior to fertilization.

If it were possible to screen such sperm (or less likely, eggs) and use only those with small numbers of deleterious mutations, it would be possible to achieve 'germ line' ends without genetic engineering. In the event that most or all sperm carried deleterious mutations, germ line engineering might be used to stabilize the genome or buttress the genome against mutations. Such futuristic models could be achieved by providing extra copies of the 'good' genes (so that mutations would have to affect *both* copies to produce a defect).

For recessive traits, prenatal diagnosis and abortion are even more problematic from a eugenic sense, since these techniques can lead to reproductive compensation and still higher gene frequencies in future generations of the deleterious genes. Neither mass genetic screening to find the at-risk population for recessive disorders nor the screening of each of their pregnancies to eliminate the 50 percent of the embryos which were carriers and the 25 percent which were homozygotes would be morally acceptable, since no one has defined heterozygotes for any recessive condition as warranting selective abortion. Thus, none of the conventional techniques used to identify high-risk pregnancies or to selectively abort affected fetuses are either universally acceptable nor very efficient methods for manipulating the genome over the long run.

In theory, germ line engineering could provide a method for efficient elimination of deleterious, recessive disorders. Presumably, universal genetic screening at birth for the genetic load each individual carries would permit the identification of those whose germ line bore an unduly high proportion of deleterious lethal or abnormal genes. Selective engineering of such germ lines, through isolation of primordial germ cells or stem cells for at-risk individuals (e.g., atomic bomb casualties or radiation-exposed workers) could in theory permit the preferential selection of 'high quality' (i.e., low genetic load) sperm, and the subsequent use of this improved population for inseminating appropriate mates. Such eugenic uses of germ line *selection* fulfill the presumptive ethical obligation to leave future generations at least as well off as our own.

By contrast, other techniques are fraught with problems. Even after successfully correcting a known genetic defect, late arising tumors in treated animals have been reported. Alterations in the germ line may also not be faithfully perpetuated in future generations because of failures in integrating at appropriate sites in the host genome. Germ line changes by insertional mutagenesis are particularly problematic, since such techniques disrupt the integrity of resident cellular genes. About 10–20 percent of transgenic mice can carry *new* deleterious recessive mutations in essential genes (Palmiter and Brinster, 1985, 343–5).

Thus, germ line engineering may generate hidden genetic damage in one generation that may show up only in subsequent ones. Disrupting the normal mechanism of genetic homeostasis, creating recessive mutations, or upsetting the normal control mechanism are but three ways that genetic engineering could result in distant harm leading to disease, disability or death in the offspring of an ostensibly genetically 'cured' individual.

Given these likelihoods, germ line engineering may only be justified if germinal changes occur secondary to otherwise morally supportable interventions.

14 Theological Concerns

Germ line alterations come closer to playing God than have any other manipulations so far construed for the new genetic technologies. Since creation is considered by some to be sacrosanct and inviolate to the point of disallowing destruction of even seriously defective fetuses, obvious parallel concerns might be voiced at germ line interventions. But not necessarily. The Roman Catholic pontiff's permissive response to somatic cell engineering would appear to leave open the possibility of considering interventions which would allow an individual who had a dominant lethal condition that would express itself say by the age of 10 to have *both* germ line and somatic cell engineering to prevent its occurrence. These steps would not only preserve one life, but would permit the fulfillment of the divine plan to permit procreation for an individual who might not otherwise have that opportunity. At the same time, the intervention would allow the affected individual free reign in his own reproduction, without fear of reintroducing the deleterious gene to yet another generation.

15 Long-Term Implications

Would not the same consequential ethics eventually permit the widespread proliferation of germ line engineering if the first experimental manipulations proved successful? The ethical requirement requires showing that a germinal intervention provides the sole method of rescuing an otherwise hopeless, ethically deserving developmental circumstance.

Is there a condition amenable only to germ line intervention which would qualify? Even the most serious genetically determined traits are rarely if ever perpetuated with 100 per cent expression in the offspring. Balanced translocations, dominantly inherited disorders, homozygous recessive conditions, and X-linked traits are passed on to only some offspring, and then only (as in the case of recessive conditions) if the partner is heterozygous for the same defect. Homozygous/homozygous crosses are extremely rare in humans, as are matings in which all offspring will invariably die (cf. lethal yellow or W phenotypes in mice). In all other circumstances, careful gamete embryo *selection* (e.g., through examination of the polar body of the newly fertilized egg) can identify the at-risk versus the normal embryo. Judicious detection and elimination of genetically defective sperm, eggs or embryos all but vitiates the need for germ line engineering.

16 Conclusions

Germ line changes which result as a secondary consequence of otherwise well-designed and ethically acceptable manipulations of somatic cells (e.g., to cure an otherwise devastating or fatal disease) can be seen as acceptable. More serious objections apply to intentional germ line interventions because of the unacceptability of using a person solely as a vehicle for creating uncertain genetic change in his descendants. It is also morally unacceptable to use the promise of future benefit to experiment on fetuses or embryos for whom other technologies exist to achieve the end of being free of major genetic defects. Although most of these technologies entail destruction of the affected embryo or fetus, others (e.g., genetic tests done on the polar body) do not.

The more difficult question of the use of germ line engineering as a technique of last resort to both somatically and germinally 'cure' an individual of a major hereditary disorder (e.g., Huntington's Chorea or retinoblastoma) is more problematic. Here, one must weigh the benefits and risks of the timing of the intervention. Earlier interventions, such as injecting genetically engineered cells at the blastocyst stage, may paradoxically leave the host still afflicted by the disorder, but with germ cells that are 'cured'. The creation of such chimeric hosts in which the primary attempt is to relieve them of suffering is again a case of 'secondary effect' and is morally defensible.

While it is ethically questionable to assume risks for future generations, it is not clear that altering the germ line to offset a near certainty of adverse consequences of normal procreation is morally contraindicated, especially if this can be achieved by zygote selection and *not* genetic modification. Similarly, the lack of assurance that the changes made to germ line cells will be faithfully expressed in offspring becomes a simple problem in experimental ethics. Where risks are profound for normal procreative choices, as in a situation where known mutagenic damage or intrinsic defective genes are involved, germ line engineering will have strong adherents. The difficulties inherent in performing the technology in addition to the risks posed by its inaccurate application are problems which could be resolved with adequate experimentation and preparation. Thus, such objections to germ line tampering or engineering (to use two perjoratives) are temporizing and insufficient to warrant the present ban on experimentation on embryos or fetuses.

It is also theoretically possible to limit the effects of germ line manipulation to a single generation, either through concurrent manipulations that limit fertility or by committing the conceptus to abstain from reproduction as one of the trade-offs of his genetic alteration. These somewhat draconian devices to limit the intergenerational impact of germ line engineering do not obviate the other major ethical concerns discussed in this paper. Germ line engineering as a directed attempt to change the genotype of future generations cannot ethically be justified. However, when such changes arise as an indirect and otherwise unavailable consequence of an approved form of somatic cell engineering, they are morally acceptable.

References

Anderson, W.F. (1985). 'Human gene therapy: scientific and ethical considerations', *Recombinant DNA Technical Bulletin*, 8, 55–63.

Anonymous (1989). 'Making mice with designer genes', *Journal of NIH Research*, I, 107.

Barinagg, M. (1989). 'Making transgenic mice: Is it really that easy?' *Science*, 245, 590–1.

Code of Federal Regulations, 45, 46.III.

Ethics Committee of the American Fertility Society (1986). 'Ethical considerations of the new reproductive technologies', *Fertility & Sterility*, 46, suppl. 1, 3S–94S.

Fowler, G., Juengst, E. T. and Zimmerman, B. K. (1989). 'Germline gene therapy and the clinical ethos of medical genetics', *Theoretical Medicine*, 151–65.

Golding, M. (1978). 'Obligations to future generations', in W. Reich (ed.), *Encyclopedia of Bioethics* (New York: Macmillan), pp. 507–12.

Hammer, R. W., Pursel, V. G. and Rexrood, C. E., Jr, et al. (1986). 'Genetic engineering of mammalian embryos', *Journal of Animal Science*, 63, 269–78.

Lipschulz, L. I. et al. (1980). 'Dibromochloropropane and its effect on testicular function in men', *Journal of Urology*, 124, 464–8.

Muller, H. (1987). 'Human gene therapy: possibilities and limitations', *Experientia*, 43, 375–8.

Orian, J. M., Tamakoshi, K., Mackay, I. R. et al. (1990). 'New murine model for hepatocellular carcinoma: transgenic mice expressing metallothionen-ovine growth hormone fusion gene', *Journal of the National Cancer Institute*, 82, 393–7.

Palmiter, R. D. and Brinster, R. L. (1985). 'Transgenic mice', *Cell*, 41, 343–5.

Rifkin, J. et al. (1983). 'Theological letter concerning the moral arguments against genetic engineering of human germline cells', reported in C. Norman, 'Clerics urge ban on cells', *Science*, 220, 1360–1.

Van Raden, P. M. and Freeman, A. E. (1985). 'Potential genetic gains from producing bulls with only sires as parents', *Journal of Dairy Science*, 68, 1425–31.

Twiss, S. (1976). 'Ethical issues in setting priorities', *Annual of the New York Academy of Science*, 245, 28–30.

Walters, L. (1986). 'The ethics of human gene therapy', *Nature*, 320, 225–7.

Weatherall, D. J. (1988). 'The slow road to gene therapy', *Nature*, 331, 13–14.

17

Is Gene Therapy a Form of Eugenics?

John Harris

> Eugenic A. *adj.* Pertaining or adapted to the production of fine offspring. B. *sb.* in *pl.* The science which treats of this. (*The Shorter Oxford English Dictionary*, 3rd edn, 1965).

> It has now become a serious necessity to better the breed of the human race. The average citizen is too base for the everyday work of modern civilization. Civilized man has become possessed of vaster powers than in old times for good or ill but has made no corresponding advance in wits and goodness to enable him to conduct his conduct rightly. (Sir Francis Galton)

If, as I believe, gene therapy is in principle ethically sound except for its possible connection with eugenics, then there are two obvious ways of giving a simple and straightforward answer to a question such as this. The first is to say "yes it is, and so what?" The second is to say "no it isn't, so we shouldn't worry." If we accept the first of the above definitions we might well be inclined to give the first of our two answers. If, on the other hand, we accept the sort of gloss that Ruth Chadwick gives on Galton's account, "those who are genetically weak should simply be discouraged from reproducing," either by incentives or compulsory measures, we get a somewhat different flavour, and one which might incline a decent person who favours gene therapy towards the second answer.

The nub of the problem turns on how we are to understand the objective of producing "fine children". Does "fine" mean "as fine as children normally are", or does it mean "as fine as a child can be"? Sorting out the ethics of the connection between gene therapy and eugenics seems to involve the resolution of two morally significant issues. The first is whether or not there is a relevant moral distinction between attempts to remove or repair dysfunction on the one hand and measures designed to enhance function on the other, such that it would be coherent to be in favour of curing dysfunction but against enhancing function? The second involves the question of whether gene therapy as a technique involves something specially morally problematic.

From *Bioethics*, vol. 7, no. 2/3 (1993), pp. 178–87.

The Moral Continuum

Is it morally wrong to wish and hope for a fine baby girl or boy? Is it wrong to wish and hope that one's child will not be born disabled? I assume that my feeling that such hopes and wishes are not wrong is shared by every sane decent person. Now consider whether it would be wrong to wish and hope for the reverse? What would we think of someone who hoped and wished that their child would be born with disability? Again I need not spell out the answer to these questions.

But now let's bridge the gap between thought and action, between hopes and wishes and their fulfilment. What would we think of someone who, hoping and wishing for a fine healthy child, declined to take the steps necessary to secure this outcome when such steps were open to them?

Again I assume that unless those steps could be shown to be morally unacceptable our conclusions would be the same.

Consider the normal practice at IVF clinics where a woman who has had say, five eggs fertilized *in vitro*, wishes to use some of these embryos to become pregnant. Normal practice would be to insert two embryos or at most three. If preimplantation screening had revealed two of the embryos to possess disabilities of one sort or another, would it be right to implant the two embryos with disability rather than the others? Would it be right to choose the implantation embryos randomly? Could it be defensible for a doctor to override the wishes of the mother and implant the disabled embryos rather than the healthy ones – would we applaud her for so doing?[1]

The answer that I expect to all these rhetorical questions will be obvious. It depends, however, on accepting that disability is somehow disabling and therefore undesirable. If it were not, there would be no motive to try to cure or obviate disability in health care more generally. If we believe that medical science should try to cure disability where possible, and that parents would be wrong to withhold from their disabled children cures as they become available, then we will be likely to agree on our answers to the rhetorical questions posed.

What is Disability?

It is notoriously hard to give a satisfactory definition of disability although I believe we all know pretty clearly what we mean by it. A disability is surely a physical or mental condition we have a strong rational preference not to be in; it is, more importantly, a condition which is in some sense a 'harmed condition'.[2] I have in mind the sort of condition in which if a patient presented with it unconscious in the casualty department of a hospital and the condition could be easily and immediately reversed, but not reversed unless the doctor acts without delay, a doctor would be negligent were she not to attempt reversal. Or, one which, if a pregnant mother knew that it affected her fetus and knew also she could remove the condition by simple dietary adjustment, then to fail to do so would be to knowingly harm her child.[3]

To make clearer what's at issue here let's imagine that as a result of industrial effluent someone had contracted a condition that she felt had disabled or harmed her in some sense. How might she convince a court say, that she had suffered disability or injury?

The answer is obvious but necessarily vague. Whatever it would be plausible to say in answer to such a question is what I mean (and what is clearly meant) by disability and injury. It is not possible to stipulate exhaustively what would strike us as plausible here, but we know what injury is and we know what disability or incapacity is. If the condition in question was one which set premature limits on their lifespan – made their life shorter than it would be with treatment – or was one which rendered her specially vulnerable to infection, more vulnerable than others, we would surely recognize that she had been harmed and perhaps to some extent disabled. At the very least such events would be plausible candidates for the description "injuries" or "disabilities".

Against a background in which many people are standardly protected from birth or before against pollution hazards and infections and have their healthy life expectancy extended, it would surely be plausible to claim that failure to protect in this way constituted an injury and left them disabled. Because of their vulnerability to infection and to environmental pollutants, there would be places it was unsafe for them to go and people with whom they could not freely consort. These restrictions on liberty are surely at least prima facie disabling as is the increased relative vulnerability.

These points are crucial because it is sometimes said that while we have an obligation to cure disease – to restore normal functioning – we do not have an obligation to enhance or improve upon a normal healthy life, that enhancing function is permissive but could not be regarded as obligatory. But, what constitutes a normal healthy life is determined in part by technological and medical and other advances (hygiene, sanitation, etc.). It is normal now, for example, to be protected against tetanus; the continued provision of such protection is not merely permissive. If the AIDS pandemic continues unabated and the only prospect, or the best prospect, for stemming its advance is the use of gene therapy to insert genes coding for antibodies to AIDS, I cannot think that it would be coherent to regard making available such therapy as permissive rather than mandatory.[4]

If this seems still too like normal therapy to be convincing, suppose genes coding for repair enzymes which would not only repair radiation damage or damage by other environmental pollutants but would also prolong healthy life expectancy could be inserted into humans. Again, would it be permissible to let people continue suffering such damage when they could be protected against it? Would it in short be OK to let them suffer?

It is not normal for the human organism to be self-repairing in this way, this must be eugenic if anything is. But if available, its use would surely, like penicillin before it, be more than merely permissive.

Of course, there will be unclarity at the margins, but at least this conception of disability captures and emphasizes the central notion that a disability is disabling in some sense, that it is a harm to those who suffer it, and that to knowingly disable another individual or leave them disabled when we could remove the disability is to harm that individual.[5]

This is not an exhaustive definition of disability but it is a way of thinking about it which avoids certain obvious pitfalls. First it does not define disability in terms of any conception or normalcy. Secondly it does not depend on *post hoc* ratification by the subject of the condition – it is not a prediction about how the subject of the condition will feel. This is important because we need an account of disability we can use for the potentially self-conscious gametes, embryos, fetuses and neonates, and for the temporarily unconscious, which does not wait upon subsequent ratification by the person concerned.

With this account in mind we can extract the sting from at least one dimension of the charge that attempts to produce fine healthy children might be wrongful. Two related sorts of wrongfulness are often alleged here. One comes from some people and groups of people with disability or from their advocates. The second comes from those who are inclined to label such measures as attempts at eugenic control.

It is often said by those with disability or by their supporters[6] that abortion for disability, or failure to keep disabled infants alive as long as possible, or even positive infanticide for disabled neonates, constitutes discrimination against the disabled as a group, that it is tantamount to devaluing them as persons, to devaluing them in some existential sense. Alison Davis identifies this view with utilitarianism and comments further that "(i)t would also justify using me as a donor bank for someone more physically perfect (I am confined to a wheelchair due to spina bifida) and, depending on our view of relative worth, it would justify using any of us as a donor if someone of the status of Einstein or Beethoven, or even Bob Geldof, needed one of our organs to survive."[7] This is a possible version of utilitarianism, of course, but not I believe one espoused by anyone today. On the view assumed here and which I have defended in detail elsewhere,[8] all persons share the same moral status whether disabled or not. To decide not to keep a disabled neonate alive no more constitutes an attack on the disabled than does curing disability. To set the badly broken legs of an unconscious casualty who cannot consent does not constitute an attack on those confined to wheelchairs. To prefer to remove disability where we can is not to prefer non-disabled individuals as persons. To reiterate, if a pregnant mother can take steps to cure a disability affecting her fetus she should certainly do so, for to fail to do so is to deliberately handicap her child. She is not saying that she prefers those without disability as persons when she says she would prefer not to have a disabled child.

The same is analogously true of charges of eugenics in related circumstances. The wrong of practising eugenics is that it involves the assumption that "those who are genetically weak should be discouraged from reproducing" or are less morally important than other persons and that compulsory measures to prevent them reproducing might be defensible.

It is not that the genetically weak should be discouraged from reproducing but that everyone should be discouraged from reproducing children who will be significantly harmed by their genetic constitution.[9]

Indeed, gene therapy offers the prospect of enabling the genetically weak to reproduce and give birth to the genetically strong. It is to this prospect and to possible objections to it that we must now turn.

In so far as gene therapy might be used to delete specific genetic disorders in individuals or repair damage that had occurred genetically or in any other way, it seems straightforwardly analogous to any other sort of therapy and to fail to use it would be deliberately to harm those individuals whom its use would protect.

It might thus, as we have just noted, enable individuals with genetic defects to be sure of having healthy rather than harmed children and thus liberate them from the terrible dilemma of whether or not to risk having children with genetic defects.

Suppose now that it becomes possible to use gene therapy to introduce into the human genome genes coding for antibodies to major infections like AIDS, hepatitis B, malaria and others, or coding for repair enzymes which could correct the most frequently occurring defects caused by radiation damage, or which could retard the ageing process and so lead to greater healthy longevity, or which might remove predispositions to heart disease, or which would destroy carcinogens or maybe permit human beings to tolerate other environmental pollutants?[10]

I have called individuals who might have these protections built into their germ line a "new breed".[11] It might be possible to use somatic cell therapy to make the same changes. I am not here interested in the alleged moral differences between germ line and somatic line therapy, though elsewhere I have argued strongly that there is no morally relevant difference.[12] The question we must address is whether it would be wrong to fail to protect individuals in ways like these which would effectively enhance their function rather than cure dysfunction, which would constitute improvements in human individuals or indeed to the human genome, rather than simple (though complex in another sense and sophisticated) repairs? I am assuming of course that the technique is tried, tested and safe.

To answer this question we need to know whether to fail to protect individuals whom we could protect in this way would constitute a harm to them.[13] The answer seems to be clearly that it would. If the gene therapy could enhance prospects for healthy longevity then just as today, someone who had a life expectancy of fifty years rather than one of seventy would be regarded as at a substantial disadvantage, so having one of only seventy when others were able to enjoy ninety or so would be analogously disadvantageous. However, even if we concentrate on increased resistance, or reduced susceptibility to disease, there would still be palpable harm involved. True, to be vulnerable is not necessarily to suffer the harm to which one is vulnerable, although even this may constitute some degree of psychological damage. However, the right analogy here seems to be drawn from aviation.

Suppose aircraft manufacturers could easily build in safety features which would render an aircraft immune to, or at least much less susceptible to, a wide range of aviation hazards. If they failed to do so we would regard them as culpable whether or not a particular aircraft did in fact succumb to any of these hazards in the course of its life. They would in short be like a parent who failed to protect her children from dangerous diseases via immunization or our imagined parent who fails to protect through gene therapy.

I hope enough has been said to make clear that where gene therapy will effect improvements to human beings or to human nature that provide protections from harm or the protection of life itself in the form of increases in life expectancy ('death postponing' is after all just 'life saving' redescribed) then call it what you will, eugenics or not, we ought to be in favour of it. There is in short no moral difference between attempts to cure dysfunction and attempts to enhance function where the enhancement protects life or health.

What Sorts of Enhancement Protect Health?

I have drawn a distinction between attempts to protect life and health and other uses of gene therapy. I have done so mostly for the sake of brevity and to avoid the more contentious area of so-called cosmetic or frivolous uses of gene therapy. Equally and for analogous reasons I have here failed to distinguish between gene therapy on the germ line and gene therapy on the somatic line. I avoid contention here not out of distaste for combat but simply because to deploy the arguments necessary to defend cosmetic uses of gene therapy would take up more space than I have available now. Elsewhere I have deployed these arguments.[14] However, the distinction between preservation of life and health or normal medical uses and other uses of gene therapy is difficult to draw and it is worth here just illustrating this difficulty.

The British Government's "Committee on the Ethics of Gene Therapy" in its report to Parliament attempted to draw this distinction. The report, known by the surname of its chairman as *The Clothier Report*, suggested "in the current state of knowledge it would not be acceptable to attempt to change traits not associated with disease."[15] This was an attempt to rule out so called cosmetic uses of gene therapy which would include attempts to manipulate intelligence.[16]

Imagine two groups of mentally handicapped or educationally impaired children. In one the disability is traceable to a specific disease state or injury, in the other it has no obvious cause. Suppose now that gene therapy offered the chance of improving the intelligence of children generally and those in both these groups in particular. Those who think that using gene therapy to improve intelligence is wrong because it is not a dimension of health care would have to think that neither group of children should be helped, and those, like Clothier, who are marginally more enlightened would have to think that it might be ethical to help children in the first group but not those in the second.[17]

I must now turn to the question of whether or not gene therapy as a technique is specially morally problematic.

What's Wrong with Gene Therapy?

Gene therapy may of course be scientifically problematic in a number of ways and in so far as these might make the procedure unsafe we would have some reason to be suspicious of it. However, these problems are ethically uninteresting and I shall continue to assume that gene therapy is tried and tested from a scientific perspective. What else might be wrong with it?

One other ethical problem for gene therapy has been suggested and it deserves the small space left. Ruth Chadwick has given massive importance to the avoidance of doubt over one's genetic origins. Chadwick suggests that someone

> who discovers that her parents had an extra gene or genes added . . . may suffer from what today in the 'problem pages' is called an 'identity crisis' . . . Part of this may be an uncertainty about her genetic history. We have stressed the importance of this knowledge, and pointed out that when one does not know where 50 per cent of one's genes come from, it can cause unhappiness.[18]

Chadwick then asks whether this problem can be avoided if only a small amount of genetic make-up is involved. Her answer is equivocal but on balance she seems to feel that "we must be cautious about producing a situation where children feel they do not really belong anywhere, because their genetic history is confused."[19] This sounds mild enough until we examine the cash value of phrases like "can cause unhappiness" or "be cautious" as Chadwick uses them.

In discussing the alleged unhappiness caused by ignorance of 50 per cent of one's genetic origin, Chadwick argued strongly that such unhappiness was so serious that "it seems wise to restrict artificial reproduction to methods that do not involve donation of genetic material. This rules out AID, egg donation, embryo donation and partial surrogacy."[20]

In elevating doubt about one's genetic origin to a cause of unhappiness so poignant that it would be better that a child who might experience it had never been born, Chadwick ignores entirely the (in fact false) truism that, while motherhood is a fact, paternity is always merely a hypothesis. It is a wise child indeed that knows her father and since such doubt might reasonably cloud the lives of a high proportion of the population of the world, we have reason to be sceptical that its effects are so terrible that people should be prevented from reproducing except where such doubt can be ruled out.

The effect of Chadwick's conclusion is to deny gay couples and single people the possibility of reproducing. Chadwick denies this, suggesting "they are not being denied the opportunity to have children. If they are prepared to take the necessary steps ('the primitive sign of wanting is trying to get') their desire to beget can be satisfied." What are we to make of this? It seems almost self-consciously mischievous. In the first place, gay couples and single women resorting to what must, *ex hypothesi*, be distasteful sex with third parties merely for procreational purposes, are unlikely to preserve the identity of their sexual partners for the benefit of their offspring's alleged future peace of mind. If this is right then doubt over genetic origin will not be removed. Since Chadwick is explicitly addressing public policy issues she should in consistency advocate legislation against such a course of action rather than recommend it.

But surely, if we are to comtemplate legislating against practices which give rise to doubt about genetic origins we would need hard evidence not only that such practices harm the resulting children but that the harm is of such a high order that not only would it have been better that such children had never been born but also better that those who want such children should suffer the unhappiness consequent on a denial of their chance to have children using donated genetic material?

Where such harm is not only unavoidable but is an inherent part of sexual reproduction and must affect to some degree or other a high percentage of all births, it is surely at best unkind to use the fear of it as an excuse for discriminating against already persecuted minorities in the provision of reproductive services.

Where, as in the case of gene therapy, such donated[21] material also protects life and health or improves the human condition, we have an added reason to welcome it.

Notes

This paper was presented at the Inaugural Congress of the International Association of Bioethics, Amsterdam, The Netherlands, 5–7 October 1992. I am grateful to the audience at that meeting and particularly to Dan Brock, Norman Daniels, Raanan Gillon, Douglas Maclean and Maurice de Wachter for helpful comments.

1 The argument here follows that of my paper "Should We Attempt to Eradicate Disability", published in the Proceedings of the Fifteenth International Wittgenstein Symposium.
2 See my discussion of the difference between harming and wronging in my *Wonderwoman & Superman: The Ethics of Human Biotechnology* (Oxford, 1992), ch. 4.
3 This goes for relatively minor conditions like the loss of a finger or deafness and also for disfiguring conditions right through to major disability like paraplegia.
4 In this sense the definition of disability is like that of "poverty".
5 See my more detailed account of the relationship between harming and wronging in my *Wonderwoman & Superman* (Oxford: Oxford University Press, 1992), ch. 4.
6 Who should of course include us all.
7 Davis, "The Status of Anencephalic Babies: should their bodies be used as donor banks?" *Journal of Medical Ethics*, 14 (1988), p. 150.
8 See my *The Value of Life* (London: Routledge, 1985 and 1990), ch. 1 and my "Not all babies should be kept alive as long as possible" in Raanan Gillon and Anne Lloyd (eds), *Principles of Health Care Ethics* (Chichester: John Wiley, 1993).
9 I use the term "weak" here to echo Chadwick's use of the term. I take "genetically weak" to refer to those possessing a debilitating genetic condition or those who will inevitably pass on such a condition. All of us almost certainly carry some genetic abnormalities and are not thereby rendered "weak".
10 Here I borrow freely from my *Wonderwoman & Superman: The Ethics of Human Biotechnology* (Oxford University Press, 1992), ch. 9, where I discuss all these issues in greater depth than is possible here.
11 Ibid.
12 Ibid., ch. 8.
13 For an elaboration on the importance of this distinction see my discussion of 'the wrong of wrongful life' in *Wonderwoman & Superman*, ch. 4.
14 Ibid., ch. 7.
15 *Report of the Committee on the Ethics of Gene Therapy*, presented to Parliament by Command of Her Majesty, January 1992. London HMSO para. 4. 22.
16 In fact intelligence is unlikely to prove responsive to such manipulation because of its multifactorial nature.
17 There would be analogous problems about attempts to block the use of gene therapy to change things like physical stature and height since it might be used in the treatment of achondroplasia or other forms of dwarfism.
18 Ruth Chadwick *Ethics, Reproduction and Genetic Control* (London: Routledge, 1987). p. 126.
19 Ibid., p. 127.
20 Ibid., p. 39.
21 I use the term 'donated' here, but I do not mean to rule out commerce in such genetic material. See *My Wonderwoman & Superman*, ch. 6.

18

Liberal Eugenics

Nicholas Agar

Francis Galton took the name for his new science of improving human stock from the Greek *eugenes* or 'good in birth'. It is hard to think of an enterprise less fortunate in birth.[1] Eugenicists throughout Europe and North America harnessed misguided views about human worth to mistaken theories of human heredity. Various combinations of encouragement for the fit and discouragement for the unfit manifestly failed to produce the perfect citizen and Galton's project was abandoned.

Recent advances in the understanding of human heredity offered by the new genetics have prompted a revival in eugenics. While old-fashioned authoritarian eugenicists sought to produce citizens out of a single centrally designed mould, the distinguishing mark of the new liberal eugenics is state neutrality.[2] Access to information about the full range of genetic therapies will allow prospective parents to look to their own values in selecting improvements for future children. Authoritarian eugenicists would do away with ordinary procreative freedoms. Liberals instead propose radical extensions of them.

There are differing views on how wide these new freedoms should be. James Watson, former head of the Human Genome Project, thinks that prospective parents should use available technologies to choose from a very wide range of offspring characteristics. He finds no problem with the selection of traits such as sexual orientation and musical ability. According to Watson, "[i]f you could find the gene which determines sexuality and a woman decides she doesn't want a homosexual child, well, let her [choose accordingly]."[3] Liberals who are less gung-ho than Watson face a tough job in arguing for constraints on individual choice. As we will see, popular suggestions such as the avoidance of disease or the securing of quality of life threaten to smuggle into individual choices substantive views about human worth. If so, citizens will end up being engineered in accordance with a dominant set of values after all, and the new eugenics will collapse into the eugenics of old.

I argue that respect for the life plans of future persons can constrain parental choice in a way that sharply distinguishes the new eugenics from its ugly ancestor. To help demonstrate this I compare genetic engineers' access to *life plans* with their access to capacities, the properties of persons that help determine success in life plans. I suggest that a program of systematic life-plan modification is beyond the reach of genetic engineers and that this inability imposes restrictions on other types of enhancement. A eugenics program appropriately sensitive to the range of potential life plans of future persons will not seek to enhance capacities with any one life plan in mind. Such a program will have the dual assets of tailoring candidate improvements to the needs of those who bear them and shielding societies from the shaping effects of dominant values.

Goods of Genetic Engineering

The weirdness of the idea of genetic engineering makes sober moral assessment difficult. Before we can get to grips with liberal arguments we need to make the topic tractable to morality. I will use the

From *Public Affairs Quarterly*, vol. 12, no. 2 (April 1998), pp. 137–55. Reprinted with permission.

notion of a *good of genetic engineering* to describe any way of shaping persons, or producing new types of persons by modifying or rearranging genes.

Goods of genetic engineering may be produced by a variety of techniques.[4] Current technology allows the testing of foetal DNA for genes linked with diseases such as cystic fibrosis and Huntington's. A sufficiently serious prognosis may prompt a decision to abort. Here the good of genetic engineering is applied in a negative way, presumably canceling out the wrong of the life that would have been lived.[5]

Other techniques might one day allow us to respond more creatively to information about genes. Human beings carry around huge resources of genetic variation; a baby girl possesses around 600 000 potentially fertilizable eggs and a man can produce around 12 trillion sperm in his lifetime.[6] The techniques of preimplantation genetics may allow the DNA of some subset of these sex cells to be inspected. As we increase the size of our sample we boost the chance that we will find the desired combination of genes.

The distant future holds the promise of still greater freedom in selecting traits. Rather than hunting out disease-free Marie Curies and Brian Laras in naturally produced DNA, twenty-fifth-century genetic engineers may be able to intervene directly in the genomes of existing individuals, splicing in genes for desired traits and snipping out those not similarly favored.

At some point in our speculation about the likely size and makeup of the category of goods of genetic engineering we move from reasonable extrapolation of existing technologies to science fiction. The most fantasized-about improvements may be forever beyond science's reach. Genes for Einsteinian intelligence, Austenian sensitivity to social detail and Wildean wit may be impossible to find, or once found, they may be impossible to manipulate. Informed scientific opinion includes a wide spectrum of views about the potential for the new genetics to support any manner of eugenic policy.[7] In this paper, for largely pragmatic reasons, I side with those who take a generous view of scientific possibilities. Science so often confounds the best predictions, and we should not risk finding ourselves unprepared for the genetic engineer's equivalent of Hiroshima. Better to have principles covering impossible situations than no principles for situations that are suddenly upon us.

There are two kinds of arrangements of goods of genetic engineering that deserve moral scrutiny. First, there is the internal arrangement. When worried about the internal arrangements of goods of genetic engineering we ask how their allocation to a given individual will promote the overall good of that individual. Second, there is the social arrangement. Here our concern is with the distribution of goods amongst different individuals and life plans in society. Will uneven allocation of goods drive some life plans out of existence or exaggerate economic inequalities?

The liberal eugenicist proposes that we arrive at the best internal and social arrangements by allowing informed prospective parents to be guided by their values in choosing enhancements.

Before I get to the details of the liberal position I make a more general point. Any acceptable program of genetic engineering offering a wide variety of goods surely lies some distance in the future. Evolutionary theorists have long known that a random mutation to a gene is unlikely either to be selectionally advantageous or to benefit its bearer. The many-trials-and-almost-as-many-errors process that is evolution by natural selection designs at great cost to its experimental subjects. Unless they are prepared to purchase improvements for a similar price in suffering, genetic engineers must be sure that the chosen technique has a very high chance of giving the desired result.

Two Distinctions in Shaping People

The liberal position is arrived at by way of a rejection of the moral importance of two conventional distinctions in shaping people. First, there is the distinction between improving people by modifying their environments and improving them by modifying their genes. Liberals see no moral difference between eugenics and improvements to people by various manipulations of the environment.[8] Parents are already free to improve intelligence and physical prowess by modifying environmental factors such as schooling or diet. The tools of genetic engineering may be novel, but in this respect they resemble experimental vitamin-enriched diets or hothouse schooling. Here is a cautious John Robertson:

> A case could be made for prenatal enhancement as part of parental discretion in rearing offspring. If special tutors and camps, training programs, even the administration of growth hormone to add a few inches in height are

within parental rearing discretion, why should genetic interventions to enhance normal offspring traits be any less legitimate?[9]

Arguments for the moral parity of genetic and environmental engineering find support in modern understanding of the parallel developmental roles of gene and environment. Old-fashioned eugenicists tended to radically overplay the importance of genes, or hereditary factors, in shaping people while underplaying the relevance of the environment. Investigators sought to trace the idleness or criminality they found running through many generations of the same family back to developmentally omnipotent 'bad' genes.[10]

This genetic determinist picture is mistaken. Traits of individuals result from the complex interaction of genes and environment.[11] A clone of Alexander the Great would not be a copy of Alexander. Short of exactly replicating the womb of Olympias of Epirus and the Macedon of the fourth century BC we would expect many of the clone's genes to express themselves in ways very different from the way they did in Alexander. Though a clone should resemble the donor of its DNA more closely than a conventionally produced child resembles its parent, the degree of similarity will be somewhat less than in the case of monozygotic twins reared in the same uterine and similar extrauterine environments.

Those interested in genetic explanations of traits must pay close attention to the impact of environmental variation on the expression of genes. Some genes produce a given phenotypic character in nearly all statistically standard contexts; others have effects that vary in response to seemingly inconsequential environmental changes. A certain trinucleotide repeat on chromosome 4 apparently leads to Huntington's Disease in any standard human environment. The story for putative genes for high intelligence or Dean Hamer's GAY1 will be much less straightforward, however.[12] Only 52 percent of genetically identical twins of homosexual men are themselves gay.[13] This almost certainly means that in a significant subset of statistically normal environments GAY1 does not lead to gayness.[14]

Genetic explanations of traits are perfectly compatible with substantive and interesting environmental explanations of them. For simplicity's sake, take the old-fashioned and surely mistaken explanation of male homosexuality in terms of close maternal bonds. This apparently paradigmatically environmental explanation of homosexuality can be conjoined with an appropriately modest genetic explanation of the kind offered by Hamer. No cautious environmentalist will hold that maternal closeness, without exception, leads to gayness. Separately, neither GAY1 nor a close relationship to a mother will be causally sufficient. Jointly, acting against a statistically standard genomic and extra-genomic background, they may very likely make a homosexual son.

The liberal linkage of eugenic freedom with parental discretion in respect of educationally or dietarily assisted improvement makes sense in the light of this modern understanding. If gene and environment are of parallel importance in accounting for the traits we currently possess, attempts to modify people by modifying either of them would seem to deserve similar scrutiny. It will turn out that some traits are more easily modifiable by changing genes; others will be more readily changed by altering a person's environment. Short of an argument that exposes a significant difference between the two sorts of trait, we should think of both types of modification in similar ways. There seems little reason to think that all morally scary changes will fall into one category or the other.

We come now to the second conventional distinction in shaping people. This distinction separates therapeutic goods of genetic engineering from eugenic goods. Therapeutic goods are those targeted at disease; the aim is for individuals functioning at a level considered normal for human beings. The purpose of eugenic goods is to produce individuals whose attributes go beyond what is considered normal.

The case for allowing prospective parents access to some therapeutic goods seems very strong indeed. Though gene therapy may potentially be a more effective means of combating diabetes than daily shots of insulin, it does not seem in a different moral category.[15] Here is where the stand against eugenics is taken. If gene therapy is medicine then it should be restricted to the treatment of disease. It may be all very well to seek to correct flaws in the execution of divine or evolutionary design, but it's a different thing altogether to shape people according to our own designs.

Liberals are united in contempt for the above reasoning. They doubt that the notion of disease is up to the moral theoretic task the therapeutic/eugenic distinction requires of it.[16] Philip Kitcher criticizes both social constructivist and objectivist biological functional accounts of disease. The first fails because it ends up doing nothing more than recapitulating dominant social prejudices. Homosexuality and left-handedness were once viewed as diseases, and authoritarian eugenicists have, in general, been swift to apply the label 'disease' to phenotypes judged non-ideal. The second sets goals for intervention that are likely often to be irrelevant to humans living in modern environments. There seems no reason why the discovery that traits such as freckles or acute musical perception have dubious natural selective pedigrees should make us place negative values on them.[17]

With the notion of disease out of the way no stable barrier separates the disease-oriented therapeutic intervention from eugenic intervention. Any interest in reducing suffering involves us in what Kitcher calls 'inescapable eugenics'.

The liberal juxtaposition of eugenics with education suggests a more suitable guide to the improving efforts of prospective parents. In allocating educational resources to an individual we do not limit ourselves to the avoidance of disease, rather we are concerned with the person's well-being, welfare or quality of life. So it should be with the goods of genetic engineering. Kitcher fashions an appropriately minimal liberal account of quality of life to guide prospective parents in selecting improvements:

> The first [dimension] focuses on whether the person has developed any sense of what is significant and how the conception of what matters was formed. The second assesses the extent to which those desires that are central to the person's life plan are satisfied: Did the person achieve those things that mattered most? Finally, the third is concerned with the character of the person's experience, the balance of pleasure and pain.[18]

We would expect the varieties of internal arrangement produced by a liberal policy to conflict with concern for quality of life less often and less markedly than those produced by authoritarian eugenicists. Parents tend to pay closer attention to the well-being of their offspring than does a state pursuing some broad program of human stock improvement.

Direction to look out for quality of life will not be entirely idle, however. Some values worthy of protection in a liberal society could have a sad impact on future lives if adopted as guides to eugenic choice. Robertson worries about allowing the procreative expression of values shaped by successful struggle against intellectual or physical disabilities.[19] Parents' ideological commitments can mislead them in other ways. According to a persistent caricature of evolutionary theory, natural selection can only build selfish and thrusting psychological dispositions into us. Two decades of work on various biological altruisms show this not to be the case; the genes of kin-helpers and discriminating cooperators fare better in the long term than those of shortsighted defectors. Over-individualistic parents are in danger of instituting a eugenic policy that matches the evolutionary parody. They will not temper the competitive urges of their offspring with kin and reciprocal altruisms. The resulting individuals are unlikely to see central desires satisfied in a world filled with psychological copies of themselves.[20]

Quality of Life and the Social Arrangements of Goods of Genetic Engineering

Earlier I distinguished between internal and social arrangements of goods of genetic engineering. For the time being I will assume concern for quality of life can guide the liberal toward appropriate internal arrangements of these goods. I now want to illustrate how problems arise in connection with the social arrangement of goods of genetic engineering.

In order to see how the advent of genetic engineering threatens to change the rules of liberal social arrangement we need to distinguish between the demands of life plan roles, on the one hand, and demands of individuals that occupy those roles, on the other. This distinction plays little role prior to genetic engineering because of a widely shared liberal assumption that in meeting the needs of a life plan we also meet the needs of the individuals, present or future, actual or potential, who pursue that plan, and vice versa. The love of art is an important component of the life plans of many current members of society. Further, we know that it is likely to be included in the life plans of at least some future citizens. So, the state aims to distribute goods in a way that does not discriminate against the plan.

Genetic engineers threaten to separate individuals from life plans. If art loving is systematically engineered out of future individuals then we can meet the needs of all individuals present or future, actual or potential, without making any provision whatsoever for the love of art.

The threat posed by the potential separation of life plan roles and occupants extends more broadly than to the love of art or any other particular life plan. A powerful pragmatic justification for liberalism stands to be undermined. Current deep differences in views about the good life mean that we cannot allow any one view to shape institutions. The worry is that one generation's eugenic fashions in genetic enhancements may forever eliminate the diversity of life plans that feeds liberalism.

It should be noted that the separation of individuals from life plans need not concern us when dealing with some worries about the social arrangement of goods of genetic engineering. An often raised worry is that a market driven eugenics will end up meeting the needs of wealthy prospective parents whilst ignoring those of poorer prospective parents. As with education, imbalances in goods of genetic engineering promise to be self-perpetuating. I do not mean to downplay this concern. However, it differs importantly from the aforementioned problems of social distribution. We can take into account the preferences of *actual individuals* rather than of *vacated life plans*, and this allows a more conventional remedy. We may intervene in the market in human improvements to extend access to prospective parents belonging to poorer sections of society.

Back to our worry about the systematic emptying of life plans. Do we have any reason to think that a dramatic reduction in life plan diversity is anything more than a theoretical possibility? In contemporary liberal societies freely taken choices do not conform with a single idea of the good life. In liberal societies of the future, differing ideas about the best life plan will surely disrupt any centrally directed eugenic pattern.

Such reasoning has not impressed recent critics of liberal eugenics.[21] They doubt that handing choice over to parents will stand in the way of the monopolizing tendencies of single ideas of the good. Some early twentieth century advocates of eugenics agreed with them.[22] They did not see a conflict between centrally determined views of the good and what they took to be 'informed choice' about improvements. Many who recoiled at the more extreme proposed means of excluding the unfit from reproduction argued that sexual selection, with its mechanism of female mate choice, could be an essentially liberal means of shaping the race in accordance with a central blueprint. Women would be encouraged to choose sexual partners with the appropriate mix of moral, intellectual and physical virtues.[23] Restrictive laws would therefore not be required to achieve the state's eugenic goals.

Here is where the injection of quality of life considerations into the liberal mix becomes especially dangerous. In spite of various legal protections, the range of life plans well adapted to a given liberal social environment is narrower than the range currently represented in it. Dominant conceptions of the good life can be relevant to individual decisions about enhancements not because they latch onto some independent facts about quality of life but because they in part constitute the environment in which the future person is to live. An individual who is not the object of prejudice stands to have a wider range of opportunities and therefore greater chance of leading a successful life, than one who is the object of prejudice.

Kitcher is sensitive to these concerns and urges that we do our best to combat prejudice. Even when our efforts are to no avail he still resists that idea that prejudice should play a role in eugenic decision-making. Kitcher advises that we should only use such tools as abortion when there is virtually no possibility for a worthwhile life. In a society that sets out to protect the diverse life plans of its citizens, challenges thrown up by the social environment to women, ethnic minorities or homosexuals do not have a substantial enough impact on quality of life to count.[24]

This response is only partially effective. It is a point often-made that natural selection satisfies rather than optimizes; a wing does not need to be perfect in order to give its possessor a high chance of evading predators, hunting down prey and thereby leaving descendants. If we restrict our attention to the analysis of foetal DNA followed by possible abortion a similarly satisfying approach on the part of parents seems to make sense. The choice is after all between a baby with quality of life prospects slightly below the norm or no baby at all.

However, an optimizing approach becomes more attractive once we consider methods that open up a wider range of choice about enhancements. Our wide view of scientific possibilities encourages us to imagine a world in which parents can identify and insert genes for traits such as great diligence and acrobatic ability, at the same time eliminating genes for homosexuality and femaleness. Once genetic engineers are in a position to offer parents-to-be this range of choice, why should they accept any reduction in quality of life prospects?

Support for this optimizing approach can be found if we return to the liberal parallel between educational and genetic enhancements. Parents will acknowledge that for most children there is a tolerably high chance of a life worth living, regardless of what decisions are taken about special schooling or diet. Yet we allow substantial latitude to vary environmental inputs to further boost the expected quality of life.

What argumentative resources does the liberal have to ensure that the social distribution of goods of genetic engineering is not only fair to individuals but neutral between morally acceptable life plans? Singer and Wells suggest the formation of a body whose task is to monitor the choices of individuals, stepping in when imbalances arise.[25] Patterns of parental choices that threaten to eliminate a morally acceptable life plan might trigger action by this body. Even if this body understands itself as preserving the diversity that sustains liberalism such measures are problematic. The liberal resists the restriction of choice in order to protect a non-liberal pattern of life plans. Can intervention to secure the favored liberal social balance of life plans be any different? Once we distinguish between life plan roles and life plan occupants it is hard to find victims of a series of optimizing parental choices.

In what follows I argue that it is correct to concentrate on internal rather than social distributions of goods of genetic engineering. Concern for future individuals will mandate capacity-enhancement that is neutral between a wide range of life plans and suboptimal with respect to any particular one. This internally justified neutrality will translate into a neutrality in respect of the social distribution of goods of genetic engineering.

Improving Capacities and Improving Life Plans

The notion of a life plan is an important constituent of many accounts of quality of life. The first two dimensions of Kitcher's account require the formation and carrying out of central elements of a plan. The following discussion contrasts attempts to improve life plans with attempts to improve capacities – those traits that help determine success in a plan.

Initially, liberals would seem capable of justifying either undertaking. There is no argument to show the global superiority of one life plan over all others, hence the barrier against substantive state-directed eugenics programs. By the light of a given set of parental values, however, there certainly are better or worse life plans. Within certain limits, the eugenic choices of parents can presumably favor the values predominating in their life plans over those that predominate in others.

Concern that internal arrangements of goods of genetic engineering contribute to a future individual's well-being directs us to evaluate capacity enhancements relative to life plans. Many people have capacities that are barely adequate, or even outright inadequate, for their life plan. By engineering in the appropriate capacity-enhancements we may bring this collection closer to the optimum for the life plan.

We need to take a closer look at how changing genes might change these two sorts of properties of persons. In what follows I highlight a difference between causal chains that lead from gene to capacity, on the one hand, and causal chains that lead from gene to life plan, on the other. A note of caution. We should certainly not expect to place these chains into their own distinct natural kinds; the differences will be rather more blurry. Though these rough and ready categories may be inadequate as a base for scientific laws, I maintain that they will be well demarcated enough to ground ethical generalizations.

The following discussion of life plans and capacities sets out to establish that while some sophisticated future genetics may be able to predict how a given genotype will combine with a specified environment to produce some significant capacities, we cannot make a similar claim in respect of life plans. No amount of information is likely to enable us to pair genotypes with life plans. A corollary is that we will be unable to predict how changes to genes will change life plans.

I will rest much on the claim that significant environmental contributions to life plans are psychologically mediated. Essential to the possession of one life plan rather than some other is the recognition by an individual that certain things matter more than certain others. There must be a *decision* to devote oneself to the harmonica or a *realization* that one's family counts for more than one's spy-novel collection. The mythical figure who spends his life unreflectively planted in front of the TV screen without ever having decided to do so has no life plan rather than one oriented toward TV soaps.

Though we must take psychological factors into consideration when describing the development of some capacities such as high intelligence this capacity is not psychologically filtered in quite the same way. I want now to get more precise about this difference.

Life plan decisions are both highly environmentally *sensitive* and environmentally *specific*. Environmental specificity comes into play in describing what life plans are available to a person. A plan can incorporate elements particular to cultural and natural environments. Many of the life plans available to a person who is born, lives and dies in urban North America are not available to a genetically identical twin who spends her life in the Thai highlands, and vice versa. The environmental sensitivity of life plans means that small changes to the environment can have far-reaching consequences. Exposure to five minutes of a television medical drama may inspire someone to be a doctor. An early encounter with a rugby ball may lead to the generation of a life plan targeted at a sporting career, or it may not. It will be next to impossible to determine beforehand what factors will be relevant.

The points about environmental sensitivity apply doubly in modern liberal societies where a highly diverse range of life plans are on offer. Nonliberal societies offer a smaller range of potential life plans to the individual. They therefore provide environments that reduce the variability resulting from this sensitivity.

There certainly are capacities that resemble life plans in terms of environmental sensitivity and specificity. It would be very difficult for a genetic engineer to select for great facility with shogi endgames. Environments that contain no shogi boards cannot be expected to give rise to individuals with highly refined shogi skills. Even in environments that are rich in shogi sets, a person with the native ability to become a great player may instead become highly proficient at chess or table tennis. Associating the game with a particularly grumpy uncle may be enough to ensure that no raw capacity is developed.

We can often work backwards from environmentally specific and sensitive capacities such as great shogi skill to find a capacity that is not psychologically mediated in the same way. Such capacities will be more proper targets for enhancement. Being intelligent or physically strong certainly requires specific gene/environment interactions. Many key environmental inputs will be psychologically filtered and without adequate schooling and nutrition, no combination of favorable genes will produce an intelligent person. Despite this I maintain that these more basic capacities are less environmentally specific and sensitive than many life plans. High intelligence is producible in a wide range of normal human environments and small changes to an environment are unlikely to block or bring about big changes to such a capacity.

We cannot make quite the same move in regard to life plans. There may, of course, be such things as proto-life plans, states that anticipate the development of properly expressed plans. The problem lies in prediction grounded in such proto plans. They can be filled out in conjunction with a modern liberal environment in many different ways. A young child with a yearning for the outdoors may end up guiding tourists on white-water rafting expeditions, planning a government's environment policy or working as a fire-spotter in a remote forest location. Success in each of these life plans will require a different mix of capacities.

Might we direct life plans by first directing capacities? Sometimes capacities do influence life plans. The knowledge that one has a natural strength in a certain area can strongly bias a person toward a life plan that makes use of the strength. However, this is not always, or even reliably, the case. We can compare advantages generated by fortunate combinations of genes with those generated environmentally. A parent successfully following a certain vocation can offer a child an environment appropriate to the successful pursuit of the same vocation. Such parents are able to impart the appropriate knowledge, provide the right contacts and so on. In spite of this the daughters of lawyers are not always, or even typically, lawyers, nor the sons of doctors, doctors.

The Eugenic Difference Principle

Were genetic engineers capable of both selecting life plans and enhancing capacities then good lives might be generated almost precisely to parental or social order. This is not the case, however. While a future genetics may allow the directed modification of some capacities, the directed generation of life plans is out of the question. We should therefore not set out to modify them. I now set out to show that conclusions about the inadvisability of seeking to shape life plans have consequences for capacity enhancement.

In what follows I draw a parallel between life-plan-respecting enhancement of capacities and John Rawls's theory of justice. Rawls's difference principle allows deviation from equal distribution of goods such as liberty and opportunity only when an unequal distribution helps everybody, most especially those occupying the worst-off positions in society. We arrive at this account by asking what arrangements rational choosers would opt for if deprived of all information about their actual positions. The imagined rational contractor cannot choose her social position and so seeks to do best by the worst off.[26]

The need for principles of justice is obvious once we observe the possibility of conflict between individuals pursuing different life plans. We see the need for similar principles governing the allocation of goods of genetic engineering, when we note how the allocation of goods to one potential life plan can impact on other potential life plans.

Capacity enhancements boosting an individual's chances of successfully pursuing a given life plan will often reduce that individual's chances of successfully pursuing alternative life plans. A stock-market trader needs to marry quickness of decision with aggression. These traits would be harmful in a poet or painter for whom reflection is demanded. Any Olympic game brings together a wide range of exceptional physiques. Having a body suitable for one discipline tends to exclude other disciplines. Larger weightlifters would be well advised not to harbour serious ambitions in horse-riding, equally equestrians should not expect to make the basketball team. At a higher level of abstraction, differing political philosophies favor potentially conflicting personality types. A communitarian will emphasize receptiveness to important local cultural traditions in the good life. Liberals may be more interested in a life plan that perhaps incorporates elements from a local culture but is capable of substantial independence from it.

We can return now to the liberal eugenicist's parallel between improvements stemming from environmental modification, and improvements stemming from modifying DNA.

Ideally capacity development is internally driven. When a person chooses for herself which capacities to improve, their development tends to be appropriately sensitive to her life plan. The resulting narrowing of the range of potential life plans will be an unavoidable part of the adapting of capacities to this chosen plan.

Both genetic engineering and parent-administered environmental engineering by education or nutrition are externally driven attempts to improve capacities. Externally driven capacity improvements can be divided into two categories. Education and diet can be selected by parents in a way that is sensitive to the child's life plan. Of course, in young children we will not find anything like a well-defined, precisely worked-out plan. Yet, almost from the beginning, there is something to guide parental efforts; some decisions about life plans have been taken. A nascent life plan may reveal itself in aversions to particular lessons or types of sporting activities. As a child's life plan fills out she will tend to take over much of the task of capacity development. Any remaining parental input will be more and more specifically targeted at the capacities required for the chosen plan.

In seeking to produce enhancements by modifying nutrition or education we can decide to act in a way that ignores the child's evolving life plan. Sometimes parents hope to live out unfulfilled components of their own life plans through their children. Enforced rigorous piano lessons or cricket training risk creating a mismatch between developed capacities and life plans.

Earlier I argued that the environmental specificity and sensitivity of life plans makes them inaccessible to genetic engineers. I suggest that this means that the manner of capacity-shaping possible for the genetic engineer necessarily falls into the second category of externally driven enhancement. The genetic engineer is forced to act in a way that ignores the individual's life plan.

Does this rule out any program of capacity-enhancement? I think not. However, in the light of the inaccessibility of life plans to genetic engineers I propose the following Rawlsian maximin constraint on capacity enhancement. Goods of genetic engineering must be allocated to an individual in a way that improves prospects associated with all possible life plans – most especially the worst off potential life plan.

Pursuit of the parallel between Rawlsian justice and genuine enhancement of life prospects allows us to respond to certain varieties of optimizing eugenics. One kind of optimizer advocates a policy resembling that of the utilitarian who countenances large gaps in the goods attaching to different positions in society to improve average or total social utility.[27] The optimizing eugenicist will accept significantly reduced prospects for a small range of life plans so long as this is compensated for by a significant boost in prospects attaching to a wider range of plans, or perhaps a huge boost for a single plan. The maximin constraint directs against this kind of reasoning. It would be wrong to gamble on future life plan choices. No capacity-enhancement will be acceptable unless it also boosts prospects associated with the least well-served life plan. The aim is to equip the person-to-be no matter what life plan she opts for.

Perhaps we can do more than just influence probabilities that certain life plans will be chosen. The discovery and potential manipulation of genes for homosexuality may enable us to produce a population either devoid of gay life plans or alternatively containing exclusively gay life plans. Success in this undertaking would presumably have consequences for capacity enhancements. The elimination of the genetic basis of the life plan might justify our designing into a fetus enhancements that are incompatible with a gay life plan, whatever those enhancements might be. Note just what we would have to do in order to use quality of life considerations to justify such a move. We would need to do much more than identify and be capable of manipulating genes such as GAY1 that may contribute to male homosexuality. Even if Hamer is right about GAY1, the elimination of the gene by itself would not rule out a gay life plan. We would be required to find and appropriately modify any gene necessary for homosexuality. Since homosexuality is likely to be multiply environmentally and genetically realizable, any such undertaking would require huge chunks of a genome to be excised.

I now anticipate a worry about the application of the eugenic maximin requirement. I observed that tailoring capacities to one life plan can disadvantage other plans. In some cases we will find life plans that are unusually well served by an individual's natural arrangement of capacities. Must the genetic engineer flatten these natural peaks in order to improve prospects associated with less well served plans? If so, the age of genetic engineering may have to do without the 'unbalanced' geniuses to whom history owes great works of art and scientific advances.

Concern for quality of life might support some smoothing out. Think again of the parallel with environmental advantages. Had a 6-year-old Mozart mixed with children of his own age rather than performing musical exhibitions throughout Europe, we would probably not now have *The Marriage of Figaro* or *Don Giovanni*. He might, instead, have become a better adjusted adult. Eighteenth-century child welfare officers, had there been such things, are likely to have used quality of life considerations to justify intervention in Mozart's upbringing. Twenty-fifth-century genetic engineers may use similar reasoning to modify some naturally produced genetic patterns.

Such a conclusion is not enforced, however. The maximin requirement applies to proposed *modifications* to a given array of potential and possible capacities. Improvements will need to be justified by their boosting prospects associated with the least well served plan. On finding that a potential person has a certain naturally endowed array of capacities we can leave it open to the parent not to intervene at all.

Earlier I sketched liberal arguments against the moral significance of the therapeutic/eugenic distinction. My Rawlsian approach makes it clear why interventions intuitively falling under the heading of therapeutic engineering often deserve more attention than those intuitively falling under the heading of eugenic engineering. The deficiencies targeted by therapeutic goods of genetic engineering impede a wide range of life plans. We have no blanket ban on modifications conventionally recognized as eugenic, however. There are likely to be ways in which we can both enhance and protect the diverse potential ends of future persons. Some improvements to physical abilities will be plan specific, thereby running the risk of ruling much out; others will support a rather wide range of plans. Adding extra centimeters to produce a better basketballer falls into the first category, increasing resistance to 'flu, more likely into the second category.

What of the fraught issue of the potential enhancement of intelligence? Uncertainty about the impact of our genetic interventions will be very important here; according to some estimates there are between 30 000 and 50 000 genes that feed into human intelligence.[28] Any intervention will require good understanding of the vast tangle of gene/gene and gene/environment interactions.

However, once this information is obtained it is not clear that intelligence is the kind of capacity that should be enhanced. Two widely held views about intelligence will have different implications.

Advocates of general intelligence or *g* propose that there is some domain general cognitive ability that explains performance across a very wide range of tasks.[29] Differences in *g* explain differences in performance in areas ranging from mathematical skill, through musical ability to reading comprehension. If this is the true view of intelligence we might well look favorably on a program of enhancement. Boosting *g* promises to improve performance across a wide range of areas without ruling out any.

There is an alternative multiple intelligence defended by Howard Gardner, according to which a range of distinct intelligence modules each accounts for performance in a relatively circumscribed area.[30] Musical intelligence will differ from mathematical intelligence which, in turn, will differ from social intelligence, and so on. This model of intelligence might require us to be considerably more choosy in our enhancing. Gardner indicates that some intelligences conflict. A study of intelligence development in children found a tendency under certain circumstances for superior artistic performance to interfere with certain spatial skills.[31] If Gardner turns out to be right, and conflicts between intelligences are ubiquitous, we should be wary of any proposed intelligence enhancements.

Clearly there is much more to be said. However, I have offered a preliminary sketch of a eugenics program that is not opposed to the diversity of life plans that characterizes liberal societies. In ensuring that the internal arrangements of goods of genetic engineering do not rule out possible life plans we guarantee that these plans will continue to be represented in society. We therefore need not fear an ideologically uniform post-enhancement world.

Is this program really a liberal one? Some liberal eugenicists will complain about the limitations on the freedom of prospective parents, arguing that there is relatively little room to improve life plans in accordance with values. I have justified these restrictions by pointing to the liberty of prospective offspring. Eugenically choosy parents are likely to produce a mismatch between capacities and life plans. Enhancing in accordance with the maximin requirement promises to expand the range of genuine life plan choices for, and therefore the liberty of, a future person.

Notes

1 Francis Galton, *Inquiries into Human Faculty and its Development* (London: J. M. Dent, 1883). For informative histories of eugenics see Daniel Kevles, *In the Name of Eugenics: Genetics and the Uses of Human Heredity* (Berkeley: University of California Press, 1985) and Diane B. Paul, *Controlling Human Heredity: 1865 to the Present* (New Jersey: Humanities Press, 1995).

2 Defenders of some version of liberal eugenics include Jonathan Glover, *What Sort of People Should There Be?* (Harmondsworth: Penguin, 1984), ch. 2 and 3; John Harris, *Wonderwoman and Superman: The Ethics of Human Biotechnology* (Oxford: Oxford University Press, 1992); Philip Kitcher, *The Lives to Come: The Genetic Revolution and Human Possibilities* (New York: Simon and Schuster, 1996); Robert Nozick, *Anarchy, State and Utopia* (Oxford: Blackwell, 1974), p. 315; John Robertson, *Children of Choice: Freedom and the New Reproductive Technologies* (Princeton: University of Princeton Press, 1994), and Peter Singer and Deane Wells, *The Reproduction Revolution: New Ways of Making Babies* (Oxford: Oxford University Press, 1984).

3 Interview with Watson in the *Sunday Telegraph* (London), 16 February 1997.

4 See Kitcher, *The Lives to Come*, ch. 5, and Jeff Lyon and Peter Corner, *Altered Fates: Gene Therapy and the* Retooling of Human Life (New York: Norton, 1996), for descriptions of the various therapies.

5 See David Heyd, *Genethics: Moral Issues in the Creation of People* (Berkeley: University of California Press, 1992), for skepticism about this way of talking.

6 Jeff Lyon and Peter Corner, *Altered Fates*, p. 492.

7 James Watson, "A Personal View of the Project," in Daniel Kevles and Leroy Hood (eds), *The Code of Codes: Scientific and Social Issues in the Human Genome Project* (Cambridge, MA: Harvard University Press, 1992), occupies the scientifically ambitious end of the spectrum. Richard Lewontin, *Biology as Ideology: The Doctrine of DNA* (New York: Harper Perennial, 1992), is more pessimistic both about scientific and moral possibilities.

8 This argument can also be found in Harris, *Wonderwoman and Superman*; Singer and Wells, *The Reproduction Revolution*, and Glover, *What Sort of People Should There Be?*

9 Robertson, *Children of Choice*, p. 167.

10 See Paul, *Controlling Human Heredity*, ch. 3.

11 For discussions of the status of genetic explanations of traits given this interactionist picture of development see Kim Sterelny and Philip Kitcher, "The Return of the Gene," *Journal of Philosophy*, 85 (1988).

12 For a popular presentation of Hamer's claim see Dean Hamer and Peter Copeland, *The Science of Desire: The Search for the Gay Gene and the Biology of Behavior* (New York: Simon & Schuster, 1994).
13 R. Grant Steen, *DNA and Destiny: Nature and Nature in Human Behavior* (New York: Plenum, 1996), p. 194.
14 Finding evidence for a causal link will be only the first step. We will know very little about the exact developmental trajectory of the gene. Hamer confesses that he has no idea how GAY1 might produce its effect.
15 Some commentators argue that there is an important moral distinction between therapies targeted at somatic cell DNA and those targeted at germ line DNA. The effects of somatic cell therapy die with the recipient of the therapy. Germ line modifications are potentially heritable. For effective argument against the moral significance of such a distinction see John Harris, *Wonderwoman and Superman*, ch. 8.
16 For a recent attack on the distinction see Kitcher, *The Lives to Come*, ch. 9.
17 Kitcher, *The Lives to Come*, pp. 212–17.
18 Ibid., p. 289.
19 Robertson, *Children of Choice*, p. 171.
20 See Gregory Kavka, "Upside Risks: Social Consequences of Beneficial Biotechnology," in Carl F. Cranor (ed.), *Are Genes Us? The Social Consequences of the New Genetics* (New Jersey: Rutgers University Press, 1994). There is a complication here. Liberals disagree about the exact relationship between concern for quality of life and parental values. Kitcher writes as if the expression of parental values takes precedence. Prospective parents should be 'encouraged' or 'urged' to look to quality of life, taking it up into their values (Kitcher, *The Lives to Come*, p. 203). Robertson and Glover paint quality of life as imposing limits on the breadth of individual eugenic choice (Robertson, *Children of Choice*, ch. 7; Glover, *What Sort of People Should There Be?*, ch. 3). In a liberal society concern for quality of life will presumably leave some latitude for parents to be guided by their values.
21 See Robert Wright, "Achilles' Helix," *New Republic* (July 9, 1990), and Troy Duster, *Backdoor to Eugenics* (London: Routledge, 1990).
22 See Paul, *Controlling Human Heredity*, pp. 36–9.
23 Sexual selection may seem an inappropriate tool for the early twentieth-century eugenicist. On the Darwinian model, sexual selection often works against conventional natural selection. The peacock's feathers are paradigms of inefficient clumsiness selected only for their appeal to mates. Traits are best purely because they are widely thought to be best. In this way sexual selection falls far short of offering any guarantee of choice-independent value.
24 Kitcher, *The Lives to Come*, p. 200.
25 Singer and Wells, *The Reproduction Revolution*, p. 188.
26 John Rawls, *A Theory of Justice* (Cambridge, MA: Harvard University Press, 1971), *Political Liberalism* (New York: Columbia University Press, 1996).
27 Rawls, *A Theory of Justice*, sections 27, 28.
28 Lyon and Gorner, *Altered Fates*, p. 543.
29 For an account of this view see Mike Anderson, *Intelligence and Development: A Cognitive Theory* (New York: Blackwell, 1992).
30 Howard Gardner, *Frames of Mind: The Theory of Multiple Intelligences* (New York: Basic Books, 1983), *Multiple Intelligences: The Theory in Practice* (New York: Basic Books, 1993).
31 Gardner, *Multiple Intelligences*, p. 96.

19

Lessons from a Dark and Distant Past

Benno Müller-Hill

Abstract

Genetic counselling bridges the interface between genetics and society. Thus a science, human genetics, meets and merges with the beliefs and demands of society. History provides frightening examples of the danger inherent in this process. Two will be discussed: (1) judgement of and measures against race mixing and (2) the policy of sterilization for carriers of supposed inherited mental disorders. There seems now to be general agreement that a genetic counsellor is not a scientific agent of the state whose job is to execute its decrees. But there seems to be less agreement whether a genetic counsellor should be nothing but a scientific expert and advertiser of the market.

Introduction

The daily burden of a genetic counsellor is heavy: she[1] has to follow the latest results of a fast developing field. The advent of the Human Genome Project (see *Human Genome News*, a monthly publication sponsored by the US Department of Energy and the National Institutes of Health since 1989) guarantees that the conceptual and technical developments will be faster here than in any other medical field. And she does not operate in a social vacuum. It has not yet been determined how legislation on the use of genetic information will affect insurers, employers and the state itself. She has to teach the client or patient both the scientific truth and the social reality and – possibly – the different values held by herself and others.

All this sounds too much to deal with. When I present here a chapter on the history of the field I can already hear the reaction: 'Forget it!' And I will not hide the fact that I am not an MD, that I have never done any genetic counselling myself and – the final blow – that I am not a professional historian of science but a molecular biologist who has worked only peripherally on problems of human genetics (Kang et al., 1987). My only credentials for this article are a book (Müller-Hill, 1988) and some articles (Müller-Hill, 1987, 1991a, 1991b) on the history of human genetics in Germany in 1933–45.

The borders between science and beliefs were and are still today ill-defined in human genetics. It may pay to define science as a sum of knowledge which has predictive power. This sum of knowledge is available to all scientists, not just some of them. For example, the maps of the four chromosomes of the fruit-fly *Drosophila melanogaster* can be used to accommodate more genes, but they will never change fundamentally or become irrelevant. All geneticists will read a DNA sequence on a gel in essentially the same way and all of them will discuss the number of open reading frames coded by such a piece of DNA in the same manner. These are examples of hard science. Thus somebody who deliberately, like Lysenko (1949), denies this network of knowledge stands outside science. The German human geneticists active during the Third Reich accepted Mendelism. They stood within science (Müller-Hill, 1988; Proctor, 1988; Weindling, 1989).

From Angus Clarke (ed.), *Genetic Counselling: Practice and Principles* (London: Routledge, 1994), pp. 133–41. Reproduced with permission.

All human geneticists will agree upon the molecular defect in sickle-cell anaemia, but there will often be disagreement where the relevant phenotypes are supposed mental defects. Here the human geneticists have to rely upon the results of psychiatry, psychology, ethnology and so on. In these fields one finds, of course, temporary agreement among the experts to a greater or lesser degree, but after some years the agreement may shift totally. Another field in which the agreement among scientists has shifted over time is the study of race, and judgements about 'racial mixing'.

The treatments or measures proposed by human geneticists also change with time. There was a time when sterilization was considered *the* treatment of choice; now it is abortion. I will discuss here the history of this issue as it has unfolded in Germany and Sweden. The role of the patient has also changed: the patient has turned into a client. This is more appropriate. The clients no longer have to accept the decisions of the counsellor; now they buy advice to help them make the best choice from what is available. Thus, the genetic counsellor no longer decides the fate of a patient: she teaches a client. Or to put it differently: she advertises the various options available in the market. But in advertising, what is truth?

The Case of Race Mixing

The notion of different races existed at least a century prior to the rediscovery of Mendel's work in 1900. At that time the community of European and US American white scientists (Kevles, 1985) shared the same low opinion of all black people. They almost all agreed that black people were unable to do abstract thinking. The only question was how profound this inability actually was. The genocide of black ethnic groups was regarded by many as normal and inevitable.

Under these conditions it is not surprising that a young German assistant professor of anatomy, Eugen Fischer, who was deeply interested in human Mendelian genetics, applied successfully for a grant in 1908 to study a small community of the offspring of white settlers and black women in one of the German African colonies – now Namibia. He studied both the physical and psychological characteristics of the members of this community. He came to the conclusion that Mendel's laws were operating for *all* phenotypes he analysed. The black–white hybrids (he called them 'bastards') were thus in their intelligence somewhere between the high white and the low black level (Fischer, 1913).

At the time when Fischer began his work, intermarriage between black women and white German settlers was against the law. The particular legal situation was thus in principle similar to the one then prevailing in several southern states of the USA. In Namibia the general situation was certainly worse: the German colonial policy was genocidal (Swan, 1991). When Germany lost its colonies a few years later during the First World War, the whole problem became almost academic for the German human geneticists. However, the French used colonial soldiers to occupy the western part of Germany. Thus about 600 coloured children were born in Germany during those years. They were all illegally sterilized in 1937–8 after being analysed by Eugen Fischer and his colleagues (Müller-Hill, 1988).

Eugen Fischer became the first director of a new institute of the Kaiser Wilhelm-Gesellschaft (now Max Planck-Gesellschaft) founded in 1927 to promote human genetics and eugenics. He and his institute had an excellent international reputation. He was president of the International Congress of Genetics held in Berlin in the same year. In 1929 he was asked by C. B. Davenport (Cold Spring Harbor) to become chairman of the committee on racial crosses (mixing) of the international Federation of Eugenic Organizations. His institute received a grant from the Rockefeller Foundation in 1932 for the work on twins done by his subdirector Otmar von Verschuer. He was elected rector of Berlin University in 1933 just before the Nazis came to power. In his rectorial speech he praised the law which led to the expulsion of Jewish professors and other civil servants as a scientific necessity. He did the same when the Nuremberg laws were announced which prohibited German–Jewish intermarriage and sexual intercourse. He was certainly not alone in defending the Nuremberg laws as arising from scientific necessity. German geneticists also compared the Nuremberg laws with the various American laws prohibiting black–white intermarriage and pointed out that the Nuremberg laws were rather lenient in comparison.

It was then and only then that the race concept held by the international community of geneticists was seen to be untenable. One could possibly argue against intermarriage of blacks and whites but it was more than difficult to defend the Nuremberg laws to Jewish colleagues. When – finally – in 1945 Nazism and its defenders fell, it became generally impossible to defend prohibitions of interracial marriage. This shift in opinion was not a shift in knowledge caused by new scientific results, but rather a shift brought about by political, social and cultural factors (Teich, 1990).

Sterilization in Germany

Sterilization was regarded as the negative measure of choice in eugenics or race hygiene. Its proponents pointed out that the operations are easy to carry out in both males and females and that the operation does not interfere with the sexual life of the person operated on. I will not attempt to give here a full historical panorama (see, for example, Kevles, 1985; Trombley, 1988). Instead I will concentrate on two countries, Germany (Bock, 1986) and Sweden (Broberg and Tyden, 1991; Lindquist, 1991).

The German eugenicists (or, as the anti-Semites among them called themselves, the race hygienicists) pushed for a law legalizing sterilization long before the Nazis came to power. There was no chance of such a law legalizing involuntary sterilization before or during the Weimar Republic. Only the Nazis advocated that. The proposed law therefore allowed only voluntary sterilization for a defined group of persons, including the schizophrenics and the feeble-minded. The realists among the German eugenicists pushed for the law as a first step. A few of them actually believed in the necessity of the patient's free choice; most others did not. When the Nazis came to power they immediately passed a law allowing sterilization in the exact words of the draft of the Weimar Republic but with two major changes: they allowed involuntary, coercive sterilization and included alcoholism as one of the conditions (Gütt et al., 1934). All private doctors who noted one of the listed defects in one of their patients had to notify officially the nearest MD active in the state-run health-care system (Schrader, 1936). This official had then to bring the case before the court. The court decision was made by two MDs and one judge. An appeal was possible. What looked to the outside as a safe and just procedure was in fact for most victims a sham. Neither the victims nor their lawyers were allowed to see the detailed diagnosis. Often the victims only learned in court that they were to be sterilized. The exact number of patients sterilized is known for the first three years, 1934–6 (62 463; 71 760; 64 646), and one can assume that the numbers did not change substantially until the beginning of the war. Thus during those years about 0.1 per cent of the German population was sterilized per year. The misery of these 350 000 persons, which was produced by coercive genetic counselling should not be underestimated or forgotten.

The community of German human geneticists also supported the sterilization policies as a means of stopping the spread of racially undesirable genes. Three different human groups were envisaged:

1 All coloured people. As stated before, all half-coloured Germans were illegally sterilized in 1937/8. The human geneticists helped in defining the criteria for selecting the victims.
2 Most Gypsies. The Gypsies living in Germany were regarded as the descendants of an originally pure Indo-Germanic tribe who, after coming to Europe, had intermarried with the lowest criminal strata of all European countries. According to this view most Gypsies were not pure Gypsies but *Mischlinge* who had to be sterilized because of their non-Gypsy genes. This policy was actively supported by the community of German human geneticists.
3 When the total annihilation of the Jews became the policy in 1941/2, discussion about the possible sterilization of all *Juden-Mischlinge* who had at least one Jewish grandparent began. Eugen Fischer was present as an honorary guest at a conference held on March 26–28 1941 in Frankfurt, where an official speaker asked for the sterilization of all quarter-Jews. Fischer's collaborator and successor von Verschuer reported on the conference in his journal (Müller-Hill, 1988). The relevant bureaucracy soon understood that the realization of the project was impossible for purely practical reasons: during the war all hospital beds were needed, the officials who would be needed were busy in the war effort, etc. These measures were therefore never implemented.

It has to be pointed out here that the criteria which defined partly coloured people, half-Gypsies or quarter-Jews were morally revolting but logically consistent. I would like to discuss this in the typical case of a part-Jew: it was only after 1800 in Germany that a substantial number of Jews left their religion to be baptized and to intermarry with non-Jewish Christian Germans. Thus a Jew was defined as the descendant of persons who had not been baptized in 1800. If a person defined by such church documents found himself pure Jewish or half-Jewish in 1940, the only legal way to avoid deportation and likely death was to claim that the legal (Jewish) father was not the biological father. Hundreds of such cases kept the German human geneticists busy. The clients who asked for help hoped, of course, that they could bribe the human geneticists in one way or another to falsify their paternity and to save their lives. The human geneticists knew that telling the truth meant suffering and possible or certain death for the client, but that lying too often would undermine their scientific reputation. The Austrian human geneticists seem to have been totally corrupt; the German ones sided with science and inhumanity. One may thus say that the German geneticists prostituted genetics: they were procurers who sold the most intimate knowledge of their patients and clients to torturers and murderers. The documentation can be found in von Verschuer's textbook of human genetics, which was published in 1941; it is worth noting that von Verschuer never had the slightest problem in his academic career in Germany after the war.

Sterilization in Sweden

One may argue that Germany is so untypical that it is not a pertinent example. So let's look at an impeccable European democracy: Sweden (Broberg and Tyden, 1991; Lindquist, 1991). In the first half of this century the Swedish government was run by social democrats. Yet Sweden was the first European country to found – in 1922 – an Institute for Race Biology at the University of Uppsala. Its director, Herman Lundborg, had close connections with the German (human) geneticists and he sympathized later with the German Nazis. He retired around the time the Nazis took power in Germany. His successor, Gunnar Dahlberg, paved the way (partly a semantic one) from the old race hygiene or eugenics to modern medical genetics.

A law legalizing sterilization in Sweden was passed in 1934 and its scope was broadened in 1941. Between 1935 and 1975, when the law was revoked, 62 888 persons, almost all of them women, were sterilized in Sweden (Broberg and Tyden, 1991). The highest number (2 351) was sterilized in 1949. Many of the sterilized were *tattare*, the Swedish name for part-Gypsies. When sterilization began in 1935, it was almost always for eugenic reasons; when it ended in 1975, it was almost entirely for medical reasons. The turning point in the reasoning was the year 1948.

During the years when more then 1 000 persons per year were sterilized (from 1942 to 1975) the incidence of Swedish sterilization was between 15 and 30 per cent of that in Nazi Germany. And this happened under a law which did not allow sterilization against a person's will! How was this possible? The victims were badly informed and mildly coerced. Lindquist's book (1991) contains interviews with several victims. They tell how they were tricked into the operation-room and how sterilization mutilated them for life.

In Lindquist's book one of the doctors who advocated sterilization is interviewed by the author (pp. 28–31). He remembers 'the time was like that. All of us thought like that... We dreamed we could improve human body and soul.... That's how the geneticist saw it then and some of them see it still today.'

Directive versus Non-Directive Counselling Today

I have tried to show that belief in the various dogmas of psychiatry, psychology, social theory, etc. led – and not only in Germany – to a treatment of patients and clients which in retrospect seems incredibly brutal and pointless. It becomes clear that directive counselling was regarded most suspiciously after the defeat of Germany and was therefore abandoned first in the USA and later in Germany too. To the best of my knowledge directive counselling is still practised only in the former eastern bloc countries. But that is a different story.

Non-directive counselling leaves the decision to the patient or client. Here the counsellor just explains all the options, as honestly as she can. The counsellor is no longer responsible for the decisions and acts of the patient or client. The genetic diagnosis poses in general no problems on the technical side. It is straightforward. The existential not the medical risks pose the problem. Is it sufficient for the counsellor just to mention them? Or should she actively try to diminish them when possible?

It is to be expected that the diagnostic power of medical genetics will increase dramatically as more and more of the human genome becomes known. I am not thinking so much about extremely rare diseases but on the contrary about common ones. So far – at least in Europe – employers and insurers have by and large resisted the temptation to get genetic information about employees or clients and to arrange contracts according to risk estimates. But times are changing (Billings et al., 1992). Can the genetic counsellor remain neutral in this development? Can she maintain that all she does is to make available (or even promote) the cheapest solution in an objective manner?

The enthusiasm of those who argue in this way is understandable. In a world in which the market and nothing but the market sets the standard, their activities are impeccable. They just sell the truth. They are also supported by philosophy. Truth is the highest value for most philosophers. Even the great Kant argued that truth is so important that you have to give the murderer the address of your friend, if he asks for it (1797). I would like to point out here that the German human geneticists did just that under the Nazis.

So what is to be done? Non-directive counselling was a step forward beyond the terrible rigidity of directive counselling. Yet it seems just one of several additional necessary steps. Let me call the next step 'Hippocratic non-directive counselling'. I would like to recall that the eighth commandment does not say 'Thou shalt tell the truth' but 'Thou shalt not bear false witness.' This implies that the counsellor has to see that justice is not lost in the process of counselling. Justice seems to me to be lost where there is no help for the weak but when they are just left to be destroyed by the forces of the market.

References

Billings, P. R., Kohn, M. A., de Cuevas, M. et al. (1992). 'Discrimination as a consequence of genetic testing', *American Journal of Human Genetics*, 50: 476–82.

Bock, G. (1986). *Zwangssterilisation im Nationalsozialismus* (Opladen: Westdeutscher Verlag).

Broberg, G. and Tyden, M. (1991). *Oönskade i Folkhemmet. Rashygien i och Sterilisering i Sverige* (Stockholm: Gidlunds).

Fischer, E. (1913). *Die Rehoboter Bastarde und das Bastardi-sierungs-problem beim Menschen* (Jena: Gustav Fischer).

Gütt, A., Rüdin, E. and Ruttke, F. (1934), *Gesetz zur Verhütung erbkranken Nachwuchses vom 14. Juli 1934* (Munich: J. F. Lehmanns).

Kang, J., Lemaire, H.-G., Unterbeck, A. et al. (1987). 'The precursor of Alzheimer's disease amyloid A4 protein resembles a cell surface receptor', *Nature*, 325: 733–6.

Kant, I. (1797). Über ein vermeintliches Recht aus Menschenliebe zu lügen', *Berlinische Blätter*, 1: 301–4. Reprinted in *Werkausgabe*, VIII (1977), Frankfurt am Main: Suhrkamp, pp. 637–43.

Kevles, D. (1985). *In the Name of Eugenics. Genetics and the Use of Human Heredity* (New York: Alfred A. Knopf and (1986) Harmondsworth: Penguin).

Lindquist, B. (1991). *Förädlade Svenskar – Drömmen om at Skapa en Bättre Mäniska* (Hässleholm: Alfabeta Bokförlag).

Lysenko, T. D. (1949). 'On the situation in biological science', in *The Situation in Biological Science*, (Moscow: Proceedings of the Lenin Academy of Agricultural Sciences of the USSR. Foreign Language Publishing House), pp. 11–50.

Müller-Hill, B. (1987). 'Genetics after Auschwitz', *Holocaust and Genocide Studies*, 2: 3–20.

——(1988). *Murderous Science. Elimination by Scientific Selection of Jews, Gypsies and Others, Germany 1933–1945* (Oxford: Oxford University Press).

——(1991a). 'Psychiatry in the Nazi era', in S. Bloch and P. Chodoff (eds), *Psychiatric Ethics*, vol. 2 (Oxford and New York: Oxford University Press), pp. 461–72.

——(1991b). 'Bioscience in totalitarian regimes: the lesson to be learned from Nazi Germany', in D. J. Roy, B. E. Wynne and R. W. Olds (eds), *Bioscience and Society*, Schering Foundation Workshop 1 (London: John Wiley) pp. 67–76.

Proctor, R. O. (1988). *Racial Hygiene. Medicine under the Nazis* (Cambridge, MA: Harvard University Press).

Schrader, E. (1936). 'Die psychologische Einstellung des Arztes zum Untersuchten bei erbbiologischer Begutachtung', *Der Erbarzt*, 3: 85–7.

Swan, J. (1991). 'The final solution in South West Africa', *Quarterly Journal of Military History*, 3: 36–55.

Teich, M. (1990) 'The unmastered past of human genetics', in M. Teich and R. Porter (eds), *Fin de Siècle and its Legacy* (Cambridge: Cambridge University Press), pp. 296–324.

Trombley, S. (1988). *The Right to Reproduce: A History of Coercive Sterilization* (London: Weidenfeld & Nicolson).

Verschuer, O. von (1941). *Leitfaden der Rassenhygiene* (Leipzig: Georg Thieme).

Weindling, P. (1989). *Health, Race and German Politics between National Unification and Nazism 1870–1945* (Cambridge: Cambridge University Press).

Note

1 The counsellor may, of course, also be male.

PART IV

Life and Death Issues

Introduction

20

The Sanctity of Life

Jonathan Glover

> I cannot but have reverence for all that is called life. I cannot avoid compassion for all that is called life. That is the beginning and foundation of morality. (Albert Schweitzer, *Reverence for Life*.)

> To persons who are not murderers, concentration camp administrators, or dreamers of sadistic fantasies, the inviolability of human life seems to be so self-evident that it might appear pointless to inquire into it. To inquire into it is embarrassing as well because, once raised, the question seems to commit us to beliefs we do not wish to espouse and to confront us with contradictions which seem to deny what is self-evident. (Edward Shils, 'The Sanctity of Life', in D. H. Labby, *Life or Death: Ethics and Options*, 1968)

Most of us think it is wrong to kill people. Some think it is wrong in all circumstances, while others think that in special circumstances (say, in a just war or in self-defence) some killing may be justified. But even those who do not think killing is always wrong normally think that a special justification is needed. The assumption is that killing can at best only be justified to avoid a greater evil.

It is not obvious to many people what the answer is to the question '*Why* is killing wrong?' It is not clear whether the wrongness of killing should be treated as a kind of moral axiom, or whether it can be explained by appealing to some more fundamental principle or set of principles.

From *Causing Death and Saving Lives* (London: Penguin, 1990), pp. 39–59. Reprinted with permission.

One very common view is that some principle of the sanctity of life has to be included among the ultimate principles of any acceptable moral system.

In order to evaluate the view that life is sacred, it is necessary to distinguish between two different kinds of objection to killing: direct objections and those based on side-effects.

1 Direct Objections and Side-effects

Direct objections to killing are those that relate solely to the person killed. Side-effects of killings are effects on people other than the one killed. Many of the possible reasons for not killing someone appeal to side-effects. (To call them 'side-effects' is not to imply that they must be less important than the direct objections.) When a man dies or is killed, his parents, wife, children or friends may be made sad. His family may always have a less happy atmosphere and very likely less money to spend. The fatherless children may grow up to be less secure and confident than they would have been. The community loses whatever good contribution the man might otherwise have made to it. Also, an act of killing may help weaken the general reluctance to take life or else be thought to do so. Either way, it may do a bit to undermine everyone's sense of security.

Most people would probably give some weight to these side-effects in explaining the wrongness of killing, but would say that they are not the whole story, or even the main part of it. People who say this hold that there are direct objections to killing, independent of effects on others. This view can be brought out by an imaginary case in which an act of killing would have no harmful side-effects.

Suppose I am in prison, and have an incurable disease from which I shall very soon die. The man who shares my cell is bound to stay in prison for the rest of his life, as society thinks he is too dangerous to let out. He has no friends, and all his relations are dead. I have a poison that I could put in his food without him knowing it and that would kill him without being detectable. Everyone else would think he died from natural causes.

In this case, the objections to killing that are based on side-effects collapse. No one will be sad or deprived. The community will not miss his contribution. People will not feel insecure, as no one will know a murder has been committed. And even the possible argument based on one murder possibly weakening my own reluctance to take life in future carries no weight here, since I shall die before having opportunity for further killing. It might even be argued that consideration of side-effects tips the balance positively in favour of killing this man, since the cost of his food and shelter is a net loss to the community.

Those of us who feel that in this case we cannot accept that killing the man would be either morally right or morally neutral must hold that killing is at least sometimes wrong for reasons independent of side-effects. One version of this view that killing is directly wrong is the doctrine of the sanctity of life. To state this doctrine in an acceptable way is harder than it might at first seem.

2 Stating the Principle of the Sanctity of Life

The first difficulty is a minor one. We do not want to state the principle in such a way that it must have overriding authority over other considerations. To say 'taking life is always wrong' commits us to absolute pacifism. But clearly a pacifist and a non-pacifist can share the view that killing is in itself an evil. They need only differ over when, if ever, killing is permissible to avoid other evils. A better approximation is 'taking life is directly wrong', where the word 'directly' simply indicates that the wrongness is independent of effects on other people. But even this will not quite do. For, while someone who believes in the sanctity of life must hold that killing is directly wrong, not everyone who thinks that killing is sometimes or always directly wrong has to hold that life is sacred. (It is possible to believe that killing is directly wrong only where the person does not want to die or where the years of which he is deprived would have been happy ones. These objections to killing have nothing to do with side-effects and yet do not place value on life merely for its own sake.) The best formulation seems to be 'taking life is intrinsically wrong'.

There is another problem about what counts as 'life'. Does this include animals? When we think of higher animals, we may want to say 'yes', even if we want to give animal life less weight than human life. But do we want to count it wrong to tread on an ant or kill a mosquito? And, even if we are prepared to treat all animal life as sacred, there are problems about plant life. Plants are living things. Is weeding the garden wrong? Let us avoid these difficulties for the moment by stating the principle in terms of human life. When we have become clearer about the reasons for thinking it wrong to kill people, we will be better placed to see whether the same reasons should make us respect animal or plant life as well. So, to start with, we have the principle: 'taking human life is intrinsically wrong.'

Can any explanation be given of the belief that taking human life is intrinsically wrong? Someone who simply says that this principle is an axiom of his moral system, and refuses to give any further explanation, cannot be 'refuted' unless his system is made inconsistent by the inclusion of this principle. (And, even then, he might choose to give up other beliefs rather than this one.) The strategy of this chapter will be to try to cast doubt on the acceptability of this principle by looking at the sort of explanation that might be given by a supporter who was prepared to enter into some discussion of it. My aim will be to suggest that the doctrine of the sanctity of life is not acceptable, but that there is embedded in it a moral view we should retain. We should reject the view that taking human life is *intrinsically* wrong, but retain the view that it is normally *directly* wrong: that most acts of killing people would be wrong in the absence of harmful side-effects.

The concept of human life itself raises notorious boundary problems. When does it begin? Is an eight-month fetus already a living human being? How about a newly fertilized egg? These questions need discussing, but it seems preferable to decide first on the central problem of why we value human life, and on that basis to draw its exact boundaries, rather than to stipulate the boundaries arbitrarily in advance. But there is another boundary problem that can be discussed first, as it leads us straight into the central issue about the sanctity of life. This boundary problem is about someone fallen irreversibly into a coma: does he still count as a living human being? (It may be said that what is important is not the status of 'human being', but of 'person'. In this chapter I write as though human beings are automatically persons. In the later discussion of abortion, there will be some attention given to those who say of a fetus that, while it is certainly a member of species *Homo sapiens*, it is not yet a person.)

3 The Boundary Between Life and Death

It was once common to decide that someone was dead because, among other things, his heart had stopped beating. But now it is well known that people can sometimes be revived from this state, so some other criterion has to be used. Two candidates sometimes proposed are that 'death' should be defined in terms of the irreversible loss of all electrical activity in the brain or that it should be defined in terms of irreversible loss of consciousness.

Of these two definitions, the one in terms of irreversible loss of consciousness is preferable. There is no point in considering the electrical activity unless one holds the (surely correct) view that it is a necessary condition of the person being conscious. It seems better to define 'death' in terms of irreversible loss of consciousness itself, since it is from this alone that our interest in the electrical activity derives. This is reinforced by the fact that, while loss of all brain activity guarantees loss of consciousness, the converse does not hold. People incurably in a vegetable state normally have some electrical activity in some parts of the brain. To define 'death' in terms of irreversible loss of consciousness is not to deny that our best evidence for this may often be continued absence of electrical activity. And, when we understand more about the neurophysiological basis of consciousness, we may reach the stage of being able to judge conclusively from the state of his brain whether or not someone has irreversibly lost consciousness.

An argument sometimes used in favour of the definition in terms of irreversible loss of consciousness is that it avoids some of the problems that nowadays arise for adherents of more traditional criteria. Glanville Williams[1] has discussed a hypothetical case that might raise legal difficulties. Suppose a man's heart stops beating and, just as the doctor is about to revive him, the man's heir plunges a dagger into his breast. Glanville Williams wonders if this would count as murder or merely as illegal interference with a corpse. If, to avoid complications, we assume that there was a reasonable expectation that the man would otherwise have been revived, the question is one of the boundary between life and death. Making irreversible loss of consciousness the boundary has the advantage, over more traditional criteria, of making the heir's act one of murder.

It may be objected that, in ordinary language, it makes sense to say of someone that he is irreversibly comatose but still alive. This must be admitted. The proposed account of death is a piece of conceptual revision, motivated by the belief that, for such purposes as deciding whether or not to switch off a respirator, the irreversibly comatose and the traditionally 'dead' are on a par. Those who reject this belief will want to reject the 'irreversible loss of consciousness' account of death. And, if they do reject it, they are not forced to revert to traditional views that give a paradoxical answer to the Glanville Williams case. It would be possible to have two tests that must be passed before someone is counted as dead, involving respiratory and circulatory activities stopping *and* brain damage sufficient to make loss of consciousness irreversible. Let us call this the 'double-test' view.

In giving an account of 'death', how should we choose between irreversible loss of consciousness and the double-test view? If we are worried about doctors being wrong in their diagnosis of irreversible loss of consciousness, the double-test view would in practice give an additional safeguard against the respirator being switched off too early. But that is a rather oblique reason, even if of some practical importance. If detecting irreversible loss of consciousness posed no practical problem, how would we then choose between the two views? Appeals to traditional usage are of no value, for what is in question is a proposal for conceptual reform. The only way of choosing is to decide whether or not we attach any value to the preservation of someone irreversibly comatose. Do we value 'life' even if unconscious, or do we value life only as a vehicle for consciousness? Our attitude to the doctrine of the sanctity of life very much depends on our answer to this question.

4 'Being Alive Is Intrinsically Valuable'

Someone who thinks that taking life is intrinsically wrong may explain this by saying that the state of being alive is itself intrinsically valuable. This claim barely rises to the level of an argument for the sanctity of life, for it simply asserts that there is value in what the taking of life takes away.

Against such a view, cases are sometimes cited of people who are either very miserable or in great pain, without any hope of cure. Might such people not be better off dead? But this could be admitted without giving up the view that life is intrinsically valuable. We could say that life has value, but that not being desperately miserable can have even more value.

I have no way of refuting someone who holds that being alive, even though unconscious, is intrinsically valuable. But it is a view that will seem unattractive to those of us who, in our own case, see a life of permanent coma as in no way preferable to death. From the subjective point of view, there is nothing to choose between the two. Schopenhauer saw this clearly when he said of the destruction of the body:

> But actually we feel this destruction only in the evils of illness or of old age; on the other hand, for the *subject*, death itself consists merely in the moment when consciousness vanishes, since the activity of the brain ceases. The extension of the stoppage to all the other parts of the organism which follows this is really already an event after death. Therefore, in a subjective respect, death concerns only consciousness.[2]

Those of us who think that the direct objections to killing have to do with death considered from the standpoint of the person killed will find it natural to regard life as being of value only as a necessary condition of consciousness. For permanently comatose existence is subjectively indistinguishable from death, and unlikely often to be thought intrinsically preferable to it by people thinking of their own future.

5 'Being Conscious Is Intrinsically Valuable'

The believer in the sanctity of life may accept that being alive is only of instrumental value and say that it is consciousness that is intrinsically valuable. In making this claim, he still differs from someone who only values consciousness because it is necessary for happiness. Before we can assess this belief in the intrinsic value of being conscious, it is necessary to distinguish between two different ways in which we may talk about consciousness. Sometimes we talk about 'mere' consciousness and sometimes we talk about what might be called 'a high level of consciousness'.

'Mere' consciousness consists simply in awareness or the having of experiences. When I am awake, I am aware of my environment. I have a stream of consciousness that comes abruptly to a halt if I faint or fades out when I go to sleep (until I have dreams). There are large philosophical problems about the meaning of claims of this kind, which need not be discussed here. I shall assume that we all at some level understand what it is to have experiences, or a stream of consciousness.

But this use of 'consciousness' should be distinguished from another, perhaps metaphorical, use of the word. We sometimes say that men are at a higher level of consciousness than animals, or else that few, if any, peasants are likely to have as highly developed a consciousness as Proust. It is not clear exactly what these claims come to, nor that the comparison between men and animals is of the same sort as the comparison between peasants and Proust. But perhaps what underlies such comparisons is an attempt to talk about a person's experiences in terms of the extent to which they are rich, varied, complex or subtle, or the extent to which they involve emotional responses, as well as various kind of awareness. Again, it is not necessary to discuss here the analysis of the meaning of these claims. It is enough if it is clear that to place value on 'mere' consciousness is different from valuing it for its richness and variety. I shall assume that the claim that being conscious is intrinsically good is a claim about 'mere' consciousness, rather than about a high level of consciousness.

If one is sceptical about the intrinsic value of 'mere' consciousness, as against that of a high level of consciousness, it is hard to see what consideration can be mentioned in its favour. The advocate of this view might ask us to perform a thought experiment of a kind that G. E. Moore would perhaps have liked. We might be asked to imagine two universes, identical except that one contained a being aware of its environment and the other did not. It may be suggested that the universe containing the conscious being would be intrinsically better.

But such a thought experiment seems unconvincing. There is the familiar difficulty that, confronted with a choice so abstract and remote, it may be hard to feel any preference at all. And, since we are dealing with 'mere' consciousness rather than with a high level of consciousness, it is necessary to postulate that the conscious being has no emotional responses. It cannot be pleased or sorry or in pain; it cannot be interested or bored; it is merely aware of its environment. Views may well differ here, but, if I could be brought to take part in this thought experiment at all, I should probably express indifference between the two universes. The only grounds I might have for preferring the universe with the conscious being would be some hope that it might evolve into some more interesting level of consciousness. But to choose on these grounds is not to assign any intrinsic value to 'mere' consciousness.

The belief that the sole reason why it is directly wrong to take human life is the intrinsic value of 'mere' consciousness runs into a problem concerning animals. Many of us place a special value on human life as against animal life. Yet animals, or at least the higher ones, seem no less aware of their surroundings than we are. Suppose there is a flood and I am faced with the choice of either saving a man's life or else saving the life of a cow. Even if all side-effects were left out of account, failure to save the man seems worse than failure to save the cow. The person who believes that the sanctity of life rests solely on the value of 'mere' consciousness is faced with a dilemma. Either he must accept that the life of the cow and the life of the man are in themselves of equal value, or he must give reasons for thinking that cows are less conscious than men or else not conscious at all.

It is hard to defend the view that, while I have good grounds for thinking that other people are conscious, I do not have adequate reasons for thinking that animals are conscious. Humans and animals in many ways respond similarly to their surroundings. Humans have abilities that other animals do not, such as the ability to speak or to do highly abstract reasoning, but it is not only in virtue of these abilities that we say people are conscious. And there is no neurophysiological evidence that suggests that humans alone can have experiences.

The alternative claim is that animals are less conscious than we are. The view that 'mere' consciousness is a matter of degree is attractive when considered in relation to animals. The philosophical literature about our knowledge of other minds is strikingly silent and unhelpful about the animal boundaries of consciousness. How far back down the evolutionary scale does consciousness extend? What kind and degree of complexity must a nervous system exhibit to be the vehicle of experiences? What kind and degree of complexity of behaviour counts as the manifestation of consciousness? At least with our present ignorance of the physiological basis of human consciousness, any clear-cut boundaries of consciousness, drawn between one kind of animal and another, have an air of arbitrariness. For this reason it is attractive to suggest that consciousness is a matter of degree, not stopping abruptly, but fading away slowly as one descends the evolutionary scale.

But the belief that 'mere' consciousness is a matter of degree is obscure as well as attractive. Is it even an intelligible view?

There are two ways in which talk of degrees of consciousness can be made clearer. One is by explaining it in terms of the presence or absence of whole 'dimensions' of consciousness. This is the way in which a blind man is less conscious of his environment than a normal man. (Though, if his other senses have developed unusual acuity, he will in other respects be more conscious than a normal man.) But if a lower degree of consciousness consists either in the absence of a whole dimension such as sight, or in senses with lower acuity than those of men, it is not plausible to say that animals are all less conscious than we are. Dogs seem to have all the dimensions of consciousness that we do. It is true that they often see less well, but on the other hand their sense of smell is better than ours. If the sanctity of life were solely dependent on degree of consciousness interpreted this way, we often could not justify giving human life priority over animal life. We might also be committed to giving the life of a normal dog priority over the life of a blind man.

The other way in which we talk of degrees of 'mere' consciousness comes up in such contexts as waking up and falling asleep. There is a sleepy state in which we can be unaware of words that are softly spoken, but aware of any noise that is loud or sharp. But this again fails to separate men from animals. For animals are often alert in a way that is quite unlike the drowsiness of a man not fully awake.

Whether or not 'mere' consciousness fades away lower down on the evolutionary scale (and the idea of a sharp boundary *does* seem implausible), there seems at least no reason to regard the 'higher' animals as less aware of the environment than ourselves. (It is not being suggested that animals are only at the level of 'mere' consciousness, though no doubt they are less far above it than most of us.) If the whole basis of the ban on killing were the intrinsic value of mere consciousness, killing higher animals would be as bad as killing humans.

It would be possible to continue to hold mere consciousness to be of intrinsic value, and either to supplement this principle with others or else to abandon the priority given to human life. But when the principle is distinguished from different ones that would place a value on higher levels of consciousness, it has so little intuitive appeal that we may suspect its attractiveness to depend on the distinction not being made. If, in your own case, you would opt for a state never rising above mere consciousness, in preference to death, have you purged the illegitimate assumption that you would take an interest in what you would be aware of?

6 'Being Human Is Intrinsically Valuable'

It is worth mentioning that the objection to taking human life should not rest on what is sometimes called 'speciesism': human life being treated as having a special priority over animal life *simply* because it is human. The analogy is with racism, in its purest form, according to which people of a certain race ought to be treated differently *simply* because of their membership of that race, without any argument referring to special features of that race being given. This is objectionable partly because of its moral arbitrariness: unless some relevant empirical characteristics can be cited, there can be no argument for such discrimination. Those concerned to reform our treatment of animals point out that speciesism exhibits the same arbitrariness. It is not in itself sufficient argument for treating a creature less well to say simply that it is not a member of our species. An adequate justification must cite relevant differences between the species. We still have the question of what features of a life are of intrinsic value.

7 The Concept of a 'Life Worth Living'

I have suggested that, in destroying life or mere consciousness, we are not destroying anything intrinsically valuable. These states only matter because they are necessary for other things that matter in themselves. If a list could be made of all the things that are valuable for their own sake, these things would be the ingredients of a 'life worth living'.

One objection to the idea of judging that a life is worth living is that this seems to imply the possibility of comparing being alive and being dead. And, as Wittgenstein said, 'Death is not an event in life: we do not live to experience death.'

But we can have a preference for being alive over being dead, or for being conscious over being unconscious, without needing to make any 'comparisons' between these states. We prefer to be anaesthetized for a painful operation; queuing for a bus in the rain at midnight, we wish we were at home asleep; but for the most part we prefer to be awake and experience our life as it goes by. These preferences do not depend on any view about 'what it is like' being unconscious, and our preference for life does not depend on beliefs about 'what it is like' being dead. It is rather that we treat being dead or unconscious as nothing, and then decide whether a stretch of experience is better or worse than nothing. And this claim, that life of a certain sort is better than nothing, is an expression of our preference.

Any list of the ingredients of a worthwhile life would obviously be disputable. Most people might agree on many items, but many others could be endlessly argued over. It might be agreed that a happy life is worth living, but people do not agree on what happiness is. And some things that make life worth living may only debatably be to do with happiness. (Aristotle:[3] 'And so they tell us that Anaxagoras answered a man who was raising problems of this sort and asking why one should choose rather to be born than not – "for the sake of viewing the heavens and the whole order of the universe".')

A life worth living should not be confused with a morally virtuous life. Moral virtues such as honesty or a sense of fairness can belong to someone whose life is relatively bleak and empty. Music may enrich someone's life, or the death of a friend impoverish it, without him growing more or less virtuous.

I shall not try to say what sorts of things do make life worth living. (Temporary loss of a sense of the absurd led me to try to do so. But, apart from the disputability of any such list, I found that the ideal life suggested always sounded ridiculous.) I shall assume that a life worth living has more to it than mere consciousness. It should be possible to explain the wrongness of killing partly in terms of the destruction of a life worth living, without presupposing more than minimal agreement as to exactly what makes life worthwhile.

I shall assume that, where someone's life is worth living, this is a good reason for holding that it would be directly wrong to kill him. This is what can be extracted from the doctrine of the sanctity of life by someone who accepts the criticisms made here of that view. If life is worth preserving only because it is the vehicle for consciousness, and consciousness is of value only because it is necessary for something else, then that 'something else' is the heart of this particular objection to killing. It is what is meant by a 'life worth living' or a 'worthwhile life'.

The idea of dividing people's lives into ones that are worth living and ones that are not is likely to seem both presumptuous and dangerous. As well as seeming to indicate an arrogant willingness to pass godlike judgements on other people's lives, it may remind people of the Nazi policy of killing patients in mental hospitals. But there is really nothing godlike in such a judgement. It is not a moral judgement we are making, if we think that someone's life is so empty and unhappy as to be not worth living. It results from an attempt (obviously an extremely fallible one) to see his life from his own point of view and to see what he gets out of it. It must also be stressed that no suggestion is being made that it automatically becomes right to kill people whose lives we think are not worth living. It is only being argued that, if someone's life is worth living, this is *one* reason why it is directly wrong to kill him.

8 Is the Desire to Live the Criterion of a Worthwhile Life?

It might be thought that a conclusive test of whether or not someone's life is worth living is whether or not he wants to go on living. The attractiveness of this idea comes partly from the fact that the question whether someone has a worthwhile life involves thinking from his point of view, rather than thinking of his contribution to the lives of other people.

This proposal would commit us to believing that a person cannot want to end his life if it is worth living, and that he cannot want to prolong his life where it is not worth living. But these beliefs are both doubtful. In a passing mood of depression, someone who normally gets a lot out of life may want to kill himself. And someone who thinks he will go to hell may wish to prolong his present life, however miserable he is. The frying pan may be worse than nothing but better than the fire. And some people, while not believing in hell, simply fear death. They may wish they had never been born, but still not want to die.

For these reasons, someone's own desire to live or die is not a conclusive indication of whether or not he has a life worth living. And, equally obviously, with people who clearly do have lives worth living, the relative strength of their desires to live is not a reliable indicator of how worthwhile they find their lives. Someone whose hopes are often disappointed may cling to life as tenaciously as the happiest person in the world.

If we are to make these judgements, we cannot escape appealing to our own independent beliefs about what sorts of things enrich or impoverish people's lives. But, when this has been said, it should be emphasized that, when the question arises whether someone's life is worth living at all, his own views will normally be evidence of an overwhelmingly powerful kind. Our assessments of what other people get out of their lives are so fallible that only a monster of self-confidence would feel no qualms about correcting the judgement of the person whose life is in question.

9 Length of Life

The upshot of this discussion is that one reason why it is wrong to kill is that it is wrong to destroy a life which is worth living.

This can be seen in a slightly different perspective when we remember that we must all die one day, so that killing and life-saving are interventions that alter length of life by bringing forward or postponing the date of death. An extreme statement of this perspective is to be found in St Augustine's *City of God*:

> There is no one, it goes without saying, who is not nearer to death this year than he was last year, nearer tomorrow than today, today than yesterday, who will not by and by be nearer than

he is at the moment, or is not nearer at the present time than he was a little while ago. Any space of time that we live through leaves us with so much less time to live, and the remainder decreases with every passing day; so that the whole of our lifetime is nothing but a race towards death, in which no one is allowed the slightest pause or any slackening of the pace. All are driven on at the same speed, and hurried along the same road to the same goal. The man whose life was short passed his days as swiftly as the longer-lived; moments of equal length rushed by for both of them at equal speed, though one was farther than the other from the goal to which both were hastening at the same rate.

The objection to killing made here is that it is wrong to shorten a worthwhile life. Why is a longer-lasting worthwhile life a better thing than an equally worthwhile but briefer life? Some people, thinking about their own lives, consider length of life very desirable, while others consider the number of years they have is of no importance at all, the quality of their lives being all that matters.

There is an argument (echoed in Sartre's short story *Le Mur*) used by Marcus Aurelius in support of the view that length of life is unimportant:

> If a god were to tell you 'Tomorrow, or at least the day after, you will be dead', you would not, unless the most abject of men, be greatly solicitous whether it was to be the later day rather than the morrow, for what is the difference between them? In the same way, do not reckon it of great moment whether it will come years and years hence, or tomorrow.[4]

This argument is unconvincing. From the fact that some small differences are below the threshold of mattering to us, it does not follow that all differences are insignificant. If someone steals all your money except either a penny or twopence, you will not mind much which he has left you with. It does not follow that the difference between riches and poverty is trivial.

There are at least two good reasons why a longer life can be thought better than a short one. One is that the quality of life is not altogether independent of its length: many plans and projects would not be worth undertaking without a good chance of time for their fulfilment. The other reason is that, other things being equal, more of a good thing is always better than less of it. This does not entail such absurd consequences as that an enjoyable play gets better as it gets longer, without limit. The point of the phrase 'other things being equal' is to allow for waning of interest and for the claims of other activities. So, unless life begins to pall, it is not in any way unreasonable to want more of it and to place a value on the prolonging of other people's worthwhile lives.

This suggests an answer to a traditional scepticism about whether people are harmed by being killed. This scepticism is stated in its most extreme form by Socrates in the *Apology*: 'Now if there is no consciousness, but only a dreamless sleep, death must be a marvellous gain.' There is clearly some exaggeration here. Death is not a dreamless sleep, but something we can treat as on a par with it. There is the doubtful suggestion that people would normally prefer a dreamless sleep to their waking lives. But, stripped of these exaggerations, there remains the valid point that being dead is not a state we experience, and so cannot be unpleasant. It was this that led Lucretius to think that the fear of death was confused:

> If the future holds travail and anguish in store, the self must be in existence, when that time comes, in order to experience it. But from this fate we are redeemed by death, which denies existence to the self that might have suffered these tribulations.

He reinforced this by a comparison with the time before birth:

> Look back at the eternity that passed before we were born, and mark how utterly it counts to us as nothing. This is a mirror that nature holds up to us, in which we may see the time that shall be after we are dead. Is there anything terrifying in the sight – anything depressing . . .?[5]

Lucretius is right that being dead is not itself a misfortune, but this does not show that it is irrational to want not to die, nor that killing someone does him no harm. For, while I will not be miserable when dead, I am happy while alive, and it is not confused to want more of a good thing rather than less of it.

Bernard Williams has suggested that a reply to Lucretius of this kind does not commit us to wanting to be immortal.[6] He argues that immortality is either inconceivable or terrible. Either desires and satisfactions change so much that it is not clear that the immortal person will still be *me*, or else they are limited by my character and will start to seem pointlessly boring: 'A man at arms can get cramp from standing too long at his post, but sentry-duty can after all be necessary. But the threat of monotony in eternal activities could not be dealt with in that way, by regarding immortal boredom as an unavoidable ache derived from standing ceaselessly at one's post.' It is true that the reply to Lucretius does not commit us to desiring immortality. But I am not convinced that someone with a fairly constant character *need* eventually become intolerably bored, so long as they can watch the world continue to unfold and go on asking new questions and thinking, and so long as there are other people to share their feelings and thoughts with. Given the company of the right people, I would be glad of the chance to sample a few million years and see how it went.

10 The 'No Trade-Off' View

In stating the principle of the sanctity of life, it seemed important not to suggest that it always took priority over other values: 'taking human life is intrinsically wrong', not 'taking human life is always wrong.' The same point holds for the acceptable principle that we have tried to extract from the sanctity of life view: 'it is wrong to destroy a life which is worth living.' There is a tacit 'other things being equal' clause. For we can hold this view while thinking that the avoidance of other things even worse may sometimes have to take priority. We can have this objection to killing without being absolute pacifists.

The alternative, which may be called the 'no trade-off' view, gives an infinite value to not killing people (whose lives are worthwhile) compared to anything else. This may be because the *act* of killing seems infinitely appalling, which is an implausible view when we think of other horrendous acts, such as torturing. Or it may be because infinite value is set on worthwhile life itself. If this second alternative is chosen, it commits us to giving the saving of life overriding priority over all other social objectives. A piece of life-saving equipment is to be preferred to any amount of better housing, better schools or higher standard of living. Neither of these versions of the no trade-off view seems particularly attractive when the implications are clear.

11 The Social Effects of Abandoning the Sanctity of Life

Sometimes the doctrine of the sanctity of life is defended in an oblique way. The social implications of widespread abandonment of the view that taking human life is intrinsically wrong are said to be so appalling that, whatever its defects, the doctrine should not be criticized.

It must be faced that there is always a real possibility of producing a society where an indifference to the lives of at least some groups of people has terrible results. The sort of attitude is exhibited clearly in some passages from letters sent by the I.G. Farben chemical trust to the camp at Auschwitz.[7]

> In contemplation of experiments with a new soporific drug, we would appreciate your procuring for us a number of women . . . We received your answer but consider the price of 200 marks a woman excessive. We propose to pay not more than 170 marks a head. If agreeable, we will take possession of the women. We need approximately 150 . . . Received the order of 150 women. Despite their emaciated condition, they were found satisfactory. We shall keep you posted on developments concerning this experiment . . . The tests were made. All subjects died. We shall contact you shortly on the subject of a new load.

If criticism of the doctrine of the sanctity of life made even a small contribution to developing such attitudes, that would be an overwhelming reason for not making any criticism. But the views to be argued for here in no way give support to these attitudes. (It is the first and most elementary test to be passed by an adequate account of the morality of killing that it should not fail to condemn them.) It is a thesis of this book that conventional moral views about killing are often intellectually unsatisfactory. The attempt to replace the unsatisfactory parts of a moral outlook may even result in something less likely to be eroded.

References

1 Glanville Williams: *The Sanctity of Life and the Criminal Law* (London, 1958), ch. 1.
2 A. Schopenhauer, *The World as Will and Representation*, translated by E. J. F. Payne (New York, 1969), Book 4, section 54.
3 *Eudemian Ethics*, 1216 a 11.
4 Marcus Aurelius, *Meditations*, trans. M. Staniforth (Harmondsworth, 1964).
5 Lucretius, *The Nature of the Universe*, trans. R. E. Latham (Harmondsworth, 1951).
6 Bernard Williams, 'The Makropulos Case', in *Problems of the Self* (Cambridge, 1973).
7 Bruno Bettelheim, *The Informed Heart* (London, 1961), ch. 6.

21

Declaration on Euthanasia

Sacred Congregation for the Doctrine of the Faith

The Congregation considers it opportune to set forth the Church's teaching on euthanasia.

It is indeed true that, in this sphere of teaching, the recent popes have explained the principles, and these retain their full force;[1] but the progress of medical science in recent years has brought to the force new aspects of the question of euthanasia, and these aspects call for further elucidation on the ethical level.

In modern society, in which even the fundamental values of human life are often called into question, cultural change exercises an influence upon the way of looking at suffering and death; moreover, medicine has increased its capacity to cure and to prolong life in particular circumstances, which sometimes give rise to moral problems. Thus people living in this situation experience no little anxiety about the meaning of advanced old age and death. They also begin to wonder whether they have the right to obtain for themselves or their fellowmen an "easy death", which would shorten suffering and which seems to them more in harmony with human dignity.

A number of Episcopal Conferences have raised questions on this subject with the Sacred Congregation for the Doctrine of the Faith. The Congregation, having sought the opinion of experts on the various aspects of euthanasia, now wishes to respond to the Bishops' questions with the present Declaration, in order to help them to give correct teaching to the faithful entrusted to their care, and to offer them elements for reflection that they can present to the civil authorities with regard to this very serious matter...

From *Declaration on Euthanasia* (Vatican City, 1980).

It is hoped that this Declaration will meet with the approval of many people of good will, who, philosophical or ideological differences notwithstanding, have nevertheless a lively awareness of the rights of the human person. These rights have often in fact been proclaimed in recent years through declarations issued by International Congresses;[2] and since it is a question here of fundamental rights inherent in every human person, it is obviously wrong to have recourse to arguments from political pluralism or religious freedom in order to deny the universal value of those rights.

I The Value of Human Life

Human life is the basis of all goods, and is the necessary source and condition of every human activity and of all society. Most people regard life as something sacred and hold that no one may dispose of it at will, but believers see in life something greater, namely a gift of God's love, which they are called upon to preserve and make fruitful. And it is this latter consideration that gives rise to the following consequences:

1. No one can make an attempt on the life of an innocent person without opposing God's love for that person, without violating a fundamental right, and therefore without committing a crime of the utmost gravity.[3]

2. Everyone has the duty to lead his or her life in accordance with God's plan. That life is entrusted to the individual as a good that must bear fruit already here on earth, but that finds its full perfection only in eternal life.

3. Intentionally causing one's own death, or suicide, is therefore equally as wrong as murder; such an action on the part of a person is to be considered as a rejection of God's sovereignty and loving plan. Furthermore, suicide is also often a refusal of love for self, the denial of the natural instinct to live, a flight from the duties of justice and charity owed to one's neighbour, to various communities or to the whole of society – although, as is generally recognized, at times there are psychological factors present that can diminish responsibility or even completely remove it.

However, one must clearly distinguish suicide from that sacrifice of one's life whereby for a higher cause, such as God's glory, the salvation of souls or the service of one's brethren, a person offers his or her own life or puts it in danger (cf. *Jn* 15: 14).

II Euthanasia

In order that the question of euthanasia can be properly dealt with, it is first necessary to define the words used.

Etymologically speaking, in ancient times *euthanasia* meant an *easy death* without severe suffering. Today one no longer thinks of this original meaning of the word, but rather of some intervention of medicine whereby the sufferings of sickness or of the final agony are reduced, sometimes also with the danger of suppressing life prematurely. Ultimately, the word *euthanasia* is used in a more particular sense to mean "mercy killing", for the purpose of putting an end to extreme suffering, or saving abnormal babies, the mentally ill or the incurably sick from the prolongation, perhaps for many years, of a miserable life, which could impose too heavy a burden on their families or on society.

It is therefore necessary to state clearly in what sense the word is used in the present document.

By euthanasia is understood an action or an omission which of itself or by intention causes death, in order that all suffering may in this way be eliminated. Euthanasia's terms of reference, therefore, are to be found in the intention of the will and in the methods used.

It is necessary to state firmly once more that nothing and no one can in any way permit the killing of an innocent human being, whether a fetus or an embryo, an infant or an adult, an old person, or one suffering from an incurable disease, or a person who is dying. Furthermore, no one is permitted to ask for this act of killing, either for himself or herself or for another person entrusted to his or her care, nor can he or she consent to it, either explicitly or implicitly. Nor can any authority legitimately recommend or permit such an action. For it is a question of the violation of the divine law, an offence against the dignity of the human person, a crime against life, and an attack on humanity.

It may happen that, by reason of prolonged and barely tolerable pain, for deeply personal or other reasons, people may be led to believe that they can legitimately ask for death or obtain it for others. Although in these cases the guilt of the individual may be reduced or completely absent, nevertheless the error of judgement into which the conscience falls, perhaps in good faith, does not change the nature of this act of killing, which will always be in itself something to be rejected. The pleas of gravely ill people who sometimes ask for death are not to be understood as implying a true desire for euthanasia; in fact it is almost always a case of an anguished plea for help and love. What a sick person needs, besides medical care, is love, the human and supernatural warmth with which the sick person can and ought to be surrounded by all those close to him or her, parents and children, doctors and nurses.

III The Meaning of Suffering for Christians and the Use of Painkillers

Death does not always come in dramatic circumstances after barely tolerable sufferings. Nor do we have to think only of extreme cases. Numerous testimonies which confirm one another lead one to the conclusion that nature itself has made provision to render more bearable at the moment of death separations that would be terribly painful to a person in full health. Hence it is that a prolonged illness, advanced old age, or a state of loneliness or neglect can bring about psychological conditions that facilitate the acceptance of death.

Nevertheless the fact remains that death, often preceded or accompanied by severe and prolonged suffering, is something which naturally causes people anguish.

Physical suffering is certainly an unavoidable element of the human condition; on the biological level, it constitutes a warning of which no one denies the usefulness; but, since it affects the human psychological makeup, it often exceeds its own biological usefulness and so can become so severe as to cause the desire to remove it at any cost.

According to Christian teaching, however, suffering, especially suffering during the last moments of life, has a special place in God's saving plan; it is in fact a sharing in Christ's Passion and a union with the redeeming sacrifice which he offered in obedience to the Father's will. Therefore one must not be surprised if some Christians prefer to moderate their use of painkillers, in order to accept voluntarily at least a part of their sufferings and thus associate themselves in a conscious way with the sufferings of Christ crucified (cf. *Mt* 27: 34). Nevertheless it would be imprudent to impose a heroic way of acting as a general rule. On the contrary, human and Christian prudence suggest for the majority of sick people the use of medicines capable of alleviating or suppressing pain, even though these may cause as a secondary effect semiconsciousness and reduced lucidity. As for those who are not in a state to express themselves, one can reasonably presume that they wish to take these painkillers, and have them administered according to the doctor's advice.

But the intensive use of painkillers is not without difficulties, because the phenomenon of habituation generally makes it necessary to increase their dosage in order to maintain their efficacy. At this point it is fitting to recall a declaration by Pius XII, which retains its full force; in answer to a group of doctors who had put the question: "Is the suppression of pain and consciousness by the use of narcotics . . . permitted by religion and morality to the doctor and the patient (even at the approach of death and if one foresees that the use of narcotics will shorten life)?" the Pope said: "If no other means exist, and if, in the given circumstances, this does not prevent the carrying out of other religious and moral duties: Yes."[4] In this case, of course, death is in no way intended or sought, even if the risk of it is reasonably taken; the intention is simply to relieve pain effectively, using for this purpose painkillers available to medicine.

However, painkillers that cause unconsciousness need special consideration. For a person not only has to be able to satisfy his or her moral duties and family obligations; he or she also has to prepare himself or herself with full consciousness for meeting Christ. Thus Pius XII warns: "It is not right to deprive the dying person of consciousness without a serious reason."[5]

IV Due Proportion in the Use of Remedies

Today it is very important to protect, at the moment of death, both the dignity of the human person and the Christian concept of life, against a technological attitude that threatens to become an abuse. Thus, some people speak of a "right to die", which is an expression that does not mean the right to procure death either by one's own hand or by means of someone else, as one pleases, but rather the right to die peacefully with human and Christian dignity. From this point of view, the use of therapeutic means can sometimes pose problems.

In numerous cases, the complexity of the situation can be such as to cause doubts about the way ethical principles should be applied. In the final analysis, it pertains to the conscience either of the sick person, or of those qualified to speak in the sick person's name, or of the doctors, to decide, in the light of moral obligations and of the various aspects of the case.

Everyone has the duty to care for his or her own health or to seek such care from others. Those whose task it is to care for the sick must do so conscientiously and administer the remedies that seem necessary or useful.

However, is it necessary in all circumstances to have recourse to all possible remedies?

In the past, moralists replied that one is never obliged to use "extraordinary" means. This reply, which as a principle still holds good, is perhaps less clear today, by reason of the imprecision of the term and the rapid progress made in the treatment of sickness. Thus some people prefer to speak of "proportionate" and "disproportionate" means. In any case, it will be possible to make a correct judgement as to the means by studying the type of treatment to be used, its degree of complexity or risk, its cost and the possibilities of using it, and comparing these elements with the result that can be expected, taking into account the state of the sick person and his or her physical and moral resources.

In order to facilitate the application of these general principles, the following clarifications can be added:

— If there are no other sufficient remedies, it is permitted, with the patient's consent, to have recourse to the means provided by the most advanced medical techniques, even if these means are still at the experimental stage and are not without a certain risk. By accepting them, the patient can even show generosity in the service of humanity.

— It is also permitted, with the patient's consent, to interrupt these means, where the results fall short of expectations. But for such a decision to be made, account will have to be taken of the reasonable wishes of the patient and the patient's family, as also of the advice of the doctors who are specially competent in the matter. The latter may in particular judge that the investment in instruments and personnel is disproportionate to the results foreseen; they may also judge that the techniques applied impose on the patient strain or suffering out of proportion with the benefits which he or she may gain from such techniques.

— It is also permissible to make do with the normal means that medicine can offer. Therefore one cannot impose on anyone the obligation to have recourse to a technique which is already in use but which carries a risk or is burdensome. Such a refusal is not the equivalent of suicide; on the contrary, it should be considered as an acceptance of the human condition, or a wish to avoid the application of a medical procedure disproportionate to the results that can be expected, or a desire not to impose excessive expense on the family or the community.

— When inevitable death is imminent in spite of the means used, it is permitted in conscience to take the decision to refuse forms of treatment that would only secure a precarious and burdensome prolongation of life, so long as the normal care due to the sick person in similar cases is not interrupted. In such circumstances the doctor has no reason to reproach himself with failing to help the person in danger.

Conclusion

The norms contained in the present Declaration are inspired by a profound desire to serve people in accordance with the plan of the Creator. Life is a gift of God, and on the other hand death is unavoidable; it is necessary therefore that we, without in any way hastening the hour of death, should be able to accept it with full responsibility and dignity. It is true that death marks the end of our earthly existence, but at the same time it opens the door to immortal life. Therefore all must prepare themselves for this event in the light of human values, and Christians even more so in the light of faith.

As for those who work in the medical profession, they ought to neglect no means of making all their skill available to the sick and the dying; but they should also remember how much more necessary it is to provide them with the comfort of boundless kindness and heartfelt charity. Such service to people is also service to Christ the Lord, who said: "As you did it to one of the least of these my brethren, you did it to me" (*Mt* 25: 40).

At the audience granted to the undersigned Prefect, His Holiness Pope John Paul II approved this Declaration, adopted at the ordinary meeting of the Sacred Congregation for the Doctrine of the Faith, and ordered its publication.

Rome, the Sacred Congregation for the Doctrine of the Faith, 5 May 1980.

FRANJO Card. ŠEPER
Prefect

✠ Jérôme Hamer, O. P.
Tit. Archbishop of Lorium
Secretary

Notes

1 Pius XII, *Address to those attending the Congress of the International Union of Catholic Women's Leagues*, 11 September 1947: *AAS* 39 (1947), p. 483; *Address to the Italian Catholic Union of Midwives*, 29 October 1951: *AAS* 43 (1951), pp. 835–54; *Speech to the members of the International Office of military medicine documentation*, 19 October 1953: *AAS* 45 (1953), pp. 744–54; *Address to those taking part in the IXth Congress of the Italian Anaesthesiological Society*, 24 February 1957: *AAS* 49 (1957), pp. 146; cf. also *Address on "reanimation"* 24 November 1957: *AAS* 49 (1957), pp. 1027–33; PAUL. VI, *Address to the members of the United Nations*

Special Committee on Apartheid, 22 May 1974: *AAS* 66 (1974), p. 346; JOHN PAUL. II: *Address to the Bishops of the United States of America*, 5 October 1979: *AAS* 71 (1979), p. 1225.

2 One thinks especially of Recommendation 779 (1976) on the rights of the sick and dying, of the Parliamentary Assembly of the Council of Europe at its XXVIIth Ordinary Session; cf. SIPECA, no. 1 (March 1977), pp. 14–15.

3 We leave aside completely the problems of the death penalty and of war, which involve specific considerations that do not concern the present subject.

4 PIUS XII, *Address* of 24 February 1957: *AAS* 49 (1957), p. 147.

5 PIUS XII, ibid., p. 145; cf. *Address* of 9 September 1958: *AAS* 50 (1958), p. 694.

Killing and Letting Die

22

The Morality of Killing: A Traditional View

Germain Grisez and Joseph M. Boyle, Jr

The Morality of Killing

In the strict sense one kills a person when, having considered bringing about a person's death as something one could do, one commits oneself to doing it by adopting this proposal instead of some alternative and by undertaking to execute it. By definition killing in the strict sense is an action contrary to the good of life. The adoption of a proposal to bring about someone's death is incompatible with respect for this good. Thus every act which is an act of killing in the strict sense is immoral. No additional circumstance or condition can remove this immorality.

This definition and moral characterization of killing in the strict sense make no distinction between intent to kill, attempt to kill, and the consummation of the undertaking by successful execution. These distinctions, which are legally significant, are morally irrelevant. If one commits oneself to realizing a certain state of affairs, by the commitment one constitutes oneself as a certain type of person. If one commits oneself to killing a person; one constitutes oneself a murderer. This remains true even if one is prevented from attempting to execute one's purpose – for example, if someone else kills the intended victim first. Even more obviously it remains true if one attempts to execute one's purpose but fails – for example, if one shoots to kill but misses the intended victim.

From *Life and Death with Liberty and Justice: A Contribution to the Euthanasic Debate* (University of Notre Dame Press, 1971), pp. 381–419. Reprinted with permission.

Although everything which is an act of killing in the strict sense is immoral, not every deadly deed is an act of killing in this sense. As we have explained, some deadly deeds carry out a consciously projected design, but the performance is not the execution of a proposal adopted by the actor's choice to bring about the death of a human individual. The examples of the enraged wife and the dutiful soldier belong here. In what follows we call this type of performance a "deadly deed" to distinguish it from a killing in the strict sense.

Finally, there are other cases of causing death, such as some killing in self-defense, which are neither killing in the strict sense nor deadly deeds as here defined. The proposal adopted or the consciously projected design carried out by persons defending themselves might not extend beyond incapacitating the attacker, but this can result in the attacker's death if the only available and adequate means to incapacitate the attacker also will result in mortal wounds...

We turn now to the consideration of cases in which one brings about one's own death. Even in ordinary language some ethically significant distinctions are made in speaking of this, for one does not call "suicide" all cases in which someone causes his or her own death. Most people who consider suicide immoral do not class martyrs and heroes as suicides, since "suicide" suggests an act of killing oneself. Yet not all who commit suicide do a moral act of killing in the strict sense.

In cases in which suicide is an act of killing in the strict sense the proposal to kill oneself is among the proposals one considers in deliberation, and this proposal is adopted by choice as preferable to alternatives. For example, a person who for some reason is suffering greatly might think: "I wish I no longer had to suffer as I am suffering. If I were dead, my suffering would be at an end. But I am not likely to die soon. I could kill myself. But I fear death and what might follow after it. I could put up with my misery and perhaps find some other way out." One thinking in this way is deliberating. In saying "I could kill myself" suicide is proposed. If this proposal is adopted, one's moral act is killing in the strict sense. As in other instances this act is incompatible with the basic good of human life, and it cannot morally be justified, regardless of what else might be the case.

One can propose to kill oneself without saying to oneself "I could kill myself." One might say something which one would accept as equivalent in meaning: "I could destroy myself," "I could rub myself out," or something of the sort. Again, one might say something which one would admit amounts to "I could kill myself" although not equivalent in meaning to it, such as "I could shoot myself," when what one has in mind is shooting oneself in the head and thereby causing death, not merely shooting oneself to cause a wound...

There are still other cases in which individuals contribute to the causation of their own deaths by acts which are morally significant but which in no way execute proposals which are properly suicidal. Typical martyrs lay down their lives. The death could be avoided if the martyr were willing to do something believed wrong or to leave unfulfilled some duty which is accepted as compelling. But the martyr refuses to avoid death by compromise or evasion of duty. Such persons do only what they believe to be morally required; the consequent loss of their own lives is willingly accepted by martyrs, neither sought nor chosen as a means to anything.

The martyr reasons somewhat as follows: "I would like to please everyone and to stay alive. But they are demanding of me that I do what I believe to be wrong or that I omit doing what I believe to be my sacred mission. They threaten me with death if I do not meet their demands. But if I were to comply with their threat, I would be doing evil in order that the good of saving my life might follow from it. This I may not do. Therefore, I must stand as long as I can in accord with my conscience, even though they are likely to kill me or torture me into submission."

Someone who does not understand the martyr's reasoning is likely to consider the martyr a suicide. But martyrs who reason thus do not propose to bring about their own deaths. The martyr bears witness to a profound commitment, first of all before the persecutors themselves. The latter can and in the martyr's view should accept this testimony and approve the rightness of the commitment. The martyr's refusal to give in does not bring about the persecutor's act of killing; the martyr only fails to win over the persecutor and to forestall the deadly deed...

Of course, we hold that suicide which is killing in the strict sense is necessarily immoral simply because it violates the basic good of human life. One who deliberately chooses to end his or her own life constitutes by this commitment a self-murderous self. But considerations which tell against even nonsuicidal acts which bring about a person's own death also argue against the moral justifiability of suicidal acts, which execute a proposal to destroy one's own life.

Considering matters from a moral point of view and from the side of the one whose life is to be ended, voluntary euthanasia is not significantly different from other cases of suicide. The proposal is to bring about death as a means to ending suffering. This proposal, if adopted and executed, is an instance of killing in the strict sense. It can never be morally justified.

Of course, a person who is in severe pain and who seeks death to escape it is likely to have mitigated responsibility or even to be drawn into acceptance without a deliberate choice, just as is the case with others whose suffering drives them to a deadly deed against themselves.

However, if an individual plans to seek euthanasia and arranges for it well in advance of the time of suffering, then the possibility that the demand for death is not an expression of deliberate choice is greatly lessened. The conditions which from the point of view of proponents of euthanasia are optimum for making a decision about the matter are precisely the conditions in which the decision is likely to be a morally unjustifiable act of killing in the strict sense.

Considering voluntary euthanasia from the point of view of the person who would carry out the killing, matters seem no better from a moral viewpoint. The performance can hardly fail to be an execution of a deliberate choice; the one carrying out the killing can hardly be driven to it, nor can anyone in the present culture accept the duty unquestioningly . . .

Nonvoluntary euthanasia also clearly proposes death as a treatment of choice. The act hardly can fail to be killing in the strict sense. And in addition to the violation of the good of life, the rights of those to be killed also will be violated – for example, by denial to them of equal protection of the laws. Nonvoluntary euthanasia would violate both life and justice . . .

The preceding treatment has been concerned with instances in which people bring about death by an outward performance. We now turn to a consideration of cases in which individuals refuse treatment for themselves or others, or withhold treatment, or fail or neglect to give it. To apply the moral theory which we articulated to such cases we must first say something about omissions.

If people act when they carry out a proposal which they have adopted by choice, certain cases of outward nonperformance must count as human actions. One can adopt a proposal and carry it out by deliberately not causing or preventing something which one could cause or prevent. One's choice not to cause or prevent something can be a way of realizing a state of affairs one considers somehow desirable. For example, one might adopt the proposal to protest against a government policy permitting the use of public funds for abortion by not paying certain taxes. In this case one aims to realize a desired state of affairs by means of nonconformance with the demands of the law. The nonconformance need involve no outward performance at all.

Omissions of this type – those in which one undertakes to realize a proposed state of affairs by not causing or preventing something – are very important for understanding the morality of withholding treatment from dying patients, refusing treatment proposed for oneself, and in general letting people die.

It clearly is possible to kill in the strict sense by deliberately letting someone die. If one adopts the proposal to bring about a person's death and realizes this proposal by not behaving as one otherwise would behave, then one is committed to the state of affairs which includes the person's death. This commitment, although carried out by a nonperformance, is morally speaking an act of killing. It involves the adoption and execution of a proposal contrary to the basic good of human life. Thus, any case in which one chooses the proposal that a person die and on this basis allows the person to die is necessarily immoral.

For example, if a child is born suffering from various defects and if the physicians and parents decide that the child, the family, and society will all be better off if the burdens entailed by the child's continued life are forestalled by its death, and if they therefore adopt the proposal not to perform a simple operation, which otherwise would be done, so that the child will die, then the parents and physicians morally speaking kill the child – "kill" in the strict sense clarified at the beginning of this chapter. The fact that there is no blood spilled, no poison injected, that the death certificate can honestly show that the child has died from complications arising from its defective condition – none of this is morally relevant. The moral act is no different from any other moral act of murder.

The same thing will be true in every instance in which a judgement is made that someone – whether oneself or another – would be better off dead, the proposal to bring about death by not causing or preventing something is considered and adopted, and this proposal is executed by outward nonperformance of behavior which one otherwise might have attempted . . .

Michael Tooley and others also have criticized those who hold that there is a significant moral difference between killing a person and letting the person die. Their criticism is that if one considers a case of killing and a case of letting die between which there is no difference except that in the one the death is brought about by a performance which causes it while in the other it is brought about by not causing or preventing something, then there is no moral difference between the two cases.

We agree. Both actions are killing in the strict sense; neither can ever be moral. However, not every instance in which someone deliberately lets another die is an action shaped by the proposal that the person whose death is accepted should die or die sooner than would otherwise be the case. We turn now to the consideration of such deliberate omissions which, considered from a moral point of view, are not acts of killing.

The fundamental point about these omissions is that one can omit to do some good or prevent some evil without adopting any proposal which either is opposed to the good or embraces (as means) the evil whose occurrence one accepts. This possibility is most obviously instantiated when one must forgo doing a certain good or preventing a certain evil because one has a duty, incompatible with doing the good or preventing the evil, to do some other good or prevent some other evil.

For example, in an emergency situation in which many people are seriously injured and the medical resources – including time and personnel – are limited, those making decisions must choose to treat some and put off the treatment of others, perhaps with fatal consequences to those not treated first. The nontreatment of those who are not treated is deliberate; even their deaths might be foreseen as an inevitable consequence and knowingly accepted when the decision to treat others is made. Yet plainly the nontreatment of those who are not treated need involve no proposal that these people should die or die more quickly than they otherwise would. Provided there is no partiality or other breach of faith with those not treated, the execution of a proposal to save others does not embrace the death of those who die, and no immorality is done...

There is another type of reason for forgoing doing good which involves no disrespect for the good which would be realized by the action. One might notice that doing the action good in itself will in fact bring about many undesirable consequences. And one might choose not to adopt the proposal to do the good in order to avoid accepting these various bad consequences. This situation is exemplified in a very important way in many instances in which potentially life-prolonging treatment is refused, withheld, or withdrawn – even in the case of a patient who is not dying – because of the expected disadvantages of accepting, carrying out, or continuing treatment...

We have articulated grounds on which someone might reasonably consider treatment undesirable: if the treatment is experimental or risky, if it would be painful or otherwise experienced negatively, if it would interfere with activities or experiences the patient might otherwise enjoy, if it would conflict with some moral or religious principle to which the patient adheres, if it would be psychologically repugnant to the patient, or if the financial or other impact of the treatment upon other persons would constitute a compelling reason to refuse treatment.

The moral legitimacy of refusing treatment in some cases on some such grounds certainly was part of what Pius XII was indicating by his famous distinction between ordinary and extraordinary means of treatment. The Pope defined "extraordinary means" as ones which involve a "great burden," and he allowed that one could morally forgo the use of extraordinary means. The conception of extraordinary means clearly is abused, however, when the proposal is to bring about death by the omission of treatment, and the difficulties of the treatment are pointed to by way of rationalizing the murderous act. If it is decided that a person would be better off dead and that treatment which would be given to another will be withheld because of the poor quality of the life to be preserved, then the focus in decision is not upon the means and its disadvantageous consequences. Rather, what is feared is that the means would be effective, that life would be preserved, and that the life itself and its consequences would be a burden.

Moreover, even when treatment is refused, withheld, or withdrawn because of an objection to the means – and without the adopting of a proposal to bring about death – there still can be a serious moral failing.

A person who refuses lifesaving or life-prolonging treatment, not on a suicidal proposal but because of great repugnance for the treatment itself, might have an obligation to maintain life longer in order to fulfill duties toward others.

For example, someone on dialysis might wish to give up the treatment because of the difficulties it involves, and some persons in this situation could discontinue treatment and accept death without moral fault. But a parent with children in need of continued care, a professional person with grave responsibilities, and many other persons who can prolong their lives at considerable sacrifice to themselves are morally bound to do so, even by this extraordinary means, because they have accepted duties which others are entitled to have fulfilled, and persons who love the goods as one ought will faithfully fulfill duties toward others at considerable cost to themselves.

Similarly, if one refuses, withholds, or withdraws lifesaving or life-prolonging treatment for another because of the grave burdens entailed by such treatment, the burdens must be grave indeed. This is especially clear in cases in which the patient is not dying – for example, cases of defective infants. One must be quite sure, at the least, that with no suicidal proposal one would in the patient's place not wish the treatment. Otherwise, one accepts moral responsibility for a very grave wrong toward the patient.

23

'Whatever the Consequences'

Jonathan Bennett

The following kind of thing can occur.[1] A woman in labour will certainly die unless an operation is performed in which the head of her unborn child is crushed or dissected; while if it is not performed the child can be delivered, alive, by post-mortem Caesarean section. This presents a straight choice between the woman's life and the child's.

In a particular instance of this kind, some people would argue for securing the woman's survival on the basis of the special facts of the case: the woman's terror, or her place in an established network of affections and dependences, or the child's physical defects, and so on. For them, the argument could go the other way in another instance, even if only in a very special one – e.g. where the child is well formed and the woman has cancer which will kill her within a month anyway.

Others would favour the woman's survival in any instance of the kind presented in my opening paragraph, on the grounds that women are human while unborn children are not. This dubious argument does not need to be attacked here, and I shall ignore it.

Others again would say, just on the facts as stated in my first paragraph, that the *child* must be allowed to survive. Their objection to any operation in which an unborn child's head is crushed, whatever the special features of the case, goes like this:

> To do the operation would be to kill the child, while to refrain from doing it would not be to kill the woman but merely to conduct oneself in such a way that – as a foreseen but unwanted consequence – the woman died. The question we should ask is not: 'The woman's life or the child's?', but rather: 'To kill, or not to kill, an innocent human?' The answer to *that* is that it is always absolutely wrong to kill an innocent human, even in such dismal circumstances as these.

This line of thought needs to be attacked. Some able people find it acceptable; it is presupposed by the Principle of Double Effect[2] which permeates Roman Catholic writing on morals; and I cannot find any published statement of the extremely strong philosophical case for its rejection.

I shall state that case as best I can. My presentation of it owes much to certain allies and opponents who have commented on earlier drafts. I gratefully acknowledge my debt to Miss G. E. M. Anscombe, A. G. N. Flew, A. Kenny and T. J. Smiley; and to a number of Cambridge research students, especially D. F. Wallace.

The Plan of Attack

There is no way of disproving the principle: 'It would always be wrong to kill an innocent human, whatever the consequences of not doing so.' The principle is consistent and reasonably clear; it can be fed into moral syllogisms to yield practical conclusions; and although its application to borderline cases may raise disturbing problems, this is true of any moral principle. Someone who thinks that the principle is laid down by a moral authority whose deliverances are to be accepted without

From *Analysis*, vol. 26, no. 3 (January 1966), pp. 83–102. Reprinted with permission.

question, without *any* testing against the dictates of the individual conscience, is vulnerable only to arguments about the credentials of his alleged authority; and these are not my present concern. So I have no reply to make to anyone who is prepared to say: 'I shall obey God's command never to kill an innocent human. I shall make no independent moral assessment of this command – whether to test the reasonableness of obeying it, or to test my belief that it *is* God's command, or for any other purpose.' My concern is solely with those who accept the principle: 'It would always be wrong to kill an innocent human, whatever the consequences of not doing so,' not just because it occurs in some received list of moral principles but also because they think that it can in some degree be recommended to the normal conscience. Against this, I shall argue that a normal person who accepts the principle must either have failed to see what it involves or be passively and unquestioningly obedient to an authority.

I do not equate 'the normal conscience' with 'the "liberal" conscience'. Of course, the principle *is* rejected by the 'liberal' majority; but I shall argue for the stronger and less obvious thesis that the principle is in the last resort on a par with 'It would always be wrong to shout, whatever the consequences of not doing so' or 'It would always be wrong to leave a bucket in a hall-way, whatever *etc.*' It is sometimes said that we 'should not understand' someone who claimed to accept such wild eccentricities as these as fundamental moral truths – that he would be making a logical mistake, perhaps about what it is for something to be a 'moral' principle. I need not claim so much. It is enough to say that such a person, if he was sincere and in his right mind, could safely be assumed to have delivered himself over to a moral authority and to have opted out of moral thinking altogether. The same could be said of anyone who accepted *and really understood* the principle: 'It would always be wrong to kill an innocent human, whatever the consequences of not doing so.' This principle is accepted by reasonable people who, though many of them give weight to some moral authority, have not abdicated from independent moral thinking. Clearly, they regard the principle as one which others might be led to accept, or at least to take seriously, on grounds other than subservience to an authority. From this fact, together with the thesis for which I shall argue, it follows that those who accept the principle (like others who at least treat it with respect) have not thought it through, have not seen what it comes to in concrete cases where it yields a different practical conclusion from that yielded by 'It is wrong to kill an innocent human unless there are very powerful reasons for doing so.' I aim to show what the principle comes to in these cases, and so to expose it for what it is.

My arguments will tell equally against any principle of the form 'It would always be wrong to . . . whatever the consequences of not doing so'; but I shall concentrate on the one principle about killing, and indeed on its application to the kind of obstetrical situation described in my opening paragraph.

I need a label for someone who accepts principles of the form: 'It would always be wrong to . . . whatever the consequences of not doing so.' 'Roman Catholic' is at once too wide and too narrow; 'intrinsicalist' is nasty; 'absolutist' is misleading; 'deontologist' means too many other things as well. Reluctantly, I settle for 'conservative'. This use has precedents, but I offer it as a stipulative definition – an expository convenience and not a claim about 'conservatism' in any ordinary sense.

Well then: when the conservative condemns the operation described in my opening paragraph, he does so *partly* because the operation involves the death of an innocent human. So does its nonperformance; but for the conservative the dilemma is asymmetrical because the two alternatives involve human deaths in different ways: in one case the death is part of a killing, in the other there is no killing and a death occurs only as a consequence of what is done. From the premiss that operating would be killing an innocent human, together with the principle: 'It would always be wrong to kill an innocent human, whatever *etc.*', it does follow that it would be wrong to operate. But the usual conservative – the one I plan to attack – thinks that his principle has *some* measure of acceptability on grounds other than unquestioning obedience to an authority. He must therefore think that the premiss: 'In this case, operating would be killing an innocent human while not-operating would involve the death of an innocent human only as a consequence' gives *some* reason for the conclusion: 'In this case, operating would be wrong.' I shall argue that it gives no reason at all: once the muddles have been cleared away, it is just not humanly possible to see the premiss as supporting the conclusion, however weakly, except by accepting the principle 'It would always be wrong *etc.*' as an unquestionable *donnée*.

The Action/Consequence Distinction

When James killed Henry, what happened was this: James contracted his fingers round the handle of a knife, and moved his hand in such a way that the knife penetrated Henry's body and severed an artery, blood escaped from the wound, the rate of oxygen-transfer to Henry's body-cells fell drastically, and Henry died. In general, someone's performing a physical action includes his moving some part or parts of his body. (The difference between 'He moved his hand' and 'His hand moved' is not in question here: I am referring to movements which he *makes*.) He does this in a physical environment, and other things happen in consequence. A description of what he *did* will ordinarily entail something not only about his movements but also, *inter alia*, about some of their upshots. Other upshots will not ordinarily be covered by any description of 'what he did', but will be counted amongst 'the consequences of what he did'. There are various criteria for drawing the line between what someone did and the consequences of what he did; and there can be several proper ways of drawing it in a given case.

This last point notwithstanding, there are wrong ways of dividing a set of happenings into action and consequences. Even where it is not positively wrong to give a very parsimonious account of 'what he did', it may be preferable to be more inclusive. If in my chosen example the obstetrician does the operation, it is true that he crushes the child's head with the consequence that the child dies, but a better account, perhaps, would say that he *kills* the child by crushing its head. There can certainly be outright wrongness at the other end of the scale: we cannot be as inclusive as we like in our account of 'what he did'. If at the last time when the operation could save the woman's life the obstetrician is resignedly writing up his notes, it is just not true that, as he sits at his desk, he is killing the woman; nor, indeed, is he killing her at any other time.

The use of the action/consequence distinction in the conservative premiss is, therefore, perfectly correct. Operating *is* killing; not-operating is not. What are we saying when we say this? By what criteria is the action/consequence distinction drawn in the present case? I shall try, by answering this, to show that in this case one cannot attach moral significance to the fact that the line drawn by the distinction falls where it does. Briefly, the criteria for the action/consequence distinction fall into two groups: those which could support a moral conclusion but which do not apply to every instance of the obstetrical example; and those which do apply to the example but which it would be wildly eccentric to think relevant to the moral assessment of courses of action. There is no overlap between the two groups.

Aspects of the Distinction: First Group

Some differences which tend to go with the action/consequence distinction, and are perhaps to be counted amongst the criteria for it, clearly do have moral significance. None of them, however, is generally present in the obstetrical example.

Given a question about whether some particular upshot of a movement I made is to be covered by the description of what I *did:*

(a) The answer may depend in part upon whether in making the movement I was entirely confident that that upshot would ensue; and this could reasonably be thought relevant to the moral assessment of my conduct. This aspect of the action/consequence distinction, however, is absent from most instances of the obstetrical example. The classification of not-operating as something other than killing does not imply that the obstetrician rates the woman's chance of survival (if the operation is not performed) higher than the child's chance of survival (if it is performed). If it did imply this then, by contraposition, not-operating would in many such cases have to be classified as killing after all.

(b) The answer may depend in part upon how certain or inevitable it was that that upshot would ensue from my movement, or upon how confidently I ought to have expected it to ensue; and that too may have a strong bearing on the moral assessment of my conduct. But it gets no grip on the obstetrical example, for in many cases of that kind there is moral certainty on both sides of the dilemma. If the conservative says that the action/consequence distinction, when correctly drawn, is always associated with morally significant differences in the inevitability of upshots of movements, then he is vulnerable to an argument by contraposition like the one in (a). He is vulnerable in other ways as well, which I shall discuss in my next section.

(c) The answer may depend in part upon whether I made the movement partly or wholly for the sake of achieving that upshot; and this is a morally significant matter. But the obstetrical example is symmetrical in that respect also: if the obstetrician crushes the child's head he does so not because this will lead to the child's death or because it constitutes killing the child, but because that is his only way of removing the child's body from the woman's.

To summarize: moral conclusions may be supported by facts (a) about what is expected, but in the example each upshot is confidently expected; (b) about what is inevitable, but in the example each upshot is inevitable; or (c) about what is ultimately aimed at, but in the example neither upshot is aimed at.

An Aside: Degrees of Inevitability

I have suggested that a conservative might say: 'The action-consequence distinction is always associated with a morally significant difference in the degree to which upshots are certain or inevitable.' This is false; but let us grant it in order to see whether it can help the conservative on the obstetrical example. I concede, for purposes of argument, that if the operation is not performed the woman will pretty certainly die, while if it is performed the child will even more certainly die.

What use can the conservative make of this concession? Will he say that the practical decision is to be based on a weighing of the comparative desirability of upshots against the comparative certainty of their achievement? If so, then he must allow that there *could* be a case in which it was right to kill the child – perhaps a case where a healthy young widow with four children is bearing a hydrocephalic child, and where her chance of survival if the operation is not performed is *nearly* as bad as the child's chance of survival if it is performed. If a professed 'conservative' allows that there could, however improbably, be such a case, then he is not a conservative but a consequentialist; he does after all base his final judgement on the special features of the case; and he has misrepresented his position by using the language of action and consequence to express his implausible views about the comparative inevitability of upshots. On the other hand, if the conservative still absolutely rules out the killing of the child, whatever the details of the particular case, then what could be his point in claiming that there is a difference in degree of inevitability? The moral significance of this supposed difference would, at best, have to be conceded to be an obscure one which threw no light on why anyone should adopt the conservative view.

A certain conservative tactic is at issue here. Miss G. E. M. Anscombe has said:

> If someone really thinks, *in advance*, that it is open to question whether such an action as procuring the judicial execution of the innocent should be quite excluded from consideration – I do not want to argue with him; he shows a corrupt mind.[3]

The phrase 'quite excluded from consideration' clearly places Miss Anscombe as what I am calling a 'conservative'. (The phrase 'a corrupt mind', incidentally, tends to confirm my view that conservatives think their position can stand the light of day, i.e. that they do not see it as tenable only by those who passively obey some moral authority.) Now, in the course of a footnote to this passage Miss Anscombe remarks:

> In discussion when this paper was read, as was perhaps to be expected, this case was produced: a government is required to have an innocent man tried, sentenced and executed under threat of a 'hydrogen bomb war'. It would seem strange to me to have much hope of averting a war threatened by such men as made this demand. But the most important thing about the way in which cases like this are invented in discussions, is the assumption that only two courses are open: here, compliance and open defiance. No one can say in advance of such a situation what the possibilities are going to be – e.g. that there is none of stalling by a feigned willingness to comply, accompanied by a skilfully arranged 'escape' of the victim.

This makes two points about the case as described: there might be nothing we could do which would have a good chance of averting a war; and if there were one such thing we could do there might be several. The consequentialist might meet this by trying yet again to describe a case in which judicially executing an innocent man *is* the only thing we could do which would have a good chance of averting a war. When he has added the details which block off the other alternatives, his invented case may well be far removed from present political likelihood; it may even be quite fantastic. Still, what does the conservative say about it?

Here is Miss Anscombe, at her most gamesome, on the subject of 'fantastic' examples:

> A point of method I would recommend to the corrupter of the youth would be this: concentrate on examples which are either banal: you have promised to return a book, but... and so on, or fantastic: what you ought to do if you had to move forward, and stepping with your right foot meant killing twenty-five young men, while stepping with your left foot would kill fifty drooling old ones. (Obviously the right thing to do would be to jump and polish off the lot.)[4]

The cards are now well stacked; but this is a game in which a conservative should not be taking a hand at all. Someone may say (i): 'In no situation could it be right to procure the judicial execution of the innocent: political probability aside, the judicial execution of the innocent is absolutely impermissible in any possible circumstances.' Or someone may say (ii): 'It is never right to procure the judicial execution of the innocent: a situation in which this would be right has never arisen, isn't going to arise, and cannot even be described without entering into the realm of political fantasy.' These are different. The former is conservatism, according to which 'the judicial execution of the innocent should be quite excluded from consideration'. The latter is not conservatism: according to it, the judicial execution of the innocent is taken into consideration, assessed in the light of the political probabilities of the world we live in, and excluded on that basis. The former is Miss Anscombe's large type; the latter, apparently, is her footnote. The difference between (i) 'In no situation could it be right...' and (ii) 'No situation is even remotely likely to occur in which it would be right...' can be masked by dismissing what is relevant but unlikely as 'fantastic' and therefore negligible. But the difference between the two positions is crucial, even if in the first instance it can be brought out only by considering 'fantastic' possibilities. The two may yield the same real-life practical conclusions, but (ii) can be understood and argued within a way in which (i) cannot. If someone accepts (ii), and is not afraid to discuss a 'fantastic' but possible situation in which he would approve the judicial execution of an innocent man, he can be challenged to square this with his contrary judgement in regard to some less fantastic situation. Whether he could meet the challenge would depend on the details of his moral position and of the situations in question. The point is that we should know where we stood with him: for example, we should know that it was *relevant* to adduce evidence about how good the chances would be of averting war in this way in this situation, or in that way in that. It is just this sort of thing which the unwavering conservative must regard as irrelevant; and that is what is wrong with his position. Miss Anscombe says: 'No one can say in advance of such a situation what the possibilities are going to be'; but the central objection to conservatism is, precisely, that it says in advance that for the judging of the proposed course of action *it does not matter* what the possibilities are going to be. Why, then, go on about them – if not to disguise conservatism as something else when the going gets tough?

I have based this paper on the obstetrical example in the hope that, without being jeered at for having 'invented' an example which is 'fantastic', I could present a kind of case in which a conservative principle would yield a practical conclusion different from any likely to be arrived at by consequentialist arguments. The claim that in these cases there would always be a morally significant difference between the woman's chance of survival and the child's could only be another attempt to get the spotlight off conservatism altogether – to get the consequentialist to accept the conservative's conclusion and forget about his principle. In the obstetrical example, the attempt is pretty desperate (though, with the aid of judiciously selected statistics, it is made often enough); with other kinds of example, used to examine this or other conservative principles, it might be easier for the conservative to make a show of insisting on the addition of details which render the examples 'fantastic'. But this does not mean that the case against conservatism is stronger here than elsewhere. It means only that the obstetrical example gives less scope than most for the 'there-might-be-another-way-out' move, or protective-coloration gambit, which some conservatives sometimes use when they shelter their position by giving the impression that it does not really exist.

A conservative might invoke inevitability, without comparing degrees of it in the consequentialist manner, by saying that if the operation is not performed the woman still has *some* chance of survival while if it is performed the child has *none*. Barring miracles, this is wrong about the woman; not barring miracles, it is wrong about the child. It could seem plausible only to someone who did not bar miracles but took a peculiar view of how they operate. Some people do attach importance in this regard to the fact that if the operation is not performed the woman may take some time to die: they seem to think – perhaps encouraged by an eccentric view of God as powerful but *slow* – that the longer an upshot is delayed the more room there is for a miraculous intervention. This belief, whatever the assumptions which underlie it, gives no help to the conservative position. For suppose the obstetrician decides to try, after operating and delivering the child, to repair its head by microsurgery. The woman's supposed 'some chance' of survival if the child's head is not crushed is of the same kind as the obstetrician's 'some chance' of saving the child after crushing its head: in each case there is what the well-informed plain man would call 'no chance', but in each case it will take a little time for the matter to be finally settled by the events themselves – for the woman to die or the obstetrician to admit failure. Would the conservative say that the obstetrician's intention to try to save the child in this way, though hopeless, completely alters the shape of the problem and perhaps makes it all right for the obstetrician to crush the child's head? If so, then what we have here is a morality of gestures and poses.

Aspects of the Distinction: Second Group

I return to the main thread of my argument. Of the remaining three aspects of the action/consequence distinction, it was not quite true to say that all are present in (every instance of) the obstetrical example; for the first of them has not even that merit. The main point, however, is that even if it were always present it would not help the conservative – though it might help us to diagnose his trouble.

(d) Someone's decision whether an upshot of a movement of mine is to be covered by his description of what I *did* may depend partly on his moral assessment of my role in the total situation. Your condemnation of me, or perhaps your approval, may be reflected in your putting on the 'action' side of the line an upshot which an indifferent onlooker would count as merely a 'consequence'. This aspect of the action/consequence distinction – if indeed it is one independently of those already discussed – cannot help the conservative who believes that a premiss using the distinction tends to *support* a moral conclusion. That belief demands a relevance relation which slopes the other way.

There seem to be just two remaining aspects to the action/consequence distinction. Certainly, there are only two which do appear in all instances of the obstetrical example. These two must be the sole justification for saying that operating would be killing while no operating would not be killing; and so they must bear the whole weight of any conservative but non-authoritarian case against killing the child.

(e) Operating is killing the child because if the obstetrician operates there is a high degree of *immediacy* between what he does with his hands and the child's dying. This immediacy consists in the brevity or absence of time-lag, spatial nearness, simplicity of causal connexions, and paucity of intervening physical objects. The relations amongst these are complex; but they are severally relevant to the action/consequence distinction, and in the obstetrical example they all pull together, creating an overwhelming case for calling the performance of the operation the *killing* of the child.

(f) Not-operating is not killing the woman because it is not *doing* anything at all but is merely *refraining* from doing something.

Since (e) and (f) are so central to the action/consequence distinction generally, it is appropriate that they should sometimes bear its whole weight, as they do in the conservative's (correct) application of the distinction to the obstetrical example. But if (e) and (f) are all there is to the premiss: 'In this case, operating would be killing an innocent human while not-operating would involve the death of an innocent human only as a consequence,' then this premiss offers no support at all to the conclusion: 'In this case, operating would be wrong.'

The matters which I group under 'immediacy' in (e) may borrow moral significance from their loose association with facts about whether and in what degree upshots are (a) expected, (b) inevitable or (c) aimed at. In none of these respects, however, is there a relevant asymmetry in the obstetrical example. The question is: why should a difference in degree of immediacy, unaccompanied by other relevant differences, be taken to support a moral discrimination? I cannot think of a remotely plausible answer which does not consist solely in an appeal to an authority.[5]

Suggestions come to mind about 'not getting one's hands dirty'; and the notion of what I call 'immediacy' does help to show how the literal and the metaphorical are mingled in some uses of that phrase. In so doing, however, it exposes the desire to 'keep one's hands clean', in cases like the obstetrical example, as a symptom of muddle or primness or, worst of all, a moral egoism like Pilate's. (To be fair: I do not think that many conservatives would answer in this way. If they used similar words it would probably not be to express the nasty sentiment I have mentioned but rather to say something like: 'I must obey God's law; and the rest is up to God.' Because this suggests a purely authoritarian basis, and because it certainly has nothing to do with immediacy, it lies beyond my present scope.)

Similarly with the acting/refraining distinction in (f). I shall argue in my next section that our criteria for this distinction do not invest it with any moral significance whatever – except when the distinction is drawn on the basis of independently formed moral judgements, and then it cannot help the conservative case for the reason given in (d). And if neither (c) immediacy nor (f) acting/refraining separately has moral significance, then clearly they cannot acquire any by being taken together.

Acting and Refraining

Suppose the obstetrician does not operate, and the woman dies. He does not kill her, but he *lets her die*. The reproach suggested by these words is just an unavoidable nuisance, and I shall not argue from it. When I say 'he lets her die', I mean only that he knowingly refrains from preventing her death which he alone could prevent, and he cannot say that her survival is in a general way 'none of my business' or 'not [even prima facie] my concern'. If my arguments so far are correct, then this one fact – the fact that the non-operating obstetrician *lets the woman die* but does not *kill her* – is the only remaining feature of the situation which the conservative can hope to adduce as supporting his judgement about what ought to be done in every instance of the obstetrical example.[6] Let us examine the difference between 'X killed Y' and 'X let Y die.'

Some cases of letting-die are also cases of killing. If on a dark night X knows that Y's next step will take him over the edge of a high cliff, and he refrains from uttering a simple word of warning because he doesn't care or because he wants Y dead, then it is natural to say not only that X lets Y die but also that he kills him – even if it was not X who suggested the route, removed the fence from the cliff-top, etc. Cases like this, where a failure-to-prevent is described as a doing partly *because* it is judged to be wicked or indefensible, are beside my present point; for I want to see what difference there is between killing and letting-die which might be a *basis for* a moral judgement. Anyway, the letting-die which is also killing must involve malice or wanton in difference, and there is nothing like that in the obstetrical example. In short, to count these cases as relevant to the obstetrical example would be to suggest that not-operating would after all be killing the woman – a plainly false suggestion which I have disavowed. I wish to criticize the conservative's argument, not to deny his premiss. So from now on I shall ignore cases of letting-die which are also cases of killing; and it will make for brevity to pretend that they do not exist. For example, I shall say that killing involves moving one's body – which is false of some of these cases, but true of all others.

One more preliminary point: the purposes of the present enquiry do not demand that a full analysis be given either of 'X killed Y' or of 'X let Y die.' We can ignore any implications either may have about what X (a) expected, (b) should have expected, or (c) was aiming at; for the obstetrical example is symmetrical in all those respects. We can also ignore the fact that 'X killed Y' loosely implies something about (e) immediacy which is not implied by 'X let Y die,' for immediacy in itself has no moral significance.

Consider the statement that *Joe killed the calf.* A certain aspect of the analysis of this will help us to see how it relates to *Joe let the calf die*. To say that Joe killed the calf is to say that

(1) Joe moved his body

and

(2) the calf died;

but it is also to say something about how Joe's moving was connected with the calf's dying – something to the effect that

(3) if Joe had not moved as he did, the calf would not have died.

How is (3) to be interpreted? We might take it, rather strictly, as saying

(3′): If Joe had moved in *any* other way, the calf would not have died.

This, however, is too strong to be a necessary condition of Joe's having killed the calf. Joe may have killed the calf even if he could have moved in other ways which would equally have involved the calf's dying. Suppose that Joe cut the calf's throat, but could have shot it instead: in that case he clearly killed it; but (3′) denies that he killed it, because the calf might still have died even if Joe had not moved in just the way he did.

We might adopt a weaker reading of (3), namely as saying

(3″): Joe could have moved in *some* other way without the calf's dying.

But where (3′) was too strong to be necessary, (3″) is too weak to express a sufficient connexion between Joe's moving and the calf's dying. It counts Joe as having killed the calf not only in cases where we should ordinarily say that he killed it but also in cases where the most we should say is that he let it die.

The truth lies somewhere between (3′), which is appropriate to 'Joe killed the calf in the only way open to him,' and (3″), which is appropriate to 'Joe killed the calf or let it die'. Specifically, the connexion between Joe's moving and the calf's dying which is appropriate to 'Joe killed the calf' but not to 'Joe let the calf die' is expressed by

(3‴): Of all the other ways in which Joe might have moved, *relatively few* satisfy the condition: if Joe had moved like that, the calf would have died.

And the connexion which is appropriate to 'Joe let the calf die' but not to 'Joe killed the calf' is expressed by

(4): Of all the other ways in which Joe might have moved, *almost all* satisfy the condition: if Joe had moved like that, the calf would have died.

This brings me to the main thesis of the present section: apart from the factors I have excluded as already dealt with, the difference between 'X killed Y' and 'X let Y die' *is* the difference between (3‴) and (4). When the killing/letting-die distinction is stripped of its implications regarding immediacy, intention etc. – which lack moral significance or don't apply to the example – all that remains is a distinction having to do with where a set of movements lies on the scale which has 'the only set of movements which would have produced that upshot' at one end and 'movements other than the only set which would have produced that upshot' at the other.

This, then, is the conservative's residual basis for a moral discrimination between operating and not-operating. Operating would be killing if the obstetrician makes movements which constitute operating, then the child will die; and there are very few other movements he could make which would also involve the child's dying. Not-operating would only be letting-die: if throughout the time when he could be operating the obstetrician makes movements which constitute not-operating, then the woman will die; but the vast majority of alternative movements he could make during that time would equally involve the woman's dying. I do not see how anyone doing his own moral thinking about the matter could find the least shred of moral significance in *this* difference between operating and not-operating.

Suppose you are told that X killed Y in the only way possible in the circumstances; and this, perhaps together with certain other details of the case, leads you to judge X's conduct adversely. Then you are told: 'You have been misled: there is another way in which X could have killed Y.' Then a third informant says: 'That is wrong too: there are two other ways... etc.' Then a fourth: 'No: there are three other ways... etc.' Then a fourth: 'No: there are three other ways... etc.' Clearly, these successive corrections put no pressure at all on your original judgement: you will not think it relevant to your judgement on X's killing of Y that it could have been carried out in any one of *n* different ways. But the move from 'X killed Y in the only possible way' to 'X killed Y in one of the only five possible ways' is of the same *kind* as the move from 'X killed Y' to 'X let Y die' (except for the latter's implications about immediacy); and the moral insignificance of the former move is evidence for the moral insignificance of the latter move also.

The difference between 'X killed Y' and 'X let Y die' is the sum total of a vast number of differences such as that between 'X killed Y' in one of the only *n* possible ways' and 'X killed Y in one of the only $n+1$ possible ways.' If the difference between '... *n* ...' and '... $n+1$ ...' were morally insignificant only because it was *too small* for any moral discrimination to be based upon it, then the sum-total of millions of such differences might still have moral significance. But in fact the differences in question, whatever their size, are of the *wrong kind* for any moral discrimination to be based upon them. Suppose you have judged X adversely, on the basis of the misinformation: 'X killed Y in the only way possible in the circumstances'; and this is then replaced, in one swoop, by the true report: 'X did not kill Y at all, though he did knowingly let Y die.' Other things being equal, would this give you the slightest reason to retract your adverse judgement? Not a bit of it! It would be perfectly reasonable for you to reply: 'The fact remains that X chose to conduct himself in a way which he knew would involve Y's death. At first I thought his choice could encompass Y's death only by being the choice of some rather specific course of conduct; whereas the revised report shows me that X's choice could have encompassed Y's death while committing X to very little. At first I thought it had to be a choice to act; I now realize that it could have been a choice to refrain. What of it?'

There are several things a conservative is likely to say at this point – all equivalent. 'When we know that the crucial choice could have been a choice to refrain from something, we can begin to allow for the possibility that it may have been a choice to refrain from doing something wrong, such as killing an innocent human.' Or: 'You say "other things being equal", but in the obstetrical example they aren't equal. By representing letting-die as a kind of wide-optioned killing you suppress the fact that the alternative to letting the woman die is killing the child.'

Replies like these are available to the conservative only if he does not need them and can break through at some other point; for they assume the very point which is at issue, namely that in every instance of the obstetrical example it would be wrong to kill the child. I think that in some cases it would indeed be wrong – (I do not press for a blanket judgement on all instances of the example – quite the contrary); and in such a case the obstetrician, if he rightly let the woman die, could defend his doing so on the basis of the details of the particular case. Furthermore, he might wish to begin his defence by explaining: 'I let the woman die, but I did not kill her'; for letting-die is in general likely to be more defensible than killing. My analysis incidentally shows one reason why: the alternatives to killing are always very numerous, and the odds are that at least one of them provides an acceptable way out of the impasse; whereas the alternative to letting-die is always some fairly specific course of conduct, and if there are conclusive objections to *that* then there's an end of the matter. All this, though, is a matter of likelihoods. It is no help in the rare cases where the alternatives to killing, numerous as they are, arguably do *not* include an acceptable way out of the impasse because they all involve something of the same order of gravity as a killing, namely a letting-die. The conservative may say: 'Where innocent humans are in question, letting-die is not of the same order of gravity as killing: for one of them is not, and the other is, absolutely wrong in all possible circumstances.' But this, like the rejoinders out of which this paragraph grew, assumes the very point which is at issue. All these conservative moves come down to just one thing: 'At this point your argument fails; for the wrongness of killing the child, in any instance of the obstetrical example, *can* be defended on the basis of your own analysis of the acting/refraining distinction – plus the extra premiss that it would always be wrong to kill the child.'

The Stress on the Specific

My argument is finished; but its strategy might be thought to be open to a certain criticism which I want to discuss.

The obstetrical example is a *kind* of situation, on every instance of which the conservative makes a certain judgement. I have argued that this judgement, as applied to many instances of the example, cannot be defended except by the unquestioning invocation of authority. This would have been damaging to the conservative position even if I had appealed only to 'fantastic' kinds of instance such as seldom or never occur; but in fact my claims have been true of many real-life instances of the obstetrical example. Still, a conservative might resist my drive towards the relatively specific, my insistence upon asking: 'What is there about *this* kind of instance which justifies your judgement upon it?' He might claim that even my opening paragraph presents so special a kind of situation that he cannot fairly be asked to find in *it* something which supports his judgement other than by a blanket appeal to his general principle that it would always be wrong to kill an innocent human. There are two ways in which he might defend this stand: they look alike, but their fatal defects are very different.

The first is by the use of a sub-Wittgensteinian argument from the nature of language. Although I have never encountered it, it is a possible and plausible objection to my strategy of argument. The conservative might say: 'Granted that facts about (a) expectation, (b) inevitability and (c) intention are irrelevant to the way the action/consequence distinction applies to the obstetrical example; it does not follow that when we apply the distinction to the example *all* we are doing – apart from (d) reflecting our already-formed moral judgements – is to report facts about (e) immediacy and (f) acting/refraining. Language and thought don't work like this. When we say: "Operating would be killing; not-operating would not be killing though it would have death as a consequence", we are not *just* talking about immediacy and specificity of options. We are using words which, *qua* words in the language, are laden with associations having to do with (a)–(d); and these associations of the words cannot simply be ignored or forgotten in a particular case. Language is not atomic in that way, and it would be at best a clumsy instrument if it were.'

I agree that we often do, and perhaps must sometimes, decide our conduct in one situation partly through verbal carry-overs from others in which similar conduct could be justified more directly. But I think that everyone will agree that the more serious a practical problem is, the greater is our obligation to resist such verbal carry-overs and scrutinize the particular problem in order to see what there is about *it* which would justify this or that solution to it. A practical problem in which human lives are at stake is a deeply serious one, and it would be an abdication from all moral seriousness to settle it by verbal carry-overs. I am not saying: 'Take pity on the poor woman, and never mind what the correct description of the situation is.' I am opposing someone who says: 'This is the correct description of the situation – never mind what its force is in this particular case.'

The second objection to my stress on the particular case, or the specific kind of case, is one which conservatives do sometimes use; and it connects with a muddle which is not special to conservatives. It goes like this: 'We must have rules. If every practical problem had to be solved on the spot, on the basis of the fine details of the particular case, the results would be disastrous. Take a situation which falls under some rule which I know to be justified in most situations. There may not be time or means for me to learn much more about the present situation than just that it does fall under the rule; the details of the case, even if I can discover them, may be too complex for me to handle; my handling of them, even if intellectually efficient, may without my knowing it be self-interested or corrupt; by deciding, however uncorruptly, not to follow the rule on this occasion, I may weaken its hold on me in other situations where it clearly ought to be followed; and even if I could be sure that I was in no such danger, I might help others into it by publicly breaking the rule.'[7]

This is all true, but it does not help the conservative. Notice first that it tells against undue attention to individual cases rather than against undue attention to limited kinds of case: its target is not the specific but the particular. Still, it could be developed into an attack on over-stressing very specifically detailed kinds of case: its opening words would then have to be replaced by: 'We must have rather general rules.' This is true too, but it is still no help to the conservative.

This argument for our bringing practical problems under rather general rules is based on the consequences of our not doing so: it points to the dangers attendant on suspending a general rule and considering whether one's practical problem might be better resolved by applying a less general one. But sometimes these dangers will be far too slight to justify doing what a given general rule enjoins in a particular situation. If the thesis under discussion is to have any practical upshot which is not ludicrous ('Never break any general rule which would enjoin the right action in more cases than not'), or vague to the point of vacuity ('Always apply some fairly general rule'), or vague to the point of vacuity ('Always apply some fairly general rule'), or merely question-begging ('Never break a rule forbidding an action which really is absolutely impermissible'), then it must allow us to raise questions of the form: 'Need we be deterred by the dangers attendant on suspending *this* rule in favour of *this* more specific rule in *this* kind of situation?' The answer will depend upon what the challenged general rule is, what the proposed substitute for it is, the intelligence and character of the agent, and the likelihood that his breaking the rule (if it comes to that) would become generally known and, if known, demoralizing to others. These matters need not be so complex as to defeat finite intelligence, or so primrose-strewn that fallen man dare not venture among them. Furthermore, they can themselves be embodied in rules carefully formulated in advance – meta-rules about the kinds of situation in which this or that ground-level general rule may be suspended in favour of this or that more specific one.

Here is a possible case. A certain obstetrician accepts the rule, 'Do not kill innocent humans', as applicable in every kind of situation he has thought of except the kind described in my opening paragraph. He wants a rule for this kind too, as a shield against the confusions, temptations and pressures of the concrete situation; and after reflection he adopts the following: 'If the child is not hydrocephalic it is not to be killed. If it is hydrocephalic it is to be killed unless either (a) the woman is bound to die within a month anyway, or (b) the woman has no other children under eighteen and she is known to be a chronic acute depressive. If (a) or (b) or both are true, the child is not to be killed.'

By preferring this rule to the more general one for instances of the obstetrical example, the obstetrician is not rendering it likely that in some situations he will flounder around not knowing what rule about killing to apply. For he has a clear enough meta-rule: 'If the only way to save a woman's life is to kill the child she is bearing, apply this rule . . . otherwise apply the rule: Do not kill innocent humans.'

The obstetrician is not satisfied with his ground-level rule for instances of the obstetrical example, and he hopes to be able to improve it. Still, he is resigned to his rule's ignoring various matters which though they are relevant to what the ideally right action would be, would involve him in the dangers of over-specificity mentioned above 'Is the woman a potential murderess or the child a mongol?' – the answers are probably unobtainable. 'In what ways would the woman's death represent a real loss to others?' – the answer, even if discoverable, could be so complex as to elude any manageable rule. 'Would either course of action bring the medical profession into undeserved but seriously damaging disrepute?' – it would be too easy for that to be unconsciously conflated with the question of which course would best further the obstetrician's own career. 'Would the child, if delivered alive, be especially helpful to students of hydrocephalus?' – asking that could be the first step on a downward path: by allowing one woman to die partly because her child will be medically interesting if alive, even an uncorrupt man may ease the way towards allowing some other woman to die partly because *she* will be medically interesting when dead.

Although he pays heed – neurotically pays far too much heed – to the conservative's warnings against over-specificity, this obstetrician arrives at a conclusion quite different from the conservative's. That is the crux. The conservative who warns against the dangers of over-specifying is trying to find a consequentialist basis for his whole position. Unlike the 'protective-coloration gambit' discussed earlier, this is legitimate enough in itself; but it simply does not yield the conservative position on the matter under discussion. For it to do so, the conservative would have to show that our obstetrician's more specific rule is *too* dangerous in the ways mentioned above; and he would have to do this without applying danger-inflating standards which would commit him also to condemning as too dangerous the suspension of the general rule: 'Never leave a bucket in a hall-way.' He may object: 'Buckets in hall-ways are not important enough to provide a fair analogy. Where something as grave as killing is in question, we should be especially sensitive to the dangers of suspending a general rule.' But then when something as grave as letting someone die is involved in applying the rule, we should be especially reluctant to accept, without good empirical evidence, popular clichés about the dangers of suspending general rules. The two points cancel out.

Of course, there are these dangers, and we should guard against them. To assess them at all precisely, though, would require more than we know of sociology, psychology and the philosophy of mind; and so our guarding against them can consist only in our keeping the urge towards specificity under some restraint, our remembering that in this matter it is not always true that the sky is the limit. The conservative who hopes to secure his position by pointing out these dangers must claim that he *can* assess them, and can discover in them a simple, sweeping pattern which picks out a certain list of general rules as the ones which ought never to be suspended by anyone in any circumstances. No one would explicitly make so preposterous a claim.

'So you do at any rate retreat from act- to rule-utilitarianism?' No. Rule-utilitarianism can be presented (1) as a quasi-mystical doctrine about the importance of rule-following 'per se', or (2) as a doctrine about the importance of rule-following because of what rule-following empirically *is*, because of what happens when people follow rules and what happens when they don't. In version (1), rule-utilitarianism is a distinct doctrine which has nothing to recommend it. In version (2), it is just part of a thorough act-utilitarianism. (In most actual presentations, there is a cloudy attempt to combine (2)'s reasonableness with (1)'s rejection of act-utilitarianism.) In this section I have been discussing what the consequences might be, for myself or others, of my suspending or breaking a given general rule. These are among, not additional to, the consequential factors whose relevance I have been urging all through the paper. There has been no retreat.

Conclusion

Principles of the form: 'It would always be wrong to . . . whatever the consequences of not doing so' seem defensible because the action/consequence distinction does often have a certain kind of moral significance. But in proportion as a situation gives real work to the rider '. . . whatever the consequences of not doing so', in proportion as it puts pressure on this rider, in proportion as the 'consequences of not doing so' give some moral reason for 'doing so' – to that extent the action consequence distinction lacks moral significance in that situation. The obstetrical example is just an extreme case: there the rider serves to dismiss the entire moral case against applying the principle; and, proportionately, the action/consequence distinction carries no moral weight at all.

The phenomenon of conservatism, then, can be explained as follows. The conservative naturally thinks that the action/consequence distinction has great moral significance because of its frequent connexion with differences concerning (a) expectation, (b) inevitability, (c) intention and (d) independently formed moral judgements. He then encounters cases like the obstetrical example, where (a)–(d) are irrelevant but where the distinction can still be applied because of facts about (e) immediacy and (f) acting/refraining. Failing to see that in these cases the distinction has lost absolutely all its moral bite, and perhaps encouraged by a mistake about 'rule-following per se', he still applies his principle in the usual way. Those who do not follow him in this he finds lax or opportunist or corrupt; and many of them half agree, by conceding to his position a certain hard and unfeeling uprightness. Both are wrong. Conservatism, when it is not mere obedience, is mere muddle.

Notes

1 K. Feeney and A. P. Barry in *Journal of Obstetrics and Gynaecology of the British Empire* (1954), p. 61. R. L. Cecil and H. F. Conn (eds), *The Specialties in General Practice* (Philadelphia, 1957), p. 410.
2 See G. Kelly, *Medico-Moral Problems* (Dublin, 1955), p. 20; C. J. McFadden, *Medical Ethics* (London, 1962), pp. 27–33; T. J. O'Donnell, *Morals in Medicine* (London, 1959), pp. 39–44; N. St John-Stevas, *The Right to Life* (London 1963), p. 71.
3 G. E. M. Anscombe, 'Modern Moral Philosophy', *Philosophy*, 33 (1958), p. 17.
4 G. E. M. Anscombe, 'Does Oxford Moral Philosophy Corrupt the Youth?', *The Listener* (February 14, 1957), p. 267. See also the correspondence in ensuing numbers, and Michael Tanner, 'Examples in Moral Philosophy', *Proceedings of the Aristotelian Society*, 65 (1964–5).
5 Conservatives use words like 'direct' to cover a jumble of factors of which immediacy is the most prominent. Pius XII has said that a pain-killing, life-shortening drug may be used 'if there exists no direct causal link, either through the will of interested parties or by the nature of things, between the induced consciousness [*sic*] and the shortening of life . . . (Quoted in St. John-Stevas, *The Right to Life*, p. 61.)
6 In a case where the child cannot survive anyway: 'It is a question of the *direct taking* of one innocent life or merely *permitting* two deaths. In other words, there is question of one *murder* against two deaths . . .' Kelly, *Medico-Moral Problems*, p. 181.
7 For a gesture in this direction, see St. John-Stevas, *The Right to Life*, pp. 14–16. See also McFadden, *Medical Ethics*, p. 133.

24

Active and Passive Euthanasia

James Rachels

Abstract

The traditional distinction between active and passive euthanasia requires critical analysis. The conventional doctrine is that there is such an important moral difference between the two that, although the latter is sometimes permissible, the former is always forbidden. This doctrine may be challenged for several reasons. First of all, active euthanasia is in many cases more humane than passive euthanasia. Secondly, the conventional doctrine leads to decisions concerning life and death on irrelevant grounds. Thirdly, the doctrine rests on a distinction between killing and letting die that itself has no moral importance. Fourthly, the most common arguments in favor of the doctrine are invalid. I therefore suggest that the American Medical Association policy statement that endorses this doctrine is unsound.

The distinction between active and passive euthanasia is thought to be crucial for medical ethics. The idea is that it is permissible, at least in some cases, to withhold treatment and allow a patient to die, but it is never permissible to take any direct action designed to kill the patient. This doctrine seems to be accepted by most doctors, and it is endorsed in a statement adopted by the House of Delegates of the American Medical Association on December 4, 1973.

> The intentional termination of the life of one human being by another – mercy killing – is contrary to that for which the medical profession stands and is contrary to the policy of the American Medical Association.
>
> The cessation of the employment of extraordinary means to prolong the life of the body when there is irrefutable evidence that biological death is imminent is the decision of the patient and/or his immediate family. The advice and judgement of the physician should be freely available to the patient and/or his immediate family.

However, a strong case can be made against this doctrine. In what follows I will set out some of the relevant arguments, and urge doctors to reconsider their views on this matter.

To begin with a familiar type of situation, a patient who is dying of incurable cancer of the throat is in terrible pain, which can no longer be satisfactorily alleviated. He is certain to die within a few days, even if present treatment is continued, but he does not want to go on living for those days since the pain is unbearable. So he asks the doctor for an end to it, and his family joins in the request.

Suppose the doctor agrees to withold treatment, as the conventional doctrine says he may. The justification for his doing so is that the patient is in terrible agony, and since he is going to die anyway, it would be wrong to prolong his suffering needlessly. But now notice this. If one simply withholds treatment, it may take the patient longer to die, and so he may suffer more than he would if more direct action were taken and a lethal injection given. This fact provides strong reason for thinking that, once the initial decision not to prolong his agony has been made, active euthanasia is actually

From *New England Journal of Medicine* (9 January 1975), pp. 78–80. Reprinted with permission.

preferable to passive euthanasia, rather than the reverse. To say otherwise is to endorse the option that leads to more suffering rather than less, and is contrary to the humanitarian impulse that prompts the decision not to prolong his life in the first place.

Part of my point is that the process of being "allowed to die" can be relatively slow and painful, whereas being given a lethal injection is relatively quick and painless. Let me give a different sort of example. In the United States about one in 600 babies is born with Down's syndrome. Most of these babies are otherwise healthy – that is, with only the usual pediatric care, they will proceed to an otherwise normal infancy. Some, however, are born with congenital defects such as intestinal obstructions that require operations if they are to live. Sometimes, the parents and the doctor will decide not to operate, and let the infant die. Anthony Shaw describes what happens then:

> When surgery is denied [the doctor] must try to keep the infant from suffering while natural forces sap the baby's life away. As a surgeon whose natural inclination is to use the scalpel to fight off death, standing by and watching a salvageable baby die is the most emotionally exhausting experience I know. It is easy at a conference, in a theoretical discussion, to decide that such infants should be allowed to die. It is altogether different to stand by in the nursery and watch as dehydration and infection wither a tiny being over hours and days. This is a terrible ordeal for me and the hospital staff – much more so than for the parents who never set foot in the nursery.[1]

I can understand why some people are opposed to all euthanasia, and insist that such infants must be allowed to live. I think I can also understand why other people favor destroying these babies quickly and painlessly. But why should anyone favor letting "dehydration and infection wither a tiny being over hours and days?" The doctrine that says that a baby may be allowed to dehydrate and wither, but may not be given an injection that would end its life without suffering, seems so patently cruel as to require no further refutation. The strong language is not intended to offend, but only to put the point in the clearest possible way.

My second argument is that the conventional doctrine leads to decisions concerning life and death made on irrelevant grounds.

Consider again the case of the infants with Down's syndrome who need operations for congenital defects unrelated to the syndrome to live. Sometimes, there is no operation, and the baby dies, but when there is no such defect, the baby lives on. Now, an operation such as that to remove an intestinal obstruction is not prohibitively difficult. The reason why such operations are not performed in these cases is, clearly, that the child has Down's syndrome and the parents and doctor judge that because of that fact it is better for the child to die.

But notice that this situation is absurd, no matter what view one takes of the lives and potentials of such babies. If the life of such an infant is worth preserving, what does it matter if it needs a simple operation? Or, if one thinks it better that such a baby should not live on, what difference does it make that it happens to have an unobstructed intestinal tract? In either case, the matter of life and death is being decided on irrelevant grounds. It is the Down's syndrome, and not the intestines, that is the issue. The matter should be decided, if at all, on that basis, and not be allowed to depend on the essentially irrelevant question of whether the intestinal tract is blocked.

What makes this situation possible, of course, is the idea that when there is an intestinal blockage, one can "let the baby die," but when there is no such defect there is nothing that can be done, for one must not "kill" it. The fact that this idea leads to such results as deciding life or death on irrelevant grounds is another good reason why the doctrine should be rejected.

One reason why so many people think that there is an important moral difference between active and passive euthanasia is that they think killing someone is morally worse than letting someone die. But is it? Is killing, in itself, worse than letting die? To investigate this issue, two cases may be considered that are exactly alike except that one involves killing whereas the other involves letting someone die. Then, it can be asked whether this difference makes any difference to the moral assessments. It is important that the cases be exactly alike, except for this one difference, since otherwise one cannot be confident that it is this difference and not some other that accounts for any variation in the assessments of the two cases. So, let us consider this pair of cases:

In the first. Smith stands to gain a large inheritance if anything should happen to his six-year-old cousin. One evening while the child is taking his bath. Smith sneaks into the bathroom and drowns the child, and then arranges things so that it will look like an accident.

In the second. Jones also stands to gain if anything should happen to his six-year-old cousin. Like Smith, Jones sneaks in planning to drown the child in his bath. However, just as he enters the bathroom Jones sees the child slip and hit his head, and fall face down in the water. Jones is delighted: he stands by, ready to push the child's head back under if it is necessary, but it is not necessary. With only a little thrashing about, the child drowns all by himself, "accidentally," as Jones watches and does nothing.

Now Smith killed the child, whereas Jones "merely" let the child die. That is the only difference between them. Did either man behave better, from a moral point of view? If the difference between killing and letting die were in itself a morally important matter, one should say that Jones's behavior was less reprehensible than Smith's. But does one really want to say that? I think not. In the first place, both men acted from the same motive, personal gain, and both had exactly the same end in view when they acted. It may be inferred from Smith's conduct that he is a bad man, although that judgement may be withdrawn or modified if certain further facts are learned about him – for example, that he is mentally deranged. But would not the very same thing be inferred about Jones from his conduct? And would not the same further considerations also be relevant to any modification of this judgement? Moreover, suppose Jones pleaded, in his own defense. "After all, I didn't do anything except just stand there and watch the child drown. I didn't kill him: I only let him die." Again, if letting die were in itself less bad than killing, this defense should have at least some weight. But it does not. Such a "defense" can only be regarded as a grotesque perversion of moral reasoning. Morally speaking, it is no defense at all.

Now, it may be pointed out, quite properly, that the cases of euthanasia with which doctors are concerned are not like this at all. They do not involve personal gain or the destruction of normal healthy children. Doctors are concerned only with cases in which the patient's life is of no further use to him, or in which the patient's life has become or will soon become a terrible burden. However, the point is the same in these cases: the bare difference between killing and letting die does not, in itself, make a moral difference. If a doctor lets a patient die, for humane reasons, he is in the same moral position as if he had given the patient a lethal injection for humane reasons. If his decision was wrong – if, for example, the patient's illness was in fact curable – the decision would be equally regrettable no matter which method was used to carry it out. And if the doctor's decision was the right one, the method used is not in itself important.

The AMA policy statement isolates the crucial issue very well: the crucial issue is "the intentional termination of the life of one human being by another." But after identifying this issue, and forbidding "mercy killing," the statement goes on to deny that the cessation of treatment is the intentional termination of a life. This is where the mistake comes in, for what is the cessation of treatment, in these circumstances, if it is not "the intentional termination of the life of one human being by another?" Of course it is exactly that, and if it were not, there would be no point to it.

Many people will find this judgement hard to accept. One reason. I think, is that it is very easy to conflate the question of whether killing is, in itself, worse than letting die, with the very different question of whether most actual cases of killing are more reprehensible than most actual cases of letting die. Most actual cases of killing are clearly terrible (think, for example, of all the murders reported in the newspapers), and one hears of such cases every day. On the other hand, one hardly ever hears of a case of letting die, except for the actions of doctors who are motivated by humanitarian reasons. So one learns to think of killing in a much worse light than of letting die. But this does not mean that there is something about killing that makes it in itself worse than letting die, for it is not the bare difference between killing and letting die that makes the difference in these cases. Rather, the other factors – the murderer's motive of personal gain, for example, contrasted with the doctor's humanitarian motivation – account for different reactions to the different cases.

I have argued that killing is not in itself any worse than letting die: if my contention is right, it follows that active euthanasia is not any worse than passive euthanasia. What arguments can be given on the other side? The most common. I believe, is the following:

"The important difference between active and passive euthanasia is that, in passive euthanasia, the doctor does not do anything to bring about the patient's death. The doctor does nothing, and the patient dies of whatever ills already afflict him. In active euthanasia, however, the doctor does something to bring about the patient's death: he kills him. The doctor who gives the patient with cancer a lethal injection has himself caused his patient's death: whereas if he merely ceases treatment, the cancer is the cause of the death."

A number of points need to be made here. The first is that it is not exactly correct to say that in passive euthanasia the doctor does nothing, for he does do one thing that is very important: he lets the patient die. "Letting someone die" is certainly different, in some respects, from other types of action – mainly in that it is a kind of action that one may perform by way of not performing certain other actions. For example, one may let a patient die by way of not giving medication, just as one may insult someone by way of not shaking his hand. But for any purpose of moral assessment, it is a type of action nonetheless. The decision to let a patient die is subject to moral appraisal in the same way that a decision to kill him would be subject to moral appraisal: it may be assessed as wise or unwise, compassionate or sadistic, right or wrong. If a doctor deliberately let a patient die who was suffering from a routinely curable illness, the doctor would certainly be to blame for what he had done, just as he would be to blame if he had needlessly killed the patient. Charges against him would then be appropriate. If so, it would be no defense at all for him to insist that he didn't "do anything." He would have done something very serious indeed, for he let his patient die.

Fixing the cause of death may be very important from a legal point of view, for it may determine whether criminal charges are brought against the doctor. But I do not think that this notion can be used to show a moral difference between active and passive euthanasia. The reason why it is considered bad to be the cause of someone's death is that death is regarded as a great evil – and so it is. However, if it has been decided that euthanasia – even passive euthanasia – is desirable in a given case, it has also been decided that in this instance death is no greater an evil than the patient's continued existence. And if this is true, the usual reason for not wanting to be the cause of someone's death simply does not apply.

Finally, doctors may think that all of this is only of academic interest – the sort of thing that philosophers may worry about but that has no practical bearing on their own work. After all, doctors must be concerned about the legal consequences of what they do, and active euthanasia is clearly forbidden by the law. But even so, doctors should also be concerned with the fact that the law is forcing upon them a moral doctrine that may well be indefensible, and has a considerable effect on their practices. Of course, most doctors are not now in the position of being coerced in this matter, for they do not regard themselves as merely going along with what the law requires. Rather, in statements such as the AMA policy statement that I have quoted, they are endorsing this doctrine as a central point of medical ethics. In that statement, active euthanasia is condemned not merely as illegal but as "contrary to that for which the medical profession stands," whereas passive euthanasia is approved. However, the preceding considerations suggest that there is really no moral difference between the two, considered in themselves (there may be important moral differences in some cases in their *consequences*, but, as I pointed out, these differences may make active euthanasia, and not passive euthanasia, the morally preferable option). So, whereas doctors may have to discriminate between active and passive euthanasia to satisfy the law, they should not do any more than that. In particular, they should not give the distinction any added authority and weight by writing it into official statements of medical ethics.

Reference

1 A. Shaw 'Doctor, Do We Have a Choice?' *New York Times Magazine*. January 30, 1972, p. 54.

25

Is Killing No Worse Than Letting Die?

Winston Nesbitt

Abstract

Those who wish to refute the view that it is worse to kill than to let die sometimes produce examples of cases in which an agent lets someone die but would be generally agreed to be no less reprehensible than if he had killed. It is argued that the examples produced typically possess a feature which makes their use in this context illegitimate, and that when modified to remove this feature, they provide support for the view which they were designed to undermine.

I want in this paper to consider a kind of argument sometimes produced against the thesis that it is worse to kill someone (that is, to deliberately take action that results in another's death) than merely to allow someone to die (that is, deliberately to fail to take steps which were available and which would have saved another's life). Let us, for brevity's sake, refer to this as the 'difference thesis', since it implies that there is a moral difference between killing and letting die.

One approach commonly taken by opponents of the difference thesis is to produce examples of cases in which an agent does not kill, but merely lets someone die, and yet would be generally agreed to be just as morally reprehensible as if he had killed. This kind of appeal to common intuitions might seem an unsatisfactory way of approaching the issue. It has been argued[1] that what stance one takes concerning the difference thesis will depend on the ethical theory one holds, so that we cannot decide what stance is correct independently of deciding what is the correct moral theory. I do not, however, wish to object to the approach in question on these grounds. It may be true that different moral theories dictate different stances concerning the different thesis, so that a theoretically satisfactory defence or refutation of the thesis requires a satisfactory defence of a theory which entails its soundness or unsoundness. However, the issue of its soundness or otherwise is a vital one in the attempt to decide some pressing moral questions,[2] and we cannot wait for a demonstration of the correct moral theory before taking up any kind of position with regard to it. Moreover, decisions on moral questions directly affecting practice are rarely derived from ethical first principles, but are usually based at some level on common intuitions, and it is arguable that at least where the question is one of public policy, this is as it should be.

From *Journal of Applied Philosopy*, vol. 12, no. 1 (1995), pp. 101–5.

2 [no part 1]

It might seem at first glance a simple matter to show at least that common moral intuitions favour the difference thesis. Compare, to take an example of John Ladd's[3], the case in which I push someone who I know cannot swim into a river, thereby killing her, with that in which I come across someone drowning and fail to rescue her, although I am able to do so, thereby letting her die. Wouldn't most of us agree that my behaviour is morally worse in the first case?

However, it would be generally agreed by those involved in the debate that nothing of importance for our issue, not even concerning common opinion, can be learned through considering such an example. As Ladd points out, without being told any more about the cases mentioned, we are inclined to assume that there are other morally relevant differences between them, because there usually would be. We assume, for example, some malicious motive in the case of killing, but perhaps only fear or indifference in the case of failing to save. James Rachels and Michael Tooley, both of whom argue against the difference thesis, make similar points,[4] as does Raziel Abelson, in a paper defending the thesis.[5] Tooley, for example, notes that as well as differences in motives, there are also certain other morally relevant differences between typical acts of killing and typical acts of failing to save which may make us judge them differently. Typically, saving someone requires more effort than refraining from killing someone. Again, an act of killing necessarily results in someone's death, but an act of failing to save does not – someone else may come to the rescue. Factors such as these, it is suggested, may account for our tendency to judge failure to save (i.e., letting die) less harshly than killing. Tooley concludes that if one wishes to appeal to intuitions here, 'one must be careful to confine one's attention to pairs of cases that do not differ in these, or other significant respects.'[6]

Accordingly, efforts are made by opponents of the difference thesis to produce pairs of cases which do not differ in morally significant respects (other than in one being a case of killing while the other is a case of letting die or failing to save). In fact, at least the major part of the case mounted by Rachels and Tooley against the difference thesis consists of the production of such examples. It is suggested that when we compare a case of killing with one which differs from it *only* in being a case of letting die, we will agree that either agent is as culpable as the other; and this is then taken to show that any inclination we ordinarily have to think killing worse than letting die is attributable to our tending, illegitimately, to think of typical cases of killing and of letting die, which differ in other morally relevant respects. I want now to examine the kind of example usually produced in these contexts.

3

I will begin with the examples produced by James Rachels in the article mentioned earlier, which is fast becoming one of the most frequently reprinted articles in the area.[7] Although the article has been the subject of a good deal of discussion, as far as I know the points which I will make concerning it have not been previously made. Rachels asks us to compare the following two cases. The first is that of Smith, who will gain a large inheritance should his six-year-old nephew die. With this in mind, Smith one evening sneaks into the bathroom where his nephew is taking a bath, and drowns him. The other case, that of Jones, is identical, except that as Jones is about to drown his nephew, the child slips, hits his head, and falls, face down and unconscious, into the bath-water. Jones, delighted at his good fortune, watches as his nephew drowns.

Rachels assumes that we will readily agree that Smith, who kills his nephew, is no worse, morally speaking, than Jones, who merely lets his nephew die. Do we really want to say, he asks, that either behaves better from the moral point of view than the other? It would, he suggests, be a 'grotesque perversion of moral reasoning' for Jones to argue, 'After all, I didn't do anything except just stand and watch the child drown. I didn't kill him; I only let him die.'[8] Yet, Rachels says, if letting die were in itself less bad than killing, this defence would carry some weight.

There is little doubt that Rachels is correct in taking it that we will agree that Smith behaves no worse in his examples than does Jones. Before we are persuaded by this that killing someone is in itself morally no worse than letting someone die, though, we need to consider the examples more closely. We concede that Jones, who merely let his nephew die, is just as reprehensible as Smith, who killed his nephew. Let us ask, however, just what is the ground of our judgement of the agent in each case. In the case of Smith, this seems to be adequately captured by saying that Smith drowned his nephew for motives of personal gain. But can we say that the grounds on which we judge Jones to be reprehensible, and just as reprehensible as Smith, are that he let his nephew drown for motives of personal gain? I suggest not – for this neglects to mention a crucial fact about Jones, namely that he was fully prepared to kill his nephew, and would have done so had it proved necessary. It would be generally accepted, I think, quite independently of the present debate, that someone who is fully prepared to perform a reprehensible action, in the expectation of certain circumstances, but does not do so because the expected circumstances do not eventuate, is just as reprehensible as someone who actually performs that action in those circumstances. Now this alone is sufficient to account for our judging Jones as harshly as Smith. He was fully prepared to do what Smith did, and would have done so if circumstances had not turned out differently from those in Smith's case. Thus, though we may agree that he is just as reprehensible as Smith, this cannot be taken as showing that his letting his nephew die is as reprehensible as Smith's killing his nephew – for we would have judged him just as harshly, given what he was prepared to do, even if he had not let his nephew die. To make this clear, suppose that we modify Jones' story along the following lines – as before, he sneaks into the bathroom while his nephew is bathing, with the intention of drowning the child in his bath. This time, however, just before he can seize the child, *he* slips and hits his head on the bath, knocking himself unconscious. By the time he regains consciousness, the child, unaware of his intentions, has called his parents, and the opportunity is gone. Here, Jones neither kills his nephew *nor* lets him die – yet I think it would be agreed that given his preparedness to kill the child for personal gain, he is as reprehensible as Smith.

The examples produced by Michael Tooley, in the book referred to earlier, suffer the same defect as those produced by Rachels. Tooley asks us to consider the following pair of scenarios, as it happens also featuring Smith and Jones. In the first, Jones is about to shoot Smith when he sees that Smith will be killed by a bomb unless Jones warns him, as he easily can. Jones does not warn him, and he is killed by the bomb – i.e., Jones lets Smith die. In the other, Jones wants Smith dead, and shoots him – i.e., he kills Smith.

Tooley elsewhere[9] produces this further example: two sons are looking forward to the death of their wealthy father, and decide independently to poison him. One puts poison in his father's whiskey, and is discovered doing so by the other, who was just about to do the same. The latter then allows his father to drink the poisoned whiskey, and refrains from giving him the antidote, which he happens to possess.

Tooley is confident that we will agree that in each pair of cases, the agent who kills is morally no worse than the one who lets die. It will be clear, however, that his examples are open to criticisms parallel to those just produced against Rachels. To take first the case where Jones is saved the trouble of killing Smith by the fortunate circumstance of a bomb's being about to explode near the latter: it is true that we judge Jones to be just as reprehensible as if he had killed Smith, but since he was fully prepared to kill him had he not been saved the trouble by the bomb, we would make the same judgement even if he had neither killed Smith nor let him die (even if, say, no bomb had been present, but Smith suffered a massive and timely heart attack). As for the example of the like-minded sons, here too the son who didn't kill was prepared to do so, and given this, would be as reprehensible as the other even if he had not let his father die (if, say, he did not happen to possess the antidote, and so was powerless to save him).

Let us try to spell out more clearly just where the examples produced by Rachels and Tooley fail. What both writers overlook is that what determines whether someone is reprehensible or not is not simply what he in fact does, but what he is prepared to do, perhaps as revealed by what he in fact does. Thus, while Rachels is correct in taking it that we will be inclined to judge Smith and Jones in his examples equally harshly, this is not surprising, since both are judged reprehensible for precisely the same reason, namely that they were fully prepared to kill for motives of personal gain. The same, of course, is true of Tooley's examples. In each example he gives of an agent who lets another die, the agent is fully prepared to kill (though in the event, he is spared the necessity). In their efforts to ensure that the members of each pair of cases they produce do not differ in any morally relevant respect (except that one is a case of killing and the other of letting die), Rachels and Tooley make them *too* similar – not only do Rachels' Smith and Jones, for example, have identical motives, but both are guilty of the same moral offence.

4

Given the foregoing account of the failings of the examples produced by Rachels and Tooley, what modifications do they require if they are to be legitimately used to gauge our attitudes towards killing and letting die, respectively? Let us again concentrate on Rachel's examples. Clearly, if his argument is to avoid the defect pointed out, we must stipulate that though Jones was prepared to let his nephew die once he saw that this would happen unless he intervened, he was not prepared to kill the child. The story will now go something like this: Jones stands to gain considerably from his nephew's death, as before, but he is not prepared to kill him for this reason. However, he happens to be on hand when his nephew slips, hits his head, and falls face down in the bath. Remembering that he will profit from the child's death, he allows him to drown. We need, however, to make a further stipulation, regarding the explanation of Jone's not being prepared to kill his nephew. It cannot be that he fears untoward consequences for himself, such as detection and punishment, or that he is too lazy to choose such an active course, or that the idea simply had not occurred to him. I think it would be common ground in the debate that if the only explanation of his not being prepared to kill his nephew was one of these kinds, he would be morally no better than Smith, who differed only in being more daring, or more energetic, whether or not fate then happened to offer him the opportunity to let his nephew die instead. In that case, we must suppose that the reason Jones is prepared to let his nephew die, but not to kill him, is a moral one – not intervening to save the child, he holds, is one thing, but actually bringing about his death is another, and altogether beyond the pale.

I suggest, then, that the case with which we must compare that of Smith is this: Jones happens to be on hand when his nephew slips, hits his head, and falls unconscious into his bath-water. It is clear to Jones that the child will drown if he does not intervene. He remembers that the child's death would be greatly to his advantage, and does not intervene. Though he is prepared to let the child die however, and in fact does so, he would not have been prepared to kill him, because, as he might put it, wicked though he is, he draws the line at killing for gain.

I am not entirely sure what the general opinion would be here as to the relative reprehensibility of Smith and Jones. I can only report my own, which is that Smith's behaviour is indeed morally worse than that of Jones. What I do want to insist on, however, is that, for the reasons I have given, we cannot take our reactions to the examples provided by Rachels and Tooley as an indication of our intuitions concerning the relative heinousness of killing and of letting die.

So far, we have restricted ourselves to discussion of common intuitions on our question, and made no attempt to argue for any particular answer. I will conclude by pointing out that, given the fairly common view that the *raison d'être* of morality is to make it possible for people to live together in reasonable peace and security, it is not difficult to provide a rationale for the intuition that in our modified version of Rachels' examples, Jones is less reprehensible than Smith. For it is clearly preferable to have Jones-like persons around rather than Smith-like ones. We are not threatened by the former – such a person will not save me if my life should be in danger, but in this he is no more dangerous than an incapacitated person, or for that matter, a rock or tree (in fact he may be better, for he *might* save me as long as he doesn't think he will profit from my death). Smith-like persons, however, *are* a threat – if such a person should come to believe that she will benefit sufficiently from my death, then not only must I expect no help from her if my life happens to be in danger, but I must fear positive attempts on my life. In that case, given the view mentioned of the point of morality, people prepared to behave as Smith does are clearly of greater concern from the moral point of view than those prepared only to behave as Jones does; which is to say that killing is indeed morally worse than letting die.

Notes

1 See, for example, John Chandler (1990), 'Killing and letting die – putting the debate in context', *Australasian Journal of Philosophy*, 68, no. 4, pp. 420–31.

2 It underlies, or is often claimed to underlie, for example, the Roman Catholic position on certain issues in the abortion debate, and the view that while 'passive' euthanasia may sometimes be permissible, 'active' euthanasia never is. It also seems involved in the common view that even if it is wrong to fail to give aid to the starving of the world, thereby letting them die, it is not as wrong as dropping bombs on them, thereby killing them.

3 John Ladd (1985), 'Positive and negative euthanasia' in James E. White (ed.), *Contemporary Moral Problems* (St Paul: West Publishing Co), pp. 58–68.

4 James Rachels (1979), 'Active and passive euthanasia' in James Rachels (ed.), *Moral Problems* (New York: Harper and Row), pp. 490–7; Michael Tooley (1983),

Abortion and Infanticide (Oxford: Clarendon Press), pp. 187–8.

5 Raziel Abelson (1982), 'There is a moral difference,' in Raziel Abelson and Marie-Louise Friquegnon (eds), *Ethics for Modern Life* (New York: St Martin's Press), pp. 73–83.

6 Tooley, *Abortion and Infanticide*, p. 189.

7 Rachels, 'Active and passive euthanasia'.

8 Ibid., p. 494.

9 Michael Tooley (1980), 'An irrelevant consideration: killing and letting die,' in Bonnie Steinbeck (ed.), *Killing and Letting Die* (Englewood Cliffs, NJ: Prentice-Hall), pp. 56–62.

26

Why Killing is Not Always Worse – and Sometimes Better – Than Letting Die

Helga Kuhse

Abstract

The philosophical debate over the moral difference between killing and letting die has obvious relevance for the contemporary public debate over voluntary euthanasia. Winston Nesbitt claims to have shown that killing someone is, other things being equal, always worse than allowing someone to die.[1] But this conclusion is illegitimate. While Nesbitt is correct when he suggests that killing is sometimes worse than letting die, this is not always the case. In this article, I argue that there are occasions when it is better to kill than to let die.

I

The conventional assumption is that killing a person is worse than allowing her to die. Beginning with James Rachels' famous article "Active and Passive Euthanasia", first published in the *New England Journal of Medicine* in 1975[2] this "difference thesis"[3] has been challenged by producing pairs of cases in which an agent who lets someone die would generally be judged to be no less reprehensible than an agent who kills. In a recent article, Winston Nesbitt argues that these pairs of cases typically contain a crucial common feature which will indeed make *these* cases of letting die the same as killing. Once this crucial feature is removed, he holds, these cases will support, rather than undermine, the difference view.

From *Cambridge Quarterly of Healthcare Ethics*, vol. 7, no. 4 (1998), pp. 371–4.

Winston Nesbitt's argument in support of the difference thesis rests on a number of contestable assumptions. In briefly retracing his argument, I shall leave these assumptions unchallenged, to show then that *even if* we accept these assumptions, Nesbitt's conclusion – that killing is worse than letting die – does not follow.

It will be adequate, for our purposes, to focus on just one of the paired examples discussed by Nesbitt: James Rachels' case of the "nasty cousins".[4] The first case involves Smith, who will gain a large inheritance should his six-year-old nephew die. One evening, Smith sneaks into the bathroom where his nephew is taking a bath, and drowns him. The second case, that of Jones, is exactly like the first case, except that as Jones is about to drown his nephew, the child slips, hits his head, and falls, face down and unconscious, into the water. Jones is delighted, and stands by as his nephew drowns.

In these examples, both men were motivated by personal gain, and both were aiming at the child's death. The only relevant difference between the cases is that Smith killed the child, whereas Jones allowed the child to die. But that difference, Rachels claims, is not morally relevant in itself, and the difference thesis is false.

Nesbitt agrees with Rachels that these examples support the common intuition that Jones is no less reprehensible than Smith, and that there is, in these cases, no difference between killing and allowing to die. The reason is, Nesbitt holds, that both agents were prepared to kill, for the sake of personal gain. After all, Jones was no less prepared to kill than Smith was – except that an accident (the child slipping, hitting his head and falling face-down in the water) obviated the need for Jones to act on his intention. "[W]hat determines whether someone is reprehensible or not", Nesbitt holds, "is not what he in fact does but what he is prepared to do, perhaps as revealed by what he in fact does" (p. 104).

This entails, Nesbitt continues, that Rachels' examples cannot show that the difference thesis is false. Both cases contain the morally relevant feature that the agent was *prepared* to kill. To test the difference thesis, this common feature must be removed. We must assume that Jones believes the difference thesis to be true, and that he was prepared to let his nephew die, but, unlike Smith, was not prepared to kill the child (p. 104). In this case, Nesbitt holds, we might indeed want to judge Smith more reprehensible than Jones.

It is this difference, the difference between an agent being prepared to kill and an agent merely being prepared to let die, that is, according to Nesbitt, morally significant – at least if we accept the widely held view that "the *raison d'etre* of morality is to make it possible for people to live together in reasonable peace and security" (p. 105).

We are not threatened, Nesbitt concludes his argument, if a person is prepared to allow another to die, but is not prepared to kill. Such a person "will not save me if my life should be in danger, but in this he is no more dangerous than an incapacitated person, or for that matter, a rock or a tree". A person who is prepared to kill, on the other hand, *is* a threat.

> If such a person should come to believe that she will benefit sufficiently from my death, then not only must I expect no help from her if my life happens to be in danger, but I must fear positive attempts on my life. In that case, given the view mentioned of the point of morality, people prepared to behave as Smith does are clearly of greater concern from the moral point of view than those prepared only to behave as Jones does; which is to say that killing is indeed morally worse than letting die. (p. 105)

II

Let us accept that Nesbitt is correct and that we should indeed be more concerned by the presence of Smith-type persons than by Jones-type persons. But what does this show? Does it show, as Nesbitt holds, that "killing is indeed morally worse than letting die," or does it show that it is worse if agents, who are motivated by personal gain, are not merely content to stand by as "nature" bestows some good on them, but are also prepared to intervene in the course of nature, to achieve their ends?

There is an illegitimate conflation in Winston Nesbitt's argument between the rightness and wrongness of actions, and the goodness and badness of agents.[5] We might thus agree that it is a bad thing for individuals to be motivated by personal gain, rather than by, say, the common good, and that it is *worse*, other things being equal, if such an agent is not only prepared to "let death happen", but to "make death happen".[6] But this is not, of course, the same as showing that killing is worse than letting die. Killing may be worse than letting die in these cases, and better than letting die in others.

Consider the following case, similar to a case that came before the Swedish courts some years ago:

> A truck driver and his co-driver had an accident on a lonely stretch of road. The truck caught fire and the driver was trapped in the wreckage of the cabin. The co-driver struggled to free him, but could not do so. The driver, by now burning, pleaded with his colleague – an experienced shooter – to take a rifle, which was stowed in a box on the back of the truck, and shoot him. The co-driver took the rifle and shot his colleague.

Was what the co-driver did morally reprehensible? Did he act wrongly? Students who are presented with this case will generally answer both questions in the negative. The reason for their intuitions is not hard to find. In this case, the agent was not motivated by personal gain, but by compassion. He acted not to benefit himself, but to benefit another. Should we feel threatened by such agents? Hardly. We should be comforted by their presence. Conversely, however, we should feel threatened, or at least abandoned, if we were surrounded by agents who believed in the difference thesis and behaved like "an incapacitated person, or . . . a rock or a tree", who would "let us die" when we sincerely wanted someone "to make us die".

Not only does Nesbitt conflate the distinction between agents and actions, he also implicitly assumes that death is always and everywhere an evil. If this view is already challenged by the above example, it has been utterly rejected in the practice of medicine by patients and doctors alike. Patients and doctors do not believe that life is always a good and will, in many cases, deliberately choose a shorter life over a longer one. Terminally or incurably ill patients standardly refuse life-sustaining treatment, and doctors allow these patients to die, for the patients' good. To put it slightly differently, while death is normally an evil, and to kill a person (or to let her die when we could save her) is harming her, this is not the case when continued life presents an intolerable burden to the person whose life it is. In short, then, doctors who are "letting" a patient die, for the patient's good, are benefiting rather than harming the patient – they are practising what is often called "passive euthanasia".

If patients can, however, be benefited by being "let die", because death is a good, then they can also be benefited by being killed – by the doctor practising "active euthanasia". Indeed, in some cases, active euthanasia will be preferable, from the patient's point of view, to passive euthanasia: being "let die" may involve unwanted protracted pain and suffering for the patient, and fail to give her the dignified death she wants. Moreover, there are patients for whom death would be a good, but who do not need life support, and whom the doctor cannot let die. This means that a doctor who is merely prepared to "let die", but not to "make die", is, once again, like an incapacitated person, a rock or a tree, who, while not preventing good befalling some patients, will merely stand by and do nothing to make the good happen for others.[7]

If the *raison d'etre* of morality is to allow people to live together in relative peace and security, what kind of motivation would we like doctors to have, and what kinds of action would we like them to perform? Clearly, we would like them to be motivated to primarily seek *our* good, rather than their own; to keep us alive, if this is in our best interests, and to "let" us die, or to "make" us die, when either one of these actions serves us best. If this is correct, the difference thesis is false. Killing is not always worse than letting die. Sometimes it is morally better.

III

James Rachels had devised the case of "the nasty cousins" to demonstrate that there is no intrinsic moral difference between killing and letting die, or active and passive euthanasia. Now, if Nesbitt is right, Rachels' example of the "nasty cousins" fails to show that the difference thesis is false. If I am right, however, Nesbitt in turn fails to establish the truth of the difference thesis. While he has shown that killing is sometimes worse than letting die, I have shown that killing is sometimes better than letting die.

This has clear implications for the public debate over (voluntary) euthanasia. Nesbitt accepts that the truth or falsity of the difference thesis may ultimately depend on the truth of the moral theory that underpins it. But, he says, "we cannot wait for a demonstration of the correct moral theory" before we attempt to make decisions on pressing moral questions, such as "active" or "passive" euthanasia (or killing a patient and letting her die). Rather, answers to practical public-policy questions are rarely derived from first ethical principles, but are, quite properly, based on common intuitions (p. 101, n. 2).

Acceptance of Nesbitt's "common intuition" view would lead one to question the contemporary blanket public-policy distinction between active and passive euthanasia: while doctors are typically permitted, by law, to "let" patients die, at the patients' request, they are almost everywhere prohibited from "making" them die. In countries like Australia, Britain and the United States, recognition of people's common intuitions would, however, lead one to the view that not only passive, but also active voluntary euthanasia should be allowed.[8]

Far from establishing the truth of the difference thesis, Winston Nesbitt has undermined the very thesis he set out support. Not only is active euthanasia no worse than passive euthanasia, and sometimes morally better; his argument also lends support to the view that public policies should allow some forms of active euthanasia.

Notes

1 Nesbitt, W. 'Is Killing No Worse Than Letting Die?' *Journal of Applied Philosophy*, 12 (1) (1995): 101–6.

2 Rachels, J. 'Active and Passive Euthanasia', *New England Journal of Medicine*, (9 January, 1975): 78–80.

3 See note 1; Nesbitt, p. 101.

4 See note 2.

5 Kuhse, H. *The Sanctity of Life Doctrine in Medicine – A Critique* (Oxford: Clarendon Press, 1987), pp. 88–90, 142, 148, 158–63. See also 'Frankena W. McCormick and the Traditional Distinction' in R. McCormick and P. Ramsey (eds), *Doing Evil to Achieve Good* (Chicago: Loyola University Press, 1978).

6 Walton, D. *On Defining Death* (Montreal: McGill–Queens University Press, 1979), pp. 118–20; Kuhse (see note 5), pp. 79–81.

7 Here it is, of course, important to not confuse the distinction between killing and letting die, or between "making happen" and "letting happen" with the distinction between actions and omissions. In distinction from a tree or a rock, an agent may act to "let happen" – for example, by telling the nurse not to attach the patient to a respirator, or by turning the respirator off. See note 5, Kuhse, chs 2 and 3.

8 Opinion polls in these countries have consistently shown strong public support for active voluntary euthanasia. For the opinions of some groups of health-care professionals see, for example, Heilig, S., 'The SFMS Euthanasia Survey: Results and Analyses', *San Francisco Medicine* (May, 1988): 24–6, 34; Ward, B. J., 'Attitudes among NHS Doctors to Requests for Euthanasia', *BMJ*, 308 (1995): 1332–4; Baume P. and O'Malley, E., 'Euthanasia: Attitudes and Practices of Medical Practitioners, *Medical Journal of Australia*, 161 (1994); 137–44; Kuhse, H. and Singer, P., Voluntary Euthanasia and the Nurse: an Australian survey, *International Journal of Nursing Studies*, 30(4) (1993): 311–22.

Severely Disabled Newborns

27

When Care Cannot Cure: Medical Problems in Seriously Ill Babies

Neil Campbell

Thankfully, most babies are born intact and healthy after a normal pregnancy, and thereafter they thrive. But a few, around 4–6 percent, are born seriously ill or become ill after birth.[1]

Illnesses in babies have two important characteristics: they are often life-threatening, and they can cause serious handicaps or chronic ill health (morbidity) in babies who survive. Advances in knowledge, organization of newborn health services, and technology are achieving cures or amelioration of many illnesses that in the past resulted in death or permanent severe handicap. With mechanical ventilators and other complex life-supporting treatment most extremely premature babies now survive. In the past most died. Complex surgery can now ensure survival of most babies with severe malformations, even those considered "monstrous".

We can take over the function of most organs, for days or weeks, when they temporarily fail. Mechanical ventilators and extra-corporeal membrane oxygenators can assume the functions of failing hearts and lungs. Hemo-filtration and dialysis can take over the functions of failing livers and kidneys, and transfusions of red blood cells, white blood cells, and blood platelets, the functions of failing bone marrow. Intravenous nutrition can take over the functions of the diseased bowel. The only major organs we cannot yet transplant are brain and bowel, given donors.

However there are still many babies for whom modern techniques are less than successful. In some, new treatments achieve little more than delaying death. In others death is averted but survival results in permanent severe handicaps or lifelong ill health. When treatment falls far short of complete success, ethical questions arise. Are such treatments in babies' and families' best interests? How can costs be justified?

This paper describes a number of newborn illnesses to show how they create ethical problems. First, however, two caveats: It is conventional to describe newborn intensive care activities in medical-technical language, implying scientific objectivity, but this language does not accurately reflect reality. Many things we do in newborn intensive care involve value judgements and some of these have ethical content. Second, medical-technical language speaks of pathology and physiology, mechanical ventilators and blood gases, drug doses and brain functions. Such language can obscure the deeper context – that of hopes and fears, joys and grief, pleasures and pains, and life and death. Scientific objectivity has its place in newborn intensive care, but much is lost if it overshadows the human values and goals it is meant to serve.

Illnesses in newborn babies can be classified into three main diagnostic groups: extreme prematurity (babies born 8–17 weeks early); birth defects, including malformations, chromosomal disorders, intrauterine infections, and inborn errors of metabolism; and acquired diseases (babies normal at the end of pregnancy, but becoming ill during or after delivery: the most important acquired diseases are birth asphyxia and bacterial infections).

This paper concentrates on aspects of extreme prematurity and representative birth defects.

From F. K. Beller and R. F. Weir (eds), *The Beginning of Human Life*, pp. 327–44. © 1994 Kluwer Academic Publishers. Reprinted with permission.

These illustrate well the ways in which newborn illnesses create ethical problems. There are many areas of ethical concern in newborn care – informed consent, "standard" versus "experimental" treatments, pain, withdrawal of treatment, costs and resource allocation, and duties to impaired survivors. This paper confines itself to placing in context the ethical questions of withdrawal of treatment and resource allocation.

Extreme Prematurity

Normal babies are born after 38 to 42 weeks of pregnancy (gestation) and average around 3400 grams in birthweight. A few babies (about 1.2%) are born far too early, and have a characteristic set of problems resulting from immaturity of organ and tissue functions. Very low birthweight (VLBW) babies are those of birthweight less than 1500g, (usually less than 32 weeks' gestation). Within this group are the tiniest babies, the extremely low birthweight (ELBW) group, less than 1000g and usually less than 28 weeks' gestation. Live-born ELBW babies represent 0.3–0.4% of all live births. There are 11,000–14,000 in the US each year.[2]

ELBW babies are usually critically ill in the hours and days after birth. Although they have a strange beauty to those experienced in their care, their skin is thin and leaks body fluids; the flesh is jellyish and bruises easily. Liver, kidneys, heart, and glands perform poorly: the babies have great difficulty even maintaining normal body warmth. They experience a variety of complex problems in the early weeks of life. Three will be described: respiratory distress syndrome (RDS), intracerebral hemorrhage, and necrotizing enterocolitis (NEC).

Respiratory distress syndrome (RDS)

Most ELBW babies develop lung disease, respiratory distress syndrome (RDS), within minutes, and their lungs are simply too immature and delicate to function normally. The baby's breathing in distressed and labored. Most affected babies must be placed on mechanical ventilators, and given extra oxygen and other life-sustaining treatments. The disease usually gets progressively worse in the first three days. Many babies die during this time. Their lungs are so affected the ventilator cannot support them, and other complications pile up. In some babies it is obvious hours in advance that they will die. In such situations, how long should care continue? Until the baby is moribund? Until the heart stops? Continuing maximal, intrusive, expensive therapies in babies who are dying is, to some, obscene. And yet, how can caregivers be sure death will occur? How much certainty is required?

In surviving babies RDS starts improving on the fourth day, but the lungs will have been injured to some extent by the physical effect of the pressure produced by the ventilator (barotrauma) and the toxic chemical effect of oxygen (oxygen toxicity). These iatrogenic injuries to the lung are called broncho-pulmonary dysplasia (BPD). BPD slows the rate of recovery from RDS. In a few babies BPD gets progressively worse over many days, and a vicious cycle is set up: the baby must remain on the ventilator and oxygen because of his/her damaged lungs, but the ventilator and oxygen, while keeping the baby alive, exacerbate the lung damage.

BPD keeps some babies on the ventilator for weeks or months. Occasional babies become respiratory cripples: they never get off the ventilator.

When it becomes clear – at a month, or six months, or a year of age – that a baby will never get off the ventilator, parents and caregivers are faced with caring for a baby with poor quality of life and a dismal long-term outlook. A point may be reached where maximal therapy cannot keep the baby comfortable. Should therapy be withdrawn? If months of ventilator dependency have gone by, should caregivers withdraw *before* the point of failing maximal therapy has been reached? Does the presence of other complications which further reduce quality of life – for example, moderate brain damage – have relevance?

Ethical problems arising from the use of mechanical ventilators are well illustrated by the example of RDS in the ELBW baby, but similar problems arise in many other serious diseases of newborn babies. A mechanical ventilator is used to assist a baby's breathing when it is inadequate. Breathing may be inadequate because the lungs are severely diseased, or because the brain is diseased or injured in such a way that it no longer drives the lungs to breathe.

The ventilator pumps oxygen into the lungs many times per minute, hour after hour, day after day. It can keep a baby alive for weeks or months, even if most of the brain is dead or the lungs hopelessly damaged and incapable of healing. Ventilators achieve excellent results in babies with diseases which *temporarily* prevent their breathing adequately: the ventilator maintains life until treatment and nature allow the baby to cope alone. Dilemmas arise if babies are kept alive by ventilators when they have no hope of eventually recovering sufficiently to cope alone. Being on a ventilator involves many painful or frightening experiences throughout each day, only partially ameliorated by sedation or analgesia. Babies on ventilators are socially and emotionally isolated: it is difficult to pick them up for feeds and cuddles, and the necessary sedation depresses their awareness.

Intracerebral hemorrhage

During the first week of life 40–50% of ELBW babies suffer bleeding of varying severity into the brain (intraventricular hemorrhage, IVH). Blood flow to the brain fluctuates widely during the unstable states ELBW babies experience in the first days after birth. During unstable episodes brain blood flow may temporarily cease, injuring areas of the brain (cerebral ischemia). Injured areas may die. When brain blood flow improves again, bleeding may occur into injured or dead areas of brain.

Small hemorrhages (small areas of ischemia) have little immediate or long-term effect on the baby. Large hemorrhages can cause sudden deterioration and, occasionally, death. When babies survive large hemorrhages, permanent serious intellectual and physical handicaps are common. Between 75% and 100% of babies with extensive intracerebral hemorrhages or ischemia have severe permanent handicaps.

The presence of areas of ischemia or hemorrhage in the brain can be seen by ultrasound or CAT scanners; ultrasound scans are usually performed daily or more often in sick ELBW babies. However, extensive ischemic areas may not be obvious to scanners in the first few days of life. Their effects may be detected only several weeks later, as the injured areas of brain dissolve or shrivel away. This process is called periventricular leukomalacia (PVL). Thus ischemic brain injuries occurring in the first few days, which will result in severe handicaps, may only be detected at several weeks of age.

Sometimes clotted blood from hemorrhagic areas of brain block the circulation of the brain's cerebrospinal fluid. The blocked fluid builds up within the spaces in the brain called the ventricles, producing hydrocephalus. The ventricles distend, further injuring the surrounding brain. Some ELBW babies with hydrocephalus need a surgical operation to insert a plastic tube into the distended ventricles, to drain the fluid blockage (ventriculo-peritoneal shunt; V-P shunt).

When an ELBW baby suddenly deteriorates in the first few days with a massive intracerebral hemorrhage, should life-supporting measures be discontinued? If so, what degree of risk of severe handicap should suffice for decision making? Only certainty? Fifty percent? When, at several weeks of age, a baby thought to have had only moderate cerebral ischemia in the first week is found to be developing extensive periventricular leukomalacia, with large areas of brain dissolving away, should life-sustaining treatment continue? At this stage the baby may be off the ventilator and other intensive life-supporting treatment. The only life-sustaining treatment the baby may be getting is scheduled feeding via a stomach tube, as he or she cannot suck or swallow. Should this scheduled feeding continue? Is it not life-supporting in the same way as is a mechanical ventilator?

The term "scheduled feeding," introduced above, requires explanation. Healthy normal babies are "demand" fed – that is, fed from breast or bottle whenever they show signs of hunger or thirst, rather than to a formal timetable or schedule. Ill babies may have no sense of hunger, nor be able to suck and swallow. For example, ELBW babies cannot suck or swallow effectively, as the brain mechanisms controlling these functions are immature and uncoordinated. Babies unconscious from brain diseases or medications do not demand feed. Also, major brain abnormalities often disturb the swallowing and sucking mechanisms. Babies with malformations of the mouth or throat also may not be able to suck and swallow. Babies with very distressed breathing from lung diseases or heart failure may be too short of breath to demand feed, or to swallow feed safely without breathing it into their lungs (aspiration).

To ensure effective nutrition in such babies, carefully planned feeding schedules, delivered by artificial means such as stomach tubes, must be prescribed. Waking and demanding, thirst and appetite, and sucking and swallowing, are replaced by scheduled feeding. For ill babies, such regimes are lifesaving. They ensure survival until the baby's recovery allows normal demand feeding. If it is acceptable to withdraw life-sustaining treatments such as mechanical ventilation from babies in whom hope for survival or meaningful life is gone, is it not also acceptable to withdraw scheduled feeding?

Necrotizing enterocolitis (NEC)

After the first week of life 2–5% of ELBW babies develop a severe inflammation of the bowel, necrotizing enterocolitis (NEC). The inflammation may be so severe that it destroys varying lengths of the bowel – from a few centimetres to the entire bowel. Some babies are overwhelmed by the inflammation and quickly die. In survivors, when parts of the bowel have been destroyed, surgical operations are required to remove them. Loss of short lengths of bowel at operation have little practical consequence, but if greater lengths of bowel are lost, the baby may be left with insufficient bowel for normal digestion.

In mild cases of NEC the inflamed bowel is rested for 2–3 weeks by stopping milk feeds. The babies' nutritional requirements are provided with intravenous nutrition. When milk feeds are recommenced, they usually succeed. In worse cases, when substantial bowel has been lost, reintroduction of feeds results in diarrhea. It may take weeks or months for the shortened bowel to recover sufficiently for normal milk feeding to succeed. During the recovery period the baby's health and growth rely on intravenous nutrition.

Occasionally babies lose so much bowel at operation that they can never recover sufficient bowel function to see them through life. Such babies will always be dependent on intravenous nutrition. In some it is obvious at the surgical operation that there is insufficient bowel for life. In others it becomes apparent only after months of intravenous nutrition and repeated failures of milk feeding.

When it is found at surgery that too much bowel has died, what should caregivers do? The baby can survive only if she is given lifelong intravenous nutrition. She will never be able to be fed normally. She is usually critically ill, on a mechanical ventilator and other life-sustaining treatments. Should they be discontinued? When it becomes apparent only after months of intravenous nutrition that the bowel will never work successfully, what should caregivers do? Once again, the baby is faced with a life of total intravenous nutrition. By this time the baby is off the ventilator, but will have developed complications of intravenous nutrition.

Intravenous nutrition is a complex, expensive procedure in which all nutrition is administered through a catheter in a vein. IV Nutrition can keep a baby healthy and growing for weeks, months, or years without oral feeds, yet life-threatening infections of the intravenous catheter are common. IV nutrition also causes liver damage, worst in the most immature babies, which can cause progressive failure of the liver over several months. Thus a baby being kept alive by intravenous nutrition because his bowel does not work can die of liver failure at 6–12 months of age, a complication of the intravenous nutrition. Liver failure is a distressing condition: the baby swells up all over (edema), the abdomen becomes tense with fluid (ascites), the blood fails to clot, and frequent, distressing hemorrhages result.

When a baby develops liver failure after months of intravenous nutrition, what should caregives do? There is little hope of recovery of either the liver or the bowel. Life with progressive liver failure is very unpleasant. Should intravenous nutrition be withdrawn? IV nutrition achieves wonderful results when babies have bowel diseases which prevent normal milk feeding for weeks or months, but which eventually get better. It creates dilemmas when it keeps babies alive with bowel diseases which will never ameliorate sufficiently for the baby to feed naturally.

Given these complex problems, what is the overall outcome for VLBW and ELBW babies? Tables 1 and 2 show typical outcome figures for all babies from a single region (Victoria, Australia). Similar figures are reported from regions in North America and Europe.

Live-born ELBW babies constitute only 0.3% of all births, but 34% of all baby deaths. Care is nowadays offered at 23 weeks' gestation (around 600 g, 17 weeks early). Few survive. By 24–25 weeks' gestation (700–799 g) around 30% survive: around 25% of survivors have severe handicaps; the chances of surviving without handicap are about 10%. By 26–27 weeks' gestation (900–999 g) 75% survive: around 10% have severe handicaps; the chances of surviving without handicap are around 40%. As organization of care and methods of treatment improve, outcomes improve. Current extremely premature babies are likely to do better than babies born five or ten years ago.

Table I VLBW and ELBW Outcomes

Birth weight, grams	*Gestational age, weeks*	*Survival rate*	*Severe handicap*	*Normal survivor*
1250–1500	29–31	> 95%	< 10%	60%
1000–1250	27–29	85%		
900–999	26–27	75%	10–15%	35–40%
800–899	25–26	45%		
700–799	24–25	30%	15–25%	5–15%
600–699	23–24	< 10%		

Table II VLBW and ELBW Babies

Victoria 1987	*61,000 292*	*Live births neonatal deaths*					
Birth weight	Total births	Live births		Percentage of all births	Neonatal deaths		Percentage of all deaths
< 1500G (VLBW)	627	467	=	0.76%	139	=	47%
< 1000G (ELBW)	294	177	=	0.3%	100	=	34%

What of costs and resources? In our state (Victoria, Australia) VLBW babies constitute 0.6% of all live-born babies, and yet they make up 53% of all admissions to neonatal intensive care units, and 83% of patient ventilator days. Thus a tiny population is responsible for a substantial workload. Estimates of costs vary from country to country and with the methods of costing used. Typical costs for ELBW babies in intensive care units are around $A1,000 per day, and average hospitalization costs around $A50,000–$A80,000 per baby. The earlier the gestation, the higher the cost. To achieve a survivor at 24 weeks in our region costs around $A300,000.

Such cost estimates include only initial hospitalization after birth. They do not include costs for subsequent hospitalization, nor lifetime costs of care for handicaps. ELBW costs compare badly with costs of other patient populations. They are more expensive than VLBW babies and mature babies needing treatment for malformations: they are far more expensive than children needing intensive care for life-threatening conditions beyond the first year of life. The care of ELBW babies diverts scarce resources from other babies, children, and adults with better potential outcomes. Should costs be taken into account in treatment decisions?

Care is nowadays often offered at 23 weeks' gestation, when the chances of survival are less than 10%, the chances of serious handicap in survivors around 30%, and the cost for each survivor between $300,000 and $400,000. Caregivers know that termination of pregnancy for serious fetal defects is performed as late as 28 weeks' gestation, legal or not. Given all these considerations, many people ask whether there is a gestation and birth size below which care should not be offered. Do caregivers really have a mandate from their society to use such large resources when returns are so poor?

Severe handicaps

In this discussion of VLBW and ELBW babies frequent reference has been made to severe handicaps (and there are many other serious illnesses in babies which also result in handicaps). Severe handicaps involve various combinations of mental deficiency, body paralysis, blindness, and deafness. Mental deficiency means varying degrees of reduced intelligence; lack of awareness of self, others, and "the meaning of life"; and lack of ability to interact socially and emotionally. Body paralysis means varying degrees of lack of control of muscles, body, and limbs, with resulting immobility and dependence on others for feeding, toileting, and other aspects of life's basics.

Survival of a baby with severe handicaps has a serious effect on his or her family. Marital breakdown is frequent, and when it occurs the mother is often left to cope as a single parent. There is a high incidence of psychiatric disturbances in affected families. Other children in the family can suffer emotional hardship and deprivation as a result. For some families, though, the care of a severely handicapped child can be an experience of moral growth and enrichment. Many parents, especially mothers, develop an extraordinary bond of love for a handicapped child, even when the child's existence leads to so much hardship. Indeed, to the outsider, the loving sacrifice by parents of self and family interests to the handicapped child is a central part of the tragedy.

It is widely held that when withdrawal of treatment is being considered, the best interests of the baby should prevail. Does a baby have interests which can be viewed in isolation, as separate from those of the family?

Birth Defects: Conditions That Can be Fixed

The list of birth defects is very long.[3] Major categories include malformations of one or more major organs or body structures, the rest of the baby being normal; chromosome abnormalities, in which every tissue of the baby is abnormal; inborn errors of metabolism, in which there are malfunctions in one or more of the body's chemical processes; and intrauterine infections, which usually affect most of the fetus's developing tissues, causing abnormal tissue function and in some cases malformations.

To illustrate ethical dilemmas, birth defects are best classified according to prognosis – what effects they have on survival and function – rather than diagnosis.

Prognostically, birth defects can be divided into those conditions which can be fixed, and those which cannot. In the former conditions, there is a very high chance of survival if all available treatment is offered. With survival there is a normal or "acceptable" life span, with no handicaps, or an "acceptable" level of handicap and no chronic ill health, or an "acceptable" level of chronicity. Obviously, much hinges on the definition of "acceptable."

More, and more serious, newborn illnesses are moving into this category. Although outcomes in this group are good, treatment is often long and arduous for the baby. Intrusive, distressing treatments are often needed, and hospitalization may continue for months. Costs can be very high, especially in babies needing prolonged mechanical ventilation, surgical operations, or intravenous nutrition. On the other hand, the average stay in hospital for mature babies with esophageal atresia (failure of the gullet to form normally), who require major chest surgery on the first day of life, is nine days. Most babies requiring bypass cardiac surgery are home within three weeks.

Birth Defects: Conditions That Cannot be Fixed

Those conditions which cannot be fixed can be categorized as follows: (1) conditions in which death is inevitable, despite all available care. Active treatment only lengthens the period before death occurs; (2) conditions in which active treatment will ensure survival, but with severe handicaps, chronic ill health, or shortened life span; and (3) conditions in which survival *might* be achieved with prolonged, intrusive, distressing treatments, but with serious handicaps, chronic ill health or shortened life span. (Classification according to prognosis is helpful in ethical discussions about *all* baby illnesses – the ELBW baby, babies with birth asphyxia or infections – not just birth defects.)

Conditions in which death is inevitable

This group includes such conditions as Potter's syndrome and its variants (renal agenesis or dysplasia with pulmonary hypoplasia), anencephaly, chromosomal abnormalities such as trisomy 18, and some complex heart malformations.

Potter's syndrome and its variants In this condition, for unknown reasons, the fetus's kidneys fail to form (renal agenesis). Fetal lung growth depends on the development of normal fetal kidneys. When the fetal kidneys fail to form, the fetal lungs fail to grow adequately. At birth Potter's syndrome babies look abnormal. They have very distressed breathing and cannot cope unless given oxygen and placed on a ventilator. These treatments are often started if the baby's condition is not recognized. Some die quickly despite ventilation and oxygen; in others survival is prolonged, but never beyond a day or so.

It is generally assumed that the lungs will never work satisfactorily, so that temporarily taking over their function with ventilators, oxygen, or extracorporeal membrane oxygenation (ECMO) is inappropriate. Babies cannot survive long-term without kidneys. It is generally assumed that it is inappropriate to temporarily take over kidney functions with renal dialysis or hemofiltration, although renal transplantation might be technically possible if donors are available. Given all of these assumptions, death is inevitable.

Are these assumptions morally sound? If a Potter's syndrome baby is placed on a ventilator before the condition is recognized, is there an ethical problem in stopping? What should be done with the baby if ventilation is withdrawn? Such babies may be conscious and aware, and death from hypoxia is frightening until unconsciousness is reached.

Potter's syndrome occurs in about 1 in 10,000 births. There are therefore approximately 370 Potter's syndrome babies born in the US each year.

Anencephaly In anencephaly there is failure of development of most of the brain (the cerebral hemispheres and much of the midbrain) together with the covering skull and scalp. Two-thirds are born dead. Most born alive die within minutes or hours; a few live for days or months. It is generally assumed that the babies have no conscious awareness and that death is inevitable. They may, however, suck, cry, grimace, and even smile.

Because death is assumed to be inevitable, most caregivers withold treatment likely to prolong life. However, recently anencephalic infants have been placed on mechanical ventilation and other life-supporting treatments, with a view to using them as sources of organs for transplantation. These babies have done better than expected. So, are assumptions about the inevitability of death soundly based? No one can say with certainty, since in the past no one has really tried to achieve survival.

Anencephaly occurs in about 3 in 10,000 births: there are about 1,100 born each year in the US, 350 of these alive at birth.

Trisomy 18 There are several chromosomal disorders, including trisomy 18, which result in profound mental insufficiency and a shortened life span. In trisomy 18 every cell in the developing fetus, from conception, has additional genetic material (an extra chromosome). This results in abnormality of all the developing tissues. The babies have an abnormal appearance. Their consciousness is depressed and it is assumed they are never aware of themselves, others, or their environment. Some have life-threatening malformations, especially of the heart or esophagus (esophageal atresia). The brain is so abnormal that its reflex nerve mechanisms controlling sucking, swallowing, and coughing do not function adequately. In some babies this results in frequent choking episodes, or blockages of the breathing passages with saliva or other secretions. Attempts at feeding often result in choking. Feeds may be breathed into the lungs (aspiration), causing pneumonia.

Half die in the first month; fewer than 10% survive the first year. It is assumed that death is inevitable from choking episodes, feeding difficulties, or pneumonia. Treatment for life-threatening malformations is therefore usually withheld. No one really knows how long life might continue if all available treatment were offered – ventilator support for poor breathing or pneumonia; surgery for life-threatening malformations, antibiotics for infections; and careful attention to nutrition. The view that death is inevitable may thus be a self-fulfilling prophesy.

What treatment should be offered to babies with trisomy 18 or other similar chromosomal abnormalities? Scheduled feeds by stomach tube, or intravenous fluids, will prolong life in some of them. In others, with choking episodes or a malformed heart, feeds and fluids may hasten death. Should caregivers clear out the throat with suction catheters when choking episodes occur? These episodes are distressing to watch, but it is assumed the baby is unaware and does not suffer. Regular sucking out of the airways can be lifesaving, but is this beneficial to the baby? Trisomy 18 occurs in about 3 in 10,000 births. There are about 1,000 per year in the US.

When death is "inevitable" It will be seen from these descriptions of conditions in which death is considered inevitable that "inevitable" is a relative term. It is not known how long such babies might live if all available treatment were given. Technically, the only major organs not currently transplantable are brain and bowel: if donors were available, and ECMO tried, an occasional Potter's syndrome baby might be salvageable. If mechanical ventilation and other active treatment were offered, anencephalics might live weeks or months. If surgery and other forms of active intervention were offered, babies with trisomy 18 might live for years. Even when active treatment is not offered, some babies with "inevitably" lethal conditions survive for weeks or months.

Nevertheless most caregivers believe that life-sustaining treatments should be withheld from these categories. Given that survival prospects are not accurately known, since no one really tries for survival, are decisions in these babies based on the "inevitability" of death, or are they rather based on "quality of life" judgements? Caregivers who view quality-of-life judgements as unacceptable criteria for deciding to withdraw treatment usually accept that life-sustaining treatments are not morally mandatory in babies for whom death is "inevitable." Perhaps these are quality of life judgements after all.

Survival with severe handicaps

This category includes conditions in which active treatment will ensure survival but with severe handicaps, shortened life span, and chronic ill health. Diagnoses included in this group are severe spina bifida and a range of chromosomal abnormalities less severe in their effects than trisomy 18.

Severe spina bifida Spina bifida (high meningomyelocoele with congenital hydrocephalus) results from failure of the brain and spinal cord to develop normally in the fetus (neural tube defect). The spinal cord carries all the nerves from the brain to all the other body structures. It is contained within the spinal column. In spina bifida one section of the spinal cord, together with the surrounding spinal column, fails to form properly. The backbone lies open with the malformed spinal cord exposed. This lesion is called a meningomyelocoele. All functions below the level of the lesion are severely abnormal, since they are normally controlled by the spinal cord nerves. Below the lesion there is no sensation: the muscles are paralyzed; organs such as urinary bladder, genitals, and lower bowel function abnormally. If the lesion is low on the back, the handicaps which result are mild. High lesions, midway up the back, result in a child who will never walk, may not be able to sit upright normally; and will have no feeling below the waist, marked disturbances (incontinence) of urine and bowel functions, and abnormal sexual function.

Most babies with meningomyelocoele also have brain malformations, i.e., hydrocephalus. In mild cases (the majority) this may require surgical operations (ventriculo-peritoneal shunts), but has no serious effects on the baby's future. In severe cases hydrocephalus can result in significant mental deficiency not correctable by surgery.

The child with a high meningomyelocoele and severe hydrocephalus has a difficult life. Surgery on the back lesion, to prevent infection, and on the head to prevent worse mental deficiency, and scheduled feeding in the early weeks of life, will ensure survival. Without these most die after weeks or months, depending on how they are cared for. Survivors spend much of their childhood in the hospital with complications. They are confined to bed or wheelchair. Their lives may be shortened by such complications as infections in the hydrocephalus shunt or kidney failure from the urinary bladder dysfunction.

The incidence of spina bifida varies from place to place, between 1 in 1,000 and 5 in 1,000 births. About one-quarter have high back lesions and serious hydrocephalus. Given the potentially poor quality of life, many caregivers practice selective treatment, withholding surgery or other lifesaving procedures from severely affected babies. However, not all such babies die: occasional babies survive, with worse handicaps than if they had been offered surgery at the beginning.

Can witholding treatment that would ensure survival be justified on the grounds of poor future quality of life? If an occasional baby might survive despite surgery's being withheld, can scheduled feeding, antibiotics, and other forms of life-prolonging care be withheld?

More than 95% of spina bifida fetuses can be detected in the womb. Termination of pregnancy can be performed if parents wish. Although this is seen by many as the answer to the ethical problems arising in babies with severe spina bifida, it is really only a shift in the ethical framework, from the ethics of withholding treatment from babies to the ethics of abortion.

Babies whose outcome is uncertain

These babies might survive after long, complex, intrusive treatment, but they might not. Survival may result in a lifetime of chronic ill health or severe handicaps. Diagnoses in this group include multiple malformation syndromes not due to chromosomal disorders, and hypoplastic left heart syndrome.

Multiple malformation syndromes There are many conditions in which babies have several major malformations. Consider a baby who has esophageal atresia (failure of the gullet to form); a major heart malformation; major abnormalities of the kidneys; and major malformations of the spine, arms, hands, and legs (VATER syndrome).

The esophagus can usually be easily repaired, but there may be annoying complications throughout childhood. Most heart defects can now be cured or improved by surgery, although some need more than one operation. The kidney abnormalities may be correctable, but there may be a risk of progressive kidney failure in childhood, with poor health and eventual need for transplantation. The spinal deformity may be correctable, but may result in a permanent marked twisting of the back. The arm, hand, and leg deformities may be improved but not corrected: walking without aids such as calipers or crutches may be difficult or impossible; the arm and hand abnormalities may make this and other functions harder. Brain function and intelligence will be normal unless diseases of the brain such as meningitis are acquired during treatment of the other conditions.

At best, such a baby will need lengthy hospitalization, with a number of surgical operations and other arduous treatments. If everything goes well, only the back, arm, hand, and leg deformities will persist as lifetime problems. At worst, complications of treatment of any of the malformations could result in death; partial success in these treatments could result in chronic ill health: kidney failure could lead to the need for transplantation; and complications of treatment causing brain damage could cause mental deficiency. Given the certainty of physical handicaps from arms, hands, legs and back, the uncertainty of survival despite months of arduous treatment, and the possibility of progressive kidney failure, could a case be made not to embark on any lifesaving treatment at the outset?

If life-threatening complications develop after weeks or months of care, how far should arduous treatment such as mechanical ventilation and surgical operations be pushed? Is a point reached where it is appropriate to say, "Enough is enough"?

Hypoplastic left heart syndrome (HLHS) This is a relatively common malformation of the heart in which the left half of the heart, the parts responsible for pumping blood around the body, fail to form properly. Babies with HLHS are usually beautiful babies. In the past they all died, most in the first week of life. Now a number of centers around the world offer surgery. Instead of dying, babies are placed on mechanical ventilators, given other complex, arduous treatment, and then have surgery to make the heart sufficiently functional to sustain life for the first year or two. If this first stage is successful, a second operation must be performed to improve long-term survival. An alternative to this two-stage treatment, advocated by some, is cardiac transplantation soon after birth.

Death rates after the first operation in various centers around the world vary from 50% to 95%, babies die hours, weeks, or months after surgery. Not many babies live to the second operation. It is too early to know how many babies will live, or for how long, after the second operation. No one knows the long-term outcome of cardiac transplantation in the first year of life, and finding donors is difficult.[4]

Before surgery was offered for HLHS, death was inevitable, but happened quickly and peacefully. With surgery, most babies still die (perhaps all will die in childhood – who knows?), but after hours, weeks, or months of intrusive, arduous treatments. Should babies and families be offered such treatment in the (so far) small hope of eventual survival? Or should it be accepted that, in some conditions, it may be better not to try? HLHS babies consume huge resources in health care systems where resources are finite. Is it fair on all that resources are used in this way? And yet, if surgeons do not try, how will advances ever be made?

Withholding Treatment

So far this paper has described a number of serious newborn illnesses to illustrate how ethical dilemmas arise, especially in relation to decisions for or against lifesaving treatment.

What happens in practice? Ways in which these problems are resolved vary around the world. In 1973 neonatologists at the Yale-New Haven Hospital (US) reported that 14% of deaths in babies followed withdrawal of treatment.[5] In 1986 Hammersmith (UK) reported a figure of 30%.[6] Our own practices are outlined below. Discussions with neonatologists in several countries lead us to believe our practices are not unusual.

We believe that withdrawal of treatment should be considered when there is little hope of survival despite all care, or when quality of life may be unacceptably poor. When such is the case, the doctor in charge must inform parents about all relevant aspects of diagnosis and prognosis and give a clear view of what he or she thinks is best.

In the context of near-certainty of death or very poor quality of life, after all necessary advice and guidance has been given, the decision whether to continue or to stop active treatment belongs to the parents. If parents decide that treatment should be continued, contrary to caregivers' views, all measures should be continued in good faith, but the doctor in charge should tactfully continue to advocate his/her views.

The baby's interests are of central importance, but we do not believe they should (or can) be separated from the interests of the family. It is appropriate for the parents and their advisers to take into account the effects of the baby's continuing defects on the rest of the family, should the baby survive.

When everyone agrees it is best to withdraw treatment, no measures likely to prolong life inappropriately should be continued. This includes oxygen, antibiotics, intravenous fluids, and scheduled feeding. When all life-sustaining treatments are withdrawn, attention to the baby's comfort is paramount. Ensuring the baby's comfort will often require analgesics and sedatives which may as a side effect shorten the baby's life.

Withdrawal of treatment at Royal Children's Hospital, Melbourne, Australia

We have studied all deaths in our unit in a recent two-year period. There were 1,362 babies admitted with complex problems during the period studied. Of these 132 (9.7%) died. Thirty-one (23.5%) of the deaths occurred despite all efforts to ensure the babies' survivals. The remaining 101 deaths (76.5%) occurred following withdrawal of life-supporting treatment.

Babies from whom treatment was withdrawn were classified in the three prognostic categories previously mentioned.

Babies in whom death was inevitable There were 42 babies in this group (41.6%). They were almost certain to die despite all available treatment; withdrawal of treatment shortened the time to the babies' deaths. In this group were extremely low birthweight babies with RDS, and lungs hopelessly disrupted by high-pressure mechanical ventilation or massive brain hemorrhages; babies born without kidneys and with lungs too small to support life (Potter's syndrome); babies with chromosomal disorders such as trisomies 18 and 13. The ELBW babies would have died within hours, as would those with Potter's syndrome. Some of the babies with chromosomal abnormalities might have lived weeks or months. The medical and ethical assumptions guiding their care were that death was inevitable and so life-prolonging treatment was burdensome and not serving their interests.

Babies who would almost certainly have survived with life-sustaining treatment but with severe handicaps and chronic ill health There were 17 babies in this group (16.8%). Diagnoses included babies with severe birth asphyxia, spina bifida with hydrocephalus, and Down's syndrome with life-threatening malformations. The medical and ethical decisions for these babies were based on judgements of the future quality of life of the babies and their families.

Babies in whom prognosis for survival was uncertain With active, prolonged, and potentially distressing treatment they might have survived, but more likely would have died. If they had survived it would have been with serious handicaps and chronic ill health. Diagnoses in this group included severe birth asphyxia, ELBW babies with serious intracerebral hemorrhages, and various serious chromosomal abnormalities.

It can be seen that withdrawal decisions were based on prognosis – whether or not babies could survive, and what the quality of survival would be – rather than diagnosis. Many forms of treatment were withdrawn. Those essential to survival were as follows: Of the 101 babies who had active treatment withdrawn, 40 (39.6%) had withdrawal of mechanical ventilation. Forty-eight babies (47.%) had scheduled feeding withheld. These were babies unable to feed from breast or bottle, so that immediate survival depended on scheduled gavage (stomach tube) feeding, gastrostomy feeding, or other special techniques. Oral feeding was not withheld from babies who "demanded" feeding and in whom oral feeding would not itself be life-threatening. Feeding was not withheld; it was simply not imposed.

Eight babies not on mechanical ventilators had oxygen therapy withdrawn. Five babies had intravenous nutrition withdrawn.

It will be clear from what has been said so far that not all babies who are going to die, or to survive with severe handicaps, are extremely tiny or immature, or "monstrous" or malformed. Some are of normal size and pleasing to look at. Not all are brain-damaged or in coma: some are conscious, aware, and responsive. Even when most of the brain is malformed or injured, babies can exhibit "normal" baby behaviors such as gazing, feeding, crying, and smiling, since these are brainstem functions.

Not all are on mechanical ventilators or other complex high-technology support. Some are breathing unaided, in ordinary baby cots, receiving no life-support treatment except oxygen or scheduled feeding and fluids, or suctioning of secretions from the throat to prevent choking. Not all are desperately ill and in the first days or weeks of life: some are stable and several months of age.

Palliative care: fluids and feeds

When life-supporting treatment is withdrawn from babies, palliative care to relieve pain or distress is essential. For many babies palliative care is straightforward: analgesics and sedatives are given even though they often incidentally shorten life. Many caregivers have ethical difficulties withholding feeds and fluids. To them feeding babies is a fundamental part of human nurturing, and seeing babies fade away dehydrated and starving seems morally repugnant.

In our experience, continuing feeds and fluids makes many dying babies worse. The dying process is prolonged. Babies who are breathless and distressed from lung disease, heart failure, or kidney failure remain distressed if fluids are continued, but symptoms improve as fluids are withdrawn and dehydration develops. Babies with abnormalities of brain or airway, which cause choking episodes and labored breathing, improve as dehydration develops and saliva and other secretions diminish. Babies with malformations of the mouth or throat, or brain abnormalities preventing them from sucking, swallowing, or coughing effectively, are made worse by feeding attempts. They may vomit and choke, or if feed is aspirated into the lungs it may cause death. Withholding feeds and fluids is sound palliative care for many dying babies.

When treatments directly supporting life, such as mechanical ventilation, oxygen, or drugs maintaining blood pressure or heart function, are withdrawn, death may follow in minutes or hours. Babies who are aware or in pain pose special problems. The symptoms resulting from withdrawal are distressing until consciousness is lost. Doses of analgesics such as morphine, sufficient to make relief of distress certain, may kill them – that is, cause immediate cessation of breathing and consciousness, whereas without analgesia they might breathe for hours. Arguments that such analgesia is not active euthanasia appear, to some bedside attendants, casuistic.

Slippery-slope arguments against euthanasia in such cases appear to many to be especially unjust. Such arguments appear to say to the baby, "As far as your interests are concerned it would be morally best if we induced a quick and painless death. But if we do, it will launch the rest of us down a slippery slope. So put up with your distress, and save us all from slippery slopes."

I have emphasized earlier that most babies with serious illnesses have good outcomes. It is these who make neonatology such a rewarding endeavor. As methods of treatment improve, further good outcomes should result, but that is not guaranteed. Unless sophisticated high-technology medicine is balanced by imagination (allowing us insight into other people's worlds), compassion, and forbearance (accepting that there are valid views other than our own), outcomes may well be worse.

Notes

1 For a brief account of medical problems in the newborn see Marshal H. Klaus and Avroy A. Fanaroff, *Care of the High-risk Neonate*, 3rd ed (Philadelphia: W. B. Saunders, 1986). For a comprehensive account see Avroy A. Fanaroff and Richard J. Martin (eds), *Neonatal-Perinatal Medicine*, 4th ed (St Louis: C. V. Mosby, 1987).

2 For comprehensive accounts of VLBW and ELBW babies see David Harvey (ed.) *The Baby under 1,000 g.*

(London: Wright, 1989); and Dharmapuri Vidyasager (ed.) *The Tiny Baby, Clinical Perinatology* 13 2 (1986).

3 For outlines of the majority of birth defects see Kenneth Jones, *Smith's Recognizable Patterns of Human Malformations*, 4th edn (Philadelphia: W. B. Saunders, 1988).

4 James H Moller and William A Neal (eds) *Fetal, Neonatal, and Infant Cardiac Disease* (Norwalk: Appleton and Lange, 1990) 35: 723–43.

5 R. S. Duff and A. G. M. Campbell "Moral and ethical dilemmas in the special care nursery." *New England Journal of Medicine*, 289 (1973) 890–4.

6 Andrew Whitelaw, "Death as an option in neonatal intensive care." *Lancet* (1986: ii): 328–31.

28

A Modern Myth: That Letting Die is not the Intentional Causation of Death

Helga Kuhse

Abstract

If a doctor kills a severely handicapped infant, he commits an act of murder; if he deliberately allows such an infant to die, he is said to engage in the proper practice of medicine. This is the view that emerged at the recent trial of Dr Leonard Arthur over the death of the infant John Pearson. However, the distinction between murder on the one hand and what are regarded as permissible lettings die on the other rests on the Moral Difference Myth, according to which deliberate lettings die in the practice of medicine are not instances of the intentional causation of death.

I argue that a doctor who refrains from preventing a handicapped infant's death, causes that infant's death and does so intentionally. He commits an act of murder. But, I suggest, not all instances of the intentional causation of death are morally wrong. To the extent that they are not, killing rather than letting die will often be the preferable option because more economical of suffering. Hence what is required is the abolition of the Moral Difference Myth and legislation to the effect that those doctors who justifiably cause a patient's death – whether by an action or by an omission – commit no offence.

> Now I wonder if I could contrive one of those convenient stories we were talking about a few minutes ago, some magnificent myth that would in itself carry conviction to our whole community, including, if possible, the Guardians themselves.
>
> Socrates in Plato: *The Republic*

From *Journal of Applied Philosophy*, vol. 1, no. 1 (1984), pp. 21–38. Reprinted with permission.

A 'magnificent myth', the Myth of Metals, lends credibility and stability to Plato's ideal state, the Republic. According to this myth, 'Mother Earth' is fashioning people differently – some have gold, others silver, bronze or iron inside them. Those with gold inside them are meant to rule; those with lesser metals, meant to be ruled. Moreover, the myth holds, gold will beget gold, silver will beget silver, and so on (although there is some room for exceptions). If believed, the myth is self-fulfilling and will become true: alleged differences 'in the nature of things' will be confirmed by social practices and fiction has become fact when, finally, the Guardians themselves believe that the myth is true.[1]

We, too, have our myths. The 'magnificent myth' I am interested in is the myth that deliberate examples of letting die in the practice of medicine are, morally and legally, different from killings. Another way of stating this myth is to say that to deliberately allow someone to die is not intentionally to cause that person's death. This 'Moral Difference Myth' lends credibility and stability to our Ideal of the Sanctity of Human life.

Like Plato's Myth of Metals, our Moral Difference Myth is backed up by religious sanctions and has strong emotional appeal. It carries conviction with many conventional thinkers and is apparently accepted by the 'Guardians' themselves – at least, that is the impression one gets when reading the summing-up by Mr Justice Farquharson of the recent trial of Dr Leonard Arthur for the attempted murder of John Pearson.[2]

But social arrangements based on myths have their price. Plato sacrifices individual freedom and autonomy for the ideal of the Republic. We allow infants to suffer for the ideal of the Sanctity of Life. The price, in either case, may be too high.

Let me unfold the most recent re-statement of the Moral Difference Myth by beginning with a description of the happenings at Derby City Hospital in 1980, which led to the Leicester court case in 1981.

On Saturday, 28 June 1980, at 7.55 a.m., Molly Pearson gave birth to a boy, John Pearson. The midwife immediately recognized Down's syndrome. This condition, also known as 'mongolism', involves permanent mental retardation. Apart from Down's syndrome, the child appeared to be healthy. When told of the child's condition, the mother wept, and one sister heard Mrs Pearson say to her husband: "I don't want it, Duck."

Some four hours after the birth of John Pearson, Dr Leonard Arthur, a senior consultant paediatrician employed by the hospital, was called in to examine the baby in the presence of the baby's parents. Apart from the typical facial characteristics of Down's syndrome, there were no clinically detectable abnormalities, a fact recorded by Dr Arthur. While there is no account of the conversation that took place between the doctor and the parents (neither gave evidence at the subsequent trial), it appears that the parents rejected the baby on account of its being afflicted with Down's syndrome because Dr Arthur noted in the records: "Parents do not wish baby to survive. Nursing care only."

Dr Arthur prescribed a narcotic analgesic, dihydrocodeine (DF 118), at a dosage of 5 mg, to be administered not less than every four hours 'as required'. The infant was given water, but no nourishment, and antibiotics were withheld when broncho-pneumonia developed. John Pearson died at 5.10 a.m. on Tuesday, 1 July, three days after his birth.

A member of the hospital staff reported the circumstances surrounding John Pearson's death to the right-to-life association 'Life', thereby initiating the events that led to Dr Arthur's prosecution. The original charge was murder, the prosecution claiming that

(1) Dr Arthur had ordered the administration of the drug DF 118 with the intention of bringing about the baby's death;
(2) the fact that Dr Arthur had ordered 'nursing care only' showed that he had intended the infant to die.

However, at an early stage during the trial it became apparent that the drug could not be proved to have caused the infant's death and Justice Farquharson reduced the charge to one of attempted murder because, as he put it, it had become "apparent that there was another possibility as to how that baby met his death, quite apart from anything that may or may not have been done by . . . Dr Arthur".[3]

A long string of eminent physicians and paediatricians appeared for the accused, giving evidence of his high professional standing and confirming that what he had done was in accordance with their general practices.

On 5 November 1981, two hours after retiring, the jury found Leonard Arthur not guilty of attempting to murder his patient, John Pearson.

Following Dr Arthur's acquittal, Nuala Scarisbrick, the Hon. Administrator of 'Life', commented:

> The verdict gives *carte blanche* to doctors to give treatment to patients who are unwanted or handicapped or both, that will result in their death. Now to be unwanted is to be guilty of a capital offence.[4]

The jury's verdict of 'not guilty' does not support Nuala Scarisbrick's conclusion about the present state of the law, because it is not clear that either the trial or the verdict has clarified the law at all. However, the case tells us something about contemporary social practices and the way in which the Moral Difference Myth helps to support the Ideal of the Sanctity of Life, an ideal which is violated by those practices.

The Sanctity of Life Ideal

Most of us believe that human life has some very special value and that it is wrong (at least prima facie) to kill other people. To the extent that we hold such beliefs, we subscribe to a cluster of principles that are central to discussions involving the value of life and the wrongness of killing. While the various ideas that life is valuable (or demands respect) are often impossibly vague and misleading,[5] this is not the case in that particular area where medicine and legal theory overlap because here we encounter not mere respect for life, but the Ideal of the Sanctity of Life. According to this Ideal all innocent human life, irrespective of its quality or kind, is absolutely inviolable and equally valuable; innocent life must never intentionally be taken and must be preserved by those charged with its protection. (Henceforth the qualification 'innocent' will be taken as read, rather than repeated each time I refer to this doctrine.)

The basic idea that human life has 'sanctity' is deeply embedded in conventional thought. Moshe Tendler, a Professor of Talmudic Law, captures an important thrust of the Judaeo-Christian tradition when he comments:

> human life is of infinite value. This in turn means that a piece of infinity is also infinite and a person who has but a few moments to live is no less of value than a person who has 60 years to live . . . a handicapped individual is a perfect specimen when viewed in an ethical context. The value is an absolute value. It is not relative to life expectancy, to state of health, or to usefulness to society.[6]

In the law, the sanctity of life is recognized in the prohibition of unlawful homicide, which retains its absolute force, irrespective of the quality or kind of life in question. As Justice Farquharson put it in his summing up:

> However serious the case may be, however much the disadvantage of a mongol . . . no doctor has the right to kill it. Doctors are . . . given no special powers to commit an act which causes death . . .[7]

But the Sanctity of Life Ideal as it underlies the law does more than prohibit killing. It also imposes on doctors the duty to preserve the lives of their patients. Doctors not only have an obligation to refrain from killing, but also an obligation to prevent death, and this obligation extends to all patients equally. This is so because on the view we are discussing, all human lives are deemed equally valuable and hence equally worthy of protection. As one legal theorist puts it, it is a fundamental tenet of Anglo-American law that

> all human lives must be regarded as having an equal claim to preservation simply because life is an irreducible value. Therefore the value of a particular life, over and above the value of life itself, may not be taken into account.[8]

This, then, is the Sanctity of Life Ideal: it holds that all human life is absolutely inviolable and equally valuable; doctors must never take human life and they must protect and prolong it when they can.

This Ideal was violated by Dr Leonard Arthur when he directed that John Pearson receive large doses of the drug DF 118 and 'nursing care only'. It is also violated by all those eminent paediatricians who, in giving evidence for the defence, stated that they treat handicapped infants in their charge similarly: that they allow handicapped infants to die if those infants are not wanted by their parents. But in deliberately allowing handicapped infants to die, doctors are intentionally terminating human lives, and they are doing so on the basis of explicit or implicit quality-of-life considerations. Excluding cases such as killings in war, legal executions and killings in self-defence, the law regards the intentional termination of life as murder. And yet, these doctors are not charged with murder and, as we know, Dr Arthur was acquitted, even of attempted murder. Why? I suggest because the Moral Difference Myth carries conviction with a large section of the community, including doctors and some of the 'Guardians' themselves.

The Moral Difference Myth

According to the Moral Difference Myth, it is one thing deliberately to kill a patient and quite another merely to let a patient die. Whereas the former is always prohibited by the law and conventional morality as an act of murder, those believing in the myth hold that the latter is not: there are times when a doctor may lawfully allow a patient to die.

In his summing-up, Justice Farquharson drew a sharp distinction between murder on the one hand and the mere 'setting of conditions' in which death may occur on the other. While he agreed that the distinction is sometimes difficult to draw, he pointed out that it is an important one in so far as it demarcates the line between unlawful homicide and the proper practice of medicine. To illustrate the difference to the jury, he gave the following four examples:

Example (1)

A Down's syndrome child is born with an intestinal obstruction. If the obstruction is not removed, the child will die. Here, Justice Farquharson said, the surgeon might say: "As this child is a mongol . . . I do not propose to operate; I shall allow nature to take its course." And, Justice Farquharson continued, "no-one could say that the surgeon was committing an act of murder by declining to take a course which would save the child."

Example (2)

A severely handicapped child, who is not otherwise going to die, is given a drug in such amounts that the drug itself will cause death. If the doctor acts intentionally, Justice Farquharson said, then "it would be open to the jury to say: yes, he was killing, he was murdering that child."

Example (3)

A patient is afflicted with terminal cancer and is suffering great pain. Increasing doses of pain-killing drugs are required to alleviate the patient's distress. The point will be reached where the pain-killing drug will cause the patient's death. This is a case, Justice Farquharson suggested, which "could never be murder. That was a proper practice of medicine."

Example (4)

A child, afflicted with an irreversible handicap and rejected by its mother, contracts pneumonia. If, in this case, the doctor withheld antibiotics and "by a merciful dispensation of providence" the child died, then, Justice Farquharson suggested, "it would be very unlikely. . that you (or any other jury) would say that the doctor was committing murder."[9]

Thus, according to Justice Farquharson, not every doctor who allows a salvageable infant to die is committing an act of murder. The distinction between 'murder' and the mere 'setting of conditions', Justice Farquharson said, is borne out by the distinction between examples (1), (3) and (4) on the one hand and example (2) on the other. What the jury had to decide was whether what Dr Arthur had done fell into the first or the second category: had he attempted to murder John Pearson, or had he merely set the conditions in which the baby's death could occur?[10]

On the basis of these comments and examples, it is difficult to imagine that many juries would have thought that Dr Arthur had murdered, or attempted to murder, John Pearson – for Justice Farquharson's comments imply that only positive acts directly intended to cause death (example 2) constitute murder and that neither deliberate letting die (examples 1 and 4) nor positive acts not directly intended to cause death (example 3) fall into this category. But this, I suggest, is wrong. Or at least – since I am not a lawyer and hence am reluctant to correct a judge's interpretation of the law – if it is a correct statement of the law, then the law is based on the Moral Difference Myth. As such, it would be drawing a distinction where no significant difference exists.

The Intentional Causation of Death

During the trial of Dr Arthur, many reputable specialists were called in and testified that both the administration of large doses of analgesic narcotics and 'nursing care only' constitute a common and acceptable medical practice in cases of handicaps, such as Down's syndrome. However, whilst it is undoubtedly correct that treatment similar to that prescribed by Dr Arthur is widely *accepted* in paediatric medicine, this does not mean that it is *acceptable* under existing laws. Rather, such treatment constitutes an infringement of the Sanctity of Life Ideal underlying those laws.

In arguing for this view, I shall take as my starting point the legal prohibition of murder and suggest that not only 'direct' killings but also 'indirect' killings and deliberately letting die fall into the category of murder. They fall into the category of murder, I shall argue, because they are all instances of the intentional causation of death – and to intentionally cause the death of a patient is, other things being equal, to commit an act of murder. As a typical Crimes Act states:

> Murder shall be taken to have been committed where the act of the accused, or the things by him omitted to be done, causing the death charged, was done or omitted with reckless indifference to human life, or with intent to kill or inflict grievous bodily harm upon some person . . .[11]

For our purposes, then, the key concepts are 'intention' and 'causation'. I shall deal with them in turn.

(a) Intention

Contrary to some ethical and theological theories, which attempt to draw a morally relevant distinction between what an agent 'directly' intends and what he merely foresees (or 'obliquely', or 'indirectly' intends), English law does not recognize the intention/foresight distinction. For legal purposes, the presumption is that "everyone must be taken to intend that which is the natural consequence of his actions."[12] This means that "[a] man can be guilty of murder although he did not intend to harm his victim, if he intended to do an act which a reasonable man would say was likely to cause death."[13] In other words, intention is presumed to include not only those consequences which an agent directly intends to bring about as an end or as a means, but also those consequences which he only obliquely intends, or merely foresees.[14] The case of *R. V. Desmond and Others* will illustrate the point.

In 1868 two Irish Fenians were imprisoned. To liberate the prisoners, one of the accused, Barrett, dynamited the prison wall. Whilst the attempt to liberate the prisoners failed, the explosion killed some people living close by. Clearly, Barrett did not intend to kill or injure anyone, either as a means or as an end. However, Barrett was convicted on the grounds that he had foreseen those deaths. As Lord Coleridge summed it up at the time: it is murder "if a man did (an) act not with the purpose of taking life but with the knowledge or belief that life was likely to be sacrificed by it".[15]

It has been suggested that more recent judicial interpretations have thrown some doubt on the traditional view that foresight is sufficient for intention.[16] However, I will not here engage in legal exegesis. Whilst questions relating to individual judicial interpretations of the law are undoubtedly of great importance in some contexts, they are not of great importance to the philosophical points I wish to make in this paper. In the philosophical arena it is important to recognize that there are convincing reasons as to why the law has, in the past, treated foresight as sufficient for intention.

One of the main arguments for this presumption (the only one I will defend in this paper) is that *even if* an intrinsic moral difference were to exist between what an agent directly intends and what he foresees – a view I do not support – this moral difference would not be relevant to the question raised at the conviction stage: did the accused *cause* the death in question and is he *responsible*, as an agent, for what he has done. Let me elaborate.

If, according to the Sanctity of Life Ideal underlying the law, human life is both inviolable and valuable, then it follows that homicide is prohibited *because* it causes death, not because the victim's death was or was not a necessary part of the agent's plan or the reason for his action. Whilst what is or is not part of an agent's plan or the reason for his action, may be relevant to the question of *why* the agent did what he did and whether he ought to be blamed or punished for what he did (something that may be relevant at the sentencing stage), it is not relevant to the question of *what* he did – to the question of intentional action. When we ask, at the conviction stage, whether an agent has committed murder, we do not want to know whether what he has done was morally justifiable (as, perhaps, in some cases of euthanasia) but rather whether in doing what he did, he acted deliberately and freely (i.e. intentionally) and is thus responsible for what he chose to bring about.[17]

The terminology of intention to cover both the directly intended and the foreseen, or obliquely intended, consequences of an action suggests itself because of the close link between those things we do intentionally and our responsibility, as agents, for what we voluntarily and deliberately bring about. It seems that the following connection between an agent's intentional action and his responsibility applies: when an agent acts intentionally, what he intends is that he bring about a certain consequence. He desires, or wants, that consequence either for its own sake or as a means to a further end. If the consequence of an agent's intentional action thereby occurs, he brought it about intentionally. The term 'intentional' therefore denotes things done with the intention of doing them. But for an agent to have brought about a consequence intentionally, it is not necessary that he desired or wanted it. Rather, what seems to be necessary for intentional action is the concept of deliberate or voluntary choice: if an agent A in doing what he intends believes that he will inevitably or very likely bring about not only P but also Q, and if he could have refrained from doing as he intends, then A has brought about P and Q intentionally because he has deliberately and voluntarily chosen to do what he could have refrained from doing. Since we are pre-eminently responsible for our intentional doings, A is responsible not only for P but also for Q.[18]

This means that both the intended and the foreseen consequences of an agent's action share a feature which any system, such as the law, concerned with assigning responsibility for prohibited consequences, must treat as crucial: that the agent could have refrained from bringing the prohibited consequence about, but that he nonetheless chose to bring it about.[19] But if this is correct, then it follows that many doctors are terminating life intentionally and are thus committing acts of murder. Take example (3) above, in which pain-killing drugs are administered in doses that cause death. This was presented by Justice Farquharson as an instance which "could never be murder" and which, he said, was an example of the proper practice of medicine. However, while it is true that the proper practice of medicine (or humanitarian concerns) would sometimes seem to require that a doctor does something which will cause a patient's foreseen death, this does not mean that the doctor is not then responsible for the death he brought about intentionally (that is, deliberately and voluntarily). If example (3) strikes many of us as one which could never be murder, this is so, I think, because we sometimes fail to distinguish between the questions of whether an agent was *justified* in bringing about a certain consequence, and whether he brought the consequence about *intentionally*. As Lord Edmund-Davies notes: "Killing both pain and patient may be good morals, but it is far from certain that it is good law."[20]

As far as the administration of the narcotic analgesic DF 118 is concerned, Dr Arthur handed a statement to the police, saying that "the [sole] intention... was to reduce any suffering on the part of the infant."[21] What is clear, though, is that what Dr Arthur had directly intended (or *why* he did what he did), as distinct from *what* he intentionally brought about, is of little import when the question of murder is at issue. Here the legal question is, simply, did the accused deliberately and voluntarily bring about death in a situation where he could have refrained from doing as he intended?

But murder ceased to be the issue when the defence was, early in the trial, able to show that the causal link between Dr Arthur's prescription of the drug DF 118 and the baby's death could not be established beyond reasonable doubt. Whilst the principal expert witness for the Crown, Professor Alan Usher, had certified that John Pearson had died of bronchial pneumonia which, he said, had been caused by the drug DF 118, subsequent histological evidence showed that there were abnormalities of the lungs, fibroelastosis of the heart and calcification of the brain. Although Professor Usher still insisted that the drug DF 118 had caused John Pearson's death, he also conceded that his initial evidence had been incomplete and inaccurate.[22] Since this raised doubts as to whether Dr Arthur's regime had caused the infant's death, Justice Farquharson withdrew the charge of murder and substituted for it the charge of attempted murder.[23] Following this, the question was no longer whether Dr Arthur had *caused* the death in question, but rather whether he *intended to cause* it. And with this, it seems, the emphasis moved more and more away from the largely objective criteria of intention and causation. The question became whether Dr Arthur had directly intended to cause the death in question and whether the treatment prescribed by the accused amounted in law to an 'attempt'.

There is no reason to doubt Dr Arthur's statement that all he (directly) intended to do, when prescribing the drug DF 118, was to "reduce any suffering on the part of the infant".[24] But since we know from Dr Arthur's records that he believed, at the time, that John Pearson was born healthy apart from his (painless) Down's syndrome, we must also ask 'what suffering was there to be reduced?'

The most plausible answer would appear to be: the suffering likely to arise from the policy of 'nursing care only', a policy which involved that the baby would not be fed and, if an infection developed, would not be treated. If the question as to why Dr Arthur had prescribed a narcotic analgesic to an apparently healthy infant had been raised, this could have led straight on to the second prong of the prosecution's initial charge of murder. This was that Dr Arthur's policy of non-treatment showed that he had intended the infant to die. Since the infant had in fact died (and may have died *because* it was not treated), the charge of murder might still have held good with regard to the charge of non-treatment. Even if doubts had arisen as to whether the drug DF 118 had caused pneumonia and John Pearson's subsequent death, John Pearson's death from pneumonia may still have been a consequence of Dr Arthur's intentional withholding of antibiotics. However, the question of whether intentional withholding of treatment, which results in a foreseen death, can ever be an instance of the intentional causation of death, or murder, was not examined at the trial. It was not examined because, as we know, by the time this question could have been raised, the charge had already been changed from 'murder' to 'attempted murder', where the issue had become whether Dr Arthur intended, and attempted, to cause death.

Whilst the question of whether a doctor can attempt to murder a patient by non-treatment could still have been raised in this context, it was not. It was not raised, partly because with the change in the charge there also came a subtle shift in emphasis; from the legal and inclusive notion of the *intentional causation* of death to the less inclusive subjective criterion of whether the accused did or did not *directly intend* to cause death when he embarked on the policy of non-treatment. But there was another reason as well: the Moral Difference Myth, which holds that killing in the practice of medicine is one thing and letting die quite another.

The Moral Difference Myth played an important role in the trial of Dr Leonard Arthur, because throughout the proceedings the view prevailed that it was, both morally and legally, permissible to allow handicapped infants to die. Only on the basis of this belief could Dr Arthur have been found not guilty of the attempted murder of John Pearson. For even if the jury believed Dr Arthur's statement to the police that when prescribing DF 118 he had intended to reduce suffering rather than to kill; and even if the jury (mistakenly) assumed that a direct intention to kill was necessary for an accused to be guilty of attempted murder; the jury would still have had to face the question of why there was likely to be any suffering to be reduced, and why the baby was not being fed in the normal manner and treated with antibiotics when it developed pneumonia. If the jury had asked these questions they would have had to conclude that the intention was that the baby should die. How then could anyone escape the conclusion that Dr Arthur was guilty of attempting to murder John Pearson? Only, it would seem, by taking the view that when a doctor lets a baby die, he does not cause its death and is not responsible for it. The baby dies, according to this view, from the disease or injury and not from what the doctor does.[25]

It is this view I wish to challenge. It rests, as I will show, on an inadequate notion of causal agency and its connection with moral and legal responsibility.

(b) Causation

For the law, causation is of primary importance because unless it can be shown that a person has caused a certain consequence, such as death, that person cannot be held legally responsible for it. In the recent trial of Dr William Waddill (Jr), for example, a California Superior Court Judge told the jury: "You may not find the defendant guilty of murder unless you are satisfied that the defendant, by act or omission, was the proximate cause of the death of Baby Girl Weaver."[26]

This quotation suggests that omissions can be causes and that an agent can cause death not only by doing something but also by doing nothing. And, indeed, this is the case. The law holds agents not only responsible for the consequences of their intentional actions, but also for the consequences of at least some of their omissions.

Legal definitions of 'homicide' and 'murder' thus typically include reference to omissions as well as to positive acts. *Black's Law Dictionary*, for example, defines 'homicide' as "the killing of one human being by the procurement, or omission, of another"[27] and, as we saw above, the New South Wales (Australia) Crimes Act states that an agent can commit murder not only by an act but also by an omission.[28]

Whilst the law thus recognizes that omissions can be causes, this view was not considered at the trial of Dr Arthur. It was not considered because by the time this question could have been discussed, Professor Usher had already conceded that John Pearson was born with a number of previously undetected abnormalities. Because of these abnormalities, doubt had arisen as to whether John Pearson's death was caused by either an act of the accused (the administration of DF 118) or – our present concern – by Dr Arthur's omission to treat.

However, even if it could not be shown beyond reasonable doubt that Dr Arthur, by an act or an omission, caused John Pearson's death, it is clear that there are many instances in the practice of medicine where the causal link between a doctor's omission to treat and a patient's subsequent death is not in doubt. Example (1) – the Down's syndrome infant born with an intestinal obstruction – is a case in point. So is, other things being equal, example (4), where a handicapped infant is allowed to die of untreated pneumonia. These cases are cited by Justice Farquharson as instances of which 'no one could say' that they constituted murder. However, for the following reasons I believe that they may well be murder.

That omissions can have consequences is most clearly seen when the act omitted is one which is normally expected to be done. Indeed, it is in circumstances such as these that we quite unhesitatingly attribute the cause of the consequence to the act omitted. If a mother does not feed her infant and the infant dies, then we say that the mother's omission is the cause of the infant's death. Similarly, if a doctor refrains from giving, say, insulin to an otherwise healthy diabetic patient and the patient dies, then we say that the doctor's omission was the cause of the patient's death. We have certain expectations as to normal functioning, or the normal course of events, and if an agent deviates from them, then we cite his omission, or his failure to do what is expected, as the cause of a consequence, such as death.

Based on this notion of normal functioning, or the normal course of events, Hart and Honoré, in their now classical account of *Causation in the Law*, emphasize that not only actions but also negative states, static conditions and omissions can be causes:

> there is no convenient substitute for statements that the lack of the rain was the cause of the failure of the corn crop, the icy condition of the road was the cause of the accident, the failure of the signalman to pull the lever was the cause of the train smash.[29]

Thus, on Hart and Honoré's account, omissions become causes when what is omitted to be done deviates from normal expectations, normal functioning and normal conditions. As they put it:

> When things go wrong and we then ask for the cause, we ask this on the assumption that the environment persists unchanged, and something "has made the difference" between what normally happens in it and what happens on this occasion.[30]

On Hart and Honoré's view, then, the distinction between omissions that have causal status and those that do not is expressed in terms of the distinction between 'causes' and 'conditions' which, in turn, is based on the difference between normal and abnormal functioning:

> and what is taken as normal for the purpose of the distinction between cause and mere conditions is very often an artefact of human habit, custom or convention. This is so because men have discovered that nature is not only sometimes harmful *if* we intervene, but it is also sometimes harmful *unless* we intervene, and have developed customary techniques, procedures and routines to counteract such harm. These have become a second 'nature' and so a second 'norm'. The effect of drought is regularly neutralized by governmental precautions in preserving water or food; disease is neutralized by inoculation; rain by the use of umbrellas. When such man-made conditions are established, deviations will be regarded as exceptional and so rank as the cause of harm. It is obvious that in such cases what is selected as the cause from the total set of conditions will often be an omission which coincides with what is reprehensible by established standards of behaviour . . .[31]

Perhaps it is this difference between normal and abnormal functioning Justice Farquharson had in mind when he drew the distinction between unlawful murder and lawful letting die in terms of the dichotomy between causing death on the one hand and the mere setting of conditions in which death may occur on the other.[32] For if it is a widely accepted practice in paediatric medicine to allow severely handicapped infants to die, then it might follow on Hart and Honoré's account that a doctor's refraining from preventing death is a mere background condition and not 'the cause' of an infant's death.

One thing did become abundantly clear during the trial: that many handicapped infants *are* deliberately being allowed to die. What is far less clear, though, is that a doctor's omission to treat is not, nonetheless, the cause of such an infant's death.

Let me begin by establishing what the policy of non-treatment or 'nursing care only' amounts to in such cases:

According to Sister Mahon, the midwife who delivered the baby, 'nursing care only' means "keeping the baby comfortable and feeding it with water . . ." For the houseman, Dr Fryatt, the term includes nourishment, but excludes treatment should an infection develop. And, again, for Sister Simcox it means the following:

> Nursing care only, if it appears on the sheet of the mother and the baby, the child goes to a

> different ward. The nurses would cherish him and remain in the ward until he died. If 'nursing care only' is prescribed, it depends on the context whether the patient survives, but in the cases of the severely deformed child, this has never happened in that hospital.[33]

As Justice Farquharson pointed out, while there was some disagreement as to what precisely the term 'nursing care only' amounted to, it was generally agreed that by the time the nurses were in fact looking after the child, it had developed pneumonia, "and by that stage... it was accepted that the child had reached the stage where, if infection overcame it, it was going to be left to die."[34]

So this is what I assume for the purposes of my subsequent discussion: that John Pearson was suffering from pneumonia, that antibiotic treatment was deliberately withheld, and that the infant's death from pneumonia was foreseen.

However, in this connection, we should also note the following: firstly, that in cases such as this, doctors are not powerlessly standing by as unsalvageable infants die, rather they *refrain* from preventing deaths that could quite easily be prevented. In other words, a doctor who refrains from preventing death has the ability and the opportunity to prevent the death, is aware of this and of the fact that were he not to refrain the infant would not die.[35] In examples (1) and (4), for example, the infants would not have died had the intestinal obstruction been removed in the first case, and had the second infant been treated with antibiotics. Similarly with John Pearson: had he not been given excessive doses of the respiratory depressant DF 118 and been treated with antibiotics, we can assume that he would not have died of pneumonia when he did. Secondly, we should note that those involved in medical decision-making and interpretations of the law not only foresee (or 'obliquely' intend) that those untreated infants will die; they actually hope for, want or desire (and therefore 'directly' intend) those infants' early deaths.

Justice Farquharson thus spoke of the "realization of hope" if a handicapped infant contracts an infection, and regarded it as a "merciful dispensation of providence" if the child then dies of such an untreated infection.[36] Professor Alexander Campbell, a witness for the defence, stated that he had, on a number of occasions, put an infant on 'nursing care only' with the intention that it should not survive.[37] A second witness, Dr Dunn, said that if he had been in charge of the treatment of John Pearson, he would have hoped that the infant "had contracted pneumonia... or had some defect..." He also stated that in cases such as this, food would be withheld "in the hope that complications would develop which would lead to death by natural causes".[38] Yet another witness, Sir Douglas Black, President of the Royal College of Physicians, agreed with his colleagues. According to him, "it would be ethical to put (a handicapped and rejected child) upon a course of management that would end in its death... I say that it is ethical that a child suffering from Down's syndrome... should not survive."[39] And a final witness, Dr Bluett, stated that if the parents decided that they did not want a child to survive, he would put that child on a regime like that prescribed by Dr Arthur, where "one hopes it would then contract an infection and die."[40]

It thus became quite clear during the trial that the practice of deliberately letting handicapped infants die is widespread in the medical community – moreover, it is endorsed by members of the community who are highly respected in both medical and non-medical circles. Whilst it is not impossible, Justice Farquharson pointed out, that such highly respected men were committing crimes, he imagined that the jury would "think long and hard before deciding that doctors of the eminence we have heard in presenting to you what medical ethics are... have evolved standards which amount to committing crime".[41]

And yet, a reasoned case can be offered for the claim that the standards which have evolved in medicine and that are apparently accepted by the general population[42] and the 'guardians' alike, are a direct infringement of the law of homicide. Refraining from preventing death is, in the cases we have discussed, always – I believe – an instance of the intentional causation of death. In other words, it is murder. To see why this is so, we need to return to the question of causation.

According to the analysis provided by Hart and Honoré, we can distinguish between 'the cause' of a consequence and the causal background conditions by relying on the distinction between normal and abnormal functioning. The authors point out that much of our interest in determining the cause of some outcome is prompted by something having gone wrong with the normal functioning of things. Thus, if we want to know why this house is now burning while normally it is not, we are asking 'what made the difference' between this house's not-burning and its burning, and it is this 'difference' that determines something's being the cause rather than a condition. Thus we would, in the present case, be satisfied in being told that the explosion of a kerosene lamp was the cause of the house's catching fire, while the presence of inflammable material and oxygen are merely conditions which exist in normal circumstances also. Frequently, as was already mentioned above, what will be selected as the cause of a consequence will be an omission because the notion of normal functioning often involves agents in performing certain actions, where failure to perform such actions will be a deviation from the norm. For example, we may ask: 'Why did the flowers die?', and the gardener's failure to water them will be cited as the cause. The gardener's omission would be the cause, according to Hart and Honoré, because it constituted "an abnormal failure of a normal condition".[43] In other words, when certain man-made normal conditions are established, deviations from them will be regarded as exceptional and so rank as the cause of harm.[44]

Hart and Honoré's analysis of negative causation – whilst correct in attributing causal status to some omissions – is ultimately too limited because we are causally (and morally) responsible not only for those omissions which constitute deviations from social norms and established practices, but for all significant refraining. However, for reasons of space I will not here be able to argue for this view (although I have done so elsewhere – nor will it be necessary for our present[45] purposes. For our purposes Hart and Honoré's more limited notion of causation – widely accepted by legal theorists – will be quite sufficient to show that if doctors discriminatorily refrain from preventing *some* infants' deaths (the deaths of those who are handicapped and unwanted by their parents), then the doctors' omissions are 'the causes' for such infants' deaths. Moreover, in so far as those doctors either directly intend, or foresee, that the infants will die as a consequence of non-treatment, these are instances of the intentional causation of death, or murder.

This is so for the following reason: it is widely recognized that we can raise the question of causation in different causal contexts. Take the case of an infant born with Down's syndrome who develops pneumonia, is not treated with antibiotics and subsequently dies. What is 'the cause' of the infant's death?

If the question is raised in the context of handicapped infants who are not wanted by their parents and whom doctors therefore allow to die, a satisfactory answer would be that the cause of this particular infant's death was pneumonia. Here the causal field, or the normal background conditions, are given by the medical history of this untreated Down's syndrome infant. And it is against these causal background conditions that we are seeking to establish what "made the difference" between the time when death occurred and when it did not. In this context, the fact that the infant contracted pneumonia will allow us to differentiate between the time when the infant died and when it did not.

However, whilst the selection of such a restricted causal field will undoubtedly be relevant for the answering of certain questions, it is not a field which we may choose when we raise the question as to the cause of an infant's death in the context of the Sanctity of Life Ideal and the law. Since it is a fundamental tenet of the law that "all human lives must be regarded as having an equal claim to preservation,"[46] the causal background conditions in this case are given by *all* the infants who contract pneumonia in a modern hospital setting. Since it is standard practice to prevent the death of all those infants who are not handicapped and are wanted by their parents, pneumonia may be the cause of death in relation to the former field of handicapped infants but cannot be the cause in relation to the latter field. It cannot be the cause in relation to the latter field since it is part of the description of that field, and being present throughout that field, it cannot differentiate one subregion from another.[47]

What, then, is 'the cause' of an untreated Down's syndrome infant's death if pneumonia is ruled out as a possible cause? It is the same as in the case of an untreated non-handicapped infant. If a doctor deliberately refrained from preventing such an infant's death, we would say that the doctor's failure to treat was the cause of that infant's death. Similarly in the case of Down's syndrome infants. If it can be shown that what differentiates those situations in which death occurs (or would have occurred) is the doctor's failure to treat, then the doctor's omission is the causal factor that allows us to distinguish those situations in which death occurs from those in which it does not, and the doctor's failure to treat is identified as the causal factor that made, or would have made, the difference between an infant's dying and not-dying. Hence, the doctor's failure to treat is the cause of death.[48]

In this connection, we do well to remind ourselves of the distinction drawn by H. L. A. Hart between causal responsibility and liability responsibility, that is, between an agent being causally responsible for a consequence, and being liable, or having to answer for the consequences of one's actions or omissions.[49] Thus it would seem that only when an agent *refrains* from preventing death is he prima facie fully accountable for it, just as accountable or morally responsible as he would have been had he brought it about by a deliberate positive action.

Precisely what is to count as 'refraining' is a topic that needs further investigation; but for our purpose it is enough to note that when doctors like Dr Leonard Arthur and the witnesses who gave evidence at the trial leave a baby to die, they have the ability, the opportunity, and the awareness to make them fully accountable or morally responsible, just as accountable and responsible as they would be were they to administer a lethal injection.

Moreover, in cases of refraining from preventing death, doctors are not only morally, but also legally, accountable for a death they failed to prevent. It is true, moral responsibility and legal liability are not always coextensive. For example, if a stranger refrains from rescuing an infant drowning in a foot of water, he is morally responsible for the death, but not liable for legal conviction or punishment because, as H. L. A. Hart notes, refusing to aid those in danger is not generally considered a criminal offence in English law.[50] However, this situation is dramatically changed in the doctor/patient relationship. Here doctors must not only refrain from taking life, they must also preserve it when they can. This is so because a special relationship (recognized by the law) characterises the doctor/patient relationship. Thus it is widely agreed that a doctor is legally obligated to provide the 'necessaries of life' for those of his patients who are dependent on them.[51] Deliberately to withhold those 'necessaries of life' is the intentional causation of death by an omission. Legally such omissions have the same status as positive actions: if it is murder in one case, so it is – other things being equal – in the other.

Conclusion

Nothing in the above account suggests that it is morally wrong to let handicapped infants die if those infants are not wanted by their parents. Nor does anything I have said suggest that such a course of action would be right. Rather, the point of my argument has been to show that not only direct killings, but also 'indirect' killings and allowing to die are cases of the intentional causation of death and thus an infringement of the Sanctity of Life Ideal and the law.

But the account has moral and legal implications: that we should abandon the convenient Moral Difference Myth which holds that letting a handicapped infant die is not an instance of the intentional causation of death or murder – and that we should reflect on a number of difficult ethical questions which have been present all along.

Does human life, irrespective of its quality or kind, have 'sanctity', i.e. is it equally valuable and inviolable and must it always be preserved by all available means; or should life and death decisions in the practice of medicine at least sometimes be based on quality-of-life considerations?

These are the fundamental questions that need to be answered first before we can arrive at morally defensible principles to instruct our life and death decisions. Whether we bring about another person's death by positive or negative means (or by killing or letting die) is ultimately but a question of method. From the moral and legal point of view, intentional killings and intentional letting die are, other things being equal, the same.

However, the question of method is crucial in two other respects. It is crucial for the Sanctity of Life Ideal itself; and it may be crucial for the patient whose life is being terminated. Let me briefly deal with these two points in turn.

A consistent application of the Sanctity of Life Ideal leads to 'vitalism', the view that it is the doctor's duty to sustain his patient's life 'even if it were decided that the patient were "better off dead"'.[52] Whilst such a position is so patently inhumane that few of us would want to defend it, it is consistent with the Sanctity of Life Ideal's two tenets: that all human life is equally valuable and inviolable. The principle's inhumanity and its disregard for the interests of individual patients is the price one has to pay if this Ideal is to be followed consistently.

In the light of the obvious inhumanity of 'vitalism', it is not surprising that this position does not have many followers. However, this is where the Moral Difference Myth comes in, a myth which initially seems to rescue the Sanctity of Life Ideal from its objectionable link with vitalism; because the Moral Difference Myth holds that it is one thing to kill a patient and quite another to let a patient die. In other words, according to the Moral Difference Myth a doctor must never kill a patient, but there are times when he may refrain from preventing death.

Now, if my above arguments have been correct, this Moral Difference Myth cannot be sustained. But the widespread belief that it marks a morally and legally relevant distinction between killing and letting die superficially lends support to the Sanctity of Life Ideal. This support, however, is bought at a price. On the basis of the Moral Difference Myth, doctors choose letting patients die as their method of bringing about death, even though killing would, under the circumstances, often be the preferable option.

Let us simply assume, for the moment, that there are times when a doctor may refrain from preventing death because continued life is not in the patient's best interest. Let us also assume that case (1) – the Down's syndrome infant born with an intestinal obstruction – is such a case. Here the doctor says (in the words of Justice Farquharson): "As this child is a mongol . . . I do not propose to operate; I shall allow nature to take its course." However, nature is not always kind. To see what happens when nature is allowed to take its course in a case like this, let us turn to the description one paediatric surgeon, Anthony Shaw, gives of the situation:

> When surgery is denied, the doctor must try to keep the infant from suffering while natural forces sap the baby's life away. As a surgeon whose natural inclination is to use the scalpel to fight off death, standing by and watching a salvageable baby die is the most emotionally exhausting experience I know. It is easy at a conference, in a theoretical discussion, to decide that such infants should be allowed to die. It is altogether different to stand by in the nursery and watch as dehydration and infection wither a tiny being over hours and days. It is a terrible ordeal for me and the hospital staff – much more so than for the parents who never set foot in the nursery.[53]

Letting die can thus be a terrible ordeal for all involved – not least for the infant for whose sake, we assume, doctors and parents are engaging in the practice of letting him or her die in the first place. The tragedy is of course, that patients, relatives and medical staff undergo these ordeals on the basis of a distinction that is, in itself, morally and legally irrelevant: the distinction between killing and letting die.

However, whilst intentional killing and intentional letting die are equivalent in so far as they are both instances of the intentional causation of death, it is clear that other extrinsic factors can make a moral difference. The point is this: whilst the administration of a lethal injection would bring a swift and painless death for the patient, letting die may be neither swift nor painless. In the much-discussed Johns Hopkins case (again involving a Down's syndrome infant with an intestinal obstruction), the dying process took 15 days.[54] The suffering involved in this is difficult to justify indeed, and it seems clear that in a case such as this a quick and painless injection would better serve the interests of the infant.

In the case of John Pearson, the letting die process took only three days. But even three days are too long if they involve those concerned in considerable unnecessary suffering. It is true, John Pearson may not have suffered as much as descriptions such as that provided by Anthony Shaw above might suggest. He was drugged with massive doses of the narcotic analgesic DF 118. However, the experience of the court proceedings and the continued belief in the Moral Difference Myth may make doctors more hesitant to administer sufficient doses of such drugs because their administration – in distinction to 'letting nature take its course' – may more easily be construed as an instance of the intentional causation of death. As a consequence, more infants may suffer for prolonged periods of time when the decision has been made to let them die. And whilst the Moral Difference Myth superficially holds the Sanctity of Life Ideal intact, the suffering of those infants is, I believe, too high a price to pay for this Ideal – an Ideal that might itself have to be questioned.

Just one final comment. Those parents and doctors who think that it is sometimes justifiable to bring about the death of a seriously handicapped infant are not moral monsters. It is clear that there are circumstances when death is the morally preferable option. So my complaint does not concern the moral dispositions of those who justifiably bring about the death of a seriously handicapped infant – it concerns the methods employed to bring those deaths about and the unarticulated and therefore frequently idiosyncratic criteria which inform life and death decisions in such cases. How can the situation be improved? By abolishing the Moral Difference Myth and recognizing that deliberately letting die is, both morally and legally, the same as deliberate killings – namely, instances of the intentional causation of death. Once this has been recognized, the real questions can be raised: under what circumstances may we intentionally cause the death of a handicapped infant; who should decide; and what is the most appropriate method of bringing death about? And if consensus can be reached on these issues, the next question, surely, must be this: how can we provide legal protection for those who do what it is sometimes right to do: intentionally cause the death of another human being? Thus what is required is not the creation of a new (and lesser) offence than that of unlawful homicide; rather, what is required is legislation to the effect that a doctor or parent who acts in accordance with accepted guidelines and brings about an infant's death commits *no* offence.[55]

And with this, we return to the beginning. Once such legislation has been introduced and has become fact, the Moral Difference Myth will truly have been banished to the realm of fiction. It will be as embarrassing for us to recount it as it was for Socrates to state his Myth of Metals: "I don't know how I'm to find the courage or the words to do so."[56]

Acknowledgements

This article was written as part of a larger study on 'Life and Death Choices for Defective Newborns', supported by the Australian Research Grants Scheme. I wish to thank the ARGS and Professor Peter Singer, Department of Philosophy, Monash University, for their support.

Notes

1 Plato: *The Republic*, Part Four (Book Three), 414–16.
2 See Transcript of the shorthand notes of the official court reporters Marten, Meredith & Co., Ltd, 36/38 Whitefriars Steet, London, EC4Y 8BJ, for the summing up by Justice Farquharson in *Regina* v *Leonard John Henry Arthur*, November 3, 4, 5, 1981, at Leicester Court, England (subsequently cited as 'Transcript').
3 Ibid., p. 3.
4 Quoted by Glover, Jonathan (1982), 'Letting people die', *London Review of Books*, vol. 4, no. 4, p. 3.
5 See, for example, William K. Frankena's excellent exposition of this vagueness in 'The ethics of respect for life' in Barker, Stephen F. (ed.), *Respect for Life in Medicine, Philosophy, and the Law* (Baltimore, MD: Johns Hopkins Press, 1977), pp. 24–62.
6 Moshe Tendler, as cited by Brody, Howard (1976) *Ethical Discussions in Medicine* (Boston, Little, Brown), p. 66.
7 Transcript, p. 16.
8 Kadish, Sanford H. (1977) Respect for life and regard for rights in the criminal law, in: Barker, *Respect for Life*, p. 72.
9 The four examples are from pp. 18–19 of the Transcript.
10 Transcript, pp. 19–20.
11 The New South Wales (Australia) Crimes Act 1900, s. 18 (1) (a); see also *Jowitt's Dictionary of English Law*, vol. 1, 1977, entry under 'homicide' pp. 918–19.
12 *Jowitt's Dictionary of English Law*, vol. II, 1977, p. 1137.
13 Ibid., p. 1212.
14 Strictly speaking, the presumption that everyone must be taken to intend that which is the natural consequence of his actions would mean that an agent intentionally brings about not only the subjectively foreseen consequences of his action, but also those which were foreseeable (even though he may not have foreseen them). However, following the English Criminal Justice Act of 1967, a court or jury is not bound to take the latter view and may decide to include only the subjectively foreseen consequences under the legal notion of intention. The latter, less inclusive notion is sufficient for our purposes. I shall, therefore, leave moot such questions as gross unthinking negligence and extreme provocation (clearly relevant for the foreseeable/foreseen distinction) and merely assume that an agent is taken to intend the foreseen consequences of his/her action. (For a discussion of the notion of 'intention' see Hart, H. L. A., Intention and Punishment,' in Hart, H. L. A. (ed.), *Punishment and Responsibility: Essays in the Philosophy of Law* (Oxford, 1965 Clarendon Press, pp. 113–35).
15 *The Times*, 28 April 1868, as cited by H. L. A. Hart, ibid., p. 119.
16 See Kenny, Anthony, 'Intention and mens rea in murder', in Hacker, P. M. S. and Raz, J. (eds), *Law, Morality and Society – Essays in Honour of H.*

L. A. Hart (Oxford, Clarendon Press, 1977) For a different view, see Baldwin, Thomas, 'Foresight and responsibility', *Philosophy*, pp. 161–74. 54, no. 209 (July 1979) pp. 347–60).

17 For a fuller discussion of the distinction between the permissibility of an action and its justifiability, see ch. III of my doctoral thesis: *The Sanctity of Life Doctrine in Medicine – A Critique*, Monash University, 1983.

18 For a more detailed defence of this view, see Chisholm, Roderick M., 'The structure of intention', *Journal of Philosophy*, 67, (1970), 633–47.

19 Hart, H. L. A. 'Intention and punishment', makes a similar point but expresses it in terms of the connection between the control an agent has over bringing/not bringing a consequence about.

20 Davies, Lord Edmund, 'On dying and dying well', *Proceedings of the Royal Society of Medicine*, 70 (1977): 73, as cited by Mason, J. K. and McCall Smith, R. A., *Law and Medical Ethics* (London: Butterworth 1983), p. 179.

21 Transcript, p. 50.

22 Ibid., pp. 45–6.

23 Ibid., p. 43.

24 Ibid., p. 50.

25 See note 3.

26 As cited by Green, O. H. 'Killing and letting die', *American Philosophical Quarterly*, 17 (1980): 195.

27 *Black's Law Dictionary*, 4th edn (1968), p. 867.

28 See note 11.

29 Hart, H. L. A. and Honore, A. M., *Causation in the Law* (London: Oxford University Press, 1959, pp. 28–9). Hart and Honore's account of negative causation has been criticized as being too limited. See, for example, Harris, John, *Violence and Responsibility*, (London: Routledge & Kegan Paul, 1980) See also note, pp. 37–42.

30 Hart, H. L. A. and Honore, A. M. *Causation in the Law*, p. 34.

31 Ibid., p. 35.

32 Transcript, pp. 20–3.

33 This and the preceding quotations are from pp. 34–35 of the Transcript.

34 Ibid., p. 35.

35 For a more extensive discussion of what it is for an agent to refrain from preventing a consequence, see, for example, Green, O. H., 'Killing and letting die', pp. 196–8.

36 Transcript, p. 44.

37 Ibid., p. 59.

38 Ibid., pp. 69 and 73.

39 Ibid., pp. 79–80.

40 Ibid., p. 86.

41 Ibid., p. 81.

42 At the time of the trial, a Mori Opinion Poll showed that 86% of almost 2000 adults polled said that a doctor should not be found guilty of murder if, with the parents' agreement, 'he sees to it that a severely handicapped baby dies', *The Times* 10 November 1981).

43 Hart, H. L. A. and Honore, A. M., *Causation in the Law*, p. 37.

44 Ibid., p. 35.

45 See ch. II of my PhD thesis, *The Sanctity of Life Doctrine in Medicine*.

46 See note 8.

47 See, for example, Mackie, J. L., 'Causes and conditions', in: Sosa, Ernest (ed.), *Causes and Conditionals* (London: Oxford University Press, 1975), pp. 15–38.

48 See also Gruzalski, Bart, 'Killing and letting die', *Mind*, 40, pp. 15–38, 91–8. (1981).

49 Hart, H. L. A. 'Postscript: responsibility and retribution', in: Hart, H. L. A. (ed.), *Punishment and Responsibility*, pp. 212–30.

50 Ibid., p. 217.

51 See, for example, Introduction, in: Steinbock, Bonnie (ed.), *Killing and Letting Die* (Englewood Cliffs, NJ: Prentice-Hall, 1980) pp. 4–9; Law Reform Commission of Canada, *Working Paper 28–Euthanasia Aiding Suicide and Cessation of Treatment* (1982), pp. 19–20.

52 Karnofsky, D. A., 'Why prolong the life of a patient with advanced cancer? *Cancer Journal for Clinicians*, 10 (1960): 9. see my 'Extraordinary means and the sanctity of life', *Journal of Medical Ethics*, 7 (June 1981), 74–82.

53 As cited by Rachels, James, 'Euthanasia, killing and letting die', in: Ladd, John (ed.), *Ethical Issues Relating to Life and Death* (Oxford University Press, 1979, p. 159).

54 Dyck, Arthur J., 'An alternative to the ethic of euthanasia', in: Reiser, Stanley Joel, Dyck, Arthur J. and Curran, William J. (eds), *Ethics in Medicine – Historical Perspectives and Contemporary Concerns* (Cambridge: MIT Press, 1977, p. 534).

55 For such a proposal, see Mason, J. K. and McCall Smith, R. A., *Law and Medical Ethics*, pp. 81–9.

56 Plato: *The Republic*, Part Four (Book Three), p. 414.

29

The Abnormal Child: Moral Dilemmas of Doctors and Parents

R. M. Hare

I was asked to make a philosophical contribution to our discussions; and any philosopher who tries to do this sort of thing is up against a serious difficulty. If he is content to act merely as a kind of logical policeman and pick up bad arguments that are put forward by other people, he will be unpopular, but may (if he is competent at his trade) establish for himself a fairly strong negative position. But if he wants to do something more constructive than that, and is going to rely on something more solid than his own intuitions and more stable than the received opinions on the subject, he will have to start from some general theory about how one argues on questions like this; and then at once he is on much shakier ground, because there is no general theory about moral argument that is universally accepted. All I can do in this situation is to tell you in outline the theory that I accept myself and then argue from that.

However, I have perhaps made my position sound shakier than it actually is; for the theory that I shall be using is one which ought to be acceptable to most of the main schools of ethics, because it relies only on certain formal characteristics of the moral words or concepts which we use in these arguments. I *think* (though obviously I shall have no time to argue) that this theory is consonant with the Christian principles that we should do to others as we wish that they should do to us, and that we should love our neighbour as ourselves; with the Kantian principle that we should act in such a way that we can will the maxim of our action to be a universal law; and with the utilitarian principle that everybody is to count as one and nobody as more than one (that is to say, that their interests are to be equally regarded). Other approaches to the theory of moral argument which lead to the same kind of principle are the so-called Ideal Observer theory, according to which what we ought to do is what a person would prescribe who was fully acquainted with the facts and impartially benevolent to all those affected; and the so-called Rational Contractor theory which says that the principles we ought to follow are those which a rational self-interested person would agree to if he did not know which end of the stick *he* was going to receive in any of the situations to be adjudicated by the principles.

All these methods come really to the same thing, that when faced with a decision which affects the interests of different people, we should treat the interests of all these people (including ourselves if we are affected) as of equal weight, and do the best we can for them. This is the fundamental principle. There are a great many other principles, some of them of great importance, which occupy a different level from this fundamental principle, and may appear to conflict with it, as they certainly do conflict on occasion with one another. I mean principles like those which forbid lying or promise-breaking or murder; or that (very important to doctors) which demands loyalty to those to whom one is under some special obligation owing to a particular relation one stands in to them (for example one's wife or one's child or one's patient).

From *Documentation in Medical Ethics*, vol. 3 (1974), pp. 365–9. This article was first given in lecture form to the London Medical Group. It is printed here by permission of the author.

However, I think it is right to subordinate all these principles to the fundamental one, because in cases of conflict between these different principles, it is only the fundamental principle that can give us any secure answer as to what we should do. The fundamental principle is the law and the prophets; although particular laws (and particular prophecies for that matter) are no doubt very important, they take their origin from the need to preserve and to do justice between the interests of people (that is, to secure to them their rights); and when there is a conflict between the principles – or even some doubt about the application of a particular principle – it is this fundamental principle which has to be brought in to resolve it.

An example that may occur to you after having heard what has been said is this: granted that the obstetrician has a special duty to his patient, the mother, and that the pediatrician has a special duty to *his* patient, the child, surely what they ought all in all to do when the interests of mother and child conflict should be governed by equal consideration for these interests and not by what branch of the profession each of them happens to have specialized in.

I am going therefore, in the hope of shedding some light on the dilemmas of doctors and parents, to ask, first of all, what are the different interests involved in the sort of case we are considering. There is first the interest of the child; but what *is* this? We can perhaps illuminate this question by asking "What if it were ourselves in that child's position – what do we prescribe for *that* case?" On the one hand it may be presumed to be in the child's interest to live, if this is possible; but if the life is going to be a severely handicapped one, it is possible that this interest in living may be at least greatly diminished. Then there is the interest of the mother, in whose interest also it is to live, and whose life may be in danger; and it is also in her interest not to have an abnormal child, which might prevent or severely impair the normal development of the rest of the family. The other members of the family have a similar interest. Against this, it is said that good sometimes comes to a family through having to bring up an abnormal child; and I can believe that this is so in some cases.

Then there are the interests (not so great individually but globally very great) which belong to those outside the family: first of all those of doctors and nurses who are concerned; then those of the rest of the staffs of hospitals, homes and other services which will be involved in looking after the child and the family. There are also the interests of all those people who *would* be looked after, or looked after better, by all these services if they did not already have too much on their hands; and there are the interests of the taxpayers who pay for it all. And lastly, there is another interest which is commonly ignored in these discussions, and which is so important that it often, I think, ought to tip the balance; but what this other interest is I shall not reveal until I have talked about those I have mentioned so far.

When I said that equal consideration ought to be given to all the interests affected, I did not mean that we should treat as equal the interest of the mother in continuing to live and that of the doctor in not being got out of bed in the middle of the night. As individuals, these people are entitled to equal consideration; but because life matters more to one than sleep to the other, that makes it right for the doctor to get out of bed and go and look after the mother. If the doctor had a car smash outside the mother's front door and she could save *his* life by getting out of bed in the middle of the night, then by the same principle she should do so. As individuals, they are equipollent; the difference is introduced by the differing importance to each of them of the various outcomes.

The number of those affected can also be important; if a GP can save a patient from a sleepless and distressful night by going along in the evening and providing a pain-killer, he will often do it, even in these days; but if a pill were not enough, and it were necessary for a whole team of nurses and an ambulance to turn out, he might decide to wait till the morning unless there were a real danger of a grave deterioration in the patient's condition. A very large number of people each of whom is affected to a small degree may outweigh one person who is affected to a greater degree. So even the fact that 60 million taxpayers will have to pay an average of 20 pence extra each a year to improve or extend the Health Service is of some moral, as well as political, importance. But I agree on the whole with those who ask us not to attach too much importance to these economic arguments; although I totally failed recently to get from an economist a straight answer to the question of the order of size of the sums involved in looking after handicapped children, I am prepared to accept for the sake of argument that they are relatively small. So let us leave the taxpayer out of it, and the rival claimants for care, and just consider the interests of the immediate family.

Here, however, we must notice the other important interest that I mentioned just now – that of the next child in the queue. For some reason that I cannot understand this is seldom considered. But try looking at the problem with hindsight. The example I am going to use is oversimplified, and I am deliberately not specifying any particular medical condition, because if I do I shall get my facts wrong. Suppose the child with the abnormality was not operated on. It had a substantial chance of survival, and, if it survived, it had a large chance of being severely handicapped. So they didn't operate, and what we now have is not that child, but young Andrew who was born two years later, perfectly normal, and leaves school next summer. Though not brilliant, he is going probably to have a reasonably happy life and make a reasonably useful contribution to the happiness of others. The choice facing the doctors and the family was really a choice between (if they didn't operate) a very high probability of having Andrew (who would not have been contemplated if they had a paralysed child in the family) and on the other hand (if they did operate) a combination of probabilities depending on the precise prognosis (shall we say a 10 per cent chance of a living normal child, a 40 per cent chance of a living but more or less seriously handicapped child, and a 50 per cent chance of a dead child plus the possibility of Andrew in the future).

If we agree with most people that family planning is right, and that therefore this family is justified in limiting its children to a predetermined number (however large), then that is the kind of choice it will be faced with, and in the situation I have imagined *was* faced with. We should try discussing with Andrew himself whether they made the right choice.

If I have characterized the choice correctly, then nearly everything is going to depend on what the prognosis was, and on our estimates of the value *to the persons concerned* of being alive and normal, and, by contrast, of being alive and defective or handicapped in some specified way. In making these value-judgements I do not see that we can do better than put ourselves imaginatively in the places of those affected, and judge as if it were our own future that was at stake. Since a sensitive doctor is bound constantly, in the course of his practice, to make this sort of imaginative judgement about what is for the best for other people, looking at it from their point of view, I do not think that it can be said that it raises any difficulties of principle; but it obviously raises very great difficulties in practice, which the sensitive and experienced doctor is as likely as anybody to be able to overcome in consultation with parents and others affected.

But the problems mostly arise from the difficulty of prognosis. That is why the work reported by Professor Smithells is so crucial. In principle it might be possible to put a numerical value upon the probabilities of the various outcomes, and having estimated how the various outcomes for the people involved affect their interests, to make a utilitarian calculation and choose the course that gives the best prospect of good and the least prospect of harm for those concerned, all in all. In practice we are bound to rely a lot on guesswork; but when guessing, it is an advantage to have a clear idea of what you are guessing *at*, and I have suggested that what we should be guessing at is what is for the best for all the parties taken together.

The prognosis, however, is always going to be pretty uncertain, and the question therefore arises of *when* the decision should be made. I suppose that it would be agreed that if there is doubt in the very early stages of pregnancy, it might be advisable to wait until the fetus had developed sufficiently to make the prognosis more certain. A hard-headed utilitarian might try to extend this principle and say that in cases of suspected abnormality we should let the child be born, operate if appropriate, and then kill the child if the operation resulted in a very severe handicap, and have another child instead. In this way we should maximize the chances of bringing into the world a human being with a high prospect of happiness. If the medical profession finds this suggestion repugnant, as it almost certainly does, and does not *want* the law changed; or if it is thought (perhaps rightly) to inflict too much mental suffering on the mother, then we shall have to be content with a far less certain procedure – that of either terminating or, if we don't terminate and then the child is born, estimating the chances *before* deciding whether to operate, and (if we do decide to operate) taking the risk, however small, of being left with a dreadfully handicapped child.

If we imagine our possible Andrew and his possible brother (the former existing only as a possible combination of sperm and ovum, the latter already existing as a fetus) – if, I say, we imagine them carrying out a prenatal dialogue in some noumenal world (and of course the supposition is just as fantastic in one case as it is in the other) and trying to arrive at a solution which will give them, taken together, the best chance of happy existence, the dialogue might go like this. Andrew points out that if the fetus is not born there is a high probability that he, Andrew, will be born and will have a normal and reasonably happy life. There is of course a possibility that the parents will change their minds about having any more children, or that one of them will die; but let us suppose that this is rather unlikely, and that there is no particular fear that the next child will be abnormal.

To this the fetus might reply "At least I have got this far; why not give me a chance?" But a chance of what? They then do the prognosis as best they can and work out the chances of the various outcomes if the present pregnancy is not terminated. It turns out that there is a slim chance, but only a slim chance, that the fetus will, if born and operated on, turn into a normal and, let us hope, happy child; that there is a considerable chance on the other hand that it will perish in spite of the operation; and that there is a far from negligible chance of its surviving severely handicapped. In that case, I think Andrew, the later possible child, can claim that he is the best bet, because the chance of the parents dying or changing their minds before he is born is pretty small, and certainly far less than the chance that the present fetus, if born, will be very seriously handicapped.

In order for the fetus to prevent Andrew winning the argument in this way, there is one move it can make. It can say, "All right, we'll make a bargain. We will say that I am to be born and operated on, in the hope of restoring me to normality. If the operation is successful, well and good. If it isn't, then I agree that I should be scrapped and make way for Andrew." I think you will see if you look at the probabilities that this compromise gives the best possible chance of having a healthy baby, and at the same time gives the fetus all the chance that it ever had of itself being that baby. But it does this at the cost of abolishing the substantial chance that there was of having this particular child, albeit in a seriously handicapped condition. I call this a *cost*, because many will argue (though I am not sure that I want to follow them) that life with a severe handicap is preferable, for the person who has it, to no life at all. Of course it depends on the severity of the handicap. And of course this policy involves so much distress for the mother that we might rule it out on that score alone, and terminate instead.

Perhaps I should end by removing what might be an obstacle to understanding. In order to expound the argument, I asked you to imagine Andrew and the fetus having a discussion in some noumenal world (and, by the way, it needn't bother you if you don't know what "noumenal" means; I only used it in order to keep my philosophical end up in the face of all your no doubt necessary medical jargon). This way of dramatizing the argument is perhaps useful though not necessary; and it carries with it one danger. We have to imagine the two possible children conducting this very rational discussion, and therefore we think of them being in a sense already grown up enough to conduct it; and that may lead us to suppose that, for either of them, to be deprived of the possibility of adulthood *after* having had this taste of it would be a very great evil. People (most of them) cling tenaciously to life (though it is a matter for argument, at what age they start to do this); and therefore to deprive a person of life is thought of as *normally* an evil. This certainly does not apply to Andrew, since he is not alive yet and so cannot be *deprived* of life in the relevant sense, though it can be *withheld* from him. I do not think it applies to the fetus as such, since it has as yet no conscious life (which is what we are talking about) and therefore cannot feel the loss of it or even the fear of that loss. If anybody thinks that fetuses *do* have conscious feelings sufficient to be put in this balance, I ask him to agree at least that their intensity is relatively small, and likewise of those of the newborn infant. So I do not think that the harm you are doing to the fetus or the unsuccessfully operated upon newborn infant by killing them is greater than that which you are doing to Andrew by stopping him from being conceived and born. In fact I think it is much less, because Andrew, unlike them, has a high prospect of a normal and happy life.

In my view as a philosopher, these are the sorts of considerations that doctors, surgeons and parents ought to be looking at when they are faced with these dilemmas.

30

Measuring Quality of Life in Theory and in Practice

Paula Boddington and Tessa Podpadec

Measuring quality of life is of concern to both philosophers and psychologists, yet the two disciplines typically approach the question in very different ways, ways so diverse that it may look as if they are engaged in such disparate activities that no dialogue between them is possible. In this paper we aim to construct the beginnings of a dialogue between the two disciplines which will show how they could serve each other and yet also show how, from the dialogue, difficult and previously unconsidered issues emerge for both sides.

The most fruitful way of looking at these differences between the two disciplines and perhaps the most fruitful way of beginning a dialogue between them is in examining the issue of *why* quality of life is being measured. Thus, this is the question on which we primarily focus, rather than giving a detailed analysis of *how* quality of life might be measured.

We are interested in how measuring quality of life stems from and leads to a differential valuing of human lives in the work of many philosophers, and how, in stark contrast, measuring quality of life is a pragmatic concern for psychologists and other social scientists which stems from an equal valuation of different human lives. We show how practitioners in the field are badly in need of a theoretical framework. One major question which then emerges is whether it is possible to have this framework and yet retain commitment to equal valuation of different human lives.

We are particularly focusing on learning difficulties as an illustration of the argument.

From *Bioethics*, vol. 6, no. 3 (1992), pp. 201–17.

What is the Purpose of Measurement?

An examination of the concerns of psychologists and philosophers regarding people with learning difficulties and questions of quality of life, or value of life, shows that the two disciplines often seem to be at completely cross purposes.

However, if the question of why the two disciplines are interested in quality of life and its measurement is asked, then it is possible to begin to see the reasons behind this divergence.

In general, philosophers are interested in what grounds the value of life, what it is that gives life the value it has, and are interested in looking at broad questions about choices between lives, and choices between life and death. For example, questions are considered concerning what sorts of people should be brought into the world, what priorities should be set concerning who should receive limited resources, and under what circumstances might it be permissible to allow a human being to die, or actively to help them on their way.

Especially as regards questions about choices between lives, some philosophers are interested in differences between different lives in terms of value and may link this to quality of life: as a rough generalization, the higher the quality of life, the greater the value. For example, Helga Kuhse and Peter Singer argue that medical resources are more effectively used on those who are judged to have higher expectation of benefiting from life, that is, those who are expected to have a higher measure of quality of life.

> Down's syndrome . . . means a reduced potential for a life with the unique features which are

> commonly and reasonably regarded as giving special value to human lives.... The possible benefits of successful surgery in the case of a Down's syndrome child are therefore, in terms of these widely accepted values, less than the possible benefits of similar surgery in a normal child.[1]

A higher valuation, in terms of expenditure of valuable resources, and in terms of what a child is thought to benefit from surgery, thus follows higher measurement of quality.

Of course, there is a wide body of opinion amongst philosophers, and we want to recognize this, but in this paper we are most concerned to consider those whose approach diverges most widely from the typical approach of psychologists and other practitioners. We go on to argue that despite this divergence, there can be a useful dialogue between those with dissimilar approaches: indeed, there should be such a dialogue. The following examples show how some moral philosophers typically differentially value different classes of people, in ways which can be connected to abilities that they are judged to have or to lack. (In turn, possession or lack of various abilities may be considered a crucial component of the quality of one's life.)

> To respect a person as an end is to value or cherish him for what he is – and that is a possessor of a rational will, where 'rational will' refers to the ability to be self-determining and rule following with all that these imply.... This is not to exclude from moral attitudes creatures which have personality only in a minimal sense, once we understand what it is to have respect for a person in the full sense ... we can then extend this attitude in a suitably modified form to whatever is thought to have traces of personality.[2]

Glover makes a claim that many people working with those with learning difficulties would find staggering in that he is prepared to consider the possibility that some lives are worth less than others:

> The idea of dividing people's lives into ones that are worth living and ones that are not is likely to seem both presumptuous and dangerous. As well as seeming to indicate an arrogant willingness to pass godlike judgements on other people's lives, it may remind people of the Nazi policy of killing patients in mental hospitals. But there is really nothing godlike in such a judgement. It is not a moral judgement we are making, if we think that someone's life is so empty and unhappy as to be not worth living. It results from an attempt (obviously an extremely fallible one) to see his life from his own point of view and to see what he gets out of it. It must also be stressed that no suggestion is being made that it automatically becomes right to kill people whose lives we think are not worth living. It is only being argued that, if someone's life is worth living, this is *one* reason why it is directly wrong to kill him.[3]

This quotation however serves to illustrate the sort of approach taken, and the kinds of questions considered, by various contemporary moral philosophers. Note, of course, that a reason given why a life should not be taken – that is, why it is of some value – is that it is worth living – that is, has some acceptable level of quality.

John Harris usefully provides an express formulation of what his account of value of life is designed to do. These include:

> (1) To have an account of the point at which, and the reasons why, the embryo or any live human tissue becomes valuable.
> (2) To recognize when and why human beings cease to be valuable *or become less valuable than others*. (our italics)[4]

Harris's agenda of ethical concerns is typical of a number of philosophers currently working in the field of applied ethics. Nowhere in this list does Harris even mention when discussing the *value* of life how quality of life may be improved, which is as we shall see, the key question for psychologists.

We do not suggest that value of life and quality of life should be conflated, but there is often a link between them. One of the most important philosophical questions to consider is how exactly the relationship between quality of life and value of life should be conceived and this is an issue we shall discuss briefly below.

Psychologists have a more pragmatic approach to quality of life, which arises from the need to determine whether the quality of life of people with learning difficulties has improved on moving from large institutions and hospitals to community-based care. As a result they are broadly interested in finding out about how quality of life of particular individuals may be improved. In contrast to some philosophers, discussed above, psychologists separate questions about the value of a life from those about the quality of a life. They simply assume that any person's life has got value, and that every person's life is of equal value. Day (1988) for example outlines:

> a vision of the future where people who are handicapped and disadvantaged are not cast out from ordinary society but are able to remain within that society as valued, contributing members.[5]

And many other workers in this field are:

> guided by the underlying principle that people with learning difficulties have the same human value and the same human rights as any other citizen.[6]

For psychologists then, there is a two-fold purpose in measuring quality of life: firstly to improve the quality of life of particular individuals in particular settings and secondly the more policy based issue of which service provisions would lead to the best quality of life for the client group in question.

Psychologists work to improve quality, hence are interested in measuring quality, because they assume value. Philosophers very often want to measure quality because they don't assume value, and reaching a certain quality will ground value, or because measuring quality may help to decide on questions of choice such as who should be given medical treatment. Where such choice is between people, and is not made on purely medical grounds, it is hard to escape the conclusion that the person who receives the treatment is more highly valued. Low quality of life for psychologists is seen as a problem which the service has to solve. For some moral philosophers, it could be said that low quality of life is potentially a problem for the person who suffers from it, in that resources, and even life itself, may be denied them.[7] Here, the philosophers under consideration seem to follow some interpretation of the text of Matthew 13:12:

> For whosoever hath, to him shall be given, and he shall have more abundance: but whosoever hath not, from him shall be taken away even that he hath.

In summary, two important features of some philosophical work that we need here to consider are the link between quality of life and value of life and the making of inter-personal comparisons. In contrast, psychologists sever the link between quality and value of life and tend to make intra-personal rather than inter-personal comparisons.

What Should Be Looked at When Measuring Quality of Life?

In the previous section we have explored the different reasons philosophers and psychologists have for wanting to measure quality of life. As we shall see in this section, this has led to different conceptualizations of what should be in any measure of the quality of life.

As stated above, psychologists are chiefly concerned with improving the quality of life for individuals. As such their measures tend to include practically based, specific items which could fairly easily be improved, rather than more abstract issues such as how happy a person considers themselves to be.

In a comprehensive review of the way in which quality of life measures have actually been used, Schalock (1988)[8] identified three overwhelmingly important aspects of quality of life:

(1) Environmental Control: ranging from control one has over daily schedule, meal planning, shopping, home decorations, money, appointments, pets, hobbies, to privacy and religion.
(2) Community Involvement: work, recreation, education.
(3) Social Relations: neighbours, people you live with, friends, family.

Other studies have also pointed to the importance of personal development, that is, increasing confidence, assertion/self-esteem, development of new skills in any assessment of quality of life.[9]

In the field of learning difficulties consideration of quality of life has largely revolved around five 'accomplishments' outlined by O'Brien (1987).[10] Here it is thought that in order to have a good quality of life one needs: to be integrated into the community; to form valued relationships; to make choices; to increase one's personal competencies; to command respect from valued members of the community. From these five accomplishments, a plethora of quality of life measures have been devised.

Emphasis on the practical side has led to a proliferation of measures, ranging from the questionnaire style measures to more innovatory approaches such as Atkinson's thematic interviewing[11] or Wilkinson's 'Being There' methodology.[12] In Wilkinson's work the quality of life of a group of men with severe learning difficulties was explored. Because of their profound communication difficulties it was not possible to ask the men directly about their quality of life, so Wilkinson spent several months attempting to get as clear a picture as possible of the men's world, in particular what they seemed satisfied with and what caused them dissatisfaction and frustration.

Psychologists have, on the whole, steered clear of tackling the theoretical issues around the question of quality of life, recognizing that it is a difficult and complex issue. Typically, Landesman recognizes

> that the *process* of defining *quality of life* and *personal life satisfaction* is likely to be fraught with difficulties and disagreements. (italics original)[13]

As a result, there is general agreement that quality of life is hard to define and even harder to measure.[14] Instead workers in this field have focused on developing and refining measures and methodologies. So, for example, it is now generally accepted that if one is using questionnaire-type measurements of quality of life that there are three types of question which should be asked:

(1) Relevance: the value that a given individual puts on a particular element of quality of life
(2) Frequency: level of engagement the person has with that element
(3) Satisfaction: whether the level of engagement is acceptable.[15]

Importantly, questions of theory are generally overtaken by discussion of appropriate methodologies. It is operationalizing quality of life that is seen as important, rather than working out definitions in any detail.

Philosophical accounts of what should be included in accounts of good lives, of what features make for quality in life, are extremely diverse. For instance, Parfit delineates three types of theory of 'what makes someone's life go best', theories that he considers to be theories of self-interest: hedonistic theories, desire-fulfilment theories, and 'objective list' theories, those which claim that certain things just are objectively good for people and so should form a part of any account of a good life.[16] Even Parfit's account is arguably incomplete. Here we shall look briefly at two different accounts, chosen because of their diversity, and also because, as we hope to show, they could both benefit from an appreciation of the work of psychology.[17]

It should be said that in the main, philosophical work does not produce such precise and detailed accounts of the elements of quality of life as does psychological work, but rather tends to focus on providing an overarching theory, out of which particular elements may drop, but which may not directly spell out all of those elements.

In *A Theory of Justice*, Rawls sets out his account of a definition of good for plans of life.[18] This could be seen as tackling only one aspect of quality of life in that it focuses on the internal aspect of how a person attempts to form their life, and leaves out external factors such as health and housing, except obliquely in so far as they affect the success of plans of life. Nonetheless, Rawls represents one typically philosophical approach in adopting Royce's thought that 'a person may be regarded as a human life lived according to a plan',[19] and in claiming that, with certain qualifications, 'we can think of a person being happy when he is in the way of a successful execution (more or less) of a rational plan of life drawn up under (more or less) favourable conditions, and he is reasonably confident that his plan will be carried through.'[20]

As part of an attempt to describe more specifically what kinds of ends these plans are likely to seek after, Rawls describes a general principle of human motivation, dubbed by him the Aristotelian Principle, which states that 'other things being equal, human beings enjoy the exercise of their realized capacities (their innate or trained abilities), and this enjoyment increases the more the capacity is realized, or the greater its complexity.'[21] He also adds 'We need not explain here why the Aristotelian Principle is true,'[22] going on to speculate about why it is presumably true, and states 'the general facts about human needs and abilities are perhaps clear enough and I shall assume that common sense knowledge suffices for our purposes here.'[23]

Important points to note here are, firstly, that Rawls is talking here of a life that is planned, at least minimally, as being the model of a satisfactory human life. Secondly, he takes a feature of human beings, important for his description of what a good life would be, that they strive after ever more complex goals based on the exercise of talents, and thirdly, he makes such a claim without any researched empirical backing of the kind that a psychologist would recognize.

The second philosophical example we examine which looks at questions of quality of life is that of Kuhse and Singer's book *Should the Baby Live?*[24] Here, the authors consider the case of how handicapped newborns should be treated, and, rejecting the idea that all human lives are of equal value, propose that the quality or expected quality of a baby's life should be taken into account. However, although various fairly predictable aspects of quality of life are at different times referred to in the text, there is no overall or systematic account of what we need to look for in assessing quality. They talk about being 'sufficiently free from pain', having a life that is 'sufficiently worthwhile', a life 'that it will find satisfying',[25] and mention as factors detracting from a good quality of life low intelligence and physical handicaps and problems such as incontinence, blindness, fits, and mobility problems.[26] The authors often focus on questions of comparison between 'normal' life and fairly severe handicaps, such as spina bifida may be, and Down's syndrome, where the reader may well think that it is obvious that life with the handicap is of a lower quality than life without. Even if this assumption is justified, it perhaps has the unfortunate result that the troubled question of what exactly makes for a life of acceptable quality is not directly or rigorously addressed. For instance, we are invited to compare the quality of a normal life with the quality of life in a coma,[27] and this does not lead us to worry about spelling out the details of any worthwhile, non-comatose life: more or less anything would do, except perhaps mental or physical agony, compared to a coma. Not a great deal of information is given on what precisely is involved in having conditions such as Down's syndrome and spina bifida, two major conditions that the authors frequently discuss. This means that there are limits placed on Kuhse and Singer's proposals and their practical application. More worryingly, there may be doubt about whether their 'chatty' sort of account of quality of life is really giving a sufficiently adequate picture to support their broad conclusions (which follow from claims such as that someone with Down's syndrome has a reduced potential for a worthwhile life). Are we perhaps simply following unexamined received wisdom here? The difference from the detailed inventories of much psychological work is striking.

The differences outlined can be explained in terms of the psychologists' overwhelming concern with empirical matters at the expense of examining theoretical issues, with exactly the reverse being so for the philosophers. Nonetheless, and importantly, we have seen in both the above two examples that philosophers are making claims with an empirical content: Rawls' Aristotelian Principle of Motivation, and Kuhse and Singer's reference to the concrete reality of desirable or undesirable features of life, to the question of what life someone 'will find satisfying', together with reference to the nature of specific conditions.

It might be tempting to suggest that philosophers and psychologists are talking different languages, and engaged in totally diverse activities.

The question then presents itself whether there is any possibility or even any point in such philosophers and psychologists communicating with each other? Or are they engaged in completely different activities? One response might be to suggest that since psychologists and philosophers have just different tasks in hand, there is no reason to expect any congruence between their work or any fruitful dialogue between them. In reply to this, we go on to show some specific ways in which a dialogue may be of great value.

What can Philosophers Learn from the Psychologists?

One important point to note initially is that many accounts of the value of life that have been produced could be argued to be biased towards those who have competence in the intellectual field, and biased against people with learning difficulties. For instance, the value of life is often explained in terms of personhood or something like it, most famously by Tooley in his discussions of abortion and infanticide.[28] These accounts of personhood in turn generally revolve around the idea of a rational, autonomous, self-conscious individual, and very often language is seen as a prerequisite. Therefore those who are seen as having limited rationality and limited or absent language may be devalued. As we shall shortly show, there are also problems in accounts or quality of life for those with communication or intellectual difficulties.

One response may be that such points show up simple disagreement about how different human beings should be valued. But before this conclusion is reached, it should be considered that the work of various psychologists can suggest that some of the philosophers' conclusions have been drawn too hastily. We go on to try to demonstrate this point.

Because of their practical remit, psychologists can offer a more thoroughly grounded account of some of the features of human beings or persons which concern philosophers. By assuming value of lives and by their quest to improve quality of whatever life a person has, psychologists have been forced to look for whatever *could* be of value in a life and hence have come up with a wider menu of quality in life than many philosophers, who can be broadly argued, very often, to be still entrenched in notions of 'the rational man' as a model of human nature and as a ground for value and quality of life.

As was shown above (pp. 273–4) philosophers, although mainly interested in providing a theoretical account, do very often make empirical claims, claims which often lack any adequate grounding in empirical research. The psychologists' operationalization of quality of life and attention to the detail of what it might involve, could help philosophers to spell out a picture of quality of life that encompassed wisdom gained from an examination of many different possibilities of living a human life, hence add to a theoretically grounded model practical insight. In the two instances studied above, Rawls' claim that something like the Aristotelian Principle seems from his observations to be true would fail him a first-year psychology exam. Why not use psychological methodology, expertise and results to substantiate such a claim? The second example examined of the work of Kuhse and Singer also shows how important conclusion are drawn from insubstantial empirical claims about what kind of life a person with a particular condition is likely to have, with little or no attempt to examine in detail the exact nature of the conditions or any individual variation, no attempt to draw on any specific data about the quality of people's lives. Neither does this appear to be based on any claim that such substantiation is unnecessary. We can only conclude that there are flaws in Kuhse and Singer's case. A very simple point to make is that psychologists and other practitioners have looked in much greater detail at the nature of the conditions Kuhse and Singer discuss.

The following will illustrate some of the concrete benefits that psychological work can offer. For example, people working with children with severe learning difficulties often use sensory stimulation as being one available route to introduce some quality into their lives. Most children will get stimulation from working out a puzzle in the course of play. One source of reward comes from getting the answer right and the sense of satisfaction that this brings. Children who will rarely or never get the answer right will miss out on this reward, with consequent frustration and dissatisfaction. By providing these children with games where rewards such as a light flashing can be attained simply by pressing a button, and so forth, it is believed that the quality of their lives may be improved to contain something which other children take for granted – that playing is a rewarding activity.

Incidentally, this raises a question of whether such simple stimulus rewards should be seen as a component in the quality of life. Psychologists here can be seen to be separating any reward from the notion of rational activity, and this may be anathema to Aristotelians and others, including any at all tempted by the notion that Utilitarianism is a 'pig' philosophy, ignoring the higher levels of human activity in its search after mere pleasure or happiness. However, such an approach, to value simple reward for its own pleasures, and to recognize the significance of this, especially perhaps for some people, could for instance be the basis of a supplement or limit to Rawls' Aristotelian Principle of Motivation. Quite a different account of what makes for a good or successful life may then be produced.

A further area where psychologists could have a lot to offer is in the field of communication difficulties. For some philosophers,[29] people without language just aren't persons and so important conclusions about the value of their lives immediately follow. Even philosophers who don't take such an extreme view might tend to think that 'we' can answer questions for this group, in particular, in making judgements about the quality of different lives. Mill's 'competent judges', allegedly having the competence to decide, on behalf of others, which pleasures are the best[30], have attracted much criticism but subtly appear in many philosophical guises. For instance, we have just seen how Kuhse and Singer, to take just one example, make judgements about the quality of the lives of babies born with certain conditions. (If it just seems obvious that of course anyone working on such an issue has no choice but to make such judgements on behalf of people falling into certain groups, the reader is asked to read on (pp. 280–1) below. In particular, many philosophers ignore the possibility of non-verbal systems of communication in relation to issues such as personhood and the resulting conclusions about value of life, in contrast to many psychologists and especially perhaps those having day-to-day contact with people without verbal skills. Moreover, if the possibility of non-verbal systems of communication is ignored, important routes to measure a person's quality of life may be missed. Again, the difference between the two disciplines may be explained pragmatically: if you *have* to interact with people, you look for whatever channels of communication you can. In this instance, if not in all, we can make the obvious corny observation that philosophy is too much of an armchair activity.

Psychologists with their unconditional value on all human life see lack of communication as a challenge to be tackled rather than an answer to a question. Recent work in psychology sees the problem as being one of relationship. Difficulties in communication are seen as being as much those of hearing as those of speaking. It is especially relevant to our purpose here to examine the unique People First Report *Service Evaluation by People with Learning Difficulties*.[31] Here, research on quality of life for people with learning difficulties was actually carried out by people with learning difficulties themselves.

> An important part of the value-system in the work of People First is that their members can relate to people with learning difficulties more easily than staff or professional researchers because they have relevant personal experience.[32]
>
> The main reason why they considered they were particularly appropriate for carrying out the work was because they felt their personal experiences had given them the ability to identify with and understand the lives of the residents.[33]

There are obvious implications in the kind of work that the People First Report has produced for the work of any moral philosopher who wishes to make claims based on judgement of quality of life: these claims must be more adequately substantiated than they typically are, avoid unfounded and vague empirical claims, and must draw on a wide and appropriate body of experience. If the readers of this article disagree with everything else we have said, we nonetheless firmly believe that this is a crucial point for work in applied ethics, and one it can ill afford to ignore.

The way in which psychologists locate difficulties in a two-way interaction helps to reply to the assumptions of many philosophers that one group is central and another group marginal and marginal because the problems reside within that group.[34]

The problems reside, at least partially, in the inability of the so-called central group to imagine and empathize with an experience which they merely vaguely think of as being very different from their own. If we even consider that a particular group, like people with learning difficulties, might not live a valued life, then we are going to have considerable difficulty imagining ourselves in their shoes and appreciating the quality of their lives. We will be bringing with us all sorts of assumptions about what, in theory, they lack and what contributes towards a valuable life. Work in this area really calls for an open mind: perhaps the remit of psychologists and other practitioners in the field to assume that all lives are of equal value is a useful way of keeping the mind open?

Imaginative steps to counter difficulties in communication can help firstly, in improving accuracy of any measures, and secondly and perhaps more fundamentally, in helping to address what should be included in any measures, in bringing other views to bear on the question of what should be included in any measures. (e.g. see the example of stimulating toys above, p. 278).

In conclusion to this section, we claim that the work of some psychologists can help to undo some of the implicit bias in the work of some philosophers against those with intellectual difficulties: in particular, helping to overcome problems with communication, and providing a much broader picture of what elements might contribute towards a good quality life.

What can Psychologists Learn from the Philosophers?

It could be argued that psychologists have little need for input from philosophy. If what they are trying to do is improve quality of life, then their measures, even if they only tap a very small portion of what might be considered to be quality of life, could be seen as meeting their needs.

Psychologists might argue that they are not tackling the question of what quality of life is in any general sense, they wouldn't claim that they had any definitive measure, but are simply working on the assumption that 'every little bit helps'.

It could however be argued that this might lead to a very limited view of what a good quality of life might entail. Without a wider view of what *could* contribute to quality of life, psychologists working in this area might be limiting themselves, and more importantly the people with whom they work, to a concept of quality of life which only includes those elements that are easily measured and easily changed. For example, the psychologists' work tends to focus on isolated elements of what goes to make up life quality without considering in any great depth how these separate elements might fit together. This contrasts with approaches such as Rawls' which is specifically concerned with plans of life, the overall shape of a good human life. Psychologists could clearly benefit from reviewing how different elements of their work relate to each other.

The above only serves to illustrate the benefits psychologists could derive from having a more clearly defined theoretical base to their work. In addition, the complete dearth of theory means that each study has to stand on its own merits, making it hard to compare or contrast different studies. In consequence, no coherent body of knowledge about what makes for a good quality of life has developed. If the theoretical base to the quality of life studies was more clearly delineated, then comparisons between the studies and accounts of how they relate to each other would be easier to make.

Philosophy could help make explicit the assumptions about quality of life psychologists are using and so perhaps enable them to question those assumptions. For example, referring back to O'Brien's five accomplishments (see p. 275) we can see that these make profound assumptions about what goes to make a good human life. Briefly, in order to live a good life we need to have contact with other human beings, to develop to our full potential and to have a sufficient measure of self-determination. These assumptions are not spelled out in any detail by those working in this area. In contrast there has been a vast body of philosophical work, from Plato and Aristotle onwards, looking at these very issues.[35]

Likewise, the 'every little bit helps' approach, outlined above, does assume one theory about the quality of life, that improving quality in one sphere of life is not going to detract from quality in another sphere. In the field of learning difficulties dimensions related to autonomy are often seen as very important when discussing quality of life. One way in which the development of autonomy is encouraged is through Self Advocacy Groups where people with learning difficulties are enabled to speak out for themselves. This has obvious benefits for the participants in that it enables them to learn various skills and to take part in an aspect of life that had been previously denied them. But given some of the measures used by psychologists, there is no guarantee that becoming involved with Self Advocacy Groups is going to give you a higher score on a quality of life measure. Indeed, it may even lead to a lower score if speaking out for yourself leads to frustration, disappointment and a growing awareness of what in life has been denied you. This is not a criticism of the concept of Self Advocacy, but serves to demonstrate the need for a global account of what constitutes a good quality of life, perhaps one where the special place of autonomy is recognized and certainly one which takes account of the way in which one's life is developing rather than focusing on isolated times with no reference to an overall plan. See, for example, Rawls' idea of looking at plans of life.

The Question of Equality between Different Lives

We have suggested that psychologists would benefit from a consideration of the theoretical work of some philosophers. Is it however possible for the psychologists to incorporate such work and still maintain their commitment to the view that all lives are of equal value? The question that presents itself is that of whether it is possible to have an adequate and sufficiently developed theory of quality of life which does not imply that some lives, lives with reduced quality or reduced potential for quality, are worth less, have less value, than others. This is a question that deserves a paper in itself, and here we simply offer a preliminary discussion of the issue.

As we have seen, psychologists tend to ignore the question of what grounds the value of human life, and assume their answer, that all human life is of equal value, whereas what value to accord to different human lives has been a major issue with which philosophers have concerned themselves.

It is often the quest for an account of why life is valuable that leads to an examination of what makes life worth living, what would give life an acceptable quality. We have also seen that the major difference between the philosophers we have been referring to (although this point does not apply to all philosophers of course) and the psychologists in question is perhaps in the psychologists' refusal to make comparisons between people in terms of value, against some philosophers' eager rush to the fray of competing and differential value. Any moral philosopher worth their salt would feel uncomfortable with any assumption of value, never being ones to give away anything of value without a heated philosophical argument. But, can a grounding be given to the value and quality of life without at once opening up the possibility of possibly pernicious comparisons between people?

Kuhse and Singer in their book *Should the Baby Live?* show, through looking at cases of extremely damaged newborns such as anencephalic babies, that it can be very difficult to insist that all human life has the same value, if this implies that the same efforts should be made to keep all humans alive.[36] If equal value is to be given to people regardless of handicap, the question may be raised of how we square this with attempts to ensure that handicapped babies are not brought into the world – for instance and perhaps least controversially by avoiding drugs in pregnancy that may cause foetal damage – and attempts to ensure that people do not acquire handicaps. Many difficult questions about the way in which we attach value to human lives, questions very often connected to judgements about the quality of those lives, need to be addressed.

The whole philosophical project of grounding the value of life arguably means that value has to be seen to be attached to some concrete aspect of an individual. It could well be claimed that there is nothing to the individual over and above these particular characteristics. So, given variation between people, the attempt to find some characteristic that we all have and which could assure us all of equal worth does not seem promising. No soul remains to modern philosophy to do this task for us. No human essence remains to any concerned to avoid the charge of speciesism: that is, the charge of according special value to human lives simply because they are members of the species *Homo sapiens*, and not because of any particular features that individual members of that species possess. Concern with the moral claims of non-human species, and concern with making moral judgements on grounds that can be shown to have moral importance and relevance, has led to an examination of what it is about any human life that gives it value.

But psychology, in practice, does seem to assume a soul or some kind of uniquely human and uniquely valuable essence, which grounds the assumption of value and justifies the quest to enhance quality of life, and which seem to reside in humans independently of any particular characteristics they have or lack. Psychology, it could be said, has in this respect divorced the life from the liver: the liver of the life has unconditioned value, the life itself may need improvement. How, if at all, this position may be held philosophically is a question for further consideration.

Notes

1 Kuhse, H. and Singer, P. *Should the Baby Live? The Problem of Handicapped Infants*, (Oxford: Oxford University Press, 1985), p. 143.

2 Downie, R. S. and Telfer, E. *Respect for Persons* (London: Allen and Unwin, 1969), p. 37.

3 Glover, J. *Causing Death and Saving Lives* (Harmondsworth: Penguin, 1977), pp. 52–3.

4 Harris, J. *The Value of Life: An Introduction to Biomedical Ethics* (London: Routledge and Kegan Paul, 1985), p. 27.

5 Day, P. R., "Not an ordinary life", *Mental Handicap*, 16 (1988), 4–7, p. 4.

6 Central Nottinghamshire Health Authority, *Declaration of Rights of Users of Facilities for People with Learning Difficulties* (1991), p. 1.

7 For example, Kuhse and Singer, *Should the Baby Live?* and James Rachels, *The End of Life* (Oxford: Oxford University Press, 1986).

8 Schalock, R. L., "The concept of quality of life in community-based mental retardation programs", *Issues in Special Education and Rehabilitation*, 5 (1988) 5–32.

9 See for example, Atkinson, D. "Moving from hospital to the community: factors influencing the life styles of people with mental handicaps", *Mental Handicap*, 16 (1988), 8–11 and O'Brien, J. "A guide to personal futures planning", in Bellamy, G. T. and Wilcox, B. (eds), *A Comprehensive Guide to the Activities Catalogue: An Alternative Curriculum for Youth and Adults with Severe Disabilities* (Baltimore: Paul Brookes, 1987).

10 O'Brien, "Personal futures planning".

11 For example, Atkinson, D. "Research interviews with people with mental handicaps", *Mental Handicap Research*, 1(1) (1988), 75–90; Atkinson, D. "With time to spare: the leisure pursuits of people with mental handicap", *Mental Handicap*, 13 (1985), 139–40; Atkinson, D. and Ward, L. "Friends and neighbours: relationships and opportunities in the community for people with a mental handicap", in Malin, N. (ed.), *Reassessing Community Care* (London: Croom Helm, 1987).

12 Wilkinson, J. " 'Being there': evaluating life quality from feelings and daily experience", in Brechin, A. and Walmsley, J. (eds), *Making Connections: Reflecting on the Lives and Experiences of People with Learning Difficulties* (London: Hodder & Stoughton in association with The Open University, 1989).

13 Landesman, S. "Quality of Life and Personal Life Satisfaction: Definition and Measurement Issues", *Mental Retardation*, 24 (1986), 141–3, p. 142.

14 See, for example, James, J., Howell, H. and Abbott, K. "Quality Matters, 1. 'Slicing the apple': maintaining and improving quality of mental handicap services", *Mental Handicap*, 17 (1989), 156–9; Saxby, H., Felce, D., Harman, M. and Repp, A. "The maintenance of client activity and staff–client interaction in small community houses for severely and profoundly mentally handicapped adults: a two year follow-up", *Behavioral Psychotherapy*, 16 (1988), 189–206; Stanley, B. and Roy, A., "Evaluating the quality of life of people with mental handicaps: a social validation study", *Mental Handicap Research*, 1 2 (1988), 197–210.

15 Stanley and Roy, "Evaluating the quality of life" pp. 200–3.

16 Parfit, D. *Reasons and Persons* (Oxford: Oxford University Press, 1986), Appendix I, pp. 493–502.

17 Rawls' account could perhaps be argued to provide the beginnings of a reasonable basis for an account of the theory underlying much psychological work on quality of life, but that is perhaps the subject of another paper.

18 Rawls, J. *A Theory of Justice* (Oxford: Oxford University Press, 1972).

19 Ibid., p. 408.

20 Ibid., p. 409.

21 Ibid., p. 426.

22 Ibid., p. 426.

23 Ibid., p. 425.

24 Kuhse and Singer, *Should the Baby Live?*

25 Ibid., all p. 89.

26 Ibid., p. 61.

27 Ibid., p. 90.

28 Tooley, M., *Abortion and Infanticide* (London: Oxford University Press, 1983).

29 See, for example, Dennett, D. "Conditions of Personhood", in his *Brainstorms* (Brighton, Manchester Press, 1978), pp. 267–85.

30 Mill, J. S. *Utilitarianism*, 4th edn (London, 1871).

31 Whittaker, A., Gardner, S. and Kershaw, J. *Service Evaluation by People with Learning Difficulties: based on the People First Report* (London, Kings Fund Centre, 1991).

32 Ibid., p. 54.

33 Ibid., p. 56.

34 See for example the quotation from Downie and Telfer, *Respect for Persons*, on page 274 of this article.

35 For fuller discussion of this point see Boddington, P. and Podpadec, T. *Questions about Need: Exploring the relationship between service provision and quality of life*, paper presented at the British Institute of Mental Handicap Annual Conference, University of Reading, 1991.

36 Kuhse and Singer, *Should the Baby Live?* ch. 2.

31

Right to Life of Handicapped

Alison Davis

In reference to your items on the bill drafted by Mr and Mrs Brahams permitting doctors to withhold treatment from newborn handicapped babies, I would like to make the following points.

I am 28 years old, and suffer from a severe physical disability which is irreversible, as defined by the bill. I was born with myelomeningocele spina bifida. Mr and Mrs Brahams suggest several criteria for predicting the potential quality of life of people like me, and I note that I fail to fulfil most of them.

I have suffered considerable and prolonged pain from time to time, and have undergone over 20 operations, thus far, some of them essential to save my life. Even now my health is at best uncertain. I am doubly incontinent and confined to a wheelchair and thus, according to the bill, I should have 'no worthwhile quality of life'.

However, because I was fortunately born in rather more tolerant times, I was given the chance to defy the odds and live, which is now being denied to handicapped newborns. Even so, my parents were encouraged to leave me in the hospital and 'go home and have another' and I owe my life to the fact that they refused to accept the advice of the experts.

Despite my disability I went to an ordinary school and then to university, where I gained an honours degree in sociology. I now work full-time defending the right to life of handicapped people. I have been married eight years to an able-bodied man, and over the years we have travelled widely in Europe, the Soviet Union and the United States. This year we plan to visit the Far East.

From *Journal of Medical Ethics*, vol. 9 (1983), p. 181. Reprinted with permission.

Who could say I have 'no worthwhile quality of life'? I am sure though that no doctor could have predicted when I was 28 days old (and incidentally had received no operation at all) that despite my physical problems I would lead such a full and happy life. I do not doubt that they were 'acting in good faith' when they advised my parents to abandon me, but that does not mean that their advice was correct.

I was pleased to see that Dr Havard considered legislation was not the right way to solve the problem, though I suspect his disquiet was rather over an infringement of the liberty of doctors than out of any concern for the rights of the handicapped. Whatever his motives, though, I feel the medical profession could go a lot farther than it has to condemn the constant undermining of the rights of handicapped people at progressively later stages in their lives. There is nothing magical about the age of 28 days after all. It is simply the currently accepted boundary of 'non-personhood' for babies with congenital defects.

This notion of 'non-personhood' denies the right of handicapped people to be recognized as equal human beings in a caring society, and it makes a mockery of the goodwill which seemingly abounded in the International Year of Disabled People.

Legislation of the type proposed could well also lead to the *de facto* decriminalization of the act of killing a handicapped person of any age, just as it did in Hitler's Germany. And if it does, woe betide any handicapped people who are too ill to defend their right to life by protesting that they are in fact happy. And woe betide us all, when we get too old to be considered 'useful' and all the friends who could have spoken in our defence have already been oh so lovingly 'allowed to die'.

Brain Death

32

A Definition of Irreversible Coma

Report of the Ad Hoc Committee of the Harvard Medical School to Examine the Definition of Brain Death

Our primary purpose is to define irreversible coma as a new criterion for death. There are two reasons why there is need for a definition: (1) Improvements in resuscitative and supportive measures have led to increased efforts to save those who are desperately injured. Sometimes these efforts have only partial success so that the result is an individual whose heart continues to beat but whose brain is irreversibly damaged. The burden is great on patients who suffer permanent loss of intellect, on their families, on the hospitals, and on those in need of hospital beds already occupied by these comatose patients. (2) Obsolete criteria for the definition of death can lead to controversy in obtaining organs for transplantation.

Irreversible coma has many causes, but *we are concerned here only with those comatose individuals who have no discernible central nervous system activity*. If the characteristics can be defined in satisfactory terms, translatable into action – and we believe this is possible – then several problems will either disappear or will become more readily soluble.

More than medical problems are present. There are moral, ethical, religious, and legal issues. Adequate definition here will prepare the way for better insight into all of these matters as well as for better law than is currently applicable.

From *Journal of the American Medical Association*, vol. 205, no. 6 (5 August 1968), pp. 85–8. Reprinted with permission.

Characteristics of Irreversible Coma

An organ, brain or other, that no longer functions and has no possibility of functioning again is for all practical purposes dead. Our first problem is to determine the characteristics of a *permanently* nonfunctioning brain.

A patient in this state appears to be in deep coma. The condition can be satisfactorily diagnosed by points 1, 2, and 3 to follow. The electroencephalogram (point 4) provides confirmatory data, and when available it should be utilized. In situations where for one reason or another electroencephalographic montioring is not available, the absence of cerebral function has to be determined by purely clinical signs, to be described, or by absence of circulation as judged by standstill of blood in the retinal vessels, or by absence of cardiac activity.

1 *Unreceptivity and Unresponsitivity*. – There is a total unawareness to externally applied stimuli and inner need and complete unresponsiveness – our definition of irreversible coma. Even the most intensely painful stimuli evoke no vocal or other response, not even a groan, withdrawal of a limb, or quickening of respiration.

2 *No Movements or Breathing*. – Observations covering a period of at least one hour by physicians is adequate to satisfy the criteria of no spontaneous muscular movements or spontaneous respiration or response to stimuli such as pain, touch, sound, or light. After the patient is on a mechanical

respirator, the total absence of spontaneous breathing may be established by turning off the respirator for three minutes and observing whether there is any effort on the part of the subject to breathe spontaneously. (The respirator may be turned off for this time provided that at the start of the trial period the patient's carbon dioxide tension is within the normal range, and provided also that the patient had been breathing room air for at least 10 minutes prior to the trial.)

3 *No Reflexes.* – Irreversible coma with abolition of central nervous system activity is evidenced in part by the absence of elicitable reflexes. The pupil will be fixed and dilated and will not respond to a direct source of bright light. Since the establishment of a fixed, dilated pupil is clear-cut in clinical practice, there should be no uncertainty as to its presence. Ocular movement (to head turning and to irrigation of the ears with ice water) and blinking are absent. There is no evidence of postural activity (decerebrate or other). Swallowing, yawning, vocalization are in abeyance. Corneal and pharyngeal reflexes are absent.

As a rule the stretch of tendon reflexes cannot be elicited; i.e., tapping the tendons of the biceps, triceps, and pronator muscles, quadriceps and gastrocnemius muscles with the reflex hammer elicits no contraction of the respective muscles. Plantar or noxious stimulation gives no response.

4 *Flat Electroencephalogram.* – Of great confirmatory value is the flat or isoelectric EEG. We must assume that the electrodes have been properly applied, that the apparatus is functioning normally, and that the personnel in charge is competent. We consider it prudent to have one channel of the apparatus used for an electrocardiogram. This channel will monitor the ECG so that, if it appears in the electroencephalographic leads because of high resistance, it can be readily identified. It also establishes the presence of the active heart in the absence of the EEG. We recommend that another channel be used for a noncephalic lead. This will pick up space-borne or vibration-borne artifacts and identify them. The simplest form of such a monitoring noncephalic electrode has two leads over the dorsum of the hand, preferably the right hand, so the ECG will be minimal or absent. Since one of the requirements of this state is that there be no muscle activity, these two dorsal hand electrodes will not be bothered by muscle artifact. The apparatus should be run at standard gains $10\mu v/mm$, $50\mu v/5mm$. Also it should be isoelectric at double this standard gain which is $5\mu v/mm$ or $25\mu v/5$ mm. At least ten full minutes of recording are desirable, but twice that would be better.

It is also suggested that the gains at some point be opened to their full amplitude for a brief period (5 to 100 seconds) to see what is going on. Usually in an intensive care unit artifacts will dominate the picture, but these are readily identifiable. There shall be no electroencephalographic response to noise or to pinch.

All of the above tests shall be repeated at least 24 hours later with no change.

The validity of such data as indications of irreversible cerebral damage depends on the exclusion of two conditions: hypothermia (temperature below 90°F [32.2°C]) or central nervous system depressants, such as barbiturates.

Other Procedures

The patient's condition can be determined only by a physician. When the patient is hopelessly damaged as defined above, the family and all colleagues who have participated in major decisions concerning the patient, and all nurses involved, should be so informed. Death is to be declared and *then* the respirator turned off. The decision to do this and the responsibility for it are to be taken by the physician-in-charge, in consultation with one or more physicians who have been directly involved in the case. It is unsound and undesirable to force the family to make the decision.

Legal commentary

The legal system of the United States is greatly in need of the kind of analysis and recommendations for medical procedures in cases of irreversible brain damage as described. At present, the law of the United States, in all 50 states and in the federal courts, treats the question of human death as a question of fact to be decided in every case. When any doubt exists, the courts seek medical expert testimony concerning the time of death of the particular individual involved. However, the law makes the assumption that the medical criteria for determining death are settled and not in doubt among physicians. Furthermore, the law assumes that the traditional method among physicians for determination of death is to ascertain the absence of all vital signs. To this extent, *Black's Law Dictionary* (4th edition, 1951) defines death as

> The cessation of life; the ceasing to exist; *defined by physicians* as a total stoppage of the circulation of the blood, and a cessation of the animal and vital functions consequent thereupon, such as respiration, pulsation, etc. [italics added]

In the few modern court decisions involving a definition of death, the courts have used the concept of the total cessation of all vital signs. Two cases are worthy of examination. Both involved the issue of which one of two persons died first.

In *Thomas vs Anderson* (96 Cal App 2d 371, 211 P 2d 478) a California District Court of Appeal in 1950 said, "In the instant case the question as to which of the two men died first was a question of fact for the determination of the trial court..."

The appellate court cited and quoted in full the definition of death from *Black's Law Dictionary* and concluded, "death occurs precisely when life ceases and does not occur until the heart stops beating and respiration ends. Death is not a continuous event and is an event that takes place at a precise time."

The other case is *Smith vs Smith* (229 Ark, 579, 317 SW 2d 275) decided in 1958 by the Supreme Court of Arkansas. In this case the two people were husband and wife involved in an auto accident. The husband was found dead at the scene of the accident. The wife was taken to the hospital unconscious. It is alleged that she "remained in coma due to brain injury" and died at the hospital 17 days later. The petitioner in court tried to argue that the two people died simultaneously. The judge writing the opinion said the petition contained a "quite unusual and unique allegation." It was quoted as follows:

> That the said Hugh Smith and his wife, Lucy Coleman Smith, were in an automobile accident on the 19th day of April, 1957, said accident being instantly fatal to each of them at the same time, although the doctors maintained a vain hope of survival and made every effort to revive and resuscitate said Lucy Coleman Smith until May 6th, 1957, when it was finally determined by the attending physicians that their hope of resuscitation and possible restoration of human life to the said Lucy Coleman Smith was entirely vain, and
>
> That as a matter of modern medical science, your petitioner alleges and states, and will offer the Court competent proof that the said Hugh Smith, deceased, and said Lucy Coleman Smith, deceased, lost their power to will at the same instant, and that their demise as earthly human beings occurred at the same time in said automobile accident, neither of them ever regaining any consciousness whatsoever.

The court dismissed the petition as a *matter of law*. The court quoted *Black's* definition of death and concluded,

> Admittedly, this condition did not exist, and as a matter of fact, it would be too much of a strain of credulity for us to believe any evidence offered to the effect that Mrs. Smith was dead, scientifically or otherwise, unless the conditions set out in the definition existed.

Later in the opinion the court said, "Likewise, we take judicial notice that one breathing, though unconscious, is not dead."

"Judicial notice" of this definition of death means that the court did not consider that definition open to serious controversy; it considered the question as settled in responsible scientific and medical circles. The judge thus makes proof of uncontroverted facts unnecessary so as to prevent prolonging the trial with unnecessary proof and also to prevent fraud being committed upon the court by quasi "scientists" being called into court to controvert settled scientific principles at a price. Here, the Arkansas Supreme Court considered the definition of death to be a settled, scientific, biological fact. It refused to consider the plaintiff's offer of evidence that "modern medical science" might say otherwise. In simplified form, the above is the state of the law in the United States concerning the definition of death.

In this report, however, we suggest that responsible medical opinion is ready to adopt new criteria for pronouncing death to have occurred in an individual sustaining irreversible coma as a result of permanent brain damage. If this position is adopted by the medical community, it can form the basis for change in the current legal concept of death. No statutory change in the law should be necessary since the law treats this question essentially as one of fact to be determined by physicians. The only circumstance in which it would be necessary that legislation be offered in the various states to define "death" by law would be in the event that great controversy were engendered surrounding the subject and physicians were unable to agree on the new medical criteria.

It is recommended as a part of these procedures that judgement of the existence of these criteria is solely a medical issue. It is suggested that the physician in charge of the patient consult with one or more other physicians directly involved in the case before the patient is declared dead on the basis of these criteria. In this way, the responsibility is shared over a wider range of medical opinion, thus providing an important degree of protection against later questions which might be raised about the particular case. It is further suggested that the decision to declare the person dead, and then to turn off the respirator, be made by physicians not involved in any later effort to transplant organs or tissue from the deceased individual. This is advisable in order to avoid any appearance of self-interest by the physicians involved.

It should be emphasized that we recommend the patient be declared dead before any effort is made to take him off a respirator, if he is then on a respirator. This declaration should not be delayed until he has been taken off the respirator and all artificially stimulated signs have ceased. The reason for this recommendation is that in our judgement it will provide a greater degree of legal protection to those involved. Otherwise, the physicians would be turning off the respirator on a person who is, under the present strict, technical application of law, still alive.

Comment

Irreversible coma can have various causes: cardiac arrest; asphyxia with respiratory arrest; massive brain damage; intracranial lesions, neoplastic or vascular. It can be produced by other encephalopathic states such as the metabolic derangements associated, for example, with uremia. Respiratory failure and impaired circulation underlie all of these conditions. They result in hypoxia and ischemia of the brain.

From ancient times down to the recent past it was clear that, when the respiration and heart stopped, the brain would die in a few minutes; so the obvious criterion of no heart beat as synonymous with death was sufficiently accurate. In those times the heart was considered to be the central organ of the body; it is not surprising that its failure marked the onset of death. This is no longer valid when modern resuscitative and supportive measures are used. These improved activities can now restore "life" as judged by the ancient standards of persistent respiration and continuing heart beat. This can be the case even when there is not the remotest possibility of an individual recovering consciousness following massive brain damage. In other situations "life" can be maintained only by means of artificial respiration and electrical stimulation of the heart beat, or in temporarily bypassing the heart, or, in conjunction with these things, reducing with cold the body's oxygen requirement.

In an address, "The Prolongation of Life," (1957),[1] Pope Pius XII raised many questions; some conclusions stand out: (1) In a deeply unconscious individual vital functions may be maintained over a prolonged period only by extraordinary means. Verification of the moment of death can be determined, if at all, only by a physician. Some have suggested that the moment of death is the moment when irreparable and overwhelming brain damage occurs. Pius XII acknowledged that it is not "within the competence of the Church" to determine this. (2) It is incumbent on the physician to take all reasonable, ordinary means of restoring the spontaneous vital functions and consciousness, and to employ such extraordinary means as are available to him to this end. It is not obligatory, however, to continue to use extraordinary means indefinitely in hopeless cases. "But normally one is held to use only ordinary means – according to circumstances of persons, places, times, and cultures – that is to say, means that do not involve any grave burden for oneself or another." It is the church's view that a time comes when resuscitative efforts should stop and death be unopposed.

Summary

The neurological impairment to which the terms "brain death syndrome" and "irreversible coma" have become attached indicates diffuse disease. Function is abolished at cerebral, brain-stem, and often spinal levels. This should be evident in all cases from clinical examination alone. Cerebral, cortical, and thalamic involvement are indicated by a complete absence of receptivity of all forms of sensory stimulation and a lack of response to stimuli and to inner need. The term "coma" is used to designate this state of unreceptivity and unresponsitivity. But there is always coincident paralysis of brain-stem and basal ganglionic mechanisms as manifested by an abolition of all postural reflexes, including induced decerebrate postures; a complete paralysis of respiration; widely dilated, fixed pupils; paralysis of ocular movements; swallowing; phonation; face and tongue muscles. Involvement of spinal cord, which is less constant, is reflected usually in loss of tendon reflex and all flexor withdrawal or nocifensive reflexes. Of the brain-stem-spinal mechanisms which are conserved for a time, the vasomotor reflexes are the most persistent, and they are responsible in part for the paradoxical state of retained cardiovascular function, which is to some extent independent of nervous control, in the face of widespread disorder of cerebrum, brain stem, and spinal cord.

Neurological assessment gains in reliability if the aforementioned neurological signs persist over a period of time, with the additional safeguards that there is no accompanying hypothermia or evidence of drug intoxication. If either of the latter two conditions exist, interpretation of the neurological state should await the return of body temperature to normal level and elimination of the intoxicating agent. Under any other circumstances, repeated examinations over a period of 24 hours or longer should be required in order to obtain evidence of the irreversibility of the condition.

Reference

1 Pius XII: The Prolongation of Life. *Pope Speaks*, 4 (1958): 393–8.

33

Is the Sanctity of Life Ethic Terminally Ill?

Peter Singer

Abstract

Our growing technical capacity to keep human beings alive has brought the sanctity of life ethic to the point of collapse. The shift to a concept of brain death was already an implicit abandonment of the traditional ethic, though this has only recently become apparent. The 1993 decision of the British House of Lords in the case of Anthony Bland is an even more decisive shift towards an ethic that does not ask or seek to preserve human life as such, but only a life that is worth living. Once this shift has been completed and assimilated, we will no longer need the concept of brain death. Instead we can face directly the real ethical issue: when may doctors intentionally end the life of a patient?

I Introduction

It is surely no secret to anyone at this Congress that I have for a long time been a critic of the traditional sanctity of life ethic. So if I say that I believe that, after ruling our thoughts and our decisions about life and death for nearly two thousand years, the traditional sanctity of life ethic is at the point of collapse, some of you may think this is mere wishful thinking on my part. Consider, however, the following three signs of this impending collapse, which have taken place – coincidentally but perhaps appropriately enough – during the past two years in which I have had the honour of holding the office of President of the International Association of Bioethics.

- On February 4, 1993, in deciding the fate of a young man named Anthony Bland, Britain's highest court threw out many centuries of traditional law and medical ethics regarding the value of human life and the lawfulness of intentionally ending it.
- On November 30, 1993, the Netherlands parliament finally put into law the guidelines under which Dutch doctors have for some years been openly giving lethal injections to patients who suffer unbearably without hope of improvement, and who ask to be helped to die.
- On May 2, 1994, twelve Michigan jurors acquitted Dr Jack Kevorkian of a charge of assisting Thomas Hyde to commit suicide. Their refusal to convict Kevorkian was a major victory for the cause of physician-assisted suicide, for it is hard to imagine a clearer case of assisting suicide than this one. Kevorkian freely admitted supplying the carbon monoxide gas, tubing and a mask to Hyde, who had then used them to end a life made unbearable by the rapidly progressing nerve disorder ALS.

These three events are the surface tremors resulting from major shifts deep in the bedrock of Western ethics. We are going through a period of transition in our attitude to the sanctity of human life. Such transitions cause confusion and division. Many factors are involved in this shift, but today I shall focus on ways in which our growing technical capacity to keep human beings alive has brought out some implications of the sanctity of life ethic that – once we are forced to face them

From *Bioethics*, vol. 9, no. 3–4 (1995), pp. 307–43. Blackwell Publishers Ltd. Reprinted with permission.

squarely – we cannot accept. This will lead me to suggest a way forward.

II Revolution by Stealth: the Redefinition of Death

The acceptance of brain death – that is, the permanent loss of all brain function – as a criterion of death has been widely regarded as one of the great achievements of bioethics. It is one of the few issues on which there has been virtual consensus; and it has made an important difference in the way we treat people whose brains have ceased to function. This change in the definition of death has meant that warm, breathing, pulsating human beings are not given further medical support. If their relatives consent (or in some countries, as long as they have not registered a refusal of consent), their hearts and other organs can be cut out of their bodies and given to strangers. The change in our conception of death that excluded these human beings from the moral community was among the first in a series of dramatic changes in our view of life and death. Yet, in sharp contrast to other changes in this area, it met with virtually no opposition. How did this happen?

Everyone knows that the story of our modern definition of death begins with "The Ad Hoc Committee of the Harvard Medical School to Examine the Definition of Brain Death" (see pp. 287–91). What is not so well known is the link between the work of this committee and Dr Christian Barnard's famous first transplantation of a human heart, in December 1967. Even before Barnard's sensational operation, Henry Beecher, chairman of a Harvard University committee that oversaw the ethics of experimentation on human beings, had written to Robert Ebert, Dean of the Harvard Medical School, suggesting that the committee should consider some new questions. He had, he told the Dean, been speaking with Dr Joseph Murray, a surgeon at Massachusetts General Hospital and a pioneer in kidney transplantation. "Both Dr Murray and I," Beecher wrote, "think the time has come for a further consideration of the definition of death. Every major hospital has patients stacked up waiting for suitable donors."[1] Ebert did not respond immediately; but within a month of the news of the South African heart transplant, he set up, under Beecher's chairmanship, the group that was soon to become known as the Harvard Brain Death Committee.

The committee was made up mostly of members of the medical profession – ten of them, supplemented by a lawyer, a historian, and a theologian. It did its work rapidly, and published its report in the *Journal of the American Medical Association* in August 1968. The report was soon recognized as an authoritative document, and its criteria for the determination of death were adopted rapidly and widely, not only in the United States but, with some modification of the technical details, in most countries of the world. The report began with a remarkably clear statement of what the committee was doing and why it needed to be done:

> Our primary purpose is to define irreversible coma as a new criterion for death. There are two reasons why there is a need for a definition: (1) Improvements in resuscitative and supportive measures have led to increased efforts to save those who are desperately injured. Sometimes these efforts have only a partial success so that the result is an individual whose heart continues to beat but whose brain is irreversibly damaged. The burden is great on patients who suffer permanent loss of intellect, on their families, on the hospitals, and on those in need of hospital beds already occupied by these comatose patients. (2) Obsolete criteria for the definition of death can lead to controversy in obtaining organs for transplantation.

To a reader familiar with bioethics in the 1990s, there are two striking aspects of this opening paragraph. The first is that the Harvard committee does not even attempt to argue that there is a need for a new definition of death because hospitals have a lot of patients in their wards who are really dead, but are being kept attached to respirators because the law does not recognize them as dead. Instead, with unusual frankness, the committee said that a new definition was needed because irreversibly comatose patients were a great burden, not only on themselves (why to be in an irreversible coma is a burden to the patient, the committee did not say), but also to their families, hospitals, and patients waiting for beds. And then there was the problem of "controversy" about obtaining organs for transplantation.

In fact, frank as the statement seems, in presenting its concern about this controversy, the committee was still not being entirely candid. An earlier draft had been more open in stating that one reason for changing the definition of death was the "great need for tissues and organs of, among others, the patient whose cerebrum has been hopelessly destroyed, in order to restore those who are salvageable". When this draft was sent to Ebert, he advised Beecher to tone it down it because of its "unfortunate" connotation "that you wish to redefine death in order to make viable organs more readily available to persons requiring transplants".[2] The Harvard Brain Death Committee took Ebert's advice: it was doubtless more politic not to put things so bluntly. But Beecher himself made no secret of his own views. He was later to say, in an address to the American Association for the Advancement of Science:

> There is indeed a life-saving potential in the new definition, for, when accepted, it will lead to greater availability than formerly of essential organs in viable condition, for transplantation, and thus countless lives now inevitably lost will be saved.[3]

The second striking aspect of the Harvard committee's report is that it keeps referring to "irreversible coma" as the condition that it wishes to define as death. The committee also speaks of "permanent loss of intellect" and even says "we suggest that responsible medical opinion is ready to adopt new criteria for pronouncing death to have occurred in an individual sustaining irreversible coma as a result of permanent brain damage." Now "irreversible coma as a result of permanent brain damage" is by no means identical with the death of the whole brain. Permanent damage to the parts of the brain responsible for consciousness can also mean that a patient is in a "persistent vegetative state", a condition in which the brain stem and the central nervous system continue to function, but consciousness has been irreversibly lost. Even today, no legal system regards those in a persistent vegetative state as dead.

Admittedly, the Harvard committee report does go on to say, immediately following the paragraph quoted above: "*we are concerned here only with those comatose individuals who have no discernible central nervous system activity*." But the reasons given by the committee for redefining death – the great burden on the patients, their families, the hospitals and the community, as well as the waste of organs needed for transplation – apply in every respect to *all* those who are irreversibly comatose, not only to those whose entire brain is dead. So it is worth asking: why did the committee limit its concern to those with no brain activity at all? One reason could be that there was at the time no reliable way of telling whether a coma was irreversible, unless the brain damage was so severe that there was no brain activity at all. Another could be that people whose whole brain is dead will stop breathing after they are taken off a respirator, and so will soon be dead by anyone's standard. People in a persistent vegetative state, on the other hand, may continue to breathe without mechanical assistance. To call for the undertakers to bury a "dead" patient who is still breathing would be a bit too much for anyone to swallow.

We all know that the redefinition of death proposed by the Harvard Brain Death Committee triumphed. By 1981, when the United States President's Commission for the Study of Ethical Problems in Medicine examined the issue, it could write of "the emergence of a medical consensus" around criteria very like those proposed by the Harvard committee.[4] Already, people whose brains had irreversibly ceased to function were considered legally dead in at least fifteen countries, and in more than half of the states of the United States. In some countries, including Britain, Parliament had not even been involved in the change: the medical profession had simply adopted a new set of criteria on the basis of which doctors certified a patient dead.[5] This was truly a revolution without opposition.

The redefinition of death in terms of brain death went through so smoothly because it did not harm the brain-dead patients and it benefited everyone else: the families of brain-dead patients, the hospitals, the transplant surgeons, people needing transplants, people who worried that they might one day need a transplant, people who feared that they might one day be kept on a respirator after their brain had died, taxpayers, and the government. The general public understood that if the brain has been destroyed, there can be no recovery of consciousness, and so there is no point in maintaining the body. Defining such people as dead was a convenient way around the problems of making their organs available for transplantation, and withdrawing treatment from them.

But does this way round the problems really work? On one level, it does. By the early 1990s as Sweden and Denmark, the last European nations to cling to the traditional standard, adopted brain death definitions of death, this verdict appeared to be confirmed. Among developed nations, only Japan was still holding out. But do people really think of the brain dead as *dead*? The Harvard Brain Death Committee itself couldn't quite swallow the implications of what it was recommending. As we have seen, it described patients whose brains have ceased to function as in an "irreversible coma" and said that being kept on a respirator was a burden to them. Dead people are not in a coma, they are dead, and nothing can be a burden to them any more.

Perhaps the lapses in the thinking of the Harvard committee can be pardoned because the concept of brain death was then so new. But twenty-five years later, little has changed. Only last year the *Miami Herald* ran a story headlined "Brain-Dead Woman Kept Alive in Hopes She'll Bear Child"; while after the same woman did bear her child, the *San Francisco Chronicle* reported: "Brain-Dead Woman Gives Birth, then Dies". Nor can we blame this entirely on the lamentable ignorance of the popular press. A study of doctors and nurses who work with brain-dead patients at hospitals in Cleveland, Ohio, showed that one in three of them thought that people whose brains had died could be classified as dead because they were "irreversibly dying" or because they had an "unacceptable quality of life".[6]

Why do both journalists and members of the health care professions talk in a way that denies that brain death is really death? One possible explanation is that even though people know that the brain dead are dead, it is just too difficult for them to abandon obsolete ways of thinking about death. Another possible explanation is that people have enough common sense to see that the brain dead are not really dead. I favour this second explanation. The brain death criterion of death is nothing other than a convenient fiction. It was proposed and accepted because it makes it possible for us to salvage organs that would otherwise be wasted, and to withdraw medical treatment when it is doing no good. On this basis, it might seem that, despite some fundamental weaknesses, the survival prospects of the concept of brain death are good. But there are two reasons why our present understanding of brain death is not stable. Advances in medical knowledge and technology are the driving factors.

To understand the first problem with the present concept of brain death, we have to recall that brain death is generally defined as the irreversible cessation of all functions of the brain.[7] In accordance with this definition, a standard set of tests are used by doctors to establish that all functions of the brain have irreversibly ceased. These tests are broadly in line with those recommended in 1968 by the Harvard Brain Death Committee, but they have been further refined and updated over the years in various countries. In the past ten years, however, as doctors have sought ways of managing brain-dead patients, so that their organs (or in some cases, their pregnancies) could be sustained for a longer time, it has become apparent that even when the usual tests show that brain death has occurred, *some brain functions continue*. We think of the brain primarily as concerned with processing information through the senses and the nervous system, but the brain has other functions as well. One of these is to supply various hormones that help to regulate several bodily functions. We now know that some of these hormones continue to be supplied by the brains of most patients who, by the standard tests, are brain dead. Moreover, when brain-dead patients are cut open in order to remove organs, their blood pressure may rise and their heartbeat quicken. These reactions mean that the brain is still carrying out some of its functions, regulating the responses of the body in various ways. As a result, the legal definition of brain death, and current medical practice in certifying brain-dead people as dead, have come apart.[8]

It would be possible to bring medical practice into line with the current definition of death in terms of the irreversible cessation of *all* brain function. Doctors would then have to test for all brain functions, including hormonal functions, before declaring someone dead. This would mean that some people who are now declared brain dead would be considered alive, and therefore would have to continue to be supported on a respirator, at significant cost, both financially and in terms of the extended distress of the family. Since the tests are expensive to carry out and time-consuming in themselves, continued support would be necessary during the period in which they are carried out, even if in the end the results showed that the person had no brain function at all. In addition, during this period, the person's organs would deteriorate, and may therefore not be usable for transplantation. What gains would there be to balance against these serious disadvantages? From the perspective of an adherent of the sanctity of life ethic, of course, the gain is that we are no longer killing people by cutting out their hearts while they are still alive. If one really believed that the quality of a human life makes no difference to the wrongness of ending that life, this would end the discussion. There would be no ethical alternative. But it would still be true that not a single person who was kept longer on a respirator because of the need to test for hormonal brain functioning would ever return to consciousness.

So if it is life with consciousness, rather than life itself, that we value, then bringing medical practice into line with the definition of death does not seem a good idea. It would be better to bring the definition of brain death into line with current medical practice. But once we move away from the idea of brain death as the irreversible cessation of *all* brain functioning, what are we to put in its place? Which functions of the brain will we take as marking the difference between life and death, and why?

The most plausible answer is that the brain functions that really matter are those related to consciousness. On this view, what we really care about – and ought to care about – is *the person* rather than the body. Accordingly, it is the permanent cessation of function of the cerebral cortex, not of the whole brain, that should be taken as the criterion of death. Several reasons could be offered to justify this step. First, although the Harvard Brain Death Committee specified that its recommendations applied only to those who have "no discernible central nervous system activity", the arguments it put forward for its redefinition of death applied in every respect to patients who are permanently without any awareness, whether or not they have some brainstem function. This seems to have been no accident, for it reflected the view of the committee's chairman, Henry Beecher, who in his address to the American Association for the Advancement of Science, from which I have already quoted, said that what is essential to human nature is:

> the individual's personality, his conscious life, his uniqueness, his capacity for remembering, judging, reasoning, acting, enjoying, worrying, and so on . . .[9]

As I have already said, when the Harvard Committee issued its report, the irreversible destruction of the parts of the brain associated with consciousness could not reliably be diagnosed if the brainstem was alive. Since then, however, the technology for obtaining images of soft tissues within the body has made enormous progress. Hence a major stumbling block to the acceptance of a higher brain definition of death has already been greatly diminished in its scope, and will soon disappear altogether.

Now that medical certainty on the irreversibility of loss of higher brain functions can be established in at least some cases, the inherent logic of pushing the definition of death one step further has already led, in the United States, to one Supreme Court judge suggesting that the law could consider a person who has irreversibly lost consciousness to be no longer alive. Here is Mr Justice Stevens, giving his judgement in the case of Nancy Cruzan, a woman who had been unconscious for eight years and whose guardians sought court permission to withdraw tube feeding of food and fluids so that she could die:

> But for patients like Nancy Cruzan, who have no consciousness and no chance of recovery, there is a serious question as to whether the mere persistence of their bodies is "life", as that word is commonly understood . . . The State's unflagging determination to perpetuate Nancy Cruzan's physical existence is comprehensible only as an effort to define life's meaning, not as an attempt to preserve its sanctity . . . In any event, absent some theological abstraction, the idea of life is not conceived separately from the idea of a living person.[10]

Admittedly, this was a dissenting judgement; the majority decided the case on narrow constitutional grounds that are not relevant to our concerns here, and what Stevens said has not become part of the law of the United States. Nevertheless, dissenting judgements are often a way of floating an idea that is "in the air" and may become part of the majority view in a later decision. As medical opinion increasingly comes to accept that we can reliably establish when consciousness has been irreversibly lost, the pressure will become more intense for medical practice to move to a definition of death based on the death of the higher brain.

Yet there is a very fundamental flaw in the idea of moving to a higher brain definition of death. If, as we have seen, people already have difficulty in accepting that a warm body with a beating heart on a respirator is really dead, how much more difficult would it be to bury a "corpse" that is still breathing while the lid of the coffin is nailed down? That is simply an absurdity. Something has gone wrong. But what?

In my view, the trouble began with the move to brain death. The Harvard Brain Death Committee was faced with two serious problems. Patients in an utterly hopeless condition were attached to respirators, and no one dared to turn them off; and organs that could be used to save lives were rendered useless by the delays caused by waiting for the circulation of the blood in potential donors to stop. The committee tried to solve both these problems by the bold expedient of classifying as dead those whose brains had ceased to have any discernible activity. The consequences of the redefinition of death were so evidently desirable that it met with scarcely any opposition, and was accepted almost universally. Nevertheless, it was unsound from the start. Solving problems by redefinition rarely works, and this case was no exception. We need to begin again, with a different approach to the original problems, one which will break out of the intellectual strait-jacket of the traditional belief that all human life is of equal value: Until last year, it seemed difficult to imagine how a different approach could ever be accepted. But last year Britain's highest court took a major step toward just such a new approach.

III Revolution by the Law Lords: The Case of Anthony Bland

The revolution in British law regarding the sanctity of human life grew out of the tragedy at Hillsborough Football Stadium in Sheffield, in April 1989. Liverpool was playing Nottingham Forest in an FA Cup semi-final. As the match started, thousands of supporters were still trying to get into the ground. A fatal crush occurred against some fencing that had been erected to stop fans getting onto the playing field. Before order could be restored and the pressure relieved, 95 people had died in the worst disaster in British sporting history. Tony Bland, a 17-year-old Liverpool fan, was not killed, but his lungs were crushed by the pressure of the crowd around him, and his brain was deprived of oxygen. Taken to hospital, it was found that only his brain-stem had survived. His cortex had been destroyed. Here is how Lord Justice Hoffmann was later to describe his condition:

> Since April 15 1989 Anthony Bland has been in persistent vegetative state. He lies in Airedale General Hospital in Keighley, fed liquid food by a pump through a tube passing through his nose and down the back of his throat into the stomach. His bladder is emptied through a catheter inserted through his penis, which from time to time has caused infections requiring dressing and antibiotic treatment. His stiffened joints have caused his limbs to be rigidly contracted so that his arms are tightly flexed across his chest and his legs unnaturally contorted. Reflex movements in the throat cause him to vomit and dribble. Of all this, and the presence of members of his family who take turns to visit him, Anthony Bland has no consciousness at all. The parts of his brain which provided him with consciousness have turned to fluid. The darkness and oblivion which descended at Hillsborough will never depart. His body is alive, but he has no life in the sense that even the most pitifully handicapped but conscious human being has a life. But the advances of modern medicine permit him to be kept in this state for years, even perhaps for decades.[11]

Whatever the advances of modern medicine might permit, neither Tony Bland's family nor his doctors could see any benefit to him or to anyone else, in keeping him alive for decades. In Britain, as in many other countries, when everyone is in agreement in these situations it is quite common for the doctors simply to withdraw artificial feeding. The patient then dies within a week or two. In this case, however, the coroner in Sheffield was inquiring into the deaths caused by the Hillsborough disaster, and Dr Howe decided that he should notify the coroner of what he was intending to do. The coroner, while agreeing that Bland's continued existence could well be seen as entirely pointless, warned Dr Howe that he was running the risk of criminal charges – possibly even a charge of murder – if he intentionally ended Bland's life.

After the coroner's warning, the administrator of the hospital in which Bland was a patient applied to the Family Division of the High Court for declarations that the hospital might lawfully discontinue all life-sustaining treatment, including ventilation, and the provision of food and water by artificial means, and discontinue all medical treatment to Bland "except for the sole purpose of enabling Anthony Bland to end his life and to die peacefully with the greatest dignity and the least distress".

At the Family Division hearing a public law officer called the Official Solicitor was appointed guardian for Bland for the purposes of the hearing. The Official Solicitor did not deny that Bland had no awareness at all, and could never recover, but he nevertheless opposed what Dr Howe was planning to do, arguing that, legally, it was murder. Sir Stephen Brown, President of the Family Division, did not accept this view, and he made the requested declarations to the effect that all treatment might lawfully be stopped. The Official Solicitor appealed, but Brown's decision was upheld by the Court of Appeal. The Official Solicitor then appealed again, thus bringing the case before the House of Lords.

We can best appreciate the significance of what the House of Lords did in the case of Tony Bland by looking at what the United States Supreme Court would not do in the similar case of Nancy Cruzan. Like Bland, Cruzan was in a persistent vegetative state, without hope of recovery. Her parents went to court to get permission to remove her feeding tube. The Missouri Supreme Court refused, saying that since Nancy Cruzan was not competent to refuse life-sustaining treatment herself, and the state has an interest in preserving life, the court could only give permission for the withdrawal of life-sustaining treatment if there were clear and convincing evidence that this was what Cruzan would have wanted. No such evidence had been presented to the court. On appeal the United States Supreme Court upheld this judgement, ruling that the state of Missouri had a right to require clear and convincing evidence that Cruzan would have wanted to be allowed to die, before permitting doctors to take that step. (By a curious coincidence, that evidence was produced in court shortly after the Supreme Court decision, and Cruzan was allowed to die.)

The essential point here is that in America the courts have so far taken it for granted that life-support must be continued, *unless* there is evidence indicating that the patient would not have wished to be kept alive in the circumstances in which she now is. In contrast, the British courts were quite untroubled by the absence of any information about what Bland's wishes might have been. As Sir Thomas Bingham, Master of the Rolls of the Court of Appeal, said in delivering his judgement:

> At no time before the disaster did Mr Bland give any indication of his wishes should he find himself in such a condition. It is not a topic most adolescents address.[12]

But the British courts did not therefore conclude that Bland must be treated until he died of old age. Instead, the British judges asked a different question: what is in the best interests of the patient?[13] In answer, they referred to the unanimous medical opinion that Bland was not aware of anything, and that there was no prospect of any improvement in his condition. Hence the treatment that was sustaining Bland's life brought him, as Sir Stephen Brown put in in the initial judgement in the case, "no therapeutical, medical, or other benefit".[14] In essence, the British courts held that when a patient is incapable of consenting to medical treatment, doctors are under no legal duty to continue treatment that does not benefit a patient. In addition, the judges agreed that the mere continuation of biological life is not, in the absence of any awareness or any hope of ever again becoming aware, a benefit to the patient.

On one level, the British approach is straightforward common sense. But it is common sense that breaks new legal ground. To see this, consider the following quotation from John Keown:

> Traditional medical ethics . . . never asks whether the patient's *life* is worthwhile, for the notion of a worthless life is as alien to the Hippocratic tradition as it is to English criminal law, both of which subscribe to the principle of the sanctity of human life which holds that, because all lives are intrinsically valuable, it is always wrong intentionally to kill an innocent human being.[15]

As a statement of traditional medical ethics and traditional English criminal law, this is right. The significance of the *Bland* decision is that it openly embraces the previously alien idea of a worthless life. Sir Thomas Bingham, for example, said:

> Looking at the matter as objectively as I can, and doing my best to look at the matter through Mr Bland's eyes and not my own, I cannot conceive what benefit his continued existence could be thought to give him . . .[16]

When the case came before the House of Lords, their Lordships took the same view. Lord Keith of Kinkel discussed the difficulties of making a value judgement about the life of a "permanently insensate" being, and concluded cautiously that:

> It is, however, perhaps permissible to say that to an individual with no cognitive capacity whatever, and no prospect of ever recovering any such capacity in this world, it must be a matter of complete indifference whether he lives or dies.[17]

In a similar vein, Lord Mustill concluded that to withdraw life-support is not only legally, but also ethically justified, "since the continued treatment of Anthony Bland can no longer serve to maintain that combination of manifold characteristics which we call a personality".[18]

There can therefore be no doubt that with the decision in the Bland case, British law has abandoned the idea that life itself is a benefit to the person living it, irrespective of its quality. But that is not all that their lordships did in deciding Tony Bland's fate. The second novel aspect of their decision is that it was as plain as anything can be that the proposal to discontinue tube feeding was *intended* to bring about Bland's death. A majority of the judges in the House of Lords referred to the administrator's intention in very direct terms. Lord Browne-Wilkinson said:

> What is proposed in the present case is to adopt a course with the intention of bringing about Anthony Bland's death ... the whole purpose of stopping artificial feeding is to bring about the death of Anthony Bland.[19]

Lord Mustill was equally explicit:

> the proposed conduct has the aim for ... humane reasons of terminating the life of Anthony Bland by withholding from him the basic necessities of life.[20]

This marks a sharp contrast to what for many years was considered the definitive view of what a doctor may permissibly intend. Traditionally the law had held that while a doctor may knowingly do something that has the effect of shortening life, this must always be a mere side-effect of an action with a different purpose, for example, relieving pain. As Justice (later Lord) Devlin said in the celebrated trial of Dr John Bodkin Adams:

> it remains the fact, and it remains the law, that no doctor, nor any man, no more in the case of the dying than of the healthy, has the right deliberately to cut the thread of human life.[21]

In rewriting the law of murder regarding the question of intention, the British law lords have shown a clarity and forthrightness that should serve as a model to many others who try to muddle through difficult questions by having a little bit of both sides. There is no talk here of ordinary and extraordinary means of treatment, nor of what is directly intended and what is merely foreseen. Instead the judges declared that Bland's doctors were entitled to take a course of action that had Bland's death as its "whole purpose"; and they made this declaration on the basis of a judgement that prolonging Bland's life did not benefit him.

Granted, this very clarity forces on us a further question: does the decision allow doctors to kill their patients? On the basis of what we have seen so far, this conclusion seems inescapable. Their Lordships, however, did not think they were legalizing euthanasia. They drew a distinction between ending life by actively doing something, and ending life by not providing treatment needed to sustain life. That distinction has long been discussed by philosophers and bioethicists, who debate whether it can make good sense to accept passive euthanasia while rejecting active euthanasia. In the *Bland* case, it is significant that while the Law Lords insist that in distinguishing between acts and omissions they are merely applying the law as it stands, they explicitly recognize that at this point law and ethics have come apart, and something needs to be done about it. Lord Browne-Wilkinson, for example, expressed the hope that Parliament would review the law. He then ended his judgement by admitting that he could not provide a moral basis for the legal decision he had reached! Lord Mustill was just as frank and even more uncomfortable about the state of the law, saying that the judgement, in which he had shared, "may only emphasize the distortions of a legal structure which is already both morally and intellectually misshapen".[22]

The law lords' problem was that they had inherited a legal framework that allowed them some room to manoeuvre, but not a great deal. Within that framework, they did what they could to reach a sensible decision in the case of Anthony Bland, and to point the law in a new direction that other judges could follow. In doing so, they recognized the moral incoherence of the position they were taking, but found themselves unable to do anything about it, beyond drawing the problem to the attention of Parliament. They could hardly have done more to show clearly the need for a new approach to life-and-death decisions.

IV Conclusion

What is the link between the problems we face in regard to the concept of brain death, and the decision reached by their Lordships in the case of Tony Bland? The link becomes clearer once we distinguish between three separate questions, often muddled in discussions of brain death and related issues:

1 When does a human being die?
2 When is it permissible for doctors intentionally to end the life of a patient?
3 When is it permissible to remove organs such as the heart from a human being for the purpose of transplantation to another human being?

Before 1968, in accordance with the traditional concept of death, the answer to the first question would have been: when the circulation of the blood stops permanently, with the consequent cessation of breathing, of a pulse, and so on.[23] The answer to the second question would then have been very simple: never. And the answer to the third question would have been equally plain: when the human being is dead.

The acceptance of the concept of brain death enabled us to hold constant the straightforward answers to questions two and three, while making what was presented as no more than a scientific updating of a concept of death rendered obsolete by technological advances in medicine. Thus no ethical question appeared to be at issue, but suddenly hearts could be removed from, and machines turned off on, a whole new group of human beings.

The *Bland* decision says nothing about questions 1 and 3, but dramatically changes the answer that British law gives to question 2. The simple "never" now becomes "when the patient's continued life is of no benefit to her": and if we ask when a patient's life is of no benefit to her, the answer is: "when the patient is irreversibly unconscious". If we accept this as a sound answer to question 2, however, we may well wish to give the same answer to question 3. Why not, after all? And if we now have answered both question 2 and question 3 by reference not to the death of the patient, but to the impossibility of the patient regaining consciousness, then question 1 suddenly becomes much less relevant to the concerns that the Harvard Brain Death Committee was trying to address. We could therefore abandon the redefinition of death that it pioneered, with all the problems that have now arisen for the brain death criterion. Nor would we feel any pressure to move a step further, to defining death in terms of the death of the higher brain, or cerebral cortex. Instead, we could, without causing any problems in the procurement of organs or the withdrawal of life-support, go back to the traditional conception of death in terms of the irreversible cessation of the circulation of the blood.[24]

Notes

1 Henry Beecher to Robert Ebert, 30 October 1967. The letter is in the Henry Beecher Manuscripts at the Francis A. Countway Library of Medicine, Harvard University, and is quoted by David Rothman, *Strangers at the Bedside* (New York: Basic Books, 1991), pp. 160–1.

2 The first draft and Ebert's comment on it are both quoted by Rothman, *Strangers at the Bedside*, pp. 162–4. The documents are in the Beecher Manuscript collection.

3 Henry Beecher, "The New Definition of Death, Some Opposing Viewpoints", *International Journal of Clinical Pharmacology*, 5 (1971), pp. 120–1 (italics in original).

4 President's Commission for the Study of Ethical Problems in Medicine, *Defining Death: A Report on the Medical, Legal and Ethical Issues in the Determination of Death* (Washington, DC: US, Government Printing Office, 1981), pp. 24, 25.

5 *Defining Death*, pp. 67, 72.

6 Stuart Youngner et al., "'Brain Death' and Organ Retrieval: A Cross-sectional Survey of Knowledge and Concepts Among Health Professionals", *Journal of the American Medical Association*, 261 (1990), 2209.

7 See, for example, the United States Uniform Determination of Death Act. Note that the Harvard committee had referred to the absence of central nervous system "activity" rather than function. The use of the term "function" rather than "activity", makes the definition of brain death more permissive, because, as the United States President's Commission recognized (*Defining Death*, p. 74), electrical and metabolic activity may continue in cells or groups of cells after the organ has ceased to function. The Commission did not

think that the continuation of this activity should prevent a declaration of death.

8 Robert Truog, "Rethinking brain death", in K. Sanders and B. Moore (eds), *Anencephalics, Infants and Brain Death Treatment Options and the Issue of Organ Donation* (Law Reform Commission of Victoria, Melbourne, 1991), pp. 62–74; Amir Halevy and Baruch Brody, "Brain Death: Reconciling Definitions, Criteria and Tests", *Annals of Internal Medicine*, 119 6 (1993), 519–25; Robert Veatch, "The Impending Collapse of the Whole-Brain Definition of Death", *Hastings Center Report*, 23 4 (1993), 18–24.

9 Henry Beecher, "The New Definition of Death, Some Opposing Views", unpublished paper presented at the meeting of the American Association for the Advancement of Science, December 1970, p. 4, quoted from Robert Veatch, *Death, Dying and the Biological Revolution* (New Haven: Yale University Press, 1976), p. 39.

10 *Cruzan v. Director, Missouri Department of Health* (1990) 110 S. Ct. pp. 2886–7.

11 *Airedale NHS, Trust v. Bland (C.A)* (19 February 1993) 2 Weekly Law Reports, p. 350.

12 Ibid., p. 333; the passage was quoted again by Lord Goff of Chieveley in his judgement in the House of Lords, p. 364.

13 Ibid., pp. 374, 386.

14 Ibid., p. 331.

15 John Keown, "Courting Euthanasia? Tony Bland and the Law Lords", *Ethics & Medicine*, 9 3 (1993), 36.

16 *Airedale NHS Trust v Bland*, p. 339.

17 Ibid., p. 361.

18 Ibid., p. 400.

19 Ibid., p. 383.

20 Ibid., p. 388.

21 *R. v. Adams* (1959), quoted by Derek Morgan, "Letting babies die legally", *Institute of Medical Ethics Bulletin*, (May 1989), p. 13. See also Patrick Devlin, *Easing the Passing: The Trial of Dr John Bodkin Adams* (London: Faber and Faber, 1986), pp. 171, 209.

22 *Aircdale NHS Trust v. Bland*, pp. 388–9.

23 For a statement of the traditional definition, see, for example, *Blacks Law Dictionary*, 4th edn (West Publishing Company, 1968).

24 This address incorporates material subsequently published in my book *Rethinking Life and Death* (Melbourne: Text, 1994; St Martin's Press, 1995).

Advance Directives

34

Life Past Reason[1]

Ronald Dworkin

We turn finally to what might be the saddest of the tragedies we have been reviewing. We must consider the autonomy and best interests of people who suffer from serious and permanent dementia, and what the proper respect for the intrinsic value of *their* lives requires. The most important cause of dementia is Alzheimer's disease, a progressive disease of the brain named after a German psychiatrist and neuropathologist, Alois Alzheimer, who first identified and described it in 1906. Patients in the late stages of this disease have lost substantially all memory of their earlier lives and cannot, except perodically and in only a fragmented way, recognize or respond to other people, even those to whom they were formerly close. They may be incapable of saying more than a word or two. They are often incontinent, fall frequently, or are unable to walk at all. They are incapable of sustaining plans or projects or desires of even a very simple structure. They express wishes and desires, but these change rapidly and often show very little continuity even over periods of days or hours.

Alzheimer's is a disease of physiological deterioration. Nerve terminals of the brain degenerate into a matted plaque of fibrous material. Though researchers have expressed some hope that treatment can be developed to slow that degeneration,[1] no such treatment has yet been established, and there is apparently little prospect of dramatically reversing very advanced brain deterioration. A specialist describes the degeneration as occurring "gradually and inexorably, usually leading to death in a severely debilitated, immobile state between four and twelve years after onset."[2] But according to the US Office of Technology Assessment, death may be delayed for as long as twenty-five years.[3]

Our discussion will focus only on the disease's late stages. I shall not consider, except in passing, the present structure of legal rights and other provisions for demented or mentally incapacitated people, or the present practices of doctors and other custodians or officials who are charged with their care. Nor shall I attempt any report of the recent research into genetic and other features of such diseases, or into their diagnosis, prognosis, or treatment. All these are the subjects of a full literature.[4] I will concentrate on the question of what moral rights people in the late stages of dementia have or retain, and of what is best for them. Is some minimum level of mental competence essential to having any rights at all? Do mentally incapacitated people have the same rights as normally competent people, or are their rights altered or diminished or extended in some way in virtue of their disease? Do they, for example, have the same rights to autonomy, to the care of their custodians, to dignity, and to a minimum level of resources as sick people of normal mental competence?

These are questions of great and growing importance. In 1990, the Alzheimer's Association estimated that four million Americans had the disease, and as Alzheimer's is a disease of the elderly, the number is expected to increase as the population continues to age. In 1989, a Harvard Medical School study estimated that 11.3 percent of the American population sixty-five or over probably had Alzheimer's. The estimated

From *Life's Dominion: An Argument about Abortion Enthanasia, and Individual Freedom* (New York: Knopf, 1993; Vintage Books, 1994), pp. 218–29. Reprinted with permission.

prevalence increased sharply with age: 16.4 percent of people between seventy-five and eighty-four were estimated to have Alzheimer's, and a stunning 47.55 percent of those over eighty-five.[5] (Other studies, using a narrower definition of the disease, suggest a significantly lesser but still alarming prevalence.[6]) The incidence of the disease is comparable in other countries. According to the Alzheimer's Disease Society in Britain, for example, 20 percent of people over eighty are afflicted, more than half a million people have the disease, and that figure will rise to three-quarters of a million in thirty years.[7] Alzheimer's cost is staggering, both for the community and for individuals. Dennis Selkoe, a leading expert on the disease, said in 1991, "The cost to American society for diagnosing and managing Alzheimer's disease, primarily for custodial care, is currently estimated at more than $80 billion annually."[8] In 1992, the annual cost of nursing home care in the United States for one individual with Alzheimer's ranged from $35,000 to $52,000.[9]

Each of the millions of Alzheimer's cases is horrible, for the victims and for those who love and care for them. A recent book dedicated "to everyone who gives a '36-hour day' to the care of a person with a dementing illness" describes the lives of some of these patients in chilling detail, not just in the final, immobile last stages, but along the way.

> Often, Mary was afraid, a nameless shapeless fear.... People came, memories came, and then they slipped away. She could not tell what was reality and what was memory of things past.... The tub was a mystery. From day to day she could not remember how to manage the water: sometimes it all ran away, sometimes it kept rising and rising so that she could not stop it.... Mary was glad when her family came to visit. Sometimes she remembered their names, more often she did not.... She liked it best when they just held her and loved her.
>
> Even though Miss Ramirez had told her sister over and over that today was the day to visit the doctor, her sister would not get into the car until she was dragged in, screaming, by two neighbors. All the way to the doctor's office she shouted for help and when she got there she tried to run away.
>
> Mr. Lewis suddenly burst into tears as he tried to tie his shoelaces. He threw the shoes in the wastebasket and locked himself, sobbing, in the bathroom.[10]

When Andrew Firlik was a medical student, he met a fifty-four-year-old Alzheimer's victim whom he called Margo, and he began to visit her daily in her apartment, where she was cared for by an attendant. The apartment had many locks to keep Margo from slipping out at night and wandering in the park in a nightgown, which she had done before. Margo said she knew who Firlik was each time he arrived, but she never used his name, and he suspected that this was just politeness. She said she was reading mysteries, but Firlik "noticed that her place in the book jumps randomly from day to day; dozens of pages are dog-eared at any given moment.... Maybe she feels good just sitting and humming to herself, rocking back and forth slowly, nodding off liberally, occasionally turning to a fresh page." Margo attended an art class for Alzheimer's victims – they all, including her, painted pretty much the same picture every time, except near the end, just before death, when the pictures became more primitive. Firlik was confused, he said, by the fact that "despite her illness, or maybe somehow because of it, Margo is undeniably one of the happiest people I have ever known." He reports, particularly, her pleasure at eating peanut-butter-and-jelly sandwiches. But, he asks, "When a person can no longer accumulate new memories as the old rapidly fade, what remains? Who is Margo?"[11]

I must now repeat an observation that I have made before: we are considering the rights and interests not of someone who has always been demented, but of someone who was competent in the past. We may therefore think of that person, in considering his rights and interests, in two different ways: as a *demented* person, emphasizing his present situation and capacities, or as a person who has *become* demented, having an eye to the course of his whole life. Does a competent person's right to autonomy include, for example, the power to dictate that life-prolonging treatment be denied him later, or that funds not be spent on maintaining him in great comfort, even if he, when demented, pleads for it? Should what is done for him then be in his contemporary best interests, to make the rest of his life as pleasant and comfortable as possible, or in the best interests of the person he has been? Suppose a demented patient insists on remaining at home, rather than living in an institution, though this would impose very great burdens on his family, and that we all agree that people lead critically better lives when they are not a serious burden to others. Is it really in his best interests, overall, to allow him to become such a burden?

A person's dignity is normally connected to his capacity for self-respect. Should we care about the dignity of a dementia patient if he himself has no sense of it? That seems to depend on whether his past dignity, as a competent person, is in some way still implicated. If it is, then we may take his former capacity for self-respect as requiring that he be treated with dignity now; we may say that dignity now is necessary to show respect for his life as a whole. Many prominent issues about the rights of the demented, then, depend on how their interests now relate to those of their past, competent selves.[12]

Autonomy

It is generally agreed that adult citizens of normal competence have a right to autonomy, that is, a right to make important decisions defining their own lives for themselves. Competent adults are free to make poor investments, provided others do not deceive or withhold information from them, and smokers are allowed to smoke in private, though cigarette advertising must warn them of the dangers of doing so. This autonomy is often at stake in medical contexts.[13] A Jehovah's Witness, for example, may refuse blood transfusions necessary to save his life because transfusions offend his religious convictions. A patient whose life can be saved only if his legs are amputated but who prefers to die soon than to live a life without legs is allowed to refuse the operation. American law generally recognizes a patient's right to autonomy in circumstances like those.[14] But when is that right lost? How far, for example, do mentally incapacitated people have a right to make decisions for themselves that others would deem not in their best interests?[15] Should Mary, the woman who couldn't recognize relatives or manage a tub, be allowed to spend or give away her money as she wishes, or to choose her own doctors, or to refuse prescribed medical treatment, or to decide which relative is appointed as her guardian? Should she be allowed to insist that she be cared for at home, in spite of her family's opinion that she would get better care in an institution?

There may, of course, be some other reason, beyond autonomy, for allowing Mary and other demented people to do as they please. For example, if they are prevented from doing as they wish, they may become so agitated that we do them more harm than good by opposing them, even though the decision they make is not itself in their interests. But do we have reason to respect their decision even when this is not so, even when we think it would be in their best interests, all things considered, to take some decision out of their hands?

We cannot answer that question without reflecting on the point of autonomy, that is, on the question of why we should ever respect the decisions people make when we believe that these are not in their interests. One popular answer might be called the *evidentiary* view: it holds that we should respect the decisions people make for themselves, even when we regard these decisions as imprudent, because each person generally knows what is in his own best interests better than anyone else.[16] Though we often think that someone has made a mistake in judging what is in his own interests, experience teaches us that in most cases we are wrong to think this. So we do better, in the long run, to recognize a general right to autonomy, which we always respect, than by reserving the right to interfere with other people's lives whenever we think they have made a mistake.

If we accepted this evidentiary account of autonomy, we would not extend the right of autonomy to decisions made by the seriously demented, who, having altogether lost the power to appreciate and engage in reasoning and argument, cannot possibly know what is in their own best interests as well as trained specialists, like doctors, can. In some cases, any presumption that demented people know their own interests best would be incoherent: when, for example, as is often the case, their wishes and decisions change radically from one bout of lucidity to another.

But in fact the evidentiary view of autonomy is very far from compelling. For autonomy requires us to allow someone to run his own life even when he behaves in a way that he himself would accept as not at all in his interests.[17] This is sometimes a matter of what philosophers call "weakness of the will." Many people who smoke know that smoking, all things considered, is not in their best interests, but they smoke anyway. If we believe, as we do, that respecting their autonomy means allowing them to act in this way, we cannot accept that the point of autonomy is to protect an agent's welfare. And there are more admirable reasons for acting against what one believes to be in one's own best interests. Some people refuse needed medical treatment because they believe that other people, who would then have to go without it, need it more. Such people act out of convictions we admire, even if we do not act the same way, and autonomy requires us to respect their decisions. Once again, the supposed explanation of the right to autonomy – that it promotes the welfare of people making apparently imprudent decisions – fails to account for our convictions about when people have that right. All this suggests that the point of autonomy must be, at least to some degree, independent of the claim that a person generally knows his own best interests better than anyone else. And then it would not follow, just because a demented person may well be mistaken about his own best interests, that others are entitled to decide for him. Perhaps the demented have a right to autonomy after all.

But we must try to find another, more plausible account of the point of autonomy, and ask whether the demented would have a right to autonomy according to it. The most plausible alternative emphasizes the integrity rather than the welfare of the choosing agent; the value of autonomy, on this view, derives from the capacity it protects: the capacity to express one's own character – values, commitments, convictions, and critical as well as experiential interests – in the life one leads. Recognizing an individual right of autonomy makes self-creation possible. It allows each of us to be responsible for shaping our lives according to our own coherent or incoherent – but, in any case, distinctive – personality. It allows us to lead our own lives rather than be led along them, so that each of us can be, to the extent a scheme of rights can make this possible, what we have made of ourselves. We allow someone to choose death over radical amputation or a blood transfusion, if that is his informed wish, because we acknowledge his right to a life structured by his own values.

The integrity view of autonomy does not assume that competent people have consistent values or always make consistent choices, or that they always lead structured, reflective lives. It recognizes that people often make choices that reflect weakness, indecision, caprice, or plain irrationality – that some people otherwise fanatical about their health continue to smoke, for example. Any plausible integrity-based theory of autonomy must distinguish between the general point or value of autonomy and its consequences for a particular person on a particular occasion. Autonomy encourages and protects people's general capacity to lead their lives out of a distinctive sense of their own character, a sense of what is important to and for them. Perhaps one principal value of that capacity is realized only when a life does in fact display a general, overall integrity and authenticity. But the right to autonomy protects and encourages the capacity in any event, by allowing people who have it to choose how far and in what form they will seek to realize that aim.

If we accept this integrity-based view of the importance of autonomy, our judgement about whether incapacitated patients have a right to autonomy will turn on the degree of their general capacity to lead a life in that sense. When a mildly demented person's choices are reasonably stable, reasonably continuous with the general character of his prior life, and inconsistent and self-defeating only to the rough degree that the choices of fully competent people are, he can be seen as still in charge of his life, and he has a right to autonomy for that reason. But if his choices and demands, no matter how firmly expressed, systematically or randomly contradict one another, reflecting no coherent sense of self and no discernible even short-term aims, then he has presumably lost the capacity that it is the point of autonomy to protect. Recognizing a continuing right to autonomy for him would be pointless. He has no right that his choices about a guardian (or the use of his property, or his medical treatment, or whether he remains at home) be respected for reasons of autonomy. He still has the right to beneficence, the right that decisions on these matters be made in his best interests; and his preferences may, for different reasons, be important in deciding what his best interests are. But he no longer has the right, as competent people do, himself to decide contrary to those interests.

"Competence" is sometimes used in a task-specific sense, to refer to the ability to grasp and manipulate information bearing on a given problem. Competence in that sense varies, sometimes greatly, even among ordinary, nondemented people; I may be more competent than you at making some decisions and less competent at others. The medical literature concerning surrogate decision making for the demented points out, properly, that competence in this task-specific sense is relative to the character and complexity of the decision in question.[18] A patient who is not competent to administer his complex business affairs may nevertheless be able to grasp and appreciate information bearing on whether he should remain at home or enter an institution, for example.

But competence in the sense in which it is presupposed by the right to autonomy is a very different matter. It means the more diffuse and general ability I described: the ability to act out of genuine preference or character or conviction or a sense of self. There will, of course, be hard cases in which we cannot know with any confidence whether a particular dementia patient is competent in that sense. But we must make that overall judgement, not some combination of judgements about specific task capability, in order to decide whether some mentally incapacitated patient has a right to autonomy.[19] Patients like Mary have no right that *any* decision be respected just out of concern for their autonomy. That may sound harsh, but it is no kindness to allow a person to take decisions against his own interests in order to protect a capacity he does not and cannot have.

So neither the evidentiary view of autonomy nor the more plausible integrity view recommends any right to autonomy for the seriously demented. But what about a patient's *precedent* autonomy? Suppose a patient is incompetent in the general, overall sense but that years ago, when perfectly competent, he executed a living will providing for what he plainly does not want now. Suppose, for example, that years ago, when fully competent, Margo had executed a formal document directing that if she should develop Alzheimer's disease, all her property should be given to a designated charity so that none of it could be spent on her own care. Or that in that event she should not receive treatment for any other serious, life-threatening disease she might contract. Or even that in that event she should be killed as soon and as painlessly as possible? If Margo had expressed any of those wishes when she was competent, would autonomy then require that they be respected now by those in charge of her care, even though she seems perfectly happy with her dog-eared mysteries, the single painting she repaints, and her peanut-butter-and-jelly sandwiches?

If we had accepted the evidentiary view of autonomy, we would find the case for respecting Margo's past directions very weak. People are not the best judges of what their own best interests would be under circumstances they have never encountered and in which their preferences and desires may drastically have changed. But if we accept the integrity view, we will be drawn to the view that Margo's past wishes must be respected. A competent person making a living will providing for his treatment if he becomes demented is making exactly the kind of judgement that autonomy, on the integrity view, most respects: a judgement about the overall shape of the kind of life he wants to have led.

This conclusion is troubling, however, even shocking, and someone might want to resist it by insisting that the right to autonomy is *necessarily* contemporary: that a person's right to autonomy is only a right that his present decisions, not past ones that he has since disowned, be respected. Certainly that is the normal force of recognizing autonomy. Suppose that a Jehovah's Witness has signed a formal document stipulating that he is not to receive blood transfusions even if out of weakness of will he requests one when he would otherwise die. He wants, like Ulysses, to be tied to the mast of his faith. But when the moment comes, and he needs a transfusion, he pleads for it. We would not think ourselves required, out of respect for his autonomy, to disregard his contemporary plea.

We can interpret that example in different ways, though, and the difference is crucial for our present problem. We might say, first, that the Witness's later plea countermanded his original decision because it expressed a more contemporary desire. That presumes that it is only right to defer to past decisions when we have reason to believe that the agent still wishes what he wanted then. On that view, precedent autonomy is an illusion: we treat a person's past decision as important only because it is normally evidence of his present wishes, and we disregard it entirely when we know that it is not. On the other hand, we might say that the Witness's later plea countermanded his original decision because it was a fresh exercise of his autonomy, and that disregarding it would be treating him as no longer in charge of his own life. The difference between these two views about the force of precedent autonomy is crucial when someone changes his mind *after* he has become incompetent – that is, when the conditions of autonomy no longer hold. Suppose that the same accident that made a transfusion medically necessary for the Witness also deranged him, and that while still plainly deranged he demands the transfusion. On the first view, we would not violate his autonomy by administering it, but on the second, we would.

Which of the two views about the force of past decisions is more persuasive? Suppose we were confident that the deranged Witness, were he to receive the transfusion and live, would become competent again and be appalled at having had a treatment he believed worse for him than dying. In those circumstances, I believe, we would violate his autonomy by giving him the transfusion. That argues for the second view about the force of past decisions, the view that endorses precedent autonomy as genuine. We refuse to give the deranged Witness a transfusion not because we think he really continues to want what he wanted before – this is not like a case in which someone who objects to a given treatment is unconscious when he needs it – but because he lacks the necessary capacity for a fresh exercise of autonomy. His former decision remains in force because no new decision by a person capable of autonomy has annulled it.

Someone might say that we are justified in withholding the transfusion only because we know that the Witness would regret the transfusion if he recovered. But that prediction would make no difference if he was fully competent when he asked for the transfusion and desperate to live at that moment, though very likely to change his mind again and be appalled tomorrow at what he has done. Surely we should accede to his request in those circumstances. What makes the difference, when we are deciding whether to honor someone's plea even though it contradicts his past deep convictions, is whether he is now competent to make a decision of that character, not whether he will regret making it later.

Our argument for the integrity view, then, supports a genuine doctrine of precedent autonomy. A competent person's right to autonomy requires that his past decisions about how he is to be treated if he becomes demented be respected even if they contradict the desires he has at that later point. If we refuse to respect Margo's precedent autonomy – if we refuse to respect her past decisions, though made when she was competent, because they do not match her present, incompetent wishes – then we are violating her autonomy on the integrity view. This conclusion has great practical importance. Competent people who are concerned about the end of their lives will naturally worry about how they might be treated if they become demented. Someone anxious to ensure that his life is not then prolonged by medical treatment is worried precisely because he thinks that the character of his whole life would be compromised if it were. He is in the same position as people who sign living wills asking not to be kept alive in a hopeless medical condition or when permanently vegetative. If we respect *their* past requests, as the Supreme Court has decided American states must do, then we have the same reasons for respecting the wishes not to be kept alive of someone who dreads not unconsciousness but dementia.

The argument has very troubling consequences, however. The medical student who observed Margo said that her life was the happiest he knew. Should we really deny a person like that the routine medical care needed to keep her alive? Could we ever conceivably *kill* her? We might consider it morally unforgivable not to try to save the life of someone who plainly enjoys her life, no matter how demented she is, and we might think it beyond imagining that we should actually kill her. We might hate living in a community whose officials might make or license either of those decisions. We might have other good reasons for treating Margo as she now wishes, rather than as, in my imaginary case, she once asked. But still, that violates rather than respects her autonomy.

Notes

1 Doctors are now investigating treatments that include reducing the presence in the brain of toxic substances that may play a role in neurodegeneration, enhancing the supply of trophic factors (which facilitate neuronal repair and growth) and neurotransmitters that are missing or deficient in Alzheimer's patients, and controlling diet-related factors such as blood glucose levels that appear to affect mental functioning in the elderly. See Dennis J. Selkoe, "Aging Brain, Aging Mind," *Scientific American*, 135 (September 1992); Robert J. Joynt, "Neurology," *Journal of the American Medical Association*, 268 (1992), 380; and Andrew A. Skolnick, "Brain Researchers Bullish on Prospects for Preserving Mental Functioning in the Elderly," *Journal of the American Medical Association*, 267 (1992), 2154.

2 Selkoe, "Amyloid Protein and Alzheimer's Disease," *Scientific American* (November 1991), 68.

3 OTA document, "Losing a Million Minds," OTA-BA-323 (1987), 14.

4 Legal provision and practices of custodial care are discussed in several of the papers contained in the OTA document, "Losing a Million Minds." For discussions of clinical diagnosis and histopathology, see, for example, Guy McKhann et al., "Clinical Diagnosis of Alzheimer's Disease: Report of the NINCDS-ADRDA Work Group Under the Auspices of

Department of Health and Human Services Task Force on Alzheimer's Disease," *Neurology*, 34 (1984), 939; Christine M. Hulette et al., "Evaluation of Cerebral Biopsies for the Diagnosis of Dementia," *Archives of Neurology*, 49 (1992), 28; Selkoe, "Amyloid Protein and Alzheimer's Disease"; and M. Farlow et al., "Low Cerebrospinal-fluid Concentrations of Soluble Amyloid β-protein Precursor in Hereditary Alzheimer's Disease," *The Lancet*, 340 (1992), 453.

5 Evans et al., "Estimated Prevalence of Alzheimer's Disease in the United States," *Milbank Quarterly*, 68 (1990), 267

6 In 1992, the continuing Framingham Study determined the prevalence of dementia in its study cohort as 23.8 percent from ages eighty-five to ninety-three. See Bachman et al., "Prevalence of dementia and probable senile dementia of the Alzheimer type in the Framingham Study," *Neurology*, 42 (January 1992), 42. For a discussion of the differences between the studies cited in this and the preceding note, see Selkoe, "Aging Brain, Aging Mind."

7 See "UK: Dementia Condition Alzheimer's Disease Will Hit 750,000 in 30 Years," *The Guardian*, July 6, 1992.

8 Selkoe, "Amyloid Protein and Alzheimer's Disease," 68.

9 See Abstract, *Journal of the American Medical Association*, 267 (May 27, 1992), 2809 (summarizing Welch et al., "The Cost of Institutional Care in Alzheimer's Disease," *Journal of the American Geriatric Society*, 40 [1992], 221).

10 Nancy L. Mace and Peter V. Rabins, *The 36-Hour Day: A Family Guide to Caring for Persons with Alzheimer's Disease, Related Dementing Illnesses, and Memory Loss in Later Life* (Baltimore: Johns Hopkins University Press, 1981, 1991).

11 See Andrew D. Firlik, "Margo's Logo," *Journal of the American Medical Association*, 265 (1991), 201.

12 I should mention another great practical problem about the relationship between a demented person and the competent person he once was. Should the resources available to a demented patient depend on what he actually put aside when he was competent, by way of insurance for his own care in that event? Insurance schemes, both private schemes and mandated public schemes, play an important part in the way we provide resources for catastrophes of different sorts. But is the insurance approach the proper model to use in thinking about provision for the demented? That must depend on whether we believe that a competent person has the appropriate prudential concern for the incompetent person he might become, and that in turn depends on knotty philosophical problems about the concept of personal identity. I cannot discuss, in this book, either that philosophical problem or any of the other serious problems about the justice of financing the extraordinarily expensive care of demented patients in different ways. I have discussed both at some length, however, in a report, "Philosophical Problems of Senile Dementia," written for the United States Congress Office of Technology Assessment in Washington, DC, and available from that office.

13 See discussion in Allen E. Buchanan et al., "Surrogate Decision-Making for Elderly Individuals Who Are Incompetent or of Questionable Competence," November 1985, a report prepared for the Office of Technology Assessment.

14 See George J. Annas and Leonard H. Glantz, "Withholding and Withdrawing of Life-Sustaining Treatment for Elderly Incompetent Patients: A Review of Appellate Court Decisions," September 16, 1985, a report prepared for the Office of Technology Assessment.

15 I am assuming, in this discussion, that it can be in a person's overall best interests, at least sometimes, to force him to act otherwise than as he wants – that it can be in a person's overall best interests, for example, to be made not to smoke, even if we acknowledge that his autonomy is to some degree compromised, considered in itself, as against his interests.

16 Buchanan et al., "Surrogate Decision-Making."

17 There is an important debate in the economic literature on the question whether it can be rational to act against one's own best interests. The better view is that it can. See, for example, Amartya Sen, "Rational Fools: A Critique of the Behavioural Foundations of Economic Theory," *Philosophy and Public Affairs*, 6, no. 4 (Summer 1977).

18 See Buchanan et al., "Surrogate Decision-Making." Questions of task-sensitive competence are plainly relevant to the issues considered in the Buchanan report. But when the argument against surrogate decision making relies on the autonomy of the demented person affected by these decisions, the overall, non-task-sensitive sense of competence is also relevant.

19 Problems are presented for this judgement of overall integrity capacity when a patient appears only periodically capable of organizing his life around a system of desires and wishes. He seems able to take command of his life sometimes, and then lapses into a more serious stage of dementia, becoming lucid again only after a substantial intervening period, at which time the desires and interests he expresses are very different, or even contradictory. It would be a mistake to say that such a patient has the capacity for autonomy "periodically." The capacity autonomy presupposes is of necessity a temporally extended capacity: it is the capacity to have and act out of a personality.

35

Dworkin on Dementia: Elegant Theory, Questionable Policy

Rebecca Dresser

In his most recent book, *Life's Dominion: An Argument About Abortion, Euthanasia, and Individual Freedom*,[1] Ronald Dworkin offers a new way of interpreting disagreements over abortion and euthanasia. In doing so, he enriches and refines our understanding of three fundamental bioethical concepts: autonomy, beneficence, and sanctity of life. It is exciting that this eminent legal philosopher has turned his attention to bioethical issues. *Life's Dominion* is beautifully and persuasively written; its clear language and well-constructed arguments are especially welcome in this age of inaccessible, jargon-laden academic writing. *Life's Dominion* also is full of rich and provocative ideas; in this article, I address only Dworkin's remarks on euthanasia, although I will refer to his views on abortion when they are relevant to my analysis.

Professor Dworkin considers decisions to hasten death with respect to three groups: (1) competent and seriously ill people; (2) permanently unconscious people; and (3) conscious, but incompetent people, specifically, those with progressive and incurable dementia. My remarks focus on the third group, which I have addressed in previous work,[2] and which in my view poses the most difficult challenge for policymakers.

I present Dworkin's and my views as a debate over how we should think about Margo. Margo is described by Andrew Firlik, a medical student, in a *Journal of the American Medical Association* column called "A Piece of My Mind."[3] Firlik met Margo, who has Alzheimer disease, when he was enrolled in a gerontology elective. He began visiting her each day, and came to know something about her life with dementia.

From *Hastings Center Report*, vol. 25, no. 6 (November–December 1995), pp. 32–8. Reprinted with permission.

Upon arriving at Margo's apartment (she lived at home with the help of an attendant), Firlik often found Margo reading; she told him she especially enjoyed mysteries, but he noticed that "her place in the book jump[ed] randomly from day to day." "For Margo," Firlik wonders, "is reading always a mystery?" Margo never called her new friend by name, though she claimed she knew who he was and always seemed pleased to see him. She liked listening to music and was happy listening to the same song repeatedly, apparently relishing it as if hearing it for the first time. Whenever she heard a certain song, however, she smiled and told Firlik that it reminded her of her deceased husband. She painted, too, but like the other Alzheimer patients in her art therapy class, she created the same image day after day: "a drawing of four circles, in soft rosy colors, one inside the other."

The drawing enabled Firlik to understand something that previously had mystified him:

> Despite her illness, or maybe somehow because of it, Margo is undeniably one of the happiest people I have known. There is something graceful about the degeneration her mind is undergoing, leaving her carefree, always cheerful. Do her problems, whatever she may perceive them to be, simply fail to make it to the worry centers of her brain? How does Margo maintain her sense of self? When a person can no longer accumulate new memories as the old rapidly fade, what remains? Who is Margo?

Firlik surmises that the drawing represented Margo's expression of her mind, her identity, and that by repeating the drawing, she was reminding herself and others of that identity. The painting was Margo, "plain and contained, smiling in her peaceful, demented state."

In *Life's Dominion*, Dworkin considers Margo as a potential subject of his approach. In one variation, he asks us to suppose that

> years ago, when fully competent, Margo had executed a formal document directing that if she should develop Alzheimer's disease ... she should not receive treatment for any other serious, life-threatening disease she might contract. Or even that in that event she should be killed as soon and as painlessly as possible. (p. 226)

He presents an elegant and philosophically sophisticated argument for giving effect to her prior wishes, despite the value she appears to obtain from her life as an individual with dementia.

Dworkin's position emerges from his inquiry into the values of autonomy, beneficence, and sanctity of life. To understand their relevance to a case such as Margo's, he writes, we must first think about why we care about how we die. And to understand that phenomenon, we must understand why we care about how we live. Dworkin believes our lives are guided by the desire to advance two kinds of interests. *Experiential* interests are those we share to some degree with all sentient creatures. In Dworkin's words:

> We all do things because we like the experience of doing them: playing softball, perhaps, or cooking and eating well, or watching football, or seeing *Casablanca* for the twelfth time, or walking in the woods in October, or listening to *The Marriage of Figaro*, or sailing fast just off the wind, or just working hard at something. Pleasures like these are essential to a good life – a life with nothing that is marvelous only because of how it feels would be not pure but preposterous. (p. 201)

But Dworkin deems these interests less important than the second sort of interests we possess. Dworkin argues that we also seek to satisfy our *critical* interests, which are the hopes and aims that lend genuine meaning and coherence to our lives. We pursue projects such as establishing close friendships, achieving competence in our work, and raising children, not simply because we want the positive experiences they offer, but also because we believe we should want them, because our lives as a whole will be better if we take up these endeavors.

Dworkin admits that not everyone has a conscious sense of the interests they deem critical to their lives, but he thinks that "even people whose lives feel unplanned are nevertheless often guided by a sense of the general style of life they think appropriate, of what choices strike them as not only good at the moment but in character for them" (p. 202). In this tendency, Dworkin sees us aiming for the ideal of integrity, seeking to create a coherent narrative structure for the lives we lead.

Our critical interests explain why many of us care about how the final chapter of our lives turns out. Although some of this concern originates in the desire to avoid experiential burdens, as well as burdens on our families, much of it reflects the desire to escape dying under circumstances that are out of character with the prior stages of our lives. For most people, Dworkin writes, death has a "special, symbolic importance: they want their deaths, if possible, to express and in that way vividly to confirm the values they believe most important to their lives" (p. 211). And because critical interests are so personal and widely varied among individuals, each person must have the right to control the manner in which life reaches its conclusion. Accordingly, the state should refrain from imposing a "uniform, general view [of appropriate end-of-life-care] by way of sovereign law" (p. 213).

Dworkin builds on this hierarchy of human interests to defend his ideas about how autonomy and beneficence should apply to someone like Margo. First, he examines the generally accepted principle that we should in most circumstances honor the competent person's autonomous choice. One way to justify this principle is to claim that people generally know better than anyone else what best serves their interests; thus, their own choices are the best evidence we have of the decision that would most protect their welfare. Dworkin labels this the *evidentiary* view of autonomy. But Dworkin believes the better explanation for the respect we accord to individual choice lies in what he calls the *integrity* view of autonomy. In many instances, he contends, we grant freedom to people to act in ways that clearly conflict with their own best interests. We do this, he argues, because we want to let people "lead their lives out of a distinctive sense of their own character, a sense of what is important to them" (p. 224). The model once again assigns the greatest moral significance to the individual's critical interests, as opposed to the less important experiential interests that also contribute to a person's having a good life.

The integrity view of autonomy partially accounts for Dworkin's claim that we should honor Margo's prior choice to end her life if she developed Alzheimer disease. In making this choice, she was exercising, in Dworkin's phrase, her "precedent autonomy" (p. 226). The evidentiary view of autonomy fails to supply support for deferring to the earlier decision, Dworkin observes, because "[p]eople are not the best judges of what their own best interests would be under circumstances they have never encountered and in which their preferences and desires may drastically have changed" (p. 226). He readily admits that Andrew Firlik and others evaluating Margo's life with dementia would perceive a conflict between her prior instructions and her current welfare. But the integrity view of autonomy furnishes compelling support for honoring Margo's advance directives. Margo's interest in living her life in character includes an interest in controlling the circumstances in which others should permit her life as an Alzheimer patient to continue. Limiting that control would in Dworkin's view be "an unacceptable form of moral paternalism" (p. 231).

Dworkin finds additional support for assigning priority to Margo's former instructions in the moral principle of beneficence. People who are incompetent to exercise autonomy have a right to beneficence from those entrusted to decide on their behalf. The best interests standard typically has been understood to require the decision that would best protect the incompetent individual's current welfare.[4] On this view, the standard would support some (though not necessarily all) life-extending decisions that depart from Margo's prior directives. But Dworkin invokes his concept of critical interests to construct a different best interests standard. Dworkin argues that Margo's critical interests persist, despite her current inability to appreciate them. Because critical interests have greater moral significance than the experiential interests Margo remains able to appreciate, and because "we must judge Margo's critical interests as she did when competent to do so" (p. 231), beneficence requires us to honor Margo's prior preferences for death. In Dworkin's view, far from providing a reason to override Margo's directives, compassion counsels us to follow them, for it is compassion "toward the whole person" that underlies the duty of beneficence (p. 232).

To honor the narrative that is Margo's life, then, we must honor her earlier choices. A decision to disregard them would constitute unjustified paternalism and would lack mercy as well. Dworkin concedes that such a decision might be made for other reasons – because we "find ourselves unable to deny medical help to anyone who is conscious and does not reject it" (p. 232), or deem it "morally unforgiveable not to try to save the life of someone who plainly enjoys her life" (p. 228), or find it "beyond imagining that we should actually kill her" (p. 228), or "hate living in a community whose officials might make or license either of [Margo's] decisions" (pp. 228–9). Dworkin does not explicitly address whether these or other aspects of the state's interest in protecting life should influence legal policy governing how people like Margo are treated.

Dworkin pays much briefer attention to Margo's fate in the event that she did not explicitly register her preferences about future treatment. Most incompetent patients are currently in this category, for relatively few people complete formal advance treatment directives.[5] In this scenario, the competent Margo failed to declare her explicit wishes, and her family is asked to determine her fate. Dworkin suggests that her relatives may give voice to Margo's autonomy by judging what her choice would have been if she had thought about it, based on her character and personality. Moreover, similar evidence enables them to determine her best interests, for it is her critical interests that matter most in reaching this determination. If Margo's dementia set in before she explicitly indicated her preferences about future care, "the law should so far as possible leave decisions in the hands of [her] relatives or other people close to [her] whose sense of [her] best interests . . . is likely to be much sounder than some universal, theoretical, abstract judgement" produced through the political process (p. 213).

Life's Dominion helps to explain why the "death with dignity" movement has attracted such strong support in the United States. I have no doubt that many people share Dworkin's conviction that they ought to have the power to choose death over life in Margo's state. But I am far from convinced of the wisdom or morality of these proposals for dementia patients.

Advance Directives and Precedent Autonomy

First, an observation. Dworkin makes an impressive case that the power to control one's future as an incompetent patient is a precious freedom that our society should go to great lengths to protect. But how strongly do people actually value this freedom? Surveys show that a relatively small percentage of the US population engages in end-of-life planning, and that many in that group simply designate a trusted relative or friend to make future treatment decisions, choosing not to issue specific instructions on future care.[6] Though this widespread failure to take advantage of the freedom to exercise precedent autonomy may be attributed to a lack of publicity or inadequate policy support for advance planning, it could also indicate that issuing explicit instructions to govern the final chapter of one's life is not a major priority for most people. If it is not, then we may question whether precedent autonomy and the critical interests it protects should be the dominant model for our policies on euthanasia for incompetent people.

Dworkin constructs a moral argument for giving effect to Margo's directives, but does not indicate how his position could be translated into policy. Consider how we might approach this task. We would want to devise procedures to ensure that people issuing such directives were competent, their actions voluntary, and their decisions informed. In other medical settings, we believe that a person's adequate understanding of the information relevant to treatment decision-making is a prerequisite to the exercise of true self-determination. We should take the same view of Margo's advance planning.

What would we want the competent Margo to understand before she chose death over life in the event of dementia? At a minimum, we would want her to understand that the experience of dementia differs among individuals, that for some it appears to be a persistently frightening and unhappy existence, but that most people with dementia do not exhibit the distress and misery we competent people tend to associate with the condition. I make no claims to expertise in this area, but my reading and discussions with clinicians, caregivers, and patients themselves suggest that the subjective experience of dementia is more positive than most of us would expect. Some caregivers and other commentators also note that patients' quality of life is substantially dependent on their social and physical environments, as opposed to the neurological condition itself.[7] Thus, the "tragedy" and "horror" of dementia is partially attributable to the ways in which others respond to people with this condition.

We also would want Margo to understand that Alzheimer disease is a progressive condition, and that options for forgoing life-sustaining interventions will arise at different points in the process. Dworkin writes that his ideas apply only to the late stages of Alzheimer disease, but he makes implementation of Margo's former wishes contingent on the mere development of the condition (pp. 219, 226). If we were designing policy, we would want to ensure that competent individuals making directives knew something about the general course of the illness and the points at which various capacities are lost. We would want them to be precise about the behavioral indications that should trigger the directive's implementation. We would want them to think about what their lives could be like at different stages of the disease, and about how invasive and effective various possible interventions might be. We would want to give them the opportunity to talk with physicians, caregivers, and individuals diagnosed with Alzheimer disease, and perhaps, to discuss their potential choices with a counselor.

The concern for education is one that applies to advance treatment directives generally, but one that is not widely recognized or addressed at the policy level. People complete advance directives in private, perhaps after discussion with relatives, physicians, or attorneys, but often with little understanding of the meaning or implications of their decisions. In one study of dialysis patients who had issued instructions on treatment in the event of advanced Alzheimer disease, a subsequent inquiry revealed that almost two-thirds of them wanted families and physicians to have some freedom to override the directives to protect their subsequent best interests.[8] The patients' failure to include this statement in their directives indicates that the instructions they recorded did not reflect their actual preferences. A survey of twenty-nine people participating in an advance care planning workshop found ten agreeing with both of the following inconsistent statements: "I would never want to be on a respirator in an intensive care unit"; and "If a short period of extremely intensive medical care could return me to near-normal condition, I would want it."[9] Meanwhile, some promoters of advance care planning have claimed that subjects can complete directives during interviews lasting fifteen minutes.[10]

We do not advance people's autonomy by giving effect to choices that originate in insufficient or mistaken information. Indeed, interference in such choices is often considered a form of justified paternalism. Moreover, advance planning for future dementia treatment is more complex than planning for other conditions, such as permanent unconsciousness. Before implementing directives to hasten death in the event of dementia, we should require people to exhibit a reasonable understanding of the choices they are making.[11]

Some shortcomings of advance planning are insurmountable, however. People exercising advance planning are denied knowledge of treatments and other relevant information that may emerge during the time between making a directive and giving it effect. Opportunities for clarifying misunderstandings are truncated, and decision-makers are not asked to explain or defend their choices to the clinicians, relatives, and friends whose care and concern may lead depressed or imprudent individuals to alter their wishes.[12] Moreover, the rigid adherence to advance planning Dworkin endorses leaves no room for the changes of heart that can lead us to deviate from our earlier choices. All of us are familiar with decisions we have later come to recognize as ill-suited to our subsequent situations. As Dworkin acknowledges, people may be mistaken about their future experiential interests as incompetent individuals. A policy of absolute adherence to advance directives means that we deny people like Margo the freedom we enjoy as competent people to change our decisions that conflict with our subsequent experiential interests.[13]

Personal identity theory, which addresses criteria for the persistence of a particular person over time, provides another basis for questioning precedent autonomy's proper moral and legal authority. In *Life's Dominion*, Dworkin assumes that Margo the dementia patient is the same person who issued the earlier requests to die, despite the drastic psychological alteration that has occurred. Indeed, the legitimacy of the precedent autonomy model absolutely depends on this view of personal identity. Another approach to personal identity would challenge this judgement, however. On this view, substantial memory loss and other psychological changes may produce a new person, whose connection to the earlier one could be less strong, indeed, could be no stronger than that between you and me.[14] Subscribers to this view of personal identity can argue that Margo's earlier choices lack moral authority to control what happens to Margo the dementia patient.

These shortcomings of the advance decision-making process are reasons to assign less moral authority to precedent autonomy than to contemporaneous autonomy. I note that Dworkin himself may believe in at least one limit on precedent autonomy in medical decision-making. He writes that people "who are repelled by the idea of living demented, totally dependent lives, speaking gibberish," ought to be permitted to issue advance directives "stipulating that if they become permanently and seriously demented, and then develop a serious illness, they should not be given medical treatment except to avoid pain" (p. 231). Would he oppose honoring a request to avoid all medical treatment, including pain-relieving measures, that was motivated by religious or philosophical concerns? The above remark suggests that he might give priority to Margo's existing experiential interests in avoiding pain over her prior exercise of precedent autonomy. In my view, this would be a justified limit on precedent autonomy, but I would add others as well.

Critical and Experiential Interests: Problems with the Model

What if Margo, like most other people, failed to exercise her precedent autonomy through making an advance directive? In this situation, her surrogate decision-makers are to apply Dworkin's version of the best interests standard. Should they consider, first and foremost, the critical interests she had as a competent person? I believe not, for several reasons. First, Dworkin's approach to the best interests standard rests partially on the claim that people want their lives to have narrative coherence. Dworkin omits empirical support for this claim, and my own observations lead me to wonder about its accuracy. The people of the United States are a diverse group, holding many different world views. Do most people actually think as Dworkin says they do? If I were to play psychologist, my guess would be that many people take life one day at a time. The goal of establishing a coherent narrative may be a less common life theme than the simple effort to accept and adjust to the changing natural and social circumstances that characterize a person's life. It also seems possible that people generally fail to draw a sharp line between experiential and critical interests, often choosing the critical projects Dworkin describes substantially because of the rewarding experiences they provide.

Suppose Margo left no indication of her prior wishes, but that people close to her believe it would be in her critical interests to die rather than live on in her current condition. Dworkin notes, but fails to address, the argument that "in the circumstances of dementia, critical interests become less important and experiential interests more so, so that fiduciaries may rightly ignore the former and concentrate on the latter" (p. 232). Happy and contented Margo will experience clear harm from the decision that purports to advance the critical interests she no longer cares about. This seems to me justification for a policy against active killing or withholding effective, non-burden some treatments, such as antibiotics, from dementia patients whose lives offer them the sorts of pleasures and satisfactions Margo enjoys. Moreover, if clear evidence is lacking on Margo's own view of her critical interests, a decision to hasten her death might actually conflict with the life narrative she envisioned for herself. Many empirical studies have shown that families often do not have a very good sense of their relatives' treatment preferences.[15] How will Margo's life narrative be improved by her family's decision to hasten death, if there is no clear indication that she herself once took that view?

I also wonder about how to apply a best interests standard that assigns priority to the individual's critical interests. Dworkin writes that family members and other intimates applying this standard should decide based on their knowledge of "the shape and character of [the patient's] life and his own sense of integrity and critical interests" (p. 213). What sorts of life narratives would support a decision to end Margo's life? What picture of her critical interests might her family cite as justification for ending her life now? Perhaps Margo had been a famous legal philosopher whose intellectual pursuits were of utmost importance to her. This fact might tilt toward a decision to spare her from an existence in which she can only pretend to read. But what if she were also the mother of a mentally retarded child, whom she had cared for at home? What if she had enjoyed and valued this child's simple, experiential life, doing everything she could to protect and enhance it? How would this information affect the interpretation of her critical interests as they bear on her own life with dementia?

I am not sure whether Dworkin means to suggest that Margo's relatives should have complete discretion in evaluating considerations such as these. Would he permit anyone to challenge the legitimacy of a narrative outcome chosen by her family? What if her closest friends believed that a different conclusion would be more consistent with the way she had constructed her life? And is there any room in Dworkin's scheme for surprise endings? Some of our greatest fictional characters evolve into figures having little resemblance to the persons we met in the novels' opening chapters. Are real-life characters such as the fiercely independent intellectual permitted to become people who appreciate simple experiential pleasures and accept their dependence on others?

Finally, is the goal of respecting individual differences actually met by Dworkin's best interests standard? Although Dworkin recognizes that some people believe their critical interests would be served by a decision to extend their lives as long as is medically possible (based on their pro-life values), at times he implies that such individuals are mistaken about their genuine critical interests, that in actuality no one's critical interests could be served by such a decision. For example, he writes that after the onset of dementia, nothing of value can be added to a person's life, because the person is no longer capable of engaging in the activities necessary to advance her critical interests (p. 230). A similar judgement is also evident in his discussion of an actual case of a brain-damaged patient who "did not seem to be in pain or unhappy," and "recognized familiar faces with apparent pleasure" (p. 233). A court-appointed guardian sought to have the patient's life-prolonging medication withheld, but the family was strongly opposed to this outcome, and a judge denied the guardian's request. In a remark that seems to conflict with his earlier support for family decision-making, Dworkin questions whether the family's choice was in the patient's best interests (p. 233). These comments lead me to wonder whether Dworkin's real aim is to defend an objective nontreatment standard that should be applied to all individuals with significant mental impairment, not just those whose advance directives or relatives support a decision to hasten death. If so, then he needs to provide additional argument for this more controversial position.

The State's Interest in Margo's Life

My final thoughts concern Dworkin's argument that the state has no legitimate reason to interfere with Margo's directives or her family's best interests judgement to end her life. A great deal of *Life's Dominion* addresses the intrinsic value of human life and the nature of the state's interest in protecting that value. Early in the book, Dworkin defends the familiar view that only conscious individuals can possess interests in not being destroyed or otherwise harmed. On this view, until the advent of sentience and other capacities, human fetuses lack interests of their own that would support a state policy restricting abortion. A policy that restricted abortion prior to this point would rest on what Dworkin calls a *detached* state interest in protecting human life. Conversely, a policy that restricts abortion after fetal sentience (which coincides roughly with viability) is supported by the state's *derivative* interest in valuing life, so called because it derives from the fetus's own interests (pp. 10–24, 168–70). Dworkin believes that detached state interests in ensuring respect for the value of life justify state prohibitions on abortion only after pregnant women are given a reasonable opportunity to terminate an unwanted pregnancy. Prior to this point, the law should permit women to make decisions about pregnancy according to their own views on how best to respect the value of life. After viability, however, when fetal neurological development is sufficiently advanced to make sentience possible, the state may severely limit access to abortion, based on its legitimate role in protecting creatures capable of having interests of their own (pp. 168–70).

Dworkin's analysis of abortion provides support, in my view, for a policy in which the state acts to protect the interests of conscious dementia patients like Margo. Although substantially impaired, Margo retains capacities for pleasure, enjoyment, interaction, relationships, and so forth. I believe her continued ability to participate in the life she is living furnishes a defensible basis for state limitations on the scope of her precedent autonomy, as well as on the choices her intimates make on her behalf. Contrary to Dworkin, I believe that such moral paternalism is justified when dementia patients have a quality of life comparable to Margo's. I am not arguing that all directives regarding dementia care should be overridden, nor that family choices should always be disregarded. I think directives and family choices should control in the vast majority of cases, for such decisions rarely are in clear conflict with the patient's contemporaneous interests. But I believe that state restriction is justified when a systematic evaluation by clinicians and others involved in patient care produces agreement that a minimally intrusive life sustaining intervention is likely to preserve the life of someone as contented and active as Margo.

Many dementia patients do not fit Margo's profile. Some are barely conscious, others appear frightened, miserable, and unresponsive to efforts to mitigate their pain. Sometimes a proposed life-sustaining treatment will be invasive and immobilizing, inflicting extreme terror on patients unable to understand the reasons for their burdens. In such cases, it is entirely appropriate to question the justification for treatment, and often to withhold it, as long as the patient can be kept comfortable in its absence. This approach assumes that observers can accurately assess the experiential benefits and burdens of patients with neurological impairments and decreased ability to communicate. I believe that such assessments are often possible, and that there is room for a great deal of improvement in meeting this challenge.

I also believe that the special problems inherent in making an advance decision about active euthanasia justify a policy of refusing to implement such decisions, at the very least until we achieve legalization for competent patients without unacceptable rates of error and abuse.[16] I note as well the likely scarcity of health care professionals who would be willing to participate in decisions to withhold simple and effective treatments from someone in Margo's condition, much less to give her a lethal injection, even if this were permitted by law. Would Dworkin support a system that required physicians and nurses to compromise their own values and integrity so that Margo's precedent autonomy and critical interests could be advanced? I seriously doubt that many health professionals would agree to implement his proposals regarding dementia patients whose lives are as happy as Margo's.

We need community reflection on how we should think about people with dementia, including our possible future selves. Dworkin's model reflects a common response to the condition: tragic, horrible, degrading, humiliating, to be avoided at all costs. But how much do social factors account for this tragedy? Two British scholars argue that though we regard dementia patients as "the problem," the patients

> are rather less of a problem than *we*. *They* are generally more authentic about what they are feeling and doing; many of the polite veneers of earlier life have been stripped away. *They* are clearly dependent on others, and usually come to accept that dependence; whereas many "normal" people, living under an ideology of extreme individualism, strenuously deny their dependency needs. *They* live largely in the present, because certain parts of their memory function have failed. *We* often find it very difficult to live in the present, suffering constant distraction; the sense of the present is often contaminated by regrets about the past and fears about the future.[17]

If we were to adopt an alternative to the common vision of dementia, we might ask ourselves what we could do, how we could alter our own responses so that people with dementia may find that life among us need not be so terrifying and frustrating. We might ask ourselves what sorts of environments, interactions, and relationships would enhance their lives.

Such a "disability perspective" on dementia offers a more compassionate, less rejecting approach to people with the condition than a model insisting that we should be permitted to order ourselves killed if this "saddest of the tragedies" (p. 218) should befall us. It supports as well a care and treatment policy centered on the conscious incompetent patient's subjective reality; one that permits death when the experiential burdens of continued life are too heavy or the benefits too minimal, but seeks to delay death when the patient's subjective existence is as positive as Margo's appears to be. Their loss of higher-level intellectual capacities ought not to exclude people like Margo from the moral community nor from the law's protective reach, even when the threats to their well-being emanate from their own former preferences. Margo's connections to us remain sufficiently strong that we owe her our concern and respect in the present. Eventually, the decision to allow her to die will be morally defensible. It is too soon, however, to exclude her from our midst.

Acknowledgment

I presented an earlier version of this essay at the annual meeting of the Society for Health and Human Values, 8 October 1994, in Pittsburgh. I would like to thank Ronald Dworkin and Eric Rakowski for their comments on my analysis.

Notes

1 Ronald Dworkin, *Life's Dominion: An Argument About Abortion, Euthanasia, and Individual Freedom* (New York: Knopf, 1993; Vintage, 1994).

2 See, for example, Rebecca Dresser, "Missing Persons: Legal Perceptions of Incompetent Patients," *Rutgers Law Review*, 609 (1994): 636–47; Rebecca Dresser and Peter J. Whitehouse, "The Incompetent Patient on the Slippery Slope," *Hastings Center Report*, 24, no. 4 (1994): 6–12; Rebecca Dresser, "Autonomy Revisited: The Limits of Anticipatory Choices," in *Dementia and Aging: Ethics, Values, and Policy Choices*, ed. Robert H. Binstock, Stephen G. Post, and Peter J. Whitehouse (Baltimore, MD: Johns Hopkins University Press, 1992), pp. 71–85.

3 Andrew D. Firlik, "Margo's Logo," *JAMA*, 265 (1991): 201.

4 See generally Dresser, "Missing Persons."

5 For a recent survey of the state of advance treatment decision-making in the US, see "Advance Care Planning: Priorities for Ethical and Empirical Research," Special Supplement, *Hastings Center Report* 24, no. 6 (1994).

6 See generally "Advance Care Planning." The failure of most persons to engage in formal end-of-life planning does not in itself contradict Dworkin's point that most people care about how they die. It does suggest, however, that people do not find the formal exercise of precedent autonomy to be a helpful or practical means of expressing their concerns about future life-sustaining treatment.

7 See generally Dresser, "Missing Persons," 681–91; Tom Kitwood and Kathleen Bredin, "Towards a Theory of Dementia Care: Personhood and Well Being," *Ageing and Society*, 12 (1992): 269–87.

8 Ashwini Sehgal et al., "How Strictly Do Dialysis Patients Want Their Advance Directives Followed?" *JAMA*, 267 (1992): 59–63.

9 Lachlan Forrow, Edward Gogel, and Elizabeth Thomas, "Advance Directives for Medical Care" (letter), *New England Journal of Medicine*, 325 (1991): 1255.

10 Linda L. Emanuel et al., "Advance Directives for Medical Care – A Case for Greater Use," *New England Journal of Medicine*, 324 (1991): 889–95.

11 See Eric Rakowski, "The Sanctity of Human Life," *Yale Law Journal*, 103 (1994): 2049, 2110–11.

12 See Allen Buchanan and Dan Brock, "Deciding for Others," in *The Ethics of Surrogate Decisionmaking* (Cambridge: Cambridge University Press, 1989), at 101–7 for discussion of these and other shortcomings of advance treatment decision-making.

13 See generally Rebecca Dresser and John A. Robertson, "Quality-of-Life and Non-Treatment Decisions for Incompetent Patients: A Critique of the Orthodox Approach," *Law, Medicine & Health Care*, 17 (1989): 234–44.

14 See Derek Parfit, *Reasons and Persons* (New York: Oxford University Press, 1985), pp. 199–379.

15 See, e.g., Allison B. Seckler et al., "Substituted Judgment: How Accurate Are Proxy Predictions?" *Annals of Internal Medicine*, 115 (1992): 92–8.

16 See generally Leslie P. Francis, "Advance Directives for Voluntary Euthanasia: A Volatile Combination?" *Journal of Medicine & Philosophy*, 18 (1993): 297–322.

17 Kitwood and Bredin, "Towards a Theory of Dementia Care," 273–4.

Voluntary Euthanasia and Medically Assisted Suicide

36

The Note

Chris Hill

An open letter to anyone who wants to understand why I've checked out. It's very personal, pretty horrible and perhaps a bit shocking. I hope that those of you who knew me well enough find it unnecessary to read this.

Well, this is it – perhaps the hardest thing you've ever had to read, easily the most difficult thing I've ever attempted to write. To understand my overwhelming sense of loss and why I chose to take my own life, you need to know a bit about my life before and after my accident. Let's take a closer look.

I was born at one of the best times in one of the world's best countries – Australia. I had more than the proverbial happy childhood. Great parents, world travel, a good education and fabulous experiences like Disneyland, swimming with a wild dolphin in the turquoise waters of the Bahamas, riding across the desert sands around the Egyptian pyramids and much more.

Later, after the travel bug had bitten good and hard, I set out on my own adventures. I can remember only a fraction of them, but many rich images come flooding back. I stood on the lip of a live volcano in Vanuatu and stared down into the vision of hell in its throat; I watched the morning sun ignite Himalayan peaks in a blaze of incandescent glory; smoked hashish with a leper in an ancient Hindu temple; danced naked under the stars with the woman I love on a tropical beach that left a trail of phosphorescent blue footsteps behind us; skied waist-deep powder snow in untracked Coloradon glades; soared thermals to 8000 feet in a hang-glider and have literally flown with the eagles. In Maryland, on midsummer nights redolent with the smell of freshly ploughed earth, I rode past fields lit by the twinkling light of a billion fireflies. I've ridden a motorcycle at 265 km/h on a Japanese racetrack and up to the 5000 metre snowline on an Ecuadorian volcano. And speaking of riding, what haven't I seen from behind the bars of a motorcycle? More than 200 000 kilometres in over a dozen countries embracing everything from some of the world's most spectacular wilderness areas to its greatest cities and vast slums containing millions of impoverished souls.

Along the way I picked up a decent education, including two university degrees, and learnt another language. All this and so much more – more than most people would experience in several lifetimes.

Perhaps most importantly of all, everywhere I've been I enjoyed the support of a caring family, the company of good friends and, more than once, the rewards of being involved in a caring relationship. They – you, if you're reading – are ultimately what made my life as rich as it was, and I thank you.

I was lucky enough to know love, and I indulged in lust. I enjoyed exotic erotica with perhaps more than a hundred women of many different nationalities in places that ranged from the bedroom to a crowded ship's deck on the Aegean Sea, fields, rivers, trees, beaches, cars and motorcycles. There's been a *ménage à trois* in various combinations and even a few outright orgies. How wonderful to have been sexually active in the pre-AIDS

From Helga Kuhse (ed.), *Willing to Listen: Wanting to Die* (Ringwood, Victoria: Penguin Books, 1994), pp. 9–17. Reprinted with permission.

era. I record this not as an exercise in testosterone-fuelled chest-beating, but to point out that sex was an important part of my life, and so that you can better understand my sense of loss.

In short, I once lived life to the max, always grateful that I had the opportunity to do just that, and always mindful to live for today because there may be no tomorrow.

Just as well, it seems. After my hang-gliding accident – how ironic that something I loved so much could destroy me so cruelly – tomorrows were nothing but a grey void of bleak despair. I was paralysed from the chest down, more than three-quarters dead. A talking head mounted on a bloody wheelchair. No more of the simple pleasures I once took for granted. No walking, running, swimming, riding motorcycles, the wonderful feel of grass, sand or mud underfoot, nothing. The simplest of everyday tasks – getting up, having a shower, getting dressed – became an enormous hassle and the source of endless frustration. That in itself was completely shattering physically and emotionally, but I lost so much more than mobility. I lost my dignity and self-respect. I would forever be a burden on those around me and I didn't want that no matter how willingly and unthinkingly family and friends assumed that burden. Every time I had to ask someone to do something for me, every time I was dragged up a damn step, was like thrusting a hot blade into the place where my pride used to be.

All that was bad enough, but there was so much more. No balance. My every action was as graceless as a toy dog nodding in the back of some beat-up car. No ability to regulate my body temperature properly – in a sense I was cold-blooded, more like a lizard than a human being. And without abdominal muscles I couldn't cough, sneeze, shout, blow out a candle or even fart.

Worse still, I couldn't shit or piss. Those body functions had to be performed manually, which meant sticking a 30-centimetre-long silicon tube up my willie four times a day so I could drain myself into a plastic bag, and sticking a finger up my arse every second day to dig out the shit. Sometimes both procedures drew blood. They always made me shudder with revulsion, but I had a powerful incentive to persevere. Autonomic dysreflexia it's called, the potentially fatal rise in blood pressure and excruciating headache that occurs if body waste isn't properly removed and backs up. I had a taste of it in hospital once, and that was enough.

Despite this regimen, there was no guarantee I wouldn't shit or piss my pants in public or wake up wallowing in it. Can you imagine living with that uncertainty? Can you imagine the shame and humiliation when it actually happened? Unbearable abominations that made me feel less than human. For me, it was no way to live.

There's more. I wept every morning when I saw myself in the mirror. I'd become a hunchback with a bloated pot belly above withered legs with muscles as soft and useless as marshmallow. It was an unbearable sight for someone who was once so grateful for being blessed with such an athletic and healthy body. Paraplegia meant that I also had to live with the constant possibility of pressure sores, ugly ulcers that can require months of hospitalization to cure. They're common. So are urinary tract infections and haemorrhoids. I suffer from both, and they also usually lead back to hospital sooner or later. I would rather die than return to hospital.

Then there was the pain in my shoulder. A damaged nerve meant that two muscles in my left shoulder didn't work and they wasted away, leaving the others to compensate and me with a pain that frequently made simple actions difficult. Then there were swollen ankles, which once meant sleeping with pillows under my feet so they could drain overnight. My chest became hypersensitive, which may sound like fun but meant that I felt like I was wearing an unbearably scratchy woollen jumper over bare skin. And after sitting in the chair for a few hours my bum, which shouldn't have had any sensation, felt like it was on fire. There were also tinea, crutch rot, headaches . . . The list of horrors was endless, and I haven't even mentioned some of the worst ones.

While at Moorong [Spinal Unit] I began to wake with pins and needles – loss of sensation – in my hands and arms. Sometimes it took hours to pass, and I began to fear losing what little I had left. That was unbearable. Tethering, nerves pinched by the scar tissue formed around the broken bones in my neck, I was told. The doctors talked about tests and surgery on my neck, wrists. Forget it. There was no way I'd return to hospital, let alone for such delicate, radical and debilitating surgery.

All my many pleasures had been stripped from me and replaced by a hellish living nightmare. The mere sight of someone standing up, a child skipping, a bicyclist's flexing leg muscles, were enough to reduce me to tears. Everything I saw and did was a stinging reminder of my condition and I cried constantly, even behind the jokes and smiles. I was so tired of crying. I never imagined that anyone could hurt so bad and cry so much. I guarantee that anybody who thinks it can't have been too bad would change their mind if they lived in my body for a day.

People kill animals to put them out of their misery if they're suffering even a tiny part of what I had to put up with, but I was never given the choice of a dignified death and I was very bitter about that. I could accept that accidents happen and rarely asked 'why me?', but I felt that the legislature's and the medical profession's attitude of life at any cost was an inhumane presumption that amounted to arrogance. And what of the dollar cost? My enforced recovery and rehabilitation cost taxpayers at least $150 000 by my rough count, money that wouldn't have been wasted had anybody bothered to ask me how I felt about the whole thing and what I'd like to do.

I had one good reason for living, of course, and her name is Lee-Ann, the best thing that ever happened to me. Wonderful Lee-Ann, without whom I would have gone insane long before now. But I wept whenever I thought of us together. What future could we have? No matter how hard I worked and how much I achieved, she would inevitably be a nursemaid in a million different ways, and I hated that, no matter that she so willingly and lovingly assumed the burden.

Nor would I condemn her to spend her nights sleeping with a sexless wooden lump twitching with spasm. That's right, sexless – impotent. Stripped of my sexuality, I felt that I'd lost part of my essence, the very core of my masculinity. I was even denied the sensual pleasure of embrace, because from the chest down I couldn't feel warmth, didn't even know if someone was touching me. I love Lee-Ann, but she deserves better than the pointless life I could offer, and I believe that I'm giving her another chance at happiness no matter how much pain I cause in the short term. Someone so desirable – open, honest, natural, loyal, with a great sense of humour and a figure the desire of men and envy of women – has a better chance than most of finding the happiness she deserves, and I hope with all my heart she finds it.

I had other reasons for living, of course – my family and friends. I remember, many years ago, lying on the verandah roof of a colonial mansion in the mountains of northern Burma. A shooting star streaked through the clear night sky and I made a wish. I wished for health, wealth and happiness for all those I loved and cared about. I repeated that wish several times in the following years and was enormously gratified to gradually see it come to pass for most of my family and friends. I'm not suggesting that my wishes had anything to do with their various successes – that was largely the result of their own efforts and the occasional dash of good fortune. But after my accident, even the joy I derived from seeing the happiness of those I cared about went sour for me. Seeing others get on with their lives, doing what I no longer could, was terribly distressing for me. I couldn't live my life vicariously through other people's satisfactions and achievements. I was a self-centred person and I'd always done what I wanted, had my own reasons for living.

Mum and Dad, you often said that you didn't care what I did as long as I was happy. I expect that many of my friends felt the same way. Well, I was terminally, unbearably unhappy with no way out – except death. I know others have come to terms with paraplegia, or even quadriplegia, and managed to lead successful, apparently normal and happy lives. I've met and been encouraged by some of them. I tips me hat to them, for they have done what I cannot. Then again, perhaps I have done what they could not. Four attempts taught me that it takes an enormous amount of courage to commit suicide. Unfortunately, I didn't find the examples of others in my position motivating or inspirational. For me, life as a para was so far from the minimum I considered acceptable that it just didn't matter. It's quality of life, not quantity, that's important.

It's a challenge, many of you said. Bullshit. My life was just a miserable existence, an awful parody of normalcy. What's a challenge without some reward to make it worthwhile?

Despite that, I gave it a go. I worked hard – harder than I ever have at anything – to try and rebuild my life. I tried picking up the threads and doing whatever I was still capable of. I went out to shops, theatres and restaurants, even a concert. I learnt to drive again, and worked. I hated every second of it with a passion I'd never felt before. What good is a picnic when you can't play with the kids and dogs and throw a frisbee? What's the point of going to a gig if you can't dance when the music grips you? I used to be a player, not a spectator, and my new existence (life seems too strong a word) was painful, frustrating and completely unsatisfying.

At least you can still work, some said. Great. I liked my job, the caring, talented and generous people I worked with and especially where we worked. But it was still just a job, and as you all know, I worked to live, not lived to work. Work was never a reason for living for me. And what of the future? Where would I go, what would I do? There's no future for a wheelchair-bound journalist, not one with my interests anyway. I'd never be able to do any of the things, like travel and adventure, that drew me to journalism in the first place and ultimately made the long office hours worthwhile.

I accepted death – embraced it eagerly, in fact, after so many months of the nightmare – without fear or regret. I had a full, rewarding and successful life by any measure, and in my last weeks I couldn't think of a single thing I'd always wanted to do but hadn't yet done. Well, actually, I guess I can think of a few things, but they don't amount to much. I'd always wanted to ride a Harley or drive a convertible Porsche, and I would have loved to have been 'stoked in the green room' – ridden a tube. Surfing would definitely have been the next sport I would have taken up. I've got a pretty good idea of the buzz it offers, and I think I would have liked it. Anyway, death is the last great adventure, and I was ready for it. I wasn't religious – how could anyone believe in a just, compassionate and almighty God after seeing and experiencing what I have? – but I felt quietly confident that whatever lay beyond had to be something more, something better, if anything.

I had one enormous regret, of course. I didn't want to hurt anyone the way I know I have.

I wish it didn't have to be this way. I didn't want to make those I love suffer, and the knowledge that I would bring awful grief to those I least wanted to hurt in the world compounded my own misery unbelievably. I'm so sorry. I hope you can find it in your hearts to forgive me. I wish you could see death as I did, as a release, something to celebrate, and be happy for me. I would rather have thrown a raging party and simply have disappeared at dawn with your blessings and understanding. Of course, it could never have happened that way. At any rate, I thank you all for making my last months as happy as they were, for your optimism and support, for the rays of light with which you pierced my gloom. My condition was permanent; I can only hope your grief fades quickly with the healing passage of time.

Chris Hill
10 February 1993

Statement

I have decided to take my own life for reasons detailed in the accompanying note. It is a fully considered decision made in a normal, rational state of mind and I have not been influenced or assisted by anyone else. Suicide is not a crime and I have the right not to be handled or treated against my will, so I absolutely forbid anyone to resuscitate or interfere with me while I continue to live, unless it is to end my suffering. Anyone who disregards this notice will be committing a civil and criminal offence against me.

In the event that I do not die, I wish to be placed under the care of Dr George Quittner at Mosman Hospital.

Chris Hill

37

When Self-Determination Runs Amok

Daniel Callahan

The euthanasia debate is not just another moral debate, one in a long list of arguments in our pluralistic society. It is profoundly emblematic of three important turning points in Western thought. The first is that of the legitimate conditions under which one person can kill another. The acceptance of voluntary active euthanasia would morally sanction what can only be called "consenting adult killing." By that term I mean the killing of one person by another in the name of their mutual right to be killer and killed if they freely agree to play those roles. This turn flies in the face of a long-standing effort to limit the circumstances under which one person can take the life of another, from efforts to control the free flow of guns and arms, to abolish capital punishment, and to more tightly control warfare. Euthanasia would add a whole new category of killing to a society that already has too many excuses to indulge itself in that way.

The second turning point lies in the meaning and limits of self-determination. The acceptance of euthanasia would sanction a view of autonomy holding that individuals may, in the name of their own private, idiosyncratic view of the good life, call upon others, including such institutions as medicine, to help them pursue that life, even at the risk of harm to the common good. This works against the idea that the meaning and scope of our own right to lead our own lives must be conditioned by, and be compatible with, the good of the community, which is more than an aggregate of self-directing individuals.

From *Hastings Center Report*, vol. 22, no. 2 (March–April 1992), pp. 52–5. Reprinted with permission.

The third turning point is to be found in the claim being made upon medicine: it should be prepared to make its skills available to individuals to help them achieve their private vision of the good life. This puts medicine in the business of promoting the individualistic pursuit of general human happiness and well-being. It would overturn the traditional belief that medicine should limit its domain to promoting and preserving human health, redirecting it instead to the relief of that suffering which stems from life itself, not merely from a sick body.

I believe that, at each of these three turning points, proponents of euthanasia push us in the wrong direction. Arguments in favor of euthanasia fall into four general categories, which I will take up in turn: (1) the moral claim of individual self-determination and well-being; (2) the moral irrelevance of the difference between killing and allowing to die; (3) the supposed paucity of evidence to show likely harmful consequences of legalized euthanasia; and (4) the compatibility of euthanasia and medical practice.

Self-Determination

Central to most arguments for euthanasia is the principle of self-determination. People are presumed to have an interest in deciding for themselves, according to their own beliefs about what makes life good, how they will conduct their lives. That is an important value, but the question in the euthanasia context is, What does it mean and how far should it extend? If it were a question of suicide, where a person takes her own life without assistance from another, that principle might be pertinent, at least for debate. But euthanasia is not that limited a matter. The self-determination in that case can only be effected by the moral and physical assistance of another. Euthanasia is thus no longer a matter only of self-determination, but of a mutual, social decision between two people, the one to be killed and the other to do the killing.

How are we to make the moral move from my right of self-determination to some doctor's right to kill me – from *my* right to *his* right? Where does the doctor's moral warrant to kill come from? Ought doctors to be able to kill anyone they want as long as permission is given by competent persons? Is our right to life just like a piece of property, to be given away or alienated if the price (happiness, relief of suffering) is right? And then to be destroyed with our permission once alienated?

In answer to all those questions, I will say this: I have yet to hear a plausible argument why it should be permissible for us to put this kind of power in the hands of another, whether a doctor or anyone else. The idea that we can waive our right to life, and then give to another the power to take that life, requires a justification yet to be provided by anyone.

Slavery was long ago outlawed on the ground that one person should not have the right to own another, even with the other's permission. Why? Because it is a fundamental moral wrong for one person to give over his life and fate to another, whatever the good consequences, and no less a wrong for another person to have that kind of total, final power. Like slavery, dueling was long ago banned on similar grounds: even free, competent individuals should not have the power to kill each other, whatever their motives, whatever the circumstances. Consenting adult killing, like consenting adult slavery or degradation, is a strange route to human dignity.

There is another problem as well. If doctors, once sanctioned to carry out euthanasia, are to be themselves responsible moral agents – not simply hired hands with lethal injections at the ready – then they must have their own *independent* moral grounds to kill those who request such services. What do I mean? As those who favor euthanasia are quick to point out, some people want it because their life has become so burdensome it no longer seems worth living.

The doctor will have a difficulty at this point. The degree and intensity to which people suffer from their diseases and their dying, and whether they find life more of a burden than a benefit, has very little directly to do with the nature or extent of their actual physical condition. Three people can have the same condition, but only one will find the suffering unbearable. People suffer, but suffering is as much a function of the values of individuals as it is of the physical causes of that suffering. Inevitably in those circumstances, the doctor will in effect be treating the patient's values. To be responsible, the doctor would have to share those values. The doctor would have to decide, on her own, whether the patient's life was "no longer worth living."

But how could a doctor possibly know that or make such a judgement? Just because the patient said so? I raise this question because, while in Holland at a euthanasia conference, the doctors present agreed that there is no objective way of measuring or judging the claims of patients that their suffering is unbearable. And if it is difficult to measure suffering, how much more difficult to determine the value of a patient's statement that her life is not worth living?

However one might want to answer such questions, the very need to ask them, to inquire into the physician's responsibility and grounds for medical and moral judgement, points out the social nature of the decision. Euthanasia is not a private matter of self-determination. It is an act that requires two people to make it possible, and a complicit society to make it acceptable.

Killing and Allowing to Die

Against common opinion, the argument is sometimes made that there is no moral difference between stopping life-sustaining treatment and more active forms of killing, such as lethal injection. Instead I would contend that the notion that there is no morally significant difference between omission and commission is just wrong. Consider in its broad implications what the eradication of the distinction implies: that death from disease has been banished, leaving only the actions of physicians in terminating treatment as the cause of death. Biology, which used to bring about death, has apparently been displaced by human agency. Doctors have finally, I suppose, thus genuinely become gods, now doing what nature and the deities once did.

What is the mistake here? It lies in confusing causality and culpability, and in failing to note the way in which human societies have overlaid natural causes with moral rules and interpretations. Causality (by which I mean the direct physical causes of death) and culpability (by which I mean our attribution of moral responsibility to human actions) are confused under three circumstances.

They are confused, first, when the action of a physician in stopping treatment of a patient with an underlying lethal disease is construed as *causing* death. On the contrary, the physician's omission can only bring about death on the condition that the patient's disease will kill him in the absence of treatment. We may hold the physician morally responsible for the death, if we have morally judged such actions wrongful omissions. But it confuses reality and moral judgement to see an omitted action as having the same causal status as one that directly kills. A lethal injection will kill both a healthy person and a sick person. A physician's omitted treatment will have no effect on a healthy person. Turn off the machine on me, a healthy person, and nothing will happen. It will only, in contrast, bring the life of a sick person to an end because of an underlying fatal disease.

Causality and culpability are confused, second, when we fail to note that judgements of moral responsibility and culpability are human constructs. By that I mean that we human beings, after moral reflection, have decided to call some actions right or wrong, and to devise moral rules to deal with them. When physicians could do nothing to stop death, they were not held responsible for it. When, with medical progress, they began to have some power over death – but only its timing and circumstances, not its ultimate inevitability – moral rules were devised to set forth their obligations. Natural causes of death were not thereby banished. They were, instead, overlaid with a medical ethics designed to determine moral culpability in deploying medical power.

To confuse the judgements of this ethics with the physical causes of death – which is the connotation of the word *kill* – is to confuse nature and human action. People will, one way or another, die of some disease; death will have dominion over all of us. To say that a doctor "kills" a patient by allowing this to happen should only be understood as a moral judgement about the licitness of his omission, nothing more. We can, as a fashion of speech only, talk about a doctor *killing* a patient by omitting treatment he should have provided. It is a fashion of speech precisely because it is the underlying disease that brings death when treatment is omitted; that is its cause, not the physician's omission. It is a misuse of the word *killing* to use it when a doctor stops a treatment he believes will no longer benefit the patient – when, that is, he steps aside to allow an eventually inevitable death to occur now rather than later. The only deaths that human beings invented are those that come from direct killing – when, with a lethal injection, we both cause death and are morally responsible for it. In the case of omissions, we do not cause death even if we may be judged morally responsible for it.

This difference between causality and culpability also helps us see why a doctor who has omitted a treatment he should have provided has "killed" that patient while another doctor – performing precisely the same act of omission on another patient in different circumstances – does not kill her, but only allows her to die. The difference is that we have come, by moral convention and conviction, to classify unauthorized or illegitimate omissions as acts of "killing." We call them "killing" in the expanded sense of the term: a culpable action that permits the real cause of death, the underlying disease, to proceed to its lethal conclusion. By contrast, the doctor who, at the patient's request, omits or terminates unwanted treatment does not kill at all. Her underlying disease, not his action, is the physical cause of death; and we have agreed to consider actions of that kind to be morally licit. He thus can truly be said to have "allowed" her to die.

If we fail to maintain the distinction between killing and allowing to die, moreover, there are some disturbing possibilities. The first would be to confirm many physicians in their already too-powerful belief that, when patients die or when physicians stop treatment because of the futility of continuing it, they are somehow both morally and physically responsible for the deaths that follow. That notion needs to be abolished, not strengthened. It needlessly and wrongly burdens the physician, to whom should not be attributed the powers of the gods. The second possibility would be that, in every case where a doctor judges medical treatment no longer effective in prolonging life, a quick and direct killing of the patient would be seen as the next, most reasonable step, on grounds of both humaneness and economics. I do not see how that logic could easily be rejected.

Calculating the Consequences

When concerns about the adverse social consequences of permitting euthanasia are raised, its advocates tend to dismiss them as unfounded and overly speculative. On the contrary, recent data about the Dutch experience suggests that such concerns are right on target. From my own discussions in Holland, and from articles on that subject, I believe we can now fully see most of the *likely* consequences of legal euthanasia.

Three consequences seem almost certain, in this or any other country: the inevitability of some abuse of the law; the difficulty of precisely writing, and then enforcing, the law; and the inherent slipperiness of the moral reasons for legalizing euthanasia in the first place.

Why is abuse inevitable? One reason is that almost all laws on delicate, controversial matters are to some extent abused. This happens because not everyone will agree with the law as written and will bend it, or ignore it, if they can get away with it. From explicit admissions to me by Dutch proponents of euthanasia, and from the corroborating information provided by the Remmelink Report and the outside studies of Carlos Gomez and John Keown, I am convinced that in the Netherlands there are a substantial number of cases of nonvoluntary euthanasia, that is, euthanasia undertaken without the explicit permission of the person being killed. The other reason abuse is inevitable is that the law is likely to have a low enforcement priority in the criminal justice system. Like other laws of similar status, unless there is an unrelenting and harsh willingness to pursue abuse, violations will ordinarily be tolerated. The worst thing to me about my experience in Holland was the casual, seemingly indifferent attitude toward abuse. I think that would happen everywhere.

Why would it be hard to precisely write, and then enforce, the law? The Dutch speak about the requirement of "unbearable" suffering, but admit that such a term is just about indefinable, a highly subjective matter admitting of no objective standards. A requirement for outside opinion is nice, but it is easy to find complaisant colleagues. A requirement that a medical condition be "terminal" will run aground on the notorious difficulties of knowing when an illness is actually terminal.

Apart from those technical problems there is a more profound worry. I see no way, even in principle, to write or enforce a meaningful law that can guarantee effective procedural safeguards. The reason is obvious yet almost always overlooked. The euthanasia transaction will ordinarily take place within the boundaries of the private and confidential doctor–patient relationship. No one can possibly know what takes place in that context unless the doctor chooses to reveal it. In Holland, less than 10 percent of the physicians report their acts of euthanasia and do so with almost complete legal impunity. There is no reason why the situation should be any better elsewhere. Doctors will have their own reasons for keeping euthanasia secret, and some patients will have no less a motive for wanting it concealed.

I would mention, finally, that the moral logic of the motives for euthanasia contain within them the ingredients of abuse. The two standard motives for euthanasia and assisted suicide are said to be our right of self-determination, and our claim upon the mercy of others, especially doctors, to relieve our suffering. These two motives are typically spliced together and presented as a single justification. Yet if they are considered independently – and there is no inherent reason why they must be linked – they reveal serious problems. It is said that a competent, adult person should have a right to euthanasia for the relief of suffering. But why must the person be suffering? Does not that stipulation already compromise the principle of self-determination? How can self-determination have any limits? Whatever the person's motives may be, why are they not sufficient?

Consider next the person who is suffering but not competent, who is perhaps demented or mentally retarded. The standard argument would deny euthanasia to that person. But why? If a person is suffering but not competent, then it would seem grossly unfair to deny relief solely on the grounds of incompetence. Are the incompetent less entitled to relief from suffering than the competent? Will it only be affluent, middle-class people, mentally fit and savvy about working the medical system, who can qualify? Do the incompetent suffer less because of their incompetence?

Considered from these angles, there are no good moral reasons to limit euthanasia once the principle of taking life for that purpose has been legitimated. If we really believe in self-determination, then any competent person should have a right to be killed by a doctor for any reason that suits him. If we believe in the relief of suffering, then it seems cruel and capricious to deny it to the incompetent. There is, in short, no reasonable or logical stopping point once the turn has been made down the road to euthanasia, which could soon turn into a convenient and commodious expressway.

Euthanasia and Medical Practice

A fourth kind of argument one often hears both in the Netherlands and in this country is that euthanasia and assisted suicide are perfectly compatible with the aims of medicine. I would note at the very outset that a physician who participates in another person's suicide already abuses medicine. Apart from depression (the main statistical cause of suicide), people commit suicide because they find life empty, oppressive, or meaningless. Their judgement is a judgement about the value of continued life, not only about health (even if they are sick). Are doctors now to be given the right to make judgements about the kinds of life worth living and to give their blessing to suicide for those they judge wanting? What conceivable competence, technical or moral, could doctors claim to play such a role? Are we to medicalize suicide, turning judgements about its worth and value into one more clinical issue? Yes, those are rhetorical questions.

Yet they bring us to the core of the problem of euthanasia and medicine. The great temptation of modern medicine, not always resisted, is to move beyond the promotion and preservation of health into the boundless realm of general human happiness and well-being. The root problem of illness and mortality is both medical and philosophical or religious. "Why must I die?" can be asked as a technical, biological question or as a question about the meaning of life. When medicine tries to respond to the latter, which it is always under pressure to do, it moves beyond its proper role.

It is not medicine's place to lift from us the burden of that suffering which turns on the meaning we assign to the decay of the body and its eventual death. It is not medicine's place to determine when lives are not worth living or when the burden of life is too great to be borne. Doctors have no conceivable way of evaluating such claims on the part of patients, and they should have no right to act in response to them. Medicine should try to relieve human suffering, but only that suffering which is brought on by illness and dying as biological phenomena, not that suffering which comes from anguish or despair at the human condition.

Doctors ought to relieve those forms of suffering that medically accompany serious illness and the threat of death. They should relieve pain, do what they can to allay anxiety and uncertainty, and be a comforting presence. As sensitive human beings, doctors should be prepared to respond to patients who ask why they must die, or die in pain. But here the doctor and the patient are at the same level. The doctor may have no better an answer to those old questions than anyone else; and certainly no special insight from his training as a physician. It would be terrible for physicians to forget this, and to think that in a swift, lethal injection, medicine has found its own answer to the riddle of life. It would be a false answer, given by the wrong people. It would be no less a false answer for patients. They should neither ask medicine to put its own vocation at risk to serve their private interests, nor think that the answer to suffering is to be killed by another. The problem is precisely that, too often in human history, killing has seemed the quick, efficient way to put aside that which burdens us. It rarely helps, and too often simply adds to one evil still another. That is what I believe euthanasia would accomplish. It is self-determination run amok.

38

Listening and Helping to Die: The Dutch Way

Pieter Admiraal

I have been a doctor for nearly forty years and am now Senior Anaesthetist at the Reinier de Graaf Gasthuis, a large 800-bed general hospital in the Dutch city of Delft. My role is not only that of a traditional anaesthetist; since the late 1960s, I have also specialized in palliative care, that is, in pain and symptom control for the incurably ill and dying and have been a member of the hospital's Terminal Care Team since it was officially set up in 1973.

As a member of that team, I also practise active voluntary euthanasia – openly and unashamedly. I practise it openly because I am fortunate to live in a country that allows doctors to do so. And I practise it unashamedly because I regard it as sometimes morally right, as not only compatible with the properly understood duties and responsibilities of a doctor, but as an act sometimes *required* by them. To fail to practise voluntary euthanasia under some circumstances is to fail the patient.

Here I want to recount the cases of two patients who requested active help in dying – Carla and Esther. Carla suffered from terminal cancer; Esther from the incurable and progressively debilitating disease, multiple sclerosis.[1]

Carla[2] was 47 years old. She was married to Henk, and the couple had four teenage children. Late in 1988, Carla noticed a painful swelling in her lower abdomen and went to her family doctor. He referred her to a gynaecologist at the Delft hospital, where I practise.

From Helga Kuhse (ed.), *Willing to Listen, Wanting to Die* (Ringwood, Victoria: Penguin Books, 1994), pp. 230–45. Reprinted with permission.

A subsequent operation revealed that the pain had been caused by a large malignant tumour on one of Carla's ovaries. By the time the operation was performed, the tumour had already grown so large that it could not be totally removed.

Carla underwent chemotherapy and by June her condition had greatly improved. She felt relatively well until March 1990, when it was found that the tumour had regrown. Chemotherapy was tried once more, but this time it was in vain.

By the middle of the year, Carla's pain had increased to such an extent that her family doctor had to prescribe opioids (morphine-like drugs). Her condition deteriorated quickly and it was not long before Carla had to be readmitted to our hospital. This is when I saw her for the first time in my role as palliative care specialist.

I told Carla that I would almost certainly be able to relieve her pain. This proved correct. A needle placed under her skin delivered a continuous infusion of morphine, and after two days Carla's pain was well controlled. She was, of course, greatly relieved. But, like many patients in her situation, she was afraid that the pain would steadily get worse and that it would, in the end, not be possible to control it.

I visited Carla at least once a day. During one of those visits, she raised the question of euthanasia: would she be helped to die when the stage had been reached where she found her condition unbearable? Her husband, Henk, was visibly upset by his wife's request. Whilst he understood that there was ultimately nothing more that could be done to save his wife's life, he had not as yet realized that he would lose her so soon. I explained to Carla that doctors at this hospital were always willing to listen, and that we did not regard the question of voluntary euthanasia as a taboo subject. But, I also pointed out to her, the final decision could not be made unilaterally by a patient or her doctor. It had to be agreed to by a team consisting of two doctors, a nurse, and one of the hospital's spiritual caregivers – the Roman Catholic chaplain, the Protestant chaplain, or the Humanist counsellor.

On the next day, Carla was already discussing the question of euthanasia with the hospital's Roman Catholic chaplain, who was sympathetic to her request.

From then on, her condition deteriorated quickly. She was vomiting constantly. For psychological reasons, Carla was still taking fluids by mouth, even though this would almost immediately lead to vomiting. To avoid this incessant vomiting, it became necessary to put a tube through her nose into her stomach. This way, we could constantly evacuate her stomach. To prevent thirst, Carla received an infusion of a saline solution. When the question arose whether she should also be fed intravenously, Carla decided against this, not wanting to prolong her life unnecessarily.

Carla lost a lot of weight and became extremely weak, unable even to move around in her bed. This made it very difficult for the nurses to prevent bedsores. While Carla lost weight, the tumour continued to grow and was soon obstructing the blood flow in her legs, causing them to swell painfully.

Right from the time of her admission to the hospital, Carla had had a room of her own. This meant that her family could visit her freely, and it became customary for Henk and one of the children to sleep in the same room. She was also frequently visited by her family doctor and his wife.

Throughout her illness, Carla remained completely alert. She was a courageous woman. Not only did she bear her own physical deterioration bravely, she also provided emotional support for her family. She was sustained by a strong Catholic faith, and was convinced that she would live on in heaven.

When the time of her death seemed near, the Catholic chaplain administered the Last Sacraments. Soon after, Carla requested us – not unexpectedly – to end her suffering. 'God could not have wanted this,' she said. By this time, her husband had also come to accept her wish to die. He had realized that it would be selfish of him not to let his wife go.

A family meeting was called. The eldest son still clung to the hope that his mother might get better and found it difficult to accept her decision. However, after Carla had talked to him privately, he too agreed with her decision.

Similarly the nurses, who had cared for Carla on a daily basis: they knew her circumstances well and respected Carla's wish to die. Then the gynaecologist, the Roman Catholic chaplain and I discussed the case, and were all of the opinion that the patient's wish should be respected.

In situations such as these, we always hesitate. A patient's request for euthanasia may, after all, be a cry for help – prompted perhaps by shortcomings in the delivery of palliative care. This was not true in Carla's case. She had received the best of care, and there was nothing more that could be done to alleviate her suffering.

Carla was visited once more by the family doctor and his wife. They had come to say farewell. Then Carla and I met with the family. It was arranged that euthanasia would be performed on the following day, and Carla signed the relevant consent form.

When the day had come, Carla once again confirmed her wish to die. Her husband, Henk, two of Carla's sisters, her parish priest, and two of the children were by her side when I administered the drugs which would give her the benign death she desired. Carla fell asleep with a smile on her face. She died eight minutes later, on 6 August 1990.

There are those who will be shocked by the case of Carla. They will be shocked because I took deliberate steps to end Carla's life. By injecting a lethal drug, they will say, I killed Carla – and killing a patient is always morally wrong. The fact that Carla was terminally ill, was suffering greatly, and desperately wanted to die, those critics might say, does not make the action morally right.

I take a contrary view: I believe it was morally proper to help Carla die in the way we did. We could have declined, of course, as some doctors do, firmly closing our ears to the patient's request for active help in dying, and Carla would have died, in a day or two, from 'natural causes'. Whilst this approach is the traditional one, I believe it has little to recommend itself from the medical or moral point of view.

As doctors we have two primary duties: to ensure the well-being of our patients, and to respect their autonomy. The first duty entails that we should seek to restore patients to health and, if we can't, that we should try to reduce their suffering. The second duty entails that we listen closely to, and respect, the wishes of our patients. Suffering, loss of control, and physical decline are subjective experiences, and nobody but the patient herself is in a position to decide when enough is enough. It would be quite improper for doctors or other health care professionals to impose their values and their understanding of pain or suffering on the patient.

Even societies which do not allow active voluntary euthanasia do grant patients the freedom to refuse medical treatment. They grant competent people the right to bring their lives to an end by requesting doctors to stop treatment, and doctors have a recognized legal duty to abide by the competent and fully informed patient's request. This is one way of ending life – sometimes referred to as 'passive voluntary euthanasia'. Here the doctor does not administer a lethal drug, but discontinues treatment and the patient will then die of so-called natural causes. Whilst people sometimes refer to these non-treatment decisions as 'passive euthanasia', I believe the term 'euthanasia' is quite misplaced here. 'Euthanasia' means 'a good death', or 'bringing about a good death'. Letting a patient die of her disease may be anything but a good death. The patient may die slowly and painfully, and in what she regards as an undignified manner.

The traditional view is that these 'passive' life-shortening acts are somehow morally better than the 'active' kind: that a doctor who respects a patient's desire to die by discontinuing life-support acts as a good doctor should; a doctor who 'actively' helps a patient like Carla to die, on the other hand, acts morally wrongly. Why?

There is now a large body of philosophical and theological literature on the moral distinction between so-called active and passive voluntary euthanasia. After having studied this sometimes rather convoluted debate, I have reached the conclusion that there is, in the end, no morally relevant difference between these two forms of euthanasia. In both cases, the doctor acts out of respect for the autonomy of the patient. In both cases life is shortened. In both cases, the doctor has performed an act which has led to the patient's death; and in both cases, the doctor must take responsibility for that action – regardless of whether this involves, say, turning off a respirator (supposedly an act of passive euthanasia), or the administration of a lethal injection. As Helga Kuhse has put it:

> Stripped of all other differences, what remains is . . . a difference that has no moral significance. In active euthanasia, the doctor initiates a course of events that will lead to the patient's death. In letting die [or passive euthanasia], the agent stands back and lets nature take her sometimes cruel course. Is letting die morally better than helping to die, or active euthanasia? I think not. Very often it is much worse.[3]

I agree. Very often passive euthanasia is morally worse than active euthanasia. It is morally worse in all those cases where we inflict on the patient a way of dying that he or she does not want, and finds unacceptable and undignified. In these cases we fail to respect the patient's autonomy; we fail to take seriously that patient's own evaluation of suffering and pain. In short, we fail to respect the patient as a self-determining person.

Fortunately, in most cases it is possible to make dying easier. Sometimes this may require the administration of opioids and sedatives in such high doses that life will be directly shortened by the medication. If this is the case, then it is even more difficult to detect any difference between this practice and active euthanasia: the patient's death is caused by the administration of a drug – just as it is in the case of active euthanasia.

I know what some people will say here. They will say that the doctor merely intended to relieve the patient's pain and that he or she did not intend to kill the patient. But to say this is once again an attempt to evade moral responsibility. Surely, doctors must be held responsible for the deaths they deliberately cause – irrespective of what they say their intentions are. Moreover, this traditional response also fails to take account of the reality of medical practice, where it is often very difficult to distinguish between the different intentions and motivations that lead doctors and patients to adopt one course of action rather than another.

Not many patients will, in the end, ask for active voluntary euthanasia.[4] In the majority of cases, it is possible to ease the dying process and to allow patients to die with dignity.

As I mentioned before, in our hospital in Delft a Terminal Care Team was officially set up in 1973. This team functions in accordance with widely accepted principles of palliative care. We always treat patients as persons, not as the carriers of symptoms or diseases. We recognize the importance of communication, and provide dying patients with an opportunity to discuss their fears of dying; we tell them about the kind of terminal care that can be offered, and we assure them that we will neither abandon them nor force medical treatment on them that they do not want.

It is sometimes suggested that one of the reasons why voluntary euthanasia has gained a foothold in the Netherlands is that palliative care is not very advanced in our country. This criticism is unjustified. While we have only two hospices, which cater specifically for those who are dying, we have integrated palliative care into the delivery of health care as a whole. Hospices in England, for example, cater for 25 per cent of dying patients. In our country, patients can receive excellent terminal care in either hospitals (40 per cent), nursing homes (10 per cent), or in their own homes (50 per cent).

Another misleading claim is that modern methods of pain control will obviate the need for active voluntary euthanasia: that patients will not ask for euthanasia if their pain is adequately controlled. This is an argument frequently voiced by opponents of voluntary euthanasia – both in the Netherlands and in other parts of the world.

Two comments need to be made on this. Firstly, it is true, great advances have been made regarding pain control. Nonetheless, it remains a sad medical fact that in some 5 per cent of cases pain cannot be controlled even with the most advanced techniques, and in some cases it can be controlled only through the continuous intravenous infusion of opioids and other drugs that will render the patient unconscious.

Secondly, pain is very seldom the sole reason why patients request euthanasia. A recent nationwide study has shown that patients ask for active euthanasia because of loss of strength and fatigue, loss of human dignity, and complete dependence. In only 5 per cent of all cases was pain the sole reason for the request.[5]

Even the best of palliative care cannot alleviate all suffering, cannot always make it bearable. Speaking about suffering in the wider sense, Dame Cicely Saunders, the founder of the modern palliative care movement and an opponent of active voluntary euthanasia, agrees: 'Sometimes unrealistic fears can be explained and eased, but a good deal of suffering has to be lived through. The very pain itself may lead to a resolution or a new vision, as came to Job.'[6] These words reflect Dame Cicely's Christian approach to life, death and suffering. I respect that view, but as a doctor I must also respect the views of patients who take a radically different approach.

Of course, we always hesitate if a patient asks for euthanasia. After all, a request for active euthanasia does not, as such, legitimate its implementation. As a first step, we will always investigate whether the patient has received adequate care and whether there is something else that can be done. But when all is said and done, we must face the fact that it is not possible to relieve all suffering. We cannot protect patients against total physical and psychological disintegration; we cannot protect some of our patients against complete loss of human dignity. We have learnt not to ignore those facts, but have come to accept that some of our patients, in spite of the best possible medical, nursing and spiritual care, will request euthanasia.

Palliative care is essential. It must always be an integral part of good medical care and voluntary euthanasia can never replace it. At our hospital and in our country we do, however, acknowledge the fact that good terminal care must incorporate at least the possibility of voluntary euthanasia. Even if a patient will never request it, the knowledge alone that we are willing to listen to requests for help in dying will alleviate much anxiety and fear, and will give many of those who are nearing the end of their lives peace of mind. And in those instances where we do perform active voluntary euthanasia, we do not regard it as separate from the delivery of terminal care, but rather as the last dignified act of terminal care.

Should active voluntary euthanasia be restricted to those who are terminally ill, that is, to those who are suffering from a disease such as cancer, likely to lead to death in a few days' time?

The notion of 'terminal illness' is slippery. In one sense of the term, we are all terminally ill. As human beings we are mortal and, one day, will have to die. Also, many life-threatening medical conditions will become 'terminal' only once we decide not to treat them. Patients who experience respiratory failure are in mortal danger, but to the extent that we are able to keep them alive with the help of a machine – for months or years perhaps – they are not terminally ill. These patients become 'terminally ill' only once the decision has been made to discontinue life-support.

This means that the notion of terminal illness cannot be employed, in a straightforward way, to justify medical end-of-life decisions. Rather, it becomes necessary to reflect on the values on which medical end-of-life decisions ought to be based. As I said before, I take it that doctors should, on the one hand, seek to maximize the patient's welfare; but that they must, on the other, respect the patient's autonomy. To respect the patient's autonomy presupposes that the patient's own evaluation of her medical situation ought to be the determinative one. The doctor might think that life with a certain condition is, or ought to be, bearable; but to the extent that the properly counselled and supported patient takes a different view, it is the patient's view which must ultimately be the determinative one.

The case of Esther will illustrate the point.

In June, 1983 I was asked to see Esther, a young patient in a denominational nursing home, who was asking for active euthanasia. Esther was suffering from multiple sclerosis, a disease of the nervous system. This disease is usually progressive and, in due course, will often completely paralyse the patient.

When I met Esther, she was sitting in an electric wheelchair, unable to walk or move on her own. She could only use her left hand to drive the wheelchair, with the assistance of a nurse. Her breathing was laboured, and she could only speak in short sentences, and with great effort. After an hour, she was completely exhausted.

She told me that she had experienced the first neurological symptoms in 1976. In 1981 she had been admitted to the nursing home, and by the beginning of 1983 she was almost completely paralysed. She had one young daughter and was divorced.

Esther had carefully informed herself about the disease and had reached the conclusion that she would wish to die once she had become completely paralysed and was totally dependent on the care of others. She knew that she would, at some stage, no longer be able to eat by herself; she would not even be able to swallow the food that somebody else had placed in her mouth. If she was not to starve to death, she would need to be fed by way of a tube leading directly into her stomach. But, Esther had decided, she would never accept tube feeding.

In 1982 Esther executed a so-called 'living will', indicating that she did not wish to be kept alive if she were no longer able to communicate her wishes. She also wrote farewell letters to her daughter, members of her family and her friends. Soon after, she had discussed with the director of the nursing home her desire to die. But, Esther said, she was told that there was nothing that could be done for her, 'for religous reasons'.

Unable to obtain help, Esther began to think about suicide; she contemplated the idea of hurling herself and her wheelchair down the stairs, but then dismissed the idea because she was not sure that it would have the desired result. Finally, a friend of hers had got in touch with me.

I visited Esther in the nursing home. When I asked her why she wanted to die, she answered:

> Would you like to live under these circumstances? I can't do anything I am completely dependent on others. I have no future, no outlook, and I'm very afraid that I will suffocate because of the aspiration of food. I've even got to call somebody if there's a fly on my face. This is senseless and cruel, and I want to die as soon as possible.

I asked her about her daughter. Would she not wish to live for the sake of her child. 'My child,' she answered, 'I've not held her in my arms for years; she never had a real mother who could walk with her in the park, feeding ducks and doing similar things ... I can't even buy a present for her; I can't educate her ... I have written a farewell letter to her, which she can read after my death, explaining why I want to die.'

Her doctor confirmed that Esther had difficulties swallowing and that there was a real danger that food would be lodged in her windpipe. This could happen at any time. The result could be pneumonia, but it might also be suffocation. It had been suggested that a feeding tube be put in place, but Esther had refused.

I asked Esther whether she was willing to stop eating, to prove her desire to die was sincere. She indicated that she was willing to do this, but then said that she thought it was very cruel of me to force her to do this. 'Why should I have to suffer first, before you help me die?'

I apologized and explained that it was necessary for me to be absolutely certain that her wish to die was sincere.

When Esther had left the room, staff of the nursing home confirmed that she had consistently expressed the desire to die and that there was no doubt that she fully understood her circumstances. But, I was told, it was out of the question that any life-shortening act would be performed on the premises.

Instead, Esther was visited by the staff psychologist. But, as soon as he mentioned green pastures, blue skies and butterflies, Esther asked him to leave her room.

After extensive consultation with Esther, her family and friends, it was decided that she would be admitted to our hospital in Delft. Esther was much relieved and, after admission, told us how happy she was that she now had the assurance that she would be helped to die.

A long meeting took place between Esther's parents, some of her friends, our head nurse, the hospital's Roman Catholic chaplain and myself. We subsequently told Esther how difficult it was for us to reach a decision: on the one hand, we respected her wish to die; on the other we were all hesitating. Since she had entered the hospital, she appeared happy and it seemed incongruous to us that she wished her life to end. We even suggested that she should consider admittance to a local nursing home in Delft, where she could stay until she felt that she did not want to go on.

Esther smiled and said: 'This is not what you have promised me – to go to another nursing home and wait for aspiration. That would only prolong my suffering. I can understand that you are hesitating, but you are not aware of what is going on in my mind.'

We were all very impressed by her honest way of speaking and her absolute self-assurance. Nonetheless, we felt it important to seek further advice and consulted Dr Kuitert, a well-known ethicist and theologian from the University of Amsterdam. He took the view that Esther's desire to die was reasonable under the circumstances, and that we should seriously consider honouring her request.

The members of the health care team, including the Roman Catholic chaplain, thought long and hard about the matter, and during the next four days each of us had long and intimate discussions with Esther. In the end, we unanimously agreed that we should honour her wish and that we would end her life.

Esther's parents and best friends came to say goodbye, and to be with her when she died. Esther told us this was the happiest day in her life since she had become ill; she could hardly wait for me to start the infusion. It was an emotional moment. We all cried. We were sad that the life of this unique person had come to an end; but we were glad that we had released her from a life that she found unbearable.

I was subsequently prosecuted for having performed an unlawful act of voluntary euthanasia – presumably because the patient had not been in the terminal phase of her illness. At the hearing, Dr Kuitert gave evidence to the effect that he believed my action was morally acceptable, justified and humane; and a second witness, the Secretary of the Dutch Medical Association, declared that my handling of the case was an example of good medical care, as accepted by the Association. The prosecution was dropped.

When it was all over, I received a letter from the management of my hospital, which congratulated me on the 'clear and satisfying verdict', and the Roman Catholic chaplain wrote: 'The verdict of the court is so unequivocally and pleasingly positive that I want to congratulate you. It is good that the question of good medical care has been answered in all clearness along this unexpected line.'

The outcome of this court case confirms that it is legally permissible for doctors to practise active voluntary euthanasia not only in situations of terminal illness, but also when a patient who is not terminally ill seeks release from a medical condition that imposes unrelievable and unbearable suffering.

Opponents of active voluntary euthanasia will regard this development as yet another step on the so-called 'slippery slope', which will ultimately lead Dutch society to some terrible disaster, where patients will be killed against their will.

I do not accept that there is a slippery slope. A clear moral and legal boundary can be drawn around the notion of consent. This notion of consent, based on respect for the patient's autonomy, is the centrepiece and backbone of the legal framework governing voluntary euthanasia in the Netherlands. Over the last ten years or so, it has served us well. No patient – no matter how ill – will have his or her life cut short, unless there is an explicit request. Active voluntary euthanasia is but one more way of delivering humane medical care.[7]

The former Bishop of Durham, Lord Jenkins, recently said that in his opinion voluntary euthanasia, under agreed conditions and surrounded by safeguards, could be part of proper medical care. In these circumstances, he felt, there was no danger of inserting a wedge to split up the curing and caring vocation of doctors, nor of encouraging doctors or relatives to press for the early removal of difficult patients. He said, 'We are working at the next stage of humanizing our mutual care for one another from conception to death.'[8]

In the Netherlands, there is after all these years no evidence of a slippery slope, or of a disturbed relationship between doctors and patients. On the contrary, the acceptance of active voluntary euthanasia has improved the relationship. Patients know that they can count on their doctors when they need them most: when, because of terminal or incurable illness they are vulnerable, and in danger of being denied the basic human right to say: 'Enough is enough. I want to die with my dignity intact. Please help me.'

Notes

1 The names in these cases are fictitious, to protect the privacy of those involved.

2 A description of this case has previously been published in Pieter V. Admiraal: 'A Physician's Responsibility to Help a Patient Die', in Robert I. Misbin (ed.), *Euthanasia: The Good of the Patient, the Good of Society* (Frederic, MD: University Publishing Group, 1992), pp. 77–8.

3 Helga Kuhse, 'The Case for Active Voluntary Euthanasia', *Law, Medicine and Healthcare*, 14 (1987), 145–8.

4 See P. J. van der Maas et al., 'Euthanasia and other medical decisions concerning the end of life', *The Lancet*, 338 (14 Sept. 1991), 669–74.

5 Ibid.

6 C. S. Saunders, 'Spiritual Pain', *Journal of Palliative Care*, 4 (1988), 29–32.

7 Helga Kuhse, in the last chapter of *Willing to Listen, Wanting to Die* (1984), outlines the Dutch regulations governing the practice of active voluntary euthanasia. There is also another discussion of the so-called 'slippery slope' argument.

8 D. E. Jenkins: 'Why not choose death in the end?', *Care of the Critically Ill*, 7, no. 6 (1991), 6.

39

Is There a Duty to Die?

John Hardwig

Many people were outraged when Richard Lamm claimed that old people had a duty to die. Modern medicine and an individualistic culture have seduced many to feel that they have a right to health care and a right to live, despite the burdens and costs to our families and society. But in fact there are circumstances when we have a duty to die. As modern medicine continues to save more of us from acute illness, it also delivers more of us over to chronic illnesses, allowing us to survive far longer than we can take care of ourselves. It may be that our technological sophistication coupled with a commitment to our loved ones generates a fairly widespread duty to die.

When Richard Lamm made the statement that old people have a duty to die, it was generally shouted down or ridiculed. The whole idea is just too preposterous to entertain. Or too threatening. In fact, a fairly common argument against legalizing physician-assisted suicide is that if it were legal, some people might somehow get the idea that they have a duty to die. These people could only be the victims of twisted moral reasoning or vicious social pressure. It goes without saying that there is no duty to die.

But for me the question is real and very important. I feel strongly that I may very well some day have a duty to die. I do not believe that I am idiosyncratic, morbid, mentally ill, or morally perverse in thinking this. I think many of us will eventually face precisely this duty. But I am first of all concerned with my own duty. I write partly to clarify my own convictions and to prepare myself. Ending my life might be a very difficult thing for me to do.

From *Hastings Center Report*, vol. 27, no. 2 (1997), pp. 34–42. Reprinted with permission.

This notion of a duty to die raises all sorts of interesting theoretical and metaethical questions. I intend to try to avoid most of them because I hope my argument will be persuasive to those holding a wide variety of ethical views. Also, although the claim that there is a duty to die would ultimately require theoretical underpinning, the discussion needs to begin on the normative level. As is appropriate to my attempt to steer clear of theoretical commitments, I will use "duty," "obligation," and "responsibility" interchangeably, in a pretheoretical or preanalytic sense.[1]

Circumstances and a Duty to Die

Do many of us really believe that no one ever has a duty to die? I suspect not. I think most of us probably believe that there is such a duty, but it is very uncommon. Consider Captain Oates, a member of Captain Scott's expedition to the South Pole. Oates became too ill to continue. If the rest of the team stayed with him, they would all perish. After this had become clear, Oates left his tent one night, walked out into a raging blizzard, and was never seen again.[2] That may have been a heroic thing to do, but we might be able to agree that it was also no more than his duty. It would have been wrong for him to urge – or even to allow – the rest to stay and care for him.

This is a very unusual circumstance – a "lifeboat case" – and lifeboat cases make for bad ethics. But I expect that most of us would also agree that there have been cultures in which what we would call a duty to die has been fairly common. These are relatively poor, technologically simple, and especially nomadic cultures. In such societies, everyone knows that if you manage to live long enough, you will eventually become incapacitated. Then you will need to decide on a time to die. The old people in these societies regularly did precisely that. Their cultures prepared and supported them in doing so.

Those cultures could be dismissed as irrelevant to contemporary bioethics; their circumstances are so different from ours. But if that is our response, it is instructive. It suggests that we assume a duty to die is irrelevant to us because our wealth and technological sophistication have purchased exemption for us . . . except under very unusual circumstances like Captain Oates's.

But have wealth and technology really exempted us? Or are they, on the contrary, about to make a duty to die common again? We like to think of modern medicine as all triumph with no dark side. Our medicine saves many lives and enables most of us to live longer. That is wonderful, indeed. We are all glad to have access to this medicine. But our medicine also delivers most of us over to chronic illnesses and it enables many of us to survive longer than we can take care of ourselves, longer than we know what to do with ourselves, longer than we even are ourselves.

The costs – and these are not merely monetary – of prolonging our lives when we are no longer able to care for ourselves are often staggering. If further medical advances wipe out many of today's "killer diseases" – cancers, heart attacks, strokes, ALS, AIDS, and the rest – then one day most of us will survive long enough to become demented or debilitated. These developments could generate a fairly widespread duty to die. A fairly common duty to die might turn out to be only the dark side of our life-prolonging medicine and the uses we choose to make of it.

Let me be clear. I certainly believe that there is a duty to refuse life-prolonging medical treatment and also a duty to complete advance directives refusing life-prolonging treatment. But a duty to die can go well beyond that. There can be a duty to die before one's illnesses would cause death, even if treated only with palliative measures. In fact, there may be a fairly common responsibility to end one's life in the absence of any terminal illness at all. Finally, there can be a duty to die when one would prefer to live. Granted, many of the conditions that can generate a duty to die also seriously undermine the quality of life. Some prefer not to live under such conditions. But even those who want to live can face a duty to die. These will clearly be the most controversial and troubling cases; I will, accordingly, focus my reflections on them.

The Individualistic Fantasy

Because a duty to die seems such a real possibility to me, I wonder why contemporary bioethics has dismissed it without serious consideration. I believe that most bioethics still shares in one of our deeply embedded American dreams: the individualistic fantasy. This fantasy leads us to imagine that lives are separate and unconnected, or that they could be so if we chose. If lives were unconnected, things that happened in my life would not or need not affect others. And if others were not (much) affected by my life, I would have no duty to consider the impact of my decisions on others. I would then be free morally to live my life however I please, choosing whatever life and death I prefer for myself. The way I live would be nobody's business but my own. I certainly would have no duty to die if I preferred to live.

Within a health care context, the individualistic fantasy leads us to assume that the patient is the only one affected by decisions about her medical treatment. If only the patient were affected, the relevant questions when making treatment decisions would be precisely those we ask: What will benefit the patient? Who can best decide that? The pivotal issue would always be simply whether the patient wants to live like this and whether she would consider herself better off dead.[3] "Whose life is it, anyway?" we ask rhetorically.

But this is morally obtuse. We are not a race of hermits. Illness and death do not come only to those who are all alone. Nor is it much better to think in terms of the bald dichotomy between "the interests of the patient" and "the interests of society" (or a third-party payer), as if we were isolated individuals connected only to "society" in the abstract or to the other, faceless members of our health maintenance organization.

Most of us are affiliated with particular others and most deeply, with family and loved ones. Families and loved ones are bound together by ties of care and affection, by legal relations and obligations, by inhabiting shared spaces and living units, by interlocking finances and economic prospects, by common projects and also commitments to support the different life projects of other family members, by shared histories, by ties of loyalty. This life together of family and loved ones is what defines and sustains us; it is what gives meaning to most of our lives. We would not have it any other way. We would not want to be all alone, especially when we are seriously ill, as we age, and when we are dying.

But the fact of deeply interwoven lives debars us from making exclusively self-regarding decisions, as the decisions of one member of a family may dramatically affect the lives of all the rest. The impact of my decisions upon my family and loved ones is the source of many of my strongest obligations and also the most plausible and likeliest basis of a duty to die. "Society," after all, is only very marginally affected by how I live, or by whether I live or die.

A Burden to My Loved Ones

Many older people report that their one remaining goal in life is not to be a burden to their loved ones. Young people feel this, too: when I ask my undergraduate students to think about whether their death could come too late, one of their very first responses always is, "Yes, when I become a burden to my family or loved ones." Tragically, there are situations in which my loved ones would be much better off – all things considered, the loss of a loved one notwithstanding – if I were dead.

The lives of our loved ones can be seriously compromised by caring for us. The burdens of providing care or even just supervision twenty-four hours a day, seven days a week, are often overwhelming.[4] When this kind of caregiving goes on for years, it leaves the caregiver exhausted, with no time for herself or life of her own. Ultimately, even her health is often destroyed. But it can also be emotionally devastating simply to live with a spouse who is increasingly distant, uncommunicative, unresponsive, foreign, and unreachable. Other family members' needs often go unmet as the caring capacity of the family is exceeded. Social life and friendships evaporate, as there is no opportunity to go out to see friends and the home is no longer a place suitable for having friends in.

We must also acknowledge that the lives of our loved ones can be devastated just by having to pay for health care for us. One part of the recent SUPPORT study documented the financial aspects of caring for a dying member of a family. Only those who had illnesses severe enough to give them less than a 50 percent chance to live six more months were included in this study. When these patients survived their initial hospitalization and were discharged about one-third required considerable caregiving from their families; in 20 percent of cases a family member had to quit work or make some other major lifestyle change; almost one-third of these families lost all of their savings; and just under 30 percent lost a major source of income.[5]

If talking about money sounds venal or trivial, remember that much more than money is normally at stake here. When someone has to quit work, she may well lose her career. Savings decimated late in life cannot be recouped in the few remaining years of employability, so the loss compromises the quality of the rest of the caregiver's life. For a young person, the chance to go to college may be lost to the attempt to pay debts due to an illness in the family, and this decisively shapes an entire life.

A serious illness in a family is a misfortune. It is usually nobody's fault; no one is responsible for it. But we face choices about how we will respond to this misfortune. That's where the responsibility comes in and fault can arise. Those of us with families and loved ones always have a duty not to make selfish or self-centered decisions about our lives. We have a responsibility to try to protect the lives of loved ones from serious threats or greatly impoverished quality, certainly an obligation not to make choices that will jeopardize or seriously compromise their futures. Often, it would be wrong to do just what we want or just what is best for ourselves; we should choose in light of what is best for all concerned. That is our duty in sickness as well as in health. It is out of these responsibilities that a duty to die can develop.

I am not advocating a crass, quasi-economic conception of burdens and benefits, nor a shallow, hedonistic view of life. Given a suitably rich understanding of benefits, family members sometimes do benefit from suffering through the long illness of a loved one. Caring for the sick or aged can foster growth, even as it makes daily life immeasurably harder and the prospects for the future much bleaker. Chronic illness or a drawn-out death can also pull a family together, making the care for each other stronger and more evident.

If my loved ones are truly benefiting from coping with my illness or debility, I have no duty to die based on burdens to them.

But it would be irresponsible to blithely assume that this always happens, that it will happen in my family, or that it will be the fault of my family if they cannot manage to turn my illness into a positive experience. Perhaps the opposite is more common: a hospital chaplain once told me that he could not think of a single case in which a family was strengthened or brought together by what happened at the hospital.

Our families and loved ones also have obligations, of course – they have the responsibility to stand by us and to support us through debilitating illness and death. They must be prepared to make significant sacrifices to respond to an illness in the family. I am far from denying that. Most of us are aware of this responsibility and most families meet it rather well. In fact, families deliver more than 80 percent of the long-term care in this country, almost always at great personal cost. Most of us who are a part of a family can expect to be sustained in our time of need by family members and those who love us.

But most discussions of an illness in the family sound as if responsibility were a one-way street. It is not, of course. When we become seriously ill or debilitated, we too may have to make sacrifices. To think that my loved ones must bear whatever burdens my illness, debility, or dying process might impose upon them is to reduce them to means to my well-being. And that would be immoral. Family solidarity, altruism, bearing the burden of a loved one's misfortune, and loyalty are all important virtues of families, as well. But they are all also two-way streets.

Objections to a Duty to Die

To my mind, the most serious objections to the idea of a duty to die lie in the effects on my loved ones of ending my life. But to most others, the important objections have little or nothing to do with family and loved ones. Perhaps the most common objections are: (1) there is a higher duty that always takes precedence over a duty to die; (2) a duty to end one's own life would be incompatible with a recognition of human dignity or the intrinsic value of a person; and (3) seriously ill, debilitated, or dying people are already bearing the harshest burdens and so it would be wrong to ask them to bear the additional burden of ending their own lives.

These are all important objections; all deserve a thorough discussion. Here I will only be able to suggest some moral counterweights – ideas that might provide the basis for an argument that these objections do not always preclude a duty to die.

An example of the first line of argument would be the claim that a duty to God, the giver of life, forbids that anyone take her own life. It could be argued that this duty always supersedes whatever obligations we might have to our families. But what convinces us that we always have such a religious duty in the first place? And what guarantees that it always supersedes our obligations to try to protect our loved ones?

Certainly, the view that death is the ultimate evil cannot be squared with Christian theology. It does not reflect the actions of Jesus or those of his early followers. Nor is it clear that the belief that life is sacred requires that we never take it. There are other theological possibilities.[6] In any case, most of us – bioethicists, physicians, and patients alike – do not subscribe to the view that we have an obligation to preserve human life as long as possible. But if not, surely we ought to agree that I may legitimately end my life for other-regarding reasons, not just for self-regarding reasons.

Secondly, religious considerations aside, the claim could be made that an obligation to end one's own life would be incompatible with human dignity or would embody a failure to recognize the intrinsic value of a person. But I do not see that in thinking I had a duty to die I would necessarily be failing to respect myself or to appreciate my dignity or worth. Nor would I necessarily be failing to respect you in thinking that you had a similar duty. There is surely also a sense in which we fail to respect ourselves if in the face of illness or death, we stoop to choosing just what is best for ourselves. Indeed, Kant held that the very core of human dignity is the ability to act on a self-imposed moral law, regardless of whether it is in our interest to do so.[7] We shall return to the notion of human dignity.

A third objection appeals to the relative weight of burdens and thus, ultimately, to considerations of fairness or justice. The burdens that an illness creates for the family could not possibly be great enough to justify an obligation to end one's life – the sacrifice of life itself would be a far greater burden than any involved in caring for a chronically ill family member.

But is this true? Consider the following case:

> An 87-year-old woman was dying of congestive heart failure. Her APACHE score predicted that she had less than a 50 percent chance to live for another six months. She was lucid, assertive, and terrified of death. She very much wanted to live and kept opting for rehospitalization and the most aggressive life-prolonging treatment possible. That treatment successfully prolonged her life (though with increasing debility) for nearly two years. Her 55-year-old daughter was her only remaining family, her caregiver, and the main source of her financial support. The daughter duly cared for her mother. But before her mother died, her illness had cost the daughter all of her savings, her home, her job, and her career.

This is by no means an uncommon sort of case. Thousands of similar cases occur each year. Now, ask yourself which is the greater burden:

(a) To lose a 50 percent chance of six more months of life at age 87?
(b) To lose all your savings, your home, and your career at age 55?

Which burden would you prefer to bear? Do we really believe the former is the greater burden? Would even the dying mother say that (a) is the greater burden? Or has she been encouraged to believe that the burdens of (b) are somehow morally irrelevant to her choices?

I think most of us would quickly agree that (b) is a greater burden. That is the evil we would more hope to avoid in our lives. If we are tempted to say that the mother's disease and impending death are the greater evil, I believe it is because we are taking a "slice of time" perspective rather than a "lifetime perspective."[8] But surely the lifetime perspective is the appropriate perspective when weighing burdens. If (b) is the greater burden, then we must admit that we have been promulgating an ethics that advocates imposing greater burdens on some people in order to provide smaller benefits for others just because they are ill and thus gain our professional attention and advocacy.

A whole range of cases like this one could easily be generated. In some, the answer about which burden is greater will not be clear. But in many it is. Death – or ending your own life – is simply not the greatest evil or the greatest burden.

This point does not depend on a utilitarian calculus. Even if death were the greatest burden (thus disposing of any simple utilitarian argument), serious questions would remain about the moral justifiability of choosing to impose crushing burdens on loved ones in order to avoid having to bear this burden oneself. The fact that I suffer greater burdens than others in my family does not license me simply to choose what I want for myself, nor does it necessarily release me from a responsibility to try to protect the quality of their lives.

I can readily imagine that, through cowardice, rationalization, or failure of resolve, I will fail in this obligation to protect my loved ones. If so, I think I would need to be excused or forgiven for what I did. But I cannot imagine it would be morally permissible for me to ruin the rest of my partner's life to sustain mine or to cut off my sons' careers, impoverish them, or compromise the quality of their children's lives simply because I wish to live a little longer. This is what leads me to believe in a duty to die.

Who Has a Duty to Die?

Suppose, then, that there can be a duty to die. Who has a duty to die? And when? To my mind, these are the right questions, the questions we should be asking. Many of us may one day badly need answers to just these questions.

But I cannot supply answers here, for two reasons. In the first place, answers will have to be very particular and contextual. Our concrete duties are often situated, defined in part by the myriad details of our circumstances, histories, and relationships. Though there may be principles that apply to a wide range of cases and some cases that yield pretty straightforward answers, there will also be many situations in which it is very difficult to discern whether one has a duty to die. If nothing else, it will often be very difficult to predict how one's family will bear up under the weight of the burdens that a protracted illness would impose on them. Momentous decisions will often have to be made under conditions of great uncertainty.

Second and perhaps even more importantly, I believe that those of us with family and loved ones should not define our duties unilaterally, especially not a decision about a duty to die. It would be isolating and distancing for me to decide without consulting them what is too much of a burden for my loved ones to bear. That way of deciding about my moral duties is not only atomistic, it also treats my family and loved ones paternalistically. They must be allowed to speak for themselves about the burdens my life imposes on them and how they feel about bearing those burdens.

Some may object that it would be wrong to put a loved one in a position of having to say, in effect, "You should end your life because caring for you is too hard on me and the rest of the family." Not only will it be almost impossible to say something like that to someone you love, it will carry with it a heavy load of guilt. On this view, you should decide by yourself whether you have a duty to die and approach your loved ones only after you have made up your mind to say goodbye to them. Your family could then try to change your mind, but the tremendous weight of moral decision would be lifted from their shoulders.

Perhaps so. But I believe in family decisions. Important decisions for those whose lives are interwoven should be made together, in a family discussion. Granted, a conversation about whether I have a duty to die would be a tremendously difficult conversation. The temptations to be dishonest could be enormous. Nevertheless, if I am contemplating a duty to die, my family and I should, if possible, have just such an agonizing discussion. It will act as a check on the information, perceptions, and reasoning of all of us. But even more importantly, it affirms our connectedness at a critical juncture in our lives and our life together. Honest talk about difficult matters almost always strengthens relationships.

However, many families seem unable to talk about death at all, much less a duty to die. Certainly most families could not have this discussion all at once, in one sitting. It might well take a number of discussions to be able to approach this topic. But even if talking about death is impossible, there are always behavioral clues – about your caregiver's tiredness, physical condition, health, prevailing mood, anxiety, financial concerns, outlook, overall well-being, and so on. And families unable to talk about death can often talk about how the caregiver is feeling, about finances, about tensions within the family resulting from the illness, about concerns for the future. Deciding whether you have a duty to die based on these behavioral clues and conversation about them honors your relationships better than deciding on your own about how burdensome you and your care must be.

I cannot say when someone has a duty to die. Still, I can suggest a few features of one's illness, history, and circumstances that make it more likely that one has a duty to die. I present them here without much elaboration or explanation.

1 A duty to die is more likely when continuing to live will impose significant burdens – emotional burdens, extensive caregiving, destruction of life plans, and, yes, financial hardship – on your family and loved ones. This is the fundamental insight underlying a duty to die.

2 A duty to die becomes greater as you grow older. As we age, we will be giving up less by giving up our lives, if only because we will sacrifice fewer remaining years of life and a smaller portion of our life plans. After all, it's not as if we would be immortal and live forever if we could just manage to avoid a duty to die. To have reached the age of, say, seventy-five or eighty years without being ready to die is itself a moral failing, the sign of a life out of touch with life's basic realities.[9]

3 A duty to die is more likely when you have already lived a full and rich life. You have already had a full share of the good things life offers.

4 There is greater duty to die if your loved ones' lives have already been difficult or impoverished, if they have had only a small share of the good things that life has to offer (especially if through no fault of their own).

5 A duty to die is more likely when your loved ones have already made great contributions – perhaps even sacrifices – to make your life a good one. Especially if you have not made similar sacrifices for their well-being or for the well-being of other members of your family.

6 To the extent that you can make a good adjustment to your illness or handicapping condition, there is less likely to be a duty to die. A good adjustment means that smaller sacrifices will be required of loved ones and there is more compensating interaction for them. Still, we must also recognize that some diseases – Alzheimer or Huntington chorea – will eventually take their toll on your loved ones no matter how courageously, resolutely, even cheerfully you manage to face that illness.

7 There is less likely to be a duty to die if you can still make significant contributions to the lives of others, especially your family. The burdens to family members are not only or even primarily financial, neither are the contributions to them.

However, the old and those who have terminal illnesses must also bear in mind that the loss their family members will feel when they die cannot be avoided, only postponed.

8 A duty to die is more likely when the part of you that is loved will soon be gone or seriously compromised. Or when you soon will no longer be capable of giving love. Part of the horror of dementing disease is that it destroys the capacity to nurture and sustain relationships, taking away a person's agency and the emotions that bind her to others.

9 There is a greater duty to die to the extent that you have lived a relatively lavish lifestyle instead of saving for illness or old age. Like most upper middle-class Americans, I could easily have saved more. It is a greater wrong to come to your family for assistance if your need is the result of having chosen leisure or a spendthrift lifestyle. I may eventually have to face the moral consequences of decisions I am now making.

These, then, are some of the considerations that give shape and definition to the duty to die. If we can agree that these considerations are all relevant, we can see that the correct course of action will often be difficult to discern. A decision about when I should end my life will sometimes prove to be every bit as difficult as the decision about whether I want treatment for myself.

Can the Incompetent Have a Duty to Die?

Severe mental deterioration springs readily to mind as one of the situations in which I believe I could have a duty to die. But can incompetent people have duties at all? We can have moral duties we do not recognize or acknowledge, including duties that we never recognized. But can we have duties we are unable to recognize? Duties when we are unable to understand the concept of morality at all? If so, do others have a moral obligation to help us carry out this duty? These are extremely difficult theoretical questions. The reach of moral agency is severely strained by mental incompetence.

I am tempted to simply bypass the entire question by saying that I am talking only about competent persons. But the idea of a duty to die clearly raises the specter of one person claiming that another – who cannot speak for herself – has such a duty. So I need to say that I can make no sense of the claim that someone has a duty to die if the person has never been able to understand moral obligation at all. To my mind, only those who were formerly capable of making moral decisions could have such a duty.

But the case of formerly competent persons is almost as troubling. Perhaps we should simply stipulate that no incompetent person can have a duty to die, not even if she affirmed belief in such a duty in an advance directive. If we take the view that formerly competent people may have such a duty, we should surely exercise extreme caution when claiming a formerly competent person would have acknowledged a duty to die or that any formerly competent person has an unacknowledged duty to die. Moral dangers loom regardless of which way we decide to resolve such issues.

But for me personally, very urgent practical matters turn on their resolution. If a formerly competent person can no longer have a duty to die (or if other people are not likely to help her carry out this duty), I believe that my obligation may be to die while I am still competent, before I become unable to make and carry out that decision for myself. Surely it would be irresponsible to evade my moral duties by temporizing until I escape into incompetence. And so I must die sooner than I otherwise would have to. On the other hand, if I could count on others to end my life after I become incompetent, I might be able to fulfill my responsibilities while also living out all my competent or semi-competent days. Given our society's reluctance to permit physicians, let alone family members, to perform aid-in-dying, I believe I may well have a duty to end my life when I can see mental incapacity on the horizon.

There is also the very real problem of sudden incompetence – due to a serious stroke or automobile accident, for example. For me, that is the real nightmare. If I suddenly become incompetent, I will fall into the hands of a medical-legal system that will conscientiously disregard my moral beliefs and do what is best for me, regardless of the consequences for my loved ones. And that is not at all what I would have wanted!

Social Policies and a Duty to Die

The claim that there is a duty to die will seem to some a misplaced response to social negligence. If our society were providing for the debilitated, the chronically ill, and the elderly as it should be, there would be only very rare cases of a duty to die. On this view, I am asking the sick and debilitated to step in and accept responsibility because society is derelict in its responsibility to provide for the incapacitated.

This much is surely true: there are a number of social policies we could pursue that would dramatically reduce the incidence of such a duty. Most obviously, we could decide to pay for facilities that provided excellent long-term care (not just health care!) for all chronically ill, debilitated, mentally ill, or demented people in this country. We probably could still afford to do this. If we did, sick, debilitated, and dying people might still be morally required to make sacrifices for their families. I might, for example, have a duty to forgo personal care by a family member who knows me and really does care for me. But these sacrifices would only rarely include the sacrifice of life itself. The duty to die would then be virtually eliminated.

I cannot claim to know whether in some abstract sense a society like ours should provide care for all who are chronically ill or debilitated. But the fact is that we Americans seem to be unwilling to pay for this kind of long-term care, except for ourselves and our own. In fact, we are moving in precisely the opposite direction – we are trying to shift the burdens of caring for the seriously and chronically ill onto families in order to save costs for our health care system. As we shift the burdens of care onto families, we also dramatically increase the number of Americans who will have a duty to die.

I must not, then, live my life and make my plans on the assumption that social institutions will protect my family from my infirmity and debility. To do so would be irresponsible. More likely, it will be up to me to protect my loved ones.

A Duty to Die and the Meaning of Life

A duty to die seems very harsh, and often it would be. It is one of the tragedies of our lives that someone who wants very much to live can nevertheless have a duty to die. It is both tragic and ironic that it is precisely the very real good of family and loved ones that gives rise to this duty. Indeed, the genuine love, closeness, and supportiveness of family members is a major source of this duty: we could not be such a burden if they did not care for us. Finally, there is deep irony in the fact that the very successes of our life-prolonging medicine help to create a widespread duty to die. We do not live in such a happy world that we can avoid such tragedies and ironies. We ought not to close our eyes to this reality or pretend that it just doesn't exist. We ought not to minimize the tragedy in any way.

And yet, a duty to die will not always be as harsh as we might assume. If I love my family, I will want to protect them and their lives. I will not want to make choices that compromise their futures. Indeed, I can easily imagine that I might want to avoid compromising their lives more than I would want anything else. I must also admit that I am not necessarily giving up so much in giving up my life: the conditions that give rise to a duty to die would usually already have compromised the quality of the life I am required to end. In any case, I personally must confess that at age fifty-six, I have already lived a very good life, albeit not yet nearly as long a life as I would like to have.

We fear death too much. Our fear of death has led to a massive assault on it. We still crave after virtually any life-prolonging technology that we might conceivably be able to produce. We still too often feel morally impelled to prolong life – virtually any form of life – as long as possible. As if the best death is the one that can be put off longest.

We do not even ask about meaning in death, so busy are we with trying to postpone it. But we will not conquer death by one day developing a technology so magnificent that no one will have to die. Nor can we conquer death by postponing it ever longer. We can conquer death only by finding meaning in it.

Although the existence of a duty to die does not hinge on this, recognizing such a duty would go some way toward recovering meaning in death. Paradoxically, it would restore dignity to those who are seriously ill or dying. It would also reaffirm the connections required to give life (and death) meaning. I close now with a few words about both of these points.

First, recognizing a duty to die affirms my agency and also my moral agency. I can still do things that make an important difference in the lives of my loved ones. Moreover, the fact that I still have responsibilities keeps me within the community of moral agents. My illness or debility has not reduced me to a mere moral patient (to use the language of the philosophers). Though it may not be the whole story, surely Kant was onto something important when he claimed that human dignity rests on the capacity for moral agency within a community of those who respect the demands of morality.

By contrast, surely there is something deeply insulting in a medicine and an ethic that would ask only what I want (or would have wanted) when I become ill. To treat me as if I had no moral responsibilities when I am ill or debilitated implies that my condition has rendered me morally incompetent. Only small children, the demented or insane, and those totally lacking in the capacity to act are free from moral duties. There is dignity, then, and a kind of meaning in moral agency, even as it forces extremely difficult decisions upon us.

Second, recovering meaning in death requires an affirmation of connections. If I end my life to spare the futures of my loved ones, I testify in my death that I am connected to them. It is because I love and care for precisely these people (and I know they care for me) that I wish not to be such a burden to them. By contrast, a life in which I am free to choose whatever I want for myself is a life unconnected to others. A bioethics that would treat me as if I had no serious moral responsibilities does what it can to marginalize, weaken, or even destroy my connections with others.

But life without connection is meaningless. The individualistic fantasy, though occasionally liberating, is deeply destructive. When life is good and vitality seems unending, life itself and life lived for yourself may seem quite sufficient. But if not life, certainly death without connection is meaningless. If you are only for yourself, all you have to care about as your life draws to a close is yourself and your life. Everything you care about will then perish in your death. And that – the end of everything you care about – is precisely the total collapse of meaning. We can, then, find meaning in death only through a sense of connection with something that will survive our death.

This need not be connections with other people. Some people are deeply tied to land (for example, the family farm), to nature, or to a transcendent reality. But for most of us, the connections that sustain us are to other people. In the full bloom of life, we are connected to others in many ways – through work, profession, neighborhood, country, shared faith and worship, common leisure pursuits, friendship. Even the guru meditating in isolation on his mountain top is connected to a long tradition of people united by the same religious quest.

But as we age or when we become chronically ill, connections with other people usually become much more restricted. Often, only ties with family and close friends remain and remain important to us. Moreover, for many of us, other connections just don't go deep enough. As Paul Tsongas has reminded us, "When it comes time to die, no one says, 'I wish I had spent more time at the office.' "

If I am correct, death is so difficult for us partly because our sense of community is so weak. Death seems to wipe out everything when we can't fit it into the lives of those who live on. A death motivated by the desire to spare the futures of my loved ones might well be a better death for me than the one I would get as a result of opting to continue my life as long as there is any pleasure in it for me. Pleasure is nice, but it is meaning that matters.

I don't know about others, but these reflections have helped me. I am now more at peace about facing a duty to die. Ending my life if my duty required might still be difficult. But for me, a far greater horror would be dying all alone or stealing the futures of my loved ones in order to buy a little more time for myself. I hope that if the time comes when I have a duty to die, I will recognize it, encourage my loved ones to recognize it too, and carry it out bravely.

Acknowledgments

I wish to thank Mary English, Hilde Nelson, Jim Bennett, Tom Townsend, the members of the Philosophy Department at East Tennessee State University, and anonymous reviewers of the *Report* for many helpful comments on earlier versions of this paper. In this paper, I draw on material in John Hardwig, "Dying at the Right Time; Reflections on (Un)Assisted Suicide" in *Practical Ethics*, ed. H. LaFollette (Oxford: Blackwell, 1996), with permission.

Notes

1 Given the importance of relationships in my thinking, "responsibility" – rooted as it is in "respond" – would perhaps be the most appropriate word. Nevertheless, I often use "duty" despite its legalistic overtones, because Lamm's famous statements has given the expression "duty to die" a certain familiarity. But I intend no implication that there is a law that grounds this duty, nor that someone has a right corresponding to it.

2 For a discussion of the Oates case, see Tom L. Beauchamp, "What Is Suicide?" in *Ethical Issues in Death and Dying*, ed. Tom L. Beauchamp and Seymour Perlin (Englewood Cliffs, NJ: Prentice-Hall, 1978).

3 Most bioethicists advocate a "patient-centered ethics" – an ethics which claims only the patient's interests should be considered in making medical treatment decisions. Most health care professionals have been trained to accept this ethic and to see themselves as patient advocates. For arguments that a patient-centered ethics should be replaced by a family-centered ethics see John Hardwig, "What About the Family?" *Hastings Center Report*, 20, no. 2 (1990): 5–10; Hilde L. Nelson and James L. Nelson, *The Patient in the Family* (New York: Routledge, 1995).

4 A good account of the burdens of caregiving can be found in Elaine Brody, *Women in the Middle: Their Parent-Care Years* (New York: Springer, 1990). Perhaps the best article-length account of these burdens is Daniel Callahan, "Families as Caregivers; the Limits of Morality" in *Aging and Ethics: Philosophical Problems in Gerontology*, ed. Nancy Jecker (Totowa, NJ: Humana Press, 1991).

5 Kenneth E. Covinsky et al., "The Impact of Serious Illness on Patients' Families," *Journal of the American Medical Association*, 272 (1994): 1839–44.

6 Larry Churchill, for example, believes that Christian ethics takes us far beyond my present position: "Christian doctrines of stewardship prohibit the extension of one's own life at a great cost to the neighbor... And such a gesture should not appear to us a sacrifice, but as the ordinary virtue entailed by a just, social conscience." Larry Churchill, *Rationing Health Care in America* (South Bend, IN: Notre Dame University Press, 1988), p. 112.

7 Kant, as is well known, was opposed to suicide. But he was arguing against taking your life out of self-interested motives. It is not clear that Kant would or we should consider taking your life out of a sense of duty to be wrong. See Hilde L. Nelson, "Death with Kantian Dignity," *Journal of Clinical Ethics*, 7 (1996): 215–21.

8 Obviously, I owe this distinction to Norman Daniels, *Am I My Parents' Keeper? An Essay on Justice Between the Young and the Old* (New York: Oxford University Press, 1988). Just as obviously, Daniels is not committed to my use of it here.

9 Daniel Callahan, *The Troubled Dream of Life* (New York: Simon & Schuster, 1993).

PART V

Resource Allocation

40

Rescuing Lives: Can't We Count?

Paul T. Menzel

On 16 September 1993, five year-old Laura Davies of Manchester, England, received small and large intestines, stomach, pancreas, liver, and two kidneys in a fifteen-hour transplant operation at Children's Hospital of Pittsburgh. The National Health Service paid for little of her care, but scores of private donors responded to newspaper publicity and her parents' appeals to provide the half-million pounds and more required for her various operations. In this case, where was medical technology taking us?

Laura died on 11 November. According to her Manchester physician at the time of the operation, however, Laura had a "better than 50–50 chance." After all, the three previous child recipients of multiple organs at Pittsburgh since the advent of a new antirejection drug in 1992 are still alive. It is thus difficult to dismiss the willingness of Laura's parents and physicians to proceed as using her for their own emotional or scientific purposes. Though surely "experimental," the surgery was the only chance Laura had.

And if anyone, either then or now in light of her death, claims that the 50–50 odds were inflated, a straightforward reply is available: maybe you're right, but let us employ this procedure, now and at other times, to see. Plucky Laura herself seemed to put the "guinea pig" charge to rest. "I'm not worried," she told reporters at a press conference. Then she ended the session with a song.

A standard objection to high expense-per-benefit care also does not apply: funded privately by response to special appeal, Laura's care does not come at the expense of anyone else whom limited funds might have saved. With a child like this and the money pouring in from donations, why should we dispute her parents' and physicians' decision? On a medical mission? Sure. Carried away? In the circumstances, seemingly not.

Still, something has been missed that is very problematic about Laura's aggressive care: in the attempt to save her, a greater number of other lives were sacrificed. It's a straightforward function of the marked scarcity of organs. Nearly half the children now on organ transplant waiting lists die before they get them. We should all be able to see the big picture: if one person at the head of the queue gets four scarce organs instead of one, four others somewhere down the queue, not one, never get any.

Both the British and the US publics seem reluctant to recognize this. Take Pennsylvania's Governor Casey last spring. At first his waiting only a few days before receiving a heart-liver transplant met with skepticism: had he been allowed to jump the queue because of his political status? The Pittsburgh transplant center quickly replied: absolutely not, he was treated as any other multiple organ failure patient would have been. Because of the multiple failure, his need was more urgent. With the political queue-jumping charge rebuffed, the critics backed off.

But if organs are scarce, and those used in multiple scarce organ transplants could virtually always have saved more lives if used on others, what can possibly justify any multiple organ transplant candidate's elevation to the top of the queue? Except in the event of an extremely rare match, only two readily understandable

From *Hastings Center Report*, 24, no. 1 (1994), pp. 22–3. Reprinted with permission.

explanations seem available, and neither justifies what was done.

One is pushing outward the medical frontier: carry out Casey's and Davies's more challenging operations despite the current sacrifice of a greater number of others' lives, and we will eventually develop new, effective forms of lifesaving. But this sort of argument represents the most extreme kind of medical adventurism. With the scarcity of organs virtually certain to continue – especially for children and infants, where we are already getting close to maximum contribution – what is the likelihood that multiple organ transplants will *ever* cease to use up on one person what could have saved several? A totally Pollyannaish view of future organ supply drives the "experimental development" argument. We should experiment with multiple scarce organ transplants only if we have good reason to believe that sometime in the future we will have ample supply. But there is every reason to think we will *never* have that!

The other readily understandable explanation is an odd view of "urgency." The Pittsburgh surgeons appear to regard the failure of both a heart and a liver as constituting more urgent need. This too falls apart upon examination. Certainly I am as close to death's door if "just" my heart fails as I am if my heart and liver both fail. Where, in "only heart failure," is there any lack of real urgency?

To say that Governor Casey or Laura Davies have greater medical need because they require two or seven organs instead of one betrays, I suppose, a kind of "Dunkirk Syndrome": thinking that the more *difficult* the rescue was, the greater was the need at the time. Admittedly, nations and doctors understandably feel in such circumstances that they have pulled off something more *miraculous* – in fact they have! But where in that pride in greater effort or thankfulness for greater luck is hidden any more urgent *need?*

So advancement of medical technology and urgent medical need utterly fail to justify multiple scarce-organ transplants. Their defense would have to invoke either of two much more difficult explanations. One is a direct, jolting challenge to the moral relevance of numbers at all in these kinds of acute care situations: there simply is no obligation to save the greater number. Such a position gets a foothold in our thinking through the claim that each and every individual deserves an equal chance of being saved; we should therefore flip coins to determine whether we will save the one or the four, not save the four right off because they are the greater number. Regardless of the merits of this view in academic philosophical terms,[1] however, it hardly fits the transplant setting. We continually strive to expand the organ pool. Why? To save more lives, obviously. If with that expanded supply we end up saving no more people than before because we use up enough of our organ bank on multiple organ recipients, what has been the point of our supply expansion efforts?

A second difficult explanation is at least anchored in some actual social reactions. Little objection to the occasional practice of using up multiple scarce organs on one recipient comes from competing single-organ patients, patients' families, or their representatives. The reason, I suspect, is that the context of waiting together on a queue is already transparently and pervasively infused with luck – the luck of the right organ and a good match arriving at the right time for one candidate, but not for another. Living continually with such grave unknowns may lead people to celebrate unselfishly when anyone gets saved. No patient begrudges another's sheer luck; all understand that there is no rhyme, reason, or desert in the outcome anyhow. Once in that laudable mindset, people may not even attend to the numbers. The many cast no challenging glance into the eyes of the few. Challenge, defense, claim – here, all are out of court. It's as if the many even consent to their own lack of rescue as long as someone is saved.

I am intrigued by this possibility of consent,[2] but I suspect that our surmisals here about the empathetic consent of organ failure patients who wait unsuccessfully on the queue are romantic and quite distort their actual feelings. Most of the real competitor potential recipients out there somewhere on the queue do not sit together in a transplant center's waiting room, directly sharing one another's fortune. In any case, why should those in the society who manage the process of organ procural and disbursement not empathize sequentially with *all* who might be saved, thereby letting the numbers of real, equally invaluable rescuable persons build up to turn their decision? Again, in terms of persuasive justifications, multiple scarce-organ transplants strike out.

Surgeons, the press, and the public need to face up to these considerations in cases like Laura Davies. How can transplant centers justify ultimately letting two or more persons somewhere down the queue likely die because they have drawn so much out of the organ bank to save one? And why should the press play along with this lifesaving delusion and publicize appeals to unknowing financial donors without telling them the morally relevant facts? If donors knew, why should they feel good about having contributed to a net *non*-lifesaving project? In the whole situation, only Laura Davies's parents, in their attachment to their child, come out clean.

Worse yet, the essential problem in the multiple scarce organ cases portends bigger trouble. It has ominous implications for the distribution of other scarce health care resources. If in multiple organ transplants we are blind to the real lives of competing potential beneficiaries, where they, too, are acutely ill, how much more blind will we be in typical contexts of distributing scarce monies where the competing beneficiaries are more distant, and certainly not on any queue of named individuals?

Let's count before we cut.

Notes

1 Frances M. Kamm, *Morality, Mortality: Death and Whom to Save From It*, vol. 1 (New York: Oxford University Press, 1993), pp. 75–122. See also J. Taurek, "Should the Numbers Count?" *Philosophy and Public Affairs*, 6, no. 4 (1977): 293–316; and Derek Parfit, "Innumerate Ethics," *Philosophy and Public Affairs*, 7, no. 4 (1978): 285–301.

2 The attempt to discern the implications of consent to risk drove most of this author's reasoning in *Strong Medicine: The Ethical Rationing of Health Care* (New York: Oxford University Press, 1990).

41

The Allocation of Exotic Medical Lifesaving Therapy

Nicholas Rescher

I The Problem

Technological progress has in recent years transformed the limits of the possible in medical therapy. However, the elevated state of sophistication of modern medical technology has brought the economists' classic problem of scarcity in its wake as an unfortunate side product. The enormously sophisticated and complex equipment and the highly trained teams of experts requisite for its utilization are scarce resources in relation to potential demand. The administrators of the great medical institutions that preside over these scarce resources thus come to be faced increasingly with the awesome choice: *Whose life to save?*

A (somewhat hypothetical) paradigm example of this problem may be sketched within the following set of definitive assumptions: We suppose that persons in some particular medically morbid condition are "mortally afflicted": It is virtually certain that they will die within a short time period (say ninety days). We assume that some very complex course of treatment (e.g., a heart transplant) represents a substantial probability of life prolongation for persons in this mortally afflicted condition. We assume that the facilities available in terms of human resources, mechanical instrumentalities, and requisite materials (e.g., hearts in the case of a heart transplant) make it possible to give a certain treatment – this "exotic (medical) lifesaving therapy," or ELT for short – to a certain, relatively small number of people. And finally we assume that a substantially greater pool of people in the mortally afflicted condition is at hand. The problem then may be formulated as follows: How is one to select within the pool of afflicted patients the ones to be given the ELT treatment in question; how to select those "whose lives are to be saved"? Faced with many candidates for an ELT process that can be made available to only a few, doctors and medical administrators confront the decision of who is to be given a chance at survival and who is, in effect, to be condemned to die.

As has already been implied, the "heroic" variety of spare-part surgery can pretty well be assimilated to this paradigm. One can foresee the time when heart transplantation, for example, will have become pretty much a routine medical procedure, albeit on a very limited basis, since a cardiac surgeon with the technical competence to transplant hearts can operate at best a rather small number of times each week and the elaborate facilities for such operations will most probably exist on a modest scale. Moreover, in "spare-part" surgery there is always the problem of availability of the "spare parts" themselves. A report in one British newspaper gives the following picture: "Of the 150,000 who die of heart disease each year [in the U.K.], Mr Donald Longmore, research surgeon at the National Heart Hospital [in London] estimates that 22,000 might be eligible for heart surgery. Another 30,000 would need heart and lung transplants. But there are probably only between 7,000 and 14,000 potential donors a year."[1] Envisaging this situation in which at the very most something like one in four heart-malfunction victims can be saved, we clearly confront a problem in ELT allocation.

From *Ethics*, vol. 79 (1969), pp. 173–86. Reprinted with the permission of the University of Chicago Press.

A perhaps even more drastic case in point is afforded by long-term haemodialysis, an ongoing process by which a complex device – an "artificial kidney machine" – is used periodically in cases of chronic renal failure to substitute for a non-functional kidney in "cleaning" potential poisons from the blood. Only a few major institutions have chronic haemodialysis units, whose complex operation is an extremely expensive proposition. For the present and the foreseeable future the situation is that "the number of places available for chronic haemodialysis is hopelessly inadequate."[2]

The traditional medical ethos has insulated the physician against facing the very existence of this problem. When swearing the Hippocratic Oath, he commits himself to work for the benefit of the sick in "whatsover house I enter."[3] In taking this stance, the physician substantially renounces the explicit choice of saving certain lives rather than others. Of course, doctors have always in fact had to face such choices on the battlefield or in times of disaster, but there the issue had to be resolved hurriedly, under pressure, and in circumstances in which the very nature of the case effectively precluded calm deliberation by the decision maker as well as criticism by others. In sharp contrast, however, cases of the type we have postulated in the present discussion arise predictably, and represent choices to be made deliberately and "in cold blood."

It is, to begin with, appropriate to remark that this problem is not fundamentally a medical problem. For when there are sufficiently many afflicted candidates for ELT then – so we may assume – there will also be more than enough for whom the purely medical grounds for ELT allocation are decisively strong in any individual case, and just about equally strong throughout the group. But in this circumstance a selection of some afflicted patients over and against others cannot *ex hypothesi* be made on the basis of purely medical considerations.

The selection problem, as we have said, is in substantial measure not a medical one. It is a problem *for* medical men, which must somehow be solved by them, but that does not make it a medical issue – any more than the problem of hospital building is a medical issue. As a problem it belongs to the category of philosophical problems – specifically a problem of moral philosophy or ethics. Structurally, it bears a substantial kinship with those issues in this field that revolve about the notorious whom-to-save-on-the-lifeboat and whom-to-throw-to-the-wolves-pursuing-the-sled questions. But whereas questions of this just-indicated sort are artificial, hypothetical, and far-fetched, the ELT issue poses a *genuine* policy question for the responsible administrators in medical institutions, indeed a question that threatens to become commonplace in the foreseeable future.

Now what the medical administrator needs to have, and what the philosopher is presumably *ex officio* in a position to help in providing, is a body of *rational guidelines* for making choices in these literally life-or-death situations. This is an issue in which many interested parties have a substantial stake, including the responsible decision-maker who wants to satisfy his conscience that he is acting in a reasonable way. Moreover, the family and associates of the man who is turned away – to say nothing of the man himself – have the right to an acceptable explanation. And indeed even the general public wants to know that what is being done is fitting and proper. All of these interested parties are entitled to insist that a reasonable code of operating principles provides a defensible rationale for making the life-and-death choices involved in ELT.

II The Two Types of Criteria

Two distinguishable types of criteria are bound up in the issue of making ELT choices. We shall call these *Criteria of Inclusion* and *Criteria of Comparison*, respectively. The distinction at issue here requires some explanation. We can think of the selection as being made by a two-stage process: (1) the selection from among all possible candidates (by a suitable screening process) of a group to be taken under serious consideration as candidates for therapy, and then (2) the actual singling out, within this group, of the particular individuals to whom therapy is to be given. Thus the first process narrows down the range of comparative choice by eliminating *en bloc* whole categories of potential candidates. The second process calls for a more refined, case-by-case comparison of those candidates that remain. By means of the first set of criteria one forms a selection group; by means of the second set, an actual selection is made within this group.

Thus what we shall call a "selection system" for the choice of patients to receive therapy of the ELT type will consist of criteria of these two kinds. Such a system will be acceptable only when the reasonableness of its component criteria can be established.

III. Essential Features of an Acceptable ELT Selection System

To qualify as reasonable, an ELT selection must meet two important "regulative" requirements: it must be *simple* enough to be readily intelligible, and it must be *plausible*, that is, patiently reasonable in a way that can be apprehended easily and without involving ramified subtleties. Those medical administrators responsible for ELT choices must follow a *modus operandi* that virtually all the people involved can readily understand to be acceptable (at a reasonable level of generality, at any rate). Appearances are critically important here. It is not enough that the choice be made in a *justifiable* way; it must be possible for people – *plain* people – to "see" (i.e., understand without elaborate teaching or indoctrination) that *it is justified*, in so far as any mode of procedure can be justified in cases of this sort.

One "constitutive" requirement is obviously an essential feature of a reasonable selection system: all of its component criteria – those of inclusion and those of comparison alike – must be reasonable in the sense of being *rationally defensible*. The ramifications of this requirement call for detailed consideration. But one of its aspects should be noted without further ado: it must be *fair* – it must treat relevantly like cases alike, leaving no room for "influence" or favoritism, etc.

IV The Basic Screening Stage: Criteria of Inclusion (and Exclusion)

Three sorts of considerations are prominent among the plausible criteria of inclusion/exclusion at the basic screening stage: the constituency factor, the progress-of-science factor, and the prospect-of-success factor.

(A) The constituency factor

It is a "fact of life" that ELT can be available only in the institutional setting of a hospital or medical institute or the like. Such institutions generally have normal clientele boundaries. A veterans' hospital will not concern itself primarily with treating nonveterans, a children's hospital cannot be expected to accommodate the "senior citizen," an army hospital can regard college professors as outside its sphere. Sometimes the boundaries are geographic – a state hospital may admit only residents of a certain state. (There are, of course, indefensible constituency principles – say race or religion, party membership, or ability to pay; and there are cases of borderline legitimacy, e.g., sex.[4]) A medical institution is justified in considering for ELT only persons within its own constituency, provided this constituency is constituted upon a defensible basis. Thus the haemodialysis selection committee in Seattle "agreed to consider only those applications who were residents of the state of Washington.... They justified this stand on the grounds that since the basic research ... had been done at ... a state-supported institution – the people whose taxes had paid for the research should be its first beneficiaries."[5]

While thus insisting that constituency considerations represent a valid and legitimate factor in ELT selection, I do feel there is much to be said for minimizing their role in life-or-death cases. Indeed a refusal to recognize them at all is a significant part of medical tradition, going back to the very oath of Hippocrates. They represent a departure from the ideal arising with the institutionalization of medicine, moving it away from its original status as an art practiced by an individual practitioner.

(B) The progress-of-science factor

The needs of medical research can provide a second valid principle of inclusion. The research interests of the medical staff in relation to the specific nature of the cases at issue is a significant consideration. It may be important for the progress of medical science – and thus of potential benefit to many persons in the future – to determine how effective the ELT at issue is with diabetics or persons over sixty or with a negative RH factor. Considerations of this sort represent another type of legitimate factor in ELT selection.

A very definitely *borderline* case under this head would revolve around the question of a patient's willingness to pay, not in monetary terms, but in offering himself as an experimental subject, say by contracting to return at designated times for a series of tests substantially unrelated to his own health, but yielding data of importance to medical knowledge in general.

(C) The prospect-of-success factor

It may be that while the ELT at issue is not without *some* effectiveness in general, it has been established to be highly effective only with patients in certain specific categories (e.g., females under forty of a specific blood type). This difference in effectiveness – in the absolute or in the probability of success – is (we assume) so marked as to constitute virtually a difference in kind rather than in degree. In this case, it would be perfectly legitimate to adopt the general rule of making the ELT at issue available only or primarily to persons in this substantial-promise-of-success category. (It is on grounds of this sort that young children and persons over fifty are generally ruled out as candidates for haemodialysis.)

We have maintained that the three factors of constituency, progress of science, and prospect of success represent legitimate criteria of inclusion for ELT selection. But it remains to examine the considerations which legitimate them. The legitimating factors are in the final analysis practical or pragmatic in nature. From the practical angle it is advantageous – indeed to some extent necessary – that the arrangements governing medical institutions should embody certain constituency principles. It makes good pragmatic and utilitarian sense that progress-of-science considerations should be operative here. And, finally, the practical aspect is reinforced by a whole host of other considerations – including moral ones – in supporting the prospect-of-success criterion. The workings of each of these factors are of course conditioned by the ever-present element of limited availability. They are operative only in this context, that is, prospect of success is a legitimate consideration at all only because we are dealing with a situation of scarcity.

V The Final Selection Stage: Criteria of Selection

Five sorts of elements must, as we see it, figure primarily among the plausible criteria of selection that are to be brought to bear in further screening the group constituted after application of the criteria of inclusion: the relative-likelihood-of-success factor, the life-expectancy factor, the family role factor, the potential-contributions factor, and the services-rendered factor. The first two represent the *biomedical* aspect, the second three the *social* aspect.

(A) The relative-likelihood-of-success factor

It is clear that the relative likelihood of success is a legitimate and appropriate factor in making a selection within the group of qualified patients that are to receive ELT. This is obviously one of the considerations that must count very significantly in a reasonable selection procedure.

The present criterion is of course closely related to item *C* of the preceding section. There we were concerned with prospect-of-success considerations categorically and *en bloc*. Here at present they come into play in a particularized case-by-case comparison among individuals. If the therapy at issue is not a once-and-for-all proposition and requires ongoing treatment, cognate considerations must be brought in. Thus, for example, in the case of a chronic ELT procedure such as haemodialysis it would clearly make sense to give priority to patients with a potentially reversible condition (who would thus need treatment for only a fraction of their remaining lives).

(B) The life-expectancy factor

Even if the ELT is "successful" in the patient's case he may, considering his age and/or other aspects of his general medical condition, look forward to only a very short probable future life. This is obviously another factor that must be taken into account.

(C) The family role factor

A person's life is a thing of importance not only to himself but to others – friends, associates, neighbors, colleagues, etc. But his (or her) relationship to his immediate family is a thing of unique intimacy and significance. The nature of his relationship to his wife, children, and parents, and the issue of their financial and psychological dependence upon him, are obviously matters that deserve to be given weight in the ELT selection process. Other things being anything like equal, the mother of minor children must take priority over the middle-aged bachelor.

(D) The potential future-contributions factor (prospective service)

In "choosing to save" one life rather than another, "the society," through the mediation of the particular medical institution in question – which should certainly look upon itself as a trustee for the social interest – is clearly warranted in considering the likely pattern of future *services to be rendered* by the patient (adequate recovery assumed), considering his age, talent, training, and past record of performance. In its allocations of ELT, society "invests" a scarce resource in one person as against another and is thus entitled to look to the probable prospective "return" on its investment.

It may well be that a thoroughly egalitarian society is reluctant to put someone's social contribution into the scale in situations of the sort at issue. One popular article states that "the most difficult standard would be the candidate's value to society," and goes on to quote someone who said: "You can't just pick a brilliant painter over a laborer. The average citizen would be quickly eliminated."[6] But what if it were not a brilliant painter but a brilliant surgeon or medical researcher that was at issue? One wonders if the author of the *obiter dictum* that one "can't just pick" would still feel equally sure of his ground. In any case, the fact that the standard is difficult to apply is certainly no reason for not attempting to apply it. The problem of ELT selection is inevitably burdened with difficult standards.

Some might feel that in assessing a patient's value to society one should ask not only who if permitted to continue living can make the greatest contribution to society in some creative or constructive way, but also who by dying would leave behind the greatest burden on society in assuming the discharge of their residual responsibilities.[7] Certainly the philosophical utilitarian would give equal weight to both these considerations. Just here is where I would part ways with orthodox utilitarianism. For – though this is not the place to do so – I should be prepared to argue that a civilized society has an obligation to promote the furtherance of positive achievements in cultural and related areas even if this means the assumption of certain added burdens.[8]

(E) The past services-rendered factor (retrospective service)

A person's services to another person or group have always been taken to constitute a valid basis for a claim upon this person or group – of course a moral and not necessarily a legal claim. Society's obligation for the recognition and reward of services rendered – an obligation whose discharge is also very possibly conducive to self-interest in the long run – is thus another factor to be taken into account. This should be viewed as a morally necessary correlative of the previously considered factor of *prospective* service. It would be morally indefensible of society in effect to say: "Never mind about services you rendered yesterday – it is only the services to be rendered tomorrow that will count with us today." We live in very future-oriented times, constantly preoccupied in a distinctly utilitarian way with future satisfactions. And this disinclines us to give much recognition to past services. But parity considerations of the sort just adduced indicate that such recognition should be given *on grounds of equity*. No doubt a justification for giving weight to services rendered can also be attempted along utilitarian lines. ("The reward of past services rendered spurs people on to greater future efforts and is thus socially advantageous in the long-run future.") In saying that past services should be counted "on grounds of equity" – rather than "on grounds of utility" – I take the view that even if this utilitarian defense could somehow be shown to be fallacious, I should still be prepared to maintain the propriety of taking services rendered into account. The position does not rest on a utilitarian basis and so would not collapse with the removal of such a basis.[9]

As we have said, these five factors fall into three groups: the biomedical factors *A* and *B*, the familial factor *C*, and the social factors *D* and *E*. With items *A* and *B* the need for a detailed analysis of the medical considerations comes to the fore. The age of the patient, his medical history, his physical and psychological condition, his specific disease, etc., will all need to be taken into exact account. These biomedical factors represent technical issues: they call for the physicians' expert judgment and the medical statisticians' hard data. And they are ethically uncontroversial factors – their legitimacy and appropriateness are evident from the very nature of the case.

Greater problems arise with the familial and social factors. They involve intangibles that are difficult to judge. How is one to develop subcriteria for weighing the relative social contributions of (say) an architect or a librarian or a mother of young children? And they involve highly problematic issues. (For example, should good moral character be rated a plus and bad a minus in judging services rendered?) And there is something strikingly unpleasant in grappling with issues of this sort for people brought up in times greatly inclined towards maxims of the type "Judge not!" and "Live and let live!" All the same, in the situation that concerns us here such distasteful problems must be faced, since a failure to choose to save some is tantamount to sentencing all. Unpleasant choices are intrinsic to the problem of ELT selection; they are of the very essence of the matter.[10]

But is reference to all these factors indeed inevitable? The justification for taking account of the medical factors is pretty obvious. But why should the social aspect of services rendered and to be rendered be taken into account at all? The answer is that they must be taken into account not from the *medical* but from the *ethical* point of view. Despite disagreement on many fundamental issues, moral philosophers of the present day are pretty well in consensus that the justification of human actions is to be sought largely and primarily – if not exclusively – in the principles of utility and of justice.[11] But utility requires reference of services to be rendered and justice calls for a recognition of services that have been rendered. Moral considerations would thus demand recognition of these two factors. (This, of course, still leaves open the question of whether the point of view provides a valid basis of action: Why base one's actions upon moral principles? – or, to put it bluntly – Why be moral? The present paper is, however, hardly the place to grapple with so fundamental an issue, which has been canvassed in the literature of philosophical ethics since Plato.)

VI More than Medical Issues are Involved

An active controversy has of late sprung up in medical circles over the question of whether nonphysician laymen should be given a role in ELT selection (in the specific context of chronic haemodialysis). One physician writes: "I think that the assessment of the candidates should be made by a senior doctor on the [dialysis] unit, but I am sure that it would be helpful to him – both in sharing responsibility and in avoiding personal pressure – if a small unnamed group of people [presumably including laymen] officially made the final decision. I visualize the doctor bringing the data to the group, explaining the points in relation to each case, and obtaining their approval of his order of priority."[12]

Essentially this procedure of a selection committee of laymen has for some years been in use in one of the most publicized chronic dialysis units, that of the Swedish Hospital of Seattle, Washington.[13] Many physicians are apparently reluctant to see the choice of allocation of medical therapy pass out of strictly medical hands. Thus in a recent symposium on the "Selection of Patients for Haemodialysis,"[14] Dr. Ralph Shakman writes: "Who is to implement the selection? In my opinion it must ultimately be the responsibility of the consultants in charge of the renal units . . . I can see no reason for delegating this responsibility to lay persons. Surely the latter would be better employed if they could be persuaded to devote their time and energy to raise more and more money for us to spend on our patients."[15] Other contributors to this symposium strike much the same note. Dr F. M. Parsons writes: "In an attempt to overcome . . . difficulties in selection some have advocated introducing certain specified lay people into the discussions. Is it wise? I doubt whether a committee of this type can adjudicate as satisfactorily as two medical colleagues, particularly as successful therapy involves close cooperation between doctor and patient."[16] And Dr M. A. Wilson writes in the same symposium: "The suggestion has been made that lay panels should select individuals for dialysis from among a group who are medically suitable. Though this would relieve the doctor-in-charge of a heavy load of responsibility, it would place the burden on those who have no personal knowledge and have to base their judgments on medical or social reports. I do not believe this would result in better decisions for the group or improve the doctor–patient relationship in individual cases."[17]

But no amount of flag-waving about the doctor's facing up to his responsibility – or prostrations before the idol of the doctor–patient relationship and reluctance to admit laymen into the sacred precincts of the conference chambers of medical consultations – can obscure the essential fact that ELT selection is not a wholly medical problem. When there are more than enough places in an ELT programme to accommodate all who need it, then it will clearly be a medical question to decide who does have the need and which among these would successfully respond. But when an admitted gross insufficiency of places exists, when there are ten or fifty or one hundred highly eligible candidates for each place in the programme, then it is unrealistic to take the view that purely medical criteria can furnish a sufficient basis for selection. The question of ELT selection becomes serious as a phenomenon of scale – because, as more candidates present themselves, strictly medical factors are increasingly less adequate as a selection criterion precisely because by numerical category-crowding there will be more and more cases whose "status is much the same" so far as purely medical considerations go.

The ELT selection problem clearly poses issues that transcend the medical sphere because – in the nature of the case – many residual issues remain to be dealt with once *all* of the medical questions have been faced. Because of this there is good reason why laymen as well as physicians should be involved in the selection process. Once the medical considerations have been brought to bear, fundamental social issues remain to be resolved. The instrumentalities of ELT have been created through the social investment of scarce resources, and the interests of the society deserve to play a role in their utilization. As representatives of their social interests, lay opinions should function to complement and supplement medical views once the proper arena of medical considerations is left behind.[18] Those physicians who have urged the presence of lay members on selection panels can, from this point of view, be recognized as having seen the issue in proper perspective.

One physician has argued against lay representation on selection panels for haemodialysis as follows: "If the doctor advises dialysis and the lay panel refuses, the patient will regard this as a death sentence passed by an anonymous court from which he has no right of appeal."[19] But this drawback is not specific to the use of a lay panel. Rather, it is a feature inherent in every *selection* procedure, regardless of whether the selection is done by the head doctor of the unit, by a panel of physicians, etc. No matter who does the selecting among patients recommended for dialysis, the feelings of the patient who has been rejected (and knows it) can be expected to be much the same, provided that he recognizes the actual nature of the choice (and is not deceived by the possibly convenient but ultimately poisonous fiction that because the selection was made by physicians it was made entirely on medical grounds).

In summary, then, the question of ELT selection would appear to be one that is in its very nature heavily laden with issues of medical research, practice, and administration. But it will not be a question that can be resolved on solely medical grounds. Strictly social issues of justice and utility will invariably arise in this area – questions going outside the medical area in whose resolution medical laymen can and should play a substantial role.

VII The Inherent Imperfection (Non-optimality) of Any Selection System

Our discussion to this point of the design of a selection system for ELT has left a gap that is a very fundamental and serious omission. We have argued that five factors must be taken into substantial and explicit account:

A *Relative likelihood of success.* – Is the chance of the treatment's being "successful" to be rated as high, good, average, etc.?[20]

B *Expectancy of future life.* – Assuming the "success" of the treatment, how much longer does the patient stand a good chance (75 per cent or better) of living – considering his age and general condition?

C *Family role.* – To what extent does the patient have responsibilities to others in his immediate family?

D *Social contributions rendered.* – Are the patient's past services to his society outstanding, substantial, average, etc.?

E *Social contributions to be rendered.* – Considering his age, talents, training, and past record of performance, is there a substantial probability that the patient will – *adequate recovery being assumed* – render in the future services to his society that can be characterized as outstanding, substantial, average, etc.?

This list is clearly insufficient for the construction of a reasonable selection system, since that would require not only *that these factors be taken into account* (somehow or other), but – going beyond this – would specify *a specific set of procedures for taking account of them.* The specific procedures that would constitute such a system would have to take account of the interrelationship of these factors (e.g., *B* and *E*), and to set out exact guidelines as to the relevant weight that is to be given to each of them. This is something our discussion has not as yet considered.

In fact, I should want to maintain that there is no such thing here as a single rationally superior selection system. The position of affairs seems to me to be something like this: (1) it is necessary (for reasons already canvassed) to *have* a system, and to have a system that is rationally defensible, and (2) to be rationally defensible, this system must take the factors *A–E* into substantial and explicit account. But (3) the exact manner in which a rationally defensible system takes account of these factors cannot be fixed in any one specific way on the basis of general considerations. Any of the variety of ways that give *A–E* "their due" will be acceptable and viable. One cannot hope to find within this range of workable systems some one that is *optimal* in relation to the alternatives. There is no one system that does "the (uniquely) best" – only a variety of systems that do "as well as one can expect to do" in cases of this sort.

The situation is structurally very much akin to that of rules of partition of an estate among the relations of a decedent. It is important *that there be* such rules. And it is reasonable that spouse, children, parents, siblings, etc., be taken account of in these rules. But the question of the exact method of division – say that when the decedent has neither living spouse nor living children then his estate is to be divided, dividing 60 per cent between parents, 40 per cent between siblings versus dividing 90 per cent between parents, 10 per cent between siblings – cannot be settled on the basis of any general abstract considerations of reasonableness. Within broad limits, a *variety* of resolutions are all perfectly acceptable – so that no one procedure can justifiably be regarded as "the (uniquely) best" because it is superior to all others.[21]

VIII A Possible Basis for a Reasonable Selection System

Having said that there is no such thing as *the optimal* selection system for ELT, I want now to sketch out the broad features of what I would regard as *one acceptable* system.

The basis for the system would be a point rating. The scoring here at issue would give roughly equal weight to the medical considerations (*A* and *B*) in comparison with the extramedical considerations (*C* = family role, *D* = services rendered, and *E* = services to be rendered), also giving roughly equal weight to the three items involved here (*C*, *D*, and *E*). The result of such a scoring procedure would provide the essential *starting point* of our ELT selection mechanism. I deliberately say "starting point" because it seems to me that one should not follow the results of this scoring in an *automatic* way. I would propose that the actual selection should only be guided but not actually be dictated by this scoring procedure, along lines now to be explained.

IX The Desirability of Introducing an Element of Chance

The detailed procedure I would propose – not of course as optimal (for reasons we have seen), but as eminently acceptable – would combine the scoring procedure just discussed with an element of chance. The resulting selection system would function as follows:

1 First the criteria of inclusion of Section IV above would be applied to constitute a *first phase selection group* – which (we shall suppose) is substantially larger than the number *n* of persons who can actually be accommodated with ELT.
2 Next the criteria of selection of Section V are brought to bear via a scoring procedure of the type described in Section VIII. On this basis a *second phase selection group* is constituted which is only *somewhat* larger – say by a third or a half – than the critical number *n* at issue.
3 If this second phase selection group is relatively homogeneous as regards rating by the scoring procedure – that is, if there are no really major disparities within this group (as would be likely if the initial group was significantly larger than *n*) – then the final selection is made by *random* selection of *n* persons from within this group.

This introduction of the element of chance – in what could be dramatized as a "lottery of life and death" – must be justified. The fact is that such a procedure would bring with it three substantial advantages.

First, as we have argued above (in Section VII), any acceptable selection system is inherently nonoptimal. The introduction of the element of chance prevents the results that life-and-death choices are made by the automatic application of an admittedly imperfect selection method.

Second, a recourse to chance would doubtless make matters easier for the rejected patient and those who have a specific interest in him. It would surely be quite hard for them to accept his exclusion by relatively mechanical application of objective criteria in whose implementation subjective judgement is involved. But the circumstances of life have conditioned us to accept the workings of chance and to tolerate the element of luck (good or bad): human life is an inherently contingent process. Nobody, after all, has an absolute right to ELT – but most of us would feel that we have "every bit as much right" to it as anyone else in significantly similar circumstances. The introduction of the element of chance assures a like handling of like cases over the widest possible area that seems reasonable in the circumstances.

Third (and perhaps least), such a recourse to random selection does much to relieve the administrators of the selection system of the awesome burden of ultimate and absolute responsibility.

These three considerations would seem to build up a substantial case for introducing the element of chance into the mechanism of the system for ELT selection in a way limited and circumscribed by other weightier considerations, along some such lines as those set forth above.[22]

It should be recognized that this injection of *man-made* chance supplements the element of *natural* chance that is present inevitably and in any case (apart from the role of chance in singling out certain persons as victims for the affliction at issue). As F. M. Parsons has observed: "any vacancies [in an ELT program – specifically haemodialysis] will be filled immediately by the first suitable patients, even though their claims for therapy may subsequently prove less than those of other patients refused later."[23] Life is a chancy business and even the most rational of human arrangements can cover this over to a very limited extent at best.

References[24]

Alexander, S., "They Decide Who Lives, Who Dies," *Life*, LIII (November 9, 1962), 102–25.

Doyle, C., "Spare-Part Heart Surgeons Worried by Their Success," *Observer* (London), (May 12, 1968).

Fletcher, J., *Morals and Medicine* (London, 1955).

Gorovitz, S., "Ethics and the Allocation of Medical Resources," *Medical Research Engineering*, V (1966), 5–7.

Lader, L., "Who Has the Right To Live?" *Good Housekeeping* (January, 1968), 85 and 144–50.

Nabarro, J. D. N., Parsons, F. M., Shakman, R. and Wilson, M. A., "Selection of Patients for Haemodialysis," *British Medical Journal* (March 11, 1967), 622–4.

Schmeck, H. M., Jr. "Panel Holds Life-or-Death Vote in Allotting of Artificial Kidney," *New York Times* (May 6, 1962), 1, 83.

Wolstenholme, G. E. W. and O'Connor, M. (eds). *Ethics in Medical Progress* (London, 1966).

Notes

1 Christine Doyle, "Spare-Part Heart Surgeons Worried by Their Success," *Observer* (May 12, 1968).

2 J. D. N. Nabarro, "Selection of Patients for Haemodialysis," *British Medical Journal* (March 11, 1967), p. 623. Although several thousand patients die in the UK each year from renal failure – there are about thirty new cases per million of population – only 10 per cent of these can for the foreseeable future be accommodated with chronic haemodialysis. Kidney transplantation – itself a very tricky procedure – cannot make a more than minor contribution here. In 1993 I learned that patients can be maintained in home dialysis at an operating cost about half that of maintaining them in a hospital dialysis unit (roughly an $8,000 minimum). In the United States, around 7,000 patients with terminal uremia who could benefit from haemodialysis evolve yearly. As of mid-1968, some 1,000 of these can be accommodated in existing hospital units. By June 1967, a world-wide total of some 120 patients were in treatment by home dialysis. (Data from a paper, "Home Dialysis," by C. M. Conty and H. V. Murdaugh. See also R. A. Baillod et al., "Overnight Haemodialysis in the Home," *Proceedings of the European Dialysis and Transplant Association*, VI [1965], 99 ff.).

3 For the Hippocratic Oath see *Hippocrates: Works* (Loeb ed; London, 1959), I, p. 298.

4 Another example of borderline legitimacy is posed by an endowment "with strings attached," e.g., "In accepting this legacy the hospital agrees to admit and provide all needed treatment for any direct descendant of myself, its founder."

5 Shana Alexander, "They Decide Who Lives Who Dies," *Life*, LIII (November 9, 1962), 102–25 (see p. 107).

6 Lawrence Lader, "Who Has the Right To Live?" *Good Housekeeping* (January 1968), 144.

7 This approach could thus be continued to embrace the previous factor, that of family role, the preceding item (*C*).

8 Moreover a doctrinaire utilitarian would presumably be willing to withdraw a continuing mode of ELT such as haemodialysis from a patient to make room for a more promising candidate who came to view at a later stage and who could not otherwise be accommodated. I should be unwilling to adopt this course, partly on grounds of utility (with a view to the demoralization of insecurity), partly on the non-utilitarian ground that a "moral commitment" has been made and must be honored.

9 Of course the difficult question remains of the relative weight that should be given to prospective and retrospective service in cases where these factors conflict. There is good reason to treat them on a par.

10 This is the symposium on "Selection of Patients for Haemodialysis," *British Medical Journal* (March 11, 1967), 622–4. F. M. Parsons writes: "But other forms of selecting patients [distinct from first come, first served] are suspect in my view if they imply evaluation of man by man. What criteria could be used? Who could justify a claim that the life of a mayor would be more valuable than that of the humblest citizen of his borough? Whatever we may think as individuals none of us is indispensable." But having just set out this hard-line view he immediately backs away from it: "On the other hand, to assume that there was little to choose between Alexander Fleming and Adolf Hitler... would be nonsense, and we should be naive if we were to pretend that we could not be influenced by their achievements and characters if we had to choose between the two of them. Whether we like it or not we cannot escape the fact that this kind of selection for long-term haemodialysis will be required until very large sums of money become available for equipment and services [so that *everyone* who needs treatment can be accommodated]."

11 The relative fundamentality of these principles is, however, a substantially disputed issue.

12 J. D. N. Nabarro, "Selection of Patients," 622.

13 See Shana Alexander, "They Decide Who Lives."

14 *British Medical Journal* (March 11, 1967), 622–4.

15 Ibid., p. 624. Another contributor writes in the same symposium, "The selection of the few [to receive haemodialysis] is proving very difficult – a true 'Doctor's Dilemma' – for almost everybody would agree that this must be a medical decision, preferably reached by consultation among colleagues" (Dr F. M. Parsons. ibid., p. 623).

16 "The Selection of Patients for Haemodialysis," (n. 10 above), 623.

17 Dr Wilson's article concludes with the perplexing suggestion – wildly beside the point given the structure of the situation at issue – that "the final decision will be made by the patient." But this contention is only marginally more ludicrous than Parson's contention that in selecting patients for haemodialysis "gainful employment in a well chosen occupation is necessary to achieve the best results" since "only the minority wish to live on charity" ibid.

18 To say this is of course not to deny that such questions of applied medical ethics will invariably involve a host of medical considerations – it is only to insist that extramedical considerations will also invariably be at issue.

19 M. A. Wilson, "Selection of Patients for Haemodialysis," p. 624.

20 In the case of an ongoing treatment involving complex procedure and dietary and other mode-of-life restrictions – and chronic haemodialysis definitely falls into this category – the patient's psychological makeup, his willpower to "stick with it" in the face of substantial discouragements – will obviously also be a substantial factor here. The man who gives up, takes not his life alone, but (figuratively speaking) also that of the person he replaced in the treatment schedule.

21 To say that acceptable solutions can range over broad limits is *not* to say that there are no limits at all. It is an obviously intriguing and fundamental problem to raise the question of the factors that set these limits. This complex issue cannot be dealt with adequately here. Suffice it to say that considerations regarding precedent and people's expectations, factors of social utility, and matters of fairness and sense of justice all come into play.

22 One writer has mooted the suggestion that: "Perhaps the right thing to do, difficult as it may be to accept, is to select [for haemodialysis] from among the medical and psychologically qualified patients on a strictly random basis" (S. Gorovitz, "Ethics and the Allocation of Medical Resources," *Medical Research Engineering*, V [1966], p. 7). Outright random selection would, however, seem indefensible because of its refusal to give weight to considerations which, under the circumstances, *deserve* to be given weight. The proposed procedure of superimposing a certain degree of randomness upon the rational-choice criteria would seem to combine the advantages of the two without importing the worst defects of either.

23 "Selection of Patients for Haemodialysis," 623. The question of whether a patient for chronic treatment should ever be terminated from the programme (say if he contracts cancer) poses a variety of difficult ethical problems with which we need not at present concern ourselves. But it does seem plausible to take the (somewhat anti-utilitarian) view that a patient should not be terminated simply because a "better qualified" patient comes along later on. It would seem that a quasi-contractual relationship has been created through established expectations and reciprocal understandings, and that the situation is in this regard akin to that of the man who, having

undertaken to sell his house to one buyer, cannot afterward unilaterally undo this arrangement to sell it to a higher bidder who "needs it worse" (thus maximizing the over-all utility).

24 I acknowledge with thanks the help of Miss Hazel Johnson, Reference Librarian at the University of Pittsburgh Library, in connection with the bibliography.

42

The Value of Life

John Harris

Suppose that only one place is available on a renal dialysis programme or that only one bed is vacant in a vital transplantation unit or that resuscitation could be given in the time and with the resources available to only one patient. Suppose further that of the two patients requiring any of these resources, one is a 70-year-old widower, friendless and living alone, and the other a 40-year-old mother of three young children with a husband and a career.

Or suppose that following a major disaster medical resources were available to save the lives of only half those for whom medical care was vital for life. Or, less dramatically, suppose that in the next two years, only half of 200 patients waiting for surgery that will alleviate severe discomfort can be accommodated in the only available hospital. Suppose further and finally that all candidates stand an equal chance of maximum benefit from any of the available treatments. Whom should we treat and what justifies our decision?

Many will think that in the first case preference should be given to the young mother rather than the old friendless widower, that this is obviously the right choice. There might be a number of grounds for such a decision. Two of these grounds have to do with age. One indicates a preference for the young on the grounds that they have a greater expectation of life if they are restored to health. The other favours the young simply because their life is likely to be fuller and hence more valuable than that of the older person. Another consideration to which many will want to give some weight is that of the number of people dependent on or even caring about a potential victim. It is sometimes also considered relevant to give weight to the patient's probable usefulness to the community or even their moral character before a final decision is made. And of course these considerations may be taken together in various combinations.

In the case of a major disaster related problems arise. If say a policy of triage[1] has identified the only group of victims to be treated, those for whom medical intervention will make the difference between life and death, but there are still not enough resources to help all such persons, then, again, many will hold that the right thing to do is help the young or those with dependants and so on first.

Those who believe that they ought to select the patient or patients to be saved on any of the above criteria will believe that they must show preference for some types or conditions of person over others. Another available strategy is of course to decline to choose between people in any way that involves preferring one patient, or one sort of person, to another. Perhaps the easiest way of declining to show such a preference is to toss a coin or draw lots to decide who shall be helped. I want to consider what might count as a good reason for preferring to help some patients rather than others where all cannot be helped and also whether our intuitive preference for saving the younger and more useful members of society can be sustained.

I The Moral Significance of Age

Many, perhaps most, people feel that, in cases like the one with which we began, there is some moral

From *The Value of Life* (London: Routledge, 1985), pp. 87–102. Reprinted with permission.

reason to save the 40-year-old mother rather than the 70-year-old widower. A smaller, but perhaps growing, group of people would see this as a sort of 'ageist' prejudice which, in a number of important areas of resource allocation and care, involves giving the old a much worse deal than the younger members of society. This is an exceptionally difficult issue to resolve. A number of the ways of thinking about the issue of the moral relevance of age yield opposed conclusions or seem to tug in opposite directions.

I want first to look at an argument which denies that we should prefer the young mother in our opening example. It is an anti-ageist argument so that is what I will call it, but it is not perhaps the usual sort of argument used to defend the rights of the old.

The anti-ageist argument

All of us who wish to go on living have something that each of us values equally although for each it is different in character, for some a much richer prize than for others, and we none of us know its true extent. This thing is of course 'the rest of our lives'. So long as we do not know the date of our deaths then for each of us the 'rest of our lives' is of indefinite duration. Whether we are 17 or 70, in perfect health or suffering from a terminal disease, we each have the rest of our lives to lead. So long as we each fervently wish to live out the rest of our lives, however long that turns out to be, then if we do not deserve to die, we each suffer the same injustice if our wishes are deliberately frustrated and we are cut off prematurely. Indeed there may well be a double injustice in deciding that those whose life expectation is short should not benefit from rescue or resuscitation. Suppose I am told today that I have terminal cancer with only approximately six months or so to live, but I want to live until I die, or at least until I decide that life is no longer worth living. Suppose I am then involved in an accident and, because my condition is known to my potential rescuers and there are not enough resources to treat all who could immediately be saved, I am marked among those who will not be helped. I am then the victim of a double tragedy and a double injustice. I am stricken first by cancer and the knowledge that I have only a short time to live and I'm then stricken again when I'm told that because of my first tragedy a second and more immediate one is to be visited upon me. Because I have once been unlucky I'm now no longer worth saving.

The point is a simple but powerful one. However short or long my life will be, so long as I want to go on living it then I suffer a terrible injustice when that life is prematurely cut short. Imagine a group of people all of an age, say a class of students all in their mid-twenties. If fire trapped all in the lecture theatre and only twenty could be rescued in time, should the rescuers shout 'youngest first!'? Suppose they had time to debate the question or had been debating it 'academically' before the fire? It would surely seem invidious to deny some what all value so dearly merely because of an accident of birth? It might be argued that age here provides no criterion precisely because although the lifespans of such a group might be expected to vary widely, there would be no way of knowing who was most likely to live longest. But suppose a reliable astrologer could make very realistic estimates or, what amounts to the same thing, suppose the age range of the students to be much greater, say 17 to 55. Does not the invidiousness of selecting by birthdate remain? Should a 17-year-old be saved before a 29-year-old or she before the 45-year-old and should the 55-year-old clearly be the last to be saved or the first to be sacrificed?

Our normal intuitions would share this sense of the invidiousness of choosing between our imaginary students by reason of their respective ages, but would start to want to make age relevant at some extremes, say if there were a 2-day-old baby and a 90-year-old grandmother. We will be returning to discuss a possible basis for this intuition in a moment. However, it is important to be clear that the anti-ageist argument denies the relevance of age or life expectancy as a criterion absolutely. It argues that even if I know for certain that I have only a little space to live, that space, however short, may be very precious to me. Precious, precisely because it is all the time I have left, and just as precious to me on that account as all the time you have left is precious to you, however much those two time spans differ in length. So that where we both want, equally strongly, to go on living, then we each suffer the same injustice[2] when our lives are cut short or are cut further short.[3]

It might seem that someone who would insist on living out the last few months of his life when by 'going quietly' someone else might have the chance to live for a much longer time would be a very selfish person. But this would be true only if the anti-ageist argument is false. It will be true only if it is not plausible to claim that living out the rest of one's life could be equally valuable to the individual whose life it is irrespective of the amount of unelapsed time that is left. And this is of course precisely the usual situation when individuals do not normally have anything but the haziest of ideas as to how long it is that they might have left.

I think the anti-ageist argument has much plausibility. It locates the wrongness of ending an individual's life in the evil of thwarting that person's desire to go on living and argues that it is profoundly unjust to frustrate that desire merely because some of those who have exactly the same desire, held no more strongly, also have a longer life expectancy than the others. However, there are a number of arguments that pull in the opposite direction and these we must now consider.

The fair innings argument

One problem with the anti-ageist argument is our feeling that there is something unfair about a person who has lived a long and happy life hanging on grimly at the end, while someone who has not been so fortunate suffers a related double misfortune, of losing out in a lottery in which his life happened to be in the balance with that of the grim octogenarian. It might be argued that we could accept the part of the anti-ageist argument which focuses on the equal value of unelapsed time, if this could be tempered in some way. How can it be just that someone who has already had more than her fair share of life and its delights should be preferred or even given an equal chance of continued survival with the young person who has not been so favoured? One strategy that seems to take account of our feeling that there is something wrong with taking steps to prolong the lives of the very old at the expense of those much younger is the fair innings argument.

The fair innings argument takes the view that there is some span of years that we consider a reasonable life, a fair innings. Let's say that a fair share of life is the traditional three score and ten, seventy years. Anyone who does not reach 70 suffers, on this view, the injustice of being cut off in their prime. They have missed out on a reasonable share of life; they have been short-changed. Those, however, who do make 70 suffer no such injustice, they have not lost out but rather must consider any additional years a sort of bonus beyond that which could reasonably be hoped for. The fair innings argument requires that everyone be given an equal chance to have a fair innings, to reach the appropriate threshold but, having reached it, they have received their entitlement. The rest of their life is the sort of bonus which may be cancelled when this is necessary to help others reach the threshold.

The attraction of the fair innings argument is that it preserves and incorporates many of the features that made the anti-ageist argument plausible, but allows us to preserve our feeling that the old who have had a good run for their money should not be endlessly propped up at the expense of those who have not had the same chance. We can preserve the conclusion of the anti-ageist argument, that so long as life is equally valued by the person whose life it is, it should be given an equal chance of preservation, and we can go on taking this view until the people in question have reached a fair innings.

There is, however, an important difficulty with the fair innings argument. It is that the very arguments which support the setting of the threshold at an age which might plausibly be considered to be a reasonable lifespan, equally support the setting of the threshold at any age at all, so long as an argument from fairness can be used to support so doing. Suppose that there is only one place available on the dialysis programme and two patients are in competition for it. One is 30 and the other 40 years of age. The fair innings argument requires that neither be preferred on the grounds of age since both are below the threshold and are entitled to an equal chance of reaching it. If there is no other reason to choose between them we should do something like toss a coin. However, the 30-year-old can argue that the considerations which support the fair innings argument require that she be given the place. After all, what's fair about the fair innings argument is precisely that each individual should have an equal chance of enjoying the benefits of a reasonable lifespan. The younger patient can argue that, from where she's standing, the age of 40 looks much more reasonable a span than that of 30, and that she should be given the chance to benefit from those ten extra years.

This argument generalized becomes a reason for always preferring to save younger rather than older people, whatever the age difference, and makes the original anti-ageist argument begin to look again the more attractive line to take. For the younger person can always argue that the older has had a fairer innings, and should now give way. It is difficult to stop whatever span is taken to be a fair innings collapsing towards zero under pressure from those younger candidates who see their innings as less fair than that of those with a larger share.

But perhaps this objection to the fair innings argument is mistaken? If seventy years is a fair innings it does not follow that the nearer a span of life approaches seventy years, the fairer an innings it is. This may be revealed by considering a different sort of threshold. Suppose that most people can run a mile in seven minutes, and that two people are given the opportunity to show that they can run a mile in that time. They both expect to be given seven minutes. However, if one is in fact given only three minutes and the other only four, it's not true that the latter is given a fairer running time: for people with average abilities four minutes is no more realistic a time in which to run a mile than is three. Four minutes is neither a fair threshold in itself, nor a fairer one than three minutes would be.

Nor does the argument that establishes seven minutes as an appropriate threshold lend itself to variation downwards. For that argument just is that seven is the number of minutes that an average adult takes to run a mile. Why then is it different for lifespans? If three score and ten is the number of years available to most people for getting what life has to offer, and is also the number of years people can reasonably expect to have, then it is a misfortune to be allowed anything less however much less one is allowed, if nothing less than the full span normally suffices for getting what can be got out of life. It's true that the 40-year-old gets more time than the 30-year-old, but the frame of reference is not time only, but time normally required for a full life.[4]

This objection has some force, but its failure to be a good analogy reveals that two sorts of considerations go to make an innings fair. For while living a full or complete life, just in the sense of experiencing all the ages of man,[5] is one mark of a fair innings, there is also value in living through as many ages as possible. Just as completing the mile is one value, it is not the only one. Runners in the race of life also value ground covered, and generally judge success in terms of distance run.

What the fair innings argument needs to do is to capture and express in a workable form the truth that while it is always a *misfortune* to die when one wants to go on living, it is not a *tragedy* to die in old age; but it is, on the other hand, both a tragedy and a misfortune to be cut off prematurely. Of course ideas like 'old age' and 'premature death' are inescapably vague, and may vary from society to society, and over time as techniques for postponing death improve. We must also remember that while it may be invidious to choose between a 30- and a 40-year-old on the grounds that one has had a fairer innings than the other, it may not be invidious to choose between the 30- and the 65-year-old on those grounds.

If we remember, too, that it will remain wrong to end the life of someone who wants to live or to fail to save them, and that the fair innings argument will only operate as a principle of selection where we are forced to choose between lives, then something workable might well be salvaged.

While 'old age' is irredeemably vague, we can tell the old from the young, and even the old from the middle-aged, so that without attempting precise formulation, a reasonable form of the fair innings argument might hold; and might hold that people who had achieved old age or who were closely approaching it would not have their lives further prolonged when this could only be achieved at the cost of the lives of those who were not nearing old age. These categories could be left vague, the idea being that it would be morally defensible to prefer to save the lives of those who 'still had their lives before them' rather than those who had 'already lived full lives'. The criterion to be employed in each case would simply be what reasonable people would say about whether someone had had a fair innings. Where reasonable people would be in no doubt that a particular individual was nearing old age *and* that that person's life could only be further prolonged at the expense of the life of someone that no reasonable person would classify as nearing old age, then the fair innings argument would apply, and it would be justifiable to save the younger candidate.

In cases where reasonable people differed or it seemed likely that they would differ as to whether people fell into one category or the other, then the anti-ageist argument would apply and the inescapable choice would have to be made arbitrarily.

But again it must be emphasized that the fair innings argument would only operate as a counsel of despair, when it was clearly impossible to postpone the deaths of all those who wanted to go on living. In all other circumstances the anti-ageist argument would apply.

So far so good. There are, however, further problems in the path of the anti-ageist argument and some of them are also problems for the fair innings argument.

Numbers of lives and numbers of years

One immediate problem is that although living as long as possible, however long that turns out to be, will normally be very important to each individual, it seems a bad basis for planning health care or justifying the distribution of resources.

Suppose a particular disease, cancer, kills 120,000 people a year. Suppose further that a drug is developed which would prolong the lives of all cancer victims by one month but no more. Would it be worth putting such a drug into production? What if, for the same cost, a different drug would give ten years' complete remission, but would only operate on a form of cancer that affects 1,000 people? If we cannot afford both, which should we invest in? Or, what if there is only one place on a renal dialysis programme and two patients who could benefit, but one will die immediately without dialysis but in six months in any event. The other will also die immediately without dialysis but with such help will survive for ten years. Although each wants the extra span of life equally badly, many would think that we ought to save the one with the longer life expectancy, that she is the 'better bet'.

All of these cases are an embarrassment for the anti-ageist argument, for our reaction to them implies that we do value extra years more. But how much more?

Extra life-time versus extra lives

> If we choose to save one person for a predicted span of sixty years, rather than saving five people each for a predicted span of ten years, we have gained ten extra life years at the cost of overriding the desires of four extra people.[6]

So far we have looked at the issue of whether we should count length of life or desire to live as the most important factor when deciding which of two people should be saved. If all things are equal, there can be no reason to prefer one to the other and so we should choose in a way that does not display preference, by lot, for example. The question that seems so difficult is what, if any, difference should length of life make to such choices?

The anti-ageist argument says that it should make no difference, but the cases we have just been examining seem to pull the other way. And if we are persuaded by such cases this seems to imply that we do think length of life or life expectancy gives additional value to lives and so constitutes a factor which must be given some weight. One consequence of this is that we should think it more important to save one 10-year-old rather than five 60-year-olds (if we take 70 as an arbitrary maximum).[7] Equally, it would be better to save one 20-year-old rather than two 50-year-old people, for we would again save ten life years by so doing. Or one 15-year-old rather than two 45-year-olds (a saving of five life years) and so on.

It is just at this point that the anti-ageist argument seems to require resuscitation, for there is surely something invidious about sacrificing two 45-year-olds to one 15-year-old. To take the 'life years' view seems to discount entirely the desires and hopes and life plans of people in middle age, whenever an importunate youngster can place herself in the balance against them. But we do not normally think it better to save a 15-year-old rather than a 45-year-old when we cannot save both, so why should we think it better to save a 15-year-old rather than *two* 45-year olds?

For those who do favour saving one 15-year-old rather than two 45-year-olds, there is another difficulty. The life-time view seems to commit us to favouring total life-time saved rather than total number of people saved, with bizarre consequences. Suppose I could prolong the lives of 121,000 people for one month? This would yield a saving of 121,000 life months. Alternatively I could develop a drug which would give ten more years of life to 1,000 people. This would yield a saving of 120,000 life months. Thus, on the time-span view, we should choose to extend the lives of 121,000 people by one month rather than 1,000 people by ten years each. So, what started out by looking as though it constituted an objection to the anti-ageist argument actually supports it in some circumstances. For, while we should favour length of life, where numbers of lives balanced against one another are equal, we should favour numbers of lives where, summed together, they yield a greater contribution to the total amount of life-time saved.

Unfortunately the force of the comparison between extending the lives of 120,000 people for one month or 1,000 for ten years was to encourage us to think that life-time saved was more important than numbers of lives saved. Its support for this conclusion now seems less decisive. What it seems to indicate is a very complicated calculus in which allocation of resources would be dependent on the amount of life-time such allocation could save. It would also lead to some bizarre orderings of priority, and not necessarily to those envisaged by enthusiasts of such a scheme.

One such enthusiast, Dr Donald Gould, produced the following scenario:

> Calculations are based on the assumption that all who survive their first perilous year ought then to live on to the age of 70 . . . In Denmark for example, there are 50,000 deaths a year, but only 20,000 among citizens in the 1–70 bracket. These are the ones that count. The annual number of life years lost in this group totals 264,000. Of these 80,000 are lost because of accidents and suicides, 40,000 because of coronary heart disease, and 20,000 are due to lung disease. On the basis of these figures, a large proportion of the 'health' budget ought to be spent on preventing accidents and suicides and a lesser . . . amount on attempting to prevent and cure heart and lung disease. Much less would be spent on cancer which is predominantly a disease of the latter half of life, and which therefore contributes relatively little to the total sum of life years lost . . . No money at all would be available for trying to prolong the life of a sick old man of 82.[8]

The first thing to note about Gould's scenario is, that while deaths before the age of 70 may be the only life years *considered to have been lost*,[9] it does not follow that there is no reason to attempt to *gain* life years by prolonging the lives of the over-seventies if that seems feasible. For example, if a reasonable prognosis is that the life of the 70-year-old could be prolonged for five years by some intervention, then that is still a gain of five life years. This can have important consequences, for it means that it would be quite wrong to write-off all care for the over-seventies. Suppose a simple procedure would add one year to the lives of all septuagenarians. This would yield a huge gain in life years spread over a whole population. Suppose, as is perhaps likely, the number of septuagenarians in Denmark was over 260,000, then the number of life years saved by adding a further year to their lives would exceed the total to be gained by all the measures to prevent accidents, suicides, heart disease and so on. This would then become the chief priority for health care spending.

Gould starts his calculations after 'the first perilous year' but this cut-off point would require justification. We might well conclude, persuaded by his general line of argument, that neonatal and postnatal care would have the first priority for resources.

The life-time position then can support a wide variety of practices and may lead to a policy of achieving small gains in lifespan for large numbers of people rather than to the sorts of substantial gains for those individuals with most to lose that its supporters seem to have principally in mind.

Threshold of discrimination It is tempting to think that we might be able to get over some of the problems of the life-time position by arguing that we can discount small gains in time as below the level of discrimination, in the sense that the benefit to the individual which accrued from living for a comparatively short period of extra time was nugatory. This might solve a few of the problems for the life-time position which arise from the necessity it imposes of favouring one group of people over another, wherever and whenever they are sufficiently numerous that the total life-time saved by rescuing them, even for a negligibly short period, exceeds that which might be saved by rescuing another smaller group who would live longer individually, but shorter collectively. However, the problem will remain wherever the amount of life-time to be saved is just enough to be worth having (or is thought so to be by those whose time it is) but seems a poor return on the investment required to procure it or in terms of other savings, including savings of longer individual life-time, that might be made instead.

People versus policies We are strongly inclined to believe that where, for example, we can prolong the lives of 120,000 people by one month or 1,000 people by ten years that we should do the latter and that it is better to use a scarce resource to save the life of someone who is likely to live on for at least ten years rather than that of someone who will die in six months in any event. This inclination makes it look as though what we must in fact value is length of life-time rather than simply saving lives. But valuing life-time can be as dangerous to our moral intuitions as is the anti-ageist argument. Again, it might be tempting to believe that a policy of devoting resources to saving individual lives for as long as possible was better than simply maximizing life-time saved. There might be a number of different grounds for such a belief. One such ground would be the expectation that procedures which could prolong individual lives by a substantial period would lead to a greater saving of life-time in the long term than would procedures which merely postponed death for a month or so. But in the absence of any strong evidence for such a conclusion this expectation would be at best an act of faith and at worse a pious hope. Is there any way out?

The fallacy of life-time views

Suppose various medical research teams to be in competition for all research funds available and that one team could demonstrate that it was capable of producing an elixir of life that would make anyone taking it immortal. Suppose further that the entire world medical research budget, if applied to this end would produce just enough elixir for one dose, and that nothing less than a full dose would have any effect at all. The life-time view suggests that all the money should go to making one person immortal rather than, say, to an alternative project by which another team could make everyone on earth live to a flourishing 80![10]

But there is an obvious fallacy in this argument which reveals a defect in the whole life-time approach. Making one person immortal will produce a saving of no more life years than would the alternative of making everyone on earth live to a flourishing 80. So long as the world itself and its population lasts as long as the immortal (and how – and where – could he last longer?) there would be no net increase in life years lived. Indeed, so long as there is either a stable or an increasing world population, from the life years point of view, it matters not at all who lives and who dies, nor does it matter how many years anyone survives. For, so long as those who die are replaced on a one-for-one or better than a one-for-one basis, there will be no loss of life years. Nor will there be any gain in life years when particular individuals live for longer. For if the overall world population is stable, then prolonging the life of particular individuals does not increase the total number of life years the world contains. And if the world population is increasing then it is highly unlikely that prolonging the lives of particular people will fuel that increase. Indeed the reverse is more likely to be the case with the survival of people beyond child-bearing age having a retarding effect on the rate of increase.

In the context of a stable or of an increasing world population, any idea that any policy which did not have the effect of increasing the population in fact made any contribution to the amount of life-time saved would be an illusion.

We do not then have always to calculate the probable net saving in life-time of any particular policy or therapy, before knowing what to do, and can revert to the more customary consideration of the numbers of lives that might be saved or lost. This, however, highlights once again the problems of whether lives that can only be saved for relatively short periods of time (that can only be prolonged by a few months say) are as worth saving as those for whom the prognosis in terms of life expectancy is much longer. A manoeuvre that seems to capture our intuitions here involves modifying the life-time view into a worthwhile life-time view.

Worthwhile life-time

While to many just staying alive may be the most important consideration, and while they may even wish to continue to live even at appalling cost in terms of pain, disability and so on even, as we have seen,[11] where their lives are hardly worth living, they of course prefer to live worthwhile lives. So that while any life might be better than no life, people generally expect medical care to concern itself not simply with preventing death but with restoring worthwhile existence.

Many sorts of thing will go to diminish the worth of life just as many and various considerations go to make life valuable and these will differ from individual to individual. For the moment we are just concerned with the question of how life expectancy operates as one of these.

If someone were sentenced to death and told that the execution would take place at dawn the next day, they would not, I imagine, be excessively overjoyed if they were then informed that the execution had been postponed for one month. Similarly if the prognosis for a particular disease were very accurate indeed, to be told that one had only seven months to live would not be dramatically less terrible than to be told one had six months to live. There are two related reasons for this. The first is simply that the prospect of imminent death colours, or rather discolours, existence and leaves it joyless. The second is that an almost necessary condition for valuing life is its open-endedness. The fact that we do not normally know how long we have to live liberates the present and leaves us apparently free to plan the future without having to be constantly aware of the futility of so doing.[12] If life had a short and finite (rather than indefinite) future, most things would not seem to be worth doing and the whole sense of the worth of life as an enterprise would evaporate.[13]

In the light of these considerations many people would not much value such short periods of remission, and support for policies which could at best produce such small gains might well be slight. However, some might well value highly the chance of even a small share of extra time. So far from emptying their life of meaning, it might enable them to 'round it off' or complete some important task or settle or better arrange their affairs. It might, so far from being of no value, be just what they needed to sort their life out and make some sort of final sense of it.

We have frequently noted the extreme difficulty involved in discounting the value of someone's life where we and they disagree about whether or not it is worth living, and we have also noted the injustice of preferring our assessment to theirs when so much is at stake for them. In view of all this it would be hard to prefer our judgement to theirs here.

Perhaps the problem would in reality be a small one. These dilemmas only arise where we cannot both help some people to live for relatively short periods *and* at the same time help others to live for much longer ones. Where there is no such conflict there is no question that we should go on helping people to stay alive for just so long as they want us to. However, the fact that hard cases are rare does not mean that we can turn our backs on them.

Fair innings or no ageism?

We have then two principles which can in hard cases pull in opposite directions. What should we do in the sorts of hard cases we have been considering? First, we should be clear that while the very old and those with terminal conditions are alike, in that they both have a short life expectancy, they may well differ with respect to whether or not they have had a fair innings. I do not believe that this issue is at all clear-cut but I am inclined to believe that where two individuals both equally wish to go on living for as long as possible our duty to respect this wish is paramount. It is, as I have suggested, the most important part of what is involved in valuing the lives of others. Each person's desire to stay alive should be regarded as of the same importance and as deserving the same respect as that of anyone else, irrespective of the quality of their life or its expected duration.

This would hold good in all cases in which we have to choose between lives, except one. And that is where one individual has had a fair innings and the other not. In this case, while both equally wish to have their lives further prolonged one, but not the other, has had a fair innings. In this case, although there is nothing to choose between the two candidates from the point of view of their respective will to live and both would suffer the injustice of having their life cut short when it might continue, only one would suffer the further injustice of being deprived of a fair innings – a benefit that the other has received.

It is sometimes said that it is a misfortune to grow old, but it is not nearly so great a misfortune as not to grow old. Growing old when you don't want to is not half the misfortune that is not growing old when you do want to. It is this truth that the fair innings argument captures. So that while it remains true, as the anti-ageist argument asserts, that the value of the unelapsed possible lifespan of each person who wants to go on living is equally valuable however long that span may be, the question of which person's premature death involves the greater injustice can be important. The fair innings argument points to the fact that the injustice done to someone who has not had a fair innings when they lose out to someone who has is significantly greater than in the reverse circumstances. It is for this reason that in the hopefully rare cases where we have to choose between candidates who differ only in this respect that we should choose to give as many people as possible the chance of a fair innings.

Notes

1 Triage is a policy for coping with disasters where resources are insufficient to provide the normal standard of care for all. It involves dividing survivors into three groups: those who will die in any event, those who will live in any event, and those for whom care will make the difference between life and death. Care is then given only to this last group. The argument is that this is the most economical use of resources where resources are insufficient to help all.
2 This may be a rash assumption because of the voluntary nature of many risks.
3 Of course if I don't value it because it is so short as to be scarcely worth having then the point does not apply in such a case.
4 I owe this objection to Tom Sorrel and am greatly in his debt here and elsewhere in this chapter for his generous and penetrating criticisms and comments.
5 No non-sexist form is available here, nor is one desirable since a different formulation would lose the resonance of the phrase.
6 Jonathan Glover, *Causing Death and Saving Lives* (Harmondsworth: Penguin, 1977), p. 221.
7 I'm assuming 70 as the full measure of life expectancy of healthy people and that all candidates are healthy in the sense that there is no reason to regard their life expectancy as less than average.
8 Quoted by Jonathan Glover (see note 6), p.221. I am indebted here and elsewhere to Glover's stimulating discussion of these matters.
9 Because any figure of life expectancy will be arbitrary and one has to be taken.
10 The elixir of life example which prompted this argument about the fallacy of life-time views in stable or increasing populations I owe to Tom Sorrel, whose formulation of it I largely use.
11 See chapter 2 in *The Value of Life* (1985), from which this extract is taken.
12 Many people have argued of course that it is always futile to plan for the future because the inevitability of our world's ultimate destruction makes everything futile.
13 For the record we should note that small gains in life-time will only seem to be worthless to those who gain them if it is known that they will be short. If the potential beneficiaries are kept in ignorance of the fact that they can be granted only a short remission then the extra time will not be clouded by the futility deriving from its short duration and the gain, though small, will be as worthwhile as any other segment of their lives of comparable duration. Of course the deception may not be justified.

43

In Defence of Ageism

A. B. Shaw

Abstract

Health care should be preferentially allocated to younger patients. This is just and is seen as just. Age is an objective factor in rationing decisions. The arguments against 'ageism' are answered. The effects of age on current methods of rationing are illustrated, and the practical applications of an age-related criterion are discussed. Ageist policies are in current use and open discussion of them is advocated.

If a 20-year-old girl and her grandmother were both drowning most of us would throw a single lifebelt to the girl and most of the grandmothers would want us to do just that. The citizen would do it because the girl had a right to live the life which the older person had already enjoyed and the doctor to save more life. The health economist would do it to save more life-years for each unit-lifebelt cost. Justice is important to the public, maximum benefit to the doctor and cost-effectiveness to the economist. Health care must be distributed in a way that achieves maximum benefit and is seen to be just. Both considerations give the young priority.

Arguments for Ageism

The British Medical Association (BMA) holds 'that no patient should be denied medical diagnosis and treatment just because of advanced age'.[1] Others disagree. Callahan has long maintained that those near the natural term of life have a duty to forgo expensive technological treatment in the interest of younger people.[2] Veatch points out that the old have already enjoyed more community support than the young.[3] Daniels believes the individual with a fixed allocation of lifetime health care would use it all in earlier years to achieve old age.[4] He would not risk premature death by refraining from using it until old age. Society is entitled to adopt the same approach.

The case for ageism is moral. Health care is a limited resource. It must be allocated in the way which achieves the greatest good for the greatest number. If all lives are of equal value more is effected by saving the one with more years left. Utilitarianism is necessary if not sufficient for ethical rationing decisions.[5]

The right to treatment must be considered as well as the benefit gained. The moral quality of a society depends in part on the lowest standard of life it permits. There is a duty to afford all citizens lives of a minimum quality and duration but no duty to bestow extreme longevity on a few individuals. Bread for all before caviare for any. Ageism uses only the objective criteria of years lived and left to live to achieve this aim. Other assessments of right to treatment often involve subjective judgements of value we should not make, certainly not as individual clinicians.[6]

The case for ageism is also economic. It would be foolish to let lifebelt-makers drown, for who will make lifebelts for the next generation? Care costs money which can only be provided by a tax-paying working population. It is in the interest of the old people of the future to spend more keeping the young and the working healthy than the

From *Journal of Medical Ethics*, 20 (1994), pp. 188–91, 194. Reprinted with permission.

retired. The economic argument for ageism is not also an argument for 'middle-ageism' as this group has much to offer the economy.[7]

Ageism is only one consideration in rationing. The girl can risk catching cold in the water while the older woman's life is saved. The cancer of the old man is more urgent than the hernia of the young man. Routine medical and nursing care is not in question. Inhumanity of any kind might temporarily benefit a majority but would change the nature of our society.[5] It would also be wrong. We are considering the use of expensive technology as in dialysis and intensive care and the emphasis which government and health authorities should place on different types of health care. Ageism must also be enlightened. Aortic valve operations on the elderly are very cost-effective if the result is death or cure instead of prolonged illness.[7]

Ageism already flourishes in British hospitals. It has long been operated openly and secretly by doctors[8] and administrators.[9] At the time of writing my cousin tells me that a surgeon would not repair the nerve to his finger because it was not worth it at 70. In Bradford there is a useful limited coronary care facility. Patients under the age of 65 with suspected myocardial infarction are routinely admitted there. Those over this age go to other wards and are transferred only if a clinical indication arises. Doctors have accepted this for many years as a just and effective method of using a limited resource. The public have never been consulted.

Objections and Answers

Need for rationing

Efficiency can abolish the need for rationing.[10] However, no country can now give state-of-the-art medical care to all its citizens.[11] There will always be two drowning and one lifebelt, however well we target and however efficiently we deliver medical care. Technical innovation yearly widens the gap between the possible and the affordable. The public always wants to pay less tax and receive more medical care. Politicians rarely want to make clear that this is impossible. Clinicians are increasingly obliged to be the rationing agents.

Economic unimportance

The elderly are relatively few and little is saved by denying them high technology medicine.[12] Health care is a precious commodity in short supply. It must all be used efficiently. In ten years from 1980 to 1990 the number of people over the age of 75 in England increased by 25 per cent from 2.7 to 3.4 million.[13] The mean length of a stay in hospital is ten days for those aged 60 to 65 years and 25 days between the ages of 80 to 85.[14] It is not a small problem. In the US half the Medicare budget is spent on the last few months of life.[15]

Biological age

The correlation between biological and chronological age is imperfect. The fit older person might derive more benefit from treatment than the unfit younger one. This is true but we see more often in hospital the 50-year-old with a 70-year-old body due to major chronic organ disease. The 50-year-old in abnormally good condition is more rare. Fewer people reach advanced age and perhaps some die without medical help.

Age in years is a factor in treatment response. Asystolic cardiac arrest over the age of 70 is death, not an occasion for resuscitation.[16] Age affects prognosis in the intensive care patient. It is true that young people are given expensive treatment which prolongs life for a very short time. This is more an argument for withholding such treatment from the young than for inflicting it on the old. If a treatment causes temporary incapacity or distress this results in damage to a greater proportion of the remaining life of an old person.

Discrimination

Why should the elderly suffer discrimination as a group? If the elderly are a group they are one which has enjoyed longer life than the rest as all men and women grow old or fail to do so. Diversion of care from the old would release resources to treat truly disadvantaged groups such as the handicapped. The old are indeed weak and need special protection. So are children, and both must have what is right, not more than is right. The dishonest and the powerful will certainly manipulate a rationing system. Food rationing in the last war was no less just and only slightly less successful because of the black market.

Injustice

It is more just to give a little care to many old people who will die soon rather than a lot of care to a few young persons. This is relevant only to an expensive resource in constant use such as dialysis. Young people are transplanted and older patients spend more time in hospital, so the argument is only partly correct. Also society owes bread to all but caviare to none.

A young person may have benefited from much medical care and an old one may never have seen a doctor before. Medicine is there for the present need of each person and the maximum future benefit of the people. Denial of treatment to those who have used up a fixed allocation would conflict with these principles.

One can turn the argument of fairness on its head and claim that the old deserve extra consideration because of the service they have given. They surely are owed love, gratitude and respect, but in times of shortage most societies give the food to the babies. Drinkers and smokers pay high taxes but they have no greater right to care than abstainers. Need and benefit should determine the allocation of care not the economic contribution made so far.

It would be unfair to the first generation of elderly who have paid for treatment were they not to get it. Ageism is already widespread but erratic and often covert. It should be open and agreed.

Value of the old

All lives are of equal value. So claims a legitimate alliance of the old and their doctors.[17] Society accepts this by awarding the same sentence for killing a young man and an old man.[18] It also awards the same medal for saving the old lady or the young one. We are not assessing the moral value of acts. We are trying to distribute limited benefit fairly. When forced to choose we give the lifebelt to the young person who will live more years and has enjoyed less life.

The value of the old lies in their wisdom and their capacity for love, which is as important as the economic value of the young. Ageism makes no assumption concerning the value of anyone. It measures years lived and left to live.

Individual right

Only the patient can decide if treatment is futile for him or her.[19] Certainly patients have a right to request treatment with one chance in a million of success or which will prolong life by an hour. Society has a duty to refuse the request in favour of more reasonable claims.

The old are ends in themselves not the means of making a just society. Choice between these ends is imposed and it must be made in the way which creates the least injustice. It is dishonest to ask why when we need to say who. Hippocrates recognized the the duty of the doctor to his patient alone, but his oath would have been different if he had faced eight patients needing his four-bedded intensive care unit. The BMA recognizes a duty to the patient in the waiting room as well as the one in the consulting room.[1]

Inaccuracy of ageism

Some refine the measurement of years by using 'QALYs'. The years of life left or saved are multiplied by a quality score derived from a value given to different disabilities.[20] There are objections to basing medical decisions on unavoidably subjective valuations of human life.[21] If it is arrogant for doctors to do this why should it be permissible for anyone else? Only the individual can decide what the value to him is of a life with various problems.[22] For some a life of disability and pain might be filled with spiritual joy. We must avoid confusing decisions based on medical fact with those based on personal values.[6]

It can be argued that someone who has had a long and miserable life has had less of a fair innings than one who has had a short and happy life. Yet it is just as arrogant to judge the value of the life someone has had as to judge the value of that which they will have. The healthy and wealthy may live in misery due to phobias and family traumas and the poor and disabled may be contended.

Dworkin points out that our grief at premature death is not greater for an infant than for a young adult.[23] The investment made by each person in life is important as well as the years left. He agrees that grief is less for an old person whose life work is largely accomplished. This is an ageist view. I would also maintain that it is more important to improve the quality of the whole future life of a child than to achieve minor gains at the end of natural life. Temporary prolongation of the life of an infant at great expense is more questionable.

Cruelty

Elderly patients admitted to hospital will fear neglect because their eightieth birthday fell the previous day. The Bradford coronary care model mentioned above should be copied. The care is targeted on the younger patients but none is denied treatment when need arises and benefit is substantial. All patients continue to be treated as individuals.

Methods of Rationing

Health care distribution is affected by factors other than need and benefit and these factors are affected by age.

Chance

It would be acceptable to spin a coin for the lifebelt only when there was no other way of deciding priority. Few would accept that medical care should be awarded by lottery. However, chance takes a hand in most human transactions. The need for fertility treatment is similar everywhere. Its availability depends on the presence of an able local specialist or the views of local general practitioners.[24] It is unfortunate but unavoidable that care should depend on proximity to specialized units. Uniform availability could be achieved only by suppressing innovation and centres of excellence. The old may suffer because travel is more exacting for them.

Queuing

The lifebelt should go to the first person seen, if other things are equal. Queuing is more acceptable in the United Kingdom than elsewhere, as anyone who has boarded a bus in Europe will know. It is reasonable to repair hernias in the order in which the patients appear but not to let patients die in the queue for cardiac surgery. Need is more important than time of arrival. The older person is more likely to die in a queue. Unless death is due to the condition requiring treatment the delay will save him from pointless disturbance shortly before death.

Market forces

The lifebelt should not go to the highest bidder but people are entitled to pay for a personal lifeguard. Why should the individual not be free to choose between tobacco and private health care? Private care is an acceptable addition to an ethically based health service. Older people can often buy private care more easily than young parents. In Britain where most care is free at the point of delivery 20 per cent more is spent on children than on adults but in the United States only a third as much.[8]

Cost effectiveness

Lifebelts must be placed where they will save most lives. Maximum benefit must be obtained from limited resources. More attention has been given to the economic appraisal of treatments than to the study of the benefits to the patients who receive those treatments.[11]

Public opinion

The public acts through its elected legislature and also by creating the atmosphere in which we all work.

The public gives priority to dread disease, visible disease such as haemophilia and emergency treatment.[8] Pressure groups also advance the claims of specific disease.

Who should take which decisions? In Oregon the public indicated the type of health care which should have priority.[15] A professional committee decided which specific interventions should be funded, influenced by the public philosophy. The public did not exclude the elderly specifically from care but it gave priority to maternity care and to preventive care for children. It also gave priority to acute fatal conditions where treatment prevented death and led to full recovery. Need, benefit and cost were therefore emphasized. Care followed by full recovery is cheap because its duration is short. In Hackney the public gave preference to dread disease and high technology.[25] Interestingly, the doctors voted according to their special interests.

In such surveys, well-designed questions must be put to a representative sample of citizens who understand the consequences of their choices, a combination difficult to achieve. It is as useful to ask an uninformed public to assess the value of medical interventions as to ask the man in the street which is the best antibiotic for his mother's pneumonia.

Ageism in Practice

I base my approach on the attitude of the Oregon public and the practice of the Bradford coronary care unit. The government and the health authorities should have some ageist emphasis when resources are allocated to doctors. Efforts are concentrated on younger people but the needs of the old are not neglected. Research into the prolongation of life should not be funded.[2] To improve life for the young elderly is laudable but to prolong life for the very old is antisocial. In this world of disease and deprivation we do not need more of us able to remember the last century but not yesterday. How useful is screening in the elderly? In those who are younger it often creates anxiety, expense, inconvenience and even risk, with little compensatory benefit. Is there evidence that it is better for the old?

Why should clinicians discuss ageism if most practise it already? We must discuss it so that a philosophy can be agreed and perhaps a code developed. As rationing becomes stricter ageism may increase and doctors will need guidance. Doctors should have complete freedom to give each patient their best advice. They need help with their new freedom to select which patient should benefit from that advice.

Callahan believes that doctors need an imposed age limitation on different treatments.[2] I oppose this on three grounds. Biological age is not the same as chronological age. Women live longer than men and different age limits might create problems. Fear might be generated by strict limits. Increasing age should be accepted as an increasingly important factor in some clinical decisions but actual age limits should be advisory. The application of any code depends on circumstances and judgement. There can be no absolutism at the bedside.

Dialysis units treat increasing numbers of patients by reducing dialysis hours or using peritoneal instead of haemodialysis. This reduces well-being and survival. Should fewer patients receive better treatment? Should older patients or those with non-renal life-shortening diseases be excluded? When patients are selected for high technology treatments doctors must consider not only how much prolongation and what kind of life are likely, but also at whose expense the prolongation and 'quality' of life are obtained.

Selection should be made on the basis of agreed guidelines rather than subjective views. Objective criteria such as age are useful. Where there is disagreement with patients the views of colleagues are helpful but a single unit may have a single approach. These painful decisions may be best arbitrated by small ethical committees derived from trained members of the research ethics committees already in being.

If the limited medical care available is to be used to best advantage age must be taken into account. Because ageism is officially condemned as unethical it flourishes unregulated in secret. Open discussion of its application would be better.

Summary

Older people have enjoyed more life and have less life left to enjoy. Age is an ethical, objective and cost-effective criterion for rationing health care. Ageism flourishes in secret. Open discussion would make its application more just.

Acknowledgement

I am grateful to S. A. Shaw, M. Ward and R. L. Woodhead for helpful discussion.

References

1 BMA. *Medical Ethics Today* (London: BMJ Publishing Group, 1993).
2 Callahan, D. *Setting Limits: Medical Goals in an Aging Society* (New York: Simon and Schuster, 1987).
3 Veatch, R. M. "Justice and the economics of terminal illness", *Hastings Center Report*, 18/4 (1988): 34–40.
4 Daniels, N. *Am I My Parents' Keeper? An Essay on Justice Between the Young and the Old* (New York: Oxford University Press, 1988).
5 Campbell, A. V. *Moral Dilemmas in Medicine*. 3rd edn (Edinburgh: Churchill Livingstone, 1984).
6 Kennedy, I. *The Unmasking of Medicine* (London: George Allen and Unwin, 1981).

7 Forster, P. The fortysomething barrier: medicine and age discrimination. *British Medical Journal*, 306 (1993), pp. 637–9.

8 Aaron, H. J. and Schwarz, W. B. *The Painful Prescription: Rationing Health Care* (Washington, DC: Brookings Institution, 1984), pp. 36–7.

9 Sims, J. Rationing comes by stealth. *Healthcare Management*, 1 (1993), pp. 23–6.

10 Relman, A. S. Is rationing inevitable? *New England Journal of Medicine*, 322 (1990), pp. 1809–10.

11 Buxton, M. Economic appraisal and prescribing choices. *Prescribers' Journal*, 33 (1993), pp. 133–8.

12 Levinsky, N. G. Age as a criterion for rationing health care. *New England Journal of Medicine*, 322 (1990), pp. 1813–15.

13 Department of Health. *Health and Personal Social Services Statistics for England, 1992* (London: HMSO).

14 Department of Health and Social Security. Office of Population Census and Surveys. *Hospital In-Patients Enquiry, 1985* (London: HMSO).

15 Kitzhaber, J. A. Prioritizing health services in an era of limits: the Oregon experience. *British Medical Journal*, 307 (1993), pp. 373–7.

16 O'Keeffe, S., Redahan, C., Keane, P. and Daly, P. Age and other determinants of survival after in-hospital cardiopulmonary resuscitation. *Quarterly Journal of Medicine*, 81 (1991), pp. 1005–10.

17 Fletcher, A. in A. Hopkins (ed.), *Measures of the Quality of Life* (London: Royal College of Physicians, 1992), p. 117.

18 Kilner, J. F. *Who Lives? Who Dies?* (London: Yale University Press, 1990).

19 Truog, R. D., Brett, A. A. and Frader, J. The problem with futility. *New England Journal of Medicine*, 326 (1992), pp. 1560–4.

20 See note 13: Williams, A. and Kind, P. The present state of play about QALYs, pp. 21–34.

21 Solomon, M. 'Futility' as a criterion in limiting treatment. *New England Journal of Medicine*, 327 (1992), p. 1239.

22 Evans, J. G. Quality of life assessments and elderly people, in A. Hopkins (ed.), *Measures of the Quality of Life*, pp. 107–16.

23 Dworkin, R. *Life's Dominion* (London: HarperCollins, 1993).

24 Redmayne, S. and Klein, R. Rationing in practice: the case of *in vitro* fertilization. *British Medical Journal*, 306 (1993), pp. 1521–4.

25 Ham, C. Priority setting in the NHS: reports from six districts. *British Medical Journal*, 307 (1993), pp. 435–8.

PART VI

Organ Donation

44

Why Give to Strangers?

Richard M. Titmuss

In Alexander Solzhenitsyn's novel *Cancer Ward* Shulubin is talking to Kostoglotov:

> 'We have to show the world a society in which all relationships, fundamental principles and laws flow directly from moral ethics, and from them *alone*. Ethical demands would determine all calculations: how to bring up children, what to prepare them for, to what purpose the work of grown-ups should be directed, and how their leisure should be occupied. As for scientific research, it should only be conducted where it doesn't damage ethical morality, in the first instance where it doesn't damage the researchers themselves.'
>
> Kostoglotov then raises questions. 'There has to be an economy after all doesn't there? That comes before everything else.' 'Does it?' said Shulubin. 'That depends. For example, Vladimir Solovyov argues rather convincingly that an economy could and should be built on an ethical basis.'
>
> 'What's this? Ethics first and economics afterwards?' Kostoglotov looked bewildered.'

The question raised by Solzhenitsyn could as well be directed at social policy institutions. What, for example, are the connections between what we in Britain conventionally call the social services and the role of altruism in modern industrial societies? And have we a convenient model for studying such relationships? Blood as a living tissue and as a bond that links all men and women so closely that differences of colour, religious belief, and cultural heritage are insignificant beside it, may now constitute in Western societies one of the ultimate tests of where the "social" begins and the "economic" ends.

From *The Lancet* (16 January 1971), pp. 123–5. Copyright © The Lancet Ltd 1971. See also Titmuss's book, *The Gift Relationship: From Human Blood to Social Policy* (London: Allen & Unwin, 1971).

The World Demand for Blood

The transfer of blood and blood derivatives from one human being to another represents one of the greatest therapeutic instruments in the hands of modern medicine. But these developments have set in train social, economic, and ethical consequences which present society with issues of profound importance.

The demand for blood and blood products is increasing all over the world. In high-income countries, in particular, the rate of growth in demand has been rising so rapidly that shortages have begun to appear. In all Western countries, demand is growing faster than rates of growth in the population aged 18–65 from whom donors are drawn. And, despite a massive research effort in the United States to find alternatives, there is often no substitute for human blood.

Many factors are responsible for this increase in demand. Some surgical procedures call for massive transfusions of blood (as many as 60 donations may be needed for a single open-heart operation, and in one American heart-transplant case over 300 pints of blood were used); artificial kidneys require substantial volumes of blood; and developments in organ transplants could create immense additional demands. Furthermore, more routine surgery is now used more frequently and is made available to a larger proportion of the population than formerly. A more violent or accident-prone world insistently demands more blood for road casualties and for war injuries (in 1968 more than 300,000 pints of blood were shipped from the USA and elsewhere to treat victims of the Vietnam war).

There seems to be no predictable limit to the demand for blood supplies, especially when one remembers the as yet unmet needs for surgical and medical treatment.

Supply of Blood

On the biological, technical, and administrative side, three factors limit the supply of blood.

Only about half of a population is medically eligible to donate blood. Furthermore, the amount any one person can give in a year is restricted – two donations in the British National Blood Transfusion Service (probably the lowest limit and the most rigorous standard in the world); five in the United States, a minimum often exceeded by paid donors, commercial blood-banks, and pharmaceutical companies using techniques such as plasmapheresis; in Japan, where 90 per cent of blood is bought and sold, the standard is even lower. These differences can be analysed as a process of redistribution of life chances in terms of age, sex, social class, income, ethnic group, and so on.

Human blood deteriorates after three weeks in the refrigerator, and this perishability presents great technical and administrative problems to those running transfusion services. But it does mean that, by measuring wastage (i.e., the amount of blood that has to be thrown away) the efficiencies of different blood collection and distribution systems can be compared.

Blood can be more deadly than any drug. Quite apart from the problems of cross-matching, storage, labelling, and so on, there are serious risks of disease transmission and other hazards. In Western countries a major hazard is serum hepatitis transmitted from carrier donor to susceptible patient. Since carriers cannot yet be reliably detected, the patient becomes the laboratory for testing "the gift". Donors, therefore, have to be screened every time they come to give blood, and the donor's truthfulness in answering questions about health, medical history, and drug habits becomes vital. Upon the honesty of the donor depends the life of the recipient of his blood. In this context we need to ask what conditions and arrangements permit and encourage maximum truthfulness on the part of the donors. Can honesty be pursued regardless of the donor's motives for giving blood? What systems, structures, and social policies encourage honesty or discourage and destroy voluntary and truthful gift relationships?

Types of Donor

To give or not to give, to lend, repay, or even to buy and sell blood are choices which lead us, if we are to understand these transactions in the context of any society, to the fundamentals of social and economic life.

The forms and functions of giving embody moral, social, psychological, religious, legal, and aesthetic ideas. They may reflect, sustain, strengthen, or loosen the cultural bonds of the group, large or small. They may inspire the worst excesses of war and tribalism or the tolerances of community.

Customs and practices of non-economic giving – unilateral and multilateral social transfers – thus may tell us much, as Marcel Mauss so sensitively demonstrated in his book *The Gift*, about the texture of personal and group relationships in different cultures. In some societies, past and present, gifts to men aim to buy peace; to express affection, regard, or loyalty; to unify the group; to fulfil a contractual set of obligations and rights; to function as acts of penitence, shame, or degradation; and to symbolize many other human sentiments. When one reads the work of anthropologists and sociologists such as Mauss and Lévi-Strauss, who have studied the social functions of giving, a number of themes relevant to any attempt to delineate a typology of blood-donors may be discerned.

From these readings and from statistics for different countries a spectrum of blood-donor types can be constructed. At one extreme is the paid donor who sells his blood for what the market will bear: some are semi-salaried, some are long-term prisoner volunteers; some are organized in blood trade-unions. As a market transaction, information that might have a bearing on the quality of the blood is withheld if possible from the buyer, since such information could affect the sale of the blood. Thus in the United States blood-group identification cards are loaned, at a price, to other sellers, and blood is illegally mislabelled and updated, and other devices are used which make it very difficult to screen out drug addicts, alcoholics, and hepatitis carriers, and so on.

At the other extreme is the voluntary, unpaid donor. This type is the closest approximation in social reality to the abstract idea of a "free human gift". There are no tangible immediate rewards, monetary or non-monetary; there are no penalties; and donors know that their gifts are for unnamed strangers without distinction of age, sex, medical illness, income, class, religion, or ethnic group. No donor type can be characterized by complete disinterested spontaneous altruism. There must be some sense of obligation, approval, and interest; some awareness of the need for the gift; some expectation that a return gift may be needed and received at some future date. But the unpaid donation of blood is an act of free will: there is no formal contract, legal bond, power situation; no sense of shame or guilt; no money and no explicit guarantee of or wish for reward or return gift.

Almost all the 1.5 million registered donors in Britain and donors in some systems in European countries fall into this category. An analysis of blood-donor motives suggests that the main reason people give blood is most commonly a general desire to help people; almost a third of the British donors studied said that their gift was in response to an appeal for blood; 7 per cent said it was to repay a transfusion given to someone they knew.

By contrast, in the United States less than 10 per cent of supplies come from the voluntary community donor. Proportionately more and more blood is being supplied by the poor, the unskilled, the unemployed, Negroes, and other low-income groups, and with the rise in plasmapheresis there is emerging a new class of exploited high blood yielders. Redistribution in terms of "the gift of blood and blood products" from the poor to the rich seems to be one of the dominant effects of the American blood-banking system.

Which System?

When we compare the commercial blood-bank, such as that found in the United States, with the voluntary system functioning as an integral part of the National Health Service in Britain we find that the commercial blood-bank fails on each of four counts – economic efficiency, administrative efficiency, price, and quality. Commercial blood-bank systems waste blood, and shortages, acute and chronic, characterize the demand-and-supply position. Administratively, there is more paperwork and greater computing and accounting overheads. The cost varies between £10 and £20 per unit in the United States, compared with £1 16*s*. (£2 if processing costs are included) in Britain. And, as judged by statistics for post-transfusion hepatitis, the risk of transfusing contaminated blood is greater if the blood is obtained from a commercial source.

Paradoxically – or so it may seem to some – the more commercialized blood-distribution becomes (and hence more wasteful, inefficient, and dangerous) the more will the gross national product be inflated. In part, and quite simply, this is the consequence of statistically "transferring" an unpaid service (voluntary donors, voluntary workers in the service, unpaid time), with much lower external costs, to a monetary and measurable paid activity involving costlier externalities. Similar effects on the gross national product would ensue if housewives were paid for housework or childless married couples were financially rewarded for adopting children or if hospital patients cooperating for teaching purposes charged medical students. The gross national product is also inflated when commercial markets accelerate "blood obsolescence"; the waste is counted because someone has paid for it.

What *The Economist* described in its 1969 survey of the American economy as the great "efficiency gap" between that country and Britain clearly does not apply to the distribution of human blood. The voluntary, socialized system in Britain is economically, professionally, administratively, and qualitatively more efficient than the mixed, commercialized, and individualistic American system.

Another myth, the Paretian myth of consumer sovereignty, has also to be shattered. In the commercial blood market the consumer is not king. He has less freedom of choice to live unharmed; little choice in determining price; is more subject to scarcity; is less free from bureaucratization; has fewer opportunities to express altruism; and exercises fewer checks and controls in relation to consumption, quality, and external costs. Far from being sovereign, he is often exploited.

What also emerges from this case-study is the significance of the externalities (the values and disvalues external to but created by blood-distribution systems treated as entities) and the multiplier effects of such externalities on what we can only call "the quality of life". At one end of the spectrum of externalities is the individual affected by hepatitis; at the other end, the market behaviour of economically rich societies seeking to import blood from other societies who are thought to be too poor and economically decadent to pay their own blood-donors.

Conclusion

We started with blood as a model for examining how altruism and social policy might work together in a modern industrial society. We might equally have chosen eye banks, patients as teaching material, fostering, or even the whole concept of the community-based distribution of welfare to those in need. All these involve in some degree a gift relationship. The example chosen suggests, firstly, that gift exchange of a non-quantifiable nature has more important functions in a complex society than the writings of Lévi-Strauss and others might indicate. Secondly, the application of scientific and technological developments in such societies is further accelerating the spread of such complexity, and has increased rather than decreased the scientific as well as the social need for such relationships. Thirdly, for these and many other reasons, modern societies require more rather than less freedom of choice for the expression of altruism in the daily life of all social groups. This requirement can be argued for on social and ethical grounds, but, as we have seen for blood donors, it can also be argued for on scientific and economic criteria.

I believe that it is a responsibility of government, acting, for example, through social policy, to weaken market forces which put men in positions where they have little opportunity to make moral choices or to behave altruistically if they wish to do so. The voluntary blood-donor system is a practical example of a fellowship relationship operating on an institutional basis, in this instance the National Health Service. It shows how social policy decisions can foster such relationships between free and equal individuals. If we accept that man has a social and biological need to help then he should not be denied the chance to express this need by entering into a gift relationship.

45

Organ Donation and Retrieval: Whose Body is it Anyway?

Eike-Henner W. Kluge

One of the most important advances in acute care medicine over the last thirty years has been the development of organ transplantation. In many instances, such as end-stage liver and heart disease, organ transplantation saves lives. In others, such as kidney disease, organ transplantation frees patients from dependence on expensive medical technology and allows them to resume an almost normal mode of existence. From a humane perspective, this makes organ transplantation very attractive.

The benefits of organ transplantation are not confined to patients. Kidney transplantation is economically more cost-effective than continued renal dialysis of patients; and as transplantation techniques become more sophisticated for other organs, similar cost savings will be realized in other areas as well. Therefore, as health-care resources are increasingly being diminished, transplantation emerges as an appealing health-care modality.

However, organ transplantation depends on the availability of organs. All countries are experiencing an acute shortage of human organs for transplantation. At any given time and in any jurisdiction, there are hundreds of people waiting for transplants.[1] Quite literally, they are waiting for a new lease on life. That is why transplant societies in all countries are doing their best to raise organ donor awareness so that more people will donate their organs; and why medical establishments and surgical teams are working to improve their techniques of organ recovery and transplantation. When the lack of a suitable organ may mean death, every organ counts and no organ may be wasted.

The responses to this organ shortage have been varied. Some countries treat human organs and bodies as commodities that belong to the individual person and that may be sold by these individuals for a valuable consideration. This lets economics decide who will have access to transplantable organs and entails that market forces determine how organ shortages are dealt with. If the shortage is severe – so goes the theory – prices for organs will go up, sellers will appear in the market-place and the shortage will thus be alleviated.

Most countries have rejected this position for several reasons. *First*, they believe that people have such a close association with their bodies that to consider bodies and organs as property is tantamount to considering the people themselves as chattels. Hence they maintain that neither bodies nor body parts may be bought or sold. *Second*, they believe that if the ownership (and hence sale) of bodies or body parts were to be allowed, this would lead to a state of affairs where the rich would take advantage of the poor by offering such high prices for human organs that the poor would be unable to resist the enticement. The poor would therefore become the walking organ banks of the well-to-do. While this might alleviate the organ shortage in the case of affluent persons in need of organs, it would do nothing about the transplantation needs and the availability of organs for the poor.

In contrast, therefore, most countries have adopted the position that while there is no ownership in human bodies, everyone has a right to decide what shall happen with her or his own body and that this right extends even beyond death. Beyond this, however, there is no general agreement. Some countries have instituted presumed consent legislation. That is to say, they have passed laws which mandate that unless people have explicitly stipulated that they do not wish to be organ donors, their organs will be retrieved once they are dead. Other countries view organ donation as a supererogatory act that cannot reasonably be expected of all persons. Consequently they have passed laws which state that specific agreement to donation is a *sine qua non* for organ retrieval, and that this agreement must come either from the potential donor during her or his lifetime or, in the case of persons who have not made a decision in this matter, from those who are legally in possession of the body after the person is dead. These usually are the next of kin.

Unquestionably, the voluntary approach to organ donation can easily exacerbate the shortage of transplantable organs simply because potential donors (or their relatives) may be reluctant to agree to donation. This reluctance may be grounded in religious precepts which construe the removal of an organ as the sacrilegious mutilation of the body and hence consider it anathema. Alternatively, the refusal may be grounded in a psychological perspective that finds organ retrieval personally offensive on aesthetic grounds. Finally, the refusal to donate may be based on a mere misunderstanding about the process of retrieval itself and the nature of death. Specifically, it may be based on the assumption that death occurs only when there is a complete and irremediable cardiovascular collapse of the body which cannot be alleviated even by mechanical ventilation. This leads to the refusal to allow organ retrieval until after all such attempts have proved unsuccessful – which effectively guarantees that the relevant organs have also deteriorated beyond the point of usefulness for transplantation.

A further contribution to the shortage of organs lies in the fact that many potential donors are simply unaware of the option of donation. Hence organs that otherwise might well be donated are never retrieved.

There is little that can be done about a refusal to donate which finds its basis in religious conviction, short of changing the tenets of the relevant religion or prohibiting adherence to the religion itself. Neither of these is morally acceptable. With due alteration of details, similar considerations apply to refusals to donate that are based on personal aesthetics.

On the other hand, organ shortages that are grounded in misinformation or in ignorance of the option of donation can be alleviated by properly focused and conducted educational campaigns. Physicians can be encouraged to raise the subject of donation with their patients, to educate them about the benefits of donation and to explain to them the nature of death. Further, transplant societies can maximize the chance of retrieving donated organs by establishing organ donor registers which list everyone who has agreed to being a donor. On the death of such a person, it would be known immediately whether that person had agreed to donation.

Furthermore, it has been suggested that all jurisdictions adopt presumed consent legislation. In this way, it is hoped, the supply of organs will be increased because refusal to donate would have to be explicitly expressed.

However, there is a readily available supply of organs wich does not require the establishment of registers or changes in the current laws. Access to this supply does not require a change in anything – except in the way in which the various transplant societies work.

More precisely, in many countries that have consent legislation, the law states that the consent of a competent person is "full" and "binding" authority for the removal of that person's organs after death for the purposes of transplantation. In legal terms, the word "full" means that if someone has given consent, then this consent is sufficient and no one else needs to be asked for permission, while the term "binding" means that others may not overrule the consent of the donor and substitute their own wishes. Such consent is usually signified by an organ donor card or an organ donor sticker on the person's driver's licence.

Almost without exception, the organ retrieval protocols of most transplant societies are out of step with these provisions. Almost invariably, they state that the consent of the next of kin is required for organ retrieval *even when there is a donor card or sticker*. They further state that if the next of kin refuse the donation, the organs will not be retrieved.

In countries which have consent legislation that recognizes the individual's right to donate, these protocols clearly violate the law. In the great scheme of things, that may not be too important. However, what *is* important is that, because of these protocols, many organs that could be retrieved and used to save lives are never recovered. In other words, because of these protocols, the current organ shortage is greater than it needs to be, people are on waiting lists when they do not have to be, and people are dying while waiting for a suitable organ.

These are preventable deaths. They are therefore tragic. They are all the more tragic because they have ramifications far beyond the immediate sphere of the donor and the prospective recipient: they have implications for the availability of health care in general. Every organ that is not retrieved represents increased health-care costs for society. Health-care resources are finite: What is given to the one is taken away from the other. Therefore the impact of this non-retrieval affects not only the person who could have received the organ but everyone in the health-care system as a whole.

These protocols also have serious ethical implications for the ethics of informed consent. What the transplant societies are in effect saying with their guidelines is that the informed donor consent will not be considered binding if the donor is no longer capable of enforcing her or his wishes. Such an attitude sends the message that organ donation really doesn't mean anything: that the wishes of others really carry the day. If that practice were to be adopted in other areas of health care, informed consent would become meaningless. In fact, it would become a farce. It is surprising that, under the circumstances, anyone bothers to donate organs at all!

The transplant societies have argued that to retrieve organs against the wishes of the next of kin runs the danger of being perceived as ghouls, and that the negative publicity that would surround such actions might well result in a drop in organ donation. That is why they have proposed the establishment of a donor register, and that the law be changed in all jurisdictions in favour of presumed consent.

Unquestionably, the establishment of organ donor registers would be useful. So would the proposed change in legislation. Unfortunately, however, neither of these comes to grips with the real issue; and more important, neither of them would change the situation.

A register is useful only if the donors who are registered actually have their organs retrieved upon death. There is nothing inherent in a register to ensure that this would take place.

As to the proposed consent legislation, it would still leave the possibility that the next of kin might say *no* to organ retrieval even though the donor him- or herself had not said *no*. Therefore unless, under presumed consent legislation, the next of kin were *not asked for their consent*, the number of organ retrievals would not go up. The same number of next of kin who now refuse consent would also refuse their consent under the new legislation. The only way to avoid this would be not to ask the next of kin (or to ignore what they might say) and simply go on the assumption that if the person had not wanted her or his organs retrieved, he or she would have said so. Therefore these proposed laws would work *only if the transplant societies acted the way they are supposed to act even under the current laws*. There is considerable justification for doubting that this would be the case.

The crux of the matter is really this: do people have the right to decide what shall be done with their body after they are dead? In particular, do they have the right to donate their organs in order to save lives? The answer may vary from society to society. However, once such a right is recognized, the ethics of informed consent entails that the donor's decision should not be overruled – or ignored – simply because others are uncomfortable with that decision. Not only does that violate the autonomous decision of the donor, it also costs lives. If others – e.g., the next of kin – are uncomfortable with the donor's decision, what is called for is not a refusal to follow the donor's last bequest but appropriate education and counselling in the ethics of donation and informed consent.

Always following the wishes of organ donors would not do away with the current shortage of organs. However, this shortage would not be so great if the donated organs were in fact retrieved, if the wishes of donors were followed – and if the ethics of informed consent were taken seriously. When every organ is a life, can one be less than ethical?

Note

1 Personal communication with various transplant organizations in Canada, US and Europe.

46

Legalizing Payment for Transplantable Cadaveric Organs

James F. Blumstein

Editors' Summary

James F. Blumstein, LLB, presents a very strongly argued case for financial incentives to relieve a shortage of organs. He argues that financial concerns help to shape medical decisions, and should not be feared. At odds with the official altruistic view of donation of organs, his commercial view is highly controversial. There is no obstacle to influencing behavior by using monetary incentives, he argues, and that this is the way other forms of care in the health care system are provided. Such incentives would relieve the shortage of organs and benefit many patients who today must wait despairingly on the lists for an available organ.

A newcomer to the field of organ transplantation has many of the experiences of an anthropologist being exposed to a new culture, a new way of thinking. There are holy totems and sacred cows that permeate the thinking and have profoundly influenced the development of public policy in the organ transplant arena. These traditional values – e.g. an almost sacrosanct altruism and hostility to financial incentives – have underpinned policy formulation in this field. It is important to re-examine and re-evaluate these entrenched ways of thinking as organ transplantation has evolved into mainstream, therapeutic medical care.

There is widespread agreement that a shortfall exists in the number of organs made available for transplantation and that lack of availability inhibits the further utilization of therapeutically promising organ transplantation techniques. Nearly 30 000 people are on waiting lists for organ transplants in the USA. These waiting lists have got longer over time, with about 200 people being added to the lists each month. Despite this quite fundamental supply-side problem, leaders in the organ transplant community have been strikingly hostile to markets and to the use of financial incentives to increase the availability of transplantable organs. There has been a strong, visceral, adverse reaction to the introduction of commerce in the field of transplantable organs. This *Weltanschauung* is reminiscent of an earlier era when the existence of a role for markets in health care was hotly contested. Shibboleth and shamanism have thrived at the expense of rigorous analysis.

In short, ideology, as much as technology, has driven organ transplantation policy. An intellectual orthodoxy, traceable to the United States Department of Health and Human Services 1986 *Report of the Task Force on Organ Transplantation, Organ Transplantation Issues and Recommendations* (OTTF Report), has permeated the field. The OTTF Report has had remarkable influence on the development of thinking and the evolution of policy. In view of the organ shortage problem, another viewpoint and frame of reference need expression.

From David C. Thomasma and Thomasine Kushner (eds), *Birth to Death: Science and Bioethics* (Cambridge: Cambridge University Press, 1996), pp. 119–32. Earlier versions of this chapter appeared in *Transplantation Proceedings*, 24 (1992), pp. 2190–7 and *Health Matrix*, 3 (1993), pp. 1–30.

Organ Transplantation Policy Values: The Ethical Foundation of Altruism

What values have underpinned organ transplantation policy in the USA? Even a superficial exposure to this field reveals an intense commitment to altruism. This is deemed a moral imperative. For example, the OTTF Report (p. 28) stated that a core value shaping organ transplantation policy was the goal of "[p]romoting a sense of community through acts of generosity." Despite the widespread recognition of the shortage of transplantable organs, there persists an insistence on the exclusion or elimination of financial incentives from all facets of organ supply, acquisition or distribution. Yet, financial incentives could enhance the availability of organs for transplantation.

Organ Transplantation Values within the Broader Health Policy Context: The Use of Incentives

A fundamental element of health policy over the last 15 years has been the recognition that competition and markets have an important role to play in the health policy arena. The values underpinning organ transplant policy are in distinct tension with those values. They also seem strangely at odds with a policy of encouraging an increased supply of transplantable organs. What are the market-oriented values that strikingly contrast with the values underpinning organ transplant policy?

Not so long ago, the use of incentives in medical care was rejected on the related grounds of ethics and effectiveness. Ethically, the objection stemmed from the ideological commitment in some quarters that unrestricted access to medical care on the basis of medical need was the appropriate normative benchmark. This was a component of the rhetorical espousal of medical care as a right. If one believes that access to medical care should be costless to users, the imposition of financial disincentives is directly in conflict with that principle. Obviously, if one starts from the premise that an individual's utilization of medical services should bear no economic consequences for the beneficiary of the treatment, the use of financial disincentives will have unacceptable distributive effects.

In terms of effectiveness, financial incentives were questioned because of the prevailing medical view that money did not affect how patients were treated. It was assumed that there was a correct course of treatment, and that was a professionally determined decision. Science, not economic incentives, drove medical care diagnosis and treatment decisions. Therefore, financial incentives could not be effective because they did not influence medical care decision-making. And, implictly, to the extent that scientific and professional judgments might indeed be influenced by financial considerations, that was an inappropriate deviation from the clinically correct scientific pathway.

The ethical issue is now seen as more richly textured than it once was. The rhetoric of rights and equality has been de-emphasized, replaced in responsible circles by concern about the role of government in providing for core services to individuals unable to afford medical care.[1] Further, there is now a broader understanding that establishing a relationship between utilization of medical resources and expenditures by patients as consumers is not always inappropriate. Medical care is not monolithic; in some areas, it may be troublesome to use financial incentives, but, with respect to other types of care, use of incentives to shape behavior might be acceptable.

With respect to effectiveness, it is now commonplace to consider the effects of incentives on conduct in the health arena. This analysis is no longer an oddity but is quite mainstream. There is a recognition that economically unrestrained decision-making in medical care, as in other areas, has consequences in terms of resource utilization. Thus, the ideological commitment to unrestricted access has run into a hardboiled economic reality: elimination of the financial dimensions from medical care decision-making increases the overall use of resources. Financial incentives influence much more than distributive values.

The existence of clinical uncertainty, reflected in the widely divergent and unexplained procedure rates among providers in seemingly similar circumstances, further suggests an appropriate role for incentives. The evidence about divergent procedure rates undermines the assumption of a monolithically correct mode of treatment. In this world of uncertainty, it is hardly inappropriate to consider financial issues in decision-making. The assumption can no longer be indulged that financial incentives undermine scientifically clear-cut clinical pathways.

Principles of competition and incentives have influenced the rest of the health policy arena in the past decade. Those principles are strikingly at odds with the strongly held, fundamental principles of altruism and communitarianism that are so widespread in the organ transplantation arena. The logical next question is what would organ transplantation policy look like if it were more compatible with mainstream trends in health policy?

The answer is that it would allow for the introduction of incentives; that is, it would permit commerce in organ transplantation. Eliminating the exclusive reliance on altruism would recognize and acknowledge the priority of overcoming organ supply shortages and yet retain fidelity to principles of autonomy and individual choice of donors or their families.

Does Organ Transplantation Warrant a Different Policy Approach from that of Mainstream Medical Care?

I have described mainstream public policy in the overall health care arena, explained how organ transplantation policy does not coincide with the mainstream, and stated what organ transplantation policy might look like if it did coincide. Does the field of organ transplantation warrant such a different policy approach from that of mainstream medical care?

The presumption for incentives in a market system

I would start with the assumption that organ transplantation policies should allow for financial incentives in the absence of convincing arguments to the contrary. Evidence from elsewhere in the health arena shows that incentives affect behavior. Evidence from abroad shows that financial incentives dramatically increase levels of transplantable organ supply. The issue is increasingly being raised and discussed favorably in professional meetings and forums. And a recent survey performed under the auspices of the United Network for Organ Sharing (UNOS) and published in the *Lancet* demonstrates that a majority of the respondents believed that some form of compensation should be offered in the USA to donors of transplantable organs; only 2 per cent of those surveyed commented that use of financial incentives would be immoral or unethical. I would require that those seeking to maintain the ban on incentives in organ transplantation persuasively make the case against commerce empirically or ethically. "In a nation whose institutions have relied on market mechanisms for making basic economic choices," governmental action that prohibits the use of incentives, which constitute a fundamental component of the market system, "bears a burden of persuasion."[2]

The advantages of a market approach

What are the advantages of the market approach that would allow individuals (or parents on behalf of their children) to enter into forward contracts while alive and in good health for the use of their organs for transplantation after their death? I want to set forth two rationales simply and succinctly and then examine, at greater length, criticisms leveled at the use of markets.

First, there is the libertarian argument in support of the use of incentives and markets. This position emphasizes respect for the autonomy of the donor (and the ability of the donor to choose), de-emphasizes paternalism, and strengthens the hand of the individual rather than the family. Payment to "donate" (a misnomer in this context) allows a person to determine his or her own organs' fate, respects the right of the buyer to contract, and recognizes the ability of the medically needy donee beneficiary to benefit from the transaction.

In addition to the libertarian argument, there is also the utilitarian argument; that is, would or could incentives increase organ supply? Permitting contracts for the sale of organs and making provision for a registry of potential donors would provide pressure to pursue transplants aggressively. A source of potential suppliers could be expected to come forward, and, once a contract had been entered into, the purchaser and the ultimate beneficiary would be forceful advocates for the effective use of transplantable organs to save lives.

Criticisms of markets

Criticisms leveled at the use of markets for increasing the supply of transplantable organs can be either empirical or ethical in character. It is worth reiterating that the burden of persuasion should lie with those advocating that market transactions remain illegal.

Empirical criticisms Many critics of the use of markets and incentives focus on an empirical claim: use of financial incentives – allowing the market to function in this area – will not result in an increase in the supply of transplantable organs. The same claim was once made about financial incentives in medicine generally. But empirical evidence now firmly refutes this. Incentives work.

Objectors raise various concerns about the state of mind of potential donors – fears, uncertainty and ignorance. These deal not with the feasibility of a system of incentives but with the price that would be needed to induce supply. It is artificial to think in terms of absolutes – people will or will not contract for anatomical "gifts." It is better to think of what inducements are needed to encourage sufficient supply so as to satisfy the demand. The issue is one of degree, not of absolutes.[3]

Some critics claim that the introduction of commercial incentives could result in reduced altruistic donating and a net reduction of organ supply. Although experiences from other countries suggest that financial incentives increase organ supply, the empirical issue is a serious and legitimate one. Since such transactions have been illegal in the USA since 1984, no reliable American data exist. Where disagreements are empirical, not ethical, in character, the appropriate scientific approach is to run a controlled experiment. Define a region, repeal the federal ban on the purchase and sale of organs for transplant in that area, and, with proper controls and monitoring, see what happens.[3]

This experimental approach is not acceptable to many market critics. They worry that the altruistic system will be undermined and that the damage will be irreversible. The thought seems to be that the use of incentives is like an incurable infectious disease – once it is unleashed, it will deal a fateful and fatal blow to the altruistic underpinnings of the existing system of organ donation, a blow from which the existing system would not recover.

This is a hard position to counter because of the absence of firm data. The evidence from India and Egypt indicates that inducements do work. Evidence from other areas of health care suggest the same thing. It is not reasonable to maintain an empirically based criticism of financial incentives and simultaneously deny society the opportunity at least to have an experiment, even if only in a region and not in the nation as a whole.

In appraising the empirical criticism, the analyst must remember that the burden of persuasion is on those seeking to outlaw market-oriented behavior in our democratic society. In the absence of firm evidence, or an experiment, we should legalize commerce in organs for transplant, as other commerce in medical care is now permitted.

Ethical criticisms

I now consider the ethical criticisms of commerce in transplantable organs. I deal with these in specific contexts, taking on the harder claims first.

The effect of markets on the distribution of organs

Much of the ethical concern regarding commerce in transplantable organs focuses on the issue of distribution: who gets the organ available for transplantation and what is the effect of a market in transplantable organs on the distribution of organs? This pair of questions focuses on the demand side of the market.

The ethical thesis is that organs are different from other commodities or services that are distributed by the market system. Organs, argue critics of markets, should be allocated by medical criteria, not by financial considerations. This claim needs to be taken seriously. Medical resources generally are not allocated solely on the basis of medical need; the question is whether organ transplantation is different from other forms of medical care generally and from comparable life-saving therapies.

In my view, the original banning of market transactions in transplantable organs stemmed from an understandable yet ultimately unsophisticated linkage of issues surrounding the demand and the supply sides of the market. A market in transplantable organs can function on the supply side and, if desired on ethical grounds, society can leave the demand side to a nonmarket form of distribution.

The concern by ethical critics of commerce in transplantable organs is with the effect of wealth inequality on the distribution of available organs. There is a special claim that, while wealth inequality is acceptable as a general matter, it is unacceptable as a basis for deciding which persons are to be recipients of organ transplants.

The problem, however, can be resolved by public subsidy for those whose inadequate level of wealth bars access. The kidney program is an example of a publicly financed program for a specific illness and a specific set of procedures. To establish a principled basis for this type of categorical public support for kidney transplantation, however, advocates must be prepared to justify a kidney transplant program in comparison to other transplant therapies, such as heart or liver transplants, which are more likely to deal with life-threatening situations and which are not funded as generously by the federal government. Also, those who make claims of special consideration for transplant programs must be prepared to demonstrate that the justification for special status for organ transplantation does not apply as persuasively to nontransplant treatments of other life-threatening illnesses (e.g. public financing of drugs such as AZT for AIDS patients). Does society have an obligation to provide a public subsidy to make available and distribute this type of life-enhancing or life-prolonging drug? And if so, must the drug be made available without a fee, so that commerce is completely eliminated in the allocation of the scarce resource? If wealth can make a difference with regard to AZT, for example, why cannot financial considerations enter into organ allocation decisions?

Special consideration for organ transplants must also distinguish not only other life-saving but also other quality-of-life-enhancing procedures. Dialysis, after all, is an alternative to kidney transplantation, albeit less desirable therapeutically. Thus, since an alternative treatment regimen exists, kidney transplantation is not necessarily a life-saving procedure. Other parts of the kidney transplantation process require a fee. Whereas kidneys cannot be paid for by the patient, and kidney donors cannot receive compensation for their beneficence, organ procurement organizations can be paid for their organ procurement efforts by hospitals. Drugs are paid for, hospital stays are paid for, physicians are compensated. Money matters in every dimension of organ transplantation. It is not so clear why ethical critics become so fastidious, so squeamish, about paying for the life-giving organ itself.

There is an irony at work here. Advocates for funding by third-party payers claim that organ transplantation is in fact ordinary and necessary medical care – mainstream, nonexperimental medicine indistinguishable from other life-saving and life-enhancing treatments. The claim for insurance coverage requires that organ transplantation be viewed as just another effective therapy, like many others covered and paid for under traditional medical insurance. The claim for third-party coverage rests on the mainstream status, the lack of specialness of organ transplants. Yet that very specialness forms the ethical foundation for the underlying hostility to commerce in transplantable organs. There is a clear tension between these two positions.

Further, for these ethical objections to commerce in organs to make sense, there must be a willingness on the part of the objectors to exalt these distributive values above overall lifesaving and quality-of-life-enhancing objectives. This is true because, for the ethical discussion, we must assume that, empirically, commerce in transplantable organs will result in an increased supply of such organs and, consequently, more saved and quality-of-life-enhanced lives from transplantation procedures.

Some have made the forthright argument that it is better not to save lives in order to maintain distributional equity. I find that argument troubling. If one assumes that a price induces more supply, and that a wealthy person's life is thereby saved, how is the poor person harmed as compared with the status quo? One must take the position that it is better to deprive the wealthy person of a transplant, which hypothetically would not otherwise be available, in order to preserve some sense of egalitarian justice. This is a difficult outcome to impose on a person in the name of fairness, since the economically disadvantaged person is not benefited in any tangible way by prohibiting the wealthier person from using his or her resources to pay for an otherwise unavailable transplantable organ.

This is a genuinely troubling ethical dilemma that is worthy of further intellectual investigation, debate and discussion. As a pragmatic matter, however, the issue can be finessed in the name of incremental reform. For the time being, at least, market-oriented reforms can be concentrated on the introduction of supply-side commercial incentives, leaving intact a nonmarket-driven system for the distribution of transplantable organs on the demand side.

The effect of markets on live donors

A second difficult question is whether a system of commerce in transplantable organs should permit payment for use of organs provided by (i.e. sold by) live donors. This ethically serious and troubling issue also can be finessed. Market-oriented reforms can focus, at least at the initial stage, on the use of markets exclusively for the sale of cadaveric organs, preferably by a forward contract.

The ethical concern with live donors is coercion, but the coercion claim may not be as much of a problem as some would argue. While there is an increase in choice, it is coercion only if we equate coercion with hard choices.

We do allow people to choose risk for a price. Life with one kidney is risky. But the question is whether this is a socially acceptable level of risk that should be subject to private choice and decision-making, or whether the risk should be banned by collective action through paternalistic governmental regulation. The risk of living with one kidney is quite moderate, equivalent to driving back and forth to work 16 miles (25 kilometers) a day. Society tolerates that level of risk in other areas, why not in the transplant area as well? Clearly the recipient/purchaser, whose health is improved, benefits. Arguably, so does the "donor"/seller, who can use the proceeds for other advantageous purposes.

One must hasten to add that, if any system of commerce is established involving live-"donor" organs, safeguards are necessary to assure voluntarism and to bar other uses of body parts via coerced, not induced, sale. Still, despite such safeguards, the paternalistic concern regarding live-"donor" organ sales is real and pervasive.

Also, there is worry about what some view as organ imperialism – the sale of organs by poor or Third World persons to provide organs for wealthy people. Rationally, the analyst may note that the sellers deem themselves better off, do not consider the risk to be excessive, and deem organ donation to be an avenue of opportunity. The skeptic may even call paternalistic objections to this activity elitist or illustrative of a certain "feel-good" morality. Yet a typical reaction is one, perhaps, of revulsion. And although this may be irrational, nonrational, or a form of symbolic hypocrisy, the objections exist and persist.

The effect of a market for cadaveric organ sale on the "donor's" family and on society

It is now appropriate to address the issue of cadaveric organ sale. There are two concerns here – the potential effect of a market in cadaveric organs on the family of the "donor" and the potentially dehumanizing effect of organ sales on society.

The family issue is a legitimate concern. By selling his or her organs during life by forward contracting for transplantation at the time of death, an individual takes charge of the disposition of his or her organs at death. In the world of estate planning, this is not unusual, rather it is the norm. By allowing sales and by enforcing these forward contracts for organ transplantation, society validates the autonomy of the individual. At the same time, society takes away the ability of the family to veto the decedent's decision to allow use of his or her organs for transplantation purposes. This undoubtedly detracts from the "silver lining" phenomenon through which family members, in the exercise of altruism, feel good about giving the organs of a loved one to save the life of another person.

The psychological satisfaction of the family in this circumstance can be considerable, but the autonomy of the patient, if it is to be adequately respected, must outweigh the family's concern. This is, of course, the normal pattern with respect to inheritance, and it is the clear determination of the existing legal regime under the United States Uniform Anatomical Gift Act, which already vests legal authority in the individual to donate his or her organs for transplantation irrespective of the wishes of the family. The family veto recognized in the transplant community is an extralegal custom not validated by existing law. Indeed, the Act was expressly drafted to overcome the family veto, giving primacy to the autonomy of the individual donor. Given the existing legal framework, which does not recognize the family veto, the supposed loss of the family's psychological well-being is a weak claim. Ultimately, the autonomy of the donor and the welfare of the beneficiaries who receive the transplantable organs must outweigh the claims of the family. The establishment of a market for cadaveric organs will take nothing from families to which they are currently legally entitled.[4]

The potentially adverse effect on society of a market in cadaveric organs stems from a concern about the commodification of human body parts. This is an abstract, hazy issue. For example, Dr Leon R. Kass, who objects to the use of markets in transplantable organs, recognizes that his objections "appeal ... largely to certain hard-to-articulate intuitions and sensibilities that ... belong intimately to the human experience of our own humanity."

One set of objections to commodification of human body parts focuses on the value of communitarianism. Establishment of a market in cadaveric organs could pose a threat to the value of altruism. I just do not see this as a transplant issue. It deals with other, broader, philosophical issues about how society should be organized and about how people should be motivated to live their lives. Advocates of communitarianism generally are suspicious of what they regard as the atomization of society that stems from reliance on markets for making economic allocation decisions. They are hostile to market transactions, and they worry that commodification of human body parts places yet another set of decisions into an economic context with which they are none too pleased to begin with. Again, I view this type of concern to be quite unrelated to organ transplantation issues per se but rather related to broader humanitarian concerns about how market economies function in general.

Significantly, in the context of a market for cadaveric organs, there is no issue of coercion as there could be in the context of live-"donor" organ sales. Similarly, there is no real issue of organ imperialism, there is no concern regarding irreversibility, and there is no problem of exploitation of the poor. According to Cohen, "[I]n the cadaver market the vendors are neither rich nor poor, merely dead."

The loss of altruism should not in itself be viewed as a problem, except if it results in reduced supply of transplantable organs. Supply is an empirical not an ethical concern. The issue is not whether or not altruism is a good thing. The question is whether market transactions should be made illegal. Advocates of markets in cadaveric organs have no desire to make altruism a felony. Altruism can coexist peacefully with a flourishing market for cadaver organs. The claim of market proponents is based upon principles of freedom, autonomy, and choice. Indeed, when one carefully examines the argument for preserving altruism by outlawing market transactions, one wonders whether the real fear is that legalization of market transactions will in fact work; that is, given a choice, people would choose to participate in a market and would abandon altruism. Unpacked, the argument to outlaw market exchanges to preserve altruism is in reality an argument to coerce altruism. This surely is a strange way of promoting the supposed good feeling of communitarian solidarity that comes from voluntary donations of the organs of a recently deceased loved one for the benefit of another human being.

To make the case against market transactions in transplantable organs, advocates must establish the unique features of organs and organ transplantation. Since, in a market economy, market-based transactions are the norm, those seeking to curtail the operation of a market must show that there are special reasons justifying the restriction. I will now argue that organs and their transplantation are not unique in this policy-relevant sense.

There are numerous other life-saving or life-enhancing therapies for which sales are not prohibited. There is no ban on the sale of alternatives to organ transplantation, such as kidney dialysis. There is no ban on the sale of substitutes for failed body parts, such as artificial organs and other artificial body parts. Thus, we are left with a gnawing concern because the transplantable organ derives from a dead human body. This is not an objection to the use of the organs of a cadaver for transplantation purposes, since a donated organ is acceptable. It is just a question of how we induce donors or families to donate those organs. Does this, as Leon Kass has suggested, really "come perilously close to selling our souls"? The UNOS-sponsored survey, which showed support for compensation for the use of transplantable organs, would certainly call that predictive judgment into question.

Analysts must balance the hazy, abstract concern about the effect on society of the use of financial incentives to motivate individuals to supply their organs for transplantation at the time of death against other, fundamental values. When life and death (for recipients) are in the balance and when libertarian values of individual autonomy are involved (for the "donor"), there is an insufficient justification for a ban on contracting while an individual is alive for the use of that individual's organs for transplantation at the time of death.

Conclusion

There are important advantages in allowing commerce in forward contracts for transplantable cadaveric organs.

There is a shift in the locus of decision-making – away from the bedside of the dying family member to an earlier time when an individual can make a determination about organ sale or donation while he or she is healthy and can act cooly and rationally.

Recognition of market transactions promotes and validates the autonomy of the individual donor/seller.

Legalization of market exchanges for cadaveric organs creates a legal and public-relations counterforce at the time of a "donor's" death so that the owner/purchaser of the organ and the potential and identified recipient of the transplantable organ can counteract the extralegal influence of the reluctant family of the potential donor and possibly of the attending physician as well.

Use of financial incentives is likely to induce a greater supply of needed transplantable organs than the current, exclusively altruistic system.

These advantages take on added significance because of the acute need for transplantable organs and the dearth of available organ supply under the current system. This is where the success of organ transplantation makes a difference. The squeamishness about markets could be indulged when the stakes were not so high. The life-saving ability of organ transplantation means that organ supply shortages are costing lives. The claim by organ transplantation experts to mainstream status within the medical community, along with third-party payment for what is now considered to be ordinary and necessary medical treatment, suggests that it is now time to emphasize the similarities between organ transplantation and other forms of life-saving and quality-of-life-enhancing medical procedures rather than emphasizing the differences. Values regarding organ transplantation fit within the mainstream. They are not unique. We have allowed this "ghettoization" of organ transplantation policy within the health policy arena to go on for too long.

At this point I would not argue for a complete, full-scale market approach. I do not now call for creation of a market for live-"donor" organs. Nor do I now call for experimenting with a market on the demand side for the distribution of transplantable organs. But I do call for a controlled supply-side experiment with the sale of cadaveric organs. Permitting the sale of cadaveric organs in advance through forward contracts, with the concomitant establishment of a computerized donor registry, would represent a reasonable, modest, incremental experiment that is well worth trying. This is especially true given the lives at stake. This would allow for a constructive blend of altruism and self-interest, and nurture the hope that this combination would help to reduce the existing shortage of transplantable organs. Upon analysis, my reluctant conclusion is that opposition to experimentation with the sale of organs is based upon prejudice, not reason.

Notes

1 See *President's Commission for the Study of Ethical Problems in Medicine and Biomedical and Behavioral Research, Securing Access to Health Care: A Report on the Ethical Implications of Differences in the Availability of Health Services* (1983), p. 18.

2 Quality, which is a concern, arguably could be monitored where patients, by contract, have agreed to the use of their organs for transplant at their death. The purchaser would have an incentive to keep the seller's organ healthy, and in most scenarios the seller would have the same incentive. This makes the organ market distinguishable from the blood sale market, where quality is a serious concern.

3 For a proposal to perform a pilot study of the effect on organ supply of a $1000 death benefit for organ donation.

4 For individuals who wish to provide this form of psychic satisfaction to members of their family, the option of delegating this choice to family members would continue to exist under the Uniform Anatomical Gift Act. The choice for altruism as the basis for an anatomical gift at death would still be available.

Suggestions for further reading

Blair, R. D. and Kaserman, D. L. The economics and ethics of alternative cadaveric organ procurement policies. *Yale Journal on Regulation* (1991), 8, 403–52.

Blumstein, J. F. Federal organ transplantation policy: A time for reassessment? *University of California at Davis Law Review* (1989), 22, 451–97.

Blumstein, J. F. and Sloan, F. A. Health planning and regulation through certificate of need: an overview. *Utah Law Review* (1978), 3.

Cohen, L. R. Increasing the supply of transplant organs: The virtues of a futures market. *George Washington Law Review* (1989), 58, 1–51.

Guttmann, R. D. The meaning of "The economics and ethics of alternative cadaveric organ procurement policies." *Yale Journal on Regulation* (1991), 8, 453–62.

Hansmann, H. The economics and ethics of markets for human organs. In *Organ Transplantation Policy: Issues and Prospects*, ed. J. F. Blumstein and F. A. Sloan

(Durham, NC: Duke University Press, 1989), pp. 57–85.

Kass, L. R. Organs for sale? Propriety, property, and the price of progress. *Public Interest* (1992), 107, 65–86.

Kittur, D. S., Hogan, M. M., Thukral, V. K., McGaw, L. J. and Alexander, J. W. Incentives for organ donation. *Lancet* (1991), 338, 1441–3.

Peters, T. G. Life or death: The issue of payment in cadaveric organ donation. *Journal of the American Medical Association* (1991), 265, 1302–5.

Radin, M. J. Market-inalienability. *Harvard Law Review* (1987), 100, 1849–937.

Schwindt, R. and Vining, A. R. Proposal for a future delivery market for transplant organs. *Journal of Health Politics, Policy and Law* (1986), 11, 483–500.

US Department of Health and Human Services. *Report of the Task Force on Organ Transplantation, Organ Transplantation Issues and Recommendations* (Washington: Government Printing Office, 1986).

Vining, A. R. and Schwindt, R. Have a heart: Increasing the supply of transplant organs for infants and children. *Journal of Policy Analysis and Management* (1988), 7, 706–10.

47

The Survival Lottery

John Harris

Let us suppose that organ transplant procedures have been perfected; in such circumstances if two dying patients could be saved by organ transplants then, if surgeons have the requisite organs in stock and no other needy patients, but nevertheless allow their patients to die, we would be inclined to say, and be justified in saying, that the patients died because the doctors refused to save them. But if there are no spare organs in stock and none otherwise available, the doctors have no choice, they cannot save their patients and so must let them die. In this case we would be disinclined to say that the doctors are in any sense the cause of their patients' deaths. But let us further suppose that the two dying patients, Y and Z, are not happy about being left to die. They might argue that it is not strictly true that there are no organs which could be used to save them. Y needs a new heart and Z new lungs. They point out that if just one healthy person were to be killed his organs could be removed and both of them be saved. We and the doctors would probably be alike in thinking that such a step, while technically possible, would be out of the question. We would not say that the doctors were killing their patients if they refused to prey upon the healthy to save the sick. And because this sort of surgical Robin Hoodery is out of the question we can tell Y and Z that they cannot be saved, and that when they die they will have died of natural causes and not of the neglect of their doctors. Y and Z do not however agree, they insist that if the doctors fail to kill a healthy man and use his organs to save them, then the doctors will be responsible for their deaths.

Many philosophers have for various reasons believed that we must not kill even if by doing so we could save life. They believe that there is a moral difference between killing and letting die. On this view, to kill A so that Y and Z might live is ruled out because we have a strict obligation not to kill but a duty of some lesser kind to save life. A. H. Clough's dictum 'Thou shalt not kill but need'st not strive officiously to keep alive' expresses bluntly this point of view. The dying Y and Z may be excused for not being much impressed by Clough's dictum. They agree that it is wrong to kill the innocent and are prepared to agree to an absolute prohibition against so doing. They do not agree, however, that A is more innocent than they are. Y and Z might go on to point out that the currently acknowledged right of the innocent not to be killed, even where their deaths might give life to others, is just a decision to prefer the lives of the fortunate to those of the unfortunate. A is innocent in the sense that he has done nothing to deserve death, but Y and Z are also innocent in this sense. Why should they be the ones to die simply because they are so unlucky as to have diseased organs. Why, they might argue, should their living or dying be left to chance when in so many other areas of human life we believe that we have an obligation to ensure the survival of the maximum number of lives possible.

Y and Z argue that if a doctor refuses to treat a patient, with the result that the patient dies, he has killed that patient as sure as shooting, and that in exactly the same way, if the doctors refuse Y and Z the transplants that they need, then their refusal

From *Philosophy*, vol. 50 (1975) pp. 81–7. Reprinted with the permission of Cambridge University Press.

will kill Y and Z, again as sure as shooting. The doctors, and indeed the society which supports their inaction, cannot defend themselves by arguing that they are neither expected, nor required by law or convention, to kill so that lives may be saved (indeed, quite the reverse) since this is just an appeal to custom or authority. A man who does his own moral thinking must decide whether, in these circumstances, he ought to save two lives at the cost of one, or one life at the cost of two. The fact that so called 'third parties' have never before been brought into such calculations, have never before been thought of as being involved, is not an argument against their now becoming so. There are of course, good arguments against allowing doctors simply to haul passers-by off the street whenever they have a couple of patients in need of new organs. And the harmful side-effects of such a practice in terms of terror and distress to the victims, the witnesses and society generally, would give us further reason for dismissing the idea. Y and Z realize this and have a proposal, which they will shortly produce, which would largely meet objections to placing such power in the hands of doctors and eliminate at least some of the harmful side-effects.

In the unlikely event of their feeling obliged to reply to the reproaches of Y and Z, the doctors might offer the following argument: they might maintain that a man is only responsible for the death of someone whose life he might have saved, if, in all the circumstances of the case, he ought to have saved the man by the means available. This is why a doctor might be a murderer if he simply refused or neglected to treat a patient who would die without treatment, but not if he could only save the patient by doing something he ought in no circumstances to do – kill the innocent. Y and Z readily agree that a man ought not to do what he ought not to do, but they point out that if the doctors, and for that matter society at large, ought on balance to kill one man if two can thereby be saved, then failure to do so will involve responsibility for the consequent deaths. The fact that Y's and Z's proposal involves killing the innocent cannot be a reason for refusing to consider their proposal, for this would just be a refusal to face the question at issue and so avoid having to make a decision as to what ought to be done in circumstances like these. It is Y's and Z's claim that failure to adopt their plan will also involve killing the innocent, rather more of the innocent than the proposed alternative.

To back up this last point, to remove the arbitrariness of permitting doctors to select their donors from among the chance passers-by outside hospitals, and the tremendous power this would place in doctors hands, to mitigate worries about side-effects and lastly to appease those who wonder why poor old A should be singled out for sacrifice, Y and Z put forward the following scheme: they propose that everyone be given a sort of lottery number. Whenever doctors have two or more dying patients who could be saved by transplants, and no suitable organs have come to hand through 'natural' deaths, they can ask a central computer to supply a suitable donor. The computer will then pick the number of a suitable donor at random and he will be killed so that the lives of two or more others may be saved. No doubt if the scheme were ever to be implemented a suitable euphemism for 'killed' would be employed. Perhaps we would begin to talk about citizens being called upon to 'give life' to others. With the refinement of transplant procedures such a scheme could offer the chance of saving large numbers of lives that are now lost. Indeed, even taking into account the loss of the lives of donors, the numbers of untimely deaths each year might be dramatically reduced, so much so that everyone's chance of living to a ripe old age might be increased. If this were to be the consequence of the adoption of such a scheme, and it might well be, it could not be dismissed lightly. It might of course be objected that it is likely that more old people will need transplants to prolong their lives than will the young, and so the scheme would inevitably lead to a society dominated by the old. But if such a society is thought objectionable, there is no reason to suppose that a programme could not be designed for the computer that would ensure the maintenance of whatever is considered to be an optimum age distribution throughout the population.

Suppose that inter-planetary travel revealed a world of people like ourselves, but who organized their society according to this scheme. No one was considered to have an absolute right to life or freedom from interference, but everything was always done to ensure that as many people as possible would enjoy long and happy lives. In such a world a man who attempted to escape when his number was up or who resisted on the grounds that no one had a right to take his life, might well be regarded as a murderer. We might or might not prefer to live in such a world, but the morality of its inhabitants would surely be one that we could respect. It would not be obviously more barbaric or cruel or immoral than our own.

Y and Z are willing to concede one exception to the universal application of their scheme. They realize that it would be unfair to allow people who have brought their misfortune on themselves to benefit from the lottery. There would clearly be something unjust about killing the abstemious B so that W (whose heavy smoking has given him lung cancer) and X (whose drinking has destroyed his liver) should be preserved to over-indulge again.

What objections could be made to the lottery scheme? A first straw to clutch at would be the desire for security. Under such a scheme we would never know when we would hear *them* knocking at the door. Every post might bring a sentence of death, every sound in the night might be the sound of boots on the stairs. But, as we have seen, the chances of actually being called upon to make the ultimate sacrifice might be slimmer than is the present risk of being killed on the roads, and most of us do not lie trembling a-bed, appalled at the prospect of being dispatched on the morrow. The truth is that lives might well be more secure under such a scheme.

If we respect individuality and see every human being as unique in his own way, we might want to reject a society in which it appeared that individuals were seen merely as interchangeable units in a structure, the value of which lies in its having as many healthy units as possible. But of course Y and Z would want to know why A's individuality was more worthy of respect than theirs.

Another plausible objection is the natural reluctance to play God with men's lives, the feeling that it is wrong to make any attempt to re-allot the life opportunities that fate has determined, that the deaths of Y and Z would be 'natural', whereas the death of anyone killed to save them would have been perpetrated by men. But if we are able to change things, then to elect not to do so is also to determine what will happen in the world.

Neither does the alleged moral difference between killing and letting die afford a respectable way of rejecting the claims of Y and Z. For if we really want to counter proponents of the lottery, if we really want to answer Y and Z and not just put them off, we cannot do so by saying that the lottery involves killing and object to it for that reason, because to do so would, as we have seen, just beg the question as to whether the failure to save as many people as possible might not also amount to killing.

To opt for the society which Y and Z propose would be then to adopt a society in which saintliness would be mandatory. Each of us would have to recognize a binding obligation to give up his own life for others when called upon to do so. In such a society anyone who reneged upon this duty would be a murderer. The most promising objection to such a society, and indeed to any principle which required us to kill A in order to save Y and Z, is, I suspect, that we are committed to the right of self-defence. If I can kill A to save Y and Z then he can kill me to save P and Q, and it is only if I am prepared to agree to this that I will opt for the lottery or be prepared to agree to a man's being killed if doing so would save the lives of more than one other man. Of course there is something paradoxical about basing objections to the lottery scheme on the right of self-defence since, *ex hypothesi*, each person would have a better chance of living to a ripe old age if the lottery scheme were to be implemented. None the less, the feeling that no man should be required to lay down his life for others makes many people shy away from such a scheme, even though it might be rational to accept it on prudential grounds, and perhaps even mandatory on utilitarian grounds. Again, Y and Z would reply that the right of self-defence must extend to them as much as to anyone else; and while it is true that they can only live if another man is killed, they would claim that it is also true that if they are left to die, then someone who lives on does so over their dead bodies.

It might be argued that the institution of the survival lottery has not gone far to mitigate the harmful side-effects in terms of terror and distress to victims, witnesses and society generally, that would be occasioned by doctors simply snatching passers-by off the streets and disorganizing them for the benefit of the unfortunate. Donors would after all still have to be procured, and this process, however it was carried out, would still be likely to prove distressing to all concerned. The lottery scheme would eliminate the arbitrariness of leaving the life and death decisions to the doctors, and remove the possibility of such terrible power falling into the hands of any individuals, but the terror and distress would remain. The effect of having to apprehend presumably unwilling victims would give us pause. Perhaps only a long period of education or propaganda could remove our abhorrence. What this abhorrence reveals about the rights and wrongs of the situation is however more difficult to assess. We might be inclined to say that only monsters could ignore the promptings of conscience so far as to operate the lottery scheme. But the promptings of conscience are not necessarily the most reliable guide. In the present case Y and Z would argue that such promptings are mere squeamishness, an over-nice self-indulgence that costs lives. Death, Y and Z would remind us, is a distressing experience whenever and to whomever it occurs, so the less it occurs the better. Fewer victims and witnesses will be distressed as part of the side-effects of the lottery scheme than would suffer as part of the side-effects of not instituting it.

Lastly, a more limited objection might be made, not to the idea of killing to save lives, but to the involvement of 'third parties'. Why, so the objection goes, should we not give X's heart to Y or Y's lungs to X, the same number of lives being thereby preserved and no one else's life set at risk? Y's and Z's reply to this objection differs from their previous line of argument. To amend their plan so that the involvement of so called 'third parties' is ruled out would, Y and Z claim, violate their right to equal concern and respect with the rest of society. They argue that such a proposal would amount to treating the unfortunate who need new organs as a class within society whose lives are considered to be of less value than those of its more fortunate members. What possible justification could there be for singling out one group of people whom we would be justified in using as donors but not another? The idea in the mind of those who would propose such a step must be something like the following: since Y and Z cannot survive, since they are going to die in any event, there is no harm in putting their names into the lottery, for the chances of their dying cannot thereby be increased and will in fact almost certainly be reduced. But this is just to ignore everything that Y and Z have been saying. For if their lottery scheme is adopted they are not going to die anyway – their chances of dying are no greater and no less than those of any other participant in the lottery whose number may come up. This ground for confining selection of donors to the unfortunate therefore disappears. Any other ground must discriminate against Y and Z as members of a class whose lives are less worthy of respect than those of the rest of society.

It might more plausibly be argued that the dying who cannot themselves be saved by transplants, or by any other means at all, should be the priority selection group for the computer programme. But how far off must death be for a man to be classified as 'dying'? Those so classified might argue that their last few days or weeks of life are as valuable to them (if not more valuable) than the possibly longer span remaining to others. The problem of narrowing down the class of possible donors without discriminating unfairly against some sub-class of society is, I suspect, insoluble.

Such is the case for the survival lottery. Utilitarians ought to be in favour of it, and absolutists cannot object to it on the ground that it involves killing the innocent, for it is Y's and Z's case that any alternative must also involve killing the innocent. If the absolutist wishes to maintain his objection he must point to some morally relevant difference between positive and negative killing. This challenge opens the door to a large topic with a whole library of literature, but Y and Z are dying and do not have time to explore it exhaustively. In their own case the most likely candidate for some feature which might make this moral difference is the malevolent intent of Y and Z themselves. An absolutist might well argue that while no one intends the deaths of Y and Z, no one necessarily wishes them dead, or aims at their demise for any reason, they do mean to kill A (or have him killed). But Y and Z can reply that the death of A is no part of their plan, they merely wish to use a couple of his organs, and if he cannot live without them... *tan pis*! None would be more delighted than Y and Z if artificial organs would do as well, and so render the lottery scheme otiose.

One form of absolutist argument perhaps remains. This involves taking an Orwellian stand on some principle of common decency. The argument would then be that even to enter into the sort of 'macabre' calculations that Y and Z propose displays a blunted sensibility, a corrupted and vitiated mind. Forms of this argument have recently been advanced by Noam Chomsky (*American Power and the New Mandarins*) and Stuart Hampshire (*Morality and Pessimism*). The indefatigable Y and Z would of course deny that their calculations are in any sense 'macabre', and would present them as the most humane course available in the circumstances. Moreover they would claim that the Orwellian stand on decency is the product of a closed mind, and not susceptible to rational argument. Any reasoned defence of such a principle must appeal to notions like respect for human life. Hampshire's argument in fact does, and these Y and Z could make conformable to their own position.

Can Y and Z be answered? Perhaps only by relying on moral intuition, on the insistence that we do feel there is something wrong with the survival lottery and our confidence that this feeling is prompted by some morally relevant difference between our bringing about the death of A and our bringing about the deaths of Y and Z. Whether we could retain this confidence in our intuitions if we were to be confronted by a society in which the survival lottery operated, was accepted by all, and was seen to save many lives that would otherwise have been lost, it would be interesting to know.

There would of course be great practical difficulties in the way of implementing the lottery. In so many cases it would be agonizingly difficult to decide whether or not a person had brought his misfortunate on himself. There are numerous ways in which a person may contribute to his predicament, and the task of deciding how far, or how decisively, a person is himself responsible for his fate would be formidable. And in those cases where we can be confident that a person is innocent of responsibility for his predicament, can we acquire this confidence in time to save him? The lottery scheme would be a powerful weapon in the hands of someone willing and able to misuse it. Could we ever feel certain that the lottery was safe from unscrupulous computer programmers? Perhaps we should be thankful that such practical difficulties make the survival lottery an unlikely consequence of the perfection of transplants. Or perhaps we should be appalled.

It may be that we would want to tell Y and Z that the difficulties and dangers of their scheme would be too great a price to pay for its benefits. It is as well to be clear, however, that there is also a high, perhaps an even higher, price to be paid for the rejection of the scheme. That price is the lives of Y and Z and many like them, and we delude ourselves if we suppose that the reason why we reject their plan is that we accept the sixth commandment.[1]

Note

1 Thanks are due to Ronald Dworkin, Jonathan Glover, M. J. Inwood and Anne Seller for helpful comments.

48

Is Xenografting Morally Wrong?

A. L. Caplan

It is tempting to think that a decision about whether or not it is immoral to use animals as sources for transplantable organs and tissues hinges only upon the question of whether or not it is ethical to kill them. But the ethics of xenografting involves more than an analysis of that question. And even the assessment of the morality of killing animals to obtain their parts to use in human beings is more complicated than it might at first glance appear to be.

To decide whether it is ethical to kill animals, a variety of subsidiary questions must be considered. Is it ethical to kill animals to obtain organs and tissues to save human lives or alleviate severe disability when it might not be ethical to kill them for food or sport?[1] Why are animals being considered as sources of organs and tissues – do alternative methods for obtaining replacement parts for human beings exist? What sorts of animals would have to be killed, how would they be killed, and how would they be stored, handled, and treated prior to their deaths?

If it is possible to defend the killing of animals for xenografting then questions as to the morality of subjecting human beings to the risks, both physical and psychological, associated with xenografting must also be weighed. In undertaking a xenograft on a human subject the focus of moral concern ought not to be solely on the animal that will be killed.

Even for those who eat meat or hunt, it might well seem immoral to kill animals for their parts if alternative sources of replacement parts were or might soon be available. The moral acceptability of xenografting will for many, including the prospective recipients of animal parts, be contingent on the presumption that there is no other plausible alternative source of transplantable organs and tissues. Unfortunately, the scarcity that is behind the current interest in xenografting is all too real.

From *Transplantation Proceedings*, vol. 24, no. 2 (April 1992), pp. 722–7. Reprinted by courtesy of the author.

Why Pursue Xenografting?

The supply of organs and tissues available from human cadaveric sources for transplantation in the United States and other nations is entirely inadequate. Many children and adults die or remain disabled due to the shortage of transplantable organs and tissues. Unless some solution is found to the problem of scarcity, the plight of those in need of organs and tissues will only grow worse and the numbers who die solely for want of an organ will continue to grow.

More than one-third of those now awaiting liver transplants die for want of a donor organ. Well over one-half of all children born with fatal, congenital deformities of the heart or liver die without a transplant due to the shortage of organs. The percentage of those who die while waiting would actually be higher if all potential candidates were on waiting lists.[2]

Some Americans are not referred for transplants because they cannot afford them. If those with organ failure from economically underdeveloped nations were wait-listed at North American and European transplant centers, the percentage of those who die while awaiting a transplant would be much larger.[3]

More than 150,000 Americans with kidney failure are kept alive by renal dialysis. The cost for this treatment exceeded five billion dollars in 1988. It would be far cheaper and, from the patient perspective as to the quality of life, far more desirable to treat kidney failure by means of transplants. But, there are simply not enough cadaveric kidneys for all who desire and could benefit from a transplant.

The supply of cadaveric organs for pancreas, small intestine, lung, heart–lung transplants for those dying of a wide variety of diseases affecting these organs is not adequate. The same story holds for bone, ligament, dural matter, heart valves, and skin. Moreover, demand for the limited supply of organs and tissues is increasing as more and more medical centers become capable of offering this form of surgery and, as techniques for managing rejection and infection improve.[4]

The shortage of organs and tissues for transplantation has led researchers to pursue a variety of alternatives in order to bridge the gap between supply and demand. Some suggest changing existing public policies governing cadaveric procurement. Others focus on locating alternatives to human cadaveric organs.

Efforts could be made to modify public policy to encourage more persons to serve as organ and tissue donors. Legislation mandating that the option of organ and tissue donation be presented whenever a person dies in a hospital setting has been enacted in the United States but, while leading to increases in both tissue and organ availability, has not been adequately implemented.[5,6] Organs and tissues are still lost because families are not approached about donation. Hospital compliance is not what it should be and the training of those who must identify potential donors and approach families is woefully lacking. Refusal rates to requests to donate are high and there exists a significant degree of mistrust and misunderstanding about donation on the part of the public.[6] Public policies could and should be changed to rectify these problems.

Other proposals to change public policy involve changing laws to permit payment to those who agree to donate or whose families consent to cadaveric donation[7,8] or to move toward a presumed consent system in which the burden of proof is placed on those who do not wish to donate to carry cards or other evidence of their nondonor status. However, cultural and religious attitudes in large segments of American society and in other societies will not support either the creation of markets, bounties, or property status for body parts[9] or the extension of state authority to the seizure of cadaveric organs and tissues.

Allowing markets may lead to criminal activities.[10] Selling irreplaceable body parts is an especially repugnant way to ask a person to earn income or benefits.[11] There is much reluctance on the part of the general public to swap the presumption of individual control over the body, either in life or death, for a policy that might benefit the common good by risking the loss of personal autonomy.[4,11] Nor has the actual experience with presumed consent laws in European nations been such as to justify enthusiasm for the likely results of a shift away from individualism and personal autonomy with respect to the control of cadavers.[12]

Even if drastic changes were made in existing public policies, other factors are working against the prospects for large increases in the human cadaveric organ supply. Improvements in emergency room access and care, the onset of the acquired immunodeficiency syndrome (AIDS) epidemic, ambivalence about cadaveric donation on the part of the public, plus laudable advances in public health measures such as mandatory seatbelt use, raising the age for legally purchasing liquor, and tougher laws against drunk driving mean that a tremendous increase in the supply of cadaveric organs is unlikely to occur no matter what public policies are adopted.

Most importantly with respect to the moral defensibility of exploring xenografting as an alternative source of organs, even if all human cadaveric organs were somehow made available for transplant, the supply would still not meet the potential demand. The hidden pool of potential transplant recipients would quickly become visible were these organs and tissues to become available.[3,6] The search for alternatives to the use of human cadaveric organs rests on the recognition that scarcity is an insurmountable obstacle.

In recent years surgeons have tried to solve the problem of shortage by using kidneys, and segments of liver, lung, and pancreas from living donors. Transplant teams in a few nations have been testing the feasibility of transplanting lobes of livers between biologically related individuals.[13,14] Teams at Stanford University and the University of Minesota have used parents as lung donors for their child. Minnesota and some other centers have been experimenting for many years with transplants of the kidney and pancreas from related and unrelated living donors.[15] Many centers around the world have performed bone marrow transplants between biologically unrelated persons.

There are serious problems with and limits to the use of living donors as alternative sources of organs and tissues. The most inviolate limit is that unmatched vital organs, such as the heart, cannot be used. Using living donors for other organs requires subjecting the donors to life-threatening risks, some pain and disfigurement, and some risk of disability. The legitimacy of consent on the part of living donors, especially among family members, is hard to assess. And, since it is not yet known whether transplanting lobes or segments of organs or unrelated bone marrow is efficacious, it is not certain that this strategy for getting more organs and tissue is a realistic option much less whether it will prove attractive to a sufficient number of actual donors.

Another alternative to human cadaveric organ transplantation is the development of mechanical or artificial organ and tissue substitutes. Kidney dialysis is one such substitute. The widely publicized efforts to create a total artificial heart, first at the University of Utah and then later at Humana Audubon Hospital in Louisville, Kentucky, represent another, albeit failed effort to create an alternative to transplantation using cadaveric hearts. New generations of mechanical hearts are in the research pipeline as are artificial insulin pumps, artificial lungs, and various types of artificial livers. But, safe, effective, and reliable artificial organs and tissues appear to still be decades away. Ironically, the immediate impact of the available forms of artificial organs is to increase the problem of allocation in the face of scarcity since these devices permit temporary "bridging" of children and adults in need of transplants, thereby increasing the pool of prospective recipients.

It is the plight of those dying of end-stage diseases for want of donor organs from both living and cadaveric human sources that has led a number of research groups to explore the option of using animals as the source of transplantable organs and tissues. Transplant researchers at Loma Linda, the University of Pittsburgh, Stanford, Columbia, and Minnesota as well as in England, China, Belgium, Sweden, Japan, and France, among other countries, are conducting research on xenografting organs and tissues. Some are exploring the feasibility of primate to human transplants. Others are pursuing lines of research that would allow them to utilize animals other than primates as sources.

It is scarcity that grounds the moral case for thinking about animals as sources of organs and tissues. In light of current and potential demand, no other options exist for alleviating the scarcity in the supply of replacement parts. If, however, society were to decide not to perform transplants or to perform only a limited number of them, then the case for xenografting would be considerably weakened. While transplant surgeons and those on waiting lists may find strategies for finding more organs or tissues attractive, another possible response to scarcity is to simply live with it. Those who advocate this response could do so on the grounds that it is not morally necessary to transplant all persons who are in need especially if doing so requires the systematic killing of animals for human purposes.[1,16,17]

Is the Problem of Scarcity Resolvable by Some Other Strategy?

Instead of pursuing the option of xenografting it is possible to argue that the answer to the problem of scarcity is that medicine should simply stop doing transplants entirely or only do as many as can be done with whatever human cadaveric organs and tissues are available. This moral stance might rest on the claim that transplants are simply too expensive and do not work well enough to justify a hunt for alternative sources to human organs. Or someone might view xenografting as unnecessary and immoral on the grounds that prevention makes far more sense than salvage and rescue in dealing with end-stage organ failure. Some forms of transplantation are notoriously expensive. A critic of the xenografting option might argue that it is not wise to spend hundreds of thousands of dollars on heart, liver, or nonrelated bone marrow transplants when the number of people requiring these treatments could be drastically reduced by decreasing the incidence of smoking, alcohol consumption, and the exposure to toxic substances in the workplace and the environment.

The arguments in favor of the "live within your means" position are not persuasive. While prevention of organ and tissue failure is surely to be preferred to rescue by means of transplants, large numbers of persons suffer organ and tissue failure for reasons that are poorly understood and, thus, not amenable to prevention. While individuals should certainly be encouraged to adopt more healthful lifestyles (including the consumption of less animal fat!) there are no proven techniques available for ensuring that people will behave wisely or prudently. Moreover, those who will need transplants in the next few decades are persons for whom prevention is too late. So, while prevention is desirable, the demand for transplants will not diminish for a significant period of time regardless of the efforts undertaken to improve public health.

Transplants are expensive, but many types of transplantation, especially for children and young adults, are very effective in providing a good quality of life for many, many years. The wisdom of doing any medical procedure cannot simply be equated with its overall cost. A more reasonable measure would be to see what is purchased for the price that is charged. If the moral value of spending money for health services is not total price but, cost per year of life saved or, cost relative to the likelihood of saving a life, then there are many other areas of health care that ought to be restricted or abandoned long before accepted forms of transplantation such as heart, liver, and kidney are deemed too expensive or not cost worthy.

Ethical Problems with the Xenograft Option

If it is true that the case for pursuing xenografting is a persuasive one then the question of whether xenografting is morally wrong shifts to an analysis of which animals will be used, how they will be kept and killed, and the risks and dangers involved for potential human recipients. Xenografting is still evolving so the ethical issues must be considered under two broad headings; issues associated with basic and clinical experimentation and, if this proves successful, those that would then be associated with the widespread use of xenografts as therapies.

Ethical issues raised by basic and clinical research

In thinking about the ethics of research on xenografting a couple of assumptions can safely be made. The number and type of animals used will be very much a function of cost, prior knowledge of the species, inbred characteristics, ease in handling, and availability. Gorillas are not going to be used in research simply because there are too few of them and they are unlikely to make compliant subjects. Rats and mice will dominate the early stages of research (as they already do) because they are relatively well understood, special-purpose bred, and cheap to acquire and maintain. Few primates will be used for basic or clinical research simply because they are too scarce, too expensive, and too complex to permit controlled study for most experimental purposes.

Even if the number of animals to be used is relatively small, the question still must be faced as to whether it is ethical to use animal models involving species such as rats, chickens, sheep, pigs, monkeys, baboons, and chimps in order to study the feasibility of cross-species xenografting? In part, the answer to this question pivots on whether or not there are plausible alternative models to the use of animals for exploring the two critical steps required for successful xenografting – overcoming immunologic rejection and achieving long-term physiologic function in an organ or tissue.

To some extent, immunologic problems can be examined without killing primates or higher animals by using lower animals or cellular models. But there would not appear to be any viable alternatives or nonhuman substitutes available for understanding the processes involved in rejection. At best it may be possible to utilize animals that have fewer cognitive and intellectual capacities for most forms of basic research with respect to understanding the immunology of xenografting.

When research gets closer to the clinical stage especially when it becomes possible to examine the extent to which xenografted organs and tissues can function post-transplant, it will be necessary to use some animals as donors and recipients that are closely related to human beings. If, in light of the scarcity of human organs, it is ethical to pursue the option of xenografting, then, it would be unethical to subject human beings to any form of xenografting that has not undergone a prior demonstration of both immunologic and physiologic feasibility in animals closely analogous to humans.

The use of animals analogous to humans for basic research on xenografting means that some form of primates must be used both as donors and as recipients. Is it ethical to kill primates, even if only a small number, to demonstrate the feasibility of xenografting in human beings? If primate and humans have the same moral status then it is hard to see how the use of primates could be justified.[1,16,18] Are humans and ape moral equivalents?

At this point, those who want to deny the validity of moral equivalence begin to look for morally significant properties uniquely present in human beings but not in primates. Strong candidates for the property that might make a moral difference sufficient to allow the killing of primates to advance human interests are language, tool, use, rationality, intentionality, consciousness, conscience, and/or empathy. The debate about the morality of killing a primate of some sort to advance human interests by saving human lives then hinges on empirical facts about what particular species of primates can or cannot do in comparison to what humans are capable of doing.[19]

It is indisputable that there are some differences in the capacities and abilities of humans and primates. Chimps can sign but humans have much more to say. Gorillas seem to reason but humans have calculus, novels, and quantum theory. Humans are capable of a much broader range of behavior and intellectual functioning then are any specific primate species.

Many who would protest the use of primates in xenografting research are keen to illustrate that primates possess many of the properties and abilities that are found to contribute moral standing to humans. The fact that one species or another of primate is capable of some degree of intellectual or behavioral ability that seems worthy of moral respect when manifest by humans does not mean that human beings are the moral equivalents of primates. It is one thing to argue that primates ought to have moral standing. It is a very different matter to argue that humans and primates are morally equivalent. One can grant that primates deserve moral consideration without conceding that, on average, the death of a human being is of greater moral significance then is the death of a baboon, a green monkey, or a chimpanzee.

Xenografting involving primates can be morally justified on the grounds that, in general, human beings possess capacities and abilities that confer more moral value upon them than do primates. This is not "speciesism"[1,20] but, rather, a claim of comparative worth that is based on important empirical differences between two classes or sets of creatures.

Perhaps there are empirical reasons to support the claim that it is worth killing primates for humans on the grounds that as groups humans have properties that confer greater moral worth and standing upon them then do other animal species. Human beings are after all moral agents while, at most, animals, even primates, are moral subjects.

Even conceding this point, there is still a problem when it comes time to kill a baboon and a chimp to see if xenografting between them is possible. Critics might ask whether scientists would be willing to kill a retarded child or an adult in a permanent vegetative state in the service of the same scientific goal? It is indisputable that human beings have on average more capacities and abilities than do animals. But there are some individual animals, many of them primates, that have more capacities and abilities than certain individual human beings who lack them due to congenital disorders or as the result of disease or injury. If it is argued that we ought to use animals instead of humans to assess the feasibility of xenografting because humans are more highly developed in terms of intellectual and emotional capacities, capacities that make a moral difference in that they are the basis for moral agency, then why should we not use a severely retarded child instead of a bright chimp or gorilla[20] as subjects in basic or clinical research? Unless those who are doing or wish to engage in basic research on xenografting can answer this question they will be open to the charge of immorality even if they kill primates or other "higher" animals in order to benefit humans who are as a species of more moral worth than are animals.

One line of response is to simply say that we are powerful and the primates are less, therefore they must yield to human purposes if we choose to experiment upon them rather than retarded children. This line of response sounds rather far removed from the kinds of arguments we expect to be mustered in the name of morality. A more promising line of attack on the view that humans and primates or other animals are morally equivalent is to examine a bit more closely why it is that we would not want to use a retarded child instead of a chimp in basic research.

Two reasons might be given for picking a chimp instead of a human being with limited or damaged capacities. We might decide not to use a human being who has lost his or her capacities and abilities out of respect for their former existence. If the person makes a conscious decision to allow his or her body to be used for scientific research prior to having become comatose or brain dead then perhaps those wishes should be honored. If no such advance notice has been given then we ought not to presume anything about what they would have wanted and should forego any involvement in medical research generally and xenografting in particular on the grounds that this is what is demanded out of respect for the persons they once were.

However, severely retarded children or those born with devastating conditions such as anencephaly have never had the capacities and abilities that confer a greater moral standing on humans as compared with animals. Should they be used as the first donors and recipients in xenografting research instead of primates?

The reason they should not has nothing to do with the properties, capacities, and abilities of children or infants who lack and have always lacked significant degrees of intellectual and cognitive function. The reason they should not be used is because of the impact using them would have upon other human beings, especially their parents and relatives. A severely retarded child can still be the object of much love, attention, and devotion from his or her parents. These feelings and the abilities and capacities that generate them are deserving of moral respect. I do not believe animals including primates are capable of such feelings.

If a human mother were to learn that her severely retarded son had been used in lethal xenografting research she would mourn this fact for the rest of her days. A baboon, monkey, or orangutan would not. The difference counts in terms of whether it is a monkey or a retarded human being who is selected as a subject in xenografting research.

It may be that parents would want to volunteer their child's organ or tissue for research or they might wish to have their baby with anencephaly serve as the first recipient of an animal organ or tissue. It may be necessary to honor such a choice. Whatever public policies are created to govern our actions toward severely retarded children or babies born with most of their brain missing, these are policies that are meant to be respectful of the sensibilities and interests of other human beings.[21] They do not find their source in some inherent property of the anencephalic infant. It is in the relationships with others, both family and strangers, that the moral worth and standing of these children are grounded.

The case for using animals, even primates, before using a human being with severely limited abilities and capacities is based on the relationships that exist among human beings, which do not have parallels in the animal kingdom. These relationships, such as love, loyalty, empathy, sympathy, family-feeling, protectiveness, shame, community-mindedness, a sense of history, and a sense of responsibility, which ground many moral duties and set the backdrop for distinguishing virtuous conduct and character, do not, despite the sociality of some species, appear to exist among animals.

If animals are to be used then what sorts of guidelines should animal care and use committees or other review bodies follow in reviewing basic research proposals? These committees must ensure that basic research is designed in such a fashion as to minimize the need for animal subjects while maximizing the opportunity to obtain generalizable knowledge. They must also ensure that the animals used are kept in optimal conditions and are handled humanely and killed without pain. These steps will be necessary in order to both respect the moral standing of the animals and to maximize the chance for generating useful knowledge from the use of these animals in research.

Perhaps the most difficult question arising when sufficient data have been obtained to make clinical trials plausible is who ought to be the first subjects in clinical xenografting trials. The baby Fae xenograft case involved an infant because the researchers felt that the scarcity of organs for infants born with congenital defects was so great that morality demanded that infants be the initial subjects selected. Many argued that this choice was mistaken since at the level of initial clinical trials it is morally wrong to use infants, children, or other human beings incapable of giving informed consent to their participation.[17]

If it is true that clinical trials involving xenografting should avoid the initial use of infants, children, and adults who lack the capacity for consent then who ought to go first? Perhaps adults who would not be otherwise eligible for transplants under existing exclusion criteria, the imminently dying, terminally ill volunteers who agree to serve, those who are brain dead, or those needing a second or third transplant when scarcity and prognosis would make it most unlikely they would receive another human organ or tissue.

Similarly, for clinical trials the question arises as to which type of organ or tissue ought be the subject of initial research efforts? Those for which the scarcity of human organs and tissues is greatest or those for which alternatives to animal organs seem the least promising? A strong case can be made that the selection of an organ or tissue to xenograft should be guided by the scarcity of human organs and tissues as well as the results achieved in animal to animal xenografting during basic research.

When clinical trials are designed for human subjects, those undertaking the research must have the qualifications and the background to make it likely that they will generate reliable and replicable results that are quickly made available in the literature. While the use of primates and human beings in research may be morally justified their use can only be justified when research is designed and conducted in circumstances most likely to maximize the changes of creating knowledge.

Those who will be recruited for clinical trials have the right to know the risks and benefits of the research that can best be inferred from animal and any other relevant studies. They should also know how many subjects will be used before the endpoint of this phase of research is reached? The measures taken for coping with any psychological issues raised by the use of animal organs for subjects must be presented. Subjects should also be told about the steps that have been taken to ensure their privacy and confidentiality to the extent they wish these preserved. It is of special importance given the high odds of failure in the initial phase of xenografting on human subjects that procedures be in place for ending the experiment if the subject wishes to withdraw from the research.

Ethical issues raised by therapy

Perhaps the most obvious moral problem that would arise if xenografting proved to be a viable source of organs and tissue for transplantation is whether prospective recipients would be able to accept animal parts when in need of transplants. Some might feel that it is unnatural to do so. But, naturalness is very much a function of familiarity. One hundred years ago surgery and anesthesia were viewed by many as unnatural. People may require support and counseling when faced with the option of xenografting but, facing death, most will probably accept a transplant and decide to deal with the naturalness issue later.

What about systematically breeding, raising, and killing animals for their parts on a large scale? Is it moral to systematically farm and kill animals for spare parts for humans? Would it be right to systematically farm and kill animals for spare parts for other animals, say companion animals?

One response to the issue of breeding and raising animals in order to have a regular supply of organs for xenografting is to argue that this practice does not raise any new or special moral issues since huge numbers of animals are currently bred, raised, and killed solely for consumption. However, animals raised for food are often raised under inhumane and brutal conditions. Nor is there much consideration given to the techniques involved in their slaughter.[1] Animals that are to be used to generate a constant source of organs and tissues for transplant must be raised under conditions that would ensure the healthiest possible animals. The moral obligation to potential recipients would seem to require that systematic farming of animals only be permitted under the most humane circumstances.

Interestingly the issue of whether it is morally permissible to systematically breed, raise, and kill animals to obtain their parts does not raise the same issues of moral equivalence between animals and humans that arise with respect to basic and clinical research. It would obviously be immoral to breed, raise, and kill humans for their parts.

The availability of animal organs for transplant on a therapeutic basis is likely to become a matter of economics. The economics of this sort of animal breeding must take into account the costs of creating the healthiest possible animals and the most painless modes of killing. However, should xenografting evolve to the point of therapy, those who perform xenografts must also strive to ensure that access to transplants is equitable.

Conclusion

The morality of using animals as sources of organs is contingent on the need to turn to animals as sources. The scarcity of organs and tissues from human sources is real, growing, and unlikely to be solved by any other alternative policies or approaches in the foreseeable future. If xenografting must be explored as an option then the moral justification for doing basic and clinical research involving animals is that it would not be possible to learn about the feasibility of overcoming immunologic and physiologic problems without using animals and that animals are to be used instead of human subjects whenever possible since human beings have more moral worth than do animals. If xenografting evolves into a therapy then provisions must be made for ensuring the welfare and health of the animals that would be bred, raised, and killed to supply organs and tissues to human beings.

References

1 Singer, P., *Animal Liberation* (New York: Random House, 1975).
2 Baum, B., Bernstein, D., Starnes V. A. et al., *Pediatrics*, 88: 203 (1991).
3 Caplan, A., *Transplant Proceedings*, 21: 3381 (1989).
4 Caplan, A., Siminoff, L. Arnold, B. et al., *Surgeon General's Workshop on Organ Donation*. (Washington, DC: HRSA, 1992).
5 Caplan, A. and Virnig, B., *Critical Care Clinics*, 6: 1007 (1990).
6 Caplan, A., *Journal of Transplant Coordination*, 1: 78, (1991).
7 Peters, T. G., *Journal of the American Medical Association*, 265: 1302, (1991).
8 Wight, J. P., *British Medical Journal* 303: 110, (1991).
9 John Paul II: Statement on Organ Transplantation. International Congress of the Society for Organ Sharing, Rome, Italy, June 20, 1991.
10 *New Scientist* (July 13, 1991).
11 Tufts, A., *Lancet*, 337: 1403 (1991).
12 Eurotransplant Foundation: *Eurotransplant Newsletter* 87: 1 (1991).
13 Raia, S., Nery, J. R. and Mies, S., *Lancet*, 26: 497 (1989).
14 Strong, R. W., Lynch, S. V., Ong, T. H. et al., *New England Journal of Medicine*, 322: 1505 (1990).
15 Elick, B. A. Der Sutherland, K. Gillingham, J. S. et al., *Transplant Proceedings* (1990).
16 Regan, T. and Singer, P., *Animal Rights and Human Obligations* (Englewood Cliffs, NJ: Prentice-Hall, 1976).
17 Caplan, A., *Journal of the American Medical Association*, 254: 3339, (1985).
18 Regan, T. and VanDe Veer, D., *And Justice for All* (Totowa, NJ: Rowman and Littlefield, 1982).
19 Jasper, J. M. and Nelkin, D., *The Animal Rights Crusade* (New York: Free Press, 1992).
20 Singer, P., *Transplant Proceedings*, 24: 28–32 (1992).
21 Caplan, A., *Bioethics* 1: 119 (1987).

49

Xenotransplantation and Speciesism

Peter Singer

Prologue

In the Netherlands a few years ago, an observer reported on the lives of some people confined in a new kind of institution. These people were not at all impaired physically, but intellectually they were well below the normal human level; they could not speak, although they made noises and gestures. In standard institutions, they had tended to spend much of their time making repetitive movements, and rocking their bodies to and fro. This institution was an unusual one, in that its policy was to allow the inmates the maximum possible freedom to live their own lives and form their own community. This freedom extended even to sexual relationships, which led to pregnancy, birth, and child rearing.

The observer's report was long and detailed, and I can only give you a few relevant highlights. First, the behavior of the inmates under these circumstances was far more varied than in the more conventional institutional settings. They rarely spent time alone, and they appeared to have no difficulty in understanding each other's gestures and grunts. They were physically active, spending a lot of time outside, where they had access to about two acres of relatively natural forest, surrounded by a wall. They cooperated in many of these activities, including on one occasion – to the consternation of the supervisors – an attempt to escape that involved carrying a large fallen branch to one of the walls, and propping it up as a kind of ladder that made it possible to climb over the wall.

From *Transplantation Proceedings*, vol. 24, no. 2 (April, 1992), pp. 728–32.

The observer was particularly interested in what he called the "politics" of the community. A defined leader soon emerged. His leadership – and it was always a "he" – depended, however, on the support of other members of the group. The leader had privileges, but also, it seemed, obligations. He had to cultivate the favor of others by sharing food and other treats. Fights would develop from time to time, but they would usually be followed by some conciliatory gestures, so that the loser could be readmitted into the society of the leader. If the leader became isolated, and allowed the others to form a coalition against him, his days as leader were numbered.

A simple ethical code could also be detected within the community. Its two basic rules, the observer commented, could be summed up as "one good turn deserves another," and "an eye for an eye and a tooth for a tooth." The breach of one of these rules apparently led to a sense of being wronged. For example when N was fighting with L, P came to L's assistance. Later, N attacked P, who gestured to L for assistance, but L did nothing. After the fight between P and N was over, N then furiously attacked L.

The mothers were with one exception competent at nursing and rearing their children. The mother–child relationships were close, and lasted many years. The death of a baby led to prolonged grieving behavior. Because sexual relationships were not monogamous, it was not always possible to tell who the father of the child was, and in fact fathers did not play a significant role in the rearing of the children.

In view of the very limited mental capacities that these inmates had been considered to possess, the observer was impressed by instances of behavior that clearly showed planning, and a high degree of self-awareness. In one example, two young mothers were having difficulty in stopping their small children from fighting. An older mother, a considerable authority figure in the community, was dozing nearby. One of the younger mothers woke her, and pointed to the squabbling children. The older mother made the appropriate noises and gestures, and the children, suitably intimidated, stopped fighting. The older mother then went back to her nap. On another occasion, after a fight, it was noticeable that the loser limped badly when in the presence of the victor, but not when alone; presumably by pretending to be more seriously hurt than he really was, he hoped for some kind of sympathy, or at least mercy, from his conqueror. A good deal of deceit also focused around sexual relationships, and to observers of human nature, this will come as no surprise. Although, as already mentioned, sexual relationships were not monogamous, there were occasions on which flirtations, leading up to sexual intercourse, were conducted with a good deal of discretion, so as not to attract the notice of a leader who would have been likely to claim exclusive sexual rights over one of his favorites.

In order to see just how far ahead these people could think, the observer devised an ingenious test of problem-solving ability. One inmate was presented with two series of five locked clear plastic boxes, each of which opened with a different key. One series of five boxes led to a food treat, whereas the other series led to an empty box. It was necessary to begin by choosing one of the two boxes that were the first in each series; and to succeed, one had to work through the five boxes to see which initial choice would lead one to the box with the treat. The inmate was able to succeed in this complex task.

Now I would like you to consider a proposal. Suppose that in view of the scarcity of organs for medical purposes, it was proposed to select some members of the community I have just described, give them an anesthetic, and then remove their hearts for transplantation into human beings whose mental capacities were normal, but who were suffering from a diseased heart and could only survive with a transplant. What would you think of such a proposal?

My guess is that your reaction to this proposal might vary according to the mental image you formed of the inmates of the community just described. I referred to them as "people," and I believe that the use of this term is justifiable, in view of the long philosophical tradition that, since at least the seventeenth-century British philosopher John Locke, has been prepared to apply the term "person" to a rational and self-conscious being, irrespective of whether that being was a member of our own species. If, however, you were led by my use of that term to assume that the people I have described were human beings suffering from some intellectual disability, you will probably have been shocked at the suggestion that we consider killing them in order to make use of their hearts. But in fact the description was not one of human beings, but of chimpanzees, living in the Amsterdam Zoo.[1] If you were able to guess this, you may not have been so shocked by the proposal. But why not? Should we be any less disturbed by the proposal, now that we know that it is not members of our own species who will be killed? That is the question I shall explore.

The exploration is in two parts. I begin with a summary statement of the principles of animal liberation, as I understand them. I shall then turn to the specific issue of the use of animals as organ donors.

Animals and Ethics

Animal liberation is a new movement, dating back to the mid-1970s, and growing out of the same period of ferment that gave rise to feminism and modern green politics. Until that time, though there were many animal welfare groups and anti-cruelty societies, they were built on the assumption that the welfare of nonhuman animals deserves protection *only* when *our* interests are not at stake. Animals remained "lower creatures." Human beings were seen as quite distinct from, and infinitely superior to, all forms of animal life. If our interests conflict with theirs, it is always their interests that have to give way.

Animal liberationists question the right of our species to assume that *our* interests must always prevail. They want to extend the basic moral ideas of equality and rights – which we apply to all *human* beings – to animals as well.

At first this sounds crazy. Obviously animals cannot have equal rights to vote, or to free speech. But the kind of equality that animal liberationists wish to extend to animals is a special kind: *equal consideration of interests*. And the basic right that animals should have is the right to equal consideration. This sounds like a difficult idea, but essentially it means that if an animal feels pain, the pain matters as much as it does when a human feels pain – if the pains hurt just as much. *Pain is pain*, whatever the species of being that experiences it.

Many people make a sharp distinction between humans and other animals. They say that all human beings are infinitely more valuable than any animals of any other species. But they don't give reasons for this view. When you think about it, it is not difficult to see that there is no morally important feature which *all* human beings possess, and *no* nonhuman animals have.

To a dispassionate Martian, it would be amusing to see how determinedly the human species, or more specifically the Western element of that species, has tried to distance itself from the other species with which it shares the planet. Only humans, we used to say, are made in the image of God, and only humans have an immortal soul. When it became apparent that those ideas lacked any basis in reason or science, we switched to saying things like: "Only humans can use tools." Then we found that chimpanzees use sticks for digging out insects, some seals will use rocks in order to break open shellfish, and various birds use thorns or small sticks to probe insects out of bark. So we said: "Only humans *make* tools." Then we discovered that chimpanzees do shape their sticks, by stripping off leaves and small branches until they get the right kind of implement for the task. So we switched ground and said: "Only humans use language" – just before several studies proved that chimpanzees and gorillas could learn hundreds of signs in the sign language used by the deaf, and could communicate in quite complex ways. Of course, we then upped the requirements for what it was to use language . . . and so the story goes.

But all of these attempts at drawing lines are really quite irrelevant to the question of justifying the things we do to animals. After all, even if no animals could use tools, or communicate by means of signs or words, we could not use these abilities to draw a line between *all* humans and the nonhuman animals. For there are many humans, too, who cannot use tools and have no language. All humans under 3 months of age, for a start. And even if they are excluded, on the grounds that they have the potential to learn to use tools and to speak, there are other human beings who do not have this potential. Sadly, some humans are born with brain damage so severe that they will never be able to use a tool or learn any form of language.

If it would be absurd to give animals the right to vote, it would be no less absurd to give that right to infants or to severely retarded human beings. Yet we still give equal consideration to their interests. We don't raise them for food, or test new cosmetics in their eyes. Nor should we. But we do these things to nonhuman animals who show greater abilities in using tools, or learning language, or doing any of the other things that use those capacities of reason that we like to believe distinguish humans from animals.

Once we understand this, it is easy to see the belief that all humans are somehow infinitely more valuable than any animal for what it is: a prejudice. Sadly, such prejudices are not unusual. Racists have a similar prejudice in favor of their own race, and sexists have the same type of prejudice in favor of their own sex.

Speciesism is logically parallel to racism and sexism. Speciesists, racists, and sexists all say: the boundary of my own group is also the boundary of my concern. Never mind what you are like, if you are a member of my group, you are superior to all those who are not members of my group. The speciesist favors a larger group than the racist, and so has a large circle of concern; but all of these prejudices are equally wrong. They all use an arbitrary and morally irrelevant fact – membership of a race, sex, or species – as if it were morally crucial.

The only acceptable limit to our moral concern is the point at which there is no awareness of pain or pleasure, and no preferences of any kind. That is why pigs have rights, but lettuces don't. Pigs can feel pain, and pleasure. Lettuces can't.

Until now the human species, especially so-called "Western civilization," has regarded our planet as a resource to be plundered for its own immediate benefit. The animal liberation movement, together with much of the environment movement, is seeking to change this attitude; to get us to see that we share the planet with other species, and that we have no God-given right to exploit them for our benefit. The change is a fundamental one, and one that threatens all the major economic forces in our society. It will not be brought about quickly or easily. But the effects of change are already visible, and the movement is growing. It rests on an argument that is so simple, and so plainly sound, that it can only continue to spread.

Animals and Organ Donation

The idea of using animals as a source for organ donation is an example of speciesism, premised as it is on the idea that animals are things for us to use as best suits our own interests, without much concern for the interests of the animals themselves. Perhaps the easiest way to see this is to ask yourself the following question: why should we be prepared to accept the use of organs from animals, but not be prepared to take them from human infants who are, and always will be, less intellectually developed than the nonhuman animals?

The human infants I have in mind fall into two categories. First, there are the anencephalics – those born with no brain, other than perhaps some brain stem. Next are the cortically dead – infants who, perhaps as a result of a brain hemorrhage soon after birth, have irreversibly lost all function in their cortex. At a recent conference at Melbourne's Royal Children's Hospital, I heard a pediatrician tell of a time when, in the hospital's intensive care ward, he had two young patients. One was healthy in every respect except one – an irreparable and lethal heart defect. The only possible treatment was a heart transplant, but no suitable donor was available, nor likely to become available. (In Australia, with a population of only 16 million, it is very rare to be able to find a suitable donor for an infant with a heart defect.) The other infant in the ward had suffered a massive brain hemorrhage and was cortically dead. The thought crossed the mind of the pediatrician, that if he could take the heart from the cortically dead baby, he could save the other one, and at least one of his patients would survive. He thought that if he asked the parents, they might see this as a way of salvaging some good out of the tragedy that had befallen their baby. But he knew that he could not do this; though a cortically dead baby can never become conscious, it is not legally dead, and to cut out its heart is, under present law, clearly murder. So the pediatrician could see that the inevitable result was going to be that both babies would die; and that is indeed what happened.

What kind of ethic can tell us that it is all right to rear sentient animals in barren cages that give them no decent life at all, and then kill them to take their organs, while refusing to permit us to take the organ of a human being who is not, and never can be, even minimally conscious? Obviously, a speciesist ethic. And that is essentially what is wrong with the present situation. My objection is not that we value the life of a normal, self-aware human being, one with a vivid awareness of the future and a desire to continue to be around next week, next month and next year, ahead of the life of an animal who lacks self-awareness and is incapable of any such future-oriented desires. Such an evaluation can be defended, without invoking an arbitrary preference for our own species. My objection is to the fact that we disregard the interests of nonhuman animals by ranking them as less worthy of our concern and respect than *any* member of our own species, no matter how limited in capacities and potential.

I therefore suggest that, before you endorse or accept the use of animals as organ sources, you ask yourself whether you are prepared to endorse or accept the use of anencephalic and cortically dead human infants. I know that there are some who do endorse this, or at least some part of it. Arthur Caplan, for instance, has persuasively argued in favor of the use of organs from fetuses and anencephalic infants.[2] He does not extend his argument to cortically dead infants. I am not sure why; perhaps he is troubled by the difficulty of establishing that cortical death really has occurred, and I know that there is still room for debate on this topic. That may be a reason for not implementing the proposal to use organs from the cortically dead until further careful study of current methods of diagnosing this state, but such obstacles have never deterred philosophers from considering the issues in a hypothetical manner, on the assumption that the technical difficulties can be overcome.

Another reason for reluctance to use cortically dead infants, even if there are no doubts about diagnosis, is that, while the cortex may be dead, the infants are, by any normal definition of the term, not dead. They are warm, pink, they breathe, sometimes unaided, they respond to touch, and so on. Of course, those who are legally brain dead satisfy many of these criteria too, although they do not breathe without assistance. But cortical death is not brain death, and I am not proposing that a cortically dead infant should be thought of, legally, ethically, or in any other sense, as a dead human being. After all, when we take a heart from a baboon, it is a warm, pink (underneath the fur) breathing animal we are killing in order to remove the heart. So if we are prepared to kill a baboon in an attempt to save the life of a human being, why aren't we prepared to kill a human being, with no potential that comes even near to equalling that of the baboon, for the same purpose?

I can think of only two ways in which someone might try to defend the view that it is better to kill the baboon than the cortically dead infant. One is that the parents of the infant may be upset by what happens to their infant in a way that the parents of the baboon will not be. Now we should not ignore the fact that baboons are mammals, and baboon mothers may and probably do suffer considerably when their infants are taken from them. But even if we overlook this fact, it remains the case that often – as in the case I mentioned – the human parents of the cortically dead infant would welcome the opportunity for some good to emerge from the death of their child. We know that this feeling has been expressed by the parents of anencephalic infants, when the possibility of the infant becoming a donor was raised.[3] So this objection does not apply to all cases in which the organs of a cortically dead infant might be used to save a life.

The second way of defending the view that it is better to kill the baboon than the cortically dead infant is by a frank defense of speciesism. This has been attempted by some of my recent critics – among them, Jeffrey Gray, Head of the Department of Psychology at the Institute of Psychiatry, University of London.[4–6] Gray's defense of speciesism is, in essence, that just as we properly give preference to our own children over the children of strangers, so we may properly give preference to the interests of members of other species. In passing, I note that Gray and others who use this kind of argument do not, for obvious reasons, make use of an intermediate step that, in other times and places, would surely have been seized on as further evidence of the case in favor of speciesism. Some of us can easily imagine our forefathers saying, just a generation or two ago: "Just as we properly give preference to the interests of members of our own race over the interests of members of other races . . ."

I agree, naturally, that parents are likely to prefer the interests of their own children to those of strangers. No doubt this preference has a biological basis. I also agree that it can be morally justifiable, under certain circumstances. Similarly, humans are likely to prefer the interests of members of their own species to those of members of other species. May be this too has a biological basis. But so what? The question is not why this preference exists, but whether this preference is justifiable.

The preference for the interests of our children can be defended on the grounds that, in recognizing the special duty of parents to look after their interests, we are promoting the greater overall welfare of children. Children thrive best in a family environment – not in large institutions, looked after by impersonal bureaucrats. Thus our support for the idea that parents should look after their own children before they look after the children of strangers works for the good of children as a whole. If we look at the fate of animals today, whether in the wild, in laboratories, or in factory farms, we cannot think that putting the interests of members of our own species ahead of the interests of members of other species works out better for all sentient beings. This naked bias in favor of our own is simply a reflection of our power over the other animals and our lack of consideration of their interests.

So the second defense of our preference for killing a baboon rather than a cortically dead infant in order to obtain a heart is no more successful than the first. I conclude that this preference is indefensible. That does not, of course, prove that it is always wrong to kill a baboon in order to obtain a heart with which one can save a human life. It might be that it is justifiable to kill both cortically dead infants *and* baboons in order to do this, or it might be that it is justifiable to kill neither, or it might be that it is justifiable to kill cortically dead infants but *not* to kill baboons. How we answer these questions, now, might also depend on the prospects of success of the transplant in each case. But if we imagine that the transplants had a very high chance of saving a life in each case, and we assume also that the parents of the infant have freely consented to the donation of the heart, then my own preference would certainly be to use the cortically dead infant before using the baboon, and I would base this preference on the higher level of awareness of the baboon.

There is, however, a more difficult question for me to answer. Suppose that we need a heart for a child who is, apart from the heart defect, healthy and much loved by her parents. Suppose that there are no anencephalic or cortically dead infant hearts available. Suppose it is a question of killing a baboon and taking her heart, or allowing the child to die? What do I say then?

Before I answer, one observation. A society that accepts the rearing of pigs in miserable conditions in intensive farms, and then allows them to be killed just because some people prefer pork to tofu, would be very odd indeed if it did not accept imposing similar suffering and death on baboons in order to save the life of a human being. That is why I have spent so much of this talk trying to put the issue of xenotransplantation in the context of a nonspeciesist ethic, one that takes seriously the interests of nonhuman animals. If anyone thinks that it is wrong to attempt to use the body parts of animals for transplantation purposes, but alright to use them for breakfast, then their way of thinking has nothing in common with mine.

Now what do I say about the case of the child or the baboon? I find it genuinely difficult. As I have already suggested, it is not speciesist to prefer the life of a being who is self-aware, and sees herself as existing over time, and who is capable of having complex future desires, to the life of a being who lacks these capacities. And it may be that a child does have these capacities and a baboon does not have them, or does not have them to nearly as high a degree. It *may* also be true that the family of the child will suffer more intensely and for a longer period if she dies than any of the baboon's family group will suffer if it dies. So considering the hypothetical choice from this perspective alone, it seems defensible to kill the baboon to save the child. At the same time, choosing the child over the baboon reinforces the attitude that animals are just things for us to use – and this is an attitude that we should strive to change. That is one reason why I do not want to see us come to rely on organs from animals as a cheap way of overcoming our health problems. Another reason is that, while in the example just given I have compared simply the death of the child with the death of a baboon, in the real world we can expect that, once organs from baboons become suitable for use in humans, there will be large colonies of baboons kept in whatever conditions can most economically be devised, as long as they are compatible with keeping the baboons alive and their organs usable. Finally, let us remember that, if we are prepared to use a baboon as a source of organs, we should be prepared to use a human of equal or inferior capacities, as long as there is no family who has greater ties to the human than the family of the baboon has to the baboon.

In a world that needlessly rears several billion animals in factory farms each year and then kills them to satisfy a mere preference of taste, it is difficult to argue persuasively against the rearing and slaughter of a few thousand animals so that their organs can be used to save people's lives. That, however, is not a reason for using animals: it is, rather, a reason for changing our views about animals. In a better world, a world that cared properly for the interests of animals, we would do our utmost to avoid choices that pit the essential interests of animals against our own, so that the issue of "the child or the baboon" does not arise. This might involve more effective ways of obtaining organs from humans who are brain dead, or cortically dead. It might involve the development of artificial organs. Or it might involve using our limited medical resources to educate people in looking after the organs with which they were born. These are ethically preferable paths to pursue.

I shall end with a quotation from Isaac Bashevis Singer, one of the great writers of our time. The passage epitomizes what is wrong with the attitude to other animals that allows us to think of them as just so much beef, or bacon – or a reservoir of hearts and kidneys:

> As often as Herman had witnessed the slaughter of animals and fish, he always had the same thought: in their behavior toward creatures, all men were Nazis. The smugness with which man could do with other species as he pleased exemplified the most extreme racist theories, the principle that might is right.[7]

References

1 De Waal, F., *Chimpanzee Politics*. (London: Jonathan Cape, 1982).
2 Caplan, A: *Bioethics*, 1: 119 (1987).
3 Ibid., p. 128.
4 Gray, J. A., *Behavioral and Brain Sciences*, 13: 22 (1990).
5 Gray, J. A., *Behavioral and Brain Sciences*, 14: 759 (1991).
6 Gray, J. A., *Psychologist*, 4: 196 (1991).
7 Singer, I. B., *Enemies, a Love Story* (New York: Farrar, Straus & Giroux, 1972).

PART VII

Experimentation with Human Subjects

50

Ethics and Clinical Research

Henry K. Beecher

HUMAN experimentation since World War II has created some difficult problems with the increasing employment of patients as experimental subjects when it must be apparent that they would not have been available if they had been truly aware of the uses that would be made of them. Evidence is at hand that many of the patients in the examples to follow never had the risk satisfactorily explained to them, and it seems obvious that further hundreds have not known that they were the subjects of an experiment although grave consequences have been suffered as a direct result of experiments described here. There is a belief prevalent in some sophisticated circles that attention to these matters would "block progress." But, according to Pope Pius XII,[1] "science is not the highest value to which all other orders of values ... should be subordinated."

I am aware that these are troubling charges. They have grown out of troubling practices. They can be documented, as I propose to do, by examples from leading medical schools, university hospitals, private hospitals, governmental military departments (the Army, the Navy and the Air Force), governmental institutes (the National Institutes of Health), Veterans Administration hospitals and industry. The basis for the charges is broad.

I should like to affirm that American medicine is sound, and most progress in it soundly attained. There is, however, a reason for concern in certain areas, and I believe the type of activities to be mentioned will do great harm to medicine unless soon corrected. It will certainly be charged that any mention of these matters does a disservice to medicine, but not one so great. I believe, as a continuation of the practices to be cited.

Experimentation in man takes place in several areas: in self-experimentation; in patient volunteers and normal subjects; in therapy; and in the different areas of *experimentation on a patient not for his benefit but for that, at least in theory, of patients in general*. The present study is limited to this last category.

Reasons for Urgency of Study

Ethical errors are increasing not only in numbers but in variety – for example, in the recently added problems arising in transplantation of organs.

There are a number of reasons why serious attention to the general problem is urgent.

Of transcendent importance is the enormous and continuing increase in available funds, as shown in Table 1.

Since World War II the annual expenditure for research (in large part in man) in the Massachusetts General Hospital has increased a remarkable 17-fold. At the National Institutes of Health, the increase has been a gigantic 624-fold. This "national" rate of increase is over 36 times that of the Massachusetts General Hospital. These data, rough as they are, illustrate vast opportunities and concomitantly expanded responsibilities.

Taking into account the sound and increasing emphasis of recent years that experimentation in

From *New England Journal of Medicine*, vol. 274, no. 24 (16 June 1966), pp. 1354–60. Reprinted with permission.

Table 1 Money available for research each year

Massachusetts	General Hospital	National Institutes of Health
1945	$ 500,000†	$ 701,800
1955	2,222,816	36,063,200
1965	8,384,342	436,600,000

*National Institutes of Health figures based upon decade averages, excluding funds for construction, kindly supplied by Dr John Sherman, of National Institutes of Health.

† Approximation, supplied by Mr David C. Crockett, of Massachusetts General Hospital.

man must precede general application of new procedures in therapy, plus the great sums of money available, there is reason to fear that these requirements and these resources may be greater than the supply of responsible investigators. All this heightens the problems under discussion.

Medical schools and university hospitals are increasingly dominated by investigators. Every young man knows that he will never be promoted to a tenure post, to a professorship in a major medical school, unless he has proved himself as an investigator. If the ready availability of money for conducting research is added to this fact, one can see how great the pressures are on ambitious young physicians.

Implementation of the recommendations of the President's Commission on Heart Disease, Cancer and Stroke means that further astronomical sums of money will become available for research in man.

In addition to the foregoing three practical points there are others that Sir Robert Plat[2] has pointed out: a general awakening of social conscience; greater power for good or harm in new remedies, new operations and new investigative procedures than was formerly the case; new methods of preventive treatment with their advantages and dangers that are now applied to communities as a whole as well as to individuals, with multiplication of the possibilities for injury; medical science has shown how valuable human experimentation can be in solving problems of disease and its treatment; one can therefore anticipate an increase in experimentation; and the newly developed concept of clinical research as a profession (for example, clinical pharmacology) – and this, of course, can lead to unfortunate separation between the interests of science and the interests of the patient.

Frequency of Unethical or Questionably Ethical Procedures

Nearly everyone agrees that ethical violations do occur. The practical question is, how often? A preliminary examination of the matter was based on 17 examples, which were easily increased to 50. These 50 studies contained references to 186 further likely examples, on the average 3.7 leads per study; they at times overlapped from paper to paper, but this figure indicates how conveniently one can proceed in a search for such material. The data are suggestive of widespread problems, but there is need for another kind of information, which was obtained by examination of 100 consecutive human studies published in 1964, in an excellent journal; 12 of these seemed to be unethical. If only one quarter of them is truly unethical, this still indicates the existence of a serious situation. Pappworth,[3] in England, has collected, he says, more than 500 papers based upon unethical experimentation. It is evident from such observations that unethical or questionably ethical procedures are not uncommon.

The Problem of Consent

All so-called codes are based on the bland assumption that meaningful or informed consent is readily available for the asking. As pointed out elsewhere,[1] this is very often not the case. Consent in any fully informed sense may not be obtainable. Nevertheless, except, possibly, in the most trivial situations, it remains a goal toward which one must strive for sociologic, ethical and clear-cut legal reasons. There is no choice in the matter.

If suitably approached, patients will accede, on the basis of trust, to about any request their physician may make. At the same time, every experienced clinician investigator knows that patients will often submit to inconvenience and some discomfort, if they do not last very long, but the usual patient will never agree to jeopardize seriously his health or his life for the sake of "science."

In only 2 of the 50 examples originally compiled for this study was consent mentioned. Actually, it should be emphasized in all cases for obvious moral and legal reasons, but it would be unrealistic to place much dependence on it. In any precise sense statements regarding consent are meaningless unless one knows how fully the patient was informed of all risks, and if these are not known, that fact should also be made clear. A far more dependable safeguard than consent is the presence of a truly *responsible* investigator.

Examples of Unethical or Questionably Ethical Studies

These examples are not cited for the condemnation of individuals; they are recorded to call attention to a variety of ethical problems found in experimental medicine, for it is hoped that calling attention to them will help to correct abuses present. During ten years of study of these matters it has become apparent that thoughtlessness and carelessness, not a willful disregard of the patient's rights, account for most of the cases encountered. Nonetheless, it is evident that in many of the examples presented, the investigators have risked the health or the life of their subjects. No attempt has been made to present the "worst" possible examples; rather, the aim has been to show the variety of problems encountered.

References to the examples presented are not given, for there is no intention of pointing to individuals, but rather, a wish to call attention to widespread practices. All, however, are documented to the satisfaction of the editors of the *Journal.*

Known effective treatment withheld

Example 1. It is known that rheumatic fever can usually be prevented by adequate treatment of streptococcal respiratory infections by the parenteral administration of penicillin. Nevertheless, definitive treatment was withheld, and placebos were given to a group of 109 men in service, while benzathine penicillin G was given to others.

The therapy that each patient received was determined automatically by his military serial number arranged so that more men received penicillin than received placebo. In the small group of patients studied 2 cases of acute rheumatic fever and 1 of acute nephritis developed in the control patients, whereas these complications did not occur among those who received the benzathine penicillin G.

Example 2. The sulfonamides were for many years the only antibacterial drugs effective in shortening the duration of acute streptococcal pharyngitis and in reducing its suppurative complications. The investigators in this study undertook to determine if the occurrence of the serious nonsuppurative complications, rheumatic fever and acute glomerulonephritis, would be reduced by this treatment. This study was made despite the general experience that certain antibiotics, including penicillin, will prevent the development of rheumatic fever.

The subjects were a large group of hospital patients; a control group of approximately the same size, also with exudative Group A streptococcus, was included. The latter group received only nonspecific therapy (no sulfadiazine). The total group denied the effective penicillin comprised over 500 men.

Rheumatic fever was diagnosed in 5.4 per cent of those treated with sulfadiazine. In the control group rheumatic fever developed in 4.2 per cent.

In reference to this study a medical officer stated in writing that the subjects were not informed, did not consent and were not aware that they had been involved in an experiment, and yet admittedly 25 acquired rheumatic fever. According to this same medical officer *more than 70* who had had known definitive treatment withheld were on the wards with rheumatic fever when he was there.

Example 3. This involved a study of the relapse rate in typhoid fever treated in two ways. In an earlier study by the present investigators chloramphenicol had been recognized as an effective treatment for typhoid fever, being attended by half the mortality that was experienced when this agent was not used. Others had made the same observations, indicating that to withhold this effective remedy can be a life-or-death decision. The present study was carried out to determine the relapse rate under the two methods of treatment; of 408 charity patients 251 were treated with chloramphenicol, of whom 20, or 7.97 per cent, died. Symptomatic treatment was given, but chloramphenicol was withheld in 157, of whom 36, or 22.9 per cent, died. According to the data presented, 23 patients died in the course of this study who would not have been expected to succumb if they had received specific therapy.

Study of therapy

Example 4. TriA (triacetyloleandomycin) was originally introduced for the treatment of infection with gram-positive organisms. Spotty evidence of hepatic dysfunction emerged, especially in children, and so the present study was undertaken on 50 patients, including mental defectives or juvenile delinquents who were inmates of a children's center. No disease other than acne was present; the drug was given for treatment of this. The ages of the subjects ranged from 13 to 39 years. "By the time half the patients had received the drug for four weeks, the high incidence of significant hepatic dysfunction... led to the discontinuation of administration to the remainder of the group at three weeks." (However, only two weeks after the start of the administration of the drug, 54 per cent of the patients showed abnormal excretion of bromsulfalein.) Eight patients with marked hepatic dysfunction were transferred to the hospital "for more intensive study." Liver biopsy was carried out in these 8 patients and repeated in 4 of them. Liver damage was evident. Four of these hospitalized patients, after their liver-function tests returned to normal limits, received a "challenge" dose of the drug. Within two days hepatic dysfunction was evident in 3 of the 4 patients. In 1 patient a second challenge dose was given after the first challenge and again led to evidence of abnormal liver function. Flocculation tests remained abnormal in some patients as long as five weeks after discontinuance of the drug.

Physiologic studies

Example 5. In this controlled, double-blind study of the hematologic toxicity of chloramphenicol, it was recognized that chloramphenicol is "well known as a cause of aplastic anemia" and that there is a "prolonged morbidity and high mortality of aplastic anemia" and that "chloramphenicol-induced aplastic anemia can be related to dose." The aim of the study was "further definition of the toxicology of the drug."

Forty-one randomly chosen patients were given either 2 or 6 gm. of chloramphenicol per day; 12 control patients were used. "Toxic bone-marrow depression, predominantly affecting erythropoiesis, developed in 2 of 20 patients given 2.0 gm. and in 18 of 21 given 6 gm. of chloramphenicol daily." The smaller dose is recommended for routine use.

Example 6. In a study of the effect of thymectomy on the survival of skin homografts 18 children, three and a half months to eighteen years of age, about to undergo surgery for congenital heart disease, were selected. Eleven were to have total thymectomy as part of the operation, and 7 were to serve as controls. As part of the experiment, full-thickness skin homografts from an unrelated adult donor were sutured to the chest wall in each case. (Total thymectomy is occasionally, although not usually part of the primary cardiovascular surgery involved, and whereas it may not greatly add to the hazards of the necessary operation, its eventual effects in children are not known.) This work was proposed as part of a long-range study of "the growth and development of these children over the years." No difference in the survival of the skin homograft was observed in the 2 groups.

Example 7. This study of cyclopropane anesthesia and cardiac arrhythmias consisted of 31 patients. The average duration of the study was three hours, ranging from two to four and a half hours. "Minor surgical procedures" were carried out in all but 1 subject. Moderate to deep anesthesia, with endotracheal intubation and controlled respiration, was used. Carbon dioxide was injected into the closed respiratory system until cardiac arrhythmias appeared. Toxic levels of carbon dioxide were achieved and maintained for considerable periods. During the cyclopropane anesthesia a variety of pathologic cardiac arrhythmias occurred. When the carbon dioxide tension was elevated above normal, ventricular extrasystoles were more numerous than when the carbon dioxide tension was normal, ventricular arrhythmias being continuous in 1 subject for ninety minutes. (This can lead to fatal fibrillation.)

Example 8. Since the minimum blood-flow requirements of the cerebral circulation are not accurately known, this study was carried out to determine "cerebral hemodynamic and metabolic changes... before and during acute reductions in arterial pressure induced by drug administration and/or postural adjustments." Forty-four patients whose ages varied from the second to the tenth decade were involved. They included normotensive subjects, those with essential hypertension and finally a group with malignant hypertension. Fifteen had abnormal electrocardiograms. Few details about the reasons for hospitalization are given.

Signs of cerebral circulatory insufficiency, which were easily recognized, included confusion and in some cases a nonresponsive state. By alteration in the tilt of the patient "the clinical state of the subject could be changed in a matter of seconds from one of altertness to confusion, and for the remainder of the flow, the subject was maintained in the latter state." The femoral arteries were cannulated in all subjects, and the internal jugular veins in 14.

The mean arterial pressure fell in 37 subjects from 109 to 48 mm. of mercury, with signs of cerebral ischemia. "With the onset of collapse, cardiac output and right ventricular pressures decreased sharply."

Since signs of cerebral insufficiency developed without evidence of coronary insufficiency the authors concluded that "the brain may be more sensitive to acute hypotension than is the heart."

Example 9. This is a study of the adverse circulatory responses elicited by intra-abdominal maneuvers:

> When the peritoneal cavity was entered, a deliberate series of maneuvers was carried out [in 68 patients] to ascertain the effective stimuli and the areas responsible for development of the expected circulatory changes. Accordingly, the surgeon rubbed localized areas of the parietal and visceral peritoneum with a small ball sponge as discretely as possible. Traction on the mesenteries, pressure in the area of the celiac plexus, traction on the gallbladder and stomach, and occlusion of the portal and caval veins were the other stimuli applied.

Thirty-four of the patients were 60 years of age or older; 11 were 70 or older. In 44 patients the hypotension produced by the deliberate stimulation was "moderate to marked." The maximum fall produced by manipulation was from 200 systolic, 105 diastolic, to 42 systolic, 20 diastolic; the average fall in mean pressure in 26 patients was 53 mm. of mercury.

Of the 50 patients studied, 17 showed either atrioventricular dissociation with nodal rhythm or nodal rhythm alone. A decrease in the amplitude of the T wave and elevation or depression of the ST segment were noted in 25 cases in association with manipulation and hypotension or, at other times, in the course of anesthesia and operation. In only 1 case was the change pronounced enough to suggest myocardial ischemia. No case of myocardial infarction was noted in the group studied although routine electrocardiograms were not taken after operation to detect silent infarcts. Two cases in which electrocardiograms were taken after operation showed T-wave and ST-segment changes that had not been present before.

These authors refer to a similar study in which more alarming electrocardiographic changes were observed. Four patients in the series sustained silent myocardial infarctions; most of their patients were undergoing gallbladder surgery because of associated heart disease. It can be added further that in the 34 patients referred to above as being sixty years of age or older, some doubtless had heart disease that could have made risky the maneuvers carried out. In any event, this possibility might have been a deterrent.

Example 10. Starling's law – "that the heart output per beat is directly proportional to the diastolic filling" – was studied in 30 adult patients with atrial fibrillation and mitral stenosis sufficiently severe to require valvulotomy. "Continuous alterations of the length of a segment of left ventricular muscle were recorded simultaneously in 13 of these patients by means of a mercury-filled resistance gauge sutured to the surface of the left ventricle." Pressures in the left ventricle were determined by direct puncture simultaneously with the segment length in 13 patients and without the segment length in an additional 13 patients. Four similar unanesthetized patients were studied through catheterization of the left side of the heart transeptally. In all 30 patients arterial pressure was measured through the catheterized brachial artery.

Example 11. To study the sequence of ventricular contraction in human bundle-branch block, simultaneous catheterization of both ventricles was performed in 22 subjects; catheterization of the right side of the heart was carried out in the usual manner; the left side was catheterized transbronchially. Extrasystoles were produced by tapping on the epicardium in subjects with normal myocardium while they were undergoing thoracotomy. Simultaneous pressures were measured in both ventricles through needle puncture in this group.

The purpose of this study was to gain increased insight into the physiology involved.

Example 12. This investigation was carried out to examine the possible effect of vagal stimulation on cardiac arrest. The authors had in recent years transected the homolateral vagus nerve immediately below the origin of the recurrent laryngeal nerve as palliation against cough and pain in bronchogenic carcinoma. Having been impressed with the number of reports of cardiac arrest that seemed to follow vagal stimulation, they tested the effects of intrathoracic vagal stimulation during 30 of their surgical procedures, concluding, from these observations in patients under satisfactory anesthesia, that cardiac irregularities and cardiac arrest due to vagovagal reflex were less common than had previously been supposed.

Example 13. This study presented a technic for determining portal circulation time and hepatic blood flow. It involved the transcutaneous injection of the spleen and catheterization of the hepatic vein. This was carried out in 43 subjects, of whom 14 were normal; 16 had cirrhosis (varying degrees), 9 acute hepatitis, and 4 hemolytic anemia.

No mention is made of what information was divulged to the subjects, some of whom were seriously ill. This study consisted in the development of a technic, not of therapy, in the 14 normal subjects.

Studies to improve the understanding of disease

Example 14. In this study of the syndrome of impending hepatic coma in patients with cirrhosis of the liver certain nitrogenous substances were administered to 9 patients with chronic alcoholism and advanced cirrhosis: ammonium chloride, diammonium citrate, urea or dietary protein. In all patients a reaction that included mental disturbances, a "flapping tremor" and electroencephalographic changes developed. Similar signs had occurred in only 1 of the patients before these substances were administered:

> The first sign noted was usually clouding of the consciousness. Three patients had a second or a third course of administration of a nitrogenous substance with the same results. It was concluded that marked resemblance between this reaction and impending hepatic coma, implied that the administration of these [nitrogenous] substances to patients with cirrhosis may be hazardous.

Example 15. The relation of the effects of ingested ammonia to liver disease was investigated in 11 normal subjects, 6 with acute virus hepatitis, 26 with cirrhosis, and 8 miscellaneous patients. Ten of these patients had neurologic changes associated with either hepatitis or cirrhosis.

The hepatic and renal veins were cannulated. Ammonium chloride was administered by mouth. After this, a tremor that lasted for three days developed in 1 patient. When ammonium chloride was ingested by 4 cirrhotic patients with tremor and mental confusion the symptoms were exaggerated during the test. The same thing was true of a fifth patient in another group.

Example 16. This study was directed toward determining the period of infectivity of infectious hepatitis. Artificial induction of hepatitis was carried out in an institution for mentally defective children in which a mild form of hepatitis was endemic. The parents gave consent for the intramuscular injection or oral administration of the virus, but nothing is said regarding what was told them concerning the appreciable hazards involved.

A resolution adopted by the World Medical Association states explicitly: "Under no circumstances is a doctor permitted to do anything which would weaken the physical or mental resistance of a human being except from strictly therapeutic or prophylatic indications imposed in the interest of the patient." There is no right to risk an injury to 1 person for the benefit of others.

Example 17. Live cancer cells were injected into 22 human subjects as part of a study of immunity to cancer. According to a recent review, the subjects (hospitalized patients) were "merely told they would be receiving 'some cells'" – "the word cancer was entirely omitted."

Example 18. Melanoma was transplanted from a daughter to her volunteering and informed mother, "in the hope of gaining a little better understanding of cancer immunity and in the hope that the production of tumor antibodies might be helpful in the treatment of the cancer patient." Since the daughter died on the day after the transplantation of the tumor into her mother, the hope expressed seems to have been more theoretical than practical, and the daughter's condition was described as "terminal" at the time the mother volunteered to be a recipient. The primary implant was widely excised on the twenty-fourth day after it had been placed in the mother. She died from metastatic melanoma on the four hundred and fifty-first day after transplantation. The evidence that this patient died of diffuse melanoma that metastasized from a small piece of transplanted tumor was considered conclusive.

Technical study of disease

Example 19. During bronchoscopy a special needle was inserted through a bronchus into the left atrium of the heart. This was done in an unspecified number of subjects, both with cardiac disease and with normal hearts.

The technic was a new approach whose hazards were at the beginning quite unknown. The subjects with normal hearts were used, not for their possible benefit but for that of patients in general.

Example 20. The percutaneous method of catheterization of the left side of the heart has, it is reported, led to 8 deaths (1.09 per cent death rate) and other serious accidents in 732 cases. There was, therefore, need for another method, the transbronchial approach, which was carried out in the present study in more than 500 cases, with no deaths.

Granted that a delicate problem arises regarding how much should be discussed with the patients involved in the use of a new method, nevertheless where the method is employed in a given patient for *his* benefit, the ethical problems are far less than when this potentially extremely dangerous method is used "in 15 patients with normal hearts, undergoing bronchoscopy for other reasons." Nothing was said about what was told any of the subjects, and nothing was said about the granting of permission, which was certainly indicated in the 15 normal subjects used.

Example 21. This was a study of the effect of exercise on cardiac output and pulmonary-artery pressure in 8 "normal" persons (that is, patients whose diseases were not related to the cardiovascular system), in 8 with congestive heart failure severe enough to have recently required complete bed rest, in 6 with hypertension, in 2 with aortic insufficiency, in 7 with mitral stenosis and in 5 with pulmonary emphysema.

Intracardiac cathetorization was carried out, and the catheter then inserted into the right or left main branch of the pulmonary artery. The brachial artery was usually catheterized; sometimes, the radial or femoral arteries were catheterized. The subjects exercised in a supine position by pushing their feet against weighted pedals. "The ability of these patients to carry on sustained work was severly limited by weakness and dyspnea." Several were in severe failure. This was not a therapeutic attempt but rather a physiologic study.

Bizarre study

Example 22. There is a question whether ureteral reflux can occur in the normal bladder. With this in mind, vesicourethrography was carried out on 26 normal babies less than forty-eight hours old. The infants were exposed to x-rays while the bladder was filling and during voiding. Multiple spot films were made to record the presence or absence of ureteral reflux. None was found in this group, and fortunately no infection followed the catheterization. What the results of the extensive x-ray exposure may be, no one can yet say.

Comment on Death Rates

In the foregoing examples a number of procedures, some with their own demonstrated death rates, were carried out. The following data were provided by 3 distinguished investigators in the field and represent widely held views.

Cardiac catheterization: right side of the heart, about 1 death per 1000 cases; left side, 5 deaths per 1000 cases. "Probably considerably higher in some places, depending on the portal of entry." (One investigator had 15 deaths in his first 150 cases.) It is possible that catheterization of a hepatic vein or the renal vein would have a lower death rate than that of catheterization of the right side of the heart, for if it is properly carried out, only the atrium is entered *en route* to the liver or the kidney, not the right ventricle, which can lead to serious cardiac irregularities. There is always the possibility, however, that the ventricle will be entered inadvertently. This occurs in at least half the cases, according to one expert – "but if properly done is too transient to be of importance."

Liver biopsy: the death rate here is estimated at 2 to 3 per 1000, depending in considerable part on the condition of the subject.

Anesthesia: the anesthesia death rate can be placed in general at about 1 death per 2000 cases. The hazard is doubtless higher when certain practices such as deliberate evocation of ventricular extrasystoles under cyclopropane are involved.

Publication

In the view of the British Medical Research Council[5] it is not enough to ensure that all investigation is carried out in an ethical manner: it must be made unmistakably clear in the publications that the proprieties have been observed. This implies editorial responsibility in addition to the investigator's. The question rises, then, about valuable data that have been improperly obtained. It is my view that such material should not be published.[6] There is a practical aspect to the matter: failure to obtain publication would discourage unethical experimentation. How many would carry out such experimentation if they *knew* its results would never be published? Even though suppression of such data (by not publishing it) would constitute a loss to medicine, in a specific localized sense, this loss, it seems, would be less important than the far-reaching moral loss to medicine if the data thus obtained were to be published. Admittedly, there is room for debate. Others believe that such data, because of their intrinsic value, obtained at a cost of great risk or damage to the subjects, should not be wasted but should be published with stern editorial comment. This would have to be done with exceptional skill, to avoid an odor of hypocrisy.

Summary and Conclusions

The ethical approach to experimentation in man has several components: two are more important than the others, the first being informed consent. The difficulty of obtaining this is discussed in detail. But it is absolutely essential to *strive* for it for moral, sociologic and legal reasons. The statement that consent has been obtained has little meaning unless the subject or his guardian is capable of understanding what is to be undertaken and unless all hazards are made clear. If these are not known this, too, should be stated. In such a situation the subject at least knows that he is to be a participant in an experiment. Secondly, there is the more reliable safeguard provided by the presence of an intelligent, informed, conscientious, compassionate, responsible investigator.

Ordinary patients will not knowingly risk their health or their life for the sake of "science." Every experienced clinician investigator knows this. When such risks are taken and a considerable number of patients are involved, it may be assumed that informed consent has not been obtained in all cases.

The gain anticipated from an experiment must be commensurate with the risk involved.

An experiment is ethical or not at its inception; it does not become ethical *post hoc* – ends do not justify means. There is no ethical distinction between ends and means.

In the publication of experimental results it must be made unmistakably clear that the proprieties have been observed. It is debatable whether data obtained unethically should be published even with stern editorial comment.

References

1 Pope Pius XII. Address Presented at First International Congress on Histopathology of Nervous System, Rome. September 14, 1952.
2 Platt (Sir Robert). *Doctor and Patient: Ethics, Morals, Government.* (London: Nutheld Provincial Hospitals Trust, 1963), pp. 62 and 63.
3 Pappworth, M. H., Personal communication.
4 Beecher, H. K., Consent in clinical experimentation: myth and reality. *Journal of the American Medical Association*, 195: 34 (1966).
5 Great Britain. Medical Research Council. *Memorandum.* 1953.

51

Equipoise and the Ethics of Clinical Research

Benjamin Freedman

Abstract

The ethics of clinical research requires equipoise – a state of genuine uncertainty on the part of the clinical investigator regarding the comparative therapeutic merits of each arm in a trial. Should the investigator discover that one treatment is of superior therapeutic merit, he or she is ethically obliged to offer that treatment. The current understanding of this requirement, which entails that the investigator have no "treatment preference" throughout the course of the trial, presents nearly insuperable obstacles to the ethical commencement or completion of a controlled trial and may also contribute to the termination of trials because of the failure to enroll enough patients.

I suggest an alternative concept of equipoise, which would be based on present or imminent controversy in the clinical community over the preferred treatment. According to this concept of "clinical equipoise," the requirement is satisfied if there is genuine uncertainty within the expert medical community – not necessarily on the part of the individual investigator – about the preferred treatment.

There is widespread agreement that ethics requires that each clinical trial begin with an honest null hypothesis.[1,2] In the simplest model, testing a new treatment B on a defined patient population P for which the current accepted treatment is A, it is necessary that the clinical investigator be in a state of genuine uncertainty regarding the comparative merits of treatments A and B for population P. If a physician knows that these treatments are not equivalent, ethics requires that the superior treatment be recommended. Following Fried, I call this state of uncertainty about the relative merits of A and B "equipoise."[3]

Equipoise is an ethically necessary condition in all cases of clinical research. In trials with several arms, equipoise must exist between all arms of the trial; otherwise the trial design should be modified to exclude the inferior treatment. If equipoise is disturbed during the course of a trial, the trial may need to be terminated and all subjects previously enrolled (as well as other patients within the relevant population) may have to be offered the superior treatment. It has been rigorously argued that a trial with a placebo is ethical only in investigating conditions for which there is no known treatment[2]; this argument reflects a special application of the requirement for equipoise. Although equipoise has commonly been discussed in the special context of the ethics of randomized clinical trials,[4,5] it is important to recognize it as an ethical condition of all controlled clinical trials, whether or not they are randomized, placebo-controlled, or blinded.

The recent increase in attention to the ethics of research with human subjects has highlighted problems associated with equipoise. Yet, as I shall attempt to show, contemporary literature, if anything, minimizes those difficulties. Moreover, there is evidence that concern on the part of investigators about failure to satisfy the requirements for equipoise can doom a trial as a result of the consequent failure to enroll a sufficient number of subjects.

From *New England Journal of Medicine*, vol. 317, no. 3 (16 July 1987), pp. 141–5. Reprinted with permission.

The solutions that have been offered to date fail to resolve these problems in a way that would permit clinical trials to proceed. This paper argues that these problems are predicated on a faulty concept of equipoise itself. An alternative understanding of equipoise as an ethical requirement of clinical trials is proposed, and its implications are explored.

Many of the problems raised by the requirement for equipoise are familiar. Shaw and Chalmers have written that a clinician who "knows, or has good reason to believe," that one arm of the trial is superior may not ethically participate.[6] But the reasoning or preliminary results that prompt the trial (and that may themselves be ethically mandatory)[7] may jolt the investigator (if not his or her colleagues) out of equipoise before the trial begins. Even if the investigator is undecided between A and B in terms of gross measures such as mortality and morbidity, equipoise may be disturbed because evident differences in the quality of life (as in the case of two surgical approaches) tip the balance.[3–5, 8] In either case, in saying "we do not know" whether A or B is better, the investigator may create a false impression in prospective subjects, who hear him or her as saying "no evidence leans either way," when the investigator means "no controlled study has yet had results that reach statistical significance."

Late in the study – when P values are between 0.05 and 0.06 – the moral issue of equipoise is most readily apparent,[9, 10] but the same problem arises when the earliest comparative results are analyzed.[11] Within the closed statistical universe of the clinical trial, each result that demonstrates a difference between the arms of the trial contributes exactly as much to the statistical conclusion that a difference exists as does any other. The contribution of the last pair of cases in the trial is no greater than that of the first. If, therefore, equipoise is a condition that reflects equivalent evidence for alternative hypotheses, it is jeopardized by the first pair of cases as much as by the last. The investigator who is concerned about the ethics of recruitment after the penultimate pair must logically be concerned after the first pair as well.

Finally, these issues are more than a philosopher's nightmare. Considerable interest has been generated by a paper in which Taylor et al.[12] describe the termination of a trial of alternative treatments for breast cancer. The trial foundered on the problem of patient recruitment, and the investigators trace much of the difficulty in enrolling patients to the fact that the investigators were not in a state of equipoise regarding the arms of the trial. With the increase in concern about the ethics of research and with the increasing presence of this topic in the curricula of medical and graduate schools, instances of the type that Taylor and her colleagues describe are likely to become more common. The requirement for equipoise thus poses a practical threat to clinical research.

Responses to the Problems of Equipoise

The problems described above apply to a broad class of clinical trials, at all stages of their development. Their resolution will need to be similarly comprehensive. However, the solutions that have so far been proposed address a portion of the difficulties, at best, and cannot be considered fully satisfactory.

Chalmers' approach to problems at the onset of a trial is to recommend that randomization begin with the very first subject.[11] If there are no preliminary, uncontrolled data in support of the experimental treatment B, equipoise regarding treatments A and B for the patient population P is not disturbed. There are several difficulties with this approach. Practically speaking, it is often necessary to establish details of administration, dosage, and so on, before a controlled trial begins, by means of uncontrolled trials in human subjects. In addition, as I have argued above, equipoise from the investigator's point of view is likely to be disturbed when the hypothesis is being formulated and a protocol is being prepared. It is then, before any subjects have been enrolled, that the information that the investigator has assembled makes the experimental treatment appear to be a reasonable gamble. Apart from these problems, initial randomization will not, as Chalmers recognizes, address disturbances of equipoise that occur in the course of a trial.

Data-monitoring committees have been proposed as a solution to problems arising in the course of the trial.[13] Such committees, operating independently of the investigators, are the only bodies with information concerning the trial's ongoing results. Since this knowledge is not available to the investigators, their equipoise is not disturbed. Although committees are useful in keeping the conduct of a trial free of bias, they cannot resolve the investigators' ethical difficulties. A clinician is not merely obliged to treat a patient on the basis of the information that he or she currently has, but is also required to discover information that would be relevant to treatment decisions. If interim results would disturb equipoise, the investigators are obliged to gather and use that information. Their agreement to remain in ignorance of preliminary results would, by definition, be an unethical agreement, just as a failure to call up the laboratory to find out a patient's test results is unethical. Moreover, the use of a monitoring committee does not solve problems of equipoise that arise before and at the beginning of a trial.

Recognizing the broad problems with equipoise, three authors have proposed radical solutions. All three think that there is an irresolvable conflict between the requirement that a patient be offered the best treatment known (the principle underlying the requirement for equipoise) and the conduct of clinical trials; they therefore suggest that the "best treatment" requirement be weakened.

Schafer has argued that the concept of equipoise, and the associated notion of the best medical treatment, depends on the judgment of patients rather than of clinical investigators.[14] Although the equipoise of an investigator may be disturbed if he or she favors B over A, the ultimate choice of treatment is the patient's. Because the patient's values may restore equipoise. Schafer argues, it is ethical for the investigator to proceed with a trial when the patient consents. Schafer's strategy is directed toward trials that test treatments with known and divergent side effects and will probably not be useful in trials conducted to test efficacy or unknown side effects. This approach, moreover, confuses the ethics of competent medical practice with those of consent. If we assume that the investigator is a competent clinician, by saying that the investigator is out of equipoise, we have by Schafer's account said that in the investigator's professional judgment one treatment is therapeutically inferior – for that patient, in that condition, given the quality of life that can be achieved. Even if a patient would consent to an inferior treatment, it seems to me a violation of competent medical practice, and hence of ethics, to make the offer. Of course, complex issues may arise when a patient refuses what the physician considers the best treatment and demands instead an inferior treatment. Without settling that problem, however, we can reject Schafer's position. For Schafer claims that in order to continue to conduct clinical trials, it is ethical for the physician to offer (not merely accede to) inferior treatment.

Meier suggests that "most of us would be quite willing to forgo a modest expected gain in the general interest of learning something of value."[15] He argues that we accept risks in everyday life to achieve a variety of benefits, including convenience and economy. In the same way, Meier states, it is acceptable to enroll subjects in clinical trials even though they may not receive the best treatment throughout the course of the trial. Schafer suggests an essentially similar approach.[5, 14] According to this view, continued progress in medical knowledge through clinical trials requires an explicit abandonment of the doctor's fully patient-centered ethic.

These proposals seem to be frank counsels of desperation. They resolve the ethical problems of equipoise by abandoning the need for equipoise. In any event, would their approach allow clinical trials to be conducted? I think this may fairly be doubted. Although many people are presumably altruistic enough to forgo the best medical treatment in the interest of the progress of science, many are not. The numbers and proportions required to sustain the statistical validity of trial results suggest that in the absence of overwhelming altruism, the enrollment of satisfactory numbers of patients will not be possible. In particular, very ill patients, toward whom many of the most important clinical trials are directed, may be disinclined to be altruistic. Finally, as the study by Taylor et al.[12] remind us, the problems of equipoise trouble investigators as well as patients. Even if patients are prepared to dispense with the best treatment, their physicians, for reasons of ethics and professionalism, may well not be willing to do so.

Marquis has suggested a third approach. "Perhaps what is needed is an ethics that will justify the conscription of subjects for medical research," he has written. "Nothing less seems to justify present practice."[4] Yet, although conscription might enable us to continue present practice, it would scarcely justify it. Moreover, the conscription of physician investigators, as well as subjects, would be necessary, because, as has been repeatedly argued, the problems of equipoise are as disturbing to clinicians as they are to subjects. Is any less radical and more plausible approach possible?

Theoretical Equipoise versus Clinical Equipoise

The problems of equipoise examined above arise from a particular understanding of that concept, which I will term "theoretical equipoise." It is an understanding that is both conceptually odd and ethically irrelevant. Theoretical equipoise exists when, overall, the evidence on behalf of two alternative treatment regimens is exactly balanced. This evidence may be derived from a variety of sources, including data from the literature, uncontrolled experience, considerations of basic science and fundamental physiologic processes, and perhaps a "gut feeling" or "instinct" resulting from (or superimposed on) other considerations. The problems examined above arise from the principle that if theoretical equipoise is disturbed, the physician has, in Schafer's words, a "treatment preference" – let us say, favoring experimental treatment B. A trial testing A against B requires that some patients be enrolled in violation of this treatment preference.

Theoretical equipoise is overwhelmingly fragile; that is, it is disturbed by a slight accretion of evidence favoring one arm of the trial. In Chalmers' view, equipoise is disturbed when the odds that A will be more successful than B are anything other than 50 percent. It is therefore necessary to randomize treatment assignments beginning with the very first patient, lest equipoise be disturbed. We may say that theoretical equipoise is balanced on a knife's edge.

Theoretical equipoise is most appropriate to one-dimensional hypotheses and causes us to think in those terms. The null hypothesis must be sufficiently simple and "clean" to be finely balanced: Will A or B be superior in reducing mortality or shrinking tumors or lowering fevers in population P? Clinical choice is commonly more complex. The choice of A or B depends on some combination of effectiveness, consistency, minimal or relievable side effects, and other factors. On close examination, for example, it sometimes appears that even trials that purport to test a single hypothesis in fact involve a more complicated, portmanteau measure – e.g., the "therapeutic index" of A versus B. The formulation of the conditions of theoretical equipoise for such complex, multidimensional clinical hypotheses is tantamount to the formulation of a rigorous calculus of apples and oranges.

Theoretical equipoise is also highly sensitive to the vagaries of the investigator's attention and perception. Because of its fragility, theoretical equipoise is disturbed as soon as the investigator perceives a difference between the alternatives – whether or not any genuine difference exists. Prescott writes, for example, "It will be common at some stage in most trials for the survival curves to show visually different survivals," short of significance but "sufficient to raise ethical difficulties for the participants."[6] A visual difference, however, is purely an artifact of the research methods employed: when and by what means data are assembled and analyzed and what scale is adopted for the graphic presentation of data. Similarly, it is common for researchers to employ interval scales for phenomena that are recognized to be continuous by nature – e.g., five-point scales of pain or stages of tumor progression. These interval scales, which represent an arbitrary distortion of the available evidence to simplify research, may magnify the differences actually found, with a resulting disturbance of theoretical equipoise.

Finally, as described by several authors, theoretical equipoise is personal and idiosyncratic. It is disturbed when the clinician has, in Schafer's words, what "might even be labeled a bias or a hunch," a preference of a "merely intuitive nature."[14] The investigator who ignores such a hunch, by failing to advise the patient that because of it the investigator prefers B to A or by recommending A (or a chance of random assignment to A) to the patient, has violated the requirement for equipoise and its companion requirement to recommend the best medical treatment.

The problems with this concept of equipoise should be evident. To understand the alternative, preferable interpretation of equipoise, we need to recall the basic reason for conducting clinical trials: there is a current or imminent conflict in the clinical community over what treatment is preferred for patients in a defined population P. The standard treatment is A, but some evidence suggests that B will be superior (because of its effectiveness or its reduction of undesirable side effects, or for some other reason). (In the rare case when the first evidence of a novel therapy's superiority would be entirely convincing to the clinical community, equipoise is already disturbed.) Or there is a split in the clinical community, with some clinicians favoring A and others favoring B. Each side recognizes that the opposing side has evidence to support its position, yet each still thinks that overall its own view is correct. There exists (or, in the case of a novel therapy, there may soon exist) an honest, professional disagreement among expert clinicians about the preferred treatment. A clinical trial is instituted with the aim of resolving this dispute.

At this point, a state of "clinical equipoise" exists. There is no consensus within the expert clinical community about the comparative merits of the alternatives to be tested. We may state the formal conditions under which such a trial would be ethical as follows: at the start of the trial, there must be a state of clinical equipoise regarding the merits of the regimens to be tested, and the trial must be designed in such a way as to make it reasonable to expect that, if it is successfully concluded, clinical equipoise will be disturbed. In other words, the results of a successful clinical trial should be convincing enough to resolve the dispute among clinicians.

A state of clinical equipoise is consistent with a decided treatment preference on the part of the investigators. They must simply recognize that their less-favored treatment is preferred by colleagues whom they consider to be responsible and competent. Even if the interim results favor the preference of the investigators, treatment B, clinical equipoise persists as long as those results are too weak to influence the judgment of the community of clinicians, because of limited sample size, unresolved possibilities of side effects, or other factors. (This judgment can necessarily be made only by those who know the interim results – whether a data-monitoring committee or the investigators.)

At the point when the accumulated evidence in favor of B is so strong that the committee or investigators believe no open-minded clinician informed of the results would still favor A, clinical equipoise has been disturbed. This may occur well short of the original schedule for the termination of the trial, for unexpected reasons. (Therapeutic effects or side effects may be much stronger than anticipated, for example, or a definable subgroup within population P may be recognized for which the results demonstrably disturb clinical equipoise.) Because of the arbitrary character of human judgment and persuasion, some ethical problems regarding the termination of a trial will remain. Clinical equipoise will confine these problems to unusual or extreme cases, however, and will allow us to cast persistent problems in the proper terms. For example, in the face of a strong established trend, must we continue the trial because of others' blind fealty to an arbitrary statistical bench mark?

Clearly, clinical equipoise is a far weaker – and more common – condition than theoretical equipoise. Is it ethical to conduct a trial on the basis of clinical equipoise, when theoretical equipoise is disturbed? Or, as Schafer and others have argued, is doing so a violation of the physician's obligation to provide patients with the best medical treatment?[4, 5, 14] Let us assume that the investigators have a decided preference for B but wish to conduct a trial on the grounds that clinical (not theoretical) equipoise exists. The ethics committee asks the investigators whether, if they or members of their families were within population P, they would not want to be treated with their preference, B? An affirmative answer is often thought to be fatal to the prospects for such a trial, yet the investigators answer in the affirmative. Would a trial satisfying this weaker form of equipoise be ethical?

I believe that it clearly is ethical. As Fried has emphasized,[3] competent (hence, ethical) medicine is social rather than individual in nature. Progress in medicine relies on progressive consensus within the medical and research communities. The ethics of medical practice grants no ethical or normative meaning to a treatment preference, however powerful, that is based on a hunch or on anything less than evidence publicly presented and convincing to the clinical community. Persons are licensed as physicians after they demonstrate the acquisition of this professionally validated knowledge, not after they reveal a superior capacity for guessing. Normative judgments of their behavior – e.g., malpractice actions – rely on a comparison with what is done by the community of medical practitioners. Failure to follow a "treatment preference" not shared by this community and not based on information that would convince it could not be the basis for an allegation of legal or ethical malpractice. As Fried states: "[T]he conception of what is good medicine is the product of a professional consensus." By definition, in a state of clinical equipoise. "good medicine" finds the choice between A and B indifferent.

In contrast to theoretical equipoise, clinical equipoise is robust. The ethical difficulties at the beginning and end of a trial are therefore largely alleviated. There remain difficulties about consent, but these too may be diminished. Instead of emphasizing the lack of evidence favoring one arm over another that is required by theoretical equipoise, clinical equipoise places the emphasis in informing the patient on the honest disagreement among expert clinicians. The fact that the investigator has a "treatment preference," if he or she does, could be disclosed; indeed, if the preference is a decided one, and based on something more than a hunch, it could be ethically mandatory to disclose it. At the same time, it would be emphasized that this preference is not shared by others. It is likely to be a matter of chance that the patient is being seen by a clinician with a preference for B over A, rather than by an equally competent clinician with the opposite preference.

Clinical equipoise does not depend on concealing relevant information from researchers and subjects, as does the use of independent data-monitoring committees. Rather, it allows investigators, in informing subjects, to distinguish appropriately among validated knowledge accepted by the clinical community, data on treatments that are promising but are not (or, for novel therapies, would not be) generally convincing, and mere hunches. Should informed patients decline to participate because they have chosen a specific clinician and trust his or her judgment – over and above the consensus in the professional community – that is no more than the patients' right. We do not conscript patients to serve as subjects in clinical trials.

The Implications of Clinical Equipoise

The theory of clinical equipoise has been formulated as an alternative to some current views on the ethics of human research. At the same time, it corresponds closely to a preanalytic concept held by many in the research and regulatory communities. Clinical equipoise serves, then, as a rational formulation of the approach of many toward research ethics; it does not so much change things as explain why they are the way they are.

Nevertheless, the precision afforded by the theory of clinical equipoise does help to clarify or reformulate some aspects of research ethics: I will mention only two.

First, there is a recurrent debate about the ethical propriety of conducting clinical trials of discredited treatments, such as Laetrile.[17] Often, substantial political pressure to conduct such tests is brought to bear by adherents of quack therapies. The theory of clinical equipoise suggests that when there is no support for a treatment regimen within the expert clinical community, the first ethical requirement of a trial – clinical equipoise – is lacking it would therefore be unethical to conduct such a trial.

Second, Feinstein has criticized the tendency of clinical investigators to narrow excessively the conditions and hypotheses of a trial in order to ensure the validity of its results.[18] This "fastidious" approach purchases scientific manageability at the expense of an inability to apply the results to the "messy" conditions of clinical practice. The theory of clinical equipoise adds some strength to this criticism. Overly "fastidious" trials, designed to resolve some theoretical question, fail to satisfy the second ethical requirement of clinical research, since the special conditions of the trial will render it useless for influencing clinical decisions, even if it is successfully completed.

The most important result of the concept of clinical equipoise, however, might be to relieve the current crisis of confidence in the ethics of clinical trials. Equipoise, properly understood, remains an ethical condition for clinical trials. It is consistent with much current practice. Clinicians and philosophers alike have been premature in calling for desperate measures to resolve problems of equipoise.

Acknowledgement

I am indebted to Robert J. Levine, MD, and to Harold Merskey, DM, for their valuable suggestions.

References

1 Levine, R. J. *Ethics and Regulation of Clinical Research.* 2nd edn (Baltimore, MD: Urban & Schwarzenberg, 1986).

2 *Idem.* The use of placebos in randomized clinical trials. *IRB: A Reviews of Human Subjects Research* (1985); 7(2): 1–4.

3 Fried, C. *Medical Experimentation: Personal Integrity and Social Policy* (Amsterdam: North-Holland Publishing, 1974).
4 Marquis, D. Leaving therapy to chance. *Hastings Center Report* (1983); 13(4): 40–7.
5 Schafer, A. The ethics of the randomized clinical trial. (1982); 307: 719–24.
6 Shaw, L. W. and Chalmers T. C. Ethics in cooperative clinical trials. *New England Journal of Medicine* (1970); 169: 487–95.
7 Hollenberg, N. K., Dzau, V. J. and Williams, G. H. Are uncontrolled clinical studies ever justified? *New England Journal of Medicine*, (1980); 303: 1067.
8 Levine, R. J. and Lebacqz K. Some ethical considerations in clinical trials. *Clinical Pharmacology and Therapeutics* (1979); 25: 728–41.
9 Klimt, C. R. and Canner, P. L. Terminating a long-term clinical trial. *Clinical Pharmacology and Therapeutics* (1979); 25: 641–6.
10 Veatch, R. M. Longitudinal studies, sequential designs and grant renewals: what to do with preliminary data. *IRB: A Review of Human Subjects Research* (1979); 1(4): 1–3.
11 Chalmers, T. The ethics of randomization as a decision-making technique and the problem of informed consent. In: T. L. Beauchamp and L. Walters (eds) *Contemporary Issues in Bioethics* (Encino, CA.: Dickenson, 1978), pp. 426–9.
12 Taylor, K. M., Margolese, R. C. and Soskolne, C. L. Physicians reasons for not entering eligible patients in a randomized clinical trial of surgery for breast cancer. *New England Journal of Medicine* (1984); 310: 1363–7.
13 Chalmers, T. C. Invited remarks. *Clinical and Pharmacological Therapy* (1979); 25: 649–50.
14 Schater, A. The randomized clinical trial: for whose benefit? *IRB: A Review of Human Subjects Research* (1985); 7(2): 4–6.
15 Meier, P. Terminating a trial – the ethical problem. *Clinical Pharmacology and Therapeutics* (1979); 25: 633–40.
16 Prescott R. J. Feedback of data to participants during clinical trials. In: H. J. Tagnon and M. J. Staquet (eds), *Controversies in Cancer: Design of Trials and Treatment* (New York: Masson, 1979), pp. 55–61.
17 Cowan, D. H. The ethics of clinical trials of ineffective therapy. *IRB: A Review of Human Subjects Research* (1981); 3(5): 10–11.
18 Feinstein, A. R. An additional basic science for clinical medicine. II. The limitations of randomized trials. *Annals of Internal Medicine* (1983); 99: 544–50.

52

The Patient and the Public Good

Samuel Hellman

These are extraordinary times in medicine. There is both a revolution in the biology relevant to medicine and a revolution in the delivery of health care. We must translate laboratory discoveries into clinical practice, and we must do so in an increasingly cost-conscious environment. Faced with this challenge, physicians appear willing to modify the traditional doctor–patient relationship. The tension between clinical research and patient care is not new, but it has increased in intensity as we try to incorporate the new biology into patient care in a cost-effective way. It has been argued that research must take precedence if we are to use the advances in biology properly and if we are to efficiently allocate health care resources. Not only will clinical investigation have to assess the medical value of the new discoveries, but it will have to determine whether the advance is worth the cost. The emphasis on controlling costs takes us farther from the traditional physician role to where, in many managed care arrangements, the physician must both take care of the patient and husband the limited resources of the group, either for use for other patients or to provide profit for the plan and the physician. How can this be done in the context of the traditional doctor–patient relationship?

As a part of the doctor–patient relationship, physicians fashion a treatment plan to the needs of each patient. As the physician learns more about each patient and the details of his or her illness, the opportunities for crafting individual patient care increase. The advances in molecular medicine will allow us to know a great deal more about the disease state in each individual patient. Already current advances in oncology offer opportunities to characterize individual patients and their tumours with molecular and genetic information, distinguishing them from others, even within current staging classifications. Molecular medicine will provide many tools for this individualization of the extent, type and virulence of the disease as well as for characterization of the host in whom the disease is resident. Each constellation of signs, symptoms, disease extent, past medical history, concomitant illness, and molecular markers of disease proclivities will affect the desirability of specific plans of management. This same phenomenon will be true in most diseases other than cancer. Because clinical investigation requires collecting patients into groups, whereas medical practice tailors treatment to individuals, these distinctions will make the role of the clinical investigator doing randomized trials more difficult.

Although it relies on altruism and informed consent, the primary ethical basis for doing randomized trials has been developed by Benjamin Freedman of McGill University who promulgates the concept of 'clinical equipoise'. This state exists when there is genuine uncertainty within the expert medical community with regard to the alternatives applied in a trial. Most important, the concept applies to the views of the medical community as a whole but not necessarily to the individual physician-investigator for an individual patient. Patient-centered care implicit in the current relationship between doctor and patient requires that patients are seen as individuals rather than as members of a group with similar characteristics. Trials require combining patients into

From *Nature Medicine*, vol. 1, no. 5 (May 1995), pp. 400–2. Reprinted with the author's permission.

categories while the tenets of patient-centered care stress personal consideration. A related conflict is emerging as managed care is used to control health costs. Can one provide individual care and at the same time be responsible for controlling costs? Peter Toon from St. Bartholomew's Hospital in London argues that the individual physician, in particular the gatekeeper in a managed care setting, can fulfill responsibilities to an individual patient and to the husbanding of scarce public resources, both within the doctor–patient relationship.[1] I disagree!

The lessons of clinical investigation can illuminate the difficulties in containing health care costs in the context of individual patient care. To demonstrate the frequent incompatibility of randomized clinical trials and patient-centered care let us consider a patient with breast cancer who might be considered a candidate for a randomized clinical trial of therapeutic alternatives directed at either local or systemic disease. The considerations can be separated into three groups: (1) the tumour, (2) the patient, and (3) the physician.

The Tumour

In order to get sufficient numbers of patients into the trial most studies consolidate patients into what are hoped to be relatively homogeneous groups. This is necessary if there are to be sufficient patients in each arm of a study for statistical analysis. For example, all stage one patients might be randomized. Stage one breast cancer includes tumours of all sizes less than two centimeters that have not spread to lymph nodes. However, there are data that indicate that two centimeters is an arbitrary cut-off in a continuum in which patients with smaller tumours do better than those having larger tumours even within stage one. Breast tumours can now be subjected to a variety of tests that appear to offer some prognostic significance. These include, ploidy, proliferative activity, the relative expression of a variety of oncogenes, tumour suppressor genes, growth factors and their receptors, as well as tumour vascularity, nuclear and cytologic grade and histological characteristics. Already these are proving to be both of prognostic importance and a useful guide to therapy. Although some of these factors may be confounding variables, it is possible to develop a profile for each patient's tumour. As the number of useful molecular markers increases, so will the ability to characterize each tumour. This emphasizes the individuality of each patient's lesion and suggests that it may not be possible to assure equipose among medical experts for each tumour although they may feel comfortable in doing so for patients with stage one tumours as a group. Further, even if it is possible for the medical experts, the physician caring for the patient may feel quite differently about each patient within the group depending on such prognostic indicators.

Women and Breast Cancer

There are anatomic differences in patients that might affect the potential benefit of treatment. Past medical history and current health status will be different for each person. Molecular medicine will further quantify the status of important host organ function. Some pre-existing conditions may proscribe a patient from the trial, but in almost all studies, patients are included with a spectrum of health states that affect the physician's view of which arm of the study may be more appropriate for the individual patient. As medical advances allow for greater knowledge of the individual they will also serve as a guide to the most desirable therapy.

There are also differences in attitudes, wishes and emotional states of individual patients. For example, how does a patient feel about breast preservation? Does her body image require the presence of the breast or alternatively is she fearful of occult disease lurking within the breast and would she prefer that it be removed? How do the burdens of daily radiation treatment affect her life? Similarly, how does she feel about reconstructive surgery? What are the patient's social circumstances? Do these affect her choice of treatments?

The Physician

There are also many differences among physicians. How enthusiastic is the physician for an answer to the trial? What is his or her view of the severity of the disease? Is the physician risk-prone or risk-averse with regard to the treatment of suspected micrometastatic disease? What is the effect of previous education and training on the physician? What about differing community standards? What has the physician learned in following prior patients in the trial? All of these will affect the physician's view of the trial. What should the physician do with his or her *a priori* opinions? One of the founders of controlled trials, Sir Bradford Hill says, "If the doctor . . . thinks even in the absence of any evidence that for the patient's benefit he ought to give one treatment rather than the other, then that patient should not be admitted to the trial. Only if, in his state of ignorance, he believes the treatment given to be a matter of indifference can he accept a random distribution of patients to the different groups."[2]

Patient-Centred Care

This example highlights the conflict between the ethical basis of trials and the requirements of patient-centered care. Freedman's notion that clinical equipoise "is satisfied if there is genuine uncertainty within the expert medical community – not necessarily on the part of the individual investigator – about the preferred treatment"[3] is in conflict with the view of many investigators. Michael Baum, a leading British surgical oncologist, in discussing breast cancer trials states.[4] "To mount national trials there has to be first of all a professional equipoise where roughly equal numbers of the profession favor either the standard treatment or the novel treatment. For a physician to enter a patient into the trial a personal equipoise must exist." This balance must exist for each patient and the patient's preferences must be considered. This is very difficult to do when treatment is determined by random assignment.

Patient-centered care requires much more than a consensus of the medical community. We must learn about the particular patient and her disease and she must be an active participant in deciding on the best course of action. This is not 'clinical equipoise'. Only rarely is a balance between alternative therapies ever reached for an individual patient. Even when it is, it may be a different balance than that reached for another patient and grouping them together may obfuscate rather than clarify. Individual patients may have different views as to the utility of different functional or cosmetic end results. McNeil and colleagues in Boston demonstrated that loss of the larynx was viewed differently when comparing firefighters with management executives and within each group there was great heterogeneity, emphasizing the range of values individual patients place on different clinical alternatives.

The Public Good and Physician Responsibility

But what of the public good? This brings us to some of the vexing questions facing medicine today. Inherent in all proposed health care reform is control of the rising costs of medical care due in large measure to the advances in diagnosis and treatment that result from technical and scientific innovation. Many of these have potential benefit but at a considerable cost. There are powerful pressures to control the rate of rise of medical expenditures by limiting the use of such techniques. There is no problem when the procedure is of no value. The bind comes with those procedures that offer possible benefit but are very expensive. Charles Fried, of the Harvard Law School, in discussing what he calls the "economic model" worries that the obligation of personal care inherent in the relationship between physician and patient would be replaced by "the physician as agent of an efficient health-care delivery system." Although physicians should participate as medical experts in judgments as to the allocation of limited resources, the issues of societal cost should not enter into a doctor's decision when caring for an individual patient. Similarly, the patient cared for by the clinical investigator must believe that the physician will not compromise her care to perform the experiment.

Questions of the public good are a responsibility of society as a whole. Physicians should participate in public discussions and decision-making about the allocation of health care resources but in a different way. The physician can participate as a citizen, expressing views about the distribution of scarce societal resources and the value of the various health outcomes. Physicians may also participate in the public discussion of health care issues as experts, providing information about the efficacy of various treatments, but the physician ought not to be given the responsibility of making important societal decisions in the context of individual patient relationships. Not only does this involve the transference of an important public policy choice to small group of individuals, but more important, it requires the physician to base treatment recommendations for an individual patient on general public policy grounds, which will compromise the character of the doctor-patient relationship.

Today financial imperatives appear to dominate medical care considerations. Simply stated, the view is that during these revolutionary times economics must pre-empt the niceties of the personal nature of the doctor–patient relationship. Most desirable are those arrangements that satisfy both but, it is suggested, we cannot afford to lose either the randomized clinical trial as a method of acquiring new knowledge or the cost-benefit analysis applied to the individual patient needed for expenditure control, at least until satisfactory alternatives are found. While however altruistically intended, I believe this notion is misguided. We lose much more than we gain if we damage the primacy of individual patient care, for this is based on the inalienable rights of human beings. These are not rights to health care but rather rights in health care. The patient is not entitled to any medical treatment, no matter how expensive, rather the patient is entitled to be treated in a particular manner by his or her physician. Society can make choices in which it balances the needs of some individuals against the needs of others. Based on this balancing, society can determine the level of health care coverage available and physicians must work within these limits. However, the ethical requirements of the doctor–patient relationship, as we now understand it, preclude the doctor from doing society's work of balancing patient and societal needs. The relationship established between the doctor and the patient is one of trust and loyalty. In fact, respect for the value of such relationships explains why maintaining the ability to choose one's doctor figured so centrally in the recent health care debate in the United States.

The doctor–patient relationship requires the fidelity of the doctor to the patient. We must not let the current transformation of health care compromise this ideal. The patient comes to the doctor in a vulnerable state – made so by illness, fear and lack of knowledge. In order to treat a vulnerable person with concern and respect, one must look out for that person's interests. Therefore the doctor treats the patient with the appropriate respect for both the patient's vulnerability and her autonomy by becoming an agent for the patient. Moreover, it is because the patient knows that the doctor is her doctor that the patient is able to relieve herself of some of the anxiety caused by illness. If the patient is unable to repose this trust in her physician (because she knows that the physician is busy balancing this patient's needs against community needs) she will lose her ally and friend and the doctor will have lost an important instrument to relieve suffering and minister to patients.

If we are to serve the individual patient and society, we must first agree on certain principles and then, within the constraints imposed by them, develop techniques to achieve our goals. There are two such principles that, if agreed upon, will allow enhancement of the public good in the context of patient-centered care. First, individual patients should not be used as a means to achieve even a societally desired end, if in so doing the individual right to personal medical care is compromised. Second, there are two roles for the physician, and they must not be confused. As an agent of society the physician must consider the greater good and be involved in the development of guidelines, directives, and limitations on practice. At the same time, we must fight against unreasonable limits on medical care. This is very important as we consider the best use of restricted resources. Once such regulations are promulgated by society, we as physicians are obligated to adhere to them. On the other hand, within those limits we are expected to act in the best interests of each patient. The responsibilities of physicians to society as a whole must be separated from our obligation to individual patients. These two different responsibilities must be undertaken in different settings with clear understanding by the physician, the patient and society as to which role is being played. Although clinical investigation and limiting health care expenditures are essential, we should not allow them to change the traditional relationship of the physician to the patient. For clinical investigation this means limiting the use of the randomized clinical trial and requiring that when it is used an individual equipoise exists for each patient. It also means separating the role of personal physician from that of the clinical investigator. These two roles residing in the same physician create conflicting goals, which have the potential to undermine the primacy of the patient. Randomized trials are already cumbersome and administratively burdened. These restrictions will make randomized trials even more difficult to perform. This does not suggest a return to non-scientific subjective methods of research but emphasizes the need to search for alternatives to random allocation that recognize the individual variables in each clinical circumstance. For the physician concerned with controlling health care expenditures this means insulating the doctor from considering societal costs when advising or treating any individual patient. While decisions about the efficient use of resources may provide limits on management options, concern about health plan expense should not enter into an individual patient management decision.

Medicine in its essence deals with a relationship between an individual doctor and a particular patient. Clinical investigation and controlling health expenditures concern society as a whole. The physician may engage in both but it would be a most unfortunate unintended consequence if altruistic concerns for the public good undermined the assurance of optimal personal treatment promulgated in patient-centered care. Revolutionary times require greater diligence in assuring the primacy of the patient in the relationship with the caring physician.

References

1 Toon, P. D. Justice for gatekeeprs, *Lancet*, 343, 585–7 (1994).

2 Hill, A. B. Medical ethics and controlled trials. *British Medical Journal*, 1, 1043–9 (1963).

3 Freedman, B. Equipose and the ethics of clinical research. *New England Journal of Medicine*, 317, 141–5 (1987).

4 Baum, M., Zikha, K. and Houghton, J. Ethics of clinical research: Lessons for the future. *British Medical Journal*, 299, 251–3 (1989).

53

Patient Access to Experimental Drugs and AIDS Clinical Trial Designs: Ethical Issues

Udo Schüklenk and Carlton Hogan

Introduction

Today's clinical AIDS research is in trouble. Principal investigators are confronted with young and frequently highly knowledgeable patients. Many of these people with AIDS (PWAs) are often unwilling to adhere to the trial protocols. These PWAs believe they are ethically justified in breaching trial protocols because they do not consider themselves *true* volunteers in such trials. PWAs argue that they do not really *volunteer* because existing legislation prevents them from buying and using experimental drugs or from testing alternative treatment strategies. Their only access to such agents is participation in clinical trials.

In this paper we address the question of whether the patients' position is ethically acceptable. At least two different ethical problems need to be analyzed in this regard. One is of a paternalistic nature, and the other claims that noncompliance with trial protocols and/or access to experimental drugs amounts to a harm in other situations. We analyze the practical implications of such patient reasoning and behavior for the predictive value of results gathered in clinical research. We conclude that the arguments that patients with terminal illnesses can present in favor of their actions are persuasive. In the last part of the article we suggest that improvements are urgently needed in protocols of clinical trials that address patient concerns and survival interests. Such improvements are possible. A possible trial design will be described briefly. The necessary changes would result in more ethical trial protocols and a predicted overall higher percentage of patient compliance than we see today. Also the predictive value of AIDS research clinical trials would increase for future patient generations.

From *Cambridge Quarterly of Healthcare Ethics*, vol. 5 (1996), pp. 400–9.

The Problem

AIDS is a disease that affects primarily relatively young people in most Western societies.[1] Many of these have a high level of education and the political determination not to become a *passive* part of a medical research process as we know it from clinical cancer trials, for instance.[2] Medical journals, AIDS policy magazines, and papers published by PWA self-organizations report that the number of patients who violate research protocols has reached staggering proportions and threatens the integrity of clinical research as such.[3] In two recently reported trials, between 40 and 80% of patients dropped out of the trial protocol altogether before the trial ended.[4] As an example, the trial that led to the approval of Zidovudine™ was supposedly a randomized, placebo-controlled double-blind trial.[5] It was revealed, however, that soon after the beginning of this trial, patients had their capsules analyzed by chemists to find out who was randomized into the placebo arm. Patients who received the active agent started sharing their drug with those who got a placebo. The trial effectively became unblinded and was not placebo controlled.[6] It was aborted prematurely because 19 patients died in the placebo arm compared to only 1 in the Zidovudine™ arm. On the basis of this study the nucleoside analogue AZT was approved by the FDA as an AIDS therapeutic and was, for the most part of the last decade, the first choice of physicians and PWAs. No other AZT trial has reproduced the results of the original study, lending support to the claim that this research either constituted bad science, as asserted by Dr Joseph Sonnabend, the medical director of the New York City's Community Research Initiative on AIDS[7] or the research was outright fraudulent, as John Lauritsen, a New York City based investigative reporter insists. Unfortunately all the problems that have plagued this and the subsequent AIDS trials have had serious real-world consequences. In a 1993 state of the art conference sponsored by the US NIH[8] an expert panel was unable to determine when, if, or how to start Zidovudine™ treatment (by far the most studied therapy to date) for most patient populations. If such basic questions remain unanswered, one has to ask if the $1 billion of AIDS research has been well spent.[9]

The editors of the medical journal *The Lancet* were certainly right when they pointed out that[10]

> Large randomized trials are becoming increasingly expensive, yet are essential to inform public health policy. Once embarked upon they should not be stopped prematurely unless, in conjunction with other studies, they provide extremely reliable and convincing evidence to guide future clinical practice.

In the next part of the paper we shed some light on the views of those people without whose voluntary participation and compliance with protocols the research clinical trials would be infeasible to conduct. What do patients think about the current world of clinical trials? What implications do their views have on their actual behavior as research subjects?

A Message From the Real World

We have already mentioned the extraordinarily high rate of patients who drop out of clinical trials. If more than every second patient walks out of trial protocols of major research clinical trial efforts, this figure alone should be reason to rethink how we conduct our medical research. This actual behavior is a clear indication that patients are unhappy or dissatisfied with the way trials are conducted on people suffering a terminal illness such as AIDS. For instance, recently a patient reported on an electronic mailing list for PWAs[11]

> I hate to say it but . . . we are no more than lab rats to these people [principal investigators]. As time passed by [in the particular study this patient participated in] my [CD4/CD8 levels] eventually dropped to almost their original levels and I gracefully bowed out of the study . . . thank you Mr. Lab Rat. . . . No more I say. Life is too precious to do this. I can honestly say that I am sorry that I did this.

Given that nothing less than the life of the participating patient is at stake in the case of AIDS and other terminal illnesses, the question needs to be addressed of whether we could have reasonably expected the just-quoted patient to stay in the trial even though he clearly realized that the drugs offered were not helping him at all. Evidence exists that patients were expected to join clinical trials that randomized them into trial arms that offered no clinical equipoise[12] by professional community standards. Bruce Nussbaum, for instance, reports that US Aids Clinical Trials Group (ACTG) trial conducted by Margaret A. Fischl, designed to test Bactrim as a possible prophylactic against *Pneumocystis carinii* pneumonia (PCP),[13] insisted on the use of a placebo control. Community doctors used PCP prophylactics successfully for several years when this trial, with the approval of the responsible Institutional Review Board (IRB), went ahead. Bactrim had then been used for nearly 20 years as a PCP prophylactic in cancer patients. He concludes his description of this particular trial: "Twenty-eight people who received placebo died in her [Dr. Fischl's] experiment to prove what virtually everyone already knew. It was senseless science. It was irresponsible, unethical science. It should have never been permitted by the Institutional Review Board that presumably approved of the trial design."[14] Hogan et al. report that ACTG trials 016 and 019 were not accessible to PWAs using PCP prophylactics until 1989.[15] Nussbaum's criticism of the IRB, even though certainly justified in a material sense, misses the mark because US IRBs are not entitled to reject research strategies *as such* on ethical grounds. This point, after all, is the reason that some authors like George Annas have argued that IRBs, as we see them operating in the United States currently, cannot fulfill the role of watchdog in any meaningful way on behalf of the research subjects. He asserts that these ethics committees are incapable of preventing discrimination or fostering equality because they are "appointed by, and work for the institution – not patients, research subjects, or the community."[16] Clinical trials such as those mentioned by Nussbaum undoubtedly violate the regulations of the 1964 code of the Declaration of Helsinki. This code requires unequivocally that in any medical study every patient, including those in the control group, should receive the best proven and therapeutic method.[17] US National Institute of Allergy and Infectious Diseases chief Dr Anthony Fauci reportedly conceded that the "randomized clinical trial routinely asks physicians to sacrifice the interests of their particular patients for the study."[18] This position violates not only the classical ethical obligations physicians have toward their patients, but also the principles of the Declaration of Helsinki. Last, but not least, such trials produce results relevant only for real-world patients who received the same substandard treatments that the trial patients received. That is, it remains unclear what the impact is on real-world patients who receive PCP prophylactics as a matter of course.

Patients as well as biostatisticians have suggested that clinical trial patient populations that do not reflect the experiences of real-world patients have very limited predictive value.[19] The results of such trials do not allow us to predict with adequate certainty how an experimental agent might work in real-world patient populations.[20] This state of affairs led a working group of the Hastings Center to propose in 1991 that prima facie at least (pregnant) women and IV drug users should be given the opportunity to join clinical trials if they wish to do so.[21] However, in the United States women, people of color, and IV drug users are underrepresented in AIDS clinical trials, even though they represent a growing proportion of the overall AIDS case load.[22] In some of the major cities in the United States AIDS is the leading cause of death for young Blacks.[23] The only access for many PWAs to a drug they believe might save their lives is ultimately to lie their way into a trial. Greg Dubbs of Stanford University went so far as to suggest, that "All you are doing [in the current clinical trials system] is finding out who can lie well. They never study how many people lie to get into their studies."[24] This attitude is also reflected in a survey undertaken by Miriam E. Cameron. What PWAs have to say about their healthcare professionals is far from flattering, to say the least.[25] Representatives of five French AIDS activist groups released a statement that reads in part:[26]

> Some people consider those who leave trials in such large numbers irresponsible in a certain manner since by their individual decision they endanger the research whose results will serve some, if not all HIV-positive persons. But self-sacrifice has its limits; rational collective logic is impossible for each individual to consider.... Substandard treatments in certain trials are to be genuinely feared. Such people, more and better informed all the time, are no longer ready to accept this phenomenon.

Even though there is some evidence in support of these PWAs' suspicion that they might be subjected to a less than ideal course of treatment in a given clinical trial,[27] the important lesson to learn from statements such as this is that if people with life-threatening illnesses do not *believe* that there is a true equipoise among the different arms onto which they might be randomized, the likelihood is high that they will try to improve their odds. This is independent of the question of whether the principal investigators *believe* that there is true clinical equipoise. Obviously, however, the overarching ethical issue is whether patients are justified in violating trial protocols for the sake of an individual advantage they might gain. The next part will discuss the ethical issues at stake.

Ethical Issues: Paternalism and Promotion of Participation in Research Clinical Trials

Current legislation in all Western societies prevents people with AIDS or other terminal illnesses from accessing and using experimental agents of their liking. This ban is based primarily on two reasons,[28] both of which are essentially ethically motivated.

(1) Patients are more likely to harm themselves with experimental drugs than benefit from the untested drugs.
(2) If patients have access to experimental agents they will not join clinical trials, thus preventing the development of successful drugs in a controlled manner and harming prospective future patient generations.

We will analyze each of these arguments to find out whether the arguments individually or combined could ethically justify preventing people from accessing experimental agents either to prevent harm to themselves or to promote their participation in clinical drug trials.

Both of these arguments assume that respect for patient autonomy is of great ethical significance, and for this reason authors putting such arguments forward try to justify the attempted overriding of patient autonomy in situations involving access to experimental drugs for people with life-threatening illnesses. We agree that respect for individual autonomy is rightly given a great deal of weight by those who try to justify the current status quo, even though we will not argue this case in the context of this paper.[29] For our purposes it is sufficient to note that those who wish to override individual autonomy acknowledge a need to justify their intended interference.

Paternalistic arguments

The first argument is obviously of a *strong* paternalistic nature. Patients are usually aware of the risks they are going to take if they use unapproved drugs. Newsletters and magazines published by and for PWAs are full of examples of articles *warning* their readers of the risks involved in taking experimental agents.[30] The justification for overriding a competent patient's decision making is the possibility of irreversible harm and the moral obligation to prevent harm.[31] Ultimately, however, as Robert Young suggested, our intervention can serve one reasonable end, that is, to preserve the patient's future dispositional autonomy by overriding occurrent or actual autonomy.[32] We tend to disagree with this type of argument. Mill's classical maxim as expressed in *On Liberty* shall serve as a defense of our interpretation.[33]

> The only purpose for which power can be rightfully exercised over any member of a civilized community against his will, is to prevent harm to others. His own good, either physical or moral, is not a sufficient warrant. He cannot rightfully be compelled to do or forbear because it will be better for him to do so, because it will make him happier, because, in the opinion of others, to do so would be wise or even right.

However, even strong paternalistic motives defended by Young would not succeed in justifying an intervention. No efficient standard therapy is currently available that can help to arrest continuing deterioration of the immune system. As of yet AIDS is defined as a terminal illness. Under such circumstances *no* future autonomy could possibly be preserved by means of our paternalistically motivated intervention. Hence, an argument based on the preservation of future autonomy as a valuable end cannot be utilized in the case of AIDS.

The strong paternalist could of course change the argument slightly. That person might point out to the PWA who wishes to use an experimental agent that despite awareness of the limited time span intervention will buy, the effort is still worthwhile. Although dispositional autonomy will not be preserved for a long period of time, preserving it even for a limited period justifies the intervention. The problem leading to a rejection of such an argumentative strategy is again a consequence of the nature of a terminal illness. A strong paternalist, like Young, interferes with the autonomous choices of persons to preserve long-term autonomy. Even in the modified situation with which we are faced, a strong paternalist fails ultimately to achieve what is intended, that is, to preserve an agent's dispositional autonomy. In the case of AIDS, for instance, the intervention must be upheld until the patient has died. If the intervention is interrupted at any time, the patient will again try to use the experimental drugs on which he puts his hopes.

Some authors have surprisingly suggested that in cases such as AIDS the intervention really is *weakly* paternalistic. Andrew F. Shorr, for instance, argued "that history has conclusively demonstrated that people facing terminal illnesses appear particularly susceptible to abuse.... Individuals may reveal a degree of desperation that clouds their judgment and thus, in some cases, undermines their ability to make completely autonomous choices."[34] Obviously Shorr's argument is missing the point. Nobody is capable at any time of making *completely* autonomous choices. Nevertheless, as a society we are usually willing to accept those choices, ingeniously described by Beauchamp and Childress as *substantially* autonomous, instead of requiring what Shorr calls completely autonomous choices.[35] Shorr and others who present similar kinds of arguments have failed to demonstrate that PWAs are incapable of making *substantially* autonomous choices. In fact, the prima facie assumption seems to be that PWAs are people who should be treated as persons. Why else would we routinely ask them to give informed consent to participation in clinical trials? It seems as if defenders of the current status quo are all too quickly willing to question the competency of terminally ill people should they decide to refuse to follow the course of action proposed by the research establishment. At the same time there would be no doubts about the competency and autonomy of, for example, PWAs should they decide to join research clinical trials instead of trying to access experimental agents.

It seems to us that paternalistically motivated arguments fail to justify current legislation that prevents people with terminal illnesses from using experimental drugs. In the next part we analyze another type of argument employed to justify the status quo.

Public health arguments

Lacking a more appropriate term to describe the second type of argument, we label them *public health arguments* (PHA). This type of argument acknowledges that paternalistic arguments are not strong enough to persuade us to leave in place the current legislation that prevents access to experimental agents. PHAs suggest that without the participation of current patients in clinical trials no clinical research will be possible, and hence no successful treatments will be developed for patient generations to come.[36] This argument can be defended on utilitarian as well as on other grounds. We do agree that, indeed, current generations have moral obligations toward future generations.[37] The question is how far-reaching can this obligation be? How much far-reaching altruistic behavior can we reasonably expect from terminally ill patients? Utilitarians such as Peter Singer have suggested on the one hand that we should always attempt "to prevent something very bad from happening, without thereby sacrificing anything of comparable moral significance." On the other hand, he also realizes that the altruism we can reasonably be expected to show is not identical with what we would see in an ideal world, simply because our capacity to act selflessly is limited. Singer proposes instead, for instance, a 10% donation of our incomes to fight the hunger in the world, which is "more than a token donation, yet is not so high as to be beyond all but saints."[38]

Brendan Minogue and his colleagues suggested that the current US legislation regulating drug approval and access to experimental agents exploits a vulnerable patient population. They argued that "just as society cannot afford to let illness go unchecked, so too it cannot afford the violation of the liberty of a small and vulnerable population. And if it happens that liberty may justifiably be violated, then surely it is not *their* [the patients'] liberty which we cannot afford to violate."[39] These virtue ethicists propose that in order to guarantee that patients are *real* volunteers in our clinical trials, we should offer them access to the desired drug without any obligation to join a trial. To do so would practically result in a clinical trial whose research subjects are *true* volunteers. These patients would participate in the trial even though they could access the very same drug without this participation. It seems reasonable to us to assume that under such circumstances the likelihood is very low that patients would resort to strategies such as those mentioned in the beginning of this paper.

AIDS treatments activists have changed their political strategy that started nearly a decade ago with a battle cry demanding *any* kinds of drugs no matter how unknown the substances' efficacy or toxicity. Scientists have seemingly tried to find a compromise between activists' demands for speeding up drug approval and scientific validity. One compromise is the replacement of clinical end points and survival with surrogate markers such as CD4 counts. Thomas Fleming rightly pointed out that before one can accept a surrogate marker as a replacement end point, one needs to be sure that "the marker fully captures the effect of treatment on the true end point."[40] Susan Ellenberg has justifiable doubts that this evidence exists for currently widely used surrogate end points such as CD4 counts. "Utilizing surrogate end points requires the assumption not only that biological activity results in clinical benefit, but that the degree of clinical benefit can be precisely predicted from the measure of biological activity. The legitimacy of such an assumption for the use of CD4 counts in AIDS trials is far from established."[41] The unexpected failure of Zidovudine™ monotherapy to delay early HIV disease[42] has led to a change of view among AIDS activists, who no longer press for the approval of experimental agents on the basis of beliefs instead of evidence. AIDS activist groups such as New York City's Treatment Action Group have begun to understand that belief-based approval amounts to a violation of the long-term interests of people with

AIDS because it prevents scientists and patients alike from *knowing* what the effect of a certain agent or treatment is on quality of life and, ultimately, on survival.[43]

The crucial question, however, is whether research interests (which often are at the same time interests of future patient generations) can be reconciled with patient autonomy. It seems that what we need are ethically designed clinical trials that meet three criteria:

(1) the patients who join them must be real volunteers;
(2) the trials must mirror real-world experiences of PWAs in order to have some predictive value for the majority of patients who have to make treatment related decisions; and
(3) the trial must not require patients to sacrifice vital survival interests.

Possibility of ethically and methodologically sound clinical trials

Many procedural and ethical problems stem directly from the conflict between patient desire for treatment and the scientific need for adherence to controlled studies until efficacy is proven. Patients may conceal their use of forbidden concomitant drugs, by sharing the active agent with recipients of the placebo or otherwise violating the trial protocol.[44] Viable alternatives to the current research strategies and trial designs have been proposed by Ellenberg et al.,[45] Byar et al.,[46] Green et al.,[47] Cooper,[48] and Hogan et al.[49] Such "strategy trials" share many common features, including relaxed eligibility criteria (thus improving generalizability), flexible on-trial clinical management guidelines, accommodations for change of treatment when necessary, and a focus on the evaluation of clinical management strategies as opposed to drug approval. This type of research has been called "pragmatic"[50] or "management"[51] research, as distinguished from "explanatory" research. Tight eligibility restrictions, inflexible management guidelines, and prompt discontinuation of noncompliant and other problematic patients make sense in the context of trying to get a drug approved. By reducing variability and selecting the optimal conditions of drug action, one maximizes the chance of seeing a benefit. But, as argued earlier, such trials do not necessarily produce the most valuable information and can further alienate the patient population. An altogether different kind of trial is needed to answer public health questions. Such issues are becoming increasingly important in the United States and other countries with large federal biomedical research establishments. Critics question the propriety of government sponsorship of pivotal trials and, in effect, procurement of approval for industry, while a backlog of unanswered research questions swells daily.

The trial design proposal of Hogan et al.[52] serves as an example. This scheme attempts to separate the interests of clinical care and approval and creates a proposal that stresses the former, at the expense of the latter, to some degree. Such a schema features a network of clinical trials that are tightly administratively coordinated. Coenrollment is encouraged rather than forbidden, and patients needing or wanting to leave a particular trial would be encouraged to enroll in a subsequent randomization, rather than being lost as is the case today. Clinically relevant treatments and combinations, as they are used in the community, would be studied. There is relatively little interest in looking at the "pure" biological activity of a single compound: AIDS is not typically treated with any form of monotherapy. Patients would be allowed to opt out of randomizations and arms of randomization, thus creating substudies of persons unwilling or unable to take specific drugs, a population that is almost entirely unstudied today.

End points would be clinical, because the diversity of treatments and the resultant potential for drug interaction makes biological activity, and hence surrogate end points, less informative for health and survival prospects. But more intensive laboratory substudies could be enrolled through sampling the larger population, allowing a better integration of pragmatic and explanatory questions. Common data items, case report forms, and follow-up schedules shared by multiple trials would reduce the burden on patient and provider alike.

Although large simple trials (LST) in cardiovascular medicine have been very successful, the complexity and number of treatments used in AIDS make a pure LST model infeasible. There are not enough patients in the world to enroll an LST for each drug and combination. Hogan's proposal adopts some of the philosophy behind LSTs, in that overall clinical benefit in a heterogeneous population is the key parameter of interest, at the same time accommodating the relatively new, incomplete, and thus complex science of HIV/

AIDS. Finally, prizing patient autonomy and explicitly trying to create trials in which patients want and are able to comply with this proposal, by virtue of its similarity to state of the art care, will correct many ethical deficiencies. This philosophy was perhaps best summed up by Dr Kinley Larntz, who said with respect to such proposals "traditionally, people who design trials came up with a question, and then attempted to recruit persons to that question. We want to have the patients, and recruit the proper questions to them."[53]

Ethical and humane AIDS trials are possible. Their creation, however, requires inclusive dialogue among patients, clinicians, advocates, and ethicists. This discussion must acknowledge the different possible types of questions, the ends to which such questions will be deployed, and the optimal designs for various purposes. Clearly, trials optimized to seek drug approval do not always meet patients' needs or those of the clinicians treating them. Equally apparent is the importance of the approval of new drugs. A greater variety of more creative and flexible trials will substantially advance the treatment of AIDS.

Notes

1 US National Research Council. *Social Impact of AIDS* (Washington, DC: National Academy Press, 1993).
2 Crimp, D. (ed.), *AIDS: Cultural Analysis, Cultural Activism* (Cambridge, MA: MIT Press, 1988).
3 Delaney, M. The case for patient access to experimental therapies. *Journal of Infectious Diseases* (1989), 59: 416–19.
4 Torres, G., ACTG 175 and delta. *Treatment Issues* (1995), 9(10): 2–3.
5 Fischl M. A., Richman, D. D. Grieco M. H. et al. The efficacy of azidothymidine (AZT) in the treatment of patients with AIDS and AIDS-related complex. *New England Journal of Medicine* (1987) 317: 185–91; Richman, D. D., Fischl, M. A., Grieco, M. H., et al. The toxicity of azidothymidine (AZT) in the treatment of patients with AIDS and AIDS-related complex. *New England Journal of Medicine* (1987) 314: 192–7.
6 Lauritsen, J., *The AIDS War* (New York: Asklepios Press, 1993).
7 Sonnabend, J., A review of AZT multi center trial-data obtained under the Freedom of Information Act by Project Inform and ACT Up. *AIDS Forum* (1989) 1(1): 9–15.
8 Sande, M. A., Arpener, C. C. J., Obiss, C. G., et al. Antiretroviral therapy for adult HIV-infected patients – recommendations from a state-of-the-art conference. *Journal of the American Medical Association* (1993); 270: 2583–9.
9 The estimate is conservative, based on TAG's *Summary of US Research Budget*. When one adds the costs of the many industry trials, the effort of the MRC in Britain. INSERM in France, the Australian European Cooperative Group, etc., the amount is probably double this figure.
10 [Anonymous]. On stopping a trial before its time. *The Lancet* (1993); 342: 1311–12.
11 AOL PWA mailing list [privileged communication].
12 As defined by Freedman, B. Equipoise and the ethics of clinical research. *New England Journal of Medicine* (1987); 317: 141–5.
13 *Pneumocystis carinii* pneumonia is a common opportunistic infection in PWAs and the cause of most AIDS-related deaths.
14 Nussbaum B., *Good Intentions. How Big Business and the Medical Establishment Are Corrupting the Fight Against AIDS, Alzheimer's, Cancer and More* (New York: Penguin, 1991).
15 Hogan, C., Hodges, J., Abrams, D. I. et al. MAPS: a proposal for more clinically relevant research in AIDS (a presentation at the Cambridge Health Technology Forum on Surrogate Markers, 1994).
16 Annas, G. J., The dominance of American law (and market values) over American bioethics. In: M. Crodin (ed.) *Meta Medical Ethics: The Philosophical Foundations of Bioethics* (Dordrecht: Kluwer, 1995).
17 Rothman K. J. and Michels K. B. The continuing unethical use of placebo controls. *New England Journal of Medicine* (1994); 331: 394–8.
18 Hellman, S. and Hellman, D. S., Of mice but not men: problems of the randomized clinical trial. *New England Journal of Medicine* (1991); 324: 1585–9.
19 Hogan, C. Test treatment strategies under real conditions. *Treatment Issues* (1995); 9(4): 7–9.
20 See note 15, Hogan.
21 Levine, C., Neveloff Dubler, N, and Levine, R. J. Building a new consensus: ethical principles and policies for clinical research on HIV/AIDS. IRB: *A Review of Human Subjects Research* (1991); 31(1–2): 1–17.
22 Mirken B. AIDS clinical trials: why they have recruiting problems. *AIDS Treatment News* (1995); 217: 1–4.
23 CDC. Update: mortality attributable to HIV infection and AIDS (25–44 years). *Morbidity and Mortality Weekly Report* (1993); 42: 481–6.
24 See note 22.

25 Cameron, M. E., *Living With AIDS – Experiencing Ethical Problems.* (Newbury Park, CA: Sage, 1993), pp. 114–27.

26 TRT-5. Concerning a clinical phase III trial on saquinavir – balancing research and health care. science. medicine. aids article 11418, posted February 22, 1995. This text was taken from an Internet newsgroup devoted to scientific aspects of the AIDS problem.

27 Novick, A., Reflections on a term of public service with the FDA anti-virals advisory committee *AIDS and Public Policy Journal* (1993) 8: 5–61.

28 Annas, G. J., Faith (healing), hope, and charity at the FDA: the politics of AIDS drug trials. In: L. O. Costin (ed.) *AIDS and the Health Care System.* (New Haven: Yale University Press, 1990), pp. 183–94.

29 We tend to agree by and large with liberal and libertarian arguments in this regard as they have been put forward by P Illingworth *AIDS and the Good Society* (London: Routledge, 1990) and R. D. Mohr AIDS, gays and state coercion. *Bioethics* (1987); 1: 35–50.

30 For example, Armington K. Evaluating new or "alternative treatments," GMHC *Treatment Issues* (1993); 7(11/12): 28–9; [Anonymous] Evaluating alternative treatments. PWAC-NY *Newsline* (1994) March 27; Hogan C. A professional patient's survival guide. *PWALive* (1994); 5(3): 19–21.

31 See note 28.

32 Young, R. *Personal Autonomy: Beyond Negative and Positive Liberty.* (Beckenham: Croom Helm, 1986).

33 Mill, J. S. *Utilitarianism Liberty. Representative Government* (London: Dent, 1960; first published *c.* 1860).

34 Short, A. F. AIDS and the FDA: an ethical case for limiting patient access to new medical therapies. *IRB: A Review of Human Subjects Research* (1992) 14(4): 1–5.

35 Beauchamp, T. L. and Childress, J. F., *Principles of Biomedical Ethics* (New York: Oxford University Press, 1994).

36 See note 34 and note 28.

37 Birnbacher, D. *Verantwortung für zukünftige Generationen* (Stuttgart: Reclam, 1988).

38 Singer, P. *Practical Ethics* (Cambridge: Cambridge University Press, 1993).

39 Minogue, B., Palmer-Fernandez, G., Udell, L. and Waller, B. N. Individual autonomy and the double-blind controlled experiment. *Journal of Medicine and Philosophy* (1995); 20: 43–55.

40 Fleming, T. R., Surrogate markers in AIDS and cancer trials. *Statistics in Medicine* (1994); 13: 1423–35.

41 Ellenberg, S. Discussion of "surrogate markers in AIDS and cancer trials." *Statistics in Medicine* (1994); 13: 1437–40.

42 Concorde Coordinating Committee. Concorde: MRC/ANRS randomized, double blind controlled trial of immediate and deferred zidovudine in symptom free HIV infection. *Lancet* (1994); 348: 871–80.

43 [Editorial]. On stopping a trial before its time. *Lancet* (1993); 342: 1311.

44 Rowlands, C., and Powderly, W. G. The use of alternative therapies by HIV-positive patients attending the St. Louis AIDS Clinical Trials Unit. *Missouri Medicine* (1991); 88: 807–10; Greenblatt, R. M., Hollander A., MacMaster, J. R., and Henke, G. J. Polypharmacy among patients attending an AIDS clinic: utilization of prescribed, unorthodox, and investigational treatments. *Journal of the Acquired Immune Deficiency Syndrome* (1991); 4: 136–43.

45 Ellenberg, S. S. Finkelstein, D. and Schoenfeld, D. A. Statistical issues arising in AIDS clinical trials. *Journal of the American Statistical Association* (1992); 87: 573–6.

46 Byar, D. P. Choenfeld D. A., Reen, S. B. et al. Design considerations for AIDS trials. *New England Journal of Medicine* (1990); 323: 1343–8.

47 Green, S. B. et al. Issues in the design of drug trials for AIDS. *Controlled Clinical Trials* (1990); 11: 80–7.

48 Cooper, E. A prospective, randomized master antiretroviral trial: a proposal for improving the quality of information on the clinical usefulness of AIDS drugs. *Second National Conference on Human Retroviruses and Related Infections* [USA, Abstract 278]. 1994.

49 See note 15.

50 Schwarz, D. and Lellouch J. Explanatory and pragmatic attitudes in therapeutical trials. *Journal of Chronic Disease* (1967); 20: 637–48.

51 Buyse, M. Regulatory vs public health requirements in clinical trials. *Drug Information Journal* (1993); 27: 977–84.

52 See note 15.

53 Larntz, K. Individually guided design. *Second CPCRA Statistical Center Clinician's Seminar*, 1992.

54

The Morality of Clinical Research: A Case Study

Torbjörn Tännsjö

Abstract

The paper is a record of a debate which took place between a group of clinicians and the author concerning a clinical trial of a drug supposed to postpone the time when HIV-patients develop AIDS. A problem with the trial was that on available (inconclusive) evidence it appeared that one patient out of 500 was killed by the drug. The question raised was whether, in view of this evidence, it was morally defensible to go on with the trial. The discussion came to involve general topics such as the appropriate role of the ideal of autonomy as well as more particular topics of quantitative and qualitative risk assessments. The main thrust of the argument is that different conceptions of rationality may provide rationales of conflicting clinical decisions. Philosophy matters to medicine.

1 Introduction

In the fall of 1991 I was contacted by a group of doctors who were conducting clinical research at an infection clinic. They were testing on their patients a new drug, ddI, which was expected to have the benefit of postponing the time when HIV-positive patients develop AIDS. The best drug known to produce such effects was at the time zidovudine. They were now trying, within a transnational program, to find out whether ddI as such might prove to be a superior drug but also, and as a matter of fact, primarily, whether it in combination with zidovudine, where the patients altered between the two drugs, would prove superior. Some evidence was forthcoming from research already conducted (in my description of the case, I will stick exclusively to the evidence then available to these doctors), to some extent neutral, to some extent hopeful, and to some extent alarming. There seemed to be little reason to believe that ddI alone was superior (or inferior) to zidovudine (neutral). There seemed to be reason indeed to believe that the combination of ddI and zidovudine did somewhat prolong the period where the patient was HIV-infected but without too serious AIDS-symptoms (hopeful), and there seemed to be reasons to believe that one patient out of 500 who received ddI was actually *killed* by the drug (alarming). The patients who were killed by the drug were not killed by it directly. The drug seemed to cause them to develop a fatal form of pancreatitis.

The doctors admitted that the problem they were now in should have been anticipated when in the first place they decided to start the trial, when their protocol was written and when the protocol was sent in to the Ethics Committee, which approved the trial. However, new evidence had been forthcoming and second thoughts had surfaced. They now asked me therefore, a professional moral philosopher, whether, from a moral point of view, it was defensible to go on with the trial. Actually, they were themselves divided over the question. Some of them wanted to go on with it, others felt inclined at least to take their patients out of it. Under the circumstances, it felt only

From *Journal of Medicine and Philosophy*, vol. 19 (1994), pp. 7–21.

natural to have a thorough discussion about the trial and even to raise again basic questions and concerns related to clinical tests of new drugs.

2 The Trial

On November 11, 1991, we held a conference together in order to try to find an answer to the question. The doctors described the trial to me in the following terms.

Patients admitted to the trial were presented with the following options. They were free not to go into the project. Then they would be treated according to practice, i.e., zidovudine would be administered to them. This is as it should be, of course, when clinical research is being conducted. If they volunteered, they would be subjected to a lottery, assigning them to one of the three arms of the trial. One third of them would be given zidovudine only, as usual, one third of them would be given ddI only, and one third of them would be allowed to alternate between zidovudine and ddI. They were informed about all the hopes and expectations about the new drug, they were informed that it was not a cure of AIDS, and they were informed, in particular, about the forthcoming evidence that there was a risk (the estimate was that one out of 500 developed a lethal form of pancreatitis) inherent in the trial. For practical reasons, the trial was not blind. The patients who entered the trial were informed in which arm of the trial they had ended up.

As a matter of fact, most of the patients who were offered inclusion in the trial volunteered. However, several dropped out of the trial when they learnt that they were going to receive zidovudine only. They had volunteered because of an intense wish to test a new drug. In spite of the fact that this was bad for the trial, they were allowed, of course, to drop out of it.

In our discussion we tried first of all to find out whether the trial conformed to the Helsinki Declaration. We found that this declaration could not help us to decide the matter, since it makes unreasonable demands on clinical research. We then had a discussion about the place of informed consent in trials such as these. We found that a reasonable respect for the autonomy of the patients did not free the doctors of their responsibility in the situation. We then tried systematically to face the question of whether, for the patients in the trial, the risk was really balanced by reasonable hope of benefits. Both quantitative and qualitative risk assessment was discussed. Eventually we failed to answer the question in a unanimous way. It might be interesting to see why. We then applied the concept of equipoise, known from the literature in the field, to each arm of the trial. Once again, we ended up without any consensus. The majority felt that the requirement of equipoise was satisfied, the minority felt that it was not. The division of opinion between the physicians seemed, in the final analysis, to depend on different *philosophical* outlook. Conflicting conceptions of rationality were involved in the discussion. A general lesson to be learnt from our discussion is then that philosophical ideas can be of the utmost clinical relevance.

Our consideration of each of these topics will now be discussed.

3 The Helsinki Declaration

The research at the clinic had been approved by an Ethics Committee. This, of course, is standard procedure in cases such as these. Unless an experiment involving human subjects be approved by the committee, it will not be conducted. This committee, like all committees of its kind, is said to take as its point of departure the World Medical Association Declaration of Helsinki: Recommendations Guiding Medical Doctors in Biomedical Research Involving Human Subjects, or, for short, The Helsinki Declaration. The question we raised, then, was the following. Does the experiment face up to the demands made by the Helsinki Declaration? We immediately ran into problems.

The trial in question was an example of what the Helsinki Declaration defines as "clinical research". This is narrowly defined in II:6 of the declaration, where it is required that clinical research can be justified "by its potential diagnostic or therapeutic value for the patient". Research that is not clinical must, according to III:2, be conducted "on volunteers – either healthy persons or patients for whom the experimental design is not related to the patient's illness". It has been pointed out that, taken literally, this means a general ban on all tests where a placebo is used. The administration of a placebo for research purposes is not in general "justified by its potential diagnostic or therapeutic value for the patient". Hence, it may only be administered to healthy persons or to patients not suffering of the relevant disease! Moreover, though not relevant in the present case, experiments conducted merely to find out about the pathogenesis of a disease are also banned by the Helsinki Declaration. They are non-therapeutic, according to II:6, and may therefore only be performed on healthy persons or on patients not having the disease one wishes to investigate (cf. Levine, 1986, p. 9). Our problem was different, however. For the sake of argument we accepted that the experiment under scrutiny was therapeutic (a question to which we were to return). However, we had problems with another paragraph in the Helsinki Declaration, II:3. According to this paragraph, concerned with clinical, therapeutic research "every patient – including those of a control group, if any – should be assured of the best proven diagnostic and therapeutic method." We concluded that this was a ban on all controlled studies of new drugs. To be sure, the patients receiving ddI rather than zidovudine were not "assured of the best proven diagnostic and therapeutic method", which was by that time – zidovudine! We found out later that even this strange aspect of the declaration has been commented on in the literature (cf. for example Wulff, Pedersen, and Rosenberg, 1990, p. 200).

We could, of course, have proceeded to an investigation of other relevant ethical codes, such as Nuremberg, CIOMS, other WMA documents, and various different national regulations. However, in view of the subtlety of the points we were raising, there was little hope that anything definite would come out of such an attempt. We decided therefore to put these paragraphs of the Helsinki Declaration, as well as other declarations, to one side, and try other approaches to our problem.

4 Could the Decision be Left to the Patients?

The doctors who wanted to go on with the trial argued that, no matter how we conceived of the risk 1 to 500 of getting killed by pancreatitis, this was not relevant to our problem. The patients themselves were given full information. When they entered the trial, they entered it as volunteers, the patients had given their informed consent. Who were we to question their decision? We ought rather to respect their autonomy (cf. Schafer, 1982).

In order to evaluate this claim we first settled for a definition of what it means to respect a patient's autonomy. We interpreted this along the lines already suggested by John Stuart Mill, i.e., as a ban on paternalism.[1] Doctors are not allowed to force patients, or take decisions on their behalf, only in the patients' own interest. There was no unanimity as to whether this is really something of value in itself,[2] but, as a rule of thumb, it is a reasonable stance, we all agreed, at least when dealing with adult patients, suffering from somatic disease, who are capable of exercising a judgment of their own.

Now, what about the patients in the trial? Did they satisfy these requirements? They were HIV-positive but mentally healthy. They were suffering from a somatic disease. Moreover, they were adults. But were they capable of exercising a judgment of their own?

Some of the more sceptical doctors at first argued that they were not. These patients, they claimed, were desperate. They would be willing to test any new drug, in the vain hope that it would prove to be a cure of AIDS. They were prepared to take unreasonable risks to this effect.

We all had to agree that this might well be so. But was this observation relevant in the present context? Did it show that they were not capable of exercising a judgment of their own? We eventually found out that we must make a distinction between, on the one hand, a person who is capable of exercising a judgment of his own, and, on the other hand, a person who is capable of reaching (in our lights) a wise judgment. The ban on paternalism is lifted only when the patient fails on both these counts. We are not allowed to force them, or take decisions on their behalf, simply because we think that their decisions are not prudent. As a matter of fact, the ban on paternalism is really intended to protect patients in situations where their view of what is best for them, and the view of the doctor or society, are at variance. We had better conclude, then, that these patients were capable of exercising a judgment of their own.

Now, did this mean that the doctors could leave the decision (and the responsibility for it) to the patients? No, we soon found out that it did not. We found it necessary to make another distinction as well, a distinction between, on the one hand, a doctor allowing a patient to exercise a judgment of his own in a troublesome situation (where his choice seems irrational to the doctor) and, on the other hand, a doctor placing a patient in a situation where he, the doctor, knows, or suspects, that the patient will make an irrational decision. The former may be unobjectionable. The doctor should, for example, not force a blood transfusion upon a patient who for religious reasons refuses to accept it, even if it means that the patient dies. But the latter is objectionable; it conforms to no reasonable rule of thumb in our medical practice. The doctor should not, if he can avoid it, put his religious patient in a situation where the patient needs a blood transfusion, if he knows that the patient will reject it. Suppose that, without treatment, a patient will die. There are two kinds of therapy available, a surgical one and a medical one. The surgical therapy succeeds in half of the cases, the medical one only in a third of the cases. In 90 percent of the cases the surgical therapy must, however, in order to succeed, be combined with blood transfusions. Suppose a doctor knows that his patient will, for religious reasons, reject a blood transfusion. The patient is willing to undergo surgery, however. He does not pay any attention whatever to probabilities. If God wishes him to survive, He will see to it that no blood transfusion is needed. Otherwise he will die, no matter what therapy is chosen, the patient believes. The doctor operates on him. As the doctor should have expected, the patient comes to need a blood transfusion but refuses to accept it and dies. Now it is not appropriate if the doctor tries the blame the death of the patient on the patient himself – or on God the Almighty. In the circumstances, the doctor should instead have chosen the medical therapy. To be sure, it is a reasonable rule of thumb to respect the theological convictions of a patient, on the grounds that medicine has no competence to assess the rationality of such convictions. However, this rule does not plausibly involve a right for the physician to suggest alternatives to patients such that, if the patient chooses them and happens to end up with serious (foreseeable) complications, he is forbidden by his theological beliefs to take necessary measures against these complications.

In a similar vein, we all agreed, eventually, that we had to face the question of whether the trial was in the best interest of the patients. We had to put ourselves in their shoes, in order to make a rational assessment of what the trial would mean to them.

5 Potential Benefits, Hazards and Discomforts

We turned to the Helsinki Declaration again. This time we looked closer at another paragraph, which looked more promising, to wit, II:2. According to this paragraph, the "potential benefits, hazards and discomforts of a new method should be weighed against the advantages of the best current diagnostic and therapeutic methods." The discussion of this problem came to involve qualitative as well as quantitative risk assessment; indeed, we ran into a deep problem concerning the concept of rationality.

How are we to do this weighing? A standard answer is that we should try to maximize expected utility. We make an account of the alternatives available. For each of the alternatives, we try to find out which are the possible outcomes. For each of these outcomes, we try to assess, both its utility (to the patient), and its probability. For each alternative we sum the products of probabilities and utilities and choose the alternative with the greatest sum.

We tried this method. Of course, when so doing, we had to simplify. We decided to assess utility solely in terms of longevity without too serious symptoms of AIDS. We had to estimate how much a patient who was killed by ddI would lose. We agreed to make a "conservative" assessment. Contrary to existing evidence, we conceded that, on average, this patient would lose as much as five years, i.e., we assumed that, on average, the patients outside the trial, who received zidovudine on a regular basis, would go on living a life without too serious symptoms of AIDS for another five years, while those who received ddI, and were killed by pancreatitis, were killed at once. When assessing probabilities we tried to make a reasonable use of all available evidence that was forthcoming. We were then faced with the following description of the case.

When a patient entered the trial he was subjected to a lottery. The probability that he would receive zidovudine only was 1/3, that he would receive ddI only was 1/3, and the probability that he would come to alternate between ddI and zidovudine, 1/3 as well. If he did not volunteer the probability was 1 that he would be treated with zidovudine only.

It seemed that if a patient would receive ddI only, he would be exposed to a slight risk of getting killed for nothing. At least this seems to be the assessment of the doctors conducting the research. But perhaps there were some possible gain. The patient, or some persons conducting the trial elsewhere, might believe that there was a plausible chance that ddI could work better than zidovudine for some patients. However, there was no *evidence* available that ddI was either superior or inferior to zidovudine. Both had known negative side-effects of various different kinds of roughly the same magnitude, but, on available evidence, only ddI seemed to kill one patient out of 500.

If the patient would receive zidovudine only, he would neither make any gain nor any loss in the trial, as compared to if he refused to enter it.

If the patient would be allowed to alternate between ddI and zidovudine, he would be exposed to a slight risk of being killed, but also to an expected benefit, measured in terms of longevity. We calculated how great this benefit must be, in order to make it rational for a patient to enter the trial.

To be sure, this cost-benefit utility calculus is awfully crude. It cannot by itself settle the case. However, if it would turn out that, on these crude assumptions, a patient in the third category had to gain a *lot* of time without too serious symptoms of AIDS, in order for it to be rational to enter the trial, then it *could* hardly be rational to enter, even if, in a particular case, the utility assessments could be more finely tuned. If this is what the crude assessment would look like, it should set off an alarm. This did not happen, however. Given our assumptions, it turned out that, if a patient in the third category, who alternated between the two drugs, gained on average more than, roughly, one week of life without too serious symptoms of AIDS, it would be rational to volunteer.[3] We found it reasonable to expect that, on average, the gain would be considerably greater than this.

This convinced a majority among us that the trial was defensible. However, a minority objected that the risk was still not worth taking. They referred to a different decision principle, a principle used by companies selling insurance (this principle has been defended in Prawitz, 1980). On this principle, there are some risks that are simply not worth taking. A company selling insurance does not sell, if it means that, should the worse come to the worst (no matter how improbable this is), the company would go bankrupt. Only after such alternatives have been eliminated is the company prepared to maximize expected utility. By the same token, these doctors argued, we ought not to try a new drug, even if it offers good hope of prolonging (somewhat) the life of a patient if, at the same time, there is a not negligible probability that it will end it at once.

The majority conceded that, in the circumstances, a 1/500 risk of getting killed is not negligible, but we objected that, if the remaining few years of a patient are of such importance, then a few more weeks should also be of considerable interest. This argument had no impact on these doctors, however. They saw, in the circumstances, a qualitative difference between, on the one hand, a patient being deprived of the last few years of his life and, on the other hand, a patient not being offered a few "extra" weeks (and even months).

The majority argued that by consistently maximizing expected utility we will in the long run achieve better results than if, consistently, we adhere to any competing principle. The minority objected, however, that this is irrelevant in situations where, because of our decision, there may not exist any long run where the method can prove its superiority.

The majority argued that, if we consider the patients as a group then, by continuing the trial, we probably do more good than harm. The minority conceded this point but argued that it was irrelevant. By focusing on the patients as a group we in the majority did not take seriously the fact that the patients were separate persons. It was wrong to sacrifice some of the patients, they argued, even if the group of patients would profit from it. We in the majority objected that, far from sacrificing individuals, we gave each a very reasonable offer, which he or she was allowed to accept or reject. The minority retorted, however, that, for reasons already stated, the offer was not reasonable. It was unethical to make it, they claimed.

The minority argued that the shaky evidential foundation of the estimate that 1 out of 500 patients might get killed by ddI was an additional reason to reject the trial. For all we know, they argued, the actual risk may well be 1/100, say. We in the majority conceded the latter point but argued that, as far as we know, it might also be 1/1000. However, 1/500 is the best estimate available. Then we ought to rely on it – and maximize expected utility.

No side in this dispute found any knock-down argument that convinced the other side.

6 Equipoise

At this point, it struck us that we had all the time been considering the rationality of entering the trial as such, the majority accepting that it could be rational for patients to enter it and the minority rejecting this. We now focused instead on each arm of the trial. It then transpired that, even among the majority, there was concern that one of the arms of the trial in particular, the one where the patients received ddI only, might be problematic. There was no evidence that ddI alone was more effective than zidovudine alone. These patients seemed to take a risk of 1 to 500 of getting killed, and they seemed to take it for nothing. Was not this objectionable? Was it reasonable to include this arm of the trial?

There is widespread agreement that ethics requires that each clinical trial begin with an honest null hypothesis, as pointed out by Robert J. Levine (Levine, 1986). A clinical trial requires what has by C. Fried been called "equipoise", a state of genuine uncertainty on the part of the clinical investigator regarding the comparative therapeutic merits of each arm in a trial (Fried, 1974). Did the doctors not know that giving only ddI to their patients was inferior to giving them only zidovudine?

This is to overstate the case. But they did have reasons to believe that the pure ddI alternative was inferior in one respect to the pure zidovudine alternative, while they had no corresponding reasons to believe that the pure zidovudine alternative was superior to the ddI alternative in any respect whatever. However, on Benjamin Freedman's interpretation of the requirement of equipoise, which we all found reasonable, this is irrelevant (Freedman, 1987). At least, this was what we in the majority thought about the situation. It was still reasonable to claim that an honest, professional disagreement among expert clinicians about the relative merits of these arms existed, at least if we were prepared, as the majority was, to play hazard with the life of the patients. And it is this state of "clinical" equipoise that is relevant, not the subjective judgment of the individual clinician, according to Freedman. For all we knew, the small disadvantage pertaining to ddI, *could* very well be balanced by some, not *yet* known, advantage pertaining to it.[4] If the trial was carried on, it would eventually be possible to say with some certainty if this was a fact or not.

The doctors in the minority were not satisfied with this, however. They felt this arm in particular should not have been included in the trial. They objected even to the third arm, where the patient altered between ddI and zidovudine. They objected that equipoise did not exist in the situation. All competent judges agreed that the patients who received ddI might get killed, and they all agreed that, on available evidence, the risk was not negligible. On their interpretation of the importance of this, there was no equipoise. On their conception of rationality, the trial would be unethical *even* if eventually it would transpire that ddI was slightly more effective than zidovudine. In their eyes, it was *obvious* that two arms of the trial, and, hence, also the trial as such, were inferior to the standard treatment.

7 Autonomy Once Again

The members of the conference were now grouped into two camps, a majority who found the trial as such, as well as each arm of it, acceptable, and who were prepared to offer it to their patients, and a minority, who found the trial as such objectionable, and who did not want to offer it to their patients. It then appeared, however, that there was one doctor in particular, who did not fully belong to any of these camps. She claimed that the pure ddI arm in particular was objectionable. She was not prepared to state any exact decision principle, to which she would plead allegiance, but she could vaguely state her position as follows. She accepted *some* hazards with the life of a patient, but only if there were a *substantial* chance of a corresponding benefit for the patient. She felt that this requirement was not satisfied for the pure ddI arm of the trial. She agreed with the minority that the trial should not be continued, and she did not want to offer the trial to her patients; however, she would have done so, she claimed, if this arm had not been there. I pointed out that there are several suggestions made by decision theorists that could serve as a rationale of her intuition (see, for example, Gärdenfors and Sahlin, 1988, and Levi, 1988). Common to these suggestions is that if our probability estimates are represented as intervals, which is a way of dealing with second-order uncertainty about them, then, when maximizing expected utility, one should take the most pessimistic value of these intervals as given. I feel myself that there is something very arbitrary about this. Moreover, as soon as we are prepared to countenance second-order probabilities other than 1 and 0, we are open to what decision theorists call a "Dutch strategy", i.e., it is possible to construct a series of bets, each of them reasonable in our lights, but such that if we accept them all, we are bound to lose (cf. van Fraassen, 1984). However, this doctor felt that there might be something to these suggestions, and it was not difficult to find a pessimistic value for the probability that a patient might get killed such that, while for the patients the pure ddI arm now turned out to be hazardous, the entire trial was worth entering into.

We in the majority tried to convince her to include her patients with the argument that, it was not she, but the lottery, who placed the patients in the pure ddI arm. Once they found themselves there – and since the trial was not blinded, they knew in which arm of the trial they had ended up – they should be allowed to decide for themselves whether to go on with the trial. As a matter of fact, the patients receiving merely ddI seemed relatively satisfied with this. At least they were happy that they were not given zidovudine only. They entertained false (in our light) expectations that ddI would cure them from AIDS. Our respect for their autonomy should allow them to stick to the trial, we suggested. It was up to these patients, when they had learnt that they would receive ddI only, to decide whether they should go on with the trial or not, and to take full (and exclusive)[5] responsibility for it.

This argument was partly accepted by this doctor. She concurred with the minority that the trial should not take place, in particular, she felt that this arm should not have been included in the trial in the first place. However, once it was there, and since the trial was going on, no matter what she felt about it, she now felt, somewhat surprisingly, that she could, for all that, offer it to her patients. After all, she too accepted that, even if one arm of the trial, the pure ddI arm, was inferior to not taking part in the trial, the trial as such (i.e., taking part in the lottery) was superior to not doing so.

8 Conclusion

Most of us who took part in the discussion felt reassured that the trial was defensible. When potential benefits, hazards and discomforts to the patients taking part in it were weighed, it transpired that, even when very conservative estimates were made of the gains and pessimistic estimates were made of the possible losses, the benefits were more substantial than the hazards and discomforts.

Those who were in the minority, however, found themselves trapped in a genuine dilemma. They felt that it was wrong to offer the trial to their patients. But they knew that, if they did not, the trial would still go on with other patients. And now their contribution to it would be that they made it scientifically less valuable. This, in turn, meant that the patients who, in their view of the matter, were sacrificed for the sake of science, were sacrificed for the sake of bad science rather than for good science.

It occurred to us all that this case is not unique. Many other trials of new drugs must raise the same problem. And so must many options of a more mundane kind in clinical *practice*. What risk of killing a patient are we allowed to take, when trying to free her of a certain inconvenience? I think of examples, such as when we want through surgery to repair the knee of an old woman. If the operation succeeds, we free her of her pain and she will become able to walk again. However, if we fail, we might not only destroy her knee completely, we might even come to kill her. Would it be ethically acceptable to offer the problem to the patient, for herself to solve? No matter *what* risks the patient was prepared to take, in order to be able possibly to walk again?

What conclusion are we to draw from this case study, and from similar examples that abound? First of all, to some of the doctors it came as a surprise – perhaps even as a shock – that subtle philosophical differences concerning the conception of rationality could have such an impact. This is as it should be, however. Philosophical differences are important, not only in this case, but in medicine in general. This is one lesson to be drawn from the case. Secondly, some of the doctors felt that there should exist some knock-down argument, that could settle the dispute over the conflicting views of rationality. They wanted me, *qua* professional philosopher, to provide it. But, of course, I could not do that. I could only state *my* reasons for siding with the majority, when they wanted to maximize expected utility. These reasons did not convince the members of the minority, however, who opted for a more cautious decisions principle. And, once again, the lesson is that this is as it should be. Our difference was philosophical and genuine, and, to my knowledge, there is no unanimity as to the correct solution of *any* genuinely philosophical question.[6] This means, however, that, within medicine we have to live with deep philosophical conflicts.

Philosophical conflicts do not strike the philosopher as very distressing. After all, intellectual conflicts are what philosophy is all about. And philosophy is a theoretical discipline. Aside from the academic world, there hardly exists any important philosophical practice. Therefore, philosophers need not disagree on serious practical matters. Medicine, however, is both theoretical and practical. And it is a disturbing but unavoidable fact that, within medicine, we have to endure irreconcilable differences of opinion on pressing practical matters, differences based on different philosophical outlooks, such as different conceptions of rationality.

Notes

1 Cf. Mill, 1962 [first published *c.* 1860], where he writes that "the only purpose for which power can be rightfully exercised over any member of a civilised community, against his will, is to prevent harm to others. His own good, either physical or moral, is not a sufficient warrant" (p. 135).

2 I have myself argued that it is not. Cf. Tännsjö, 1989, about this.

3 The mathematics is straightforward. The reader can easily, if he or she pleases, check my calculation.

4 The majority case should be strengthened if it was argued that it is not the state of indifference among clinicians that is relevant, but rather indifference (or equipoise) by the potential subjects. However, for reasons already stated, even we in the majority were reluctant to grant patients the right to exercise *this* kind of autonomy.

5 Note that exclusive responsibility does not follow from full responsibility. Two persons may each be fully responsible for one and the same event. Cf. Nozick, 1974, p. 130, about this.

6 It might be questioned whether the problem as to what conception of rationality is the most plausible one is a genuine one. Some may want to take up a nihilistic stance to this problem and argue that there is no fact of the matter in virtue of which one decision-principle is more plausible than another. As psychologists have shown, people are different, some people are more risk-aversive than others, and this is something they express in their adherence to one principle rather than the other. It would be absurd, however, to say that one conception is closer to the truth than the other. In the present context I will not try to assess the plausibility of this diagnosis. I notice only that, even if it would turn out to be correct, the conflicts over rationality, within medicine, would remain.

References

Freedman, B. (1987), 'Equipoise and the ethics of clinical research', *New England Journal of Medicine*, 317, 141–5.

Fried, C. (1974), *Medical Experimentation, Personal Integrity and Social Policy* (Amsterdam: North-Holland Publishing).

Gärdenfors, P. and Sahlin, N.-E. (1988), 'Unreliable probabilities, risk-taking, and decision-making', in Peter Gärdentors and Nils-Eric Sahlin (eds.), *Decision, Probability, and Utility – Selected Readings* (Cambridge: Cambridge University Press), pp. 313–35.

Levi, I. (1988), 'On indeterminate probabilities', in Peter Gärdentors and Nils-Eric Sahlin (eds.), *Decision, Probability, and Utility – Selected Readings* (Cambridge: Cambridge University Press), pp. 287–312.

Levine, R. J. (1986), *Ethics and Regulation of Clinical Research*, 2nd ed (Baltimore, MD: Urban & Schwarzenberg).

Mill, J. S. (1962) [first published *c.* 1860], 'On Liberty', in *Utilitarianism*, ed. Mary Warnock (London and Glasgow: Collins Fontana), pp. 126–250.

Nozick, R. (1974), *Anarchy, State and Utopia* (Oxford: Blackwell).

Prawitz, D. (1980), 'Rationalitet och kärnkraft', *Filosofisk tidskrift*, no. 1, 1–14.

Schafer, A. (1982), 'The ethics of the randomized clinical trial', *New England Journal of Medicine*, 307, 719–24.

Tännsjö, T. (1989), 'Against personal autonomy', *International Journal of Applied Philosophy* 4, 45–56.

van Fraassen, B. C. (1984), 'Belief and the will', *Journal of Philosophy*, 81, 235–56.

Wulff, H. R., Pedersen, S. A. and Rosenberg, R. (1990), *Philosophy of Medicine. An Introduction*, 2nd edn (Oxford: Blackwell).

Experimentation with Animals

55

Duties Towards Animals

Immanuel Kant

Baumgarten speaks of duties towards beings which are beneath us and beings which are above us. But so far as animals are concerned, we have no direct duties. Animals are not self-conscious and are there merely as a means to an end. That end is man. We can ask, 'Why do animals exist?' But to ask, 'Why does man exist?' is a meaningless question. Our duties towards animals are merely indirect duties towards humanity. Animal nature has analogies to human nature, and by doing our duties to animals in respect of manifestations which correspond to manifestations of human nature, we indirectly do our duty towards humanity. Thus, if a dog has served his master long and faithfully, his service, on the analogy of human service, deserves reward, and when the dog has grown too old to serve, his master ought to keep him until he dies. Such action helps to support us in our duties towards human beings, where they are bounden duties. If then any acts of animals are analogous to human acts and spring from the same principles, we have duties towards the animals because thus we cultivate the corresponding duties towards human beings. If a man shoots his dog because the animal is no longer capable of service, he does not fail in his duty to the dog, for the dog cannot judge, but his act is inhuman and damages in himself that humanity which it is his duty to show towards mankind. If he is not to stifle his human feelings, he must practise kindness towards animals, for he who is cruel to animals becomes hard also in his dealings with men. We can judge the heart of a man by his treatment of animals. Hogarth depicts this in his engravings ('The Stages of Cruelty', 1757). He shows how cruelty grows and develops. He shows the child's cruelty to animals, pinching the tail of a dog or a cat; he then depicts the grown man in his cart running over a child; and lastly, the culmination of cruelty in murder. He thus brings home to us in a terrible fashion the rewards of cruelty, and this should be an impressive lesson to children. The more we come in contact with animals and observe their behaviour, the more we love them, for we see how great is their care for their young. It is then difficult for us to be cruel in thought even to a wolf. Leibniz used a tiny worm for purposes of observation, and then carefully replaced it with its leaf on the tree so that it should not come to harm through any act of his. He would have been sorry – a natural feeling for a humane man – to destroy such a creature for no reason. Tender feelings towards dumb animals develop humane feelings towards mankind. In England butchers and doctors do not sit on a jury because they are accustomed to the sight of death and hardened. Vivisectionists, who use living animals for their experiments, certainly act cruelly, although their aim is praiseworthy, and they can justify their cruelty, since animals must be regarded as man's instruments; but any such cruelty for sport cannot be justified. A master who turns out his ass or his dog because the animal can no longer earn its keep manifests a small mind. The Greeks' ideas in this respect were high-minded, as can be seen from the fable of the ass and the bell of ingratitude. Our duties towards animals, then, are indirect duties towards mankind.

From *Lectures on Ethics*, trans. Louis Infield (New York: Harper & Row, 1963), pp. 239–41. Written about 1790; first published in German in 1924; this translation first published in 1930.

56

A Utilitarian View

Jeremy Bentham

What other agents then are there, which, at the same time that they are under the influence of man's direction, are susceptible of happiness? They are of two sorts: 1. Other human beings who are styled persons. 2. Other animals, which, on account of their interests having been neglected by the insensibility of the ancient jurists, stand degraded into the class of *things*.[1]

Note

1 Under the Gentoo and Mahometan religions, the interests of the rest of the animal creation seem to have met with some attention. Why have they not, universally, with as much as those of human creatures, allowance made for the difference in point of sensibility? Because the laws that are have been the work of mutual fear; a sentiment which the less rational animals have not had the same means as man has of turning to account. Why *ought* they not? No reason can be given. If the being eaten were all, there is very good reason why we should be suffered to eat such of them as we like to eat: we are the better for it, and they are never the worse. They have none of those long-protracted anticipations of future misery which we have. The death they suffer in our hands commonly is, and always may be, a speedier, and by that means a less painful one, than that which would await them in the inevitable course of nature. If the being killed were all, there is very good reason why we should be suffered to kill such as molest us: we should be the worse for their living, and they are never the worse for being dead. But is there any reason why we should be suffered to torment them? Not any that I can see. Are there any why we should *not* be suffered to torment them? Yes, several. The day has been, I grieve to say in many places it is not yet past, in which the greater part of the species, under the denomination of slaves, have been treated by the law exactly upon the same footing as, in England for example, the inferior races of animals are still. The day *may* come, when the rest of the animal creation may acquire those rights which never could have been withholden from them but by the hand of tyranny. The French have already discovered that the blackness of the skin is no reason why a human being should be abandoned without redress to the caprice of a tormentor. It may come one day to be recognized, that the number of the legs, the villosity of the skin, or the termination of the *os sacrum*, are reasons equally insufficient for abandoning a sensitive being to the same fate. What else is it that should trace the insuperable line? Is it the faculty of reason, or, perhaps, the faculty of discourse? But a full-grown horse or dog is beyond comparison a more rational, as well as a more conversable animal, than an infant of a day, or a week, or even a month, old. But suppose the case were otherwise, what would it avail? the question is not, Can they *reason?* nor, Can they *talk?* but, Can they *suffer?*

First published *c.*1820. From *An Introduction to the Principles of Morals and Legislation*, section XVIII, IV.

57

All Animals are Equal[1]

Peter Singer

In recent years a number of oppressed groups have campaigned vigorously for equality. The classic instance is the Black Liberation movement, which demands an end to the prejudice and discrimination that has made blacks second-class citizens. The immediate appeal of the black liberation movement and its initial, if limited, success made it a model for other oppressed groups to follow. We became familiar with liberation movements for Spanish-Americans, gay people, and a variety of other minorities. When a majority group – women – began their campaign, some thought we had come to the end of the road. Discrimination on the basis of sex, it has been said, is the last universally accepted form of discrimination, practiced without secrecy or pretense even in those liberal circles that have long prided themselves on their freedom from prejudice against racial minorities.

One should always be wary of talking of "the last remaining form of discrimination". If we have learnt anything from the liberation movements, we should have learnt how difficult it is to be aware of latent prejudice in our attitudes to particular groups until this prejudice is forcefully pointed out.

A liberation movement demands an expansion of our moral horizons and an extension or reinterpretation of the basic moral principle of equality. Practices that were previously regarded as natural and inevitable come to be seen as the result of an unjustifiable prejudice. Who can say with confidence that all his or her attitudes and practices are beyond criticism? If we wish to avoid being numbered amongst the oppressors, we must be prepared to rethink even our most fundamental attitudes. We need to consider them from the point of view of those most disadvantaged by our attitudes, and the practices that follow from these attitudes. If we can make this unaccustomed mental switch we may discover a pattern in our attitudes and practices that consistently operates so as to benefit one group – usually the one to which we ourselves belong – at the expense of another. In this way we may come to see that there is a case for a new liberation movement. My aim is to advocate that we make this mental switch in respect of our attitudes and practices towards a very large group of beings: members of species other than our own – or, as we popularly though misleadingly call them, animals. In other words, I am urging that we extend to other species the basic principle of equality that most of us recognize should be extended to all members of our own species.

All this may sound a little far-fetched, more like a parody of other liberation movements than a serious objective. In fact, in the past the idea of "The Rights of Animals" really has been used to parody the case for women's rights. When Mary Wollstonecraft, a forerunner of later feminists, published her *Vindication of the Rights of Women* in 1792, her ideas were widely regarded as absurd, and they were satirized in an anonymous publication entitled *A Vindication of the Rights of Brutes*. The author of this satire (actually Thomas Taylor, a distinguished Cambridge philosopher) tried to refute Wollstonecraft's reasonings by showing that they could be carried one stage further. If sound when applied to women, why should the

From *Philosophic Exchange* (1974), pp. 103–16.

arguments not be applied to dogs, cats and horses? They seemed to hold equally well for these "brutes"; yet to hold that brutes had rights was manifestly absurd; therefore the reasoning by which this conclusion had been reached must be unsound, and if unsound when applied to brutes, it must also be unsound when applied to women, since the very same arguments had been used in each case.

One way in which we might reply to this argument is by saying that the case for equality between men and women cannot validly be extended to nonhuman animals. Women have a right to vote, for instance, because they are just as capable of making rational decisions as men are; dogs, on the other hand, are incapable of understanding the significance of voting, so they cannot have the right to vote. There are many other obvious ways in which men and women resemble each other closely, while humans and other animals differ greatly. So, it might be said, men and women are similar beings, and should have equal rights, while humans and nonhumans are different and should not have equal rights.

The thought behind this reply to Taylor's analogy is correct up to a point, but it does not go far enough. There *are* important differences between humans and other animals, and these differences must give rise to *some* differences in the rights that each have. Recognizing this obvious fact, however, is no barrier to the case for extending the basic principle of equality to nonhuman animals. The differences that exist between men and women are equally undeniable, and the supporters of Women's Liberation are aware that these differences may give rise to different rights. Many feminists hold that women have the right to an abortion on request. It does not follow that since these same people are campaigning for equality between men and women they must support the right of men to have abortions too. Since a man cannot have an abortion, it is meaningless to talk of his right to have one. Since a pig can't vote, it is meaningless to talk of its right to vote. There is no reason why either Women's Liberation or Animal Liberation should get involved in such nonsense. The extension of the basic principle of equality from one group to another does not imply that we must treat both groups in exactly the same way, or grant exactly the same rights to both groups. Whether we should do so will depend on the nature of the members of the two groups. The basic principle of equality, I shall argue, is equality of consideration; and equal consideration for different beings may lead to different treatment and different rights.

So there is a different way of replying to Taylor's attempt to parody Wollstonecraft's arguments, a way which does not deny the differences between humans and nonhumans, but goes more deeply into the question of equality, and concludes by finding nothing absurd in the idea that the basic principle of equality applies to so-called "brutes". I believe that we reach this conclusion if we examine the basis on which our opposition to discrimination on grounds of race or sex ultimately rests. We will then see that we would be on shaky ground if we were to demand equality for blacks, women, and other groups of oppressed humans while denying equal consideration to nonhumans.

When we say that all human beings, whatever their race, creed or sex, are equal, what is it that we are asserting? Those who wish to defend a hierarchical, inegalitarian society have often pointed out that by whatever test we choose, it simply is not true that all humans are equal. Like it or not, we must face the fact that humans come in different shapes and sizes; they come with differing moral capacities, differing intellectual abilities, differing amounts of benevolent feeling and sensitivity to the needs of others, differing abilities to communicate effectively, and differing capacities to experience pleasure and pain. In short, if the demand for equality were based on the actual equality of all human beings, we would have to stop demanding equality. It would be an unjustifiable demand.

Still, one might cling to the view that the demand for equality among human beings is based on the actual equality of the different races and sexes. Although humans differ as individuals in various ways, there are no differences between the races and sexes *as such*. From the mere fact that a person is black, or a woman, we cannot infer anything else about that person. This, it may be said, is what is wrong with racism and sexism. The white racist claims that whites are superior to blacks, but this is false – although there are differences between individuals, some blacks are superior to some whites in all of the capacities and abilities that could conceivably be relevant. The opponent of sexism would say the same: a person's sex is no guide to his or her abilities, and this is why it is unjustifiable to discriminate on the basis of sex.

This is a possible line of objection to racial and sexual discrimination. It is not, however, the way that someone really concerned about equality would choose, because taking this line could, in some circumstances, force one to accept a most inegalitarian society. The fact that humans differ as individuals, rather than as races or sexes, is a valid reply to someone who defends a hierarchical society like, say, South Africa, in which all whites are superior in status to all blacks. The existence of individual variations that cut across the lines of race or sex, however, provides us with no defence at all against a more sophisticated opponent of equality, one who proposes that, say, the interests of those with ratings above 100. Would a hierarchical society of this sort really be so much better than one based on race or sex? I think not. But if we tie the moral principle of equality to the factual equality of the different races or sexes, taken as a whole, our opposition to racism and sexism does not provide us with any basis for objecting to this kind of inegalitarianism.

There is a second important reason why we ought not to base our opposition to racism and sexism on any kind of factual equality, even the limited kind that asserts that variations in capacities and abilities are spread evenly between the different races and sexes: we can have no absolute guarantee that these abilities and capacities really are distributed evenly, without regard to race or sex, among human beings. So far as actual abilities are concerned, there do seem to be certain measurable differences between both races and sexes. These differences do not, of course, appear in each case, but only when averages are taken. More important still, we do not yet know how much of these differences is really due to the different genetic endowments of the various races and sexes, and how much is due to environmental differences that are the result of past and continuing discrimination. Perhaps all of the important differences will eventually prove to be environmental rather than genetic. Anyone opposed to racism and sexism will certainly hope that this will be so, for it will make the task of ending discrimination a lot easier; nevertheless it would be dangerous to rest the case against racism and sexism on the belief that all significant differences are environmental in origin. The opponent of, say, racism who takes this line will be unable to avoid conceding that if differences in ability did after all prove to have some genetic connection with race, racism would in some way be defensible.

It would be folly for the opponent of racism to stake his whole case on a dogmatic commitment to one particular outcome of a difficult scientific issue which is still a long way from being settled. While attempts to prove that differences in certain selected abilities between races and sexes are primarily genetic in origin have certainly not been conclusive, the same must be said of attempts to prove that these differences are largely the result of environment. At this stage of the investigation we cannot be certain which view is correct, however much we may hope it is the latter.

Fortunately, there is no need to pin the case for equality to one particular outcome of this scientific investigation. The appropriate response to those who claim to have found evidence of genetically-based differences in ability between the races or sexes is not to stick to the belief that the genetic explanation must be wrong, whatever evidence to the contrary may turn up: instead we should make it quite clear that the claim to equality does not depend on intelligence, moral capacity, physical strength, or similar matters of fact. Equality is a moral ideal, not a simple assertion of fact. There is no logically compelling reason for assuming that a factual difference in ability between two people justifies any difference in the amount of consideration we give to satisfying their needs and interests. The principle of the equality of human beings is not a description of an alleged actual equality among humans: it is a prescription of how we should treat humans.

Jeremy Bentham incorporated the essential basis of moral equality into his utilitarian system of ethics in the formula: "Each to count for one and none for more than one." In other words, the interests of every being affected by an action are to be taken into account and given the same weight as the like interests of any other being. A later utilitarian, Henry Sidgwick, put the point in this way: "The good of any one individual is of no more importance, from the point of view (if I may say so) of the Universe, than the good of any other."[2] More recently, the leading figures in contemporary moral philosophy have shown a great deal of agreement in specifying as a fundamental presupposition of their moral theories some similar requirement which operates so as to give everyone's interests equal consideration – although they cannot agree on how this requirement is best formulated.[3]

It is an implication of this principle of equality that our concern for others ought not to depend on what they are like, or what abilities they possess – although precisely what this concern requires us to do may vary according to the characteristics of those affected by what we do. It is on this basis that the case against racism and the case against sexism must both ultimately rest; and it is in accordance with this principle that speciesism is also to be condemned. If possessing a higher degree of intelligence does not entitle one human to use another for his own ends, how can it entitle humans to exploit non-humans?

Many philosophers have proposed the principle of equal consideration of interests, in some form or other, as a basic moral principle; but, as we shall see in more detail shortly, not many of them have recognized that this principle applies to members of other species as well as to our own. Bentham was one of the few who did realize this. In a forward-looking passage, written at a time when black slaves in the British dominions were still being treated much as we now treat nonhuman animals, Bentham wrote:

> The day *may* come when the rest of the animal creation may acquire those rights which never could have been witholden from them but by the hand of tyranny. The French have already discovered that the blackness of the skin is no reason why a human being should be abandoned without redress to the caprice of a tormentor. It may one day come to be recognised that the number of the legs, the villosity of the skin, or the termination of the *os sacrum*, are reasons equally insufficient for abandoning a sensitive being to the same fate. What else is it that should trace the insuperable line? Is it the faculty of reason, or perhaps the faculty of discourse? But a full-grown horse or dog is beyond comparison a more rational, as well as a more conversable animal, than an infant of a day, or a week, or even a month, old. But suppose they were otherwise, what would it avail? The question is not, Can they reason? nor Can they *talk*? but, *Can they suffer*?[7]

In this passage Bentham points to the capacity for suffering as the vital characteristic that gives a being the right to equal consideration. The capacity for suffering – or more strictly, for suffering and/or enjoyment or happiness – is not just another characteristic like the capacity for language, or for higher mathematics. Bentham is not saying that those who try to mark "the insuperable line" that determines whether the interests of a being should be considered happen to have selected the wrong characteristic. The capacity for suffering and enjoying things is a prerequisite for having interests at all, a condition that must be satisfied before we can speak of interests in any meaningful way. It would be nonsense to say that it was not in the interests of a stone to be kicked along the road by a schoolboy. A stone does not have interests because it cannot suffer. Nothing that we can do to it could possibly make any difference to its welfare. A mouse, on the other hand, does have an interest in not being tormented, because it will suffer if it is.

If a being suffers, there can be no moral justification for refusing to take that suffering into consideration. No matter what the nature of the being, the principle of equality requires that its suffering be counted equally with the like suffering – in so far as rough comparisons can be made – of any other being. If a being is not capable of suffering, or of experiencing enjoyment or happiness, there is nothing to be taken into account. This is why the limit of sentience (using the term as a convenient, if not strictly accurate, shorthand for the capacity to suffer or experience enjoyment or happiness) is the only defensible boundary of concern for the interests of others. To mark this boundary by some characteristic like intelligence or rationality would be to mark it in an arbitrary way. Why not choose some other characteristic, like skin color?

The racist violates the principle of equality by giving greater weight to the interests of members of his own race, when there is a clash between their interests and the interests of those of another race. Similarly the speciesist allows the interests of his own species to override the greater interests of members of other species.[5] The pattern is the same in each case. Most human beings are speciesists. I shall now very briefly describe some of the practices that show this.

For the great majority of human beings, especially in urban, industrialized societies, the most direct form of contact with members of other species is at meal-times: we eat them. In doing so we treat them purely as means to our ends. We regard their life and well-being as subordinate to our taste for a particular kind of dish. I say "taste" deliberately – this is purely a matter of pleasing our palate. There can be no defence of eating flesh in terms of satisfying nutritional needs, since it has been established beyond doubt that we could satisfy our need for protein and other essential nutrients far more efficiently with a diet that replaced animal flesh by soy beans, or products derived from soy beans, and other high-protein vegetable products.[6]

It is not merely the act of killing that indicates what we are ready to do to other species in order to gratify our tastes. The suffering we inflict on the animals while they are alive is perhaps an even clearer indication of our speciesism than the fact that we are prepared to kill them.[7] In order to have meat on the table at a price that people can afford, our society tolerates methods of meat production that confine sentient animals in cramped, unsuitable conditions for the entire durations of their lives. Animals are treated like machines that convert fodder into flesh, and any innovation that results in a higher "conversion ratio" is liable to be adopted. As one authority on the subject has said, "cruelty is acknowledged only when profitability ceases."[8] So hens are crowded four or five to a cage with a floor area of twenty inches by eighteen inches, or around the size of a single page of the *New York Times*. The cages have wire floors, since this reduces cleaning costs, though wire is unsuitable for the hens' feet; the floors slope, since this makes the eggs roll down for easy collection, although this makes it difficult for the hens to rest comfortably. In these conditions all the birds' natural instincts are thwarted: they cannot stretch their wings fully, walk freely, dust-bathe, scratch the ground, or build a nest. Although they have never known other conditions, observers have noticed that the birds vainly try to perform these actions. Frustrated at their inability to do so, they often develop what farmers call "vices", and peck each other to death. To prevent this, the beaks of young birds are often cut off.

This kind of treatment is not limited to poultry. Pigs are now also being reared in cages inside sheds. These animals are comparable to dogs in intelligence, and need a varied, stimulating environment if they are not to suffer from stress and boredom. Anyone who kept a dog in the way in which pigs are frequently kept would be liable to prosecution, in England at least, but because our interest in exploiting pigs is greater than our interest in exploiting dogs, we object to cruelty to dogs while consuming the produce of cruelty to pigs. Of the other animals, the condition of veal calves is perhaps worst of all, since these animals are so closely confined that they cannot even turn around or get up and lie down freely. In this way they do not develop unpalatable muscle. They are also made anaemic and kept short of roughage, to keep their flesh pale, since white veal fetches a higher price; as a result they develop a craving for iron and roughage, and have been observed to gnaw wood off the sides of their stalls, and lick greedily at any rusty hinge that is within reach.

Since, as I have said, none of these practices cater for anything more than our pleasures of taste, our practice of rearing and killing other animals in order to eat them is a clear instance of the sacrifice of the most important interests of other beings in order to satisfy trivial interests of our own. To avoid speciesism we must stop this practice, and each of us has a moral obligation to cease supporting the practice. Our custom is all the support that the meat industry needs. The decision to cease giving it that support may be difficult, but it is no more difficult than it would have been for a white Southerner to go against the traditions of his society and free his slaves; if we do not change our dietary habits, how can we censure those slaveholders who would not change their own way of living?

The same form of discrimination may be observed in the widespread practice of experimenting on other species in order to see if certain substances are safe for human beings, or to test some psychological theory about the effect of severe punishment on learning, or to try out various new compounds just in case something turns up. People sometimes think that all this experimentation is for vital medical purposes, and so will reduce suffering overall. This comfortable belief is very wide of the mark. Drug companies test new shampoos and cosmetics that they are intending to put on the market by dropping them into the eyes of rabbits, held open by metal clips, in order to observe what damage results. Food additives, like artificial colorings and preservatives, are tested by what is known as the "LD_{50}" – a test designed to find the level of consumption at which 50 per cent of a group of animals will die. In the process, nearly all of the animals are made very sick before some finally die, and others pull through. If the substance is relatively harmless, as it often is, huge doses have to be force-fed to the animals, until in some cases sheer volume or concentration of the substance causes death.

Much of this pointless cruelty goes on in the universities. In many areas of science, nonhuman animals are regarded as an item of laboratory equipment, to be used and expended as desired. In psychology laboratories experimenters devise endless variations and repetitions of experiments that were of little value in the first place. To quote just one example, from the experimenter's own account in a psychology journal: at the University of Pennsylvania, Perrin S. Cohen hung six dogs in hammocks with electrodes taped to their hind feet. Electric shock of varying intensity was then administered through the electrodes. If the dog learnt to press its head against a panel on the left, the shock was turned off, but otherwise it remained on indefinitely. Three of the dogs, however, were required to wait periods varying from 2 to 7 seconds while being shocked before making the response that turned off the current. If they failed to wait, they received further shocks. Each dog was given from 26 to 46 "sessions" in the hammock, each session consisting of 80 "trials" or shocks, administered at intervals of one minute. The experimenter reported that the dogs, who were unable to move in the hammock, barked or bobbed their heads when the current was applied. The reported findings of the experiment were that there was a delay in the dogs' responses that increased proportionately to the time the dogs were required to endure the shock, but a gradual increase in the intensity of the shock had no systematic effect in the timing of the response. The experiment was funded by the National Institutes of Health and the United States Public Health Service.[9]

In this example, and countless cases like it, the possible benefits to mankind are either nonexistent or fantastically remote; while the certain losses to members of other species are very real. This is, again, a clear indication of speciesism.

In the past, argument about vivesection has often missed this point, because it has been put in absolutist terms: would the abolitionist be prepared to let thousands die if they could be saved by experimenting on a single animal? The way to reply to this purely hypothetical question is to pose another: would the experimenter be prepared to perform his experiment on an orphaned human infant, if that were the only way to save many lives? (I say "orphan" to avoid the complication of parental feelings, although in doing so I am being overfair to the experimenter, since the nonhuman subjects of experiments are not orphans.) If the experimenter is not prepared to use an orphaned human infant, then his readiness to use nonhumans is simple discrimination, since adult apes, cats, mice, and other mammals are more aware of what is happening to them, more self-directing and, so far as we can tell, at least as sensitive to pain, as any human infant. There seems to be no relevant characteristic that human infants possess that adult mammals do not have to the same or a higher degree. (Someone might try to argue that what makes it wrong to experiment on a human infant is that the infant will, in time and if left alone, develop into more than the nonhuman, but one would then, to be consistent, have to oppose abortion, since the fetus has the same potential as the infant – indeed, even contraception and abstinence might be wrong on this ground, since the egg and sperm, considered jointly, also have the same potential. In any case, this argument still gives us no reason for selecting a nonhuman, rather than a human with severe and irreversible brain damage, as the subject for our experiments.)

The experimenter, then, shows a bias in favor of his own species whenever he carries out an experiment on a nonhuman for a purpose that he would not think justified him in using a human being at an equal or lower level of sentience, awareness, ability to be self-directing, etc. No one familiar with the kind of results yielded by most experiments on animals can have the slightest doubt that if this bias were eliminated the number of experiments performed would be a minute fraction of the number performed today.

Experimenting on animals, and eating their flesh, are perhaps the two major forms of speciesism in our society. By comparison, the third and last form of speciesism is so minor as to be insignificant, but it is perhaps of some special interest to those for whom this paper was written. I am referring to speciesism in contemporary philosophy.

Philosophy ought to question the basic assumptions of the age. Thinking through, critically and carefully, what most people take for granted is, I believe, the chief task of philosophy, and it is this task that makes philosophy a worthwhile activity. Regrettably, philosophy does not always live up to its historic role. Philosophers are human beings and they are subject to all the preconceptions of the society to which they belong. Sometimes they succeed in breaking free of the prevailing ideology: more often they become its most sophisticated defenders. So, in this case, philosophy as practiced in the universities today does not challenge anyone's preconceptions about our relations with other species. By their writings, those philosophers who tackle problems that touch upon the issue reveal that they make the same unquestioned assumptions as most other humans, and what they say tends to confirm the reader in his or her comfortable speciesist habits.

I could illustrate this claim by referring to the writings of philosophers in various fields – for instance, the attempts that have been made by those interested in rights to draw the boundary of the sphere of rights so that it runs parallel to the biological boundaries of the species *Homo sapiens*, including infants and even mental defectives, but excluding those other beings of equal or greater capacity who are so useful to us at mealtimes and in our laboratories. I think it would be a more appropriate conclusion to this paper, however, if I concentrated on the problem with which we have been centrally concerned, the problem of equality.

It is significant that the problem of equality, in moral and political philosophy, is invariably formulated in terms of human equality. The effect of this is that the question of the equality of other animals does not confront the philosopher or student as an issue in itself – and this is already an indication of the failure of philosophy to challenge accepted beliefs. Still, philosophers have found it difficult to discuss the issue of human equality without raising, in a paragraph or two, the question of the status of other animals. The reason for this, which should be apparent from what I have said already, is that if humans are to be regarded as equal to one another, we need some sense of "equal" that does not require any actual, descriptive equality of capacities, talents or other qualities. If equality is to be related to any actual characteristics of humans, these characteristics must be some lowest common denominator, pitched so low that no human lacks them – but then the philosopher comes up against the catch that any such set of characteristics which covers *all* humans will not be possessed *only by humans*. In other words, it turns out that in the only sense in which we can truly say, as an assertion of fact, that all humans are equal, at least some members of other species are also equal – equal, that is, to each other and to humans. If, on the other hand, we regard the statement "All humans are equal" in some nonfactual way, perhaps as a prescription, then, as I have already argued, it is even more difficult to exclude nonhumans from the sphere of equality.

This result is not what the egalitarian philosopher originally intended to assert. Instead of accepting the radical outcome to which their own reasonings naturally point, however, most philosophers try to reconcile their beliefs in human equality and animal inequality by arguments that can only be described as devious.

As a first example, I take William Frankena's well-known article "The Concept of Social Justice."[10] Frankena opposes the idea of basing justice on merit, because he sees that this could lead to highly inegalitarian results. Instead he proposes the principle that:

> all men are to be treated as equals, not because they are equal, in any respect but simply because they are human. They are human because they have emotions and desires, and are able to think, and hence are capable of enjoying a good life in a sense in which other animals are not.

But what is this capacity to enjoy the good life which all humans have, but no other animals? Other animals have emotions and desires, and appear to be capable of enjoying a good life. We may doubt that they can think – although the behavior of some apes, dolphins and even dogs suggests that some of them can – but what is the relevance of thinking? Frankena goes on to admit that by "the good life" he means "not so much the morally good life as the happy or satisfactory life," so thought would appear to be unnecessary for enjoying the good life; in fact to emphasize the need for thought would make difficulties for the egalitarian since only some people are capable of leading intellectually satisfying lives or morally good lives. This makes it difficult to see what Frankena's principle of equality has to do with simply being *human*. Surely every sentient being is capable of leading a life that is happier or less miserable than some alternative life, and hence has a claim to be taken into account. In this respect the distinction between humans and nonhumans is not a sharp division, but rather a continuum along which we move gradually, and with overlaps between the species, from simple capacities for enjoyment and satisfaction, or pain and suffering, to more complex ones.

Faced with a situation in which they see a need for some basis for the moral gulf that is commonly thought to separate humans and animals, but can find no concrete difference that will do the job without undermining the equality of humans, philosophers tend to waffle. They resort to high-sounding phrases like "the intrinsic dignity of the human individual";[11] They talk of the "intrinsic worth of all men" as if men (humans?) had some worth that other beings did not,[12] or they say that humans, and only humans, are "ends in themselves," while "everything other than a person can only have value for a person."[13]

This idea of a distinctive human dignity and worth has a long history; it can be traced back directly to the Renaissance humanists, for instance to Pico della Mirandola's *Oration on the Dignity of Man*. Pico and other humanists based their estimate of human dignity on the idea that man possessed the central, pivotal position in the "Great Chain of Being" that led from the lowliest forms of matter to God himself; this view of the universe, in turn, goes back to both classical and Judeo-Christian doctrines. Contemporary philosophers have cast off these metaphysical and religious shackles and freely invoke the dignity of mankind without needing to justify the idea at all. Why should we not attribute "intrinsic dignity" or "intrinsic worth" to ourselves? Fellow-humans are unlikely to reject the accolades we so generously bestow on them, and those to whom we deny the honor are unable to object. Indeed, when one thinks only of humans, it can be very liberal, very progressive, to talk of the dignity of all human beings. In so doing, we implicitly condemn slavery, racism, and other violations of human rights. We admit that we ourselves are in some fundamental sense on a par with the poorest, most ignorant members of our own species. It is only when we think of humans as no more than a small subgroup of all the beings that inhabit our planet that we may realize that in elevating our own species we are at the same time lowering the relative status of all other species.

The truth is that the appeal to the intrinsic dignity of human beings appears to solve the egalitarian's problems only as long as it goes unchallenged. Once we ask *why* it should be that all humans – including infants, mental defectives, psychopaths, Hitler, Stalin and the rest – have some kind of dignity or worth that no elephant, pig, or chimpanzee can ever achieve, we see that this question is as difficult to answer as our original request for some relevant fact that justifies the inequality of humans and other animals. In fact, these two questions are really one: talk of intrinsic dignity or moral worth only takes the problem back one step, because any satisfactory defence of the claim that all and only humans have intrinsic dignity would need to refer to some relevant capacities or characteristics that all and only humans possess. Philosophers frequently introduce ideas of dignity, respect and worth at the point at which other reasons appear to be lacking, but this is hardly good enough. Fine phrases are the last resource of those who have run out of arguments.

In case there are those who still think it may be possible to find some relevant characteristic that distinguishes all humans from all members of other species, I shall refer again, before I conclude, to the existence of some humans who quite clearly are below the level of awareness, self-consciousness, intelligence, and sentience, of many nonhumans. I am thinking of humans with severe and irreparable brain damage, and also of infant humans. To avoid the complication of the relevance of a being's potential, however, I shall henceforth concentrate on permanently retarded humans.

Philosophers who set out to find a characteristic that will distinguish humans from other animals rarely take the course of abandoning these groups of humans by lumping them in with the other animals. It is easy to see why they do not. To take this line without rethinking our attitudes to other animals would entail that we have the right to perform painful experiments on retarded humans for trivial reasons; similarly it would follow that we had the right to rear and kill these humans for food. To most philosophers these consequences are as unacceptable as the view that we should stop treating non-humans in this way.

Of course, when discussing the problem of equality it is possible to ignore the problem of mental defectives, or brush it aside as if somehow insignificant.[14] This is the easiest way out. What else remains? My final example of speciesism in contemporary philosophy has been selected to show what happens when a writer is prepared to face the question of human equality and animal inequality without ignoring the existence of mental defectives, and without resorting to obscurantist mumbo-jumbo. Stanley Benn's clear and honest article "Egalitarianism and Equal Consideration of Interests"[15] fits this description.

Benn, after noting the usual "evident human inequalities" argues, correctly I think, for equality of consideration as the only possible basis for egalitarianism. Yet Benn, like other writers, is thinking only of "equal consideration of human interests". Benn is quite open in his defence of this restriction of equal consideration:

> not to possess human shape *is* a disqualifying condition. However faithful or intelligent a dog may be, it would be a monstrous sentimentality to attribute to him interests that could be weighed in an equal balance with those of

human beings ... if, for instance, one had to decide between feeding a hungry baby or a hungry dog, anyone who chose the dog would generally be reckoned morally defective, unable to recognize a fundamental inequality of claims.

This is what distinguishes our attitude to animals from our attitude to imbeciles. It would be odd to say that we ought to respect equally the dignity or personality of the imbecile and of the rational man ... but there is nothing odd about saying that we should respect their interests equally, that is, that we should give to the interests of each the same serious consideration as claims to considerations necessary for some standard of well-being that we can recognize and endorse.

Benn's statement of the basis of the consideration we should have for imbeciles seems to me correct, but why should there be any fundamental inequality of claims between a dog and a human imbecile? Benn sees that if equal consideration depended on rationality, no reason could be given against using imbeciles for research purposes, as we now use dogs and guinea pigs. This will not do: "But of course we do distinguish imbeciles from animals in this regard," he says. That the common distinction is justifiable is something Benn does not question; his problem is how it is to be justified. The answer he gives is this:

> we respect the interests of men and give them priority over dogs not *insofar* as they are rational, but because rationality is the human norm. We say it is *unfair* to exploit the deficiencies of the imbecile who falls short of the norm, just as it would be unfair, and not just ordinarily dishonest, to steal from a blind man. If we do not think in this way about dogs, it is because we do not see the irrationality of the dog as a deficiency or a handicap, but as normal for the species. The characteristics, therefore, that distinguish the normal man from the normal dog make it intelligible for us to talk of other men having interests and capacities, and therefore claims, of precisely the same kind as we make on our own behalf. But although these characteristics may provide the point of the distinction between men and other species, they are not in fact the qualifying conditions for membership, or the distinguishing criteria of the class of morally considerable persons; and this is precisely because a man does not become a member of a different species, with its own standards of normality, by reason of not possessing these characteristics.

The final sentence of this passage gives the argument away. An imbecile, Benn concedes, may have no characteristics superior to those of a dog; nevertheless this does not make the imbecile a member of "a different species" as the dog is. *Therefore* it would be "unfair" to use the imbecile for medical research as we use the dog. But why? That the imbecile is not rational is just the way things have worked out, and the same is true of the dog – neither is any more responsible for their mental level. If it is unfair to take advantage of an isolated defect, why is it fair to take advantage of a more general limitation? I find it hard to see anything in this argument except a defence of preferring the interests of members of our own species because they are members of our own species. To those who think there might be more to it, I suggest the following mental exercise. Assume that it has been proven that there is a difference in the average, or normal, intelligence quotient for two different races, say whites and blacks. Then substitute the term "white" for every occurrence of "men" and "black" for every occurrence of "dog" in the passage quoted; and substitute "high IQ" for "rationality" and when Benn talks of "imbeciles" replace this term by "dumb whites" – that is, whites who fall well below the normal white IQ score. Finally, change "species" to "race." Now reread the passage. It has become a defence of a rigid, no-exceptions division between whites and blacks, based on IQ scores, *not withstanding an admitted overlap* between whites and blacks in this respect. The revised passage is, of course, outrageous, and this is not only because we have made fictitious assumptions in our substitutions. The point is that in the original passage Benn was defending a rigid division in the amount of consideration due to members of different species, despite admitted cases of overlap. If the original did not, at first reading, strike us as being as outrageous as the revised version does, this is largely because although we are not racists ourselves, most of us are speciesists. Like the other articles, Benn's stands as a warning of the ease with which the best minds can fall victim to a prevailing ideology.

Notes

1 Passages of this article appeared in a review of *Animals, Men and Morals*, edited by S. and R. Godlovitch and J. Harris (London: Gollanez and Taplinger, 1972) in the *New York Review of Books*, April 5, 1973. The whole direction of my thinking on this subject I owe to talks with a number of friends in Oxford in 1970–1, especially Richard Keshen, Stanley Godlovitch, and, above all, Roslind Godlovitch.

2 *The Methods of Ethics*, 7th edn, p. 382.

3 For example, R. M. Hare, *Freedom and Reason* (Oxford, 1963) and J. Rawls, *A Theory of Justice* (Harvard, 1972); for a brief account of the essential agreement on this issue between these and other positions, see R. M. Hare, "Rules of War and Moral Reasoning," *Philosophy and Public Affairs*, I, no. 2 (1972).

4 *Introduction to the Principles of Morals and Legislation*, ch. XVII.

5 I owe the term "speciesism" to Dr Richard Ryder.

6 In order to produce 1 lb of protein in the form of beef or veal, we must feed 21 lb of protein to the animal. Other forms of livestock are slightly less inefficient, but the average ratio in the US is still 1:8. It has been estimated that the amount of protein lost to humans in this way is equivalent to 90% of the annual world protein deficit. For a brief account, see Frances Moore Lappe, *Diet for a Small Planet* (New York: Friends of the Earth/Ballantine, 1971), pp. 4–11.

7 Although one might think that killing a being is obviously the ultimate wrong one can do to it, I think that the infliction of suffering is a clearer indication of speciesism because it might be argued that at least part of what is wrong with killing a human is that most humans are conscious of their existence over time, and have desires and purposes that extend into the future – see, for instance, M. Tooley, "Abortion and Infanticide", *Philosophy and Public Affairs*, 2, no. 1 (1972). Of course, if one took this view one would have to hold – as Tooley does – that killing a human infant or mental defective is not in itself wrong, and is less serious than killing certain higher mammals that probably do have a sense of their own existence over time.

8 Ruth Harrison, *Animal Machines* (London: Stuart, 1964). This book provides an eye-opening account of intensive farming methods for those unfamiliar with the subject.

9 *Journal of the Experimental Analysis of Behavior*, 13, no. 1 (1970). Any recent volume of this journal, or of other journals in the field, like the *Journal of Comparative and Physiological Psychology*, will contain reports of equally cruel and trivial experiments. For a fuller account, see Richard Ryder, "Experiments on Animals" in *Animals, Men and Morals.*

10 In R. Brandt (ed.), *Social Justice* (Englewood Cliffs, NJ: Prentice-Hall, 1962); the passage quoted appears on p. 19.

11 Frankena in Brandt, *Social Justice*, p. 23.

12 H. A. Bedau, "Egalitarianism and the Idea of Equality" in *Nomos IX: Equality*, ed. J. R. Pennock and J. W. Chapman (New York 1967)

13 G. Vlastos, "Justice and Equality" in Brandt, *Social Justice*, p. 48.

14 For example, Bernard Williams, "The Idea of Equality", in *Philosophy, Politics and Society* (second series) ed. P. Laslett and W. Runciman (Oxford: Blackwell, 1962), p. 118; J. Rawls, *A Theory of Justice*, pp. 509–10.

15 *Nomos IX: Equality*; the passages quoted are on pp. 62ff.

58

Vivisection, Morals and Medicine: An Exchange

R. G. Frey and Sir William Paton

Note

If one wishes to accept that some painful animal experimentation can be justified on grounds that benefit is conferred, one is faced with a difficult moral dilemma argues the first author, a philosopher. Either one needs to be able to say why human lives of any quality however low should be inviolable from painful experimentation when animal lives are not; or one should accept that sufficient benefit can justify certain painful experiments on human beings of sufficiently low quality of life. Alternatively, one can reject the original premise and accept antivivisectionism.

Morals and Medicine

R. G. Frey

I am not an antivivisectionist, and I am not in part for the same reason most people are not, namely, that vivisection can be justified by the benefits it confers. I do not believe it is widely realized, however, to what those who employ this reason are committed. Since many medical people also employ it to justify animal experiments, I think some discussion of the most important of these commitments is in order here. That members of the medical profession will almost certainly find this commitment repugnant in the extreme is perhaps reason enough for making sure that they are aware of it and of why they are in need of some means of avoiding it. (In order to stress this commitment, I am going only to sketch some matters and to avoid some others which, in a fuller treatment of vivisection, would have to be explored. My remarks are non-technical and will be familiar to those knowledgeable of recent controversies involving utilitarianism and the taking of life and of the work on vivisection of Peter Singer, one of the utilitarians involved in these controversies.)

From *Journal of Medical Ethics*, vol. 9 (1983), pp. 94–7, 102–4. Reprinted by courtesy of Professor R. G. Frey.

I

Most people are not antivivisectionists, I suspect, because they think that some benefit or range of benefits can justify experiments, including painful ones, on animals. Increasingly, there are some things such people do not think; for example, that they are committed (i) to regarding simply anything – another floor polish, another eye shadow, for which animals have suffered – as a benefit, (ii) to approving of simply any experiment whatever on animals, in the hallowed name of research, (iii) to foregoing criticism of certain experiments as trivial or unnecessary or a (mere) PhD exercise, (iv) to halting the search for alternatives to the use of animals or to refraining from criticism of scientists who, before commencing experiments, conduct at best a perfunctory search for such alternatives, (v) to approving of (extravagant) wastage, as when twenty rabbits are used where five will do, and (vi) to refraining, in the case of some painful experiments, from a long, hard look at whether even *this* projected benefit is really important and substantial enough to warrant the infliction of *this* degree of pain.

Who benefits? Sometimes animals do, and sometimes both humans and animals do; but, not infrequently, indeed, perhaps typically, the experiments are carried out on animals with an eye to human benefit.

Some antivivisectionists appear to reject this appeal to benefit. I have in mind especially those who have, as it were, a two-stage position, who begin by objecting to painful animal experiments and eventually move on to objecting to animal experiments per se. Among other reasons for this move, two are noteworthy here. First, vivisectionists may well seek to reduce and eliminate the pain involved in an experiment, for example by redesigning it, by dropping parts of it, by adopting different methods for carrying it out, by the use of drugs and pain-killers (and by fostering new developments in drugs, pain-killers, and genetic engineering), by painlessly disposing of the animals before they come to feel post-operative pain, and so on. The point, of course, is not that the vivisectionist must or will inevitably succeed in his, or her, aim but rather that, if he did, or to the extent that he does, the argument from pain would, or does, cease to apply. Thus, giving up painful experiments may well not be the only or the only effective way of dealing with the pain they involve. So, it is tempting to shift to a condemnation of animal experiments per se, which at once reduces the manoeuvrings of the vivisectionist over pain to nothing. Second, and, to a great many antivivisectionists, possibly even more importantly, the pain argument has nothing to say to the countless millions of painless and relatively painless animal experiments performed each year throughout the world; and these, I should have thought, vastly outnumber the painful ones. So, in order to encompass them in one's antivivisectionism, it is once again tempting to shift to a condemnation of animal experiments per se.

The above in no way denies, of course, that the antivivisectionist may want to deal first with painful experiments, before turning to look at any others; but turn he will, if those I have talked to are representative. For, in the end, *it is the use of animals as experimental subjects at all*, not just or possibly even primarily their use as subjects of painful experiments, that I have found lies at the bottom of their antivivisectionism.

To the vivisectionist, the antivivisectionist would appear to think that *no* benefit is important and substantial enough to justify painful animal experiments and, eventually, that *no* benefit is important and substantial enough to justify animal experiments. And this position, the vivisectionist will think, is very unlikely to recommend itself to many people. It is obvious why. Would your view of Salk vaccine simply be turned on its head, if it came to light that it was tested on monkeys or that some monkeys suffered pain (perhaps even intense pain) in the course of testing it or that it is made by cultivating strains of a virus in monkey tissue?

It would be silly to pretend that all animal experiments are of vast, stupendous importance; it would be equally silly, however, to deny that benefit has accrued to us (and sometimes to animals) through animal experimentation. (Often, the problem is that a series of experiments, at different times, by different people, enable still someone else to build upon those experiments to yield a benefit; for this reason, it is not always easy to tell of a particular experiment what its ultimate significance will be). If informed, concerned people do not want animal research carried out without guidelines as to animal welfare, since animals are not merely another piece of equipment, to be manipulated however one will, neither do they want our laboratories closed down until, assuming such a time comes, all experiments can be carried out on bacteria, or, more generally, on non-animal subjects.

II

I believe this vivisectionist I have sketched represents what a great many people think about animal experimentation and antivivisectionism. To be sure, it represents what they think only in its most general outline; but even this much shows the central role the appeal to benefit plays in their thinking.

Now there is a feature of this appeal which, though perfectly straightforward, is nevertheless not widely appreciated, a feature which has implications for the medical profession. Michael W Fox, a long-serving member of the animal welfare movement, comes out against antivivisectionism.[1] 'Some antivivisectionists would have no research done on animals. This is a limited and unrealistic view since in many cases it is the only way to test a new vaccine or drug which could save many lives – human and animal. Often the drugs being tested will treat or alleviate disease in both animal and human.' Fox might have posed a sterner test for himself and vivisectionists generally if he had drawn the example so that the vaccine benefited only humans but was tested, and tested painfully, only on animals; but this is by the way. The important point is Fox's entirely false presumption that the only alternative to not testing the vaccine and reaping the benefit is to test it upon animals; it could, of course, be tested upon human beings. There is absolutely nothing about the appeal to benefit which precludes this; so far as this appeal is concerned, if securing the benefit licenses (painful) experiments on animals, it equally licenses (painful) experiments on humans, since the benefit may be secured by either means. Moreover, we must not forget that we have already a powerful reason *for* human experiments: we typically experiment upon animals with an eye towards benefiting humans, and it seems only sensible, if we want to find out the effect of some substance upon humans, that we test it upon humans. This is especially true, as doubts increasingly arise about whether extrapolations from the animal to the human case are not very prone to error and to the effects of in-built differences between animals and humans. (The saccharin controversy is sometimes cited as a case in point.) In some cases, such extrapolations may be positively dangerous; I have in mind cases where a substance has far less marked or severe effects in animals than in humans. (I have heard thalidomide, and what testing was done with it, cited in this connection.)

What I am saying, then, is that someone who relies upon the appeal to benefit to justify (painful) experiments on animals needs one more shot in his locker, if he is to prevent the appeal from justifying (painful) experiments upon humans. Specifically, he needs some reason which demarcates humans from animals, and which shows why we are not justified in doing to humans what we in our laboratories do to animals.

A great many things could be said at this point (the claim that animals do not feel pain is hardly one of them, since, whatever else may be said about this claim, the experiments in question could be painless), but I do not have space for even a few of them. I propose to leap, therefore, to what I think would be widely held, upon reflection, to be the reason to allow the appeal to benefit in the case of animals but to disallow it in the case of humans. Quite simply, human life, it will be said, is more valuable than animal life. Not only is this something which is widely thought, but it is also something which even such a fervent defender of animal liberation as the philosopher Peter Singer accepts.[2]

What is the source of this greater value? To some, it may be traced to their religious beliefs; but to the ever increasing numbers of non-believers, which I presume include some medical people as well as others, this appeal to religion is unavailable. I am not myself religious, and I cannot in good faith maintain that humans have souls but animals do not, that humans have been granted dominion over the beasts of the earth, that human life is sacred or sanctified whereas animal life is either not similarly blessed or blessed to a far less extent, and so on. So, what is left? One might try to appeal to some non-religiously grounded principle of respect or reverence for life; but, prima facie, such a principle does not cede human life greater value than animal life but rather enjoins us to revere life or living things per se. Accordingly, a person who adopts the appeal to benefit and who accepts a respect or reverence-for-life view still has no reason for thinking the benefit may only be secured through animal and never through human experiments.

Ultimately, though many twists and turns of argument have to be disposed of first, I think the non-religious person who thinks that human life is more valuable than animal life will find himself forced back upon our complex make-up to find the source of that value. What I mean is this. If we ask ourselves what makes our lives valuable, I think we shall want to give as answers such things as the pleasures of friendship, eating and drinking, listening to music, participating in sports, obtaining satisfaction through our job, reading, enjoying a beautiful summer's day, getting married and sharing experiences with someone, sex, watching and helping our children to grow up, solving quite difficult practical and intellectual problems in pursuit of some goal we highly prize, and so on. Within this mixed bag, there are some activities we may well share with animals; but our make-up is complex, and there are dimensions to us which there are not to animals. When we think in these terms, of dimensions to us which there are not to animals, we are quite naturally led to cede our lives more value *because of the many more possibilities for enrichment they contain.*

To think in this way is very common; it is, I believe, the way many non-religious people find greater value in human life. It should be obvious, however, that those who think this way must eventually confront an undeniable fact: not all human lives have the same enrichment or scope for enrichment. (There are babies, of course, but most people seem happy to regard them as leading lives which have the relevant potentialities for enrichment.) Some people lead lives of a quality we would not wish upon even our worst enemies, and some of these lives have not the scope for enrichment of ordinary human lives. If we regard the irreversibly comatose as living human lives of the lowest quality, we must nevertheless face the fact that many humans lead lives of a radically lower quality than ordinary human lives. We can all think of numerous such cases, cases where the lives lack enrichment and where the scope, the potentialities for enrichment are severely truncated or absent, as with spina bifida children or the very, very severely mentally enfeebled.

If we confront the fact that not all human life has the same quality, either in terms of the same enrichment or the same scope for enrichment, and if we are thinking of the value of life in these terms, then we seem compelled to conclude that not all human life has the same value. And, with this conclusion, the way is open for redrawing Fox's vaccine example in a way that makes it far less apparent that we should test the vaccine on animals. For, as opposed to testing it on quite ordinary and healthy animals, with a reasonably high quality of life, the alternative is to test it on humans whose quality of life is so low *either* as to be exceeded by the quality of life of the healthy animals *or* as to approach their quality of life. On the former alternative, and it is as well to bear in mind that a great many experiments are performed upon healthy, vigorous animals, we would have a reason to test the vaccine on the humans in question; on the latter alternative, we would again find ourselves in need of a reason for thinking it justified to test the vaccine on animals but not on humans.

III

Where, then, are we? If we are not to test the vaccine on humans, then we require some reason which justifies testing it on animals but not on humans. If we purport to find that reason in the greater value of human life, then we must reckon with the fact that the value of human life is bound up with and varies according to its quality; and this opens the way either for some animals to have a higher quality of life than some humans or for some humans to have so low a quality of life as to approach that of some animals. Either way, it is no longer clear that we should test the vaccine on animals.

So, in order to make this clear, what is needed, in effect, is some reason for thinking that a human life, no matter how truncated its scope for enrichment, no matter how low its quality, is more valuable than an animal life, no matter what its degree of enrichment, no matter how high its quality. (Bear in mind that those who have this need are those who, for whatever reason, are not religious and so cannot escape the need that way.) I myself have and know of nothing with which to satisfy this need; that is, I have and know of nothing which enables me to say, *a priori*, that a human life of any quality, however low, is more valuable than an animal life of any quality, however high. Perhaps some readers think that they can satisfy this need; certainly, I am receptive to suggestions.

In the absence of something with which to meet the above need, we cannot, with the appeal to benefit, justify (painful) animal experiments without justifying (painful) human experiments. We seem to have, then, two directions in which we may move. On the one hand, we may take the fact that we cannot justify animal experiments without justifying human experiments as a good reason to re-examine our whole practice of (painful) animal experiments. The case for antivivisectionism, I think, is far stronger than most people allow: so far as I can see, the only way to avoid it, if you are attracted by the appeal to benefit and are not religious, is *either* to have in your possession some means of conceding human life of any quality greater value than animal life of any quality *or* to condone experiments on humans whose quality of life is exceeded by or equal to that of animals. If you are as I am and find yourself without a means of the required sort, then the choice before you is either antivivisectionism or condoning human experiments. On the other hand, we may take the fact that we cannot justify animal experiments without justifying human experiments as a good reason to allow some human experiments. Put differently, if the choice before us is between antivivisectionism and allowing human experiments, can we bring ourselves to embrace antivivisectionism? For, consider: we find ourselves involved in this whole problem because we strongly believe that some benefit or range of benefits can justify (painful) animal experiments. If we choose antivivisectionism, we may very well lose the many benefits obtained through vivisection, and this, at times, even if we concede, as we must, that not every experiment leads to a Salk vaccine, may be a serious loss indeed. Certainly, it would have been a serious loss in the past, if we had had to forgo the benefits which accrued through (and which we presently enjoy as a result of) vivisection. Scientific research and technological innovation have completely altered the human condition, occasionally in rather frightening ways, but typically in ways for which most people are thankful, and very few people indeed would look in the face the benefits which medical research in particular has conferred upon us, benefits which on the whole have most certainly involved vivisections. If the appeal to benefit exerts its full attraction upon us, therefore, we may find ourselves unable to make the choice in favour of antivivisectionism, especially if that meant a good deal of serious research in serious affairs of health had either to be stopped until suitable, alternative experimental subjects were developed for a full range of experiments or, if nothing suitable for a full range of experiments were developed, to be stopped entirely.

Accordingly, we are left with human experiments. I think this is how I would choose, not with great glee and rejoicing, and with great reluctance; but if this is the price we must pay to hold the appeal to benefit and to enjoy the benefits which that appeal licenses, then we must, I think, pay it.

I am well aware that most people, including most medical people, will find my choice repugnant in the extreme, and it is easy to see how I can appear a monster in their eyes. But I am where I am, not because I begin a monster and end up choosing the monstrous, but because I cannot in good faith think of anything at all compelling that cedes human life of any quality greater value than animal life of any quality. It might be claimed by some that this shows in me the need for some religious beliefs, on the assumption that some religious belief or other will allow me to say that any human life is more valuable than any animal life. Apart from the fact that this appears a rather strange reason for taking on religious beliefs (for example, believing in the existence of God and of God's gifts to us in order to avoid having to allow experiments on humans), other questions about those beliefs, such as their correctness and the evidence for their truth, intrude. I may well find that I cannot persuade myself of the beliefs in question.

Is there nothing, then, that can now be cited which, even if we accept that we are committed to allowing human experiments, would nevertheless serve to bar them? I think all I can cite – I do not by this phraseology mean to undercut the force of what follows – are the likely side-effects of such experiments. Massive numbers of people would be outraged, society would be in an uproar, hospitals and research centres would come under fierce attack, the doctor–patient relationship might be irrevocably affected, and so on. (All of us will find it easy to carry on with the list.) Such considerations as these are very powerful, and they would have to be weighed very carefully, in deciding whether actually to perform the experiments. Perhaps their weight would be so great that we could not proceed with the experiments; certainly, that is possible.

But what I meant by saying that such important side-effects of human experiments are 'all I can cite' in the present context is this: it is an utterly contingent affair whether such side-effects occur, and their occurrence is not immune to attempts – by education, by explaining in detail and repeatedly why such experiments are being undertaken, by going through, yet again, our inability to show that human life is always more valuable than animal life, etc. – to eliminate them. It is this last fact especially, that such things as outrage and harm to the doctor–patient relationship can be affected by education, information, and careful explanation, that poses a danger to those who want actually to bar human experiments by appeal to side-effects. So, I do not play down the importance of side-effects in deciding whether actually to perform human experiments, I only caution that they do not provide a once-and-for-all bar to such experiments, unless they survive any and all attempts to mitigate and eliminate them.

References

1 Fox, M. *Returning to Eden: Animal Rights and Human Obligations* (New York: Viking Press, 1980), p. 116.

2 Singer, P. *Animal Liberation* (London: Jonathan Cape, 1976).

Commentary from a Vivisecting Professor of Pharmacology

Sir William Paton

It would be best to start by summarizing what (for this comment) I take to be the essential points of Dr Frey's interesting, and I believe novel, argument. (1) A major justification of animal experiment, commonly accepted, is the benefit that results. (2) This justification is rejected by some, initially on the grounds that the benefit does not justify the pain inflicted; but when it is noted that experiments may be painless, or that steps are taken to minimize the pain, the fundamental ground of rejection is revealed by a shift to the statement that the use of animals for these purposes is *absolutely* wrong. (3) Those who argue this way will accept the loss of the benefits. (4) But is it necessary to forgo these benefits? Why not, in order to retain them, be willing to use man for these experiments? (5) If it is said against this that man is more valuable than animals, in what way is this so? (6) Dr Frey does not believe in 'souls', nor does he accept the 'dominion' of man, and he can only identify 'capacity for enrichment' as a suitable defining characteristic of humanity. (7) He finds that this criterion does not separate man from animals; for instance, he concludes that some animals may possess *more* of this capacity than some humans (for example, the very, very severely mentally enfeebled or spina bifida children). (8) He therefore accepts (with great reluctance) that human experiment should be permissible, with due precaution, in order to obtain the benefits concerned. (9) While acknowledging that the side-effects of such experiment (society's outrage, damage to doctor–patient relations) might prevent particular experiments, their occurrence would be 'utterly contingent', and would not negate the general principle of permissibility.

It is not always clear whether Dr Frey himself holds the views expressed, or is doing no more than presenting them for discussion. In the latter spirit, anything which follows refers to what Dr Frey happens to be voicing, and not to whatever may be his actual opinions.

Before coming to the specific question of human experiment, two general points arise. The first concerns the method of argument. It is an old one: that of reviewing a section of experience (in this case, experience of other people's opinion; reports regrettably hearsay, about experimental work – thalidomide, saccharin, and experience of the life of animals and of handicapped humans); and then of abstracting from this experience particular propositions which then become the subject of the discourse. A single instance (the tree in the quad, or the visual experience of a red patch) has sometimes sufficed to create such a proposition. This is a blameless, indeed common activity. The problem comes with 're-entry' to the experiential world. The proposition may be combined with others to yield further propositions. One such result here is: 'It is not possible to say, *a priori*, that a human life of any quality, however low, is more valuable than an animal life of any quality, however high.' (Dr Frey does not put it so bluntly, but says only that nothing enables *him* to say this. I believe, however, that he is not merely wishing to report on his own psychological state, but wishes the proposition to be considered generally.) What *use* is this proposition? None that I can see. It explicitly assumes that there are scales of human and animal life, and explicitly compares the lower extreme of one with the upper extreme of the other; yet it gives no criterion as to where (or whether) the scales end. Even given these, and comparing (say) an anencephalic fetus with a favourite sheep-dog, over which people could make up their minds, all that has been done is to discuss extreme cases. What then? Few would accept that because a particular instance of animal life is more valuable than a particular instance of human life, therefore no human life is more valuable than animal life. The general proposition merely ends by regurgitating the sort of special case from which it originated.

This links with a second general point, the general philosophical mayhem created by continuity. The type of argument by which Dr Frey fails to find a 'dimension' by which humans differ from animals is one that can also be used to fail to distinguish between light and dark, sweet and sour, motion and immobility. Yet this does not prevent (for instance) the specification of a well-lit factory or an efficient dark-room, or the formulation of successful cooking recipes, or the measurement of velocity. The idea of continuity in the 'scale of creation' is an old and cogent one. It is true that individual species represent discrete steps, but within each species, variation is such as to blur the absolute demarcation in respect of any chosen character between neighbours. Dr Frey could have gone further, and added that no one has yet produced any logically rigorous principle of division at any point in the scale from the inanimate, through bacteria, protozoa, vegetables, insects and animals to man – whether reproduction, complexity, or evidence of responsiveness, purposiveness or sentience is considered. Even the leech will respond to morphine. But the recognition of continuity does not debar the drawing of *operational* divisions.

This brings us to the specific question of whether such operational distinctions can, or cannot, be drawn between humans and animals, particularly distinctions to which 'value' can be attached. Dr Frey's strongest candidate is 'self-enrichment', exemplified chiefly by a capacity for enjoyable experience. But he has to reject this as a discriminant between man and animal because he believes that a very, very severely mentally enfeebled person or a spina bifida child has less capacity for enrichment than a healthy animal. It is a comment on moral philosophy today that 'capacity for enrichment' should be advanced as the strongest index of value in human activity. In such a context, one cannot expect that other indices, such as capacity for goodness, altruism, responsibility, or forgiveness, would be admissible. But one need not resort to these. There is one respect in which the human has come increasingly to distance himself from the animal – namely the capacity to accumulate his experience by the spoken and (especially) by the written and printed word. This means that successive generations build on their predecessors' achievements, not (as with a crystal, an anthill, or a coral reef) more and more of the same, but continually changing what they build. The scratches in the Lascaux caves lead to the Renaissance; Pythagorean harmonics in time grow up to the Bach fugue; Archimedes' method of exhaustion, transmuted in the seventeenth century to the calculus, becomes O-level mathematics for today's schoolboy. Man's mastery of the environment, initially little more than adequate for survival, is now so great as to arouse his deepest sense of responsibility and his deepest questions of meaning and purpose. Nor must this human capacity be linked only to the 'normal' human in perfect health. Human achievement owes much to the deformed, diseased, epileptic and insane; but perhaps only those familiar with the handicapped know that achievement is not restricted to geniuses, but can pervade all levels of personal and social relationships. (There is the medical point, too, that one must not assume a present handicap to be necessarily permanent: the cretin used to be a striking example of severe handicap, seemingly irreversible in 1890, but curable by 1900. Phenylketonuria provides a more recent example.)

If we accept that man can accumulate his experience (not only that of other men: he can and does accumulate his experience of animals) how does that affect the argument? It is not necessary to argue that an absolute distinction from the animal has been found. Indeed there is some evidence (though it remains inconclusive) for vestiges of a capacity to build a language and to frame abstract thought in the higher primates, although it is hard to see evidence of the use of these for progressive cumulation. But all that is needed is to recognize a quantitative distinction between man and animal sufficiently great to be accepted in practice as qualitative. That this is the case seems to me, whether or not the reasons are articulated, the general consensus. The capacity to accumulate, and thus to build on the past and to look to the future, is a quality, too, to which value can be attached, and a value which looks beyond personal enjoyment to the needs of other individuals. This constitutes an answer to the question (5) in my initial summary of Dr Frey's argument, and a rebuttal to (6) and (7), after which (8) and (9) lapse.

One might stop there, but Dr Frey's paper – from which an uninformed reader might suppose that no human experiment had hitherto taken place – calls for something more. One can now identify three approaches to such experiment: (a) The one argued above, which gives a greater value to the human than to the animal; this does not debar human experiment, but only introduces a coefficient to be applied to the choices to be made. (b) At the opposite extreme is an equation of human and animal value. This, too, fails to debar human experiment. The question becomes instead that of choosing animals or human beings for experiments, presumably simply by practical criteria such as scientific suitability (large animals such as man would need much larger apparatus), cost, and availability. The question of availability is interesting; it would entail consent on the part of a human subject. How does one obtain the consent of an animal? It is not possible for a human to speak for it, for that would deny the postulated human–animal equivalence. The question illustrates the crucial character of one's view of human and animal relationships. (c) In between, it seems, is Dr Frey's position, which appears to accept that there *are* different scales of value for human beings and animals, but argues that they overlap. Thus Beethoven is more valuable than a mouse, but the severely handicapped human is of less value than a healthy 'higher' animal. The implications of this are not worked out; but such a calculus would appear to legitimize the use especially of the diseased and mentally deficient. I doubt if this is what he intends.

More important, perhaps, is to make clear how much human experiment has been, and is being, done. I do not believe Dr Frey would have written as he has if he had adequately consulted the original medical literature, or medical scientists. Human experiment has a long and honourable, though still unwritten history. Some is severely ad hoc: experiments on effects of acceleration on the human body, leading to ejector seats; or on oxygen poisoning, high pressure, carbon dioxide poisoning, and the 'bends', to make diving safer. Some is to help to improve medical understanding: the cardiologist first passing a cardiac catheter on himself; self-curarization; the paralysis of nerves by local anaesthesia, or nerve section, or vascular occlusion, to throw light on neurological problems. Much takes place in pharmacological work: early trials of metabolism, pilot studies on dose-level, analyses of mechanism of action. Unlike animal experiment no licence is needed, no annual return of the numbers of human experiments is needed, and no government office counts them. Thus it is not easy to estimate their number. But some indication is given by a single issue of just one monthly journal, the *British Journal of Clinical Pharmacology*, which contained 20 papers, covering 124 experiments on normal human subjects (both young and old) and 99 experiments on patients. Scale this up, and one may well doubt if there is scope for much more human experiment than is already conducted.

Dr Frey's argument raises yet other issues. One can well argue that if no distinction can be drawn between man and animals, then neither can it be drawn between the animal and the vegetable world. So one could ask, as one contemplates the insectivorous plant *Drosera*, responsive to sun, rain, and the nutrients of the soil, and exquisitely sensitive to chemicals, and watches it close a leaf around and digest an insect caught on its hairs, 'Can anyone say that this plant is *less* enriched by its experience than a lion as it devours a buck, or a man enjoying his dinner?' But this merely emphasizes again the importance of one's view of man's relation to the rest of creation. But these are not the issues at the heart of the debate about animal experiment. In practice, I take the most important to be the assessment of the scientific value of an experiment, of the knowledge or benefit to be gained, and of the suffering (if any) involved, and the question of how to balance these. It is ultimately a moral problem, and a question of responsibility borne both by the scientist and by the rest of society in the characteristically human task of removing ignorance and minimizing suffering.

Response

R. G. Frey

Professor Paton would have us believe that man's capacity to accumulate his experience by the spoken, written and printed word confers greater value on his life; but this generalization does not help over the problem I posed.

A medical scientist engaged in serious work needs to perform experiments on retinas, experiments which in the end involve loss of sight and not in some accidental fashion; he may use the retinas of perfectly healthy rabbits or those of severely mentally enfeebled humans. To put the matter somewhat elliptically, the scientist can blind the rabbits or blind the humans. How is this choice to be made? Presumably, Professor Paton would point to the humans and maintain that they belong to a species that has the capacity to make significant advances on any number of fronts as a result of accumulated experience; but exactly how does this fact help with the case before us? These same mentally enfeebled humans belong to a species capable of producing Beethovens, Mozarts and Schuberts, but that in no way makes *them* composers or confers on *their* lives any value. So exactly how is the fact that our species has been capable of great wonders supposed to help out in the cases of those humans far removed from any such wonders? Professor Paton writes: 'Few would accept that because a particular instance of animal life is more valuable than a particular instance of human life, therefore no human life is more valuable than animal life.' Of course not; nor did I suggest anything so silly. But the people to be used by the scientist are not fully normal humans but seriously defective ones, who are still such – they have eyeballs – as to be suitable experimental subjects. Clearly, Professor Paton has given us no reason for not carrying out the experiment upon the humans in question; for, to repeat, the mere fact that my species can produce a Beethoven does not per se make *my* life any more valuable than that of a mouse.

Professor Paton writes at one point about our having to obtain the consent of human subjects and of our having no means of obtaining consent from animals; but I should have thought he was unwise to make much of this. Animals may not be able to consent, but that does not appear to stop Professor Paton using them as experimental subjects; whereas, though it makes no sense to speak of obtaining the consent of the severely mentally enfeebled, I presume he would recoil from *their* use as subjects for blinding. Why? What makes him hesitate in their case but go ahead in the case of rabbits? My strong suspicion is that he intuitively accepts human life as more valuable than animal life, even when all the grandiose talk of our capacities and accomplishments is inapplicable, and it would be interesting to know how he justifies this intuition.

Professor Paton speaks of my use of hearsay, my failure to consult medical reports, my making it appear as if no human experiments have been performed; well, here is his chance to nail down his accusations. I can point to a number of instances where rabbits with good eyesight have knowingly been blinded in the course of experimental work; I ask him if he can point to a single instance where a human subject, with otherwise good or perfect eyesight, has knowingly been blinded by a medical experimenter. If he can, then let him name names; if he cannot, then he might justly be accused of having failed to take my point, which, as readers will know, is that we do not do to defective humans all that we presently do in our laboratories to quite healthy animals. My interest is in why we do not. If the justification is that we think human life of greater value than animal life, then we must be prepared to face the facts, at least on the grounds I suggested, that (i) not all human life is of the same value and (ii) some human life has a value so low as to be exceeded by some animal life.

PART IX

Ethical Issues in the Practice of Health Care

Confidentiality

59

Tarasoff v. Regents of the University of California

Tobriner, Justice

On October 27, 1969, Prosenjit Poddar killed Tatiana Tarasoff. Plaintiffs, Tatiana's parents, allege that two months earlier Poddar confided his intention to kill Tatiana to Dr Lawrence Moore, a psychologist employed by the Cowell Memorial Hospital at the University of California at Berkeley. They allege that on Moore's request, the campus police briefly detained Poddar, but released him when he appeared rational. They further claim that Dr Harvey Powelson, Moore's superior, then directed that no further action be taken to detain Poddar. No one warned the plaintiffs of Tatiana's peril.

Plaintiffs' complaints predicate liability on two grounds: defendants' failure to warn plaintiffs of the impending danger and their failure to bring about Poddar's confinement... Defendants, in turn, assert that they owed no duty of reasonable care to Tatiana...

We shall explain that defendant therapists cannot escape liability merely because Tatiana herself was not their patient. When a therapist determines, or pursuant to the standards of his profession should determine, that his patient presents a serious danger of violence to another, he incurs an obligation to use reasonable care to protect the intended victim against such danger. The discharge of this duty may require the therapist to take one or more of various steps, depending upon the nature of the case. Thus it may call for him to warn the intended victim or others likely to apprise the victim of the danger, to notify the police, or to take whatever other steps are reasonably necessary under the circumstances.

From *551 Pacific Reporter*, 2nd series (1976), 334–61 (extracts).

1. Plaintiff's Complaints

Plaintiffs, Tatiana's mother and father, filed separate but virtually identical second amended complaints. The issue before us on this appeal is whether those complaints now state, or can be amended to state, causes of action against defendants. We therefore begin by setting forth the pertinent allegations of the complaints.

Plaintiffs' first cause of action, entitled "Failure to Detain a Dangerous Patient," alleges that on August 20, 1969, Poddar was a voluntary outpatient receiving therapy at Cowell Memorial Hospital. Poddar informed Moore, his therapist, that he was going to kill an unnamed girl, readily identifiable as Tatiana, when she returned home from spending the summer in Brazil. Moore, with the concurrence of Dr Gold, who had initially examined Poddar, and Dr Yandell, assistant to the director of the department of psychiatry, decided that Poddar should be committed for observation in a mental hospital. Moore orally notified Officers Atkinson and Teel of the campus police that he would request commitment. He then sent a letter to Police Chief William Beall requesting the assistance of the police department in securing Poddar's confinement.

Officers Atkinson, Brownrigg, and Halleran took Poddar into custody, but, satisfied that Poddar was rational, released him on his promise to stay away from Tatiana. Powelson, director of the department of psychiatry at Cowell Memorial Hospital, then asked the police to return Moore's letter, directed that all copies of the letter and notes that Moore had taken as therapist be destroyed, and "ordered no action to place Prosenjit Poddar in 72-hour treatment and evaluation facility."

Plaintiffs' second cause of action, entitled "Failure to Warn On a Dangerous Patient," incorporates the allegations of the first cause of action, but adds the assertion that defendants negligently permitted Poddar to be released from police custody without "notifying the parents of Tatiana Tarasoff that their daughter was in grave danger from Posenjit Poddar." Poddar persuaded Tatiana's brother to share an apartment with him near Tatiana's residence; shortly after her return from Brazil, Poddar went to her residence and killed her.

2. *Plaintiffs can state a cause of action against defendant therapists for negligent failure to protect Tatiana.*

The second cause of action can be amended to allege that Tatiana's death proximately resulted from defendants' negligent failure to warn Tatiana or others likely to apprise her of her danger. Plaintiffs contend that as amended, such allegations of negligence and proximate causation, with resulting damages, establish a cause of action. Defendants, however, contend that in the circumstances of the present case they owed no duty of care to Tatiana or her parents and that, in the absence of such duty, they were free to act in careless disregard of Tatiana's life and safety.

In analyzing this issue, we bear in mind that legal duties are not discoverable facts of nature, but merely conclusory expressions that, in cases of a particular type, liability should be imposed for damage done.

In the landmark case of *Rowland v. Christian* (1968). Justice Peters recognized that liability should be imposed "for an injury occasioned to another by his want of ordinary care or skill" as expressed in section 1714 of the Civil Code. Thus, Justice Peters, quoting from *Heaven v. Pender* (1883) stated: "'whenever one person is by circumstances placed in such a position with regard to another... that if he did not use ordinary care and skill in his own conduct... he would cause danger of injury to the person or property of the other, a duty arises to use ordinary care and skill to avoid such danger.'"

We depart from "this fundamental principle" only upon the "balancing of a number of considerations"; major ones "are the foreseeability of harm to the plaintiff, the degree of certainty that the plaintiff suffered injury, the closeness of the connection between the defendant's conduct and the injury suffered, the moral blame attached to the defendant's conduct, the policy of preventing future harm, the extent of the burden to the defendant and consequences to the community of imposing a duty to exercise care with resulting liability for breach, and the availability, cost and prevalence of insurance for the risk involved."

The most important of these considerations in establishing duty is foreseeability. As a general principle, a "defendant owes a duty of care to all persons who are foreseeably endangered by his conduct, with respect to all risks which make the conduct unreasonably dangerous." As we shall explain, however, when the avoidance of foreseeable harm requires a defendant to control the conduct of another person, or to warn of such conduct, the common law has traditionally imposed liability only if the defendant bears some special relationship to the dangerous person or to the potential victim. Since the relationship between a therapist and his patient satisfies this requirement, we need not here decide whether foreseeability alone is sufficient to create a duty to exercise reasonably care to protect a potential victim of another's conduct.

We note that a relationship of defendant therapists to either Tatiana or Poddar will suffice to establish a duty of care; as explained in section 315 of the Restatement Second of Torts, a duty of care may arise from either "(a) a special relation... between the actor and the third person which imposes a duty upon the actor to control the third person's conduct, or (b) a special relation... between the actor and the other which gives to the other a right of protection."

The courts hold that a doctor is liable to persons infected by his patient if he negligently fails to diagnose a contagious disease or, having diagnosed the illness, fails to warn members of the patient's family.

Since it involved a dangerous mental patient, the decision in *Merchants Nat. Bank & Trust Co. of Fargo v. United States* comes closer to the issue. The Veterans Administration arranged for the patient to work on a local farm, but did not inform the farmer of the man's background. The farmer consequently permitted the patient to come and go freely during nonworking hours; the patient borrowed a car, drove to his wife's residence and killed her. Notwithstanding the lack of any "special relationship" between the Veterans Administration and the wife, the court found the Veterans Administration liable for the wrongful death of the wife.

In their summary of the relevant rulings Fleming and Maximov conclude that the "case law should dispel any notion that to impose on the therapists a duty to take precautions for the safety of persons threatened by a patient, where due care so requires, is in any way opposed to contemporary ground rules on the duty relationship. On the contrary, there now seems to be sufficient authority to support the conclusion that by entering into a doctor–patient relationship the therapist becomes sufficiently involved to assume some responsibility for the safety, not only of the patient himself, but also of any third person whom the doctor knows to be threatened by the patient." (Fleming and Maximov, *The Patient or His Victim: The Therapist's Dilemma* (1974).)

Defendants contend, however, that imposition of a duty to exercise reasonable care to protect third persons is unworkable because therapists cannot accurately predict whether or not a patient will resort to violence. In support of this argument amicus representing the American Psychiatric. Association and other professional societies cites numerous articles which indicate that therapists, in the present state of the art, are unable reliably to predict violent acts; their forecasts, amicus claims, tend consistently to overpredict violence, and indeed are more often wrong than right. Since predictions of violence are often erroneous, amicus concludes, the courts should not render rulings that predicate the liability of therapists upon the validity of such predictions.

We recognize the difficulty that a therapist encounters in attempting to forecast whether a patient presents a serious danger of violence. Obviously we do not require that the therapist, in making that determination, render a perfect performance; the therapist need only exercise "that reasonable degree of skill, knowledge, and care ordinarily possessed and exercised by members of [that professional specialty] under similar circumstances." Within the broad range of reasonable practice and treatment in which professional opinion and judgment may differ, the therapist is free to exercise his or her own best judgment without liability; proof, aided by hindsight, that he or she judged wrongly is insufficient to establish negligence.

In the instant case, however, the pleadings do not raise any question as to failure of defendant therapists to predict that Poddar presented a serious danger of violence. On the contrary, the present complaints allege that defendant therapists did in fact predict that Poddar would kill, but were negligent in failing to warn.

Amicus contends, however, that even when a therapists does in fact predict that a patient poses a serious danger of violence to others, the therapist should be absolved of any responsibility for failing to act to protect the potential victim. In our view, however, once a therapist does in fact determine, or under applicable professional standards reasonably should have determined, that a patient poses a serious danger of violence to others, he bears a duty to exercise reasonable care to protect the foreseeable victim of that danger. While the discharge of this duty of due care will necessarily vary with the facts of each case in each instance the adequacy of the therapist's conduct must be measured against the traditional negligence standard of the rendition of reasonable care under the circumstances. As explained in Fleming and Maximov, *The Patient or His Victim: The Therapist's Dilemma* (1974): "the ultimate question of resolving the tension between the conflicting interests of patient and potential victim is one of social policy, not professional expertise.... In sum, the therapist owes a legal duty not only to his patient, but also to his patient's would-be victim and is subject in both respects to scrutiny by judge and jury."

The risk that unnecessary warnings may be given is a reasonable price to pay for the lives of possible victims that may be saved. We would hesitate to hold that the therapist who is aware that his patient expects to attempt to assassinate the President of the United States would not be obligated to warn the authorities because the therapist cannot predict with accuracy that his patient will commit the crime.

Defendants further argue that free and open communication is essential to psychotherapy; that "Unless a patient ... is assured that ... information [revealed by him] can and will be held in utmost confidence, he will be reluctant to make the full disclosure upon which diagnosis and treatment ... depends." The giving of a warning, defendants contend, constitutes a breach of trust which entails the revelation of confidential communications.

We recognize the public interest in supporting effective treatment of mental illness and in protecting the rights of patients to privacy and the consequent public importance of safeguarding the confidential character of psychotherapeutic communication. Against this interest, however, we must weigh the public interest in safety from violent assault.

We realize that the open and confidential character of psychotherapeutic dialogue encourages patients to express threats of violence, few of which are ever executed. Certainly a therapist should not be encouraged routinely to reveal such threats; such disclosures could seriously disrupt the patient's relationship with his therapist and with the persons threatened. To the contrary, the therapist's obligations to his patient require that he not disclose a confidence unless such disclosure is necessary to avert danger to others, and even then that he do so discreetly, and in a fashion that would preserve the privacy of his patient to the fullest extent compatible with the prevention of the threatened danger.

The revelation of a communication under the above circumstances is not a breach of trust or a violation of professional ethics; as stated in the Principles of Medical Ethics of the American Medical Association (1957), section 9: "A physician may not reveal the confidence entrusted to him in the course of medical attendance... *unless he is required to do so by law or unless it becomes necessary in order to protect the welfare of the individual or of the community.*" (Emphasis added.) We conclude that the public policy favoring protection of the confidential character of patient–psychotherapist communications must yield to the extent to which disclosure is essential to avert danger to others. The protective privilege ends where the public peril begins.

For the foregoing reasons, we find that plaintiffs' complaints can be amended to state a cause of action against defendants Moore, Powelson, Gold, and Yandell and against the Regents as their employer, for breach of a duty to exercise reasonable care to protect Tatiana.

CLARK, Justice (dissenting).

Until today's majority opinion, both legal and medical authorities have agreed that confidentiality is essential to effectively treat the mentally ill, and that imposing a duty on doctors to disclose patient threats to potential victims would greatly impair treatment. Further, recognizing that effective treatment and society's safety are necessarily intertwined, the Legislature has already decided effective and confidential treatment is preferred over imposition of a duty to warn.

The issue whether effective treatment for the mentally ill should be sacrificed to a system of warnings is, in my opinion, properly one for the Legislature, and we are bound by its judgment. Moreover, even in the absence of clear legislative direction, we must reach the same conclusion because imposing the majority's new duty is certain to result in a net increase in violence.

Overwhelming policy considerations mandate against sacrificing fundamental patient interests without gaining a corresponding increase in public benefit.

The importance of psychiatric treatment and its need for confidentiality have been recognized by this court. "It is clearly recognized that the very practice of psychiatry vitally depends upon the reputation in the community that the psychiatrist will not tell" (Slovenko, *Psychiatry and a Second Look at the Medical Privilege* (1960)).

Assurance of confidentiality is important for three reasons.

Deterrence from Treatment

First, without substantial assurance of confidentiality, those requiring treatment will be deterred from seeking assistance. It remains an unfortunate fact in our society that people seeking psychiatric guidance tend to become stigmatized. Apprehension of such stigma – apparently increased by the propensity of people considering treatment to see themselves in the worst possible light – creates a well-recognized reluctance to seek aid. This reluctance is alleviated by the psychiatrist's assurance of confidentiality.

Full Disclosure

Second, the guarantee of confidentiality is essential in eliciting the full disclosure necessary for effective treatment. The psychiatric patient approaches treatment with conscious and unconscious inhibitions against revealing his innermost thoughts. "Every person, however well-motivated, has to overcome resistances to therapeutic exploration. These resistances seek support from every possible source and the possibility of disclosure would easily be employed in the service of resistance." (Goldstein & Katz, *supra*). Until a patient can trust his psychiatrist not to violate their confidential relationship, "the unconscious psychological control mechanism of repression will prevent the recall of past experiences." (Butler, *Psychotherapy and Griswold: Is Confidentiality a Privilege or a Right?* (1971)).

Successful Treatment

Third, even if the patient fully discloses his thoughts, assurance that the confidential relationship will not be breached is necessary to maintain his trust in his psychiatrist – the very means by which treatment is effected. "[T]he essence of much psychotherapy is the contribution of trust in the external world and ultimately in the self, modelled upon the trusting relationship established during therapy" (Dawidoff, *The Malpractice of Psychiatrists*, 1966). Patients will be helped only if they can form a trusting relationship with the psychiatrist. All authorities appear to agree that if the trust relationship cannot be developed because of collusive communication between the psychiatrist and others, treatment will be frustrated.

Given the importance of confidentiality to the practice of psychiatry, it becomes clear the duty to warn imposed by the majority will cripple the use and effectiveness of psychiatry. Many people, potentially violent – yet susceptible to treatment – will be deterred from seeking it; those seeking it will be inhibited from making revelations necessary to effective treatment; and, forcing the psychiatrist to violate the patient's trust will destroy the interpersonal relationship by which treatment is effected.

Violence and Civil Commitment

By imposing a duty to warn, the majority contributes to the danger to society of violence by the mentally ill and greatly increases the risk of civil commitment – the total deprivation of liberty – of those who should not be confined. The impairment of treatment and risk of improper commitment resulting from the new duty to warn will not be limited to a few patients but will extend to a large number of the mentally ill. Although under existing psychiatric procedures only a relatively few receiving treatment will ever present a risk of violence, the number making threats is huge, and it is the latter group – not just the former – whose treatment will be impaired and whose risk of commitment will be increased.

Both the legal and psychiatric communities recognize that the process of determining potential violence in a patient is far from exact, being fraught with complexity and uncertainty. In fact precision has not even been attained in predicting who of those having already committed violent acts will again become violent, a task recognized to be of much simpler proportions.

This predictive uncertainty means that the number of disclosures will necessarily be large. As noted above, psychiatric patients are encouraged to discuss all thoughts of violence, and they often express such thoughts. However, unlike this court, the psychiatrist does not enjoy the benefit of overwhelming hindsight in seeing which few, if any, of his patients will ultimately become violent. Now, confronted by the majority's new duty, the psychiatrist must instantaneously calculate potential violence from each patient on each visit. The difficulties researchers have encountered in accurately predicting violence will be heightened for the practicing psychiatrist dealing for brief periods in his office with heretofore nonviolent patients. And, given the decision not to warn or commit must always be made at the psychiatrist's civil peril, one can expect most doubts will be resolved in favor of the psychiatrist protecting himself.

60

Confidentiality in Medicine: A Decrepit Concept

Mark Siegler

Medical confidentiality, as it has traditionally been understood by patients and doctors, no longer exists. This ancient medical principle, which has been included in every physician's oath and code of ethics since Hippocratic times, has become old, worn-out, and useless; it is a decrepit concept. Efforts to preserve it appear doomed to failure and often give rise to more problems than solutions. Psychiatrists have tacitly acknowledged the impossibility of ensuring the confidentiality of medical records by choosing to establish a separate, more secret record. The following case illustrates how the confidentiality principle is compromised systematically in the course of routine medical care.

A patient of mine with mild chronic obstructive pulmonary disease was transferred from the surgical intensive-care unit to a surgical nursing floor two days after an elective cholecystectomy. On the day of transfer, the patient saw a respiratory therapist writing in his medical chart (the therapist was recording the results of an arterial blood gas analysis) and became concerned about the confidentiality of his hospital records. The patient threatened to leave the hospital prematurely unless I could guarantee that the confidentiality of his hospital record would be respected.

This patient's complaint prompted me to enumerate the number of persons who had both access to his hospital record and a reason to examine it. I was amazed to learn that at least 25 and possibly as many as 100 health professionals and administrative personnel at our university hospital had access to the patient's record and that all of them had a legitimate need, indeed a professional responsibility, to open and use that chart. These persons included 6 attending physicians (the primary physician, the surgeon, the pulmonary consultant, and others); 12 house officers (medical, surgical, intensive-care unit, and "covering" house staff); 20 nursing personnel (on three shifts); 6 respiratory therapists; 3 nutritionists; 2 clinical pharmacists; 15 students (from medicine, nursing, respiratory therapy, and clinical pharmacy); 4 unit secretaries; 4 hospital financial officers; and 4 chart reviewers (utilization review, quality assurance review, tissue review, and insurance auditor). It is of interest that this patient's problem was straightforward, and he therefore did not require many other technical and support services that the modern hospital provides. For example, he did not need multiple consultants and fellows, such specialized procedures as dialysis, or social workers, chaplains, physical therapists, occupational therapists, and the like.

Upon completing my survey I reported to the patient that I estimated that at least 75 health professionals and hospital personnel had access to his medical record. I suggested to the patient that these people were all involved in providing or supporting his health-care services. They were, I assured him, working for him. Despite my reassurances the patient was obviously distressed and retorted, "I always believed that medical confidentiality was part of a doctor's code of ethics. Perhaps you should tell me just what you people mean by 'confidentiality'!"

From *New England Journal of Medicine*, vol. 307, no. 24 (8 December 1982), pp. 1518–21. Reprinted with permission.

Two Aspects of Medical Confidentiality

Confidentiality and third-party interests

Previous discussions of medical confidentiality usually have focused on the tension between a physician's responsibility to keep information divulged by patients secret and a physician's legal and moral duty, on occasion, to reveal such confidences to third parties, such as families, employers, public-health authorities, or police authorities. In all these instances, the central question relates to the stringency of the physician's obligation to maintain patient confidentiality when the health, well-being, and safety of identifiable others or of society in general would be threatened by a failure to reveal information about the patient. The tension in such cases is between the good of the patient and the good of others.

Confidentiality and the patient's interest

As the example above illustrates, further challenges to confidentiality arise because the patient's personal interest in maintaining confidentiality comes into conflict with his personal interest in receiving the best possible health care. Modern high-technology health care is available principally in hospitals (often, teaching hospitals), requires many trained and specialized workers (a "health-care team"), and is very costly. The existence of such teams means that information that previously had been held in confidence by an individual physician will now necessarily be disseminated to many members of the team. Furthermore, since health-care teams are expensive and few patients can afford to pay such costs directly, it becomes essential to grant access to the patient's medical record to persons who are responsible for obtaining third-party payment. These persons include chart reviewers, financial officers, insurance auditors, and quality-of-care assessors. Finally, as medicine expands from a narrow, disease-based model to a model that encompasses psychological, social, and economic problems, not only will the size of the health-care team and medical costs increase, but more sensitive information (such as one's personal habits and financial condition) will now be included in the medical record and will no longer be confidential.

The point I wish to establish is that hospital medicine, the rise of health-care teams, the existence of third-party insurance programs, and the expanding limits of medicine all appear to be responses to the wishes of people for better and more comprehensive medical care. But each of these developments necessarily modifies our traditional understanding of medical confidentiality.

The Role of Confidentiality in Medicine

Confidentiality serves a dual purpose in medicine. In the first place, it acknowledges respect for the patient's sense of individuality and privacy. The patient's most personal physical and psychological secrets are kept confidential in order to decrease a sense of shame and vulnerability. Secondly, confidentiality is important in improving the patient's health care – a basic goal of medicine. The promise of confidentiality permits people to trust (i.e., have confidence) that information revealed to a physician in the course of a medical encounter will not be disseminated further. In this way patients are encouraged to communicate honestly and forthrightly with their doctors. This bond of trust between patient and doctor is vitally important both in the diagnostic process (which relies on an accurate history) and subsequently in the treatment phase, which often depends as much on the patient's trust in the physician as its does on medications and surgery. These two important functions of confidentiality are as important now as they were in the past. They will not be supplanted entirely either by improvements in medical technology or by recent changes in relations between some patients and doctors toward a rights-based, consumerist model.

Possible Solutions to the Confidentiality Problem

First of all, in all nonbureaucratic, noninstitutional medical encounters – that is, in the millions of doctor–patient encounters that take place in physicians' offices, where more privacy can be preserved – meticulous care should be taken to guarantee that patients' medical and personal information will be kept confidential.

Secondly, in such settings as hospitals or large-scale group practices, where many persons have opportunities to examine the medical record, we should aim to provide access only to those who have "a need to know." This could be accomplished through such administrative changes as dividing the entire record into several sections – for example, a medical and financial section – and permitting only health professionals access to the medical information.

The approach favored by many psychiatrists – that of keeping a psychiatric record separate from the general medical record – is an understandable strategy but one that is not entirely satisfactory and that should not be generalized. The keeping of separate psychiatric records implies that psychiatry and medicine are different undertakings and thus drives deeper the wedge between them and between physical and psychological illness. Furthermore, it is often vitally important for internists or surgeons to know that a patient is being seen by a psychiatrist or is taking a particular medication. When separate records are kept, this information may not be available. Finally, if generalized, the practice of keeping a separate psychiatric record could lead to the unacceptable consequence of having a separate record for each type of medical problem.

Patients should be informed about what is meant by "medical confidentiality." We should establish the distinction between information about the patient that generally will be kept confidential regardless of the interest of third parties and information that will be exchanged among members of the health-care team in order to provide care for the patient. Patients should be made aware of the large number of persons in the modern hospital who require access to the medical record in order to serve the patient's medical and financial interests.

Finally, at some point most patients should have an opportunity to review their medical record and to make informed choices about whether their entire record is to be available to everyone or whether certain portions of the record are privileged and should be accessible only to their principal physician or to others designated explicitly by the patient. This approach would rely on traditional informed-consent procedural standards and might permit the patient to balance the personal value of medical confidentiality against the personal value of high-technology, team health care. There is no reason that the same procedure should not be used with psychiatric records instead of the arbitrary system now employed, in which everything related to psychiatry is kept secret.

Afterthought: Confidentiality and Indiscretion

There is one additional aspect of confidentiality that is rarely included in discussions of the subject. I am referring here to the wanton, often inadvertent, but avoidable exchanges of confidential information that occur frequently in hospital rooms, elevators, cafeterias, doctors' offices, and at cocktail parties. Of course, as more people have access to medical information about the patient the potential for this irresponsible abuse of confidentiality increases geometrically.

Such mundane breaches of confidentiality are probably of greater concern to most patients than the broader issue of whether their medical records may be entered into a computerized data bank or whether a respiratory therapist is reviewing the results of an arterial blood gas determination. Somehow, privacy is violated and a sense of shame is heightened when intimate secrets are revealed to people one knows or is close to – friends, neighbors, acquaintances, or hospital roommates – rather than when they are disclosed to an anonymous bureaucrat sitting at a computer terminal in a distant city or to a health professional who is acting in an official capacity.

I suspect that the principles of medical confidentiality, particularly those reflected in most medical codes of ethics, were designed principally to prevent just this sort of embarrassing personal indiscretion rather than to maintain (for social, political, or economic reasons) the absolute secrecy of doctor–patient communications. In this regard, it is worth noting that Percival's Code of Medical Ethics (1803) includes the following admonition: "Patients should be interrogated concerning their complaint in a tone of voice which cannot be overheard." We in the medical profession frequently neglect these simple courtesies.

Conclusion

The principle of medical confidentiality described in medical codes of ethics and still believed in by patients no longer exists. In this respect, it is a decrepit concept. Rather than perpetuate the myth of confidentiality and invest energy vainly to preserve it, the public and the profession would be better served if they devoted their attention to determining which aspects of the original principle of confidentiality are worth retaining. Efforts could then be directed to salvaging those.

61

Confidentiality and the AMA's New Code of Ethics: An Imprudent Formulation?

Helga Kuhse

Abstract

The Australian Medical Association's modification of the absolute rule requiring confidentiality in the doctor–patient relationship may be seen as a coming-of-age of the organization. However, the change remains controversial: there are no guidelines as to when breaches of confidentiality are justified; and it is uncertain whether the new formulation will actually protect the public interest.

The Australian Medical Association (AMA) is not known for its radical stance on social and ethical issues. This makes it all the more remarkable that the AMA has, in its 1996 revised Code of Ethics,[1] dared to touch the hoary chestnut of confidentiality. Ever since Hippocratic times, the maintenance of confidentiality in the doctor–patient relationship has been regarded as a primary, often absolute, obligation. As stated in the World Medical Association's International Code of Ethics: "A physician shall preserve absolute confidentiality on all he knows about his patient even after the patient has died."[2]

The revised AMA Code does not require absolute confidentiality. After telling doctors that they should not divulge information without the patient's permission, the Code states: "Exceptions may arise where the health of others is at risk or you are required by order of a court to breach patient confidentiality."[1]

This departure from the absolutism of the past was the subject of fierce debate. Praised by one commentator as "a lovely step towards recognizing that although the individual patient in front of you is paramount, there are other people who need help, too,"[3] it was condemned not only by health care consumer and civil liberties groups,[4] but also by the Doctors' Reform Society.[4, 5]

It was not surprising that groups concerned with individual patients' rights would criticize the Code. But why did the revision attract criticism from the Doctors' Reform Society as well? After all, this appears to be a public interest initiative, and the Doctors' Reform Society generally takes a broader perspective than the AMA – not focusing predominantly on the health interests of individual, identifiable patients, but on the good of the community as a whole.[6]

An initially plausible case for the insertion of the exception clause was put by then AMA Federal Vice-President Keith Woollard, who had chaired the Ethics, Science and Social Issues Committee (since renamed the Ethics and Public Health Committee) charged with revision of the Code. Giving examples of impaired airline pilots and crane drivers and of severely depressed patients, who may be a threat to others, Woollard argued that there are occasions when a doctor must breach patient confidentiality in order to protect innocent third parties.[4, 7, 8]

Is breaching patient confidentiality ever justified?

It is easy to agree with Woollard that the principle of confidentiality should not be understood as being absolute without exceptions. Certainly, there are cases where a breach of patient confidentiality appears justified or even morally required.

From *Medical Journal of Australia*, vol. 165 (16 September 1996), pp. 327–9.

Take the famous 1976 *Tarasoff* case in the United States, where a male patient confided in his psychotherapist that he intended to kill a young woman, Tatiana Tarasoff. The psychotherapist maintained confidentiality and did not warn the unsuspecting woman, who was subsequently killed by the patient.[9] Similarly, take the following case: a psychiatrist used hypnosis in helping a pilot recall details about his responsibility for a commercial plane crash. The therapist thought it would be risky for the pilot to fly again and advised against it. The pilot did not heed the advice of the doctor, who maintained strict confidentiality. Six months later, the pilot made an error of judgement and crashed a plane on a transatlantic flight, causing many deaths.[10]

Examples such as these suggest that we should welcome the modified AMA Code. The change makes it clear that doctors have obligations not only to their patients, but also to others, and that they are responsible not only for the harm they do, but also for (at least some of) the harm they fail to prevent. The fact that the AMA has explicitly done away with an absolute rule that put strict limits on a doctor's responsibilities might even, perhaps somewhat optimistically, be seen as a coming-of-age of the AMA – the public recognition of the fact that the moral life of doctors is more complex than can be captured in simple rules without exceptions, rules such as "never breach patient confidentiality", "never deliberately hasten death", and so on. In this sense, the change in the AMA's Code is to be welcomed. But more needs to be said.

Does confidentiality matter anyway?

There are various reasons why confidentiality and trust in the doctor–patient relationship are widely regarded as morally significant. For example, the duty to uphold patient confidentiality might be defended as a corollary of respecting patient autonomy, or because it is seen as an important element in achieving the general medical goals of effective diagnosis and treatment. If patients did not trust their doctors and feared disclosure of sensitive information without their consent, they would be unlikely to confide in their doctors.

As there are thus good reasons for maintaining confidentiality, it would be helpful if doctors were to receive some guidance as to when disclosure is justified. In this regard, the AMA Code is not very helpful: apart from reminding doctors that there may be legal requirements of disclosure, it merely states that "[e]xceptions may arise where the health of others is at risk." Does this mean that doctors are justified in breaching confidentiality whenever there is a slight risk to the health or well-being of others, or only when the risk is very significant – for example, when some innocent others might be likely to lose their lives? The Code does not say.

Of course, Woollard is quite right when he points out that it is very difficult, in a Code of Ethics, to provide clear guidelines as to when confidentiality may (or should) be breached.[8] Professional codes, as distinct from detailed laws, must be brief and can do little more than articulate broad ethical principles and rules. However, once again more needs to be said.

Will the revised Code protect the public interest?

It is not only important that a code articulate the correct ethical principles and values, it is also important that it be formulated so as to achieve the desired result. The question is whether the new formulation will, in fact, achieve the intended effect of protecting the public interest. If the balance is wrong between the obligation to protect patient confidentiality and the obligation to protect the public good, much can be lost. Indeed, Con Costa (national President of the Doctors' Reform Society), despite agreeing with Woollard that the obligation to protect patient confidentiality is not absolute,[5] also believes (if I understand him correctly) that the AMA has got the emphasis wrong, in so far as the Code is too cavalier about possible breaches of confidentiality. Costa's point appears to be that if doctors are known to be cavalier about maintaining patient confidentiality, they will be seen by patients to be "dobbers" and will no longer have access to sensitive information. Consequently, they will not be able to dissuade at-risk patients from engaging in behaviour, such as driving cranes and buses or flying commercial jets, that might endanger not only their own lives but also those of others.[5]

Thus, where the AMA may have erred is not in moving away from an absolute principle of confidentiality, but rather in the way it has addressed the issue of exceptions. In the words of Costa: "[W]hat the AMA is proposing on doctor–patient confidentiality is overkill. We would be throwing away the baby with the bath-water. Those patients a doctor actually might be able to influence to modify their behaviour in the wider public interest will stay away from the consulting rooms."[5]

I fear Costa may be right. Indeed, public comments by Woollard on confidentiality exacerbate, rather than ameliorate, this fear. After discussing some cases where it might, indeed, be proper to breach patient confidentiality, Woollard points out that various Australian States already impose a requirement of notification in the case of HIV and some other infections, and have devised legal mechanisms which will sometimes allow curtailment of behaviour that constitutes a risk for others. "Considered in that light," Woollard continues, "the recent statement . . . that the AMA was considering recommending that doctors notify partners of those infected with HIV infection may not be such a radical proposal." While Woollard made it clear that this recommendation would cover only cases "where an HIV positive individual continued a sexual relationship with the partner or partners remaining unaware of the infection",[8] this is, in my opinion, not only a radical proposal, but also a potentially dangerous one, as it may not serve the interests of those it seeks to protect.

What happens now?

Codes of ethics are not only one hallmark of a profession, they are also an informal but powerful public statement of intent by professionals to the communities they serve. A medical code of ethics that is not specific about when confidentiality may be breached could signal to patients that it would be unwise to reveal all.

There is no doubt that harm to identifiable others can sometimes be prevented by doctors' breaching confidentiality. However, the question is whether this should lead one to formulate a general rule to allow disclosure in any but the most exceptional circumstances. While a rule that allows breaches of confidentiality whenever a significant harm is at stake will prevent harm some of the time, it may not work well over time. Take the rule against exceeding a certain speed limit. While my exceeding the speed limit on my way to hospital may minimize harm to the seriously injured person in my car, it is doubtful that a general rule that allows speeding whenever it will prevent harm to an individual would serve society well. Very often, more harm may result from weakening a given rule or law rather than by retaining it in its absolute formulation.

The point is that if known breaches of confidentiality are likely to prevent individuals from seeking treatment or to hinder them from seeking treatment in a timely fashion, then a rule requiring disclosure is likely to do more harm than good. This would lead one to devise a more stringent rule that emphasizes the value of confidentiality, making it clear that any disclosure will not only be exceptional, but will also need to be justified. Such a rule might work best in the long term. For example, it would not only save the lives of particular individuals some of the time, but also, by strongly supporting the value of confidentiality, protect the lives of as yet unidentifiable others.

It is ultimately an empirical question whether a strict or a more relaxed requirement of confidentiality will best protect the interests and rights of all those affected. The claims and counterclaims have not been adequately tested, although the few available studies appear to support the view that a strong, but not absolute, requirement of confidentiality will work best.[11] If so, professional medical associations might be well advised to formulate their codes accordingly and refrain from unwittingly creating the impression that doctors are justified in breaching confidentiality whenever "the health of others is at risk". Such a formulation may well prove imprudent.

References

1 Australian Medical Association *AMA Code of Ethics* (Canberra AMA, 1996).
2 World Medical Association *International Code of Medical Ethics* The World Medical Association handbook of declarations (The World Medical Association, 1985).
3 Ragg, M. Code of ethics falls short of the ideal. *Australian Doctor* (1996 Feb. 9), 20.
4 Lamont, L. Ethics code worries doctors, *Sydney Morning Herald* (1996 Jan, 4), 3.
5 Costa, C. Dobbing doctors risk losing their patients' trust, *Sydney Morning Herald* (1996 Jan. 4), 9.
6 Chapman, S. Doctors as Delilahs new ethics code causes row. *British Medical Journal* (1996), 12: 78.
7 Chan, G. GPs to divulge patients' secrets. *The Australian* (1996 Jan 3), 1.

8 Woollard, K. When keeping a secret threatens other lives. *Australian Medicine* (1995 Nov.), 20; 4.

9 *Tarasoff v. Regents of the University of California*. 17 Cal 3d 425 (1976); 131 *California Reporter* 14 (1976 Jul. 1).

10 Raginsky, B. B. Hypnotic recall of aircrash cause. *International Journal of Clinical Experimental Hypnosis*, 1969: 17: 1–19.

11 Beauchamp, T. and Childress, J. F. *Principles of Medical Ethics*, 4th edn (Oxford: Oxford University Press, 1994), pp. 422–3.

Truth-telling

62

On a Supposed Right to Lie from Altruistic Motives

Immanuel Kant

IN the work called *France*, for the year 1797, Part VI., No. 1, on Political Reactions, by *Benjamin Constant*, the following passage occurs, p. 123:–

"The moral principle that it is one's duty to speak the truth, if it were taken singly and unconditionally, would make all society impossible. We have the proof of this in the very direct consequences which have been drawn from this principle by a German philosopher, who goes so far as to affirm that to tell a falsehood to a murderer who asked us whether our friend, of whom he was in pursuit, had not taken refuge in our house, would be a crime."

The French philosopher opposes this principle in the following manner, p. 124: – "It is a duty to tell the truth. The notion of duty is inseparable from the notion of right. A duty is what in one being corresponds to the right of another. Where there are no rights there are no duties. To tell the truth then is a duty, but only towards him who has a right to the truth. But no man has a right to a truth that injures others." The πρῶτον ψεῦδος here lies in the statement that "*To tell the truth is a duty, but only towards him who has a right to the truth.*"

It is to be remarked, first, that the expression "to have a right to the truth" is unmeaning. We should rather say, a man has a right to his own *truthfulness* (*veracitas*), that is, to subjective truth in his own person. For to have a right objectively to truth would mean that, as in *meum* and *tuum* generally, it depends on his *will* whether a given statement shall be true or false, which would produce a singular logic.

Now, the *first* question is whether a man – in cases where he cannot avoid answering Yes or No – has the *right* to be untruthful. The *second* question is whether, in order to prevent a misdeed that threatens him or some one else, he is not actually bound to be untruthful in a certain statement to which an unjust compulsion forces him.

Truth in utterances that cannot be avoided is the formal duty of a man to everyone, however great the disadvantage that may arise from it to him or any other; and although by making a false statement I do no wrong to him who unjustly compels me to speak, yet I do wrong to men in general in the most essential point of duty, so that it may be called a lie (though not in the jurist's sense), that is, so far as in me lies I cause that declarations in general find no credit, and hence that all rights founded on contract should lose their force; and this is a wrong which is done to mankind.

If, then, we define a lie merely as an intentionally false declaration towards another man, we need not add that it must injure another; as the jurists think proper to put in their definition (*mendacium est falsiïoquium in praejudicium alterius*). For it always injures another; if not another individual, yet mankind generally, since it vitiates the source of justice. This benevolent lie *may*, however, by *accident* (*casus*) become punishable even by civil laws; and that which escapes liability to punishment only by accident may be condemned as a wrong even by external laws. For instance, if you have *by a lie* hindered a man who is even now

This essay was first published in a Berlin periodical in 1797. From *Critique of Practical Reason and Other Works on the Theory of Ethics*, trans. T. K. Abbott, 6th edn (London, 1909), pp. 361–3.

planning a murder, you are legally responsible for all the consequences. But if you have strictly adhered to the truth, public justice can find no fault with you, be the unforeseen consequence what it may. It is possible that whilst you have honestly answered. Yes to the murderer's question, whether his intended victim is in the house, the latter may have gone out unobserved, and so not have come in the way of the murderer, and the deed therefore have not been done; whereas, if you lied and said he was not in the house, and he had really gone out (though unknown to you), so that the murderer met him as he went, and executed his purpose on him, then you might with justice be accused as the cause of his death. For, if you had spoken the truth as well as you knew it, perhaps the murderer while seeking for his enemy in the house might have been caught by neighbours coming up and the deed been prevented. Whoever then *tells a lie*, however good his intentions may be, must answer for the consequences of it, even before the civil tribunal, and must pay the penalty for them, however unforeseen they may have been; because truthfulness is a duty that must be regarded as the basis of all duties founded on contract, the laws of which would be rendered uncertain and useless if even the least exception to them were admitted.

To be *truthful* (honest) in all declarations is therefore a sacred unconditional command of reason, and not to be limited by any expediency.

63

Should Doctors Tell the Truth?

Joseph Collins

This is not a homily on lying. It is a presentation of one of the most difficult questions that confront the physician. Should doctors tell patients the truth? Were I on the witness stand and obliged to answer the question with "yes" or "no," I should answer in the negative and appeal to the judge for permission to qualify my answer. The substance of this article is what that qualification would be.

Though few are willing to make the test, it is widely held that if the truth were more generally told, it would make for world-welfare and human betterment. We shall probably never know. To tell the whole truth is often to perpetrate a cruelty of which many are incapable. This is particularly true of physicians. Those of them who are not compassionate by nature are made so by experience. They come to realize that they owe their fellow-men justice, and graciousness, and benignity, and it becomes one of the real satisfactions of life to discharge that obligation. To do so successfully they must frequently withhold the truth from their patients, which is tantamount to telling them a lie. Moreover, the physician soon learns that the art of medicine consists largely in skillfully mixing falsehood and truth in order to provide the patient with an amalgam which will make the metal of life wear and keep men from being poor shrunken things, full of melancholy and indisposition, unpleasing to themselves and to those who love them. I propose therefore to deal with the question from a pragmatic, not a moral standpoint.

"Now you may tell me the truth," is one of the things patients have frequently said to me. Four types of individuals have said it: those who honestly and courageously want to know so that they may make as ready as possible to face the wages of sin while there is still time; those who do not want to know, and who if they were told would be injured by it; those who are wholly incapable of receiving the truth. Finally, those whose health is neither seriously disordered nor threatened. It may seem an exaggeration to say that in forty years of contact with the sick, the patients I have met who are in the first category could be counted on the fingers of one hand. The vast majority who demand the truth really belong in the fourth category, but there are sufficient in the second – with whom my concern chiefly is – to justify considering their case.

One of the astonishing things about patients is that the more serious the disease, the more silent they are about its portents and manifestations. The man who is constantly seeking assurance that the vague abdominal pains indicative of hyperacidity are not symptoms of cancer often buries family and friends, some of whom have welcomed death as an escape from his burdensome iterations. On the other hand, there is the man whose first warning of serious disease is lumbago who cannot be persuaded to consult a physician until the disease, of which the lumbago is only a symptom, has so far progressed that it is beyond surgery. The seriousness of disease may be said to stand in direct relation to the reticence of its possessor. The more silent the patient, the more serious the disorder.

The patient with a note-book, or the one who is eager to tell his story in great detail, is rarely very ill. They are forever asking, "Am I going to get well?" and though they crave assistance they are often unable to accept it. On the other hand, patients with organic disease are very chary about asking point blank either the nature or the outcome of their ailment. They sense its gravity, and the last thing in the world they wish to know is the truth about it; and to learn it would be the worst thing that could happen to them.

This was borne in upon me early in my professional life. I was summoned one night to assuage the pain of a man who informed me that he had been for some time under treatment for rheumatism – that cloak for so many diagnostic errors. His "rheumatism" was due to a disease of the spinal cord called locomotor ataxia. When he was told that he should submit himself to treatment wholly different from that which he had been receiving, the import of which any intelligent layman would have divined, he asked neither the nature nor the probable outcome of the disease. He did as he was counselled. He is now approaching seventy and, though not active in business, it still engrosses him.

Had he been told that he had a disease which was then universally believed to be progressive, apprehension would have depressed him so heavily that he would not have been able to offer the resistance to its encroachment which has stood him in such good stead. He was told the truth only in part. That is, he was told his "rheumatism" was "different"; that it was dependent upon an organism quite unlike the one that causes ordinary rheumatism; that we have preparations of mercury and arsenic which kill the parasite responsible for this disease, and that if he would submit himself to their use, his life would not be materially shortened, or his efficiency seriously impaired.

Many experiences show that patients do not want the truth about their maladies, and that it is prejudicial to their well-being to know it, but none that I know is more apposite than that of a lawyer, noted for his urbanity and resourcefulness in Court. When he entered my consulting room, he greeted me with a bonhomie that bespoke intimacy but I had met him only twice – once on the golf links many years before, and once in Court where I was appearing as expert witness, prejudicial to his case.

He apologized for engaging my attention with such a triviality, but he had had pain in one shoulder and arm for the past few months, and though he was perfectly well – and had been assured of it by physicians in Paris, London, and Brooklyn – this pain was annoying and he had made up his mind to get rid of it. That I should not get a wrong slant on his condition, he submitted a number of laboratory reports furnished him by an osteopath to show that secretions and excretions susceptible of chemical examinations were quite normal. His determination seemed to be to prevent me from taking a view of his health which might lead me to counsel his retirement. He was quite sure that anything like a thorough examination was unnecessary but he submitted to it. It revealed intense and extensive disease of the kidneys. The pain in the network of nerves of the left upper-arm was a manifestation of the resulting autointoxication.

I felt it incumbent upon me to tell him that his condition was such that he should make a radical change in his mode of life. I told him if he would stop work, spend the winter in Honolulu, go on a diet suitable to a child of three years, and give up exercise, he could look forward confidently to a recovery that would permit of a life of usefulness and activity in his profession. He assured me he could not believe that one who felt no worse than he did should have to make such a radical change in his mode of life. He impressed upon me that I should realize he was the kind of person who had to know the truth. His affairs were so diversified and his commitments so important that he *must* know. Completely taken in, I explained to him the relationship between the pain from which he sought relief and the disease, the degeneration that was going on in the excretory mechanisms of his body, how these were struggling to repair themselves, the procedure of recovery and how it could be facilitated. The light of life began to flicker from the fear that my words engendered, and within two months it sputtered and died out. He was the last person in the world to whom the truth should have been told. Had I lied to him, and then intrigued with his family and friends, he might be alive today.

The longer I practice medicine the more I am convinced that every physician should cultivate lying as a fine art. But there are many varieties of lying. Some are most prejudicial to the physician's usefulness. Such are: pretending to recognize the disease and understand its nature when one is really ignorant; asserting that one has effected the cure which nature has accomplished, or claiming that one can effect cure of a disease which is universally held to be beyond the power of nature or medical skill; pronouncing disease incurable which one cannot rightfully declare to be beyond cessation or relief.

There are other lies, however, which contribute enormously to the success of the physician's mission of mercy and salvation. There are a great number of instances in support of this but none more convincing than that of a man of fifty who, after twenty-five years of devotion to painting, decided that penury and old age were incompatible for him. Some of his friends had forsaken art for advertising. He followed their lead and in five years he was ready to gather the first ripe fruit of his labor. When he attempted to do so he was so immobilized by pain and rigidity that he had to forgo work. One of those many persons who assume responsibility lightly assured him that if he would put himself in the hands of a certain osteopath he would soon be quite fit. The assurance was without foundation. He then consulted a physician who without examining him proceeded to treat him for what is considered a minor ailment.

Within two months his appearance gave such concern to his family that he was persuaded to go to a hospital, where the disease was quickly detected, and he was at once submitted to surgery. When he had recovered from the operation, learning that I was in the country of his adoption, he asked to see me. He had not been able, he said, to get satisfactory information from the surgeon or the physician; all that he could gather from them was that he would have to have supplementary X-ray or radium treatment. What he desired was to get back to his business which was on the verge of success, and he wanted assurance that he could soon do so.

He got it. And more than that, he got elaborate explanation of what surgical intervention had accomplished, but not a word of what it had failed to accomplish. A year of activity was vouchsafed him, and during that time he put his business in such shape that its eventual sale provided a modest competency for his family. It was not until the last few weeks that he knew the nature of his malady. Months of apprehension had been spared him by the deception, and he had been the better able to do his work, for he was buoyed by the hope that his health was not beyond recovery. Had he been told the truth, black despair would have been thrown over the world in which he moved, and he would have carried on with corresponding ineffectiveness.

The more extensive our field of observation and the more intimate our contact with human activity, the more we realize the finiteness of the human mind. Every follower of Hippocrates will agree that "judgment is difficult and experience fallacious." A disease may have only a fatal ending, but one does not know; one may know that certain diseases, such as general paresis, invariably cause death, but one does not know that tomorrow it may no longer be true. The victim may be reprieved by accidental or studied discovery or by the intervention of something that still must be called divine grace.

A few years ago physicians were agreed that diabetes occurring in children was incurable; recently they held that the disease known as pernicious anemia always ended fatally; but now, armed with an extract from the pancreas and the liver, they go out to attack these diseases with the kind of confidence that David had when he saw the Philistine approach.

We have had enough experience to justify the hope that soon we shall be able to induce a little devil who is manageable to cast out a big devil who is wholly out of hand – to cure general paresis by inoculating the victim with malaria, and to shape the course of some varieties of sleeping sickness by the same means.

I am thankful for many valuable lessons learned from my early teachers. One of them was an ophthalmologist of great distinction. I worked for three years in his clinic. He was the most brutally frank doctor I have known. He could say to a woman, without the slightest show of emotion, that she was developing a cataract and would eventually be blind. I asked a colleague who was a co-worker in the clinic at that time and who has since become an eminent specialist, if all these patients developed complete opacity of the crystalline lens.

"Not one half of them," said he. "In many instances the process is so slow that the patient dies before the cataract arrives; in others it ceases to progress. It is time enough for the patient to know he has cataract when he knows for himself that he is going blind. Then I can always explain it to him in such a way that he does not have days of apprehension and nights of sleeplessness for months while awaiting operation. I have made it a practice not to tell a patient he has cataract."

"Yes, but what do you tell them when they say they have been to Doctor Smith who tells them they have cataract and they have come to you for denial or corroboration?"

"I say to them, 'You have a beginning cloudiness of the lens of one eye. I have seen many cases in which the opacity progressed no farther than it has in your case; I have seen others which did not reach blindness in twenty years. I shall change your glasses, and I think you will find that your vision will be improved.' "

And then he added, "In my experience there are two things patients cannot stand being told: that they have cataract or cancer."

There is far less reason for telling them of the former than the latter. The hope for victims of the latter is bound up wholly in early detection and surgical interference. That is one of the most cogent reasons for bi-yearly thorough physical examination after the age of forty-five. Should we ever feel the need of a new law in this country, the one I suggest would exact such examination. The physician who detects malignant disease in its early stages is never justified in telling the patient the real nature of the disease. In fact, he does not know himself until he gets the pathologist's report. Should that indicate grave malignancy no possible good can flow from sharing that knowledge with the patient.

It is frequently to a patient's great advantage to know the truth in part, for it offers him the reason for making a radical change in his mode of life, sometimes a burdensome change. But not once in a hundred instances is a physician justified in telling a patient point blank that he has epilepsy, or the family that he has dementia præcox, until after he has been under observation a long time, unless these are so obvious that even a layman can make the diagnosis. We do not know the real significance of either disease, or from what they flow – we know that so many of them terminate in dementia that the outlook for all of them is bad. But we also know that many cases so diagnosticated end in complete recovery; and that knowledge justifies us in withholding from a patient the name and nature of his disorder until we are beyond all shadow of doubt.

Patients who are seriously ill are greedy for assurance even when it is offered half-heartedly. But those who have ailments which give the physician no real concern often cannot accept assurance. Not infrequently I have been unable to convince patients with nervous indigestion that their fears and concern were without foundation, and yet, years later when they developed organic disease, and I became really concerned about them, they assured me that I was taking their ailments too seriously.

There was a young professor whose acquaintance I made while at a German university. When he returned he took a position as professor in one of the well-known colleges for women. After several years he consulted me for the relief of symptoms which are oftentimes associated with gastric ulcer. It required no elaborate investigation to show that in this instance the symptoms were indicative of an imbalance of his nervous system. He refused to be assured and took umbrage that he was not given a more thorough examination each time that he visited me. Finally he told me that he would no longer attempt to conceal from me that he understood fully my reasons for making light of the matter. It was to throw him off the track, as it were. No good was to be accomplished from trying to deceive him; he realized the gravity of the situation and he was man enough to confront it. He would not show the white feather, and he was entitled to know the truth.

But the more it was proffered him, the greater was his resistance to it. He gave up his work and convinced his family and friends that he was seriously ill. They came to see me in relays; they also refused to accept the truth. They could understand why I told the patient the matter was not serious, but to them I could tell the facts. It was their right to know, and I could depend upon them to keep the knowledge from the patient and to work harmoniously with me.

My failure with my patient's friends was as great as with the patient himself. Fully convinced his back was to the wall, he refused to be looked upon as a lunatic or a hypochondriac and he decided to seek other counsel. He went from specialist to naturopath, from electrotherapist to Christian Scientist, from sanatorium to watering place and, had there been gland doctors and chiropractors in those days, he would have included them as well. Finally, he migrated to the mountains of Tennessee, and wooed nature. Soon I heard of him as the head of a school which was being run on novel pedagogic lines; character-building and health were the chief aims for his pupils; scholastic education was incidental. He began writing and lecturing about his work and his accomplishments, and soon achieved considerable notoriety. I saw him occasionally when he came north and sometimes referred to his long siege of ill-health and how happily it had terminated. He always made light of it, and declared that in one way it had been a very good thing: had it not been for that illness he would never have found himself, never have initiated the work which was giving him repute, happiness, and competency.

One summer I asked him to join me for a canoe trip down the Allegash River. Some of the "carrys" in those days were rather stiff. After one of them I saw that my friend was semi-prostrated and flustered. On questioning him, I learned that he had several times before experienced disagreeable sensations in the chest and in the head after hard manual labor, such as chopping trees or prying out rocks. He protested against examination but finally yielded. I reminded myself how different it was fifteen years before when he clamored for examination and seemed to get both pleasure and satisfaction from it, particularly when it was elaborate and protracted. He had organic disease of the heart, both of the valve-mechanism and of the muscle. His tenure of life depended largely on the way he lived. To counsel him successfully it was necessary to tell him that his heart had become somewhat damaged. He would not have it. "When I was really ill you made light of it, and I could not get you interested. But now, when I am well, you want me to live the life of a dodo. I won't do it. My heart is quite all right, a little upset no doubt by the fare we have had for the past two weeks, but as soon as I get back to normal I shall be as fit as you are, perhaps more so."

We returned to New York and I persuaded him to see a specialist, who was no more successful in impressing him with the necessity of careful living than I was. In despair, I wrote to his wife. She who had been so solicitous, so apprehensive, and so deaf to assurance during the illness that was of no consequence wrote, "I am touched by your affectionate interest, but Jerome seems so well that I have not the heart to begin nagging him again, and it fills me with terror lest he should once more become introspective and self-solicitous. I am afraid if I do what you say that it might start him off again on the old tack, and the memory of those two years frightens me still."

He died about four years later without the benefit of physician.

No one can stand the whole truth about himself; why should we think he can tolerate it about his health, and even though he could, who knows the truth? Physicians have opinions based upon their own and others' experience. They should be chary of expressing those opinions to sick persons until they have studied their psychology and are familiar with their personality. Even then it should always be an opinion, not a sentence. Doctors should be detectives and counsellors, not juries and judges.

Though often it seems a cruelty, the family of the patient to whom the truth is not and should not be told are entitled to the facts or what the physician believes to be the facts. At times, they must conspire with him to keep the truth from the patient, who will learn it too soon no matter what skill they display in deception. On the other hand, it is frequently to the patient's great advantage that the family should not know the depth of the physician's concern, lest their unconcealable apprehension be conveyed to the patient and then transformed into the medium in which disease waxes strong – fear. Now and then the good doctor keeps his own counsel. It does not profit the family of the man whose coronary arteries are under suspicion to be told that he has angina pectoris. If the patient can be induced to live decorously, the physician has discharged his obligation.

I recall so many instances when the truth served me badly that I find it difficult to select the best example. On reflection, I have decided to cite the case of a young man who consulted me shortly after his marriage.

He was sane in judgment, cheerful in disposition, full of the desire to attract those who attracted him. Anything touching on the morbid or "unnatural" was obviously repellent to him. His youth had been a pleasant one, surrounded by affection, culture, understanding, and wealth. When he graduated he had not made up his mind what he wanted to do in the world. After a year of loafing and traveling he decided to become an engineer. He matriculated at one of the technical schools, and his work there was satisfactory to himself and to his professors.

He astonished his intimates shortly after obtaining a promising post by marrying a woman a few years older than himself who was known to some of them as a devotee of bohemian life that did not tally with the position in society to which she was entitled by family and wealth. She had been a favorite with men but she had a reputation of not being the "marrying kind."

My friend fell violently in love with her, and her resistance went down before it. His former haunts knew him no more, and I did not see him for several months. Then, late one evening, he telephoned to say that it was of the greatest importance to him to consult me. He arrived in a state of repressed excitement. He wanted it distinctly understood that he came to me as a client, not as a friend. I knew, of course, that he had married. This, he confessed, had proved a complete failure, and now his wife had gone away and with another woman, one whom he had met constantly at her home during his brief and tempestuous courtship.

I attempted to explain to him that she had probably acted on impulse; that the squabbles of early matrimony which often appeared to be tragedies, were adjustable and, fortunately, nearly always adjusted.

"Yes," said he, "but you don't understand. There hasn't been any row. My wife told me shortly after marrying me that she had made a mistake, and she has told me so many times since. I thought at first it was caprice. Perhaps I should still have thought so were it not for this letter." He then handed me a letter. I did not have to read between the lines to get the full significance of its content. It set forth briefly, concretely, and explicitly her reasons for leaving. Life without her former friend was intolerable, and she did not propose to attempt it longer.

He knew there were such persons in the world, but what he wanted to know from me was, Could they not, if properly and prudently handled, be brought to feel and love like those the world calls normal? Was it not possible that her conduct and confession were the result of a temporary derangement and that indulgent handling of her would make her see things in the right light? She had not alienated his love even though she had forfeited his respect; and he did not attempt to conceal from me that if the tangle could not be straightened out he felt that his life had been a failure.

I told him the truth about this enigmatic gesture of nature, that the victims of this strange abnormality are often of great brilliancy and charm, and most companionable; that it is not a disease and, therefore, cannot be cured.

In this instance, basing my opinion upon what his wife had told him both in speech and in writing, I was bound to believe that she was one of the strange sisterhood, and that it was her birthright as well as her misfortune. Such being the case, I could only advise what I thought might be best for their mutual and individual happiness. I suggested that divorce offered the safest way out for both. He replied that he felt competent to decide that for himself; all that he sought from me was enlightenment about her unnatural infatuation. This I had only too frankly given him.

Two days later his body with a pistol wound in the right temple was found in a field above Weehawken.

That day I regretted that I had not lied to him. It is a day that has had frequent anniversaries.

64

On Telling Patients the Truth

Roger Higgs

That honesty should be an important issue for debate in medical circles may seem bizarre. Nurses and doctors are usually thought of as model citizens. Outside the immediate field of health care, when a passport is to be signed, a reference given, or a special allowance made by a government welfare agency, a nurse's or doctor's signature is considered a good warrant, and false certification treated as a serious breach of professional conduct. Yet at the focus of medical activity or skill, at the bedside or in the clinic, when patient meets professional there is often doubt. Is the truth being told?

Many who are unfamiliar with illness and its treatment may well be forgiven for wondering if this doubt has not been exaggerated. It is as if laundry-men were to discuss the merits of clean clothes, or fishmongers of refrigeration. But those with experience, either as patients or professionals, will immediately recognize the situation. Although openness is increasingly practised, there is still uncertainty in the minds of many doctors or nurses faced with communicating bad news; as for instance when a test shows up an unexpected and probably incurable cancer, or when meeting the gaze of a severely ill child, or answering the questions of a mother in mid-pregnancy whose unborn child is discovered to be badly handicapped. What should be said? There can be few who have not, on occasions such as these, told less than the truth. Certainly the issue is a regular preoccupation of nurses and doctors in training. Why destroy hope? Why create anxiety, or something worse? Isn't it 'First, do no harm'?[1]

From Michael Lockwood (ed.) *Moral Dilemmas in Modern Medicine* (Oxford: Oxford University Press, 1985), pp. 186–202, 232–3. Reprinted with permission.

The concerns of the patient are very different. For many, fear of the unknown is the worst disease of all, and yet direct information seems so hard to obtain. The ward round goes past quickly, unintelligible words are muttered – was I supposed to hear and understand? In the surgery the general practitioner signs his prescription pad and clearly it's time to be gone. Everybody is too busy saving lives to give explanations. It may come as a shock to learn that it is policy, not just pressure of work, that prevents a patient learning the truth about himself. If truth is the first casuality, trust must be the second. 'Of course they wouldn't say, especially if things were bad,' said the elderly woman just back from out-patients, 'they've got that Oath, haven't they?' She had learned to expect from doctors, at the best, silence; at the worst, deception. It was part of the system, an essential ingredient, as old as Hippocrates. However honest a citizen, it was somehow part of the doctor's job not to tell the truth to his patient . . .

It is easier to decide what to do when the ultimate outcome is clear. It may be much more difficult to know what to say when the future is less certain, such as in the first episode of what is probably multiple sclerosis, or when a patient is about to undergo a mutilating operation. But even in work outside hospital, where such dramatic problems arise less commonly, whether to tell the truth and how much to tell can still be a regular issue. How much should this patient know about the side effects of his drugs? An elderly man sits weeping in an old people's home, and the healthy but exhausted daughter wants the doctor to tell her father that she's medically unfit to have him back. The single mother wants a certificate to say that she is unwell so that she can stay at home to look after her sick child. A colleague is often drunk on duty, and is making mistakes. A husband with venereal disease wants his wife to be treated without her knowledge. An outraged father demands to know if his teenage daughter has been put on the pill. A mother comes in with a child to have a boil lanced. 'Please tell him it won't hurt.' A former student writes from abroad needing to complete his professional experience and asks for a reference for a job he didn't do.[2] Whether the issue is large or small, the truth is at stake. What should the response be?

Discussion of the apparently more dramatic situations may provide a good starting-point. Recently a small group of medical students, new to clinical experience, were hotly debating what a patient with cancer should be told. One student maintained strongly that the less said to the patient the better. Others disagreed. When asked whether there was any group of patients they could agree should never be told the truth about a life-threatening illness, the students chose children, and agreed that they would not speak openly to children under six. When asked to try to remember what life was like when they were six, one student replied that he remembered how his mother had died when he was that age. Suddenly the student who had advocated non-disclosure became animated. 'That's extraordinary. My mother died when I was six too. My father said she'd gone away for a time, but would come back soon. One day he said she was coming home again. My younger sister and I were very excited. We waited at the window upstairs until we saw his car drive up. He got out and helped a woman out of the car. Then we saw. It wasn't mum. I suppose I never forgave him – or her, really.'[3]

It is hard to know with whom to sympathize in this sad tale. But its stark simplicity serves to highlight some essential points. First, somehow more clearly than in the examples involving patients, not telling the truth is seen for what it really is. It is, of course, quite possible, and very common in clinical practice, for doctors (or nurses) to engage in deliberate deceit without actually *saying* anything they believe to be false. But, given the special responsibilities of the doctor, and the relationship of trust that exists between him and his patient, one could hardly argue that this was morally any different from telling outright lies. Surely it is the *intention* that is all important. We may be silent, tactful, or reserved, but if we intend to deceive, what we are doing is tantamount to lying. The debate in ward or surgery is suddenly stood on its head. The question is no longer 'Should we tell the truth?' but 'What justification is there for telling a lie?' This relates to the second important point, that medical ethics are part of general morality, and not a separate field of their own with their own rules. Unless there are special justifications, health-care professionals are working within the same moral constraints as lay people. A lie is a lie wherever told and whoever tells it.

But do doctors have a special dispensation from the usual principles that guide the conduct of our society? It is widely felt that on occasion they do, and such a dispensation is as necessary to all doctors as freedom from the charge of assault is to a surgeon. But if it is impossible to look after ill patients and always be open and truthful, how can we balance this against the clear need for truthfulness on all other occasions? If deception is like a medicine to be given in certain doses in certain cases, what guidance exists about its administration?

My elderly patient reflected the widely held view that truth-telling, or perhaps withholding, was part of the tradition of medicine enshrined in its oaths and codes. Although the writer of the 'Decorum' in the Hippocratic corpus advises physicians of the danger of telling patients about the nature of their illness '... for many patients through this cause have taken a turn for the worse',[4] the Oath itself is completely silent on this issue. This extraordinary omission is continued through all the more modern codes and declarations. The first mention of veracity as a principle is to be found in the American Medical Association's 'Principles of Ethics' of 1980, which states that the physician should 'deal honestly with patients and colleagues and strive to expose those physicians deficient in character or competence, or who engage in fraud and deception'.[5] Despite the difficulties of the latter injunction, which seems in some way to divert attention from the basic need for honest communication with the patient, here at last is a clear statement. This declaration signally fails, however, to provide the guidance that we might perhaps have expected for the professional facing his or her individual dilemma.

The reticence of these earlier codes is shared, with some important exceptions, by medical writing elsewhere. Until recently most of what had been usefully said could be summed up by the articles of medical writers such as Thomas Percival, Worthington Hooker, Richard Cabot, and Joseph Collins, which show a wide scatter of viewpoints but do at least confront the problems directly.[6] There is, however, one widely quoted statement by Lawrence Henderson, writing in the *New England Journal of Medicine* in 1955.[7] 'It is meaningless to speak of telling the truth, the whole truth and nothing but the truth to a patient... because it is... a sheer impossibility... Since telling the truth is impossible, there can be no sharp distinction between what is true and what is false.'...

But we must not allow ourselves to be confused, as Henderson was, and as so many others have been, by a failure to distinguish between truth, the abstract concept, of which we shall always have an imperfect grasp, and *telling* the truth, where the intention is all important. Whether or not we can ever fully grasp or express the whole picture, whether we know ultimately what the truth really is, we must speak truthfully, and intend to convey what we understand, or we shall lie. In Sissela Bok's words 'The moral question of whether you are lying or not is not *settled* by establishing the truth or falsity of what you say. In order to settle the question, we must know whether you *intend your statement to mislead*.'[8]

Most modern thinkers in the field of medical ethics would hold that truthfulness is indeed a central principle of conduct, but that it is capable of coming into conflict with other principles, to which it must occasionally give way. On the other hand, the principle of veracity often receives support from other principles. For instance, it is hard to see how a patient can have autonomy, can make a free choice about matters concerning himself, without some measure of understanding of the facts as they influence the case; and that implies, under normal circumstances, some open, honest discussion with his advisers.[9] Equally, consent is a nonsense if it is not in some sense informed...

Once the central position of honesty has been established, we still need to examine whether doctors and nurses really do have, as has been suggested, special exemption from being truthful because of the nature of their work, and if so under what circumstances... It may finally be decided that in a crisis there is no acceptable alternative, as when life is ebbing and truthfulness would bring certain disaster. Alternatively, the moral issue may appear so trivial as not to be worth considering (as, for example, when a doctor is called out at night by a patient who apologizes by saying, 'I hope you don't mind me calling you at this time, doctor', and the doctor replies, 'No, not at all.'). However... occasions of these two types are few, fewer than those in which deliberate deceit would generally be regarded as acceptable in current medical practice, and should regularly be debated 'in public' if abuses are to be avoided.[10] To this end it is necessary now to examine critically the arguments commonly used to defend lying to patients.

First comes the argument that it is enormously difficult to put across a technical subject to those with little technical knowledge and understanding, in a situation where so little is predictable. A patient has bowel cancer. With surgery it might be cured, or it might recur. Can the patient understand the effects of treatment? The symptom she is now getting might be due to cancer, there might be secondaries, and they in turn might be suppressible for a long time, or not at all. What future symptoms might occur, how long will she live, how will she die – all these are desperately important questions for the patient, but even for her doctor the answers can only be informed guesses, in an area where uncertainty is so hard to bear.

Yet to say we do not know anything is a lie. As doctors we know a great deal, and *can* make informed guesses or offer likelihoods. The whole truth may be impossible to attain, but truthfulness is not. 'I do not know' can be a major piece of honesty. To deprive the patient of honest communication because we cannot know everything is, as we have seen, not only confused thinking but immoral. Thus deprived, the patient cannot plan, he cannot choose. If choice is the crux of morality, it may also, as we have argued elsewhere, be central to health. If he cannot choose, the patient cannot ever be considered to be fully restored to health.[11]

This argument also raises another human failing – to confuse the difficult with the unimportant. Passing information to people who have more restricted background, whether through lack of experience or of understanding, can be extremely difficult and time-consuming, but this is no reason why it should be shunned. Quite the reverse. Like the difficult passages in a piece of music, these tasks should be practiced, studied, and techniques developed so that communication is efficient and effective. For the purposes of informed consent, the patient must be given the information he needs, as a reasonable person, to make a reasoned choice.

The second argument for telling lies to patients is that no patient likes hearing depressing or frightening news. That is certainly true. There must be few who do. But in other walks of life no professional would normally consider it his or her duty to suppress information simply in order to preserve happiness. No accountant, foreseeing bankruptcy in his client's affairs, would chat cheerfully about the Budget or a temporarily reassuring credit account. Yet such suppression of information occurs daily in wards or surgeries throughout the country. Is this what patients themselves want?

In order to find out, a number of studies have been conducted over the past thirty years.[12] In most studies there is a significant minority of patients, perhaps about a fifth, who, if given information, deny having been told. Sometimes this must be pure forgetfulness, sometimes it relates to the lack of skill of the informer, but sometimes with bad or unwelcome news there is an element of what is (perhaps not quite correctly) called 'denial'. The observer feels that at one level the news has been taken in, but at another its validity or reality has not been accepted. This process has been recognized as a buffer for the mind against the shock of unacceptable news, and often seems to be part of a process leading to its ultimate acceptance.[13] But once this group has been allowed for, most surveys find that, of those who have had or who could have had a diagnosis made of, say, cancer, between two-thirds and three-quarters of those questioned were either glad to have been told, or declared that they would wish to know. Indeed, surveys reveal that most *doctors* would themselves wish to be told the truth, even though (according to earlier studies at least) most of those same doctors said they would not speak openly to their patients – a curious double standard! Thus these surveys have unearthed, at least for the present, a common misunderstanding between doctors and patients, a general preference for openness among patients, and a significant but small group whose wish not to be informed must surely be respected. We return once more to the skill needed to detect such differences in the individual case, and the need for training in such skills.

Why doctors have for so long misunderstood their patients' wishes is perhaps related to the task itself. Doctors don't want to give bad news, just as patients don't want it in abstract, but doctors have the choice of withholding the information, and in so doing protecting themselves from the pain of telling, and from the blame of being the bearer of bad news. In addition it has been suggested that doctors are particularly fearful of death and illness. Montaigne suggested that men have to think about death and be prepared to accept it, and one would think that doctors would get used to death. Yet perhaps this very familiarity has created an obsession that amounts to fear. Just as the police seem over-concerned with violence, and firemen with fire, perhaps doctors have met death in their professional training only as the enemy, never as something to come to terms with, or even as a natural force to be respected and, when the time is ripe, accepted or even welcomed.

Undeniably, doctors and nurses like helping people and derive much satisfaction from the feeling that the patient is being benefited. This basic feeling has been elevated to major status in medical practice. The principle of beneficence – to work for the patient's good – and the related principle of non-maleficence – 'first do no harm' – are usually quoted as the central guiding virtues in medicine. They are expanded in the codes, and underlie the appeal of utilitarian arguments in the context of health care. 'When you are thinking of telling a lie,' Richard Cabot quotes a teacher of his as saying, 'ask yourself whether it is simply and solely for the patient's benefit that you are going to tell it. If you are sure that you are acting for his good and not for your own profit, you can go ahead with a clear conscience.[14] But who should decide what is 'for the patient's benefit'? Why should it be the doctor? Increasingly society is uneasy with such a paternalistic style. In most other walks of life the competent individual is himself assumed to be the best judge of his own interests. Whatever may be thought of this assumption in the field of politics or law, to make one's own decisions on matters that are central to one's own life or welfare and do not directly concern others would normally be held to be a basic *right*; and hardly one to be taken away simply on the grounds of illness, whether actual or merely potential.

Thus if beneficence is assumed to be the key principle, which many now have come to doubt, it can easily ride roughshod over autonomy and natural justice. A lie denies a person the chance of participating in choices concerning his own health, including that of whether to be a 'patient' at all. Paternalism may be justifiable in the short term, and to 'kid' someone, to treat him as a child because he is ill, and perhaps dying, may be very tempting. Yet true respect for that person (adult or child) can only be shown by allowing him allowable choices, by granting him whatever control is left, as weakness gradually undermines his hold on life. If respect is important then at the very least there must be no acceptable or effective alternative to lying in a particular situation if the lie is to be justified...

However, a third argument for lying can be advanced, namely, that truthfulness can actually do harm. 'What you don't know can't hurt you' is a phrase in common parlance (though it hardly fits with concepts of presymptomatic screening for preventable disease!) However, it is undeniable that blunt and unfeeling communication of unpleasant truths can cause acute distress, and sometimes long-term disability. The fear that professionals often have of upsetting people, of causing a scene, of making fools of themselves by letting unpleasant emotions flourish, seems to have elevated this argument beyond its natural limits. It is not unusual to find that the fear of creating harm will deter a surgical team from discussing a diagnosis gently with a patient, but not deter it from performing radical and mutilating surgery. Harm is a very personal concept. Most medical schools have, circulating in the refectory, a story about a patient who was informed that he had cancer and then leapt to his death. The intended moral for the medical student is, keep your mouth shut and do no harm. But that may not be the correct lesson to be learned from such cases (which I believe, in any case, to be less numerous than is commonly supposed). The style of telling could have been brutal, with no follow-up or support. It may have been the suggested treatment, not the basic illness, that led the patient to resort to such a desperate measure. Suicide in illness is remarkably rare, but, though tragic, could be seen as a logical response to an overwhelming challenge. No mention is usually made of suicide rates in other circumstances, or the isolation felt by ill and warded patients, or the feelings of anger uncovered when someone takes such precipitate and forbidden action against himself. What these cases do, surely, is argue, not for no telling, but for better telling, for sensitivity and care in determining how much the patient wants to know, explaining carefully in ways the patient can understand, and providing full support and 'after-care' as in other treatments.

But even if it is accepted that the short-term effect of telling the truth may sometimes be considerable psychological disturbance, in the long term the balance seems definitely to swing the other way. The effects of lying are dramatically illustrated in 'A Case of Obstructed Death?'[15] False information prevented a woman from returning to healthy living after a cancer operation, and robbed her of six months of active life. Also, the long-term effect of lies on the family and, perhaps most importantly, on society, is incalculable. If trust is gradually corroded, if the 'wells are poisoned', progress is hard. Mistrust creates lack of communication and increased fear, and this generation has seen just such a fearful myth created around cancer.[16] Just how much harm has been done by this 'demonizing' of cancer, preventing people coming to their doctors, or alternatively creating unnecessary attendances on doctors, will probably never be known.

There are doubtless many other reasons why doctors lie to their patients; but these can hardly be used to justify lies, even if we should acknowledge them in passing. Knowledge is power, and certainly doctors, though usually probably for reasons of work-load rather than anything more sinister, like to remain 'in control'. Health professionals may, like others, wish to protect themselves from confrontation, and may find it easier to coerce or manipulate than to gain permission. There may be a desire to avoid any pressure for change. And there is the constant problem of lack of time. But in any assessment, the key issues remain. Not telling the truth normally involves telling lies, and doctors and nurses have no *carte blanche* to lie...

If the importance of open communication with the patient is accepted, we need to know when to say what. If a patient is going for investigations, it may be possible at that time, before details are known, to have a discussion about whether he would like to know the details. A minor 'contract' can be made. 'I promise to tell you what I know, if you ask me.' Once that time is past, however, it requires skill and sensitivity to assess what a patient wants to know. Allowing the time and opportunity for the patient to ask questions is the most important thing, but one must realize that the patient's apparent question may conceal the one he really wants answered. 'Do I have cancer?' may contain the more important questions 'How or when will I die?' 'Will there be pain?' The doctor will not necessarily be helping by giving an extended pathology lesson. The informer may need to know more: 'I don't want to avoid your question, and I promise to answer as truthfully as I can, but first...' It has been pointed out that in many cases the terminal patient will tell the doctor, not vice versa, if the right opportunities are created and the style and timing is appropriate. Then it is a question of not telling but listening to the truth.[17]

If in spite of all this there still seems to be a need to tell lies, we must be able to justify them. That the person is a child, or 'not very bright', will not do. Given the two ends of the spectrum of crisis and triviality, the vast middle range of communication requires honesty, so that autonomy and choice can be maintained. If lies are to be told, there really must be no acceptable alternative. The analogy with force may again be helpful here: perhaps using the same style of thinking as is used in the Mental Health Act, to test whether we are justified in removing someone's liberty against their will, may help us to see the gravity of what we are doing when we consider deception. It also suggests that the decision should be shared, in confidence, and be subject to debate, so that any alternative which may not initially have been seen may be considered. And it does not end there. If we break an important moral principle, that principle still retains its force, and its 'shadow' has to be acknowledged. As professionals we shall have to ensure that we follow up, that we work through the broken trust or the disillusionment that the lie will bring to the patient, just as we would follow up and work through bad news, a major operation, or a psychiatric 'sectioning'. This follow-up may also be called for in our relationship with our colleagues if there has been major disagreement about what should be done.

In summary, there are *some* circumstances in which the health professions are probably exempted from society's general requirement for truthfulness. But not telling the truth is usually the same as telling a lie, and a lie requires strong justification. Lying must be a last resort, and we should act as if we were to be called upon to defend the decision in public debate, even if our duty of confidentiality does not allow this in practice. We should always aim to respect the other important principles governing interactions with patients, especially the preservation of the patient's autonomy. When all is said and done, many arguments for individual cases of lying do not hold water. Whether or not knowing the truth is essential to the patient's health, telling the truth is essential to the health of the doctor–patient relationship.

Notes

1 *Primum non nocere* – this is a Latinization of a statement which is not directly Hippocratic, but may be derived from the *Epidemics* Book 1 Chapter II: 'As to diseases, make a habit of two things – to help, or at least do no harm.' *Hippocrates*, 4 vols (London: William Heinemann, 1923–31), vol. I, trans. W. H. S. Jones.

2 Cases collected by the author in his own practice.

3 Case collected by the author.

4 Quoted in Reiser, Dyck, and Curran (eds), *Ethics in Medicine, Historical Perspectives and Contemporary Concerns* (Cambridge, MA: MIT Press, 1977).

5 American Medical Association, 'Text of the American Medical Association New Principles of Medical Ethics', *American Medical News* (August 1–8 1980), 9.

6 To be found in Reiser et al. (see n. 4 above).

7 Lawrence Henderson, 'Physician and Patient as a Social System', *New England Journal of Medicine*, 212 (1935).

8 Sissela Bok, *Lying: Moral Choice in Public and Private Life* (London: Quartet, 1980).

9 Alastair Campbell and Roger Higgs, *In That Case* (London: Darton, Longman and Todd, 1982).

10 John Rawls, *A Theory of Justice* (Cambridge, MA: Harvard University Press, Belknap Press, 1971).

11 (See n. 9 above).

12 Summarized well in Robert Veatch, 'Truth-telling I' in *Encyclopaedia of Bioethics*, ed. Warren T. Reich (New York: Free Press, 1978).

13 The five stages of reacting to bad news, or news of dying, are described in *On Death and Dying* by Elizabeth Kubler-Ross (London: Tavistock, 1970). Not everyone agrees with her model. For another view see a very stimulating article 'Therapeutic Uses of Truth' by Michael Simpson in E. Wilkes (ed.), *The Dying Patient* (Lancaster: MTP Press, 1982). 'In my model there are only two stages – the stage when you believe in the Kubler-Ross five and the stage when you do not.'

14 Quoted in Richard Cabot, 'The Use of Truth and Falsehood in Medicine; an experimental study', *American Magazine*, 5 (1903), 344–9.

15 Roger Higgs, 'Truth at the last – A Case of Obstructed Death?' *Journal of Medical Ethics*, 8 (1982), 48–50, and Roger Higgs, 'Obstructed Death Revisited', *Journal of Medical Ethics*, 8 (1982), 154–6.

16 Susan Sontag, *Illness as Metaphor* (New York: Farrar, Straus and Giroux, 1978).

17 Cicely Saunders, 'Telling Patients', *District Nursing* (now *Queens Nursing Journal*) (September 1963), 149–50, 154.

Informed Consent and Patient Autonomy

65

On Liberty

John Stuart Mill

The object of this essay is to assert one very simple principle, as entitled to govern absolutely the dealings of society with the individual in the way of compulsion and control, whether the means used be physical force in the form of legal penalties, or the moral coercion of public opinion. That principle is, that the sole end for which mankind are warranted, individually or collectively, in interfering with the liberty of action of any of their number, is self-protection. That the only purpose for which power can be rightfully exercised over any member of a civilized community, against his will, is to prevent harm to others. His own good, either physical or moral, is not a sufficient warrant. He cannot rightfully be compelled to do or forbear because it will be better for him to do so, because it will make him happier, because, in the opinions of others, to do so would be wise, or even right. These are good reasons for remonstrating with him, or reasoning with him, or persuading him, or entreating him, but not for compelling him, or visiting him with any evil in case he do otherwise. To justify that, the conduct from which it is desired to deter him must be calculated to produce evil to someone else. The only part of the conduct of anyone, for which he is amenable to society, is that which concerns others. In the part which merely concerns himself, his independence is, of right, absolute. Over himself, over his own body and mind, the individual is sovereign.

It is perhaps hardly necessary to say that this doctrine is meant to apply only to human beings in the maturity of their faculties. We are not speaking of children, or of young persons below the age which the law may fix as that of manhood or womanhood. Those who are still in a state to require being taken care of by others, must be protected against their own actions as well as against external injury. For the same reason, we may leave out of consideration those backward states of society in which the race itself may be considered as in its nonage. The early difficulties in the way of spontaneous progress are so great, and there is seldom any choice of means for overcoming them; and a ruler full of the spirit of improvement is warranted in the use of any expedients that will attain an end, perhaps otherwise unattainable. Despotism is a legitimate mode of government in dealing with barbarians, provided the end be their improvement, and the means justified by actually effecting that end. Liberty, as a principle, has no application to any state of things anterior to the time when mankind have become capable of being improved by free and equal discussion. Until then, there is nothing for them but implicit obedience to an Akbar or a Charlemagne, if they are so fortunate as to find one. But as soon as mankind have attained the capacity of being guided to their own improvement by conviction or persuasion (a period long since reached in all nations with whom we need here concern ourselves), compulsion, either in the direct form or in that of pains and penalties for non-compliance, is no longer admissible as a means to their own good, and justifiable only for the security of others.

It is proper to state that I forgo any advantage which could be derived to my argument from the idea of abstract right, as a thing independent of utility. I regard utility as the ultimate appeal on all

First published in 1859.

ethical questions; but it must be utility in the largest sense, grounded on the permanent interests of a man as a progressive being. Those interests, I contend, authorized the subjection of individual spontaneity to external control, only in respect to those actions of each which concern the interest of other people. If anyone does an act hurtful to others, there is a *prima facie* case for punishing him, by law, or, where legal penalties are not safely applicable, by general disapprobation. There are also many positive acts for the benefit of others, which he may rightfully be compelled to perform: such as to give evidence in a court of justice; to bear his fair share in the common defense, or in any other joint work necessary to the interest of the society of which he enjoys the protection; and to perform certain acts of individual beneficence, such as saving a fellow-creature's life, or interposing to protect the defenseless against illusage, things which whenever it is obviously a man's duty to do, he may rightfully be made responsible to society for not doing. A person may cause evil to others not only by his actions but by his inaction, and in either case he is justly accountable to them for the injury. The latter case, it is true, requires a much more cautious exercise of compulsion than the former. To make anyone answerable for doing evil to others is the rule; to make him answerable for not preventing evil is, comparatively speaking, the exception. Yet there are many cases clear enough and grave enough to justify that exception. In all things which regard the external relations of the individual, he is *de jure* amenable to those whose interests are concerned, and, if need be, to society as their protector. There are often good reasons for not holding him to the responsibility; but these reasons must arise from the special expediencies of the case: either because it is a kind of case in which he is on the whole likely to act better, when left to his own discretion, than when controlled in any way in which society have it in their power to control him; or because the attempt to exercise control would produce other evils, greater than those which it would prevent. When such reasons as these preclude the enforcement of responsibility, the conscience of the agent himself should step into the vacant judgment seat, and protect those interests of others which have no external protection; judging himself all the more rigidly, because the case does not admit of his being made accountable to the judgment of his fellow-creatures.

But there is a sphere of action in which society, as distinguished from the individual, has, if any, only an indirect interest; comprehending all that portion of a person's life and conduct which affects only himself, or if it also affects others, only with their free, voluntary, and undeceived consent and participation. When I say only himself, I mean directly, and in the first instance; for whatever affects himself, may affect others through himself; and the objection which may be grounded on this contingency, will receive consideration in the sequel. This, then, is the appropriate region of human liberty. It comprises, *first*, the inward domain of consciousness; demanding liberty of conscience in the most comprehensive sense; liberty of thought and feeling; absolute freedom of opinion and sentiment on all subjects, practical or speculative, scientific, moral, or theological. The liberty of expressing and publishing opinions may seem to fall under a different principle, since it belongs to that part of the conduct of an individual which concerns other people; but, being almost of as much importance as the liberty of thought itself, and resting in great part on the same reasons, is practically inseparable from it. *Secondly*, the principle requires liberty of tastes and pursuits; of framing the plan of our life to suit our own character; of doing as we like, subject to such consequences as may follow: without impediment from our fellow-creatures, so long as what we do does not harm them, even though they should think our conduct foolish, perverse, or wrong. *Thirdly*, from this liberty of each individual, follows the liberty, within the same limits, of combination among individuals; freedom to unite, for any purpose not involving harm to others: the persons combining being supposed to be of full age, and not forced or deceived.

No society in which these liberties are not, on the whole, respected, is free, whatever may be its form of government; and none is completely free in which they do not exist absolute and unqualified. The only freedom which deserves the name, is that of pursuing our own good in our own way, so long as we do not attempt to deprive others of theirs, or impede their efforts to obtain it. Each is the proper guardian of his own health, whether bodily, or mental and spiritual. Mankind are greater gainers by suffering each other to live as seems good to themselves, than by compelling each to live as seems good to the rest.

66

From *Schloendorff v. New York Hospital*

Benjamin N. Cardozo

Every human being of adult years and sound mind has a right to determine what shall be done with his own body; and a surgeon who performs an operation without his patient's consent commits an assault, for which he is liable in damages. (*Pratt* v. *Davis*, 224 Ill. 300; *Mohr* v. *Williams*, 95 Minn. 261.) This is true except in cases of emergency where the patient is unconscious and where it is necessary to operate before consent can be obtained.

From B. N. Cardozo, *Schloendorff* v *N. Y. Hospital* 211 NY, 127, 129, 105 N. E. 92, 93 (1914) as it appears in *Experimentation with Human Beings* ed. Jay Katz (New York: Russell Sage Foundation, 1972), p. 526.

67

Autonomy, Futility, and the Limits of Medicine

Robert L. Schwartz

Surgeon: I don't seem to understand; why, precisely, have you come to see me today?

Patient: I am here because I need to have my right arm amputated, and I have been told that you are one of the finest surgeons in town.

Surgeon: That is, of course, correct. Tell me, though – I do not see a referral here – what makes you think that you need your arm amputated?

Patient: It is the only way I can expiate my sins. I could describe those sins to you in detail, and I could tell you why this is the only way I can seek expiation, but that hardly seems appropriate or necessary. In any case, I am sure that the only way I can expiate them is by having my right arm amputated.

Surgeon: Do I understand this? You came to see me because you want a good surgeon to amputate your right arm so that you can expiate your sins.

Patient: Exactly; I knew you would understand. By the way, I am fully insured.

Surgeon: Are you crazy? You've come to a surgeon just because you want your arm lopped off?

Patient: I would be crazy if I went any place else. I mean, you wouldn't recommend a butcher or a chiropractor, would you?

Surgeon: I'm sorry; your request is simply unacceptable. My values do not permit me to provide the services you seek. I just don't think it would be right.

Patient: Wait just a minute. I am not hiring you for your ability to make moral judgments. I am hiring you because of your technical skill in removing limbs. We are talking about my arm, my life, and my values. I have decided I need the surgery and I ask you merely to respect my autonomy and to apply your medical skill so that my values can be served. If you want to expiate your sins in some other way, that's just fine with me. I don't want your religious and ethical peccadillos to interfere with a high-quality technical medical service that I am paying you to provide for me.

Most of us find the surgeon's surprise at this patient's request understandable, and it is hard to imagine any surgeon acceding to this patient's demand. On the other hand (the one left), the patient is right – the surgeon is denying his technical skill because his values are different from those of the patient, whose values the surgeon does not respect.[1] The autonomy of the patient is being limited by the values of the doctor whose own interests, other than his interest in practicing medicine according to his own ethical values, would remain unaffected by his decision to provide the service.

Autonomy and Patient Control of Medical Decision Making

Autonomy is the authority to make decisions in accord with one's own values, unrestrained by the

From *Cambridge Quarterly of Healthcare Ethics*, vol. 2 (1992), pp. 159–64.

values of others who do not suffer the consequences of the decision. Ordinarily, the principle of autonomy authorizes patients to make healthcare decisions unrestrained by the values of their physicians, others in the healthcare industry, or the rest of society. Despite this, even the strongest supporters of the primacy of the principle of autonomy in healthcare decision making – even those who believe that autonomy virtually always trumps beneficence – would be likely to support (or even require) the surgeon's decision *not* to offer surgery in this case. But why?

The principle of autonomy has never been understood to authorize patients to choose from among an unrestricted range of alternatives. As Fenella Rouse points out in the next note on the *Wanglie* case, autonomy has often been misconstrued and improperly applied by courts in cases involving medical decision making. In any case, there are at least three kinds of limitations on the exercise of autonomy by those making healthcare choices. First, patients may not require that they be treated by nonmedical means. Second, patients may not require that they be given scientifically futile treatment. Finally, and most significantly, patients may not require that they be treated in ways that are inconsistent with the ends of medicine, that is, in ways that are outside of the scope of medicine.

First, for example, a tense and depressed streetcar operator is not denied autonomy by our healthcare system if he is not given the option of choosing three weeks on the beach in Tahiti as a cure for his condition, even though it may well be effective. Three weeks on the beach in Tahiti is simply not a medical means of treatment – it is not among the medical alternatives for the treatment of that (or any other) condition.

Second, where the issue is one of scientific futility, i.e., whether a medical procedure will have the scientific consequences that are expected, the issue is left entirely to the medical profession. Physicians are not required to prescribe pasque-flower tea for the treatment of cancer, for example, because, as a scientific matter, there is simply no efficacy in treatment by pasque-flower tea. From a purely scientific perspective, the treatment of cancer by pasque-flower tea really is futile.

Unlike beach rest, amputation is within the therapeutic arsenal of the medical profession; it is a medical procedure. Unlike pasque-flower tea as a cure for cancer, surgical amputation is a proven effective way of removing a limb; thus, it is not futile in a scientific sense. Despite this, though, we would not allow the patient in the opening vignette to demand that his arm be amputated because patients are not permitted to demand surgery that is inconsistent with the definition of the scope of medical practice accepted by the surgeon.[2] In their exercise of autonomy, patients may choose only from among reasonable medical alternatives. The hard question is how doctors, patients, and others define which medically and scientifically proven procedures are among the reasonable medical alternatives.

The Wanglie Case

The limitations on a patient's autonomy to choose healthcare has come to the forefront of the bioethics debate over the past year. In December 1989, Helga Wanglie, an 87-year-old retired school teacher in Minneapolis, tripped on a rug in her home and fractured her hip.[3] One month later, after surgery in one hospital, she was transferred to Hennepin County Medical Center, where her doctors determined she needed assistance in breathing and placed her on a ventilator. Three months later, in May 1990, she was transferred to yet another hospital to see if she could be weaned from her ventilator. While there, she suffered cardiac arrest and was resuscitated, but only after she suffered severe and irreversible brain damage that put her in a persistent vegetative state. She was moved back to Hennepin County Medical Center, where she was maintained on a ventilator and fed through a gastrostomy tube. Mrs Wanglie remained in a persistent vegetative state for several months before her physicians determined that the continuation of high-tech medical intervention was inappropriate. In essence, the doctors determined that the care Mrs Wanglie was receiving was no longer among the reasonable medical alternatives for a person in her condition – it was, to her doctors, morally analogous to amputating a limb to expiate sins.

Mrs Wanglie's husband and her two children disagreed. As Mrs Wanglie's husband pointed out, "Only He who gave life has the right to take life." He also pointed out, "I am a pro-lifer. I take the position that human life is sacred."[4] He and the children agreed that Mrs Wanglie would want treatment continued, even if the doctors believed that there were no chance of recovery. This was, as the family pointed out, a determination based on the patient's values, and there was no reason to defer to the doctors' collective ethical judgment.

The physicians and the hospital searched in vain for some healthcare facility in Minnesota that would be willing to take Mrs Wanglie and continue to provide her care. None came forward. Frustrated by what they considered the continued inappropriate use of medicine, the hospital sought a court order appointing a conservator to replace Mr Wanglie to make healthcare decisions for Mrs Wanglie. On 1 July 1991, the trial court judge refused to issue an order and effectively confirmed Mr Wanglie's right to continue to make healthcare decisions for his wife of 53 years.[5] Three days after the order was issued, Mrs Wanglie died "of natural causes." Her hospitalization cost nearly 1 million dollars, which was paid by Medicare and her private medigap insurance carrier. Neither objected to the care for financial or cost-benefit reasons, and the cost properly did not enter into the judicial analysis of the case.

Asking the Wrong Question: Substitute Decision Makers and the Wanglie Court

Unfortunately, the litigation in this case obscured the real issue. The hospital's decision to seek a conservatorship did nothing more than raise the issue of whether Mr Wanglie was the best decision maker for his wife. The lawsuit asked nothing more than whether Mr Wanglie was the most able to apply his wife's values to the medical facts in this case.[6] Indeed, the hospital supplied no evidence that anyone else would be more likely to be able to determine and apply Mrs Wanglie's values. To the extent that the litigation focused on how best to carry to fruition Mrs Wanglie's autonomy, not on the limits of that autonomy, the hospital was left without a prayer of success.

The real question, however, should not have been what Mrs Wanglie would have desired (or what was in her "best personal medical interest") – there was no reason to doubt her family on that point – but whether the continuation of ventilator support and gastrostomy feeding were among the reasonable medical alternatives that should have been available to Mrs Wanglie or her surrogate decision maker, whoever that might be. The question, really, was whether the provision of this kind of treatment in this kind of case was outside the limits of medicine and, thus, beyond her power of choice.

Mrs Wanglie's healthcare providers should have argued that medical practice simply did not include providing a ventilator and gastrostomy feeding under circumstances of this case, and that no surrogate decision maker – whether it be Mr Wanglie or another substituted by the court – should be able to choose this option. If, for example, Mr Wanglie requested that his wife be frozen and cryopreserved so that she could be brought back to life and "cured" when there were sufficient advances in the science of her underlying ailments, there is no doubt that this request would not have to be honored by Mrs Wanglie's medical team. A request for cryopreservation, like a request for surgery that a patient believes will expiate his sins, may well reflect the true desires of the patient, but it is a request that asks something that is beyond the limits of medicine.[7] Why is the Wanglie family request in this case any different? The real question in the *Wanglie* case was whether the continuation of life-sustaining treatment for an 87-year-old woman in a persistent vegetative state with no hope of return to sentience constitutes treatment outside of the limits of medicine.

Although the question of the propriety of treatment for Mrs Wanglie has been discussed as if it were a question of "futility," there is no doubt that the treatment was *not* futile in the purely scientific sense. The treatment was designed to keep Mrs Wanglie alive, and it served this end effectively. Those who have viewed the *Wanglie* case as one dealing with futility in a scientific sense have brought the wrong perspective to the case. The question is not whether the treatment offered would successfully do what Mrs Wanglie's family said she desired – keep her alive – but whether keeping her alive, under the circumstances, was beyond the proper scope of medicine. Like most questions in medicine, this is not purely a question of science or a question of values, but a hybrid question.

The Role of the Physician in Healthcare Decision Making

Even when the question is not a purely scientific one, even when it involves a determination of whether medical treatment justifies the quality of life that results, our society has generally left to physicians the determination of whether a particular treatment is among the reasonable medical alternatives. There are, of course, problems with this approach.[8] Why should physicians have the exclusive authority to define the extent of their own professional conduct? Does this lead to too much variation from doctor to doctor and from hospital to hospital? Could doctors decide that providing treatment to HIV-positive patients is beyond the limits of medicine? Leaving the question of what constitutes a reasonable medical alternative in the hands of Dr Kevorkian yields a very different result than leaving that same question in the hands of the doctors who are associated with the right-to-life movement. As the national debate over euthanasia has demonstrated, doctors disagree over the appropriate scope of medicine with as much vigor, and probably with more concern, than the rest of us.

In the end, though, that is exactly why these decisions should be left to physicians. If a patient who desires a particular course of treatment can find a healthcare provider – *any* healthcare provider – who believes that the proposed course of treatment is within the realm of reasonable medical alternatives, that patient will have access to that course of treatment. It is only when a patient desires treatment that not a single healthcare provider believes to be within the limits of medicine that the patient will be denied that course of treatment. If a patient seeks amputation for the expiation of sins, for example, it is unlikely that the patient will find any surgeon willing to perform the task. When there is universal agreement among healthcare providers that the patient's request seeks something beyond the limits of medicine, that should constitute very strong evidence that the request is inappropriate.

The Wanglie family could not find any healthcare provider in Minnesota who would offer the medical services the family thought appropriate. Although the technical services that were sought (the ventilator, for example) were clearly within the scope of medical practice, there was no healthcare provider in Minnesota who believed that the provision of those services in Mrs Wanglie's circumstance was within the range of reasonable medical alternatives – at least, no one who was capable of providing the services was willing to do so. In effect, the court required Hennepin County Medical Center to provide a service that was, in the universal conclusion of Minnesota healthcare providers, inappropriate.

Asking the Right Question: The Courts and Ethics Committees

Courts focus only on the best way to serve the autonomy of patients; after all, the courts are largely responsible for making the principle of autonomy the guiding principle for medical decision-making. The *Wanglie* court was simply unable to get beyond the question of who could best identify the values and interests of the patient and move on to the question of whether the proposed treatment was within the limits of medicine. The court did not decide that continued use of the ventilator and the continued gastrostomy feedings were reasonable medical alternatives for Mrs Wanglie; it did not address these questions at all. Similarly, in October 1991, an Atlanta judge finessed the same issue in just the same way when she determined in the *Jane Doe* case that a 13-year-old with a degenerative neurologic condition must be continued on a treatment dictated by her father, who believed in miracles, despite the testimony of her pediatric neurologist that it was "ethically and morally unconscionable" to do so.[9]

If the courts continue to miss the real issue in these cases, as they will, that issue will have to be addressed in some other forum where there is both the moral and medical sophistication to understand the limits of medicine and the sensitivity to understand (and help define) society's reasonable expectations of medicine. Within their roles as educators, as mediators, and as sources for discussion of exactly these questions, broadly interdisciplinary ethics committees seem particularly well suited to the task. When a court is forced to face a determination by such a committee that a particular treatment, in a particular case, is beyond the limits of medicine – even though this treatment is exactly what the patient desires, even though the treatment employs a clearly medical procedure, and even though the treatment is not scientifically futile – that court may be forced to take the real question seriously.

Notes

1 One might argue that the surgeon's only real concern is over the competency of the patient, but there is no reason outside of this medical request itself to question that competency. Indeed, we accept the fact that competent people can make unusual requests – requests that the vast majority of us find strange – and still be competent. We are even more likely to find unusual behavior (such as various kinds of abstinence and abnegation) consistent with competence when the behavior is religious, or quasi-religious, as it is here. In any case, there is very little left to any meaningful notion of competence if we determine a patient's competence to choose a particular form of treatment solely by reference to the treatment choice he makes.

2 Analogously, the American Medical Association has found it unacceptable to have physicians administer lethal doses of drugs to execute condemned prisoners, even if the condemned prisoners request the administration of the drugs because the alternative methods of execution are more painful or degrading. Although the administration of the relevant drugs is appropriately limited to physicians, their use *for this purpose* is simply outside of the scope of medicine, whatever the prisoner-patient may desire.

3 A great deal has been written about the *Wanglie* case. Several relevant articles are found in the July–August 1991 issue of the *Hastings Center Report*, which includes a summary of the facts prepared by Ronald Cranford of the Department of Neurology at the hospital in which Mrs Wanglie remained a patient at her death. The facts are fleshed out in various newspaper articles: Colen. Fight over life. *Newsday* (1991 Jan. 29): City p. 57; Belkin. As family protests, hospital seeks an end to woman's life support. *New York Times* (1991 Jan. 10): Sec. A, p. 1; Steinbrook. Hospital or family: who decides right to die? *Los Angeles Times* (1991 Feb. 17): Part A, p. 1.

4 See note 3. Colen (1991): 57.

5 *Conservatorship of Wanglie*, No. PX-91-283 (Minn., Hennepin Co. Dist. Ct., July 1, 1991).

6 The hospital argued that Mr Wanglie should be disqualified from making the decision for his wife because his decision was not in the "patient's best *personal medical interest*." Cranford. Helga Wanglie's ventilator. *Hastings Center Report* (1991; Jul.–Aug.): 23–4.

7 The courts have been unsympathetic to those who seek cryopreservation, as you might guess. For a description of the case of Thomas Donaldson, who did not convince a court to allow the removal and freezing of his head before his certain death from a brain tumor, see Corwin. Tumor victim loses bid to freeze head before death. *Los Angeles Times* (1990 Sep. 15): Sec. A, p. 28. As one might expect, the case was subsequently turned into an episode of *L. A. Law* (#7D08, copyright 1990).

8 To the extent these problems flow from the use of a "futility" exception to normal requirements of consent, they are cogently and thoughtfully expressed in Scofield. Is consent useful when resuscitation isn't. *Hastings Center Report* (1991; Nov.–Dec.): 28–6. As Scofield points out (in the context of CPR);

> In reality the futility exception is a dishonest solution to the tragic choice that decisions to limit treatment represent. It purports to represent, but in fact departs from the fundamental values consent is intended to serve. It will not generate the conversation we need if we are to attain consensus about limiting treatment; nor will it make physicians sensitive in their dealings with patients, especially dying patients. It promotes a model of consent that is antithetical to setting limits in a democratic, caring manner. (p. 30)

9 Colen. Judge bars letting girl in coma die. *Newsday* (1991 Oct. 18): News p. 4.1.

68

Abandoning Informed Consent

Robert M. Veatch

Consent has emerged as a concept central to modern medical ethics. Often the term is used with a modifier, such as *informed* or *voluntary* or *full*, as in loosely used phrases like "fully informed and voluntary consent." In some form or another, modern ethics in health care could hardly function without the notion of consent.

While we might occasionally encounter an old-guard retrograde longing for the day when physicians did not have to go through the process of getting consent, by and large consent is now taken as a given, at least at the level of theory. To be sure, we know that actual consent is not obtained in all cases and even when consent is obtained, it may not be adequately informed or autonomous. For purposes of this discussion, we shall not worry about the deviations from the ideal; rather the focus will be on whether consent ought to be the goal.

This consensus in favor of consent may turn out to be all too facile. *Consent* may be what can be called a transition concept, one that appears on the scene as an apparently progressive innovation, but after a period of experience turns out to be only useful as a transition to a more thoroughly revisionary conceptual framework.

This paper will defend the thesis that consent is merely a transitional concept. While it emerged in the field as a liberal, innovative idea, its time may have passed and newer, more enlightened formulations may be needed. Consent means approval or agreement with the actions or opinions of another; terms such as *acquiescence* and *condoning* appear in the dictionary definitions. In medicine, the physician or other health care provider will, after reviewing the facts of the case and attempting to determine what is in the best interest of the patient, propose a course of action for the patient's concurrence. While a few decades ago it might have been considered both radical and innovative to seek the patient's acquiescence in the professional's clinical judgment, by now that may not be nearly enough. It is increasingly clear if one studies the theory of clinical decision-making that there is no longer any basis for presuming that the clinican can even guess at what is in the overall best interest of the patient. If that is true, then a model in which the clinician guesses at what he or she believes is best for the patient, pausing only to elicit the patient's concurrence, will no longer be sufficient. Increasingly we will have to go beyond patient consent to a model in which plausible options are presented (perhaps with the professional's recommendation regarding a personal preference among them, based on the professional's personally held beliefs and values), but with no rational or "professional" basis for even guessing at which one might truly be in the patient's best interest. To demonstrate that the concept of consent will no longer be adequate for the era of contemporary medicine, some work will be in order. After briefly summarizing the emergence of the consent doctrine, we will look at what we learn from axiology – the philosophical study of the theory of the good – that calls into question the adequacy of *consent* as a way of legitimating clinical decisions. This, I suggest, will provide a basis for demonstrating why experts in an area such as medicine ought not to be expected to be able to guess correctly what course is in the patient's interest, and therefore should not

From *Hastings Center Report*, vol. 25, no. 2 (March–April 1995), pp. 5–12.

be able to propose a course to which the patient's response is mere consent or refusal.

The History of Consent

The history of consent reveals that it is a relatively recent phenomenon.[1] None of the classical documents in the ethics of medicine had anything resembling a notion of consent, informed or no. Autonomy of decision making, especially lay decision-making, was not in the operating framework. For example, neither the Hippocratic oath nor any of the other Hippocratic writings says anything about consent or any other form of patient participation in decision-making.[2] The oath explicitly prohibits even disclosure of information to patients. Up until the revision of 1980, the American Medical Association's published *Current Opinions* did not include any notion of consent either. To this day the AMA *Opinions* permit physicians to treat without consent when the physician believes that consent would be "medically contraindicated."[3] Consent is essentially a twentieth-century phenomenon, but one that has its roots in post-Reformation affirmation of the individual and the liberal political philosophy and related judicial system derived from it rather than in professional physician ethics.[4]

While classical medical ethics had no doctrine of informed consent, what can be called modern medicine did begin making limited room for the notion. Wide recognition of the importance of patient concurrence in a medical intervention first arose in research involving human subjects. The Nuremberg Code gives pride of place to the consent requirement.[5] In clinical medicine explicit consent has, at least until very recently, been reserved for more controversial treatments and for choices that are perceived as "ethically exotic." Consent is frequently invoked for treatment decisions in which the patient is seen as drawing on ethical and other values coming from outside medicine. Often this arises more in the refusal of consent than approvals of treatment. For instance, patients are now sometimes given the opportunity to refuse consent for certain death-prolonging interventions during a terminal illness.

Sometimes the consent notion gets a bit muddled – as when patients are asked to "consent" to DNR (do-not-resuscitate) orders. The idea of consenting to an "order" is strange, but the idea of consenting to nontreatment is even more so. A more appropriate language would refer to refusal of consent to resuscitation rather than consenting to nonresuscitation.

Modern medicine has reluctantly made room for the consent doctrine and has recognized, at least in theory, the right of patients to consent and refuse consent to certain kinds of treatment. Usually explicit consent is reserved for these more complex and exotic decisions. It is still common to hear people distinguish between treatments for which consent is required and those for which it is not. Surely it would be better to speak of those for which consent must be explicit and others that still require consent even though the consent can be implied or presumed. For example, many would probably say that routine blood drawings of modest amounts of blood can be done without consent. This would more appropriately be described as being done without explicit consent and with no specific information needing to be transmitted. The mere extending of the arm should count as an adequate consent.

Likewise, when a physician writes a prescription, he or she is supposed to review the alternatives and choose the best medication, select a brand name or generic equivalent, choose a route of administration, a dosage level, and length of use of the medication. The patient may signal "consent" simply by accepting the prescription and getting it filled at the local pharmacy.

Up until now no one has seriously questioned the adequacy, from the left, of an approach that permits explicit consent for special and complex treatment, including research and surgery, and implicit or presumed consent for more routine procedures. More careful analysis reveals that, in fact, the consent model buys into more of the traditional, authoritarian understanding of clinical decision-making than many people realize. As in the days prior to the development of the consent doctrine, the clinician is still supposed to draw on his or her medical knowledge to determine what he or she believes is in the best interest of the patient and propose that course of treatment. Terms such as "doctor's orders" may have been replaced by more appropriate images, but the physician is still expected to determine what is "medically indicated," the "treatment of choice," or what in the "clinical judgment" of the practitioner is best for the patient. The clinician then proposes that course, subject only to the qualification that through either word or action, the patient signals approval of the physician-determined plan.

Consent and the Theory of the Good

Current work on the theory of medical decision-making and in axiology makes increasingly clear that this pattern no longer makes sense. It still rests on the outdated presumption that the clinician's moral responsibility is to do what is best for the patient, according to his or her ability and judgement, and that there is some reason to hope that the clinician can determine what is in the patient's best interest. The idea in medical ethics of doing what is best for the patient has achieved the status of an unquestioned platitude, but like many platitudes, it may not stand the test of more careful examination. On several levels the problems are beginning to show.

The best interest standard in surrogate decisions

The "best interest standard" has become the standard for surrogate decision-making in cases in which the wishes of the patient are not known and substituted judgment based on the patient's beliefs and values is not possible. But the best interest standard, if taken literally, is terribly implausible. In fact, no decision-maker is held to it in practice.

Two problems arise. First, since such judgments are increasingly recognized to be terribly complex and subjective, it is now widely accepted that the surrogate need not choose literally what is best. It would be extremely difficult to determine whether the absolute best choice has been made. Surely, the opinion of the attending physician cannot serve as a definitive standard. A privately appointed, parochial ethics committee might be better, but still surely is not definitive. If every surrogate decision were taken to court, we still would not have an absolute assurance that the best choice had been made.

Fortunately, we generally do not hold parents and other surrogates to a literal best interest standard when they make decisions for their wards. We expect, tolerate, even encourage a reasonable range of discretion. That is why it makes sense to replace the best interest standard with a "standard of reasonableness" or what could be called a "reasonable interest standard."[6]

There is a second reason why the best interest standard is inappropriate for surrogate decisions. Often surrogates have legitimate moral obligations to people other than the patient. Parents, for example, are pledged to serve the welfare of their other children. When best interests conflict, it is logically impossible to fulfill simultaneously the best interest standard for more than one child at the same time. Surely, all that is expected is that a reasonable balance of the conflicting interests be pursued.

Problems with best interest in clinician judgments

Although the problems with the best interest standard in surrogate decisions are more immediately apparent, a more fundamental and important problem with best interest arises when clinicians are held to the best interest standard in an ethic of patient care. For a clinician to guess at what is the best course for the patient, three assumptions must be true regarding a theory of the good. First, the clinician must be expected to determine what will best serve the patient's medical or health interest; second, the clinician must be expected to determine how to trade off health interests with other interests; and third, the clinician must be expected to determine how the patient should relate the pursuit of her best interest to other moral goals and responsibilities, including serving the interests of others and fulfilling any moral duties she may have that happen to conflict with her interest. An examination of the theories of the good and the morally right will reveal that it is terribly implausible to expect a typical clinician to be able to perform any one of these tasks completely correctly, let alone all three of them. If the clinician cannot be expected to guess at what serves the well-being of the patient and determine when patient well-being should be subordinated to other moral requirements, then there is no way that he or she can be expected to propose a course of treatment to which the patient would offer mere consent.

Alternative Theories of the Good

To understand the limits on the ability of the clinician to propose a course that will maximize patient well-being, we need to examine briefly current theories of the good. Axiology – the study of theories of the good or valuable – is a field of normative philosophical ethics that is in considerable turmoil. Fortunately, for our purposes, any plausible contemporary theory leads to the same radical conclusion: there is no reason to believe that a physician or any other expert in only one component of well-being should be able to determine what constitutes the good for another being.

Determining what it means to say something is in someone's best interest turns out to be a very difficult task. Establishing the proper criteria for determining that one course or another maximizes the good for an individual is even harder. One major philosophical contributor to this debate suggests that there are at least three major groups of answers to the question of what is in someone's best interest.[7] Hedonistic theories hold that what best serves someone's interest is that which makes the person's life happiest. Desire-fulfillment theories hold that what is best for someone is what would in one way or another fulfill his or her desires (recognizing that one's desires may include many ends other than happiness). There is no reason to assume that a clinician – a specialist in one relatively narrow aspect of well-being and a relative stranger to the patient – should be able to guess either at what would make the patient most happy or what would fulfill a patient's desires.

The third group of theories of the good is collectively referred to as objective list theories. As summarized by Parfit, "According to this theory, certain things are good or bad for people, whether or not these people would want to have the good things, or to avoid the bad things. The good things might include moral goodness, rational activity, the development of one's abilities, having children and being a good parent, knowledge, and the awareness of true beauty."[8] Other people's lists of objective goods may differ, but, as Bernard Gert has argued, there is a remarkable convergence on the items for the list, as long as the items are kept quite general.

Most uses of the concept of best interests in health care ethics appear to rely on some theory of objective goods. If a physician is expected to determine what is in the patient's best interest and then present it to the patient for consent, there must be a presumption of a good that is, in some sense, objective, knowable by one who is committed to pursuing the patient's welfare. When the standard of best interest is used by a court or a theorist dealing with surrogacy decisions for patients whose personal wants, desires, preferences, and beliefs are not known, surely there is operating some notion that the good of the patient is objective and external to the patient.

What is striking here is that even with objective list theories, there is an enormous gap between what it would take to know what is "objectively in a patient's interest" and what the usual clinician can be expected to know about the patient. For example, many objective list theories include among the things that are good for people such items as spiritual well-being, freedom, sense of accomplishment, and "deep personal relationships."[9] Holders of such objective list theories claim that these are good for people regardless of whether they make people happy and, in contradistinction to desire-fulfillment theories, whether the individual desires these or even knows they are possible.

Certainly a physician is normally not in a good position to determine whether a medical intervention will contribute to the patient's sense of accomplishment or to that individual's "deep personal relationships." If this is true even for an objective theory of the good, there will be no way for the health professional to know whether the patient's good is served with a medical intervention without asking the patient. To put it bluntly, the only way to know whether an intervention is good medicine is to ask the patient.

Our conclusion seems clear: regardless of the theory of the good chosen, there is no reason to assume that the health professional can be expected to know what will promote the best interest of the patient. This conclusion seems clear on its face for hedonistic and desire-fulfillment theories of the good. It is less obvious but equally true even for objective theories of the good.

Elements of Well-Being

The problem can be made more clear by formulating an account of what could be called the spheres or elements of well-being. Regardless of the theory of the good, we can understand what promotes the good for persons better by asking what the elements are that contribute to one's well-being. Another way of putting the question would be to ask in what areas one's limited amount of personal resources – time, money, energy, and material – ought to be invested in order to maximize well-being.

The main elements of well-being

Several elements can be identified. These would surely include some concern with medicine or what could be called one's organic well-being. Closely related, but distinct, would be psychological well-being. It would be a terrible distortion to assume that well-being involved only the organic and psychological, however. Reasonable persons would devote considerable attention and resources to other elements, including the social, legal, occupational, religious, aesthetic, and other components that together make up one's total well-being. There is no reason to assume that each of these components is the same size. By trading off emphasis on different components one should be able to increase or decrease the size of the whole. Well-being is not a zero-sum game.

The problem is central to the concern about the concept of consent. It is unrealistic to expect experts in any one component to be able to speak knowledgeably about well-being in its other components. If this is true, then it makes no sense to expect them to come up with a proposed intervention that will promote the total well-being of the individual.

The subcomponents of organic or medical well-being

One obvious response is to back off from the claim that the goal of medicine is to promote total well-being. A more modest formulation of the end of medicine would be that it should promote not the total well-being of the patient, but the health, the medical good, of the patient.

While this is surely more realistic, it still raises two serious problems. First, even if the health professional were to limit concern to the component of health narrowly construed to mean organic well-being, this component of well-being cannot be thought of as a single, univocal good. There are several, often competing goods in the medical realm. Indeed, organic well-being has subcomponents, including the preservation of life, cure of disease, relief of suffering, and promotion of health.

If a physician is to attempt to use "clinical judgment" to choose what will serve the medical good of the patient, he or she will have to have a definitively correct account of what the relationship is among these medical goods and how they should be traded off against one another. Unless someone is prepared to argue not only that there is a definitively correct relationship among these various medical goods, but also that the physician ought to be able to identify that definitively correct relationship, even the more modest goal of recommending what is *medically* best for the patient in order for the patient to consent to it will be illusory.

There is a second, even more serious problem with the strategy of expecting clinicians to recommend the medically best course and having the patient consent or refuse consent for that recommendation. At best such a strategy will produce what is *medically* best for the patient. However, a realistic goal for a person is to maximize total well-being (subject to possible moral constraints requiring one to take into account the well-being of others and to act in ways that are morally required). Assuming that resources are not infinite, no rational person wants to maximize his or her health. Assuming decreasing marginal utility, it would be irrational to expect that one could maximize the amount of one's total well-being by maximizing the amount of one of its components. Health professionals not only have to figure out how to balance the various medical goods against one another; they also have to realize that rational patients do not want that goal pursued, at least if it comes at the expense of goods in other spheres and lowers the patient's total well-being.

The example of v-tach

An example may help illustrate the difficulty. A forty-year-old man is diagnosed as having moderately severe polyfocal ventricular arrhythmia consisting of PVCs at a rate of over 600 per hour with occasional runs of v-tach. Other than being able to perceive the arrhythmias, he is asymptomatic. There is some reason to believe that these unstable heart rhythms could lead to a serious episode of ventricular fibrillation and even death, but many people are known to suffer such arrhythmias indefinitely without any adverse effect. There are four classes of medications on the market that can be used to suppress the arrhythmias: membrane-stabilizing agents, beta-blockers, repolarization inhibitors, and calcium channel blockers. Some of the classes have subclasses. Although they all suppress PVCs, there is no definitive evidence that suppressing them lowers the mortality risk. In each class of agents there are many different drugs, each with slightly different desired effects and side effects. There are many different dose levels and routes of administration. There are different manufacturers, different costs, and different risk profiles involved. Some clinicians are sufficiently concerned about the side effects that they recommend to their patients that no medication be used. Other clinicians use modest pharmacological intervention with low risk and proportionally low suppression of the arrhythmias. Others more aggressively suppress the PVCs, believing that on balance more good is done. The choices involve matters that are not trivial. The side effects range from nausea, vomiting, diarrhea, headache, and ringing in the ears, to unwanted changes in heart rhythm, a lupus erythematosus-like syndrome, coma, and even death. The dose forms range from a simple one-a-day capsule to more complex combinations taking different medications at several different times a day. The costs range from nothing to several hundred dollars a year for the rest of the patient's life. There are easily over a hundred possible courses of action, each of which has its own unique combination of advantages and disadvantages and might be favored depending on the patient's idiosyncratic circumstances and values and what one considers to be the correct theory of the good.

A patient will have his arrhythmia discovered by a physician, who will assess the options and recommend either no medication, or some variant of conservative or more aggressive medication. That physician will opt for one (or more) of the classes of drugs, some route of administration, dose range, cost, and profile of side effects and will write the prescription, subject, whether the patient realizes it or not, to the consent of the patient. Perhaps some of the variables in the decision will be discussed with the patient and the patient will be given a chance to object.

What the patient may not know is that another equally competent clinician with different instincts about how aggressive to be, which risks are worth taking, and what tradeoffs with nonmedical well-being should be made, will choose some other course and propose it for patient consent. Many of the hundred therapeutic regimens could be perceived as plausible by responsible clinicians. The correct choice will depend on the tradeoffs among the various medical goods and between the medical and nonmedical goods, including a judgment about how the patient should spend marginal dollars. In such a situation it is simply hubristic for clinicians to believe that, out of the hundreds of subtle value tradeoffs to be made, they can come up with just the course that will maximize the patient's well-being.

Why Experts Should Not Propose a Course for Patient Consent

It should now be clear why it makes no sense to continue to rely on consent as the mode of transaction between professionals and their clients. In order for a physician to make an initial estimate of which treatment best served the patient's interest, he or she would first have to develop a definitive theory of the relationship among various medical goods and pick the course that best served the patient's medical good. Then the clinician would have to estimate correctly the proper relationship between the patient's medical good and all other components of the good so that the patient's overall well-being was served.

Even if this could be done, there is a final problem. In virtually any moral theory the well-being of the individual is only one element. Plausible consequentialist theories (such as utilitarianism) also insist that the good of other parties be taken into account. Plausible nonconsequentialist theories, including Kantian theories, natural law theories, much of biblical ethics, and all other deontological theories, hold that knowing what will be in the best interests of persons does not necessarily settle the question of the right thing to do. Many patients may purposely want to consider options that do not maximize their well-being. A patient may acknowledge, for example, that his well-being would be served if he lived longer, but choose to sacrifice his interests to conserve resources for his offspring. A pregnant woman might conclude, for another example, that her interests would be served if she had an abortion, but that such a course would still be morally wrong. Both of these people would rationally not choose the course of action that admittedly maximized their personal well-being. Even if physicians can figure out what maximizes medical well-being and how medical well-being should be related to other elements of well-being, that still does not necessarily lead to the course that is right, all things considered. To know what is "good medicine" and what should be recommended for the patient's assessment and consent, one needs to know how to answer all three of these questions. There is no basis for assuming that physicians have any special expertise in answering any of them.

Why Physicians Should Guess Wrong

This may simply establish that physicians are no better than the rest of us at guessing what counts as the medical good, how the medical good relates to total good, and whether the patient's total good should be promoted. A defender of the emerging process of informed consent might respond by pointing out that physicians should at least be considered to be as good as any other lay person in answering these value theory questions. Since physicians clearly have technical expertise, if they are as good as anyone else at answering the value theory questions, would not efficiency suggest that the physician could combine her technical knowledge of the patient's case with the physician's ordinary level of wisdom when it comes to making value judgments? This could lead to a recommended course of action for the patient. As long as the patient can decline, would that not be the most efficient way to maximize the patient's welfare?

There are two problems here. First, this democratic theory of value which holds that professional experts are as good as others at guessing what maximizes the good can, at best, lead to a general estimate of what the typical person would consider to be good. If, however, any plausible value theory includes elements that are unique to the individual, then merely figuring out what would be good for the general person will not be good enough. We need to know what is good for this particular person. We need not hold to the liberal position that the individual is the best predictor of what serves his or her interest. All we need to acknowledge is that experts in a particular area are not the best at this task.

This leads to a second problem with relying on the claim that experts in one component of well-being should be as good as anyone else at determining the total good for the patient. Experts in any one component of well-being predictably will answer the questions about what maximizes interests in an atypical fashion. This is not because they are self-serving, trying to increase utilization of their services. I assume, perhaps naively, that most health professionals are altruistic and do a good job most of the time of holding self-interest in check.

The problem is more theoretical and more fundamental. Anyone who has given his or her life to an area of professional specialization ought to be expected to value the contributions of that area in an atypical way. Cardiologists ought to believe atypically that cardiology does good for people. Presumably that is one reason why people choose to go into a professional field. But this means if they ask themselves what medical intervention will best promote the overall well-being of the patient, they predictably will give an answer different from the one that would be given by lay people, including the patient himself. They often, but not always, will overvalue the benefits of their field. If one were seriatim to ask experts in each of the components of well-being what portion of an individual's total resources should be invested in their component and then sum the collective recommendations, it is likely that the total would exceed 100 percent.

Specialists not only make the value tradeoffs atypically, they also make the moral tradeoffs atypically. In short, if clinicians are asked to guess at what will serve the best interest of the patient, they ought to come up with the wrong answer. In so far as the consent process involves a clinician using personal judgment to guess at what would be best for the patient, it still rests on the false assumption that clinicians can, at least tentatively, estimate what specific treatment interventions are in the individual patient's interests.

This should make clear why relying on the consensus of medical experts does not provide an adequate way to figure out what the "treatment of choice" should be for the patient with the cardiac arrhythmia. One might make the move of holding the clinician to the "professional standard" of choosing to recommend the drug that the majority of her colleagues similarly situated would have chosen. The most this move could do is tell us what people with the dominant value profile of the medical profession would choose under similar circumstances. It does not tell us what persons with the typical value profile of the average lay person would choose, let alone what one with the value profile of the individual patient would choose. The consensus of the profession does not provide an adequate basis for deciding what the "treatment of choice" is and what should be recommended to patients.[10] The idea that a clinician can determine what is a "medically indicated" treatment for a patient rests on a confused understanding of what the skills of a physician can be expected to provide.[11] If the clinician cannot be expected to figure out what is best for the patient, then he or she cannot obtain a valid consent to a recommended treatment of choice.

Choice: The Liberal Alternative

If consent is no longer adequate as a mechanism for assuring that the patient's beliefs and values will help shape decisions about what a patient ought to do, what are the alternatives? Adherents to medical ethical systems that emphasize autonomy may prefer the concept of choice to that of consent. In this alternative the patient would be presented with a list of plausible treatment options, together with a summary of the potential benefits and risks of each. It is important to emphasize that choice is conceptually different from consent and potentially could replace consent as the basis for patient involvement in health care decisions.

This "liberal" solution, however, faces serious, probably insurmountable problems. First, if the choices that are plausible for the patient are contingent on the beliefs and values of the patient, then the professional cannot be sure that all plausible options are being presented unless he or she has knowledge of the patient's beliefs and values – knowledge that we have argued is normally unavailable. Second, some options (for example, suicide) may be so offensive to some practitioners that they ought not to present them. Third, it is increasingly recognized that even the description of the "facts" necessarily must incorporate certain value judgments, such that even the clinician of good will cannot give a value-free account of the likely outcomes of the alternatives. In short, while the choice alternative may go part of the way toward giving the patient more active control, it is naive to believe it will be able to solve the problems with the consent model.

Pairing Based on "Deep Values"

There is another alternative worth considering. If a clinician is skilled and passionately committed to maximizing the patient's welfare, and knows the belief and value structure and socioeconomic and cultural position of the patient quite well, there would be some more reason to hope for a good guess. Unfortunately, not only is that an ever-vanishing possibility, even knowing the value system of the patient well probably would not be sufficient. The value choices that go into a judgment about what is best for another are so complex and subtle that merely knowing the other's values and trying to empathize will probably not be enough. There is ample evidence that unconscious value distortions will not only influence the clinician's judgment about what is best, but even influence the very interpretation of the scientific data.

There might be more hope if the patient were to choose her cadre of well-being experts (lawyers, accountants, physicians) on the basis of their "deep" value systems. That way when unconscious bias and distortion occur, as inevitably they must, they will tip the decision in the direction of the patient's own system.

I say "deep" value system because I want to make clear that I am not referring to the cursory assessment of the professional's personality, demeanor, and short-term tastes. That would hardly suffice. If, however, there were alignments, "value pairings," based on the most fundamental worldviews of the lay person and professional, then there would be some hope. This probably would mean picking providers on the basis of their religious and political affiliations, philosophical and social inclinations, and other deeply penetrating worldviews. To the extent that the provider and patient were of the same mind set, then there is some reason that the technically competent clinician could guess fairly well what would serve the patient's interest.

The difficulty in establishing a convergence of deep values cannot be underestimated. Surely it would not be sufficient, for instance, to pair providers and patients on the basis of their institutional religious affiliations. Not all members of a religious denomination think alike. But there is reason to hope that people can establish an affinity of deep value orientations, at least for certain types of medical services. For example, certain institutionalized health care delivery systems are now organizing around identifiable value frameworks, recruiting professional and administrative staff on the basis of commitment to that value framework, and then announcing that framework to the public so as to attract only those patients who share the basic value commitment of the institution. A hospice is organized around such a constellation of values. It recruits staff committed to those values and attracts patients who share that commitment. When hospice-based health care providers present options to patients they should admit that they do not present all possible options. (They do not propose an aggressive oncology protocol, for instance; most would not present physician-assisted suicide or active mercy killing.) They should also admit that when they explain options and their potential benefits and harms they do so in ways that incorporate a tone of voice or body language that reflects their value judgments. Patients, however, need be less concerned about this value encroachment than if they were discussing options with a provider who was deeply, instinctively committed to maximally aggressive life preservation. There will be biases, but they will be less corrupting of the patient's own perspective.

Other delivery systems are beginning to organize around deep value orientations: feminist health centers, holistic health clinics, and the National Institutes of Health Clinical Center all announce at least their general value orientations to potential patients.

Providing an institutional framework for pairing based on deep value convergence in more routine health care may be more difficult, but not impossible. HMOs could be organized by social and religious groups that could formally articulate certain value commitments. A Catholic HMO, like a Catholic hospital, could articulate to potential members not only a set of values pertaining to obstetrical and gynecological issues, but also a framework for deciding which treatments are morally expendable as disproportionally burdensome. A liberal Protestant health care system would announce a different framework; a libertarian secular system still another. A truly Protestant health care system, for example, would probably reflect the belief that the lay person is capable of having control over the "text." The medical record, accordingly, would plausibly be placed in the patient's hands just as the Bible is.

Such value pairings will obviously not be a total matching, but they should at least place provider and patient in the same general camp. Moreover, organizing health care delivery on the basis of explicit value pairings would put both provider and patient on notice that values are a necessary and essential part of health care decision-making, a part that cannot be avoided and cannot be handled adequately by merely obtaining the consent of the patient to a randomly assigned provider's guess about what would be best.

With such an arrangement the problems that arise with use of consent for the normal random pairing of lay people and professionals is mitigated. The clinician has a more plausible basis for guessing what would serve the interests of the patient and, more importantly, will let a system of beliefs and values influence the presentation of medical information in a way that is more defensible. To be sure, such deep value pairing will not eliminate the problem of the necessary influence of beliefs and values on communication of medical facts, but it will structure the communication so that the inevitable influence will resemble the influence that the patient would have brought to the data were he or she to become an authority in medical science.

Barring such radical adjustment in the basis for lay-professional pairings, there is no reason to believe that the process of consent will significantly advance the lay person's role in the medical decision-making process. The concept of consent will have to be replaced with a more radical, robust notion of active patient participation in the choice among plausible alternatives – either by getting much greater information to the patient or by actively selecting the professional on the basis of convergence of "deep" value systems.

References

1 Robert M. Veatch, "Three Theories of Informed Consent: Philosophical Foundations and Policy Implications," *The Belmont Report: Ethical Principles and Guidelines for the Protection of Human Subjects of Research* (Washington, DC: National Commission for the Protection of Human Subjects of Biomedical and Behavioral Research, DHEW Publication No. (05)78-0014), pp. 26–1 through 26–66; President's Commission for the Study of Ethical Problems in Medicine and Biomedical and Behavioral Research, *Making Health Care Decisions: A Report on the Ethical and Legal Implications of Informed Consent in the Patient-Practitioner Relationship*, vol. 1 (Washington, DC: US Government Printing Office, 1982); Ruth Faden and Tom L. Beauchamp in collaboration with Nancy P. King, *A History and Theory of Informed Consent* (New York: Oxford University Press, 1986); Jay Katz, *The Silent World of Doctor and Patient* (New York: Free Press, 1984).

2 Ludwig Edelstein, "The Hippocratic Oath: Text, Translation and Interpretation," *Ancient Medicine: Selected Papers of Ludwig Edelstein*, ed. Owsei Temkin and C. Lilian Temkin (Baltimore: Johns Hopkins University Press, 1967), pp. 3–64.

3 American Medical Association, *Current Opinions of the Council on Ethical and Judicial Affairs of the American Medical Association: Including the Principles of Medical Ethics and Rules of the Council on Ethical and Judicial Affairs* (Chicago: American Medical Association, 1989), p. 32.

4 Schloendorff v. New York Hospital (1914), discussed in Jay Katz, *Experimentation with Human Beings: The Authority of the Investigator, Subject, Professions, and State in the Human Experimentation Process* (New York: Russell Sage Foundation, 1972), p. 526.
5 *Encyclopedia of Bioethics*, s.v. "Nuremberg Code, 1946."
6 Robert M. Veatch, "Limits of Guardian Treatment Refusal: A Reasonableness Standard," *American Journal of Law & Medicine*, 9, no. 4 (Winter 1984): 427–68; Robert M. Veatch, *Death, Dying, and the Biological Revolution*, rev. edn (New Haven: Yale University Press, 1989).
7 Derek Parfit, *Reasons and Persons* (Oxford: Clarendon Press, 1984), pp. 493–503.
8 Parfit, *Reasons and Persons*, p. 499; see also Bernard Gert, "Rationality, Human Nature, and Lists," *Ethics*, 100 (1990): 279–300.
9 See David DeGrazia, "Sketch of a Tentative Value Theory for Human Persons," photocopy, 11 November 1991, for an objective list that includes deep personal relationships.
10 Robert M. Veatch, "Consensus of Expertise: The Role of Consensus of Experts in Formulating Public Policy and Estimating Facts," *Journal of Medicine and Philosophy*, 16 (1991): 427.
11 Robert M. Veatch, "The Concept of 'Medical Indications,'" in *The Patient–Physician Relation: The Patient as Partner* (Bloomington: Indiana University Press, 1991), pp. 54–62.

69

Rational Desires and the Limitation of Life-Sustaining Treatment[1]

Julian Savulescu

Abstract

It is accepted that treatment of previously competent, now incompetent patients can be limited if that is what the patient would desire, if she were now competent. Expressed past preferences or an advance directive are often taken to constitute sufficient evidence of what a patient would now desire. I distinguish between desires and rational desires. I argue that for a desire to be an expression of a person's autonomy, it must be or satisfy that person's rational desires. A person rationally desires a course of action if that person desires it while being in possession of all available relevant facts, without committing relevant error of logic, and "vividly imagining" what its consequences would be like for her. I argue that some competent, expressed desires obstruct autonomy. I show that several psychological mechanisms operate to prevent a person rationally evaluating what future life in a disabled state would be like. Rational evaluation is difficult. However, treatment limitation, if it is to respect autonomy, must be in accord with a patient's rational desires, and not merely her expressed desires. I illustrate the implications of these arguments for the use of advance directives and for the treatment of competent patients.

> That suicide may often be consistent with interest and with our duty to ourselves, no one can question, who allows that age, sickness or misfortune may render life a burden, and make it worse even than annihilation. I believe that no man ever threw away life, while it was worth keeping. For such is our natural horror of death, that small motives will never be able to reconcile us to it.[2]

From *Bioethics*, vol. 8, no. 3 (1994), pp. 191–222.

Two hundred years after Hume wrote these words, society has begun to accept that continued life can be worse than "annihilation" and that it is not necessary, nor even desirable, to prolong all lives as long as is biologically possible. "Quality of life," we now realize, is important too. "Living wills", "advance directives", "respect for autonomy", "shared decision-making" and "the right to die" help to ensure, we hope, that the days are over when a person is compelled to live a life which has become a burden.

But there is naive optimism in Hume's second belief "that no man ever threw away life, while it was worth keeping". There are good reasons to believe that normal people, when evaluating whether it is worth living in a disabled state in the future, will undervalue that existence, even in terms of what they judge is best. I will examine the evidence for this claim and look at the implications for the limitation of life-sustaining treatment of formerly competent but now incompetent patients, and, more briefly towards the end, of competent patients.

It has been argued that life-sustaining treatment ought to be limited when such treatment limitation shows respect for a patient's autonomy or promotes a patient's best interests. I will examine what constitutes autonomy and, more briefly, best interests. My point is that being autonomous involves making a certain kind of judgement about how one would like one's life to go over time. It involves making some quite complex evaluations. Which of a person's desires are expressions of her autonomy may not be transparent to casual observation. Indeed, some expressed desires actually prevent a person achieving what she judges to be best for herself. We need to look more carefully and critically at a person's desire to die before we can say that the satisfaction of it shows respect for her autonomy.

Questions of treatment limitation can be considered from many perspectives: that of the patient, his family or society. I will consider only the patient perspective. I use the term "treatment limitation" to cover all cases of withdrawal, withholding or other limitation of treatment. Within the following sets, I use the terms interchangeably: "preference" and "desire", "autonomy" and "autonomous desire" as a desire which is a reflection of a person's autonomy.

The President's Commission Report

The President's Commission Report argues that treatment of incompetent patients ought to be limited if the patient in question would now desire to have treatment limited, if he were competent. This, it is said, shows respect for the patient's former autonomy. If there is no evidence concerning what the patient would desire, treatment can be limited if it is not in the best interests of the patient.

> [D]ecisionmaking for incapacitated patients should be guided by the principle of substituted judgement which promotes the underlying values of self-determination and well-being better than the best interests standard does.[3]

This is based on the guiding principle of the Commission that "a competent patient's self-determination is and should be given greater weight than other people's views of that individual's well-being."[4]

How are we to determine what a person "would now desire"? It has been claimed that a patient's past preference on a related issue or an advance directive constitute sufficient evidence for what a patient would now desire. I will argue that this sense of "what a patient would now desire" is insufficient to determine whether life-sustaining treatment should be limited. It reflects a superficial understanding of what constitutes autonomy. In order to respect former autonomy, we must ask not, "What would the patient now desire if she were competent?" but rather, "What would she now rationally desire if she were competent?" I will argue that self-determination is reflected by a person's own rational hypothetical desire.

Part I. What is Autonomy?

The word, "autonomy", comes from the Greek: *autos* (self) and *nomos* (rule or law).[5] Autonomy is self-government or self-determination.[6] "Self-determination" entails forming a plan for how one's life is to go through time, choosing a course according to what one judges is best for oneself. Autonomous choice fundamentally involves evaluation. It is not mere desiring; rather, it is the weighing and evaluation of alternatives by a person, and the selection of that alternative which best suits that person's judgement for how she wants her life to go.

Self-determination thus entails forming desires for how one's life is to go through time. These desires constitute what has been called a "life-plan". As Robert Young puts it, "[t]he term 'plan' here is intended to refer merely to whatever it is that a person broadly wants to do in and with his or her life – thus covering career, life-style, dominant pursuits and the like."[7]

Consider the simple case of a person, P, faced with only two options: A and B. Imagine that A is suffering from a painful cancer of the knee and B is having one leg amputated. For P's preference for, say, A over B to be a reflection of his autonomy, it must be the result of an evaluation which judges that A is better for P than B. I will argue that being self-determining entails that this evaluation must involve at least three elements: (1) knowledge of relevant, available information concerning each of the states of affairs A and B, (2) no relevant, correctable errors of logic in evaluating that information, and (3) vivid imagination by P of what each state of affairs would be like for P. Call those desires which satisfy these three conditions, rational desires. That is,

> P rationally desires some state of affairs, that q, iff (if and only if) P desires that q while in possession of all relevant, available information, without making relevant, correctable error of logic and vividly imagining what each state of affairs would be like for P.[8]

I will argue that:

> One necessary condition for a desire to be an expression of a person's autonomy is that it is a

rational desire or that it satisfies a rational desire.

An argument for rational desiring

The paradigm of P autonomously choosing between A and B entails that, having appreciated the nature of A and B, P judges that one is better for her, fits better her "life-plan", than the other. Why is appreciation of the nature of A and B important? It will not do when imagining what A is like, to imagine some state of affairs which is more like B, or some other state of affairs. If P were to choose A under these circumstances, what P would really want is B, or something else entirely.

To appreciate A and B as they are, P must know what each is like. P must have relevant, available information. If the cancer will cease to be painful after a certain stage, or if amputation means that P can still get around with an artificial leg, it is relevant for P to know these facts.

In processing this information, it is important not to make any errors of logic. P is trying to decide whether to have the amputation. Suppose that P is provided with information and reasons in the following way.

(1) There is a risk of dying from anaesthesia. (true)
(2) I will require an anaesthetic if I am to have an amputation. (true)

Therefore, if I have an amputation, I will die. (false)

Logic is important so that P can utilize available facts properly. False beliefs which arise from correctable errors of logic corrupt P's appreciation of the nature of the options, and so reduce the autonomy of his choice.

Not all false beliefs corrupt P's appreciation of the alternatives in a way that matters. If P falsely believes that the anaesthetic will be a gas, when it will be an intravenous infusion with the same risks and benefits, then this false belief is irrelevant to her evaluation of the anaesthetic.[9]

What if P desires to not use all the information available or to commit errors of logic? What if P wants only to know whether an operation will cause pain or not? P does not want to know what its likely benefits are. Should these be presented to her?

The default answer is that such a person should be compelled to confront available information and any errors of logic. It is only then that she can be self-determining and get what she really wants.

However, there is one exception. Some people really do not want to know all the facts. They might not want to know the risk of death which an operation entails. That desire ought to be respected *if it has been evaluated in the right way*. Has the person stood back and imagined the possible implications of such a stance? If she has, then this desire may inherit autonomy from the parent evaluation. If, however, such a reaction is driven only by fear or dread, then it is not an expression of autonomy.

In addition to the provision and logical evaluation of information, the evaluative sense of the concept of self-determination requires that alternative states of affairs be "vividly imagined". What constitutes "vivid imagination"?

The concept of choice entails that at least two alternatives are available. But it is necessary to distinguish between subjectively and objectively available alternatives. Two objective alternatives may exist with only one subjective alternative.

Consider the converse of Locke's case.[10] A person in a room is led to believe that the room is locked, when in fact one door is open. This person has two objective alternatives (leave or stay) but only one subjective alternative (stay).

It is only after a person has presented herself with subjective alternatives that she can choose the one which she judges is best. One cannot logically be self-determining if one believes that the path one sets upon is the only path available. As far as demonstrating that a choice is autonomous, it is not enough to show that objective choices exist. There must be some evidence that subjective choice exists.[11]

In order to be self-determining, then, it is necessary to present at least two alternatives to oneself. However, being autonomous requires more than this. Imagine that P wants to do A. P believes that he could also do B. However, it is A that P wants to do, and P does not think about B. In one sense, it can be said that P has *chosen* to do A, but is doing A an expression of P's *self-determination*? Self-determination is an active process of actually determining the path of one's life. In order to judge what is best for himself, P must think and imagine what it would be like for her if A and B obtained, and what the consequences, at least in the short term, of each of these would be for her. Thus, not only must P know what A and B are like, but she must also imagine what A and B would be like *for her*. I call this vivid imagination.

Depression is one condition which may reduce one's capacity to be autonomous. The depressive loses the ability to "live life". At the level of decision-making, this manifests itself as an inability to present alternatives in the vivid colours of reality. Once depression has lifted, some describe the experience as being one where a "veil" descended on their life. Such people may be cognizant of facts, but they are unable to engage in the process of vivid imagination which brings meaning to our choices.[12]

Two objections to vivid imagination

1 Uncertainty and the unknown It might be argued that my requirement for vivid imagination is too strong. We do not require that our choices be made with knowledge of what the outcome will be. Such knowledge may not be available. The paradigm case is that of explorers such as Captain Cook or Columbus. These men could not have vividly imagined the outcome of their explorations, but surely their decision to explore the unknown could have been autonomous?[13]

I am not suggesting that one must vividly imagine what an alternative is like before one can autonomously choose that alternative; I am only suggesting that one must imagine it *as far as is possible*. These explorers were faced with many different courses of action. The results of some of these were clearly imaginable (like staying at home and reading a book), while the results of others were largely unpredictable (like exploring the Pacific). One can autonomously choose to explore the unknown. However, one must gather as many facts as possible about the unknown, if one is to choose to explore it autonomously.

We are in some ways like these explorers. There are various courses of action open to us, and various outcomes are possible with each course of action. Under conditions of uncertainty, we must present to ourselves a "reasonable range of alternatives" for each course of action entertained. A "reasonable range of alternatives" is that range defined by P's rational beliefs about what courses of action are open to P (and their probabilities of producing various outcomes).[14] P's beliefs are rational if they are based on an appreciation of all relevant facts available at the time to P, evaluated by P without any errors of logic being committed. We must vividly imagine these alternatives, as far as is possible.

Contrast this with an example of non-autonomously choosing the unknown. Imagine that John is considering setting out to explore an uncharted part of the interior of Africa. Although this area has not been mapped, it is known from natives who have been there that it is infested with tsetse flies. These flies cause a fatal sleeping sickness. John knows this fact, but does not vividly imagine what it would be like to be in a dense jungle infested with tsetse flies. It is not that he wants to die. He is merely a person who can't be bothered thinking carefully about the consequences of his actions. John's desire to explore the interior of Africa without appropriate precautions frustrates what he really wants: to chart the interior of Africa and stay alive.

2 Impulsiveness and choosing to ignore available facts It might be objected that we are in many ways like John. We often choose impulsively and choose to ignore available facts, yet we do not believe that the impulsiveness of our choice precludes it from being autonomous.[15] If this is so, then vivid imagination of the alternatives is not necessary.

It is true that a person can autonomously choose to lead an impulsive life. What matters is whether she evaluates the impulsive life, whether she imagines in broad and general strokes, what it is to live an impulsive life, and what other lives are like. She can only then *autonomously* choose to live the impulsive life.

The impulsive explorer comes in two versions. In one version, at some prior point she stands back from her life and evaluates it as the best overall for her. She sees people living their lives like accountants, or crude short-sighted utilitarians, scrutinizing the value of every possible option. She decides that spontaneity is more important. This impulsive explorer is autonomous. Autonomy of choice can be inherited if the parent choice was autonomous.

In the second version, the impulsive explorer never stands back and engages in vivid imagination of the alternatives. She never evaluates her life. She is not self-determining.

Two senses of rational desiring

A rational desire can be described in an actual (non-counterfactual) sense: (1) as a desire which *does* satisfy or *has* satisfied the three evaluative conditions, or in a hypothetical (counterfactual) sense: (2) as a desire which *would* satisfy the three conditions. I favour the actual (non-counterfactual) reading.

Consider the happy follower. This person is happy simply being one of the herd. She passively does as others do, lets her friends and family decide for her, leads the most unoriginal of existences. This person can be autonomous, if she has chosen her life for a reason. Such a person may find choice burdensome, or realize that she is a bad chooser. Or perhaps she enjoys the pleasure others feel in choosing for her. If she stands back and evaluates her life as good for one of these reasons, she may be autonomous in being a follower. But if there has been no such reflection, no such deliberate choice, no such conscious planning, then her life is the paradigm of lack of autonomy.

It may be true of this latter person that *if* she had confronted her life, she would have endorsed it. However, it is necessary for self-determination that she *determine* her life, that she *actually* chooses a certain life according to what she judges best, not that she would have chosen that life under certain ideal conditions.

It might be objected that few people have rational desires. Clearly, we hardly ever go through the process of collecting information, logically evaluating it and vividly imagining the alternatives in a formal, overt and organized way. Evaluation is often fractured over time, and in the background of our minds. Yet I believe that we do engage in this kind of evaluation. We do form considered judgements about what is best for ourselves.

Autonomy as a dispositional concept

It is important to recognize that to be autonomous it is not necessary that we are *always* evaluating states of affairs rationally, in the way I have described. Firstly, as I have shown, a desire can inherit autonomy if it springs from an overall plan or desire which is itself rational and autonomous.

However, there is a second way in which we are often autonomous at a certain time in the absence of having a rational desire at that time. Autonomy is a dispositional concept.[16] When we say that P is autonomous, we mean that P has a disposition to behave (under certain conditions)[17] in a certain way. That is, P is autonomous if P *would* behave in way A if circumstances C were present. More specifically, P is autonomous if, under certain conditions, P would bring about what she rationally evaluates to be best for herself. That is, P would act, and perhaps also form other desires, so as to realize her rational desires for how she would like her life to go. Thus, while it is necessary that a person rationally evaluate states of affairs *at some point* in order to be autonomous, it is not true that she is only autonomous when she is actually rationally desiring some end.

Being autonomous thus requires both: (1) forming a rational desire for what is best for ourselves, and (2) having a disposition to realize our rational desires, that is, having a disposition (or tendency) to bring about what we judge to be best for ourselves.

The account of rational desiring I have provided is like some accounts of valuing.[18] However, valuing is a dispositional concept.[19] (I still value freedom when I am anaesthetized, yet I may have no desires at that time. So values must not necessarily be actual desires.) The relationship between valuing and rational desiring can be put this way;

> P values that q iff P would rationally desire that q in C.

"To value" is the dispositional verb to which the corresponding occurrent or episodic verb is "to rationally desire". Valuing captures the dispositional sense of being autonomous.

Ulysses and the Sirens: an example of obstructive desire

I have argued that a rational desire is a desire formed under conditions of awareness of available information, evaluated without error of logic and after engaging in a process of vivid imagination. Call a desire which does not satisfy these three conditions, a non-rational desire. Some non-rational desires frustrate the satisfaction of our rational desires, that is, obstruct the expression of our autonomy. Call these irrational or obstructive desires.

An example of obstructive desire is seen in the case of Ulysses and the Sirens. Ulysses was to pass "the Island of the Sirens, whose beautiful voices enchanted all who sailed near. [They] . . . had girls' faces but birds' feet and feathers . . . [and] sat and sang in a meadows among the heaped bones of sailors they had drawn to their death," so irresistible was their song. Ulysses desired to hear this unusual song, but also wanted to avoid the usual fate of sailors who succumbed to this desire. So he contrived to plug his men's ears with beeswax and instructed them to bind him to the mast of his ship. He told them: "if I beg you to release me, you must tighten and add to my bonds". As he passed the island, "the Sirens sang so sweetly, promising him foreknowledge of all future happenings on earth." Ulysses shouted to his men to release him. However, his men obeyed his previous orders and only lashed him tighter. They passed safely.[20]

Before sailing to the Island of the Sirens, Ulysses made a considered evaluation of what he judged was best. His order that he would remain shackled was an expression of his autonomy. In the grip of the Sirens' song, Ulysses' strongest desire was that his men release him. This may have been his only desire. But it was an irrational desire. Moreover, this desire obstructed the expression of his autonomy.

We see in this case how it is necessary to frustrate some of a person's desires if we are to respect his autonomy.

One objection

How, it might be objected, can Ulysses' desire to be released obstruct his autonomy when he has no other desire at the time of hearing the Sirens?

Ulysses did rationally desire to live and he will rationally desire to live, but he now irrationally desires to move closer to the Island. This last desire entails dying.[21] His past and future rational desires are reflections of a settled disposition to stay alive. Ulysses has this disposition at the time of hearing the Sirens, though it fails to issue in a present desire. It is out of respect for autonomy in its dispositional sense that we believe Ulysses ought to be lashed tighter to the mast.[22] It is out of respect for Ulysses' values that we restrain him.

PART II. "No Man Ever Threw Away Life, While it was Worth Keeping"

It is difficult for a person to evaluate future states in which she suffers a significant physical disability. In such cases, there are several hurdles to forming a desire which expresses our autonomy. Obstructive desires often arise. I will now review the evidence for these claims.

Consider the following case.

Mrs X was a woman in her mid-forties with severe diabetes, and many complications of that disease, including severe vascular disease. She was admitted to hospital with pain in her foot. The circulation of blood to her foot was so poor that it required amputation. The necessity of amputation was explained to her. She, however, refused to have an amputation. She did not want to be bed- or wheelchair-bound and dependent on her husband, she said. It was carefully explained to her that most amputees were able to walk independently on an artificial leg. She did not believe that she would be able to walk on a prosthesis. She would, she said, rather die. Amputees were brought in to the ward to show that it was possible to independently ambulate with an artificial leg. Other attempts were made to dispel any false belief about amputation. She, however, remained unmoved. She was discharged home. Sometime later, she was rushed to hospital. Gangrene had developed in her foot. She was in septic shock. She became delirious. It became obvious that she would die without amputation. On death's door, the medical staff cajoled her into "consenting" to an above knee amputation, though it appeared clear to all that this was not what she had wanted and that she was at the time incompetent to consent to operation. Her amputation went well (from a medical point of view), her infection cleared and she went to a rehabilitation hospital. When one of her doctors saw her a year later, she had had a second amputation. Remarkably, she was walking on bilateral prostheses. He asked her how she was going with the amputations. "Fine," she remarked to his astonishment. "But you never even wanted the first amputation." "Yes", she replied, "but that was because I never believed that *I* would be able to walk with an amputation. It was being stuck in a wheelchair that I dreaded. But now I can get around by myself and it's not so bad."

Why did this woman refuse amputation?

The problem was not merely one of lack of information, although information could have been more effectively presented. Let us assume that all the facts had been made available. Mrs X had at least one relevantly false belief: that *she* would not be independent after an amputation. This belief was not supported by the information available to her. However, she made a second evaluative error: she failed to vividly imagine what life as an amputee would be like for her.[23]

Before I address why these evaluative errors might have occurred, I will show that in some respects Mrs X is not an unusual case. Many people utlimately adapt to disability following life-threatening illness.

Adaptation to disability

People suffering painful or disabling illnesses often adapt to a significant decrement in function. Following a large review of the medical literature, De Haes and Van Knippenberg conclude:

> It is commonly assumed that cancer and cancer treatment have a severe, negative impact on the QOL [quality of life] of patients . . . However, no differences were found with respect to most QOL indicators: satisfaction with family, friends, work, income, values, activities, community, local government, health, the overall quality of life; psychological functioning; anxiety, depression, positive well-being, general mental well-being; daily activities; and work satisfaction. Interestingly, survived cancer patients have reported more satisfaction with care from their partner and others than have healthy controls.[24]

There were no differences between normal and mastectomy, chemotherapy or melanoma patients over a wide range of subjective indicators of quality of life. Cancer patients judged their situation more positively and more like 'normals' than patients with skin disease.[25] Patients with chronic renal failure on dialysis subjectively rank their life quality only 6% below the average of the normal population.[26] Kidney transplant recipients rank their subjective quality of life more highly than the general population rates theirs.[27] Brickman, Coates and Janoff-Bulman found that recent lottery winners were no happier than control groups. Paraplegics were less happy, though still above the midpoint of the scale.[28]

Some victims of personal tragedy even derive something positive from their experience. One polio victim remarked:

> Far away from the hospital experience, I can evaluate what I have learned . . . I know my awareness of people has deepened and increased, that those who are close to me can want me to turn all my heart and mind and attention to their problems. I could not have learned *that* dashing all over the tennis court.[29]

Interviews with women with breast cancer revealed similar experiences:

> I have much more enjoyment of each day, each moment. I am not so worried about what is or isn't or what I wish I had. All those things you get so entangled with don't seem to be part of my life right now.
>
> You take a long look at your life and realize that many things you thought were important before are totally insignificant . . . What you do is put things in perspective. You find out things like relationships are really the most important things you have – the people you know and your family – everything is just way down the line. It's very strange that it takes something serious to make you realize that.[30]

Taylor concludes:

> victims of life-threatening attacks, illness, and natural disaster sometimes seem from their accounts . . . to have benefited from it . . . Studies of chronic illness or conditions, such as cancer, diabetes, severe burns, cystic fibrosis, or hemophilia, and investigations of coping with the loss of a child or a spouse reveal that most people experiencing such events are able to say that their lives are as good as or better than they were before the events.[31]

It is possible to portray an overly rosy picture of serious illness. Many people do not find meaning in their illness. But many at least appear to adapt.[32]

Hurdles to evaluation: loss aversion and contrast

If it is true that many people, like Mrs X, will ultimately adapt to their disability, is there any reason to believe that they will, like Mrs X, fail to rationally evaluate those states of disability? The psychological coding mechanisms of *contrast* and *loss-aversion* tend to prevent rational evaluation.

Maintenance of a state and frequent repetition of a stimulus result in adaptation. Exposure to repeated stimulation thus tends to produce a neutral subjective state, or null state. Contrasting states become the primary determinants of experience.[33] The principle of contrast states that the experience of a given stimulus or state is determined to a significant extent by its contrast to the null or present adapted state (size and rate of change of difference are important).

Consider an example. In one experiment, subjects were asked to describe the facial expression of a woman seen in a photograph. The face was "enigmatically unemotional". Before viewing this photograph, however, subjects were shown another photograph which expressed a strong emotion. The target face was judged by subjects to express a moderately intense *contrasting* emotion.[34] Tversky and Griffin have shown that perceived levels of happiness behave in a similar way.[35]

Thus, it is not the level of a person's function, but the change from whatever level she has adapted to which is important in determining a person's evaluation of that state. Although many paraplegics ultimately adapt to their level of function, becoming a paraplegic is a terrible event because one moves rapidly from a normal state to a paralysed state. One paraplegic stated in a television interview, "You probably think that I am unhappy but you are wrong. And I used to think that I knew what suffering was, but I was wrong."[36]

The phenomenon of *loss aversion* also distorts the evaluative experience. This is the psychological phenomenon where "losses loom larger than gains." The dread Mrs X had of dependency may be one example.

Consider another example. Participants in an experiment were indifferent between the following prospects: (1) equal chances to win $20 or lose $5, with a 0.5 chance to win or lose nothing and (2) equal chances to win $60 or lose $15, and a 0.5 chance to win or lose nothing. "Here, a chance to win $60 rather than $20 was needed to compensate for the risk of losing $15 rather than $5 – a ratio of 4:1 between matched differences of losses and gains."[37]

From experiments such as these, it has been concluded that "[w]hen left to their own devices . . . decision makers focus myopically at problems one at a time, and their choices appear to be dominated by the anticipated emotional consequences of individual losses."[38]

People often also focus on the present and near future, and discount the more distant future. They are biased to the present and near future.[39]

It would be expected, then, that people, prior to injury, will concentrate "myopically" on the loss of becoming disabled, and ignore the value of their adapted state. Kahneman and Varey conclude:

> In dealing with unfamiliar states, however, most people probably have a more accurate view of the utility of the transition than of the steady state. As a consequence, adaptation will tend to be neglected or underestimated and differences between states correspondingly exaggerated.[40]

This is in agreement with Tversky and Griffin's conclusions:

> A common bias in the prediction of utility is a tendency to overweight one's present state or mood . . . A related source of error is the failure to anticipate our remarkable ability to adapt to new states . . . People generally have a reasonable idea of what it is like to lose money or to have a bad cold, but they probably do not have a clear notion of what it means to go bankrupt, or to lose a limb.[41]

The implication here is that people may have a good idea about treatment decisions relating to familiar problems, like having a cold, a sprained or broken limb. But as treatment decisions pertain to more unfamiliar states, people will have more difficulty in imagining what these states will be like. The evidence is that, prior to experiencing them, they will systematically underrepresent their utility. The President's Commission appears to fail to appreciate the difficulty facing patients who make decisions concerning unfamiliar states:

> The Commission has found no reason for decisions about life-sustaining therapy to be considered differently from other treatment decisions. A decision to forego such treatment is awesome because it hastens death, but that does not change the elements of decision-making capacity and need not require greater abilities on the part of the patient.[42]

While the Commission is right that such decisions are not different to other decisions about unfamiliar states (such as those involving serious disability), they are different to the everyday health care decisions which people make about familiar health problems.

Mrs X failed to vividly imagine what it would be like to adapt to a disabled state. Loss aversion, contrast and discounting of the future prejudice appreciation of future life with disability. Importantly, false beliefs about dependency may persist even after presentation of evidence to the contrary. Kahneman and Miller describe the "well-documented" phenomenon of "the perseverance of discredited beliefs".[43] "The message . . . is that traces of an induced belief persist even when its evidential basis has been discredited."[44]

In conclusion, the process of vivid imagination so necessary for evaluation is no easy or straightforward process to engage in. It involves not only the provision of much information, but the overcoming of several innate psychological hurdles.

PART III. Limitations of Treatment of Incompetent Patients

Should Mrs X's leg have been amputated when she was incompetent?

The President's Commission Report argues that the limitation of treatment of formerly competent but now incompetent patients should attempt to achieve two goals: promotion of well-being and respect for autonomy.[45] Respect for self-determination becomes embodied in the notion of "substituted judgement". Substituted judgement attempts to arrive at a hypothetical or counterfactual preference – what the patient would prefer, were she competent now. Treatment is only to be in accordance with the best interests standard if we cannot form a substituted judgement.

How are we to determine what a patient would prefer?

Buchanan and Brock claim that there must be "sufficient evidence". Exactly what constitutes sufficient evidence is left somewhat unclear. They seem to equate it with the expression of a past preference for a related issue (including an advance directive). The manner in which they restrict the use of substituted judgement provides support for this contention. Substituted judgements do *not* represent "a surrogate exercise of the right of self-determination" if: (1) individuals "have not clearly expressed the relevant preferences prior to the onset of incompetence or because they have expressed relevant but contradictory preferences" and (2) patients have never been competent.[46]

Which desires will count as reflecting a patient's autonomy according to the President's Commission? Firstly, the principal (person making the directive) should be legally competent. Secondly, "[a] statute might require evidence that the person has the capacity to understand the choice embodied in the directive when it is executed." This capacity will be assessed in lay terms by lay people. "Furthermore, the standard they are asked to attest to may be as low as that used in wills, unless specified differently." The principal should also understand the seriousness of the step being taken. The Commission recommends that the principal "have had a discussion with a health care professional about a directive's potential consequences".[47]

The loaded concept in these accounts is "competence". If competence to make a life and death choice means that the patient must be in possession of the available facts, without committing relevant errors of logic and vividly imagining the relevant states of affairs, then it is *ex hypothesi* true that a competent patient will make an autonomous choice.[48] However, the notions of competence and autonomy, although related, are generally though to be separate.[49] I will not address the notion of competence. It suffices to say that unless the notions of competent choice and autonomous choice are collapsed, it will be possible that a competent person will express a non-autonomous desire.

If this is right, it will not do to look only to a past competent preference if we wish to respect an incompetent patient's former autonomy. Some desires, even some competent desires, frustrate a person's autonomy. We need also to ask: was the desire obstructive?

Consider the case of Mrs X. She rationally desired to live independently (let us assume). Amputation and a prosthetic leg would have allowed her to live independently. Her false belief (that she would be dependent after an amputation) led her to desire to die. This desire prevented her from getting what she rationally desired (and valued). Her expressed desire to die was obstructive.

Moreover, it would be wrong to conclude from this expressed past desire that she would now at the time of being incompetent, rationally desire to die if she were competent. She would now rationally desire to be treated.

False belief is not always present. But other evaluative failings are equally important. If Mrs X had failed to vividly imagine what it would be like to adapt to life with a prosthetic leg, her previous desire to die would have been irrational and quite possibly obstructive.

The important question, then, is: was Mrs X's past desire an expression of her *autonomy*? Buchanan and Brock claimed that "acting in accordance with a patient's prior preferences" shows "a respect for the patient's former autonomy".[50] This claim is not necessarily true. Some preferences, and even some preferences of competent persons, frustrate autonomy. In order to determine whether a desire is rational or obstructive requires considerable evaluation, and certainly more than that suggested by the President's Commission.

In order to form a substituted judgement, we must ask not what would the patient desire, but what *would* the patient *rationally desire*? A person's past rational desires give us a clue as to what this person's "life-plan" is, and so to what she would now rationally prefer.

In the case where a past desire to die now is obstructive, and it is clear that the patient would now *rationally* desire to live, then respect for autonomy requires that we treat the patient.

In many cases, it will not be possible to clarify whether a past desire was an expression of a person's autonomy. In health care, there is often a presumption of competence: a person is presumed to be competent until proven otherwise. What will *not* do is to presume that a competent person's desire is autonomous, in so far as treatment limitation decisions are concerned. There are too many factors operative which can interfere with the required evaluation.

Moreover, it is possible that some people have never rationally evaluated their lives and lack entirely a rational life plan. Without a plan, without making certain evaluations, a person cannot be autonomous.

What ought to be done, then, when it is not clear what the patient would now rationally desire or if the patient lacks the relevant rational desires?

The following principle is reasonable: in the case that a person has no relevant rational desires or as we become more unclear what the patient would now rationally desire, treatment should promote that patient's best interests.

These principles apply to advance directives. If there are reasons to believe that such a directive was not an expression of the patient's autonomy, then it is appropriate to disregard such a directive and assess the situation afresh.

Consider an example from The *Hastings Center Report*.[51] A 32-year-old, HIV-positive man presented with shortness of breath. He was diagnosed as having *Pneumocystis* pneumonia. Upon being told his diagnosis, the man produced a living will forbidding artificial ventilation "under any circumstances" and endowing his friend with Enduring Power of Attorney (or equivalent). The friend left. Upon commencement of antibiotic treatment, the patient had an unexpected anaphylactic reaction, rendering him incompetent. The doctor, who "believe[d] strongly in patient autonomy", was faced with a dilemma: the patient required immediate intubation or he would die. He was likely to require such intubation only until the anaphylaxis resolved. However, such intubation had been expressly forbidden by the patient. His proxy was not contactable. What should the doctor do?

This is a case where the meaning of the past desire is unclear. It is likely that the patient did not intend to forbid artificial ventilation in a case of drug-related anaphylaxis. Indeed, it is likely that he would rationally desire to be ventilated in these circumstances.

I am arguing for something stronger. I am arguing that there is still a case for artificial ventilation to be given even if the patient has expressly forbidden that "artificial ventilation in cases of anaphylaxis" be instituted *if* that desire was based on inadequate information, either about artificial ventilation or anaphylaxis and their consequences, or inadequate imagination or feeble reflection. I am claiming that such deficiencies may be common. It is necessary then to go beyond what people have said, or written, to how they have lived their lives, what they have thought important, what their goals and rational desires are, that is, to what they have rationally evaluated is the best life for themselves. It is important to know what they value.

When is limitation of treatment in a patient's best interests?

If we do not know what this person values or if she has no values, then she ought to be treated according to her best interests. But how are we to define interests?

The President's Commission defines "interests" in terms of "more objective, societally shared criteria" of "welfare." The following factors are important:

> the relief of suffering, the preservation or the restoration of functioning, and the quality as well as the extent of life sustained. An accurate assessment will encompass consideration of present desires, the opportunities of future satisfactions, and the possibility of developing or regaining the capacity for self-determination.[52]

This is all rather superficial. What precisely is meant by "quality of life"? More rigorous accounts are available. Derek Parfit has distinguished three theories of well-being: Hedonistic Theories, Desire-Fulfilment Theories and Objective List Theories.[53]

The classical doctrine of Hedonism describes only one valuable mental state – happiness or pleasure – and one negative mental state – unhappiness or pain. More recent accounts argue that there are many mental states aside from pleasure which are valuable.

Desire-Fulfilment Theories claim that a person's life goes well when her desires are satisfied.

The Objective List approach to well-being claims that certain activities are objectively good. Parfit argues that being morally good, engaging in rational activity, developing one's abilities, having children and being a good parent (and presumably engaging in other meaningful human relationships), gaining knowledge and being aware of "true" beauty are examples of such activities.[54]

Each of these theories has problems.[55] Parfit argues that while each of these three elements (desire satisfaction, happiness, valuable activity) is necessary for a good life, no one in isolation is sufficient for a valuable life. What makes a life go well is to have all three together.[56] On this approach, an example of what is good for someone is to be engaged in fulfilling, meaningful human relationships, wanting to be so engaged and gaining pleasure from these relationships.

There are problems still with this account. However, the aim of this paper is to show when a person's interests ought to be invoked, and not how we should construe interests.

Two points are important. Firstly, the account makes clear that there is a difference between a person's (narrowly construed) medical interests. Restoring the hearing of a member of the deaf community may make him better off medically (from the point of view of his health), but if it will alienate him from his community and he strongly desires not to have the operation, the operation may not be in his overall best interests.

Secondly, one item missing from Parfit's list of objectively valuable activities is that activity which is an expression of a person's autonomy. Promoting a person's interests is thus interconnected with respecting her autonomy.[57] However, even if autonomous activity is valuable, the account makes clear that autonomous activity is only *a part* of what makes a person's life go well. A person's interests ought not be equated with satisfaction of autonomous desires. A person can autonomously choose a way of life which makes her life go less well overall than it could. Satisfaction of autonomous desire is not the only good in life.

Consider an example. A Jehovah's Witness refuses a blood transfusion and suffers serious brain damage which fundamentally impairs her ability to get what she wants, to carry on social relations, etc. She has made her life go badly. If her choice is to be justified, it will have to be in terms of her autonomy, not in terms of her interests.

When should treatment be limited in a person's best interests? On this account, life would be not worth living when it fell below a certain threshold where a person could no longer engage in a reasonable spectrum of valuable activity, could no longer gain happiness from that life and no longer satisfy her desires to engage in worthwhile activity.

There are lives which are so bad. A life with late stage Huntington's Chorea is one example. However, from empirical studies of patients with paraplegia, it appears that such people are able to lead fulfilling lives.[58]

Limitation of Treatment of Competent Patients

> An advance directive does not, however, provide self-determination in the sense of active moral agency by the patient on his or her behalf ... [A]lthough self-determination is involved when a patient establishes a way to project his or her wishes into a time of anticipated incapacity, it is a sense of self-determination lacking in one important attribute: active, contemporaneous personal choice. Hence a decision not to follow an advance directive may sometimes be justified when it is not acceptable to disregard a competent patient's contemporaneous choice. Such a decision would most often rest on a finding that the patient did not adequately envision and consider the particular situation within which the actual medical decision must be made.[59]

The point made here by the President's Commission is that an advance directive which was formed by a person who failed to adequately envision the situation at hand does not provide self-determination. It can be disregarded *because it is not an instance of active, contemporaneous choice*. Implied, then, is that (competent) active, contemporaneous choice ought to be respected, *even when* that choice is the result of evaluation which does not adequately envision the situation at hand. I will argue that we ought not to respect all competent contemporaneous choices. Consider an example.

J is a man in a situation very like that of Mrs X. He, however, has no false beliefs. He believes that he will be able to walk independently on an artificial leg. He finds this abhorrent. An attempt is made to bring in amputees to talk to him about their lives. He refuses to see them. He has made his decision, he says, and we do not have the right to interfere.

J's wife subsequently reveals that J was involved in a car accident 10 years ago. As a result, J was critically ill. At the time, it was clear that if he was treated, he would be left a paraplegic. J desired to die. However, his doctors treated him against his will. He was left a paraplegic. Initially, J was depressed and continued to want to die, but gradually he adapted. He came to find life very fulfilling, participating in the "Para-Olympics". Some years later, a new surgical technique involving the use of a "nerve growth factor" was developed for conditions of spinal injury. After being operated on, J was able to regain the use of his legs. J's wife claims that he is now deliberately suppressing this information. He is an attention-seeker, she claims, and always tries to make his situation look as bad as possible to manipulate the sympathy of others. "He pulled the same stunt last time," she says. "He doesn't really want to die. He just wants you all running around after him, like I do everyday."

A person's evaluation of what is best for himself can change. A person can judge that p is best now, but later judge that not-p is best.[60] But imagine that J's wife can give us good reasons why she believes that J would now rationally desire to live, that J values life as a paraplegic more than death. (His past behaviour provides valuable clues.) J's desire to die is then obstructive.[61]

What ought to be done when a competent person's desire obstructs the expression of his autonomy?

If a person's expressed desire is obstructive, steps should be taken to facilitate the expression of his rational desires. Exactly how this can be done is a matter for psychological investigation.

In some cases, it will not be possible to set the conditions which will facilitate autonomous choice. A young trauma victim, rushed to hospital, may refuse to have some urgent, life-saving operation, like having a bleeding spleen removed. She may not believe that if her spleen is removed, she will completely recover. Or she might claim to "not like operations". There may not be time to present enough information in a way that promotes adequate evaluation. It is reasonably to operate on this young person if there is a reasonable expectation that with appropriate information and reflection, she would consent. In some cases, we ought to satisfy a person's rational, hypothetical desire (her values), rather than her actual desire. If we wish to respect autonomy, it is more important to respect a person's values than satisfy an obstructive actual desire.

The situation becomes more complicated when an obviously obstructive desire is resistant to change, even after considerable counselling and provision of information. My own feeling is that, if we wish to respect autonomy, such desires ought to be overridden. This is contentious.

Another difficult situation arises when we suspect, but do not know, that an expressed desire is obstructive. Or we may believe that this person has never formed a rational life-plan, that she has failed entirely to rationally evaluate *anything*. Such a person is not autonomous. One possible solution is to treat her according to her interests.

It might be objected that such a policy is liable to paternalistic abuse. We may, in these cases, abide by competent persons' desires *as a matter of policy*. But the justification for this lies not necessarily with respect for this patient's autonomy, but elsewhere.

Two Objections

1. Respect only articulated desires?

It might be agreed that in cases like that of Ulysses, where a person has expressed two conflicting desires, the desire which better promotes autonomy ought to be respected. However, it might be argued that if a competent person, like J, expresses a desire to die, and there is *no contrary desire articulated*, then that desire ought to be presumed to be autonomous.

There are two reasons why we ought not respect only articulated desires.

Firstly, being autonomous does not entail that one has a rational desire at the moment. Being autonomous does entail having a certain disposition, but this disposition will not always be "momentarily actualized", as Ryle put it,[62] in the form of a desire. Assume that when I am deeply asleep, I have no desires. *A fortiori*, at that time I do not desire my freedom. But if I were awoken by the gunshots of a revolution, I *would* desire my freedom. When I am asleep, I still value my freedom, but I do not at that time rationally desire it.

The less my valuing of, say, freedom manifests itself in an actual desire, the less chance there is for someone to witness my desiring freedom. I may still value freedom, but few may ever have heard me *articulate* that value.

Secondly, some of a person's desires are *never* articulated. Some rational desires remain unarticulated. Is this claim plausible?

What determines whether a person articulates her desires or not? A lot depends on what sort of person she is: is she the kind of person who articulates her thoughts and beliefs to others? Is she the sort of person who thinks in terms of words, sentences and "propositions"? Or is she a person who does not verbalize in her own mind her experiences? Moreover, articulation of desire has nothing necessarily to do with whether the desire is rational or not. There is no reason to believe that rational desires will necessarily be articulated. There is no reason to believe that all people who value freedom will have articulated this value at some point in time.

A related objection can be levelled at articulated desires: how do we *know* that Mrs X *rationally desired* living independently?[63] Why wasn't *this* desire obstructive? The answer turns on how we can come to know whether the three evaluative conditions were satisfied. There is not space to address this important issue. I suspect that the answer is, in part, in the realm of the psychologist. However, we *can* know that some of a person's desires are rational. Ulysses' men, confronted with two conflicting desires, knew what he judged was best, what he rationally desired. It was clear, without him *fully articulating* it, what Ulysses' *plan* was. Though his instructions were brief, his intentions were clear. Our plans may not be so clear, but they are, I believe, intelligible. And they are often intelligible to a greater extent than we articulate them.

It is of course possible that Mrs X has not rationally evaluated her life at any stage. I think this unlikely, but if so, she ought to be treated according to her interests.

2. *Autonomy and false beliefs*

> Every creature that lives and moves shall be food for you... But you must not eat the flesh with life, which is the blood, still in it. (Gen 9:3–5)

> Abstain from... fornication, from anything that has been strangled and from blood. (Acts 15: 19–21)

Jehovah's Witnesses interpret these passages as forbidding blood transfusion.

A Jehovah's Witness (JW) is involved in a car accident. He requires a blood transfusion if he is to live. He refuses to have the blood transfusion. He would prefer to die. Should his desire be respected?

I have argued that Mrs X's false belief distorts her appreciation of treatment options available to her. It precludes her choice to die from being autonomous. However, not giving blood to JW is said to respect his autonomy. Yet JW (let us assume) holds a false belief: if he receives a blood transfusion, he'll go to Hell. Why is the refusal of treatment of JW an expression of his autonomy, and that of Mrs X not? Aren't they both under a misapprehension as to a matter of relevant fact? Why does, "If I have an amputation, I'll be confined to a wheelchair", make Mrs X's refusal non-autonomous, whereas 'If I get blood, I'll be confined to Hell' ' doesn't make the Witness' refusal non-autonomous?[64]

a. Instrumental irrationality JW may be instrumentally irrational, that is, mistaken about the appropriate means to his ends. Assume that the Bible only forbids the consumption of animal blood. Assume also that JW rationally desires (in the narrow sense in which I have defined it) to live in accordance with the dictates of the Bible. JW mistakenly believes that the Bible forbids blood transfusion, when the Bible is only referring to certain dietary practices. His desire not to receive blood is the result of false belief about what the Bible says. His desire will cause him to die. It is thus an obstructive desire. It prevents him achieving what he judges is best: *living* in accordance with the Bible. His *instrumental* irrationality frustrates his autonomy. This kind of JW is like Mrs X.[65]

b. Instrumentally valuable false beliefs A person can rationally (in both my sense and a broader sense) choose to hold false beliefs. Knowing that I must fight courageously in battle to survive, I might form the false belief that I am the incarnation of a great Hindu Warrior. Or I may be dying of some disease. In order to put on a brave face for my family, I cause myself to believe that death will not be the end. Indeed, a person can rationally cause himself to act irrationally.[66] Desire based on false belief is often instrumentally irrational; however, it is not *necessarily* instrumentally irrational.

If it is the case that JW's false belief serves some useful purpose, then this provides some reason to hold this belief. For instance, the belief that Witnesses have in bodily purity sets them apart from other sects. If holding this false belief is necessary for their identity as members of this discrete sect, and being a member confers great advantages not easily found elsewhere (feelings of solidarity, uniqueness, camaraderie, loyalty, etc.), then each person would have a reason to hold the false belief.

As I argued before, autonomy can be inherited from a parent evaluation. If JW autonomously chose to be a member of this sect, having appreciated what it entails, including the risk of death from blood loss, and holding this false belief is *necessary* if one is to be a member of this sect, then holding this false belief is an expression of his autonomy.

To what degree the false belief is necessary in either of these two senses is an open question.

c. Descriptive and non-descriptive beliefs One can have beliefs about descriptive and non-descriptive statements or claims. Descriptive statements are pure statements of fact. Non-descriptive statements are not pure statements of fact, but may in part be "expressions of attitudes, prescriptions or something else non-descriptive".[67] A belief about a descriptive statement is meant to describe the way the world is. Examples might be "I believe that the cat is on the mat" or "I believe that Rome is further north than Athens." Beliefs about descriptive statements are verifiable by empirical investigation of the world. That is, my belief is false if the cat is *not* on the mat, and so on.

I will call beliefs about descriptive statements, descriptive beliefs. One way to interpret religious belief is as descriptive belief, that is, as representing the way the world is. This would include the belief that there *is* a place, Heaven and another, Hell, there *is* a being, God, and so on. On this interpretation, JW is expressing a descriptive belief: if he gets a blood transfusion, he will actually go to Hell, which is supposed to be a place of fire and eternal torment, inhabited by beings with horns on their heads and tails, holding small pitchforks.

As far as being an empirical hypothesis about the way the world is, there is no good reason to believe that such descriptions of the world represent true propositions. Available evidence suggests that there is no Hell of any description. If held in this descriptive manner, religious belief distorts one's grasp on the nature of the world. In this case, the JW's belief would be like that of Mrs X; his desire to die would not be autonomous.

Compare the following statements: (1) I ought to hand in the money I found. (2) The painting is beautiful. (3) God exists.

(1) represents a moral statement. There is division about whether moral statements are descriptive or non-descriptive. I will not enter that debate. A non-descriptive account of (1) is that the statement expresses in part some attitude on the part of the speaker. The meaning of the statement is not fixed by properties of actions, the world or other descriptive criteria.[68]

It seems to me that if non-descriptivism is a coherent account of the meaning of moral statements, then it may also be a coherent account of other statements. I have in mind statements like (2). It is possible to agree on all the facts concerning a painting: what colours it employs, the type of brush strokes, the subject, the quality of the canvas, and so on, and yet disagree about whether it is beautiful. The expression that something is beautiful is, at least in part, the expression of a certain attitude.

But if this is right, it is possible that religious statements, although ostensibly purporting to report some property or fact about the world, may be non-descriptive statements.[69] Statements "reporting" religious fact may be like statements "reporting" aesthetic fact. (3) may be like (2). Statement (3) may represent, not a mere statement of fact or the description of a property, but an expression of an attitude, a commitment to a way of life, an adherence to an ideal. On this reading, religion is a construct which gives meaning to people's lives, rather than an empirical statement about the nature of the world. JW's belief, B, that if he receives blood, he'll go to Hell, can thus be viewed as a belief about a non-descriptive statement. The following statements all represent a similar attitude or commitment about which we can have beliefs: "If I receive blood, it will be very bad," "If I receive the blood, I'll go to Hell," "I ought not to receive the blood."

Since non-descriptive statements do not describe properties of the world, they cannot be assessed for their truth or falsehood by empirical examination of the world or of the people in it.

Just as there is no property or descriptive criterion of a painting that will establish that the painting is beautiful, so too there is no property of the world that will establish that God exists. To say to JW that B is false is like saying to a small clique of painters that their paintings are ugly. They might reply, "But we think that they are beautiful." There is no fact of the matter which will settle that the paintings are "truly beautiful". Beauty is in the eye of the beholder, at least for the non-descriptivist.

Nor is there any necessary irrationality or failure of rational evaluation in dying for a non-descriptive construct. It is no more non-autonomous to die for one's religion than it is to die for one's country.

There is, then, not one kind of Jehovah's Witness, but many. Some are irrational and non-autonomous, while others are as autonomous as the next man, or woman. What respect for autonomy requires depends on how a particular Witness holds his belief.

Conclusion

The President's Commission, along with many contemporary bioethicists, accepts that treatment of previously competent but now incompetent patients can be limited if that is what the patient would desire, if she were now competent. If this hypothetical desire cannot be determined, then treatment can be limited if it is not in the patient's best interests. On this approach, a past preference on a related issue or an advance directive constitute sufficient evidence of what a patient would now desire, if she were competent.

I have distinguished between desiring and rational desiring. One necessary condition for a desire to be fully autonomous is that it is a rational desire or that it satisfies a rational desire. A person rationally desires a state of affairs if that person desires that state of affairs while being in possession of all available relevant facts, without committing relevant error of logic, and vividly imagining what a reasonable range of states of affairs associated with each course of action would be like for him or her.

Not all desires are expressions of a person's autonomy. Some competent, expressed desires obstruct one's autonomy. In evaluating a life of suffering and disability, there are several psychological mechanisms which tend to prevent adequate evaluation of those states. The process of vivid imagination so necessary for rational evaluation is no easy or straightforward process to engage in. When deciding whether to live or die, there are many hurdles to forming a desire which is an expression of our autonomy.

In relation to limitation of treatment of incompetent patients, I conclude: (1) If past desires (including those expressed in advance directives) are to be full expressions of a person's former autonomy, they must have been formed by a person who was in possession of all relevant, available information, who did not commit relevant logical errors and who was vividly acquainted with the lives on offer. (2) In the realm of decisions about states of significant disability, it ought not be presumed that past competent desires (including advance directives) were necessarily autonomous. (3) Past competent desires (including advance directives) ought to be evaluated to examine whether they were the expression of a person's autonomy. (4) In order to respect a now incompetent patient's former autonomy, it is not enough to know what a patient would now desire if she were competent. We must know what she would rationally desire. (5) Treatment of an incompetent person ought to be limited if limitation is what she would rationally desire. Evidence of what a patient would now rationally desire is what she did rationally desire. (6) If it is clear that allowing a patient to die is a violation of his former autonomy (as reflected by what he or she rationally desired), then he or she ought not be allowed to die. This may entail acting contrary to an expressed past preference (including an advance directive), if that preference was irrational (obstructive). (7) As our degree of belief that a past expressed desire (including an advance directive) was not autonomous increases, and we are not confident that we know what the patient would now rationally desire, treatment should promote an incompetent patient's best interests.

My arguments have implications for the limitation of treatment of competent patients. My conclusions in this regard are: (1) Care providers ought to ensure that the conditions under which a patient can choose autonomously are secured. This includes provision of information, purging of errors of logic and facilitation of imagination of options on offer. (2) When it is clear that a competent desire is obstructive, and what the person would rationally desire can be confidently estimated, then it is best if we wish to respect autonomy to override the obstructive desire in favour of what the patient would rationally desire. (3) Cases where an obstructive desire persists, or where a person has failed to rationally evaluate the relevant states of affairs, or it is unclear whether the expressed desire is obstructive are complex. If we elect to obey a competent desire, we must recognize that we may not be respective, and may even be frustrating, this patient's autonomy.

Notes

1 Thanks to two anonymous referees who reviewed an earlier draft. Their detailed comments greatly improved the paper. I am also indebted to Helga Kuhse, Justin Oakley, Cora Singer, Robert Young, Professor R. M. Hare, Hilary Madder and, most of all, to Peter Singer, for their pains and the many invaluable comments which they gave me. This paper was written with the support of a National Health and Medical Research Council of Australia Medical Scholarship.

2 David Hume, "Of Suicide", in P. Singer (ed), *Applied Ethics* (Oxford: Oxford University Press, 1986), p. 26.

3 President's Commission for the Study of Ethical Problems in Medicine and Biomedical and Behavioral Research, *Deciding to Forego Life-Sustaining Treatment: A Report on the Ethical, Medical and Legal Issues in Treatment Decisions* (March 1983), p. 136.

4 Ibid., p. 27.

5 G. Dworkin, *The Theory and Practice of Autonomy* (Cambridge: Cambridge University Press, 1988), p. 12.

6 R. Young, *Personal Autonomy: Beyond Negative and Positive Liberty*, (London: Croom Helm, 1986), p. 8.

7 Ibid., p. 8. The term "life-plan" is used on p. 78.

8 This account is like Brandt's account of rational desires (*A Theory of the Good and the Right* (Oxford: Clarendon Press, 1979), pp. 111ff). One important difference is that Brandt's is a counterfactual account. Young also appeals to a similar notion of rational desire (*Personal Autonomy*, p. 10 and pp. 43–5).

9 I assume she does not have an intrinsic distaste for intravenous infusions.

10 In Locke's case, the person believes the door is open when in fact it is locked. (J. Locke, *An Essay concerning Human Understanding*, ed. A. S. Pringle-Pattinson Oxford: Clarendon Press, 1924), Book II, Chapter xxi, sec. 10).

11 Kahneman and Varey note: "A basic tenet of psychological analysis is that the contents of subjective experience are coded and interpreted representations of objects and events. An objective description of stimuli is not adequate to predict experience because coding and interpretation can cause identical physical stimuli to be treated as different and different ones to be treated as identical." (D. Kahneman and C. Varey, "Notes on the psychology of utility", in J. Elster and J. E. Roemer, *Interpersonal Comparisons of Well-Being* (Cambridge: Cambridge University Press, 1991), p. 141.)

12 If the reader does not accept the preceding argument, then his or her favoured account of autonomous desiring should be inserted.

13 This formulation of the objection is Robert Young's.

14 I will not discuss the more complex problem of which of all the possible courses of action open to an agent ought to be entertained for a choice to be autonomous.

15 This formulation of the objection is again Robert Young's. Dan Brock puts the problem in the form of "impetuous Adam". (See D. Brock, "Paternalism and Autonomy", *Ethics*, 98 (April 1988), 550–65.) My response is similar to that of Feinberg (*Harm to Self* (New York: Oxford University Press, 1986), p. 109).

16 Professor Hare convinced me of this (personal communication). I use "dispositional concept" in Ryle's sense (G. Ryle, *The Concept of Mind*, (Harmondsworth: Penguin, 1963), p. 43, 113–20). Young also argues that autonomy has an important dispositional sense (*Personal Autonomy*, p. 8).

17 I will not discuss these in detail. Examples might be that the person is not asleep, under anaesthesia, not in the grip of psychotic illness, not under the influence of certain drugs, not being coerced by others, etc.

18 See for example, G. Watson, "Free Agency", *Journal of Philosophy*, 72 (1975) and D. Gauthier, *Morals by Agreement* (Oxford: Clarendon Press, 1986).

19 P desires that q iff P would desire that q under conditions C. See: M. Smith, "Valuing: Desiring or Believing?" in D. Charles and Lennon, D. (eds), *Reduction, Explanation and Realism* (Oxford University Press, 1995).

20 R. Graves, *The Greek Myths*, vol. 2 (Harmondsworth: Penguin, 1960), p. 361.

21 One editor asked whether Ulysses knows that he will die at the time he commands his men to move closer to the Island. If he does, his desire is more clearly irrational. But let us assume that he does not know this at the time. Let us assume that the Sirens' song removes this belief or makes it inaccessible. It might be objected that Ulysses is not then irrational because he does not know that he will die in moving closer to the Sirens. However, Ulysses' desire is still irrational because it has not been made by vividly imagining the

relevant alternatives. The Sirens' song causes Ulysses' mind to be dominated by one alternative.

22 I thank Professor Hare for this objection and for drawing to my attention this crucial distinction between disposition and desire.

23 I will not address the relationship between these two errors. It may be that the false belief caused the failure of imagination *or* that the failure in imagination caused the false belief. Her *dread* of amputation may have prevented her believing she would walk.

24 J. C. J. M. De Haes and F. C. E. Van Knippenberg, "Quality of life of cancer patients: a review of the literature". In N. K. Aaronson and J. Beckmann (ed), *The Quality of Life of Cancer Patients* (New York: Raven Press, 1987), p. 170. These results represent the cumulation of a series of studies – see de Haes and Van Knippenberg for specific references.

25 Ibid. for specific references.

26 P. Menzel, *Strong Medicine* (Oxford: Oxford University Press, 1990), p. 82. Menzel also shows that these patients will prefer to shorten their lives by 50% to be cured of their disease, p. 81. These findings together may suggest that these patients value normality more than normal people do.

27 Ibid., p. 82, n. 11.

28 P., Brickman, D. Coates, and R. Janoff-Bulman, "Lottery winners and accident victims: is happiness relative?" *Journal of Personality and Social Psychology*, 36(8) (1978), 917–27 as quoted in D. Kahneman and C. Varey, "Notes on the psychology of utility", in J. Elster and J. E. Roemer, *Interpersonal Comparisons of Well-Being* (Cambridge: Cambridge University Press, 1991).

29 From Heinrich and Kriefel cited in E. Goffman, *Stigma: Notes on the Management of Spoiled Identity* (Englewood Cliffs, NJ: Prentice-Hall, 1963) as cited in S. E. Taylor, *Positive Illusions* (Basic Books, 1989), p. 161.

30 All quotations are from S. E. Taylor, "Adjustment to threatening events: A theory of cognitive adaptation", *American Psychologist*, 38 (1983), 1161–73 as quoted in Taylor, *Positive Illusions*, pp. 195–6.

31 Ibid, p. 166. She quotes from several different sources (see text for full references).

32 Kahneman and Varey ("Psychology of Utility", pp. 136–7) argue that adaptation is a normal phenomenon.

33 Ibid. pp. 136–7.

34 J. A. Russell, and B. Fehr, "Relativity in the perception of emotion in facial expressions", *Journal of Experimental Psychology: General*, 116(3) (1987), 223–37, as quoted in Kahneman and Varey, "Psychology of Utility", p. 139.

35 For more recent experiments illustrating the significance of contrast effects, see A. Tversky and D. Griffin, "Endowment and contrast in judgements of well-being" in F. Strack, M. Argyle and N. Schwarz (eds), *Subjective Well-Being* (Oxford: Pergamon, 1991), pp. 101–18.

36 Kahneman and Varey, "Psychology of Utility", p. 144.

37 Ibid., p. 149.

38 Ibid., p. 149.

39 See D. Parfit, *Reasons and Persons* (Oxford: Clarendon Press, 1984), Part III for a discussion of the rationality of this bias. I am not arguing that these attitudes or psychological responses *necessarily* preclude autonomy. I am not arguing that one cannot be autonomously loss- or risk-averse, or "live for the moment". But to be autonomous and hold these attitudes and biases, they must at some point have been evaluated in the right way and endorsed. Most people have not evaluated their biases.

40 "Psychology of Utility", p. 144.

41 "Endorsment", pp. 113–14.

42 President's Commission, p. 45.

43 D. Kahneman and D. T. Miller, "Norm Theory: Comparing Reality to Its Alternatives", *Psychological Review*, 93(2), (1986), 136–53. The quote is on p. 148.

44 Ibid., p. 148.

45 President's Commission, p. 132.

46 A. Buchanan and D. Brock, "Deciding for Others", *Milbank Quarterly*, 64(Suppl. 2), (1986), 17–94.

47 President's Commission, p. 149.

48 I here assume that a desire's being rational is *sufficient* for its being autonomous. This is an oversimplification. Other necessary conditions must be satisfied for a desire to be autonomous.

49 T. L. Beauchamp and J. F. Childress, *Principles of Biomedical Ethics* (New York: Oxford University Press, 1989), p. 83. Beauchamp and Childress describe a competent person as one who possesses certain abilities or capacities, pp. 79–85. They claim that it "seems a plausible hypothesis that an autonomous person is necessarily a competent person", p. 83. The more relevant question for me is: is a competent person *necessarily* autonomous?

50 Buchanan and Brock, "Deciding for Others", p. 70.

51 L. M. Silverman, et al. "Whether No Means No", *Hastings Center Report*, (May–June 1992), 26–7.

52 President's Commission, p. 135.

53 See D. Parfit, *Reasons and Persons*, pp. 493–502 and J. Griffin, *Well-Being* (Oxford: Clarendon Press, 1986).

54 Parfit, *Reasons and Persons*, p. 499.

55 See Parfit (*Reasons and Persons*) and Griffin (*Well-Being*).

56 Parfit, *Reasons and Persons*, p. 502.

57 A point forcefully made by Robert Young.

58 Clearly not all paraplegics later find life worth living. There is some uncertainty about whether *this* person's life will be worth living as a paraplegic. This issue is dealt with in my "Treatment Limitation Decisions under Uncertainty: the Value of Subsequent Euthanasia", *Bioethics*, 8(1), (Jan. 1994).

59 President's Commission, p. 137.

60 Better than vivid imagination is actual experience. Still, there are factors which can interfere with rational evaluation based on experience. We may focus on only one aspect of that experience or unjustifiably generalize from one aspect, and so on.

61 Third party evaluations of what a patient values raise problems. There is a suggestion of antipathy between J and his wife. She may want him to be punished. We must keep clear that our aim is to determine what the patient values. Third party evaluations constitute just one line of evidence.

62 *Concept of Mind*, p. 84.

63 Another related question is: if one can rationally desire death, then one must have vividly imagined what death is like. Is this possible? Imagination of what being dead is like ought only occur to the extent that it can occur. One way in which being dead can be imagined is as the absence of certain states of affairs.

64 This objection is Peter Singer's.

65 The importance of the instrumentality, and the example given, was raised by one referee.

66 See Derek Parfit's "Could It Be Rational to Cause Oneself to Act Irrationally?" in *Reasons and Persons*, pp. 12–13.

67 R. M. Hare, *Moral Thinking* (Oxford: Clarendon Press, 1981), p. 208.

68 Ibid., p. 70.

69 Professor Hare gives a detailed non-descriptivist interpretation of religious statements in "The Simple Believer", "Appendix: Theology and Falsification" and "Religion and Morals" in his *Essays on Religion and Education* (Oxford: Clarendon Press, 1992). I thank Professor Hare for very valuable discussion on these points.

PART X

Special Issues Facing Nurses

70

One Nurse's Story: What I Had to Do for My Patient Mac

Barbara Huttmann

"Murderer," a man shouted. "God help patients who get *you* for a nurse."

"What gives you the right to play God?" another one asked.

It was the Phil Donahue show, where the guest is a fatted calf and the audience a 200-strong flock of vultures hungering to pick at the bones. I had told them about Mac, one of my favorite cancer patients. "We resuscitated him 52 times in just 1 month. I refused to resuscitate him again. I simply sat there and held his hand while he died."

There wasn't time to explain that Mac was a young, witty, macho cop who walked into the hospital with 32 pounds of attack equipment, looking as if he could single-handedly protect the whole city, if not the entire state. "Can't get rid of this cough," he said. Otherwise, he felt great.

Before the day was over, tests confirmed that he had lung cancer. And before the year was over, I loved him, his wife, Maura, and their three kids as if they were my own family. All the nurses loved him. And we all battled his disease for six months without ever giving death a second thought. Six months isn't such a long time in the whole scheme of things, but it was long enough to see him lose his youth, his wit, his macho, his hair, his bowel and bladder control, his sense of taste and smell, and his ability to do the slightest thing for himself. It was also long enough to watch Maura's transformation from a young woman into a haggard, beaten old lady.

When Mac had wasted away to a 60-pound skeleton kept alive by liquid food we poured down a tube, IV solutions we dripped into his veins, and oxygen we piped to a mask on his face, he begged us: "Mercy . . . for God's sake, please just let me go."

Reprinted with permission from *Newsweek*, (August 8, 1983).

Miracles

The first time he stopped breathing, the nurse pushed the button that calls a "code blue" throughout the hospital and sends a team rushing to resuscitate the patient. Each time he stopped breathing, sometimes two or three times in one day, the code team came again. The doctors and technicians worked their miracles and walked away. The nurses stayed to wipe the saliva that drooled from his mouth, irrigate the big craters of bedsores that covered his hips, suction the lung fluids that threatened to drown him, clean the feces that burned his skin like lye, pour the liquid food down the tube attached to his stomach, put pillows between his knees to ease the bone-on-bone pain, turn him every hour to keep the bedsores from getting worse, and change his gown and linen every 2 hours to keep him from being soaked in perspiration.

At night I went home and tried to scrub away the smell of decaying flesh that seemed woven into the fabric of my uniform. It was in my hair, the upholstery of my car – there was no washing it away. And every night I prayed that Mac would die, that his agonized eyes would never again plead with me to let him die.

Every morning I asked his doctor for a "no code" order. Without that order, we had to resuscitate every patient who stopped breathing. His doctor was one of several who believe we must extend life as long as we have the means and knowledge to do it. To not do it is to be liable for negligence, at least in the eyes of many people, including some nurses. I thought about what it would be like to stand before a judge, accused of murder, if Mac stopped breathing and I didn't call a code.

And after the 52nd code, when Mac was still lucid enough to beg for death again, and Maura was crumpled in my arms again, and when no amount of pain medication stilled his moaning and agony, I wondered about a spiritual judge. Was all this misery and suffering supposed to be building character or infusing us all with the sense of humility that comes from impotence?

Had we, the whole medical community, become so arrogant that we believed in the illusion of salvation through science? Had we become so self-righteous that we thought meddling in God's work was our duty, our moral imperative, and our legal obligation? Did we really believe that we had the right to force "life" on a suffering man who begged for the right to die?

Such questions haunted me more than ever early one morning when Maura went home to change her clothes and I was bathing Mac. He had been still for so long, I thought he at last had the blessed relief of coma. Then he opened his eyes and moaned, "Pain . . . no more . . . Barbara . . . do something . . . God, let me go."

Death

The desperation in his eyes and voice riddled me with guilt. "I'll stop," I told him as I injected the pain medication.

I sat on the bed and held Mac's hands in mine. He pressed his bony fingers against my hand and muttered, "Thanks." Then there was one soft sigh and I felt his hands go cold in mine. "Mac?" I whispered, as I waited for his chest to rise and fall again.

A clutch of panic banded my chest, drew my finger to the code button, urged me to do something, anything . . . but sit there alone with death. I kept one finger on the button, without pressing it, as a waxen pallor slowly transformed his face from person to empty shell. Nothing I've ever done in my 47 years has taken so much effort as it took not to press that code button.

Eventually, when I was as sure as I could be that the code team would fail to bring him back, I entered the legal twilight zone and pushed the button. The team tried. And while they were trying, Maura walked into the room and shrieked, "No . . . don't let them do this to him . . . for God's sake . . . please, no more."

Cradling her in my arms was like cradling myself, Mac, and all those patients and nurses who had been in this place before who do the best they can in a death-denying society.

So a TV audience accused me of murder. Perhaps I am guilty. If a doctor had written a no-code order, which is the only *legal* alternative, would he have felt any less guilty? Until there is legislation making it a criminal act to code a patient who has requested the right to die, we will all of us risk the same fate as Mac. For whatever reason, we developed the means to prolong life, and now we are forced to use it. We do not have the right to die.

71

Ethical Dilemmas for Nurses: Physicians' Orders Versus Patients' Rights

E. Joy Kroeger Mappes

The American Hospital Association in a widely promulgated statement entitled "Patient's Bill of Rights," makes explicit a number of the generally recognized rights of hospitalized patients.[1] Among the rights expressly articulated in the AHA statement is a cluster of rights closely associated with a more general right, the right of self-determination. The "self-determination cluster" includes: (1) the right to information concerning diagnosis, treatment, and prognosis; (2) the right to information necessary to give informed consent; and (3) the right to refuse treatment. The AHA statement duly recognizes several other important patient rights but, importantly, fails to explicitly recognize the patient's right to adequate medical care.[2] Surely, if the purpose of a statement of patients' rights is to catalogue patients' rights, we ought not to overlook this one. After all, the patient has agreed to enter the hospital setting precisely for the purpose of obtaining medical treatment. To the extent that adequate medical care is not forthcoming, the patient has been done an injustice. That is, the patient's right to adequate medical care has been violated.

This paper explores two types of ethical dilemmas related to patients' rights that arise for the hospital nurse.[3] (1) The first set of dilemmas is related to the patient's basic right to adequate medical care. (2) The second set of dilemmas is related to the cluster of rights closely associated with the patient's right of self-determination. Dilemmas arise for a nurse if adequate medical care for a patient would be jeopardized by following the expressed or understood orders of a physician. Dilemmas also arise for a nurse if the patient's right to self-determination would be violated by following the expressed or understood orders of a physician. In each case, the logic of the dilemma is similar. The dilemma arises because the nurse's apparent obligation to follow the physician's order conflicts with his or her obligation to act in the interest of the patient. To carry out the physician's order would be to act against the interest of the patient. To act in the interest of the patient would be to disobey the physician's order.[4] I will argue that when this conflict arises the nurse's obligation to the patient is overriding and that nurses must act and be allowed and encouraged to act to protect the rights of the patient.

T. A. Mappes and J. S. Zembaty (eds), *Biomedical Ethics* (New York: McGraw-Hill, 1981), pp. 95–102.

I Nursing Dilemmas and the Patient's Right to Adequate Medical Care

In a hospital the primary responsibility for a patient's care rests with a physician. Physicians determine the medical diagnosis, treatment, and prognosis of patients' illnesses and write orders to arrive at and effect these determinations. In general, physicians' orders govern what a patient is to do and what is to be done for a patient, i.e., the degree of activity, diet, medication, diagnostic and treatment procedures to be performed. Nurses carry out physicians' orders themselves, delegate tasks to others, or make the orders known to those responsible for carrying them out. They are not generally allowed by law to diagnose or prescribe.[5]

Although this is a greatly oversimplified picture of what goes on, as anyone familiar at all with the functioning of a hospital will realize, at least some of the complexities involved in the interaction among physicians, nurses, and patients in a hospital setting will emerge as we proceed.

The complexity of the ethical dilemmas arising for nurses regarding the patient's right to adequate medical care can best be understood by examining various examples. The following are suggested as being not atypical of situations arising in hospitals:

1 A patient who has had emphysema for a number of years is admitted to a cardiac unit for observation with a tentative diagnosis of myocardial infarction. Oxygen is ordered in a concentration commonly given for patients with this diagnosis. The nurse, knowing that oxygen is contraindicated for patients with emphysema, must decide whether to carry out or question the order through appropriate channels.
2 A patient admitted to the hospital for a diagnostic work-up has been on a special and fairly extensive drug therapy regimen. This regimen is common to patients of a particular private physician, seemingly regardless of their diagnosis. The private physician orders the drug therapy program continued after admission. However, accepted medical practice would ordinarily call for ceasing as many drugs as is safely possible, thus avoiding unnecessary variables in arriving at an accurate diagnosis. In general the private physician is viewed by other physicians as incompetent. The nurse is aware that the orders do not reflect good medical practice, but also realizes that she[6] will be dealing with this physician as long as she works at that hospital. The nurse must decide whether to follow the orders or refuse to carry out the orders, attempting through channels to have the orders changed.
3 A frail patient recovering from recent surgery has been receiving intra-muscular antibiotic injections four times a day. The injection sites are very tender, and though the patient now is able to eat without problems, the intern refuses to change the order to an oral route of administration of the antibiotic because the absorption of the medication would be slightly diminished. The nurse must decide whether to follow the order as it stands or continue through channels to try to have the order changed.
4 A nurse on the midnight shift of a large medical center is closely monitoring a patient's vital signs (blood pressure, pulse rate, respiratory rate). The physicians have been unable to diagnose the patient's illness. In reviewing the patient's record, the nurse thinks of a possible diagnosis. The patient's condition begins to worsen and the nurse phones the intern-on-call to notify him of the patient's condition. The nurse mentions that the record indicates that diagnosis X is possible. The intern dismisses the nurse's suggested diagnosis and instructs the nurse to follow existing orders. Concerned that the patient's condition will continue to deteriorate, the nurse contacts her supervisor who concurs with the intern. The patient's blood pressure gradually but steadily falls and the pulse increases. The nurse has contacted the intern twice since the initial call but the orders remain unchanged. The nurse must decide whether to pursue the matter further, e.g., calling the resident-on-call and/or the patient's private physician.[7]

What are the obligations of nurses in such cases? Under what circumstances are nurses obligated to rely on their judgment and to question the physician's order? To what extent must nurses pursue the questioning when, in their view, the patient's right to adequate medical care is being violated? It is often taken for granted that when the medical assessments of physician and nurse differ, "the physician knows best." In order to see both why this is thought, perhaps correctly so, to be generally true and yet why it is surely not always true, it is necessary to consider some of the factors that account for the difference in physician and nurse assessments.

A nurse's assessment of what constitutes adequate medical treatment may differ from a physician's assessment for at least three reasons. (*a*) There is a difference in the amount and the content of their formal training. Physicians generally have a number of years more formal training than nurses, though that difference is not as great as it once was. More nurses now continue formal training in various ways, i.e., by pursuing graduate work and/or by becoming nurse practitioners, nurse clinicians, or nurse anesthetists. In addition, proportionately more nurses than ever before are college graduates. However, a physician's formal training is more extensive and detailed. Moreover, and perhaps most importantly, physicians are explicitly trained in the diagnosis and treatment of illness, with the emphasis of the training placed on the hard sciences. Nurses are trained to be knowledgeable about illness in general, the symptoms and treatment of illness, and the complications and side effects of various forms of therapy. While this formal training includes both the hard sciences and the social (primarily behavioral) sciences, there is an emphasis on the behavioral sciences. Nurses are trained to concentrate on the overall well-being of the patient. (*b*) There may be a difference in the length or concentration of their experience. For example, nurses who have worked in special care units (in medical and surgical cardiac units, burn units, renal units, intensive care units) for a number of years acquire a great deal of knowledge which may not be possessed by interns, and perhaps even residents and non-specialty private physicians. Nurses who have worked for years in small community hospitals may well be more knowledgeable in some areas than some physicians. (*c*) There may be a difference in their knowledge of the patient. Nurses often have more detailed knowledge about patients than do physicians, who often see a patient only once a day. Nurses who are "at the bedside" are thus in a position to recognize small changes as they happen. Because of the possibility of more detailed knowledge, nurse assessments may be more accurate than physician assessments. Where physician and nurse assessments differ then, it is not necessarily the case that the physician's assessment is the correct one simply because of the amount and content of the physician's formal training. Physicians do make mistakes and, when they do, nurses must be in a position to protect the patient.[8]

Ethical dilemmas of the kind typified in the above four examples arise when to follow physician's orders would be to act against the medical interest of the patient. Given the fact that the *basic* obligation of both the physician and the nurse is to act in the medical interest of the patient, it is rather striking that anyone should suppose that the nurse's obligation to follow the physician's orders should ever take precedence. What, after all, is the foundation of the nurse's obligation to follow the physician's orders? Presumably, the nurse's obligation to follow the physician's orders is grounded on the nurse's obligation to act in the medical interest of the patient. The point is that the nurse has an obligation to follow physicians' orders because, ordinarily, patient welfare (interest) thereby is ensured. Thus when a nurse's obligation to follow a physician's order comes into *direct* conflict with the nurse's obligation to act in the medical interest of the patient, it would seem to follow that the patient's interests should always take precedence.

For instance, Example 1 provides a clear case of a medically unsound order. In fact, it is such a clear case that a nurse not questioning the order would be judged incompetent. The medically unsound order may be the result of a medical mistake or of medical incompetence. If the order is the result of an oversight, the physician is likely to be grateful when (if) a nurse questions the order. If the order is a result of incompetence, the physician is not likely to be grateful. Whatever the reason for the medically unsound order, the nurse is obligated to question an order if it is clearly medically unsound. The nurse must refuse to carry out the order if it is not changed, and to press the matter through channels in order to protect the medical interest of the patient. Example 2 is similar to Example 1 in that it involves a medical practice that is clearly unsound. If the orders are questioned, the physician here again is not likely to be grateful. Indeed, since the physician's practice may ultimately be at stake, the pressures brought to bear on a nurse may be overwhelming, particularly if the physician's colleagues choose to defend him or her. It is undeniable, however, that medical incompetence is not in the best medical interest of patients, and thus that a nurse's obligation is to question the order. It is of course true that a nurse acting on behalf of the patient in this situation may pay a heavy price, perhaps his or her job, for protecting the medical interests of patients. However, the nurse's moral obligation is no less real on this account.

With Example 3 the murkiness begins, since it does not provide a clear case of unsound medical practice, though perhaps it presents us with a case in which the physician is operating with a too-narrow view of good medical practice. As I mentioned earlier, nurses often are more concerned with the overall well-being of the patient. Physicians often are concerned only with identifying the illness, treating it, and determining how responsive the illness is to the treatment. To the extent that Example 3 resembles Example 1, i.e., the lumps are very bad and the difference in the absorption of the medication in the two routes of administration is small, the nurse has an obligation to question the order. Example 4 is like Example 3 in that it does not provide a clear case of a medically unsound order. However, in Example 4, much more is at stake. Since life itself is involved, any decision must be considered very carefully. The problem here is not a problem of weighing or balancing but a problem of being either right or wrong. Both Examples 3 and 4 force a nurse to assess this question: "How strong are my grounds for thinking that the orders are not in tune with the patient's best medical interest?" The murkiness comes in knowing exactly when the physician's order is in direct conflict with the patient's medical interest. As the last two examples illustrate, it can be very difficult to know exactly what is in the best medical interest of the patient. To the extent that the nurse has carefully considered the situation and is sure that his or her view is in accord with good medical care, the order should be questioned. The less sure one is, the less clear it becomes whether the order should be questioned and the matter pressed through channels.

In arguing the above, I am not advocating uncritical questioning. Clearly, questioning at some point must cease. Otherwise, hospitals could not function efficiently and as a result the medical interest of all patients would suffer. But if there is little or no opportunity for nurses and other health professionals to contribute their knowledge to the care of the patient, or if they are directly or indirectly discouraged from contributing, it would seem that they will find it difficult, if not impossible, to fulfill their obligations with respect to the patient's right to adequate medical care.

II Nursing Dilemmas and the Patient's Right of Self-Determination

The complexity of the ethical dilemmas arising for nurses regarding the patient's right of self-determination can best be understood by examining various cases. Again, the following are suggested as being not atypical of situations arising in hospitals:

1 A patient is scheduled for prostate surgery (prostatectomy) early in the morning. Because he is generally unaware of what is happening to him due to senility, he is judged incompetent to give informed consent for surgery. The patient's sister visits him in the evenings, but the physicians have not been available during those times for her to give consent. The physicians have asked the nurses to obtain consent from the patient's sister. When she arrives the evening before surgery is scheduled, the nurses explain to her that her brother is to have surgery and what it would entail. The sister had not been told that surgery was being considered and questions its necessity for her brother who has not experienced any real problems due to an enlarged prostate. She does not feel she can sign the consent form without talking with one of his physicians. Should the nurses encourage her to sign the consent form, as the physicians have requested, or call one of the physicians to speak with the patient's sister?
2 A patient in the cardiac unit who was admitted with a massive myocardial infarction begins to show signs of increased cardiac failure. The patient and the family have clearly expressed their desire to the medical and nursing staff to refrain from "heroics" should complications arise. The patient stops breathing and the intern begins to intubate the patient, requests the nurse's assistance, and orders a respirator. Should the nurse follow orders or attempt to convince the intern to reconsider, calling the resident-on-call should the intern refuse?
3 A patient is hospitalized for a series of diagnostic tests. The tests, history, and physical pretty clearly indicate a certain diagnosis. The physicians only tell the patient that they are not yet sure of the diagnosis, reassuring the patient that he is in good hands. Each day after the physicians leave, the patient asks the nurse, coming in to give medications, what the tests have shown and what his diagnosis is. When the nurse encourages the patient to ask the physicians these questions, he says he feels intimidated by them and that when he does ask questions they simply say that everything will be fine. Should the nurse reinforce what the physicians have said or attempt to convince the physicians that the patient has a right to information about his illness, pressing the matter through channels if they do not agree?
4 A patient suffering from cancer is scheduled for surgery in the morning. While instructing the patient not to eat or drink after a certain hour, the nurse realizes that the patient is unaware of the risks involved in having the surgery and of those involved in not having the surgery. In talking further, the nurse sees clearly that the option of not having surgery was never presented and that the patient has only a vague idea of what the surgery will entail. She also appears to be unaware of her diagnosis. The patient has signed the consent form for surgery.

Should the nurse proceed in preparing the patient for surgery, or, proceeding through channels, attempt to provide for a genuinely informed consent for the surgery?

What are the obligations of nurses in examples such as these? To what extent must nurses pursue questioning when, in their view, the patient's right of self-determination is being violated? Unless we are willing to say that a patient upon entering a hospital surrenders the right of self-determination, it seems clear that physicians' orders, explicit and implied, should be questioned in all of the above examples. After all, in each of the above examples, one of the rights expressly outlined by the American Hospital Association is in danger of being abridged. The rights involved are (or should be) known by all to be possessed by all. Here a difference in the formal training and knowledge based on experience is not relevant in any difference between a physician's and a nurse's assessment. No formal training in medicine is necessary to arrive at the conclusion that the patient's right of self-determination is endangered.

The tension that exists for nurses in situations typified in the above four examples is not really that of a moral dilemma, but rather, a tension between doing what is morally right and what is least difficult practically, a tension common in everyday life. The problem is not that the nurse's obligation is unclear, but that in actual situations fulfilling this moral obligation is extremely difficult. What we must consider now in some detail are the social forces that make it so difficult for a nurse to act on behalf of the patient.

III Nursing Dilemmas and the Importance of a Classist and Sexist Context

I have argued that when following a physician's order would violate the patient's right to adequate medical care or the patient's right of self-determination, the nurse's moral obligation is to question the order. If necessary, the matter should be pressed through channels. It is well and good to say what nurses should do. It is quite another thing, given the forces at work in the everyday world in which nurses must work, to expect nurses to do what they ought to do.

To begin with, we must recognize that there is an important class difference between physicians and nurses, the difference between the upper middle class or upper class of physicians and the lower middle class of nurses.[9] A large proportion of physicians both start out and end their lives in the upper class. Though the economic status of a physician is not as high as that of a high-level corporation executive, the social status of a physician is very high because of the prestige of the profession of medicine in the United States today.[10] Physicians have a high social status in American society and they understand and identify with people who have a similarly high status.[11] "Physicians talked with physicians; nurses talked with nurses," is an observation of one sociological study.[12] Generally physicians do not understand or identify with nurses (or with most patients), in part because of a difference in social status. Correspondingly, there is an educational difference between physicians and nurses. As mentioned earlier, the formal educational training necessary for a physician is generally much longer than that necessary for a nurse, and their training differs in content.

The differences in the composition of each profession on the basis of sex is clear. Most physicians are male (93.1 percent) and most nurses are female (97.3 percent).[13] In accordance with traditional sex roles, physicians are encouraged to be decisive and to act with authority. Studies indicate that physicians view themselves as omnipotent.[14] Nurses are encouraged to be tactful, sensitive, and diplomatic. Tact and diplomacy are necessary to make a physician feel in control. Put another way, nurses' recommendations for patient treatment must take a particular form. These recommendations must appear to be initiated by the physician. Nurses are expected to take the initiative and are responsible for making recommendations, but at the same time must appear passive.[15] Nurses who see their roles, partially at least, as one of consultant must follow certain rules of the "game."[16] If they refuse to follow the rules, they will be made to suffer consequences such as snide remarks, ostracism, harassment, or job termination.

Again, in accordance with traditional sex roles, nurses in hospitals are viewed much the same as are wives and mothers in the family. This is the view of nursing held both by society and by physicians. Nurses as women are expected to be subservient to physicians as men, to provide "tender loving care" to whoever may be in need, and to be responsible and competent in the absence of physicians but to relinquish that responsibility upon request, i.e., when physicians are present.[17]

As in society, women in hospitals (here women nurses) are typically viewed as sex objects, a situation which encourages physicians to discount the input of nurses with regard to patient care. The observation that women are viewed by male physicians as sexual objects was prevalent in a project which studied the discriminatory practices and attitudes against women in forty-one United States medical schools as seen from questionnaires completed by 146 women medical students. As the author notes, "The open expression of the notion that any woman – even if she is a patient – is fair game for lecherous interests of all men (including physicians) is in some ways the most distressing fact of these student observations."[18] Responses showing the prevalent attitude of physicians toward women in general or toward women as patients included: "[I] often hear demeaning remarks, usually toward nurses offered by clinicians...." "[There is] superficial discussion of topics related to women... Basic assumption: women are not worth serious consideration." "[The] most frequent remarks concern female patients – women's illnesses are assumed psychosomatic until proven otherwise."[19] Perhaps the most frequent response of women medical students depicting the attitudes of male medical students, professors, and clinicians centered around the use of slides in class of parts of women's anatomy and slides of nude women from magazine centerfolds. Those slides were introduced by medical-student colleagues or instructors often to bait women medical students or belittle them. One student relates, "My own experience with [a professor who had included a "nudie" slide in his lecture] was an interesting and emotional comment ending on, 'Men need to look down on women, and that's why I show the slide.' "[20] The response of the male members of the class to the slides was generally one of unmitigated laughter and approval. With such a negative and restricted view of women as persons, nurses, not to mention all women, are at a disadvantage in dealing with most male physicians.

Another aspect of the sexism that permeates the physician–nurse relationship is reflected in divergent standards of mental health for men and women. A study of thirty-three female and forty-six male psychiatrists, psychologists, and social workers showed that they held a different standard of mental health for women and men. The standard agreed upon for mentally healthy men was basically the same as the standard for mentally healthy adults. The standard for mentally healthy women included being more easily influenced, less objective, etc., in general characteristics which are less socially desirable.[21] Women then who are mentally healthy women are mentally unhealthy adults and women who are mentally healthy adults are mentally unhealthy women. This is clearly a "no win" situation for all women. Women nurses are no exception.

It is the just described classist and sexist economic and social context of the physician–nurse relationship that often inhibits the nurse from effectively functioning on behalf of the patient. Nurses have a moral responsibility to act on behalf of the patient, but in order to expect them to carry out that responsibility, changes must be made in the workplace. Nurses must be in a position to act to protect the rights of patients. They must be allowed and encouraged to do so. Therefore, those operating and managing hospitals and those responsible for hospital policies must establish policies which make it possible for nurses to protect patients' rights without risking their present and future employment. Those operating and managing hospitals cannot eradicate classism and sexism, but they must be aware of the impact it has on patient care, for again the ultimate goal of everyone connected with hospitals is adequate medical care within the framework of patients' rights. As potential patients it is important to all of us.[22]

Notes

1 The statement can be found, for example, in *Hospitals*, vol. 4 (Feb. 16, 1973).

2 I am aware of the difficulties in determining what constitutes adequate medical care. For example, is adequate medical care determined solely by reference to past and present medical practices, by the established wisdom of knowledgeable health professionals, or by knowledgeable recipients of medical care? And how is the standard for knowledgeability determined? I am presuming that problems such as these, though difficult, are not insoluble. I am also aware of the related difficulty in distinguishing medical care from health care. And what distinguishes medical care and health care from nursing care? In this paper, "medical care" will refer to the diagnosis and treatment of illness. Health professionals, then, who aid physicians in

the process of diagnosing and treating illness, aid in providing medical care.

3 A large majority of all working nurses work in hospitals.

4 The International Code of Nursing Ethics is ambiguous in addressing such a dilemma. The relevant section (#7) of the code merely states: "The nurse is under an obligation to carry out the physician's orders intelligently and loyally and to refuse to participate in unethical procedures." What exactly is the nurse supposed to do when to carry out the physician's orders is in effect to participate in unethical procedures? The most recent (1976) version of the *Code of Nurses* (available from the American Nurses' Association) adopted by the American Nurses' Association directly addresses this problem. Section 3 states, "The nurse acts to safeguard the client and the public when health care and safety are affected by the incompetent, unethical, or illegal practice of any person." The interpretive statement of section 3 begins, "The nurse's primary commitment is to the client's care and safety. Hence, in the role of client advocate, the nurse must be alert to and take appropriate action regarding any instances of incompetent, unethical, or illegal practice(s) by any member of the health-care team or the health-care system itself, or any action on the part of others that is prejudicial to the client's best interests."

5 The area of practice which is solely that of the nurse and the area of practice which is solely that of the physician is presently in a state of flux. The submissive role that nursing has held in relation to the physician's practice of medicine is being rejected by the nursing profession. Nurse practice acts, which regulate the practice of nursing, in many states reflect the change toward an expanded and more independent role for nurses. For example, a definition of a nursing diagnosis, as distinct from a medical diagnosis, is a part of some nurse practice acts. Daniel A. Rothman and Nancy Lloyd Rothman, *The Professional Nurse and the Law* (Boston: Little, Brown, 1977), pp. 65–81.

6 The overwhelming majority of nurses are women and the overwhelming majority of physicians are men. Because the examples are intended to reflect the hospital situation as it exists, I will use the feminine pronoun to refer to nurses and the masculine pronoun to refer to physicians.

7 In an actual case of this description, the intern dismissed the nurse's diagnosis by asking if her woman's intuition told her that diagnosis X was the correct one. The nurse's decision was to not pursue the matter and early in the morning the patient sustained a cardiac arrest and was unresponsive to resuscitation efforts by the resuscitation team.

8 Obviously, nurses also make mistakes, but physicians are clearly in a position to protect the patient when they become aware of nurses' mistakes.

9 Vicente Navarro, "Women in Health Care," *New England Journal of Medicine*, 292 (Feb. 20, 1975), p. 400.

10 Barbara Ehrenreich and John Ehrenreich, "Health Care and Social Control," *Social Policy*, 5 (May/June 1974), p. 33.

11 Raymond, S. Duff and August Hollingshead, *Sickness and Society* (New York: Harper & Row, 1968), p. 371.

12 Ibid., p. 376.

13 Navarro, p. 400.

14 Robert L. Kane and Rosalie, A. Kane, "Physicians' Attitudes of Omnipotence in a University Hospital," *Journal of Medical Education*, 44 (August 1969), pp. 684–90, and Trucia Kushner, "Nursing Profession: Condition Critical," *Ms*, 2 (August 1973), p. 99.

15 Kushner, p. 99.

16 Leonard, I. Stein, "The Doctor–Nurse Game," in Edith R. Lewis (ed.) *Changing Patterns of Nursing Practice: New Needs, New Roles* (New York: American Journal of Nursing Company, 1971), p. 227.

17 JoAnn Ashley, *Hospitals, Paternalism, and the Role of the Nurse* (New York: Teachers College, 1976), p. 17.

18 Margaret A. Campbell, *Why Would a Girl Go into Medicine?* (Old Westbury, NY: Feminist Press, 1973), p. 73.

19 Ibid., p. 74.

20 Ibid., p. 26.

21 Inge K. Broverman, Donald M. Broverman, Frank, E. Clarkson, Paul S. Rosenkrantz, and Susan R. Vogel, "Sex-Role Stereotypes and Clinical Judgments of Mental Health," *Journal of Consulting and Clinical Psychology*, 34 (February 1970), pp. 1–7.

22 I wish to thank Jorn Bramann, Marilyn Edmunds, Jane Zembaty, and especially Tom Mappes for their helpful comments on earlier versions of this paper.

72

In Defense of the Traditional Nurse

Lisa H. Newton

When a truth is accepted by everyone as so obvious that it blots out all its alternatives and leaves no respectable perspectives from which to examine it, it becomes the natural prey of philosophers, whose essential activity is to question accepted opinion. A case in point may be the ideal of the "autonomous professional" for nursing. The consensus that this ideal and image are appropriate for the profession is becoming monolithic and may profit from the presence of a full-blooded alternative ideal to replace the cardboard stereotypes it routinely condemns. That alternative, I suggest, is the traditional ideal of the skilled and gentle caregiver, whose role in health care requires submission to authority as an essential component. We can see the faults of this traditional ideal very clearly now, but we may perhaps also be able to see virtues that went unnoticed in the battle to displace it. It is my contention that the image and ideal of the traditional nurse contain virtues that can be found nowhere else in the health care professions, that perhaps make an irreplaceable contribution to the care of patients, and that should not be lost in the transition to a new definition of the profession of nursing.

A word should be said about what this article is, and what it is not. It is an essay in philosophical analysis, starting from familiar ideas, beliefs, and concepts, examining their relationships and implications and reaching tentative conclusions about the logical defensibility of the structures discovered. It is not the product of research in the traditional sense. Its factual premises – for example, that the "traditional" nursing role has been criticized by those who prefer an "autonomous professional" role – are modest by any standard, and in any event may be taken as hypothetical by all who may be disposed to disagree with them. It is not a polemic against any writer or writers in particular, but a critique of lines of reasoning that are turning up with increasing frequency in diverse contexts. Its arguments derive no force whatsoever from any writings in which they may be found elsewhere.

From *Nursing Outlook*, vol. 29, no. 6 (June 1981), pp. 348–54. Reprinted with permission from Mosby-year Book, Inc.

Role Components

The first task of any philosophical inquiry is to determine its terminology and establish the meanings of its key terms for its own purposes. To take the first term: a *role* is a norm-governed pattern of action undertaken in accordance with social expectations. The term is originally derived from the drama, where it signifies a part played by an actor in a play. In current usage, any ordinary job or profession (physician, housewife, teacher, postal worker) will do as an example of a social role; the term's dramatic origin is nonetheless worth remembering, as a key to the limits of the concept.

Image and ideal are simply the descriptive and prescriptive aspects of a social role. The *image* of a social role is that role as it is understood to be in fact, both by the occupants of the role and by those with whom the occupant interacts. It describes the character the occupant plays, the acts, attitudes, and expectations normally associated with the role. The *ideal* of a role is a conception of what that role could or should be – that is, a conception of the norms that should govern its work. It is necessary to distinguish between the private and public aspects of image and ideal.

Since role occupants and general public need not agree either on the description of the present operations of the role or on the prescription for its future development, the private image, or self-image of the role occupant, is therefore distinct from the public image or general impression of the role maintained in the popular media and mind. The private ideal, or aspiration of the role occupant, is distinct from the public ideal or normative direction set for the role by the larger society. Thus, four role-components emerge, from the public and private, descriptive and prescriptive, aspects of a social role. They may be difficult to disentangle in some cases, but they are surely distinct in theory, and potentially in conflict in fact.

Transitional Roles

In these terms alone we have the materials for the problematic tensions within transitional social roles. Stable social roles should exhibit no significant disparities among images and ideals: what the public generally gets is about what it thinks it should get; what the job turns out to require is generally in accord with the role-occupant's aspirations; and public and role-occupant, beyond a certain base level of "they-don't-know-how-hard-we-work" grumbling, are in general agreement on what the role is all about. On the other hand, transitional roles tend to exhibit strong discrepancies among the four elements of the role during the transition; at least the components will make the transition at different times, and there may also be profound disagreement on the direction that the transition should take.

The move from a general discussion of roles in society to a specific discussion of the nursing profession is made difficult by the fact that correct English demands the use of a personal pronoun. How shall we refer to the nurse? It is claimed that consistent reference to a professional as "he" reinforces the stereotype of male monopoly in the professions, save for the profession of nursing, where consistent reference to the professional as "she" reinforces the stereotype of subservience. Though we ought never to reinforce sex and dominance stereotypes, the effort to write in gender-neutral terms involves the use of circumlocutions and "he/she" usages that quickly becomes wearisome to reader and writer alike. Referring to most other professions, I would simply use the universal pronouns "he" and "him", and ignore the ridiculous accusations of sexism. But against a background of a virtually all-female profession, whose literature until the last decade universally referred to its professionals as "she", the consistent use of "he" to refer to a nurse calls attention to itself and distracts attention from the argument.

A further problem with gender-neutral terminology in the discussion of this issue in particular is that it appears to render the issue irrelevant. The whole question of autonomy for the nurse in professional work arises because nurses have been, and are, by and large, women, and the place of the profession in the health care system is strongly influenced by the place of women in society. To talk about nurses as if they were, or might as well be, men, is to make the very existence of a problem a mystery. There are, therefore good reasons beyond custom to continue using the pronoun "she" to refer to the nurse. I doubt that such use will suggest to anyone who might read this essay that it is not appropriate for men to become nurses; presumably we are beyond making that error at this time.

Barriers to Autonomy

The first contention of my argument is that the issue of autonomy in the nursing profession lends itself to misformulation. A common formulation of the issue, for example, locates it in a discrepancy between public image and private image. On this account, the public is asserted to believe that nurses are ill-educated, unintelligent, incapable of assuming responsibility, and hence properly excluded from professional status and responsibility. In fact they are now prepared to be truly autonomous professionals through an excellent education, including a thorough theoretical grounding in all aspects of their profession. Granted, the public image of the nurse has many favorable aspects – the nurse is credited with great manual skill, often saintly dedication to service to others, and, at least below the supervisory level, a warm heart and gentle manners. But the educational and intellectual deficiencies that the public mistakenly perceives outweigh the "positive" qualities when it comes to deciding how the nurse shall be treated, and are called upon to justify not only her traditionally inferior status and low wages, but also the refusal to allow nursing to fill genuine needs in the health care system by assuming tasks that nurses are uniquely qualified to handle. For the sake of the quality of health care as well as for the sake of the interests of the nurse, the public must be educated through a massive educational campaign to the full capabilities of the contemporary nurse; the image must be brought into line with the facts. On this account, then, the issue of nurse autonomy is diagnosed as a public relations problem: the private ideal of nursing is asserted to be that of the autonomous professional and the private image is asserted to have undergone a transition from an older subservient role to a new professional one but the public image of the nurse ideal is significantly not mentioned in this analysis.

An alternative account of the issue of professional autonomy in nursing locates it in a discrepancy between private ideal and private image. Again, the private ideal is that of the autonomous professional. But the actual performance of the role is entirely slavish, because of the way the system works – with its tight budgets, insane schedules, workloads bordering on reckless endangerment for the seriously ill, bureaucratic red tape, confusion, and arrogance. Under these conditions, the nurse is permanently barred from fulfilling her professional ideal, from bringing the reality of the nurse's condition into line with the self-concept she brought to the job. On this account, then, the nurse really is not an autonomous professional, and total reform of the power structure of the health care industry will be necessary in order to allow her to become one.

A third formulation locates the issue of autonomy in a struggle between the private ideal and an altogether undesirable public ideal: on this account, the public does not want the nurse to be an autonomous professional, because her present subservient status serves the power needs of the physicians; because her unprofessional remuneration serves the monetary needs of the entrepreneurs and callous municipalities that run the hospitals; and because the low value accorded her opinions on patient care protects both physicians and bureaucrats from being forced to account to the patient for the treatment he receives. On this account, the nurse needs primarily to gather allies to defeat the powerful interest groups that impose the traditional ideal for their own unworthy purposes, and to replace that degrading and dangerous prescription with one more appropriate to the contemporary nurse.

These three accounts, logically independent, have crucial elements of content in common. Above all, they agree on the objectives to be pursued: full professional independence, responsibility, recognition, and remuneration for the professional nurse. And as corollary to these objectives, they agree on the necessity of banishing forever from the hospitals and from the public mind that inaccurate and demeaning stereotype of the nurse as the Lady with the Bedpan: an image of submissive service, comforting to have around and skillful enough at her little tasks, but too scatterbrained and emotional for responsibility.

In none of the interpretations above is any real weight given to a public ideal of nursing, to the nursing role as the public thinks it ought to be played. Where public prescription shows up at all, it is seen as a vicious and false demand imposed by power alone, thoroughly illegitimate and to be destroyed as quickly as possible. The possibility that there may be real value in the traditional role of the nurse, and that the public may have good reasons to want to retain it, simply does not receive any serious consideration on any account. It is precisely that possibility that I take up in the next section.

Defending the "Traditional Nurse"

As Aristotle taught us, the way to discover the peculiar virtues of any thing is to look to the work that it accomplishes in the larger context of its environment. The first task, then, is to isolate those factors of need or demand in the nursing environment that require the nurse's work if they are to be met. I shall concentrate, as above, on the hospital environment, since most nurses are employed in hospitals.

The work context of the hospital nurse actually spans two societal practices or institutions: the hospital as a bureaucracy and medicine as a field of scientific endeavor and service. Although there is enormous room for variation in both hospital bureaucracies and medicine, and they may therefore interact with an infinite number of possible results, the most general facts about both institutions allow us to sketch the major demands they make on those whose function lies within them.

To take the hospital bureaucracy first: its very nature demands that workers perform the tasks assigned to them, report properly to the proper superior, avoid initiative, and adhere to set procedures. These requirements are common to all bureaucracies, but dramatically increase in urgency when the tasks are supposed to be protective of life itself and where the subject matter is inherently unpredictable and emergency prone. Since there is often no time to re-examine the usefulness of a procedure in a particular case, and since the stakes are too high to permit a gamble, the institution's effectiveness, not to mention its legal position, may depend on unquestioning adherence to procedure.

Assuming that the sort of hospital under discussion is one in which the practice of medicine by qualified physicians is the focal activity, rather than, say, a convalescent hospital, further contextual requirements emerge. Among the prominent features of the practice of medicine are the following: it depends on esoteric knowledge which takes time to acquire and which is rapidly advancing; and, because each patient's illness is unique, it is uncertain. Thus, when a serious medical situation arises without warning, only physicians will know how to deal with it (if their licensure has any point), and they will not always be able to explain or justify their actions to nonphysicians, even those who are required to assist them in patient care.

If the two contexts of medicine and the hospital are superimposed, three common points can be seen. Both are devoted to the saving of life and health; the atmosphere in which that purpose is carried out is inevitably tense and urgent; and, if the purpose is to be accomplished in that atmosphere, all participating activities and agents must be completely subordinated to the medical judgments of the physicians. In short, those other than physicians, involved in medical procedures in a hospital context, have no right to insert their own needs, judgments, or personalities into the situation. The last thing we need at that point is another autonomous professional on the job, whether a nurse or anyone else.

Patient Needs: The Prime Concern

From the general characteristics of hospitals and medicine, that negative conclusion for nursing follows. But the institutions are not, after all, the focus of the endeavor. If there is any conflict between the needs of the patient and the needs of the institutions established to serve him, his needs take precedence and constitute the most important requirements of the nursing environment. What are these needs?

First, because the patient is sick and disabled, he needs specialized care that only qualified personnel can administer, beyond the time that the physician is with him. Second, and perhaps most obviously to the patient, he is likely to be unable to perform simple tasks such as walking unaided, dressing himself, and attending to his bodily functions. He will need assistance in these tasks, and is likely to find this need humiliating; his entire self-concept as an independent human being may be threatened. Thus, the patient has serious emotional needs brought on by the hospital situation itself, regardless of his disability. He is scared, depressed, disappointed, and possibly, in reaction to all of these, very angry. He needs reassurance, comfort, someone to talk to. The person he really needs, who would be capable of taking care of all these problems, is obviously his mother, and the first job of the nurse is to be a mother surrogate.

That conclusion, it should be noted, is inherent in the word "nurse" itself: it is derived ultimately from the Latin *nutrire*, "to nourish or suckle;" the first meaning of "nurse" as a noun is still, according to *Webster's New Twentieth Century Unabridged Dictionary* "one who suckles a child not her own." From the outset, then, the function of the nurse is identical with that of the mother, to be exercised when the mother is unavailable. And the meanings proceed in logical order from there: the second definitions given for both noun and verb involve caring for children, especially young children, and the third, caring for those who are childlike in their dependence – the sick, the injured, the very old, and the handicapped. For all those groups – infants, children, and helpless adults – it is appropriate to bring children's caretakers, surrogate mothers, nurses, into the situation to minister to them. It is especially appropriate to do so, for the sake of the psychological economies realized by the patient: the sense of self, at least for the Western adult, hangs on the self-perception of independence. Since disability requires the relinquishing of this self-perception, the patient must either discover conditions excusing his dependence somewhere in his self-concept, or invent new ones, and the latter task is extremely difficult. Hence the usefulness of the maternal image association: it was, within the patient's understanding of himself "all right" to be tended by mother; if the nurse is (at some level) mother, it is "all right" to reassume that familiar role and to be tended by her.

Limits on the "Mother" Role

The nurse's assumption of the role of mother is therefore justified etymologically and historically but most importantly by reference to the psychological demands of and on the patient. Yet the maternal role cannot be imported into the hospital care situation without significant modification – specifically, with respect to the power and authority inherent in the role of mother. Such maternal authority, includes the right and duty to assume control over children's lives and make all decisions for them; but the hospital patient most definitely does not lose adult status even if he is sick enough to want to. The ethical legitimacy as well as the therapeutic success of his treatment depend on his voluntary and active cooperation in it and on his deferring to some forms of power and authority – the hospital rules and the physician's sapiential authority, for example. But these very partial, conditional, restraints are nowhere near the threat to patient autonomy that the real presence of mother would be; maternal authority, total, diffuse, and unlimited, would be incompatible with the retention of moral freedom. And it is just this sort of total authority that the patient is most tempted to attribute to the nurse, who already embodies the nurturant component of the maternal role. To prevent serious threats to patient autonomy, then the role of nurse must be from the outset, as essentially as it is nurturant, unavilable for such attribution of authority. Not only must the role of nurse not include authority; it must be incompatible with authority: essentially, a subservient role.

The nurse role, as required by the patient's situation, is the nurturant component of the maternal role and excludes elements of power and authority. A further advantage of this combination of maternal nurturance and subordinate status is that, just as it permits the patient to be cared for like a baby without threatening his autonomy, it also permits him to unburden himself to a sympathetic listener of his doubts and resentments, about physicians and hospitals in general, and his in particular, without threatening the course of his treatment. His resentments are natural, but they lead to a situation of conflict, between the desire to rebel against treatment and bring it to a halt (to reassert control over his life), and the desire that the treatment should continue (to obtain its benefits). The nurse's function speaks well to this condition: like her maternal model, the nurse is available for the patient to talk to (the physician is too busy to talk), sympathetic, understanding, and supportive; but in her subordinate position, the nurse can do absolutely nothing to change his course of treatment. Since she has no more control over the environment than he has, he can let off steam in perfect safety, knowing that he cannot do himself any damage.

The norms for the nurse's role so far derived from the patient's perspective also tally, it might be noted, with the restrictions on the role that arise from the needs of hospitals and medicine. The patient does not need another autonomous professional at his bedside, any more than the physician can use one or the hospital bureaucracy contain one. The conclusion so far, then is that in the hospital environment, the traditional (nurturant and subordinate) role of the nurse seems more adapted to the nurse function than the new autonomous role.

Provider of Humanistic Care

So far, we have defined the hospital nurse's function in terms of the specific needs of the hospital, the physician, and the patient. Yet there is another level of function that needs to be addressed. If we consider the multifaceted demands that the patient's family, friends, and community make on the hospital once the patient is admitted, it becomes clear that this concerned group cannot be served exclusively by attending to the medical aspect of care, necessary though that is. Nor is it sufficient for the hospital-as-institution to keep accurate and careful records, maintain absolute cleanliness, and establish procedures that protect the patient's safety, even though this is important. Neither bureaucracy nor medical professional can handle the human needs of the human beings involved in the process.

The general public entering the hospital as patient or visitor encounters and reacts to that health care system as an indivisible whole, as if under a single heading of "what the hospital is like." It is at this level that we can make sense of the traditional claim that the nurse represents the "human" as opposed to "mechanical" or "coldly professional" aspect of health care, for there is clearly something terribly missing in the combined medical and bureaucratic approach to the "case": they fail to address the patient's fear for himself and the family's fear for him, their grief over the separation, even if temporary, their concern for the financial burden, and a host of other emotional components of hospitalization.

The same failing appears throughout the hospital experience, most poignantly obvious, perhaps, when the medical procedures are unavailing and the patient dies. When this occurs, the physician must determine the cause and time of death and the advisability of an autopsy, while the bureaucracy must record the death and remove the body; but surely this is not enough. The death of a human being is a rending of the fabric of human community, a sad and fearful time; it is appropriately a time of bitter regret, anger, and weeping. The patient's family, caught up in the institutional context of the hospital, cannot assume alone the burden of *discovering and expressing the emotions* appropriate to the occasion; such expression, essential for their own regeneration after their loss must originate somehow within the hospital context itself. The hospital system must, somehow, be able to share pain and grief as well as it makes medical judgments and keeps records.

The traditional nurse's role addresses itself directly to these human needs. Its derivation from the maternal role classifies it as feminine and permits ready assumption of all attributes culturally typed as "feminine" tenderness, warmth, sympathy, and a tendency to engage much more readily in the expression of feeling than in the rendering of judgment. Through the nurse, the hospital can be concerned, welcoming, caring, and grief-stricken; it can break through the cold barriers of efficiency essential to its other functions and share human feeling.

The nurse therefore provides the in-hospital health care system with human capabilities that would otherwise be unavailable to it and hence unavailable to the community in dealing with it. Such a conclusion is unattractive to the supporters of the autonomous role for the nurse, because the tasks of making objective judgments and of expressing emotion are inherently incompatible; and since the nurse shows grief and sympathy on behalf of the system, she is excluded from decision-making and defined as subordinate.

However unappealing such a conclusion may be, it is clear that without the nurse role in this function, the hospital becomes a moral monstrosity, coolly and mechanically dispensing and disposing of human life and death, with no acknowledgement at all of the individual life, value, projects, and relationships of the persons with whom it deals. Only the nurse makes the system morally tolerable. People in pain deserve sympathy, as the dead deserve to be grieved; it is unthinkable that the very societal institution to which we generally consign the suffering and the dying should be incapable of sustaining sympathy and grief. Yet its capability hangs on the presence of nurses willing to assume the affective functions of the traditional nursing role, and the current attempt to banish that role, to introduce instead an autonomous professional role for the nurse, threatens to send the last hope for a human presence in the hospital off at the same time.

The Feminist Perspective

From this conclusion it would seem to follow automatically that the role of the traditional nurse should be retained. It might be argued, however, that the value of autonomy is such that any non-autonomous role ought to be abolished, no matter what its value to the current institutional structure.

Those who aimed to abolish black slavery in the United States have provided a precedent for this argument. They never denied the slave's economic usefulness; they simply denied that it could be right to enslave any person and insisted that the nation find some other way to get the work done, no matter what the cost. On a totally different level, the feminists of our own generation have proposed that the traditional housewife and mother role for the woman, which confined women to domestic life and made them subordinate to men, has been very useful for everyone except the women trapped in it. All the feminists have claimed is that the profit of others is not a sufficient reason to retain a role that demeans its occupant. As they see it, the "traditional nurse" role is analogous to the roles of slave and housewife – it is derived directly, in fact, as we have seen, from the "mother" part of the latter role – exploitative of its occupants and hence immoral by its very nature and worthy of abolition.

But the analogy does not hold. A distinction must be made between an autonomous person – one who, over the course of adult life, is self-determining in all major choices and a significant number of minor ones, and hence can be said to have chosen, and to be responsible for, his own life – and an autonomous *role* – a role so structured that its occupant is self-determining in all major and most minor role-related choices. An autonomous person can certainly take on a subordinate role without losing his personal autonomy. For example, we can find examples of slaves (in ancient world at least) and housewives who have claimed to have, and shown every sign of having, complete personal integrity and autonomy with their freely chosen roles.

Furthermore, slave and housewife are a very special type of role, known as "life-roles." They are to be played 24 hours a day, for an indefinite period of time; there is no customary or foreseeable respite from them. Depending on circumstances, there may be *de facto* escapes from these roles, permitting their occupants to set up separate personal identities (some of the literature from the history of American slavery suggests this possibility), but the role-definitions do not contemplate part-time occupany. Such life-roles are few in number; most roles are the part-time "occupational roles," the jobs that we do eight hours a day and have little to do with the structuring of the rest of the twenty-four. An autonomous person can, it would seem, easily take up a subordinate role of this type and play it well without threat to personal autonomy. And if there is excellent reason to choose such a role – if, for example, an enterprise of tremendous importance derives an essential component of its moral worth from that role – it would seem to be altogether rational and praiseworthy to do so. The role of "traditional nurse" would certainly fall within this category.

But even if the traditional nurse role is not inherently demeaning, it might be argued further, it should be abolished as harmful to the society because it preserves the sex stereotypes that we are trying to overcome. "Nurse" is a purely feminine role, historically derived from "mother", embodying feminine attributes of emotionality, tenderness, and nurturance, and it is subordinate – thus reinforcing the link between femininity and subordinate status. The nurse role should be available to men, too, to help break down this unfavorable stereotype.

This objective to the traditional role embodies the very fallacy it aims to combat. The falsehood we know as sexism is not the belief that some roles are autonomous, calling for objectivity in judgment, suppression of emotion, and independent initiative in action, but discouraging independent judgment and action and requiring obedience to superiors; the falsehood is the assumption that only men are eligible for the first class and only women are eligible for the second class.

One of the most damaging mistakes of our cultural heritage is the assumption that warmth, gentleness, and loving care, such as are expected of the nurse, are simply impossible for the male of the species, and that men who show emotion, let alone those who are ever known to weep, are weaklings, "sissies," and a disgrace to the human race. I suspect that this assumption has done more harm to the culture than its more publicized partner, the assumption that women are (or should be) incapable of objective judgment or executive function. Women will survive without leadership roles, but it is not clear that a society can retain its humanity if all those eligible for leadership are forbidden, by virtue of that eligibility, to take account of the human side of human beings: their altruism, heroism, compassion, and grief, their fear and weakness, and their ability to love and care for others.

In the words of the current feminist movement, men must be liberated as surely as women. And one of the best avenues to such liberation would be the encouragement of male participation in the health care system, or other systems of the society, in roles like the traditional nursing role, which permit, even require, the expressive side of the personality to develop, giving it a function in the enterprise and restoring it to recognition and respectability.

Conclusions

In conclusion, then, the traditional nurse role is crucial to health care in the hospital context; its subordinate status, required for its remaining features, is neither in itself demeaning nor a barrier to its assumption by men or women. It is probably not a role that everyone would enjoy. But there are certainly many who are suited to it, and should be willing to undertake the job.

One of the puzzling features of the recent controversy is the apparent unwillingness of some of the current crop of nursing school graduates to take on the assignment for which they have ostensibly been prepared, at least until such time as it shall be redefined to accord more closely with their notion of professional. These frustrated nurses who do not want the traditional nursing role, yet wish to employ their skills in the health care system in some way, will clearly have to do something else. The health care industry is presently in the process of very rapid expansion and diversification, and has created significant markets for those with a nurse's training and the capacity, and desire, for autonomous roles. Moreover, the nurse in a position which does not have the "nurse" label, does not need to combat the "traditional nurse" image and is ordinarily accorded greater freedom of action. For this reason alone it would appear that those nurses intent on occupying autonomous roles and tired of fighting stereotypes that they find degrading and unworthy of their abilities, should seek out occupational niches that do not bear the label, and the stigma, of "nurse."

I conclude, therefore: that much of the difficulty in obtaining public acceptance of the new "autonomous professional" image of the nurse may be due, not to public ignorance, but to the opposition of a vague but persistent public ideal of nursing; that the ideal is a worthy one, well-founded in the hospital context in which it evolved; and that the role of traditional nurse, for which that ideal sets the standard, should therefore be maintained and held open for any who would have the desire, and the personal and professional qualifications, to assume it. Perhaps the current crop of nursing school graduates do not desire it, but there is ample room in the health care system for the sort of "autonomous professional" they wish to be, apart from the hospital nursing role. Wherever we must go to fill this role, it is worth going there, for the traditional nurse is the major force remaining for humanity in a system that will turn into a mechanical monster without her.

PART XI

Ethicists and Ethics Committees

73

When Philosophers Shoot from the Hip

James Rachels

These days moral philosophers often find themselves in the heady position of being called upon by newspapers to comment on the latest public controversies. Being treated as quotable experts by the media may be old stuff for economists, and a few other academic types, but it is a new experience for philosophers, a visible result of the applied ethics movement that began twenty years ago. Sometimes the newspapers want columns of commentary. The op-ed page, pioneered by the *New York Times*, has now become a regular feature of most large metropolitan dailies. Op-ed columns aren't much like articles in *Bioethics*, but for the general public they are a good substitute. They allow enough space, and writing them allows one enough time, for serious reflection.

Sometimes, however, the newspapers want something different. The telephone rings, and a reporter rattles off a few "facts" about something somebody is supposed to have done. Ethical issues are involved – something alarming is said to have taken place – and so the "ethicist" is asked for a comment to be included in the next day's story, which may be the first report the public will have seen about the events in question.

Usually when this happens the reporters aren't interested in detailed analysis or lengthy qualifications. A short, pithy quote is what's wanted. Nor are the reporters eager to hear reassurances that the alarming events really aren't alarming. That doesn't make good copy. What makes good copy is the idea that the events being reported are morally troubling, or worse. And frequently philosophers are willing to provide just such comments. The story then appears, with a pronounced moral slant: "Such-and-such has happened, and the ethicists say it's bad." More often than not, this combination of reporters' interests and philosophers' snap judgments has a conservative effect. The new developments are viewed as troubling against the background, not of careful analysis, but of accepted wisdom.

In March 1990 a story appeared in American newspapers about a Los Angeles couple who had decided to have another child in the hope that the baby's bone-marrow cells could be used to save the life of their teenaged daughter. Abe and Mary Ayala, who are in their forties, had not intended to have an additional child; in fact, Abe Ayala had had a vasectomy. But their 17-year-old daughter, Anissa, was dying of leukemia, and a bone-marrow transplant was her only hope. After two years of searching in vain for a suitable donor, they decided to have another child because there was a one-in-four chance that the new family member would be a suitable donor. So Abe Ayala had his vasectomy reversed and Mary Ayala became pregnant. The baby, a girl named Marissa, was born on April 6 and she is indeed a compatible donor. The transplant procedure, which will be accomplished sometime in the fall, will involve little risk for the baby, and Anissa's chances of surviving will rise from zero to between 70 and 80 percent.

The Ayalas were understandably elated to learn that Anissa's life might be saved. However, the newspaper stories prominently featured quotations from medical ethicists who labeled their decision "troublesome" and even "outrageous": "The ideal reason for having a child," said a well-known

From *Bioethics*, vol. 5, no. 1 (1991), pp. 67–71

figure in the field, "is associated with that child's own welfare – to bring a child into being and to nurture it. One of the fundamental precepts of ethics is that each person is an end in himself or herself, and is never to be used solely as a means to another person's end without the agreement of the person being used." The Ayalas' baby "is not seen as an end in itself, but as a means to another end. The fact that the other end is laudable doesn't change that." Another expert was quoted as saying that the Ayalas' decision means "we're willing to treat people like objects" – and, he added, "I don't think we ought to do that."[1]

The Ayalas are real people, not characters in a made-up classroom example, and they didn't care much for the ethicists' comments. Mrs Ayala said that the ethicists ought to be worrying more about the shortage of marrow donors, and less about their decision. Anissa herself was asked what she thought about all this, and she said that she was "sort of troubled" by the criticism, but added that "We're going to love our baby."

If Anissa were trained in philosophy, she might find the criticisms less troubling. She might observe that people have always had babies for reasons other than the "ideal" one. Real life rarely measures up to philosophers' expectations. People have children so that the children can share in the family's work, to please the grandparents, or just because it's expected of them. They sometimes have second children because they don't want the first to be an "only child". None of this is strange or unusual; it's just the way life is. What is important is, as Anissa insists, that once born the children are loved and nurtured within good families. Anissa might also point out that her mother, in fact, had wanted another baby anyway – it was only her father's wish to have no more children. And finally, she might express some appropriate scepticism about the idea that an individual "is never to be used solely as a means to another person's end without the agreement of the person being used." Does this mean that, if Anissa already had a baby sister, the baby could not be used as a donor because the baby was not old enough to give permission? Should Anissa herself be left to die, for the sake of respecting this principle? Perhaps the ethicist quoted in the *New York Times* thinks so; he was quoted as saying "It's outrageous that people would go to this length."

Curiously, there is an argument, proceeding from principles endorsed by the most conservative pro-life advocates, that supports the Ayalas' decision. This argument invokes the idea that we are confering a benefit on someone by bringing them into existence. The new baby, not Anissa, seems the really big winner here: after all, if her parents had not decided to have her, the baby would have not got to exist. Those who oppose abortion sometimes ask: Aren't you glad your mother didn't have an abortion? The answer, of course, is that most of us are happy that our mothers didn't do that; otherwise we wouldn't be here now. The people who ask this question think that something follows about the morality of abortion, although it isn't clear what; but they usually fail to notice that we could just as well ask: Aren't you glad that your parents didn't practice birth control? (Orthodox Catholics, at least, are consistent on this point.) We should be equally happy that contraceptives were not used by our parents, and for the same reason: otherwise, we wouldn't be here now. Similarly, Anissa's little sister might someday be asked: Aren't you glad that your parents decided to have you? Aren't you fortunate that Anissa needed those stem cells? Perhaps this means that conservatives who take a pro-life view ought to be happy with the Ayalas' decision, rather than being critical of it.

It might be doubted, however, that this is a sound argument. The idea that we are conferring a benefit on someone by bringing them into existence is easily disputed. I would rather rest my defense of the Ayalas' decision on a different sort of reasoning. First we may consider two separate questions:

1 Suppose a couple, before having any children at all, is trying to decide whether to have one child or two. They slightly prefer having only one. But then they are told that if they have only one child it will die when it is a teenager. However, if they have two, both will probably live full lives. Would it be wrong for the couple to decide, for this reason, to have two children?
2 Suppose a couple already has two children, one a teenager dying of leukemia, and the other an infant who is the only available bone-marrow donor. The infant cannot give its permission, of course, but then again it would not be harmed at all by the procedure. Would it be wrong, under these circumstances, to use some of the infant's stem-cells to save the teenager's life?

It seems to me that it would be easy enough to argue that the answer to both these questions is no. Then the inference to the permissibility of the Ayalas' decision would be obvious.

But this is a peripheral point. My subject here is in the performance of philosophers – "ethicists" – as commentators on public events. Sometimes they do what we might think philosophers ought to do: challenge the prevailing orthodoxy, calling into question the assumptions that people unthinkingly make. But just as often they function as orthodoxy's most sophisticated defenders, assuming that the existing social consensus must be right, and articulating its theoretical "justification". And when all else fails, there is another familiar argument that can be relied upon: the slippery slope. Any departure from business-as-usual can be pronounced "troubling" because of what it might lead to. The Ayalas' decision was also criticized on this ground. It was said that it might lead to "fetus farming," or to abortions so that the aborted fetus can be used for life-saving purposes.

Of course we don't know exactly what will happen to the Ayala family, or to social values, in consequence of decisions such as theirs. But two comments seem relevant. First, there is nothing new about their sort of decision. In the publicity surrounding the Ayala case, it was revealed that other families have been making similar decisions for quite some time. Dr Robertson Parkman, head of the division of research immunology and marrow transplantation at Los Angeles Children's Hospital, told a reporter that he personally knows of cases going back to 1974 in which families have had additional children to obtain marrow transplants. But until now there has been little publicity about it. The new publicity also revealed that, in previous cases, medical ethicists have been able to do much more than complain about such decisions after the fact. In 1986 a California woman, Phyliss Baker, who had had a tubal ligation, asked a physician to reconnect her Fallopian tubes so that she could have another child. The physician, knowing that Mrs Baker was trying to save the life of her 3-year-old son, who needed a marrow transplant, consulted a bioethicist and then refused to do the operation. The physician's and the bioethicist's moral scruples were preserved, and Travis, the 3-year-old, died.[2]

Second, the recent history of medical ethics is dotted with episodes in which ethicists have reacted with alarm to new developments, predicting dire consequences that never occurred. Greg Pence's new book, *Classic Cases in Medical Ethics*, recounts several such episodes.[3] A review of these cases suggests caution, lest our quick-and-easy comments today look silly tomorrow. In 1978, for example, Louise Brown was the first baby to be born as a result of *in vitro* fertilization. This important event prompted alarmed and highly critical responses from physicians, theologians, and philosophers that are embarrassing to look back upon today. Pence reminds us of a whole series of exaggerated statements and predictions: terrible consequences were sure to follow for the parents, the child, and society. But today Louise is a, happy, rambunctious child, and so are many others like her.

What will happen to the Ayalas? One plausible scenario is that Anissa will be saved, the new baby will grow up happy – or at least with the same mixture of happiness and unhappiness as the rest of us – and the Ayalas, like the Browns, will forever after think that ethicists are jerks. If terrible consequences transpire, then of course it might turn out that they were wrong. But in their particular circumstances, I do not see how they could have been wrong to weigh their daughter's life more heavily than the philosophers' vague fears.[4]

Notes

1 *The New York Times* (17 February, 1990), 1.

2 *The Birmingham News* (16 April, 1990), 4D.

3 Gregory E. Pence, *Classic Cases in Medical Ethics* (New York: McGraw-Hill, 1990). This book is a valuable corrective in another way as well: Pence demonstrates how the facts about these cases are often very different than philosophers assume them to be.

4 This article is based on one section of a paper presented at a conference on "Moral Philosophy in the Public Domain", at the University of British Columbia in June 1990. The complete paper appears in a volume of essays growing out of the conference, edited by Earl Winkler.

74

Ethics Consultation as Moral Engagement

Jonathan D. Moreno

I want to examine what the role of the "ethicist" should be in the clinical setting. In using the term ethicist I am obviously not limiting myself to those who have qualifications in academic philosophy. To do so would be to circumscribe the range of concern too severely, because the qualified academic moral philosopher may often lack other necessary credentials (including the rather nebulous "clinical experience"), whereas the humanistically cultivated health care provider may be a competent student of moral philosophy. Further, "clinical setting" refers to nursing homes and ambulatory care clinics, as well as hospital inpatient services.

I will begin by presenting some doubts about what might be called the "received view" of the role of the moral expert as a health care consultant. Then I will review the literature on moral experts and moral expertise and proceed to apply the results of that review to the notion that there are some who are expert in ethical decision making in health care. I will try to show that certain conclusions that can be drawn from this rather circumscribed topic have implications for the very conception of the relationship between moral theory and clinical ethics.

Moral Experts in Health Care: The Received View

A respected writer and clinical ethics consultant, Terrence F. Ackerman, has articulated the received view of the function of the ethics consultant[1] The general idea is that the ethics consultant is a "facilitator of moral inquiry". For Ackerman this formulation has several implications. First, since moral inquiry is an effort to develop plans for dealing with problematic situations that can evoke a shared social commitment, the determination of morally appropriate behavior requires the contributions of other members of the moral community who participate in reflective moral inquiry. Thus the ethics consultant cannot simply step in and announce that he or she has "the right answers".

Second, the ethics consultant may nevertheless make recommendations to health care providers "about the morally appropriate course of action in a particular situation". These recommendations are founded on the ethicist's belief that these are courses of action that would be endorsed by other reflective members of the moral community. Third, the ethics consultant should facilitate moral investigation by the health professionals themselves. And fourth, the consulting ethicist should be wary of being placed in inappropriate roles, such as that of moral policeman or secular clergyman.

There is much in Ackerman's analysis with which I am in thorough agreement, particularly his emphasis on the role of the moral community. Ultimately, however, this approach fails to come to grips with the true complexity of the ethics consultant's role or the relationship of moral theory to clinical decision making. Among these issues are the theoretical problems with social consensus as a source of authority for moral decision making.[2] More troubling still in the context of Ackerman's

From *Bioethics*, vol. 5, no. 1 (1991), pp. 44–56.

formulation is the notion that the ethics consultant's recommendation must square with some imagined result of the moral community's reflection. How is the consultant's belief in this congruence to be sustained? Which moral community is the relevant one? What if the result of that imaginatively projected reflection is itself indecision? Is the ethics consultant no more than a "middle man" between the health care providers and the ideal moral community? Must the reflective moral community adopt the same framework of principles as the ethics consultant to be legitimate, or the other way around? Clearly this account cries out for further explanation.

Underlying the received view is the assumption that, if only we could get clear on the business of moral expertise, it would be a straightforward matter to use the rich resources of moral philosophy to treat tough ethical dilemmas encountered in clinical medicine. In what follows I will try to show that even a more full-bodied conception of ethical expertise must fall short in the clinical setting unless it is liberated from the prevalent notion that clinical ethics is essentially the application of moral theory to problems in the delivery of health care, or that the role of the clinical ethicist is that of a Socratic "facilitator". I argue that what is required is a substantial reconstruction of the notion of clinical ethics and of our understanding of the ethics consultant's role.

Are There Moral Experts?

Of the many vexed philosophical problems, this is one about which modern philosophers are particularly divided. Though many authors have articulated doctrines that touch upon the question of moral expertise, I confine my discussion to some who have addressed it most directly. I begin by presenting two arguments against the notion that there can be moral expertise, arguments that tend to crop up frequently in one form or another in the literature.

The first argument is the one that Socrates entertains. It is an argument from analogy with other disciplines to the effect that, since there are recognized experts in other disciplines that most people consider to have something to do with objective matters but none in morality, one has reason to believe that morality is not objective.[3] If there is nothing to be objective about there can be no experts.

The second argument appears in Kant and in another version in Ryle: Morality is not the kind of thing in which there can be competence, expert or otherwise, because moral virtue is not a skill. Rather, to be moral is to have a concern for persons, a concern that can obtain as a feature of an individual's character regardless of his or her non-moral qualities like intelligence or judgment.[4] To think otherwise is to commit a category mistake.

The first or "no moral experts" view can be countered by showing that the doubt that there are moral experts is unfounded. Often this doubt is characterized by the charge that the advice of so-called moral experts is equivocal. Terrance McConnell sketches three responses.[5] The first is that moral experts possess general moral principles but not the factual knowledge to apply them; therefore their expertise is not obvious because its application requires knowledge from two fields, only one of which is within the ethicist's realm of expertise. The second response is that some ethicists do in fact give unequivocal advice. And the third is that experts in other fields also often fail to provide unequivocal answers to problems in which they are supposed to be expert. Further, even conflicting expert opinions or points of view among experts does not distinguish ethics from other fields in which it is generally agreed that there is something to be expert about.

Of these three responses only the first does more than leave open the possibility that there are in fact moral experts. The other two have nothing to say about the content of this expertise. A response to the second or Kant–Ryle argument against the idea that there are moral experts gives some more detail on this score. Robert W. Burch contends that the view that morality is a matter of character rather than skill depends on too superficial an understanding of what character is all about.[6] For, to the extent that the person of good character is necessarily good at certain things, this will include an ability to discern what is right and wrong and the capacity to be resolute in not taking the easy way out. Moreover, experience suggests that these are not traits that appear *ex nihilo* but require a great deal of hard work. The question whether "resoluteness" can properly be considered a matter of expertise is one to which I must return. Finally, that few are in a position to learn from those possessed of these skills can be attributed to the difficulty of the subject as easily as to the non-existence of its teachers.

These responses to the two arguments against the idea of moral expertise leave us with some ideas about what that expertise might plausibly be like: it involves at least (1) the knowledge of general principles and theories of morality, (2) analytic skills such as discernment and insight, and (3) the strength of will not to take the easy way out. Certainly there is room for doubt about each of these elements. Those problems will emerge in the course of examining the implications of this catalogue of elements of moral expertise for the role of the ethicist in health care.

Ethical Expertise in Health Care

Arthur Caplan has warned about the limitations of "ethical engineering" in the clinical setting, or the tendency to think that in practice one can provide solutions to troubling ethical issues merely by straightforward deductions from general moral principles.[7] Others, including James Nickel, have called this "strong applied ethics".[8] Elsewhere,[9] Caplan relates an anecdote that can be used to illustrate the futility of such a scholastic approach. In a situation that appeared to relate to the problem of scarce medical resources, health care providers worried that patients with respiratory problems aggravated by summer heat were straining the resources of an emergency room, which had only two oxygen units. Caplan reports that he dutifully consulted the medical ethics texts to see what they had to say about resource allocation. Of course he found not one guideline but various criteria, and seemed no better off than the medical staff without the benefit of those theoretical resources. Caplan then asked the staff if Medicare/Medicaid would cover the cost of air conditioners for those afflicted patients, and it was discovered that this was indeed the case, thus "solving" the resource allocation problem.

This anecdote illustrates the limitations of the first substantive qualification for moral expertise in bioethics, the knowledge of general principles of morality. In this instance Caplan knew the principles that could cover the allocation problem, but there were a number of them and none was evidently logically prior or morally superior. Nevertheless, a rigid ethical engineer might simply have selected his or her favorite criterion of distribution and mechanically applied it to the specific problem.

Yet from a different angle Caplan's solution did exhibit another of the three substantive characteristics of clinical expertise in ethics, that of discernment. While Caplan's own report of this incident is somewhat self-deprecating, the fact is that the health care providers did not come up with his structural question themselves, perhaps because they were too close to the human suffering the problem had engendered. The detachment of the non-provider on the spot also helps give the discerning disposition a chance to express itself. Caplan also exhibited another of the three proposed characteristics of the ethics expert: he could have taken the easy way out by playing the role of philosopher that the emergency room undoubtedly expected him to play. When he returned with a query about bureaucratic regulations he risked being seen at least as naive, at worst as attempting to avoid a tough ethical issue by blaming the problem on financing arrangements.

It could even be argued that Caplan's approach did instance awareness of ethical principles far more basic than those that generated criteria of distribution of scarce resources. In particular, Caplan was surely aware of the principle of equity. It is plausible to suppose that, whether he was fully aware of it or not, his reluctance to select one criterion over another had something to do with his sense that the results of applying any distribution criterion would not comport as well with this basic ethical principle as a result that treated similarly situated patients in a similar fashion. It is most revealing that his solution accomplished exactly that. Hence the result was both ethically and strategically satisfactory.

There are two observations I want to make about the foregoing. First, in order for the three characteristics of moral expertise I have adduced to be plausible, they must be seen as complementary. Sometimes one characteristic will be more in evidence than another. Second, possession of the first two can confidently be said to depend to some significant degree upon formal study of moral philosophy; and I think a good case can be made that while strength of will is not simply, or even mainly, a matter of education, there is something to the quasi-Socratic, psychological claim that it is hard for people to turn away from what they are rationally persuaded is the right thing to do. Thus, in order for the inclusion of resoluteness on my list of characteristics to be plausible, strength of will must have an ineliminable cognitive dimension.

But why should resoluteness be regarded as a characteristic of expertise per se? Here I want to say that, though it is not strictly a characteristic of expertise, strength of will is a characteristic of the efficacious expert. I take it that this point is undeniable, since those with specialized knowledge who are invited to intervene can hardly be regarded as effective if they sit on their hands for fear of provoking controversy. To the extent that effective intervention is expected of the true expert, irresoluteness will disqualify an individual from such regard.

I have not attempted to "prove" that my list of elements of moral expertise is "correct", though I believe that it captures the elements of other lists of essential characteristics of ethical experts that have been put forward by such philosophers as Peter Singer.[10] Further, by emphasizing the third quality, strength of will, an additional point is made: the moral expert in the clinical setting often confronts situations in which there is more pressure to "take a stand" than does the moral philosopher in the seminar room. I use the term "take a stand" both in the sense of opposition to institutional routines and pressures, and in the sense of articulating a decisive position.[11] Finally, I believe that this list reflects characteristics that individuals effective as ethicists in health care settings tend to possess. But this is an empirical claim for which I can as yet offer only anecodotal evidence.

This having been said, there is a final problem about moral expertise in health care that I want to surface, one that I have found troubling in my own experience in an inner-city medical center under enormous social and financial stress. To illustrate this problem I will turn again to Caplan's anecdote: it could be argued that his ethical *cum* bureaucratic solution ultimately helped perpetuate, or at least helped distract attention from, social arrangements that, in a very general sense, are themselves responsible for the health problems of many poor people.

Now I do not think many would want to take the Leninist position that the present generation should be sacrificed so that the revolution will not be delayed and future generations will benefit. So, in its extreme form, this is not a result of health care ethics that most will want to give up. But there is something to be said for the view that it is a distraction from underlying social problems, that clinical ethics enables social institutions to focus on short-term "ethical fixes". Thus we tend to focus on questions such as, "Should all impaired infants be treated?" instead of "Should all pregnant women have access to prenatal care?"; "Should drug-addicted pregnant women be incarcerated?" instead of "Should there be enough space in addiction treatment programs for all women of child-bearing age?"; and, "Should all elderly people be refused certain forms of technological intervention?" instead of "Should there be universal health insurance?" The point is not that all ethical problems result from structural shortcomings, but that concentration on the former distracts attention from the latter.

This interesting criticism of the role of clinical ethics is not directed at ethical experts per se, though one might argue that their presence is an integral part of the distraction. However, I will not pursue this issue. Restated in light of the foregoing, I want to pursue a related charge: even if the notion of ethical expertise has content, and even if it is not on the whole more detrimental to society than beneficial to have these people participating in "ethics consults" and sitting on ethics committees, there is still something very odd about their role.

Toward Reconstruction in Clinical Ethics

There are three respects in which the activity of clinical ethics, and therefore the ethicist's role, is crucially different from doing moral philosophy. These differences may be relevant to other forms of the applied philosophy of professional ethics, too, so long as it is done *in situ*, that is, so long as it is conducted with the knowledge that it is likely to affect professional conduct in specific cases.

My purpose is to show that these differences are so important that applied ethics as such – or what Frances Myrna Kamm has called "*applying* applied ethics"[12] – cannot simply be considered "moral philosophy applied". Because this is not appreciated there has been no satisfactory analysis of the role of the "bioethicist" or clinical ethicist, whose activities cannot be understood as simply an extension of the traditional role of the moral philosopher. The qualitative difference between moral philosophy and the application of ethics to specific clinical situations in turn imposes different requirements on those who practice in this field. These are large claims that cannot thoroughly be defended here, but perhaps I can at least sketch out the territory relevant to a reconstructed conception of clinical ethics.

There are at least three respects in which moral philosophy and clinical ethics represent qualitatively different activities. First, at the level of practice, since moral philosophers in the Western tradition are suspicious of the moral authority of consensus about moral questions, they are necessarily critics of cultural practices. As a teacher the moral philosopher has social license to ply this critical trade with students, whose intellectual horizons are thought to be broadened by this encounter. In fact, if moral philosophers do nothing else with their students but take this critical position, calling upon a wide range of learning in the process, then that represents the satisfactory performance of their duties. The Socratic tradition authorizes the critical style as a respectable, if not always constructive, pedagogy.

Now bioethicists are also critics of certain cultural practices, namely, those that have to do with the delivery of health care. They are expected to have insightful and sometimes even unsettling things to say about the way doctors relate to patients, or about the priorities evident in current systems of resource allocation, and so on. But if the ethicists were *only* critics they would not be welcome for long in health care institutions, but would be derided as inhabitants of an "ivory tower" with nothing helpful to contribute. Rather, ethicists are expected to take a position, give advice, express an educated opinion, or at the very least offer constructive options. This, after all, is the very essence of what it is to be an *applied* ethicist. Again, it is precisely the unwillingness to take a position that is interpreted as lack of resolve in clinical situations such as clinical ones, which are not academic and in which some decision must be made.

I am alluding to a familiar experience, even a shocking one, for many philosophers who first make their way around a hospital. As classroom moral philosophers they are allowed to hedge, even expected to do so, but as clinical ethicists this behavior meets with hostility. This is not a trivial difference, for it shows that detachment cannot be the dominant feature of the practice of applied ethics, though it might be for moral philosophy. Again, this difference follows from the different approach to consensus: western moral philosophy initially requires detachment from received wisdom and permits the philosopher to adopt such an attitude indefinitely; the ethicist, on the other hand, is not permitted to dwell in detachment but must become engaged.

In reply, it could be said that a sort of Socratic detachment in which moral inquiry is facilitated is and must remain at the heart of what clinical ethics is all about, for this is the unique contribution that philosophers can make to health care decision making.[13] But my own experience suggests that the more clinical the context the less welcome is an exercise that only succeeds in heightening intellectual frustration. Normally when the ethics consultant is called the ethical problem is already all too clear to the health care providers, and they are in need of a plan of action, sometimes desperately so.

I am not claiming that moral philosophers never become engaged, that they always and unremittingly adopt a critical posture. In fact, this may be true of only a very few of them. My contention is that moral philosophers in their practical role as teachers (and not as authors constructing original arguments), are not *required* to be more than enlightened and enlightening critics (though of course they are often allowed and even encouraged to be more). By contrast, I argue this is not true of applied ethicists in the clinical setting, who *are* required to be more than critics. At the other extreme, the danger that engagement will turn ethicists into preaching moralists is met only in so far as the ethicist is prepared always to re-evaluate his or her own views, and this involves adopting the critical posture again.

The second important reason that clinical ethics cannot simply be understood as moral philosophy applied has to do with the historic development of the great moral theories. Bioethics, particularly as it was finding its philosophical feet in the 1970s, has frequently adopted a methodology that entailed the following steps: coming across a "hard case" in which ordinary "common sense" yielded inconclusive moral intuitions; reaching for an important moral theory or two, usually some version of Kantianism and consequentialism; and applying the theories to the hard case. If the theories yielded the same results one could at least be satisfied with this commonality; but if the theories yielded different results one was thrown back on theoretical justification. Since the latter is not a bioethical but a moral philosophical task, the bioethicist's choice of a solution often had an arbitrary air.

More importantly, the recognition that the above methodology would not always yield satisfactory results in terms of the hard cases undermined confidence in the moral philosophies themselves. Around this time important philosophers, especially Alasdair MacIntyre[14] and Richard Rorty[15] presented forceful anti-foundational arguments. MacIntyre's approach, in particular, emphasized the conflicts between systems of moral discourse around hard cases like abortion.

In my view, this way of thinking about moral philosophies, broadly understood, rests on a misunderstanding, and the assessment of a moral philosophy or form of moral life should not rest solely, or even mainly, on its treatment of the so-called "hard case". One reason for this is that the great moral philosophies were not designed to address specific conceptual dilemmas, but to create panoramic views of the good life, the "great souled human being", the just society, or the right mode of conduct. The instances in which those philosophies in their classical expressions do tackle specific cases have not generally been regarded as their finest hours: recall Kant's application of his moral philosophy to the problem of telling the truth about someone's whereabouts in the presence of an enemy bent on murder. While it is of course possible to derive standards, guidelines or criteria from them, the theories are usually rich enough to admit various interpretations: consider, for example, the familiar difficulties in deciding which of several alternatives "maximizes utility" even after all the data is in. It is true that the hard case helps chart the limits of a system of moral belief, but because it stimulates the moral theory to express its richness, the exercise often produces ambiguous and therefore ultimately unsatisfying results.

For the clinical ethicist moral theory provides some orientation, but only in a broad and general sense, for it can also prove disorienting once the various theories' multiple implications for the hard case are discerned, as they will be when the theory is used to throw light on some particular case. Thus, again, applied moral philosophy is not simply moral philosophy applied. Clinical ethics is like a river with many tributaries, and moral philosophy is only one, though major, tributary.

A hackneyed response to the realization that there is no royal road to bioethical truth through moral theory is that there are "no answers", a refrain heard more often in the 1970s when the approach described was more common. But the point is that moral philosophy cannot in itself provide "the answers", or at least not to the genuinely hard cases, and I think there is a reason for this additional to the one I have just discussed.

The reason is that the hard cases are such precisely because they reveal the points at which systems of moral belief rub up against each other. In homogeneous societies the limits of the belief systems may not be noticed or may not engender great public controversy, but in pluralistic societies such as ours "the answers" must satisfy constituents of moral points of view that differ, though these differences are often only at the edges. Because the differences are so intractable they tend to exaggerate the contrasts between the moral theories.

In such a situation the ethicist is in a position to do more than teach, criticize and analyze. Because he or she is conversant with the nature of moral belief in a general sense, the ethicist is well-placed to discern hitherto unrecognized ways in which rival belief systems might be "stretched" (e.g., the adult child who wants "everything done" for her parent with multiple system failure but will consent to a do-not-resuscitate order to avoid vegetative existence); reasonably modified (e.g., the surgeon who agrees to delay a risky corrective procedure for a heart defect for an infant with numerous uncorrectable anomalies in order to assess the child's pulmonary potential); or even defensibly constrained (e.g., the practice of obtaining court orders to transfuse children of Jehovah's Witnesses). As the ethicist becomes more directly engaged in this process he or she assumes a role in the "political" processes that are an essential part of the management of rivalries among communal values.

Beyond a certain point it is useless to wonder whether the clinical ethicist should participate in these processes or not. As soon as the individual identified as the "moral expert" leaves the seminar room or library for the hospital conference room or nursing station the transformation from moral philosopher to ethicist has been accomplished. That is, when the moral philosopher no longer trades only in theory and hypothesis but participates in institutional decision making about particular cases. In these circumstances the clinical ethicist must adopt the sanguine posture that the moral philosopher's intellectual abilities can be brought to bear, but not without some further skills required of participants in human institutions. Thus the outstanding question is, what skills besides moral expertise does the ethicist require? While this question invites a study in itself, I will close with some brief suggestions.

It is often said that the non-physician ethicist must be familiar with the language of health care in order to be effective. But there are at least three other sorts of skill that are required for ethicists to play their inherently political role effectively. Probably they all suggest a level of formal training that few ethicists can claim, if any, but it would be surprising if the best clinical ethicists did not have sound intuitions in these directions. First, the ethicist should be a skilled participant-observer, able to identify informal social structures and arrangements and to assess his or her developing role in them. Second, the ethicist should understand the dynamics of small group behavior, with an ability to recognize the interplay between sociometric structures and decisional outcomes. Third, the ethicist should be a competent mediator, familiar with negotiating strategies and having sound interpersonal skills.[16]

These proposals, and especially the last, will strike many as Machiavellian. The error lies in a failure to appreciate the depth and significance of the shift from moral philosopher to ethicist, a profound change in role that has in my view been seriously underestimated. But so long as the moral philosopher elects to pursue this new role in the midst of the *agora*, or a public place like a hospital, the only alternatives to the deliberate acquisition of these skills are blindness to the social complexities of the situation and fumbling efforts to retain academic detachment. If the ethicist in the clinical setting chooses to deny the subtlety of the undertaking by clutching the mantle of moral philosophy, that will rightly be interpreted as arrogance or naiveté. Neither would reflect well on the philosophical traditions that remain our touchstone.

Acknowledgement

A version of this paper was presented to the Kennedy Institute Scholars Luncheon Seminar at Georgetown University in Washington, DC, and to the Conference on Method in Philosophy and the Sciences at the New School for Social Research in New York, both during the fall of 1989. I am grateful to the participants in these forums. Special thanks to Andrew Altman and David DeGrazia for their extensive comments on an earlier form of this paper, and to two anonymous reviewers.

Notes

1 Terrence F. Ackerman, "Conceptualizing the Role of the Ethics Consultant: Some Theoretical Issues" in John C. Fletcher, Norman Quist, and Albert R. Jonsen (eds), *Ethics Consultation in Health Care* (Ann Arbor, MI: Health Administration Press, 1989), pp. 37–52. See also Terrence F. Ackerman, "Moral Problems, Moral Inquiry, and Consultation in Clinical Ethics" in Barry Hoffmaster, Benjamin Freedman, and Gwen Fraser (eds), *Clinical Ethics: Theory and Practice* (Clifton, NJ: Humana Press, 1989), pp. 141–60; and "The Role of an Ethicist in Health Care" in Gary R. Anderson and Valerie A. Glesnes-Anderson (eds), *Health Care Ethics: A Guide for Decision Makers* (Rockville, MD: Aspen Publications, 1987), pp. 308–20.

2 Jonathan D. Moreno, "Ethics by Committee: The Moral Authority of Consensus", *Journal of Medicine and Philosophy*, 13: 411–32 (1988).

3 This is a summary of the account found in Robert W. Burch, "Are There Moral Experts?" *Monist*, 58: 646–58 (1974).

4 I am relying on the formulation of Terrance E. McConnell, "Objectivity and Moral Expertise", *Canadian Journal of Philosophy*, 14: 193–216 (1984).

5 Ibid.

6 Burch, "Are There Moral Experts?"

7 Arthur Caplan, "Ethical Engineers Need Not Apply: The State of Applied Ethics Today", *Science, Technology and Human Values*, 6: 24–32 (1980).

8 James W. Nickel, "Philosophy and Policy" in David M. Rosenthal and Fadlou Shehadi (eds), *Applied Ethics and Ethical Theory* (Salt Lake City: University of Utah Press, 1988), pp. 139–48.

9 Arthur Caplan, "Can Applied Ethics Be Effective in Health Care and Should It Strive To Be?", *Ethics*, 13: 311–19 (1983).

10 See Peter Singer, "Moral Experts", *Analysis*, 32: 115–17 (1972); and "How Do We Decide?", *Hastings Center Report*, 12(3): 9–11 (1982).

11 An anonymous reviewer pointed this distinction out to me.

12 Frances Myrna Kamm, "Ethics, Applied Ethics, and Applying Applied Ethics", in Rosenthal and Shehadi (eds), *Applied Ethics*, pp. 62–87.

13 This criticism I owe to Edmund Pellegrino.

14 Alasdair MacIntyre, *After Virtue* (Notre Dame, IN: University of Notre Dame Press, 1981).

15 Richard Rorty, *Philosophy and the Mirror of Nature* (Princeton, NJ: Princeton University Press, 1979).

16 Ackerman reaches similar conclusions. The difference between us is the significance each of us attributes to the fact that these personal skills are substantial departures from those normally required of the moral philosopher.

75

Ethics Committees: Decisions by Bureaucracy

Mark Siegler

The rise of institutional ethics committees (IECs) is, unfortunately, a sign of the times. Their development symbolizes the dreary, depressed, and disorganized state to which American medicine has fallen. Not only have physicians lost political and economic power; they have even lost the autonomy to reach medical decisions. Good physicians have always incorporated technical judgments, ethical reflections, and patient wishes in reaching difficult decisions. However, the increased frequency of ethical problems has encouraged some physicians and ethicists to suggest that these decisions may be too complex for practitioners and are best made by committees.

Concerns about IECs

IECs threaten to undermine the traditional doctor–patient relationship and to impose new and untested administrative and regulatory burdens on patients, families, and physicians. Their existence may shift the focus of decision-making from the office or bedside to the conference room or executive suite.

Such committees may expand the number of participants in the decision from those directly involved in the case to an unmanageable collection of noninvolved professional and moral "experts," including other physicians, nurses, lawyers, hospital administrators, ethicists, clergy, community representatives, and patient advocates. These committees also may have serious conflicts of interest between their responsibility to the individual patient and their efforts to minimize hospital risk, to develop sound hospital policies, and perhaps even to allocate economic resources most efficiently.

Most troubling of all, they may remove or at least attenuate the decision-making authority of the physician who is responsible – medically, morally, and legally – for the patient's care. Some physicians may abdicate their medical responsibility by delegating difficult clinical-ethical decisions, an intrinsic part of medical practice, to such committees. In contrast to individual physicians, committees lack specific medical knowledge, have not been trained in the ethic of caring, have little responsibility or accountability for decisions, and have not been sanctioned by the patient to make such decisions. Thus, to delegate decision-making to the IEC may be unethical for physicians and hospitals. Christine Cassel has put the point nicely:

> The coming together of many different perspectives and areas of expertise may provide the "crucible" in which the best (i.e., most humane and most just) decisions are made. But a committee can also provide the setting in which immoral decisions can be made for which no one has ultimate responsibility. This is most likely to occur in a setting where most persons on the committee are relatively removed from the clinical setting, where conflict of interest with administrative needs exists, and where the group dynamic is bureaucratized. Such a committee is no longer a crucible for the tempering of apparently conflicting values, but rather a

From *Hastings Center Report* (June 1986), pp. 22–4. Reprinted with permission.

> bureau whose primary value is not the anguish of moral dilemma but the efficiency of decision making, abiding by rules and adhering to regulations and legal proscriptions.[1]

To justify the existence of IECs, their proponents have suggested many possible roles for them, including: (1) developing educational programs on bioethical matters; (2) providing an interdisciplinary forum for discussions about bioethical issues; (3) advising persons who seek counsel from the committee; and (4) assessing and evaluating hospital policies that relate to bioethical matters.[2] In addition, many supporters of IECs state categorically that such committees should not make patient care decisions.[3] Despite the rhetoric that forswears the use of IECs as decision-making bodies, I fear that these committees will, directly or indirectly, become increasingly involved in patient care decisions and will thus usurp the role and responsibility of those who should be making such decisions.

Can Decision Making Be Avoided?

My concerns may seem unjustified or at least excessive in view of these guidelines and other statements. In a recent article Norman Fost and Ronald E. Cranford note:

> The most controversial role of an ethics committee is as a consulting group for urgent decisions about withholding, withdrawing, or continuing life-sustaining medical care... While some might advocate investing decision-making authority in such committees, there has been little experience with such a role. The majority of existing ethics committees surveyed by the President's Commission [in 1982] did not view themselves as primary decision makers. This has also been our experience as we have worked with at least 20 hospital ethics committees around the country. The majority have emphasized their consultative, advisory, informational, and consensus-development roles rather than primary decision making.[4]

Nevertheless, they conclude:

> Hospital ethics committees are increasingly becoming a part of decision making involving life support in critically ill patients.

Fost and Cranford wish to draw a fine distinction between "investing decision-making authority in such commitees" and having such committees "increasingly [become] a part of decision making involving life support in critically ill patients." This is a distinction without a substantial difference. Further, Fost and Cranford may be technically correct when they note that "the majority of existing ethics committees surveyed by the President's Commission did not view themselves as primary decision makers," although, in fact, 31 percent of committees surveyed said that one of their "actual" functions was to "make final decisions about life support." In addition, those hospital committees surveyed noted that other "actual" functions included: (1) "to provide counsel and support to physicians" (69 percent); (2) "to make ethical/social policy for care of critically ill" (38 percent); (3) "to review ethical issues in patient care decisions" (56 percent); and (4) "to determine medical prognosis" (25 percent).

Clearly, there are many ways in which ethics committees can become "involved" implicitly or explicitly in clinical decisions and can influence patient–physician decisions, even if *only* 31 percent of the committees surveyed reported that they actually made final decisions about life support. Thus, hospital ethics committees can constrain and modify physician–patient decisions in at least the following ways:

1 By developing rules, regulations, and institutional policies that limit the prudential clinical-ethical discretion that normally could be exercised by the responsible physician;
2 By reviewing physician decisions retrospectively (presumably for the purpose of approving or disapproving the decision);
3 By consulting on cases and by having the opinion of the committees carry the authority of the institution;
4 By serving occasionally as a quasi-judicial body that actually makes decisions and thus wrests the authority from the physician;
5 By influencing physicians to make the "right" decision through moral suasion and group power.

Fost has cited one example of a disagreement between an attending pediatrician and a neonatologist that was brought to the attention of a hospital ethics committee. Although the committee did not vote or issue a formal recommendation, its discussion "appeared to show a slim majority favoring continuing treatment." Fost writes: "The committee chairman said to the attending, 'Of course, the committee has no power to make decisions; the choice is still up to you.' To which the attending replied, 'Poppycock!' Understandably, he felt enormous social pressure to continue treatment and knew that he would be going upstream against colleagues if he chose otherwise."[5]

An Alternative to Committees

Ethics committees should divorce themselves absolutely from involvement in patient decision-making and from ethics consultations and should not even review and criticize decisions that have been made previously. Other appropriately constituted hospital and medical committees (including the quality assurance committee, the morbidity and mortality committee, and the medical-legal affairs committee) should continue to monitor and correct deficiencies in patient care, including those associated with clinical-ethical decisions.

The principal role of ethics committees should be a broadly conceived program of education. Ethics committees should develop and coordinate institutional resources in clinical ethics and should also develop formal training programs for physicians, nurses, and staff from all clinical disciplines in order to train them in the knowledge and behavioral skills required to make sound decisions in their own area of expertise. The ultimate goal of institutional ethics committees should be to put themselves out of business after having completed this ambitious training program and provided for the training of new personnel.

I would be greatly reassured if I thought that institutional ethics committees were a short-term, stop-gap measure designed to train a sufficient number of clinicians to assume the task of making sound clinical-ethical decisions. This is not the way most bureaucracies function, and I suspect that we are more likely to see a progressive bureaucratization of institutional ethics committees with all that this entails, including newsletters, new journals, and national organizations.

In place of ethics committees, I encourage the formation of many small advisory groups possessing great clinical expertise in their own particular specialty and composed primarily of involved clinicians but with occasional representation of other experts. These advisory groups would be organized in those clinical units that were regarded as "high-risk ethical areas." Thus, a large hospital might have separate advisory groups in, for example, its burn unit, medical oncology service, neurosurgical ICU, respiratory ICU, neonatal ICU, AIDS clinic, emergency room, and in the transplantation surgery unit. For medical centers that perform several types of transplantation there might be a separate advisory group for each team.

Each of these clinical disciplines is extremely complex and presents very different types of clinical-ethical dilemmas. Only a very few trained clinicians (physicians or nurses) would be so presumptuous as to think that their particular clinical training had prepared them to take care of the entire range of medical problems from medical oncology to neonatal intensive care and liver transplantation. A superb operating room nurse would probably be uncomfortable and ill-prepared if he were assigned to a neurology unit. Furthermore, if the operating nurse specialized in open heart surgery procedures, he might not be entirely competent as the scrub on a neurosurgery case.

Clinicians realize that even though cellular biochemistry and organ physiology are similar in all patients, profound differences remain between the basic sciences of medicine and the clinical application of these sciences to the care of individual patients. Similarly, ethical principles such as beneficience, truth telling, and autonomy that are taken as basic by various philosophic and religious groups often must be applied with great subtlety and discretion, based on clinical experience, in particular clinical situations.

IECs, on the other hand, often think they are capable of analyzing, adjudicating, and resolving the most delicate and complex clinical matters. I think they are wrong. The goal of such committees should be to develop clinicians from each of the clinical disciplines who have both the cognitive knowledge in ethics and law and the clinical experience to assist their colleagues in reaching sound clinical-ethical decisions.

References

1 Christine Cassel, "Deciding to Forego Life-Sustaining Treatment: Implications for Policy in 1984," *Cardozo Law Review* (May 1985) pp. 287–302.

2 See, for example, American Hospital Association, "Hospital Committees on Biomedical Ethics," Chicago, 1984. Also, President's Commission, *Deciding to Forego Life-Sustaining Treatment* (March 1983, Washington, DC), pp. 439–57.

3 See, in addition to the AHS guidelines, the American Medical Association's "Guidelines for Ethics Committees in Health Care Institutions," *Journal of the American Medical Association*, 253 (1985), 2698–9.

4 Norman Fost and Ronald E. Cranford, "Hospital Ethics Committees: Administrative Aspects," *Journal of the American Medical Association*, 253 (1985), 2687–92.

5 Norman Fost, "What Can a Hospital Ethics Committee Do For You?" *Contemporary Pediatrics* (February 1986), p. 125.

76

Truth or Consequences: The Role of Philosophers in Policy-Making

Dan W. Brock

My reflections here are based principally on my experience during the 1981–2 academic year as staff philosopher on the President's Commission for the Study of Ethical Problems in Medicine, as well as participation in various capacities in other policy-making or advising bodies in biomedical ethics at both state and national levels. My central thesis is that there is a deep conflict between the goals and constraints of the public policy process and the aims of academic scholarly activity in general and philosophical activity in particular. I shall support this thesis by developing several related aspects of the conflict.

Truth is the central virtue of scholarly work. Scholars are taught to follow arguments and evidence where they lead without regard for the social consequences of doing so. Whether the results are unpopular or in conflict with conventional or authoritative views, determining the truth to the best of one's abilities is the goal. In philosophy, especially, nothing is to be immune from question and criticism; all assumptions are open to and must withstand critical scrutiny. Now it would be silly to maintain that philosophers always succeed in this unconstrained quest for the truth, either in the sense that their quest is unconstrained or that they reach the goal of the truth. We often fail to recognize the problematic nature of particular assumptions or views and so fail to subject them to the criticism they deserve. Like our colleagues in the natural and social sciences, we can become wedded to particular views or general theories so that we fail to recognize or acknowledge the difficulties facing them. At any time, much is simply beyond the grasp of our best efforts.

When philosophers become more or less direct participants in the policy-making process and so are no longer academics just hoping that an occasional policy-maker might read their scholarly journal articles, this scholarly virtue of the unconstrained search for the truth – all assumptions open to question and follow the arguments wherever they lead – comes under a variety of related pressures. What arises is an intellectual variant of the political problem of "dirty hands" that those who hold political power often face. I emphasize that I do not conceive of the problem as one of pure, untainted philosophers being corrupted by the dirty business of politics. My point is rather that the different goals of academic scholarship and public policy call in turn for different virtues and behavior in their practitioners. Philosophers who steadfastly maintain their academic ways in the public policy setting are *not* to be admired as islands of integrity in a sea of messy political compromise and corruption. Instead, I believe that if philosophers maintain the academic virtues there they will not only find themselves often ineffective but will as well often fail in their responsibilities and act wrongly. Why is this so?

The central point of conflict is that the first concern of those responsible for public policy is, and ought to be, the consequences of their actions for public policy and the persons that those policies affect. This is not to say that they should not be concerned with the moral evaluation of those consequences – they should; nor that they must be moral consequentialists in the evaluation of the

From *Ethics* vol. 97 (July 1987), pp. 786–91.

policy, and in turn human, consequences of their actions – whether some form of consequentialism is an adequate moral theory is another matter. But it is to say that persons who directly participate in the formation of public policy would be irresponsible if they did not focus their concern on how their actions will affect policy and how that policy will in turn affect people.

The virtues of academic research and scholarship that consist in an unconstrained search for truth, whatever the consequences, reflect not only the different goals of scholarly work but also the fact that the effects of the scholarly endeavor on the public are less direct, and are mediated more by other institutions and events, than are those of the public policy process. It is in part the very importence in terms of major, direct effects on people's lives of most academic scholarship that makes it morally acceptable not to worry much about the social consequences of that scholarship. When philosophers move into the policy domain, they must shift their primary commitment from knowledge and truth to the policy consequences of what they do. And if they are not prepared to do this, why did they enter the policy domain? What are they doing there?

Let me be more specific about some of the forms this conflict between scholarly and policy goals and virtues has taken in my own experience. No philosopher that I am aware of has ever been an omnipotent philosopher king or queen – able to make public policy however he or she sees fit. Instead, I think my own experience is more typical. I worked with nonphilosophers on the professional staff of a presidential commission, and the staff worked for the commissioners who were political appointees out of the office of the president. We published ten book-length reports on different issues in biomedical ethics, each of which had several staff members assigned to it. The Commissioners had the final word on what our reports would say. Thus, though I had my own views about what they should say, those views would only have any effect if I was able to persuade other staff members working on a particular project, and in turn the Commissioners, of them. I and the two other staff philosophers who preceded and followed me were, quite rightly, not accorded the role of moral authorities to whom appeals were made for the right answers; our impact lay instead in our ability to persuade.

The staff were also often more expert than our "bosses," the Commissioners, on many of the problems on which we worked. In our case, as elsewhere in the policy and political world, this was to a large extent inevitable and appropriate since the staff was selected for their professional expertise in the area of the Commission's responsibilities and worked full time on our projects, while the Commissioners retained their other usual professional responsibilities and spent only a small portion of their time on Commission work. Staff sometimes believed that Commissioners held particular views on indefensible grounds. If our reports were to say what we thought they should say, we had to bring the Commissioners around to our views. It was in the resulting context of debate and dialogue that I and other staff members often found ourselves looking to what the consequences on others would be of making a particular argument or taking a particular position, instead of simply at whether we considered the argument or position sound. The goal often became to persuade or even to manipulate others in order to reach a desired outcome instead of a common search for the truth. There is space to give only one example.

In our report on decisions about life-sustaining treatment, we addressed briefly a number of distinctions that commonly play a role in the reasoning underlying those decisions, distinctions such as between killing and allowing to die, between a physician's or a disease's being the cause of death, and so forth. I believe that on common understandings of the kill/allow to die distinction, the difference is not in itself morally important, and that stopping life-sustaining treatment is often killing, though justified killing. Needless to say, many of the Commissioners did not share this view. They believed that killing was far more seriously wrong than allowing to die, and that stopping life support was allowing the patient to die of his disease, not causing his death and killing. We shared the conclusion that stopping life-sustaining treatment at the request of a competent patient was morally permissible, but I believed that their reasons for this conclusion were confused and unsound and that I might have some success in convincing them of this. My philosophical instincts urged me to attack the confusion and to follow the argument wherever it led.

But what would be the consequences of convincing them either that allowing to die is in itself no different morally than killing and/or that stopping life support was killing? A quite plausible case could be, and was, made that this could throw into question their acceptance of the moral permissibility of stopping life support. Could one then responsibly attack what seemed confusions in their view when the result of doing so might well be to lead them to an unwarranted and worse conclusion – and a conclusion, it is important to add, that could produce important adverse consequences in suffering and loss of self-determination for real people? I want to stress that this attention to the consequences of criticizing a position or defending one in a particular way became a significant factor in our work. The example I have cited was not an isolated case but only one instance of a common phenomenon. I believe that when a philosopher or anyone else accepts the role and responsibilities of participating directly in the policy-making process, it would be morally wrong and irresponsible not to give substantial weight in this way to the consequences likely to flow from one's actions in that role. Doing so, however, leads to manipulative attitudes toward others that I am not comfortable with and fosters playing a little fast and loose with the truth as best one understands it, in a way that is inimical to the scholarly academic enterprise.

There are related aspects of this general conflict. Philosophers are viewed as somewhat strange beasts in governmental and policy circles. It is never clear to many others exactly what they do or what are the criteria for their having done it well. There is particular skepticism about whether academics in general, and especially philosophers, understand how the "real" political world works and the constraints it puts on policy making and policy. All of this means that philosophers have a credibility problem in policy circles that leads to pressure for some cutting and trimming in at least the voicing of one's more extreme, unconventional, or radical views. To voice and press views that others will find outrageous, however much one may be convinced of them, is to risk using up one's credibility and to risk not being heard, or even losing the opportunity to speak, on other occasions when one might have a significant impact. Once again, the effect is to make philosophers look over their shoulders at what effect pressing their views will have on others, independent of whether they believe them to be sound.

It is not just the inherent conservativeness of policy-makers and bureaucrats that creates pressure not to voice views that others will find extreme or bizarre. An important part of the policy-maker's job is to "sell" a position or policy to others in the policy and political process. Ultimately, it must be sold to all others affected by and affecting the process, including the public. That makes the "packaging" of a policy proposal often extremely important to its fate. The particular formulation and defense of a policy that is likely to move it most successfully through the policy arena may differ substantially from what a philosopher believes its correct formulation and defense to be. For example, philosophers who believe that infanticide is morally permissible would be ill advised to use that as the basis of an attack in the public policy arena on the Reagan administration's so-called Baby Doe regulations.

On this point, as elsewhere for the general scholarly-policy conflict I am sketching, the contrast should not be overstated. Philosophers in their academic scholarship are not indifferent to whether they convince others of their views. But the attempt of scholars to persuade others is not just a process of coalition building to gain allies. What is important is that other scholars are persuaded by their own assessment of one's arguments and evidence.

A related aspect of moral philosophers' credibility problem lies in their own uncertain views of the nature of their enterprise, as much as others' views of it. For many philosophers, basic moral principles cannot ultimately be established as true, objectively correct, and so forth. Rather, the deepest moral conflicts and disagreements may admit of no rational resolution. But if so, then philosophers' grounds for using their expertise or title to press their own views on moral questions may in turn be uncertain. Yet they inevitably will do so, even if neither they nor others construe their role to be provider of the moral truth and of solutions to moral problems. One can hold, as I do, some form of coherentist view of justification in ethics without slipping into a radical moral skepticism or subjectivism, but for many nonphilosophers coherentism never seems a fully convincing or adequate account of moral justification.

A further aspect of the scholarly-policy contrast I have been sketching is what Norman Daniels has called the priorities problem, and what I will call the agenda problem.[1] The problem is what is to be taken as fixed or given for the purpose of setting or changing policy and what is to be taken as open to modification and so on the policy agenda. The scholarly philosophical virtues I have sketched above are intended to leave nothing fixed or given, and beyond criticism, revision, or rejection. This leads the philosopher toward a maximally wide agenda; no change is too far-reaching if persuasive argument supports it. For seasoned policy-makers and bureaucrats, on the other hand, who have lost as many battles as they have won and who are constantly subject to the competing forces and interest groups active in the policy process, all is not immediately possible. Many issues are not on their agenda because they are not politically feasible, or because it is not an opportune time for them, or because efforts must be focused on other, higher-priority issues. Incrementalism and resistance to change may be endemic to policymakers and bureaucracies.

The interaction that ensues from this conflict about the policy agenda has some beneficial consequences for both philosophy and policy. For policy, philosophers can contribute to a desirable widening of the policy agenda. Though philosophers may want to set agendas that are unrealistically wide, policy-makers and bureaucrats may otherwise construe them unnecessarily narrowly. For philosophy, the result may be analyses of policy issues reflecting a more realistic understanding of the constraints of political reality. Nevertheless, philosophers' credibility problem can be exacerbated as they are seen as unrealistic, "head in the clouds," "ivory tower" academics. And more to my general point here, this mutual adjustment process can lead philosophers to a narrowing of vision and acceptance of fixed points that is contrary to the scholarly, philosophical virtues.

I have sketched a variety of respects in which the characteristic aims, virtues, and commitments of philosophical scholarship are in conflict with those of public policy-making. Does this imply that philosophers should avoid the policy process like the plague? I think not. Some aspects of the conflicts I have cited are beneficial either for policy and/or philosophy. In many respects that I have not touched on here the experience can lead to better applied ethics – perhaps most obviously in giving philosophers enough experience in a particular area of applied ethics to gain a clear understanding of its moral issues and problems. Far too often, philosophers fail to be as effective as they might be because they lack adequate sustained exposure and understanding of the area, such as medicine or business, in which they seek to do applied ethics. Moreover, there are many valuable roles, though I have not detailed them here, that I believe at least some philosophers are both professionally and personally well suited to play. Despite the philosophy–policy conflict I have been developing here, I believe that philosophers who are fortunate enough to have the opportunity to use their analytical and critical skills at influential points in the policy process often can help improve and illuminate thinking and practice in ways that produce real and significant benefits for those affected by the policies. I, at least, found that to be a deeply satisfying aspect of my own experience in the policy world. However, I believe the scholarly – policy conflicts that I have cited here do give reason for thinking that philosophers' forays into the world of policy should best be limited and temporary, not full time and permanent. The philosophical virtues that enable philosophers to make effective, valuable, and distinctive contributions to the policy process are probably best maintained if their primary base and commitment remain in academic philosophy.

Reference

1 Norman Daniels, "Conflicting Objectives and the Priorities Problem," in *Income Support*, ed. P. Brown, C. Johnson, and P. Vernier (Totowa, NJ: Rowman & Littlefield, 1981).

Index

Index